APPLIED
AND
DECORATIVE ARTS

APPLIED AND DECORATIVE ARTS
A Bibliographic Guide

Second Edition

DONALD L. EHRESMANN

LIBRARIES UNLIMITED, INC.
Englewood, Colorado
1993

LIBRARIES UNLIMITED, INC.
P.O. Box 6633
Englewood, CO 80155-6633

Library of Congress Cataloging-in-Publication Data

Ehresmann, Donald L., 1937-
   Applied and decorative arts : a bibliographic guide / Donald L. Ehresmann. -- 2nd ed.
    xxxvii, 629 p. 17x25 cm.
    ISBN 0-87287-906-2
    1. Decorative arts--Bibliography. I. Title.
Z5956.A68E47   1992
[NKJ1110]
016.745--dc20   92-28156
                                                  CIP

CONTENTS

CHAPTER ONE—APPLIED AND DECORATIVE ARTS—GENERAL (*Continued*)

CHAPTER THREE—FOLK ART (*Continued*)

CHAPTER FOUR—ARMS AND ARMOR **66**

CHAPTER FIVE—CERAMICS (*Continued*)

CHAPTER FIVE—CERAMICS (*Continued*)

CHAPTER SIX—CLOCKS, WATCHES, AUTOMATA, AND SCIENTIFIC INSTRUMENTS (Continued)

CHAPTER NINE—FURNITURE (*Continued*)

CHAPTER NINE—FURNITURE (*Continued*)

CHAPTER TEN—GLASS (*Continued*)

CHAPTER SIXTEEN—METALWORK (*Continued*)

CHAPTER SIXTEEN—METALWORK (*Continued*)

CHAPTER SIXTEEN—METALWORK (*Continued*)

CHAPTER SIXTEEN—METALWORK (*Continued*)

CHAPTER EIGHTEEN—TEXTILES (*Continued*)

CHAPTER EIGHTEEN—TEXTILES (*Continued*)

CHAPTER ONE

APPLIED AND DECORATIVE ARTS—GENERAL

BIBLIOGRAPHIES

1   Chafer, Denis, ed. **The Arts Applied. A Catalogue of Books**. London, Weinreb, 1975. 319p. illus. index. LC 77-355058.

Sales catalog (B. Weinreb, no. 29) of a collection of nearly 2,000 books and original drawings on the applied and decorative arts. Emphasis is on interior design and decoration. Descriptive annotations make it useful to scholars interested in the drawings—a miscellany of various countries and periods, but mostly English eighteenth and nineteenth centuries—and the earlier books.

2   Franklin, Linda Campbell. **Antiques and Collectibles. A Bibliography of Works in English 16th Century to 1976**. Metuchen, N.J., Scarecrow Press, 1978. 1091p. illus. index. ISBN 0810810921.

Comprehensive, classified bibliography of 10,783 books and periodicals in English on the applied and decorative arts, popular and folk art, crafts, and a host of other classes of objects that are collected. The emphasis is on the lower end of the spectrum of antique collecting and is a valuable compilation of literature on "collectibles," e.g., flags, cigar labels, barbed wire, beer cans, etc. Unfortunately not annotated. Locations for major works indicated by abbreviations at the ends of the entries.

3   Lackschewitz, Gertrud. **Interior Design and Decoration: A Bibliography. Compiled for the American Institute of Decorators**. New York, New York Public Library, 1961. 86p. index. LC 61-7059.

Classified bibliography of books on interior design and decoration. Contents: I, History of Architecture and the Decorative Arts; II, Interior Design and Decoration from the Middle Ages to the 19th Century; III, 20th-century Forms and Concepts of Design; IV, Theory and Practice of Interior Design and Decoration; V, Decorative Elements, Materials, and Accessories; Periodical and Periodical Indexes.

See also the catalogs of the Bibliothèque Forney, Paris (FA 238).

DIRECTORIES

4   **British Antiques Yearbook**. 1968/69-. London, Antiques Yearbooks, 1968-. illus.

Annual guide to antique dealers in Great Britain. Lists names, addresses and telephone numbers. Supplements the listings in *International Art and Antiques Yearbook* (6).

5   **Guide Européen de l'antiquaire, de l'amateur d'art et du bibliophile**. 1949/1951-. Paris, Guide Emer, 1949-.

Biannual guide to antique and art dealers of the world with emphasis on France. Includes antiquarian and rare book dealers.

6   **International Art and Antiques Yearbook. 1949/50-**. London, Tantivy Press: Antique Yearbooks, 1949-. illus. index.

Annual directory of antique dealers, art dealers, and antiquarian and rare book dealers throughout the world with particular emphasis on western Europe. Sections on packers and shippers, auction and sales rooms, antique fairs, antique periodicals and associations.

7   **World Design Sources Directory. Repertoire des sources d'information en design 1980. An Icograda ICSID Publication**. Edited by the Centre de Création Industrielle. Oxford, New York, Pergamon Press, 1980. 188p. index. ISBN 0080256767.

Directory of 250 public and private organizations concerned with industrial and graphic design throughout the world. Compiled by questionnaire (pp. 8-9). Supplies address, telephone number, date of establishment, status, director, number of persons employed, activities, documentation services and documentation resources.

See also: *Internationales Kunst-Adressbuch. International Directory of Arts...* (FA 299) and *International Who's Who in Art and Antiques* (FA 298).

DICTIONARIES AND ENCYCLOPEDIAS

8   Aprá, Nietta. **Dizionario enciclopedico dell'antiquariato**. Milan, Mursia, 1969. 572p. illus. (Dizionari enciclopedici, 1). LC 75-464036.

Comprehensive dictionary of the applied and decorative arts. Includes a selection of artists. Bibliographical references in some entries.

9   Benedictus, David. **The Antique Collector's Guide**. New York, Atheneum, 1981. 264p. illus. ISBN 0689111460.

General dictionary covering styles, objects, ornamental patterns and motifs with emphasis on Britain. Glossary of names gives basic biographical data for major designers and craftsmen. Chronological chart. Hints for further reading, p. 254.

10   Bernasconi, John R. **The Collectors' Glossary of Antiques and Fine Arts**. 3rd ed. London, Estates Gazette, 1971. 595p. illus. ISBN 0900361344.

Handbook for collectors with concise definitions to terms arranged in sections by media and types of objects. Glossary of general terms, pp. 497-521. Tables of silver date letters, pp. 522-71.

11   Boger, Louise A., and Batterson H. Boger. **The Dictionary of Antiques and the Decorative Arts; a Book of Reference for Glass, Furniture, Ceramics, Silver, Technical Terms, Etc.** New York, Scribner's, 1967. 662p. illus. LC 67-18131.

First published in 1957. Comprehensive dictionary of terms and subjects relating to the applied and decorative arts. Well-illustrated with line drawings and plates of museum pieces and items accessible to the collector. Good, classified bibliography of books, mostly in English, pp. 566-662.

12   Bosc, Ernest. **Dictionnaire de l'art, de la curiosité et du bibelot**. Paris, Firmin-Didot, 1883. 695p. illus. Reprint: New York, Garland, 1979. LC 78-50225.

Older dictionary covering terms and subjects relating to arms and armor, ceramics, glass, gold and silver, jewelry, metalwork and musical instruments. A useful feature for the specialist is the list of nineteenth-century collectors, pp. 671-90.

13   Bradford, Ernle. **Dictionary of Antiques**. London, English Universities Press, 1963. 151p. illus. LC 63-25207.

      Pocket-sized dictionary covering terms relating to ornament, technique, material, styles and objects of the decorative and applied arts. Appendices give lists of major designers, craftsmen and artists.

14   Cameron, Ian, and Elizabeth Kingsley-Rowe, eds. **Collins Encyclopedia of Antiques**. London, Collins, 1973. 400p. illus. Reprint as *The Encyclopedia of Antiques*. New York, Greenwich House, 1982. ISBN 0517381974.

      First American edition was titled: *The Random House Encyclopedia of Antiques*. Comprehensive dictionary with over 5,000 entries relating to European and American applied and decorative arts between 1400 and 1875. Emphasis is on objects accessible to the collector. Bibliography of basic books, pp. 391-98. Glossary of ceramic marks and silver date letters.

15   **The Complete Color Encyclopedia of Antiques**. L. G. G. Ramsey, ed. New York, Hawthorn, 1975. 704p. illus. LC 74-7888.

      First published as *The Complete Encyclopedia of Antiques* (London, The Connoisseur; New York, Hawthorn) from material adapted from the *The Concise Encyclopedia of Antiques* (16) and *The Concise Encyclopedia of American Antiques* (98). A comprehensive handbook of European and American applied and decorative arts with emphasis on objects accessible to the collector. Contents: 1, The Aesthetic Movement; the Arts and Crafts Movement; Art Nouveau; Art Deco, etc.; 2, Antiquities; 3, Arms and Armour; 4, Barometers, Clocks and Watches; 5, Carpets and Rugs; 6, Coins and Medals; 7, Ethnographica; 8, Furniture; 9, Glass; 10, Jewelry; 11, Metalwork; 12, Mirrors; 13, Needlework and Embroidery; 14, Pottery and Porcelain; 15, Prints; 16, Scientific Instruments; 17, Silver. Classified bibliography, pp. 669-78.

16   **The Connoisseur's Complete Period Guides to Houses, Decoration, Furnishing and Chattels of the Classic Periods**. Edited by Ralph Edwards and L. G. G. Ramsey. London, The Connoisseur, 1968. 1536p. illus. index. LC 70-369442.

      Originally published in five volumes as *The Concise Encyclopedia of Antiques* edited by L. G. G. Ramsey, (London, The Connoisseur, New York, Hawthorn, 1954-61). Comprehensive encyclopedia of Western applied and decorative arts from 1500 to 1860 with emphasis on English and American works. Arrangement is by periods, with essays on the various media by experts in the field of collecting. Some of the chapters have bibliographical footnotes and short bibliographies at their end.

17   Coysh, A. W. **The Antique Buyer's Dictionary of Names**. New York, Praeger, 1970. 278p. LC 70-125355.

      Dictionary with brief biographies of craftsmen, decorators, and designers active in Europe, the United States, and Japan from the Renaissance to the mid-twentieth century. Arrangement is by medium and class of object, e.g., bronzes, furniture, glass, netsuke, pottery, silhouettes, etc. making it handy for collectors who specialize. No bibliography.

18   Fleming, John, and Hugh Honour. **The Penguin Dictionary of Decorative Arts**. New ed. London, Viking, 1989. 935p. illus. ISBN 0670820474.

      First edition published as *Dictionary of the Decorative Arts* (New York, Harper & Row, 1977. 896p. illus. ISBN 0060119365). A companion volume to *The Penguin Dictionary of Architecture* (ARCH 19). Comprehensive dictionary of over 4,000 entries with emphasis on furniture and furnishings in Europe from the Middle Ages and in North America from colonial times to the present. Includes brief biographies of leading craftsmen and designers. Some entries have bibliographies. Glossaries of ceramic marks, silver hallmarks, makers' marks on silver and pewter. One of the best dictionaries covering the terminology of the applied and decorative arts.

19   Grassi, Luigi et al. **Dizionario di antiquariato**. Turin, UTET, 1989. 4v. illus. ISBN 880204290X.

Comprehensive dictionary of the applied and decorative arts from antiquity to the early twentieth century designed for the collector. Entries cover media, techniques, objects, styles, periods, ornaments, etc. Comprehensive, classified bibliography in volume 4, pp. 229-287.

20   Harling, Robert, ed. **Studio Dictionary of Art and Decoration**. rev. and enl. ed. New York, Viking, 1973. 583p. illus. LC 73-1024.

Published in Britain as *Dictionary of Design and Decoration* (London, Collins, 1973). General dictionary of design covering the applied and decorative arts and architecture. Entries vary from brief definition of terms to biographies of major designers running to several pages. Much of the material derives from the pages of *House and Garden*. No bibliography.

21   Havard, Henry. **Dictionnaire de l'ameublement**. Paris, Librairies-Imprimeries Réunies, 1887-90. 4v. illus. LC 02-50.

The great nineteenth-century encyclopedia of the applied and decorative arts from the thirteenth century to the nineteenth century still valuable for its treatment of French developments and for the numerous references to documentary records, e.g., inventories, archives, letters, etc. Many cuts in the text and a collection of chromolithographic plates.

22   Jervis, Simon. **The Facts on File Dictionary of Design and Designers**. New York, Facts on File, 1984. ISBN 0871968916.

Published in Britain as *The Penguin Dictionary of Design and Designers*. (London, Allen Lane, 1984. 533p. ISBN 0713912324)

Dictionary covering Europe and North America from 1450 to the present. Biographies of designers, craftsmen, and artists who worked in or for the decorative and applied arts and definitions of styles, concepts, motifs, etc. Emphasis is on ceramics, furniture, interior decoration, and metalwork. No bibliography.

23   Macdonald-Taylor, Margaret S. **A Dictionary of Marks: Metalwork, Furniture, Ceramics; the Identification Handbook for Antique Collectors**. New York, Hawthorn, 1962. 318p. illus. index. LC 62-17114.

Pocket-sized handbook of major marks found on American and British metalwork, English and French furniture, and English, European and Oriental ceramics. List of basic books, pp. 309-310.

24   Mountfield, David. **The Antique Collectors' Illustrated Dictionary**. London, Hamlyn, 1974. 273p. illus. ISBN 0600301540.

Popular but comprehensive dictionary of short entries defining terms used in the field of antique collecting (to circa 1850). Covers objects, ornamental motifs, technical terms and classes or types of antiques. Well illustrated with color plates and line drawings. No bibliography.

25   Morgan, Ann Lee, ed. **Contemporary Designers**. Detroit, Gale, 1984. 658p. illus. ISBN 6810320363.

Dictionary of approximately 600 artists and designers from around the world who were alive in 1960. Signed entries provide biographical information, list of exhibitions, list of writings by the designer and a selected bibliography of works on the designer.

26   Osborne, Harold, ed. **The Oxford Companion to the Decorative Arts**. Oxford, Clarendon, 1975. 865p. illus. LC 75-331784. Paperback reprint: New York, Oxford Univ. Press, 1985. ISBN 0192818635.

Companion to the *Oxford Companion to Art* (FA 319). Comprehensive dictionary of the applied and decorative arts of all periods and countries. Articles cover techniques, materials, types of objects, styles and cultures. Compiled and written by a team of British experts. Bibliographical references are to a list of 940 books, pp. 851-65. One of the best one-volume reference works on the applied and decorative arts.

27   Pegler, Martin M. **The Dictionary of Interior Design**. New York, Fairchild, 1983. 217p. illus. ISBN 087005473.

First published in 1964 (New York, Crown, LC 66-15127). General dictionary of the applied and decorative arts as they relate to interior decoration. Short entries cover major artists, styles, school, objects and decorative motifs. Illustrated with line drawings. No bibliography. *See also*: Dizik, A. Allen *Concise Encyclopedia of Interior Design*. 2nd ed. (New York, Van Nostrand Reinhold, 1988. 220p. Illus. ISBN 0442221096).

28   Phillips, Phoebe, ed. **The Collectors' Encyclopedia of Antiques**. New York, Crown, 1973. 704p. illus. index. LC 73-76934.

Comprehensive encyclopedia of Western applied and decorative arts with emphasis on the eighteenth and nineteenth centuries. Signed articles by a team of British specialists. Arrangement is by broad class of object: Arms and Armour; Bottles and Boxes; Carpets and Rugs; Ceramics; Clocks, Watches and Barometers; Embroidery and Needlework; Furniture; Glass; Jewellery; Metalwork; Musical Instruments; Silver; Toys and Automata. Each section has its own table of contents, glossary and special section on care and repair, bibliography and list of collections in Britain and the United States.

29   **The Random House Encyclopedia of Antiques**. New York, Random, 1973. 302p. illus. ISBN 0394488113.

British ed.: *Collins Encyclopedia of Antiques* (London, Collins, 1973). Comprehensive encyclopedia of some 5,000 entries covering the applied and decorative arts from the fifteenth century to circa 1875. Emphasis is on objects accessible to the average collector.

Dictionary of ceramic marks, pp. 385-87, silver date marks, pp. 388-90. Classified bibliography of works in English, pp. 391-98. Companion volume (75) covers the period from 1875 to 1939.

30   Savage, George. **Dictionary of Antiques**. 2nd ed. New York, Mayflower Books, 1978. 534p. illus. ISBN. 0831700114.

Comprehensive dictionary designed for the collector and dealer. Entries cover objects, materials, techniques, styles, schools, major artists and artisans from the Renaissance to the nineteenth century. Intended as a companion to the author's *Dictionary of 19th Century Antiques and Later (76)*. Select and classified bibliography of books, mostly in English, pp. 504-534.

31   Seling, Annemarie, ed. **Keysers Antiquitätenlexikon**. 3rd ed. Munich, Keyser, 1969. 328p. illus. LC 77-391175.

Comprehensive dictionary of the applied and decorative arts directed to the needs of the European collector. More than 2,000 entries cover styles, techniques, materials, objects and major artists and designers. Well illustrated. Appendix with outline history of style in applied arts as an aid to identification.

32   Seling, Helmut, ed. **Keysers Kunst-und Antiquitätenbuch**. Heidelberg and Munich, Keyser, 1967-70. 3v. illus. LC 75-274937.

Comprehensive handbook of the applied and decorative arts for collectors. First volume covers books, paintings and frames, boxes and miniatures, prints, faience, glass, tapestries, furniture, Oriental carpets, Far Eastern decorative arts, sculpture, porcelain, silver and pewter. Second volume covers coins, medals, arms and armor, drawings, jewelry, clocks and watches, scientific instruments, and modern art. Third volume covers folk furniture, folk painting, folk prints, autographs, old maps, bookbindings, bronzes, copper and brass, old toys, and ancient, pre-Columbian, African and Oceanic applied arts. Well illustrated. Chapters are written by various German specialists.

33   Stoutenburgh, John Leeds. **Dictionary of Arts and Crafts**. New York, Philosophical Library, 1956. 259p. LC 56-13756.

Dictionary of technical terms related to the applied arts and to various crafts.

34   Wills, Geoffrey. **A Concise Encyclopedia of Antiques**. New York, Van Nostrand Reinhold, 1976. 304p. illus. index. ISBN 0442294883.

Popular dictionary of terms used in the field of antique collecting with particular attention given to British antiques. Part one is a concise survey of the history of applied and decorative arts in Britain and America from 1500 to 1890. Part two is divided into separate dictionaries by media: furniture, pottery and porcelain, glass, silver, and copper, bronze, pewter and other metals. Broad selection of illustrations: color plates of historic interiors, black and white plates of individual pieces and reproductions of contemporary designs. No bibliography.

GENERAL HISTORIES AND HANDBOOKS

35   Ball, Victoria K. **Architecture and Interior Design: Europe and America from the Colonial Era to Today**. New York, Wiley, 1980. 442p. illus. index. ISBN 0471051616.

History of interior design from the eighteenth century to the present with emphasis on developments in America. Designed as a textbook. Bibliographical notes and classified bibliography of basic books and articles in English, pp. 399-409.

36   Bossert, Helmuth T. **Geschichte des Kunstgewerbes aller Zeiten und Volker...** Berlin, Wasmuth, 1928-35. 6v. illus. index. LC 30-18231.

The most comprehensive history of the applied and decorative arts produced to date. The work of a team of eminent German scholars. Extraordinary number and variety of illustrations including plates of museum pieces, drawings of techniques and processes, reproductions of historic interiors and many watercolor renderings of pieces. Contents: Band I: H. Kühn, Kunstgewerbe der Eiszeit; A. van Scheltema, Das alteuropäische Kunstgewerbe der jüngeren Stein- Bronze- und vorrömischen Eisenzeit; H. Kühn, Das Kunstgewerbe der Völkerwanderunszeit; G. Boroffka, Kunstgewerbe der Skythen; P. Bosch-Gimpera, Das spanisch-portugiesische Kunstgewerbe vom Neolithikum bis zur Römerzeit; E. Baumgärtel, Das prähistorische Kunstgewerbe Nordakfrikas; F. Matz, Das Kunstgewerbe Alt-Italiens; H. Bossert, Das Kunstgewerbe des ägäischen Kulturkreises; P. Hambruch, Das Kunstgewerbe in Australien, in der Südsee und Indonesien; H. Meinhard, Das Kunstgewerbe der niederen Völker Vorder- und Hinterindien. Band II: A. Byhan and E. Krohn, Das Kunstgewerbe der Völker Nord-, Mittel und Vorderasiens; H. Baumann, Afrikanisches Kunstgewerbe; E. Baumgärtel, Kunstgewerbe auf den Kanarischen Inseln; W. Krickeberg, Das Kunstgewerbe der Eskimo und Nordamerikanischen Indianer; F. Krause, Das Kunstgewerbe der Naturvölker Südamerikas; H. Doering, Altperuanisches Kunstgewerbe; H. Doering, Das Kunstgewerbe der alten Kulturvölker Nordwestargentiniens, Ecuadors und Columbiens; F. Röck,

Kunstgewerbe von Mexiko, Mittelamerika und Westindien. Band II: H. Bossert, Das prähistorische Kunstgewerbe Vorder- und Hinterindeins, Chinas, Japans, und Koreas; M. Feddersen, Das Kunstgewerbe Ostasiens; E.& R. Waldschmidt, Das Kunstgewerbe Süd- und Hochasiens; E. Unger, Das Kunstgewerbe des Alten Orients. Band IV: W. von Jenny, Die Übergangszone zwischen Asien und Europa; H. Findeisen, Kunstgewerbe nordasiastischer Grenzlande; W. Wolf, Das ägyptische Kunstgewerbe; V. Müller, Das phönizische Kunstgewerbe, Das palästinensische Kunstgewerbe, Das karthagische Kunstgewerbe, Phönizisches Kunstgewerbe in Spanien; A. Ippel, Das griechische Kunstgewerbe; F. Matz, Das Kunstgewerbe der römischen Kaiserzeit; H. Bossert, Das altarabische und altabessinische Kunstgewerbe; H. Glück, Islamisches Kunstgewerbe; E. Kühnel, Der maurische Westen. Band V: A. Mahr, Das irische Kunstgewerbe; W. F. Volbach, Das christliche Kunstgewerbe der Spätantike und des frühen Mittelalters im Mittelmeergebiet; W. Zaloziecky, Das byzantinische Kunstgewerbe in der mittelalterlichen und spätmittelalterlichen Periode; P. Metz, Das Kunstgewerbe von der Karolingerzeit bis zum Beginn der Gotik; H. Kohlhaussen, Gotisches Kunstgewerbe. Band VI: E. W. Braun, Das Kunstgewerbe der Renaissance; F. Hepner, Barock und Rokoko; W. Holzhausen, Das Kunstgewerbe des Klassizismus im 18. und 19. Jahrhundert; T. Riewerts, Die Entwicklung des Kunstgewerbes seit der Mitte des 19. Jahrhunderts; H. Bossert, Volkskunst in Europa. Table of contents of the entire set is at the end of Band VI. Bibliographies are given at the end of each chapter or section. Although out of date in details, this work has never been equaled in the breadth of it scope—it gives unusual weight to the applied and decorative arts of the non-Western world—and many chapters are deeply insightful distillations by scholars who were founders in their fields, i.e., F. Matz, M. Feddersen, W. von Jenny, W. Wolf, H.Glück, A. Mahr, W. F. Volbach, W. Zaloziecky and H. Kohlhaussen.

37   Bucher, Bruno, ed. **Geschichte der technischen Künsten**. Stuttgart, Spemann, 1875-93. 3v. illus. index. LC 10-1939.
       Old, standard history of the applied and decorative arts throughout the world from antiquity to the nineteenth century. Collaborative work by a team of leading German scholars. Contents: Erster Band: I, Email von B. Bucher; II, Glasmalerei von B. Bucher; III, Mosaic von B. Bucher; IV, Lackmalerei von B. Bucher;V, Miniatur von B. Bucher; VI, Glyptik von H. Rollett; VII, Formschneidekunst von F. Lippmann und B. Bucher. Zweiter Band: VIII, Kupferstich von B. Bucher; IX, Goldschmiedekunst von A. Ilg und B. Bucher. Dritter Band: X, Kunstgewerbliche Eisenarbeiten von J. Stockbauer; XI, Bronze, Kupfer, Zinn von B. Bucher; XII, Der Bucheinband von F. Luthmer; XIII, Lederwerk von B. Bucher; XIV, Die Möbel von J. Stockbauer; XV, Glas von B. Bucher; XVI, Textilkunst von A. Riegl; XVII, Keramik von B. Bucher. Bibliographical footnotes.

38   Drury, Elizabeth, ed. **Antiques: Traditional Techniques of the Master Craftsmen: Furniture, Glass, Ceramics, Gold, Silver and Much More**. New York, Doubleday, 1986. 224p. illus. index. ISBN 0385231288.
       Comprehensive history of the techniques and materials used in woodwork, glass, ceramics, and metalwork in the West from antiquity to the early twentieth century. Illustrated with many representative pieces and by drawings demonstrating the various techniques and views of past practices. The vast majority of pieces illustrated are in British museums. Bibliography of books in English, p. 218. In spite of its British bias this a very useful work of synthesis.

39   Lehnert, Gustav, et al., eds. **Illustrierte Geschichte des Kunstgewerbes**. Berlin, Oldenbourg, n.d. 2v. illus. index. LC 13-3249.
       Scholarly, comprehensive history of the applied arts written by a team of German experts. Volume one covers Western ceramics, bronze, gold and silver, terra cotta, engraved gems, glass, wood, mosaic, and stained glass from ancient times through the Renaissance. Volume two covers the same arts to the early twentieth century and the applied and decorative arts of Islam and the

Far East. Illustrated with museum pieces. Comprehensive bibliography, v. 2, pp. 795-817, of books and periodical articles in all languages is classified by chapters.

40   Lucie-Smith, Edward. **The Story of Craft. The Craftsman's Role in Society**. Ithaca, N.Y., Cornell Univ. Press, 1981. 292p. illus. index. ISBN 0801414288.

Survey history of the applied and decorative arts worldwide from earliest times to the present. Emphasis is on the position of the craftsman in society, the technical and economic aspects of the skilled and artistic crafts. Many valuable illustrations of workplaces, tools and technical applications. Contents: 1, What Is Craft?; 2, The Beginnings; 3, The Ancient World; 4, The Eastern World; 5, The Islamic World; 6, The European Middle Ages; 7, Renaissance Attitudes; 8, Craft against Art; 9, The Industrial Revolution; 10, The Decline of Craft; 11, The British Arts and Crafts Movement; 12, The Arts and Crafts Movement in America; 13, Art Nouveau and Jugendstil; 14, Art Deco versus the Bauhaus; 15, The Survival of Craft; 16, Craft Today. Bibliography of basic books in English, pp. 282-84.

41   Marangoni, Guido, and Alberto Clementi. **Storia dell'arredamento**. 2d ed. Milan, Societa Editrice Libraria, 1952. 3v. illus.

Comprehensive history of the applied and decorative arts in Western Europe and the United States from antiquity to 1950 with emphasis on the stylistic development of interior decoration. Volume one covers the period from antiquity to 1500, volume two the period from 1500 to 1850, and volume three the period 1850 to 1950. Particularly useful for the numerous illustrations of contemporary interiors. Brief bibliography at the end of volume three.

42   McCorquodale, Charles. **History of the Interior**. New York, Paris, The Vendome Press, 1983. 224p. illus. index. ISBN 0865650322.

British edition: *The History of Interior Decoration* (Oxford, Phaidon, 1983). History of the permanent fixtures of domestic interiors from antiquity to 1980. Many illustrations of interiors, most without furnishings. Contents: 1, The Classical World: Greece and Rome; 2, Byzantium and the Middle Ages; 3, Renaissance and Mannerism; 4, The Age of the Baroque; 5, Europe and the Rococo, 1700-1750; 6, Neo-classicism; 7, The Age of Revivals; 8, Arts and Crafts; 9, The Twentieth Century. Glossary, bibliography of books in all languages, pp. 221-22.

43   Morant, Henry de. **Histoire des arts décoratifs, des origines a nos jours**. Paris, Hachette, 1970. 574p. illus. index. LC 70-575081.

Comprehensive survey of the applied and decorative arts from prehistoric times to 1970. Last Chapter: Le Design et les tendances actuelles is written by Gérald Gassiot-Talabot and is a critical essay on European design since the Second World War. The non-Western world is divided into areas and countries, the West into periods, and each chapter is subdivided by media. The text is factual and emphasis is placed on the evolution of styles. Biographical dictionary of the artists mentioned in the text, list of museums with important collections of the applied and decorative arts, and comprehensive, classified bibliography, pp. 525-39, lists books in all languages.

44   Praz, Mario. **An Illustrated History of Furnishings from the Renaissance to the 20th Century**. New York, Braziller, 1964. 396p. illus. index. Reprint: New York, Braziller, 1982. LC 81-85473.

Erudite and richly evocative history of the applied and decorative arts as they are featured in interior design from antiquity to the beginning of the twentieth century. Illustrated with 400 plates of paintings and prints illustrating period interiors accompanied by long commentaries that are both descriptive and aesthetically critical. A leading Italian historian and critic of the applied arts, Praz writes from the belief that furnishings reveal more about the varying personalities of the occupants than do painting, sculpture, or even architecture. Extensive bibliographical references in the notes. A standard and classic work.

45   Thornton, Peter. **Authentic Decor: The Domestic Interior 1620-1920**. New York, Viking, 1984. 408p. illus. index. ISBN 067014229X.

Comprehensive history of interior decoration in Europe and America from 1620 to 1920. Richly illustrated with paintings and photographs showing historic interiors and with designs of interiors including ground plans and details of features and ornaments. The illustrations have detailed descriptive notes. Divided into sections of 50 years each with an introductory essay that sketches the overall development of interior decoration during the half century. Bibliographical references in the footnotes. One of the richest compendiums of illustrations of historic interiors with a highly informative and often insightful text.

ANCIENT APPLIED AND DECORATIVE ARTS

46   Kayser, Hans. **Ägyptisches Kunsthandwerk**. Braunschweig, Klinkhardt & Biermann, 1969. 354p. illus. index. LC 70-437760. (Bibliothek für Kunst- und Antiquitätenfreunde, Band XXVI).

Comprehensive and authoritative handbook of ancient Egyptian decorative arts directed to the collector. Includes 311 black-and-white illustrations. Contents: Ägyptisches Kunsthandwerk; Stein; Töpferton; Ägyptische Fayence; Glas; Metalle; Schmuck; Metallgeräte; Holz und Elfenbein; Flechterei und Weberei. Within each section the text is subdivided by periods. Comprehensive, classified bibliography, pp. 345-50.

See also A. Lucas, *Ancient Egyptian Materials and Industries* (ARCH 169).

47   La Baume, Peter. **Römisches Kunstgewerbe zwischen Christi Geburt und 400**. Braunschweig, Klinkhardt & Biermann, 1964. 330p. illus. index (Bibliothek für Kunst- und Antiquitätenfreunde, Band 18). Reprint, 1987. ISBN 3781402304.

Comprehensive collector's handbook of the applied and decorative arts of ancient Rome. Covers the period from the birth of Christ to circa A.D. 400. Arrangement is by type or class of object, e.g., drinking cups, bottles, tablets, boxes, lamps, statuettes, arms and armour, toys. Nearly 300 illustrations of objects of the type accessible to serious collectors. Selected bibliography, pp. 317-320.

48   Strong, Donald, and David Brown, eds. **Roman Crafts**. New York, New York Univ. Press, 1976. 256p. illus index. ISBN 0814778011.

Essays by various British scholars on the techniques and materials of ancient Roman applied and decorative arts including sculpture, painting and mosaic. Classified bibliographies of books and periodical articles given at the end of each essay. Well-illustrated with plates of objects in museums and private collections, and drawings showing the manipulation of the various materials. Contents: 1: Silver and Silversmithing by David Sherlock; 2: Bronze and Pewter by David Brown; 3: Enamelling by Sarnia Butcher; 4: Jewellery by Reynold Higgins; 5: Minting by David Sellwood; 6: Pottery by David Brown; 7: Pottery Lamps by D. M. Bailey; 8: Terracottas by Reynold Higgins; 9: Glass by Jennifer Price; 10: Ironmaking by Henry Cleere; 11: Blacksmithing by W. H. Manning; 12: Woodwork by Joan Liversidge; 13: Textiles by J. P. Wild; 14: Leatherwork by J. W. Waterer; 15: Marble Sculpture by Donald Strong; 16: Stuccowork by Roger Ling; 17: Wall Painting by Pamela Pratt; 18: Wall and Vault Mosaics by Frank Sear; 19: Floor Mosaics by David S. Neal.

49   Gusman, Pierre. **L'art décoratif de Rome de la fin de la république au IVe siecle.** Paris, Librarie centrale d'art et d'architecture, 1908. 3v. illus. LC 10-2595.

Corpus of plates with descriptive notes and bibliographical references. Covers ornaments on architecture and sculpture, furniture and jewelry.

MEDIEVAL APPLIED AND DECORATIVE ARTS

50   Labarte, Jules. **Handbook of the Arts of the Middle Ages and Renaissance as Applied to the Decoration of Furniture, Arms, Jewels, Etc.** London, John Murray, 1855. 443p. illus. LC 12-3219.

Translation of condensed version of the author's three-volume history. Important today as a source for nineteenth-century Neo-Gothicism, particularly in England. Contents: I, Sculpture; II, Painting and Caligraphy; III, Engraving (on metalwork); IV, Enamels; V, Damascene Work; VI, The Lapidary's Art; VII, The Goldsmith's Art; VIII, The Keramic Art; IX, Glass; X, The Armourer's Art; XI, The Locksmith's Art; XII, Clockwork; XIII, Ecclesiastical and Domestic Furniture; XIV, Oriental Art. Many of the references to documentary sources found in the French edition are included in this edition in the footnotes. Large number of woodcut illustrations. Bibliographical references in the footnotes.

51   Labarte, Jules. **Histoire des arts industriels au moyen age et a l'époque de la renaissance.** Paris, A. Morel, 1872-75. 3v. illus. LC 12-3218R26.

Important, early history of the applied and decorative arts in western Europe from the beginning of the Middle Ages to the sixteenth century. Still valuable for the numerous references to inventories and other documentary sources. Includes manuscript illumination, mosaics and stained glass. Contents: Volume I: Sculpture, orfèvrerie. Volume II: Orfévrerie (l'époque ogivale, seizième siècle); Peinture (Ornamentation des manuscrits, peinture sur verre, mosaique, peinture en matières textiles). Volume III: Emaillerie, Damasqinerie, Art céramique, Verrerie, Art de l'armurier, Horologie, Mobil civil et religieux. Illustrated with engraved and color photo-graveur plates. Bibliographical references in the footnotes. Subject index to entire work in the third volume.

52   Vaboulis, Petros. **Byzantine Decorative Art.** Athens, Astir, 1977. 19p. (text), 184p. (plates).

Collection of plates of works, many in color, of Byzantine manuscript illumination, textiles, metalwork, enamels, and relief carving compiled by a contemporary Greek artist working in the traditional icon style. Many of the plates are free renditions of historical pieces. Brief bibliography at the end of the introductory essay by Kostas E. Tsiropouloos. Text in Greek and English.

RENAISSANCE AND BAROQUE APPLIED AND DECORATIVE ARTS

Bibliographies

53   De Winter, Patrick W. **European Decorative Arts 1400-1600: An Annotated Bibliography.** Boston, Hall, 1988. 543p. index. ISBN 081618612X.

Comprehensive, classified and annotated bibliography of over 2,000 books; exhibition, auction, and museum catalogs; and periodical articles on all aspects of the history of the decorative arts in Western Europe from 1400 to 1600. The annotations make specific reference to the coverage of the applied and decorative arts between 1400 and 1600 in works of a more general scope. The listings of periodical literature in De Winter's bibliography is a valuable supplement to titles listed in A&D under Renaissance in the general sections and under the specific media.

General Histories and Handbooks

54   Aprá. Nietta. **The Louis Styles: Louis XIV, Louis XV, Louis XVI.** London, Orbis, 1972. 64p. illus. ISBN 0856131253.

Pictorial survey of the applied and decorative arts of eighteenth-century Europe with emphasis on French furniture.

55   Thornton, Peter. **Seventeenth Century Interior Decoration in England, France and Holland.** New Haven, London, Yale Univ. Press, 1978. 427p. illus. index. ISBN 0300021933.

In the series: "Studies in British Art"; published for the Paul Mellon Centre for Studies in British Art, Yale University. Important, comprehensive history of interior decoration and furnishings in England, France and Holland during the seventeenth century. Well-illustrated with paintings and prints of interiors accompanied by descriptive captions. Contents: I, France and Aristocratic Fashion; II, The Spread of the French Ideal; III, The Architectural Framework; IV, The Upholster's Task; V, The Upholsterer's Materials; VI, The Upholsterer's Furnishings; VII, Beds, Cloths of Estate and Couches; VIII, Upholstered Seat-furniture; IX, Tables and Cup-boards; X, Other Furniture and Decorative Features; XI, Lighting; XII, Specific Rooms and Their Decoration. Extensive bibliographical references in the notes. A standard work and a model for subsequent handbook/histories of interior decoration.

See also the museum catalogs: *The Irwin Untermeyer Collection,* The Metropolitan Museum of Art, New York (Cambridge, Ma., Harvard Univ. Press, 1956-1969. 6v. illus.), *The Wrightsman Collection,* Metropolitan Museum of Art, New York (Greenwich, Conn., New York Graphics Society, 1960-1970. 5v. illus.). Note: The individual volumes of these important catalogs are listed separately under their appropriate headings in this bibliography. See index for complete listings.

MODERN APPLIED AND DECORATIVE ARTS (19th and 20th Centuries)

General Histories and Handbooks

56   Anscombe, Isabelle. **A Woman's Touch: Women in Design from 1860 to the Present Day.** New York, Viking Penguin, 1984. 216p. illus. index. ISBN 0670778257.

Survey history of the participation of women in the development of design in western Europe and America from 1860 to 1980. Concentrates on the house and its furnishings. Contents: 1, The Blessed Damozel; 2, Not a Lady Among Us; 3, Two Laughing Comely Girls; 4, The Heyday of Decorators; 5, From Icon to Machine; 6, Something Colourful, Something Joyful; 7, Equipment and Couture; 8, The Rational Woman; 9, The Simple Life; 10, Art and Industry; 11, The Return to Formality. Useful chronology of world events, decorative arts in general, and the decorative arts and women. List of women's publications in the decorative arts, select bibliography, pp. 207-210, and bibliographical footnotes.

57   Collins, Michael. **Towards Post-Modernism: Decorative Arts and Design since 1851.** Boston, Little, Brown, 1988. 176p. illus. index. ISBN 0821216872.

Survey history of European and American design from 1851 to the early 1980s. Contents: 1, Ornament with Everything: The Nineteenth-century Eclectics; 2, The Whiplash: Art Nouveau; 3, Form without Ornament: The Modern Style; 4, Free Flow: The 1950s; 5, Pop and Liquorice Allsorts: The 1960s to Post-Modernism. Dictionary with brief biographies of the major personalities. Select bibliography, p. 171.

58   Conway, Hazel, ed. **Design History: a Student Handbook**. London, Boston, Allen & Unwin, 1987. 226p. illus. index. ISBN 0047090197.
      Contents: Design History Basics by Hazel Conway; The Study of Dress and Textiles by Josephine Miller; Ceramic History by Jonathan Woodham; Furniture History by Pat Kirkham; Interior Design by Rowan Roenisch and Hazel Conway; Industrial Design by John Heskett; Graphic Design History by Jeremy Aynsley; Environmental Design by Hazel Conway. Bibliography, pp. 181-192.

59   Ferebee, Ann. **A History of Design from the Victorain Era to the Present; a Survey of the Modern Style in Architecture, Interior Design, Industrial Design, Graphic Design, and Photography**. New York, Van Nostrand Reinhold, 1970. 128p. illus. LC 68-16033.
      Illustrated survey of interior, industrial and graphic design and photography from the mid-nineteenth century to the present in western Europe and America. Large collection of illustrations featuring groups of objects, e.g., telephones, chairs, andposters, arranged in chronological order.

60   Garner, Philippe, ed. **The Encyclopedia of Decorative Arts, 1890-1940**. New York, Van Nostrand, 1978. 320p. illus. ISBN 0442225776.
      Well-illustrated survey of the applied and decorative arts in Europe and the United States from 1890 to 1940. Work of a team of British experts. Contents: I, Styles and Influences in the Decorative Arts, 1890-1940: Art Nouveau, Art Deco, Modernism, Surrealism and Neo-Baroque, Revivalism, Industrial Design; II, Designs and Designers 1890-1940: France, United Kingdom, United States, Germany and Austria, Belgium, The Netherlands, Scandinavia, Italy and Spain, Eastern Europe; III, The Background to the Decorative Arts 1890-1940: The Great Exhibitions, Photography and the Decorative Arts, Literature and the Decorative Arts. Glossary, list of major craftsmen and designers, bibliography of basic books and periodical articles, pp. 310-12.

61   Sparke, Penny. **Design in Context**. London, Bloomsbury, 1987. 256p. illus. ISBN 07475-0072X.
      Pictorial survey of design in the West from 1750 to 1985 with emphasis on the relationship between industry and culture. Excellent illustrations of the major examples of industrial design and the contexts in which they were made and used. Classified bibliography of books in English, p. 255.

Nineteenth Century

62   Apra, Nietta. **Empire Style**. New York, World, 1973. 64p. illus. ISBN 0529050188.
      Survey of the applied and decorative arts of Europe between 1804 and 1815 with emphasis on furniture. Bibliography of basic works in all languages, p. 14.

63   Bourgeois, Emile. **Le style empire, ses origines et ses caractères**. Paris, Laurens, 1930. 131p. illus. index.
      History of neo-classical decorative art from its origins in Tuscan art of the eighteenth century through the second decade of the nineteenth century with emphasis on French interior decoration and furniture. Bibliographical footnotes.

64   Gere, Charlotte. **Nineteenth-century Decoration: the Art of the Interior**. New York, Abrams, 1989. 409p. illus. index. ISBN 0810913828.
      Comprehensive, well-illustrated survey of interior design and decoration in Europe and America during the nineteenth century. Divided into two main parts; the first treats the interior of four classes of houses: town house, country house, conservatory, and cottage. The second part is a

history of interior decoration by 20-year subdivisions. Both parts feature excellent illustrations of interiors, both those preserved today and those represented in paintings, photographs and other works of art. Fully descriptive captions accompany the plates. Appendices with "The Working Library of a Nineteenth-century Architect and Designer," i.e., hypothetical list of books published during the nineteenth century and a dictionary with short biographies of major artists, designers and architects. Bibliography of basic works, pp. 402-403.

65   Groer, Léon de. **Decorative Arts in Europe 1790-1850**. New York, Rizzoli, 1986. 356p. illus. LC 85-42864.

Richly illustrated survey of the applied and decorative arts of Western Europe from 1790 to 1850 with emphasis on France. Contents: I: Imitation of the Antique; II: Interior Decoration and Furnishing; III: Neoclassical Furniture; IV: Neoclassical Furniture in the Rest of Europe: Influences and National Characteristics; V: Gothic, Renaissance, Louis XV and Louis XVI Revival Furniture; VI: Architects, Ornamentalists, Manufacturers and Furniture Makers; VII: Lights and Lighting; VIII: Bronzes, Pendulum Clocks and Decorative Vases; IX: Curtains, Wall Hangings, Wallpaper and Carpets. Classified bibliography of books in all languages, pp. 346-49.

66   Klein, Dan, and Margaret Bishop. **Decorative Art 1880-1980**. Oxford, Phaidon, 1986. 263p. illus. index. ISBN 0714880256.

Collector's handbook/history of European and American applied and decorative arts from the Arts and Crafts Movement to the 1980s. Illustrated with pieces sold at Christie's. Prices listed at the end.

67   Lichten, Frances. **Decorative Art of Victoria's Era**. New York, Scribner's, 1950. 274p. illus. index. LC 50-9758.

Popular history of English and American art of the Victorian era arranged by broad cultural classes, e.g., "World of Industry," and illustrated chiefly with engravings from contemporary books and pamphlets. Bibliography, pp. 265-70, is chiefly a list of Victorian illustrated books on the decorative arts.

68   Mackay, James A. **Turn-of-the-Century Antiques: An Encyclopedia**. New York, Dutton, 1974. 320p. illus. ISBN 0525495045.

Popular, collector's dictionary of European and American applied and decorative arts from 1890 to 1910. Entries cover: artist and designers, styles and schools, techniques, media and objects. Although the emphasis is on Art Nouveau, there is much information on and illustrations of pieces in late Victorian styles. Bibliography, pp. 314-19, is a comprehensive, classified list of books in all languages.

69   Meurer, Bernd. **Industrielle Asthetik: zur Geschichte und Theorie der Gestaltung**. Giessen, Anabas, 1983. 264p. illus. index. (Werkbund-Archiv, Band 9) ISBN 3870380837.

Scholarly history of design with emphasis on theory and developments in the German-speaking countries. Contents: Industrialisierung des Entwerfens: Handwerk: Ursprung des Entwerfens; Entwurfstätigkeit innerhalb der Manufaktur; Industrie und Propaganda; Industrie-Kultur: Klassizistischer Entwurfswille und höfische Kultur; Historismus; Jugendstil; Industrielle Gestaltung: Zum Beispiel Eisenbahn, Ballon Frame, Modularkoordination und Chicago School; Sachlichkeit und Wilhelminismus—Industriekultur al gesellschaftliches Projek; Kulturelle Bewegungen nach dem Ersten Weltkrieg; Alltagskultur im deutschen Faschismus; Industrielle Konsumismus; Schönheit heute; Exkurs 1: Ausbildung und Berufsfeld der Designer; Exkurs 2: Aus dem Alltag der Designer. Bibliographical footnotes and classified bibliography of books and periodical articles in all languages, pp. 249-57.

70   Mundt, Barbara. **Historismus: Kunstgewerbe zwischen Biedermeier und Jugendstil.** Munich, Keyser, 1981. 392p. illus. index. ISBN 3874051412.

Important history/handbook of the applied and decorative arts in Europe from the end of Neoclassicism to the beginning of Art Nouveau. Emphasis is on the history of style and the interests of collectors. Contents: Einleitung: Historische Grundlagen, Kulturgeschichte, Die industrielle Revolution, Handwerker-Entwerfer; Die Kunstgewerbeform, Die Weltausstellungen; Stilenwicklung im Historismus: Später Klassizismus, Neogotik, Zweites Rokoko, Stilpluralismus um 1850, Neurenaissance, Neubarock und drittes Rokoko, Orienteinfluss, Gegenbewegungen: Naturalismus, Gegenbewegungen: Form ohne Ornament; Die Kunst im Hause: Inneneinrichtung; Sammelgebiete: Möbel, Textil, Steingut, Steinzeug, Fayence, Prozellan, Glas, Gold- und Silberschmiedekunst, Schmuck, Mode; Hinweise für Sammler. Comprehensive bibliography of books and periodical articles in all languages, pp. 377-84. Not only a valuable collector's handbook but also an excellent history of the historicism in nineteenth-century European art.

71   Naylor, Gillian. **The Arts and Crafts Movement: A Study of Its Sources, Ideals, and Influence on Design Theory.** Cambridge, Mass., M.I.T. Press, 1971. 208p. illus. index. Reprinted, 1980. ISBN 026264018X.

Scholarly study of the Arts and Crafts Movement in Britain and America with emphasis on its theoretical basis. Contents: 1, The Sources: Pugin, The 1835 Committee, Henry Cole and the Summerly Venture, The Great Exhibition; 2, Ruskin's 'New Road': The True Functions of the Workman, Involvement, The St. George's Guild; 3, Theory into Practice: William Morris: The Pre-Raphaelites and Design, The Formation of the Firm, Definitions of the Design Process, The Democracy of Art, The Kelmscott Press; 4, Guilds and Guildsmen: Mackmurdo and the Century Guild; The Art-Workers' Guild; The Arts and Crafts Exhibition Society, Walter Crane; 5, Guildsmen and Industry: Pottery, Furniture, Glass and Textiles; Silver and Metalwork, The National Association for the Advancement of Art and Its Application to Industry; 6, Ashbee and the Craft of the Machine: The Guild of Handicraft at Chipping Campden, Frank Lloyd Wright; 7, Towards an Efficiency Style: Lethaby and the Central School; European Interpretations; 8, Consolidation or Eclipse. Select bibliography, pp. 195-198, and specialized bibliography in the notes.

See also Naylor, Gillian, et al. *The Encyclopedia of Arts and Crafts: The International Arts Movement, 1850-1920*(New York, Dutton, 1989. 192p. illus. ISBN 05252448048).

See also the exhibition catalog: *"The Art That Is Life": The Arts & Crafts Movement in America, 1875-1920* by W. Kaplan, et al., (Boston, New York Graphics Society, 1986. 424p. illus. ISBN 087846278).

72   Norbury, John. **The World of Victoriana: Illustrating the Progress of Furniture and Decorative Arts in Britain and America, 1837-1901.** London, Hamlyn, 1972. 128p. illus. index. ISBN 0600391213.

Popular survey of American and British decorative arts of the Victorian era. Covers furniture, interior decoration, glass, ceramics and textiles. Brief bibliography of basic books.

73   **The Random House Collector's Encyclopedia: Victoriana to Art Deco.** New York, Random House, 1974. 302p. illus. LC 74-5380.

Popular dictionary covering western European and American decorative arts from the middle of the nineteenth century to the 1930s. Covers artists, designers, crafts, styles, materials, techniques, objects, major works and movements. Illustrated with objects of the type accessible to the average collector. Bibliography, pp. 297-302, is arranged according to the entries and lists chiefly books in English.

74   Savage, George. **Dictionary of 19th Century Antiques and Later Objets d'Art**. London, Barrie & Jenkins, 1978. 401p. illus. ISBN 0214202550.

Comprehensive dictionary covering the applied and decorative arts of the nineteenth and early twentieth centuries. Follows the format and complements the author's: *Dictionary of Antiques* (30). Bibliography, pp. 389-401.

75   Wichmann, Siegfried. **Jugendstil Art Nouveau: Floral and Functional Forms**. Boston, Little, Brown, 1984. 238p. illus. index. ISBN 0821216074.

History of applied and decorative arts in the Art Nouveau style in Europe and America with emphasis on the Jugendstil in German-speaking countries and on origins and influence of plant forms in Art Nouveau decoration. Contents: Plants and Their Movements—an Art Nouveau Theme; The Lamp as Sculpture and the Lamp as Flower; Geological and Submarine Motifs and Themes; Form and Movement in Glass; Plant and Floral Models and the Abstract Play of Line; Bentwood Furniture: Form and Function; The Aesthetics of the Machine; Cube and Square: A Functional Design Unit. Bibliography of basic works, pp. 228-230.

76   Woodhouse, Charles P. **The Victoriana Collector's Handbook**. New York, St. Martin's, 1970. 237p. illus. index. LC 70-156345.

Popular collector's handbook of the decorative arts of the Victorian era with emphasis on England. Covers ceramics, furniture, glass, jewelry and metalwork with chapters on collecting and Victorian artists and craftsmen. Appendix with assay marks.

See also Wood, Violet. *Victoriana: A Collector's Guide* (London, Bell, 1960. 175p. illus. index).

Twentieth Century

77   Attfield, Judy, and Pat Kirkham. **A View from the Interior: Feminism, Women and Design**. London, Women's Press, 1989. 246p. illus. index. ISBN 0704341107.

Collected essays on various aspects of feminism in European and American design in the twentieth century. Contents: Part One. Images of Difference: 1, Objectifying Gender: The Stiletto Heel by Lee Wright; 2, Representations of Women and Race in the Lancashire Cotton Trade by Z. Munby; 3, Tarting Up Men: Menswear and Gender Dynamics by J. Ash; 4, From Alcatraz to the OK Corral: Images of Class and Gender by J. Boys. Part Two. Women as Designers: 5, Women Textile Designers in the 1920s and the 1930s: Marion Dorn, a Case Study by C. Boydell; 6, Pottery Women: A Comparative Study of Susan Vera Cooper and Millicent Jane Taplin by C. Buckley; 7, Women Architects by L. Walker. Part Three. Women in Design Production: 8, 'If You Have No Sons': Furniture-making in Britain by P. Kirkham; 9, Powerful Women: Electricity in the Home, 1919-40 by S. Worden; 10, Sexual Division of Labour in the Arts and Crafts Movement by A. Callen; 11, The Arts and Crafts Alternative by L. Walker; 12, The Inter-war Handicrafts Revival by P. Kirkham. Part Four. A Place of Their Own: 13, A View from the Interior by A. Ravetz; 14, The Designer Housewife in the 1950s by A. Partington; 15, Inside Pram Town: A Case Study of Harlow House Interiors, 1951-61 by J. Attfield; Appendix: Women at the Archive of Art and Design by M. Sweet. Bibliography in the notes.

78   Bayley, Stephen, et al. **Twentieth-century Style and Design**. New York, Van Nostrand, 1986. 320p. illus. index. ISBN 0442230087.

Well-illustrated history of design including architecture, urban design, decorative arts and industrial design in Europe and America from 1900 to 1985. Brief biographies of major personalities with references to their writings. Select bibliography, pp. 306-307.

79   Battersby, Martin. **The Decorative Twenties**. Revised and edited by Philippe Garner. New York, Watson-Guptill, 1988. 224p. illus. index. ISBN 0823012735.

First published in 1969 (New York, Walker). Pictorial survey of the applied and decorative arts of Europe and America during the 1920s. Contents: Martin Battersby: A Biography by Philippe Garner; Part I. The Decorative Arts in France: 1, The Sources of Art Deco, 2, The Art Deco Designers, 3, Decorative Painting, 4, The New Modernism, 5, Glass and Ceramics, 6, Book Production and Posters, 7, Textiles, Wallpapers and Carpets, 8, Fashion. Part II. The Decorative Arts in England and America: 9, Interior Decoration, 10, Associations, Societies and Exhibitions, 11, Furniture, 12, Glass and Ceramics; 14, Posters, 15, Textiles and Wallpapers. Updated bibliography, pp. 221-222.

80   Battersby, Martin. **The Decorative Thirties**. Revised and edited by Philippe Garner. New York, Watson-Guptill, 1988. 224p. illus. index. ISBN 0823012743.
First published in 1971 (New York, Walker). Pictorial survey of the applied and decorative arts in Europe and America during the 1930s with emphasis on interior decoration. Contents: Martin Battersby: The Literature by Philippe Garner; 1, The Background, 2, The Depression and Its Impact on the Decorative Arts; 3, Decorative Style Interiors; 4, Art and Industry; 5, Interior Furnishing; 6, Decorative Painters; 7, The Surrealist Influence on Decoration; 8, Period Revivalism; 9, Fashion; 10, Hollywood Style. Updated bibliography, pp. 220-221.

81   Bayer, Patricia. **Art Deco Interiors. Decoration and Design Classics of the 1920s and 1930s**. Boston, Little, Brown, 1990. 224p. illus. index. ISBN 0821218131.
Well-illustrated survey of European and American interiors in the Art Deco style. Illustrations include original designs, contemporary photographs of Art Deco interiors and photographs of restored Art Deco interiors. Contents: 1, The Art Deco Interior; 2, Showcase Interiors; 3, French Interiors; 4, Streamline Moderne; 5, Art Deco in Public Places; 6, The Art Deco Interior Revived. List of museums. Comprehensive, classified bibliography, pp. 216-18.

82   Borsi, Franco. **The Monumental Era: European Architecture and Design 1929-1939**. New York, Rizzoli, 1987. 207p. illus. index. ISBN 084780805X.
Richly illustrated survey of architecture and interior design in Europe during the decade 1929-1939, the so-called Modern Style. Contents: 'Ecupalinos ou l'architecte'; Architecture and Revolution: Fascist Italy-Nazi Germany-Communist Russia; The Monumental Order: Classicism-Gothic-Cubism, Volumes-Surfaces-Proportion; National Spirit: England-Germany and Austria-Italy, Belgium-Holland-Scandinavia-France; Materials; Conclusion-Perspectives. Bibliographical references in the notes; bibliography, pp. 201-202, is a list with introduction of books in all languages.

83   Brunhammer, Yvonne. **The Art Deco Style**. New York, St. Martin's Press, 1984. 175p. illus. index. ISBN 0312052243.
Illustrated survey of Art Deco architecture, interior design, and applied arts. Contents: The Origins of Art Deco; Art Deco in France; The 1925 Exhibition; Furniture; Floor and Wall Decoration; The Applied Arts: Metalwork, Dinanderie and Enamel, Silverwork, Door Furniture, Clocks, Ceramics, Glass, Sculpture, Jewellery, Bookbinding, Lighting.

84   Collins, Michael, and Andreas Papadakis. **Post-Modern Design**. New York, Rizzoli, 1989. 288p. illus. index. ISBN 0847811360.
Richly illustrated survey of post-modern design in interiors, furniture, metalwork, ceramics, and textiles. Contents: 1, The Origins of Post-Modernism; II, Post-Pop Design; III, Post-Modernism; IV, Post-Modern Design in America: Robert Venturi; V, Charles Jencks, Michael Graves, Robert Stern, Charles Moore, Stanley Tigerman, Symbolic Objects by Charles Jencks; VI, Deconstruction, Deconstructivism & Late-Modernism; VII, Paolo Portoghesi & Aldo Rossi. The Sympathy of Things by Paolo Portoghesi; VIII, Arata Isozaki & Hans Hollein; IX, Secondary

Post-Modernism Design; Conclusion; Post-Modernism and Consumer Design by Volker Fischer. Selected bibliography, p. 286.

85   Calloway, Stephen. **Twentieth-Century Decoration**. New York, Rizzoli, 1988. 408p. illus index. ISBN 0847808866.

Richly illustrated history of interior decoration in Europe and America during the twentieth century. Chronological arrangement with introductory essay for each period followed by illustrations of interiors from photographs, paintings, and designs for interiors with descriptive notes. Occasional bibliographical reference in notes to the introductory essays.

86   **Encyclopédie des arts décoratifs et industriels modernes au XXème siècle**. Paris, Office Central d'Éditions et de Librairies, 1927. 12v. illus. Reprint: New York, Garland, 1977. LC 77-3273r852.

Published following the famous Paris Exposition Internationale des Art Décoratifs of 1925 and as such is a major source for the Art Deco style. First volume is a history of modern art, architecture and decorative arts; second volume covers interior decoration divided into architecture, sculpture and painting; third volume covers decorative arts in stone, wood, metal, ceramic and glass; fourth volume covers furniture and associated interior fixtures; fifth volume covers accessories in marquetry, incrustation, lacquer, enamel, and bronzes and medals; sixth volume covers textiles; seventh volume covers the art of the book; eighth volume covers jewelry, musical instruments, sporting goods, automobiles, railway cars, boats etc.; ninth volume covers costumes and related assessories; tenth volume covers theatre, photography and film; eleventh volume covers city planning and landscape design; twelfth volume covers technical aspects of art in wood, stone, metal, etc.

87   Fehrman, Cherie, and Kenneth Fehrman. **Postwar Interior Design: 1945-1960**. New York, Van Nostrand Reinhold, 1987. 198p. illus. index. ISBN 0442226179.

History of European and American interior design from 1945 to 1960 with emphasis on high art furniture design. Contents: Part 1: Major Influences on Postwar Interior Design; Part 2: The Designers and Manufacturers: Charles Eames, Eero Saarinen, George Nelson, Harry Bertoia, Hans and Florence Knoll, Gilbert Rohde, Isamu Moguchi, Arne Jacobsen, Borge Mogensen, Hans J. Wegner, Russel J. Wright, The Italians, Supplemental Designers; Part 3: Materials and Methods of Construction; Part 4: The Furniture and Designs. Appendices with list of manufacturers and distributors and chronological charts. Bibliography of books in English, p. 194.

88   Fischer, Volcker, ed. **Design Heute. Maßstäbe: Formgebung zwischen Industrie und Kunst-Stück**. Munich, Prestel, 1988. 325p. illus. index. ISBN 3791308548.

Important pictorial survey of twentieth-century industrial design, chiefly in Europe, with five essays on various aspects of the interaction between design and industrial production. Contents: "Design Heute"; Leitbilder: Stühle und Lampe im 20. Jahrhundert; Formkonzepte der Gegenwart; High-Tech; Trans-High-Tech; Alchimia/Memphis; Postmoderne; Minimalismus; Archetypen; Dieter Rams & Stefan Wewerka; Holger Scheel; Neobarocke Maßstäbe by M. Thun; Micro-Architektur; Banal-Design; Maßstab, Rolex und Manhattan by V. Albus; Schrumpftechnik und Stilblüten by J. Gros. Includes 619 plates with descriptive notes. Bibliographical references in the notes.

89   McClinton, Katharine M. **Art Deco: A Guide for Collectors**. 1st rev. ed. New York, Potter, 1986. 278p. illus. index. ISBN 0517545993.

Popular collector's handbook of Art Deco furniture, silver, ceramics, glass, textiles, metalwork, jewelry and graphics. Illustrated with objects of the type accessible to the average collector and gives suggestions on where and how to buy. Bibliography of basic books and periodical articles.

See also Hillier, Bevis, *Art Deco of the 20s and 30s*, (New York, Schocken, 1985. 168p. illus. index. ISBN 0805207856).

90   Sempach, Hans J. **Style 1930: Elegance and Sophistication in Architecture, Design, Fashion, Graphics, and Photography**. New York, Universe Books, 1972. 175p. illus. ISBN 0876631537.

Introductory essay with collection of plates with descriptive notes. Brief biographies of major personalities. Emphasis is on European design of the early 1930s. No bibliography.

91   Sparke, Penny. **An Introduction to Design and Culture in the Twentieth Century**. Boston, Allen & Unwin, 1986. 269p. illus. index. ISBN 0047410142.

Survey history of twentieth-century design in Europe and America. Contents: Part One: Proto-Design, 1900-1917: 1, Mass Production and the Mass Market; 2, New Products for New Life Styles; 3, Theory and Design in the Twentieth Century; 4, Promoting Design. Part Two: Modern Design, 1918-1945: 5, Democracies and Dictatorships; 6, The Industrial Designer; 7, From Mass to Mass Style; 8, New Materials, New Forms. Part Three: Modern Design, from 1945 to the Present: 9, The Admass Society; 10; Educating Designers; 11, Design and the Company; 12, Anti-Design. Biographical dictionary of major personalities and good, general bibliography, pp. 237-255.

92   Tate, Allen, and C. Ray Smith. **Interior Design in the 20th Century**. New York, Harper & Row, 1986. 577p. illus. index. ISBN 0060465840.

History/handbook of interior design designed as a textbook with a comprehensive history of interior design in America from the industrial revolution to 1980 (Part 3). Suggestions for further reading at the end of each chapter.

AMERICAN APPLIED AND DECORATIVE ARTS (U.S. and Canada)

Bibliographies

93   Ames, Kenneth L., and Gerald W. R. Ward, eds. **Decorative Arts and Household Furnishings in America, 1650-1920: an Annotated Bibliography**. Winterthur, Del., Henry Francis du Pont Winterthur Museum; Charlottesville, Distributed by the University Press of Virginia, 1989. 392p. ISBN 0912724196.

Comprehensive, annotated bibliography of literature of the applied and decorative arts in the United States from 1650 to 1920. Focus is on the material culture of Euroamericans. The work of a team of specialists, each section has an introduction that sketches the state of research. Includes books, catalogs and periodical articles. Descriptive annotations. Contents: Introduction by K. L. Ames; References and Surveys by N. Thompson, K. L. Ames, and B. G. Garson; Architecture-Domestic Architecture by D. Schuyler; Furniture: American Furniture to 1820 by B. M. Ward and G. W. R. Ward; American Furniture, 1820-1920 by K. L. Ames; Metals: American Silver and Gold by B. M. Ward and G. W. R. Ward; Pewter and Britannia Metal by B. M. Ward; Brass, Copper, Iron, and Tin by D. A. Federsen; Ceramics and Glass: American Ceramics by E. P. Denker; Continental and Oriental Ceramics in America by E. Paul Denker; English Ceramics in America by G. L. Miller and A. S. Martin; American Glass by K. Nelson; Textiles: Floor Coverings by R. Roth, Needlework by S. B. Swan; Quilts by S. Roach-Lankford; Textiles by A. D. Hood; Timepieces—Clocks and Watches by T. S. Michie; Household Activities and Systems: Kitchen Artifacts and Housework by D. R. Braden; Plumbing, Heating, and Lighting by U. G. Dietz;

Artisans and Culture: Craftsmen by E. S. Cooke Jr.; The Arts and Crafts Movement in America by C. R. Robertson.

94   Ames, Kenneth L. "The Stuff of Everyday Life: American Decorative Arts and Household Furnishing," in: **Material Culture: A Research Guide,** edited by Thomas J. Schlereth. Lawrence, Kan., Univ. of Kansas Press, 1985. ISBN 0700602747.

Essay on the state of research in the applied and decorative arts of America that gives a good overview of the various foci of interest, e.g., the collecting orientation, the art orientation, orientations of history and theory, and a summary of the major contributions in the history of the various "genres," e.g., periods, styles, regions, materials and functions. Particularly thorough for studies on furniture.

95   Saint-Pierre, Louise. **Bibliographie québécoise de l'sartisanat et des métiers d'art, 1689-1985**. Quebec, Centre de Formation de de Consultations en Métier d'Art: Cégep de Limoilou, 1986. 205p. illus. index. ISBN 2920790013.

Comprehensive, classified and annotated bibliography of books, periodical articles, exhibition and museum catalogs on all aspects of the applied and decorative arts in French-speaking Canada. Emphasis is on the traditional arts of Quebec and includes the arts of Native American peoples. Covers publications between 1689 and 1984. In addition to the annotations, the entries are further described by the use of a numerical code. Contents: Generalites; Familles: Bois, Cuir et fourrure, Encre et colorant, Métaux précieux, Métal non précieux, Nouveaux matériaux, Pierre (béton et plâtre), Silicate, Textile, Autres matériaux, Design, Gestion-marketing; Ouvrages specialises: Catalogues d'exposition, Mémoires et thèses, Collections; Périodiques; Documents Audio-visuels; Bibliographies generales; 2iéme partie: Les Autochtones: Generalities, Familles; Ouvrages Specialises; Documents audio-visuels; Bibliographies generales. Thorough subject index.

96   Sokol, David M. **American Decorative Arts and Old World Influences: A Guide to Information Sources**. Detroit, Gale, 1980. 294p. index. (Art and Architecture Information Guide Series, v. 14). ISBN 0810314657.

Comprehensive, annotated bibliography of over 1,000 books and periodical articles on all aspects of the applied and decorative arts in the United States with emphasis on the literature since 1940.

See also B. Karpel, *Arts in America: A Bibliography*. Volume 1: *Art of the Native Americans, Architecture, Decorative Arts, Design, Sculpture, Art of the West*. (FA 209).

Indexes

97   **The Index of American Design**. Teaneck, N.J., Somerset House, 1980. Mircofiche in ten parts with printed *Consolidated Catalog to the Index of American Design*. ISBN 0914146947.

Color microfiche reproduction of over 15,000 renderings of all sorts of American applied and decorative arts including folk and popular arts assembled by the Federal Art Project and the Works Progress Administration in the 1930s. The collection is now part of the National Gallery of Art in Washington, D.C. Contents:

    Part 1, Textiles, Costume and Jewelry
    Part 2, The Art and Design of Utopian and Religious Communities
    Part 3, Architecture and Naive Art
    Part 4, Tools, Hardware, Firearms and Vehicles
    Part 5, Domestic Utensils
    Part 6, Furniture and Decorative Accessories
    Part 7, Wood Carving and Weathervanes
    Part 8, Ceramics and Glass

Part 9, Silver, Copper, Pewter and Toleware

Part 10, Toys and Musical Instruments

The entries in the catalog provide date of manufacture, name of the maker and original owner, place where it was made or where it came from, item's owner at the time the rendering was made, name of the artist of the rendering and the renderings accession number in the *Index of American Design*. An invaluable resource for research into the traditional applied and decorative arts of the United States. Selections from the *Index* are published in Christensen (101) and Hornung (104).

Dictionaries and Encyclopedias

98   Comstock, Helen, ed. **The Concise Encyclopedia of American Antiques**. New York, Hawthorn Books, n.d. 2v. illus. index. LC 58-5628.

Popular enyclopedia consisting of essays on the various media by experts in the antique collecting field. Good selection of plates. Each chapter concludes with a bibliography of basic books.

99   Drepperd, Carl W. **A Dictionary of American Antiques**. Garden City, N.Y., Doubleday, 1952. 404p. illus. LC 52-11623.

Comprehensive dictionary of American applied and decorative arts from early Colonial times to the nineteenth century. Directed to the collector, the entries cover styles, objects, ornament and major peronalities. General bibliography, pp. 398-404.

100   Phipps, Frances. **The Collector's Complete Dictionary of American Antiques**. Garden City, N.Y., Doubleday, 1974. 640p. illus. ISBN 0385033370.

Popular but comprehensive dictionary of terms relating to the collecting of American antiques from early Colonial times to the end of the nineteenth century. Brief history of the applied and decorative arts is followed by separate dictionaries under the following headings; Rooms— Their Placement and Use; Crafts, Trades, and Useful Professions; Weights and Measures; Terms Used by Joiners and Cabinetmakers; Woods and Their Preferred Uses; Paints, Dyes, Finishes, Varnishes; Cleaning, Polishing, and Repairing; Metals—Antique Formulae and Uses; Pottery, Porcelain and Minerals; Glass; Furnishings Made Here or Imported for Use (including Apparel, Armorial Bearings, Jewelry, and Textiles and Leather). Entries often contain short excerpts from earlier printed sources. This is an unusual and useful feature but these sources are given in very abbreviated fashion.

General Histories and Handbooks

101   Christensen, Erwin C. **The Index of American Design**. New York, Macmillan, 1950. 229p. illus. index. LC 50-10215.

Pictorial survey of American applied, popular and folk art consisting of some 400 illustrations recorded in the *Index of American Design* at the National Gallery of Art. Subject list, pp. 209-17, covers the entire collection, not solely those watercolors reproduced. Bibliography, pp. 219-21, lists basic books. This work has been reprinted in Hornung (104).

102   Cooper, Wendy. **In Praise of America: American Decorative Arts, 1650-1830; Forty Years of Discovery Since the 1929 Girl Scouts Loan Exhibition**. New York, Knopf, 1980. 280p. illus. index. ISBN 0394509943.

Important collection of essays published in association with an exhibition marking the fortieth anniversary of the Girl Scouts Loan Exhibition, which was a landmark in the appreciation of American applied and decorative arts. The essays concentrate on issues and new information since the 1929 exhibition. Contents: Introduction (with views of 1929 exhibition); 1, Search and

Re-Search: The Documented Object; 2, Form and Fabric: The Art of the Upholstered Object; 3, American Patronage: Special Commissions; 4, Craftsmen and Ornament: Economics in Fashion and Workmanship; 5, Regionalism: Old and New Approaches; 6, Design with a Difference: Production Outside of Major Style Centers; 7, The Classical Impulse: Early Nineteenth-Century Style in America. Bibliographical footnotes.

103   Garrett, Elisabeth D. **The Antiques Book of American Interiors: Colonial & Federal Styles.** New York, Crown, 1980. 158p. illus. index. ISBN 0517541726.
       Collected essays from *Antiques* magazine on historic interiors of the Colonial and Federal periods in The William Paca House, Annapolis, Jonathan Sayward House, York, Maine; Winterthur Museum, Wilmington, Delaware; Middleton Place, Charleston, South Carolina; historic houses in Salem, Massachusetts; The Lindens, Washington, D.C.; Harrison Gray Otis House, Boston; The Hys-Kiser House, Antioch, Tennessee; and the White House, Washington, D.C. Good color illustrations.

104   Hornung, Clarence P. **Treasury of American Design.** New York, Abrams, n.d. 2v. illus. index. LC 76-142742.
       Popular, pictorial survey of American "articles of daily use from Colonial times to the end of the nineteenth century." Grouped in broad classes—for example, objects associated with the sea, tavern, etc.—but also has chapters on specific classes like cigar store Indians. No bibliography.

105   Mayhew, Edgar de N., and Minor Myers. **A Documentary History of American Interiors: From the Colonial Era to 1915.** New York, Scribner's, 1980. 399p. illus. index. ISBN 06841-62938.
       History of interior decoration in America from the seventeenth century to 1912, particularly useful for the profusion of references to documentary sources—many recording prices—and the numerous illustrations from contemporary sources of historic interiors that supplement the material in Peterson (106) and Seale (107). Bibliographical footnotes and comprehensive, classified bibliography, pp. 389-392.

106   Peterson, Harold L. **American Interiors from Colonial Times to the Late Victorians: A Pictorial Source Book.** New York, Scribner's, 1971, 1978. u.p. 205 plates. LC 78-71679.
       First published under the title: *American at Home.* Valuable collection of views of interiors in America from 1659 to 1787 found in contemporary paintings, drawings, prints and photographs. Appendix of interiors of inns and taverns from the same period. Plates are accompanied by descriptive notes. No bibliography.

107   Seale, William. **The Tasteful Interlude: American Interiors through the Camera's Eye, 1860-1917.** 2d ed. Nashville, Tenn., American Association for State and Local History, 1981. 256p. illus. index. ISBN 091005049X.
       Valuable collection of plates taken from photographs of American interiors, mostly domestic, from 1860 to 1917. Notes describing the decorations and furnishings accompany the plates. Invaluable for the restorations of period rooms.

108   Stillinger, Elizabeth. **The Antiques Guide to Decorative Arts in America, 1600-1875.** New York, Dutton, 1972. 463p. illus. LC 77-158605.
       Popular collector's handbook covering furniture, ceramics, glass, metalwork and silver. Illustrated with types of pieces accessible to the average collector. Classified bibliography of basic books, pp. 459-63.

109   Winkler. Gail C., and Roger Moss. **Victorian Interior Decoration: American Interiors, 1830-1900.** New York, H. Holt, 1986. 257p. illus. index. ISBN 0030079896.

History of interior decoration in America from 1830 to 1900 with a valuable collection of views of interiors from contemporary works of art and photographs. Glossary of terms, select bibliography, pp. 241-245, and additional references in the notes.

See also the exibition catalog: *The American Craftsman and the European Tradition, 1620-1820*, F. J. Puig and M. Conforti, eds. (Minneapolis, Minn., Minneapolis Institute of Arts, 1989. 295p. illus. ISBN 0912964383).

Modern (19th and 20th Centuries)

110   Boris, Eileen. **Art and Labor: Ruskin, Morris, and the Craftsman Ideal in America.** Philadelphia, Temple Univ. Press, 1986. 261p. illus. index. ISBN 087722384X.

Study of the history of the spread and development of English ideals of the unity of art and craft in America during the nineteenth century. Contents: I, The English Example: John Ruskin, William Morris, and the Craftsman Ideal; 2, The Arts and Crafts Movement: Its English Origin and American Trends; 3, The Arts and Crafts Societies in America; 4, The Social Meaning of Design: The House Beautiful and the Craftsman Home; 5, Schooling Taste: Art and Manual Training in the Public Schools; 6, Women's Culture, Women's Crafts; 7, Women's Culture as Art and Philanthropy: The Revival of the Textile Arts; 8, "A Factory as It Might Be": Art Manufacturing and the New Feudalism; 9, The Communal Impulse: Back to the Land with Arts and Crafts.

111   Meikle, Jeffrey L. **Twentieth Century Limited: Industrial Design in America, 1925-1939.** Philadelphia, Temple Univ. Press, 1979. 249p. illus. index. ISBN 0877221588.

Scholarly history of American industrial design from 1925 to 1930 with emphasis on the work of Norman Bel Geddes, Raymond Loewy and Walter Dorwin Teague. Contents: 1, A Consumer Society and Its Discontents; 2, Machine Aesthetics; 3, The New Industrial Designers; 4, Selling Industrial Design; 5, Industrialized Design; 6, Everything from a Match to a City; 7, The Practical Ultimate; 8, From Depression to Expression; 9, A Microcosm of the Machine-Age World. Bibliographical references in the notes.

112   Pulos, Arthur J. **American Design Ethic: A History of Industrial Design to 1940.** Cambridge, Mass., M.I.T Press, 1983. 441p. illus. index. ISBN 0262160854.

Important history of industrial design in America from the late eighteenth century to 1940. Large number of plates with descriptive and critical captions including numerous views of industrial installations, interiors, and advertisements as well as examples of industrial design. Contents: The Colonies; The Young Republic; The Democracy; The Aristocracy; The New Century; The Machine Age; The Design Decade; Epilogue: From Affluence to Conscience. Bibliography, pp. 426-432.

See also the exhibition catalogs: *"The Art That Is Life": The Arts and Crafts Movement in America, 1875-1920*, by W. Kaplan (Boston, Museum of Fine Arts, 1987. 410p. illus. LC 86-63192), *In Pursuit of Beauty: Americans and the Aesthetic Movement*, by D. B. Burke (New York, Metropolitan Museum of Art, 1986. 511p. illus. ISBN 0870994670), *From Architecture to Object: Masterworks of the American Arts & Crafts Movement*, S. Schwartz, ed. (New York, Dutton, 1989. 156p. illus. ISBN 0525249400), and *American Arts & Crafts: Virtue in Design*, by L G. Bowman (Los Angeles, Calif., Los Angeles County Museum of Art, 1990. 255p. illus. ISBN 082121847).

Canada

113 Lessard, Michel, and Huguette Marquis. **Encyclopedie des antiquities du Quebec.** Montreal, Les Editions de l'Homme, 1971. 526p. illus. LC C71-4511.

Comprehensive handbook of the applied and decorative arts in Quebec (i.e., of French-speaking Canada) directed to the collector. Illustrated with plates of pieces in museums, historic houses and private collections. Contents: 1, Pourquoi s'intéresser aux vieilles choses; 2, L'antiquité québécoise; 3, Les styles français et leur influence au Québec; 4, Les styles anglo-américains et leur influence; 5, Les types de meubles au Québec; 6, Les objets de bois autres que les pièces de mobilier; 7, Céramique québécoise; 8, Le verre; 9, Les lampes et autres instruments d'éclairage; 10, Fonderie, forge et ferblanteries; 11, Argenterie et étain au Québec; 12, Les outlis de fabrication domestique; 13, Les jouets anciens du Québec; 14, Les armes à feu et les armes blanches; 15, Papiers, volumes, timbres, monnaies, médailles et boutons; 16, Les oeuvres d'art; 17, Restauration et entretien; 18, Perspective de la recherche en quebecensia. Comprehensive, classified bibliography, pp. 511-518.

114 Lessard, Michel, and Huguette Marquis. **Encyclopédie de la Maison Québécoise.** Montreal, Les Editions de l'Homme, 1972. 728p. illus. index. ISBN 0775903256.

Important history/handbook of traditional French Canadian architecture and interior furnishings. Contents: I, Architecture domestique et constructeurs; II, L'habitation domestique au carrefour de plusieurs cultures; III, Adaption à l'hiver et aux matériaux; IV, La maison d'inspiration française (1680-1780); V, Le modèle "Québécois" (1760-1900); VII, Mansardes et habitats vernaculaires américains (1780-1900); VIII, Recherches et expérimentation (1880-1945); IX, Internationalisme et Pèlerinage aux sources (1945-1970); X, L'habitat urbain (1700-1970); XI, Dépendances et besoins; XII, Perspective de recherche et politique de conservation. Glossary and comprehensive bibliography, pp. 713-724.

115 Webster, Donald B., ed. **The Book of Canadian Antiques**. New York and Toronto, McGraw-Hill, 1974. 352p. illus. index. LC 74-10381.

Comprehensive history of Canadian applied and decorative arts consisting of essays by various experts including chapters on dating and identification, restoration and care, fakes and investment in Canadian antiques. Contents: French-Canadian Furniture by J. Palardy; Quebec Sculpture and Carving by J. Trudel; Furniture of English Quebec by D. B. Webster; Nova Scotia Furniture by G. E. G. MacLaren; New Brunswick Furniture by H. G. Ryder; Ontario Furniture by P. Shackelton; Ontario-German Decorative Arts by A. Lynn McMurray; Silver by H. Ignatieff; Pewter and Copper by D. B. Webster; Tureenware and Wooden Utensils by U. Abrahamson; Toys and Games by J. Holmes; Guns and Gunmakers by S. J. Gooding; Decorative Ironwork by N. Wilson; Tools of the Trades by L. Russell; Pottery—Earthenware and Stoneware by D. B. Webster; Nineteenth-century British Ceramic Imports by E. Collard; Glass and the Glass Industry by J. Holmes; Handweaving and Textiles by H. B and D. K. Burnham; Prints and Early Illustrations by M. Allodi; Books and Broadsides by E. G. Firth; Photography and Photographers by R. Greenhill. List of museums and collection and classified bibliography of books and catalogs, pp. 343-46.

EUROPEAN APPLIED AND DECORATIVE ARTS

General Histories and Handbooks

116 Alexandre, Arsene. **Histoire de l'art décoratif du XVI siècle a nos jours**. Preface by Roger Marx. Paris, Laurens, 1892. 336p. illus. LC 01-6156.

Survey of western European applied and decorative arts from the sixteenth century to 1890 with very good chromolithographs by Alfred Léon Lemercier. Contents: Les arts du bois; Les arts du métal; La terre et le verre; Les arts du tissue.

117 Kohlhaussen, Heinrich. **Europäisches Kunsthandwerk**. Frankfurt am Main, Umschau, 1969-72. 3v. illus. LC 72-366786.

Comprehensive, scholarly history of western European applied and decorative arts from the early Middle Ages to the end of the Baroque Period. Volume one covers Romanesque; volume two, Gothic; and volume three, the Renaissance and Baroque periods. Each volume has an introductory eassy followed by a collection of plates with descriptive notes which have bibliographies. General classified bibliographies at the end of each volume.

118 Molinier, Emile. **Histoire générale des arts appliqués a l'industrie du Ve a la fin du XVIIIe siècle**. Paris, Levy, 1896-1919. 6v. illus. LC 01-22039r28.

Volume 5 never published. Comprehensive history of European applied and decorative arts from the fifth through the seventeenth centuries. Contents: Tome 1, Les ivoires; Tome 2, Les meubles du moyen age et de la renaissance; Tome 3, Le mobilier au XVIIe et au XVIIIe siècle; Tome 4, L'orfèvrerie religieuse et civile au Ve a la fin du XVe siècle; Tome 6, Les tapisseries par Jules Guiffrey. An old, standard work still valuable especially for the references to documentary sources.

119 Pazaurek, Gustav E. **Guter und Schlecter Geschmack im Kunstgewerbe**. Stuttgart and Berlin, Deutsche Verlags-Anstalt, 1912. 365p. illus. index.

Comprehensive and authoritative study of good and bad taste in European applied and decorative arts from the Middle Ages to the beginning of the twentieth century. Important both as a reflection of turn-of-the-century aesthetics and as a methodological study. Contents: I. Materialfragen; II, Zweckform und Technik; III, Kunstform und Schmuck; Kitsch. Bibliographical references in the footnotes.

See also Labarte (50, 51).

See also the museum catalogs: *The James A. de Rothschild Collection at Waddesdon Manor* (Fribourg, Office du Livre, 1967-1975. 7vs. illus.), *Decorative Arts from the Samuel H. Kress Collection at the Metropolitan Museum of Art*, by C. C. Dauterman, James Parker and Edith A. Standen (London, Phaidon, 1964. 303p. illus. index), *The Irwin Untermeyer Collection* (Cambridge, Mass., Harvard Univ. Press for the Metropolitan Museum of Art, 1956-69. 6v. illus. index.), and *The Wrightsman Collection*, by F. J. B. Watson (New York, Metropolitan Museum of Art, 1966-70. 5v. illus.).

National Histories and Handbooks

Australia

120 Forge, Suzanne. **Victorian Splendor: Australian Interior Decoration, 1837-1901**. Melbourne, New York, Oxford Univ. Press, 1981. 160p. illus. index. ISBN 0195542991.

History of Australian interior decoration from 1837 to 1901 illustrated with contemporary paintings, photographs, and illustrations of various historic house-museums. Contents: 1, The

Drawing Room; 2, The Dining-Room; 3, The Entrance Hall; 4, The Library; 5, The Billiard-Room; 6, The Bedroom; 7, The Kitchen; 8, The Bathroom; 9, Mynda; 10, Madeville Hall; 11, Labassa; 12, Rouse Hill House; 13, The Acacias; 14, Wardlow; 15, An Approach to Restoration; 16, Wallpapers; 17, Floor and Floor Coverings; 18, Stencilling; 19, Wood-graining; 20, Marbling. Glossary, bibliographical notes, and general bibliography, pp. 158-59.

Austria

121 Gmeiner, Astrid, and Gottfied Pirhofer. **Der Österreichische Werkbund: Alternative zur klassischen Moderne in Architektur, Raum- und Produkgestaltung.** Vienna, Salzburg, Residenz, 1985. 258p. illus. index. ISBN 3701704279.

  Scholarly history of the Austrian Werkbund. Contents: Die Perspektive der Tradition; Der österreichische Beitrag zur Deutschen Werkbund-Ausstellung in Köln; Die Werkbund-Tätigkeit in den Kriegsjahren; Die Identitätssuche in den Nachkriegsjahren; Zwischen Tradition und Neubegin—Die Herausforderung der Neuen Sachlichkeit; "Haus und Garten"—Neue Wiener Wohnkultur; Die organisatorische Erneuerung—Der intellektuelle Beitrag von Josef Frank—Die Österreichische Werkbundausstellung 1930; Positionen einer liberalen Moderne—Die Wiener Werkbundsiedlung 1932; Der Zerfall der österreichischen Moderne; Svaz ceskeho dila—Der Tschechische Werkbund; Von der Kunstarbeit zum Werkstattbund—Die ungarische Architektur zwischen zwei Werkbund-Gründungen. Appendix with biographies of major figures. Extensive bibliographic footnotes.

122 Kallir, Jane. **Viennese Design and the Wiener Werkstätte.** New York, Braziller, 1986. 152p. illus. ISBN 0807611549.

  Survey history of design in the Austrian capital from historicism to the beginnings of expressionism. Contents: I, Background: In Search of the Total Artwork; II, A Brief History of the Wiener Werstätte; III, Architecture and the Grand Ideal; IV, Fashion and Related Developments; V, The Graphic Arts and the Birth of Expressionism. Bibliography of basic works, p. 147, and further references in the notes.

123 Schweiger, Werner. **Wiener Werkstatte: Design in Vienna, 1903-1932.** New York, Abbeville Press, 1984. 272p. illus. ISBN 0896594408.

  Well-illustrated history of the Wiener Werkstätte from its founding to its dissolution in 1932. Contents: Part I: The History of the Wiener Werkstätte; Part II: Exhibition Work, Construction, Graphic Design, Class, Ceramics and China, The WW Look. Bibliographical references in the notes and general bibliography, pp. 255-257.

124 Wilkie, Angus. **Biedermeier.** New York, Abbeville Pr., 1987. 216p. illus. index. ISBN 0896597490.

  Richly illustrated survey of interior decoration in the Biedermeier period with emphasis on furniture. Contents: 1. Domestic Life and the Viennese Interior; 2, Biedermeier Design; 3, Centers of Production; 4, Furniture Categories, 5, Decorative Objects; 6, Painting. Bibliography of basic books, pp. 211-213.

Denmark

125 Gelfer-Jorgensen, Miriam. **Dansk Kunsthandvaerk, 1730-1850: Rokoko, Klassicisme.** Copenhagen, Gylendal, 1973. 23p. illus. LC 74-304735.

  Pictorial survey of Danish silver, ceramics, furniture and textiles of the period 1730 to 1850. Bibliographical references in the notes.

126   Miller, Viggo S. **Dansk kunstindustri**. Copenhagen, Rhodos, 1969-70. 2v. illus. LC 79-417525.

Comprehensive, well-illustrated history of Danish applied and decorative arts from 1850 to 1950. First volume covers the period 1850 to 1900; the second 1900 to 1950. English summary. Bibliography in the footnotes.

127   Nielsen, Kay R. **Dansk antikviteter**. Copenhagen, Reitzel, 1963. 2v. illus. index. LC 65-30994.

Comprehensive handbook of Danish applied and decorative arts from the Middle Ages to the mid-nineteenth century. Volume one covers furniture; volume two covers clocks, ceramics, glass, silver and pewter. Brief bibliography of basic books in Danish is given on p. 70 in volume two. A useful pocket handbook for the collector.

France

Dictionaries and Encyclopedias

128   Arminjon, Catherine, and Yvonne Brunhammer, et al. **L'art de Vivre; Decorative Arts and Design in France 1789-1989**. New York, Vendom Press, 1989. 256p. illus. index. LC 88-63278.

Collection of essays on the history of French applied and decorative arts from the Revolution to the present with emphasis on social context. Contents: Two Centuries of French Style by David R. McFadden; National, International, and Universal Exposition and the French Decorative Arts by Yvonne Brunhammer; Les Grands Magazines by Suzanne Tise; Domestic Elegance: The French Home by Madeline Deschamps; The Art of Dining by Catherine Arminjon; French Taste in Fashion: Myth and Reality by France Grand; Bijouterie and Joaillerie by Evelyne Possémé; Forty Years of French Design by Raymond Guidot. Particularly useful for illustrations of historic interiors, advertisements and samples. No bibliography.

129   Arminjon, Catherine, and Nicole Blondel. **Objets civils domestiques: principes d'analyse scientique: vocabulaire**. Paris, Imprimerie nationale, 1984. 632p. illus. index. ISBN 21108-08128.

Part of the subseries: "Principes d'analyse scientifique" in the Inventaire général des monuments et des richesses artistiques de la France (FA 1523). Important, comprehensive dictionary of objects of French domestic life from the Middle Ages to the twentieth century. Includes objects representative of all levels of French society. Nearly 3,000 illustrations of objects in the museums of France. Arrangement is by classes of objects. Definitions of major types of objects have bibliographical references. General bibliography, pp. xv-xxiii.

130   Vial, Henri, Adrien Marcel, and André Girodie. **Les artistes décorateurs du bois; répertoire alphabétique des ébénistes, menuisiers, sculpteurs, doreurs sur bois, etc...** Paris, Bibliothèque d'Art et d'Archéologie, 1912-1922. 2v. illus. LC VA37-154.

Comprehensive dictionary of French artists working in wood during the seventeenth and eighteenth centuries. The majority are furniture makers, but important biographical information is provided on the less well-known interior decorators and sculptors working in wood. Contents: v. 1: A-L; v. 2: M-Z with supplement. General bibliography, v. 1, pp. xxvi-xxvii.

131   Viollet-le-Duc. Eugene E. **Dictionnaire raisonné du mobilier français de l'époque carlovingienne à la renaissance**. Paris, Morel, 1868-75. 6v. illus. index. Reprint: Paris, Grund, 1926. LC 31-24686.

Important encyclopedia of French applied and decorative arts of the Middle Ages and Renaissance. Contents: T. 1, Meubles; t. 2, Ustensiles, Orfèvrerie, Instruments de musique, Jeux, passe-temps, Outils, outillage; t. 3-4, Vêtements, bijous de corps, objets de toilette, Armes de guerre offensives et défensives. Arranged in dictionary form within the volumes. A scholarly source much out of date but still valuable as a pioneering, classic work affording insight into the neo-Gothic taste of its influencial author.

General Histories and Handbooks

132   Oglesby, Catherine. **French Provincial Decorative Art**. New York, Scribner's, 1951. 214p. illus. index. LC 51-13137.

Popular history/handbook of French provincial furniture, ceramics, metalwork and textiles. Bibliography of basic books, pp. 212-214.

Middle Ages and Renaissance

133   Geck, Francis J. **French Interiors & Furniture: The Gothic Period**. Boulder, Colo., Stureck Educational Services, 1988. 128p. illus. ISBN 0933471084.

Pictorial survey of interior decoration and furnishings in France during the Gothic period (1137-1498), an outgrowth of lectures given at the University of Colorado. Illustrations are reproduced from photocopies and include a great many details of decorative motifs. Glossary of terms, chronology, biographies of major personalities and general bibliography, pp. 126-27. In the same series: *French Interiors and Furniture: The Period of Henry II* (1985), and *French Interiors and Furniture: The Period of Henry IV (1986)*.

Baroque-Neoclassicism

134   Eriksen, Svend. **Early Neo-classicism in France: The Creation of the Louis Seize Style in Architectural Decoration, Furniture and Ormolu, Gold and Silver, Sèvres Porcelain in the Mid-eighteenth Century**. London, Faber and Faber, 1974. 432p. illus. ISBN 0571087175.

Scholarly history and analysis of early Neoclassicism as manifested in the applied and decorative arts of the Louis XVI style. Extensive use of documentary sources. Descriptive catalog with 499 plates. Repertory of biographies of major artists and designers with bibliographies. Appendices with transcripts and translations of pertinent texts.

135   Fregnac, Claude. **Les styles français, de Louis XIII a Napoleon III**. Paris, Hachette, 1975. 223p. illus. index. ISBN 2010022726.

Survey of interior decoration and furnishings from the seventeenth century to 1870. Contents: La décor des appartements; Le mobilier; les objets d'ameublement. Well-illustrated with views of historic interiors in contemporary works of art and photographs with detailed descriptive captions.

136   Gonzalez-Palacios, Alvar. **The French Empire Style**. London, Hamlyn, 1966. 157p. illus. LC 77-569199.

Popular survey of French Empire architecture, sculpture, painting, furniture, metalwork, porcelain and textiles. Good collection of color plates. No bibliography.

137   Savage, George. **French Decorative Art, 1638-1793**. New York, Praeger, 1969. 189p. illus. index. LC 79-81560.

Comprehensive introduction to the applied and decorative arts in France between 1638 and 1793 by a leading British connoisseur. Emphasis is on works commissioned by the crown.

Contents: I, Versailles and the French Court Style; 2, The Progression of Styles; 3, Designers and Orne- manistes; 4, Furniture; 5, Metalwork and Small Sculpture; 6, Ceramics; 7, Tapisserie; 8, The Decoration of the Interior. Appendices with a summary of the Directoire style, extracts from the Livre-Journal of Lazare Duvaux, extracts from the 1882 sales catalog of the Duke of Hamilton and extracts from the sale in 1928 of much of the contents of the Hermitage. Brief, unclassified bibliography. Footnotes with references to documentary sources.

138 Strange, Thomas A. **An Historical Guide to French Interiors ... During the Last Half of the Seventeenth Century, the Whole of the Eighteenth Century and the Earlier Part of the Nineteenth.** London, Methuen, 1950. 370p. illus.

Popular illustrated survey concentrating on restored interiors featuring furniture, wall decorations and objets d'art. No bibliography.

139 Verlet, Pierre. **The Eighteenth Century in France: Society, Decoration, Furniture.** Rutland, Vt., Tuttle, 1967. 291p. illus. LC 67-4313.

Authoritative survey of French eighteenth century applied and decorative arts with emphasis on the social context. Written by a leading French expert in the history of furniture and ceramics. Contents: I, Society in the Eighteenth Century: Customers and Dealers, The Growth of Luxury, Precedence among the Rich, Traditionalists and Innovators, Paris and the Provinces, The Influence of Versailles and the Problem of Styles; II, Distribution and Decoration of Apartments: Mural Decorations, Decoration of Windows and Doors, The Chimney-piece, Floor-decoration; III, Architectural Furniture: Consoles and Table-supports, Seat-furniture, Beds, Large Furniture; IV, Furniture of Comfort and Elegance: Sièges Courants (circulating chairs), Small Furniture, Furnishing Bronzes; V, The Inventories: Jacques Verberckt, rue Basse du Rempart, Paris, 1771; The Maréchal de Contades at Montgeoffroy; The Prince de Condé at The Palais de Bourbon. Bibliographical references in the notes.

See also S. F. Kimball. *The Creation of the Rococo* (ARCH 846).

Modern (19th and 20th Centuries)

140 Brunhammer, Yvonne, and Suzanne Tise. **Artiste décorateurs: The Decorative Arts in France, 1900-1942: La Société des artistes decorateurs.** New York, Rizzoli, 1990. 288p. illus. index. ISBN 0847812510.

Well-illustrated and authoritative survey of French applied and decorative arts from 1900 to 1942. The 332 illustrations feature a large number of photographs of interiors. Plates have detailed notes. Arranged chronologically: 1900-1914; 1919-1924; 1925; 1926-1929; 1930; 1931-1942. Bibliographical references in the notes.

Germany

General Histories and Handbooks

141 Dexel, Thomas. **Gebrauchsgerättypen. Das Grebrauchsgerät Mitteleuropas von der römischen Zeit bis ins 19. Jahrhunderts.** Braunschweig, Klinkhardt & Biermann, 1980-1981. 2v. illus. ISBN 378140157X.

Comprehensive history of utilitarian objects in various materials from ancient Roman times to the nineteenth century with emphasis on pieces produced in German-speaking lands. This unusual and very important work is a history of the forms of objects stressing the relationship between forms and functions and the interrelationship of forms in different media. Well-illustrated with museum pieces and works of art showing the use of various types of objects. First volume covers the earlier history to the late Middle Ages and objects in wood and ceramic. Second volume covers altar development and objects in metal. Contents: Band I: Archaeologica Iranica; Römuisches Gerät; Gerät vom Früh-zum Hochmittelalter; Gerät aus Holz; Gerät as Ton. Band II: Schalenformen: Teller, Platten, Schüssel, Becher, Eimer, Mörser, Grapen, Driebeinschüssel, Lavabos, Dosen, Büchsen, Kasten; Topfformen: Schulter-und Kugeltopf; Flaschenformen: Platt-oder Feldflaschen, Scraubflaschen; Kannen- und Krugformen: Messingkannen, gefusste Kannen, Birnförmige, konische und zylindrische Zinnkannen und-krüge; Gerät für Tee und Kaffee, Kannen und Krüge aus getriebenem Messing und Kupfer; Leuchter. The author employs the same method in his history of glass (1426). Bibliographies at the end of each volume.

142 Klingenburg, Karl-Heinz. **Vom Steinbeil bis zum Schönen Brunnen. Angewandte Kunst in Deutschland bis zur Mittelalter.** Berlin, Zentralinstitut fur Formgesaltung, 1964. 462p. illus. (Abriss der Angewandten Kunst, 1).

Comprehensive history of German applied and decorative arts from prehistoric times to the end of the Middle Ages written with emphasis on the relationship between design and function. Corpus of 311 plates with descriptive notes. Contents: I, Urgesellschaft: Steinzeit, Bronzezeit, Eisenzeit; II, Zerfall der Urgesellschaft und Beginn des Feudalismus; III, Mittelalterlicher Feudalismus (Romanik); IV, Mittelalterlicher Feudalismus (Gotik). Comprehensive bibliography, pp. 454-59.

143 Kohlhaussen, Heinrich. **Geschichte des deutschen Kunsthandwerks.** Munich, Bruckmann, 1955. 591p. illus. index. (Deutsche Kunstgeschichte, Band V). LC A56-2530.

Comprehensive and authoritative history of the applied and decorative arts in German-speaking countries from the early Middle Ages to the mid-twentieth century. Contents: Einleitung; Frühzeit; Ottonisches Zeitalter; Romanische Kunst (Stauferzeit); Frühgotik; Hochgotik; Spätgotik; Renaissance (Anfang 16. Jahrhundert bis um 1630); Barock und Rokoko: Manufaktur-Fayencen, Porzellan, Möbel, Goldscmiedekunst, Das barocke Ornament; Seit 1780. Comprehensive, classified bibliography, pp. 577-580. A standard work.

Modern (19th and 20th Centuries)

Bibliographies

144 Burckhardt, Lucius. **The Werkbund: Studies in the History and Ideology of the Deutscher Werkbund, 1907-1933.** London, Design Council, 1980. 117p. illus. ISBN 0850721083.

Important collection of essays on the history and theory of the German Werkbund. First published in 1977. Contents: Between Art and Industry—The Deutscher Werkbund by J. Posener; Werkbund and Jugendstil by J. Posener; The Artists' Colony on the Mathildenhöhe by H. Kruft; Berlin at the Turn of the Century: A Historical and Architectural Analysis by G. Peschken and T. Heinisch; The New Life-Style by O. Birkner; Public Parks by I. Maass; "Everyone Self-Sufficient"—The Urban Garden Colonies of Leberecht Migge by I. M. Hülbusch; Distant Goals, Great Hopes: the Deutscher Werkbund 1918-1924 by W. Pehnt; Finding the Norm and Standard, Constructing for Existenzminimum—The Werkbund and New Tasks in the Social State by H. Eckstein; The Deutscher Werkbund from 1907 to 1933 and the Movements for the "Reform of Life and Culture" by J. Petsch; The Thirties and the Seventies: Today We See Things Differently by L. Burckhardt; The Österreichischer Werkbund and Its Relations with the Deutscher Werkbund by F. Achleitner; The Foundation of the Schweizer Werkbund and l'Oeuvre by O. Birkner. Bibliographical notes at the end of each essay.

145 Campbell, Joan. **The German Werkbund: The Politics of Reform in the Applied Arts.** Princeton, N.J., Princeton Univ. Press, 1978. 350p. illus. index. ISBN 0691052506.

Based on the author's dissertation (Queens University, Ontario). Scholarly history of the German Werkbund with emphasis on political relationships. Contents: I, The Founding of the Werkbund; II, The Evolution of the Werkbund to 1914; III, Cologne 1914; IV, The Werkbund at War; V, Revolution and Renewal: 1918-1929; VIII, The Disintegration of the Weimar Werkbund: 1930-1932; IX, The Werkbund and National Socialism. Appendices with documents including recent interviews and correspondence with leading political and artistic figures.

146   Günther, Sonja. **Interieurs um 1900**. Munich, Wilhelm Fink, 1971. 178p. illus. index.
Scholarly study of German interior and furniture design in the years around 1900 with emphasis on the works of Bernhard Pankok, Bruno Paul and Richard Riemerschmid in the Vereinigten Werksätten für Kunst im Handwerk, Darmstadt. Contents: I, Die Gründung und die Grundsätze der Vereinigten Werkstätten; II, Die Beiträge von Bernhard Pankoko, Bruno Paul und Richard Riemerschmid für die Vereinigten Werkstätten bis 1900; III, Die Tätigkeit von Richard Riemerschmid, Bernhard Pankok und Bruno Paul auf der Pariser Weltanschauung von 1900; IV, Die Tätigkeit von Richard Riemerschmid, Bruno Paul und Bernhard Pankok auf der Weltanschauung St. Louis 1904; VI, Zur weiteren Entwicklung von Bernhard Pankok, Bruno Paul und Richard Riemerschmid. Comprehensive, classified bibliography, pp. 136-48, includes archival and documentary sources. Appendix with catalog of the works of the three designers exhibited in Paris and St. Louis.

147   Haskett, John. **Design in Germany, 1870-1918**. London, Trefoil, 1986. 160p. illus. index. ISBN 0862940834.
Survey history of design in Germany between the Franco-Prussian War and World War I. Contents: 1, The Unification of Germany ?; 2, The Applied Arts in the Gründerzeit; 3, Unity and Diversity; 4, Cultural Pessimism and the Germanic Ideology; 5, New Initiatives in Cultural Reform; 6, Jugendstil; 7, The Role of Government; 8, Developments in German Industry; 9, Worships and the Adaptation of Craft Ideals; 10, The Third German Applied Arts Exhibition, Dresden; 11, The German Werkbund; 12, Ideal and Reality; 13, The First World War. Bibliographical references in the notes.

148   Günther, Sonja. **Das deutsche Heim: Luxusinterieurs und Arbeitermöbel von der Gründerzeit bis zum "Dritten Reich."** Giessen, Anabas, 1984. 184p. illus. index. ISBN 3870381094 (Werkbund-Archiv, 12).
History of interior decoration and furniture in Germany from 1844 to 1944. Contents: Produktion von Luxusmöbel als Präsentation deutschen Wohlstandes und Schwierigkeiten bei der Versogung mit Konsumgütern für alle—Wohungen von 1844-1900; Deutsche Luxusgüter als Weltreisende aud Dampfern und Aufruf intellektueller Gruppen zur Einfachheit der Lebenshaltung—Wohungen von 1900-1933; Verordnung von Einfachhait und Luxus der Verordner—Wohnungen im "Dritten Reich"; Wohnverhältnisse seit der Industrialisierung— Zusammenfassung. Bibliographical footnotes and very comprehensive bibliography, pp. 156-180.

149   Günther, Sonja. **Innenraum des "Dritten Reiches": Interieurs aus den Vereinigten Werkstätten für Kunst im Handwerk für Reprasentanten des "Dritten Reiches."** 2nd ed. Berlin, S. Gunther, 1979. 148p. illus.
Scholarly study of interior design during the Third Reich with particular attention paid to the designs for interiors and furniture in The Führerwohnung, Berlin, the Fuhrerbau, Munich, the German Embassy, London, the Neuen Reichskanzlei, Berlin, and the Foreign Ministry, Berlin. Bibliographical references in the footnotes.

150   Junghanns, Kurt. **Der Deutsche Werkbund: sein erstes Jahrzent**. Berlin, Henschelverlag, 1982. 191p. illus. index. ISBN 388520097X.

Well-illustrated and documented history of the German Werkbund from its founding in 1907 to the outbreak of the First World War. Contents: Zeitumstände; Karl Schmidt; Hermann Muthesius; Zur Vorgesichte des Werkbundes; Gründung; Ziel und Arbeitsweise; Die Entwicklung der Werkbundgedanken; Die Opposition; Werkbund und Arbeiterklasse; Die Werkbundkrise; Weltkrieg und Novemberrevolution. Collection of plates illustrating the full range of Werkbund design and valuable collection of contemporary documents, some hitherto unpublished. General bibliography, pp. 184-187, and bibliographical references in the notes.

151 Naylor, Gillian. **The Bauhaus Reassessed: Sources and Design Theory**. New York, Dutton, 1985. 198p. illus. index. ISBN 0525243593.

Scholarly history of the Bauhaus with emphasis on the theory of design. Contents: Part I. Sources: 1, Educational Theory, 2, Craft and Industry, 3, The Werkbund; Part II. The Bauhaus in Weimar: 1, War and Revolution; 2, The Cathedral of Socialism; 3, The Workshops; Johannes Itten and the Basic Course; 5, Claims for Art: Kandinsky and Klee, Van Doesburg and Moholy-Nagy; 6, Crisis and Consolidation; Part III. The Bauhaus in Dessau: 1, Dessau: The Great Transformation; 2, Dessau and Architecture; 3, From Workshop to Laboratory; 4, Hannes Meyer: Formalism or Functionalism?; 5, Confrontation and Collapse. Bibliographical footnotes and select bibliography, pp. 192-194.

152 Passarge, Walter. **Deutsche Werkkunst der Gegenwart**. 2d ed. Berlin, Rembrandt, n.d. 222p. illus. LC 46-34656.

Comprehensive history of the applied and decorative arts in German-speaking lands of the 1920s and 1930s, written by a leading theorist and art historian (See FA 705). Contents: Einleitung; Edelmetall; Email; Metall: Messing, Kupfer, Bronze, Zinn, Eisen; Keramik; Glas; Textilkunst; Bucheinband; Holz und Elfenbein; Körbe und Bastarbeiten. No bibliography.

153 Scheidig, Walther. **Crafts of the Weimar Bauhaus, 1919-1924: an Early Experiment in Industrial Design**. New York, Reinhold, 1967. 150p. illus. LC 66-25545.

Popular introduction to the applied and decorative arts of the Weimer Bauhaus. Contains 92 plates with brief, descriptive captions. Basic bibliography, pp. 147-48.

154 Selle, Gert. **Design-Geschichte in Deutschland: Produktkultur al Entwurf und Erfahrung**. Cologne, Dumont, 1987. 350p. illus. index. ISBN 3770119274.

Revised edition of: *Geschichte des Designs in Deutschland von 1870 bis Heute* (Cologne, Dumont, 1978). Comprehensive, scholarly history of industrial design in Germany from 1870 to the present, particularly valuable for the extensive use of quotes from contemporary writings. Contents: I, Form, Geschichte, Erfahrung; II, Fabrikation und Ästhetik—Der Aufbruch in das Industriezeitalter; III, Maschinelle Produktion, Massendesign und Gegenstadserfahrung; IV, Entwurf und Wirklichkeit der Moderne—Entwicklung und Deutung der gegenständlichen Kultur zwischen den Weltkriegen; V, Der Weg ins Zeitalter der Automation und des Massenkomforts. Extensive, classified bibliography, pp. 310-342.

155 Thiekotter, Angelika, and Eckhard Siepmann, eds. **Packeis und Pressglas: von der Kunstgewerbebewegung zum Deutschen Werkbund: eine wissenschaftliche Illustrierte**. Giessen, Anabas-Verlag, 1987. 368p. illus. index. (Werkbund-Archiv, Band 16) ISBN 3870381264.

Scholarly history of German art and design from 1851 to 1914 in the form of essays by various scholars and extracts from earlier writers. Excellent collection of illustrations emphasizing the role of design in German society. Contents: Teil I: Die Kunstgewerbebewegung im Zeitalter der Weltausstellungen 1851-1900. Grundlagen; Die Morgenröte des preussischen Kunstgewerbes; Von der Barrikade zum Kristallpalast; Die Weltausstellungen; Surreallismus der Gründerzeit; Der Gespenstertanz der Surrogate; Der "Kampf um den Stil"—Die Deutsche Kunstgewerbebewegung; Martin Gropius' Bau. Teil II: Von der Kunstgewerbebewegung zum Deutschen Werkbund 1895-1914. Ein elektrischer Frühling; Unterricht im Kunstgewerbe; "Brüder zu Sonne, zur Freiheit"—Kunstgewerbebewegung, Werkbund und Arbeiterkultur; Versuchsanordnungen: Naturwissenschaft, Technik und Jugendstil; Werkbund und Wirtschaft—Krisenerscheinungen. Bibliographical references in the notes.

156   **Die Zwanziger Jahre des Deutschen Werkbunds herausgegeben vom Deutschen Werk-bund und dem Werkbund-Archiv.** Giesse, Anabas, 1982. 360p. illus. index. ISBN 3870380969. (Werkbund-Archiv, Band 10).
      Comprehensive history of the German Werkbund during the 1920s. Contains valuable documents and interviews with major personalities. Contents: Berlin; Die Werkbundsiedlung in Stuttgart-Weissenhof; Der Münchner Bund; Das Neue Frankfurt und der Werkbund; Der Schweizer Werkbund; Der Übergang zum Untergang; Lebensbeschreibungen; Lebens-selbst-beschreibungen.
      See also the exhibition catalog: *Product—Design—History: German Design from 1820 down to the Present Era* (New York, Universe Books, 1986. 339p. illus. ISBN 0876635036).

Great Britain

General Histories and Handbook

157   Lavine, Sigmund A. **Handmade in England. The Tradition of British Craftsmen.** New York, Dodd Mead, 1968. 148p. illus. index. LC 68-16179.
      Popular survey of British applied and decorative arts with emphasis on the craftsmen. Covers furniture, glass, ceramics and silver. Brief bibliography, p. 135.

158   Sitwell, Sacheverell. **British Architects and Craftsmen, a Survey of Taste, Design, and Style During Three Centuries, 1600 to 1830.** 4th ed. London, New York, B. T. Batsford, 1948. 196p. illus. LC 50-18073.
      Survey of British interior decoration between 1600 and 1830 emphasizing major buildings and their decorations. Written by an influencial writer and connoisseur. Contents: I, Elizabethan and Jacobean Building; II, Inigo Jones; III, Sir Christopher Wren; IV, The Craftsmen; V, Sir John Vanbrugh; VI, Hawksmoor and the Baroque; VII, Gibbs and the Rococo; VIII, Kent and the Palladians; IX, Adam; X, Non-Adam; XI, The Regency. Occasional bibliographical footnote.

159   Strange, Thomas A. **English Furniture, Decoration, Woodwork and Allied Arts During the Last Half of the Seventeenth Century, the Whole of the Eighteenth Century, and the Earlier Part of the Nineteenth.** New York, Scribner's, 1950. 369p. illus. Reprint: London, Studio, 1986. ISBN 1851700700.
      Popular illustrated survey of English furniture and interior decoration. Illustrations feature restored interiors and major pieces of furniture and wall decoration. No bibliography.

160   Yarwood, Doreen. **English Interiors: Pictorial Guide and Glossary.** Guildford, Surrey, Butterworths, 1983. 191p. illus. ISBN 0718825438.
      Combination of a survey of English interiors from 1300 to the present and a dictionary covering objects, styles, decorative patterns and motifs. Illustrated with line drawings. Chronological list of selected historic houses in Britain. List of museums with period rooms. List of basic books, p.192. ˙

Baroque and Rococo (17th and 18th Centuries)

161   Beard, Geoffrey W. **Georgian Craftsmen and Their Work**. South Brunswick, N. J., A. S. Barnes, 1967. 206p. illus. index. LC 67-20199.

Survey of British interior decoration during the eighteenth century. Emphasis is on the work of little-known carvers, plasters, etc. Contents: Part One: The Age of Orders, 1700-1760: I, The Virtuosi of York; II, The Italian Plasterers; III, Iron and Paint; IV, Great Fine Houses; V, Visions and Revivals; Part Two: A Regiment of Artificers, 1760-1800: I, Launching a Style; II, "The Ingenious Mr. Rose"; III, Something Like Truth; IV, In the Best Manner; V, Rivals and Claimants. Appendices with lists of craftsmen of the Georgian period and specimen cost of interior decoration in the eighteenth century. Classified bibliography, pp. 190-197, and bibliographical references in the footnotes.

162   Gloag, John. **Georgian Grace: A Social History of Design from 1660-1830**. London, Adam and Charles Black, 1956. 426p. illus. index. Reprint: London, Spring Books, 1967. LC 68-94580.

Comprehensive history of the applied and decorative arts in Great Britain from 1660 to 1830 with emphasis on the social context affecting the design of interior and exterior architectural design and furnishings. Very valuable collection of reproductions of contemporary views, designs, etc. Contents: Part I: The Background: 1, The Growth of Educated Patronage; 2, The Architectural Bones; 3, The Georgian Scene; 4, Ornamental Conventions and Waves of Taste; Part II: The Accompaniments to Life: 1, "Fill Every Glass"; 2, A Dish of Tea; 3, Pray Be Seated; 4, Bed and Bedroom; 5, "The Toilet Stands Display'd"; 6, Writing and Reading; 7, Music in the Drawing-room, Fiddles in the Kitchen; 8, Chimney-piece and Chimney-corner; 9, "Let Us Take the Road"; 10, Epitaph. Appendices with biographies of principle designers, architects and furniture-makers; list of books on furniture published between 1660 and 1830; essays on the society of dilettanti; the Society of Arts; The Gunning Sisters; Georgian grace in the American colonies and transcripts of selected advertisements. Bibliography in the form of "Books Referred to in the Text," pp. 19-59.

Modern (19th and 20th Centuries)

163   Coulson, Anthony J. **A Bibliography of Design in Britain, 1851-1970**. London, Design Council, 1979. 291p. index. ISBN 0850720915.

Comprehensive, classified and annotated bibliography of books and periodical literature related to the history of design in Britain between 1851 and 1970. The annotations precede groups of similar titles. Coverage includes monographic literature on major designers, organizations, schools and styles. A valuable guide for research in modern British design; the comments on broader areas are often pregnant with future directions for design history.

164   Anscombe, Isabelle, and Charlotte Gere. **Arts & Crafts in Britain and America**. New York, Van Nostrand Reinhold, 1983. 232p. illus. index. ISBN 0442208081.

Survey history of the Arts and Crafts Movement in Britain and America. Contents: 1, Morris and His Circle; 2, 'Towards a Free Style'; 3, The Establishment of the Guilds; 4, 'Art and the Handicraftsman'; 5, Arts and Crafts and the Beginnings of Modernism; 6, Liberty and Company; 7, The Emergence of a 'Polychromatic' Idiom. Bibliography of basic works, pp. 226-239.

165   Boe, Alf. **From Gothic Revival to Functional Form: A Study in Victorian Theories of Design**. New York, Da Capo Press, 1979. 183p. illus. index. ISBN 0306775441.

Reprint of 1st ed. published in 1957 by Oslo Univ. Press as no 6. of Oslo Studies in English. Bibliography, pp. 158-164.

Important, pioneering study of the theoretical basis for the history of design in Great Britain from Neogothicism to the Arts and Crafts Movement. Contents: I, The Background: Early Victorian Commercial Design in the Great Exhibition of 1851; II, Gothic Reforms: August Northmore Welby Pugin; III, Part 1: 1835-1851: Parliamentary Reports and the Reform Group, Part II: 1851: Criticism by Principle, Part III: The Eighteen-Fifties: Departmental Activities and a New Literature of Design; IV, The Ethics of Ornament: John Ruskin; V, Handicraft, Legend, and the Beauty of the Earth: William Morris; VI, Aestheticism, Symbolic Ornament, and Functional Form: E. W. Godwin, The Arts and Crafts, and Christopher Dresser. Appendices with letter from Pugin to A. N. Didron and "General Principles" by Owen Jones. Good, classified bibliography, pp. 158-164, and further references to specialized literature in the notes.

166 Cooper, Jeremy. **Victorian and Edwardian Decor: from the Gothic Revival to Art Nouveau.** New York, Abbeville, 1987. 256p. illus. index. ISBN 0896597687.

Richly illustrated survey of interior design in Britain from 1830 to 1915. Contents: 1, A Matter of Style: Artists at Home, The Taste for the Exotic, The Renaissance Style; Early Victorian Revivals, New Materials; 2, A. W. N. Pugin: From Regency to Reformed Gothic; Pugin Furniture, Pugin Interiors, Pugin Plagiarist; 3, William Burges: Burges Interiors; Burges Furniture, Burges at Home, Burges' Assistants; 4, Geometric Gothic: The Muscular Goth, John Pollard Seddon, Alfred Waterhouse 'Hints on Household Taste', Bruce Talbert, Charles Bevan Commercial Design; 5, From 'Nankin' to Bedford Park: Jeckyll and Whistler, Early Godwin Furniture, Later Godwin Furniture, Christopher Dresser, Richard Norman Shaw, Collinson & Lock, Aesthetic Variety Cottier and Edis; 6, Morris and Company: Earl 'Morris' Furniture, the 'Rossetti' Chair, Morris & Co., Philip Webb, Stained Glass, Textiles and Tiles, Later Morris & Co. Furniture, Stanmore Hall; 7, The Arts and Crafts Movement: The Century Club, C.R. Ashbee and the Guild of Handicraft; W. R. Lethaby and Kenton & Co., Ernest Gimson, Cotswold Craftsmen, C. F. A. Voysey, Walter Cave, Edwin Lutyen and Frank Brangwyn; 8, The 'New Art': Mackintosh Interiors, Scottish Furniture, George Walton, English 'New Art' Furniture, Omega and Others; 9, Heal's and Liberty's: Early Ambrose Heal Furniture, Pre-War Heals'. Liberty's, Outside Designers at Liberty's. List of public collections of Victorian and Edwardian furniture, bibliography of books and periodical articles, pp. 248-49, and additional bibliography in the notes.

167 Cooper, Nicholas. **The Opulent Eye: Late Victorian and Edwardian Taste in Interior Design.** London, The Architectural Press, 1977. 258p. illus. index. ISBN 051390048.

Collection of plates from photographs made by H. Bedford Lemere (1864-1944) of interiors in London between 1890 and 1911. Most of the photographs are of upper-class domestic settings but there are a few businesses, churches and gardens. The meticulous detail of Lemere's photographs and the descriptive notes by Nicholaus Cooper make the *Opulent Eye* an important source for the history of British interior design around 1900.

168 Gloag, John. **Victorian Comfort: A Social History of Design from 1830-1900.** Newton Abbot, David & Charles, 1973. 252p. illus. index. LC 75-308490.

First published in 1961 (London, A. & C. Black). Comprehensive history of the applied and decorative arts in Britain during the Victorian era. Emphasis is on the social context of furniture and other furnishings in the various settings of the time. Illustrated with a large number of images from contemporary advertisements, catalogs, magazines, etc. Contents: 1, The Victorian Scene; 2, Home; 3, Comfort and Elegance; 4, The Cosy Hearth; 5, Comfort in Travel: The Road; 6, Comfort in Travel: The Railway; 7, Comfort and Pleasure; 8, Comfort and Conscience; 9, Memorials and Monuments. Bibliography consists of references to the sources of the illustrations.

169 MacCarthy, Fiona. **British Design since 1880: A Visual History.** London, Lund Humphries, 1982. 229p. illus. index. ISBN 0853314616.

Survey history of British design from 1880 to 1980. Arrangement is by decades with concluding chapters on British design books and exhibition catalogs, British design collections and index of designers.

See also the author's *A History of British Design 1830-1970* (London, Allen & Unwin, 1972. 136p. illus. index. ISBN 004745007X).

170   Pevsner, Nikolaus. **An Enquiry into Industrial Art in England.** Cambridge, Cambridge Univ. Press, 1937. 234p. illus. index. LC 38-1487r48.

Important study of English industrial design during the 1920s and 1930s written by a leading art historian and specialist in the history of English art. Based in part on visits to various art schools and societies. Contents: Part I: Data: Survey of Trades Investigated; Metalwork; Electric and Gas Fittings; Furniture; Textiles; Wallpapers; Pottery; Glass; Silver and Electro-plate; Hollow-ware; Plastic Mouldings; Wireless Cabinets; Jewellery; Leather Goods; Packaging; Printing; Motor-cars. Part II: Conclusions: Ratio between Good and Bad in England and Abroad; Sequences of Trades According to Artistic Quality of Products; Reasons for Differences of Artistic Quality; Size of Manufacturing Unit; Organization of Manufacturing Unit; Old and New Industries; Objects for Use for Adornment; Hand-made and Machine-made Articles; Boom and Slump; The Creator of Designs; The Aesthetic Value of Cheap and Expensive Articles; The Taste of the Public; The Social Problem; Suggestions for Improvements; I, Art Education; II, Exhibitions— Prizes—Registration of Design; III, Other Public Institutions—Private Institutions—Publications; The Duties of the Consumer; The Duties of the Manufacturer and the Retailer. Bibliographical references in the footnotes.

171   Service, Alastair. **Edwardian Interiors: Inside the Homes of the Poor, the Average, and the Wealthy.** London, Barrie & Jenkins, 1982. 159p. illus. ISBN 0091470005.

History of interior decoration in Britain during the reign of Edward VII (1901-10) with many informative photographic views of interiors and references to economic factors. Arrangement is by dwelling: cottages, suburban houses, small country houses, flats and mansion blocks, green streets and garden cities, houses of businessmen and professionals, country mansions, town mansions. Selected bibliography, pp. 156-157, and further references in the notes.

172   Stansky, Peter. **Redesigning the World: William Morris, the 1880's, and the Arts and Crafts.** Princeton, N.J., Princeton Univ. Press, 1985. 293p. illus. index. ISBN 0691066167.

Scholarly study of the activity of William Morris in the field of design. Contents: I, William Morris and the Arts and Crafts in the 1880's; II, The Century Guild; III, The Art Worker's Guild; IV, The Arts and Crafts Exhibition Society; Conclusion. Comprehensive, classified bibliography, pp. 274-281, and further bibliography in the footnotes.

173   Thackara, John, ed. **New British Design.** London, Thames and Hudson, 1986. 111p. illus. ISBN 0500274460.

Pictorial survey of British design 1980-1986. Includes jewelry, ceramics, glass, industrial design, furniture and interiors, graphic design, and fashion and textile design. Commentary by Peter Dormer. Directory of designers and manufacturers. No bibliography.

174   Watkinson, Ray. **William Morris as Designer.** London, Studio Vista, 1979. ISBN 02897-08990.

Introductory monograph on the work of William Morris as a designer. Contents: 1, Life and Background; 2, The Firm; 3, Precursors; 4, Stained Glass; 5, Pattern Design; 6, Printing; 7, The Arts and Crafts Movement. Bibliography, pp. 80-81.

Italy

General Histories and Handbooks

175   Chiesa, G. **Il Cinquecento: Mobili, arti decorative, costume**. Milan, Gorlich, 1972. 96p. illus.

————. **Il Quattrocento: Mobili, arti decorative, costume**. Milan, Gorlich, 1972. 96p. illus.

————. **Il Seicento: Mobili, arti decorative, costume**. Milan, Gorlich, 1973. 111p. illus.
Pictorial survey of the applied and decorative arts of Italy in the sixteenth, fifteenth and seventeenth centuries with emphasis on furniture and interiors. Good collection of plates of museum pieces and historic interiors.

176   Cito Filomarino, Anna M. **L'arredamento in Italia ieri e oggi**. Milan, Gorlich, 1972. 2v. illus. LC 73-33343.
Comprehensive history of Italian applied and decorative arts from the Middle Ages to the twentieth century with particular emphasis on interior decoration.

Modern (19th and 20th Centuries)

177   Albera, Giovanni, and Nicolas Monti. **Italian Modern, a Design Heritage**. New York, Rizzoli, 1989. 240p. illus. index. ISBN 0847810348.
Pictorial survey of Italian industrial design from the end of the Second World War to the 1980s. Concise text discussing the development by decades is followed by 90 pages of color illustrations with descriptive captions. Appendix with list of suppliers of many of the products illustrated. Few bibliographical references in the footnotes.

178   Horn, Richard. **Memphis. Objects, Furniture, and Patterns**. Philadelphia, Running Press, 1986. 143p. illus. index. ISBN 0894714473.
Pictorial survey of the design products of the Memphis/Milano, the Italian design collaborative founded in 1981. All plates are in color. Contents: 1, Lamps; 2, Chairs; 3, Sofas; 4, Tables; 5, Storage Pieces; 6, Pièces de Résistance; 7, Ceramics, Glass, Silver; 8, Electronics; 9, Patterns; 10, Interiors; 11, Wearables. Appendix with addresses of suppliers. Bibliography, p. 140.

179   Sambonet, Guia. **Alchimia 1977-1987**. Turin, Umberto Allemandi, 1986. 127p. illus. ISBN 8842200751.
Text in Italian and English. Pictorial survey of the furniture, interiors, graphics and other works of design by the Alchimia group of Italian designers formed in 1977 by Alessandro and Adriana Guerriero. Contains 198 plates with descriptive notes. Biographies of the designers. General bibliography, p. 127, and list of exhibitions, pp. 116-117.

180   Fossati, Paolo. **Il design in Italia, 1945-1972**. Turin, Einaudi, 1972. 255p. illus.
Survey of Italian post-war design through the work of ten major designers: Franco Albini, Bruno Munari, Carlo Scarpa, Ernesto N. Rogers, Marco Zanuso, Ettore Sottass, Achille Castiglioni, Alberto Rosselli, Roberto Sambonet, and Enzo Mari. Bibliographical references in the notes.

181   Gregotti, Vittorio. **Il disegno del prodotto industriale: Italia 1860-1980**. Milan, Electa, 1982. 429p. illus. index. LC A51-4474.
Pictorial survey of Italian industrial design from 1860 to 1980. Divided into three periods: 1860-1918; 1919-1945; 1946-1980, each with introductory essay followed by plates with detailed descriptive and analytical notes. Comprehensive, classified bibliography, pp. 356-363.

182 Sparke, Penny. **Design in Italy: 1870 to the Present**. New York, Abbeville Press, 1988. 240p. illus. index. ISBN 0896598845.

Pictorial survey of design history in Italy from 1870 to 1987. Comprehensive, classified bibliography, pp. 233-236, and further bibliography in the notes.

183 Wichmann, Hans. **Italien: Design, 1945 bis Heute**. Basel, Boston, Birkhauser, 1988. 388p. illus. index. (Industrial Design-Graphic Design, Band 4) ISBN 3764319690.

Well-illustrated survey of Italian industrial and graphic design since the end of the Second World War. Introductory essays followed by plates with descriptive captions. Contents: Italien: Design 1945 bis Heute by H. Wichmann; Das italienische Design nach dem Zeiten Welkrieg by V. Gregotti; Kunstindustrie; Mobel Design; Eleganz und Weltoffenheit; Industrial Design; Graphic Design; Stimmen Italiens zum italienischen Design (extracts from the writings of designers); Daten und Fakten (illustrated outline of Italian design history); Kurzviten iatlienischer Designer (with bibliographies). Comprehensive, classified bibliography, pp. 375-388.

Netherlands

184 Berendsen, Anne. **Het Nederlandse interieur: Binnenhuis, meubelen, tapijten, koper, tin, zilver, glas, porcelein enaardewerk van 1450-1820**. Utrecht, W. de Haan, 1950. 264p. illus. index.

Survey of Dutch interior decoration and furnishings from 1450 to 1820.

Norway

185 Hopstock, Carsten. **Norwegian Design, from Viking Age to Industrial Revolution**. Oslo, Dreyer, n.d. 212p. illus. LC 59-20547.

Comprehensive history of the applied and decorative arts in Norway from the early Middle Ages to the mid-nineteenth century. Contents: Viking Times and Middle Ages, c. 800 to 1550; Renaissance, c. 1550-1650; Baroque and Rococo, c. 1650-1780; Louis XVI and Empire, c. 1780 to 1850. Descriptive captions to the plates. Includes folk art. Still the most comprehensive history available in English.

See also K. Berg, ed. *Norges Kunsthistorie* (FA1679).

Poland

186 Bochnak, Adam. **Decorative Arts in Poland**. Warsaw, Arkady, 1972. 331p. illus. index. LC 72-17120.

Pictorial survey of the applied and decorative arts in Poland from the Romanesque to the middle of the twentieth century. Brief text followed by a large collection of plates. No bibliography.

Scotland

187 Finlay, Ian. **Scottish Crafts**. London, Harrap; New York, Chanticleer, 1948. 128p. illus. index. LC 49-7870. Reprint: East Ardsley, Wakefield, Eng., EP Pub., 1976. ISBN 07185811711.

Pictorial survey of the applied and decorative arts in Scotland from the early Middle Ages to the nineteenth century. Contents: I, Architecture; II, Sculpture; III, Bone-carving and Wood-work; IV, Metalwork; V, Textiles; VI, Ceramics and Glass; VII, Manuscripts and Books. No bibliography.

Spain

188 Sanchez Mesa, Martin D. **L'arredamento spagnolo**. Milan, Fabbri, 1967. 158p. illus. LC 68-111877.

Popular, pictorial survey of Spanish applied and decorative arts from the Middle Ages through the nineteenth century.

189 **Historia de las artes aplicadas e industriales en Espana**. Madrid, Catedra, 1982. 658p. illus. ISBN 8437603730.

Coordinator: Antonio Bonet Correa. Comprehensive history of the applied and decorative arts in Spain from earliest times to the present. Work is by a team of Spanish experts. Contents: I. Metales: 1, Hierro, Rejeria, 2, Plateria, 3, Armas y armaduras, 4, Relojes, 5, Objetos metalicos, 6, Medallas; II, Maderas: 7, Carpinteria de lo Blanco; 8, Mobiliaro, III, Cueros: 9, Cordobanes y Guadamecies, 10, Encaudernacion; IV, Textiles: 11, Telas, Alfombras, Tapices, 12, Bordados, Pasamanerias y Encajes; V, Papeles: 13, Papeles pintados, 14, Naipes; VI, Piedras Duras: 15, El Arte de la Piedras duras; VII, Marfiles: 16, La Talla del Marfil; VIII, Artes del Fuego: 17, Vidrio y cristal; 18, Vidrieras, 19, Esmaltes; 20, Cerámica, 21, CerÄmica (siglos XIII-XIX); IX, Distintos Materiales: 22, Abanicos, 23 Juguetes. Comprehensive, classified bibliography, pp. 639-658.

190 Von Bargbahn, Barbara. **Age of Gold, Age of Iron: Renaissance Spain and Symbols of Monarchy, the Imperial Legacy of Charles V and Philip II, Royal Castles, Palace-Monasteries, Princely Houses**. Lanham, Md., University Press of America, 1985. 2v. illus. index. LC 85-20400. ISBN 0819147397.

Scholarly study of the interior decorations in the various royal residences in Spain during the sixteenth century. Volume I: Text; volume II: Illustrations. Contents of volume one: I, Royal Alcazares: Toledo, Segovia, Seville, Granada; II, The Monastery-Complex of Yuste and the Escorial; III, The Spanish Monarchy and Portugal; IV, The Library of the Escorial; V, Later Decoration at the Escorial la Fresneda and the "Casitas" of the Princes. Volume two has 1,400 illustrations with descriptive notes. Bibliographical references in the notes.

191 Williams, Leonard. **The Arts and Crafts of Older Spain**. Chicago, A. C. McClurg & Co., 1908. 108. 3v. illus. index. LC 08-15871.

Comprehensive survey of the applied and decorative arts of Spain from the Middle Ages to the end of the nineteenth century. Volume 1 covers metalwork; volume 2, furniture, ivory, pottery, glass; volume 3, textiles including lace.

Sweden

192 Frick, Gunilla. **Svenska slöjdföreningen och konstindustrin före 1905**. Stockholm, Nordiska Museet, 1978. 315p. illus. index. (Nordiska Museets Handlingar, 91) ISBN 9171081488.

Scholarly history and study of the applied and decorative arts in Sweden during the nineteenth century with focus on the establishment of an art industry for the new middle class and the place of the Slöjdföeningen (Artists and Craftsmen Art Industry Association). Contents: 1, Svenska konstindustri under 1800-talet; 2, Svenska Slöjdföreningen grundas. Versamheten under de först 25 åren. Medlemmar. Skolan; 3, Scenska Slöjdföreningens verksamhet inriktas på konstidustri; 4, Svenska Slöjdföreningens Museum; 5, Föreningen för konstslöjd. Pristävlingar och lotteri; 6, Mönster för konstindustri och slöjd. Summary in German, pp. 247-72. Comprehensive, classified bibliography, pp. 296-309.

193 Plath, Iona. **The Decorative Arts of Sweden**. New York, Dover, 1966. 218p. illus. index. LC 65-20487.

Pictorial survey of the applied and decorative arts in Sweden from the Middle Ages to 1950. Covers textiles, ceramics, metalwork, glass, wood and wall paintings.

194 Stavenow, Ake, and Ake H. Huldt. **Design in Sweden**. New York, Bedminster Press, 1961. 268p. illus. index. LC 62-6157.

Pictorial survey of design in Sweden from 1900 to 1960 with emphasis on design since World War II. Contents: Swedish Design: A Survey in Words and Pictures; The Designer at Work; Design in Closeup: Traditional Handicraft; Public Environment—and at Home; For the Table; Art Handiwork, Industrial Design. Good selection of plates illustrating individual pieces, designers at work and settings. No bibliography.

Switzerland

195 Erni, Peter. **Die gute Form: eine Aktion des Schweizerischen Werkbundes: Dokumentation und Interpretationen**. Baden, LIT, 1983. 157p. illus. ISBN 3906700011.

Well-illustrated survey of design in Switzerland from the 1920s to 1980. Emphasis is on the place of Swiss design in the international context. Contents: Zwanzig Jahre prätentiöse Bescheidenheit; Authentische Dinge: zweckmässig, dauerhaft und rein; Häretische Dinge: üppig, bodenständig oder exaltiert; Die gegenstandlose Welt und die Gegenstände des täglichen Bedarfs; Sparsam und ordentlich: Nationaltugenden und der Geist des Kapitalismus; Die Konkurrenz schläft nicht; Die sündigen Gewänder des profanen Geschmacks: Ethik; Die Missionare des Guten: SWB; Demokratisieren wir den Luxus: Die gute Form zerfällt; Utopisches Potential: Rationaliisierung und Wunschproduktion. Selected bibliography, p. 155.

196 Luthi, Max. **Bürgerliche Innendekoration des Spätbarok und Rokoko in der deutschen Schweiz**. Zurich, O. Fussli, 1927. 92p. illus.

Useful pictorial survey of Swiss interior decoration and major works of furniture and objets d'art of the eighteenth century. Comprehensive bibliography, pp. 80-89.

ORIENTAL APPLIED AND DECORATIVE ARTS

General

197 Cohn-Wiener, Ernst. **Das Kunstgewerbe des Ostens**. Berlin, Verlag fur Kunstwissenschaft, n.d. 256p. illus. index.

Older, once standard history of Near Eastern, Middle Eastern and Far Eastern applied and decorative arts from antiquity through the nineteenth century. Bibliography, pp. 255-56, is a classified list of books chiefly in German.

198 Kümmel, Otto. **Ostasiatisches Gerät**. Berlin, Cassirer, 1925. 62p. (text) 140 plates. LC 25-13035.

An old, survey history of Far Eastern applied and decorative arts written by a leading German scholar. Many of the essays remain today important for their insights into the aesthetics of Oriental decoration and the decorative arts. Covers ceramics, lacquer, furniture, bronzes and other metalwork. Classified bibliography of books in all languages, p. 62. Plates are grouped as follows: Chinesische Sakralbronzen; Buddhistisches Kultgerät; Schreibgerät; Teegerät; Räuchergerät; Waffen; Hausgerät; Musikinstrumente.

China

199 Feddersen, Martin. **Chinese Decorative Arts; a Handbook for Collectors and Connoisseurs.** New York, T. Yoseloff, 1961. 286p. illus. index. LC 61-9623.

Comprehensive collector's history/handbook of Chinese applied and decorative arts from early dynastic times to the end of the nineteenth century written by a leading authority. Contents: 1, Historical Survey; 2, Ceramics; 3, Metalwork (excluding mirrors); 4, Bronze Mirrors; 5, Jade; 6, Ivory, Bone, Horn, Tortoiseshell, Mother-of-Pearl, Amber; 7, Glass; 8, Textiles; 9, Iconography; 10. Marks. Comprehensive, classified bibliography, pp. 253-72.

See also Soame Jenyns and William Watson, *Chinese Art* (FA1868) and Margaret Medley, *A Handbook of Chinese Art for Collectors and Students* (FA1869).

Islam

200 Kühnel, Ernst. **The Minor Arts of Islam.** Ithaca, N.Y., Cornell University Press, 1971. 255p. illus. index. LC 75-110331.

Translation of 2d ed. of *Islamische Kleinkunst*. Some misspellings and misprints. Comprehensive, authoritative history/handbook of Islamic applied and decorative art. Chapters on books, pottery, glass, metalwork, ivory, wood and stone carving and stucco. Appendices with formula for converting Muslim into Christian dates, list of public collections of Islamic art, and classified and annotated bibliography, pp. 247-50.

201 Wulff, Hans E. **The Traditional Crafts of Persia; Their Development, Technology, and Influence on Eastern and Western Civilizations.** Cambridge, Mass., M.I.T Press, 1966. 404p. illus. LC 66-22642.

Comprehensive, scholarly history of the applied and decorative arts and crafts of Iran with emphasis on those that survive to modern time. Illustrations include many useful photographs of contemporary craft activities. Contents: I, Metalworking Crafts; 2, Woodworking Crafts; 3, Building Crafts and Ceramic Crafts; 4, Textile Crafts and Leather Crafts; 5, Agriculture and Food-Treating Crafts. Comprehensive bibliography, pp. 305-314, and additional bibliography in the footnotes.

See also the museum handbook: *A Handbook of Muhammadan Art*, by M. S. Dimand. 3rd ed. (New York, Metropolitan Museum of Art, 1958. 380p. illus.).

See also G. Migeon, *Les arts plastiques et industriels* (FA1789).

Japan

202 Bowes, James Lord. **Japanese Marks and Seals...** London, Sotheran, 1882. 379p. illus. index. Reprint: Ann Arbor, Mich., Ars Ceramica, 1976. ISBN 0893440027.

Old, but still useful, index of marks and seals found on Japanese pottery, illuminated manuscripts, printed books, lacquer, enamel, metalwork, wood, ivory, etc. "The Zodiacal Cycle and Year Periods," pp. 342-53.

203 Feddersen, Martin. **Japanese Decorative Art: A Handbook for Collectors and Connoisseurs.** London, Faber and Faber, 1962. 296p. illus. LC 64-2765.

Translation of *Japanisches Kunstgewerbe*. (Braunschweig, Klinkhardt & Biermann, 1960. LC A61-874). Comprehensive handbook/history of Japanese applied and decorative arts from earliest dynastic times to the end of the nineteenth century. Introductory essay sketching the overall development is followed by chapters on ceramics, metalwork, lacquer, netsuke, textiles, leather, basketry and iconography. Comprehensive bibliography of books in all languages, pp. 267-83.

204   Lee, Sherman E. **Japanese Decorative Style**. New York, Abrams, 1961. 161p. illus. index. LC 61-9910.

Published in association with an exhibition organized by the Cleveland Museum of Art in 1961. Provides an authoritative introduction to Japanese decorative style as illustrated in 176 works of painting, prints, and the decorative arts. Descriptive notes to the plates. Bibliography, pp. 155-58, lists books and periodical articles in Japanese and Western languages.

205   Smith, Lawrence. **Japanese Decorative Arts from the 17th to the 19th Centuries**. London, Trustees of the British Museum, 1982. 128p. illus. index. ISBN 0714114219.

Popular introductory survey of Japanese traditional decorative arts of the seventeenth through the nineteenth centuries featuring pieces in the British Museum. Contents: 1, Introduction; 2, Metalwork; 3, Sculpture and Decorative Carving; 4, Lacquer; 5, Ceramics; 6, Postscript— Textiles and the Hidden Artifacts of Japan. Bibliography of basic books in English, p. 126.

206   Turk, Frank. **Japanese Objets d'Art**. New York, Sterling, 1963. 156p. illus. index. LC 63-11584.

Popular handbook for the beginning collector of Japanese decorative arts with chapters on the historical background, periods and styles, and subject matter. Glossary and brief bibliography of general works.

207   Yamada, Chisaburoh F., ed. **Decorative Arts of Japan**. Tokyo, Kodansha International, 1964. 262p. illus. LC 63-22011.

Pictorial survey of Japanese ceramics, metalwork, lacquer, and textiles by a team of Japanese experts. Well illustrated with color plates of major museum pieces with descriptive captions. Chronological table. No bibliography.

See also Arts of Japan (FA1888) and *Heibonsha Survey of Japanese Art* (FA1892).

AFRICAN APPLIED AND DECORATIVE ARTS

208   Jeferson, Louise E. **The Decorative Arts of Africa**. New York, 1973. 191p. illus. LC 72-12055

Pictorial survey of traditional decorative arts in sub-Sahara Africa. Contents: 1, Symbols, Patterns, and Motifs; 2, Dress; 3, Ceremonial Costume; 4, Fabrics; 5, Hair Styles; 6, Body Decoration; 7, Metalwork; 8, Carving; 9, Basketry and Pottery; 10, Beadwork; 11, Wall Decoration. Illustrated with artisans at work and works of the decorative arts in the social context. Bibliography of general books in English, pp. 188-189. List of African Studies Centers in America and Britain.

209   Trowell, Kathleen M. **African Design**. New York, Praeger, 1960. 78p.text. illus. index. LC 60-71832.

Survey of traditional African applied and decorative arts. Contents: I, The Craftsman's Aim; II, Wall Decoration; III, Patterns on Mats and Screens; IV, Textile Design; V, Ornamental Basketry; VI, Beadwork; VII, The Decoration of Hides and Leather; VIII, Cicatrization and Body Painting; IX, Calabash Patterns; X, Decoration on Wood; XI, Ornamental Ivory Carving; XII, Decorative Metal Work; XIII, Pottery Design; XIV, Motifs in African Design. Occasional bibliographical footnotes.

CHAPTER TWO

ORNAMENT

BIBLIOGRAPHIES

210 Debes, Dietmar. **Das Ornament, Wesen und Geschichte: Ein Schriftenverzeichnis.** Leipzig, Seeman, 1956. 101p. LC 58-29583.

Classified bibliography of 2,026 books and periodical articles on all aspects of the history and nature of ornament. Selectively annotated. Contents: Allgemeines (Lexika, Kataloge); Wesen des Ornaments; Unterricht im Ornamentieren; Volkskunst; Allgemeine Ornamentsammlungen; Allgemeine Darstellung und Geschichte; Vor- und Frühgeschichte; Alter Orient; Antike; Mittelalter; Renaissance-Manierismus; Barock-Rokoko; Zopfstil-Klassizismus; 19./20. Jahrhundert; Aussereuropäische Ornamentik; Ornamentik der Naturvölker. Thoroughly indexed. Very useful guide to the older literature.

DICTIONARIES AND ENCYCLOPEDIAS

211 Lewis, Philippa, and Gillian Darley. **Dictionary of Ornament.** London, Macmillan, 1986. 319p. illus. ISBN 0333405641.

General dictionary of the ornament, pattern and ornamental motifs found in the applied and decorative arts of Europe and North America from the Renaissance to the present. Includes entries on major artists and designers and materials and techniques particularly important for the history of ornament. Well illustrated. Bibliography of basic works in English, pp. 17-18.

212 Stafford, Maureen, and Dora Ware. **An Illustrated Dictionary of Ornament.** New York, St. Martin's, 1974. 246p. illus. index. LC 74-21095.

Comprehensive, popular dictionary of world ornament covering types, motifs, geographical and period styles. Illustrated with line drawings. List of basic books in English, pp. 243-44.

GENERAL HISTORIES AND HANDBOOKS

213 Bossert, Helmuth T., ed. **Ornament in Applied Art...** New York, Weyhe, 1924. 35p. (text), 122 plates. index. LC 25-1788. Another edition: *An Encyclopedia of Colour Decoration from the Earliest Times to the Middle of the XIXth Century...* New York, Weyhe, 1928. 34p. (text), 120 plates.

Last true descendant of the great nineteenth-century encyclopedias of ornament begun by Jones (219). Collection of collotypes and halftones in color of world ornament. Particularly useful for those on non-Western and Western folk ornament. Many of the latter appear again in the author's works on folk art (243, 272).

214 Evans, Joan. **Pattern: A Study of Ornament in Western Europe from 1180 to 1900.** Oxford, Clarendon Press, 1931. 2v. illus. index. Reprint: New York, Hacker, 1975. ISBN 0878171517.

Important, scholarly history of ornament from the Gothic period to the beginning of the twentieth century with particular reference to the cultural context. Particularly thorough for the Middle Ages. Contents: Volume 1: I, The Mistress Art: 1, Gothic Decoration, 2, Traditional Motives, 3, Arcades and Tracery, 5, Curvilinear Gothic, 6, Perpendicular Gothic, 7, Flamboyant Gothic; II, Speculum Naturae: 1, The Vision of Nature; 2, Forest and Chase, Medieval Pastoral, 4, Garden and Orchard, 5, Birds and Beasts, 6, Everyday Life, 7, Naturalism of the Renaissance, 8, Botany; III, The Mark of the Individual: 1, Heraldic Use, 2, The Tournament; 3, Decorative Heraldry, 4, Renaissance Heraldry, 5, Imprese, 6, Cyphers, 7, The Decline of Heraldy, IV, Literature and Decoration: 1, Beasts and Grotesques, 2, Epic and Romance, 3, Literary Illustration, 4, Renaissance Literature, 5, Inscriptions; 6, Allegory and Emblems; V, The Romance of Distance: 1, Textile Patterns, 2, Arabic Inscriptions; 3, Ogival Brocades, 4, Moresques, 5, Voyages. Volume 2: VI, The New Age: 1, The Italian Renaissance, 2, Triumphs, 3, The French Renaissance, 4, French Classicism, 5, Spain and the North, 6, Italian Baroque, 7, Le Grand Monarque, 8, Baroque outside Italy; VII, The Far East: 1, The Far East, 2, Exotic Styles; VIII, Les Amateurs: 1, The Picturesque, 2, Rocaille; IX, The Return to Antiquity: 1, The Grand Tour; 2, Rome and Greece; 3, French Classicism, 4, Nineteenth-century Classicism; X, The Return to Nature: 1, The Romantic Pastoral, 2, Rousseau, 3, Flowers, 4, Nineteenth-century Naturalism, 5, L'Art Nouveau; XI, The Romance of the Past: 1, The Gothic Rivival, 2, Gothic Romance, 3, Nineteenth-century Gothic, 4, Eclectic Archaeology; XII, The Age of Theory: 1, Philosophy and Industrialism, 2, The Search for Principles, 3, Evoi. Extensive bibliographical footnotes.

215   Glazier, Richard. **A Manual of Historic Ornament**. 4th ed. New York, Van Nostrand Reinhold, 1983. 184p. illus. index. ISBN 0442229992.

First published in 1899. Handbook of world ornament from antiquity to the end of the nineteenth century, with a collection of 200 line drawings. Particular attention is given to ancient civilizations. For its time, Glazier's handbook was among the best inexpensive manuals and was extensively used by design students.

216   Gombrich, Ernst H. **The Sense of Order. A Study in the Psychology of Decorative Art**. Ithaca, N.Y., Cornell Univ. Press, 1979. 411p. illus. index. LC 77-83898. Reprinted, 1984. ISBN 0801492491.

Based on the Wrightsman Lectures delivered at the Institute of Fine Arts, New York University. Important study of the psychology of perception in the history of ornamental art worldwide from earliest times to the present. Contents: Part One: Theory and Practice; I, Issues of Taste; II, Ornament as Art; III, The Challenge of Constraints; Part Two: The Perception of Order; IV, The Economy of Vision; V, Towards an Analysis of Effects; VI, Shapes and Things; Part Three: Psychology and History; VII, The Force of Habit; VIII, The Psychology of Styles; IX, Designs as Signs; X, The Edge of Chaos; Epilogue: Some Musical Analogies. Extensive bibliographical references in the notes.

217   Hamlin, Alfred D. F. **A History of Ornament**. New York, Century, 1916-23. 2v. illus. index. Reprint: New York, Cooper Square, 1973. LC 72-92374.

An old, once-standard history of world ornament from antiquity to the twentieth century. Contents: Volume 1: Ancient and Medieval Ornament; Volume 2: Renaissance and Modern Ornament. Illustrated with plates and line drawings. Bibliographies at the end of each chapter.

218   Hulme, Frederick E. **The Birth and Development of Ornament**. London, S. Sonnenschein, New York, Macmillan, 1893. 340p. illus. Reprint: Detroit, Gale, 1974. ISBN 0810340267.

Important, early history of ornament in Europe from ancient Egypt to the nineteenth century with a chapter on the ornament of the non-Western world. Illustrated with 177 plates of ornamental works of art and details of motifs. Occasional bibliographical reference in the footnotes.

219   Jones, Owen. **The Grammar of Ornament...** London, Quaritch, 1910. 157p. illus. Reprint: London, Studio Editions, 1986. ISBN 185170048X.

First published in 1856 (London, Day and Son) with contributions by Christopher Dresser, J. B. Waring, Matthew Digby Wyatt and others. A pioneering work in the history of ornament inspired by the popularity of the Crystal Palace Architectural Museum (Owen was responsible for the design of the ancient Egyptian, Greek and Roman courts). Illustrated with beautiful chromolithographs useful as sources for the study of nineteenth-century historicism and as sources for color and pattern for designers. Contents: 1, Ornament of Savage Tribes; 2, Egyptian Ornament; 3, Assyrian and Persian Ornament; 4, Greek Ornament; 5, Pompeian Ornament; 6, Roman Ornament; 7, Byzantine Ornament; 8, Arabian Ornament; 9, Turkish Ornament; 10, Moresque Ornament from the Alhambra; 11, Persian Ormnament; 12, Indian Ornament; 13, Hindoo Ornament; 14, Chinese Ornament; 15, Celtic Ornament; 16, Medieval Ornament; 17, Renaissance Ornament; 18, Elizabethan Ornament; 19, Italian Ornament; 20, Leaves and Flowers from Nature. Bibliographies at the end of each chapter.

220   Meyer, Franz S. **A Handbook of Ornament...** Chicago, Wilcox & Follett, 1945. 548p. illus. index. Reprint: New York, Dover, 1975. LC 75-325928.

First published in 1888. Old, comprehensive handbook of ornament. Part one treats the elements of ornament; part two, applied ornament; part three, ornament on decorative objects. Within the parts the brief text and numerous illustrations are arranged by formal qualities.

221   Racinet, Albert C. A., ed. **L'ornement polychrome; deux cents vingt planches en couleur** ... Paris, Firmin Didot, 1888. 2v. illus. index. Reprinted as: *Handbook of Ornaments in Color* (New York, Van Nostrand Reinhold, 1978, LC 77-25047).

First published in 1869 (Paris, Didot Freres). Inspired by Jones' *Grammar of Ornament* (219). Corpus of chromolithographs of ornament from antiquity to the nineteenth century.

222   Rettelbusch, Ernst. **Stilhandbuch: Ornamentik, Mobel, Innenausbau von den ältesten Zeiten bis zum Biedermeier.** 9th ed. Stuttgart, Hoffman, 1974. 254p. illus. ISBN 387346022X.

Collection of line drawings of ornament and ornamented works of the decorative arts from antiquity to the late Empire style, i.e., Biedermeier style. Captions in English, French, and German, but notes to the illustrations in German only. Bibliography, p. vi.

223   Speltz, Alexander. **Styles of Ornament, Exhibited in Designs, and Arranged in Historical Order...** New York, Grosset and Dunlap, 1935. 647p. illus. index. LC 36-12494. Reprint: New York, Dover, 1959.

Comprehensive pictorial history of ornament from ancient Egypt through Neoclassicism. Brief text introduces each period followed by collection of line drawings with captions indicating source. Alphabetical list of sources, pp. 627-29.

224   Wersin, Wolfgang von. **Das Elementare Ornament und seine Gesetzlichkeit. Eine Morphologie des Ornaments.** Ravensburg, 1940. 100p. LC 43-32034.

Important, scholarly study of the design principles inherent in ornament worldwide from prehistoric times to the twentieth century. Contents: I. Teil: Von der Natur des Ornaments: Ornament als abstrakte Ausdrucksform; Polarität al Inhalt des Ornaments. Einheit im Gegensatz; Rhythmus; Dynamik; Ordnung. II. Teil: Versuch einer Gliederung des Ornaments: Über die Berechtigung einer gliederden Übersicht; Die zwei Hauptgruppen: Rhythmisches und dynamisches Ornament; Das elementare Ornament; Grundlagen der Gliederung des rhythmischen Ornaments; Die drei Grundgattungen des rhytrhmischen Ornaments. III. Teil: Von der Bestimmung des Ornaments. Beziehungen und Abgrenzungen: Ornament als Mittel der Gestaltung; Das

Typische im Ornament; Ornamentals Schmuck; Ornament und Symbol; Ornament und Stil; Ornament und Naturdarstellug; Ornament und Material und Technik.

ANCIENT AND MEDIEVAL ORNAMENT

225 Audsley, William J. **Medieval Ornamental Styles**. Secaucus, N.J., Chartwell Books, 1988. various pagings. ISBN 155213375.

Reprint of the author's *Polychromatic Decoration as Applied to Buildings in the Medieval Styles* (London, H. Sotheran, 1882).

Collection of 36 color plates of medieval ornament. Most are taken from specific medieval sources, but others are the free interpretations of the author. All are intended to guide contemporary artists in correctly imitating medieval colors and ornament styles in interior decoration and as such are valuable sources for ecclesiastical English neo-Gothic interior decoration. Introduction provides practical hints: processes of painting, preparing and transferring the design, executing the design, principles of decorating design and coloring.

226 Bronsted, Johannes. **Early English Ornament; the Sources, Developement and Relationship to Foreign Styles of Pre-Norman Ornamental Art in England...** London, Hachette; Copenhagen, Levin & Munksgaard, 1924. 352p. illus. index. LC 25-23105.

Important, scholarly history of the ornament found on English art from the seventh century A.D. to the Norman Conquest. Emphasis is on the relationship between Anglo-Saxon art and Scandinavian art. Contents: I, From the Introduction of Christianity to the Encounter with the Scandinavian Style about A.D. 900: 1, North of England; 2, The South of England; 3, Scandinavia; II, The Period from about 900 A.D. till the Conquest: 1, The North of England; 2, The South of England; 3, Scandinavia; III, Southern Europe: Oriental Animal Ornament in the Pre-Norman Period. Bibliographical references in the footnotes.

227 Dehli, Arne. **Selections of Byzantine Ornament**. New York, W. Helburn, 1890. 2v. in 1. LC 44-422717.

Collection of 100 plates illustrating specimens of Byzantine ornament found in sites in Italy.

228 Fottova-Samalova, Pavla. **Egyptian Ornament**. London, A. Wingate, 1963. 162p. illus. LC 64-2811.

Popular survey of ancient Egyptian ornament illustrated with plates and line drawings taken from various works of architecture and the applied and decorative arts. No bibliography.

229 Grabar, André. **La decoration byzantine**. Paris and Brussels, Van Oest, 1928. 44p. illus. LC 39-718.

In the series: Architecture et Arts Décoratifs. Survey by a leading scholar of ornament in Byzantine art and architecture from the fourth century to the fifteenth century. Contains 32 plates with descriptive notes. Bibliography, p. 41, lists basic books on Byzantine art.

230 Heideloff, Carl A. von. **Les Ornements du moyen age**. Die ornamentik des Mittelalters. Eine Sammlung auserwahter Verzierungen und Profile byzantinischer und deutscher Architektur... Nuremberg, J. A. Stein, 1846-47. 4v. in 1. LC 10-29095.

Collection of plates illustrating Byzantine and German medieval architectural ornament. Important as a source for medieval revivalism in the nineteenth century.

231   Leeds. E. T. **Celtic Ornament in the British Isles down to 700 A.D.** Oxford, England, Clarendon, 1933. 170p. illus. index. LC 34-2029.

Survey of the development of ornament in Celtic Britain from the la Tène period to the late eighth century A.D. Contents: I, The Beginnings; II, The British Development; III, Early British Numismatic Art; IV, The Celts as Delineators of Human and Animal Figures and as Plastic Artists; V, The Coming of Rome; VI, The Revival. Bibliographical footnotes.

232   Petrie, Flinders. **Decorative Patterns of the Ancient World.** London, Quaritch, 1930. 88 plates. LC 32-2670. Reprint: New York, Dover, 1990. ISBN 0517022176.

Pictorial survey of ornament from ancient Egypt through la Téne Celtic. Consists of plates of line drawings detailed with brief notes.

233   Pugin, Augustus Charles. **Gothic Ornaments, Selected from Various Ancient Buildings in England and France...** New and rev. ed. Cleveland, Ohio, Carl Wendelin Kuehny, 1931. 92 plates.

First published in 1840 (London, Bohn). Highly influencial collection of drawings of medieval architectural ornament taken from various buildings dating from the eleventh to the sixteenth centuries. For the role of Pugin in the Gothic revival *see* ARCH 938, 940, 949, 950, 1019.

234   Ulbert, Thilo. **Studien zur dekorativen Reliefplastik des ostlichen Mittelmeeraumes.** Munich, Universität, Institut für Byzantinisk und Neugriechische Philologie, 1969. 140p. illus. (Miscellanea Byzantina Monacensia, Heft 10).

Based on the author's thesis, *Freiburg im Breisgau*. Extensive bibliography in the notes, pp. 89-137. For ancient architectural ornament *see also*: ARCH 239-247, 310-312. For medieval architectural ornament *see also*: ARCH 425, 426, 428.

RENAISSANCE—MODERN ORNAMENT

235   Berliner, Rudolf. **Ornamentale Vorlageblätter des 15. bis 18. Jahrhunderts.** Leipzig, Klinkhardt & Biermann, 1924-26. 182p. (text), 450 plates in 4 v. index. Reprinted, 1981. ISBN 3781402002.

Important history/handbook of European engraved ornament design from the beginning of engraving in the fifteenth century to the beginning of the nineteenth century. The corpus of 450 plates is accompanied by a scholarly catalog that includes references to specialized literature and long notes that constitute an important history of the genre. The engravings were selected from print collections in Amsterdam, Basel, Berlin (Kunstbibliothek and Kupferstichkabinett), Braunschweig, Bremen (Kunsthalle), Veste Coburg, Dresden (Kunstgewerbe museum, Kupferstichkabinett and Sammlung Friedrich), Florence (Uffizi), Frankfurt am Main, Hamburg (Kunsthalle), Leipzig (Kunstgewerbemuseum), London (British Museum and Victoria and Albert Museum), Munich (Graphische Sammlung, Bayerisches Nationalmuseum, Staatsbibliothek), Münster (Landesmuseum), Nuremberg (Germanisches Nationalmuseum), Oxford (Christ Church), Paris (Bibliothèque nationale and Musée des Arts Décoratifs), Stuttgart, Vienna (Albertina, Kunsthistorisches Museum, Österrichisches Museum), and Wolfenbüttel. Fully indexed. A standard work; invaluable tool for the history of prints and of ornament.

236   Durant, Stuart. **Ornament, from the Industrial Revolution to Today.** Woodstock, N.Y., Overlook Press, 1986. 336p. illus. index. ISBN 0879512199.

Important history of ornament in Europe and America from the 1840s to the present. Richly illustrated with views of interiors, details of architecture and a great number of details of ornamental motifs. Contents: 1, Encyclopedias of Ornament; 2, Nature and Ornament; 3, Geometrical Ornament; 4, The Gothic Revival; 5, Eclecticism; 6, Orientalism; 7, 'The Cult of Japan'; 8, 'Primitivism'; 9, The Arts and Crafts Movement; 10, Art Déco—the Evolution of a Style; 11, Modernism; 12, 1940 to the Present: Revival. Appendix with brief biographies of major designers. Bibliographical footnotes, many with useful annotations, and good classified bibliography of books in all languages, pp. 310-319.

237 Guilmard, Désiré. **Les maitres ornemanistes, dessinateurs, peintures, architectes, sculpteurs et graveurs; écoles française, italienne, allemande, et des Pays-Bas (flamande & hollandaise)...** Paris, Plon, 1880-81, 560p. illus. index. Reprint: Amsterdam, S. Emmering, 1968. LC 68-141921.

Important dictionary of European decorative and graphic artists from the fifteenth to the end of the eighteenth centuries. Arrangement is by country (écoles) subdivided by period. Entries on individual artists provide biographical information and a valuable catalog of the artists' ornament prints, some of which are published in Bartsch (*Le peintre graveur,* Vienne, Degen, 1803-21, 21v.), but many are unpublished suites of prints in various print collections in France and Belgium. Collection of 180 plates are a representative sample of the work of the major artists and of distinctive genres. Indexes by artist and motif at the end of each chapter.

238 Kroll, Franz-Lothar. **Das Ornament in der Kunsttheorie des 19. Jahrhunderts.** Hildesheim, New York, Olms, 1987. 304p. illus. (Studien zur Kunstgeschichte, Band 42) ISBN 3487078368.

Important, scholarly study of the position of ornament in the theory of art and art history of the nineteenth century. Only recently has the analysis of ornament again become a focus of the art historiography (*see* Gombrich 216). In the nineteenth century, and particularly in the writings of many of the "founders" of art history, it played a major role. Contents: I, Ornament-Deutung als Ornament-Kritik? Die Kunstliterature seit der Renaissance; II, Das Ornament als Kunstform: Hegel—Boetticher—Schinkel; III, Das Ornament im System der ästhetik: Friedrich Theodor Vischer; IV, Die Entwicklung des islamischen Ornaments: Karl Schnaase und Franz Kugler; V, Das Ornament als Zweckform: Gottfried Semper; VI, Das Ornament als Stilträger: Alois Riegl; VII, Weltgeschichte des Ornaments: Wilhelm Worringer; VIII, Psychologie des Ornaments: Theodor Lipps und Wilhelm Wundt; IX, Ornament, Industrie, Nature: John Ruskin und William Morris; X, Ornamenttheorie und Künstlerästhetik: Henry van de Velde und Adolf Loos; XI, Das Ornament im System der Künste: August Schmarsow; XII, Europäisches Denken und islamisches Ornament: Die Kunstliteratur der Gegenwart. Bibliographical footnotes and comprehensive, classified bibliography, pp. 157-193.

ORIENTAL ORNAMENT

239 Rawson, Jessica. **Chinese Ornament: The Lotus and the Dragon.** New York, Holmes & Meier, 1984. 240p. illus. ISBN 084190227.

Published to accompany an exhibition of the same title at the British Museum. Comprehensive survey of ornament in all Oriental cultures as illustrated in works of the applied and decorative arts. Contents: I, Architectural Decoration in Asia; 2, Lotus and Peony Scrolls; 3, Animal Ornament; 4, Flowers and Frames; 5, Chinese Motifs in Iranian and Turkish Art. Appendix surveys lotus and papyrus designs in ancient Egypt, Mesopotamia and Greece. Maps, list of Chinese dynasties, glossary and comprehensive bibliography, pp. 228-235.

240 Jarry, Madeleine. **Chinoiserie: Chinese Influence on European Decorative Art, 17th and 18th Centuries**. New York, Vendome Press, 1981. 221p. illus. index. ISBN 0865650187.

Important, well-illustrated survey of the influence of Chinese ornament and works of applied and decorative arts on European applied and decorative arts in the seventeenth and eighteenth centuries. Contents: I, Textiles and Painted Wallpapers; II, Ceramics; III, Furniture; IV, Objets d'Art; V, George IV of England Exoticism. Bibliographical references in the footnotes and general bibliography, p. 197.

241 Jones, Owen. **The Grammar of Chinese Ornament: Selected from Objects in the South Kensington Museum and Other Collections**. 1887. 15p. 100 plates. Reprint: New York, Portland House, 1987. ISBN 0517641542.

Collection of 100 chromolithographic plates of Chinese ornament taken from various objects of the decorative arts. Descriptions of the plates often offer valuable insights into the principles of the particular patterns but do not adequately identify the object from which the ornament is derived. In the eight-page introduction the author applies to Chinese ornament the "propositions" described in detail in his *Grammar of Ornament* (219).

See also the author's *Chinese Design & Pattern in Full Color* (New York, Dover, 1981. 48p. illus. ISBN 0486242048).

242 Rostovtzeff, Michael Ivanovitch. **The Animal Style in South Russia and China**. New York, Hacker Art Books, 1973. 112p. illus. LC 75-143361.

Pioneering study of the origin and early development of animal ornament in Scythian and Sarmatian cultures of the Black Sea region and the Han and Chou Dynasties in China. Contents: I, The Sythian Period; II, The Sarmatian Period; III, Origin of the Scythian Animal Style and the Animal Style of China of the Chou Dynasty; IV, Animal Style in China in the Time of the Han Dynasty. Contains 33 plates. Bibliographical references in the notes.

PRIMITIVE ORNAMENT

243 Bossert, Helmuth T. **Folk Art of Primitive Peoples; Six Hundred Decorative Motifs in Color, Forming a Survey of the Applied Art of Africa, Asia, Australia, and Oceania, North-Central, and South America**. New York, Praeger, 1955. 15p. 40 plates. LC 55-11523.

Pictorial survey of traditional ornament of the non-Western world. Brief introductory essay. No bibliography.

244 Lehmann, Johannes. **Die Ornamente der Natur-und Halbkulturvölker**. Frankfurt am Main, J. Lehmann, 1920. 160p. illus.

Pictorial survey of the ornament used in the art and architecture of the native peoples of Oceania, Australia, Malaysia, Indonesia, China, Japan, India, Africa and North and South America. Illustrated with drawings grouped in two parts. First part presents general ormanent types with analysis of their formal qualities; second group illustrates ornaments by cultural group. Introductory essay: "Beitrag zu Entwicklung der Ornamente und ihre Verwertung für Kunstgewerbe und Architektur." Comprehensive, classified and annotated bibliography, pp.15-34, is keyed to the illustrations.

245 Williams, Geoffrey. **African Designs from Traditional Sources**. New York, Dover, 1971. 22p. 200 plates. ISBN 0486227529. Dover Pictorial and Archive Series.

Useful collection of designs taken from various traditional works of Black African decorative arts intended as a resource for contemporary artists and designers. Bibliography, pp. xxi-xxii.

246   Caraway, Caren. **African Designs of the Congo, Nigeria, the Cameroons and the Guinea Coast**. Owings Mill, Md., Stemmer House, 1986. 140p.
Collection of designs taken from various works of West African decorative arts intended as a resource for contemporary artists and designers.

CHAPTER THREE

FOLK ART

BIBLIOGRAPHIES

247 **Internationale Volkskundliche Bibliographie. International Folklore Bibliographie. Bibliographie internationale des arts et traditions populaires.** v. 1-. Basel, Societe Suisse des Traditions Populaires, 1942-. Edited by Robert Wildhaber. Succeeds: *Volkskundliche Bibliographie* (Strasbourg and Berlin, 1917-41).

Comprehensive annual bibliography covering all aspects of folk and popular culture including folk art. Lists books, catalogs and periodical articles in all languages. A standard reference work for research in the field of folk art.

GENERAL HISTORIES AND HANDBOOKS

248 **Art populaire; travaux artistiques et scientifiques du 1er congrès international des arts populaires.** Paris, Editions Duchartre, 1932. 2v. illus. LC 22-30049.

Important collection essays on various aspects of world folk art based on reports given at the first international congress of popular art in Prague in 1928. Contents: Tome I: I, Definitions—Origines—Generalites; II, Monographiies Nationales et Regionales: Allemagne, Canada, Congo belge, Danemark, Egypte, Equateur, Espagne,Estonie, Etats-Unis, France, Grèce, Hongrie, Indes Néerlandaises, Lettonie, Norvège, Nouvelle-Calédonie, Pays-Bas, Pologne, Roumanie, Russie, Suède, Suisse, Techécoslovaque; III, Etudes sur les Techniques: L'architecture, Le travail du bois,Le metal et les bijoux, La ceramique. Tome II: III, Etudes sur les techniques: Le textile: Le costume, Ornements du costume, Tapis et tissage, Divers; La Musique; La Danse et le theatre. Important collection of plates. Bibliographical references in the footnotes.

See also the museum guide: *Hamburgisches Museum für Volkerkunde: Führer durch die Sammlungen,* by J. Zwernemann (Munich, Prestel, 1984. 199p. illus. ISBN 3791307002).

See also the exhibition catalog: *The Spirit of Folk Art: The Girard Collection at the Museum of International Folk Art,* by H. Glassie (New York, Abrams, 1989. 276p. illus. index. ISBN 089013193).

AMERICAN FOLK ART

Bibliographies

249 Bronner, Simon J. **A Critical Bibliography of American Folk Art.** Bloomington, Ind., Folklore Publications Group, 1978. 112p. index. (FPG Monograph Series, v. 3). LC 78-113721.

Classified and annotated bibliography of 704 books and periodical articles on folk art in the United States. Folk art is defined by the compiler as "art in traditional society and traditional art in contemporary society" thus works by so-called naive modern and contemporary artists are included. Emphasis is on painting and sculpture with few citations of works dealing with the crafts in folk culture. For further expressions of the author's definition of folk art see his: "Recent Folk

Art Publications: A Review Essay," *Mid-South Folklore*, 6 (1978), pp. 27-30. An expanded edition appeared in 1980 as: *Bibliography of American Folk and Vernacular Art* with 1,138 entries.

250   Bronner, Simon J., ed. **American Folk Art: A Guide to Sources**. New York, Garland, 1984. 313p. illus. index. ISBN 0824090063 (Garland Reference Library of the Humanities, vol. 464).

Comprehensive bibliography of books and periodical literature on the broad aspects of American folk art, the work of a team of experts. Contents: A, Background and History by S. J. Bronner; B, Art Criticism and Aesthetic Philosophy by M. O. Jones and V. Greenfield; C, Grenres (Panting, Sculpture, Furniture, Textiles, Ceramics, Metals) by K. L. Ames; D, Biographies by S. S. Faulds and A. Skillman; E, Region and Locaity by C. K. Dewhurst and M. MacDowell; F, Ethnicity and Religion by R. T. Teske; G, Afro-Americans by E. W. Metcalf; H. Workers and Trades by D. D. Fanelli and S. J. Bronner; I, Symbol, Image, and Theme by E. Eff; J, Collectors and Museums by E. M. Adler; K, Educators and Classrooms by K. G. Congdon; L, Films by W. Ferris; M, Topics on the Horizon (Public Folk Art, Folk Art and the Aging, Folk Art and Gender, Commercialization, Popularization and Modernization) by S. J. Bronner. Each section is introduced by an essay giving an over view of the state of research. The titles are also fully annotated.

251   Sink, Susan. **Traditional Crafts and Craftsmanship in America: A Selected Bibliography**. Washington, D.C., American Folklife Center, Library of Congress, 1983. 84p. index. (Publications of the American Folklife Center, no. 11). LC 84-127666.

Comprehensive bibliography of some 1,000 books, periodical articles and unpublished dissertations published from 1852 to 1983 on all aspects of traditional crafts in the United States including folk and naive art. Entries are not annotated but bear the call numbers of the Library of Congress. The subject headings in the index offer some substitute for lack of a classification system.

Research Guides

252   Ames, Kenneth L., et al. **Material Culture: a Research Guide**. Lawrence, Ks., University of Kansas Press, 1985. 224p. index. ISBN 0700602747.

Collected essays on the methods and problems of research in a broad variety of aspects of material culture including folk art and craft. Bibliographical references in the notes. Contents: Material Culture and Cultural Research by T. J. Schlereth; Learning from Looking by P. F. Lewis; The Power of Things (on vernacular architecture) by D. Upton; The Stuff of Everyday Life, American Decorative Arts, Household Furnishings by K. L. Ames; The History of Technology and the Study of Material Culture by C. W. Pursell, Jr.; Visible Culture Research by T. J. Schlereth; A Guide to General Research Resources by T. J. Schlereth (with list of bibliographies and serial literature).

253   Brunvand, Jan H. **The Study of American Folklore: An Introduction**. 3rd. ed. New York, Norton, 1985. 620p. illus. index. ISBN 0393954951.

Comprehensive guide to the study and reserach of Amerucan folklore including folk art and architecture. Contents: I, Introduction: 1, The Field of Folklore, 2, The Study of Folklore, 3, Bearers of American Folk Tradition; II, Verbal Folklore: 4, Folk Speech and Naming, 5, Proverbs and Proverbial Phrases, 6, Riddles and Other Verbal Puzzels, 7, Rhymes and Folk Poetry, 8, Myths and Motifs, 9, Legends and Anecdotes, 10, Folktales, 11, Folksongs, 12, Ballads, 13, Folk Music; III. Customary Folklore: 14, Superstitions, 15, Customs and Festivals, 16, Folk Dances and Dramas, 17, Folk Gestures, 18, Folk Games; IV, Material Folk Traditions: 19, Folklife, 20, FolkArchitecture, 21, Folk Crafts and Art, 22, Folk Costumes, 23, Folk Foods. Each chapter concludes with an extensive bibliography.

See also Dorson, Richard. *Handbook of American Folklore.* (Bloomington, Ind., Indiana Univ. Press, 1983).

Histories and Handbooks

254   Andrews, Ruth, ed. **How to Know American Folk Art**. New York, Dutton, 1977. 204p. illus. index. ISBN 0525474609.

Collected essays on various aspects of American folk art. Contents: Preface by R. Andrews; Introduction by L. C. Jones; Early New England Gravestone by A. Neal; The Wildfowl Decoy by A. Earnest; Redware and Stoneware Folk Pottery by W. C. Ketchum; Folk Art of Spanish New Mexico by R. J. Stroessner; American Folk Painting by. M. Black; American Country Furniture by R. Bishop; American Quilts by J. Hostein; Pennsylvania German Folk Art by F. S. Weiser,; American Folk Sculpture by F. Fried; American Folk Art in the Twentieth Century by M. J. Gladstone. Bibliographies at the end of each chapter.

255   Bishop, Robert et al. **Folk Art: Paintings, Sculpture & Country Objects**. New York, Knopf, 1983. 478p. illus. index. ISBN 0394714938.

In the series: "The Knopf Collectors' Guides to American Antiques." Well-illustrated collector's guidebook. Arrangement is by media: paintings, sculpture, country household objects, and subdivided by types of objects, e.g. portraits, signs, decoys, baskets, lighting fixtures, tools. Each of the 360 objects are featured with illustrations in color and descriptions that include comment on the place of the object in the history of folk art and estimates of the rarity of the object. Price ranges of the objects is supplied through a list at the end of the work. Useful advice on collecting, list of museums and other collections of American folk art and selected bibliography, pp. 442-44.

256   Christensen, Erwin O. **American Crafts and Folk Arts**. Washington, D.C., R. B. Luce, 1964. 90p. illus. LC 64-19601.

Popular survey from Colonial times to end of the nineteenth century. Chapters on American Indian crafts, the iconography of the American eagle, and European folk art transplanted in America.

257   Ericson, Jack T., ed. **Folk Art in America: Painting and Sculpture**. New York, Mayflower Books, 1978. 175p. illus. index. ISBN 0831734124.

Collection of articles that appeared in the magazine *Antiques* between 1935 and 1977. Contents: What Is Primitive and What Is Not? by C.W. Drepperd; What Is American Folk Art? A Symposium; Artisan and Amateur in American Folk Art by H. Cahill; Print to Primitive by J. Lipman; Engraved Sources for American Overmantle Panels by N. F. Little; Liberty and Considerable License by L. C. Jones; How Pictures Were Used in New England Houses, 1825-1850 by B. T. Rumford; Benjamin Greenleaf, New England Limner by J. Lipman; Isaac Sheffield, Connecticut Limner by E. deN. Mayhew; The Conversation Piece in American Folk Art by N. F. Little; J. Evans, Painter by N. and G. Savage; Joseph Goodhue Chandler (1813-1884) by J. W. Keefe; J. A. Davis by N. and G. Savage; Sheldon Peck by M. E. Balazs; The Landscape of Change, Views of Rural New England by J. E. Canton; Mary Ann Willson by N.F. Karlins; Noah North (1809-1880) by N. C. Muller and J. Oak; John S. Blunt by R. Bishop; John Haley Bellamy by V. Stafford; Schimmel the Woodcarver by Milton E. Flower; Aaron Mountz by Milton Flower; Pierre Joseph Landry by L. B. Bridaham; Figures and Figureheads: The Maritime Collection of the State Bank and Trust Company, Boston by W. D. Garrett; Cushing and White's Copper Weather Vanes by M. Kaye; Winged Skull and Weeping Willow by V. W. Allen; Massachusetts Gravestones by D. Farber. Bibliography of basic books, pp. 171-172.

258   Hemphill, Herbert W., and Julia Weissman. **Twentieth Century American Folk Art and Artists**. New York, Dutton, 1974. 237p. illus. index. ISBN 0525224734.

Survey of American folk art, or naive art, from 1900 to 1970 with emphasis on the work of known painters and sculptors. Contains much valuable biographical material not available elsewhere. Index to the artists, classified bibliography of basic works, pp. 232-233.

259   Horwitz, Elinor. **Contemporary American Folk Artists**. Philadelphia and New York, Lippincott, 1975. 144p. illus. index. ISBN 0397316267.

Collection of biographies of ten painters, six carvers, and seven environmental artists working in 1970 in folk traditions or who were untutored, so-called naive artists. Suggestions for further reading, p. 139, and list of museums with outstanding folk art collections, p. 140.

260   Jones, Michael Owen. **Exploring Folk Art: Twenty Years of Thought on Craft, Work, and Aesthetics**. Ann Arbor, Mich., U.M.I. Research Press, 1987. 219p. illus. index. ISBN 0835718158.

In the series: "American Material Culture and Folklife." Collected essays by an important scholar of American material culture and folk art, many are important efforts to reevaluate the definition of folk art and its relationship to material culture. Contents: 1, Violations of Standards of Excellence and Preference in Utilitarian Art; 2, A Strange Rocking Chair: The Need to Express, the Urge to Create; 3, Re-dos and Add-Ons: Private Space vs. Public Policy; 4, Modern Arts and Arcane Concepts: Expanding Folk Art Study; 5, The Proof Is in the Pudding: The Role of Sensation in Food Choice as Revealed by Sensory Deprivation; 6, Creating and Using Argot at the Jayhawk Cafe: Communication, Ambience, and Identity; 7, A Feeling for Form, as Illustrated by People at Work; 8, Aesthetics at Work: Art and Ambience in an Organization; 9, Aesthetic Attitude, Judgment and Response: Definitions and Distinctions; 10, The Material Culture of Corporate Life; 11, Preaching What We Practice: Pedagogical Techniques Regarding the Analysis of Objects in Organizations. References, pp. 205-214, is an unclassified but useful list of recent publications on American folk art and material culture.

261   Jones, Michael Owen. **The Hand Made Object and Its Maker**. Berkeley and Los Angeles, University of California Press, 1975. 261p. illus. LC 73-93055.

Study of contemporary American craftsman based chiefly on interviews with "Charley," a chairmaker in the 1950s and 1960s. Text reproduces handwriting; this together with the "homey" titles of the chapters hides the important insights presented. Contents: 1, A Strange Rocking Chair; 2, The Bookcase Masterpiece and the New Design; 3, It all Ended up the Wrong Way; 4, Make It Look Older, More Antique; 5, Like Somebody Hugging You; 6, It Takes Half a Fool to Make Chairs; 7, The Beauty Part and the Lasting Part. Bibliographical references with commentary in the notes.

262   Lipman, Jean, and Eve Meulendyke. **American Folk Decoration**. New York, Oxford University Press, 1951. 163p. illus. index. Reprint: New York, Dover, 1972. LC 51-11035.

History/handbook of American folk art with advice on how to imitate historical pieces. Good selection of illustrations. Contents: 1, Decorated Furniture; 2, Decorative Accessories; 3, Ornamented Tinware; 4, Stenciled and Painted Fabrics; 5, Architectural Decoration; 6, Coach and Sign Painting; 7, Fractur Designs. Classified bibliography, pp. 157-59.

263   Lipman, Jean, and Alice Winchester. **The Flowering of American Folk Art, 1776-1876**. New York, Viking, 1974. 288p. illus. LC 73-6081.

Written to accompany an exhibition of major works of American folk art at the Whitney Museum of American Art. Highly influential work in establishing the aesthetic value of American folk art, particularly painting. Today criticized for its historical definition of folk art. Contents:

Pictures: Painted, Drawn and Stitched: Portraits, Landscapes and Seascapes, Scenes from Daily Life, Religious, Literary and Historical Subjects, Still Life, Cutouts and Samplers, Penmanship, Fractur and Presentation Pieces; Sculpture in Wood, Metal, Stone and Bone: Portraits, Ship Figureheads and Sternboards, Weathervanes and Whirligigs, Cigar-store Figures and Other Shop Signs, Decoys, Toys, Household Ornaments; Decoration for Home and Highway: Overmantels, Fireboards, Cornices, Walls and Floors, Tavern Signs; Furnishings: Furniture, Accessories. Appendix with biographies of artists. Classified bibliography of books and periodical articles, pp. 284-287.

264 Lipman, Jean, Elizabeth V. Warren, and Robert Bishop. **Young America: A Folk-Art History**. New York, Hudson Hills Press, 1986. 199p. illus. index. ISBN 093392075X.

Survey of folk art in America designed to accompany a traveling exhibition of the American Museum of Folk Art. Contents: Foreword: Finding and Defining Folk Art in the Early Days by Jean Lipman; Introduction: Between the Wars by Elizabeth V. Warren; 1, House and Garden; 2, Church and School; 3, On the Farm; 4, In Town; 5, On the Road; 6, At Sea; 7, War; 8, Weddings, Births, and Deaths; 9, Work; 10, Play; Afterword: Rediscovering American Folk Art—Yesterday, Today, and Tomorrow by Robert Bishop. General bibliography, pp. 190-192.

265 Ketchum, William. **All-American Folk Art and Crafts**. New York, Rizzoli, 1986. 256p. illus. index. ISBN 0847807657.

Richly illustrated survey of American folk art that is concerned with patriotic themes. Contents: Stars and Stripes Forever; The Original Americans; Faces of America; Fathers of the Nation; In God We Trust; The American Eagle; Liberty, the Great Lady; Home Sweet Home; Working the Land; Building the Nation; Down to the Sea in Ships; Celebrating America. List of public collections of American folk art. Selected bibliography of general works, pp. 249-250.

266 Polley, Robert L., ed. **America's Folk Art**. New York, Putnam, 1968. 192p. illus. LC 68-31615.

Popular survey of American folk arts and crafts of the eighteenth and nineteenth centuries. Chapters treat media (i.e., glass, ceramics, metalwork, painting) and classes of objects (i.e., lighting devices, weathervanes, toys, and guns). Appendix with list of major museums and collection. No bibliography.

See also the museum catalog: *American Folk Paintings: Paintings and Drawings Other Than Portraits from the Abby Aldrich Rockefeller Folk Art Center* (Boston, Little Brown, 1988. 449p. illus. index. ISBN 0821216201).

See also the exhibition catalogs: *Beyond Necessity: Art in the Folk Tradition: An Exhibition from the Collections of Winterthur Museum at the Brandywine River Museum*, by K. L. Ames (Winterthur, Del., Winterthur Museum, 1977. 131p. illus. ISBN 0912724056), *American Folk Art; from the Traditional to the Naive*, by L. Rhodes (Cleveland, Oh., Cleveland Museum of Art, 1978. 117p. illus. ISBN 0910386420), *An American Sampler: Folk Art from the Shelburne Museum* (Washington, D.C., National Gallery of Art, 1987. 211p. illus. ISBN 0894681044), *American Folk Art: The Herbert Waide Hemphill, Jr. Collection* (Milwaukee, Wis., Milwaukee Art Museum, 1981. 112p. illus.), *American Folk Art: Expressions of a New Spirit*, by R. Bishop, et al. (New York, Museum of American Folk Art, 1983. 146p. illus. ISBN 0912161831), *Unexpected Eloquence: The Art in American Folk Art*, by H. Rose (NewYork, R. Saroff in association with Edith C. Blum Art Institute, Bard College, 1990. 128p. illus. ISBN 1878352024).

Canada

267   Bird, Michael. **Canadian Folk Art**. Toronto, Oxford Univ. Press, 1982. 121p. illus. index. ISBN 0195404246.

Pictorial survey of the folk and traditional arts and crafts of Canada from early colonial times to the end of the nineteenth century. Contents: 1, Paintings, Drawings, and Paper Cut-outs; 2, Sculpture; 3, Toys and Games; 4, Textiles; 5, Furniture; 6, Architecture; 7, Gravemarkers; 8, Religious Objects; 9, Household Articles; 10, Decorated Boxes. Glossary and classified bibliography of basic works, pp. 119-121.

268   McKendry, Blake. **Folk Art: Primitive and Naive Art in Canada**. Toronto, Methueun; New York, Facts on File, 1983. 288p. illus. index. ISBN 0458968005.

History of folk art in Canada from early Colonial times to the present. Also includes so-called naive art, i.e., the art of modern artists, often uneducated provincial artists, who work without knowledge of academic techniques and styles. Contents: 1, Interest and Recognition; 2, Definitions and Sources, 2, Primitive, 4, Naive; 5, Provincial; 6, Folk-Culture Artifacts; 7, Themes and Directions. Comprehensive, classified bibliography, pp. 265-270, and additional bibliography in the notes.

See also Lessard (113, 114) and Webster (115).

See also the exhibtion catalog: *From the Heart: Folk Art in Canada.* Canadian Centre for Folk Culture Studies of the National Museum of Man (Toronto, McClelland and Stewart, 1983. 256p. illus. ISBN 071090218).

Latin America

269   Cordero Iniguez, Jaun. **Bibliografia eucatoriana de artesanias y artes populares.** Cuenca, Ecuador, Centro Interamericano de Artesanias y Artes Populares, 1980. 373p. index. LC 81-120228.

Unclassified, annotated bibliography of 1,000 books and periodical articles on all aspects of folk art and popular art in Eucador. Includes music as well as the visual arts. Comprehensive dictionary index.

270   Rubin de la Borbolla, Daniel F. **Arte popular mexicano**. Mexico, Fondo de Cultura Economica, 1974. 302p. illus. LC 75-527407.

Scholarly study of folk art in Mexico from pre-Columbian times to the present with emphasis on the economic aspects. Contents; Arte popular: definición; Characterísticas del arte popular; El arte popular precolombino; España; Interculturación; El trasplante y otros fenómenos; Arte popular: el Virreinato; El arte popular y la Revolución industrial; El arte popular mexicano: observaciones finales; Reflexiones finales. General bibliography, pp. 295-99.

271   Toneyama, Kojin. **The Popular Arts of Mexico**. New York, Tokyo, Weatherhill, Heibonsha, 1974. 225p. illus. ISBN 0834810301.

Sumptuously illustrated survey of contemporary folk art in Mexico in the form of the author's travel journal to Nayarit, Guerro, Michoacán, Mexico City, Puebla, Oaxaca, Chiapas, and Veracruz. Three hundred six plates encompass all folk art and crafts as well as theater, dance, and festivals. Appendix with essay on techniques by Carlos Espejel. No bibliography.

See also the museum catalog: *Folk Treasures of Mexico: The Nelson A. Rockefeller Collection in the San Antonio Museum of Art and the Mexican Museum, San Francisco,* by M. Oettinger (New York, Abrams, 1990. 223p. illus. index. ISBN 0810911825).

EUROPEAN FOLK ART

General Histories and Handbooks

272   Bossert, Helmuth T. **Peasant Art in Europe...** London, Benn, 1927. 44p. (text), 132 plates. index. LC 28-11634.
Pictorial survey arranged by country. List of dated examples. General bibliography, pp. 40-43.

273   Hansen, H. J., ed. **European Folk Art in Europe and the Americas.** New York and Toronto, McGraw-Hill, 1967. 281p. illus. index. LC 68-16683.
Well-illustrated survey of European and American folk art and architecture, the work of a team of international experts. Contents: Northern Europe: Norway, Sweden, Finland, Iceland, Denmark; The British Isles: Scotland, England, Ireland; Central Europe: The Low Countries, Germany, Austria, Czechoslovakia, Switzerland; Western Europe: France, Portugal, Spain; Southern Europe: Italy, Yugoslavia, Greece; Eastern Europe: Hungary, Bulgaria, Rumania, Poland, The Soviet Union; The New World: North America, South America; Folk Art on the Market. Genera; bibliography, pp. 261-62.
See also the museum catalog: *Europäische Volkstrachter* by H. Nixdorff (Berlin, Museum für Volkerkunde, 1977- v. 1-).

National Histories and Handbooks

Austria

274   Haberlandt, Michael. **Werke der Volkskunst mit besonderer Berücksichtung Öster-reichs.** Vienna, J. Lowey, 1914. 2v. illus. index.
Collected essays on a broad range of topics in the folk art of Austria-Hungary. Contents Band I: Die Werke des Johann Georg Kieninger by M. Haberlandt; Ein Werk der Volkskunst im Lichte der Kunstforschung by J. Strzygowski; Wahrsagekarten der Willdensteiner Ritterschaft by W. von Molthein; Prähistorisches in der Volkskunst Osteuropas by A. Haberlandt; Ein altes Werk der Habaner Keramik by J. Tvrdy; Zwei alte Votivbilder in Riffian bei Meran by O. Menghin; Ein Schraubentaler der Salburger Emigranted by W. von Molthein; Ein Hirtenbecher aus Sardinien by M. Haberlandt; Der vFund von Schwanenstadt by H. Ubell; Der Alpacher Möbelstil by K. von Radinger; Der Renaissancefund von Poysdorf by W. von Molthein; Hangezeichnete Webereibücher aus Tirol by F. Donat; Figurale Bienenstöcke aus Mähren und Böhmen by M. Haberlandt. Band I: Die Holzschnitzerei im Grídener Tale by A. Haberlandt; Trintätsdarstellungen mit dem Dreigesichte by K. von Spiess; Oberösterreiches Hohlgals mit Emailfarbenbemalung by A. Ritter von Walcher; Figurale Tonplastik aus Mähren by J. Tvry; Ein Bilstock mit Darstellung der Klosterneuburger Schleierlegende by O. Menghin; Frühhistorisches in der galizischen Volkskunst by F. Adama van Scheltema; Ölbild mit Darstellung der europäischen Nationen by M. Haberlandt. Bibliographical references in the footnotes.

275   Holme, Charles, ed. **Peasant Art in Austria and Hungary.** London, Paris, New York, The Studio, 1911. 54p. (text), 816 plates. LC 11-35972.
Pictorial survey of folk art in Austria, Hungary, Rumania, Croatia and Slovenia. Essays by various experts accompanied by collection of plates illustrating peasant houses and examples of various crafts. No bibliography.

276   Schmidt, Leopold. **Volkskunst in Österreich.** Vienna and Hanover, Forum Verlag, 1966. 200p. illus. index. LC 67-76390.

Comprehensive and authoritative history/handbook of folk art in Austria with important investigations of the basic principles and functions of folk art. Contents: Kategorien der Volkskunst: Grundstoffe; Grundformen; Form und Sinn; Das Land und seine Volkskunst: Hoff und Haus; Gerät und Geschirr; Textile und Tracht; Brauchkunst; Volkskunst, Volkskünstler. One hundred twenty black and white and 24 color plates with descriptive captions. Comprehensive, classified bibliography, pp. 189-196.

Bulgaria

277 Boschkov, A. **Die bulgarische Volkskunst**. Recklinghausen, Bongers, 1972. 384p. illus. index.

Comprehensive history/handbook of Bulgarian folk arts covering costume, furniture, ceramics and metalwork. Well illustrated, including maps. Brief bibliography of basic books.

See also the exhibition catalog: *Bulgarian Folk Art* ed. by D. Korbanova (Sofia, National Ethnographic Museum, 1980. 247p. illus. LC 80-481814/r84).

Czechoslovakia

278 Hasalova, Vera, and Jaroslav Vajdis. **Folk Art of Czechoslovakia**. New York, Arco, 1974. 294p. illus. index. ISBN 0668035102.

Comprehensive survey of folk art in Czechoslovakia from the Middle Ages to the present. Contents: I, Background and Development; II, Art in the Life of the People; III, Settlements and Village Homes; IV, Form and Ornament; V, Drawing, Graphics, and Painting; VI, Sculptural Works in Folk Culture; VII, The Specific Character of Czech and Slovak Folk Art in a European Context. Bibliography, pp. 291-293, is divided into books in the Czech language and books in English.

See also the museum catalog: *Europäische Volkstrachten* v. 1: Tschechoslowakei, by H. Nixdorff (Berlin, Museum für Volkerkunde, 1977. 333p.).

279 Mrlian, Rudolf, ed. **Slovak Folk Art**. Prague, Artia, 1953-54. 2v. illus. LC 55-2669.

Pictorial survey of Slovak folk art covering architecture, costume and embroideries, ceramics and pottery, wood carving and painting. Brief introductory essay in English and Czech followed by plates with descriptive notes in both languages. No bibliography.

280 Sourek, Karel. **Folk Art in Pictures**. London, Spring, n.d. 45p. (text), 271 illus. LC A58-80.

Popular pictorial survey covering all classes of folk art in Czechoslovakia with examples dating from the seventeenth century through the twentieth century. No bibliography.

Denmark

281 Uldall, Kai. **Dansk folkekunst**. Copenhagen, Thaning & Appel, 1963. 298p. illus. index. LC 66-32747.

Comprehensive, authoritative history/handbook of Danish folk art covering furniture, ceramics, metalwork, textiles and costume. Bibliography of basic books, pp. 297-98.

For Danish folk furniture *see*: Steensberg, Axel, and Grith Lerche. *Danske Bondemobler: Danish Peasant Furniture* (1394).

France

282   Cuisenier, Jean. **French Folk Art**. Tokyo, New York, Kodansha International, 1977. 310p. illus. index. ISBN 087011297X.

Translation of: *L'art populaire en France* (Fribourg, Office du Livre, 1976). Comprehensive handbook of French folk art by a leading expert. Contents: 1, The Territory and the Works; 2, Genres and Materials; 3, Obstacles and Illusions; 4, Pathways; 5, Models; 6, Sources; 7, Tradition and Innovation. Comprehensive bibliography of books, periodicals and exhibition catalogs, pp. 255-96, and references to specialized, periodical literature in the footnotes. List of museums of folk art in France. Well illustrated with descriptive notes to the plates.

283   Ducharte, Pierre L., and Rene Saulnier. **L'imagerie populaire; les images de toutes provinces francaises du XVe siecle au second Empire**. Paris, Libraire de France, 1925. 447p. illus. index.

Scholarly dictionary of the subject matter found in popular and provincial French art. Although based upon and illustrated by popular graphics, this work is very useful for the study of French folk art motifs and subjects. Bibliography of basic books, pp. 443-45.

See also the exhibition catalogs: *Cinq siècles d'imagerie française* (Paris, Editions des Musées Nationaux, 1973. 335p. illus.), *French Popular Imagery: Five Centuries of Prints* (London, Arts Council of Great Britain, 1974. 147p. illus. ISBN 0728700336), *Hier pour demain: arts, traditions et patrimone: exposition: Galerie Nationales du Grand-Palais* (Paris, Ministere de la Culture et de la Communication, 1980. 245p. illus. ISBN 2711801632).

Germany

284   Brauneck, Manfred. **Religiöse Volkskunst: Votivgaben, Andachtsbilder, Hinterglas, Rosenkranz, Amullette**. Cologne, DuMont, 1978. 387p. illus. ISBN 3770109678.

Comprehensive scholarly history of religious folk art in German-speaking lands from the Middle Ages to the present with emphasis on the long tradition of ex voto art. Contents: I, Religiöse Volkskunst: ihr Zusammenhang mit Brauchtum und Kult; II, Ex Voto; III, Andacht und Gebet; IV, Amulette. Comprehensive bibliography, pp. 371-87, and references to specialized literature in the notes. Descriptive notes to the plates.

285   Brückner, Wolfgang. **Deutschland, vom 15. bis zum 20. Jahrhundert**. Munich, Callwey, 1969. 284p. illus. index.

Comprehensive, popular survey of German folk art covering furniture, costume, textiles, metalwork and ceramics. Bibliography, pp. 236-45, provides a thorough listing of basic books, catalogs, and periodical articles published up to 1965.

286   Karlinger, Hans. **Deutsche Volkskunst**. Berlin, Propylaen, 1938. 505p. illus. index. LC 39-13354.

Important corpus of 448 black-and-white and 20 color plates of German folk art in all media with descriptive notes. Introduction (128 pages) and an authoritative survey from the twelfth century to the end of the nineteenth century. General bibliography, p. 450, and bibliographical references to the illustrations in the notes.

287   Lehmann, Otto. **Deutsches Volkstum in Volkskunst und Volkstracht**. Berlin, W. de Gruyter, 1938. 125p. illus. index. LC 41-34512.

Survey of German folk art with emphasis on folk art as an expression of folk culture and on German regional folk costumes. Contents: Volkskunst und Volkstracht als Funktion des

Volkleben; Volkunst und Volkstracht im Volkstum der deutschen Stämme (survey by regions); Ergebnisse. Bibliographical references in the footnotes.

288   Meyer-Heisig, Erich. **Deutsche Volkskunst**. Munich, Prestel, 1954. 17p. (text) 102 plates. LC 55-1770.
Authoritative survey of German folk art based upon the superlative collection in the Germanisches Nationalmuseum in Nuremberg. Contents: Haus und Stube; Die Möbel; Geräte für Haus und Arbeit; Arbeiten der Töpfer; Trascht und Schmuck; Die Gewebe und ihre Auszier; Gestaltung für das Brauchtum des Jahres-und Lebenslaufes; Werke der Andacht und des Volksglaubens. Contains 102 black-and-white plates with descriptive captions.

289   Schlee, Ernst. **German Folk Art**. Tokyo, New York, Kodansha International, 1980. 316p. illus. index. ISBN 0870113569.
Lavishly illustrated, comprehensive history/handbook of folk art in the German-speaking lands. Contents: Types of Folk Art; House Decoration; House Interiors (including furniture); Minor Objects (boxes); Painted Glasses, Window-Panes and Bakery Moulds; Metals; Ceramics; Textiles; Costume and Ornament; Religious Folk Art; Miscellaneous Folk-Art Objects; Folk Art as Art. Descriptive notes to the plates with references to specialized literature. Excellent, comprehensive but unclassified bibliography, pp. 300-09.

290   Schwedt, Elke. **Volkskunst und Kunstgewerbe: Überlegungen zu einer Neuorientierung der Volkskunstforschung**. Tübingen, Schloss: Tübinger Vereinigung für Volkskunde, 1970. 187p. illus. (Untersuchungen des Ludwig-Uhland-Instituts der Universität Tübingen, Bd. 28.)
Important study of the perception of folk art and the place of folk art in the broad context of popular culture. Contents: I, Wertungsprobleme: 1, Praedisposition der Forschung, 2, Volkskunst und Kunstindustrie, 3, Vom "alten Volkskunstgeist"; II, Definitions probleme: 1, Vom "Reservat" der Volkskunst, 2, Kunstgewerbe al Residualetikett, 3, Volkskunst nach ihrem Ende; III, Versuch einer Bestandsaufnahme: 1, Vorüberlegungen, 2, Die Exploration, 3, Ergebnisse in Fragestellungen; IV, Versuch einer Systematik: 1, Kunst-Kommunikation in der Populärkultur, 2, Konsumtionsforschung, 3, Kreativitätsforschung. Comprehensive bibliography, pp. 153-179, and bibliographical references in footnotes.

291   Speiss, Kurt von. **Bauernkunst, ihre Art und Sinne**. 2nd ed. Berlin, Stubenrauch, 1943. 338p. illus. index. LC AF47-54.
Scholarly history of German folk art especially important for the analysis of the iconology of the ornamental subjects and programs. Contents: I, Einführung; II, Stoff und Bearbeitung: 1, Holzarbeiten; 2, Lederarbeiten; 3, Gewebe und ihre Auszier; 4, Töpferarbeiten; 5, Glasarbeiten; 6, Metallarbeiten; III, Inhalt: 1, Der Kampf zweier Gegner; 2, Verkehren; 3, Der Baum; 4, Lebenswasser; 5, Das Feuer; 6, Salz; IV, Ausdruck. Comprehensive, classified bibliography, pp. 324-30.
See also the exhibition catalogs: *Volkskunst aus Deutschland, Österreich und der Schweiz* (Cologne, Kunstgewerbemuseum der Stadt Köln, 1968. 374p. illus.), *Volkskunst und Volkshandwerk: 75 Jahre*, Museum für Deutsche Volkskunde, Berlin (Berlin, Museum für Deutsche Volksunde, Bildarchiv, 1969. 82p. 16 plates); and the museum guides: T. Kohlmann, *Die Meisterwerke aus dem Museum*, Museum für Deutsche Volkskunde Berlin (Stuttgart, Belser, 1980. 125p. illus. ISBN 3763020144), and B. Deneke, *Volkskunst: Führer durch d. volkundl.* Sammlungen German. National Museum Nürnberg (Munich, Prestel, 1979. 159p. illus. ISBN 3791304674).
For German folk ceramics *see*: M. Brauneck. *Volkstümliche Hafnerkeramik im deutschsprachigen Raum* (785) and E. Meyer—*Heisig. Deutsche Bauerntöpferei* (786). For German folk furniture *see*: M. Baur-Heinhold. *Alte Bauernstuben: Dösen, Küchen, Kammern von den Alpen*

bis zur See (1294), Deneke, Bernward. *Bauernmöbel; ein Handbuch fur Sammler und Liebhaber* (1295), and Schmidt, Leopold, *Bauernmöbel aus Sudeutschland, Oesterreich und der Schweiz* (1296).

Great Britain

292 Ayres, James. **British Folk Art**. Woodstock, N.Y., Overlook Press, 1977. 144p. illus. index. ISBN 0879510609.
Popular survey of British folk art. Contents: Methods and Materials; Ecce Signum, The Travellers; Ships and the Mariner; The Pictorial Arts; Inside the Home; Domestic Crafts; Craft Industries. Bibliography of basic books, p. 138.

293 Lambert, Margard, and Enid Marx. **English Popular Art**. 2d ed. London, Merlin, 1951. 120p. illus. index. ISBN 0850363721.
Popular survey of folk and popular art in England from the Middle Ages to the present. Chapters on carvings, metal signs and ornaments, painting, textiles, pottery, glass and printing. No bibliography.

Hungary

294 Gink, Karoly, and Ivor S. Kiss. **Folk Art and Folk Artists in Hungary**. Budapest, Corvina, 1968. 112p. illus. LC 72-5032.
Popular survey covering costume, ceramics, furniture, metalwork and textiles. No bibliography.

295 Hofer, Janus, and Edit Fél. **Hungarian Folk Art**. Oxford, London, New York, Oxford Univ. Press, 1979. 638p. illus. ISBN 0192114484.
Well-illustrated handbook of Hungarian folk art from earliest times to the present. Contents: The Peasant World of Objects; The Meaning of Beautiful Objects; The Making and Acquisition of Objects of Folk Art; Periods in the History of Folk Art: Early Styles; Periods in the History of Folk Art: Development of New Styles; Folk Art in the Last 150 Years; Distinctive Features of Hungarian Folk Art. Corpus of illustrations arranged by environment, e.g., churches, graveyards, villages, etc., and by object type, e.g., pottery, costume, jewelry, etc. Bibliography of basic works, p. 61-63.

296 **Hungarian Decorative Folk Art**. 2nd ed. Budapest, Corvina, 1955. 36p. (text) 208 plates. LC 55-43700.
Popular pictorial survey with brief introduction followed by plates with descriptive captions. No bibliography.

Italy

297 Holme, Charles, ed. **Peasant Art in Italy**. London, Paris, New York, The Studio, 1913. 39p. (text), 449 plates. LC 14-2882.
Important collection of plates of Italian folk art. Introductory essay emphasizes the folk art of the Abruzzi, women's craft, peasant jewelry and the "presepe." No bibliography.

298 Toschi, Paolo. **Arte popolare italiana**. Rome, Bestetti, 1960. 451p. illus. LC A60-2447.
Comprehensive, authoritative history of folk art in Italy. Contents: Arte dei Pastori e della vita agricola; Mobili; Tappeti e tessuti; Oreficeria, ricami, ornamenti del costume; Ceramiche e

vetri; Ferri, battuti, rami-insegne, arte marinara; Maschere teatro, feste popolari; Religiosita popolare; Stampe popolare. 553 plates. Summary in English. Comprehensive, classified bibliography, pp. 439-448.

Norway

299 Anker, Peter. **Folkekunst in Norge**. Oslo, Cappelen, 1975. 228p. illus. ISBN 8202032539.

Comprehensive, scholarly history of folk art in Norway from the Middle Ages to the twentieth century. Contents: 1, Hva er folkekunst ?; 2, Bygdekunsten og bygdehåndverket; 3, Hus og innredning; 4, Bohave og briksting; 5, Middelalderens folkekuntst og den sene middelaldertradisjonen; 6, Treskurd i nyere tid; 7, Billedvev og åklevev; 8, Rosemalingen; 9, Folkekunstens billedrike. Motiver og formprinsipper. Illustrated only with line drawings. Comprehensive, unclassified bibliography, pp. 224-229.

300 Ellingsgard, Nils. **Norsk rosemå**. Oslo, Orske Sammlaget, 1981. 263p. illus. index. ISBN 8252120245.

Comprehensive, well-illustrated history of Norwegian painted folk art (Rosemaling—Rose painting after the chief decorative motif) during the eighteenth and nineteenth centuries. Covers furniture and interiors. Contents: I: Innleiing; Materielle vilkår og føresternader; Stilhistorisk bakgrunn; Frå by til byd; Rosemålaren som biletkunstnar; Materialar og teknikkar; II: Flatbygdene på Austlandet; Osterdalen; Gundbrandsdalen; Valdres; Hallingdal; Numedal; Telemark; Aust-Agder; VestAgder; Rogalund; Hordaland; Sogn og Fjordane; Møre og Romsdal; Trøndelag; Rosemålinga blømer av. Bibliogrpahy, pp. 248-49. Summary in English, pp.250-60.

See also Miller, Margaret M. *Norwegian Rosemaling: Decorative Painting on Wood* (New York, Scribner's, 1974. 211p. illus. ISBN 0684129434).

301 Hauglid, Roar. **Native Arts of Norway**. New York, Praeger, 1965. 175p. illus. index. LC 67-21845/r83.

Concise, popular survey of Norwegian folk art. Contents: Woodcarving by R. Hauglid; Rose Painting by R. Asker; Nowegian Art Weaving by H. Engelstad; Folk Costumes by G. I. Traetteberg. Plates have descriptive captions. No bibliography.

302 Stewart, Janice S. **The Folk Arts of Norway**. 2d ed. New York, Dover, 1972. ISBN 0486228118.

First published in 1953 (Univ. of Wisconsin Press). Useful, popular introduction to the folk art of Norway. Contains 152 illustrations with brief, descriptive captions. Contents: 1, Of Vikings & Farmers; 2, In the Peasant Home; 3, Carving; 4, Rosemaling; 5, Metalworking; 6, Weaving; 7, Embroidery; 8, Costumes. Basic bibliography, pp. 231-235.

Poland

303 Czarnecka, Irena. **Folk Art in Poland**. Warsaw, Polonia, 1957. 9p. (text). 234 plates.
Pictorial survey of Polish folk art. No bibliography.

304 Jackowski, Aleksander, and Jadwiga Jarnuszkiewicz. **Folk Art of Poland**. Warsaw, Arkady, 1968. 476p. illus. LC 75-314490.

Pictorial survey of folk art in Poland from the Middle Ages to 1960. A 22-page introduction is followed by 521 plates arranged by types of objects with short descriptive notes. Bibliography, pp. 475-77, has separate list of periodicals.

305   Prokropek, Marian. **Guide to Folk Art and Folklore in Poland**. Warsaw, Arkady, 1980. 269p. illus. index. ISBN 8321330142.

Informative, pocket-sized guide book to the folk art found in the various provinces of Poland. Introduction discusses the layout of villages, architecture, kinds of farmsteads, rural dwelling houses, farm buildings, industrial architecture, public buildings, sacred architecture, sculpture, painting, ceramics, folk decoration and ornament, textiles and costumes. The 2,500 localities in the catalog give abbreviated information with selected illustrations. Appendix of maps.

306   Schauss, H. Joachim. **Contemporary Polish Folk Artists**. New York, Hippocrene Books, 1987. 204p. illus. ISBN 0870522957.

Pictorial survey of 24 contemporary Polish folk artists; majority are sculptors. Entries include portrait of the artist, transcripts from interviews with the author and autobiographical statements. No bibliography.

Rumania

307   **Folk Art in Rumania**. Bucharest, Rumanian Institute for Cultural Relations with Foreign Countries, 1955. 23p. (ext), 186 p. (illus). LC 52-23646r61.

Pictorial survey covering Rumanian folk interiors (including churches), traditional costumes, jewelry, textiles and pottery. No bibliography. Brief introductory text followed by plates with descriptive captions.

Russia

308   Pronin, Alexander, and Barbara Pronin. **Russian Folk Arts**. South Brunswick, N.J., A. S. Barnes, 1975. 192p. illus. index. ISBN 049801276X.

Popular survey of the folk art of the Soviet Republic of Russia (Great and Little Russia) covering icons, lubki, lacquer ware, wood and bone carving, ceramics, metalwork and textiles from the ninth through the nineteenth centuries. Glossary of Russian terms. General bibliography of books in Russian and English, p. 184.

309   Razina, Tatyana, Natalia Cherkasova, and Alexander Kantsedikas. **Folk Art of the Soviet Union**. New York, Abrams, 1990. 459p. illus. ISBN 0810909448.

Lavishly illustrated survey of the various ethnic and traditional folk arts of the Soviet Union. Includes all media including folk sculpture and painting. Brief introductory text illustrated with color plates is followed by a collection of small black and white illustrations; all are pieces in various museums in the Soviet Union. Contents: Folk Art in the Russian Soviet Federated Republic: Russian Folk Art, Karelian Folk Art, Folk Art in the Volga and Kama Areas, Folk Art in Siberia, Folk Art in the Far North and Far East; Folk Art in the Caucasus: Folk Art in the North Caucasus, Folk Art in Georgia, Folk Art in Azerbaidzhan, Folk Art in Armenia; Ukrainian, Byelorussian, and Moldavian Folk Art; Folk Art in the Baltic Area: Folk Art of Lithuania, Folk Art in Latvia, Folk Art in Estonia; Folk Art in Central Asia and Kazakhstan: Uzbek Folk Art, Tadzhik Folk Art, Turkmen Folk Art, Kirghiz Folk Art, Kazakh Folk Art. No bibliography.

See also the exhibition catalog: *Folk Art of the Soviet Union: Reflections of a Rich Cultural Diversity of the Fifteen Republics* by M. Longenecker (San Diego, Mingei International Museum of World Folk Art, 1989. 167p. illus. ISBN 0914155067).

Spain

310 Pelauzy, Maria A. **Artesania popular española**. Barcelona, Blume, 1977. 239p. illus. index. ISBN 8470310453.

Pictorial survey of folk art in Spain with emphasis on the work of the folk artists and craftsmen of today. Divided by media including: textiles, basket weaving, ceramics, metalwork, leather, wood carving, glass, jewelry, theater, wax modeling, dough modeling and paper. Special chapter on ex votos. Excellent illustrations including many showing contemporary practices. Glossary of terms, list of museums, and collection of folk art in Spain. No bibliography.

311 Subias Galter, Juan. **El arte popular en Espana**. Barcelona, Editorial Seix Barral, 1948. 623p. illus. LC 49-27113.

Comprehensive history/handbook of Spanish folk art and architecture. Contents: I, Arquitectura popular; II, Esgrafiados; III, El mueble; IV, El guadameci; V, La cerámica; VI, los vidros; VII, Forja y repujado; VIII, Rejidos, bordados y encajes; IX, El traje; X, Las joyas; XI, Los abanicos; XII, Los juguetes; XIII, Cincelado, modelado y escultura; XIV, La estamperia. Descriptive notes to the over 500 plates. Bibliographical references in the text.

Sweden

312 Jacobsson, Bengt. **Svensk folkonst**. Lund, Signum, 1983-1985. 2v. illus. index. ISBN 9185330558.

Comprehensive, scholarly history of folk art in Sweden. Well illustrated with individual pieces, historic interiors and contemporary works of art illustrating folk art, customs and life. Contents: Del 1: Byggnadens yttre utsmyckning; Byggnadens inre utsmycckning; Dekor på redskap och husgeråd; Pyntat på färden. Del 2: Vad är folkkonst?; Folkkonsten—ett kulturellt fenomen; Folkkonstens myter; Folkkonstens formbildning; Rumsliga och sociala aspekter. Comprehensive bibliographies at the end of each volume.

Switzerland

313 Baud-Bovy, Daniel. **Peasant Art in Switzerland**. London, The Studio, 1924. 72p. (text), 431 plates. LC 24-14035.

Important collection of plates illustrating Swiss folk interiors, furniture, costume, metalwork, pottery and textiles. Includes works of art depicting Swiss folk art and architecture. Bibliography, pp. xvii-xix.

314 Creux, Rene. **Volkskunst in der Schweiz**. 2d ed. Paudex, Éditions de Fontainemore, 1976. 327p. illus. LC 72-558264.

Well-illustrated survey of folk art in Switzerland, consisting of essays by a team of Swiss experts. Contents: Personnalité géographique de la Suisse; Suisse alémanique; Suisse rhétique; Suisse française; Suisse italienne; Les origines; L'architecture rurale; Le mobilier de la maison paysanne; Les meubles peints; Les poêles en faïence et les motifs de leurs carreaux; La céramique; La poterie d'étain; Le verre peint et le verre gravé; L'art de la boissellerie; Les moules à biscuits et les marques à pain; De l'ornementation des sacs de farine; Les instruments domestiques; Les instruments de travail; Le métal travaillé; Les enseignes; Traineaux décorés; Le costume; Coffrets peints; Les arts du textile; Papiers découpes; Pages d'écriture et imagerie; L'art religieux et les images de dévotion; Ex-voto; Présence de la mort dans l'art populaire; Les masques; Images dans la pierre et dans le bois; La peinture; Jeux d'adultes et art forain; Cartes à jouer; Les jouets. General bibliography, p. 322.

See also the exhibition catalogs: *Swiss Folk Art: Organized by the Pro Helvetia Foundation* by R. Wildhaber (Washington, D.C., Smithsonian Institution, 1968. 152p. illus. LC 70-572805), and *Schreibkunst: Schulkunst und Volkskunst in der deutschsprachigen Schweiz 1548 bis 1980* by O. Batschmann (Zurich, Kunstgewerbemuseum der Stadt Zürich, 1981. 179p. illus.).

Yugoslavia

315   Pantelic, Nikola. **Traditional Art and Crafts in Yugoslavia**. Belgrad, Jugoslavenks Revija, 1984. 199p. illus. index.

Well-illustrated survey of Yugoslavian folk art with 204 plates with descriptive captions. Informative text is divided into chapters on the various geoethnographic areas and the various media, i.e., jewelry, textiles, stone carving, pottery, painting, woodcarving, metalwork and dough sculpture. Comprehensive bibliography, pp. 194-95; nearly all titles in Slavic.

See also the exhibition catalog: *Yugoslav Folk Art* (Belgrade, Ethnographic Museum of Belgrade, 1980. 112p. illus.).

ORIENTAL FOLK ART

China

316   Berliner, Nancy Zeng. **Chinese Folk Art: The Small Skills of Carving Insects**. Boston, Litte, Brown, 1986. 254p. illus. index. ISBN 0821216155.

Well-illustrated, popular survey of Chinese folk arts and crafts. Contains 227 illustrations with descriptive captions. Contents: Symbols and Legends; Papercuts; Shadow Puppets; Embroidery; Dye-Resist Printed Fabrics; Woodblock Prints; Folk Art Today; Chronology. Excellent, comprehensive bibliography listing works in English and Chinese, pp. 243-46, and bibliographical references in the notes.

317   Chavannes, Edouard. **The Five Happinesses: Symbolism in Chinese Popular Art**. New York, Weatherhill, 1973. 152p. illus. ISBN 0834800764.

Originally published in *Journal Asiastique* (1901). Brief essay on the symbolism of various decorative motifs and ornament in Chinese popular arts and crafts with 47 drawings with descriptive notes. General bibliography, pp. 151-152, and bibliographical references in the text and notes.

See also Chin, Chi-lin. *L'esthetique de l'art populaire chonois: la poupée porte-bonheur: Aesthetic Features of Chinese Folk Art: The Good Luck Dolly* (Paris, Librairie You-Feng: Musée Kwok On, 1989. 178p. illus. ISBN 2906658308).

See also the exhibition catalog: *Chinese Folk Art in American Collections, from Early 15th Century to Early 20th Century,* by T. Y. Ecke (Honolulu, Univ. Press. of Hawaii, 1977. 159p. illus.).

India

318   Mode, Heinz A. and Subodh Chandra. **Indian Folk Art**. New York, Alpine Fine Arts, 1985. 312p. illus. index. ISBN 0881680109.

Comprehensive, well-illustrated survey of Indian folk art in all media. Contains 396 plates. Contents: Significance and Characteristic Features of Indian Folk Art; Region I: Central India: Early Art in Hill and Jungle; Region II: North-western India: Site of the Earliest Urban Civilization in India; Region III: Northern India: Country of Two Rivers; Region IV: Southern India: Folk Art in the Country of the Dravidians. Comprehensive, classified bibliography, pp. 300-307.

319 Mookerjee, Ajiit. **Folk Art of India**. New Delhi, Clarion Books, 1986. 123p. illus. ISBN 8185120013.

Pictorial survey of contemporary folk art of India including dolls and toys, textiles, drawings and paintings, metal, wood, and ivory, pottery and basketry, and jewelry. Glossary of terms and good bibliography, pp. 121-23.

See also the museum catalog: *National Handicrafts and Handlooms Museum, New Delhi* by J. Jyotindra (Ahmedabad, Mapin, Middletown, N.J., Grantha Corp., 1989. 221p. illus. ISBN 0944142230).

See also the exhibition catalog: *Unknown India: Ritual Art in Tribe and Village*, by S. Kramrisch (Philadelphia, Philadelphia Museum of Art, 1968. 127p. illus. LC 68-14542/r84).

Japan

320 Munsterberg, Hugo. **The Folk Arts of Japan**. Rutland, Vt., Tuttle, 1958. 168p. illus. index. LC 58-7496.

Popular survey of Japanese folk pottery, baskets, lacquer, metalwork and textiles as well as sculpture, painting and architecture. No bibliography.

321 Muraoka, Kageo, and Kichiemon Okamura. **Folk Arts and Crafts of Japan**. New York and Tokyo, Weatherhill/Heibonsha, 1973. 164p. illus. (Heibonsha Survey of Japanese Art, No. 26).

Survey of Japanese folk art emphasizing works dating from the seventeenth through the nineteenth centuries. Good selection of plates. No bibliography. For the series *see*: FA1892.

322 Saint-Gilles, Amaury. **Mingei: Japan's Enduring Folk Arts**. Rutland, Vt., Tuttle, 1989. 260p. illus. ISBN 0804816069.

Popular but quite comprehensive handbook of the folk arts of contemporary Japan arranged by class or type of object, further subdivided by province. Text is appreciative and autobiographical. Illustrated with line drawings and small collection of color plates. No bibliography.

See also the exhibition catalogs: *Mingei: Japanese Folk Art from the Brooklyn Museum Collection* by R. Moes (New York, Universe, 1985. 191p. illus. ISBN 08766634811), *Mingei: Folk Arts of Old Japan, by H. Munsterberg* (New York, Abrams, 1965. 143p. illus. LC 65-19378), *Folk Traditions in Japanese Art*, by V. and T. Hauge (Washington, D.C., International Exhibitions Foundation, 1978. 272p. illus. ISBN 0883970058), *Yo no bi: the Beauty of Japanese Folk Art* by W. J. Rathbun (Seattle, Wash., Seattle Art Museum, 1983/133p. illus. index. ISBN 0932216129).

CHAPTER FOUR

ARMS AND ARMOR

DICTIONARIES AND ENCYCLOPEDIAS

General

323 Gelli, Jacopo. **Guida del raccoglitore e dell' amatore di armi antiche**. Milan, Hoepli, 1968. 434p. illus. LC 77-407935.

First published in 1900. Pocket-sized dictionary covering all aspects of European arms and armour. Illustrated with line drawings and drawings of armourers' marks. Comprehensive bibliography of the older literature, pp. 429-34.

324 Stone, George C. **A Glossary of the Construction, Decoration, and Use of Arms and Armor in All Countries and in All Times**. Portland, Me., Southworth, 1934. 694p. illus. LC 34-38895. Reprint: New York, Jack Brussel, 1961.

Comprehensive dictionary of world arms and armour with entries varying in length from a few lines to many pages. Nearly all have bibliographical references to the list of books, pp. 687-94. Contains 875 illustrations of pieces in museums and the author's collection. Valuable resource for definitions of parts and types of arms and armour.

325 Tarassuk, Leonid and Claude Blair. **The Complete Encyclopedia of Arms and Weapons**. New York, Simon & Schuster, 1982. 544p. illus. ISBN 067142557X.

Translation of: *Enciclopedia ragionata delle armi* (Milan, Mondador, 1979). Comprehensive encyclopedia of world arms and armor from antiquity to the twentieth century. Work of an international team of experts. Covers all aspects with entries varying from a few lines to several pages. Well illustrated with color and black and white plates. Comprehensive, classified bibliography, pp. 435-43.

326 Wilkinson-Latham, Robert. **Phaidon Guide to Antique Weapons and Armour**. Englewood Cliffs, N.J., Prentice-Hall, 1984. 256p. illus. index. ISBN 0136619355.

Popular survey of European and American arms and armour from the early Middle Ages to the twentieth century. Organized into broad groups: armour, staff weapons, swords, daggers and bayonets, bows, and firearms. Well illustrated with color plates of pieces, reproductions of works of art depicting arms and armour, and drawings of details. General bibliography, p. 252. Appendix with list of principal collections of arms and armour in Europe and America.

Dictionaries of Armorers

327 Gardner, Robert E. **Small Arms Makers: A Directory of Fabricators of Firearms, Edged Weapons, Crossbows and Polearms**. New York, Crown, 1963. 378p. illus. index. LC 62-20058.

Comprehensive dictionary of makers of small arms, e.g., pistols, rifles, swords, and daggers, with particularly thorough coverage of American makers. Data in the entries is derived from printed and other documentary sources and often includes original values and numbers of arms. Repertory of marks in facsimile. Comprehensive, classified bibliography, pp. 375-78.

328   Gyngell, Dudley S. H. **Armourers' Marks: Being a Compilation of the Known Marks of Armourers, Swordsmiths and Gunsmiths.** London, Thorsons, 1959. 131p. illus. LC 59-41997.

Concise dictionary of the marks of European armourers arranged by country. Marks given in facsimiles. Indexes by town and name of armourer. No bibliography.

329   Stockel, Johan F. **Haandskydevaabens Bedommelse.** Copenhagen, Nordlundes bogtrykkeri, 1938-43. 2v. illus. index. LC 44-18923.

Comprehensive, scholarly dictionary of European armourers' marks and other control marks used on arms and armor. Danish text with summary translations in German, English, French. Glossaries. The standard reference work on armourers' marks.

GENERAL HISTORIES AND HANDBOOKS

330   Ashdown, Charles H. **Arms and Armour.** New York, Dodge, n.d. 384p. illus. index. LC A10-1. Reprinted as *An Illustrated History of Arms & Armour.* (Hertfordshire, England, Wordsworth Editions, 1988. ISBN 185326914X).

Survey of arms and armour from prehistoric times to the introduction of gunpowder. Illustrated with line drawings, many taken from contemporary works of art. Contents: I, Weapons of Prehistoric Man; II, The Assyrian; III, The Roman; IV, Saxon and Danes; V, The Norman Period to 1180; VI, The Chain Mail Period, 1180-1250; VII, Chain Mail Reinforced, 1250-1325; VIII, The Cyclas Period, 1325-1335; IX, The Studded and Plinted Armour Period, 1335-1360; X, The Camail and Jupon Period, 1360-1410; XI, The Surcoatless Period, 1410-1430; XII, The Tabard Period, 1430-1500; XIII, The Transition Period, 1500-1525; XIV, Maximillian Armour, 1525-1600; XV, The Half-Armour Period after 1600; XVI, Weapons of the Early Middle Ages; XVIII, Projectile-Throwing Engines; XVIII, German, Italian, and Other Influences upon European Armour; XIX, The Introduction of Gunpowder and Its Influence upon Armour. No bibliography.

331   Reid, William. **Weapons through the Ages.** New York, Crescent Books, 1986. 280p. illus. index. ISBN 0517617714.

First published in 1976 as: *The Lore of Arms* (London, Mitchell Beazley, 1976) and *Arms through the Ages* (New York, Harper & Row). General history of weapons including arms and armour from ancient times to the present with emphasis on technological developments. Large number of colored drawings of the mechanisms of various weapons, especially firearms. Bibliography, pp. 269-270, is a classified list of mostly books in English. A condensed version without the bibliography and many of the illustrations was published as: *The Lore of Arms; a Concise History of Weaponry* (New York, Facts on File, 1984. 256p. illus. ISBN 087196855X).

332   Tavard, Christian Henry. **Le Livre des armes et armures: de l'Antiquité au Grand Siècle.** Paris, Hier et Demain, 1977. 379p. illus. ISBN 2720600415.

Richly illustrated history of Western arms and armour from ancient times to the early nineteenth century. Contents: Les armes offensives: Les armes de choc et de coup. les armes d'Hast, les armes blanches ou tranchantes, les armes de jet et de trait, les armes a feu primitives; Les armes defensives: les casques, les boucliers, de l'armure de cuir a la cotte de mailles, les armures de plates de fer, les armures de plates de fer, les armures équestres, survivance de l'armure. Bibliography of books and articles mostly in French, pp. 376-378.

See also Kelly and Schwabe (995) and T. N. Dupuy. *The Evolution of Weapons and Warfare* (Indianapolis, Ind., Bobbs-Merrill, 1980. 350p. illus. index. ISBN 0672520508).

ANCIENT ARMS AND ARMOR

333   Bonnet, H. **Die Waffen der Völker des alten Orients.** Berlin, Leipzig, J. C. Hinrichs, 1926. 223p. illus. index. Reprint: Gutersloh, Prisma, 1977. LC 78-380269.

Old standard history of the arms and armor of the civilizations of the ancient Near East from Sumer to Assyria. Contents: Schlagstock und Keule; Die Streitaxt; Dolch; Schwert; Das Krummschwert; Speer; Wurfholz; Scleuder; Bogen und Pfeil; Köcher und Bogentasche; Schild; Helm; Panzer. Includes 1,107 illustrations of arms and armour and drawings derived from depictions of arms and armor in works of art. Bibliographical references in the footnotes.

See also Salonen, Erkki. *Die Waffen der alten Mesopotamier; eine lexikalische und kulturegeschichtliche Untersuchung* (Helsinki, Societas Orientalis Fennica, 1965. 215p. illus. Studia Orientalis Edidit Societas Orientalis Fennica, 33. LC 67-9).

334   Couissin, Paul. **Les armes romaines; essai sur les origines et l'évolution des armes individuelles du légionnaire romain.** Paris, H. Champion, 1926. 569p. illus. index.

Comprehensive, scholarly history of Roman arms (including helmets and shields) from the earliest times to end of the fifth century. Divided into six periods (Des Origines à Servius Tullius; De Servius Tullius à Camille; De Camille à Marius; Marius, César, Auguste; D'Auguste à Alexandre Sévère; De Maximin à la chute de Rome) and subdivided by type or class of arms, e.g., lance, épée, bouclier, casque, cuirasse, jambarts. Bibliographical footnotes give excellent coverage of the older literature as does the "Index bibliographique," pp. xvii-xxiv. An old standard work.

335   Oakeshott, R. Ewart. **The Archaeology of Weapons: Arms and Armour from Prehistory to the Age of Chivalry.** London, Butterworth Press, 1960. 358p. illus. index. LC 60-11279.

Comprehensive, authoritative history of Western arms and armor from the prehistoric Bronze Age to the fifteenth century. Contains 22 plates of pieces in British and continental museums and 179 figures in the text, many based upon depictions in works of art. Contents: Part One. The Prehistoric Age: I, "The Pitiless Bronze"; II, Iron Comes to Europe: The Hallstat People; III, The Gauls. Part Two. The Heroic Age: IV, The Great Migrations; V, Rome in Decline: The Gothic Cavalry; VI, The Bog-Deposits of Denmark; VII, The Arms of the Migration Period. Part Three. The Vikings: VIII, Swords in the Viking Period; IX, The Vikings at War; X, From Charlemagne to the Normans. Part Four. The Age of Chivalry: XI, The "Gay Science" of Chivalry; XII, Sword Types and Blade Inscriptions 1100-1325; XIII, Sword Hilts and Fittings; XIV, The Sword in War; XV, "The Complete Arming of a Man," 1100-1325; XVI, Armour and the Longbow in the Fourteenth and Fifteenth Centuries; XVIII, Swords and Daggers in the Fourteenth and Fifteenth Centuries. Selected bibliography, pp. 351-52

336   Robinson, H. Russell. **The Armour of Imperial Rome.** New York, Scribner's, 1975. 200p. illus. index. ISBN 0684139561.

Comprehensive, well-illustrated history of ancient Roman armor. Illustrations include actual pieces, reconstructions of how full sets were worn, and numerous illustrations of works of ancient Roman art that show armor. Contents: Part I: The helmet (Galea or Cassis): 1, The jockey-cap helmet of Montefortino type, 2, The jockey-cap helmet of Coolus type, 3, The Agen/Port Gallic helmets, 4, Helmets of Imperial-Gallic type; 5, Helmets of Imperial-Italic type, 6, Helmets of the Auxiliary Infantry, 7, Helmets of the Auxiliary Cavalry, 8, Cavalry sports helmets, 9, Officers' helmets, 10, Helmet crests, 11, The helmet lining; Part II: Body armour (Lorica): 1, The muscle cirass, 2, Scale armour (lorica squamata), 3, Lamellar armour, 4, Mail (lorica hamata), 5, Laminated armour (lorica segmentata), 6, Greaves (ocreae), 7, Horse armour; The Roman saddle. Bibliographical notes at the end of each chapter.

337   Snodgrass, Anthony M. **Early Greek Armour and Weapons, from the End of the Bronze Age 600 B.C.** Edinburgh, Edinburgh University Press, 1964. 280p. illus. index. LC 65-506.

Authoritative history of ancient Greek arms and armor up to the Archaic period. Thirty-seven plates of actual pieces and representations of arms and armor in works of art. Contents: 1, The Helmet; 2, The Shield; 3, Body-Armour; 4, The Sword; 5, The Spear; 6, The Bow and Arrow; 7, Miscellanea; 8, The Literary Evidence; 9, Conclusions. Bibliographical references in the notes.

338   Snodgrass, Anthony M. **Arms and Armour of the Greeks.** London, Thames and Hudson, 1967. 151p. illus. index. LC 67-20632.

Authoritative survey of ancient Greek arms and armour from the Myceneans to the first century B.C. Sixty plates of actual pieces and depictions of arms and armor in works of art. Contents: I, The Mycenaeans; II, The Dark Age; III, The Age of the Hoplite; IV, The Great Wars; V, Macedon. Bibliographical references in the footnotes.

339   Wolf, Walther. **Die Bewaffnung des altägyptischen Heeres.** Leipzig, J. C. Hinrichs, 1926. 108p. illus. index. Reprint: Leipzig, Zentralantiquariat der Deutschen Demokratischen Republik, 1978. LC 79-342296.

Scholarly history of the arms and armor of the ancient Egyptian army based on extant pieces, representations in works of art and documentary evidence. Contents: Die Quellen; Die Vor- und Frühzeit; Das Alte Reich und die Zeit zwischen Altem und Mittlerem Reich; Das Mittlere Reich und die Hyksoszeit; Das Neue Reich. Contains 22 plates with descriptive notes. Bibliographical references in the footnotes.

MEDIEVAL ARMS AND ARMOR

340   Edge, David, and John Miles Paddock. **Arms & Armor of the Medieval Knight: An Illustrated History of Weaponry in the Middle Ages.** New York, Crescent Books, 1988. 189p. illus. index. ISBN 0517644681.

Illustrated survey of the arms and armour of the Western Middle Ages from the seventh century to the middle of the sixteenth century. Many illustrations of arms and armour in contemporary medieval art. Appendix with illustrations of construction, glossary of terms, but no bibliography.

341   Nicolle, David. **Arms and Armour of the Crusading Era, 1050-1350.** White Plains, N.Y., Kraus International Pubs., 1987. 2v. illus. ISBN 0527671282.

Important catalog of European and Islamic arms and armor from 1050 to 1350. Contains 1,632 entries arranged chronologically and by region, including actual pieces and a large number of depictions of arms and armor in works of art in an array of media. Descriptive entries are keyed to the line drawings in the second volume. Various subdivisions of the catalog are introduced with an essay that traces the overall history. Dictionary of terms precedes the illustrations in volume two. Comprehensive, classified bibliography including unpublished sources, v. 2, pp. 964-1017, and bibliographical references in the notes to the essays in volume one.

342   Norman, A. Vesey B. **The Medieval Soldier.** New York, Crowell, 1971. 278p. illus. ISBN 0690528213.

General history of the life of the medieval soldier. Contents: Part I: The Beginnings of Feudalism; 1, The Lombards; 2, The Franks; 3, The Vikings; 4, The Saxons; Part II: Feudalism and Chivalry; 5, Feudalism; 6, Organization; 7, Chivalry and Knighting; 8, The Military Orders; 9, The Crusades; 10, Crusading Campaigns; 11, Arms and Armour of the Crusaders; 12,

Crusaders' Ships. Good, classified bibliography of books and periodical articles in all languages, pp. 259-262.

See also P. Contamine. *La guerre au Moyen Age.* (Paris, Presses Universitaires de France, 1980. 516p. illus. index. ISBN 2130363083); F. Kottenkamp, *The History of Chivalry and Armor: With Description of the Feudal System, the Practices of Knighthood, the Tournament, and Trials by Single Combat.* (New York, Portland House, 1988. 110p. illus. index. ISBN 0517671077); L. Funcken, *The Age of Chivalry* (Englewood Cliffs, N.J., Prentice-Hall, 1983. 3v. illus. index. ISBN 0130462764).

See also the exhibition catalog: *The Art of Chivalry: European Arms and Armor from the Metropolitan Museum of Art,* by H. Nickel, et al. (New York, American Federation of the Arts, 1982. 179p. illus. ISBN 0917418670).

AMERICAN ARMS AND ARMOR

343 Neumann, George C. **The History of Weapons of the American Revolution**. New York, Harper & Row, 1967. 373p. illus. index. LC 67-20829.

Comprehensive, authoritative history of the firearms and edged weapons used in the American Revolutionary War. Brief introductory essays are followed by a large number of illustrations of pieces with detailed, descriptive notes. Contents: 1, Firearms Come of Age...Last of the Pikes; 2, Eighteenth-Century Warfare...Lines of Muskets; 3, The American Revolution...Any Lock, Stock, and Barrel—That Fires; 4, Muskets and Other Shoulder Arms; 5, The Long Rifle; 6, Pistols; 7, Swords; 8, Polearms. Appendices with list of European rulers 1600-1800, references dates, measurement definitions, and glossary of terms. Comprehensive, classified bibliography, pp. 365-69.

344 Peterson, Harold L. **Arms and Armour in Colonial America, 1526-1783**. Harrisburg, Pa., Stackpole, 1956. 350p. illus. index. LC 56-11273.

Comprehensive, scholarly history of arms and armor in colonial America. Contains 310 plates of pieces and depictions of arms and armor. Contents: Book I: The Age of Colonization and Exploration: 1, Firearms; 2, Ammunition and Equipment; 3, Edged Weapons; 4, Armor. Book II: The French Wars and the Revolution 1689-1783: 5, Firearms; 6, Ammunition and Equipment; 7, Edged Weapons; 8, Armor. Appendix with extracts from documents dating from 1540 to 1779. Comprehensive, classified bibliography, pp. 337-45, and additional bibliography in the notes. A standard work on early American arms and armor.

EUROPEAN ARMS AND ARMOR

345 Aroldi, Aldo M. **Armi e armatore italiane fino al XVIII secolo**. Milan, Bramante, 1961. 543p. illus. index. LC 62-11803.

Comprehensive history of arms and armor in Italy from prehistoric times to the nineteenth century. Contains 383 black and white and 70 color plates. Contents: La preistoria; I primi secoli della storia; L'età medioevale; Milano durante i Communi e le Signorie; Decadimento dell'armatura; Le armi; Conclusione. Glossary of terms and repertory of makers. Comprehensive bibliography, pp. 535-44.

346 Blair, Claude. **European and American Arms, c. 1100-1850**. New York, Crown, 1962. 134p. illus. index. LC 62-11803.

Authoritative survey of European and American edged weapons and firearms from 1100 to 1850. Contains 647 plates with descriptive notes and additional line drawings illustrating details designed to aid in identification. Contents: I, Swords and Daggers; II, Staff-Weapons; III,

Projectile Weapons: Sling and Bow; IV, Projectile Weapons: Firearms and Other Guns; V, Combined Weapons; VI, The Decoration of Arms. Selected bibliography, pp. 123-127, and additional bibliography in the footnotes.

347 Blair, Claude. **European Armour, 1066 to c. 1700**. New York, Macmillan, 1959. 248p. illus. index. LC 59-24447.

Popular but informative survey of European armor from 1066 to 1700 supported by a good selection of illustrations of pieces of armor and representations of armor in works of art. Contents: 1, The Age of Mail, c. 1066-c. 1250; 2, The Introduction of Plate Armour, c. 1250-c. 1330; 3, Early Plate Armour, c. 1330-c. 1410; 4, The Great Period, c. 1410-c. 1500; 5, The Sixteenth Century, c. 1500-c. 1600; 6, The Decline, c. 1600-c. 1700; 7, Tournament Armour; 8, The Decoration of Armour; 9, The Shield; 10, Horse Armour; 11, The Making of Armour. Appendix with notes on the weight of armor and useful dictionary on the details of armor. Bibliography, pp. 230-33, with additional references in the notes.

348 Boccia, Lionello G., and E. T. Coelho. **L'arte dell'armatura in italia**. Milan, Bramante, 1967. 549p. illus. index. LC 68-119207.

Well illustrated and authoritative handbook of Italian arms and armor from the late Middle Ages to the middle of the eighteenth century. Introductory essay is followed by 471 plates of pieces of arms and armor and depictions in contemporary works of art with detailed notes that include facsimiles of marks and bibliographies of specialized literature. Plates are arranged in periods: L'armatura bianac (1380-1500); Laa guerre d'Italia (1480-1530); La Grande Maniera (1530-1590); L'armatura d'uso (1550-1600); I motivi a tessuto (1540-1620); La lunga trasformazione (1600-1750). Bibliography, pp. 545-49.

349 Boeheim, Wendelin. **Handbuch der Waffenkunde. Das Waffenwesen in seiner historischen Entwicklung vom Beginn des Mittelalters bis zum Ende des 18. Jahrhunderts**. Leipzig, Seemann, 1890. Reprint: Graz, Akedemische Druck- und Verlagsanstalt, 1966. 694p. illus. index. LC 67-78549.

Old, once-standard history/handbook of western European arms and armor from the beginning of the Middle Ages to the end of the eighteenth century. Still an important source for illustrations, particularly for dated examples. Contents: I, Die Schutzwaffen; II, Die Angriffswaffen; III, Die Turnierwaffen; IV, Bemerkungen für Freunde und Sammler von Waffen; V, Kunst und Technik im Waffenschmiedwesen; VI, Dier hervorragendsten Waffensammlungen; VII, Die Beschau- und Meisterzeichen und die Namen der Waffenschmiede mit ihren Marken. Bibliographical footnotes.

350 Boeheim, Wendelin. **Meister der Waffenschmiedekunst vom XIV. bis ins XVII. Jahrhundert; eine Beitrag zur Geschichte der Kunst und des Kunsthandwerks**. Berlin, W. Moeser, 1897. 246p. illus. index.

Pioneering work on European armorers from the fourteenth century to the middle of the seventeenth century. Includes biographies of 100 individuals and families with references to sources and facsimiles of marks. Twenty plates of signed pieces.

351 Bruhn de Hoffmeyer, Ada. **Arms and Armour in Spain. A Short Survey**. Volume 1: *The Bronze Age to the End of the High Middle Ages*. Madrid, Instituto de Estudios Sobre Armas Antiquas, 1972. 199p. illus. index. LC 74-193975r88.

Authoritative survey of Spanish arms and armor from the Bronze Age to the end of the thirteenth century. Bibliographical references in the footnotes.

352 Calvert, A. F. **Spanish Arms and Armour**. London, Lane, 1907. 142p. illus. LC 07-41545.

Survey of Spanish arms and armor from the early Middle Ages to the nineteenth century based on the collection of the Royal Armory in Madrid. Contains 248 plates arranged in chronological order. Occasional bibliographical footnotes.

353 Demmin, August. **Die Kriegswaffen in ihren geschichtlichen Entwicklungen von den ältesten Zeiten bis auf die Gegenwart**. 4th ed. Leipzig, Seemann, 1893. 2v. illus. index. Reprint: Hildesheim, Ohlms, 1964. LC 66-97580.

Pioneering and still useful history of the development of arms and armor in the West from prehistoric times to the end of the nineteenth century. English translation of first edition: *An Illustrated History of Arms and Armour from the Earliest Period to the Present* (London, 1877). Expansion of the author's earlier work: *Die Kriegswaffen in ihrer historischen Entwicklung von der Steinzeit bis zur Erfindung des Zündnadelgewehres* (Leipzig, Seemann, 1869). Text arranged in outline form with numbered illustrations of pieces of arms and armor in chronological order with brief descriptive text. Appendix with dictionary of major armorers and their marks.

354 Ffoulkes, C. **The Armourer and His Craft from XIth to XVIth Century**. London, Methuen, 1912. 199p. illus. index. Reprints: New York, B. Blom, 1967. LC 67-13328; and New York, Ungar, 1967. LC 67-25838. New York, Dover, 1988. ISBN 0486258513.

An old standard history of the European armorer from the early Middle Ages to the end of the Renaissance based on extensive use of documentary sources. Still valuable for the many extracts from sources in the text, the thirteen appendices, and for much information on techniques and materials. Contents: The Armourer; Tools, Appliances, Etc.; Iron and Steel; The Craft of Armor; The Decoration of Armor; The Cleaning of Armor; The Use of Fabrics and Linen; The Use of Leather; The Wearing of Armor; The Armorers' Company of the City of London; List of European Armorers; Short Biographies of Notable Armorers; List of Armorers' Marks; Polyglot Glossary of Words Dealing with Armor and Weapons. Bibliographical references in the footnotes.

355 Hewitt, John. **Ancient Armor and Weapons in Europe**. Oxford and London, Parker, 1855-60. 3v. illus. index. Reprint: Graz, Akademische Druck—und Verlagsanstalt, 1967. LC 67-105989.

An old, once-standard history of European arms and armor from prehistoric times to the end of the seventeenth century. Reprint has preface by Claude Blair with excellent overview of the early history of writing on arms and armor. Volumes one and two cover ancient and medieval periods; volume 3, originally a supplement, covers the fifteenth, sixteenth and seventeenth centuries. Illustrations are nearly all derived from contemporary representations of arms and armor and have detailed descriptive notes. Bibliographical references in the footnotes. Bibliography of the writings of John Hewitt at the end of the preface (introduction) in volume one.

356 Laking, Guy F. **A Record of European Armor and Arms through Seven Centuries**. London, Bell. 1920-22. 5v. illus. index. LC 20-13583.

Comprehensive history from the eleventh century through the seventeenth century. Volume one provides a general history; subsequent volumes treat the development of major types. Well illustrated with museum pieces and works of art illustrating arms and armor. Appendices with notes on forgeries and armor in English churches. Comprehensive bibliography, v. 5, pp. 275-304, lists books and periodical articles in all languages. A standard work on European arms and armor.

357 Martin, Paul. **Arms and Armor, from the 9th to the 17th Century**. Rutland, Vt., Tuttle, 1968. 298p. illus. index. LC 67-28906.

Survey of European arms and armor from the early Middle Ages to the end of the Renaissance. Contents: I. Armor in Europe: The Early Stages of Chivalry; The Era of the Coat of Mail and Tunic; The Reinforced Hauberk; The Period of the White Harness; The Emblazoned Tunic; Renaissance Armor; The Decline of Armor; Head Defence; Horse Armor (the Bard); Jousts and Tourney; Armorers and Craftsmen; II, Weapons: The Sword, the Belt and the Dagger; The Buckler, Shield and Targew; The Saddle and the Spurs; The Lance, Banner and Pennon; Staff-weapons; Missile Weapons; The Bow and Crossbow; Tactics and Weapons in Warfare. General bibliography, pp. 289-92.

358 Nickel, Helmut. **Arms and Armor Through the Ages**. Rev. ed. London, Collins, 1971. 122p. illus. index. LC 72-188098.

Pictorial survey of world arms and armor from ancient times to the end of the nineteenth century based on pieces in the collections of the Metropolitan Museum of Art in New York written by a well-known expert. Illustrations include depictions of arms and armor in works of art. Brief list of books in English, p. 120.

359 Nickel, Helmut. **Ullstein Waffenbuch. Eine kulturhistorische Waffenkunde mit Markenzeichen**. Frankfurt/Main and Berlin, Ullstein, 1974. 323p. illus. index. ISBN 3550074494.

Authoritative survey of world arms and armor with particular attention given to Continental arms and armor from the Middle Ages to the eighteenth century. Contents: Das Schild; Der Harnisch; Die Blankwaffen; Die Fernwaffen. Appendices with repertory of marks and list of major museum collections of arms and armor. Comprehensive, classified bibliography, pp. 312-16.

360 Oakeshott, R. Ewart. **European Weapons and Armour: From the Renaissance to the Industrial Revolution**. London, Butterworth Press, 1980. 288p. illus. index. ISBN 0718821262.

Authoritative survey of European armor and edged weapons from the 1400s to the nineteenth century with a chapter on American swords. Contains 24 plates of examples with descriptive captions and 114 line drawings illustrating types and features. Chapters are finely subdivided so the work can be used much like an encyclopedia. Contents: I, The Developing Power of the Handgun; 2, Staff-Weapons; 3, Mace, War-Hammer and Horseman's Axe; 4, Armour: 1400-1525; Helmets: 1400-1525; 7, The Two-Hand Sword; 8, The Curved and Single-Edged Swords of the Sixteenth Century; 9, Sword and Rapier in the Seventeenth Century; 10, The Military Sword of the Seventeenth Century; 11, Armour in Decline; 12, Helmets in the Sixteenth and Seventeenth Centuries; 13, The Dagger: 1500-1650; 14, The Smallsword. Appendix with essay on tournament armor and American swords in the nineteenth century. Brief bibliographies at the ends of chapters.

361 Reitzenstein, Alexander von. **Der Waffenschmied. Vom Handwerk der Schwertschmiede, Plattner und Buchsenmacher**. Munich, Prestel, 1964. 96p. illus. LC 55-83393.

Authoritative introduction to German edged weapons, armor, and firearms of the fifteenth and sixteenth centuries with 57 excellent quality plates of major museum pieces and contemporary illustrations depicting arms and armor. Basic bibliography, p. 88.

362 Thomas, Bruno, Ortwin Gamber, and Hans Schedelmann. **Arms and Armor of the Western World**. New York, McGraw Hill, 1964. 251p. illus. LC 64-22727.

Pictorial survey of western European arms and armor from the thirteenth to the nineteenth centuries. Brief introductory essay followed by a good selection of plates of major museum pieces with detailed catalog entries. Glossary of terms and additional notes on major armorers with bibliographical references.

See also the museum catalogs:

Budapest—*The Treasures of the Hungarian National Museum: Arms and Armor*, by F. Temesváry (Budapest, Corvina, 1982. 71p. illus. ISBN 9632075218).

Churburg—*The Armoury of the Castle of Churburg*, by O. Trapp (London, Methuen, 1929. 370p. illus.).

Cleveland—*Catalogue of the Severence Collection of Arms and Armor in the Cleveland Museum of Art*, by H. I. Gilchrist (Cleveland, Ohio, Cleveland Museum of Art, 1924).

Dresden—*Princely Arms and Armor: A Selection from the Dresden Collection*, by J. Schöbel (London, Barrie & Jenkinsm 1975. 255p. illus.).

London—*Inventory and Survey of the Armouries of the Tower of London*, by C. J. Ffoulkes (London, H.M.S.O., 1915. 2v. illus.); *European Armor in the Tower of London*, by A. R. Dufty (London, H.M.S.O., 1968. 75p. illus. LC 68-115491r895); *European Arms and Armor*, by J. Mann (6th ed. London, Trustees of the Wallace Collection, 1962. 2v. illus. LC 65-5602); *Treasures from the Tower of London: An Exhibition of Arms and Armor*, by A.V. B. Norman and G. M. Wilson (Norwich, Sainsburg Centre for the Visual Arts, 1982. 131p. illus. ISBN 0946009015).

New York—*The Bashford Dean Collection of Arms and Armor in the Metropolitan Museum of Art*, by C.O. von Kienbusch and S. V. Grancsay (Portland, Me., Southworth Press, 1933. 27p. illus.).

Paris—*Armes et armures anciennes et souvenirs historiques les plus précieux. Musée de l'armée* (Paris, Hotel des Invalides, 1917-27. 2v. illus.), *Les Armures des rois de France au Musée de l'Armée*, by J.-P. Reverseau (Saint-Julien-du-Sault, Éditions F. P. Lobies, 1982. 142p. illus.).

Vienna—*Katalog der Waffensammlung in der Neuen Burg*, by A. Grosz and B. Thomas (Vienna, Kunsthistorisches Museum, 1936. 291p. illus.), *Katalog der Leibrüstkammer. Der Zeitraum von 500 bis 1530. Führer durch das Kunsthistorisches Museum.* (Vienna, Anton Schroll, 1976, 264p. illus.).

Waddesdon Manor—*Arms, Armor and Base-Metalwork* by C. Blair (London, National).

ORIENTAL ARMS AND ARMOR

Bibliographies

363 Creswell, K. H. C. **A Bibliography of Islamic Arms and Armor.** London, Royal Asiatic Society, 1956. 79p. LC 57-59222.

Classified and annotated bibliography of 497 books and periodical articles on all aspects of Islamic arms and armor. This material has been incorporated in the author's comprehensive bibliography: *A Bibliography of the Architecture, Arts and Crafts of Islam to 1960* (FA 162).

General Histories and Handbooks

364 Holstein, Prosper P. H. **Contribution a l'étude des armes orientales.** Paris, Lévy, 1931. 2v. illus. index.

Comprehensive, scholarly history of the arms of the Near and Middle East with a catalog of the author's collection. Contents of volume one: Première Partie: Inde, A, Le sabre; B, Armes diverses. Deuxième Partie: Archipel Malais: A, Le Kriss; B, De quelque autres armes blanches de l'archipel Malais; C, De Quelques peuplades curieuses de l'archipel Malais et leurs arms. Second volume is a detailed catalog of the Hostein collection. Contains 36 plates and 154 figures in volume one; 84 plates in volume two. General bibliography, v. 1, pp. ii-xxiii, and further bibliography in the footnotes and catalog.

365   Robinson, H. Russell. **Oriental Armour**. New York, Walker, 1967. 257p. illus. index. LC 67-13231.

Authoritative survey of Oriental armor illustrated with 32 plates of museum pieces and 110 drawings derived from depictions in works of art. Contents: I, The Origins of Oriental Armour; II, Persia; III, Turkey; IV, The Middle East; V, India, Ceylon, Philippine Islands; VI, China, Korea, Tibet, Bhutan; VII, Japan. Important glossary of terms in various Oriental languages. Select bibliography, pp. 216-17.

India

366   Egerton, Wilbraham E. **Indian and Oriental Armour**. Harrisburg, Pa., Stackpole Books, 1968. 178p. illus. index. LC-16504.

Reprint of work published in 1896 as a catalog of the collections of arms and armor exhibited in London in 1880 and now mostly in the Victoria and Albert Museum and the Armouries of the Tower of London. First part is "A Sketch of the Military History of India"; the second part is the descriptive catalog arranged by ethnic groups: Aboriginal and Non-Aryan Tribes of Central India and the Andaman Island; Aborigonal and Dravidian Races of Southern India; Hill Tribes of Assam and the North-East Frontier; British and Native Burma and Siam; Malayan Peninsula and the Indian Archipelago; Nepal; The Rajputs; The Mahrattas, Mahomedan Arms of the Deccan and Mysore; Northwestern India—the Punjab, Sind; Northwest Frontier, Afghanistan, Persia, China, etc.; Arms Used for Athletic and Sacrificial Purposes. Appendices with essays on artillery, Arab arms and a catalog of the arms in the private collection of Lord Egerton.

367   Pant, G. N. (Gayatri Nath). **Indian Arms and Armour**. New Delhi, Army Educational Stores, 1978-. LC 78-903904.

Comprehensive history of arms and armour in India from prehistoric times to the end of the eighteenth century. Contents: v. 1: Pre-and-protohistoric weapons and archery; v. 2, Swords and armour; v. 3, Human armour and shield. Volume 4 will cover Horse and Elephant armour. Bibliographies in each volume.

Japan

368   Anderson, L. John. **Japanese Armour: An Illustrated Guide to the Work of the Myochin and Saotome Famillies from the 15th to the 20th Century**. Harrisburg, Pa., Stackpole Books, 1968. 84p. illus. LC 68-31180.

Popular but informative survey of Japanese armor with special attention to the works of the famous Myochin and Saotome families of armourers. Contents: Japanese Armor: History, The Age of Battles; The Myochin Family and Their Work; The Saotome Familly; The Warrior Class System. Contains 70 black and white plates with detailed descriptive notes. Bibliography of books and articles in English, p. 82.

369   Bottomley, Ian, and Anthony Hopson. **Arms and Armor of the Samurai: The History of Weaponry in Ancient Japan**. New York, Crescent Books, 1988. 192p. illus. ISBN 0517644673.

Well illustrated and informative history of the arms and armor of the Japanese Samurai from its origins in prehistoric times to the end of the Edo Period. Contents: 1, The Origins of the Warrior Class; 2, The Samurai during the Gempei Wars; 3, The Kamakura and the Nambokucho Periods; 4, Civil Unrest: The Ashikaga Shogunate; 5, The Evolution of Modern Armor; 6, The Arrival of the Southern Barbarians; 7, Japan in Isolation: The Edo Period. Bibliography of basic works in English and Japanese.

EDGED WEAPONS

General Histories and Handbooks

370 Connolly, Peter, ed. **Sword and Hilt Weapons**. New York, Weidenfeld & Nicolson, 1989. 239p. illus. index. ISBN 1555842909.

Well-illustrated introduction to the history of swords and daggers from ancient times to the end of the Second World War. Essays by leading British and American experts. Contents: I, Stone, Bronze and Iron by A. Harding; 2, Greece and Rome by P. Connolly; 3, Barbarians and Christians by A. North; 4, The Renaissance Spirit by D. LaRocca; 5, From Rapier to Smallswords by A. North; 6, Seventeenth-Century Europe by A. North; 7, Eighteenth- and Nineteenth Century Europe by A. North; 8, Combination Weapons by A. North; 9, American Swords and Knives by F. Wilkinson; 10, World Wars I and II by F. Wilkinson; 11, Swords of Islam by A. North; 12, Japanese Swords by V. Harris; 13, China and Central Asia by T. Richardson; 14, India and Southeast Asia by F. Wilkinson; 15, African Hilt Weapons by C. Spring; 16, Pre-Conquest America by M. Coe. Classified bibliography, pp. 227-229.

371 Seitz, Heribert. **Blankwaffen**. Braunschweig, Klinkhardt & Biermann, 1965-68. 2v. illus. index. LC 67-35206. (Bibliothek fur Kunst- und Antiquitätenfruende, Band 4-4A).

Comprehensive, authoritative history of European and American edged weapons from prehistoric times to the end of the nineteenth century. Contains 350 black and white plates and 16 in color illustrating major museum pieces and many works of art depicting edged weapons in use. Contents: Band I: Vorgeschichte und klassisches Altertum; Das Mittelalter; Das Mittelalterliche Erbe und Die Renaissance; Die Schlagwaffen; Band II: Das Barock und das Rokoko; Der Neuklassizismus und das Empire; Die Romantik und das 19. Jahrundert. Each volume concludes with a comprehensive, classified bibliography. A standard work.

372 Wagner, Eduard. **Cut and Thrust Weapons**. London, Spring Books, 1967. 491p. illus. index. LC 67-112910.

Comprehensive handbook on the identification of the various types of European edged weapons from ancient times to the end of the nineteenth century. Particular emphasis is given to the weapons of the Austro-Hungarian military. Detailed descriptions of the plates, some with bibliographical references. Bibliography, pp. 489-491, is alphabetical list of books chiefly in German.

373 Wilkinson, Frederick J. **Edged Weapons**. Garden City, N.Y. Doubleday, 1970. 256p. illus. index. LC 72-113989.

Popular survey of edged weapons from prehistoric times to World War II. Emphasis is on the sword. Contents: From Flint to Steel; The Evolution of the Sword; Rapiers; Smallsword; Knives and Daggers; Hunting Weapons; Polearms; Hand Bows; Crossbows; Naval and Military Swords; Bayonets; African and South Asian Weapons; Japanese Weapons; Indian Weapons; German Weapons; Construction and Decoration. No bibliography.

See also the museum catalogs: *Catalog of Eureprean Daggers including the Ellis, De Dino, and Reubell Collection*, by B. Dean (New York, Metropolitan Museum of Art, 1929. 196p. illus.), *Waffen im schweizerischen Landesmuseum Nand 1: Griffwaffen*, by H. Schneider (Zurich, Füssli, 1980).

See also the price guide: *The Price Guide to Antique Edged Weapons*, by L. Southwick (Woodridge, Suffolk, Antique Collectors Club, 1982. 280p. illus. index. ISBN 0902028944).

American Edged Weapons

374   Neumann, George C. **Swords & Blades of the American Revolution**. Harrisburg, Pa., Stackpole Books, 1973. 288p. illus. LC 72-126665, ISBN 0811717208.

Authoritative, well-illustrated handbook of the edged weapons of the American Revolutionary War. Contents: 1, Blades in the Early Colonies; 2, Cold Steel on the Battlefield; 3, Lines of Bayonets; 4, The Flashing Sword; 5, Stately Polerams; 6, Knives and Daggers; 7, The Belt and Camp Axe. Chapters 1 and 2 give broad overview. Chapters 3-7 each have introductory essays illustrated with drawings, followed by a large number of photographic plates of individual pieces with descriptive captions. Comprehensive bibliography, pp. 280-84.

European Edged Weapons

375   Boccia, Lionello G., and Eduardo T. Coelho. **Armi bianche italiane**. Milan, Bramante, 1975. 462p. illus.

Comprehensive history of Italian edged weapons from the thirteenth century to the nineteenth century with emphasis on decoration. Brief introductory essay followed by 800 plates with descriptive captions.

376   Oakeshott, R. Ewart. **The Sword in the Age of Chivalry**. New York, Praeger, 1965. 152p. illus. index. LC 65-14185.

Authoritative introduction to the history of the sword in the Western Middle Ages. Contains 48 plates of swords with descriptive captions and an additional 134 figures in the text that include drawings taken from works of English medieval art. Contents: 1, Swords of Group I (1050-1350); 2, Swords of Group II (1350-1550); 3, Pommel-Forms; 4, Cross-Guards; 5, Grip and Scabbard. Appendix with lists of inscriptions on blades. Bibliography, pp. 144-145.

Japanese Edged Weapons

377   Hara, Shinkichi. **Die Meister der japanischen Schwertzierarten**. 2d. ed. 2v. illus. Hamburg, Museum für Kunst und Gewerbe, 1931.

Important, comprehensive handbook/history of Japanese swords with repertory of makers and their marks and history of decorative forms. Bibliographical references in the footnotes.

378   Robinson, B. W. **The Arts of the Japanese Sword**. London, Faber and Faber, 1970. 110p. illus. index LC 70-587865.

Authoritative introduction to the history of the Japanese sword. Contains 108 plates with descriptive captions. Contents: Part One: The Blade. Introduction, Evolution and History of the Japanese Sword; The Smith and His Work: Making a Blade; Nomenclature and Expertise: Judging a Blade; The Five Traditions; The Chief Schools of Japanese Swordsmiths; The Greatest Swordsmiths of Japan. Part Two: The Mounts: Evolution of Styles; Materials and Technique; Mounting of Katana and Wakizashi; Mounting of Tachi; Mounting of Daggers; The Chief Schools of Japanese Sword-furniture Makers; The Greatest Sword-furniture. Appendices: A, The Year-periods; B, The Numerals and the 'Ten Stems' and the 'Twelve Signs'; C, The Provinces; D, Care and Cleaning; E, Characters Used in the Names of Swordsmiths and Makers of Sword-fittings.

See also Ogasawara, Nobuo. *Japanese Swords,* 3rd ed. (Osaka, Hoijusha, 1975. 128p. illus. Hoikusha Color Books, 22).

379   Sato, Kanzan. **The Japanese Sword**. Tokyo, New York, Kodansha International, 1983. 210p. illus. index. ISBN 0870115626.

Well illustrated and informative survey of the Japanese sword. Contents: 1, The Development of the Japanese Sword; 2, The Appreciation of Fine Swords; 3, The Mounts of a Japanese Sword; 4, Metal Sword-Fittings; 5, The Making of a Japanese Sword; 6, Sword Appraisal; 7, Essentials of Sword Care. Bibliography, pp. 202-05, has separate annotated section on works in English.

See also the museum and exhibition catalogs: *The Baur Collection Geneva: Japanese Sword Fittings and Associated Metalwork*, by B. W. Robinson (Geneva, Collections Baur, 1980), *Das Schwert des Samurai: Exponate aus dem Sammlungen des Staatlichen Museums für Völkerkunde zu Dresden un des Museums für Völkerkunde zu Leipzig*, by L. Icke-Schwalbe. (Berlin, Militarverlag, 1977. 95p. illus.), *Japanese Sword-Mounts in the Collections of Field Museum, Chicago*, by H. C. Gunsaulus (Chicago, Field Museum, 1923. 195p. illus. Reprint: New York, Kraus, 1968), *Court and Samurai in an Age of Transition: Medieval Paintings and Blades from the Gotoh Museum, Tokyo* (New York, Japan Society, 1990. 127p. illus. ISBN 091330428X), and *Nippon-to: Art Swords of Japan*, by W. A. Compton, et al. (New York, Japan Society, 1976).

FIREARMS

Dictionaries and Encyclopedias

380 Hogg, Ian V. **The Complete Encyclopedia of the World's Firearms**. New York, A & W Publishers, 1978. 320p. illus. ISBN 0894790315.

Well-illustrated dictionary of firearms from 1830 to 1975 with a 56-page introduction tracing the history of firearms from the late Middle Ages to the twentieth century. Entries are largely devoted to major designers, manufacturers and types of firearms. Illustrations include diagrams of internal mechanisms, facsimiles of trademarks as well as photographs of handguns, rifles and small caliber automatic weapons. Appendices include tables of technical specifications and an illustrated glossary. No bibliography.

381 Peterson, Harold L., ed. **Encyclopedia of Firearms**. New York, Dutton, 1964. 367p. illus. index. LC 64-25937.

Comprehensive dictionary encompassing all aspects of the manufacture and use of firearms including types, mechanisms, materials and makers. Longer entries have bibliographies. Illustrated with plates and line drawings.

382 Schedelmann, Hans. **Die grossen Buchsenmacher: Leben, Werke, Marken**. Braunschweig, Klinkhardt & Biermann, 1972. 325p. illus. index. LC 73-304998.

Comprehensive, scholarly handbook of European and American gunsmiths from the fifteenth to the nineteenth centuries. Biographies are grouped by centuries. Gunsmiths known only by their initials are at the end of the century groups. Entries give basic biographical data, lists of pieces in major museum collections and references to specialized literature. Contains 392 plates of signed or marked pieces with many details of marks. Comprehensive bibliography, pp. 322-25. Standard reference work on gunsmiths.

General Histories and Handbooks

383 Blackmore, Howard L. **Guns and Rifles of the World**. New York, Viking, 1965. 134p. illus. LC 65-17169.

Pictorial survey of European and American handguns and rifles from the earliest examples to the end of the nineteenth century. Written by a well-known authority. Contains 869 plates with descriptive notes and an additional number of drawings illustrating details of mechanisms and ammunition. Contents: 1, The Hand-Gun; 2, The Matchlock; 3, Wheellocks; 4, Flintlocks; 5, Percussion Locks; 6, Breechloaders; 7, Multi-Shot Guns; 8, Air, Steam and Electric Guns. Select bibliography, pp. 125-26.

384 Hayward, John F. **The Art of the Gunmaker**. New York, St. Martin's Press, 1962-64. 2v. illus. index. LC 62-5869 rev.

Comprehensive, authoritative history of European and American gun making from 1500 to 1830. Volume one covers European firearms from 1500 to 1660; volume two European and American firearms from 1660 to 1830. Both volumes are divided by country and time and have concluding chapters on ornament and design and appendices with descriptions of the chief mechanisms used in the periods covered by the two volumes. Plates with descriptive notes. Bibliographical references in the notes.

385 Lindsay, Merrill. **One Hundred Great Guns: An Illustrated History of Firearms**. New York, Walker, 1967. 379p. illus. index. LC 67-23653.

Sumptuously illustrated survey of European and American firearms from the sixteenth century to the early twentieth century. Emphasis is placed on pieces of unusual artistic or technological sophistication. Dictionary of gun maker with facsimiles of marks. Contents: 1, The Invention of Gunpowder: Fact and Fiction; 2, Machines before Guns; 3, The Gonne: Being a Summary of the Earliest Weapons Using Gunpowder, Including Cannon, Hand Cannon, Pot de Fer and Totenorgel; 4, The Matchlock—The Arquebus; 5, The Wheel Lock; 6, The Snaphaunce; 7, The Miquelet or Mediterranean Lock; 8, The True Flintlock or French Lock; 9, Fulminating Powders and Transitional Weapons; 10, True Percussion; 11, Breech Loading; 12, The Comic History of Bullets; 13, The Sealed Breech: Pinfire, Needlefire, Rimfire, Center Fire; 14, Revolvers; 15, The Single Shot Rifle; 16, Magazine Repeaters; 17, Double-Barreled; 18, Self-Loaders: Full and Semi-Automatics; 19, Rockets and Blue Sky; 20, "Shooters" and "Decorators." Comprehensive bibliography, pp.310-365.

386 Muller, Heinrich. **Guns, Pistols, Revolvers: Hand-firearms from the 14th to the 19th Centuries**. New York, St. Martin's Press, 1980. 224p. illus. ISBN 0312353928.

Well-illustrated survey of European and American hand guns. Plates feature museum pieces with important decoration. Descriptive captions to the plates. Contents: The Discovery of Gunpowder; The First Hand-Firearms; Firing-iron and Matchlock; Pistols, Breechloaders and Organ Guns; Science and Weapons; Technology at the Time of the Renaissance; The Craft of the Gunmaker; Leonardo da Vinci and the Wheel Lock; Shooting Prize Competitions and Shooting Festivals; Muskets-Carbines-Wheel Lock Pistols; Barrel-bores—Grooves—Inserted Barrels; Hand-firearms in Costly Guise; Snap Lock and Miquelet Lock; Deer Hunting Rifles and Sporting Guns; Superstition and Protective Magic; Combination Weapons; Repeating Small-arms and Breechloaders; Gun Barrels of Horseshoe Iron and Damascus Barrels; Powder Testing Devices; Plug and Socket Bayonets; Manufacture and Technology of Arms Production; Standing Armies and Line Tactics; The Flintlock; Drill and Shooting with Military Flintlock Weapons; Military and Civil Pistols; Blunderbusses, Priming-powder; Magazines and Concealed Flintlocks; Air Guns and Electrical Ignition; Industrial Weapons Production; National Civil Armies and New Tactics; Percussion Locks; Dilating and Expanding Projectiles; Needle-fire Small-arms; Pepperboxes and Cylinder Revolvers; Pistol Duels and Duelling Pistols; Breechloaders and Metallic Cartridges; Repeating Arms. Basic bibliography, pp. 215-17.

387 **Pollard's History of Firearms**. Rev. ed. New York, Macmillan, 1983. 559p. illus. index. LC 84-19437.

General editor Claude Blair with contributions by various British experts. Comprehensive history of world firearms from the invention of gun powder to the present. Supersedes: *A History of Firearms* by Hugh C. Pollard (London, G. Bles, 1926. 320p. illus. index. Reprint: New York, Burt Franklin, 1973. ISBN 0833746766). Large number of plates and drawings illustrating pieces in museums and private collections, details of mechanisms and decoration, and works of art illustrating firearms. Contents: A Memoire of Hugh Pollard; 1, Early Firearms by C. Blair; The Sixteenth Century by C. Blair; The Seventeenth Century by C. Blair; The Eighteenth Century and the End of the Flintlock by H. L. Peterson; 5, The Percussion System by H. L. Blackmore; 6, Early Breech-Loading Firearms by H. L. Blackmore; 7, Early Repeating Firearms by H. L. Peterson; 8, Muzzle-Loading Revolvers by A. W. F. Taylerson; 9, Breech-Loading and Repeating Firearms Other Than Revolvers 1810-70 by H. L. Peterson; 10, Firearms Oher Than Revolvers and Automatic Pistols 1870-1918 by C. H. Roads; 11, Cartridge Revolvers down to 1918 by A.W.F. Taylerson; 12, Automatic Pistols down to 1918 by C. H. Roads; 13, Genearl Survey of Firearms: 1918 to the Present by C. H. Roads with I. Hogg; 14, Scottish Firearms by W. Reid; 15, Oriental and Levantine Firearms by Z. Zygulski; 16, The Manufacture and Proof of Firearms by A. W. F. Taylerson; 17, The Decoration of Firearms by I. Graboska; 18, Firearms Accessories by H. L. Blackmore. Appendices with glossary, essays on air, spring, and gas guns, and miniature firearms. Comprehensive bibliography complied by A. R. North, pp. 538-44.

388   Wilkinson-Latham, Robert. **Antique Guns in Color**. New York, Arco , 1978. 215p. illus. index. ISBN 0668044675.

General survey of firearms in Europe and North America from the invention of gunpowder to 1865. Illustrated with 118 color plates with brief descriptive notes. Glossary of terms. No bibliography.

See also the author's: *Antique Firearms* (Garden City, N.Y. Doubleday, 1969. 256p. illus. index).

American Firearms

Dictionaries of Gun Makers

389   Satterlee, Leroy D., and Arcadi Gluckman. **American Gun Makers**. Buffalo, N.Y., 1940. 186p. illus.

————. **Supplement to American Gun Makers.** Buffalo, N.Y., Ulbrich Co., 1949. 66p. Reprint of both: Harrisburg, Pa., Stackpole Books, 1953. 246p. LC 53-5668.

Comprehensive dictionary of American gun makers from early Colonial times to the end of the nineteenth century. Entries vary from simply place and date to longer entries with references to documentary sources.

General Histories and Handbooks

390   Brown, M. L. **Firearms in Colonial America: The Impact on History and Technology, 1492-1792.** Washington, D.C., Smithsonian Institution Press, 1980. 450p. illus. index. ISBN 0874742900.

Comprehensive, authoritative history of firearms used and made in the American colonies. Illustrations include manufacturing machinery and techniques as well as many illustrations of actual pieces. Contents: I, Genesis of the Gun; II, Cross, Sword and Arquebus; III, Flintlocks, Merchants and Saints; IV, Firearms in the Emerging Colonies; V, Firearms in the Expanding Colonies; VI, Firearms in the Developing Colonies; VII, Muskets, Powder and Patriots; VIII, Firearms and the Road to Independence; IX, Firearms in the New Republic. Nine appendices with documentary material. Comprehensive, classified bibliography, pp. 411-15, and extensive bibliography in the notes. Standard work on early American firearms.

391   Butler, David F. **United States Firearms: The First Century, 1776-1875**. New York, Winchester Press, 1971. 249p. illus. index. LC 77-146062.

Comprehensive history of firearms made in the United States between 1776 and 1875 with emphasis on technological and mechanical aspects. Important source for data on dimensions, ammunition size and ballistic tests. No bibliography.

392   Russell, Carl P. **Guns on the Early Frontiers: A History of Firearms from Colonial Times through the Years of the Western Fur Trade**. New York, Bonanza, 1957. 395p. illus. index. Reprinted: Lincoln, Neb., Univ. of Nebraska Press, 1980. ISBN 0803238576.

Comprehensive, authoritative history of firearms in America from the beginning of European settlement to the early nineteenth century. Emphasis is on the technical aspects. Contents: I, Arming the American Indian; II, Personal Weapons of the Traders and Trappers; III, Trade Muskets and Rifles Supplied to the Indians; IV, Military Arms of the Fur-Trade Period; V, Powder, Ball, and Accessories; VI, Small Cannon of the Traders and the Military. Comprehensive bibliography, pp. 357-81.

393   Serven, James E. **200 Years of American Firearms**. Chicago, Follett, 1975. 224p. illus. ISBN 0695805991.

Popular pictorial survey of American guns and rifles from 1776 to 1976. Illustrations feature many examples of familar types and serves as a resource for collectors. No bibliography.

European Firearms

394   Ffoulkes, Charles J. **The Gun-Founders of England**. Cambridge, N.Y., Cambridge University Press, 1937. 133p. illus. index. Reprint: York, Pa., G. Shumway, 1969. ISBN 08738-7031X, LC 70-89561.

Scholarly history of the production of cannons in England from the fourteenth to the nineteenth centuries. Contents: 1, Introduction; 2, Manufacture; 3, Guns of Iron and Brass; 4, Gun-foundries in London and Calais; 5, Foundries of Douai and Woolwich; 6, Foundries of Sussex; 7, The Carron Foundry; 8, Powder and Shot; 9, Proof and Range. Appendices with extracts from documents, repertory of gun-founders in England and on the continent. Basic bibliography, pp. 126-28, and additional bibliography in footnotes and in the repertory.

395   Jackson, Herbert J., and Charles E. Whitelaw. **European Hand Firearms of the Sixteenth, Seventeenth and Eighteenth Centuries**. London, Holland Press; Chicago, Quadrangle, 1960. 108p. illus. index. LC 60-980.

First published in 1923. Collector's survey of European pistols from the sixteenth through the eighteenth centuries emphasizing the development of the major types. Contents: I, Wheel-Locks and Match-Locks of the XVIth and XVIIth Centuries; II, Snaphaunce and Transition Weapons and Locks; The Flint-Lock in the XVIIth Century; IV, XVIIth Century Gunsmiths; V, Types of XVIIIth Century Flint-Lock Weapons; VI, The Flint-Lock of the First Half of the XVIIIth Century; VII, Examples of Early XVIIIth Century Firearms; VIII, Firearms in the Latter Part of the XVIIIth Century; IX, The Period of Transition from Flint to the Percussion System; X, Some Hints on the Cleaning and Keeping of Firearms. Appendix: "A Treatise on Scottish Firearms" by C. E. Whitelaw. Bibliographical references in the notes.

CHAPTER FIVE

CERAMICS

BIBLIOGRAPHIES

396 Campbell, James E. **Pottery and Ceramics: A Guide to Information Sources**. Detroit, Gale Research Co., 1978. 241p. index. ISBN 08910312743.

Comprehensive bibliography of books and periodical articles in all languages on all aspects of ceramic history and technology. Contents: 1, Reference Works; 2, General Histories, Dictionaries, and Encyclopedias; 3, Ancient and Pre-Columbian Ceramics; 4, Eastern Ceramics; 5, Western Ceramics: The Middle Ages to the 20th Century; 7, Ceramics of the United States; 8, Contemporary World Ceramics; 9, Ceramic Collections; 10, Ceramic Marks; 11, Technical Works on Ceramic Materials and Processes; 12, Ceramic Periodicals; 13, Ceramic Organizations and Societies; 14, Museum Collections in the United States.

397 Champfleury, Jules F. H. **Bibliographie céramique; nomenclature analytique de toutes les publications faites en Europe et son Orient sur les arts et l'industrie céramiques depuis le XVIe siècle jusqu'à nos jours**. Paris, Quantin, 1881. 352p. LC 06-14255.

Old but thorough classified bibliography of books and periodical articles on all aspects of world ceramics, with the exception of ancient Greek, Roman, and Gallo-Roman. Part one covers general works and is arranged alphabetically; part two treats works on various countries and civilizations and is arranged geographically. Entries in part two are annotated. A standard reference work for specialized research.

398 Solon, Louis M. E. **Ceramic Literature: An Analytical Index to the Works Published in All Languages on the History and the Technology of the Ceramic Art...** London, Griffin, 1910. 660p. LC 10-21651.

Annotated bibliography of books, periodicals and catalogs on all aspects of ceramics. Main part, an annotated list by author, is followed by a classified list of the same works. A supplement was published in the *Transactions of the Ceramic Society* (Stoke-on-Kent, v. VI, 1911-12, pp. 65-104). A useful tool for gaining access to older literature, particularly on the history of ceramic technology.

TECHNIQUE

399 Leach, Bernard H. **A Potters Book**. 3rd ed. London, Faber and Faber, 1976. 296p. illus. index. ISBN 0571049273.

Comprehensive handbook of the design and technique of Oriental and Western pottery illustrated with line drawing diagrams and plates. Appendix with glossary of terms, tools and materials.

400 Morley-Fletcher, Hugo, ed. **Techniques of the World's Great Masters of Pottery and Ceramics**. Oxford, Phaidon: Christie's, 1984. 192p. illus. index. ISBN 0714880108.

Collection of essays by a group of British experts on the history of ceramics with emphasis on the interrelationship between material and technological innovation and style history. Contents: 1, The Lustre Tradition; 2, Sèvres: Luxury for the Court; 3, The Blue and White Tradition; 4, The Influence of Japan and the Kakiemon Style; 5, The Observation of Nature; 6, The Debt to Metalwork; 7, The Revival of Craft Pottery; 8, Wares: Useful and Decorative. Bibliography, p. 187, is a list of books in English.

401   Parsons, Claudia S. M., and F. H. Curl. **China Mending and Restoration**. London, Faber and Faber, 1963. 435p. illus.index. LC 64-4526.

Comprehensive and authoritative handbook on the techniques and materials used in the restoration of ceramics. Contents: 1, Riveting; 2, Restoring; 3, Overpainting, Gilding and Glazing; 4, Glass Repair. Comprehensive, classified bibliography, pp. 421-26.

402   Rhodes, Daniel. **Clay and Glaze for Potter**. Rev. ed. Philadelphia, Chilton, 1973. 330p. illus. LC 72-12887.

Technical handbook of the materials and techniques used in ceramic glazes. Although the emphasis is on present-day techniques, there is reference to and illustrations of historical examples. Bibliography, p. 325.

DICTIONARIES AND ENCYCLOPEDIAS

General

403   Barber, Edwin A. **The Ceramic Collectors' Glossary**. New York, Walpole Society, 1914. 119p. illus. Reprint: New York, Da Capo, 1967, 1967. LC 67-27448.

General dictionary of ceramic terms covering techniques, materials, ornament, and types. Illustrated with line drawings. Still useful for older and antiquated terms.

404   Boger, Louise A. **The Dictionary of World Pottery and Porcelain**. New York, Scribner's, 1971. 533p. illus. LC 72-123829.

Popular dictionary designed for the collector. Covers potters, marks and signatures, types of ceramics, techniques and processes, places, countries, styles and periods. Short entries with informative notes and good illustrations of pieces typical of those accessible to the average collector. Bibliography of basic books in all languages, pp. 525-33.

405   Cinotti, Mia. **Dizionario della ceramica dalla preistoria all'Ottocento**. Milan, Ideal-Standard, 1967. 253p. illus. LC 76-372706.

Comprehensive dictionary covering all aspects of world ceramics including techniques and materials, styles, periods, countries and centers. General bibliography, pp. 241-53, lists basic books in all languages.

406   Fournier, Robert. **Illustrated Dictionary of Pottery Form**. New York, Van Nostrand Reinhold, 1981. 257p. illus. ISBN 0442261129.

General dictionary of the types of ceramic objects. Although the intention of the work is to be a resource for contemporary ceramicists, there is much historical material and numerous illustrations of traditional ceramics useful to the collector. Bibliographical references to a fairly comprehensive list of basic reference works, pp. ix-xii.

407   Garnier, Edouard. **Dictionnaire de la céramique; faïences-gres poteries...** Paris, Libraire de l'art, 1893. 258p. illus. LC F-3126.

Comprehensive dictionary of ceramics covering makers, places, types and terms, with an alphabetical list of marks and signatures. Appendix with figurative marks. Older, pioneering work of interest chiefly to the scholar and antiquarian.

408 Haggar, Reginald G. **The Concise Encyclopedia of Continental Pottery and Porcelain.** New York, Praeger, 1968. 533p. illus. LC 68-28656.

Comprehensive dictionary of continental European pottery and porcelain, a companion to the author's *Concise Dictionary of English Pottery and Porcelain* (513). Covers periods, countries, centers, artists, decorative motifs and techniques. Plates illustrate museum pieces. Entries on major manufacturers give facsimiles of marks and signatures. Bibliographies accompany the major entries. Classified bibliography of books in all languages, pp. 523-33.

409 Jervis, William P., comp. **The Encyclopedia of Ceramics...** New York, Canal Street, n.d. (c. 1902). 673p. illus. index. Microfiche reprint: Chicago, Library Resources, 1970. (Microbook Library of American Civilization, LAC 15889).

Older, popular dictionary covering countries, styles, materials, techniques, centers and objects. List of marks of major American and European factories, pp. 657-73.

410 Minghetti, Aurelio. **Ceramisti**. Milan, Istituto Editoriale Italiano B. C. Tosi, 1939. 451p. illus. (Encyclopedia biographica e bibliographica "Italiana" serie XLI)

Biographical dictionary of ceramic makers from the eleventh century to the early twentieth century. Biographical references given in most entries.

411 Savage, George, and Harold Newman. **An Illustrated Dictionary of Ceramics**. New York, Van Nostrand Reinhold, 1974. 320p. illus. LC 73-17999.

Comprehensive dictionary of ceramic terminology. Over 3,000 terms realting to the materials, techniques, processes, styles, patterns and shapes of ceramic ware from antiquity to the twentieth century. List of principal marks of European factories, pp. 7-18.

Dictionaries of Marks and Signatures

412 Behse, Arthur. **Porzellanmarken—Brevier fur Sammler und Kunsthandler.** 3rd ed. Braunschweig, Klinkhardt & Biermann, 1965. 50p. illus. LC 66-74730.

Pocket-size dictionary of European porcelain marks illustrated with facsimiles. General bibliography, pp. 49-50.

413 Burton, William, and Robert L. Hobson. **Handbook of Marks on Pottery & Porcelain.** Rev. ed. London, Macmillan, 1928. 213p. illus. index. LC 29-15592.

Pocket-sized dictionary of ceramic marks covering Europe, the Orient and America. Arranged geographically with brief introduction to each country.

414 Chaffers, William. **Marks and Monograms on European and Oriental Pottery and Porcelain...** 15th rev. ed. London, Reeves, 1965. 2v. illus. index. LC 66-38182.

Comprehensive dictionary of ceramic marks arranged by country then by place, giving facsimiles of the marks. Short histories and descriptions at the beginning of each section. Bibliographies are given at the end of some sections. First volume covers continental European and Oriental ceramics; second volume concentrates on British ceramics. In this edition the second volume has been greatly expanded by G. A. Godden. Appendices at the end of volume 2 give notes on auction prices with quotations from auctioneer's catalogues of sales of English ceramics during fifty-five years and a section on advice to collectors by F. Litchfield. In spite of inaccuracies, still the most used dictionary of ceramic marks. For a condensed version *see* Chaffers, William,

Collector's Hand-Book of Marks and Monograms on Pottery & Porcelain... 4th. Revised by Frederick Litchfield, London, Reeves, 1965. 2v. illus. index. LC 66-74730.

415 Cushion, John P., and William B. Honey. **Handbook of Pottery and Porcelain Marks.** 4th rev. ed. London, Faber and Faber, 1980 272p. illus. index. ISBN 0571049222.

Comprehensive dictionary of ceramic marks of Europe and the Orient, with especially good coverage of British marks. Illustrated with facsimiles of marks and signatures. Arranged by country with a brief introduction to each and a useful general introduction on the historical use of ceramic marks. Appendices provide dating letters for Wedgwood, Minton, and Staffordshire ceramics.

416 Graesse, Johann G. T., and E. Jaennicke. **Führer für Sammler von Porzellan und Fayence, Steinzeug, Steingut usw...** 26th ed. Braunschweig, Klinkhardt & Biermann, 1990. 862p. illus. index. ISBN 3781402665.

Comprehensive handbook of marks on all kinds of world ceramics. Originally published in French in 1864 (Dresden, Schönfeld). An old standard handbook updated through numerous revisions, the last two by Arthus and Luise Behse. Two part arrangement: first covers European ceramic marks, second East Asian ceramic marks. The parts are further divided by country. Thoroughly indexed by types of marks, factories, and artists. Comprehensive bibliography of books and periodical articles, pp. 753-60, has been kept up to date.

417 Neuwirth, Waltraud. **Porzellanmaler Lexikon 1840-1914.** Braunschweig, Klinkhardt & Biermann, 1977. 2v. illus.

Comprehensive dictionary of artists who executed painted decoration on European porcelain manufactured between 1840 and 1914. Arranged by artists' names, the entries give basic biographical data, description of types of decoration and bibliographical references. Includes facsimiles of signatures. Many illustrations of pieces of decorated porcelain but also works of art that were copied as porcelain decoration. List of monogram marks at the end of second volume. Standard work on porcelain painters of nineteenth century historicism.

418 Zühlsdorff, Dieter. **Markenlexikon: Porzellan und Keramik Report 1885-1935.** v. 1-. Stuttgart, Arnoldsche Verlag, 1988- illus. ISBN 3925369007 (v.1).

Comprehensive dictionary of marks on porcelain and other ceramic ware dating between 1885 and 1935. Includes biographies of cermacists, information of firms, workshops and schools, and a glossary of terms. To date the first volume covering continental Europe (Europe-Festland, 1988. 756p. illus.) has appeared. The series is planned for four volumes. This work promises to fill an important gap in reference tools in the history of modern ceramics.

GENERAL HISTORIES AND HANDBOOKS

419 Berges, Ruth. **From Gold to Porcelain; the Art of Porcelain and Faience.** New York, Yoseloff, 1964. 239p. illus. index. LC 63-18243.

Popular history of world ceramics with emphasis on the beginning and early development of western European porcelain and faience. Illustrated with museum pieces. Chapter on music themes in porcelain. Basic bibliography, pp. 226-27.

420 Chaffers, William. **The New Keramic Gallery....** 3rd ed. London, Reeves and Turner, 1926. 2v. illus. LC 27-16433.

Collection of plates illustrating world ceramics designed as a compendium to the author's *Marks and Monograms* (405).

421 Charleston, Robert J., ed. **World Ceramics: An Illustrated History**. New York, McGraw-Hill, 1968. 352p. illus. index. LC 68-24604.

Well-illustrated survey of world ceramics written by a leading authority. Brief section on African, Oceanian and pre-Columbian ceramics. No bibliography.

422 Cox, Warren E. **The Book of Pottery and Porcelain**. rev. ed. New York, Crown, 1970. 2v. illus. index. LC 75-127511.

General survey of world ceramics from antiquity to the early twentieth century. Many poor quality illustrations of museum pieces. No bibliography.

423 Hannover, Emil. **Pottery and Porcelain, a Handbook for Collectors...** London, Benn, 1925. 3v. illus. index. LC 25-1787.

An old, once-standard collector's handbook covering world ceramics from ancient Egypt to the end of the nineteenth century. Volume one covers earthenware and stoneware of Europe and the Near East; volume two, Far Eastern ceramics; volume three, European porcelain. Good bibliographies of the early literature at the end of each volume.

424 Marryat, Joseph. **History of Pottery and Porcelain**. 3rd ed. London, Murray, 1868. 549p. illus. index.

Old, once-standard history of European pottery and porcelain from the early Middle Ages to the nineteenth century, illustrated with drawings and color plates, many of pieces in the author's famous collection. Contents: I, Spanish Pottery; II, Italian Pottery; III, Italian Pottery: Paintings and Forms; IV, Italian Pottery: Manufactories; V, Italian Pottery: Collections; VI, French Pottery; VII, German, Dutch, and Flemish Pottery; VIII, English Pottery; IX, Porcelain: Hard Paste. Oriental; X, Porcelain: Hard Paste. European; XI, Porcelain: Hard Paste. European; XII, English Porcelain: Soft Paste; XIII, French Porcelain; XIV, Manufactures of Italy and Spain. Appendices with list of private collections valuable for the history of connoisseurship. Bibliographical references in the footnotes.

425 **Masterpieces of Western and Near Eastern Ceramics**. Robert J. Charleston, general editor. Tokyo, Kodansha, 1979-80. 8 vs. illus. index. LC 78-55079.

Corpus of magnificently reproduced plates of major museum pieces illustrating the history of ceramics in Europe and the Near East from ancient times to circa 1800. Contents:

Volume I: *Ancient Near Eastern Pottery* by John R. Hennessy

Volume II: *Greek and Roman Pottery* by Robert M. Cook and Robert Charleston

Volume III: *Pre-Columbian Pottery* of the Americas by David M. Boston

Volume IV: *Islamic Pottery* by Robert J. Charleston

Volume V: *Italian Ceramics* by Giuseppe Liverani

Volume VI: *French Ceramics* by Henri-Pierre Fourest

Volume VII: *English and Dutch Ceramics* by Robert J. Charleston and D. F. Lunsingh Scheurleer

Volume VIII: *German and Austrian Ceramics* by Günter Reinheckel

Plates are accompanied by descriptive notes and proceeded by an introductory essay. All volumes have bibliographies of books in all langauges. Text in English and Japanese.

See also the exhibition catalog: *Keramik aus 5000 Jahre aus dem Hejtens-Museum Düsseldorf* by A. Klein (Düsseldorf, Hetjens-Museum, 1969).

PRE-COLUMBIAN CERAMICS

General Histories and Handbooks

426   Bushnell, G. H. S., and Adrian Digby. **Ancient American Pottery**. London, Faber and Faber, 1955. 51p. (text) 80p. (illus.) index. LC 56-1604.

Concise survey of pre-Columbian pottery in Central and South America from the second millenium B.C. to the Spanish conquest. Includes some pieces from the southwestern United States. Contents: 1, Introduction; 2, The Southwest of the U.S.; 3, The Pottery of Central America; 4, South America. Classified bibliography, pp. 47-48.

427   Lehmann, Henri. **Pre-Columbian Ceramics**. New York, Viking, 1962. 127p. illus. index. LC 61-5481.

Introduction to pre-Columbian ceramics in North America, Meso-America, Central America and South America written by a leading French expert. Contents: Part One. General and Technical: 1, Definition of the Term "Pre-Columbian"; 2, Technology; 3, Typology. Part Two. History of Ceramics in the Various Civilizations: 1, Meso-American Zone (Mexico and Guatemala); 2, Central America; 3, Andean Zone; 4, Caribbean Zone; 5, The Amazon; 6, The United States. Part Three. Collections and Collectors: 1, Forgeries and Principal Workshops; 2, The Market and Price Fluctuations; 3, Principle Collections of the World. Classified bibliography, pp. 122-25.

See also Sanchez Montañés, Emma. *La cerámica precolombina: el barroque los indios hicieron arte*. Madrid, Ediciones Anaya, 1988. 127p. illus. index. ISBN 8420729604 (Biblioteca iberoamericana, no. 6).

428   Wuthenau, Alexander von. **The Art of Terra Cotta Pottery in Pre-Columbian Central and South America**. New York, Crown, 1967. 203p. illus. index. LC 75-103627.

Concise but authoritative survey of pre-Columbian ceramics from the earliest times to the Post-classical period. Contents: A. The Principal Problems: I, Chronology; II, The Techniques; III, The Sites; IV, The Objects and Their Significance; V, The Artist and His Origins. B. The Artistic Achievement; C. Figurative Representations in the Various Regions of Mexico: I, The South: Guerro and Morelos; II, The Central Plateau; III, Puebla and Oaxaca; IV, The East: The Gulf Coast and the Hinterland; V, The West; VI, The Maya Region; VII, Connections with El Salvador, Colombia and Ecuador; and a Brief Glimpse at the Rest of the World; Final Note: The Códice Sierra; Conclusion. Well-selected, basic bibliography, pp. 192-95.

See also the museum catalog: *Ceramiche precolombiane. Museo internazionale delle ceramiche in Faenza, Catalogo generale delle raccolte* v. 2, by A. Guarnotta (Casalecchio di Reno, Bologna, Grafis Edizioni, 1985. 365p. illus.) and the catalog of the Hans Wolf Collection, *Keramik aus Schwarz-Afrika und Alt-Amerika: die Sammlung Hans Wold, Zurich-Ceramics from Black-Africa and Ancient America: The Hans Wolf Collection*, Zurich. by K. F. Schaedler. (Zurich, Edition Primart, 1985. 345p. illus. ISBN 3907550013).

See also David M. Boston, *Pre-Columbian Ceramics* (417).

Central America

429   Foncerrada de Molina, Marta. **Vasijas pintadas mayas en contexto arqueologico**. Mexico, Universidad Nacional Autonoma de México, 1979. 364p. illus. index. (Estudios y fuentes del arte en México, 39). ISBN 9685825955.

Comprehensive, scholarly catalog of 534 painted, pre-Columbian Maya ceramics arranged by place of discovery. The fifty sites are alphabetically arranged except for El Salvador, which is appended at the end. Each piece is illustrated in a drawing or photographic reproduction, a few in color. The catalog entries provide a detailed description of the piece and specific information is provided under nine headings at the end. The ninth heading covers references to specialized literature. General bibliography, pp. 355-362. A standard reference work that provides invaluable information on the context of Maya ceramics.

430   Kerr, Justin. **The Maya Vase Book: A Corpus of Rollout Photographs.** 2v. illus. New York, Kerr Associates, 1989, 1990. ISBN 0962420808.

Important collection of photographic reproductions of the paintings on the outside of Maya vases photographed with a special camera that produces a continuous frieze-like illustration. Essays are appended to both volumes: v. 1: The History of the Study of Maya Vase Painting by M. E. Miller; A Brief Note on the Name of the Vision Serpent by L. Schele; Hieroglyphs on Maya Vessels by D. Stuart; The Hero Twins: Myth and Image by M. D. Coe. v. 2: The Primary Standard Sequence in Chochola Style Ceramics by M. Grube; The God N/Step Set in the Primary Sequence by B. MacLeod; Notes on the Maya Vision Quest through Enema by B. Stross and Justin Kerr. Essays have bibliographical references.

431   Lothrop, Samuel K. **Pottery of Costa Rica and Nicaragua.** New York, Museum of the American Indian, Heye Foundation, 1926. 2v. illus. (Contributions from the Heye Museum, v. 8) LC 26-12897.

Comprehensive history/handbook of pre-Columbian ceramics in Costa Rica and Nicaragua. Contents: Volume One: Part I—Historical Background: I, Tribes and Languages; II, Material Culture; III, Manners and Customs; IV, Religion. Part Two—The Pacific Area; I, General Consideration of the Archaeology; II, Geological Man; III, Ceramics: Nicoya Polychrome Ware; IV, Nicoya Polychrome Ware: Modeled Forms; V, Nicoya Polychrome Ware: Painted Decoration; VI, Nicoya Polychrome Ware: Painted Decoration—continued; VII, Nicoya Polychrome Ware: Painted Decoration—continued; VIII, Under-slip Incise Ware; IX, Luna Ware; X, Intermediate Wares. Volume two: Part II—The Pacific Area; XI, Monochrome Wares; XII, Miscellaneous Pottery Objects; Part III—The Highland Region; I, General Features; II, Polychrome Ware; III, Simple Painted Wares; IV, Monochrome Wares; IV, Monochrome Ware; V, Appliqué Wares; VI, Miscellaneous Pottery Types; VII, Boruca; Part IV—Summary and Conclusions; I, Summary; II, Pottery Types and Historic Peoples; III, Cultural Relations and Chronology; IV, Interrelationship of Middle America and South America; Appendix I: Archaeological Sites; Appendix II: Memorial of Our Lord the King, Giving a Description and Characteristics of the Province of Costa Rica. Year 1610; Appendix III: Report of Fray Francisco de San José, Apostolic Missionary, to the President of the Audiencia of Guatemala, Concerning the Subject of Talamanca and the Houses and Tribes of the Térrabas Indians; Appendix IV, Notes on Las Mercedes, Costa Rica Farm, and Anita Grande, by Alanson Skinner. Chronologically arranged bibliography, v. 2, pp. 468-87, and bibliographical references in the footnotes. A classic and pioneering work written from an anthropological standpoint.

432   Noguera, Eduardo. **La cerámica arqueológica de Mesoamérica.** 2d ed. Mexico, Universidad Nacional Attónoma de México, Instituto de Investigaciones plates Históricas, 1975. 570p. illus. LC 77-480824.

Comprehensive, scholarly and archaeological history/handbook of pre-Columbian ceramics in Central America. Contents: La estratigrafía; Técnicas de excavación; Fabricación de la cerámica; La decoración; Descripción de la cerámica; I, El horizonte preclásico; II, El horizonte clásico; III, El horizonte histórico; IV, Cerámica Mixteca; V, Cerámica de Monte Albán; VI, Culturas del Golfo; VII, La cerámica Huasteca; VIII, Cerámicas del occidente de México; IX, Cerámicas del notre de México; X, Cerámica Maya. Comprehensive bibliography, pp. 381-95, and additional bibliography in the footnotes.

433   Snarskis, Michael J. **La cerámica precolombina en Costa Rica**. San Jose, Costa Rica, Instituto Nacional de Seguros, 1982. 136p. illus. LC 83-839036.

Concise survey of the pre-Columbian ceramics in Costa Rica. Text in Spanish and English. Good plates with descriptive captions. Contents: Introduction; Archaeological Zones of Costa Rica; Chronology; Archaeologists in Costa Rica; Ceramic Technology and Nomenclature; Guanacaste-Nicoya; Central Highlands-Atlantic Watershed; Diquis. Bibliography of books and periodical articles listed by author, pp. 133-135.

See also the exhibition catalogs: *Old Gods and Young Heroes: The Pearlman Collection of Maya Ceramics*, by M. D. Coe (Jersusalem, Israel Museum, Maremont Pavillion of Ethnic Arts, 1982. 128p. illus.), *Lords of the Underworld: Masterpieces of Classic Maya Ceramics*, by M.D. Coe (Princeton, N.J., Art Museum, 1978. 142p. illus. ISBN 0691039178), *Art of Costa Rica: Pre-Columbian Painted and Sculpted Ceramics from the Arthur M. Sackler Collections*, by P. Clifford (Washington, D.C., Arthur M. Sackler Foundation, AMS Foundation, 1985. 307p. illus. ISBN 0913291013).

North America [*See also* Native American Pottery]

Bibliographies

434   Farrington, William. **Prehistoric and Historic Pottery of the Southwest: A Bibliography**. Santa Fe, N.M., Sunstone Press, 1975. 24p.illus. ISBN 0913270458.

Classified bibliography of basic books and periodical articles on the pottery of the native American peoples of the Southwest designed as an introductory guide for beginning students.

See also Oppelt (756).

435   Brody, J. J. **Mimbres Painted Pottery**. Santa Fe, N.M., School of American Research, 1977. 253p. illus. index. ISBN 0826304524.

Scholarly study of the pottery made between A.D. 1000 and 1250 in southern New Mexico by the Mimbres Indians. Collection of 198 plates with descriptive captions. Contents: 1, Introduction; 2, The Discovery of the Mimbres; 3, The Physical Environment; 4, The Swarts Ruin: A Typical Mimbres Village; 5, The Human Environment; 6, Mimbres Painted Wares: Continuity and Change; 7, The Potters and Their Wares; 8, Pottery Painting: Form and Structure of Mimbres Black-on-White; 9, Representation Paintings; 10, Ethnoaesthetic and Other Aesthetic Considerations. Bibliography, pp. 243-49.

436   Brody, J. J., et al. **Mimbres Pottery: Ancient Art of the American Southwest: Essays**. New York, Hudson Hills Press, 1983. 128p. illus. ISBN 0933920466.

Published to accompany an exhibition organized by the American Federation of the Arts. Contents: Mimbres Painting: An Artist's Perspective by T. Berlant; The Mimbres Culture by S. LeBlanc; The Evolution of Mimbres Pottery by C. J. Scott; Mimbres Painting by J. J. Brody. Excellent collection of plates. General bibliography, p. 128.

South America

437   Bankes, George. **Peruvian Pottery**. Aylesbury, Shire Publications, 1989. 72p. illus. index. ISBN 0747800138.

Concise, informative introduction to the pre-Columbian pottery of Peru with particular attention to technique and with a chapter on the continuation of earlier traditions in present day Peru. Contents: 1, Peru and Her People; 2, Chronology of Peruvian Pottery; 3, The Technology of Pre-Hispanic and Modern Pottery; 4, Iconography of Pre-Hispanic Pottery; 5, Modern Peruvian Pottery; 6, Museums; 7, Further Reading (general bibliography, pp. 69-70).

438   Blasco Bosqued, Concepcion, and Luis J. Ramos Gomez. **Ceramica Nazca**. Valladolid, San José de Calasanz, 1980. 282p. illus. index. ISBN 8260015297.

Comprehensive, scholarly history of ancient Nazca pottery based on a close study of pieces in Spanish museum collections. Contents: I, Consideraciones generales; II, Caracteristicas technicas; III, La decoracion: motivos geometricos, Tipos de motivos geometricos; IV, Los motivos vegetales; V, Animales naturalistas; VII, Cabezas cortadas; VIII, Animales fantasticos; IX, Personajes fantasticos; X, Las formas: Tipologias realizadas, Las formas del Museo de America, Conservacion y restauracio de ceramicas Nazcas. Bibliographical references in the footnotes.

439   Menzel, Dorothy, et al. **Paracas Pottery of Ica: A Study in Style and Time**. Berkeley, Calif., Univ. of California Press, 1964. 399p. illus. (University of California. Publications in American Archaeology and Ethnology, v. 50).

Scholarly, archaeological study of Ocucaje-style Paracas pottery, circa 700 B.C.-A.D. 100 based on the author's own excavated pieces and pieces in various museums and private collections. Material is divided into ten successive phases and concludes with an analysis of Phase "1" of Nazca style pottery to demonstrate the continuity between Paracas- and Nazca-style pottery. Comprehensive bibliography, pp. 305-307, and additional references in the notes.

See also the authors': *Pottery Style and Society in Ancient Peru: Art as a Mirror in the Ica Valley, 1350-1570* (Berkeley, Calif., Univ. of California Press, 1976. 275p. illus. ISBN 05200-29704).

440   Salazar Bondy, Sebastian. **La cerámica peruana prehispanica**. Mexico City, Universidad Nacional Autonoma de Mexico, 1964. 25p. (text), 40p. illus.

Introduction to the ceramics of pre-Columbian Peru with emphasis on the Nazca figurative vessels in the Museo Nacional de Arqueologia, Lima. Contents: Introducción; Arte y aqueologia; Una clasificatión estilística; Estilo inicial: Chavin; Estilo clásicos: Nazca; Estilo clásicos: Tiahuanaco; Estilos regionales; Estilos imperial: Inca; Astillas de un naufragio. Basic bibliography, p. 21.

See also the museum catalogs: *Chimu, pre-Spanish Pottery from Peru: Catalogue of the Chimu Collection of the Rijksmuseum voor Volkenkunde (1882-1986)*, by Th. P. M. Kop Jansen and Th. J. J. Leyenaar. (Leiden, R-M-V, 1986. 171p. illus. ISBN 9071310310), *Ancient Peruvian Ceramics: The Nathan Cummings Collection*. by A. R. Sawyer (New York, Metropolitan Museum of Art; Greenwich, Conn., New York Graphics Society, 1966. 144p. illus. index. LC 65-16883), *Cerámica prehispanica norperuana: estudio de la ceramica Chimu de la coleccion del Museo de America de Madrid*, by C. Martinez (Oxford, B.A.R., 1986. 2v. illus.) and the exhibition catalogs: *Les Vases péruviens de la collection de LL. MM. le roi Albert et la reine Elisabeth de Belgique*, by E. della Santa (Bruxelles, Musées Royaux d'Art et d'Histoire, 1962. 193p. illus. LC 65-134), *Ancient Peruvian Ceramics from the Kehl and Nena Markley Collection*. by A. R. Sawyer (University Park, Pa., Museum of Art, The Pennsylvania State University, 1975. 90p. illus.), *Le Perou precolombien de Chavin aux Incas: Petit Palais* (Paris, Petit Palais, 1978. 108p. illus.), *Colombia before Columbus: The People, Culture, and Ceramic Art of Prehispanic Colombia* by A. J. Labbe (New York, Rizzoli, 1986. 208p. illus. ISBN 0847807703), and *Art of the Andes: Pre-Columbian Sculptured and Painted Ceramics from the Arthur M. Sackler Collections*, by P. A. Clifford (Washington, D.C., AMS Foundation, 1983. 344p. illus. ISBN 0913291005).

ANCIENT AND MEDIEVAL CERAMICS

[Note: Only general histories and handbooks are included here. Works dealing with ancient Greek vase painting will be included in a separate volume on painting.]

441 Pritchard, Alison C., ed. **The Many Dimensions of Pottery: Ceramics in Archaeology and Anthropology.** Amsterdam, Universiteit van Amsterdam, 1984. 797p. illus. ISBN 9070319071.

Collected essays based on lectures given at an international symposium in Lhee, Netherlands (1982) on various aspects of pottery in historical and archaeological studies, with particular emphasis on ethnoarchaeological perspectives. Of direct interest here are: The Reconstruction of Production Techniques for Relief-Decorated Terra Sigillata by B. Hoffman and H. Juranek; Modeling Ceramic Production and Organizational Change in the Pre-Hispanic Valley of Oaxaca, Mexico by G. Feinman et al.; Types of Potter's Wheels and the Spread of the Spindle Wheel in Germany by H. W. Löbert. Bibliographical references at the end of each essay.

442 Chesterman, James. **Classical Terracotta Figures.** London, Ward Lock, 1974. 99p. illus. index. ISBN 0706318781.

Survey of figure sculpture in terracotta from Minoan Crete to sixth century A.D. Rome. Chapter of forgeries and other advice for collectors, lists of dealers and public collections. Bibliography of basic works in English, p. 90-91.

Egypt

443 Kaczmarczyk, Alexander, and Robert E. M. Hedges. **Ancient Egyptian Faience.** Warminster, Aris & Philipps, 1983. 587p. illus. index. ISBN 0856682217.

Technical study of the materials and techniques used in the production of faience in ancient Egypt from predynastic to Roman times. Contents: I, The Objects and Their Analysis; II, The Elemental Composition of Faience Glazes; III. The Production and Nature of Individual Colours; IV, The Composition of Faience Bodies; V, Geographical and Historical Consideration. Appendices provide a precis of Egyptian faience technology, summary of x-ray fluorescence analyses of individual objects discussed in the work, and concordance of objects and recovery sites. Bibliography of 283 titles, pp. 566-84.

444 Wallis, Henry. **Egyptian Ceramic Art...** London, MacGregor Co., 1900. 37p. illus. LC 43-41632.

Important, older survey of ancient Egyptian pottery and other ceramic arts. Brief historical sketch followed by twelve plates of pieces ranging in date from the XI dynasty to early Coptic times. Detailed descriptive notes to the plates. No bibliography.

See also the exhibition catalog: *Umm El-Gaab: Pottery from the Nile Valley before the Arab Conquest*, by J. Bouviau (Cambridge, New York, Cambridge Univ. Press, 1981. 142p. illus. ISBN 0521284155).

Ancient Near East

445 Amiran, Ruth. **Ancient Pottery of the Holy Land; from Its Beginnings in the Neolithic Period to the Iron Age.** New Brunswick, N.J., Rutgers Univ. Press, 1970. 305p. illus. ISBN 813506344.

Important history of ceramics in Palestine from the Neolithic to the early Iron Age. Contents: 1, The Neolithic Period; 2, The Chalcolithic Period; 3, The Early Bronze Period; 4, The Early Bronze I; 5, The Early Bronze II, 6, The Early Bronze III; 7, The Early Bronze IV; 8, The Middle Bronze I Period; 9, The Middle Bronze II A and II B-C Periods; 10, The Late Bronze I, II A and II B Periods; 11, The Iron I, II A-B and II C Periods; 12, Selected Types of Ammonite

Pottery; 13, Selected Types of Pottery of Ezion-Geber; 14, Cult Vessels. Extensive bibliographical footnotes.

446   Andrae, Walter. **Coloured Ceramics from Ashur and Earlier Ancient Assyrian Wall-Paintings**. London, Paul, Trench, Trubner, 1925. 78p. 36 plates. LC 26-8537.

Scholarly introduction to and catalog of the polychromed ceramics, both architectural and utilitarian, excavated at Ashur by the Deutsche Orient-Gesellschaft between 1903 and 1914. Contents: Coloured Ceramics from Ashur; Wall Paintings from Kar-Tukulti-Enurta; Pictures in Coloured Glaze on Brick Orthostats; Earthenware Vases with Paintings in Coloured Enamel; Enamelled Terra Cotta Figures; Enamelled Knob-Plates and Knobs; Conclusion. Plates reproduce watercolors made during excavation. Bibliographical references in the catalog entries and the footnotes to the introduction.

447   Fukai, Shinji. **Ceramics on Ancient Persia**. New York, Weatherhill, Kyoto, Tankosha, 1981. 54p. illus. ISBN 0834815230.

Survey of pre-Islamic ceramics of Iran illustrated with pieces in Japanese collections. Contents: 1, The Emergence of Glaze in the Elam Kingdom; 2, The Azerbaijan Region in the First Millenium B.C.; 3, The Acaemenid Dynasty; 4, The Parthian Dynasty; 5, The Sassanian Dynasty; Personal Ornaments and Other Objects. Bibliographical footnotes.

448   Yon, Narguerite. **Dictionnaire illustré multilingue de la céramique du Proche Orient ancien**. Lyon, Maison de l'Orient, 1981. 310p. illus. index. (Collection de la Maison de l'Orient, no. 10) ISBN 2903264007.

Scholarly polyglot dictionary of the terms used by scholars in French, German, English, Greek and Italian in describing the ceramics of the various cultures of the ancient Near East. Many of the terms are illustrated by pieces and/or representations in contemporary art. Entries have bibliographical references to list of basic scholarly works. Polyglot indexes.

Minoan and Mycenean

449   Dugas, Charles. **La ceramique des Cyclades**. Paris, E. de Boccard, 1925. 292p. illus. index. (Bibliotheque des Écoles francaises d'Athènes et de Rome...fasc. 129).

Scholarly history of ancient Cycladic pottery from 3,000 to 550 B.C. Contents: I, L'Invention des motifs géométriques; II, L'Influence Créto-Mycénienne; III, L'Esprit décoratif dans la céramique des Cyclades;Conclusion; Résumé chronologique. Bibliographical references in the footnotes.

450   Furumark, Arne. **Mycenaean Pottery: Analysis and Classification**. Stockholm, Kungl. Vitterhets Historie och Antikvitets Akademien, 1941. 2v. illus. (Skrifter utgivna av Svenska Institutet i Athen, XX,1) Reprint: 1972. LC 73-167705.

Comprehensive scholarly history and analysis of ancient Minoan, Mycenaean and Cycladic pottery. Contents: Introduction; Technique; Shape; Decoration: Antecedents and Sources: Minoan Decoration, Antecedents and Sources: Middle Helladic Decoration, The Elements of Mycenaean Decoration; Pictorial Decoration; The Successive Styles of Mycenaean Decoration; Catalogue of Vessel Types; Index to Sites and Publications of Finds. Bibliographical footnotes, bibliographical references in the catalog, and alphabetical list of major works, pp. 665-71.

451   Vermeule, Emily, and Vassos Karagegeorghis. **Mycenaean Pictorial Vase Painting**. Cambridge, Mass., Harvard Univ. Press, 1982. 417p. illus. index. ISBN 0674596501.

Scholarly history of ancient Mycenaean pottery with pictorial painted decoration; emphasis on the development of the style and description of regional variations. Catalog of pieces discussed with specialized literature. Contents: I, Introduction; II, Sources and Distribution of Pictorial Painting: A Historical Sketch; III, Cyprus and the East: Early Pictorial; IV, Cyprus and the East: Middle Pictorial; V, Cyprus and the East: Ripe Pictorial; VI, Cyprus and the East: Pastoral; VII, The Greek Mainland: Early Pictorial; VIII, The Greek Mainland: Middle Pictorial; VIII, The Greek Mainland: Ripe Pictorial; X, The Greek Mainland: Transitional; XI, The Greek Mainland: Late Pictorial; XII, Rhodes and the Dodekanese; XIII, Asia Minor and the Near East; XIV, Individual Vase Painters. Appendix with essay on representations of chariots and harnesses in Mycenaean vase painting by M. A. Littauer and J. H. Crouwel. Selected bibliography, pp. 189-192.

452   Higgins, Reynold A. **Greek Terracottas**. London, Methuen, 1967. 169p. illus. index. LC 67-31958.

In the series: "Methuen's Handbooks of Archaeology." Standard survey history of ancient Greek terracotta sculpture. Contents: 1, Technical Processes; 2, The Earliest Terracottas, 7000-2000 B.C.; 3, The Middle Bronze Age, 2000-1550 B.C.; 4, The Late Bronze Age, 1550-1050 B.C.; 5, The Dark Ages, 1100-700 B.C.; 6, The Seventh and Sixth Centuries B.C.; 7, The Fifth and Fourth Centuries B.C.; 8, The Hellenistic Period, 220 B.C.-A.D. 100; 9, Epilogue. Comprehensive bibliography, pp. 135-157.

See also the author's *Greek Terracotta Figures* (London, British Museum, 1969. LC 77-356439).

453   Lacy, A. D. **Greek Pottery in the Bronze Age**. London, Methuen, 1967. 303p. illus. index. LC 67-108472.

Scholarly history of pottery in Crete, mainland Greece and the Cyclades during the Bronze Age. Contents: 1, The Neolithic Era, 6600-3000 B.C.; 2, The Minoan Era, 3000-1100 B.C.; 3, The Helladic Era; 4, The Mycenaean Era, 1580-1100 B.C.; 5, The Cyclades and Cycladic Pottery in the Bronze Age; 6, The Dorian Invasion, 1200-1100 B.C. Bibliography, pp. 288-90, is an unclassified list of books and periodical articles in all languages.

454   Morris, Desmond. **The Art of Ancient Cyprus**. Oxford, Phaidon, 1985. 368p. illus. index. ISBN 0714822809.

Comprehensive, well-illustrated survey and analysis of the ceramics of the Bronze Age in Cyprus. Covers both vessels and figures. Based on the author's private collection. Comprehensive bibliography, pp. 360-63.

Greece

455   Buschor, Ernst. **Griechische Vasen**. Munich, Piper, 1940. 213p. illus. LC 46-39521.

Survey of ancient Greek vases with emphasis on both the art of the painter and the craft of the potter. Work of a leading historian and theorist of ancient Greek art (*see* FA 685). Chronological arrangement covering the period from the eleventh century to the early fourth century. Index of pieces discussed by type of vase. No bibliography.

456   Folsom, Robert S. **Handbook of Greek Pottery: A Guide for Amateurs**. Greenwich, Conn., New York Graphic Society, 1967. 213p. illus. index. LC 68-25740.

Popular history of ancient Greek ceramics from 1050 to 145 B.C., written in outline form and directed to the beginning collector. Select bibliography of major books in English; an appendix explains the terminology of the shapes of ancient Greek pottery.

457   Lane, Arthur. **Greek Pottery**. 3rd ed. London, Faber, 1971. 64p. illus. LC 75-852836.

Brief outline history of ancient Greek pottery. Contents: 1, How Greek Pots Were Made and Painted; 2, Use, Shapes, and Ornament; 3, Historical Outline; 4, Notes on the Illustrations. Selected bibliography, 59-61.

Rome

458 Ballardini, Gaetano. **L'eredita ceramistica dell'antico mondo romano...** Rome, Istituto Poligrafico dello Stato, 1964. 303p. illus. index. LC 68-141986.
Scholarly history of ancient Roman ceramics from Roman times to the early Middle Ages. Includes oil lamps, ceramic pipes, androof tiles as well as tableware. Contents: Parte Prima: Tecniche e cimeli; Parte Seconda: I Figuli nelle associazoni di lavoro e i trattati didascalici dell'alto medio evo. Bibliographical references in the extensive notes. A standard work on ancient Roman ceramics.

459 Charleston, Robert J. **Roman Pottery**. London, Faber & Faber, 1955. 48p. illus. index. LC 55-2952.
Survey of the basic types of ancient Roman pottery. Contents: 1, Introduction; 2, Red-gloss pottery; 3, Glazed pottery; 4, 'Coarse' pottery. Table of shapes, bibliographical footnotes, and classified bibliography of books and periodical articles, pp. 41-44.

460 Hayes, J. W. **Late Roman Pottery**. London, British School at Rome, 1972. 477p. illus. index. LC 74-155758.
Comprehensive, scholarly history of the ceramics of ancient Rome from the second to the seventh century A.D. Contents: I, Introduction; II, African Red Slip Ware; III, Other African Wares; IV, African Lamps; V, Candarli Ware; VI, 'Late Roman C' Ware; VII, Cypriot Red Slip Ware; VIII, Egyptian Red Slip Ware; IX, Gaulish 'T/S. Grise'; X, Other Late Roman Wares; XI, Distribution; Conclusion. Appendixes: 1, Late Roman Pottery: Site Bibliography; 2, African Red Slip Ware: Concordance of Vessel Forms; 3, Last Roman Pottery: Concordance of Stamp Types on Main Wares. Many maps show distribution of the various wares. Bibliographical footnotes and select bibliography, pp. xix-xxv. Supplement to *Late Roman Pottery*, by J. W. Hayes (London, British School at Rome, 1980) continues the pagination of the original to 551p. and has additional illustrations and index.

461 Oswald, Felix. **Index to Potter's Stamps on Terra Sigillata "Samian Ware."** Liverpool, Author, 1931. Reprinted: Farnborough, Gregg Press, 1964. 428p. LC A32-1986.
The 1964 reprint includes addenda from the edition of 1936. Scholarly index of potter's marks (i.e., marks of the owners of the workshops) found on ancient Roman terra sigillata (Samian ware), arranged by name of potter. References are given to dates and examples. A standard reference work.

462 Oswald, Felix and T. Davies Pryce. **An Introduction to the Study of Terra Sigillata.** London, Longmans, Green and Co., 1920. 286p. illus. index. LC20-17389. Reprint: London, Gregg Press, 1966.
Authoritative history of ancient Roman terra sigillata ware. Contains 85 plates of line drawings of pieces in collections around the world. Contents: I, Introductory; II, General Description: i, Italian Terra Sigillata, ii, Provincial Terra Sigillata; III, Dated Sites; IV, Stamps of Well-Attested Potters; Vessels Decorated in Moulded Relief; VI, Origin and Development of the Decorative Designs of Provincial Terra Sigillata; VII, Details of Chronological Significance; VIII, Plain Forms; IX, Miscellaneous Sigillata Fabrics; X, The Origin and Evolution of Terra Sigillata. Comprehensive, classified bibliography, pp. 245-72. Reprint has new preface and corrigenda and addenda.

See also the museum handbook: C. Johns, *Arrentine and Samian Pottery* (London, British Museum, 1971. 31p. illus. LC 78-875957).

Byzantine and Medieval

463 Haslam, Jeremy. **Medieval Pottery in Britain**. 2d. ed. Aylesbury, Buckshire, U.K., Shire, 1984. 64p. illus. index. (Shire Archaeology, 6) ISBN 0852636709.
    Thumbnail sketch of the history of medieval pottery in Britain from 850 to 1500. Contents: Glossary and Techniques; 1, Introduction; 2, Saxo-Norman Pottery (AD 850 to 1150); 3, Medieval Pottery (1100 to 1500); 4, Some Regional Types: Oxford and London; 5, Some Regional Types: Other Areas; 6, Kilns; 7, Museums; 8, Further Reading.

464 McCarthy, Michael R., and Catherine N. Brooks. **Medieval Pottery in Britain, AD 900-1600**. Leicester, Leicester Univ. Pr., 1988. 521p. illus. index. ISBN 0718512715.
    Comprehensive, scholarly history of medieval pottery in Britain directed to archaeologists and historians. First part covers pottery technology, production, distribution, and relationship between pottery and society. Second part is a select gazetteer of sites and their main pottery types. Illustrated with plates of museum pieces, drawings of reconstructed pieces, maps and illustrations of the use of pottery in contemporary works of art. Full scholarly apparatus including comprehensive bibliography, pp. 479-505.

465 Rice, David Talbot. **Byzantine Glazed Pottery**. Oxford, Clarendon Press, 1930. 120p. illus. index. LC 31-3589.
    History of Byzantine glazed pottery including tiles by a leading expert in Byzantine art history. Contents: Introduction by Bernard Rackham; Classification and Discussion; The Forms; Designs; Monograms; Geographical; The Problems; Appendices: Island Ware, Collection. Chronological tables. Comprehensive and annotated bibliography, pp.105-07.

466 Wallis, Henry. **Byzantine Ceramic Art**. London, Quaritch, 1907. 40p. (text), 41 plates. LC A12-1367.
    Brief survey of Byzantine ceramics with emphasis on Constantinople and Italy. Important collection of plates.

MODERN CERAMICS

467 Cameron, Elisabeth. **Encyclopedia of Pottery and Porcelain: The Nineteenth and Twentieth Centuries**. London and Boston, Faber and Faber, 1986. 366p. illus. LC GB85-26079.
    Comprehensive, popular dictionary covering all aspects of modern ceramics. Bibliographical references given at the end of each entry.

468 Hillier, Bevis. **Pottery and Porcelain, 1700-1914: England, Europe and North America**. New York, Meredith, 1968. 386p. illus. index. LC 68-27001.
    Survey of European and American pottery and porcelain between 1700 and 1914 which seeks to integrate ceramics with social and economic history. Contents: 1, Social Status of the Potter; 2, The End of the Baroque; 3, Porcelain; 4, The Rococo; 5, Folk Pottery; 6, Wedgewood, Neo-Classicism and the Industrial Revolution; 7, The French Revolution; 8, North America; 9, Marketing; 10, Revivals—Gothic and Otherwise; 11, Artist Potters in England; 12, Collectors; 13, Repairs, Reproductions and Fakes; 14, Art Nouveau. Well-selected, basic bibliography, pp. 361-68, and further references in the notes.

469 Preaud, Tamara, and Serge Gauthier. **Ceramics of the 20th Century**. New York, Rizzoli, 1982. 216p. illus. index. ISBN 0847804364.

Translation of *Ceramique, art du XXe siècle* (Fribourg, Office du Livre, 1982). Well-illustrated survey of ceramic art worldwide during the twentieth century. Contents: Factories, Artists, Potters, Techniques. List of recent exhibitions. Bibliography, pp. 205-06, is an alphabetical list of books in all languages.

For a pictorial survey of art ceramics of the 1960s and 1970s *see*: H. Storr-Britz, *Internationale Keramik der Gegenwart*. Contemporary International Ceramics (Cologne, DuMont, 1980. 244p. illus. index. ISBN 3770112288).

AMERICAN CERAMICS

United States

Bibliographies

470 Strong, Susan R. **History of American Ceramics: An Annotated Bibliography**. Metuchen, N.J., Scarecrow Press, 1983. 184p. index. ISBN 0810816369.

Classified and annotated bibliography of books published up to 1983 on the history of ceramics in the United States from colonial time to 1966.

471 Weidner, Ruth I. **American Ceramics before 1930: A Bibliography**. Westport, Conn. Greenwood Press, 1982. 279p. index. ISBN 0313228310.

Classified bibliography of nearly 3,000 books and periodical literature on the history of ceramics in the United States from Colonial times to 1930. Emphasis is on art pottery between the Civil War and World War II.

For the older literature and much obscure but useful material *see* Branner, John C. *A Bibliography of Clays and the Ceramic Arts* (Columbus, Ohio, American Ceramic Society, 1906. 451p.).

Histories and Handbooks

472 Barber, Edwin A. **Marks of American Potters...** Philadelphia, Patterson and White, 1904. 174p. illus. index. Reprint: Southhampton, N.Y., Cracker Barrel Press, 1973. LC 70-21077.

Dictionary with over 1,000 marks reproduced in facsimile. Contents: Pennsylvania Potteries; New Jersey Potteries; New York Potteries; New England Potteries; Ohio Potteries; Potteries of the Southern States; Potteries of the Western States. Each region is introduced with a brief historical sketch. Short commentaries on major factories. Old, but still a basic reference tool.

473 Barber, Edwin A. **The Pottery and Porcelain of the United States; an Historical Review of American Ceramic Art from the Earliest Times to the Present Day**. New York, Putnam, 1909. 621p. illus. index. Reprint: Watkins Glen, N.Y., Century House, 1971. LC 79-96939.

First published in 1893 and still the most comprehensive history of ceramics in the United States. Pioneering work by a champion of American ceramics at a time when they were disregarded by European writers. Still valuable for its comprehensive overview and collection of illustrations. List of marks and signatures, pp. 392-414. A combined reprint with the author's *Marks of American Potters* (472) was published by Feingold & Lewis, 1976.

474 Clark, Garth. **American Ceramics, 1876 to the present**. rev. ed. New York, Abbeville, Press, 1987. illus. index. ISBN 0896597431.

Revised edition of: *A Century of Ceramics in the United States, 1878-1978* (New York, Dutton, 1979. ISBN 0525078207). Published in association with exhibition: "A Century of Ceramics in the United States, 1878-1978" at the Everson Museum of Art, Syracuse, New York. History of ceramics in the United States with emphasis on studio pottery and its emergence out of the 1876 Centennial Exhibition. The author presents the view that expressionistic ceramics are the only true American ceramics, ceramics in other styles are derivative of European ceramics. Section with biographies of major studio potters; bibliography, pp. 345-61, is a list of books and periodical articles.

475   Cunningham, Jo. **The Collector's Encyclopedia of American Dinnerware**. Paducah, Kent., Collector Books, 1982. 319p. illus. index. ISBN 0891451994.

Guide to the identification and evaluation of American mass-produced ceramic dinnerware produced by firms active in the last 100 years. Entries are chiefly dedicated to the wares of particular factories (Bennington, Haeger, Pfaltzgraff, Red Wing, Steubenville, etc.) with a few covering classes of ware (children's pieces) and regional pottery (western stoneware). Well illustrated with actual pieces, advertisements and photographs of marks. Glossary of terms. Separately printed price guide is attached to back cover. No bibliography.

476   Denker, Ellen, and Bert Denker. **The Warner Collector's Guide to North American Pottery and Porcelain**. New York, Warner Books, 1982. 256p. illus. index. ISBN 04469766318.

Collector's handbook that classifies American ceramics into 50 categories of redware, stoneware, porcelain and art pottery, subdivided by place and style. Price ranges given for each piece.

477   Derwich, Jenny B., and Mary Latos. **Dictionary Guide to United States Pottery and Porcelain (Nineteenth and Twentieth Century)**. Franklin, Mich., Jenstan, 1984. 276p. illus. index. ISBN 0961262400

Dictionary of pottery and porcelain makers—individuals and firms—active in the United States in the nineteenth and twentieth centuries. Contains useful information garnered through correspondence with potters and their descendants. Alphabetical arrangement by name of potters and firms.

478   Ketchum, William. **The Pottery and Porcelain Collector's Handbook; a Guide to Early American Ceramics from Maine to California**. New York, Funk & Wagnalls, 1971. 204p. illus. index. LC 71-137487.

Handbook of American ceramics designed as an introduction and guide for collectors. Arrangement is by type of ceramic body and region. Appendix provides a list of early American potteries. Has useful information on pottery from the Western states. Illustrated with works typical of those accessible to the average collector.

479   Ketchum, William C. **Pottery & Porcelain**. New York, Knopf, 1983. 478p. illus. index. ISBN 0394714946.

In the series: "The Knopf Collectors' Guide to American Antiques." For format *see:* W. Ketchum, *Chests, Cupboards, Desks...* (1174).

480   Lehner, Lois. **Complete Book of American Kitchen and Dinner Wares**. Des Moines, IA, Wallace-Homestead, 1980. 239p. illus. index. ISBN 087069300X.

Dictionary of American mass producers of pottery and porcelain dinner and kitchen wares with emphasis on the products of the late nineteenth and twentieth centuries. Entries for the larger firms list patterns with dates introduced, dates discontinued, or give lists of date codes. Plates feature patterns and complete sets. Appendix with marks. Bibliography, pp. 218-219, is chiefly a list of articles in popular collector's magazines.

481 Levin, Elaine. **The History of American Ceramics, 1607 to the Present; from Pipkins and Bean Pots to Contemporary Forms.** New York, Abrams, 1988. 351p. illus. index. ISBN 0810911728.

Pictorial survey of ceramics in the United States with emphasis on the development of modern studio art pottery. Contents: I, From Folk Pottery to Industry 1600-1876; II, The Art Pottery Movement 1876-1918; III, Art Deco: The Dominance of Sculpture 1918-1942; IV, The Vessel Revival 1930-1955; V, Abstract Expressionism: Its Effects and Ramifications 1955-1965; VI, Clay for an Age of Contradictions 1965-1975; VII, Post-Modernism 1975-1987. Bibliography, pp. 343-46, provides a classified list of books and periodical articles.

482 Schwartz, Marvin. **Collector's Guide to Antique American Ceramics.** Garden City, N.Y., Doubleday, 1969, 134p. illus. index. LC 69-10989.

Popular history of ceramics in United States from 1650 to 1910 emphasizing the Eastern states and directed to beginning collectors. Arranged by types, with a short introductory history and a section on advice to the collector. Illustrated chiefly with pieces in the Brooklyn Museum's outstanding collection of American ceramics.

483 Spargo, John. **Early American Pottery and China.** New York, Century, 1926. 393p. illus. index. LC 26-19815 Reprint: Rutland, Vt., Tuttle, 1974. ISBN 0804811350.

Important early history of ceramics in America from Colonial times through the nineteenth century. Chronological list of potters and selected list of marks.

Canada

484 Collard, Elizabeth. **Nineteenth-Century Pottery and Porcelain in Canada.** 2d ed. Montreal, McGill University Press, 1984. 477p. illus. index. ISBN 0773503927.

Comprehensive history of ceramics in Canada during the nineteenth century. Contents: The Tide of Imports: Toils and Hazards; How Pottery and Porcelain Were Sold; The Earthenwares; The Porcelains; Printed Earthenware with Canadian Views and Emblems; Canadian Compete. Appendices with discussion of marks and list of potters. Bibliographical footnotes. A standard work.

Latin America

485 Duarte, Carlos F. **La Cerámica la epoca colonial venezolana.** Caracas, E. Armitano, 1980. 309p. illus. LC 82-225976.

Well-illustrated and comprehensive history of ceramics in Venezuela from the Spanish conquest to 1875. Includes foreign ceramics imported into the country. List of museums and comprehensive bibliography, pp. 301-06.

486 Lujan Munoz, Luis. **Historia de la mayolica en Guatemala.** Guatemala, Instituto de Antropologia e Historia, Ministerio de Educacion, 1975. 78p. illus. LC 84-129634.

Concise survey of the production of majolica in Guatemala from the first Spanish colonies to the twentieth century. Contents: I, Introduccion; II, Trasplante de la mayolica española a Guatemale; III, La mayolica en Santiago de Guatemala; IV, La mayolica en la nueva Guatemala; V, La mayolica en San Miguel Totonicaoan; VI, Intento de periodificacion y tipologia de la mayolica en Guatemala; VII, Consideracionees sobre la produccion de mayolica en Guatemala; VIII. Appendices with chronological list of majolica potters active in Guatemala between 1585 and 1937 and lists of names of potters active in Guatemala City and San Miguel Totonicapan. Basic bibliography, pp. 46-49.

487   Pileggi, Aristides. **Ceramica no Brasil e no mundo**. Sao Paulo, Martins, 1958. 290p. illus. index. LC 61-30502.

General survey of ceramics produced in Brasil from pre-Columbian times to 1950. Chapters one and two are devoted to a history of world ceramics; chapter three is a history of Brazilian ceramics divided into pre-Columbian, colonial and contemporary sections; chapter four is a discussion of manufacturing processes in Brazil; chapter five a glossary of technical terms. General bibliography, p. 201.

488   Rivero, Manuel R. **Lozas y porcelanas en Venezuela**. Caracas, n.p. 1972. 150p. illus. LC 72-225341.

Pictorial history of pottery and porcelain in Venezuela from early colonial times to the present. Includes both indigenous products and products imported. General bibliography, pp. 149-50, and further bibliography in the notes.

EUROPEAN CERAMICS

General Works

489   Dexel, Walter. **Keramik. Stoff und Form**. Berlin and Braunschweig, Klinkhardt & Biermann, 1958. 141p. illus. index. LC A59-3167.

Important survey of European ceramics from prehistoric times to the middle of the twentieth century that concentrates on the overall form of ceramic vessels and how that form is influenced by technique and function. Contents: I, Technik der Keramik; Hauptarten der Keramik; II, Zur Frage der Formentstehung bei der Keramik; III, Vom Wesen keramischer Formen; IV, Versuch einer systematischen Ordnung der keramischen Hauptformen; V, Zur Kunstkeramik der Gegenwart; VI, Gebrauchskeramik aus Manufakturen und Fabriken. No bibliography.

490   Honey, William B. **European Ceramic Art, From the End of the Middle Ages to about 1815**. 2nd ed. London, Faber and Faber, 1963. 2v. illus. LC 68-128038.

Important, comprehensive history/handbook of European ceramics from the fifteenth century to circa 1815. Volume one is a concise, stylistic survey with 192 well-selected plates with descriptive notes; volume two is a comprehensive dictionary of factories, artists, terms, etc. The entries in the dictionary have very useful bibliographies listing specialized literature. Illustrations include facsimiles of marks with a repertory of marks by letters and names in the appendix of volume two.

491   Morley-Fletcher, Hugo, and Roger McIlroy. **Christie's Pictorial History of European Pottery**. Oxford, Phaidon: Christie's, 1984. 319p. illus. index. ISBN 0714880094.

Well-illustrated survey of western European pottery and porcelain from the Middle Ages to the early nineteenth century. Features pieces sold at Christie's. Maps, glossary, brief bibliography, p. 307, and list of prices.

492   Tardy (firm). **Les poteries, les faïences et les porcelaines européenes...** Paris, Tardy, 1953-55. 2v. illus. index. LC 62-32073 rev.

General handbook/history arranged by countries giving an historical survey for each and repertory of the chief marks. Illustrated with works accessible to the collector.

See also the price guide: *Warman's English & Continental Pottery & Porcelain: an Illustrated Price Guide*, by S. D. Badgale and A. D. Bagdale (Willow Grove, Pa., Warman Pub. Co., 1987. 464p. illus. index. ISBN 0911594116).

France

493 Cushion, John P. **Pocket Book of French & Italian Ceramic Marks**. London, Faber & Faber, 1965. 199p. illus. LC 66-36391.

Useful pocket-size dictionary of major French ceramic marks reproduced in facsimiles.

494 Ernould-Gandouet, Marielle. **La céramique en France au XIXe siècle...** Paris, Grund, 1969. 192p. illus. index. LC 76-415743.

Survey of French ceramic ware of the nineteenth century with emphasis on the broad cultural context; features unusual ceramic objects, such as clocks and dolls together with dinnerware. Contents: I, En préambule; II, Céramique de toujours; III, L'Ar du Temps; IV, La Conquête du Siècle; V, Poteries de France; VI, La Faïence fine; VIII, La Porcelaine; IX, Le Grès; X, Les Nouveautés du Siècle. Repertory of major marks in both photographic and facsimile reproductions. General bibliography, pp. 188-190.

495 Fontaine, Georges. **La céramique française**. Paris, Presses Universitaires de France, 1965. 186p. illus. index. LC 66-72503.

Survey of French ceramics from the sixteenth through the nineteenth centuries. Illustrated with museum pieces. Chronological table listing the major factories. Bibliography, p. 182, is a comprehensive and classified list of books including many monographs.

496 Peyre, Roger R. **La céramique françcaise: fayences, porcelaines, biscuits, grès, dates de la fondation des ateliers, caractéristiques, marques et monogrammes...** Paris, E. Flammarion, 1910. 310p. illus. index. LC 10-7833.

Once-standard history/handbook of French ceramics including porcelain, faience, soft paste and stoneware. Still an important source of factual information on the operations of various centers and workshops. Repertory of major marks and signatures.

Germany, Austria, and Switzerland

Bibliographies

497 Staehelin, Walter A. **Bibliographie der schwiezerischen Keramik vom Mittelalter bis zur Neuzeit**. Basel, Hirzen-Verlag, 1947. 39p.

Comprehensive, classified bibliography of 350 books and periodical articles on all aspects of Swiss ceramics published through 1947. Continued by: Früh, Margit, *Bibliographie der schweizerischen Keramik, 1947-1968* (n.p. Keramik- Freunde der Schweiz, 1960. 24p.), for titles published between 1947 and 1968.

Dictionaries

498 Cushion, J. P. **Pocket Book of German Ceramic Marks and Those of Other Central European Countries**. London, Faber and Faber, 1961. 184p. illus. index. LC 62-2187.

Companion to the author's pocket-size dictionary on French marks (493).

499 Pazaurek, Gustav E. **Deutsche Fayence- Porzellan- Hausmaler**. 2nd ed. Stuttgart, Hiersmann, 1971. 2v. illus. index. LC 72-329340.

First published in 1925. Comprehensive, scholarly history/handbook of German painted porcelain and faience. Arranged by place, it emphasizes major painters who worked independently of factories during the seventeenth and eighteenth centuries. Chapter on Biedermeier period painters. Facsimiles of signatures and extensive bibliographical footnotes. A standard work on German ceramic painters.

General Histories and Handbooks

500   Ducret, Siegfried. **German Porcelain and Faience**. New York, Universe, 1962. 466p. illus. index. LC 62-13886.

Comprehensive, authoritative pictorial survey of porcelain and faience in the German speaking countries from the seventeenth century to the present but with emphasis on the eighteenth century. Particular attention is given to technical achievements of the major factories. The various manufactories are introduced by a brief historical essay and that is followed by a good collection of plates—many in excellent color—with descriptive notes. Abbreviated list of porcelain and faience marks with facsimiles. Comprehensive, unclassified bibliography of recent publications, pp. 452-56.

Modern Ceramics

501   Klinge, Ekkart. **Deutsche Keramik Heute**. Düsseldorf, Kunst & Handwerk, Verlagsanstalt Handwerk, 1984. 212p. illus. ISBN 3878641125.

Collected biographies of German ceramic artists active in the 1980s. Entries give basic biographical data, portrait of the artist and illustrations of three or four recent works with descriptive captions. Bibliography, p. 212, has no list of exhibition catalogs.

502   Pelka, Otto. **Deutsche Keramik, 1900-1925**. Munich, Dry, 1984. 63p. illus. index. ISBN 392252124X.

First published in 1925 as *Deutsche Keramik der Gegenwart* (Reutlingen, Ensslin & Laiblin). Important essay on German art ceramics of the period 1900 to 1925. Bibliographical references in the footnotes.

503   Reineking von Bock, Gisela. **Keramik des 20**. Jahrhunderts, Deutschland. Munich, Keyser, 1979. 356p. illus. index. ISBN 3874051188.

History of art ceramics in Germany during the twentieth century. Introduction sketches the stylistic development by decades, discusses technical aspects—with glossary of terms and photographs of electron microscopic examinations of various materials—and gives advice to the collector concerning restoration, evaluation and descriptions of five renown private collections (Gottfried Cremer, Gertrud and Karl Funks-Kaiser, J. W. Hinder, Hans Thiemann, and H. T. and I. Wolf). Comprehensive dictionary of German art potters with basic biographical data, description of work, signatures and references to specialized literature. Signatures are given in photographs and facsimiles. Comprehensive, classified bibliography, pp. 349-52, has extensive list of exhibition catalogs and periodicals.

See also the exhibition catalogs: *Meister der deutschen Keramik, 1900 bis 1950*, by G. Reineking-von Bock (Cologne, Kunstgewerbemuseum, 1978. 329p. illus. ISBN 78365757), *Keramik in der Weimarer Republik, 191-1933: die Sammlung Tilmann Buddensieg im German-isches Nationalmuseum*, ed. by T. Buddensieg (Nuremberg, Das Nationalmuseum, 1985. 184p. illus.), and *Keramik und Bauhaus*, by K. Weber (Berlin, Kupfergraben Verlagsgesellschaft, 1989. 286p. illus. ISBN 3891814046).

Great Britain

504   Cushion, John P. **Pocket Book of British Ceramic Marks**. 3rd ed. London, Faber, 1983. 431p. ISBN 0571131085.

Useful pocket-sized dictionary of major ceramic marks, illustrated with facsimiles.

505   Godden, Geoffrey A. **Encyclopedia of British Pottery and Porcelain Marks**. New York, Crown, 1964. 765p. illus. LC 64-22014.

Comprehensive dictionary of British ceramic marks arranged alphabetically by the name of the maker, designer, factory, place or region and illustrated with facsimiles of marks and occasional photographs of marked pieces. Appendix with list of unidentified marks. Glossary of terms. Chronologically arranged bibliography, pp. 741-44.

506   Godden, Geoffrey A. **English China**. London, Barrie & Jenkins, 1985. 362p. illus. index. ISBN 0091583004.

Collectors handbook of British ceramics written by a major dealer and collector. Following a brief chronological survey and glossary of terms are chapters on various types of English pottery and porcelain: blue and white porcelain, London porcelain, Lowestoft porcelain, Caughley and Worcester porcelain, Chamberlain—Worcester porcelain, Coalport porcelain, Miles Mason of London, Minton pottery, Ridgway porcelain, Parian figures. Introduction on factory marks and general hints on collecting. Classified bibliography, pp. 353-57, list books, periodical articles are referenced in the text.

507   Godden, Geoffrey A. **The Handbook of British Pottery and Porcelain Marks**. New York, Praeger, 1968. 197p. illus. index. LC 68-19134.

Pocket-sized handbook of British ceramics marks arranged alphabetically by name of maker with index by initials. Separate chronological list of Staffordshoire potters since 1780.

508   Godden, Geoffrey A. **An Illustrated Encyclopedia of British Pottery and Porcelain**. New York, Crown, 1966. 390p. illus. index. LC 66-23065.

Useful collection of plates intended as a companion to the author's *Encyclopedia of British Pottery and Porcelain Marks* (505).

509   Godden, Geoffrey A. **Victorian Porcelain**. New York, Universe, 1970. 22p. illus. ISBN 087663126X.

Brief survey of British porcelain made between 1840 and the beginning of Art Nouveau. Brief bibliography of basic works.

510   Honey, William B. **English Pottery and Porcelain**. 6th ed. rev. by R. J. Charleston. London, A. and C. Black, 1969. 287p. illus. index. LC 76-484125.

First published in 1933. An old, standard history of ceramic ware in England from the late Middle Ages to 1930. Contents: Part I: Earthenware and Stoneware to the End of the Eighteenth Century; Part II: English Porcelain of the Eighteenth Century; Part III: Nineteenth Century Pottery and Porcelain. Chapter on collecting and excellent, classified bibliography of books and periodical articles (updated to 1960), pp. 271-77.

511   Hughes, Bernard, and Therle Hughes. **English Porcelain and Bone China, 1743-1850**. New York, Praeger, 1968. 254p. illus. index. LC 68-21583.

Survey of English porcelain and bone china from 1748 to 1850 written for the collector and with particular attention to materials and techniques and the insight their study affords to matters of dating and provenance. Contents: 1, The Story of Porcelain; 2, Glazes; 3, Cobalt Blue;

4, Overglaze Enamels; 5, Transfer-Printed Ceramics; 6, Chelsea: 1743-83; 7, Bow: 1745-75; 8, Longton Hall: 1749-60; 9, Derby: 1749-1848; 10, Bristol Soft-Paste: 1748-52; 11, Worcester: 1751-83; 12, Later Worcester: 1783-1852; 13, Caughley: 1775-99; 14, Liverpool: 1756-1841; 15, Lowestoft: 1757-1802; 16, Nantgarw and Swansea: 1813-23; 17, Madeley: 1825-40; 18, Plymouth and Bristol under Cookworthy: 1763-73; 19, Bristol under Champion: 1773-81; 20, New Hall: 1781-1830; 21, Spode: 1796-1847; 22, Coalport: 1795-1865; 23, Minton: 1796-1858; 24, Rockingham: 1820-54; 25, Davenport, Wedgwood and Other Bone China Manufacturers. Illustrations feature especially pieces in the Victoria and Albert Museum. Facsimiles of marks append to most chapters. Classified bibliography, pp. 244-48.

512   Hughes, George B. **Victorian Pottery and Porcelain**. New York, Macmillan, 1960. 184p. illus. index. LC 60-930.

Comprehensive survey of ceramic ware produced in Greta Britain during the nineteenth century with emphasis on the technical innovations that characterized the production of the second half of the century. Contents: 1, Basaltes and Egyptian Black; 2, Terra-cotta; 3, Pearl Ware; 4, Staffordshire Blue; 5, Bone China; 6, Felspar Porcelain and Stone China; 7, Ironstone China; 8, Parian Ware; 9, Slip Ware and Welsh Ware; 10, Decoration; 11, Lustre Ware; 12, Colour Picture Prints on Staffordshire Pottery; 13, Lithophane Pictures; 14, Worcester; 15, Derby, Rockingham, Coalport and Madeley; 16, Leeds and Other Yorkshire Potteries; 17, Pinxton, Torksey, Nantgarw and Swansea; 18, Spode and Copelannd; 19, Minton, Wedgwood, Davenport and Other Staffordshire Potters; 20, Liverpool; 21, Sunderland Pottery; 22, Chesterfield Brown Ware and Spirit Flasks; 23, Belleek; 24, Figures; 25, Art Potteries; 26, Registration Marks. Brief bibliography, p. 173.

513   Mankowitz, Wolf, and Reginald G. Haggar. **The Concise Encyclopedia of English Pottery and Porcelain**. 2nd ed. New York, Praeger, 1968. 312p. illus. LC 68-28655.

Comprehensive dictionary of English pottery and porcelain covering factories, manufactories, artists, techniques, materials, and ornament. Illustrated with both museum pieces and pieces of the type accessible to the collector and many facsimiles of marks and signatures. Appendices with lists of museums in Britain and America having good collections of English ceramics, engravers for pottery and porcelain decoration, and British potters on foreign soil. Classified bibliography, pp. 300-11.

514   Sandon, Henry. **British Pottery and Porcelain**. New York, Arco, 1969. 175p. illus. LC 72-108999.

General introduction to the history of British pottery and porcelain directed to the beginning collector. Contents: I, Medieval and Post Medieval; 2, Delftware; 3, Slipware; 4, Stonewares and Saltglaze; Astbury, Whieldon and Wedgwood; 6, Other Eighteenth Century Earthenware Factories; 7, Eighteenth Century Porcelain; 8, Nineteenth Century Pottery and Porcelain; 9, The Twentieth Century. Appendices with list of museums with collection of British ceramics, concise repertory of marks, and selected bibliography, p. 160.

See also Savage, George, *English Pottery and Porcelain*. New York, Universe, 1961. 431p. illus. LC 61-11039.

Italy

515   Cairola, Aldo. **Ceramica italiana dalle origini a oggi**. Rome, Editalia, 1981. 301p. illus. index. ISBN 8870600130.

Well-illustrated, comprehensive history of ceramics in Italy from ancient times to 1981. Chapters describing ancient, medieval, Renaissance, Baroque, Rococo and modern ceramics are followed by a glossary of terms, dictionary of major makers and appendices with reprints of documents relative to the history of ceramic technology in Italy, e.g., Vannoccio di Biringuccio, De Pirotecnia (1560), Niccolo Piccopasso, I tre libri dell'arte del Vasaio (1857), the winners of the Premio Faenza (1938-1981), the Ceramisti Ammessi al Premio Faenza (1961-1981).

516   Gardelli, Giuliana. **Ceramiche del medioevo e del Rinascimento**. Ferrara, Belriguardo, 1986. 316p. illus. index. LC 87-110768.

Handbook of Italian ceramics from the thirteenth to the seventeenth centuries based on 119 pieces in Italian private collections. Most are central Italian majolica. Collections of ceramics in Italy. Bibliography, pp. 293-94.

Scandinavia

517   Hernmarck, Carl. **Fajans och poslin; svenska keramik fore 1850**. Stockholm, Wahlstrom & Widstrand, 1959. 164p. illus. index. LC 62-67457.

Pictorial survey of Swedish ceramics dating before 1850 written by a leading expert on Swedish decorative arts. Bibliography of basic works.

518   Martenson, Gunnar G. **Gammal findlandsk keramik**. Helsinki, Soderstrom, 1958. 164p. illus. index. LC A59-7458. rev.

Pictorial survey of Finnish ceramics with brief list of marks and bibliography of basic works.

Spain and Portugal

519   González Marti, Manuel. **Cerámica del Levante español, siglos medievales**. Barcelona, Labor, 1944-52. 3v. illus. index. LC 46-21770.

Scholarly history of Spanish medieval ceramics. Contents: t. 1: Loza; t. 2: Alicatados y azulejos; t. 3: Azulejos, "socarrats" y retablos. Comprehensive indexes and bibliographies at the end of each section.

520   Llubia Munne, Luis M. **Cerámica mediieval española**. Barcelona, Labor, 1967. 194p. illus. index. LC 73-270660.

Survey of the production of ceramics in Spain from the seventh century to the end of the fifteenth century including that of the Moors. Contents: Prólogo; Introducción: Terminología cerámica en general; 1, Dominación visigoda; 2, Dominación musulmana; 3, Dominación cristiana: Andalucía, Aragón, Castilla, Cataluña, Valencia, Baleares y Murcia. General bibliography, pp. 185-191.

521   Valente, Vasco. **Ceramica artistica portuense dos seculos XVIII e XIX**. Porto, Machado, n. d. 244p. illus. index.

Comprehensive history/handbook of Portuguese porcelain and pottery from the eighteenth century to 1947. Contents: I, A porcelana, sua introduçao na Europa; II, Ensaios para o fabrico da porcelana em Portugal; III, "Real Fabrica de Porcelana, Vidro e Processos chimos" (Vista Alegre); IV, Recompensas concedidas à fábrica da Vista Alegre; V, Relaçao das ilustraçoes; VI, Bibliografia (alphabetical list, pp. 103-105, further bibliography in the notes). Facsimiles of marks at the end of each section in part III.

Eastern European Countries

522   Csányi, Károly. **Geschichte der ungarischen Keramik, des Porzellans und ihre Marken**. Budapest, Verlag des Fonds fur Bildende Kunste, 1954. 153p. illus. index. LC 55-33362.

Handbook/history of ceramics in Hungary from the Middle Ages to the twentieth century. Each section has discussion of marks, and Marktafeln, pp. 67-116, has reproductions of 935 marks. Contents: I, Die mittelalterlichen TongefÄsse in Ungarn; II, Die Hafnerkeramik und ihre Meistermarken; III, Die Fayencen von Ungarn und ihre Marken; V, Die ungarnischen Porzellane und ihre Marken; VI, Die Marken der neueren Fayence-, Steingut, Porzellan-und bleiglasierten Erzeugnisse. Classified bibliography, pp. 124-26.

523   Strauss, Konrad P. **Die Geschichte der Topferkunst vom Mittelalter bis zur und die Kunsttopferein in Alt-Livland** (Estland und Lettland). Basel, P. H. Heitz, 1969. 272p. illus. index. LC 79-519605.

Scholarly history of ceramics produced in Estonia, Latvia and Lithuania from the early Middle Ages to the twentieth century. Bibliographical references in the footnotes.

See also Meyer, *Böhmisches Porzellan und Steingut (695)*.

ORIENTAL CERAMICS

Islamic Ceramics

524   Butler, Alfred J. **Islamic Pottery; a Study Mainly Historical**. London, Benn, 1926. 179p. illus. index. LC 27-18040.

Older, scholarly history of Islamic ceramics from the beginnings to the sixteenth century with particular attention given to Egyptian lustreware. Excellent collection of plates illustrating museum pieces. Bibliography, pp. xxi-xxiv, of the basic older literature. A similar work: Riviere, Henri. *La ceramique dans l'art musulman*. Paris, E. Levy, 1913. 2v. illus.

525   Fehérvári, Geza. **Islamic Pottery; A Comprehensive Study Based on the Barlow Collection with a Foreword by Sir Harry Garner**. London, Faber and Faber, 1973. 191p. illus. LC 74-152879.

Scholarly history of Islamic pottery based on 300 pieces, mainly Turkish, in the former Barlow Collection (now dispersed). Eight pieces not in the Barlow Collection are included. Contents: I, The Early Islamic Period; II, The Medieval Islamic Period; III, The Later Islamic Period. General bibliography, pp. 181-83, and specialized literature in the footnotes.

526   Lane, Arthur. **Early Islamic Pottery; Mesopotamia, Egypt and Persia**. London, Faber and Faber, 1947. 52p. (text), 100p. (illus). index. LC 48-9602.

Brief but authoritative survey of Islamic pottery from the seventh through the fourteenth centuries. Contents: 1, The Islamic Scene; 2, The Umayyad Caliphs (661-750 A.D.): The Sources of Islamic Ornament: and Earlier Contributions to the Potter's Technique; 3, First Contacts with China: the Abbasid School of Mesopotamia in the 9th and 10th Centuries; 4, Painted Wares of the Samarkand Region and Persia; 5, Egyptian Lustre-painted and Carved Pottery of the Fatimid Period (969-1171); 6, Common Pottery: the Ceramic Underworld of Islam; 7, The Saljuq Turks and the New Epoch of Pottery of Islam; 8, Saljuq Carved, Moulded, and Silhouette-painted Pottery: 12-13th Centuries; 10, The 'Minai' and 'Lajvardina' Painted Wares of Persia: 12-14th Centuries; 11, Under-glaze Painting: Egypt, Mesopotamia, and Persia: 12th-13th Centuries. Basic bibliography, p. 49.

527   Lane, Arthur. **Later Islamic Pottery**. 2nd ed. London, Faber and Faber, 1971. 133p. illus. index. LC 72-179330.

Sequel to the author's *Early Islamic Pottery...* (526). Contents: 1, The 14th-century Mongol Style; 2, 15th-Century Blue and White; 3, Turkish Pottery; 4, Persia: Safavid Period (1502-1722) and Later; 5, Late Persian Polychrome Wares; 6, Late Persian Blue-and White; 7, Late Persian Lustre-painted Ware; 8, Late Persian Monochrome Wares; 9, Marks. Appendix with extracts from contemporary documents referring to Persian pottery. Comprehensive bibliography, pp. 124-27, and further literature in the footnotes.

528   Watson, Oliver. **Persian Lustre Ware**. London, Faber and Faber, 1985. 209p. illus. index. ISBN 0571132359.

In the series "Faber Monographs on Pottery and Porcelain." Comprehensive, scholarly history of lustreware ceramics made in Persia from the late twelfth to the mid-fourteenth century with emphasis on attributions, style and function. Contents: 1, Introduction; 2, The Ceramic Background; 3, Technique; 4, Attribution to Production Sites; 5, The Monumental Style; 6, The Miniature Style; 7, The Kashan Style; 8, Il-Khanid Wares; 9, Figures; 10, Tiles; 11, Images, Inscriptions and the Use of Lustre Tiles; 12, Later Lustre Ware. Appendices with lists of potters, buildings with lustre tiles, and dated pieces. Comprehensive bibliography, pp. 201-206, and bibliographical references in the footnotes.

See also the collection catalogs: *Islamic Pottery of the Eight to the Fifteenth Century in the Keir Collection*, by E. Grube (London, Faber and Faber, 1976. 378p. illus.) and *Nishapur: Pottery of the Early Islamic Period*, by C. K. Wilkinson (New York, Metropolitan Museum of Art; Greenwich, Conn., New York Graphics Society, 1973. 374p. illus.) and the exhibition catalog: *Ceramics from the World of Islam*, by E. Atil (Washington, D.C., Smithsonian Institution, 1973. 225p. illus.).

See also: R. J. Charleston, *Islamic Pottery* (420) and A. U. Pope, *Survey of Persian Art...* vs. I, II, IV-VI (FA 1796).

Far Eastern Ceramics

General Works

529   Honey, William B. **The Ceramic Art of China, and Other Countries of the Far East**. London, Faber and Hyperion Press, 1945. 238p. illus. index. LC 45-10141.

Comprehensive survey of the Chinese pottery and porcelain with chapters on Korea and Japan by a leading British expert and former Keeper of the Department of Ceramics at the Victoria and Albert Museum. Contents: I, Introduction; II, China: Chinese Pottery before the Han Period; The Han Period and the Adoption of Lead Glaze; The Development of Stoneware and Porcelain: Han: Six Dynasties: T'ang; Tomb-Figures and Others: Han: Six Dynasties: T'ang; Ming; The T'ang Period: The Sung Period; The Ming Period: The Ch'ing Period; III, Indo-China: Siam, Annam; IV, Corea: Silla Period; Koryu Period; Yi Period; V, Japan. Appendices with note on spelling and pronunciation of Chinese names, repertory of marks; glossary of hinese names for shapes, colors, etc., list of patterns and subjects used as decoration of Chinese porcelain, and essay on forgeries and copies. Comprehensive bibliography with introductory notes, pp. 218-26.

530   Koyama, Fujio, and John Figgess. **Two Thousand Years of Oriental Ceramics**. New York, Abrams, 1961. 379p. illus. LC 60-10344.

Pictorial survey of the ceramics of China, Japan, Korea and Southeast Asia from prehistoric times to the nineteenth century. Brief text provides outlines of the development in the major periods and regions. Large collection of plates have descriptive notes. General bibliography of books in English, Japanese and Chinese, p. 379. Contents: An Outline History of Chinese Ceramics from Ancient Times To the T'ang Period; Sung Pottery and Porcelain; Ceramic Production in China during the Yüan, Ming, and Ch'ing Periods; The Development of Japanese Ceramics before 1600 A.D.; The Development of Japanese Ceramics after 1600 A.D.; A Short Survey of the Development of Korean Ceramics; Ceramics of Annam, Thailand, and the Ryukyus.

531   **Oriental Ceramics, the World's Great Collections.** Tokyo, Kodansha, 1980-1982. 11v. illus. index.

First published as a limited edition 1974-1979. Sumptuously illustrated surveys of the masterpieces of Oriental ceramics in the great museums around the world. Contents:

v.   1: *Tokyo Museum.* ISBN 0870114409
v.   2: *National Museum of Korea, Seoul.* ISBN 0870114417
v.   3: *Museum Pusat, Jakarta.* ISBN 0870114425
v.   4: *Iran Bastan Museum, Teheran.* ISBN 0870114433
v.   5: *The British Museum, London.* ISBN 087011441
v.   6: *Percival David Foundation of Chinese Art, London.* ISBN 087011445X
v.   7: *Musée Guimet, Paris.* ISBN 0870114468
v.   8: *Museum of Far Eastern Antiquities, Stockholm.* ISBN 070114476
v.   9: *The Freer Gallery of Art, Washington, D.C.*
v. 10: *Museum of Fine Arts, Boston.* ISBN 0870114492
v. 11: *The Metropolitan Museum of Art, New York.*

532   Penkala, Maria. **Far Eastern Ceramics; Marks and Decoration.** The Hague, Mouton, 1963. 263p. illus. index. LC 65-375.

Important, comprehensive handbook of Far Eastern ceramics, arranged by countries and consisting of brief introductory histories followed by repertories of marks. Glossary of Chinese, Korean, and Japanese terms. Comprehensive bibliography, pp. 235-41.

China

General Histories and Handbooks

533   Addis, J. M. **Chinese Ceramics from Datable Tombs: and Some Other Dated Material: A Handbook.** London; New York, Sotheby Parke Bernet, 1978. 184p. illus. ISBN 08566670391.

Important corpus of plates illustrating works of Chinese ceramics that have come from datable tombs. Each piece is described in detail with bibliographical references. Contents: Part One: Three Kingdoms to Five Dynasties 220-907; Part Two: Sung 960-1279; Part Three: Yüan 1271-1368; Part Four: Early Ming 1368-1424; Part Five: Early Ming: the Sung Sheng Family Group of Tombs; Part Six: Middle and Late Ming 1436-1644; Part Seven: Dragons from Ming Tombs with Some from the Ming Imperial Palace in Peking.

534   Beurdeley, Michel, and Cecile Beurdeley. **A Connoisseur's Guide to Chinese Ceramics.** New York, Evanston; San Francisco and London, Harper & Row, 1974. 318p. illus. index. LC 74-1792. Reprinted: New York, Alpine Fine Arts Collection, 1984. ISBN 0881689939.

Well-illustrated, comprehensive survey of Chinese ceramics from prehistoric times to the early twentieth century. Contents: I, Neolithic Period; II, The Shang-Yin Period; III, The Zhou (Chou) Period; IV, The Qin (Ch'in) and Han Periods; V, Period of the Six Dynasties; VI, The Sui Dynasty; VII, The Tang (T'ang) Dynasty and the Five Dynasties; VIII, The Song (Sung) and Jin (Chin) Dynasties; IX, The Liao Dynasty; X, The Mongol Yuan (Yüan) Dynasty; XI, The Ming Dynasty; XII, From Ming to Qing (Ch'ing). Transitional Period; XIII, The Qing (Ch'ing) Dynasty; XIV, Export Ware; XV, Chinese Porcelain of the 19th and early 20th Centuries. Appendices with transcription of Chinese, glossary and discussion of materials and technique. Comprehensive bibliography arranged by chapters, pp. 305-10.

535   Dexel, Thomas. **Frühe Keramik in China. Die Entwicklung der Hauptformen vom Neolithikum bis in die T'ang-Zeit.** Braunschweig, Klinkhardt & Biermann, 1973. 84 p.text, 80 p. plates. LC 73-344817.

Scholarly study of the development of early Chinese ceramics with emphasis on forms of vessels. Covers the period from circa 4000 B.C. to A.D. 1000. Corpus of outline drawings augments the plates of pieces in museums. Classified bibliography of books and periodical literature in all languages, pp. 82-84.

536 Du Boulay, Anthony. **Christie's Pictorial History of Chinese Ceramics**. Oxford, Phaidon, Christie's, 1984. 319p. illus. index. ISBN 0714880159.

Comprehensive history of Chinese ceramics from the Han dynasty to the nineteenth century featuring pieces sold at Christie's, for which the prices at the time of the sale is given in a list at the end. Contents: 1, Early Wares; 2, Song and Yuan Dynasties; 3, Yingqing and Underglaze Blue and Red Wares; 4, Ming Monochromes and Wares Decorated in Enamel Colours; 5, Transitional Wares, Blue and White, Wucai and Famille Verte; 6, Yongzheng, Qianlong and Famille Rose; 7, Export Porcelain. Map showing sites of kilns, glossary of terms and bibliography of basic works in English, p. 307.

537 Garney, Wanda. **China, Ancient Kilns and Modern Ceramics**. Canberra, Australia, Australian National Univ. Pr., 1983. 144p. illus. index. ISBN 0708113133.

Survey of Chinese ceramics by province with emphasis on sites of kilns and present-day practices. Covers the sixteen provinces: Honan, Shansi, Shantung, Hopeh, Kansu, Shenshi, Liaoning, Sinkiang, Szechwan, Kiangsu, Chekiang, Hunan, Kwangsi, Kiangsi Chuang, Fukien, Kwangtung. The history of ceramics in each province is described and illustrated with representative pieces, views of archaeological sites and photographs of contemporary ceramic production. Useful for identification of contemporary Chinese ceramics. General bibliography, pp. 137-38.

538 Goidsenhaven, J. P. van. **La céramique chinoise: Commentaires sur son évolution**. Brussels, Connaissance, 1954. 213p. index. LC 54-22710.

Important history of the Chinese ceramics from prehistoric times to 1912 written by a leading French expert. Emphasis is on the changes in the bodies and glazes of ceramic ware. Contains 114 plates of pieces from major European private collections. Contents: Des Neolithiques aux Han; La Dynastie des Han; Des Han aux T'ang; De l'Epoque des T'ang; Les Song; La Dynastie des Yuan; La Dynastie des Ming; La Dynastie des T'sing. Unclassified bibliography, pp. 197-200.

539 Gulland, W. G. **Chinese Porcelain...** 2nd ed. London, Chapman & Hall, 1902. 2v. illus. index. LC 03-12857r51.

Comprehensive collector's handbook of Chinese porcelain from the early sixteenth century to circa 1875. Out-of-date in many areas but still useful for the detailed description of types of glazes, bodies, and painted decorations used in historic Chinese porcelains and for the 411 plates of pieces mostly in English private collections at the turn of the century.

540 Hetherington, Arthur L. **The Pottery and Porcelain Factories of China; Their Geographical Distribution and Periods of Activity...** London, Paul, Trench, Trubner; New York, Dutton, 1921. 15p. map.

Useful list, by provinces, of the major factories, with dates of activity. Second list by dynasty. Map with locations of the factories.

541 Hobson, Robert L. **Chinese Pottery and Porcelain; an Account of the Potter's Art in China from Primitive Times to the Present Day**. London and New York, Cassell, 1915. 2v. illus. index. Reprint: New York, Dover, 1976. ISBN 0486232530.

An old, standard history Chinese ceramics out-of-date in many areas but still a useful overview of the sequences of styles and for the basic characteristics of the various types of pottery nd porcelain. Includes 134 plates of pieces in museums and private collections with descriptive captions. Contents: Volume I: 1, The Primitive Periods; 2, Han Dynasty; 3, The T'ang Dynasty; 4, The Sung Dynasty; 5, Ju, Kuan, and Ko Wares; 6, Lung-Ch'üan Yao; 7, Ting Yao; 8, Tz'u Chou Ware; 8, Chün Wares and Some Others; 10, Mirabilia; 11, Porcelain and its Beginnings; 12, Ching-Te Chen; 13, The Yüan Dynasty; 14, Kuangtung Wares; 15, Yi-Hsing Ware; 16, Miscellaneous Potteries; 17, Marks on Chinese Pottery and Porcelain. Volume 2: 1, Ming Dynasty; 2, Hsüan Te; 3, Ch'eng Hua and Other Reigns; 4, Chia Ching and Lung Ch'ing; 5, Wan Li and other Reigns; 6, The Technique of Ming Porcelain; 7, Miscellaneous Porcelain Factories; 8, The Ch'ing Dynasty; 9, K'ang Hsi Blue and White; 10, K'ang Hsi Polychrome Porcelains; 11, K'ang Hsi Monochromes; 12, Yung Cheng Period; 13, Ch'ien Lung; 14, European Influences in the Ch'ing Dynasty; 15, Nineteenth Century Porcelains; 16, Porcelain Shapes in the Ch'ing Dynsaty; 17, Motives of the Decoration; 18, Forgeries and Imitations. Bibliographical references in the footnotes.

542   Li, Chih-yen and Cheng Wen. **Chinese Pottery and Porcelain.** Beijing, Foreign Languages Pr., 1985. 209p. illus. ISBN 0835111857.

Survey of Chinese ceramics from prehistoric times to circa 1980 with emphasis on the relationship between ceramics and Chinese culture and on the technology of ceramic production. Contents: I, Pottery Comes into People's Lives; Neolithic Pottery; 2, Pottery from the Shang and Zhou to the Qin and Han Dynasties; 3, Invention and Refinement of Porcelain; 4, Ceramics Flourish in the Sui and Tang Dynasties and the Period of the Five Dynasties and Ten Kingdoms; 5, The Art of Porcelain in the Song and Yuan Dynasties; 6, Pottery and Porcelain of the Liao and Kin Dynasties; 7, Ceramic Craftsmanship Excels in the Ming and Qing Dynasties; 8, Decline of Chinese Porcelain in the One Hundred Years before Liberation; 9, Blossoming of Ceramic Art in New China; 10, Chinese Pottery and Porcelain in World Culture. Valuable table listing the ancient kiln sites discovered in China.

543   Medley, Margaret. **The Chinese Potter: a Practical History of Chinese Ceramics.** 3rd ed. Oxford, Phaidon, 1989. 288p. illus. index. ISBN 071482593X.

Comprehensive survey of Chinese ceramics from prehistoric time to the present. Emphasis is on technical development and the social and economic dimensions. Contents: 1, The Basic Technology; 2, The Period of Discovery and Innovation; 3, Development and Variations. List of reign marks and glossary of terms. Bibliographical references in the notes. General, classified bibliography, pp. 282-84.

544   Mino, Yutaka, and Patricia Wilson. **An Index to Chinese Ceramic Kiln Sites from the Six Dynasties to the Present.** Toronto, Royal Ontario Museum, 1973. 103p. illus. maps. LC 74-167138.

Important geographical index of the locations of kilns in China from earliest times to the end of the nineteenth century. Arranged in two parts: the first arranges the kilns by types of glaze; the second by province. Within provinces the kilns are grouped by dynasty. Name of kiln is given in Chinese characters and transliterated. Brief comment on the type of ware produced. Good maps. Bibliography, pp. 67-68, list books in Chinese.

545   Sato, Masahiko. **Chinese Ceramics.** New York, Weatherhill, 1981. 255p. illus. index. ISBN 0834810417.

Concise but fact-filled survey of the history of Chinese ceramics from prehistoric times to the end of the Ching (Qing) dynasty. Emphasis is on the qualities of the ceramic body, glaze and form. Contents: 1, Painted Pottery and Black Pottery; 2, From Black Pottery to Gray Pottery;

3, The Beginning of Ash-Glazed Stoneware; 4, Proto-Porcelain; 4, Green and Brown Lead-Glazed Earthenware; 6, The Rise of the Yue Kilns; 7, The Beginning of Northern Celadon; 8, From Celadon to White Ware; 9, The Revival of Lead-Glazed Earthenware; 10,. Tang Three-color Ware; 11, Tang Black Ware, White Ware, and Celadon; 12, Southern Celadon; 13, The Beginning of Song Ceramics: Ding Ware; 15, Cizhou Ware; 16, Ru Celadon; 17, Jun Celadon; 18, Southern White Porcelain; 19, Qingbai Ware of Jingdezhen; 20, Temmoku of the North; 21, Temmoku of the South; 22, Longquan Celadon; 23, Celadon of the Southern Song Official Kilns; 24, The Emergence of Blue-and-White Ware; 25, Yonglle and Xuande Wares; 26, Chengua Ware; 27, Hongzhi and Zhengde Ware; 28, Jiajing, Longqing, and Wanli Wares; 29, Various Types of Ming Unofficial Wares; 30, Late Ming and Early Qing Unofficial Kilns; 31, Thed Revival of Official Kilns in the Qing Dynasty; 32, Qing Blue-and-White Ware; 33, Qing Enameled Porcelains; 34, Qing Monochrome Wares. Illustrated mainly with pieces in Japanese museums and collections. Bibliography, pp. 247, has a particularly thorough list of Japanese and Chinese sources.

546   Thiel, Albert W. R. **Chinese Pottery and Stoneware**. New York, Nelson, 1953. 204p. illus.LC A54-3538.

Concise survey of Chinese ceramics from the Han dynasty to the end of the Ch'ing dynasty directed to the collector and enthusiast and illustrated with pieces from the author's famous collection. Chapter "Advice to the Collector." No bibliography.

547   Vainker, S. J. **Chinese Pottery and Porcelain from Prehistory to the Present**. London, Trustees of the British Museum, 1991. 240p. illus. index. ISBN 0714114480.

Well-illustrated history of Chinese ceramics based on pieces in the collections of the British Museum. Contents: I, Ceramics in the Neolithic and Bronze Age; 2, Funerary Art and Functional Vessels: The Han and Six Dynasties; 3, Foreign Influences and Chinese Traditions: the Tang Dynasty; 4, The Classical Period: The Song Dynasty; 5, The Worldwide Export of Porcelain: the Yuan, Ming and Qing Dynasties; 6, Later Architectural and Popular Ceramics: 1500 Onwards; 7, Imperial Porcelains from Jingdezhen: the Yuan, Ming and Qing Dynasties. Appendices with valuable discussions of clays, glazes and firing techniques. Comprehensive bibliography, pp. 228-32, with useful section of site reports.

548   Valenstein, Suzanne G. **A Handbook of Chinese Ceramics**. Rev. and enl. ed. New York, Metropolitan Museum of Art; New York, Abrams, 1989. 331p. illus. ISBN 0870995146.

First published in 1975. Introductory survey of Chinese ceramics based on pieces in the Metropolitan Museum of Art. Contents: Early Periods; Shang Dynasty; Chou Dynasty; Ch'in and Han Dynasties; Six Dynasties; Sui Dynasty; T'ang Dynasty; Five Dynasties; Northern Sung, Chin and Southern Sung Dynasties; Yüan Dynasty; Ming Dynasty; Ch'ing Dynasty; The 20th Century. Map and glossary. Bibliographical references in the notes, general bibliography, pp. 313-14.

See also the museum catalogs: *Chinese Ceramics. The Baur Collection*, by J. Ayers (Geneva, Collections Baur, 1968-74. 4v. illus. LC 74-390031), *Percival David Foundation of Chinese Art. Illustrated Catalogue* (London, Percival David Foundation of Chinese Art, 1953-73. 6v. illus.), the collection catalog: *Chinese Ceramics, Bronzes and Jades in the Collection of Sir Alan and Lady Barlow*, by M. Sullivan (London, Faber and Faber, 1963. 173p. illus. LC 63-24839), and the museum guides: *Chinese Ceramics in the Ashmolean Museum: an Illustrated Handbook to the Collections*, by M. Tregear (Oxford, The Museum, 1979. 40p. illus. ISBN 0900090588), *Chinese Ceramics in the Topkapi Saray Museum*, by R. Krahl (3v. illus. London, Sotheby's Publications, 1986. ISBN 0856671843), the exhibition catalogs: *Chinese Ceramics in Japanese Collections: T'ang through Ming Dynasties*, by S. Hayashiva and H. Trubner (New York, Asia Society, 1977. 135p. illus. ISBN 0878480498), and *Chinese Ceramics: the Kroger Collection*, by J. Ayers (London, Sotheby, 1985. 180p. illus. ISBN 0856673013), *Seventeenth-*

century Chinese Porcelain from the Butler Family Collection, by M. Butler, Maragaret Medley, Stephen Little (Alexandria, VA, Art Services International, 1990. 208p. illus.).

Particular Periods

549   Gray, Basil. **Sung Porcelain and Stoneware**. London, Faber and Faber, 1984. 205p. illus. index. ISBN 0571130488.

In the series: "Faber Monographs on Pottery and Porcelain." Comprehensive, scholarly history of Sung dynasty by a leading British expert. Contents: 1, Historical Background; 2, The Yüeh-yao Kilns: Five Dynasties to Early Sung; 3, The Yao-chou Kilns of Shensei: and Their Imitations; 4, Ting-yao and the White Wares of Northern Sung and Chin; 5, Chün-yao; 6, Tz'u-chou Wares; 7, The Brown Wares of North and South China; 8, Kuan Ware; 9, Ch'ing-pai Wares; 10, Lung-ch'üan Wares; 11, Technique; 12, The Export of Chinese Stonewares and Porcelain. Comprehensive, classified bibliography, pp. 196-99, and extensive references to specialized bibliography in the footnotes.

See also the author's earlier survey: *Early Chinese Pottery and Porcelain*. London, Faber and Faber, 1953. 48p. (text), 75p. (plates). index. LC 53-27387. Authoritative introduction to Chinese ceramics from the Shang through Yüan dynasties, illustrated with major museum pieces. General bibliography, p. 46.

550   Hobson, Robert L. **The Wares of the Ming Dynasty**. Rutland, Vt., Tuttle, 1962. 208p. illus. index. ISBN 0804806233.

First published in 1923 (London, Benn). An old, standard history of Ming ceramics based upon documentary accounts. Now largely out-of-date for chronology and attributions.

551   Jenyns, Soame. **Ming Pottery and Porcelain**. 2d ed. London, Faber, 1988. 237p. illus. index. ISBN 0571148417.

Authoritative survey of Ming ceramics with emphasis on the products of the Imperial factories. Contents: 1, Introduction to the First Edition; 2, A General Survey; 3, The Period of Transition from the Yüan to the Ming; 4, The Reigns of Hung Wu (1368-98), Chien Wên (1399-1402) and Yung Lo (1403-24); 5, The Reigns of Hung Hsi (1425) and Hsüan Tê (1425-35); 6, The Reigns of Chêng T'ung (1436-49), Ching T'ai (1450-7), T'ien Shun (1457-64) and Ch'êng Hua (1465-87); 7, The Reigns of Hung Chih (1488-1505) and Chêng Tê (1506-21); 8, The Reigns of Chia Ching (1522-66) and Lung Ch'ing (1567-72); 9, The Reigns of Wan Li (1573-1620), T'ai Ch'ang (1620), Tien Ch'i (1621-7) and Ch'ung Chêng (1628-44); 10, Export and Provincial Wares. Appendix with Ming dynasty reign marks and dates. General bibliography, pp. 229-30.

552   Laufer, Berthold. **Chinese Pottery of the Han Dynasty**. Leiden, Brill, 1909. 339p. illus. index. Reprint: Rutland, Vt., Tuttle, 1962. LC 62-14935.

Classic history of Han dynasty ceramics by a leading expert on the history of early Chinese art. Contents: I, Introductory; II, Pottery Prior to the Han Dynasty; III, Description of Han Pottery—Imitative Forms; IV, Description of Han Pottery—Vessels; V, Notes on Ornamentation; VI, Inscriptions. Appendices discuss Han roofing tiles, mortuary pottery of the Sung dynasty and later periods. Bibliographical references in the footnotes.

553   Medley, Margaret. **Yüan Porcelain and Stoneware**. New York, Pitman, 1974. 139p. illus. index. ISBN 0273070849.

Authoritative, scholarly history of Chinese ceramics during the Yüan dynasty (1271-1368). Contents: 1, Historical and Stylistic Setting; 2, The White Wares of Jao-Chou; 3, Underglaze Blue and Copper Red Decorated Wares; 4, Lung-Ch'üan Celadons; 5, Northern Celadon, Chün and Ting; 6, Tz'u-Chou and Related Black Wares; 7, Chi-Chou and the Minor Southern Kilns.

Illustrated with pieces in major museums. General bibliography, pp. 135-36, and specialized literature in the footnotes.

554   Plummer, James M. **Temmoku: a Study of the Ware of Chien**. Tokyo, Idemitsu Art Gallery, 1972. 109p. illus. index. LC 73-160368.
Scholarly introduction to the black stoneware made in Fuchien province during the Sung dynasty and introduced in Japan where it was known as Temmoku and brought with it the Tea Ceremony. Contents: I, Introduction; II, Shifting Boundaries and Changing Names; III, Journey into Sung; IV, The Kiln Sites; V, The Saggar and the Bowl; VI, Inscriptions; VII, The Chien Potters Bow Out. Bibliography of works in Chinese, Japanese and Western languages, pp. 95-100, the Tea Ceremony.

555   Tregear, Mary. **Song Ceramics**. London, Thames and Hudson, 1982. 262p. illus. index. LC 81-84083.
Comprehensive, scholarly history of Chinese ceramics during the Song (Sung) dynasty (960-1278). Contents: Introduction: Survey of the Development of Ceramics; I, Ding Ware and the First Great White-Stoneware Kilns of the Song Dynasty; II, Cizhou-Type Wares: The Most Widespread Popular Stonewares of the Northern Song Dynasty; III, Yaozhou Greenware: The Heir to the Great Yue Tradition; IV, Jun, Ru and Guan Wares: New Styles of Glazing for Stoneware; V, Jingdezhen: The Beginning of the Oldest and Greatest Tradition of Porcelain in the World; VI, Longquan Ware: The Great Greenware of the Southern Song Dynasty and the Kilns It Influenced; VIII, Trade and the Influence of Song Ceramics on the Ceramic Cultures of Foreign Lands. Each chapter ends with a "catalogue," i.e., a collection of small plates with descriptive captions that supplement the major pieces illustrated in large plates in the text. Classified bibliography, pp. 239-241.

556   Watson, William. **Tang and Liao Ceramics**. London, Thames and Hudson, 1984. 283p. illus. index. LC 83-24630.
Comprehensive history of Chinese ceramics of the T'ang and Liao dynasties based on archaeological evidence since 1949 and published almost exclusively in Chinese journals. Contents: I, Prolegomena: History, Tang Style in Painting and Buddhist Art; Pre-Tang Ceramic History, Uses for Ceramics in the Tang Dynasty; II, Techniques: Earthenware and Its Decoration, High-Fired Ware and its Glazes, Kilns, Areas of Production; III, Ceramic Types: Their Ornament and Dating; IV, Figurines; V, Liao Ceramics: The Liao Dynasty, Kilns, Ceramic Shapes; VI, Tang and Five Dynasties Ceramics outside China; Epilogue. Each section concludes with a catalog of small illustrations with descriptive captions that supplement the major pieces illustrated in large plates in the text. Bibliography, pp. 269-274, has section devoted to museum and exhibition catalogs.
See also Prodan, Mario, *The Art of the T'ang Potter* (London, Thames and Hudson, 1968. 186p. illus. index). Pictorial survey of the Chinese ceramics during the T'ang dynasty with emphasis on the large size funerary figures. Brief text with descriptive caption to the 154 plates. General bibliography, p. 179.

557   Yang, Gen et al. **The Ceramics of China: the Yangshao Culture—the Song Dynasty**. Beijing, China, Science Press; London, Methuen, 1985. 179p. illus. ISBN 041354740X.
Pictorial survey of Chinese ceramics from earliest times through the Sung dynasty with particular reference to the products of the Yangshao culture and with emphasis on technical aspects. Chemical analysis of bodies and glazes are provided. Contains 171 plates, many in color, of pieces in collections in mainland China. Important group of plates of pieces recovered in recent excavation in Shaanxi province. Contents: 1, Pottery of the Neolithic Age; 2, The Evolution of

Porcelain from Pottery; 3, Porcelain-Firing in the Sui, Tang and Five Dynasties; 4, Porcelain-Firing in the Song Dynasty.

China Trade Ceramics

558   Guy, John. **Oriental Trade Ceramics in South-East Asia, Ninth to Sixteenth Centuries.** Singapore; New York, Oxford University Press, 1985. 161p. illus. index. ISBN 0195825934.

In the series: "Oxford in Asia Studies in Ceramics." Scholarly history of trade in glazed stoneware and porcelain in Southeast Asia from the ninth to the sixteenth centuries. Contents: 1, Early Chinese Contacts with South-East Asia; 2, South-East Asia as Entrepot; 3, The Expansion of China's Trade with South-East Asia; 4, Fourteenth-century Trade Ceramics and the Mongol Contribution; 5, Early Ming Policies and South-East Asia Trade; 6, Vietnamese Trade Ceramics; 7, Thai Ceramics and International Trade; 8, Some Concluding Remarks. Bibliography, pp. 145-159, and bibliographical footnotes. Catalog of Chinese, Vietnamese, and Thai wares in Australian collections.

See also the exhibition catalog: *Chinese Blue & White Ceramics*. National Museum, Singapore. by S. T. Yeo and J. Martin. (Singapore, Arts Orientalis, 1978. 315p. illus. LC 78-943767) and the museum catalog: *Sino-Thai Ceramics in the National Museum, Bangkok, Thailand and in Private Collections*, by N. V. Robinson (Bangkok, Dept of Fine Arts, 1982. 354p. illus. index. Lc 83-916130).

Japan

See also Heibonsha Survey of Japanese Art, 29: The Art of Japanese Ceramics (FA 1892).

559   Gorham, Hazel H. **Japanese and Oriental Ceramics**. Rutland, Vt., Tuttle, 1970. 256p. illus. index. LC 70-130416.

Survey of Japanese ceramics with particular attention paid to distinguishing Japanese from Chinese and old from modern reproductions. Contents: 1, Introduction; 2, Cha no yu and Its Influence on Japanese Ceramics; 3, Clays, Kilns and Potters' Methods; 4, Pre-historic and Early Potteries; 5, Celadons—Forerunners of Porcelain; 6, Imari Kilns and Potters; 7, Seto Kilns and Potters; 8, Kutani Kilns and Potters; 9, Kyoto and Neighboring Kilns and Potters; 10, Tokyo Kilns and Potters; 11, Korean Wares—Brief Historical Outline; 12, How to Buy and Appreciate Japanese Wares; 13, Japanese Ceramics in Religion and Superstition; 14, Ceramic Designs and Symbols; 15, Inscriptions on Ceramics. Selected bibliography of titles in English, pp. 237-41.

560   Klein, Adalbert. **A Connoisseur's Guide to Japanese Ceramics**. London, Alpine Fine Arts Collection, 1984. 275p. illus. index. ISBN 0881681326.

Well-illustrated history of Japanese ceramics from the fifth millennium B.C. to the present. Contents: Ceramics of the Early Period; Pottery of the Heian Period, Medieval Pottery, The Pottery of the "Six Old Kiln"; Tea Wares; Legends in the History of Japanese Pottery; Porcelain; Kyoto Pottery; Pottery of the Eighteenth Century; Pottery of the Nineteenth Century; Repetitions of Their Own Traditional Style; The Pottery of the Twentieth Century; On the Technology of Japanese Pottery; Conclusion. Appendices with maps, chronological table, list of marks, glossary of terms, names and dates of reigning emperors, and comprehensive, classified bibliography of books and articles in Japanese (transliterated) and Western languages, pp. 257-260.

561   Koyama, Fujio. **The Heritage of Japanese Ceramics**. New York, Weatherhill, 1973. 256p. illus. index. ISBN 0834815133.

Survey of Japanese ceramics from prehistoric times to the present with emphasis on continuity of traditional ceramics in Japanese culture. Excellent, large size plates with detailed descriptive notes. Contents: Part One: The Heritage of Japanese Ceramics: 1, The Dawn of the Potter's Art, 2, The Rise of the Six Ancient Kilns; 3, The Glories of the Tea Ceremony, 4, The Flowering of the Ceramic Tradition, 5, The Riches of Porcelain, 6, Some Master Potters and Their Successors; Part Two: The Enduring Tradition: A Photo Essay. Appendix with chronological list of kiln sites. Selected bibliography, p. 248, lists books in English.

562 Mikami, Tsugio. **The Art of Japanese Ceramics**. New York, Weatherhill, 1972. 185p. illus. LC 77-162681. (Heibonsha Survey of Japanese Art, 29)

Popular survey of Japanese ceramics from prehistoric times to the late Edo period with a chapter on the place of ceramics in Japanese life. For the series *see*: FA1892.

563 Miller, Roy A. **Japanese Ceramics after the Japanese Text by Seiichi Okuda and Others...** Tokyo, Shuppan; Rutland, Vt., Tuttle, 1960. 240p. illus. index. LC 60-16172.

Well-illustrated survey of Japanese ceramics from prehistoric times to 1950. Contents: 1, Early Earthenware; 2, Early Pottery; 3, Medieval Wares; 4, Mino and Allied Pottery; 5, Karatsu and Allied Pottery; 6, Raku Ware; 7, Early Japanese Porcelains; 8, The Arita Porcelains; 9, Ninsei and His Heirs.

564 Mitsuoka, Tadanari. **Ceramic Art of Japan**. 5th ed. Tokyo, Japan Travel Bureau, 1960. 184p. illus. index. LC 60-10373.

First published in 1949 as the 8th volume in the Tourist Library of Japan. A concise but authoritative survey of Japanese ceramics from prehistoric Jomon earthenware to the work of Japanese potters of the immediate post-World War II era. Special attention is given to the work of known potters such as Kenzan in the eighteenth century and Mizukoshi-Yosobei in the nineteenth century. Maps showing the location of kilns and potters' villages in the various regions of Japan.

565 Munsterberg, Hugo. **The Ceramic Art of Japan: A Handbook for Collectors**. Rutland, Vt., Tuttle, 1964. 272p. illus. index. LC 63-20586.

Survey of Japanese ceramics from prehistoric times to the present. Includes folk pottery and chapter on collecting Japanese ceramics. General bibliography, pp. 265-66.

566 Penkala, Maria. **A Survey of Japanese Ceramics: A Handbook for the Collector**. Schiedam, Interbooks International, 1980. 296p. illus. LC 81-1-3767.

Collector's introduction to Japanese ceramics by a leading expert. Plates feature pieces in Dutch museums. Contents: Buddhism in Japan; The cha-no-yu; the Six Old Kilns; Japanese Porcelain; Japanese Deities and Symbols; Japanese Crests; Marks; Border Patterns. Comprehensive bibliography, pp. 285-88.

567 Sanders, Herbert H. **The World of Japanese Ceramics**. New York, Kodansha, 1978. 267p. illus. index. ISBN 087011042X.

Comprehensive survey of the materials and technique of Japanese arts ceramics with emphasis on work produced since the Second World War. Contents: Japanese Potters; Tools and Materials; Forming Process; Decorating Processes; Underglazes, Glazes and Overglaze Decoration; Tea and the Japanese Potter; Technical Information for the Potter. Glossary of technical terms. Many informative plates showing the techniques and materials—including the various colored glazes of Japanese art ceramics. Appendix with chemical analysis of representative wares.

See also the exhibition catalog: *Ceramic Art of Japan; One Hundred Masterpieces from Japanese Collections* (Seattle, Wash., Seattle Art Museum, 1972. 172p. illus. LC 74-189738),

Japanische Keramik: Kunstwerke historischer Epochen und der Gegenwart, by A. Klein (Düsseldorf, Hetjens-Museum, 1979. 229p. illus. index. LC 80-493780), *Japanese Ceramics*, by R. Moes (Brooklyn, N.Y., Brooklyn Museum of Art, 1979) and the collection catalog: *The Baur Collection, Geneva: Japanese Ceramics*, by J. Ayers (Geneva, Collections Baur, 1982. 150p. illus. ISBN 288031004X), *Japanese Ceramics from the Morse Collection* by H. Seizo (Boston, Museum of Fine Arts, 1980).

568 **Famous Ceramics of Japan**. Tokyo and New York, Kodansha; distributed by Harper & Row, v 1- , 1981-.
    v. 1: *Nabeshima* by M. Imaisumi (1981) ISBN 08700114158
    v. 2: *Agano & Takatori* by G. Kozuru (1981) ISBN 0870114519
    v. 3, v. 4: *Folk Kilns I, II*, 2 vs. by H. Mizuo and K. Okamura (1981) ISBN 0870114166
        & 0870114778
    v. 5: *Kakiemon* by T. Nagatake (1981) ISBN 0870114786
    v. 6: *Imari* by T. Nagatake (1982) ISBN 0870114875
    v. 7: *Tokoname* by Y. Sawada (1982) ISBN 0870115022
    v. 8: *Oribe* by T. Murayama (1982) ISBN 08700115308
    v. 9: *Karatsu* by T. Nakazato (1983) ISBN 0870115510
    v.10: *Kiseto and Setoguro* by S. Furukawa (1983) ISBN 0870115677
    v.11: *Hagi* by R. Kawano (1983) ISBN 0870115944
    v.12: *Shino* by R. Kuroda (1984) ISBN 0870116312
Important series of brief monographs on various types and manufactories of Japanese ceramics. Excellent color plates with descriptive notes.

569 Stitt, Irene. **Japanese Ceramics of the Last 100 Years**. New York, Crown, 1974. 256p. illus. index. ISBN 0517516640.
    Comprehensive survey of Japanese ceramics produced since 1868 with emphasis on the commercial wares made for export to the West. Includes folk ceramics. Contents: Introduction; Domestic Wares and Export Wares in Traditional Styles (Arita, Imari, Kyoto, Kutani and Satmsum wares, etc.,); For Export Only (Nippon wares, Noritake wares, Occupied Japan wares, etc.). Glossary. Bibliography, pp. 207-08, lists titles in English.
    See also the exhibition catalog: *Erde und Feuer: traditionelle japanische Keramik der Gegenwart*, by G. Jahn and A. Petersen-Brandhorst (Munich, Hirmer; Deutsches Museum, 1984. 273p. illus. ISBN 3777437808).

Korea

570 Akaboshi, Goro, and Heiichiro Nkamaru. **Five Centuries of Korean Ceramics: Pottery and Porcelain of the Yi Dynasty**. New York, Weatherhill, 1975. 159p. illus. ISBN 0834815141.
    Pictorial survey of Korean ceramics of the Yi dynasty, 1392-1910. Contents: 1, Korean Pottery before the Yi Dynasty; 2, The Culture of Yi-Dynasty Korea; 3, Yi-Dynasty Pottery in Japan; 4, Yi Wares and the Tea Ceremony; 5, Rediscovery of Yi-Dynasty Pottery: Soetsu Yanagi; 6, Classification and Terminology of Yi-Dynasty Pottery. Chapters have brief but informative text followed by plates. Detailed commentaries on the plates at the end. No bibliography.

571 Covell, Jon E. H. C. **The World of Korean Ceramics**. Seoul, Korea, Si-sa Yong-o-sa; Honolulu, Hawaii, Dae-Won-Sa, 1986. 128p. illus. index. ISBN 0872960226.
    Popular survey of Korean ceramics from prehistoric times to the present with emphasis on the relationship between ceramics and Korean society. Particularly useful chapter on modern Korean ceramic production. Bibliography, p. 124 has separate list of major exhibition catalogs.

572   Gompertz, G. St. G. M. **Korean Celadon and Other Wares of the Koryo Period**. London, Faber and Faber, 1963. 102p. illus. index. LC 66-3383.

Authoritative survey of Korean ceramics of the Koryo Period: A.D. 918-1392. Contents: Introduction and Aesthetic Approach; 1, The History of Koryo Wares; 2, Early Kyro Celadons and Their Relationship with Yüeh Ware; 3, Hsü Ching's Record of Koryo Ceramic Wares; 4, The Koryo Celadon Glaze; 5, Celadon Roof-Tiles for a Royal Pavilion; 6, Koryo Inlaid Celadon Ware; 7, Black Koryo Ware; 8, Koryo White Porcelain; 9, Cyclical Year-marks, Iron Painting, Gilding and Copper-red. Chronological summary, p. xvii. Appendix with note and map on Koryo kiln sites. Comprehensive, classified bibliography, pp. 91-96. For sequel *see* (573).

573   Gompertz, G. St. G. M. **Korean Pottery and Porcelain of the Yi Period**. New York, Praeger, 1968. 106p. illus. index. LC 68-22780r84.

Authoritative history of Korean ceramics of the Yi Period: 1392-1910 based on documentary research and visits to kiln sites. Contents: 1, The History of Yi Wares; 2, Punch'ong ware; 3, Early Yi Bowls; 4, White Porcelain; 5, Painted Decoration in Underglaze Iron and Copper; 6, Blue-and-White Porcelain; 7, Black-glazed and Other Wares; 8, The Potter's Craft and Pottery Wares Which Have Been Identified from Their Special Names, Uses and Shapes. Chronological summary, pp. xix-xx. Comprehensive, classified bibliography, pp. 95-97.

574   Honey, William B. **Corean Pottery**. London, Faber and Faber, 1957. 19p. (text), 96p. (illus.). index. LC 48-9606.

Popular survey of Korean ceramics from earliest time to 1910 written by a leading British connoisseur. Illustrated with museum pieces. Basic bibliography, p. 17.

575   Kim, Chae-won, and G. M. Gompertz, eds. **The Ceramic Art of Korea**. New York, Yoseloff, 1961. 222p. illus. LC 61-19038.

Pictorial survey of Korean ceramics from 57 B.C. to 1920. A brief introduction which outlines the history of Korean ceramics is followed by an excellent collection of plates with descriptive notes.

See also the exhibition catalog: *The Art of the Korean Pottery: Silla Koryo, Y.* (New York, Asia Society, 1968. 131p. illus.)

Southeast Asia

576   Brown, Roxanna M. **The Ceramics of South-east Asia. Their Dating and Identification**. 2d ed. Singapore, New York, Oxford Univ. Press, 1988. 129p. (text), 63p. (plates). index. ISBN 0195888898.

Important survey of the ceramics of Southeast Asia from the ninth century to the early twentieth century designed as a guide for collectors. Contents: 1, Vietnamese Ceramics; 2, The Go-sanh Kilns; 3, Khmer Wares; 4, The Sukhotai and Sawankhalok Kilns; 5, The Northern Kilns. Bibliography of books and periodical articles in all languages, pp. 113-124.

577   Shaw, J. C. **Northern Thai Ceramics**. Kula Lumpur, New York, Oxford Univ. Press, 1981. 270p. illus. index. ISBN 0195804759.

Survey of Thai ceramics of the late middle ages with emphasis on production in Sukothai and Lanna. Contents: 1, Of Thailand and Thais; 2, Sukothai and Ayuthya; 3, Northern Thailand or Lana; 4, The Coming of Potters to Sukothai; 5, The Kilns of Kalong; 6, Sankampaeng Ceramics; 7, The Potters of Paan; 8, Other Northern Kilns; 9, Haripunchai Pottery, 10, Usage; 11, The Potters of Lanna. Chronological table, glossary, and bibliography of basic works, pp. 94-98.

578   Spinks, Charles Nelson. **The Ceramic Wares of Siam**. 3rd ed. Bangkok, Siam Society, 1978. 211p. illus. LC 80-911395.

Important history of ceramics in Thailand during the fourteenth through sixteenth centuries. Contents: I, The Coming of the Thai; II, Sukhodaya's Relationship with the Yuan Court; III, Chinese Ceramic Influences at Sukhodaya; IV, The Chaliang Monochromes; V, The Rise of the Svargaloka Kilns; VI, Svargaloka Painted Wares; VIII, Svargaloka Figurines; IX, The Ceramic Export Trade; X, Unconventional Uses of Ceramics; XI, The Later Kilns of Northern Siam; XII, The Rediscovery of Thai Ceramics; XIII, Thai Kiln Construction and Potting Methods; XIV, A Simplified Grammar of Thai Ceramic Forms. Comprehensive bibliography, pp. 183-202.

See also the exhibition catalog: *Southeast Asia Ceramics: Ninth through Seventeenth Centuries*, by D. F. Frasché (New York, Asia Society—John Weatherhill, 1976. 144p. illus.).

PORCELAIN

General Histories and Handbooks

579   Atterbury, Paul, ed. **The History of Porcelain**. London, Orbis, 1982. 256p. illus. index. ISBN 0856133442.

Well-illustrated survey of the history of porcelain worldwide. The work of a team of British experts. Very useful plates with original pattern books juxtaposed with actual pieces of porcelain. Contents: 1, The Origins of Porcelain by R. Gray; 2, Quing Dynasty Porcelain for the Domestic Market by G. Lang; 3, Korean and Annamese Porcelain by G. Lang; 4, Japanese Porcelain by O. Impey; 5, China and the West by G. Godden; 6, The Development of European Porcelain by P. Raffo; 7, Eighteenth-Century English Porcelain by M. Schleger; 8, The Development of Bone China by T. Lockett; 9, Porcelain of the Victorian Era by P. Atterbury; 10, Popular Nineteenth-Century Porcelain by N. Riley; 11, Art Porcelain by J. Hawkins; 12, Twentieth-Century Studio Porcelain by L. Levine; 13, Industrial Porcelain by J. Welbourne; Appendix: Forgeries and Deceptions by D. Battie. Glossary of terms. Bibliography, pp. 244-47, is classified by chapter and emphasizes books in English.

580   Burton, William. **A General History of Porcelain...** London and New York, Cassell, 1921. 2v. illus. index. LC 22-14500.

An old, standard history but still a useful overview. Volume one covers the porcelain of China, Japan, Korea, Persia, Italy, Spain, Portugal and France. Volume two covers the porcelain of the minor factories of France and the porcelain of England, Germany, Norway and Sweden and other European countries. Basic bibliography, v. 2. pp. 207-208.

581   Dillon, Edward. **Porcelain...** London, Methuen, 1904. 419p. illus. index. LC 06-14772.

An old, standard history of world porcelain. Still valuable as a work of connoisseurship, especially in regard to materials, and for the comprehensive bibliography of the older literature, pp. xxvi-xxxiii. Contents: I, Introductory and Scientific; II, Materials: Mixing, Fashioning, and Firing; III, Glazes; IV, Decoration by Means of Colour; V, The Porcelain of China. Introductory—Classification—The Sung Dynasty—the Mongol or Yuan Dynasty; VI, The Porcelain of China. The Ming Dynasty; VII, The Porcelain of China. The Manchu of Tsing Dynasty; VIII, The Porcelain of China. Marks; IX, The Porcelain of China. King-te-chen and the Père D'Entrecolles; X, The Porcelain of China. Forms and Uses—Descriptions of the Various Wares; XI, The Porcelain of Korea and of the Indo-Chinese Peninsula; XII, The Porcelain of Japan; XIII, From East to West; XIV, The First Attempts at Imitation in Europe; XV, The Hard-Paste Porcelain of Germany. Böttger and the Porcelain of Meissen; XVI, The Hard-Paste Porcelain of Germany. Vienna—Berlin—Höchst—Fürstenburg—Frankenthal—Fulda—Strassburg. The Hard and Soft

Pastes of Switzerland, Hungary, Holland, Sweden, Denmark, and Russia; XVII. The Soft-paste Porcelain of France. Saint-Cloud—Lille—Chantilly—Mennecy—Paris—Vincennes—Sèvres; XVIII, The Hard-paste Porcelain of Sèvres and Paris; XIX, The Soft and Hybrid Porcedlain of Italy and Spain; XX, English Porcelain. The Soft-paste Porcelain of Chelsea and Bow; XXI, English Porcelain. The Soft Paste of Derby, Worcester, Caughley, Coalport, Swansea, Nantgarw, Lowestoft, Liverpool, Pinxton, Rockingham, Church Gresley, Spode, and Belleek; XXII, English Porcelain. The Hard Paste of Plymouth and Bristol; XXIII, Contemporary European Porcelain. Appendices with essay and brief list of marks.

582   Schmidt, Robert. **Porcelain as an Art and Mirror of Fashion...** London, Harrap, 1932. 336p. illus. index. LC 33-573.
　　　General history of porcelain, both Oriental and European, from its beginnings to the early nineteenth century. Emphasis is on the relationship between porcelain and the overall culture at the time, with particular attention given to the relationship between porcelain decoration and figurines and the style of contemporary painting and other arts. Chapter on table decorations and altar sets is still a useful overview of the great porcelain services of the eighteenth century. Bibliography, pp. 311-317, is an annotated list of books in English.

American Porcelain (U.S. and Canada)

583   Frelinghuysen, Alice Cooney. **American Porcelain, 1770-1920.** New York, Metropolitan Museum of Art, Harry Abrams, 1989. 320p. illus. index. ISBN 0810911787.
　　　Comprehensive history of porcelain made in America from 1770 to 1920 published in conjunction with an exhibition of the same name at the Metropolitan Museum of Art. A 70-page introductory essay sketches development. Catalog of the 121 pieces shown in the exhibition provides full descriptive entries, excellent color plates and references to the specialized literature. General and comprehensive, but unclassified bibliography, pp. 303-309. Further bibliography in the notes to the introduction. Although restricted to the pieces exhibited, the catalog is by far the most informative and comprehensive treatment of the aesthetic high points of American porcelain.

584   Schwartz, Marvin D., and Richard Wolfe. **A History of American Art Porcelain.** New York, Renaissance Editions, 1967. 93p. illus. LC 66-30197.
　　　Popular survey of art porcelain, i.e., figurines and presentation pieces from the eighteenth century to the 1960s. Bibliography, p. 93, lists major books with brief annotations.

European Porcelain

General Works

585   Charles, Rollo. **Continental Porcelain of the Eighteenth Century.** London, and Toronto, Benn, 1964. 198p. illus. index. LC 65-1933.
　　　Introductory survey of the golden age of European porcelain by a well-known connoisseur still valuable for it balanced treatment of technique and style, regional and national styles and role of major personalities. Contents: 1, Porcelain in the Eighteenth Century; 2, The Material; 3, Making and Decorating Porcelain; 4, The Porcelain Trade; 5, Porcelain Figures; 6, Meissen: Boettger; 7, Meissen: Herold; 8, Meissen: Kaendler; 9, Meissen: 1750 Onwards; 10, Independent Decorators; 11, Vienna; 12, Höchst; 13, Fürstenberg; 14, Berlin; 15, Nymphenburg; 16, Franken-thal; 17, Ludwigsburg; 18, Other Factories in Germany; 19, Switzerland; 20, Rouen and St. Cloud; 21, Chantilly; 22, Mennecy; 23, Vincennes-Sèvres: History; 24, Vincennes-Sèvres: Productions; 25, Tournai; 26, Other French Factories; 27, Holland; 28, Scandinavia and Russia; 29, Medici

Porcelain; 30, Venice and North Italy; 31, Doccia; 32, Capodimonte, Madrid, Naples. General bibliography, pp. 187-88.

586   Danckert, Ludwig. **Manuel de la porcelaine européene. Le vade-mecum de l'amateur et du professionnel.** 2d ed. Paris, Office du Livre, 1973. 448p. illus. LC 75-528579.

   First published as: *Handbuch des Europäischen Porzellans* (Munich, Prestel, 1954). Comprehensive dictionary of European porcelain manufactories and their marks. Includes potters, modelers, decorators, and terms relating to the technique and decoration of porcelain. A particularly useful feature is the alphabetical index of marks with facsimiles. The single most comprehensive of the pocket-size dictionaries of European porcelain.

587   Ducret, Siegfried. **Porzellan der europäischen Manufacturen im 18.** Jahrhundert. Zurich, Silva, 1971. 136p. illus. index. LC 72-302796.

   Survey of continental porcelain of the eighteenth century written by a leading authority. Arrangement is by countries subdivided by centers. Illustrated with major museum pieces.

588   Fay-Hallé, Antionette and Barbara Mundt. **Porcelain of the Nineteenth Century.** London, Trefoil Books, 1983. 302p. illus. index. ISBN 0862940273.

   Comprehensive, scholarly history of European porcelain during the nineteenth century. Well-illustrated with many color and black and white plates of major museum pieces. Contents: I, The Techniques of Nineteenth-Century Porcelain; II, 1800-1830: The Triumph of Painting; III, 1830-1850: From Art Institute to Industrial Manufactory; IV, 1850-1880: Historicism; V, Eclecticism and Art Nouveau; Conclusion. The five sections are further divided by countries. Catalog of porcelain marks, map of factories, classified bibliography of books and periodical articles, pp. 290-95.

589   Jedding, Herman. **Europäisches Porzellan.** Munich, Keyser, 1971. 194p. (text), 316p. (plates) index. ISBN 3874050076.

   Comprehensive handbook/history of European porcelain. First volume covering the period from the beginnings to 1800; the only one published. Introductory essay sketching the history of porcelain in the period, followed by a dictionary of major artists, manufactories and terms and concludes with a large corpus of plates with detailed descriptive captions. Facsimiles of marks are provided in the dictionary sections. Appendices with list of major collections of porcelain with bibliographical references to their catalogs—a most valuable feature—and a summary of auction prices between 1965 and 1970. Classified bibliography at the conclusion.

590   Meister, Peter W. and Horst Reber. **European Porcelain of the 18th Century.** Ithaca, N.Y., Cornell Univ. P., 1983. 320p. illus. index. ISBN 0801414431. LC 81-66539.

   Translation of *Europäisches Porzellan*. Comprehensive, scholarly history of European porcelain during the eighteenth century. Well illustrated with color and black and white plates of museum pieces. Contents: The Term Porcelain and Its Use in the Seventeenth and Eighteenth Centuries; Chinese Porcelain and the West; Manufactories as Artistic Centers; Artists and Artisans; History of Porcelain Style in the Eighteenth Century; Porcelain as an Article of Use in the Eighteenth Century; Iconography of European Porcelain of the Eighteenth Century; Important Customers and Patrons of Porcelain in the Eighteenth Century; Eighteenth Century Porcelain in the Nineteenth and Twentieth Centuries. Bibliographical references in the notes and classified bibliography of books in all languages, pp. 297-304.

591   Olivar-Daydi, Marcel. **La porcelana en Europa desde sus orígines hasta principios del siglo XIX.** Barcelona, Barral, 1952-53. 2v. illus. LC 53-20258.

Comprehensive history of porcelain in Europe from the beginnings to the early nineteenth century. Arrangement is by country subdivided by manufactory. Illustrated with plates of museum pieces with descriptive notes. Bibliographical references in the footnotes. Particularly useful are the chapters on Portuguese and Spanish porcelain.

592 Schnorr von Carolsfeld, Ludwig, and Erich Kollmann. **Porzellan der europaischen Fabriken**. 6th ed. Braunschweig, Klinkhardt & Biermann, 1974. 2v. illus. index. (Bibliothek fur Kunst und Antiquitätenfreunde, Band 3). LC 75-582828.

Comprehensive history/handbook of European porcelain of the eighteenth century with particularly full treatment of the production in the German-speaking countries. Illustrated with museum pieces and pieces in major private collections. Contents: Band 1: Meissen; Wien; Berlin; Fürstenberg; Höchst. Band 2 : Frankenthal; Ludwigsburg; Nymphenburg; Die kleinen deutschen Porzellanfabriken; Böhmen; Hausmaler; Französisches Porzellan; Schweizer Porzellan; Englisches Porzellan; Italienisches und spanisches Porzellan; Holländisches Porzellan; Belgisches Porzellan; Dänisches Porzellan; Schwedisches Porzellan; Russisches Porzellan; Polen; Ungarn. Bibliographical references in the footnotes and at the end of both volumes. A standard handbook designed for museums and advanced private collectors.

593 Hofmann, Friedrich H. **Das Porzellan der europäischen Manufakturen im XVIII Jahrhundert; eine Kunst-und Kulturegeschichte**. Berlin, Propylaen, 1932. 537p. illus. index. (Propyläen Kunstgeschichte, Supplement-und Sonderbände, I(6)). LC 85-0255.

Comprehensive, authoritative history of European porcelain from its beginnings to the present. First published in 1932 as a supplement volume in the original Propyläen Kunstgeschichte. Contents: Vorwort; Das chinesische Porzellan und die ersten Nachahmungen in Europa: Die Erfindung des Porzellans in Dresden; Dar Arkanum und die Arkanisten; Die Manufakturen und ihre wirtschaftliche Entwicklung; Technische Grundlagen und Organisation des Fabrikbetriebes: Die Künstler: Modelleure und Maler; Vorbilder und Einflüsse; Verkaufsmethoden, Reklame, Markenwesen; Motive der Porzellanplastik: Formen: Geschirr, Geräte, Galanterien; Dekor und Staffierung; Angewandte Porzellankunst; Vom Empire zum Art déco; Die Porzellankunst des Empire: Vom Biedermeier bis zur neueren Zeit: 1830-1930; Technische Voraussetzungen, Die Manufakturen, Stilentwicklungen in der neueren Porzellankunst. Text followed by large corpus of excellent plates with full, descriptive notes including bibliographical references. Concise dictionary of marks. Comprehensive, classified bibliography, pp. 353-360.

594 Wynter, Harriet. **An Introduction to European Porcelain**. New York, Crowell, 1972. 255p. illus. index. ISBN 851401279.

General survey of European porcelain for the collector with emphasis on the social background of the use of porcelain. Geographical arrangement with concise repertory of major factories and their marks at the end of each chapter. Chapter on copies, forgeries and fakes, and classified bibliography, pp. 244-47.

Belgium

595 Delplace de Formanoir, Lucien. **Considerations su les porcelains de Tournai 1750-1830**. Paris, Tournai, Casterman, 1970. 282p. illus. LC 72-308825.

Comprehensive history/handbook of porcelain produced in Tournai from the 1750s to the early twentieth century. Includes porcelain sculpture. Contents: I, Les Prémices; II, La Production; III, La Léthagie; IV, La Révélation; V, Commentaires à propos de quelques réalisations de la manufacture: a, La source des décors, b, Copies de Porcelaine de Chine, c, Productions de J. Duvivier, d., Service de table à quadrillages, e, Service aux oiseaux de Buffon, f, Décor des prix

de tir; VI, Observations diverses; VII, Conclusion; Produits catalogués; Documents et renseigne-
ments divers. Produits catalogués contains plates of 156 pieces with descriptive captions. Bibliographical footnotes.

See also Soil de Moriamé, Eugéne J. *La manufacture imperiale et royale de porcelaine de
Tournay.* Tournai, Casterman, 1937. 382p. illus. LC AC3927 and Backer, J. de, *La porcelaine de
Tournai: le camieu bleu.* Tournai, J. de Backer, 1983. 246p. illus. LC 84-121986.

France

Dictionaries

596 Grollier, Charles de. **Manuel de l'amateur de porcelaines, manufactures françaises,
suivi du répertoire alphabétique et systématique de toutes les marques connues.** Paris, A.
Picard, 1922. 296p. illus.

Comprehensive dictionary of French porcelain marks, arranged alphabetically by initial
letter and systematically by device. General bibliography, pp. xvii-xviii. A standard dictionary of
French porcelain marks.

597 Tardy (firm). **Les Porcelaines françaises...** Paris, Tardy, 1967. 839p. illus. LC 68-85450.

Pocket-sized handbook of French porcelain from the beginnings to the twentieth century.
Arrangement is by place. Entries give concise history of the manufactory and facsimiles of marks.
Fully indexed. List of museums with porcelain collections.

General Histories and Handbooks

598 Chavagnac, Xavier R. M., and Gaston A. Grollier. **Histoire des manufactures françaises
de porcelaine...** Paris, Picard, 1906. 966. illus. index. LC 24-1712.

Old, standard history of French porcelain from the beginnings in soft paste during the
seventeenth century to the end of the nineteenth century. Still unmatched for the breadth of
coverage. Arrangement is chronological subdivided by place and/or manufactory. The larger
manufactories are further subdivided by periods. Facsimiles of marks are given throughout the
texts and in a repertory at the end of the work. Extensive references to documents, often with long
extracts. The few plates illustrate plans and view of manufactories. Extensive bibliographical
footnotes. Remains an indispensable work because of the documentary material and history of
marks and signatures.

599 Frégnac, Claude, ed. **Les porcelainiers du XVIIIe siècle français.** Paris, Hachette, 1964.
333p. illus.

In the series: "Collection Connaissances des arts "Grands artisans d'autrefois."
Well-illustrated survey of French eighteenth-century porcelain with essays on the major
manufactories by various French experts. Contents: La manufacture de Rouen et les débuts de la
porcelaine française by R. Weigert; La manufactures de Saint-Cloud by R. Weigert; La manufactures de Chantilly by P. Chapus; La manufactures de Mennecy by G. Poisson; La manufacture de
Vincennes puis de Sèvres by G. Poisson; La manufacture de Vincennes puis Sèvres by P. Chapus;
Les manufactures de Strasbourg et de Niderviller by J. Fischer; Les manufactures de Limoges et
Paris by J. Giacomotti; Répertoire des principales manufactures de porcelaine française avec leurs
marques. Brief bibliography, p. 334.

600 Honey, William B. **French Porcelain of the 18th Century.** 2d. ed. London, Faber and
Faber, 1972. 79p. (text), 104p. (illus.) index. LC 72-181111r86.

In the series: "Faber Monographs on Pottery and Porcelain." Survey of eighteenth-century French porcelain with emphasis on the early soft-paste wares. Contents: Introduction; Rouen; Saint-Cloud; Chantilly; Mennecy, Sceaux and Bourg-la-Reine; Vincennes and Sèvres; Other Soft-pastes: Tournay, Arras and Saint-Amand-Les-Eaux; Strasburg and other Factories in the East of France; Paris and Miscellaneous Factories Making Hard-paste; Forgeries; Marks; Miscellany. General bibliography, pp. 70-71.

601   Savage, George. **Seventeenth and Eighteenth Century French Porcelain**. New York, Macmillan, 1960. 243p. illus. index. Reprint: London, New York, Spring Books, 1969. ISBN 600036499X.

Comprehensive history/handbook by a leading British expert. Contents: I, A Survey of French Decorative Art in the Seventeenth and Eighteenth Centuries; II, The Earliest French Porcelain; III, The Chantilly Factory; IV, The Later Soft Porcelain Factories; V, Vincennes-Sèvres; VI, Hard Porcelain in France; VII, The Factories of Alsace and Lorraine; VIII, The Later Paris Factories; IX, Tournai and St. Amand-les-Eaux; X, Forgeries. Appendix with glossary of marks, and letters, artists marks. Bibliography of basic books in English and French, pp. 232-233.

602   Tilmans, Emile. **Porcelaines de France**. Paris, Editions Mondes, 1952. 320p. illus. index. LC 54-36365.

Survey history of French porcelain from the eighteenth century to the present. Divided by manufactory with concise repertory of marks in facsimiles at the end of each chapter. Comprehensive, classified bibliography of the older literature, pp. 310-312.

Major Centers and Manufactories

Limoges

603   Albis, Jean d', and Céleste Romanet. **La porcelaine de Limoges**. Paris, Sous le Vent, 1980. 255p. illus. index. ISBN 2858890250.

Comprehensive history of porcelain produced in Limoges and the nearby region from the eighteenth century to the 1920s. Contents: Introduction: Histoire de l'assiette; Histoire de la porcelaine; Découverte du kaolin à Saint-Yrieix; I, Fabriques du XVIIIe siècle: le comte d'Artois; La Seynie; Une favrique inconnue à Saint-Yrieix; Monnerie; Etienne Baignol; François Alluad, père; II,, Les fabriques limousines du XIXe siècle à nos jours: François Allaud, fils; Pierre Tharaud; Fabriques rurales; Nivet, puis Martin; Aaron & Valin; Ruaud; Henri Ardant, puis R. Laporte; L'Association; Lesme; Jean Pouyant, puis La Céramique; Jouhanneaud & Dubois; William Guérin, puis Guérin Pouyant Elite Ltd; Gibus, Margaine & Redon; Léon Sazerat; Haviland & Co; Théodore Haviland; Charles Field Haviland, puis G.D.A.; H. Jouhanneuad, puis Bernardaud, Vignaud Frères; C. Ahrenfeldt; Al. Lanternier; Labesse; Balleroy Frères; Legrand & Cie; Lafarge & Cie; Robert Haviland & C. Parlon; Société Porcelainière; George Boyer; III, Le Style Limoges: Evolution des technique de fabrication et de décoration depuis le XVIIIe; La lithophanie. Vases et scukptures d'église; Impératifs économiques et évolution du style; 1873, Bracquemond et la révolution du style; G. D. A. et l'Art Nouveau de Bing; Les "grand feu" de Camille Thaaraud; La porcelaine Art Déco. Appendices with documents, glossary, list of marks with facsimiles and general bibliography, pp. 235-37. An important well-illustrated work that fills a need for information about the complex later production of porcelain—the Havilands—in Limoges that was exported worldwide.

604   Gaston, Mary F. **The Collector's Encyclopedia of Limoges Porcelain**. Paducah, Ky., Collector Books, 1980. 190p. illus. index. ISBN 0891451323.

Handbook of the hard paste porcelain produced in Limoges between 1860 and 1930 for export to the United States. Emphasis is on the products of manufactories other than Haviland. Includes factory, decorator, and exporter and importer marks. Marks are arranged alphabetically and illustrated in facsimile. Good collection of color plates featuring many hand painted pieces by nonprofessional decorators. Includes price list of the pieces illustrated. For Haviland porcelain *see*: H. Young, *Grandmother's Haviland*. 2d. ed. Des Moines, Iowa, Wallace-Homstead, 1970. 200p. illus. index.

Paris

605   De Plinval de Guillebon, Regine. **Porcelain de Paris.** Fribourg, Office du Livre, 1972. 350p. illus. index. LC 73-309584.

Comprehensive, well-illustrated history of porcelain made in Paris from 1770 to 1850. Contents: Le XVIIIe siècle: Priviléges, lutte contre la manufacture royale de Sèvres, les manufactures à Paris entre 1770 et 1800, Le financement, Les ouvriers, La technique, La production et l'évolution du style, Les formes, le décor; Les XIXe siècle: Les manufactures et ateliers de décoration entre 1800 et 1850, Le financement, les ouvriers, Les expositions industrielles et commerciales, La technique, La production et l'évolution du style, Les formes, Le décor; Historique des manufactures; Le commerce; Les influences; Répertoire des marques; Sources. Contains 243 plates—tipped-in colour plates and black and white—have detailed, descriptive captions. Bibliography, pp. 337-39, with section of specialized works. Repertory of marks has good illustrations of actual marks as well as the usual facsimiles.

See also the author's *La Porcelaine a Paris sous le Consulat et l'Empire.* (Geneva, Droz, 1985. 239p. illus. index).

Sèvres

606   Brunet, Marcelle, and Tamara Préaud. **Sèvres: des origines á nos jours.** Fribourg, Office du Livre, 1978. 391p. illus. index. LC 80-450399. ISBN 2851090631.

Well-illustrated, concise survey of Sèvres porcelain from the eighteenth century to 1978. Introduction on technique, followed by part, devoted to the three centuries, each with a brief history and a catalog—the most valuable parts of the book—of representative pieces with descriptive notes. Chapter on marks and signatures with facsimiles. Comprehensive bibliography, pp. 347-352, with a full list of exhibition catalogs.

607   Dauterman, Carl C. **Sèvres porcelain: Makers and Marks of the Eighteenth Century.** New York, Metropolitan Museum of Art, 1986. 262p. illus. ISBN 0870992279.

Comprehensive dictionary of artists and artisans at work in or for the porcelain manufactories of Vincennes and Sèvres during the eighteenth century. More than 1,200 names are included, with 200 newly discovered. Based on archival sources and marks on actual pieces. The author has made a particular effort to decipher the significance of the many incised marks that are largely ignored in other guides to Sèvres porcelain.

608   Eriksen, Svend, and Geoffrey de Bellaigue. **Sèvres Porcelain: Vincennes and Sèvres, 1740-1800.** Boston, Faber and Faber, 1987. 379p. illus. index. ISBN 057109354X.

Comprehensive, well-illustrated history of Sèvres porcelain of the eighteenth century. First part covering the early years—to 1759—is written by the Danish expert Svend Eriksen; the second part, covering the period from 1759 to 1800, is written by the French expert Geoffrey de Bellaigue; a third part, dealing with marks and forgeries, is written by Eriksen. Both authors contribute the detailed notes to the plates. Comprehensive bibliography, pp. 359-64, and further bibliography in the notes and at the end of the notes to the plates.

See also Garnier, Edouard, *The Soft Porcelain of Sèvres*. Secaucus, N.J., Chartwell Books, 1988. 37p. (text), 50p. (plates). ISBN 1555213561.

609 Nordenfalk, Carl A. J. **Sèvres et les cinq sens**. Stockholm, Nationalmuseum, 1984. 120p. illus. index. (Nationalmusei skriftserie; n.s. 2). ISBN 9171002642.

Important study of the artistic and iconographic sources of the decoration on several famous Sèvres presentation porcelains featuring allegories of the seven senses. Contents: Première Partie: Arrière-Plans; Second Partie: Le Cadeau de Louis XVIII à la cour d'Espagne; Troisième Partie: La Coupe dite des sebs; Quatrième Partie: D'autres versions; Appendice I: Le programme de Bongniart (Alexandre 1800-1847); Appendice II: Le texte du catalogue de l'exposition de 1826; Appendice II: Les emblèmes décoratifs. Bibliography in the notes.

610 Verlet, Pierre, Serge Grandjean and Marcelle Brunet. **Sèvres**. Paris, Le Prat, 1953. 2v. illus. index. LC 53-39479.

Comprehensive history/handbook on Sèvres porcelain from its beginnings to the twentieth century. Second volume is an important dictionary of marks on Sèvres porcelain. Descriptive notes accompany the plates. Contents: Volume one: Le XVIIIe siècle: I, Histoire, II, La techniques; III, Les oeuvres; IV, Le style; V, Le succès et ses conséquences by P. Verlet; Les XIXe et XXe siècles by S. Grandjean. Volume two: Les marques de Sèvres by M. Brunet. A standard work on Sèvres porcelain.

See also the museum catalogs: *Wallace Collection*, London, England. Sèvres Porcelain. (London, Trustees of the Wallace Collection, 1975, James A. de Rothschild Collection at Waddesdon Manor), *Sèvres Porcelain* by S. Eriksen (Fribourg, Office du Livre, 1968) and the exhibition catalogs: *Musée Céramique, Sèvres. Les Grands services de Sèvres,* (Paris, Editions du Musées Nationaux, 1951), and *The Royal Collections* (Great Britain) Gallery, London, England. *Sèvres Porcelain from the Royal Collection* (London, The Gallery, 1979). For Sèvres porcelain in the twentieth century *see* the exhibition catalog *Porcelaines de Sèvres au XXe siècle.,Musée national de ceramique, Sèvres* (Paris, Ministere de la Culture et de la Communication, 1987. 131p. illus. index. ISBN 2711821153).

Germany, Austria, and Switzerland

611 Honey, William B. **German Porcelain**. London, Faber and Faber, 1947. 56p. illus. LC 47-7173.

In the series: "Faber Monographs on Pottery and Porcelain." Reissued in 1967. Brief survey of German eighteenth-century porcelain with particular emphasis on the aesthetic difference between original pieces and later imitations. Classified bibliography, pp. 49-51.

612 Newman, Michael. **Die deutschen Porzellan-Manufakturen im 18**. Jahrhundert. Braunschweig, Klinkhardt & Biermann, 1977. 2v. illus. (Bibliothek für Kunst- und Antiquitätenfreunde, Band 50). LC 78-359324/r80.

Comprehensive history of the origin of porcelain in Europe and the development of porcelain in the various manufactories in the German-speaking territories during the eighteenth century. Incorporates recent information culled from archives and other documentary sources. Designed for the collector and the historian. Illustrations include many rare pieces and pieces in private collection together with famous works on public view. Contents: Band I: Meissen; Die Hausmaler; Wien; Höchst; Fürstenberg; Berlin. Band II: Neudeck-Nymphenburg; Frankenthal; Ludwigsburg; Ansbach; Kelsterbach; Die rheinischen Manufakturen: Ottweiler, Pfalz-Zweibrücken, Baden-Baden; Fulda; Kassel; Würzburg; Die Thüringer Manufakturen: Gotha, Kloster Veilsdorf, Volkstedt, Wallendorf, Limbach und Grossbreitenbach, Ilmenau, Gera, Rauenstein. Comprehensive, classified bibliographies at end of both volumes.

613 Savage, George. **18th Century German Porcelain**. London, Salisbury Square, 1958. 242p. illus. index. LC 59-232.

Survey history/handbook of German eighteenth-century porcelain arranged by centers with chapter on collecting. List of marks with facsimiles. Bibliography of basic books, pp. 226-27.

614 Schönberger, Arno. **Deutsches Porzellan**. Munich, Prestel, 1949. 36p. (text), 56 plates. LC 50-30461.

Pictorial survey of German porcelain of the eighteen and early nineteenth centuries by a leading authority. Features major museum pieces.

615 Ware, George W. **German and Austrian Porcelain**. New York, Crown, 1963. 244p. illus. index. LC 64-1631.

Popular history/handbook of German and Austrian porcelain from its beginnings to the twentieth century. Contents: I, General History of Porcelain; II, The Production of Porcelain; III, Major Porcelain Factories; IV, Other Porcelain Factories; V, Suggestions for the Amateur. Appendix with a list of auction and collection catalogs and glossary of terms. Selected marks in facsimiles. Classified bibliography of books in English and German, pp. 227-28.

See also the catalog of the *Pauls-Eisenbeiss Collection*, Riehen, Switzerland. *German Porcelain of the 18th Century*, by P. W. Meister (London, Barrie and Jenkins, 1972. 2v. illus. ISBN 0214653463).

Major Centers and Manufactories

Berlin

616 Jarchow, Margarete. **Berliner Porzellan im 20. Jahrhundert**. Berlin Porcelain in the 20th Century. Berlin, Reimer, 1988. 343p. illus. index. ISBN 3496010541.

Comprehensive history of Berlin porcelain of the twentieth century. Text in German and English. Introductory chapter discussing the technology of modern porcelain production is followed by chapters on the manufactory during the Weimar Republic, The Third Reich, times since the Second World War, and the various classes of porcelain objects made in Berlin with a fine collection of plates. Appendices with biographies of artist-designers with bibliographical references, reproductions of the 1930 sales catalog showing dinner service forms (1765-1930), a detailed oeuvre catalog of the products of the Berlin manufactory from 1914 to 1984, and a glossary of marks and signatures with facsimiles. Bibliographical references in the notes.

617 Kollman, Erich. **Berlin Porzellan**. 2d ed. Munich, Klinkhardt & Biermann, 1987. 2v. illus. index. ISBN 3781402649.

Revised by Margarete Jarchow. Comprehensive, scholarly history of the porcelain manufactory at Berlin from its beginnings to the 1930s with extensive use of documentary sources. Band I: text; Band II: plates. Contents of Band I: Versuche der Porzellanherstellung in Preußen; Die "Fabrique de Porcelaine de Berlin" von Johann Ernst Gotzkowsky; Die Königliche Porzellanmanufaktur; Die Staatliche Porzellan-Manufaktur Berlins nach 1918; Plastik; Tafelgeschirre; Kaffee- Tee und Schokoladengeschirre; Vasen; Möbel; Toilettegeräte, Galantierien und anderes; Malerei; Das technische Porzellan; Nachwort; Marken; Markentafeln. Appendices with extracts from documents supported by illustrations of actual pages. Plates in Band II are grouped according to the arrangement of the text in Band I. Excellent quality black and white and color plates with detailed, descriptive notes. The standard work on Berlin porcelain

618 Schade, Günter. **Berlin Porzellan**. 2d ed. Leipzig, Koehler & Amelang, 1986. 228p. illus. ISBN 3733800052.

History of porcelain manufacturing in Berlin from its beginnings in 1751 to 1970. Contents: 1, Zur Geschichte des Porzellans; 2, Zur Technologie der Porzellanherstellung; 3, Erste Versuche der Porzellanherstellung in Brandenburg-Preussen am Anfang des 18. Jahrhunderts; 4, Die erste Berliner Porzellanmanufaktur Wilhelm Kaspar Wegelys (1751-1757); 5, Die Porzellanmanufaktur Johann Ernst Gotzkowskis (1761-1763); 6, Die Witschaftliche und technische Entwicklung der Königlichen Porzellanmanufaktur im 18. und 19. Jahrhundert; 7, Die Entwicklung der Geschirrformen im 18. Jahrhundert; 8, Die Entwicklung der Porzellangeschirre vom Klassizismus bis zum Biedermeier; 9, Die Entwicklung des figürlichen Porzellans bis zum Klassizismus; 10, Historismus und Jugendstil. Bibliographical references in the notes, general bibliography, pp. 215-16.

Frankenthal

619 Heusser, Emil. **Porzellan aus Straßburg und Frankenthal im 18.** Jahrhundert. Landau in der Pfalz, PVA, 1988. 328p. illus. index. ISBN 3876291461. First published in 1922 (Landau, Pfälzischen Verlagsanstalt).

Comprehensive, authoritative history of porcelain made at Strasbourg and Frankenthal during the eighteenth century with extensive use of archival and other documentary sources. Contents: I, Die Hannongsche Porzellanerzeugung in Straßburg und in Frankenthal; II, Die Künstler und Handwerker unter den Hannongs 1751 bis 1762 und ihre Erzeugnisse; III, Die Hannongschen Fabrikmarken; IV, Die Unterscheidung der Hannongschen Porzellane von Straßburg und von Frankenthal; Der kurfürstliche Betrieb unter Direktor Bergdoll 1762 bis 1775; Der kurfürstliche Betrieb 1775 bis 1793 unter Direktor Feylner; VII, Die Porzellanfabrik während der Kriegsereignisse 1794 bis 1797 und von da bis zur Auslösung; VIII, Geschichte der Porzellanformen von Straßburg und Frankenthal und das Formenverzeichnis. Chart with facsimiles of marks with notes. General bibliography, p. 299, specialized literature in the footnotes.

See also Friedrich H. Hofmann *Frankenthaler Porzellan* (2v. Munich, 1911), and the exhibition catalogs: *Frankenthaler Porzellan* by R. Tressel and K. Schultz (Frankenthal, Neues Rathaus, 1955.) and *Frankenthaler Porzellan* by S. Fauck (Ludwigshafen, Stadtsmuseum, 1970).

Fürstenberg

620 Ducret, Siegfried. **Fürstenberger Porzellan.** 3v. illus. index. Braunschweig, Klinkhardt & Biermann, 1965.

Comprehensive, scholarly history of Furstenberg porcelain of the second half of the eighteenth century. Extensive use of documentary evidence. Contents: v. 1: Geschichte der Fabrik has lists of artists and craftsmen in chronological order, and artists and modelers listed by their specialties, general index of all artists and artisans working at Fürstenberg between 1746-1800, analysis of the archives and general bibliography, p. 309); v. 2. Geschirre (with chapters on the forms, painted decoration and design of Fürstenberg porcelain with corpus of 343 plates); v. 3, Figures (covers the major modelers of figures and has section on auction sales and index of marks and signs). The standard work on Fürstenberg porcelain and a paradigm for the study of all great centers of porcelain production.

621 Wolff-Metternich, Beatrix von. **Fürstenberg Porzellan.** Braunschweig, Klinkhardt & Biermann, 1976. 94p. illus. index. LC 77-467130.

Concise survey of Furstenberg porcelain of the eighteenth and early nineteenth centuries.

See also the exhibition catalog: *Fürstenberger Porzellan, Tradition und Gegenwart,* by E. Klinge (Düsseldorf, Hetjens-Museum, 1970).

Höchst

622 **Die Kurmainzische Porzellanmanufaktur Höchst.** Munich, Klinkhardt & Biermann, 1986- ISBN 3781402444 (vol. 2).

Comprehensive, scholarly history of the ceramic production of Höchst during the eighteenth and early nineteenth centuries. To date Band II: Fayencen by H. Reber (334p. illus. index) has appeared. Contents: Die Höchster Figuren—Ikonographie und Stilgeschichte; Formen und Farbigkeit der Höchster Fayencen; Die Gegenstände der Höchster Fayencemalerei; Die Höchster Blumenmaler; Nachbemerkung zur Chronologie der Höchster Fayencen. Comprehensive bibliography, pp. 324-25, and further bibliography in the footnotes.

Johann Peter Melchoir, 1742-1825

623 Oppenheim, Michel. **Johann Peter Melchior als Modellmeister in Höchst.** Frankfurt am Main, Woeller, 1957. 135p. illus. LC A58-3285.

Scholarly monograph on the work of Johann Peter Melchior as modeler of porcelain figurines at the factory of Höchst between 1767 and 1779. Emphasis is on distinguishing Melchior's style from that of other modelers. Contents: Johann Peter Melchior 1747-1767; Melchiors Tätigkewit in Höchst 1767-1779; Die von Melchior signierten Porzellane; Urkundlich gesicherte Modelle Melchiors; Ausformungen in Porzellann nach Originalen von Melchior; Zuweisungen an Melchior; Andere Modellmeister in Höchst. Summary in English and French. Bibliographical references in the notes.

See also the exhibition catalog: *Höchster Porzellan aus der Sammlung des Historischen Museums* by L. Döry (Frankfurt am Main, Historisches Museum, 1963).

Ludwigsburg

624 Lahnstein, Peter. **Das Ludwigsburger Porzellan und seine Zeit.** 2d. ed. Stuttgart, Berlin, Cologne, Mainz, Kohlhammer, 1980. 143p. illus. ISBN 3170043188.

Authoritative history of the porcelain produced in Ludwigsburg during the eighteenth century with emphasis on its place in the general culture of the Grand Duchy of Wurttemberg. Contents: Kulturgeschichtliche Betrachtungen; Landesgeschichtliche Betrachtungen; Die Ludwigsburger Porzellan-Manufaktur. Selected bibliography, pp. 140-141, and further bibliography in the notes.

See also the exhibition catalog: *Ausstellung Alt-Ludwigsburger Porzellan.* Stuttgart, Württembergisches Landesmuseum. (Stuttgart, Druck Thurmhaus-Druckerei, 1959. 184p. illus.).

Meissen

625 Adam, Len and Yvonne Adams. **Meissen Portrait Figures.** London, Barrie & Jenkins, 1987. 224p. illus. index. ISBN 0712615474.

Well-illustrated survey of Meissen figurines manufactured during the eighteenth century. Contents: Court Life; Country Life; Religion; Mythology; Street Traders; Artisans; People from Distant Lands; Satire; Italian Comedy. Appendices with list of modelers and other artists, list of museums with important collections of Meissen figurines. Basic bibliography, p. 222.

626 Albiker, Karl. **Die Meissener Porzellantiere im 18. Jahrhundert.** Berlin, Deutscher Verein für Kunstwissenschaft, 1935. 125p. illus. (Forschungen zur deutschen Kusntgeschichte, Bd. 10). LC AC38-2704.

Scholarly history of the animal figurines made at Meissen during the eighteenth century with important corpus of 330 plates. Contents: Einführung: Das Tier in der Neuzeit, Dresden,

Porzellan; Meissner Porzellantierplastik: Kirchner, Kirchner und Kändler; Klassizismus. Appendix with essay on dating. Bibliography in the footnotes.

627 Charleston, Robert J. **Meissen and Other European Porcelain**. Fribourg, Office du Livre, 1971. 316p. illus. index. LC 72-192633r905.

Scholarly catalog of the James de Rothschild Collection at Waddesdon Manor which includes 63 pieces of eighteenth century Meissen, 3 pieces of eighteenth century Frankenthal porcelain, a pair of Doccia cups on shell, 4 sets of "Girl in a Swing" Chelsea porcelain, 32 pieces of Oriental porcelain. The latter are catalogued by John Ayers. Bibliographical references in the entries and footnotes.

628 Goder, Willi, et al. **Johann Friedrich Böttger: die Erfindung des europäischen Porzellans**. Stuttgart, Kohlhammer, 1982. 359p. illus. index. ISBN 3170073621.

Comprehensive study of Johann Friedrich Böttger and his discovery of true porcelain at Meissen. Well illustrated. The work of a team of German experts. Contents: Das Kurfürstentum Sachsen and der Wende vom 17. zum 18. Jahrhundert; Das ostasiatische Porzellan und die Bemühungen um seine Nacherfindung in Europa; Johann Friedrich Böttger—Stationen seines Lebens; Die technische Entwicklung von Böttgersteinzeug und Böttgerporzellan; Die Anfänge der Porzellanmanufaktur Meissen; "Das rothe und das weisse Porcellain." General bibliography, pp. 316-18, and specialized literature in the footnotes.

See also the exhibition catalog: *Johann Friedrich Böttger zum 300, Geburtstag: Meissen Frühzeit und Gegenwart. Staatliche Kunstsammlung Dresden.* (Dresden, Staaliche Kunstsammlung, 1982. 331p. illus.).

629 Honey, William B. **Dresden China: an Introduction to the Study of Meissen Porcelain**. New York, Tudor Pub. Co., 1946. 219p. illus. LC 46-6202.

Authoritative introduction to Dresden, i.e., Meissen, porcelain of the eighteenth century by a leading British connoisseur. Contents: I, Introduction; II, Böttger's Stoneware and Porcelain; III, Meissen under Augustus the Strong: 1720-33; IV, Meissen under Count Brühl: 1733-56; V, Meissen during the Seven Years War: Frederick the Great: 1756-63; VI, Later Productions: 1763 onwards; VII, Meissen Porcelain Painted Outside the Factory ('Hausmalerei'). Repertory of major marks and select bibliography with introductory note, pp. 175-76.

630 Jedding, Hermann. **Meissener Porzellan des 18. Jahrhunderts**. Munich. Keyser, 1979. 184p. illus. index. ISBN 3874051161.

Comprehensive handbook of Meissen porcelain of the eighteenth century. Introductory essays discuss the discovery of porcelain under Böttger and the development of style and decoration from Chinese style to the German floral patterns. These are followed by a list of craftsman, artisans and artists active in Meissen and a analysis of the marks of Meissen eighteenth century wares. The bulk of the work is a large collection of plates with detailed commentary in both captions and text on the same page as the plates. Special section on Hausmaler pieces. Glossary, appendices with inventories and list of prices from the eighteenth century and a list of prices paid for Meissen porcelain at international auction houses from 1877 to 1978. A very successful collector's guide and handbook.

631 Jedding, Hermann. **Meissener Porzellan des 19. und 20**. Jahrhunderts, 1800-1933. Munich, Keyser, 1981. 190p. illus. ISBN 3874051331.

Continuation of the author's work on the eighteenth century (630) using the same format. Introductory essays are titled: Marcolini 1774-1814: Klassizismus/Empire; Kühn 184-1870:Biedermeier/Historismus; Die Tehniker 1870-1912: Gründerzeit/ Jugendstil; Pfeiffer 1913-1933: Kunst der zwanziger Jahre; Organisatoren—Techniker—Künstler 1800-1933; Die Meissener

Kurschwerter seit 1800. These are followed by a collection of plates with commentary. Appendix with auction prices from 1979 and 1980. Bibliography, pp. 189-190.

632 Just, Johannes. **Meissener Jugendstilporzellan. Meissen Porcelain of the Art Nouveau Period**. London, Orbis, 1985. 164p. illus. index. ISBN 085613712X.

Well-illustrated survey of Meissen porcelain produced in the Art Nouveau Style (Jugendstil). Covers figurines, presentation pieces, and table ware. Contents: A Neglected Chapter in the History of Meissen Porcelain; The Meissen Porcelain Manufactory on the Threshold of a New Century; New Developments in Ceramic Technology; The Conflict over Artistic Concept; The Manufactory and the Artists; Shapes and Decorations; The Historical Significance of Meissen Jugendstil Porcelain. List of artists with brief biographies. General bibliography, p. 164.

633 Morely-Fletcher, Hugo. **Antique Porcelain in Color: Meissen**. Garden City, N.Y., Doubleday, 1971. 119p. illus. LC 74-134440.

Concise history of Meissen porcelain in the eighteenth and nineteenth centuries with good color plates of museum pieces with descriptive captions.

634 Röntgen, Robert E. **The Book of Meissen**. Exton, PA, Schiffer, 1984. 333p. illus. index. ISBN 0887400140.

Collector's history and handbook of Meissen porcelain with emphasis on wares produced since 1814. Contents: Glossary; Meissen Today; History of the Manufactory; Red Stoneware; Sculptural Art; Tableware; Painting and Decorations; Medals and Coins, Lithopanes, Tiles, Knick-knack, Technical Porcelain; Outside Painting, Imitations and Copies of Meissen Porcelain; Onion Patter; Marks on Meissen Porcelain; Imitations of Meissen Marks; Dresden China; Technology. Useful information and plates on imitations and reproductions including an extensive section on marks. Bibliography, pp. 328-330.

635 Walcha, Otto. **Meissen Porcelain**. New York, Putnam, 1981. 516p. illus. index. ISBN 399117490.

Comprehensive history of porcelain produced at Meissen from the beginnings under Böttger to immediate post-World War II years with emphasis on documentary sources for the history of the factory. Written by a former curator of the archives in Meissen.

Contents: 1, The Invention of European Porcelain; 2, The Albrechtsburg Manufactory and Porcelain in the Böttger Period; 3, The First Manufactory Reforms: 1719; 4, Johann Gregorius Höroldt—The Early Day; 5, The Development of Painting under Höroldt and His Fellow Craftsmen; 6, Porcelain Design from Irminger to Kaendler; 7, The Year of Reform; 8, The Great Period of Meissen; 9, The Domination of Form; 10, The Manufactory between the Silesian Wars; 11, The Manufactory during the Seven Year's War; 12, The Manufactory after the State Reform of 1763; 13, The Influence of Meissen Porcelain in the Eighteenth Century; 14, Classicism and the Meissen ; 15, The Manufactory in the First Half of the Nineteenth Century; 16, The Manufactory Moves to New Premises; 17, The Meissen State Porcelain Manufactory, 1918-1945; 18, The Meissen Porcelain Manufactory in the Postwar Years; 19, The VEB Staatliche Porzellan-Manufaktur Meissen. Corpus of 259 plates, chronology of Meissen porcelain manufactory, chronological survey of forms and decorations of Meissen ware, with illustrations, outline of marks, glossary of terms, and comprehensive, classified bibliography, pp. 504-509. Extensive section on catalogues. A standard history of Meissen.

636 Zimmermann, Ernst. **Die Erfindung und Frühzeit des Meissener Porzellan: ein Beitrag zur Geschichte der deutschen Keramik**. Berlin, De Gruyter, 1978. 328p. illus. index. LC 78-379493.

First published in 1908. Pioneering work on discovery of true, i.e., hard paste, porcelain at Meissen. Contents: I, Die ersten Erfindungsversuche; II, Die Erfindung; III, Die Meissner Manufaktur als Steinzeugfabrik (1709-1713); IV, Das Böttgersteinzeug; V, Die Meissnner Manufaktur als Porzellanfabrik (1713-1719); VI, Das Böttgerporzellan; VII, Fortsetzung des Böttgerschen Erbes. Extensive bibliography in the notes.

See also the exhibition catalogs: *Meissener Porzellan, Ausstellung im Bayerischen National-almuseum, München*, by R. Rückert (Munich, Hirmer, 1966. 208p. illus.), *Meissener Porzellan des 18 Jahrhunderts in Hamburger Privatbesitz*, by H. Jedding. Museum für Kunst und Gewerbe, Hamburg (Hamburg, Museum für Kunst und Gewerbe, 1982. 252p. illus.).

Johann Gregorius Höroldt, 1696-1775

637 Seyffarth, Richard. **Johann Gregorius Höroldt. Vom Porzellanmaler zum 1. Arkanisten der Könglichen Porzellan-Manufaktur Meißen**. Dresden, VEB, 1981. 292p. illus. LC 83-120488.

Scholarly history of the Meissen manufactory under the leadership of Johann Gregorius Höroldt, 1720-1731, with extensive use documentary evidence. Contents: Die Höroldtperiode; Die Goldmalerei in Meißen; Die Höroldtmalerei; Christoph Conrad Hunger; Carl Heinrich Keil; Graf Hoym—Leamire und das Ende der Höroldtperiode; Höroldt—Nitzschner; Höroldt—Kändler; Höroldt als Arkanist; Das Testament Höroldts. Chronologically arranged bibliography, pp. 287-91.

Johann Joachim Kaendler, 1706-1775

638 Gröger, Helmuth. **Johann Joachim Kaendler der Meister des Porzellans**. Dresden, Wolfgang Jess Verlag, 1956. 215p. illus. index.

Scholarly monograph on Kaendler as designer of porcelain sculptor. Contents: I, Die Aufgabe; II, Herkunft und Vorbereitung; III, Der starke Anfang: Das erste Jahrhrzent Kaendlers in Meissen 1731 bis 1741; IV, Die hohe Zeit: 1742 bis 1763; V, Der Großbildhauer; VI, Jahre der künstlerischen Beschränkung: 1764 bis 1775; VII, Werkstatt und Verwaltung; VIII, Ausklang; IX, Zeittafel der Haupt- oder Leitwerke; X, Abbildungen; XI, Quellen.

Nymphenburg

639 Hofmann, Friedrich H. **Geschichte der bayerischen Porzellan-Manufactur Nymphenburg**. Leipzig, Hiersemann, 1923. 3v. illus. index. LC 42-48759.

Comprehensive, scholarly history of Nymphenburg porcelain beginning in 1748 to the end of state control in 1862. Contents: Buch I, Wirtschaftsgeschichte und Organization: I, Die kurfürstliche Fabrik in Neudeck, II, Die Fabrik in Nymphenburg während des 18. Jahrhunderts, III, Die Fabrik als "Kunstanstalt" im 19. Jahrhundert; Buch II: Werkbetrieb und Personal: I, Technische Einrichtungen und Werkbetrieb, II, Künstler und Arbeiter bei der "Gestaltung"; III, Die Malerstube; Buch III, Produktion und Verschleiss: I, Die plastische Produktion, II, Geschirr und Geräte, III, Der Verschleiss. Appendix with table of marks. Bibliography in the footnotes. The standard work on Nymphenburg porcelain.

640 Woeckel, Gerhard P. **Die Tierplastik der Nymphenburger Porzellan-Manufaktur: Bestandskatalog 1905-1920**. Munich, Berlin, Deutschen Kunstverlag, 1978. 342p. illus. index. ISBN 3422006966.

Comprehensive, scholarly history and handbook of the porcelain and majolica animal figurines produced at the Nymphenburg factory between 1905 and 1920. Introduction discusses the place of Nymphenburg animal porcelains in the broader context of German porcelain production in the early twentieth century and as a facet of the Art Nouveau style. Catalog examines in detail all 165 animal figures recorded in the factory registers between 1905 and 1920. Arranged by artist, the entries begin with a biography of the sculptor-modeler, catalogs detail each animal figure with bibliographical references. All pieces are illustrated, some in stunning color.

Franz Anton Bustelli, 1723-1763

641   Rückert, Rainer. **Franz Anton Bustelli**. Munich, Hirmer, 1963. 35p. illus. LC 66-80959.

Well-illustrated, forty-four plate introduction to the porcelain sculpture of Bustelli written by a leading expert on German porcelain of the eighteenth century. Brief list of basic books, p. 35.

See also Hofmann, Friedrich H., *Franz Anton Bustelli: der Meister-Modelleur von Nymphenburg, 1754 bis 1763*. Munich, Residenzmuseum, 1965. 47p. illus. LC 85-853690.

Switzerland

642   Pelichet, Edgar. **Merveilleuse porcelaine de Nyon**. Lausanne, Éditions du Grand-Pont, 1973. 225p. illus. index. LC 75-510969.

Comprehensive, scholarly, well-illustrated history of the porcelain of Noyon of the eighteenth and early nineteenth centuries with extensive use of documentary information. Contents: Découvrir la Porcelaine de Noyon: 1, Les hommes; 2, L'entreprise; 3, L'art. Connaitre la Porcelain de Noyon: 4, Dates, gens et chiffres; 5,La fabrique; 6, Les formes; 7, Les décors. Appendices with extracts from documents and comprehensive bibliography.

Vienna

643   Hayward, John F. **Viennese Porcelain of the Du Paquier Period**. London, Rockliff, 1952. 218p. illus. LC 52-3546.

Scholarly study of the porcelain made in the Vienna factory under the direction of Claude Innocent Du Paquier from 1718 to 1744, distinguished by a high aesthetic sensitivity to the relationship between the porcelain and contemporary art and architecture. Contents: I, Vienna and the Viennese Porcelain in the Early Eighteenth Century; 2, Contemporary Sources of Information; 3, The Foundation and History of the Factory; 4, The First Period of the Factory, 1718-25; 5, The Middle Period, 1725-35; 6, Chinoiseries and Decoration in the Oriental Manner, 1725-35; 7, The Development of Laub- und Bandelwerk and of "Deutsche Blumen," 1725-35; 8, Landscape and Figure Subject Decoration, 1725-35; 9, The Schwarzlot-Decorated Services; 10, The Last Period, 1735-44; 11, The Artists of the Du Paquier Factory; 12, The Outside Decorators (Hausmaler); 13, Figure Sculpture; 14, The Recognition of Du Paquier Porcelain; 15, The Sources of Du Paquier Ornament. Appendices with extracts from documents. Bibliographical references in the notes.

See also the museum catalog: *Wiener Porzellan aus der Manufaktur du Paquiers (1718-1744)*. Vienna, Österreichisches Museum für Angewandte Kunst. (Vienna, Verlag des Museums, 1952. 18p. (text), 56 plates).

644   Neuwirth, Waltrad. **Wiener Porzellan**. Vienna, Waltraud Neuwirth, 1979. 612p. illus. index, ISBN 390028080.

Comprehensive collector's handbook of Viennese porcelain from 1744 to the twentieth century. Chapter on marks is in German, English and French. Contents: Einleitung: Kunstfälschung, Kunstverfälschung, Kunstbetrug; Kennzeichen auf Wiener Porzellan (Marks and Signs on Viennese Porcelain, Marques et signes de la Porcelaine Viennoise); Porzellanfiguren; Tafelgeschirr und-gerät; Mechanische Vervielfältigungsmethoden; Technologie: Analysen; Originalrezepte der Wiener Porzellanmanufaktur; Mitarbeiter-Kennzeichen der Wiener Porzellanmanu-faktur. Bibliographical references in the text via abbreviations listed, pp. 12-16.

645   Neuwirth, Waltraud. **Wiener Keramik: Historismus, Jugendstil, Art Déco**. Braunschweig, Klinkhardt & Biermann, 1974. 508p. illus. index. LC 75-527341.
    Comprehensive history/handbook of Viennese porcelain of the late nineteenth and early twentieth centuries (to 1938). Contents: Die Situation der Wiener Keramik im späten 19. Jahrhundert; Die Wiener Manufaktur Friedrich Goldscheider; Wiener Keramik 1898-1938. The bulk of the book is filled by a very important dictionary of Viennese firms, modelers, designers and decorators. Repertory of marks and signatures in both facsimiles and photographic reproductions. Comprehensive, classified bibliography, pp. 491-93.

Würzburg

646   Ducret, Siegfried. **Das Würzburger Porzellan des 18**. Jahrhunderts, 1775-1780. Braunschweig, Klinkhardt & Biermann, 1968. 186p. illus. index. LC 68-111879.
    Scholarly examination of Wurzburg porcelain which was produced in the short span of five years during the eighteenth century. Introductory chapter discusses the history of the manufactory in light of archival material and illustrates actual documents. In a chapter on the persons associated with Wurzburg porcelain, the author has recovered the outlines of the identity of this manufactory that have long been vague. Equally groundbreaking is the chapter on the analysis of the material of Wurzburg ware. Chapters cover various forms of porcelain made at Wurzburg with detailed discussion of the production of figurines. Bibliography in the notes.

Zurich

647   Ducret, Siegfried. **Die Zürcher Porzellanmanufaktur und ihre Erzeignisse im 18. und 19**. Jahrhundert. Zurich, Füssli, 1958-59. 2v. illus. index. LC 59-18810.
    Comprehensive, scholarly history of porcelain manufactory in Zurich during the eighteenth and nineteenth centuries by a leading expert on European porcelain. Combines a rare blend of archival work and connoisseurship. The chapters of volume one cover the foundation of the Zurich factory, the organization, the buildings and other facilities, the raw materials, the personalities and personnel, advertisement, stock books, prices charged between 1769 and 1780, the porcelain lottery of 1775, the famous service made for Cloister Einsiedeln, the liquidation of the factory, the various aspects of the decoration and forms of Zurich porcelain including special attention to the influence of the Swiss painter Salomon Gessner, fakes, marks, dating, the relationship of Zurich porcelain and other contemporary porcelain manufactories, and end with a chapter on Zurich porcelain during the nineteenth century. The second volume is dedicated to figurative porcelain made at Zurich. Chapters include important analysis of the value and purposes of porcelain sculpture in the eighteenth century, the classes of subjects depicted and detailed treatment of the creations of the modelers: J. J. Meyer, Josef Nees, Valentin Sonneschein, J. W. Spengler, and Gabriel Klein, and concludes with chapters on special subjects such as William Tell, dogs, medallions, fakes, marks and an index of forms. Bibliographical references throughout in the notes.

Great Britain

648   Charleston, R. J., ed. **English Porcelain, 1745-1850**. London, Benn, 1965. 183p. illus. index. LC 65-8705.
    Important collection of essays on various types of English porcelain manufactured between 1745 and 1850 written by a team of British experts. Contents: Chelsea by J. V. G. Mallet; Bow

by H. Tait; Derby by A. L. Thorpe; Longton Hall by B. Watney; Worcester by F. A. Barrett; Liverpool by B. Watney; Caughley and Coalport by F. A. Barrett; Lowestoft by G. C. Bolster; Pinxton by A. L. Thorpe; Swansea and Nantgarw by R. Charles; Rockingham by A. A. Eaglestone and T. A. Lockett; Plymouth and Bristol by N. Elphinstone; New Hall (hardpaste) by G. E. A. Grey; New Hall (bone-china) and Other Nineteenth-century Staffordshire Factories: Herculaneum by R. J. Charleston. List of museums and historic houses in Britain and America with good collections of British porcelain. General bibliography, pp. 171-72.

649   Godden, Geoffrey. **British Porcelain: An Illustrated Guide**. New York, Potter, 1974. 456p. illus. LC 73-88984.
    Collector's encyclopedia of British porcelain from the beginnings to the twentieth century. Entries on the major manufactories are arranged alphabetically by place. Particularly useful are the photographs of the backs of plates and bottoms of vessels that show not only marks but also peculiarities of the undersides such as stilt marks, foot rims, etc. Select bibliography, pp. 446-48, is a comprehensive and classified list of major monographs.

650   Godden, Geoffrey. **Eighteenth-century English Porcelain: A Selection from the Godden Reference Collection**. London, New York, Granada, 1985. 426p. illus. index. ISBN 0246126051.
    Handbook of English eighteenth century porcelain written by a major dealer and collector. Arrangement is by factory in chronological order. Three pieces of each type from the author's collection are described and illustrated with the aim of facilitating identification and discerning aesthetic qualities.
    Much of the text is autobiographical including the sections on collecting in general that are added at the end of the work. Most useful are the many illustrations of details of the pieces including the marks on and the form of the bottoms.

651   Savage, George. **18th Century English Porcelain**. London, Salisbury Square, 1952. 435. illus. index. LC 52-1412.
    Survey of English eighteenth-century porcelain with emphasizes tests of authenticity and provenance possible through simple examination of the bodies and glazes of pieces. Throughout the text are the results of scientific analysis from specialized publications. Contents: Part I: A Review of the Art and the Technics of Eighteenth-century Porcelain; Part II: Dramatis Personae: Some Biographies: Nicholas Sprimont of Chelsea; Wlliam Duesbury of Derby; William Littler of Longton Hall; Thomas Frye and the Bow Factory; Dr. John Wall and the Worcester Factory; William Cockworthy of Plymouth; Part III: The Wares of the Porcelain Factories: Chelsea; The Derby Factory; Pinxton; Longton Hall Porcelain; The Bow Factory; Lowestoft; The Bristol Birthplace of Worcester Porcelain; Worcester; Caughley; Liverpool; English True Porcelain. Appendices discuss the composition of the porcelain of Meissen, Sèvres, Tournai, theatre in porcelain, forgeries and fakes, reproduction of the Chelsea catalog of 1756.

652   Watney, Bernard. **English Blue and White Porcelain of the Eighteenth Century**. 2d ed. London, Faber and Faber, 1973. 145p. illus. index. LC 64-54899.
    Survey of English porcelain with blue underglaze decoration directed to the collector. Contents: 1, Cobalt; 2, Bow; 3, Limehouse, Lund's Bristol and Worcester; 4, The First Two Staffordshire China Factories; 6, Derby; 7, Lowestoft; 8, Caughley; 9, Plymouth, Bristol and New Hall. Bibliographical references in the footnotes, general, classified bibliography of books and articles, pp. 138-140.

Major Centers and Manufactories

Belleek

653 Degenhardt, Richard K. Belleek. **The Complete Collector's Guide and Illustrated Reference**. New York, Portfolio Press, 1978. 207p. illus. index. LC 78-72893.

Collector's history and handbook of Belleek pottery and porcelain from the foundation of the factory in 1857 to 1970. Chapter on the production of Parian ware, marks on Belleek and reproduction of the 1904 catalog.

See also An Illustrated Guide to Irish Belleek Parian China. (Los Angeles, E. J. Lease, 1969. 85p. illus. LC 74-12597. Bibliography, p. 207).

Bristol

654 Mackenna, F. Severene. **Champion's Bristol Porcelain**. Leigh-on-Sea, F. Lewis, 1947. 107p. illus. index. LC 48-635.

Concise history of the production of porcelain by Richard Champion in Bristol from the 1760s to his emigration to Virginia in 1784. Chapters on the various types of Champion's porcelain including figurines and biscuit plaques. Contains 116 plates of pieces with descriptive captions. Photographs of 12 marks. Chronological list of books, p. 104.

Davenport

655 Lockett, T. A. **Davenport Pottery and Porcelain 1794-1887**. Rutland, Vt., Tuttle, 1972. 112p. illus. index. ISBN 0804810796.

Concise history and collector's handbook of Davenport pottery and porcelain. Contents: Part One: Family and Firm; Part Two: The Wares: Earthenwares (Cream-coloured, White Stoneware, Canesware, Black basalt, Coloured-body, Transfer Printed, Stone china); Porcelain (Dessert Wares, Teawares, Ornamental Wares—Vases); Marks.

Derby

656 Barrett, Franklin A., and Arthur L. Thorpe. **Derby Porcelain, 1750-1848**. London, Faber and Faber, 1971. 206p. illus. index. LC 78-8894002.

Comprehensive history of Derby porcelain from 1750 to 1848. Contents: 1, Andrew Planché 1750-56; 2, William Duesburg I 1756-69; 3, Chelsea-Derby Period 1770-84: Introduction; 4, Chelsea-Derby Period 1770-84: Figures; 5, Chelsea-Derby 1770-84: Useful Decorative Ware; 6, The Later Figures 1786-1848; 7, Useful and Decorative Wares 1786-1848. Appendices with biographies of persons employed at the factory; factory and workers' marks; list of pattern books; description of physical characteristics and chemical composition; extracts of documents including sales catalogs and articles of agreement; list of groups and single figures; and list of figures attributed to Andrew Planché. Bibliographical references in footnotes, general bibliography, pp. 199-200.

See also P. Bradshaw. *Derby Porcelain Figures, 1750-1848* (London, Faber and Faber, 1990).

657 Twitchett, John, and Betty Bailey. **Royal Crown Derby**. London, Barrie & Jenkins, 1976. 224p. illus. index. ISBN 0214200442.

Comprehensive history of the pottery and porcelain made in Derby from 1848 to 1970 with particular attention to the wares of the Royal Crown Derby Porcelain Company (1890-1970). Chapters on the history of the various firms, techniques and materials used, Désiré Leroy, list of

Derby shapes with numbers, pattern books, figures, biographies of designers, modelers, painters and gilders. List of marks and year ciphers. Brief list of books, p. 218.

Lowestoft

658   Godden, Geoffrey A. **The Illustrated Guide to Lowestoft Porcelain**. New York, Praeger, 1969. 164p. illus. index. LC 77-88897.

Comprehensive collector's handbook of Lowestoft porcelain (the true soft-paste ware made in the East Anglian town of Lowestoft, not the imitation, Chinese export ware). Contents: I, General History and Marks; II, Pre-1770 Blue and White Porcelains; III, Post-1170 Porcelain; IV, The Artist and Work People; V, Dated Lowestoft Porcelains; VI, Lowestoft Forms. Appendices with sales records and discussion of fakes and false attributions. Bibliography with essay, pp. 157-59.

Minton

659   Godden, Geoffrey A. **Minton Pottery and Porcelain of the First Period, 1793-1850**. New York, Praeger, 1968. 168p. illus. index. LC 68-31671.

History of less well-known early phase of Minton pottery based on a study of company records and other documents. Contents: I, General Survey; II, Marks; III, Useful Table-wares; IV, Ornamental Wares; V, Figures; VI, Artists, Designers and Modelers; Appendix I: Accounts of Minton Wares Sold to Richard Egan, Messrs Wedgwoods, and Messrs Chamberlains of Worcester; Appendix II: Summary of Staff, 1831; Appendix III: Copy Letters, 1836-1840. Brief bibliography, p. 164.

Staffordshire

660   Godden, Geoffrey. **Staffordshire Porcelain**. London and New York, Granada, 1983. 593p. illus. index. ISBN 0246114940.

Comprehensive, well-illustrated history/handbook on porcelain made in Staffordshire by various manufactories from 1760 to the present. Contents: 1, Social Conditions and General Styles, a Résumé by R. G. Haggar; 2, Porcelain Comes to the Potteries: pre-1760 Period by A. R. Mountford; 3, The Baddley-Littler Porcelains? c. 1777-c.1785 by G. Godden; 4, James Neale's Porcelains, c. 1783-1790 by G. Godden; 5, New Hall Porcelains (c. 1781-1835) by D. Holgate; 6, The Turner Porcelains, c. 1786-c. 1805 by D. Holgate and G. Godden; 7, Bone China, a General Survey by R. G. Haggar; 8, Spode Porcelains, c. 1797-1833, and the Succeeding Firms by R. Copeland; 9, The Minton Porcelain, 1793 to the Present Day by G. Godden; 10, The Davenport Porcelains, 1794-1887 by T. A. Lockett; 11, Miles Mason's Porcelains, c. 1803-1813, and Continued by His Son by R. G. Haggar; 12, The Ridgway Porcelains, 1808-1856 by G. Godden; 13, The Machin Porcelains, c. 1809-1840 by. P. Miller; 14, Wedgwood Bone China of the First Period, 1812-1829 by J. K. des Fontaines; 15, The 'London'-shape Teawares by P. Miller; 16, Charles Bourne, the Foley Potteries, Fenton, c. 1817-c. 1830 by G. Godden; 17, The Hicks & Meigh Porcelains, c. 1817-1835 by G. Godden; 18, The Hilditch Porcelains, c. 1811-1867 by P. Helm; 19, H & R Daniel of Stoke, c. 1822-1846 by G. Godden; 20, John Yates and the Yates & May Porcelains, c. 1822-1843 by G. Godden; 21, The Samuel Alcock Porcelains, c. 1822-1859 by Dr. Geoffrey and Mrs. Alma Barnes; 22, Staffordshire Porcelain: the Main Developments after 1851 by P. Atterbury; 23, Working and Living Conditions of Nineteenth-Century Potters in Staffordshire by F. Celoria. Appendices with potteries in separate townships, check-list of Staffordshire porcelain manufacturers, design registration system, list of patterns and their numbering system. Comprehensive, classified bibliography with introduction, pp. 246-553. A most valuable collector's handbook.

Swansea

661   Jones, A. E (Jimmy), and Leslie Joseph. **Swansea Porcelain: Shapes and Decoration**. Cambridge, D. Brown, 1988. 274p. illus. index. ISBN 0905928849.

Well-illustrated collector's handbook of Swansea porcelain from the beginnings in 1764 to the closing of the manufactory in 1826. First part gives a survey history of the manufactory; second part profiles biographies of the major artists and designers (William Billingsley, Thomas Baxter, David Evans, Henry Morris, William Pollard, George Beddow, De Junic, James Brindley); the third and fourth parts are illustrated catalogs of pieces grouped by shapes and patterns of decoration. Repertory of marks. Appendices documents plans of the factory and includes a chronology of Cambrian pottery. Bibliography of basic books, pp. 269-70.

662   Nance, Ernest M. **The Pottery & Porcelain of Swansea & Nantgarw**. London, Malvern Wells, Worcs., Batsford, 1942. 579p. illus. index. LC 43-9038.

Comprehensive history of the pottery and porcelain manufactories at Swansea and Nantgarw from the beginnings until 1823. Contents: I, The Early Days of Potting in Swansea; II, The Work of George Hasynes; III, The Partnership of George Haynes and Lewis Weston Dillwin; IV, The Partnership between Lewis Weston Dillwyn and the Veingtons; V, The Cambrian Pottery under T & J Bevington & Company and T. & J. Bevington; VI, The Return of Lewis Weston Dillwyn to the Cambrian Pottery. China Works Surrendered to Dillwyn in 1821 or 1822; VII, Lewis Llewelyn Dillwyn's Period; VIII, Evans & Glasson and D. J. Evans & Company; IX, The Glamorgan Pottery; X, Beginnings of the Manufacture of Porcelain at Nantgarw; XI, The Manufacture of Porcelain at Swansea; XII, The Return of William Billingsley to Nantgarw; XIII, Young's Tenure of the Nantgarw Factory; XIV, Marks. Appendices with biographies of major personalities, discussions of special wares. Comprehensive, classified bibliography, pp. 547-553. The standard work on Swansea and Nantgarw porcelain with extensive use of documentary materials. Plates are some of the earliest to show photographs of marks.

Worcester

663   Barrett, Franklin A. **Worcester Porcelain and Lund's Bristol**. 2d ed. London, Faber and Faber; New York, Pitman, 1966. 92p. illus. LC 66-73450.

In the series: "Faber Monographs on Pottery and Porcelain." Concise survey of Worcester porcelain during the eighteenth century. Contents: 1, Lund's Bristol China Works and the Origins of China Manufacture at Worcester; 2, Worcester—The Early Productions; 3, Worcester After the Chelsea Migration; 4, Black and Other Enamel Printing; 5, Underglaze Blue Decoration; 6, Figures and Kindred Productions; 7, 'Outside Decoration'; 8, The Later Worcester Wares. List of marks with key. Brief bibliography, p. 49, with early exhibition and collection catalogs.

664   Branyon, Lawrence, Neal French, and John Sandon. **Worcester Blue and White Porcelain 1751-1790**. London, Barrie & Jenkins, 1981. 367p. illus. index. ISBN 0091440602.

Comprehensive handbook of porcelain with blue and white underglaze decoration produced in Worcester from 1751 to 1790. Introduction sketching the history and technique of Worcester blue and white porcelain is followed by a comprehensive repertory of pieces arranged by pattern. Entries give the range of dates for the type of piece, degree of rarity, marks and shapes, and concludes with a commentary. Bibliography of books, p. 364.

665   Godden, Geoffrey A. **Caughley and Worcester Porcelain, 1775-1800**. Woodbridge, Suffolk, Antique Collectors' Club, 1981. 336p. illus. index. ISBN 0907462014.

History/handbook of early porcelain made at Caughley and Worcester written by a major dealer and collector. Based in part on archaeological finds from the sites of the two factories.

Contents: I, General History and Marks; II, Caughley Oriental Style Patterns; III, The Fisherman Pattern; IV, European Designs in Underglaze Blue; V, The Chamberlain Trade with Caughley; VI, Designs Other Than Blue and White; VII, Check List of Articles Made at Caughley; VIII, Post-1799 Caughley-Coalport Porcelains; IX, Caughley or Worcester? Appendices with excerpts from documentary sources. Brief list of books, p. 163.

666 Sandon, Henry. **The Illustrated Guide to Worcester Porcelain, 1751-1793**. London, Barrie and Jenkins, 1980. 96p. illus. index. ISBN 0091421101.

Important history/handbook of the earliest phase of porcelain production in Worcester based on the extensive archaeological evidence from excavations at the site of the old factories. Contents: I, Warmstry House—Its History; II, Warmstry House—The Excavation and Production Methods; III, The Ware; IV, Checklist of Worcester Shapes; V, Identifying Worcester—Marks and Fakes. Excellent bibliographical essay, pp. 91-92.

Wedgwood

Bibliography

667 Heilpern, Gisela. **Josiah Wedgwood, Eighteenth-Century English Potter: A Bibliography**. Carbondale, Ill., Southern Illinois Univ. Press, 1967. 66p. (Bibliographic Contributions no. 3).

Comprehensive bibliography of books and periodical articles on Josiah Wedgwood, his life, family, business partners and his work as a maker of pottery and porcelain. Covers literature to circa 1960 and is based largely on the holdings of the library of Southern Illinois University in Carbondale. Contents:I, Works by Josiah Wedgwood; II, Works about Josiah Wedgwood; III, Josiah Wedgwood's Business Partner, Thomas Bentley; His Modelers; His Friends; IV, A Selected Bibliography of General Books on Pottery Containing Material on Josiah Wedgwood and Wedgwood; V, A Selected Bibliography of Periodical Articles about Josiah Wedgwood, Wedgwood Ware, Exhibitions, etc.; VI, A Selected List of Josiah and Sarah Wedgwood's Portraits in Books and Periodicals.

Dictionaries

668 Reilly, Robin and George Savage. **The Dictionary of Wedgwood**. Woodbridge, Eng. Antique Collectors' Club, 1980. 414p. illus. ISBN 0902028855.

Comprehensive dictionary covering all aspects of the products of the Wedgwood manufactory from its beginnings to the present. Entries cover artists, designers, and craftsmen, styles, decoration, subjects, types and forms of Wedgwood ware. Appendices with chronology of Wedgwood, list of marks with facsimiles and family tree of the Wedgwoods. Comprehensive, classified bibliography including sales catalogs, pp. 412-414.

Histories and Handbooks

669 Batkin, Maureen. **Wedgwood Ceramics, 1846-1959**. London, R. Dennis, 1982. 244p. illus. index. ISBN 0903685116.

Comprehensive history of the ceramic ware produced by Wedgwood between 1846 and 1959 using archival and other documentary information. Large collection of illustrations including documents, advertisements, original designs and large plates illustrating sets of wares in particular patterns of styles. Contents: Introduction to Wedgwood in the 19th and 20th Centuries; I, Parian; II, Jasper and Dry Body Wares; III, Majolica; IV, Emile Lessore and his Followers; V, Victorian Art Wares; VI, Victorian Tablewares; VII, Tiles; VIII, John Goodwin and His Influence; IX,

Alfred and Louise Powell; X, Millicent Taplin and Handcraft Painting; XI, Veronese Wares; XII, Victor Skellern and the Development of Freelance Design during the 1930s; XIII, 20th Century Sculpture; XIV, Keith Murray; XV, Commemorative and Advertising Wares; XVI, Norman Wilson. Appendix with repertory of marks with many reproduced by photographs, and dictionary of selected artists, designers, modelers, painters and guilders. Classified bibliography, pp. 242-44, with section on exhibition catalogs.

670   Buten, David. **18th Century Wedgwood: A Guide for Collectors & Connoisseurs**. New York, Methuen, 1980. 192p. illus. index. ISBN 0416005616.
        Well-illustrated handbook for collectors on Wedgwood porcelain produced in the eighteenth century. The most important feature is the 198 plates with detailed descriptive captions. Contents: Chronology; 1, Queen's Ware; 2, Variegated Ware; 3, Pearly Ware; 4, Black Basalt; 5, Jasper; 6, Cane Ware; 7, Rosso Antico. Comprehensive, unclassified bibliography, pp. 186-87.

671   Mankowitz, Wolf. **Wedgwood**. London, Batsford, 1953. 283p. illus. index. LC 54-16484.
        Once-standard handbook for collectors; important for attention given to the earliest products and to the queensware of the founder Josiah Wedgwood. Illustrations include many pages from the catalogs of Wedgwood. Contents: 1, Coloured Glazed Wares, 1754-1764; 2, Cream-coloured Ware, 1760; 3, The White Body, 1773-1796; 5, Dry Bodies, 1776-1810; 6, Bone China, 1812-1822; 7, Emile Lessore, 1858-1875 Repertory of marks in facsimiles and appendix with transcript of the 1779 Wedgwood and Bentley Catalogue. Select bibliography, p. 275.

672   Reilly, Robin. **The Collector's Wedgwood**. Huntington, N.Y., Portfolio Press, 1980. 312p. illus. index. ISBN 0253286107.
        Well-illustrated, concise history/handbook of Wedgwood pottery and porcelain from 1759 to the present, with emphasis on early and later wares in the art ceramics category. Contents: The Wedgwood Story; Wedgwood Wares: I, Earthenware; II, Stoneware; III, Porcelain; How Wedgwood Is Made; Collecting Wedgwood; The Care of Wedgwood. Glossary and general bibliography, p. 312.

673   Reilly, Robin. **Wedgwood. The First Comprehensive History of the World's Greatest Pottery Firm**. 2v. illus. London, Macmillan, 1989. ISBN 0333346491 (vol. 1) ISBN 0333455711 (vol. 2).
        Extraordinary comprehensive history/handbook of Wedgwood china. Contents: Volume One. I, Josiah Wedgwood and His Work: 1, Antecedents and Apprenticeship 1730-1759, 2, The Foundations 1759-1768, 3, The Great Partnership 1768-1780, 4, Last Achievements 1781-1795; II, Wedgwood Ware 1759-1795: 5, Colours and Glazes, 6, Queen's Ware: Creamware and Pearl Ware, 7, Variegated Wares, 8, Terracotta and Other White Compositions, 9, Black Basaltes, 10, Cane, 11, Roos Antico, 12, Jasper. Appendices: A, Josiah Wedgwood's Code; B, Sadler & Green; C, Engine-turning; D, Josiah Wedgwood's 'Price Book of Workmanship'. Volume Two. I, The Successors: 1, The Unwanted Inheritance 1795-1843, 2, Travellers 1809-1842, 3, The Age of Comfort 1844-1895, 4, Taste, Fashion and Design 1795-1910, 5, Years of Resolution 1895-1930; 6, The Last Etruria 1930-1938, 7, A New Age: Barlaston 1939-1967, 8, Epilogue: The Great Expansion 1967-1986. II, Modern Production: 9, The Earthenwares, 10, The Dry Bodies and Other Stonewares, 11, Lustre, 12, Stone China, Bone China and Porcelains. Appendices: A, Production Processes; B, Wedgwood Trademarks; C, The 2 February 1805 Mark; D, The Wedgwoods of Etruria; E, Cameos and Intaglios 1773-1795; F, Medals 1773-1795; G. Portrait Medallions: Antique Subjects; H, Portrait Medallions: Modern Subjects 1771-1967; J, Tablets, Plaques and Medallions 1769-1795; K, Busts 1774-1967; L, Figures 1769-1795. Comprehensive, classified

bibliography, v. 2, pp. 783-790, includes unpublished materials and sales records. Specialized literature in the notes. Standard work on Wedgwood.

See also the museum catalog: *Masterpieces of Wedgwood in the British Museum*, by A. Dawson (Bloomington, Ind., Indiana Univ. Pr., 1984. 160p. illus.ISBN 0253336880).

Italy

674   Ferrari, Oreste. **Porcellane italiane del Settecento**. Milan, Vallardi, 1982. 168p. illus. index. LC 84-192192.

Collector's survey of Italian eighteenth-century porcelain. Contents: Porcellane italiane del Settecento; Le origini—La manifattura medicea; Le manifattura venete: Vezzi, Hewelcke, Cozzi, Le Nove, Este; Le manifattura piemontesi; La manifattura di Doccia; Le manifatture romane; La manifattura Capodimonte; La manifattura di Buen Retiro; La Real Fabbrica di Napoli. One hundred pages of plates with descriptive captions. Classified bibliography, pp. 169-70.

675   Lane, Arthur. **Italian Porcelain with a Note on Buen Retiro**. London, Faber and Faber, 1954. 79p. illus. index. LC 55-19772.

Concise but authoritative survey of Italian porcelain from the late sixteenth century to the early nineteenth century. Contents: 1, The Medici Porcelain (1575-87) and Other Early Experiments; 2, Venice: the Vezzi Factory; 3, Later Venetian Factories; 4, Vinovo (1776-1820) and of the North-western Factories; 5, Doccia; 6, The Bourbon Factories. Classified bibliography, pp. 74-75, and further bibliography in the footnotes.

676   Morazzoni, Giuseppe. **Le porcellaine italiane**. 2nd ed. Milan, Gorlich, 1960. 2v. illus. LC A62-208.

Comprehensive handbook of Italian porcelain from its beginnings in the late sixteenth century to the early nineteenth century. First volume text: Le porcellane de' Medici; Le manifatture venete; Le manifatture del Piemonte; Doccia; Le manifatture romane; Le fabbriche borboniche; Le porcellane lombardi dell'Ottocento. Second volume includes plates of museum pieces and pieces in private collections. Brief, general bibliography with specialized literature in the footnotes. A standard handbook of Italian porcelain.

See also the museum guide book: *Eighteenth-century Italian Porcelain* by Clare Le Corbeiller. (New York, Metropolitian Museum of Art, 1985. 32p. ISBN 0870994212).

Major Centers and Manufactories

Capodimonte

677   Caròla-Perrotti, Angela. **Le Porcellane dei Borbone di Napoli. Capodimonte e real fabbrica Ferdinandea 1743-1806**. Naples, Guida Editori, 1986. 633p. illus. ISBN 8870427897.

Comprehensive, authoritative, well-illustrated handbook of porcelain made in Naples from 1743 to 1806. Catalog of 615 pieces. Contents: Capodimonte: Capodimonte rivisitata; Vita e vicissitudini di un'attività durata un Regno: La Real Manifattura delle Porcellane a Capodimonte; Il salottino de porcellana di Portici: I, Il vasellame, II, Le plastiche. Giuseppe Gricci e la produzione plastica di Capodimonte, III, Tabacchiere e pomi di bastone, IV, La produzione di ogetti di arredo, V, Oggetti problematici, VI, Fortuna delle porcellane di Capodimonte. Real Fabbrica Ferdinandea: Omaggio a Domenico Venuti, Intendente della Real Fabbrica Ferdinandea e procuratore della cultura napoletana: I, Il periodo Perez, II, Dall'arrivo Domenico Venuti al 1790: la grande produzione vascolare, III, La produzione vascolare del decennio 1790-1800, IV, La produzione plastica, V, Galanterie, VI, Gli ultimi anni della direzione Nicolas 1800-1806, VII, Oggetti di arredo, VIII, Sezione didattica. Arte presepiale e dipinti. Comprehensive bibliography, pp. 621-29, and additional references in the catalog entries.

678   Cocchi, Vittore. **Domenico Venuti e le porcellane di Capodimonte**. Cortona, Calosci, 1982. 52p. illus. LC 83-122443.

Survey of the porcelain made at Capodimonte under Domenico Venuti (1742-1814) with particular reference to documentary sources. Bibliographical references in the footnotes.

679   Frothingham, Alice W. **Capodimonte and Buen Retiro Porcelains: Period of Charles II**. New York, Hispanic Society, 1955. 55p. illus. (Hispanic Notes & Monographs: Essays, Studies and Brief Biographies) LC 55-13562. *see* (693).

680   Romano, Elena. **La porcellana di Capodimonte: Storia della Manifattura Borbonica**. Naples, L'Arte Tipograpfia, 1959. 252p. illus. index. LC A60-4657.

Comprehensive, scholarly history of Capodimonte and Naples porcelain from 1743 to 1806. Contents: Parte Prima: La Fabbrica di Capodimonte (1743-1759): I, L'ambiente artistico della Napoli sttecentesca; II, La Real fabbrica di Capodimonte; III, Problemi tecnici della produzione; IV, O modellatori: Giuseppe e Stefano Gricci; V. I pittori: G. Casellie discepoli; VI, Il capolavoro: Il salottino della regina Maria Amalia; Parte Sceconda: La fabbrica di Napoli (1771-1806): I, Il clima storico ed artistico; II, La fabbrica di Napoli; III, Problemi tecnici; IV, Direttori e artefici; V, I pittori; V. Ill modellatori; VII, Il capolavoro: La Caduta dei giganti; Conclusione. Illustrated with museum pieces. Bibliographical notes.

681   Spinosa, Nicola. **Le porcellane di Capodimonte**. Milan, Rusconi, 1983. 190p. illus. LC 84-125149.

Concise history/handbook of Capodimonte porcelain consisting of a brief introductory essay followed by plates of major museum-quality pieces with descriptive notes. Included is the boudoir of Maria Amalia di Sassonia now in the Naples Museo Nazionali. Bibliographical note, pp. 26-27.

682   Stazzi, Francesco. **Capodimonte**. Milan, Görlich, 1972. 344p. illus. index. LC 73-327733.

Comprehensive, history/handbook of porcelain production at Capodimonte during the eighteenth century. Contents: Vicende storiche dell'impressa ceramica; I principali artefici di Capodimonte (Schepers, Caselli, Gricci). Good collection of plates with descriptive captions. Chronological list of books, pp. 209-11.

See also the museum catalog: *Le porcellande dei Borboni di Napoli. Capodimonte e Real Fabbrica Ferdinandea, 1743-1806* by A. Carola-Perrott (Naples, Mus. Archeol. Naz. di Napoli, 1986-87. 629p. illus.).

Doccia

683   Lankheit, Klaus. **Die Modellsammlung der Porzellanmanufaktur Doccia: ein Dokument italienischer Barockplastik**. Munich, Bruckmann, 1982. 240p. illus. index. ISBN 3765418552.

Important scholarly study of the collection of models for figurines in the Doccia factory in the eighteenth century with a translation into German of the inventory of models made circa 1780. Contents: I, Modellsammlung und Inventar der Manufaktur Doccia als Bild- und Schriftquelle zur Kunst des 18. Jahrhunderts: 1, Die Porzellanmanufaktur Doccia; 2, Die Modellsammlung; 3, Die Beschreibung des Inventars; 4, Die Bedeutung des Inventars; II. Das Inventar: 1, Vorbemerkungen zu Edition; 2, Der Wortlaut des Textes mit Erläuterungen. Bibliographical references in the footnotes.

684 Liverani, Giuseppe. **Il Museo delle porcellane di Doccia**. n.p. Società Ceramica Italiana Richard-Ginori, 1967. 266p. illus. LC 70-372293.

History of Doccia porcelain from 1737 to the end of the nineteenth century featuring pieces in the Museo delle Manifattura Ginori in the Villa at Doccia. Brief introductory essays sketching the history of Doccia porcelain with references to documents followed by a good collection of 170 plates with descriptive noted that include bibliographical references. General bibliography, pp. 57-61.

Netherlands

685 Rust, W. J. **Nederlands Porselein**. Amsterdam, De Lange, 1952. 178p. illus. LC A53-4149. Reprinted: Schiedam, Interbooks International, 1978.

Comprehensive history of porcelain manufacturing in the Netherlands from the beginnings in the middle of the eighteenth century until the middle years of the nineteenth century. Contents: I, Vervaardiging van Europees porselein; II, Ontstaan en verbreiding van de porseleinfabricage in Europa; III, Vormen en versieringen van het Europees porselein; IV, Weesper porselein; V, Loosdrtechts porselein; VI, Hasags porselein; VII, Porselein uit Ouder-Amstel; VIII, Nederlands porselein sind 1809. Brief list of books, pp. 167-68. Resumé in French.

686 Schrijver, Elka. **Hollands porselein**. Bussum, Van Dishoeck, 1966. 85p. illus. index. LC 68-93565.

Popular survey of Dutch porcelain of the eighteenth and nineteenth centuries. List of major marks. Basic bibliography, pp. 81-82.

See also Sypesteyn, Catharinus Henri C. A. van. *Het Oud-Hollandsch Porselein* Hilversum, J. W. Ebert, 1933. 77p. illus. index and *English and Dutch Ceramics* (425).

Scandinavia

Denmark

687 Grandjean, Bredo L. **Kongelig dansk porcelain, 1884-1980**. Copenhagen, Gyldendahl, 1983. 230p. illus. ISBN 8700342726.

Concise history of Royal Danish porcelain from 1884 to 1980. Covers both porcelain wares and art ceramics produced by the factory. Contents: Flytningen fra Kobmagergade til Smallegade; Arnold Krogs forste arbejeder; Underglasurmaleriet; Udstillingerne teknik; Signerede arbejder i underglasurteknik o. 1889-1972; Underglasurdekorationsafdelinen for Kurant Kunst; Krystal-glasurer og flydeglasurer; Juliane Marie porcelain; Porcelaesskulptur: Henning, Thylstrup og Malinowski; Gråt porcelaen; Craquelé; Forsogsproduktionen i Kina 1921-22; Dekorationrer i trykteknik; Jernporcelaen; Mat porcelaen; Blanc de Chine; Pourpre de Chine; Andre nedsynkn-ingsfarver; Bordstellenes udvikling. Catalog of works arranged by type. Good collection of plates and dictionary of artists and designers. Bibliography in the notes.

688 Grandjean, Bredo L. **Kongelig dansk porcelain, 1775-1884**. Copenhagen, Thaning & Appel, 1962. 311p. illus. index. Reprinted: Copenhagen, Gyldendal, 1983. LC 84-109952.

Comprehensive history of Royal Danish porcelain from 1775 to 1884 based in part on information in documents. Contents: I, Historie og administration; II, Teknik; III, Kunstnerne og produktionnen; IV, Katalog; V, Porcelanets forhandling; VI, Maerker; VII, Bilag. The catalog list pieces by periods subdivided by type of ware or decoration. Comprehensive, classified bibliography, pp. 301-303, and further bibliography in the notes. The standard work on Danish porcelain.

689 Grandjean, Bredo L., Dyveka Helsted, and Meret C. Bodelsen. **The Royal Copenhagen Porcelain Manufactory 1775-1975**. Copenhagen, The Manufactory, 1976. 134p. illus. ISBN 8798034219.

Published to mark the bicentenary of the factory. Concise survey. Contents: The Royal Factory. The Period 1775-1790 by B. L. Grandjean; Arnold Krog and the Porcelain by D. Helsted; Sèvres-Copenhagen. Crystal Glazes and Stoneware at the Turn of the Century by M. Bodelsen; The Royal Copenhagen Porcelain Manufactory in Pictures (plates illustrating the current operations and products). Bibliographical references in the notes to each chapter.

690 Winstone, H. V. F. **Royal Copenhagen**. London, Stacey International; Atlantic Highlands, N.J., Humanities Press, 1984. 160p. illus. index. ISBN 0905743377.

Well-illustrated survey of Royal Danish porcelain from its beginnings to 1980. Contents: 1, A Royal Heritage; 2, True Porcelain; 3, The Royal Vases; 4, Early On-glaze Enamelled Wares; 5, Flora Danica; 6, Blue and White; 7, Figures; 8, Interregnum; 9, Revival; 10, Crystal Glazes, Stoneware and Art Faience; 11, The Modern Factory. Appendices with list of artists' signatures, recipes for clays, and list of factory marks. Classified bibliography, pp. 155-56, and specialized literature in the footnotes.

See also the exhibition catalog: *200 Years of Royal Copenhagen Porcelain*. Smithsonian Institution, Washington, D.C. (Washington, D.C., The Institution, 1974. 44p. illus. LC 79-311284).

Sweden

691 Dahlbäck-Lutteman, Helena. **Svenskt porslin: Fajans, porslin och flintgods 1700-1900**. Västerås, ICA Bokförlag, 1980. 248p. illus. index. ISBN 9153405757.

Comprehensive history of porcelain, faience, and stoneware made in Sweden between 1700 and 1900. First part covers the history of faience from 1730 to circa 1780; second part porcelain from 1766 to 1788; the third part stoneware from 1770 to 1840; the four part the industrial product of all three wares from 1850 to 1900; the fifth part is a survey of the chief manufactories: Rörstrand, Marieberg, Stralsund; Pålsjö and Växjö; Sölvesborg, Vänge-Gustavsberg; Ulfsunda; Löfnäs; Gustafsberg; Högnäs; Tillinge, Boda and Nittsjö; Malmö. Good selection of plates and photographic reproductions of marks.

692 Hernmarck, Carl. **Marieberg: en lysande representant för svenskt sjuttonhundratal**. Stockholm, Walström & Widstrand, 1946. 253p. illus. index. LC 53-25705.

Comprehensive history of the porcelain of Marieberg during the eighteenth century. Contents: Mariebergsfabrikens tillkomst och utveckling under Ehrenreichs ledning; Marieberg under Pierre Berthevins ledning; Marieberg på Henrik Stens och hans efterföljares tid; Marieberg; Mariebergssignaturer; Fabrikssignaturer frå olika perioder; Målarsignaturer; Drejare- och modellörsignaturer. Appendix with repertory of marks. General bibliography, pp. 232-33, and further bibliography in the notes. The standard work on Marieberg porcelain written by a leading Swedish historian of the applied and decorative arts of the eighteenth century.

Spain and Portugal

693 Frothingham, Alice W. **Capodimonte and Buen Retiro Porcelains**. New York, Hispanic Society of America, 1955. 55p. illus. index. (Hispanic Notes & Monographs; Essays, Studies, and Brief Biographies) LC 55-13562.

Concise history of the porcelain manufactory at Buen Retiro (circa 1740-1808) with emphasis on the transfer of techniques, styles, and artists from the Capodimonte factory near Naples.

694   Valente, Vasco. **Porcelana artistica portuguesa**. Porto, F. Machado, 1949. 111p. illus.

Comprehensive handbook of Portuguese porcelain of the eighteenth and early nineteenth centuries. Contents: I, Fábrica de Massarelos; II, Fábrica de Miragaia; III, Reais Fábrica do Cavaquinho; IV, Fábrica de Santo Antonio do Vale de Piedale; V, Documentos; VI, Relação das estampas. Contains 79 plates with facsimiles of marks.

See also the exhibition catalog: *Portugal and Porcelain*, Metropolitan Museum of Art, New York. (Lisbon, Ministry of Culture in association with Fabrica de Porcelana da Vista Alegre, 1984. 89p. illus.).

Eastern European Countries

695   Meyer, Hans. **Böhmisches Porzellan und Steingut**. Leipzig, K. W. Hiersemann, 1927. 336p. illus.

Comprehensive, scholarly history of porcelain and biscuit ware produced in Bohemia from the mid-eighteenth to the mid-nineteenth century with extensive use of documents. Text emphasizes the various designers and decorators working in the Bohemian manufactories. Contents: Rabensgrün; Schlaggenwald; Klösterle; Prag; Teinitz; Giesshübel; Pirkenhammer; Elbogen; Dallwitz; Altrohlau; Unterchodau; Die übrigen Fabriken; Haus- und Winkelmaler. List of private collections and museums. Bibliographical references in the footnotes. Appendix with facsimiles of principal marks.

696   Poche, Emanuel. **Bohemian Porcelain**. Prague, Artia, n. d. 70p. (text), 160p. (plates). LC 57-2988.

Popular history of Bohemian porcelain from its beginnings to the end of the nineteenth century. Illustrated with museum pieces. Brief list of marks and selected bibliography, p. 71.

697   Lukomsij, Georgii. **Russisches Porzellan 1744-1923**. Berlin, E. Wasmuth, 1924. 24p. illus. LC 26-1500.

Pictorial survey of Russian porcelain featuring selected museum pieces. No bibliography.

698   Ryszard, Stanislaw R. **Porzellan vom Barock zum Empire**. Warsaw, Arkady, 1964. 311p. illus. index.

Comprehensive history of Polish porcelain from the beginnings in the eighteenth century to the early nineteenth century.

699   Rozembergh, A. **Les marques de la porcelaine russe: Periode imperiale**. Paris, Champion, 1926. 31p. (text), 76p. (plates). LC 57-51565.

Handbook of marks on Russian porcelain from 1750 to 1850, with a brief introductory history. Illustrated with museum pieces. No bibliography.

See also the catalog of the Marjorie Merriweather Post Collection: *Russian Porcelains; the Gardner, Iiusupov, Batenin...Factories* by M. C. Ross (Norman, Okla., Univ. of Oklahoma Press, 1968. 427p. illus.) and *Russian Porcelain in the Hermitage Collection* by L. Nikiforova (Leningrad, Aurora, 1973. 24p. 164 plates. LC 75-512699)

See also Csànyi, *Geschichte der ungarnischen Keramik, des Porzellans und ihre Marken* (522).

Oriental Porcelain

700 Garner, Harry. **Oriental Blue and White**. 3d ed. London, Faber and Faber; New York, Praeger, 1970. 86p. illus. index. LC 77-550085.

Authoritative introduction to the history of blue and white porcelains of China, Japan and Korea. Contents: 1, Introduction; 2, Origin of Blue and White; 3, The Late 14th and 15th Centuries; 4, Classical Reigns of the 15th Century; 5, The 16th Century; 6, The End of the Ming Dynasty; 7, The Reign of K'ang Hsi; 8, Yung Cheng and the Subsequent Reigns of the Ch'ing Dynasty; 9, Provincial Chinese Blue and White; 10, Korean Blue and White; 11, Japanese Blue and White; 12, The Dating and Attribution of Oriental Blue and White. Appendix with list of marks. Updated bibliography, pp. 83-84.

China

701 Beurdeley, Michel, and Guy Raindre. **Qing Porcelain: Famille Verte, Famille Rose 1644-1912**. New York, Rizzoli, 1987. 315p. illus. index. ISBN 0847807371.

Comprehensive, authoritative, and well-illustrated history/handbook of Chinese porcelain of the Ch'ing dynasty (1644-1912)with emphasis on the famous Famille verte and Famille rose wares exported to the West. Contains 385 illustrations with descriptive captions. Contents: Classical Qing Porcelain: I, The Reign of the First Qing Emperor, Shunzhi (1644-1661) Transitional Porcelain; II, Jingdezhen and the Manufacture of Porcelain; III, The Reign of Kangxi (1662-1722); IV, Biscuit Wares; V, The Reign of Emperor Yongzheng (1723-1735); VI, The Reign of Emperor Qianlong (1735-1795); VII, So-called Imperial Porcelain and the Guyuexuan Wares; VIII, Monochrome Porcelain; IX, Nineteenth-Century Ceramics; Export Porcelain: X, The Porcelain Trade of the East India Company; XI, Nineteenth-century Export Porcelain for Brazil and the United States; XII, Porcelain for South-east Asia and the Middle East. Provincial Factories: XIII, Blanc-de Chine from Fujian; XIV, Stonewares from Yixing; XV, Stonewares from Guangdong Province. Mounted Porcelain: XVI, Chinese Porcelain Mounted in Gold, Silver and Gilt Bronze. Appendices with advice for collectors, glossary of technical terms, mythology and symbolism, list of emperors, repertory of marks. Select bibliography, pp. 305-06.

702 Feng, Hsien-ming. **Problems Concerning the Development of Chinese Porcelain**. London, Victoria and Albert Museum in association with the Oriental Ceramic Society, 1978. 20p. illus. (Chinese Translations No. 8).

Translation of review of an exhibition of archaeological finds in the People's Republic of China published in Wen-wu in 1973. Important summary of the recent finds and interpretation of their significance for the history of Chinese porcelain, particularly the transition from pottery to porcelain. Serves as a postscript to the author's survey published as Chinese Translations, No. 2.

703 Gompertz, F. St. G. M. **Chinese Celadon Wares**. L2d rev. & exp. ed. Boston, Faber and Faber, 1980. 216p. illus. index. LC 80-670113.

Authoritative introduction to the history of Chinese celadon porcelain. Contents: Introduction; 1, The Origin of Celadon; 2, Yüeh Ware; 3, Some Unidentified Celadons—from T'ang to Sung; 4, Ju and Other Northern Wares; 5, Southern Kuan; 6, Lung-Ch'üan Ware; 7, Celadon of the Yüan and Ming Periods; 8, The Ch'ing Celadons. Bibliography, pp. 69-70.

See also the exhibition catalog: *Ice and Green Clouds: Traditions of Chinese Celadon* by Y. Mino (Bloomington, Ind., Indiana Univ. Press, 1986. 240p. illus. ISBN 0936260165).

704 Jenyns, Soame. **Later Chinese Porcelain: the Ch'ing Dynasty, 1644-1912**. 4th ed. London, Faber and Faber, 1971. 111p. illus. LC 72-190459.

First published in 1951. Important history of Ch'ing porcelain with emphasis on wares made for the domestic market. Contents: i, The Letters of Père d'Entre-colles from Ching-Te Chen; 2, The Period of Transition, 1620-83; 3, The Directorship of T'sang Ying-Hsüan and the Years That Followed, 1683-1726; 4, The Directorship of Nien Hsi-Yao, 1726-36; 5, The Directorship of T'ang Ying (1736-49 or 1755); 7, The Period of Decline, 1749 (or 1653)-1912; 7, The Porcelain of the Provincial Kilns; Appendixes: I, Ku Yüeh Hüan (Ancient Moon Terrace); II, The nien hao. Hall-marks, and Marks of Commendation; III, Ch'ing Dynasty Reign Marks and Dates. General bibliography, pp. 102-03.

See also the museum guide: R. Kerr. *Chinese Ceramics: Porcelain of the Quing Dynasty, 1644-1911.* (London, Victoria and Albert Museum, 1986. 142p. illus. ISBN 0948107170).

705 Lion-Goldschmidt, Daisy. **Ming Porcelain**. New York, Rizzoli, 1978. 291p. illus. index. ISBN 0847801810.

Well-illustrated, authoritative history of porcelain made in China during the Ming dynasty (1368-1644). Contents: I, The Ming Dynasty; II, The Characteristics of Ming Porcelain; III, The General Development of Ming Pottery; IV, The Yüan Dynasty (1279-1368): The Beginnings of the Ming Dynasty; V, The Hsüan-Tê Period and the Mid-Fifteenth Century (1426-87); VI, The Late Fifteenth and Early Sixteenth Centuries (1488-1521); VII, The Period of Chia-Ching (1522-66); VIII, The Last Ming Emperors: The T'ien ch'i (1621-27) and Ch'ung-Chen (c. 1628-44) Periods: The Transitional Period (c. 1630-c. 1680); X, Ming Pottery Other Than Ching-Tê Chên. The plates within the chapters illustrate major museum pieces; collection of small illustrations of secondary pieces end each chapter. All plates and illustrations have descriptive captions. Glossary of technical terms. Comprehensive, classified bibliography, pp. 276-81, includes large section on museum and exhibition catalogs. High quality of the plates matched by that of the text.

706 Williamson, George C. **The Book of Famille Rose**. Rutland, Vt., Tuttle, 1970. 231p. illus. ISBN 0804808805.

Comprehensive history/handbook of Chinese famille rose porcelain designed for the collector. Contents: I, Introductory; II, The Jesuit Letters; III, Books, Catalogues and Articles; IV, Famille Rose Decoration; V, Eggshell Porcelain and Opaque Glass; VI, What Is Meant by Famille Rose; VII, Hints on Classification; VIII, Chinese Taste; IX, Armorial China; X, Chinese Porcelain Decorated in Europe; XI, Figures; XII, Collections and Collectors; XIII, Hints to Collectors; XIV, Bargains. Appendices discuss ormolu mounts on Chinese porcelains, Chinese wall-papers, and resemblance between porcelain and silver. No bibliography.

707 Zimmermann, Ernst. **Chinesisches Porzellan**. Seine Geschichte, Kunst, und Technik. 2d. ed. Leipzig, Klinkhardt & Biermann, 1923. 2v. illus. index. LC 37-12355.

Old, standard history by one of the leading experts in the history of porcelain in the interwar years. Contents: Band I: Text. I, Quellen, Literatur und Bestände; II, Die Ersten Anfänge der chinesischen Keramik; III, Die Zeit der Handynsatie (206 vor bis 220 n. Chr.); IV, Die Zeit der T'angdynastie (618-906); V, Die Zeit der Sungdynastie (960-1279); VI, Die Zeit der Monogolen-herrschaft (1280-1367); VII, Die Porzellanfabrikation von King-Tê Tschên in der Zeit der Mingdynastie (1368-1643); VIII, Die Porzellanfabrikation zu King-Tê Tschên in der Zeit der Ts'ingdynastie (1644-1912); IX, Die übrige Keramik Chinas in der Zeit der Ming- und Ts'ing Dynastie (1368-1912); X, Die Technik des chinesischen Porzellans; XI, Die Datierungsmarken des chinesischen Porzellans von King-Tê Tschên; XII, Verzeichnis der wichtigeren Werke und Arbeiten über die chinesische Keramik (the most comprehensive bibliography of the older literature). Band II: Plates of pieces in chronological order with descriptive notes.

See also the museum catalog: *Kuo li ku kung po wu yüan. Porcelain of the National Palace Museum* (Hong Kong, Cafa, 1961-69. 3v. illus.).

Chinese Export Porcelain

708   Godden, Geoffrey A. **Oriental Export Market Porcelain and Its Influence on European Wares**. London, Granada; Brooklyn Heights, N.Y., Beekman, 1979. 384p. illus. index. ISBN 0246110570.

Comprehensive history/handbook of Oriental export porcelain with chapters on the influence of Oriental wares on European porcelain production. Contents: 1, The East India Company's Porcelain Trade; 2, The 'Private Trade' Imports; 3, The Earl of Elgin, East Indiaman; 4, The Blue and White Porcelains; 5, The Enamelled Wares; 6, The Armorial, Crested and Initialled Wares; 7, The Special Designs and the Figure and Animal Models; 8, Blanc de Chine; 9, The American Market Wares; 10, The Japanese Porcelains; 11, The Influence of Oriental Wares on European Porcelains; 12, European Decorated Oriental Porcelains. Illustrated with pieces in private collections and in the trade. Selected bibliography of books in English, pp. 376-380.

709   Gordon, Elinor. **Collecting Chinese Export Porcelain**. Pittstown, N.J., Main Street Press, 1984. 158p. illus. index. ISBN 0915590506.

Popular survey of Chinese porcelain made specifically for export to the West from the seventeenth century to the early 1800s based on pieces in the author's collection. Good introduction to pieces made for the American market. Contents: I, British and Continental European Armorial Services; II, Floral Decoration; III, Blue and White Decoration; IV, Mythological and Religious Decoration; V, European and Oriental Genre Scenes; VI, Blac de Chine; VII, Animal Forms; VIII, Assorted Forms; IX, "Fitzhugh" Decoration; X, Order of the Society of Cincinnati China; XI, American Ship Designs; XII, American Family Services; XIII, American Eagle Designs. Selected bibliography, pp. 154-55.

See also the author's collected articles from *Antiques: Treasures from the East: Chinese Export Porcelain for the Collector*. Rev. ed. (Pittstown, N.J., Main Street Pr., 1984. 191p. illus. index. ISBN 0915590581).

710   Howard, David S. **Chinese Armorial Porcelain**. London, Faber and Faber, 1974. 1,034p. illus. index. ISBN 0571098118.

Monumental handbook of Chinese porcelain exported to the West with armorial devices between 1695 and 1820. Contents: Introduction; 1, The Honourable East India Company; 2, Canton; 3, The Porcelain and Its Painting; 4, The Armigerous Families; 5, Heraldry and Chinese Painters; 6, Collections and Salesroom; 7, The Classification of Styles; Illustrated Services, Styles A to Y; An Alphabetical List of the Services Not Illustrated. The "Classification of Styles" is a dictionary catalog of the porcelain services with detailed description of the heraldry. Nearly 2,000 are illustrated and an additional 1,000 mentioned. Appendices with supplementary material. A standard reference work.

711   Jorg, C. J. A. **Porcelain and the Dutch China Trade**. The Hague, Nijhoff, 1982. 372p. illus. index. ISBN 9024790913.

Scholarly history of the importation of porcelain from China by the Dutch East India Company based on extensive use of archival sources. Contents: I, The China Trade of the Dutch East India Company: 1, The Seventeenth Century, 2, The Direct Trade, 1729-34, 3, The China Trade under Batavia, 1735-56, 4, The Direct Trade, 1757-95; II, Life and Trade in Canton: 1, Introduction, 2, The Ships, 3, The Factory Building, 4, Daily Life, 5, Relations with Chinese Merchants and Mandarins, 6, Trade and Merchandise; III, The Porcelain Trade of the Dutch East India Company: 1, The Porcelain Trade up to 1729, 2, The Porcelain Trade with China, 1929-95; IV, The Porcelain: 1, Introduction, 2, The Decoration, 3, The Types of Porcelain; Conclusions. Eleven appendices with extracts from various documents, e.g., lists of ships, personnel, inventories, sales records. Comprehensive bibliography, pp. 307-14, and additional bibliography in the notes.

712   Lunsingh Scheurleer, D. F. *Chinese Export Porcelain; chine de commande*. London, Faber and Faber, 1974. 256p. illus. index. LC 74-82704.

Authoritative history and handbook of Chinese porcelain made in the seventeenth through the nineteenth centuries for export to the West. Written by a Dutch expert and emphasis is on the European trade. Good collection of illustrations including details of motifs and marks. Appendix with list of collections in the Netherlands. Comprehensive, classified bibliography, pp. 233-43.

713   Macintosh, Duncan. **Chinese Blue & White Porcelain**. 2d ed. London, Bamboo Pub., 1986. 181p. illus. index. ISBN 1870076001.

First published in 1977. Collector's history/handbook of Chinese blue and white porcelain from the fourteenth century to the nineteenth century with particular reference to export wares. Contents: 1, Origins: The Fourteenth Century; 2, The Classical Period: The Fifteenth Century; 3, Late Ming Wares: The Sixteenth Century; 4, New Developments: The Seventeenth Century; 5, Later Blue and White: The Eighteenth and Nineteenth Centuries; 6, Provincial Ming Wares and Exports to Southeast Asia; 7, Blue and White and the West. Appendices with discussion of manufacturing techniques, glossary with definitions of decorative motifs and marks, and advice for the collector. General bibliography, pp. 175-76, and further bibliography in the notes.

714   Mudge, Jean M. **Chinese Export Porcelain for the American Trade, 1758-1835**. 2d ed. Newark, Del., Univ. of Delaware Pr., 1981. 284p. illus. index. LC 79-4713.

First published in 1963. Comprehensive study of the American-China trade in porcelain with thorough examination of documentary and cataloging the various forms of decoration.

715   Phillips, John G. **China-trade Porcelain; An Account of Its Historical Background, Manufacture, and Decoration, and a Study of the Helena Woolworth McCann Collection**. Cambridge, Mass., Harvard Univ. Press, 1956. 234p. illus. LC 56-11749.

Survey of Chinese export porcelain based on the Helena Woolworth McCann Collection. Bibliography, pp. 222-24.

See also the catalog of the additions to the part of the McCann Collection now in the Metropolitan Museum of Art, New York: *C. Le Corbeiller, China Trade Porcelain: Patterns of Exchange; Additions to the Helena Woolworth McCann Collection* (New York, Metropolitan Museum of Art, 1974. 134p. illus.).

716   Schiffer, Herbert, Peter Schiffer and Nancy Schiffer. **China for America. Export Porcelain of the 18th and 19th Centuries**. Exton, Pa.,   Schiffer, 1980. 223p. illus. index. ISBN 0916838234.

Collector's guide to Chinese porcelain made for export to America between 1780 and 1880. Contents: Early Chinese-American Commerce with Porcelain; Armorial Decorations; Monogrammed Decorations; Eagle Decorations; Masonic and Political Decorations; Marine Decorations; Western Landscape Decorations; Chinese Landscape Decorations; Floral Decorations. Comprehensive bibliography of books and periodical articles in English, pp. 214-17.

See also the exhibition catalogs: *Directly from China: Export Goods for the American Market, 1784-1830*. Salem, MA, Peabody Museum of Salem, 1985. 120p. illus.; *Blue and White: Chinese Porcelain and Its Impact on the Western World*, by J. Carswell (Chicago, David and Alfred Smart Gallery, 1985. 184p. illus. ISBN 093557003) and the collection catalog: *China for the West: Chinese Porcelain & Other Decorative Arts for Export Illustrated from the Mottahedeh Collection*, by D. S. Howard (London, Sotheby Parke Bernet, 1978. 2v. illus. ISBN 0856670359).

Japan [*See also* Ceramics, Japan]

717 Arts, P. L. W. **Japanese Porcelain: A Collector's Guide to General Aspects and Decorative Motifs**. Lochem-Poperinge, 1983. 178p. illus. ISBN 9060870271.

Useful, clearly organized handbook for collectors of Japanese porcelain dating between the middle of the seventeenth century and the beginning of the nineteenth century. First two chapters discuss the history and technique of Japanese porcelain. These are followed by a well-illustrated catalog of the main types of Japanese porcelain: Blue-and-White, Imari, Kakiemon, Kutani, and Nabeshima and a repertory of the decorative motifs found on Japanese porcelain arranged by classes. Appendix with list of marks. General bibliography of 68 titles.

718 Feddersen, Martin. **Japanische Porzellan; ein Brevier**. Braunschweig, Klinkhardt & Biermann, 1960. 48p. illus.

Brief survey of Japanese porcelain from its beginnings in the seventeenth century to the mid-nineteenth century, illustrated with major museum pieces.

719 Jenyns, Soame. **Japanese Porcelain**. London, Faber and Faber, 1965. 351p. illus. LC 65-13447.

Authoritative history of Japanese porcelain by the leading Western expert. Contents: 1, The Export Trade and Its Influence on the Japanese Porcelain Kilns; 2, The Imari and Other Artia Wares; 3, The Early Blue and White Porcelain of Japan; 4, Sakaida Kakiemon and the First Enamelled Porcelain; 5, The Kutani Wares of Kaga and Some Related Kilns; 6, The Porcelain of Nabeshima, Hirado and Some Less Important Factories; 7, Chinese Porcelain Made for the Japanese Market and the Work of Japanese Studio Potters in the Chinese Tradition. Comprehensive bibliography, pp. 321-23. A standard work.

See also the author's: *Japanese Pottery* (London: Faber and Faber, 1971. 380 p. ISBN 0571087094).

720 Schiffer, Nancy N. **Japanese Porcelain, 1800-1950**. West Chester, Pa., Schiffer Pub., 1986. 295p. illus. index. ISBN 0887400744.

Collector's handbook to Japanese porcelain with emphasis on the late nineteenth and early twentieth centuries. Contents: Japanese Political History and the West; History of Porcelain in Japan; Arita and Imari; Hirado; Kakiemon; Nabeshima; Kutani; Satsuma; Kyoto and Kyoto-Satsuma; Seto and Nagoya. Basic bibliography, pp. 289-91.

See also the museum catalog: *Early Japanese Porcelain: Arita Porcelain in the Dresden Collection*, by F. Reichel (London, Orbis, 1981. 156p. illus. ISBN 0856133922) and the exhibition catalogs: *Japanische Porzellan der Edo-Zeit*. (Düsseldorf, Hetjens-Museum, Deutsches Keramikmuseum, 1983); *Two Hundred Years of Japanese Porcelain* (Kansas City, William Rockhill Nelson Gallery of Art, 1970), *The Burghley Porcelains: an Exhibit from the Burghley House Collection Based on the 1688 Inventory and 1690 Devonshire Schedule*. ed. by A. Munroe and N. N. Noble (New York, Japan Society, 1986. 284p. illus. ISBN 0913304247), *Porcelain for Palaces: the Fashion for Japan in Europe, 1650-1750*, by J. Ayers et al (London, Ceramic Society, 1990. 328p. illus. ISBN 0903421240).

Particular Types and Manufactories

Kutani

721 Nakagawa, Sensaku. **Kutani Ware**. New York, Kodansha International, 1979. 181p. illus. index. ISBN 0870113224.

In the series: "Japanese Arts Library." Well-illustrated survey of the Kutani ceramic wares from the 1660s to the end of the nineteenth century. Based in part on archeological and archival information. Contents: 1, Old Kutani: The Sites of the Kilns, The Dates of Production, The Men Responsible, Types of Vessels, Types of Body and Overglaze, Types of Ware Excavated, The Decorations, Patterns on Recently Excavated Fragments, Inscriptions, Future Research; 2, Kutani Wares: The Kasugayama Kiln, The Minzan Kiln, The Wakasugi Kiln, The Ino Kiln, The Yoshidaya Kiln, Aoya Gen'emon, The Miyamotoya Kiln, The Sano Kiln, The Matsuyama Kiln, The Rendaiji Kiln, The Eiraku Kiln, Kutani Shoza, The Post-Restoration Kutani. Glossary, maps, and annotated bibliography, pp. 171-75.Van

Nippon and Noritake

722   Patten, Joan F. **The Collector's Encyclopedia of Nippon Porcelain.** Paducah, Ky., Collector Books, 1979. 319 p. illus. index. ISBN 08914553083.

Collector's handbook of Nippon chinaware made for export to the United States between the two World Wars. Especially valuable for the numerous illustrations of pieces together with their marks and reproductions of advertisements and catalogs. For chinaware made by the Noritake company *see* the author's *Collector's Encyclopedia of Noritake.* (Paducah, Ky., Collector Books, 1984. 197p. illus. index. ISBN 0891452443).

POTTERY, FAIENCE, MAJOLICA, STONEWARE

General Histories and Handbooks

723   Bergesen, Victoria. **Majolica: British, Continental and American Wares 1851-1915.** London, Barrie & Jenkins, 1989. 224p. illus. index. ISBN 071262077X.

Comprehensive history of European and American majolica from 1851 to 1915. Includes color and glazed ceramic decoration on furniture and interiors. Contents: 1, Introduction; 2, Minton Majolica; 3, Wedgwood Majolica; 4, Other Major British Majolica Manufacturers; 5, American Majolica; 6, Continental Majolica; 7, Majolica Tiles and Architectural Ceramics; 8, Collecting and Identification; Appendix A, Minor British Majolica Manufacturers; B, Minor American Majolica Manufacturers; C, Designers, Modelers and Decorators of British Majolica; D, List of Shapes and Pattern Numbers: Minton, Wedgwood, George Jones, Copeland, Griffen, Smith & Co.; E, Annotated bibliography.

724   Caiger-Smith, Alan. **Tin—Glaze Pottery in Europe and the Islamic World. The Tradition of 1000 Years in Maiolica, Faience and Delftware.** London, Faber and Faber, 1973. 128p. illus. index. ISBN 0571093493.

Comprehensive history of tin-glazed pottery, i.e., faience, in the Islamic world and Europe from the ninth century to the end of the eighteenth century with emphasis on the technical aspects written by a potter. Contents: 1, Mesopotamia; 2, Egypt; 3, Persia; 4, Moorish Spain; 5, Hispano-Moresque Pottery; 6, Italian Maiolica; 7, The Spread of Maiolica; 8, French Faience; 9, The Netherlands; 10, Central Europe; 11, The British Isles; 12, Faience of the Eighteenth Century; 13, Tin Glaze since 1800; 14, Methods and Men. Appendices with chemical analysis of clay bodies and glazes, many of theme historical. General bibliography, pp. 226-228.

725   Caiger-Smith, Alan. **Lustre Pottery: Technique, Tradition and Innovation in Islam and the Western World.** London and Boston, Faber and Faber, 1985. 246p. illus. index. ISBN 0571135072.

Comprehensive history of ceramics decorated with reduced-pigment lustre which were particularly common in early Islamic pottery, and of Spanish and Italian majolica written by a potter. Contents: 1, Irag: The First Lustred Pottery; 2, Early Figurative Lustre of Iraq; 3, Egyptian Lustre of the Fatimid Period; 4, Syrian Lustre; 5, Persian Lustre: Seljuk, Il-Khanid, Safavid; 6, Moorish Lustre of Andulucía; 7, Hispano-Moresque Lustre; 8, Lustre in Italy: Deruta and Gubbio; 9, Rival; 10, Post-revival; 11, Alchemy and Symbol; 12, The Technique of Reduced-Pigment Lustre; 13, Old Technical Methods; 14, The Science of Lustre: Questions and Answers. Although the emphasis is on technique there is much information and valuable illustrations relative to the history of Islamic pottery in general. Comprehensive, unclassified bibliography, pp. 237-241.

726   Cooper, Emmanuel. **A History of Pottery**. 3rd ed. Radnor, Pa., Chilton Trade Book Publishing, 1988. 224p. illus. index. ISBN 080197982X.

Popular history of ceramics worldwide from earliest times to the present. Contents: 1, The Early Civilizations; 2, The Greek and Roman; 3, The Far East; 4, Islamic Countries; 5, Europe (c AD 500-1850); 6, Great Britain (until 1700); 7, Great Britain (1700-1850); 8, Ancient America (until AD 1500); 9, Modern Tribal and Primitive Societies; 10, Modern America (1500-1860); 11, The Arts and Crafts Movement (1850-1910); 12, The Twentieth Century; 13, New Directions. Glossary of terms, list of museums with pottery collections. Classified bibliography of books in English, pp. 217-219.

727   Savage, George. **Pottery Through the Ages**. London, Cassell, 1963. 246p. illus. index. LC 64-6041.

General history of world pottery from ancient Egypt to 1800 written for the general reader, collector and enthusiast. Contents: 1, Egypt and Mesopotamia; 2, Greece, Rome and Byzantium; 3, China and Far East; 4, Persia and the Middle East; 5, Turkey and the Near East; 6, Spain and Portugal; 7, The Pottery of Italy; 8, Germany and the Austrian Empire; 9, France and Belgium; 10, Dutch Pottery; 11, Scandinavian Pottery; 12, English Pottery. General bibliography, p. 223, and bibliographies of specialized literature at the end of the chapters.

American Pottery, Etc. (U.S. and Canada)

728   Evans, Paul. **Art Pottery of the United States: An Enyclopedia of Producers and Their Marks**. New York, Scribner's, 1974. 353p. illus. index. ISBN 0684140292.

Comprehensive handbook of studio art pottery in the United States with reproductions of the marks of major makers and manufactures. Covers the period between 1876 and the Great Depression. Chapters on individual art potteries arranged alphabetically by name of pottery. List of museums with important collections of art pottery. Bibliographical references in the major entries and list of general works, p. 345.

729   Greer, Georgeanna H. **American Stoneware: The Art of and Craft of Utilitarian Potters**. Exton, Pa., Schiffer, 1981. 286p. illus. index. LC 81-51449.

Comprehensive handbook to American stoneware from early Colonial times to the twentieth century. Discusses the European background, technology—with illustrations of potters at work and their tools—and gives a good overview with representatives of mid-western and southern examples together with the more commonly recognized pieces of northeastern states.

730   Henzke, Lucille. **American Art Pottery**. Camden, N.J., T. Nelson, 1970. 336p. illus. index. LC 70-11371.

Popular survey of American nineteenth century ceramic figurines, tiles, and hand-painted pottery. Arranged by companies and provided with lists of artist's marks and signatures.

731   Ketchum, William C. **American Country Pottery. Yellowware and Spongeware**. New York, Knopf, 1987. 148p. illus. index. ISBN 0394752449.

Popular survey of American yellowware and spongeware pottery manufactured during the late nineteenth and early twentieth centuries. Contents: The Manufacture of Yellowware and Spongeware; Yelloware Manufacturers; Yellowware Forms; Spongewrae Manufacturers; Spongeware Forms. Appendix with list of makers. Basic bibliography, p. 147-48.

732   Ketchum, William C. **American Redware**. New York, H. Holt, 1991. 147p. illus. ISBN 0805012621.

Popular survey of redware pottery made in the United States during the nineteenth century and the early twentieth century. Contents: Redware Pottery Manufacture; 2, Products of the Redware Potteries; Massachusetts; 4, New Hampshire and Vermont; 5, Connecticut, Rhode Island, and Maine; 6, New York and New Jersey; 7, Pennsylvania; 8, Virginia, Maryland, and West Virginia; 9, Redware of the South; 11, Western Redware. Appendix with repertory of marks. General bibliography, pp. 135-37.

733   Kovel, Ralph M., and Terry H. Kovel. **The Kovels' Collector's Guide to American Art Pottery**. New York, Crown, 1974. 320p. illus. index. ISBN 0517516764.

Popular encyclopedia of American manufactures making art pottery from circa 1875 to circa 1975, with facsimiles of marks and signatures. Includes tile makers. Bibliographical references accompany most entries. Numerous illustrations of collectibles.

734   Lehner, Lois. **Complete Book of American Kitchen and Dinner Wares**. Des Moines, Ia., Wallace-Homestead Book Co., 1980. 240p. illus. Index.

Comprehensive dictionary of American manufacturers of whiteware with useful information on early twentieth century makers ignored in other sources.

See also Jo Cunningham, *The Collector's Encyclopedia of American Dinnerware* (Paducah, Ky., Collector's Books, 1982).

735   Ramsay, John. **American Potters and Pottery**. New York, Tudor, 1947. 309p. illus. index. Reprint: Ann Arbor, Mich., Ars Ceramica, 1976. ISBN 089344006X.

Popular history of pottery in the United States through the late nineteenth century with emphasis on commercial products. Checklist of major potters is still the most extensive. Illustrated with pieces typical of those accessible to the average collector.

736   Rebert, M. Charles. **American Majolica, 1850-1900**. Des Moines, Ia., Wallace-Homestead Book Co., 1981. 86p. illus. index. ISBN 0870693433.

Collector's handbook of American nineteenth- and twentieth-century majolica.

737   Stradling, Diana, and G. Garrison Stradling, eds. **The Art of the Potter: Redware and Stoneware**. New York, Universe, 1977. 158p. illus. index. ISBN 0876632851.

Fifty-six articles from *Antiques* magazine on American redware and stoneware grouped in six categories: Unearthing the Past, Redware—The Germanic Influence, Redware—The English Influence, Redware—New England, Stoneware—New York and West, The Potters Craft.

738   Webster, Donald B. **Decorated Stoneware Pottery of North America**. Rutland, Vt., 1971. 232p. illus. index. LC 71-134032.

Popular history/handbook covering painted and incised pottery in the United States and Canada from Colonial times to the end of the nineteenth century. Arrangement is by motif. Illustrated with pieces typical of those accessible to the average collector. Bibliography of basic books and periodical articles, pp. 229-30.

Major Regional Studies

739 Barber, Edwin A. **Tulip Ware of the Pennsylvania-German Potters: An Historical Sketch of the Art of Slip-Decoration in the United States**. New introduction by Henry J. Kauffman. 1903. 233p. illus. index. Reprint: New York, Dover, 1970. LC 74-111904.

A pioneering work in the study of the folk art of the Pennsylvania Germans. Contents: I, The Settlement of Eastern Pennsylvania by the Germans; II, The Pennsylvania-German Dialect and Literature; III, Slip-Decorations in Europe and America; IV, Tools and the Processes of Manufacture; V, Varieties of Slip Ware; VI, Decorative Subjects of the Pennsylvania-German Potters; VII, The Tulip in Decoration; VIII, Earthenware Utensils of the Pennsylvania Germans; IX, Slip Potters of Eastern Pennsylvania. Eighteenth Century; X, Slip Potters of Eastern Pennsylvania. Early Nineteenth Century; XI, Gift Pieces; XII, Unidentified Slip-Decorated Ware Found in Pennsylvania; XIII, Miscellaneous Inscriptions; XIV, Slip-Decorations as Practised by American Potters. Bibliographical footnotes.

740 Bivins, John, Jr. **The Moravian Potters in North Carolina**. Chapel Hill, N.C., Univ. of North Carolina Press, 1972. 300p. illus. index. ISBN 0807811912.

Comprehensive history of the pottery produced by Moravians in North Carolina from 1753 to the 1830s. Contents: Introduction: The Moravians by Francis Griffin; 1, A Complex Tradition; 2, The Potters: The Masters; 3, The Potters: The Apprentices and Journeymen; 4, Clay, Wheel, and Kiln: the Materials, Tools, and Techniques; 5, The Pottery; 6, The Pottery: The Slip-Decorated Ware. Glossaries of technical terms and Moravian(i.e., German) terms. General bibliography, pp. 289-90, with references to archival collections.

741 Branin, M. Lelyn. **The Early Makers of Handcrafted Earthenware and Stone Ware in Central and Southern New Jersey**. Rutherford, N.J., Fairleigh Dickinson Univ. Press, 1988. 266p. illus. index. ISBN 0838632351.

Comprehensive history of the pottery produced in central and southern New Jersey during the eighteenth and nineteenth centuries. Contents: The Coxe Pottery at Burlington; Kempell at Ringoes; The Morgan Pottery at Cheesequake; Eighteenth-Century Monmouth County Potters; The Nornor Pottery at Queenstown (Princeton); Early Potters in the Trenton Area; Early New Brunswick Potters; The McCullys and Others at Trenton; The Price Pottery at the Roundabouts (Sayreville); Warne & Letts at Cheesequake; The Seigles in Warren County; Prudden and Meeker in Morris County; Later Burlington County Potteries; The Potteries at Old Bridge; Mounty Holly Potteries; Snowden and Wingender at Haddonfield; Nineteenth-century New Brunswick Potteries; Bridgeton and Cumberland County; Hill-Fulper at Flemington; Bordentown and Crosswicks Potteries; Salem County Potteries; Van Wickle at Manasquan; Washington and South River; The Raisner Pottery in Lambertville; Nineteenth-Century Monmouth County Potteries; Camden and Gloucester Counties; The Sourland Mountain Potteries; The Congress Pottery at South Amboy; The Perth Amboy Potteries; The Slamander Works at Woodbridge; Furman at Cheesequake; Abial Price at Middletown Point; Atlantic and Cape May County Potteries; The Rue Pottery at Matawan; The Province and Bay View Potteries. Appendices with manufacturing statistics, inventories and wills, pages from the catalog of *Pottery*, and floor plans of some potteries. General bibliography, p. 256, and further literature in the footnotes.

742 Branin, M. Lelyn. **The Early Potters and Potteries of Maine**. Middletown, Conn., Wesleyan Univ. Press, 1978. 262p. illus. ISBN 0819550221.

Scholary history of pottery—mostly redware—made in Maine during the nineteenth century. Contents: 1, Introduction; 2, Imports, Reproductions, and Art Ware, 3, Hollis and Other York County Potteries; 4, Potteries in the Alfred-Sanford Area; 5, Buxton and Limington; 6, Early Redware at Portland; 7, Early Stoneware at Portland; 8, Portland Stoneware after 1850; 9, Gorham and Windham; 10, Kittson and Hill in Bridgton; 11, Oxford and Androscoggin Counties; 12, Early Potteries of Old Yarmouth; 13, Brunswick, Topsham, and Bath; 14, The Corliss Pottery at Woolwich; 15, Redware at Wiscasset; 16, Earthenware at Hallowell and Augusta; 17, Stoneware at Gardiner and Farmingdale; 18, Belfast, Winslow, and Vassalboro; 19, Bodge at Fayette and Wayne; 20, The Potters at Winthrop; 21, The Saffords and Coburn at Monmouth; 22, Farmington and New Sharon; 23, The Philbrick Pottery at Skowhegan; 24, The Stoneware Manufactory at Bangor; 25, Wakdoboro, Thomaston, and Ellsworth; 26, Earthenware and Tile at Orrington; 27, Other Penobscot County Potteries. Appendices with lists of potters and facsimiles of the marks and excerpts from daybooks and other sources. Bibliographical references in the footnotes.

743 Burrison, John A. **Brothers in Clay: The Story of Georgia Folk Pottery**. Athens, Ga., Univ. of Georgia Press, 1983. 326p. illus. index. ISBN 0820306576.
Scholarly history and study of folk pottery in Georgia written by a folklorist with particular attention to the continuing tradition in the Meaders family of White County. Includes interviews with potters and their customers. Contents: Part One: The Potter's World Human Dimensions of Craftsmanship; Part Two: Green Glazes and Groundhog Kilns: Profile of a Tradition; Part Three: Potsherds of the Past: Selective Statewide Survey. Bibliographical references in the notes, selected bibliography, pp. 305-307, is an exhaustive list of books and periodical articles on all aspects of Georgia folk pottery.

744 Ketchum, William C. **Potters and Potteries of New York State, 1650-1900**. Syracuse, N.Y., Syracuse Univ. Press, 1987. 626p. illus. index. ISBN 0815624131.
First published as: *Early Potters and Potteries of New York State*. New York, Funk and Wagnalls, 1970. 278p. illus. index.
Comprehensive history of pottery made in New York State from 1650 to 1900 based on extensive use of archival and other documentary sources. Contents: 1, The Potters' Methods and Wares; 2, Forms by New York Potters; 3, Manhattan Potters of the Seventeenth and Eighteenth Centuries; 4, Nineteenth-century Manhattan Potters; 5, Kings County; 6, Queens and Richmond Counties; 7, The Ancient Kilns of Long Island; 8, Pot Works of the Hudson Valley; 11, Ellenville and Athens; 13. Troy and Vicinity; 14, Lansingburgh; 15, West Troy; 16, The Potters of Saratoga County; 17, Washington County; 18, Potteries of the Adirondack Region; 19, Redware Kilns of the Upper Mohawk; 21, Utica; 22, Potters of Onondaga County; 23, Stoneware of the Finger Lakes Area; 24, Cayuga and Seneca County Redware; 25, Redware Potteries of the Ontario County Area; 26 The Clark Branches: Lyons, Mount Morris, and Rochester; 27, The Hart Kilns: Fulton, Sherburne, and Ogdensburg; 28, Stoneware of the Southern Tier; 29, Redware Kilns of Rural Erie County; 30, Buffalo; 31, Redware of Genesee and Niagara Counties; 32, Chautauqua and Cattaraugus Redware. Appendices with list of potters and their marks. Comprehensive, classified bibliography, pp. 581-608, includes unpublished material.

745 Lehner, Lois. **Ohio Pottery and Glass Marks and Manufacturers**. Des Moines, Ia., Wallace-Homstead Book Co., 1978. 113p. illus. index. ISBN 0870691686.
Dictionary of persons and companies active in the production of pottery and glass in Ohio from the earliest times to 1970 with facsimiles of their marks and signatures. Entries give basic information including references to registries and other documents. Bibliographical reference through footnotes. Classified bibliography, pp. 109-111, includes company histories and articles in collector's magazines.

746 Sweezy, Nancy. **Raised in Clay: The Southern Pottery Tradition**. Washington, D.C., Smithsonian Institution Press, 1984. 280p. ISBN 0874748607. illus.
Comprehensive history of pottery made in the southern states during the nineteenth and early twentieth centuries. Designed to accompany an exhibition at the Smithsonian Institution.

Introductory chapters tracing the history and the technology of southern pottery are followed by entries describing 35 individual potteries divided by types.

747 Turnbaugh, Sarah P., ed. **Domestic Pottery of the Northeastern United States, 1625-1850.** Orlando, Fla., Academic Press, 1985. 319p. illus. index. ISBN 0127038701.

History and interpretation of ceramics production and consumption in northeastern United States from 1625 to 1850. Chapters are written by various experts. Emphasis is on the social aspects of ceramics. Contents: 1, Introduction ; 2, Cultural Pluralism and Pots in New Amsterdam-New York City; 3, Traditional Patterning of Earthenware Entries and the Form of the Probate Inventory in Seventeenth-Century Plymouth Colony, 4, Ceramics and the Colonial System: The Charlestown Example; 5, Re-Creating Ceramic Production and Tradition in a Living History Laboratory; 6, Changing Redware Production in Southern New Hampshire; 7, Product Standardization and Increasing Consumption Demands by an Eighteenth-Century Industrial Labor Force; 8, Production Continuity and Obsolescence of Traditional Redwares in Concord, New Hampshire; 9, Ceramic Production in the Exchange Network of an Agricultural Neighborhood; 10, Eclecticism as a Response to Changing Market Conditions in Connecticut; 11, Regional Variation and Drift: Late Eighteenth- and Early Nineteenth-Century Requa-McGee Site Coggle-Edged Trail Slipware; 12, Imitation, Innovation, and Permutation: The Americanization of Bay Colony Lead-Glaze Redwares; 13, The Demise of Traditional Pottery Manufacture on Sourland Mountain, New Jersey, during the Industrial Revolution; 14, The Founding of a Dynamic Family Industry: Hews, Redware Potters of Massachusettes; 15, The Pottery-making Trade in Colonial Philadelphia: The Growth of an Early Urban Industry. Comprehensive bibliography, pp. 285-305.

748 Watkins, Lura W. **Early New England Potters and Their Wares**. 1950. Reprint: Hamden, Conn., Archon Books, 1968. 291p. illus. index. LC 68-26937.

Comprehensive history of pottery in New England from colonial times to the early twentieth century. Emphasis is on the traditional pottery in red earthenware and in stoneware. Contents:I, Techniques; II, Seventeenth-Century Potters; III, James Kettle Shard Pile; IV, The Provincial Potters of Charlestown; V, A Potter's Daybook; VI, A Woman Introduces Stoneware; VII, Redware Potting from Boston to the Cape; VIII, Excavations on the Bayley Sites of 1723-1799; IX, The Osborns of Danvers and Other Essex County Potters; X, The Quaker Potters of Bristol County; XI, Stoneware Potting in Eastern Massachusetts; XII, Some Potteries of Central and Western Massachusetts; XIII, The Whately and Ashfield Group; XIV, Pioneer Craftsmen of New Hampshire; XV, The Clarks of Lyndeboro and Concord; XVI, North of Concord; XVII, Redware Potters of Vermont; XVIII, Vermont Stoneware Potteries; XIX, Early Maine Potteries; XX, The Maine Industry After 1800; XXI, Early Connecticut Redware and the Goshen Group; XXII, The States Family of Greenwich and Stonington; XXIII, Potters of New London County; XXIV, Hartford and New Haven Potteries; XXV, Pots and Dishes of Norwalk; XXVI, Rhode Island; XXVII, Bennington and Kindred Developments; XXVIII, The Art Potteries; XXIX, Redware Forms. Appendixes with documents relating to the Parkers of Charlestown and a check list of New England potters. Comprehensive, classified bibliography, pp. 271-76, includes numerous references to local histories, magazine articles and manuscripts.

Major Manufactories

Bennington

749 Barrett, Richard C. **Bennington Pottery and Porcelain**. New York, Crown, 1958. 342p. illus. LC 58-8312.

Comprehensive collectors' handbook of the pottery and porcelain made in the Bennington, Vermont factory from 1793 to 1858. Contains 45 plates with descriptive captions. Contents: I:

Functional Items: 1, Pitchers; 2, Table Ware; 3, Kitchen and Household Accessories; II: Fancy Articles: 4, Vases, Ewers, Cologne Bottles and Trinket Boxes; 5, Statuettes and Figures; 6, Animals and Birds; 7, Novelty Items. No bibliography.

Van Briggle

750   Arnest, Barbara M., ed. **Van Briggle Pottery. The Early Years.** Colorado Springs, Colo., Colorado Springs Fine Arts Center, 1975. 70p. illus. LC 74-30990.

Published to accompany an exhibition dedicated to the production of Van Briggel art pottery between 1900 and 1912. Introduction: "Van Briggle: Several Perspectives" makes extensive use of documentary sources. Appendix gives biographies of Artus Van Briggle and Anne Lawrence Gregory, a bibliography of interviews and correspondence and a history of Van Briggle markings. "Early Van Briggle in Color" is a catalog of 300 pieces displayed at the exhibition. "Catalogue of Van Briggle Designs" is a collector's repertory of 750 designs.

751   Nelson, Scott H., et al. **A Collector's Guide to Van Briggle Pottery.** Indiana, Pa., Halldin Pub. Co., 1986. 178p. illus. ISBN 0961643609.

Contents: I, The History of the Van Briggle Pottery: Artus Van Briggle, The Anne Van Briggle Period, The Influence of Maria Storer, The Later Years; II, Characteristics of Van Briggle Pottery: Bottom Markings; Van Briggle Glazes and Colors; Van Briggle Designs and Designers; Tiles; Plates; Specialty Items; Van Briggle Pottery in Collections; Value of Van Briggle Pottery; III. Catalog (line drawings of pieces arranged in chronological order with descriptive captions).

Canada

752   Webster, Donald B. **Early Canadian Pottery.** Greenwich, Conn., New York Graphics Society, 1971. 256p. illus. index. LC 75-162722.

Well-illustrated survey of pottery in Canada from colonial times to the end of the nineteenth century. Contents: 1, The Production of Earthenware; 2, Quebec. The French Period; 3, Quebec—the Later 18th and 19th Centuries; 4, Ontario Earthenware; 5, Earthenware of the Martimes; 6, Miniatures, Toys and Whimseys; 7, Salt-glazed Stoneware; 8, Manufacturing—Rockingham and Yellow-ware; 9, Whitewares and Porcelain; 10, The Archaeology of Potteries. Glossary and unclassified list of books, pp. 249-50.

Regional Studies

753   Antonelli, Marylu, and Jack Forbes. **Pottery in Alberta: The Long Tradition.** Edmonton, Univ. of Alberta Press, 1978. 189p. illus. LC 74-304211

Popular history of the pottery making industry during the twentieth century in Alberta. The considerable amount of information is unfortunately presented without proper references. No bibliography.

754   Newlands, David L. **Early Ontario Potters: Their Craft and Trade.** Toronto and New York, McGraw-Hill, 1979. 245p. illus. index. ISBN 0070829721.

Comprehensive history/handbook of pottery made in Ontario from the eighteenth century to the end of the nineteenth century. Contents: 1, Introduction; 2, The Potter's Craft; 3, The Ontario Pottery Industry; 4, Potteries of Eastern Ontario; 5, Kilns of Prince Edward and Hastings Counties; 6, Potteries of East Central Ontario; 7, The Workshops of York County; 8, Potters of West Central Ontario; 9, Kilns of the Georgian Bay-Lake Simcoe Region; 10, Pottery of Waterloo County; 11, Pottery Shops of Perth and Huron Counties; 12, Potteries and Potters of Brant County; 13, Factories of the City of Hamilton-Wentworth County Region; 14, Workshops of the Niagara

Peninsula; 15, Pot Shops of the North Shore of Lake Erie; 16, Potteries of Southwestern Ontario. Appendices with advice on collecting, glossary of ceramic terms and list of marks in photographic reproductions. Selected bibliography, pp. 236-37. Plates include reproductions of advertisements and views of potteries from old photographs.

Native American Pottery

Bibliographies

755   Muth, Marcia. **Indian Pottery of the Southwest: A Selected Bibliography**. Santa Fe, N.M., Sunstone Press, 1990. 32p. illus. ISBN 0865340676.

Concise bibliography of books and articles on traditional Native American pottery of the southwest designed as an introductory guide for students.

756   Oppelt, Norman T. **Southwestern Pottery: an Annotated Bibliography and List of Types and Wares**. 2d ed. Metuchen, N.J., Scarecrow Pess, 1988. 325p. illus. index. ISBN 0810821192.

Annotated bibliography of books and periodical articles on prehistoric and historic pottery of the southwestern region of the United States. Titles are listed by author. The List of Pottery Types and Wares is an index to the titles in the bibliography.

See also Farrington (434).

Histories and Handbooks

757   Barry, John W. **American Indian Pottery: An Identification and Value Guide**. rev. ed. Florence, Ala., Books Americana, 1984. 214p. illus. index. ISBN 0896890473.

Collector's handbook of native American pottery both pre-historic and contemporary with emphasis on contemporary production in the southwest. Contents: I, The Railroad—Introducing Southwest Pottery Arts; II, Pueblos of the Southwest; III, Archaeology—a New Era; IV, Pre-historic Pottery Section: New England, Midwest, Southwest; V, Contemporary and Historic Pottery Section: Hopi, Acoma, Laguna, Zia, San Filipe, Santa Ana, Santo Domingo, Cochiti, Jemez, Pecos, Tesuque, Nambe and Pojoaque, Santa Clara, San Ildefonso, San Juan, Taos and Picuris, Sandia, Isleta, Ysleta-Tigua, Navajo, Zuni, Papago, Yuman, Catawba, Cherokee, Coushatta, Pamunkey. Basic bibliography, pp. 205-06.

758   White, John K. **Pottery Techniques of Native America: An Introduction to Traditional Technology**. Chicago, Univ. of Chicago Press, 1976. 52p. illus. ISBN 0226698157.

Important introduction to the techniques used by North American Indians to create pottery vessels. Special attention is given to the traditions of the Cherokee and other Native American tribes of the Southeast. Text is illustrated with examples from the collection of the Field Museum of Natural History in Chicago and by color microfiche illustrations showing the sequences of movement in creation of a vessel. Basic bibliography, pp. 51-52.

Hopi Pottery

759   Allen, Laura G. **Contemporary Hopi Pottery**. Flagstaff, Ariz., Museum of Northern Arizona, 1984. 127p. illus. ISBN 0897340558.

Introduction to the traditional pottery made today by the Hopi Indians with a chapter on the history of Hopi ceramics of the historic period and catalog of the collection in the Museum of Northern Arizona. Good selection of plates. Bibliography, pp. 126-27.

See also the museum catalogs: *Historic Hopi Ceramics: the Thomas V. Keam Collection of the Peabody Museum of Archaeology and Ethnology, Harvard University: Catalog*, by E. L.

Wade and L. S. McChesney (Cambridge, Mass., Peabody Museum, 1981. 604p. illus. ISBN 0873657985) and *A Reference Manual for Historic Hopi Ceramics: The Thomas V. Keam Collection*, by L. S. McChesney (Cambridge, Mass., Peabody Museum, 1982. 203p.).

Pueblo Pottery

760   Babcock, Barbara A. **The Pueblo Storyteller: Development of a Figurative Ceramic Tradition**. Tuscon, Ariz., Univ. of Arizona Press, 1986. 201p. illus. index. ISBN 0816508704.

Well-illustrated survey of terra cotta figurines of Pueblo Indian storytellers and their listeners that became popular among Pueblo ceramics beginning in the 1960s. Contents: Part I: The Storyteller Tradition in Pueblo Culture: The Figurative Tradition; the Invention of the Storyteller; The Revival of Pueblo Figurative Ceramics; The Regenerative Power of the Story-teller; Part II: Color Plates; Part III: Pueblo Storyteller Potters: Biographical Survey of the Artists; Part IV. Reference Material (glossary and comprehensive bibliography).

761   Frank, Larry, and Francis H. Harlow. **Historic Pottery of the Pueblo Indians, 1600-1880**. 2d ed. West Chester, Pa., Schiffer Pub., 1990. 160p. illus. ISBN 0887402275.

Well-illustrated collector's handbook of the pottery made by the Pueblo Indians from 1600 to 1880. Contains 166 plates, some in color, with descriptive notes. Contents: Part One. Historic Pottery of the Pueblo Indians: The Pueblo Indians as Potters; Forms of Pueblo Pottery and Their Preservation; The Making of Pueblo Pottery; Pottery Styles, Quality, and Trends; Pueblo Pottery Types and Dating; Key Characteristics of Pueblo Pottery. Part Two. Types of Pueblo Pottery of the Historic Period: Northern Tiwa Pueblo; Tewa Pueblos; Northeast Keres Pueblos; Puname Pueblos; Other Pottery-making Pueblos; Acoma and Laguna Pueblos; Zuni Area; Hopi Area. Annotated bibliography, pp. 158-160.

See also L. P. Frank. *Historic Pottery of the Pueblo Indians, 1600-1880*. (Boston, New York Graphics Society, 1974. 160p. illus. ISBN 0821205862).

762   Guthe, Carl E. **Pueblo Pottery Making: A Study at the Village of San Idelfonso**. New Haven, Conn., Yale Univ. Press, 1925. 88p. illus. LC 25-9216. (Papers of the Southwestern Expedition, no. 2).

The first scholarly study of the pottery production in the San Idelfonso Pueblo with much invaluable information on technique and materials. Contents: Raw Materials; Collection and Preparation; Paraphernalia; Moulding; Sun-Drying; Scraping; Slipping and Polishing; Painting; Firing; Painting of Designs; Symbolism. Basic bibliography, p. 89.

See also The Pottery of San Ildefonso Pueblo, by K. M. Chapman (Albuquerque, N.M., Univ. of New Mexico Press, 1970. 260p. illus. index. LC 79-99565).

763   Harlow, Francis H. **Historic Pueblo Indian Pottery: Painted Jars and Bowls of the Period, 1600-1900**. Sante Fe, N.M., Museum of New Mexico Press, 1970. 50p. illus.

Authoritative handbook of Pueblo pottery made between 1600 and 1900, illustrated with twenty illustrations of drawings with descriptive notes designed to aid the collector in dating and placing the various types. Arrangement is by type of ware and by tribal group. No bibliography.

764   Trimble, Stephen A. **Talking with Clay: The Art of Pueblo Pottery**. Santa Fe, N.M., School of American Research, 1987. 116p. illus. index. ISBN 0933452152.

Popular survey of contemporary Pueblo pottery. Contents: 1, Talking with the Clay: Technique; 2, Mountain Villages: Tao and Picuris; 3, The Red and the Black: Tewa Pueblos; 4, Storyteller and Birds: Middle Rio Grande Pueblos; 5, Clay Made from History: Acoma, Laguna, and Zuni; 6, The Legacy of Sikyatki: Hopi; Conclusion: One with the Clay: Economics and Tradition. "Note on Sources," pp. 109-12, is a useful, annotated bibliography.

See also the museum catalog: *Pottery of the Pueblos of New Mexico, 1700-1940* by J. Batkin (Colorado Springs, Colo., Taylor Museum of the Colorado Springs Fine Arts Center, 1987, 215p. illus. index. ISBN 0916537080); the collection catalogs: *Pueblo Indian Pottery: 50 Reproductions in Color from Specimens in the Famous Collection of the Indian Arts Fund* by K. M. Chapman (Nice, C. Szwedzicki, 1933-36. 2v. illus.) and *Beauty from the Earth: Pueblo Indian Pottery from the University Museum of Archaeology and Anthropology* by J. J. Brody and R. Allen (Philadelphia, Univ. of Pennsylvania, Museum of Archaeology and Anthropology, 1990. 99p. illus.).

Navajo Pottery

765 Hartman, Russell P. **Navajo Pottery: Traditions & Innovations**. Flagstaff, Ariz., North-land Press, 1987. 113p. illus. index. ISBN 0873584309.

Popular survey of the traditional pottery of the Navajo Indians from early historic times to the present. Emphasis is on revival of ancient techniques and decoration in the post-World War II period. Contents: 1, The Navajo People: A Historical Overview; 2, Navajo Pottery: A Cultural and Social Perspective; 3, Navajo Pottery Technology; 4, Historic Navajo Pottery; 5, Decline and Survival of the Pottery Tradition; 6, The Revitalization of Navajo Pottery; 7, Contemporary Pitch-Coated Navajo Pottery; 8, Reaching Beyond Traditions.9, Summary and Predictions. Basic bibliography, pp. 103-06.

Native American Potters

766 Blair, Mary E., and Laurence R. Blair. **Margaret Tafoya: A Tewa Potter's Heritage and Legacy**. Westchester, Pa., Schiffer Pub., 1986. 199p. illus. index. ISBN 0887400809.

Monograph of the life and work of Margaret Tafoya (b. 1904), the most famous of the Tewa Pueblo Indian potters. Contains 31 color illustrations of pieces by Tafoya and many black and white illustrations of the potter at work, her family and scenes of Pueblo Indian life. Contents: 1, History; 2, Margaret Tafoya's Life 1904; 3, The Making of Traditional Santa Clara Pottery; 4, The Descendents. Comprehensive bibliography, pp. 191-94.

767 Peterson, Susan. **Lucy M. Lewis, American Indian Potter**. Tokyo, New York, Kodansha International, 1984. 218p. illus. index. ISBN 0870116851.

Well-illustrated monograph of the life and work of the Acoma Indian potter, Lucy M. Lewis (b.c. 1890). Contains 351 color illustrations and includes many informative scenes of pottery making by Lucy and her family. Contents: The Setting; Lucy, Lady of Acoma; Lucy's Potter Children; Lucy's Pottery Heritage; Making Pottery; Gallery of Lucy's Pots; Lucy's Awards; Modern Potters Emerge from the Past by B. P. Dutton. Comprehensive bibliography, pp. 209-214.

768 Peterson, Susan. **The Living Tradition of Maria Martinez**. Tokyo, New York, Kodansha International, 1981. 300p. illus. index. ISBN 0870114972.

Well-illustrated monograph on the life and pottery of Maria Martinez, one of the most celebrated Pueblo Indian potters. Contains 337 color plates with brief captions including many scenes of Maria at work, scenes of Pueblo Indian life and customs. Contents: Maria—a Meeting by Bernard Leach; Maria; Black Pottery; Maria and Santana; Making Pots; Barbara; Firing; Appendix: A Brief Historical Note on Burnished Black and Matt Pottery. Comprehensive bibliography, pp. 289-96.

See also Maria: The Potter of San Ildefonso by A. Marriott (Norman, Okla., Univ. of Oklahoma Press, 1948. 294p. illus. index. LC 48-2101).

European Pottery, Etc.

General Works

769   Penkala, Maria. **European Pottery, 5000 Marks on Majolica, Faience and Stoneware.** 2nd ed. Rutland, Vt., Tuttle, 1969. 472p. illus. index. LC 69-19602.
Dictionary of 5,780 marks on European pottery, arranged by countries with brief introductions. Marks reproduced in facsimile.

770   Klein, Adalbert. **Fayencen Europas.** Braunschweig, Klinkhardt & Biermann, 1980. 412p. illus. index. LC 81-452855.
Comprehensive history/handbook of European faience and majolica ware from the fifteenth century to the nineteenth century. Does not include the German-speaking countries, the subject of a separate volume by the author (788). Geographical arrangement with bibliographies at the end of each section. One of the best collector's handbooks.

771   Morley-Fletcher, Hugo, and Roger McIlroy. **Christies' Pictorial History of European Pottery.** Oxford, England, Phaidon/Christies, 1984. ISBN 0714880094.
Collector's handbook of all forms of nonporcelain ceramics in Europe from 1400 to 1800. Arrangement is by country. Many illustrations—nearly 2000—of pieces available on the art market during the previous fifteen years with lists and dates of their auction prices.

772   Weiss, Gustav. **Ullstein Fayencebuch. Eine Kunst—und Technikgeschichte der Fayencen mit Markenverzeichnis.** Frankfurt/Main and Berlin, Ullstein, 1970. 319p. illus. index. LC 77-569251.
Comprehensive and authoritative history/handbook of Euopean faience, with emphasis on history of manufacture and technique. Well illustrated with museum pieces. Basic bibliography.
See also the museum catalogs: Faience I. *Niederlande, Frankreich, England,* by B. Tietzel (Cologne Kunstgewerbemuseum, 1980). *Europäische Fayencen,* by M. Bauer (Frankfurt am Main, Museum für Kunsthandwerk, 1977), *Majolica. Spanische und Italienische Keramik von 14. bis 18. Jahrhundert,* by T. Hausmann (Berlin, Kunstgewerbemuseum, 1976).

France

Dictionaries

773   Curtil, Henri. **Marques et signatures de la faïence française.** Paris, Massin, 1969. 152p. illus. LC 71-550456.
Pocket-sized dictionary of marks found on French faience. Marks are illustrated in facsimile.

774   Lesur, Adrien. **Les poteries et les faïences françaises.** 2nd ed. Paris, Tardy, 1969-74. 5v. illus. index. LC 70-429720.
Comprehensive handbook of French pottery and faience, arranged by regions and centers of production. Large corpus of plates and repertory of marks.
See also Tardy (firm). *Les faïences françaises: historique, caractéristiques du décor, couleurs, pâtes, émail, production, marques...* (Paris, Tardy, 1949. 289p. illus. index. LC 49-29935/L).

General Histories and Handbooks

775   Chompret, Jean, Jean Bloch, Jacques Guerin, and Paul Alfossa. **Répertoire de la faïence française**. Paris, S. Lapina, 1933-35. 2v. illus. index.

Published in association with an exhibition at the Musée des Arts Décoratifs, Paris. Corpus of 610 plates (originally published in 5 folios) of pieces of French faience from the sixteenth to the early nineteenth centuries arranged by place. Text comprised of essays on various manufactories by a team of French experts. Useful bibliography of the older literature, pp. 287-288.

776   Fay-Hallé, Antoinette, and Christine Lahaussois. **Le grand livre de la faïence française**. Fribourg, Office du Livre, 1986. 242p. illus. index. ISBN 2826400487.

Richly illustrated history of French faience from the seventeenth and eighteenth centuries. Brief text followed by collection of plates illustrating museum pieces with detailed, descriptive notes. Contents: I, Des origines au XVIIe siècle; II, Le triomphe du camaieu bleu. 1700-1730; III, La polychromie de grand feu à partir de 1730; IV, La faïence à décor de petit feu. Seconde moitié du XVIIe siècle. Classified bibliography, pp. 236-237, includes exhibition catalogs.

777   Fourest, Henry P. **L'ouvre des faïence français du XVIe a la fin du XVIIIe siècle**. Paris, Hachette, 1966. 332p. illus. LC 67-79023.

Authoritative history of French faience from the sixteenth century to the end of the eighteenth century. Illustrated with pieces representative of the highest artistic quality in European and American collections and with many valuable designs and comparative works of art. Contents: Les origines de la faïence française; Le style Louis XIV; Le style Louis XV—la faïence de grand feu; le style Louis XV—la faience de petit feu. Repertory of major manufactories and their marks. Bibliography of books and periodical articles, pp. 328-29.

778   Giacommoti, Jeanne. **French Faience**. New York, Universe, 1963. 266p. illus. index. LC 63-18339.

Comprehensive history of French faience during the seventeenth and eighteenth centuries with exceptional plates illustrating many pieces in smaller museums and private collections. Contents: Part 1, Faience in France, Origins and Technique; Primitive Faience; Nevers and Loire Valley; Rouen and Normandy; Brittany; Paris and the Surrounding Factories; The Northern and Eastern Districts; The Central Region; Provence; The South-east Region; The South-west Region; Charente. Part 2: Strasbourg; Niderviller; Marseille; Aprey; Meillonas; Sceaux. General bibliography, p. 258. List of marks, pp. 259-63.

779   Lane, Arthur. **French Faience**. 2nd ed. New York, Praeger, 1970. 51p.(text) 104 p. illus. index. LC 75-133087.

Survey of French faience of the seventeenth and eighteenth centuries written by a recognized British authority. Illustrated with museum pieces and pieces in major private collections. Contents: 1, The Technical Nature of Faience; 2, The Medieval Beginnings; 3, Italian Modes in the 16th Century; 4, Faience 'Blanche' Made for Common Use; 5, Nevers in the 17th Century; 6, Faience as a Fine Art; a Prelude to the 18th Century; 7, Rouen and the Factories of the North; 8, Moustiers and Marseilles: the Factories of the South; 9, Strasbourg and the Factories of Eastern France; 10, Avery, Meillonas, and Sceaux. General bibliography, p. 45.

780   Tilmans, Emile. **Faïence de France**. Paris, Editions Mondes, 1954. 326p. illus. index. LC A56-121/R56.

Pictorial survey of French faience and majolica from the fifteenth century to the present. Contents: Tableau chronologique de l'activité faïencière du XVe au XIXe siècle; Lexique de quelques termes techniques; Faïences de France. Techniques. Histoire; Marques d'inventaire d'ouvriers et de décorateurs; Les précurseurs; Les faïenceries françaises et leurs marques; Faïences domestiques; Faïences patriotiques et révolutionnaires; Faïences contemporaines. Brief text followed by good collection of plates with descriptive captions. Most useful is the dictionary of regions and ateliers which includes facsimiles of marks. General bibliography, pp. 307-308.

See also the exhibition catalog: *La Faïence française de 1525 à 1820*, by C. B. Metman (Paris, Palais du Louvre, 1923. 515p. illus.) and *Faïences francaises: XVIe-XVIIIe siècles* (Paris, Ministere de la Culture et de la Communication, 1980. 321p. illus. ISBN 2711801535).

Beauvais Ware

781   Cartier, Claudine, et al. **La céramique du Beauvaisis du moyen-age au XVIIIe siècle**. Paris, Musée National de Céramique de Sèvres, 1973.48p. illus. LC 81-109015r90.

Catalog of exhibit of 397 pieces of pottery made in Beauvais and vicinity from the Carolingian Period to the end of the eighteenth century. General bibliography, p. 48, and bibliographical references in the notes to the introduction.

Palissy Ware

782   Gibbon, Alan. **Céramiques de Bernard Palissy**. Paris, Sequier, 1986. 133p. illus. index. ISBN 2906284084.

Well-illustrated introductory monograph on the ceramic art of Bernard Palissy; 104 plates, many in color, with brief descriptive captions. Contents: I, La céramique française au XVe siècle; La dominante italienne; Début du siècle: Lyon; Le milieu du siècle: Rouen; La fin du siècle: Nevers; Les foyers annexes. II. Bernard Palissy la rupture française; Le potier; Le savant, l'écrivain. III, Esthétique des céramiques de Bernard Palissy; Les plats aux poissons ou l'esprit naturaliste; Les décors abstraits ou l'esprit géometrique; Les décors allégoriques ou l'esprit mythologique; Les décors religieux ou l'esprit mystique. IV, Ecoles et disciples de Bernard Palissy: onde de choc; Le premier cercle: Paris 1570-1590; Le second cercle: Avon 1580-1620; Le troisième cercle: Manerbe-Le Pré d'Auge 1580-1650; Le dernier cercle: Anvers-Londres; Conclusion. Bibliography of books, p. 133.

783   Morley, Henry. **Palissy the Potter: The Life of Bernard Palissy of Saintes**. London, Chapman & Hall, 1852. 494p. illus. index.

Only monograph in English on Bernard Palissy (1509-1589) and still a source of valuable information if used with caution. Contents: Book I: The Field of Labour, 1509-1537; Book II: The Potter, 1538-1557; Appendix to Book I; Book III: The Reformer, 1557-1562; Appendix to Book III; Book IV: The Naturalist, 1562-1580; Appendix to Book IV; Book V: "White Already to Harvest," 1580-1589; Appendix. Appendices have extracts from Palissy's writings.

See also Sauzay, Alexandre de and Henri Delange. *Monographie de l'oeuvre de Bernard Palissy suive d'un choix de ses continuateurs ou imitateurs*. Paris, Quai Voltaire, 1862, E. Dupuy. Bernard Palissy. *L'Homme—l'artiste—la savant—l'écrivain*. 2nd. ed. (Paris, 1902. 342p. reprint: Geneva, Slatkine Reprints, 1970.) and L. Audiat. *Bernard Palissy. étude sur sa vie et ses travaux*. (Paris, 1868. 480p. Reprint: Geneva, Slatkine Reprints, 1970).

See also the museum catalog: *La Céramique française: Bernard Palissy et le fabriques du XVIe siècle by M. J. Ballot (Paris, Albert Morancé, 1924. 39p. illus.)*.

Germany, Austria, and Switzerland

General Histories and Handbooks

784 Stoehr, August. **Deutsche Fayencen und Deutsches Steingut. Ein Handbuch fur Sammler und Liebhaber**. Berlin, Schmidt, 1920. 596p. illus. index. (Bibliothek fur Kunst- und Antiquitätensammler, Band 20). LC 23-12476.

Older, scholarly history/handbook of German faience and stoneware. Superseded by Klein (788) except for the material on stoneware which is still valuable today. Bibliographies of the specialized literature at the beginning of each chapter or section.

Folk Pottery

785 Brauneck, Manfred. **Volkstümliche Hafnerkeramik im deutschsprachigen Raum**. Munich, Kunst & Antiquitäten, 1984. 148p. illus. index. ISBN 3921811317.

Collectors' handbook of folk ceramics in German-speaking lands from the eighteenth and nineteenth centuries. First part describes the technical aspects of German folk ceramics; second part provides an overview of the development in the various regions. Illustrated with pieces in museums. Comprehensive, classified bibliography, pp. 131-142.

786 Meyer-Heisig, Erich. **Deutsche Bauerntöpferei**. Munich, Prestel, 1955. 159p. illus. LC A56-2060.

Survey of German folk ceramics by a leading authority. Illustrated with museum pieces, the work has chapters on technique, history and the major regions of folk ceramic production in the German-speaking world. Notes have definitions of terms, lists of museums and bibliographical commentary. General bibliography, pp. 69-71, lists books and periodical articles.

Faience

787 Huseler, Konrad. **Deutsche Fayencen, ein Handbuch der Fabriken, ihrer Meister und Werke**. Stuttgart, Hiersemann, 1956-58. 3v. illus. index. LC A57-1246.

Scholarly history/handbook of German faience. Volume one is a comprehensive handbook of the products of the various regions and manufactories with a chapter of technique. Volume two is an art history of German faience from the sixteenth century to the end of the eighteenth century with biographies of major painters and sections on dating, collecting, faience sculpture, the role of color, and models. Volume three contains a corpus of plates, biographical dictionary and dictionary of marks. Comprehensive bibliography in volume 3, pp. 435-41, includes museum and exhibition catalogs plus the best guide to the specialized, older literature on German faience. A standard work.

788 Klein, Adalbert. **Deutsche Fayencen; ein Handbuch für Sammler und Liebhaber**. Braunschweig, Klinkhardt & Biermann, 1975. 367p. illus. index. (Bibliothek für Kunst- und Antiquitätenfreunde, Band 20). LC 75-517527.

Comprehensive history/handbook of German faience from the sixteenth to the end of the eighteenth centuries by a leading authority on faience. Arranged by regions with concluding chapters on technique and collecting. Contents: Einführung; Frühe Fayence im deutschen Kultur-bereich; Hanau und Frankfurt; Berlin und Nordwestdeutschland; Thüringen und Sachsen; Der Westen; Süddeutschland-Nördlicher Teil; Süddeutschland—Südlicher Teil; Der Südwesten; Norddeutschland; Der Nordosten; Deutsche Fayencenmaler; Fayencentechnik—Die Manufaktur; Kachelöfen; Zur Beurteilung von Fayencen. General bibliography, pp. 362-63, and bibliographies of specialized literature at end of sections within chapters.

789 Stahl, Siegfried. **Deutsche Fliesen**. Fayence-Fliesen des 18. Jahrhunderts. Braunschweig, Klinkhardt & Biermann, 1977. 402p. illus. index. ISBN 3781401251.

Comprehensive, scholarly history/handbook of Germany faience tiles of the eighteenth century. Contents: 1, Herkunft, Herstellung und Bemalung; 2, Fliesenbemalung und ihre graphischen Vorbilder; 3, Gekachelte Räume in deutschen Schlössern des 18. Jahrhunderts; 4, Die Fayencemanufakturen, in denen Fliesen hergestellt wurden; 4.1, Hanau und Frankfurt/Main; 4.2, Kassel; 4.3, Braunschweig; 4.4, Dorotheenthal; 4.5, Dresden; 4.6, Ansbach; 4.7, Nürnberg; 4.8, Bayreuth; 4.9, Erfurt; 4.10, Crailsheim; 4.11, Zerbst; 4.12, Hannoversch-Münden; 4.13, Öttingen-Tiergarten-Schrattenhofen; 4.14, Köthen; 4.15, Wrisbergholzen; 4.16, Das Porzellanzimmer in Aystetten; 4.17, Fulda; 4.18, Schrezheim; 4.19, Magdeburg; 4.20, Stralsund; 4.21, Lesum. Appendices with repertory of distinctive corner designs and technical data on tiles representative of the various manufactories. Bibliographical references in the notes.

Stoneware

790 Falke, Otto von. **Das rheinisches Steinzeug**. 2v. illus. index. Berlin-Schöneberg, 1908. Reprint: Osnabrück, Zeller, 1977. 2v. in 1. ISBN 3535024161.

Authoritative history of German decorated stoneware of the Middle Ages and Renaissance. Contents: I, Einleitung; II, Die Herstellung des Steinzeugs; III, Töpfer, Formstecher und Händler; IV, Die Frühzeit des rheinischen Steinzeugs im Mittelalter; V, Cöln-Frechen; VI, Siegburg; VII, Raeren; VIII, Der Esterwald; IX, Urkunden. The standard work on the golden age of German stoneware written by a leading expert in the applied and decorative arts; filled with information on technique as well as clear delineation of the production of the major centers and extensive use of documentary material. Bibliographical references in the footnotes.

791 Gaimster, David R. M., Mark Redknap, and Hans-Helmut Wegner. **Zur Keramik des Mittelalters und der beginnenden Neuzeit im Rheinland: Medieval and Later Pottery from the Rhineland and Its Markets**. Oxford, England, B.A.R., 1988. 358p. illus. ISBN 0860545679.

Collection of twenty essays, most delivered at a colloquium held at Koblenz in 1987, on various aspects of the production of pottery in the Rhineland during the Middle Ages and the Renaissance. The majority are scholarly treatments of archaeological evidence and/or analysis of trade. German and English text. Bibliographies at the end of each essay and in the footnotes.

792 Horschik, Josef. **Steinzeug: 15. bis 19. Jahrhundert, von Bürgel bis Muskau**. Dresden, VEB, 1978. 496p. illus. index. LC 79-342595.

Comprehensive history of stoneware produced in Saxony, Thuringia, and Silesia from the fifteenth to the nineteenth centuries. Arrangement is by regional types, e.g., Waldenburg, Altenburg, Bürgel, Annaberg, Freiberg, Muskau, Triebe, Bunzlau. Contains 285 plates with detailed descriptive notes. Large repertory of hundreds of additional pieces arranged by type with descriptive captions. Comprehensive bibliography, pp. 489-494. A paradigmatic handbook for the history of stoneware.

793 Kerkhoff-Hader, Barbel. **Lebens-und Arbeitsformen der Topfer in der Südwesteifel: ein Beitrag zur Steinzeugforschung im Rheinland**. Bonn, Rohrscheid, 1980. 352p. illus. ISBN 3792804042. (Rheinisches Archiv, 110).

Scholarly study, based on the author's dissertation (University of Bonn, 1976), of the production of stoneware in the region of the Eifel between Bitburg, Wittlich, and Trier (chief center at Speicher) during the eighteenth and nineteenth centuries. Includes all types including roof tiles and smoking pipes. Based on detailed and extensive study of archival material; presents a mass of information on the potters' villages, families, organizations, methods and materials and commercial relationships. Contents: Einführung; Allegeminer Überblick; Die Entwicklung des

Krugbäckergewerbes; Das Krugbäckeranwesen; Das Arbeitsmaterial; Die Herstellung von Steinzeug; Das Leben in der Gruppe; Die Ware; Der Handel mit "steinen Geschirr"; Die Irden- und Ziegelbäckerei im Abriss; Die Pfeifenbäckerei im Abriss; Ergebnisse. Comprehensive bibliography, pp. 268-78, and further bibliography and in the footnotes.

794 Koetschau, K. **Rheinisches Steinzeug.** Munich, 1924. 53p (text), 73 plates. LC 35-20454.

Important collection of plates of sixteenth- and seventeenth-century Rhenish stoneware with an introductory essay by a leading expert. Contents: I, Allgemeine Charakteristik—Forscher und Sammler; II, Die Technik des Rheinischen Steinzeugs; III, Die Arten der Steinseuggefässe; IV, Die Kölner unf Frechner Werkstätten; V, Die Siegburger Werkstätten; VI, Die Raerener Werkstätten; VII, Die Werkstätten des Westerwaldes. No bibliography.

795 Kroll, Joachim. **Creussener Steinzeug.** Braunschweig, Klinkhardt & Biermann, 1980. 321p. illus. index. LC 80-151012.

Comprehensive history/handbook of the stoneware, decorated in relief and colors made in Creussen during the seventeenth and early eighteenth centuries. Creussen ware is viewed as the apex of stoneware art. Contents: 1, Creussen—Lage, geschichtliche Entwicklung, Wirtschaft; 2, Creussener Ton und seine Verarbeitung; 3, Creussener Fayence; 4, Die Vests al Krugmacher; 5, Die Familie Speckner; 6, Weitere Creussener Hafner und Krugmacher; 7, Was kostete ein Creussener Krug; 8, Humpen mit Kerbschnittmuster; 9, Apostelkrüge; 10, Jagdkrüge; 11, Planetenkrüge; 12, Kurfürstenkrüge; 14, Hochzeits- und Familienkrüge; 14, Humpen mit abweichenden Dekors; 15, Kannen; 16, Flaschen; 17, Varia. Notes to the plates. Bibliographical references in the notes, basic books, p. 319.

See also the exhibition catalogs: *Deutsches Steinzeug der Renaissance-und Barockzeit.* Hetjens-Museum, Düsseldorf—Deutsches Keramikmuseum (Düsseldorf, Das Museum, 1979. 194p. illus.) and *Steinzeug* by G. Reineking von Bock (Cologne, Kunstgewerbemuseum, 1971).

Bunzlau Pottery

796 Müller, Heide, Ekkehard and Inge Lippert. **Bunzlauer Geschirr: Grebrauchsware zwischen Handwerk und Industrie.** Berlin, Reimer, 1986. 415p. illus. ISBN 3496010363.

Comprehensive, scholarly history/handbook of the pottery made in the region of Bunzlau from the middle of the nineteenth century to 1985. "Katalog" provides detailed descriptions of the products of the individual firms, list of the names of potters and repertory of marks and examination of the technologies employed, the training of potters and other workers, and commercial aspects. Contents: Lebens- und Arbeitsbedingungen der Töpfer; Herstellungsverfahren des Bunzlauer Geschirrs; Dekore; Formen des Bunzlauer Geschirrs; Die "Großen Töpfe" von Bunzlau und Naumburg/Q.; Der Gebrauch von Bunzlauer Geschirr; Handel und Absatz; Verkaufspreise; Bunzlau und seine Konkurrenz; Preußische Gewerbeförderung; Die Keramischen Fachschule Bunzlau; Aktion "Bunzlauer Braunzeug"; Bau- und Industriekeramik; "Bunzlauer Geschirr" nach 1945; Katalog. Comprehensive bibliography, pp. 218-228.

797 Späth, Kristine. **Töpferei in Schlesien.** Bunzlau und Umgebung. 2d ed. Bad Windsheim, Delp, 1981. 124p. illus. ISBN 3768901726.

History of Silesian pottery between the two World Wars that includes high quality industrial production and studio pottery. Contents: I, Bunzlau; II, Naumburg/Queis: Die Arbeit in einer schlesischen Töpferwerkstelle, Die Arbeit im Brennhaus, Ausstellungsplakat von 1912, Vom Vertrieb der Topfwaren, Der "Töpferstolz" Die soziale Stellung der Töpfergesellen; Redende Teller; Die Keramische Fachschule in Bunzlau und ihre kurze aber wechselvolle Geschichte; Die

Aktion Bunzlauer Braunzeug der Keramischen Fachschule. Appendix with price list of Bunzlau-Naumburg ware dated 1936. General bibliography, pp. 122-23.

Mettlach Pottery

798 Kirsner, Gary. **The Mettlach Book**. 2d ed. Coral Springs, Fla., Glentiques, 1987. 335p. illus. index. ISBN 0961413018.

Comprehensive collector's handbook of the ceramics made by the firm of Villeroy & Boch at Mettlach in the Saarland. Particular attention is given to the production for export between 1880 and 1910. Introduction traces the history of the factory at Mettlach. Catalog is subdivided by type of ware: steins, plaques, beakers, punch bowls, pokals, vases, early wares, chronolith wares, present day production. Representative pieces are described in table form listing mold number, size, type of decoration, and value. Appendix with advice for collectors.

See also Post, Anton. *Mettlach Steinzeug, 1885-1905*. Wheeling, Ill., H. J. Ammelounx, 1975. 368p. illus. for a compilation of the Mettlach catalogs and price lists from 1885 to 1905 of the Villeroy & Boch Company, Mettlach, Germany, R. H. Mohr, *Mettlach Steins and Their Prices: Including Plaques, Beakers, Punch Bowls, Pokals, Coasters*. rev. 7th ed. Rockford, Ill., Mohr, 1978. 145p. illus., and the exhibition catalog: *Villeroy & Boch, 1748-1985: Art et industrie ceramique*, by A. Fay-Halle and F. Heisbourg-Sulbout (Paris, Éditions de la Reunion des Musées Nationaux, 1985. 209p. illus. ISBN 2711820203).

Great Britain

General Histories and Handbooks

799 Godden, Geoffrey. **British Pottery**. New York, Potter, 1975. 452p. illus. index. LC 74-14332.

Popular collector's handbook/history of British pottery from the seventeenth century to 1970. Companion to the author's *British Porcelain: An Illustrated Guide* (649). Contents: Slip-wares; Delft-type Wares; Stonewares; Salt-Glazed Wares; Veined Wares; Red-Wares; Wieldon-type Wares; Sussex Wares; Wedgwood; Wedgwood-styled Wares; Creamwares; Basalt; Jasper; Turner's Body; Ironstone-type Bodies; Lustre Decoration; Mocha Decoration; William Ridgway Earthenware; Printing; Pratt and Colour-printing; Pratt-type Wares; Majolica Wares; Staffordshire Figures; Doulton Wares; The Martin Brothers; William De Morgan; The Art Potteries: Della Robia, Linthorpe, Ault, Barum, Aller Vale and Farnham, Ruskin, Bernard Moore, Elton; Art Nouveau; Maw & Co.; Pilkington's Royal Lancastrian; Moorcroft; "Cheap Line''; Art Deco and the 1920s and 1930s: Poole, Powell Decorated Wedgwood, Gwendolen Parnell, Charles Vyse, Henry Parr, Coronation Wares; Studio Pottery; Modern Commercial Pottery. Useful chiefly for the large number of illustrations arranged to facilitate identification of a broad spectrum of wares.

800 Hodgkin, John E., and Edith Hodgkin. **Examples of Early English Pottery, Named, Dated, and Inscribed**. London, Cassell, 1891. 187p. illus. Reprint: Yorkshire, E. P. Pub., 1973. LC 75-320112.

Collection of 685 examples of dated and inscribed English pottery from the sixteenth through the seventeenth centuries. Arrangement is by type of ware. Inscription given in facsimile and each piece is briefly described.

801 Hughes, George B. **English and Scottish Earthenware, 1660-1860**. New York, Macmillan, 1961. 238p. illus. index. LC 61-1648.

General history of English and Scottish pottery from 1660 to 1860 directed to the collector. Text features excerpts from contemporary—mostly nineteenth-century advertisements. 1, Tin-enamelled Earthenware; 2, Salt-Glazed Stoneware: Brown; 3, Staffordshire Salt-Glazed Stoneware: White; 4, Variegated Earthenwares: Marbled, Agate and Tortoiseshell; 5, Red and Cane-Coloured Stonewares; 6, Egyptian Black Stoneware and Basaltes; 7, Jasper; 8, Cream-Coloured Earthenware; 9, Transfer-printed Earthenware; 10, The Stone Chinas; 11, Chimney Ornaments; 12, Lustre and English Majolica; 13, Scottish Pottery.

802   Rackham, Bernard, and Herbert Read. **English Pottery**. London, Benn, 1924. 142p. illus. index. Reprint: Wakefield, E. P. Publishing, 1972. LC 73-150451.

Authoritative survey of English pottery from the Middle Ages to the end of the eighteenth century. Includes 115 plates with brief, descriptive captions. Contents: I, Introduction ; II, The Middle Ages and Tudor Times; III, The English Tradition; IV, Foreign Strains: Majolica and Delft; V, Foreign Strains: Stoneware; VI, Staffordshire: The Rise of Industrialism; VII, Minor Industrial Potteries: Leeds and Liverpool; VIII, The Influence of Porcelain; IX, The Neo-classical Age; X, Conclusion. Appendix with notes on the potters of Wotham by J. W. L. Glaisher. Bibliographies at the end of each section.

803   Rackham, Bernard. **Medieval English Pottery**. 2nd ed. London, Faber and Faber, 1972. 39p. (text), 96p. (plates). index. ISBN 0571047653.

First published in 1948. A pioneering work in the history of medieval pottery. Covers English pottery, earthenware and stoneware of the twelfth through the fifteenth centuries. Collection of plates of well-chosen museum pieces with descriptive captions. General bibliography, pp. 33-35, and references to specialized literature in the footnotes.

Turner Pottery

804   Hillier, Bevis. **Master Potters of the Industrial Revolution. The Turners of Lane End.** London, Cory, Adams & Mackay, 1965. 96p. illus. index. LC 66-70629.

Survey of the pottery produced in London at the end of the eighteenth and beginning of the nineteenth centuries by John Turner (1738-87) and his sons William and John. Extensive use of documentary sources. Contents: 1, Brewood and Stoker; 2, Lane End; 3, The Wares; 4, Modelers and Decorators; 5, Porcelain; 6, The Gerverot Beaker; 7, The French Revolution; 8, The London Partnership; 9, The End of the Factory; 10, The Industrial Revolution. Bibliographical references in the notes.

Wemyss Pottery

805   Davis, Peter, and Robert Rankine. **Wemyss Ware. A Decorative Scottish Pottery**. Edinburgh and London, Scottish Academic Press, 1986. 173p. illus. index. ISBN 0707303540.

Well-illustrated survey of the popular, gaily painted pottery table and decorative ware made at Fife between 1882 and 1930. Contents: I, The Fife Pottery in Its Scottish Context; II, Establishing Wemyss Ware; III, Management, Potting & Firing; IV, Working Conditions; V, Commercial Aspects; VI, The Decorators; VII, Wemyss Decorations; VIII, Bovey Tracey Period & Wemyss-Like Wares; IX, List of Wemyss Decorations; X, Markings; XI, Notes on Price Lists & Catalogues; XII, Chronology. Brief bibliography, p. 57. Contains 356 plates with descriptive captions.

English Delftware (Faience)

806 Garner, F. H., and Michael Archer. **English Delftware**. 2d rev. and enl. ed. London, Faber and Faber, 1972. 103p. (text), 253p. (plates). index. ISBN 0571047564.

In the series: "The Faber Monographs on Pottery and Porcelain." Comprehensive history of Delftware in England from the sixteenth to the middle of the eighteenth centuries. Contents: 1, Origins and Method of Manufacture; 2, Seventeenth-Century Delftware; 3, An Introduction to Eighteenth-Century Delftware; 4, The Attribution of Eighteenth-Century Delftware from Lambeth, Bristol and Liverpool; 5, The History of the London Pot-Houses; 6, The History of the Brislington and Bristol Pot-houses; 7, The History of the Liverpool Pot-Houses; 8, The Wincanton Pot-house and Its Delftware; 9, The Irish Pot-houses and Their Delftware; 10, The Glasgow Pot-house and Its Delftware; 11, The Manufacturer of Delftware in America. Comprehensive, classified bibliography, pp. 83-86. Standard work.

See also the older history: *English Delft Pottery* by R. G. Mundy (London, Jenkins, 1928. 127p. illus. index).

807 Lipski, Louis L. **Dated English Delftware: Tin-Glazed Earthenware, 1600-1800**. Edited and augmented by Michael Archer; contributions by Robert J. Charleston, M. K. Stammers, and Douglas C. Harrod. London, Sotheby Publications, 1984. 447p. illus. index. ISBN 0856671827.

Important corpus of dated pieces of English faience of the seventeenth and eighteenth centuries. Arranged by type then by date. Concluding chapter on pieces inscribed at a later date. Each piece is illustrated and described. Introductory essay for each type or category. General bibliography given at the end of the introduction. An indispensable handbook for collector and historian.

Stoneware

808 Oswald, Adrian, R. J. C. Hildyard, and R. C. Hughes. **English Brown Stoneware, 1670-1900**. London, Faber and Faber, 1982. 308p. illus. index. ISBN 057119050.

In the series: "The Faber Monographs on Pottery and Porcelain." History/handbook of English brown stoneware from the late sixteenth century to the end of the nineteenth century. Emphasis is on the products of common use: mugs, jugs, teapots, etc. The refined stoneware with improved bodies made in the factories of Turner, Adams, Wedgwood and Herculaneum are not included. Arrangements is by region. Includes much information culled from documents and excavations. Appendices with survey of Scottish stoneware, list of dated hunting mugs, and list of dated Derbyshire pieces. Comprehensive, classified bibliography, pp. 289-30, includes periodical articles.

Printed Pottery

809 Coysh, A. W., and R. K. Henrywood. **The Dictionary of Blue and White Printed Pottery, 1780-1880**. Woodbridge, Suffolk, England, Antique Collectors' Club, 1982. 420p. illus. index. ISBN 0907462065.

Comprehensive dictionary covering all aspects of European pottery using the transfer printed technique between 1780 and 1880. Although the entries include makers, manufactories and types of ware, the majority are patterns and motifs typical of transfer ware. Many of these patterns are identified by name on the reverse and these marks are reproduced along with the pottery. Appendix I is a index of potters initial marks, appendix II a list of illustrated nineteenth century books used as sources for patterns. General bibliography, pp. 419-420. A very useful reference work to the complex world of nineteenth-century popular pottery.

810   Williams-Wood, Cyril. **English Transfer-Printed Pottery and Porcelain: A History of Over-Glaze Printing**. London, Faber and Faber, 1981. 249p. illus.index. ISBN 0571116949.

Comprehensive history of use of the technique of transferring an engraved or etched print to decorated pottery and porcelain in England during the eighteenth and early nineteenth centuries. Contents: 1, Introduction; 2, Invention of Transfer Printing: Pouncing; Japanning and Enamelling; John Brooks in Birmingham; Battersea Enamel Works; 3, Transfer Printing on Glazed Porcelain; 4, The Northern School of Transfer Printing; 6, The Dissemination—Free-Lance Transfer Printers; 7, The Dissemination—Potteries and Factories; 8, Aberrations and Vagaries. Glossary of terms, comprehensive, classified bibliography, pp. 240-243.

Art Pottery

811   Haslam, Malcom. **English Art Pottery, 1865-1915**. Woodbridge, Suffolk, Antique Collectors' Club, 1975. 214p. illus. index. ISBN 09002002826X.

Collector's history/handbook of British art ceramics of the so-called Aesthetic Movement, featuring extracts from contemporary art magazines, e.g., *The Studio*, that describe the products of the various factories and artists-designers (Doulton; Martinware & Brannam; Minton Art Pottery; Painted Pottery; De Morgan; Della Robia; Watcombe; Brannam; Elton, Linthorpe; Burmantofts; Edwardian; Martinware). Large collection of plates illustrating typical pieces, many with details showing marks and signatures. Contents: The Art Pottery Movement; Artistic Stoneware; Painted Pottery of the Aesthetic Movement; Pre-Raphaelite Pottery; Art Pottery from the West Country; Form and Colour; From Art Pottery to Studio Pottery. No bibliography.

Michael Cardew, 1901-1982

812   Clark, Garth. **Michael Cardew. A Portrait**. Tokyo, New York, Kodansha International, 1976. 228p. illus. index. ISBN 0870112775.

Appreciative monograph on the art pottery of Michael Cardew with 82 plates of pieces dating between 1938 and 1976. "Workshop Appendix" discusses the technical aspects of the four workshops that Cardew directed. Bibliography, pp. 225-26.

Bernard Leach, 1887-1979

813   Hogben, Carol, ed. **The Art of Bernard Leach**. New York, Watson-Guptill, 1978. 192p. illus. ISBN 0823002632.

Contents: Foreword and Introduction by C. Hogben; Leach as Author by E. Mullins; Writings; Tributes; Bernard Leach: Chronology; Pots; Drawings and Etchings; Descriptions of the Illustrations; Select Bibliography, pp. 185-86. Appendices with "Review 1909-1914" and "A Potter's Outlook" (1928).

Italy

814   Ballardini, Gaetano. **Corpus della maiolicha italiana**. Rome, Libreria dello Stato, 1933-35. 2v. illus. index. (Bollettino d'Arte, Pubblicazione Annuale, N. 1). Reprinted, 1988.

Important handbook of Italian majolica to 1535 confined to dated examples in museums and private collections in Europe and America. Contents: volume 1: Le maioliche datate fino al 1530; volume 2: Le maioliche datate dal 1531 al 1535. Volume one catalogs 255 pieces, volume two catalogs 2,219 pieces. A standard reference work on early Italian majolica. Bibliographical footnotes.

815 Ballardini, Gaetano. **La maiolicha italiana dalle origini alla fine del Cinquecento**. Florence, Babera, Alfoni e Venturi, 1938. 64p. illus. index. Reprinted: Florence, Faenza, 1975. LC 75-406525.

Popular, pictorial survey of Italian majolica from the Middle Ages to the end of the seventeenth century. No bibliography.

816 Brosio, Valentino. **Porcellane e maioliche italiane dell' Ottocento**. Milan, Vallardi, 1960. 139p. illus. index. LC A61-3713.

Popular survey of Italian porcelain and faience of the eighteenth century. Brief introductory essay followed by selection of plates illustrating museum pieces. Brief bibliography of books in Italian.

817 Chompret, J. **Repertoire de la majolique italienne**. Paris, Editions Nomis, 1949. 227p. illus. index. LC A51-1293r53.

Comprehensive, scholarly handbook of Italian majolica from the fifteenth century through the eighteenth century. Contents; volume one: text; volume two: 1,100 plates. Both text and plates are arranged by center of production. Brief bibliography, v 1, p. 210, lists books consulted; additional bibliography in the footnotes.

818 Conti, Giovanni. **L'arte della maiolica in Italia**. Milan, Bramante, 1973. 387p. illus. LC 73-309617.

Authoritative survey of Italian majolica from its beginnings to the end of the nineteenth century. Well-illustrated with pieces in museums and major private collections. Arranged by centuries; brief introductory essays on technique, function, forgeries and collectors are followed by an outline of events and documents in the manufacture of majolica from 1115 and 1908, and a corpus of plates of 517 pieces. Comprehensive, chronologically arranged bibliography, pp. 379-81, and additional bibliography in the footnotes.

819 Falke, Otto von. **Majolike**. 2nd ed. Berlin, G. Reimer, 1907. 208p. illus. index. LC 13-9925.

Old, scholarly history of Italian majolica of the fifteenth and sixteenth centuries with emphasis on pieces in the Berlin Kunstgewerbe Museum. First published in 1896. A classic pioneering work by a great authority in the history of medieval and Renaissance decorative arts.

820 Liverani, Giovanni. **Five Centuries of Italian Majolica**. New York, McGraw-Hill, 1960. 258p. illus. index. LC 59-13206.

Authoritative survey of Italian majolica from the fifteenth century to the early twentieth century. Selection of excellent plates. Brief bibliography of basic books and periodical articles.

821 Rackham, Bernard. **Italian Maiolica**. New York, Pitman, 1952. 35p. (text), 96p. (illus). illus. index. LC 53-16488.

Popular but authoritative survey of Italian tin-glazed pottery from the fifteenth century to 1800. Illustrated with pieces in British museums and great private collections. Contents: 1, Historical Setting. Origins, Technique; 2, Aesthetics of Maiolica; 3, Local Distribution of the Potteries, Development of Design. The Early Wares. Tuscany and Faenza; 4, The Early Renaissance. Introduction of Lustre; 5, The Pictorial School. Castel Durante and Urbino; 6, Sgraffiato Ware; 7, Later Maiolica: 1550-1800. Bibliography of basic books, pp. 32-33.

See also the museum catalogs: *Catalogue of the Italian Majolica in the Walters Art Gallery*, by J. Prentice von Erdbert and M. C. Ross (Baltimore, Md., Walters Art Gallery, 1952. 58p. illus.), *Italienische Majolika: Katalog der Sammlung*, by J. Lessmann (Braunschweig, Herzog Anton Ulrich-Museum; Berlin, Wasmuth, 1979. 623p. illus.), *Catalogo delle maioliche* (Museo Nazionale del Bargello) by G. Conti. (Florence, Centro Di., 1971. 154p. illus.), *Majolika: spanische und italienische Keramik vom 14. bis zum 18. Jahrhundert,* by T. Hausmann (Berlin, Mann, 1972. 422p. illus.), *Catalog of Italian Majolica* by B. Rackham (London, Victoria and Albert Museum, 1977. 2v. illus.), *Catalogue des majoliques des musées nationaux—Musées du Louvre et de Cluny, Musée national de céramique à Sèvres, Musée Adrien-Dubouché à Limoges,* by J. Giacomotti (Paris, Éditions des Musées Nationaux, 1974. 517p. illus.), *Ceramic Art of the Italian Renaissance,* by T. Wilson (London, Trustees of the British Museum, 1987. 192p. illus. index. ISBN 0292711158) and the exibition catalogs: *Italian Renaissance Maiolica from the William A. Clark Collection,* by W. M. Watson (London, Scala Books, 1986. 191p. illus), *Italian Maiolica from Midwestern Collections* by B. Cole (Bloomington, Ind., Indiana University Art Museum, 1977. 101p. illus.), *Una collezione di maioliche del Rinascimento,* by G. Conti (Milan, Galleria Carla Silvestri, 1984. 100p. illus.).

Regional Histories and Handbooks

Cafaggiolo

822   Cora, Galeazzo, and Angiolo Fanfani. **La maiolica di Cafaggiolo.** Florence, Centro Di, 1982. 191p. illus. ISBN 8870380521.

Well-illustrated, authoritative handbook/history of majolica manufactured in Caffaggiolo during the sixteenth century. Introductory essay: "La manifattura di Cafaggiolo e il suo tempo" followed by 154 plates of pieces arranged in chronological order and with detailed descriptive captions. Includes views of the undersides of marked and signed pieces. Appendix has valuable dictionary of potters. Comprehensive bibliography, pp. 188-189.

Deruta

823   De Mauri, L. **Le maioliche di Deruta: Una pagina di storia dell'arte umbra.** Milan, Bottega di Poesia, 1924. 61p. illus. LC NUC87-725860.

Survey of majolica produced in Deruta froom the thirteenth century to early twentieth century with emphasis on the period between 1400 and 1600. References to documentary sources.

See also the exhibition catalog: *Antiche maioliche di Deruta* by G. Guaitini (Perugia, Provincia di Perugia, 1980. 160p. illus.).

Ferrara

824   Magnani, Romolo. **La ceramica ferrarese tra Medioevo e Rinascimento.** Ferrara, Belriguardo, 1981. 2v. illus. LC 81-150979.

Comprehensive, scholarly history of ceramics produced in Ferrara in the fifteenth and sixteenth centuries with emphasis on the characteristic sgraffito ware and the relationship of its decoration to contemporary painting and sculpture.

Florence

825   Cora, Galeazzo. **Storia della maiolica di Firenze e del Contado.** Florence, Sansoni, 1973. 2v. illus. index. LC 73-336189.

Comprehensive, scholarly, and well-illustrated history of majolica produced in Florence and vicinity during the fourteenth and fifteenth centuries. Extensive use of documentary sources and results of recent excavations. Volume one: text divided into 21 chapters and includes information on more than 650 potters; volume two: 365 plates with reproductions of marks and list of documents. A standard work.

826 Davillier, Charles. **Les origines de la porcelaine en Europe: Les Fabriques italiennes du XVe au XVIIe siècle avec une étude spécial sur les porcelaines des Médicis.** Paris, J. Rouam; London, Remington & Co., 1882. 140p. illus.

Still a fundamental study of the efforts to imitate Oriental porcelain in Italy, particularly under the patronage of the Medici, during the sixteenth and seventeenth centuries. Catalog of pieces and list of documents. Illustrated with line drawings.

Liguria

827 Marzinot, Federico. **Ceramica e ceramisti di Liguria.** Genoa, SAGEP, 1979. 383p. illus. index.

Comprehensive history of ceramics and ceramicists in Liguria from prehistoric times to the twentieth century. Includes 443 plates with descriptive captions. Appendix with 57 marks in facsimile and 16 marks in photographic reproduction. Bibliographical references in the footnotes.

Milan

828 Baroni, Costantino. **Maioliche di Milano.** Milan, Libreria Lombarda, 1940. 71p. illus.

Survey of majolica produced in Milan from the fourteenth century through the eighteenth century with emphasis on pieces in the Castello Sforzesco.

Naples

829 Mosca, Luigi. **Napoli e l'arte ceramica dal XII al XX secolo con marche e piante di antiche fabbriche.** 2d ed. Naples. Fausto Fiorentino, 1963. 257p. illus. index. LC 75-566252.

First published in 1908 (Naples, R. Ricciardi). Survey of ceramics produced in Naples and vicinity from the twelfth to the twentieth centuries.

Pesaro

830 Berardi, Paride. **L'antica maiolica di Pesaro dal XIV al XVII secolo.** Florence, Sansoni, 1984. 356p. illus. index. LC 84-192856.

Comprehensive history of majolica produced in Pesaro from the fourteenth century to the end of the seventeenth century with emphasis on the socio-economic context. List of potters.

Siena

831 Francovich, Riccardo. **La ceramica medievale a Siena e nella Toscana (sec. XIV-XV).** Florence, All'Insegna del Giglio, 1982. 332p. illus. (Ricerche di Archaeologia Altomedievale e Medievale, 5-6).

Scholarly, archaeological study of Sienese majolica of the fourteenth and fifteenth centuries. Contents: I, Abreviazioni bibliografiche (comprehensive bibliography); II, Introduzione; III, I documenti; IV, I caratteri generali della ceramica senese; V, Le tipologie della "maiolica arcaica" e dell' "ingubbiata e graffita"; VI, I retrovamenti in area urbana; VII, Studio delle caratteristiche mineralogico-petrografiche e chemiche delle coperte e dei biscotti di alcuni reperti provenicuti da una fornace di Siena. Bibliographical footnotes.

Venice

832 Bartolotto, Angelica A. **Storia della ceramica a Venezia dagli albori alla fine della Repubblica.** Florence, Sansoni, 1981. 430p. illus. LC 82-111098.

Comprehensive history of pottery and porcelain production in Venice from the ninth century to the early nineteenth century. Extensive use of documents; large collection of plates with descriptive captions. Contents: I, Le Fonti (excellent essay on sources and bibliography); II, Testimonianze ritrovate; III, La techniche piu antiche. Terracotta, terracotta verniciata e mezzamaiolica dal IX secolo al XVI; IV, La maiolica del primo periodo tra influssi orientali e tendenze classicheggianti; V, La maiolica del secondo periodo dal manierismo dell'istoriato alla sobrietà del compendaiario e oltre; VI, La porcellana Dura, conquista del moderno imprenditore- i Latesini, canto del cigno dell'antica corporazione. Comprehensive bibliography, pp. 406-413.

Netherlands

833   Havard, Henry. **La céramique hollandaise. Histoire des faïences de Delft, Haarlem, Rotterdam, Arnhem, Utrecht, etc. et des porcelaines de Weesp, Loosdrecht, Amsterdam et la Haye**. Amsterdam, Vivat, 1909. 2v. illus. index. LC 08-056399.
    An old, standard history by a leading connoisseur. Covers Dutch pottery and ceramics from the Middle Ages to the nineteenth century with chapter on Dutch porcelains of de Weesp, Loosdrecht, Amsterdam and the Hague. Contents: I, Le précurseurs; II, Les origines de la faïencerie de Delft; III, Haarlem; IV, La faïence de Delft—première période; V, La Gilde de Saint-Luc a Delft; VI, La faïence de Delft—seconde période; VII, La faïence de Delft—troisième période; VIII, La province de Hollande; IX, Utrecht, la Gueldre, le Gooi; X, Le Théières rouges; XI, La porcelaine hollandaise. Bibliographical references in the footnotes.

834   Jonge, C. H. de. **Delft Ceramics**. New York, Praeger, 1970. 168p. illus. index. LC 68-24042.
    Based on the author's *Oud-Nederlandsche Majolica en Delftsch Aardwerk* (1947). Pictorial survey of Delft faience from the seventeenth century to the end of the nineteenth century. Contents: I, The Technique; II, The Transition from Northern Dutch Majolica to Delft Faience; III, Tiles and Plaques: 1600-1700. Frederik van Frijtom; IV, 'Wapengoet en Porceleyn'—"Kaapsche Schotels." Delft Faience 1650-1700; V, Blue Delft: 1670-1730; VI, Red Delft Teapots: 1672-1731; VII, Polychrome Delft Faience Fired at High Temperature: 1670-1730; VIII, Polychrome Delft Faience on Dark Brown, Olive-Green or Black Background. Nevers Blue Faience: 1670-1740; IX, Tile Pictures and Plaques. Rooms Tiled with Blue, Polychrome and Back Delft Faience: 1680-1740; X, Polychrome Delft Faience Fired at Low Temperatures: 1680-1750; XI, Blue and Polychrome Delft Faience Fired at High Temperatures after 1730; XII, White Delft: 1600-1800. Appendix with list of potteries and marks reproduced in facsimiles. Basic bibliography, p. 168.

835   Korf, Dingeman. **Nederlandse majolica**. Haarlem, De Haan, 1981. 257p. illus. index. LC 81-189016. ISBN 9022842738.
    Comprehensive history/handbook of Dutch majolica of the sixteenth and seventeenth centuries. Includes tiles. Chapters on technique, dating and overview of the style of Dutch faience and majolica are followed by chapters with detailed descriptions of pieces—some fragmentary— grouped by the type of decoration. Pieces are shown in cross section and with measurements. Bibliography, pp. 255-57, and bibliographical references in the notes.

836   Neurdenburg, Elisabeth, and Bernard Rackham. **Old Dutch Pottery and Tiles**. London, Benn, 1923. 155p. illus. index. LC 83-14932.
    Scholarly, but in part out-of-date, history of Dutch earthenware from the Middle Ages to the end of the eighteenth century with emphasis on tiles. Contents: 1, Introduction; 2, The Process of Manufacture; 3, Dutch Red Earthenware and Tiles; 4, Dutch Maiolica of the 16th and 17th Centuries; 5, Dutch Tiles; 6, Dutch Tile-picture; 7, Delft Earthenware; its Origins and Study; 8, Blue-and White Delft. De Keizer, Pijnacker, Frijtom and Other Potters and Pottery-painters of the 17th Century; 9, Samuel van Eeenhoorn and Rochus Hoppesteyn; 10, Lambertus van Eeenhorn

and Louwijs Fictoor; 11, Blue-and White and Purple Delft of the 18th Century; 12, Polychrome Delft of the Grand Feu. Lambertus van Eeenhorn and Louwijs Fictoor; 13, The "Rose" Factory. Verhaast and Other 17th-century Potters; 14, Delft Ware with Coloured Ground. Imitations of Foreign Earthenware; 15, Grand feu Polychrome Ware of the 18th Century; 16, The Beginnings of Muffle-kiln Painting. Hoppesteyn, Pijnacker, and others; 17, The Muddle-kiln. The Influence of Porcelain Technique; 18, The Red Teapots of Delft; 19, The Decline; 20, The Place of Dutch Earthenware in the History of European Pottery. Appendix with list of Delft potters in 1764. Basic bibliography, pp. 147-48.

837   Rackham, Bernard. **Early Netherlands Maiolica**. London, Bles, 1926. 136p. illus. index. LC 37-31758.
    Authoritative survey of Dutch polychromatic earthenware, including tiles, of the sixteenth and seventeenth centuries. Chapter on the seventeenth century includes England. Illustrated with museum pieces and illustrations of pottery in contemporary paintings. Bibliography of basic books and periodical article, p. 131-32.

Delft Ware

Dictionaries

838   Justice, Jean. **Dictionary of Marks and Monograms of Delft Pottery**. London, Jenkins, 1930. 171p. illus. LC 31-8665.
    Repertory of marks on Dutch faience illustrated with facsimiles.

Histories and Handbooks

839   Fourest, Henry P. **Delftware. Faience Production at Delft**. New York, Rizzoli, 1980. 201p. illus. index. ISBN 0847803228.
    Early edition: Paris, Presses universitaires de France, 1957. 117p. illus. LC A58-3123. Comprehensive, well-illustrated history of faience produced in Delft during the seventeenth and eighteenth centuries. Contents: I, Dutch Faience before Production began at Delft; II, Materials and Manufacture; III, Historical Setting: Trade Guilds, Masters, Trade Problems; IV, Seventeenth and Early Eighteenth Centuries; V, The Rapid Rise of Production in the Early Eighteenth Century; VI, The Evolution of Styles and Shapes; VII, 'Peasant Delft'; VIII, Figurines, Trompe-l'oeil and Full Relief; IX, Ornamental Plaques; X, Dutch Tiles; XI, Dutch Faience Other Than Delftware; XII, The Role and Influence of Delftware in Europe. Repertory of marks and comprehensive, classified bibliography, pp. 195-96, with good coverage of exhibition catalogs.

840   Lunsingh Scheurleer, D. F. **Delft: niederlandische Fayence**. Munich, Klinkhardt & Biermann, 1984. 379p. illus. index. ISBN 3781402118.
    Comprehensive, authoritative history of Netherlandish faience and majolica from the late Middle Ages to the early nineteenth century with emphasis on the production at Delft in the seventeenth and eighteenth centuries. Contents: Einleitung: Zur Verwendung nordniederländischen Majolika und Delfter Fayence, Zur Literatur über niederländischen Fayencen; Technik; Vorläufer und Frühformen der niederländischen Fayence; Delfter Fayence—Hanwerksgeschichte; Nordniederländische Majolika 1550 bis 1650; Delfter Fayence 1640/50 bis um 1725; Delfter Fayence 1725/30 bis zum Ende des 18. Jahrhunderts: Formen und Dekore, Die Manufakturen, Tafelgeschirr, Tee-, Schokoladen- und Kaffeeservices, Delfter Gebrauchsfayence, Rauchergegenstände und Objekte mit Raucherdarstellungen; Weiße Delfter Fayence; Vasen und Schrankaufsätze; Tulpenvasen; Delfter Blaudekore 1640/50 bis um 1725; Delfter Baudekore 1725/30 bis gegen Ende des 18. Jahrhunderts; Delfter Fayencen mit polychromen Scharffeuerdekoren; Delfter

Fayencen mit petit-feu oder Muffelfarbendekor; Delfter Fayencen mit einfarbigem Fond; Delfter Bauernfayence, Kleinplastiken, Mitglied des Hauses Oranien, historische und politische Ereignisse auf Delfter Fayencen; Friesische Fayencen; Delfter Fayence und das Ausland; Fayencen aus anderen niederländischen Städten; Niederländische Creamware. Comprehensive, unclassified bibliography, pp. 345-360, has exhaustive list of exhibition catalogs. See introduction for bibliographical essay. A standard work on Delft faience.

See also the museum catalog: *Delfts Aardewerk*, by M. A. Heukensfeldt Jansen (Amsterdam, Rijksmuseum, 1961) and the exhibition catalog: *Nederlands-Dutch Silver 1580-1830*, by A. L. den Baauwen (Amsterdam, Rijksmuseum, 1979).

Portugal

841 Santos, Reynaldo dos. **Faiança portuguesa**. Porto, Galaica, 1960. 169p. illus. index. LC 61-43631.

Pictorial history of Portuguese faience of the sixteenth and seventeenth centuries with particular emphasis on the influence of Chinese porcelain. Section on the seventeenth century is divided into quarter centuries and features a number of dated pieces. One hundred black and white plates and twenty-five color plates with descriptive notes. No bibliography.

Alcora

842 Codina, E. **Aportación documental a la historia de la Real Fábrica de Loza Fina de Alcora**. Catellón de la Plana, Sociedad Castellonense de Cultura, 1980. 70p. index. ISBN 840004553X.

Unillustrated history of the faience manufactory at Alcora during the eighteenth century based on documentary sources. List of names of potters and painters and list of inventories dating between 1729 and 1789.

Scandinavia

843 Frohne, J. W. **Danske fajancer...** Copenhagen, Schultz, 1911. 157p. illus. index. LC 46-41846.

Old, once-standard history of Danish faience of the eighteenth and early nineteenth century. Contents: I, Kong Christian VI.s Kakelovnsfabrik bag Blaataarn 1738-1754; II, Fajancerfabriken i St. Kongensgade 1722-1772; III, Kastrup Fajances-og Stentøjsfabrik 1755- ca. 1814; IV, Johan Frederik Classens Fajance-og Ovnfabrik paa Osterbro; V, Ovnfabriken paa Vesterbro 1787-1812; VI, Fajancefabrikerne paa Mors, Gudumlund og Oland; VII, Bornholms Fajance- og Stentøjsfabrik 1792-1800; VIII, Slesvig Bys Fajancefabrik 1755-1814; IX, Criseby's og Eckernförde's Fajancefabriken 1758- ca. 1785; X, Kiels Fajancefabrik 1758- ca. 1780; XI, Rendsborgs Fajance- og Stentøjsfabriker 1765- ca. 1830; XII, Kellinghusens Fajance- og Stentøjsfabriker 1765- ca. 1830; XIII, Stockelsdorffs Fajancefabrik 1771- ca. 1786. Appendix with the privilegium of 1727 for the factory at St. Kongensgade. Bibliographical references in the footnotes.

844 Uldall, Kai. **Gammel Dansk Fajence**. Copenhagen, Thaning & Appels, 1961. 300p. illus. index. LC 68-79933.

Comprehensive, scholarly history/handbook of Danish faience from the beginnings until the early nineteenth century. Contents: St. Kongensgadefabriken; Blåtårnfabriken; Osterbrofabriken; Morsofabriken; Bornholmfabriken; Gudumlundfabriken; Olandfabriken; Antvorskov-og Hesbjergfabrikerne; Slevigfabriken; Criseby-Eckernforde-, Kiel- og Stockelsdorffabrikerne; Rendsborgfabriken; Kellinghusenfabrikerne; Altonafabriken; Anden Fajencetilvirkning, ovnfabriker. Repertory of marks. Notes contain much important documentary information and extensive bibliography.

Spain

845 Frothingham, Alice W. **Lustreware of Spain**. New York, Hispanic Society of America, 1951. 310p. illus. index. LC 51-10259.

Comprehensive, scholarly history of lustreware made in Spain from the tenth through the eighteenth centuries by a leading expert on Spanish applied and decorative arts. Contents: I, Lustreware of Andalucía (10th-15th Century); II, Lustreware of Valencia (14th-18th Century); III, Lustreware of Aragón, Cataluña, and Sevilla (15th-17th century). Emphasis is on the style of the decoration and the relationship between the ceramic and Spanish culture. Comprehensive bibliography, pp. 291-97, and further bibliography in the notes.

846 Frothingham, Alice W. **Tile Panels of Spain: 1500-1650**. New York, Hispanic Society of America, 1969. 106p. illus. LC 71-5770.

Important, scholarly history of ceramic tile panels made in Spain between 1500 and 1650 based on extensive use of archival information. Contents: I, Francisco Niculoso and His Work at Sevilla; II, Sevillian Panels in Italo-Flemish and Genoese Styles; III, Panels of Talavera de la Reina; IV, Spanish Tile Panels in the New World. Included are tile panels on both exteriors and interiors. Comprehensive bibliography, pp. 93-95, and further bibliography in the notes.

847 Van de Put, A. **Hispano-Moresque Ware of the XV Century. A Contribution to Its History and Chronology based upon Armorial Specimens**. London, Chapman & Hall, 1904. 105p. illus.

Study of fifteenth century lustreware made in Valencia featuring 34 pieces with armorial devices of various Spanish, Italian, and French families. The author published a sequel expanding into a general history of Valencian lustreware: *Hispano-Moresque Ware of the Fifteenth Century. Supplemenatry Studies and Some Later Examples* (London, Art Worker's Quarterly, 1911, 108p. illus.).

See also the museum catalog: *Catalogue of Hispano-Moresque Pottery in the Collection of the Hispanic Society of America*, by A. W. Frothingham (New York, Hispanic Society of America, 1936. 291p. illus. index).

Talavera Pottery

848 Martinez Caviro, Balbina. **Cerámica de Talavera**. Madrid, Instituto Diego Velazquez, 1969. 50p. illus.

Introductory survey of the pottery produced in Talavera from the sixteenth century to the nineteenth century. Forty-eight plates with descriptive notes. Contents: I, Introduccion; II, La Ceramica Talaverna durante el siglo XVI; III, La Cerámaica de Talavera de la Reina durante el siglo XVII; IV,La Cerámica de Talavera de la Reina durante el siglo XVIII; V, La Loza Talaverana del siglo XIX. Basic bibliography, p. 37.

849 Frothingham, Alice W. **Talavera Pottery with a Catalogue of the Collection of the Hispanic Society of America**. New York, Hispanic Society of America, 1944. 191p. illus. index.

In the series: Hispanic Notes & Monographs, Catalogue Series. Authoritative survey of Renaissance and Baroque ceramics of Talavera. Includes large-scale works in glazed tiles as well as ceramic table ware. Contents: I, Medieval and Renaissance Pottery; II, Seventeenth-Century Pottery; III, Eighteenth-Century Pottery; IV, Catalogue of Talavera Pottery in the Collection of the Hispanic Society of America; V, Catalogue of Spanish Imitations of Talavera Pottery in the Collection of the Hispanic Society of America. Extensive bibliography in the notes.

Oriental Pottery

China [see Oriental Ceramics, China]

Japan

850 Kidder, Jonathan E. **Prehistoric Japanese Arts: Jomon Pottery**. Tokyo and Palo Alto, Calif., Kodansha, 1968. 308p. illus. index. LC 68-17458.

Comprehensive, scholarly, and well-illustrated history of Japanese prehistoric pottery. Contents: Earliest Jomon; Early Jomon; Middle Jomon; Late Jomon; Latest Jomon; Notes on Decorative Techniques by T. Esaka; Jomon Design Incidence Chart by T. Esaka; List of Collections; Carbon 14-dated Sties by T. Esaka; Jomon Chronology by T. Esaka; Lomon Shape Incidence Chart by T. Esaka; Map of Archaeological Sites; Archaeological Site List; Jomon Shape Development Chart. Bibliography, pp. 296-300.

See also N. Egami, *The Beginings of Japanese Art*. (Heibonsha Survey of Japanese Art, 2) FA 1892.

Particular Periods and Types

851 Andacht, Sandra. **Treasury of Satsuma**. Des Moines, Ia., Wallace-Homstead, 1981. 160p. illus. index. ISBN 0870693182.

Popular collector's handbook/history of Satsuma ware with emphasis on that produced in the late nineteenth and early twentieth centuries. Contents: 1, Historical Background; 2, Tea and Cha No Yu; 3, Prominent Westerners; 4, Satsuma Wares; 5, Potting and Decoration; 6, The Awaji School; 7, The Kyoto School; 8, The Tokyo School and the Moderns; 9, Satsuma Decorated Blanks; 10, The Mon and Other Marks; 11, Comparison Study and Value Determination; 12, Satsuma Style. Appendix with facsimiles of marks and reproductions of catalogs and advertisements of American importers of Satsuma ware; Glossary. General bibliography, p. 156.

See also by the same author: Andacht, Sandra. *Satsuma: An Illustrated Guide*. Des Moines, Ia., Wallace-Homstead Book Co., 1978. 67p. illus. index. ISBN 0870692275.

852 Cort, Louise A. **Shigaraki, Potters' Valley**. Tokyo, New York, Kodansha, 1979. 428p. illus. index. ISBN 080113828.

Comprehensive, scholarly history of the ceramics—earthenware and stoneware—made in Shigaraki from the thirteenth century to the 1960s. Based on archival study, close examination of pieces and by experience living and working with potters in Shigaraki. Contents: 1, Introduction; 2, Imperial Bounty; 3. Medieval Wares; 4, Tea-Storage Jars; 5, Tea-Ceremony Wares; 6, Kyoto and Shigaraki; 7, Official Tea Jars; 8, Glazed Domestic Wares; 9, Response to Westernization; 10, The Hibachi Era; 11, Shigaraki Today. Appendices: a, Morita Kyuemon's Diary; B, Shigaraki in 1872; C., A Shigaraki Woman's Life; D., Shigaraki in Omi by Kawai Kanjiro; E, Shigaraki Kiln Sites; F, Shigaraki Clays. Comprehensive bibliography, pp. 403-412, with Japanese titles translated. Specialized bibliography in the notes.

853 Moeran, Brian. **Lost Innocence: Folk Craft Potters of Onta, Japan**. Berkeley, Calif., Univ. of California Press, 1984. 252p. illus. index. ISBN 050046927.

Comprehensive, scholarly, sociological study of the tradition of folk pottery in Japan. Contents: 1, The Japanese Folk Craft Movement; 2, The Fieldwork Community; 3, Social Organization of a Pottery Community; 4, Ecological Aspects of Social Structure; 5, Labor

Cooperation; 6, Environmental and Social Change; 7, The Economic Development of a Potting Household; 8, The Decline of Community Solidarity; 9, Theory and Practice in Japanese Folk Crafts. Comprehensive bibliography, pp. 235-46, and bibliographical references in the footnotes.
See also L. Philip. *The Road through Miyama*. New York, Random House, 1989. 264p. illus. ISBN 039457818X.

Account of the author's two-year residence in Miyama, the potters' village established in 1640 by Shiamzu Mitsuhisa, Lord of Satsuma, with Korean potters. Since the author also served as a potter's apprentice, this richly evocative record contains much information concerning contemporary pottery practice.

854 Rhodes, Daniel. **Tamba Pottery, the Timeless Art of a Japanese Village**. Tokyo, Kodansha, 1970. 180p. illus. ISBN 870111183.

Survey of the stoneware made in Tamba region from the Kamakura period to the present with emphasis on the continuation of traditional methods today. Contents: Old Tamba; The Momoyama and Edo Periods; Tamba in Recent Times; Notes on the Six Ancient Kilns. General bibliography, pp. 179-80.

Japanese Potters

855 Leach, Bernard. **Hamada Potter**. Tokyo, New York, Kodansha; distributed by Harper & Row, 1975. 305p. illus. index. ISBN 087011252X.

Comprehensive study of the life and work of Shoji Hamada, one of the leading potters in modern-day Japan, written by a leading British ceramicist and expert on Japanese stoneware. Well-illustrated with photographs of the potter at work and 88 plates of his work dating between 1927 and 1961 with descriptive notes. Text is largely a dialogue between Hamada and Leach and includes transcripts of correspondence.

856 Kawahara, Masahiko. **The Ceramic Art of Ogata Kenzan**. Tokyo, New York, Kondansha; distributed by Harper & Row, 1985. 151p. illus. ISBN 0870117173.

Well-illustrated monograph on the ceramics of Ogata Kenzan (1699-1743), the greatest of Japan's potters during the Edo period. Contents: Introduction: before and after Kenzan; 1, Kenzan and the Tradition of Kyoto Ceramics; 2, The Life of Ogata Kenzan; 3, Technique and Style of Kenzan Ware; 4, Dated Kenzan Ware and the Kenzan Signature. Glossary of terms, places and personalities. Annotated bibliography, pp. 147-49.
See also B. Leach, *Kenzan and Its Tradition*. London, Faber and Faber, 1966.

857 Peterson, Susan. **Shoji Hamada: A Potter's Way and Work**. Tokyo, New York, Kodansha; distributed by Harper & Row, 1974. 239p. illus. index. ISBN 0870112287.

Life and work of Shoji Hamada with emphasis on the great potter's technique. Many plates showing the potter and his assistants at work with notes describing the techniques.

African Pottery

858 Drost, Dietrich. **Töpferei in Afrika. Technologie**. Berlin, Akademie-Verlag, 1967. 289p. illus. index (Veröffentlichungen des Museums für Volkerkunde zu Leipzig, Heft 15) LC 67-107702.

Scholarly study of the technique and materials of ceramic ware produced in Subsahara Africa directed to the task of identification and classification. Contents: Erster Abschnitt: Der Rohstoff und seine Verarbeitung; Zweiter Abschnitt: Die Gefässherstellung; Dritter Abschnitt: Das Ornamentierungstechniken; Vierter Abschnmitt: Trocknen und Brand; Fünfter Abschnitt:

Schlussbetrachtungen (with English Summary). Comprehensive bibliography, pp. 261-75, is unfortunately unclassified. Further bibliography references in the text.

See also the exhibition catalogs: *Afrikanische Keramik: traditionelle Handwerkskunst südlich der Sahara*, ed. by M. Kecskesi (Munich, Hirmer, 1984. 408p. illus. ISBN 3777437700), *The Potter's Art in Africa*. by W. Fagg and J. Picton (London, Trustees of the British Museum, 1978. 47p. illus. ISBN 0714115452), *Keramik aus Westafrika: Einführung in Herstellung und Gebrauch* by A. Stossel (Munich, Galerie Biedermann, 1981. 36p. illus.), and *Keramik aus Schwarz-Afrika und Alt-Amerika: die Sammlung Hans Wolf-Zurich: Ceramics from Black-Africa and Ancient America: the Hans Wolf Collection-Zurich...* by K. F. Schaedler (Zurich, Edition Primart AG Zurich, 1985. 345p. illus. ISBN 3907550013).

Australian Pottery

859 Graham, Marjorie. **Australian Pottery of the 19th and Early 20th Century**. Sydney, David Ell Press, 1979. 176p. illus. index. LC 80-456009.

Popular, well-illustrated history of Australia pottery to the 1930s arranged by regions: New South Wales, Tasmania, Victoria, South Australia, Queensland, Western Australia. Select bibliography, p. 171.

860 Hood, Kenneth. **Australian Pottery**. South Melbourne, Australia, Macmillan, 1972. 173p. illus. index. LC 73-163201.

Biographies of 20 contemporary Australian studio potters. Well illustrated with black and white and color plates of pieces and photographs of the potters. Descriptive notes to the plates. Bibliography, p. 173, consists mainly of periodical articles.

861 Timms, Peter. **Australian Studio Pottery & China Painting**. Melbourne, New York, Oxford University Press, 1986. 192p. illus. index. ISBN 0195546598.

Comprehensive history of art pottery and the painting of ceramics in Australia during the nineteenth and twentieth centuries. The five chapters: 'An Agreeable Pastime for Persons of Leisure'; 'Distinct National Aspirations'; 'A Large Clan of Slightly Eccentric Habits'; 'Artwares'; 'The Precious Seed,' are followed by biographies of potters, designers and decorators. The larger entries have bibliographical references. Bibliographical references in the notes.

CHAPTER SIX

CLOCKS, WATCHES, AUTOMATA, AND SCIENTIFIC INSTRUMENTS

BIBLIOGRAPHIES

862 Baillie, Granville H. **Clocks and Watches; an Historical Bibliography.** London, N. A. G. Press, 1951. 414p. illus. index. LC 53-357. Reprint: Toronto, Movements in Time, 1978.

Comprehensive bibliography of books and periodical articles on all aspects of mechanical timepieces up to the year 1800. Entries are arranged chronologically and have annotations. Subject and author index.

863 Tardy (firm). **Bibliographie générale de la mesure du temps.** 2d ed. Paris, Tardy, 1980. 391p.

Comprehensive bibliography of books and periodical articles in Western languages on all aspects of measuring time, including clocks and watches. Preface by Paul Ditisheim.

DICTIONARIES AND ENCYCLOPEDIAS

864 Baillie, Granville H. **Watchmakers and Clockmakers of the World.** 3rd ed. London, N. A. G. Press, 1951. 388p. illus. Reprinted 1976. LC 78-107368.

Comprehensive dictionary of some 35,000 watch and clock makers active to 1825. Brief biographical entries also give initials and monograms used by the makers. No bibliography. Supplemented by Loomes (869). The standard reference work on watch and clock makers.

865 Brunton, Eric. **Dictionary of Clocks and Watches.** New York, Crown, 1963. 201p. illus. LC 63-14437.

Popular dictionary covering all aspects of clocks and watches including terms, major makers, famous clocks, types of time pieces and parts of mechanisms. Illustrated with line drawings and plates of museum pieces. Bibliography, pp. 199-201, is a good annotated list of basic books in English.

866 **The Country Life International Dictionary of Clocks.** Consultant editor Alan Smith. New York, Putnam, 1979. 350p. illus. index. ISBN 0399123385.

Comprehensive dictionary of clocks from all countries and times but with emphasis on western Europe and America during the eighteenth and nineteenth centuries. Contents: 1, The History and Styles of Clocks; II, The Mechanical Parts of Clocks; III, Tools, Materials and Workshop Methods; IV, International Clockmaking with a Selection of Important Makers; V, Sundials and Astronomical Instruments. Bibliography, pp. 339-42, is a classified list of books in all langauges. An excellent all-around reference work for the collector and enthusiast.

867 Kiegeland, Burkhardt, ed. **Bruckmann's Uhrenlexikon.** 2d ed. Munich, Bruckmann, 1980. 304p. illus. ISBN 376541850.

Authoritative dictionary covering all aspecst of world clocks and watches, with special emphasis on material of interest to the collector and historian. The work of a team of German specialists. Covers mechanisms, materials, styles and forms, and major makers. Well illustrated with major museum pieces.

868 Lloyd, H. Alan. **The Collector's Dictionary of Clocks**. South Brunswick, N. J. A. S. Barnes, 1965. 214p. illus. LC 65-24848.

Popular dictionary of world clocks and watches, with emphasis on artistic and mechanical aspects. Includes automata. Entries cover types of mechanisms, forms of clocks, major clock and watch makers, styles and countries. Good selection of plates representative of pieces accessible to the private collector. Bibliography of basic works, pp. 204-206.

869 Loomes, Brian. **Watchmakers and Clockmakers of the World**. London, N. A. G. Press, 1976. 263p. ISBN 0719800803.

Supplement to Baillie (864) that adds 35,00 entries to the same number in Baillie. Revises Baillie and extends coverage to 1875. Entries give dates and location of the makers.

GENERAL HISTORIES AND HANDBOOKS

870 Bassermann-Jordan, Ernst von. **The Book of Old Clocks and Watches**. 4th ed. Fully revised by Hans von Bertele. New York, Crown, 1964. 522p. illus. index. LC 63-2111.

Translation of Uhren: *Ein Handbuch für Sammler und Liebhaber*. (Braunschweig, Klinkhardt & Biermann, 1961). Comprehensive, scholarly history/handbook with chapters on the conception, division, and measurement of time, history of timepiece mechanisms and detailed chapters on the development of particular parts. Includes water clocks and sand glasses. Well illustrated; plates with descriptive captions. Good classified bibliography, pp. 497-503, of books and periodical articles in all languages. A standard work particularly important for the history of German clocks and watches. Supersedes the author's earlier work: *Bassermann-Jordan, Ernst von. Alte Uhren und ihre Meister*. Leipzig, W. Dieber, 1926. 179p. illus. index.

871 Britten, Frederick J. **Britten's Old Clocks and Watches and Their Makers: A Historical and Descriptive Account of the Different Styles of Clocks and Watches of the Past in England and Abroad...** 8th ed. edited by Cecil Clutton. New York, Dutton, 1973. 532p. illus. index. LC 73-82531.

First published as *Former Clock and Watchmakers and Their Work* (1894); 2d through 7th eds. published under the title of: *Old Clocks and Watches*. A comprehensive history of clocks and watches in the West from the earliest examples in the late Middle Ages to 1970. Arranged by centuries, countries, and technical and mechanical types. Appendices with glossary of terms, extensive list of makers and their marks, and thorough bibliography of books and periodical articles in all languages with addenda to the eighth edition, pp. 326-31. Britten's is a classic in the history of clocks and watches.

872 Brusa, Giuseppe. **L'arte dell'orologeria in Europa: Sette secoli di orologi meccanici**. Busto Arsizio, Bramante, 1978. 491p. illus. index. LC 79-360210.

Comprehensive history of clocks and watches in Europe from the fourteenth century to the twentieth century with emphasis on technical aspects. Extensive use of documentary sources. Many illustrations of timepieces in contemporary works of art. Illustrated with museum pieces with detailed notes. Excellent glossary of technical terms.

873 Bruton, Eric. **The History of Clocks and Watches**. New York, Rizzoli, 1979. 288p. illus. index. LC 76-65958.

Well-illustrated history of clocks and watches from the Middle Ages to 1970 with a good balance between artistic and technological aspects. Contents: I, The Earliest Clocks; II, The Advent of Clockwork; III, Domestic Clocks; IV, European Mechanical Clocks; V, The Time at Sea; VI, The Development of the Watch; VII, Mass Production; VIII, The Technological Age; IX, Watches for the People; X, The Science of Time; XI, Great Clocks of the World. Glossary of terms. Bibliography, pp. 278-80, is an unclassified list of mostly books in English. By the same author: *Clocks and Watches* (Feltham, Malyn, 1968. 140p.), *Clocks and Watches, 1400-1900* (New York, Praeger, 1967. 208p. LC 67-14706).

874 Chapuis, Alfred. **De horologiis in arte; L'horloge et la montre a travers les ages, d'apres les documents du temps.** Lausanne, Scriptar, 1954. 154p. illus. LC 56-26117.

Important compendium of illustrations of works of art that depict clocks and watches dating from the late Middle Ages to the end of the nineteenth century. Includes chapter on the Far East.

875 Gélis, Edouard. **L'horlogerie ancienne; histoire, décor et technique.** Paris, Grund, 1950. 254p. illus. index. LC 51-27388.

Comprehensive, authoritative history/handbook of watches and clocks of the fifteenth through the eighteenth centuries. Part one is a history of watch and clock making with emphasis on decorative case work. Part two is a catalog of 130 pieces in the author's collection. The catalog entries are fully descriptive and contain bibliographical references. General bibliography, pp. 241-244.

876 Guye, Samuel, and Henri Michel. **Time & Space; Measuring Instruments from the 15th to the 19th Century.** New York, Praeger, 1971. 289p. illus. index. LC 77-111070.

Comprehensive, well-illustrated history of instruments used to measure time and space including clocks and watches from ancient times to the early nineteenth century. Divided into two parts: clocks and watches and measuring instruments. Second part includes, globes, armillary spheres, astrolabes, sundials, clepsydras and hour-glasses, topographical instruments. No bibliography.

877 Jagger, Cedric. **The World's Great Clocks & Watches.** London, Hamlyn, 1977. 256p. illus. index. ISBN 0600340279.

Well-illustrated survey of clocks and watches throughout the world from the first timekeeping devices in antiquity to the end of the nineteenth century. Useful chapters on the rudiments of clockwork and collectors and collecting. Bibliography, p. 254.

878 Meis, Reinhard. **Die alte Uhr: Geschichte—Technik—Stil.** 2v. illus. Braunschweig, Klinkhardt & Biermann, 1978. LC 79-346256.

Comprehensive, authoritative history of Western clocks and watches from the late Middle Ages to the twentieth century. First volume is dedicated to technical developments; volume two to the casements and their decoration. A new standard work.

879 Willsberger, Johann. **Zauberhafte Gehäuse der Zeit. Die schonen Uhren aus 6 Jahrhunderten.** Düsseldorf, Econ-Verlag, 1974. 180p. illus. ISBN 3430196655.

Pictorial survey of European clocks and watches chosen for the artistic significance of their cases.

See also the museum catalog: Die Uhrensammlung-Nathan-Rupp im Historischen Museum Basel. by H. C. Ackermann. (Munich, Callwey, 1984. 333p. illus), the museum guide: *Clocks and Watches.* by H. Tait. (London, British Museum Publications, 1983. 72p. illus.), and the exhibition catalog: *Northern European Clocks in New York Collections.* By C. Vincent (New York, Metropolitan Museum of Art, 1972. 25p. illus.) and *Die Uhr: Zeitmesser und Schmuck in fünf*

Jahrhunderts by A. Leiter and A. Helfrich-Dörner. (Kornwestheim, Alfred Reichert, 1967. 359p. illus.).

Clocks

880   Cipolla, Carlo M. **Clocks and Cultures, 1300-1700**. London, Collins, 1967. 192p. illus. index. LC 67-77490.

Unorthodox social history of clocks with emphasis on the relationship between clocks and time measurement and broad cultural changes. Author links the rise of clocks to the urbanization of late medieval Europe. Fascinating chapter on the influence of Western clocks in China and Japan. General bibliography, pp. 166-181.

881   Fleet, Simon. **Clocks**. New York, Putnam, 1961. 128p. illus. LC 61-12199.

Popular survey of clocks from antiquity to the twentieth century. No bibliography.

882   Krombholz, Lothar. **Frühe Hausuhren mit Gewichtsantrieb. Der Beginn der mechanischen Zeitrechnung**. Munich, 1984. 169p. illus. (Bibliothek für Kunst-und Antiquitätenfreunde, LVII) ISBN 3781402320.

Comprehensive, scholarly history of weight-driven clocks in Europe from 1300 to 1530. Contents: Die Räderuhr—Ein Wunder des erfinden Genies; Zeitgenössische Beschreibungen früher Räderuhren; Der Aufbau der Werkskörper früher Uhren: A, Der Flachbau, B, Die prismatischen Werksköper; Die Weisung der Zeit (Indikationen); Mechanismus und Räderwerk; Schlusswort. Text followed by plates of 89 examples with descriptive captions. General bibliography, p. 169.

883   Lloyd, H. Alan. **Old Clocks**. 4th red. rev and enl. London, Benn, 1970. 216p. illus.index. LC 78-528441.

First published under the title: *Some Outstanding Clocks over Seven Hundred Years, 1250-1950*. Popular survey with emphasis on technical features. Well illustrated with major museum pieces. Basic bibliography, pp. 169-70. Appendices: I, "Giovanni de Dondi's Horological Masterpiece 1364"; II, "The Original Greenwich Clocks." Glossary of terms.

884   Tardy, Henri L. **La pendule dans le monde. Part 4: Europe du nord, centrale, orientale et méditerranéene, Japon**. 5th red. Paris, Tardy, 1985. 615p. illus.

Comprehensive history of clockmaking outside of France (for volume on France *see* 925) with a large corpus of illustrations of pieces in museums and private collections. Captions in French and English.

885   Tyler, Eric J. **European Clocks**. New York, Hawthorn, 1969. 258p. illus. index. LC 69-12962.

Popular history from earliest examples to the twentieth century. Glossary of technical terms and brief bibliography of basic books. Good guide to museums and public collections in Europe.

See also the price guides: *Clocks*. by T. Curtis. (New York, Coward-McCann, 1983. 254p. illus. ISBN 0698112385) and *The Price Guide to Collectable Clocks, 1840-1940*. by A. and R. Shenton. 2d ed. (Woodbridge, Antique Collectors's Club, 1985. 250p. illus. ISBN 0907462669).

Carriage Clocks

886 Allix, C., and P. Bonnert. **Carriage Clocks: Their History, Decoration and Mechanism.** Woodbridge, Antique Collectors' Club, 1974. 482p. illus. index. ISBN 090202825.

Comprehensive collector's history/handbook of carriage clocks of the eighteenth to the twentieth centuries with emphasis on French and British pieces. Contents: I, The First Spring-Driven Clocks; II, The Beginning, Late 18th and Early 19th Century; III, Later Manufacture, 19th and 20th Century; III, Saint-Nicolas-d'Aliermont, Past and Present; V, Paris Today and Yesterday; VI, The Carriage Clock Industry in the Franche-Comté; VII, Case Styles. The Names, Shapes and Sizes of Standard French Carriage Clocks; VIII, The Rarer French Carriage Clocks; IX, English Work and Workmen; X, Swiss Carriage Clocks; XI, Germany and the Austro-Hungarian Empire; XII, American Carriage Clocks; XIII, Japan, Italy and the Argentine. Appendices with extracts from writings on Paul Garnier, the Paris Exposition Universelle, 1889; M. A. Pitcher on the French Carriage Clock after 1900, the Japy Factory at Badevel, Nail and Cork by D. S. Torrens, Rule of Thumb by D. S. Torrens and description of the Société des Horlogers. Glossary of terms and comprehensive, classified bibliography, pp. 453-466, including many references to monographic literature not included in *Applied and Decorative Arts.*

See also: J. Fanelli. *A Century of Fine Carriage Clocks* (Bronxville, N.Y., Clock Trade Enterprises, 1987. 224p. illus. index. ISBN 0916316041).

Church Clocks

887 Edwardes, Ernest L. **Weight Driven Chamber Clocks of the Middle Ages and Renaissance.** Cheshire, John Sherratt & Sons, 1965. 160p. illus. index. ISBN 0854270183.

Authoritative survey of European weight driven clocks from the thirteenth through the sixteenth centuries with emphasis on the place of mechanical time-keeping in medieval society. Illustrated with clock works, cases and representations of clocks in contemporary works of art. Appendix with detailed notes on more important pieces including a modern reconstruction of the astronomical clock by Giovanni de' Dondi, 1364. Bibliographical references in the footnotes.

888 Ungerer, Alfred. **Les horloges astronomiques et monumentales.** Strasbourg, Ungerer, 1931. 514p. illus. index.

Comprehensive, authoritative history of large clocks—mostly in churches and public buildings and most with astronomical or decorative clockwork—in Europe from antiquity to the twentieth century. Emphasis is on the tower clocks of Europe from the fifteenth through the seventeenth centuries which, are discussed in a large catalog divided by country and subdivided by place. Large entry devoted to the famous astronomical clock in Strasbourg Cathedral. Illustrations of both the faces and movements. General bibliography, pp. 503-09, and references to specialized literature in the catalog entries. A standard work on tower clocks.

Longcase Clocks

889 Bruton, Eric. **The Longcase Clock.** New York, Arco, 1964. 246p. illus. index. Reprint: New York, Scribner's, 1977. ISBN 0684162474.

Comprehensive handbook/history of the European and American longcase clock from 1660 to the nineteenth century. Contents: 1, The Birth of the Pendulum Clock; 2, The First Pendulum Clock; 3, Development of the Longcase Clock; 4, Timekeeping, Striking and Chiming; 5, Shapes and Wood for Cases; 6, Dials and Hands; 7, Moon Dials, Calendars and other Special Indications; 8, Thirty-house and One-hand Clocks; 9, Development of the Regulator; 10, Special Clocks to Cottage Clocks; 11, The Famous Makers; 12, An Ancient Workshop and Restoration Today; 13, European Longcase Clocks; 14, North American Clocks and Makers; 15, Valuing and Setting-up a Clock. Appendix I: Pendulum Calculations; II: Dating by General Style. Basic bibliography, pp. 238-39.

890 Edwardes, Ernest L. **The Grandfather Clock**. Cheshire, John Sherratt & Son, 1971. 215p. illus. index. ISBN 085427054X.

Authoritative history of British longcase clocks from the seventeenth century to the early nineteenth century. Contents: I, Movements; 2, Dials and Hands; Casework; Conclusion. Appendix One: Notes on Certain Clocks Illustrated; Appendix Two: The Long Case Movement; Appendix Three: Glossary. The glossary consists of many very long entries, particularly on parts of mechanisms, that include much additional historical information and often important practical advice concerning repair and care. Bibliography in the footnotes.

891 Loomes, Brian. **Grandfather Clocks and Their Cases**. Newton Abbot, David & Charles; New York, Arco, 1985. 352p. illus. index. ISBN 0688063300.

Comprehensive, well-illustrated history of British grandfather clocks from the seventeenth century to the early nineteenth century. Emphasis is on the artistic development of case work and decorative details and dials. Contains 433 black and white plates with descriptive captions. Contents: 1, Cases, Movements and Dials—The Terminology; 2, The Early Eight-day Longcase; 3, Early Country Work; 4, Mid-century and Later in the North; 5, Mid-century and Later in the South; 6, White Dials (1770-1870); 7, Scotland; 8, Ireland; 9, Special, Complicated and Unusual Clocks; 10, Fakes. Basic bibliography, p. 347.

See also: T. Robinson. *The Longcase Clock* (Woodbridge, Suffolk, Antique Collector's Club, 1981. 467p. illus. index. ISBN 0907462073).

Watches

892 Baillie, Granville H. **Watches: Their History, Decoration and Mechanism**. London, Methuen, 1929. 383p. illus. index. Reprint: London, N. A. G. Press, 1979. ISBN 719801400.

Popular history of watches with emphasis on the artistic aspect of form and decoration. Includes Oriental watches. Useful summary in the form of a chronology of watches. Comprehensive bibliography of the older literature, pp. xvi-xxiii.

893 Clutton, Cecil, and George Daniels. **Watches: A Complete History of the Technical and Decorative Development of the Watch**. 3d rev. and enl. ed. London, Southeby Parke Bernet, 1979. 312p. illus. index. ISBN 0713407158.

First edition under the title *Watches* (New York, Viking, 1965. 159p. LC 65-15108).

Authoritative survey of the history of European and American watches from 1500 to 1900 with emphasis on mechanisms. Biographical dictionary of major watch makers. Contents: I, Historical; Mechanical 1500-1750; The Precision Watch 1750-1830; The Modern Watch 1830-1960; II, Performance of Early Watches; III, Technical; IV, Biographical Notes

894 Cuss, T., and P. Camerer. **The Country Life Book of Watches**. London, Country Life, 1967. 128. illus. index. LC 67-112524.

Popular survey of watches from 1500 to 1900, well illustrated with artistically and technologically important pieces. No bibliography.

895 Kahlert, Helmut, Richard Muhe, and Gisbert L. Brunner. **Wristwatches: History of a Century's Development**. West Chester, Pa., Schiffer Pub., 1986. 399p. illus. index. ISBN 0887400701.

Comprehensive collector's handbook of wristwatches with large collection of illustrations of movements, cases and advertisements. Although directed to the collector, the text is highly informative for the history of watch technology and the history of the wristwatch in consumer culture. Chapter on collecting wristwatches. Appendix with facsimiles of trademarks. Comprehensive bibliography, pp. 142-45.

896   Meis, Reinhard. **Pocket Watches: From the Pendant Watch to the Tourbillon.** West Chester, Pa., Schiffer Pub., 1987. 316p. illus. index. ISBN 0887400841.

Translation of: *Taschenuhren, von der Halsuhr zum Torbillon. (Munich, Callwey, 1985). Comprehensive, authoritative history of the pocket watch from the sixteenth century to the twentieth century. Introductory text followed by 905 illustrations of pocket watches with detailed, descriptive captions. Select bibliography, pp. 53-54. Price guide by G. Converse tipped in at back.*

See also the catalog of the James Arthur Collection: *The Lure of the Clock: An Account of the James Arthur Collection of Clocks and Watches at New York University.* by D. W. Hering (New York, New York Univ. Pr., 1932. 114p. illus.; Addendum published 1934. 21p.).

See also the price guide: *The Official Price Guide to Watches.* by C. Shugart and T. Engle. 10th. ed. (New York, House of Collectibles, 1990. 574p. illus. ISBN 0876378084).

AMERICAN CLOCKS AND WATCHES

Dictionaries

897   Sposato, Kenneth A. **The Dictionary of American Clock & Watch Makers.** White Plains, N.Y., K.A. Sposato, 1983. 190p. ISBN 0961283203.

Dictionary of 7,600 clock and watch makers active in the United States from Colonial times to the beginning of the twentieth century. Entries are brief after the model of Baillie (864) with location(s) and dates. For the major makers references to a list (pp. 191-92) of basic books is supplied.

Histories and Handbooks

898   Bailley, Chris. **Two Hundred Years of American Clocks and Watches.** Englewood Cliffs, N.J., Prentice-Hall, 1975. 255p. illus. index. ISBN 0139351302.

Comprehensive history of American clock and watches, illustrated with pieces in the American Clock and Watch Museum in Bristol, Conn. and in private collections.

899   Distin, William H., and Robert Bishop. **The American Clock: A Comprehensive Pictorial Survey, 1723-1900, with a Listing of 6,153 Clockmakers.** New York, E. P. Dutton, 1976. 359p. illus. index. Reprint: New York, Bonanza Books, 1983. ISBN 0517413590.

Survey of American longcase, mantle and wall clocks from 1723 to 1900 with a list of over 6,000 clockmakers active in America. Entries in the list provide only basic biographical data. More valuable for the collector is the collection of 661 plates. Selected bibliography, p. 352.

900   Drepperd, Carl W. **American Clocks & Clockmakers.** 2nd ed. Boston, Branford, 1958. 312p. illus. index. LC 58-2993.

Important handbook of American clocks and clockmakers from the Colonial period to the early twentieth century. Directory of clockmakers, based in part on Britten (871) and Nutting (1184), has been supplemented with information from documentary sources.

901   Harris, H. G. **Nineteenth Century American Clocks.** Buchanan, N.Y., Emerson Books, 1981. 256p. illus. index. LC 81-65124.

Popular survey of American made clocks of the nineteenth century directed to the collector and restorer. Particularly valuable for the detailed descriptions of various movements and references to major makers. Contents: 1, Acquiring an Old Clock; 2, Tall Case Clocks; 3, Shelf Clocks; 4, Wall Clocks; 5, Movements and Mechanisms; 6, Restoration of Cases: Restorers and Suppliers of Materials & Tools; 7, Preservation of Movements; 8, Some Famous Makers. Glossary of terms, dates of interest and general bibliography, p. 251.

902   Palmer, Brooks. **The Book of American Clocks**. New York, Macmillan, 1950. 318p. illus. LC 50-11068.
　　Pictorial survey of American clocks from the earliest examples to the twentieth century. Brief introductory essay provides a short history; this is followed by more than 300 illustrations arranged chronologically, glossary of terms, and a list of more than 6,000 names of American clockmakers with basic biographical data and bibliographical references. Bibliography of basic books, pp. 317-18.

903   Palmer, Brooks. **A Treasury of American Clocks**. New York, Macmillan, 1967. 371p. illus. LC 67-28469.
　　Companion to the author's earlier work: *The Book of American Clocks* adding additional plates and names to the list of clockmakers. Plates are arranged by case type. Chapter on clockmakers' labels.

904   Schwartz, Marvin D. **Collector's Guide to Antique American Clocks**. New York, Doubleday, 1975. 175p. illus. index. ISBN 0385029225.
　　General handbook for collectors designed to aid in the identification of pieces available to the average collector. List of major clockmakers and manufacturers.

905   Thomson, Richard. **Antique American Clocks & Watches**. Princeton, N.J., Van Nostrand Reinhold, 1968. 192p. illus. index. LC 68-29920.
　　Concise history and handbook of American clocks and watches before 1850 written for the beginning collector. Contents: 1, The Beginnings of Timekeeping; 2, Our English Heritage; 3, Pennsylvania Clockmaking; 4, New England Clockmaking—the Boston School; 5, Connecticut Clockmaking—The Terry School; 6, Connecticut Clockmaking—Yankee Clocks; 7, The Early American Watchmakers; 8, The Waltham Story; 9, The Watch Factories. No bibliography.

906   Tyler, E. J. (Eric John). **American Clocks and Watches**. New York, Dutton, 1981. 209p. illus. index. ISBN 0525932127.
　　History of American clocks and watches from Colonial times to the late nineteenth century intended for the collector. Has chapters on imitations and reproductions, repairs, restoration of cases, and hints on how to collect. Appendixes with list of marks and trademarks, clockmaking in Connecticut, and the Ansonia Factory in New York. Bibliography, pp. 172-180.
　　See also the author's *The Craft of the Clockmaker*. (New York, Crown, 1874. 96p. illus. index) which emphasizes the construction of preindustrial clocks in America.
　　See also the museum handbook: *Clocks*. by D. H. Shaffer. (The Smithsonian Illustrated Library of Antiques. New York, Cooper-Hewitt Museum, 1980. 128p. illus. index) and the museum catalog: *The American Clock, 1725-1865: The Mabel Brady Garvan and Other Collections at Yale University*. by E. A. Battison and P. E. Kane. (Greenwich, Conn., New York Graphics Society, 1973. 207p. illus. index).
　　See also the price guide: *American Clocks and Clockmakers*. by Robert W. Swedberg. (Radnor, Pa., Wallace-Homstead, 1989. 179p. illus. index. ISBN 0870695258).

Watches

907   Faber, Edward, et al. **American Wristwatches: Five Decades of Style and Design**. West Chester, PA, Schiffer, 1988. 277p. illus. index. ISBN 0887401465.

Comprehensive, illustrated history/handbook of American wristwatches from circa 1915 to the 1960s directed to the collector. Illustrations of many pieces and a selection of contemporary advertisements. Descriptive captions. Includes novelty watches. Appendix with histories of watch companies. Basic bibliography, p. 275.

See also the price guide: *Identification and Price Guide to American Pocket Watches from Beginning to End.* by R. Ehrhardt and W. F. Meggers. (Kansas City, Mo., Heart of America Press, 1987. 480p. illus. ISBN 0913902535).

Regional Histories and Handbooks

908   Burrow, G. Edmond. **Canadian Clocks and Clockmakers**. Oshawa, Ontario, Kalabi Enterprises, 1973. 506p. illus. LC 74-181881.

Checklist of clock and watchmakers active in Ontario, Quebec, Nova Scotia, and New Brunswick from early colonial times to the early twentieth century. Includes a chapter on clocks made by Seth Thomas for Canadian dealers.

909   Carlisle, Lillian B. **Vermont Clock and Watchmakers, Silversmith, and Jewelers**. Burlington, Vt., By the author, 1970. 313p. illus. index. ISBN 0877920087.

Dictionary of some 1,000 craftsmen active in Vermont between 1778 and 1878. Illustrations of pieces, marks, and facsimiles of advertisements.

910   Chandlee, Edward E. **Six Quaker Clockmakers**. Philadelphia, Historical Society of Pennsylvania, 1943, 260p. illus. index.

Important biographies of Abel Cottey, Benjamin Goldsmith, Ellis, and Isaac Chandlee, five generations of clockmakers active in Pennsylvannia, Maryland and Virginia between 1709 and 1811.

911   Conrad, Henry C. **Old Delaware Clockmakers**. Wilmington, Del., Historical Society of Delaware, 1898. 34p. illus.

Short biographies of some twenty clockmakers active in Delaware in the eighteenth and nineteenth centuries.

912   Drost, William E. **Clocks and Watches of New Jersey**. Elizabeth, N.J., Engineering Pub., 1966. 291p. illus. index. LC 66-26780.

History/handbook of clock and watchmakers active in New Jersey between 1710 and 1966.

913   Eckhardt, George H. **Pennsylvania Clocks and Clockmaking: An Epic of Early American Science, Industry, and Craftsmanship**. New York, Devin-Adair Co., 1955. 229p. illus. index. LC 55-7743.

Popular history/handbook of Pennsylvania clocks made between 1682 and 1850 with list of Philadelphia clockmakers and those working outside Philadelphia. Chapters on care, repair and appraisal. Includes Pennsylvania German folk clocks. Occasional bibliographical reference in footnote.

914   Gibbs, James W. **Buckeye Horology: A Review of Ohio Clock and Watch Makers**. Columbia, Pa., Art Crafters Printing Co., 1971. 128p. illus. index. ISBN 088289059X.

Repertory of Ohio clock and watchmakers arranged by county. Information derived from local historical archives. Appendix with reproductions of newspaper advertisements.

915   Gibbs, James W. **Dixie Clockmakers**. Gretna, La., Pelican Pub. Co., 1979. 191p. illus. index. LC 78-2204.

Biographical dictionary of clockmakers active in Delaware, Maryland, District of Columbia, Virginia, North Carolina, Alabama, Florida, Georgia, Kentucky, Louisiana, Mississippi, Tennessee, and West Virginia.

916   Hoopes, Penrose R. **Connecticut Clockmakers of the Eighteenth Century**. 2d ed. New York, Dover, 1974. 182p. illus. index. ISBN 048622922X.

History/handbook of early Connecticut clocks and clockmakers. Contains the biographies of seventy-nine clockmakers plus an additional seven in the appendix.

917   Langdon, John E. **Clock and Watchmakers and Allied Workers in Canada, 1700 to 1900**. Toronto, Anson-Cartwright Editions, 1976. 195p. illus. ISBN 0919974023.

Comprehensive directory of clock and watchmakers active in Canada between 1700 and 1900. Entries give basic biographical data and include bibliographical references. Information was culled in large part from advertisements, directories, newspapers and unpublished archival documents. Standard reference work.

918   Parsons, Charles S. **New Hampshire Clocks and Clockmakers**. Exeter, Pa., Adams Brown Co., 1976. 356p. illus. ISBN 0917900006.

Authoritative history/handbook of New Hamphsire clocks and their makers with thorough consideration of the case work. Repertory of 285 clockmakers.

919   Wood, Stacy B. C., Jr., Stephen E. Kramer III, and John J. Snyder, Jr. **Clockmakers of Lancaster County and Their Clocks, 1750-1850**. New York, Van Nostrand Reinhold, 1977. 224p. illus. index. LC 76-30279r852.

Authoritative history/handbook of clocks and clockmakers of Lancaster County, Pennsylvania. First part is a biographical directory of some 94 clockmakers active between 1750 and 1850 based on documentary evidence; second part surveys the history of case work; concluding parts comprise plates with detailed captions.

Major Clock and Watchmakers

920   Hindle, Brooke. **David Rittenhouse**. Princeton, N.J., Princeton Univ. Press, 1964. 94p. illus. index. Reprint: New York, Arno, 1980. LC 79-3120.

Scholarly biography of the multifarious Rittenhouse, who made a number of complicated clocks.

921   Husher, Richard W., and Walter W. Welch. **A Study of Simon Willard's Clocks**. Nahant, MA, By the authors, 1980. 292p. illus. ISBN 0960394400.

Comprehensive monograph on Simon Willard with emphasis on the technical aspects of his clocks. Contents: 1, The Thirty Hour Grafton Wall Clock; 2, Willard Shelf Clocks; 3, The Improved Timepiece or Banjo Clock; 4, The Regulator Banjo Clock; 5, Gallery Clocks; 6, The Patented Alarm or Lighthouse Clock; 7, Tall Case Clocks; 8, Tower Clocks; 9, Clockwork Roasting Jack; 10, Orrery. Appendices with bills of sale and letters to Paul Revere and general bibliography with commentary, pp. 283-85.

922 Roberts, Kenneth D. **Eli Terry and the Connecticut Shelf Clock**. Bristol, Conn., Ken Roperts Pub. Co., 1973. 320p. illus. index. LC 72-97556.

Comprehensive monograph on the clocks of Eli Terry (1772-1852) who was instrumental in the development of the Connecticut industry making wooden movement shelf clocks in the early decades of the nineteenth century. Extensive use of and extracts from documentary sources. Contents: I, Success with Plymouth Tall Clocks; II, Introduction of the Shelf Clock; III, The Five-Wheeled Train Movement; IV, The Patent Suit: Terry vs. Thomas; V, Chauncey Jerome: The Promoter; VI, Ephraim Downs: Clockmaker & Miller; VII, Samuel Terry: Clockmaker's Clockmaker; VIII, Clockmaking in the Neighboring Towns. Bibliographical essay, pp. 289-93. Appendix with list of Connecticut shelf clock firms through 1833.

923 Willard, John W. **Simon Willard and His Clocks**. 1911. Reprint: New York, Dover, 1968. 128p. illus. LC 68-23802.

First published in 1911 as: *A History of Simon Willard, Inventor and Clockmaker*. Life of Simon Willard, his sons, and grandsons, clockmakers in Massachusetts in the last decades of the eighteenth century and early decades of the nineteenth century based upon archival sources. Chapter on Simon Willard's clocks with appendix containing check list of documented pieces. Bibliographical references in the footnotes. Emphasis is on history and genealogy; general treatment of clocks.

EUROPEAN CLOCKS AND WATCHES

France

Dictionaries

924 Develle, Edmond. **Les horloges blésois au XVIe et au XVIIe siècle**. Blois, Rivière, 1913. 373p. illus. LC 13-16356. Reprint: Nogent-le-Roi, Librarie des Arts et Metiers, 1978.

Authoritative handbook of the clockmakers of Blois.

925 Tardy (firm). **Dictionnaire des horlogers francais...** Paris, Tardy, 1971-72. 2v. illus. LC 72-302813.

Comprehensive dictionary of French clock and watchmakers from 1300 to 1880. Contains over 23,000 names. Entries supply basic biographical data and facsimiles of marks and signatures, and for major personalities, portraits. Over 1,000 illustrations with emphasis on major signed pieces.

926 Thiout, Antoine, and Claudius Cote. **Les horloges lyonnais de 1550 à 1650**. Paris, Rapilly, 1927. 253p. illus.

Old, but still important handbook of the watch and clockmakers of the Lyonais in the sixteenth and seventeenth centuries.

Histories and Handbooks

927 Edley, Winthrop. **French Clocks**. New York, Walker, 1967. 83p. illus. LC 67-23091.

Popular survey of French domestic clocks from the sixteenth century to 1789 with chapter on collecting. No bibliography.

928 Maurice, Klaus. **Die französische Pendule des 18**. Jahrhunderts. Ein Beitrag zu ihrer Ikonologie. Berlin, de Gruyter, 1967. 124p. index. LC 68-75515.

Scholarly study of the imagery of French clock cases of the eighteenth century. Contents: I, Die Räderuhr als Attribut; II, Die Monumentalisierung der Zeit; III, Die Räderuhr als Analogon der Welt; IV, Die französische Pendule; V, Die Uhr als Denkmal. Contains 59 plates of clocks and contemporary designs for clock cases. Appendix with essay on the clock makers guild of Paris. Comprehensive bibliography, pp. 109-115, and bibliographical references in the footnotes.

929   Tardy (firm). **La pendule française des origines à nos jours.** 3rd ed. Paris, Tardy, 1967. 2v. illus. index. LC 68-90858.

Comprehensive history/handbook of French clocks from the late Middle Ages to the twentieth century. Contents: Pt. I: De l'horloge gothique à la pendule Louis XV; Pt. II: Du Louis XIV à nos jours; Pt. III: Provinces et étranger; Table alphabétique des horlogers d'art, d'antiquaires et de réparateurs; Principaux musées possédant des pièces d'horlogerie. Must be used with caution for dates and attributions. Very useful corpus of plates.

930   Thiout, Antoine. **Traité de l'horlogerie méchanique et pratique. Suivi des lettres de Mossoteau de Saint-Vincent et Julien Le Roy et de la réponse d'Antoine Thiout.** Paris, Moette, 1941. 2v. Reprint: Paris, Éditions du Palais Royal, 1972. 2v. in 1. LC 73-335699.

Important treatise on clockmaking based chiefly on correspondence between Julien Le Roy and Mossoteau de Saint-Vincent.

Abraham-Louis Breguet, 1747-1823

931   Daniels, George. **Art of Breguet.** London, Sotheby Parke Bernet, 1974. 394p. illus. index. ISBN 0856670049.

Comprehensive, well-illustrated monograph on the watchmaking science and art of Breguet. Contents: Part One: Abraham-Louis Breguet; The House of Breguet; Workshop Practice; Part Two: Versatility and Evolution of Style; Colour Plates; Principal Types and Styles; Series Production; Part Three: Mechanical Techniques. Illustrated with color plates of major pieces, numerous black and white plates of mechanisms and line drawings showing details of movements. Glossary. A standard work on Breguet.

932   Salomons, David L. **Breguet.** London, David Salomons, 1921. 233p. illus.

Older monograph with an important collection of 106 plates of Breguet watches and clocks and description of 87 watches taken from their certificates. Appendices have important documents relating to Breguet's certificates, correspondence and exhibition.

Pierre le Roy, 1717-1785

933   Ditisheim, Paul, Roger Lallier, and L. Reverchon. **Pierre le Roy et la Chronométrie.** Paris, Tardy, 1940. LC AF47-3092.

The Clock of Philip of Burgundy

934   Bassermann-Jordan, Ernst von. **The Clock of Philip the Good of Burgundy.** Leipzig, Diebener, n.d. 43p. illus.

Brief monograph on the cathedral-shaped timepiece made circa 1430 for Duke Philip the Good of Burgundy, the oldest spring-actuated, wheel-clock with fusee.

Germany

935   Bobinger, Maximilian. **Kunstuhrmacher in Alt-Augsburg**. Augsburg, Hans Rösler Verlag, 1969. 128p. illus. index. (Abhandlungen zur Geschichte der Stadt Augsburg. Schiftenreihe der Stadtarchivs Augsburg, Band 18). LC 78-521152.

Scholarly history of the clock and watch makers of Augsburg from the sixteenth century to the middle of the eighteenth century with extensive references to documentary sources. Contents: Erster Teil: Johann Reinhold, Georg Roll und ihr Kreis; Zweiter Teil: Die Generationen der Muschmann. Bibliographical references in the footnotes.

936   Maurice, Klaus. **Die deutsche Räderuhr. Zur Kunst und Technik des mechanischen Zeitmessers in deutschen Sprachraum**. 2vs. illus. Munich, Beck, 1976. ISBN 3406062970.

Extraordinarily comprehensive history of German clocks from the fourteenth century to the twentieth century by a leading authority. Contents: v. 1: Text: I, Symbolische Bedeutung und Indikationen der Räderuhr; II, Monumentale astronomische Uhren; III, Planetarische Uhren; IV, Gehäuse und Werktypen des 16. Jahrhunderts; V, Zentren des Uhrmacherhandwerks bis zur Mitte des 17. Jahrhunderts; VI, Die technische Entwicklung von 1658-1815; VII, Die Uhren im 18. Jahrhundert; VIII, Produktion und Präzision in der Uhrenherstellung im 19. Jahrhundert. Volume two has 1,184 plates with detailed catalog. Bibliographical references in margin notes. The most exhaustive national history in horology.

937   Maurice, Klaus. **Von Uhren und Automaten**. Munich, Prestel, 1968. 96p. illus. (Bibliothek des Germanischen Nationalmuseum Nürnberg zur Deutschen Kunst- und Kulturgeschichte, Band 29). LC 70-379113.

Well-illustrated history of German clocks, watches, and automata from the late Middle Ages to the nineteenth century. Illustrated with major museum pieces. Contents: Vorwort; Sonnenuhren; Wasseruhren; Sanduhren; Die Räderuhr; Die Zunft der Uhrmacher; Der Urhrmacher am Werktisch; Die verschiedenen Studenzählungen; Klagen über Uhren und Uhrmacher; Die Räderuhr in ihrer Symbolik; Kugellauffuhren—Perpetuum Mobile; Automaten; Sphähren und Planetarien; Kunstkammern. Bibliography of basic works, pp. 95-96.

Black Forest Clocks

938   Kochmann, Karl. **The Black Forest Cuckoo Clock: European Clockmaking**. 2d ed. Greensboro, N.C., S. LaRose, Inc., 1983. 240p. illus. ISBN 0933396155.

Collector's and restorer's handbook of Black Forest cuckoo clocks with detailed instructions and illustrations on repair and restoration. Includes case work. Plates—uniformly poor quality—show representative pieces, advertisements by manufacturers and importers and views of production activities.

939   Tyler, E. J. **Black Forest Clocks**. London, NAG Press, 1977. 120p. illus. index. ISBN 0719801001.

Popular history—first in English—of clocks made in the Black Forest region of Germany during the eighteenth, nineteenth and twentieth centuries. Emphasis is on the mass-produced clocks other than the cuckoo clocks exported to Britain. Contents: 1, The Clocks and Their Makers; 2, The Development of the Traditional Black Forest Clock; 3, The Factories 1851-1946; 4, The Factory-made Clocks; 5, Marketing the Product; 6, Repairing Black Forest Clocks; 7, The Black Forest Today; Appendix 1: List of Makers; Appendix 2: Papers from Inside Black Forest Clocks; Appendix 3: Agencies in London; Appendix 4: List of Museums. General bibliography, p. 118.

See also the museum catalog: *Das Wuppertaler Uhrenmuseum*. by J. Abeler. (Berlin and New York, W. de Gruyter, 1971. 86p. illus.) and the exhibition catalog: *The Clockwork Universe:*

German Clocks and Automata 1550-1650 by K. Maurice and O. Mayr (New York, Neale and Watson Academic Publications, 1980. 321p. illus.).

Great Britain

940 Bird, Anthony. **Illustrated Guide to House Clocks**. New York, Arco, 1973. 313p. illus. index. LC 72-96575.

Comprehensive history of English domestic clocks from the beginnings until the middle of the nineteenth century. Directed to the collector and emphasizing the development of the clock mechanisms. Contents: 1, The Background of English Horology; 2, Pre-clockwork Time Measurement; 3, Early Mechanical Clocks; 4, The Bob Pendulum; 6, The Royal Pendulum; 7, Spring-Driven Clocks; 8, Later Lantern and Thirty-hour Clocks; 9, Finding the Longitude; 10, Long-case Clock Development from Queen Anne to Queen Victoria; 11, From Bracket to Mantel; 12, Tavern and Travelling Clocks; 13, Clock Care and Maintenance; 14, Restoration and Faking; 15, English Influence and Decline. No bibliography.

941 Cescinsky, Herbert, and Malcomb R. Webster. **English Domestic Clocks**. Feltham, England, and New York, Spring, 1969. 354p. illus. index. LC 70-579806.

Comprehensive collector's handbook of English house clocks from the seventeenth century to the early nineteenth century. Contents: I, The Problem of the Measurement of Time; II, The Law of the Pendulum; III, The Regulation of Domestic Clocks; IV, The Mechanism of Clocks; V, Brass Lantern or "Birdcage" Clocks; VI, The Development of Long-case Clock Dials; VII, The Development of Clock Hands; VIII, The Development of the Spandrel-Corners of Clock Dials; IX, Long-Case Clocks from 1670 to 1740; X, Lacquered Cases of Long Clocks; XI, Long-case Clocks 1760 to 1800; XII, The Decline of the Long-case Clock; XIII, Chippendale and Sheraton Clock Cases; XIV, Bracket Clocks from 1670 to 1800; XV, Mural and Cartel Clocks. List of clockmakers mentioned in the text. An old standard collector's handbook illustrated with pieces in the trade and private collection and many details of hands, dials, etc. that remain earmarks for dating and provenance.

942 Daniels, George. **English and American Watches**. London and New York, Abelard-Schuman, 1967. 128p. illus. index. LC 66-15599.

Popular history of British and American clocks from the sixteenth century to circa 1965. Appendices with technical descriptions of major mechanical features and list of major markers.

943 Dawson, Percy G., C. B. Drover, and D. W. Parkes. **Early English Clocks: A Discussion of Domestic Clocks up to the Beginning of the Eighteenth Century**. London, Antique Collectors' Club, 1982. 550p. illus. index. ISBN 0902028596.

Comprehensive, authoritative history of English clocks from the sixteenth century to the early eighteenth century. Well illustrated with many details and views of movements and cases. Equal emphasis is given to the clockwork and the cases. Contents: I, The Period up to the Early Seventeenth Century; II, The Clockmakers' Company and Associated Matters; III, The Lantern Clock; IV, Clock Movements during the Architectural Period; V, Clock Cases during the Architectural Period; VI, Later Weight-driven Movements; VII, Later Longcases; VIII, Later Spring-driven Clocks; IX, Later Spring Clock Cases; X, Cases for Weight-driven Clocks of Short Duration; XI, Some Special Clocks. Basic bibliography, pp. 544-45.

944 Jagger, Cedric. **The Artistry of the English Watch**. Newton Abbot, David & Charles, 1988. 160p. illus. index. ISBN 0804870225.

Well-illustrated survey of British watches from the sixteenth century to the early nineteenth century concentrating on the artistic embellishment of the case and exposed parts of the movements. Contents: 1, Background to a Beginning; 2, Sources of Inspiration; 3, The Formative Years; 4, Fashions in English Watches—The Main Trends; 5, The Personal Touch; 6, Materials and Techniques for Enriching the Watch; 7, Postscript—The Best of Both Worlds. Appendices with essay on working methods, areas of art on the watch movement; repertory of watch decorators, watch pillars, and a catalog of watch imagery. Summarized bibliography, p. 153.

945 Loomes, Brian. **Complete British Clocks**. Newton Abbot, North Pomfret, VT., David & Charles, 1978. 256p. illus. index. ISBN 0715375679.
    Comprehensive history of British clocks from the seventeenth century to 1870. Contents: 1, The Cream of Crafts; 2, Lantern Clocks; 3, The Pendulum; 4, The London Longcase; 5, Clocksmiths and their Work; 6, Provincial Eight-Day Longcase Clocks; 7, Clocks with Painted Dials; 8, Clocks for the Wall; 9, Table Clocks; 10, Casework; 11, Collecting and Investing; 12, Outstanding Makers and Outstanding Work. General bibliography, pp. 251-52.

Italy

Dictionaries

946 Morpurgo, Enrico. **Dizionario degli orologiai italiani**. Rome, "La Clessidra," 1950. 239p. illus. LC A51-2741.
    Authoritative, comprehensive dictionary of Italian clock and watchmakers from 1300 to 1880. Comprehensive, classified bibliography of books and major periodical articles, pp. 213-18.

Histories and Handbooks

947 Simoni, Antoni. **Orologi italiani dal Cinquecento all' Ottocento**. Milan, Vallardi, 1965. 172p. illus. index. LC 67-124548.
    Popular history of Italian clocks of the sixteenth through the eighteenth centuries. Illustrated with museum pieces. Brief list of basic books in Italian.

Netherlands

Dictionaries

948 Morpurgo, Enrico. **Nederlands klokken- en horloge makers vanaf 1300**. Amsterdam, Scheltema & Holkema, 1970. 152p. illus. index. LC 78-504861.
    Authoritative, comprehensive dictionary of Dutch clock and watchmakers from 1300 to 1880. Illustrated with major signed pieces; has facsimiles of marks and signatures. Bibliography, pp. 148-52.

Histories and Handbooks

949 Sellink, J. L. **Dutch Antique Domestic Clocks, ca. 1670-1870, and Some Related Examples**. Leiden, Stenfert, 1973. 60p. (text), 300p. (illus. index. LC 73-177830.
    Concise history of Dutch clocks featuring examples in the Oegstgeest Museum of Clocks including examples of early clocks—before Huygen's patent of 1657—and examples made in The Hague, Amsterdam and Haarlem, Zaandam clocks, Groninger and Frisian stoelkloks and staartklots. Bibliography, p. 365.

Norway

950   Ingstad, Olav. **Urmakerkunst: Norge fra midten av 1500-aree til laugstidens slutt.** Oslo, Gyldendal, 1980. 464p. illus. LC 80-497249.

Comprehensive and authoritative history of clock and watchmaking in Norway from the middle of the sixteenth century to the middle of the nineteenth century. Arrangement is by region and place. Comprehensive, classified bibliography, pp. 429-36.

Russia

951   Chenekal, Valentin L. **Watchmakers and Clockmakers in Russia, 1400 to 1850.** London, Antiquarian Horological Society, 1972. 64p. illus. (Antiquarian Horological Society Monographs, 6). ISBN 0901180084.

Concise dictionary of Russian clock and watchmakers active between 1400 to 1850 with a select group of plates of major pieces.

Spain

Dictionaries

952   Basanta Campos, Jose L. **Relojeros de Espana: Diccionario bio- bibliografico.** Ponteve-dra, Paredes, 1972. 151p. illus. LC 73-327348.

Comprehensive, authoritative dictionary of Spanish clock and watchmakers from the late Middle Ages to 1970 illustrated with major, signed pieces and facsimiles of marks and signatures.

Histories and Handbooks

953   Montañés Fontenia, Luis. **Relojes españoles.** 2d ed. Madrid, Prensa Española, 1968. 352p. illus. index.

Comprehensive, scholarly history of Spanish clocks and clockmaking. Contents: Relojes fuera de serie; La relojería en la corte; Panorama de la relojería en el Noroeste; Relojería popular catalana; Otros relojes y relojeros españoles. Bibliographical references in the footnotes, and comprehensive, classified bibliography, pp. 189-198.

Sweden

954   Sidenbladh, Elis T. **Urmakarei Sverige under aldre tider, anteckningar.** 2nd ed. Stockholm, Nordiska Museet, 1947. 256p. illus. (Nordiska Museets handlingar, 28). LC 84-237908r84.

Comprehensive, authoritative dictionary of Swedish clock and watchmakers illustrated with pieces in the Nordiska Museet in Stockholm.

Switzerland

955   Jaquet, Eugene, and Alfred Chapuis. **Technique and History of Swiss Watch.** London and New York, Spring, 1970. 272p. illus. index. LC 70-22401.

Comprehensive, authoritative history of Swiss watchmaking with equal emphasis on artistic form and mechanism. Contents: 1, The Beginnings of Watch-making in Switzerland; 2, The Introduction of the Watch Industry to the Jura, andIits Development; 3, The 18th Century; 4, Decoration of the Watch and of the Movement from 1700 to 1850; 5, The Commerce of Watch-making; 6, The 19th Century and the Beginnings of the Mechanical Manufacturer of the Modern Watch; 7, Chronometry; 8, The Later Evolution of the Modern Watch; 9, Development of the Swiss Watch Industry from 1945 to 1968. Index of Swiss watchmakers and other craftsmen up to 1900, pp. 268-72.

956   Tardy, (firm). **Les plus belles pendules suisses**. Paris, Tardy, 1984. 127p. illus.

Pictorial survey of Swiss clocks from the sixteenth century to the twentieth century with emphasis on casework. Text in French and English. Contains 78 high quality plates, many in color, with descriptive captions. Contents: Introduction; Les horloges de style de l'Europe Centrale; Horloges à poids neuchâteloises Louis XIII; Pendules neuchâteloises Louis XIV; Pendules neuchâteloises Louis XV; Pendules neuchâteloises Louis XVI; Pendules neuchâteloises 1830-1840; Le décors; Pendule cage; Signatures; Mouvements; Cadrans et aiguilles; Chronomètres longue ligne et régulateurs. Comprehensive bibliography, pp. 8-10.

ORIENTAL CLOCKS AND WATCHES

957   Mody, N. H. N. A. **A Collection of Japanese Clocks**. London, Paul, Trench, Trubner, 1932. 46p. illus. Reprint: Rutland, VT, Tuttle, 1967 under the title: *Japanese Clocks*. 46p. text, 135 plates. LC 67-21931.

Unique work. Handbook/history of Japanese clocks from the eighteenth century to the early twentieth century. Brief introductory chapters on time measurement, the Japanese calendar, Japanese clocks followed by catalog of 135 plates illustrating pieces and works of art showing clocks. Descriptive entries in Japanese and English. Clocks are grouped as "lantern clocks," "bracket clocks," "pillar clocks," and miscellaneous clocks which include pocket watches.

See also O. Kurz, *European Clocks and Watches in the Near East*. Studies of the Warburg Institute, vol. 34 (1975).

AUTOMATA (including Music Boxes)

Automata

958   Bailly, Christian. **Automata. The Golden Age 1848-1914**. New York, Harper & Row, 1987. 359p. illus. index. ISBN 0856673455.

Sumptuously illustrated survey of French automata 1848-1914. Contents: 1, The Automata Industry of Paris; 2, The Master Automaton-Makers: Théroude, Bontems, Vichy, Roullet & Decamps, Phalibois, Lambert, Renou; 3, Inside the Magic: Restorations, Function and Mechanisms, Musical Movements; 4, Makers' Catalogues in Facsimile. Bibliography, p. 357, is a list of books in French.

959   Chapuis, Alfred, and Eduard Gelis. **Le monde des automates; etude historique et technique**. Paris, E. Gelis and Neuchatel, A. Chapuis, 1928. 2v. illus. index. Reprint: Geneva, Slatkine, 1984. ISBN 2051005184.

Comprehensive history of automata from antiquity to the early twentieth century written by a leading expert. Contents: I, Premières figures articulées, Automates primitifs; II, L'ecole d'Alexandrie; III, Les Automates Byzantins et Musulmans; IV, Les Automates hydrauliques postérieurs au XVe siècle; V, Les Automates au Moyen-âge et au début des Temps Modernes; VI, Les Automates dans la religion chrétienne; VII, Les Jaquemarts et autres Automates des grandes hologes; VIII, Les Jacquemarts et autres Automates inspirés de ceux des grandes horloges; IX, Hologes de Table et Pièces d'Orfèvrerie à Automates; X, Les Automates dans les horloges et les pendules d'appartement; XI, Les Horloges en bois avec Automates; XII, Horloges, Pendules et Pièces de fantaisie avec figurines ou scènes animées; XIII, Les Tableux mécaniques; XIV, Les Théatres d'Automates; XV, Les Girouettes Mécaniques; XVI, Les Jouets Automates; XVII,

Montres et Tabatières; XVIII, Les Oiseaux Chantants; XIX, Les Animaux Mécaniques; XX, Les Automates Magiciens et Escamoteurs; XXI, Les Constructeurs d'Androïdes; XXII, Les Machines et Têtes parlantes; XXIII, Les Automates et Androïdes Marchants; XXIV, Les Androïdes Ecrivans et Dessinateurs; XXV, Les Androïdes Musiciens; XXVI, Les Faux Automates; XXVII, L'Automatisme dans l'orthopédie; XXVIII, L'Automate et la Littérature. Comprehensive, unclassified bibliography, v. 2, pp. 333-341. A classic work, still a standard in the history of automata. The breadth of the selection of illustrations has not been matched.

960   Droz, Edmond and Alfred Chapuis. **Automata. A Historical and Technological Study.** New York, Central Book Company, 1958. 426p. illus. index. LC A58-4506.
   Translation of: *Les automates; figures artificielles d'hommes et d'animaux.* (Neuchatel, Editions du Griffon, 1949). Authoritative survey of the history of automata from antiquity to the nineteenth century. Contents: I, Early Automata and Articulated Masks; II, Automata in Antiquity from the Arabs to the Renaissance; III, Some Large Clocks with Automata; IV, Old Chamber Clocks and Pieces of Jewellery with Automata; V, Later Clocks with Automata; VI, Wooden Clocks and Small Novelty Clocks; VII, Mechanical Pictures and Picture-Clocks; VIII, Mechanical Toys; IX, Watches and Snuff-Boxes with Automata; X, Singing Birds; XI, Mechanical Animals; XII, Sooth-Sayers, Magicians and Conjurers; XIII, Mechanical Music and Automaton Musicians; XIV, Automaton Writers and Draughtsmen; XV, Walking and Talking Automata; XVI, Automaton; XVII, Animated Displays; XVIII, Trick Machinery, Fake Automata Plays and Semi-Automata; XIX, Robots and Automation. Bibliographical references in the notes.

Music Boxes

961   Chapuis, Alfred. **Histoire de la Boite à musique et de la musique mécanique.** Lausanne, 1955. 319p. illus. index. LC A56-2283.
   Comprehensive, scholarly history of the music box and other musical clockwork from the earliest pieces from the sixteenth century to the end of the nineteenth century written by one of the greatest experts in the history of clocks, watches and automata. Contents: I, Quelques considérations sur la production du son et ses caractéristiques; II, Débuts de la musique mécanique—Les carillons mécaniques; III, Les orgues mécaniques.—Les maitres d'Augusbourg; IV, Un tourant: le début du XVIIIe siècle.—Engramelle.—Les maitres français et viennois; V, Les pendules à musique; VI, Orgues de Barbarie et orgues de foire.—Orchestrions; VII, Un album original; VIII, Une merveille de mécanique ancienne: le Componium de T. N. Winkel; X, Un chef d'orchestre mécanique; XI, Pianos et violons mécaniques; XII, Quel fut l'inventeur de la "musique à peigne"; XIII, Les premiers types de pièces à musique; XIV, L'industrie de la boite à musique à Genève à partir de 1815; XV, Principaux types primitifs de movements à musique; cachets, bijoux, montres et anciennes tabatières; XVI, Développement de la musiqwue à peigne en dehors de Gèneve: Vallée de Joux, Canton de Neuchâtel, Sainte-Suzanne en France; XVII, Les débuts à Sainte-Croix; XVIII, La fabrication de la boite à musique en Suisse vers 1867.—Progès de la région de Sainte-Croix; XIX, Genève et Ste-Croix à l'Exposition nationale de 1896. Autres expositions.—A propos des accordeurs; XX, La technique de la boite à musique; XXI, Principaux types de boites à musique; XXII, Quelques exemples anciens d'application de la musique à peigne à des objets de fantasisie; XXIII, Les pièces à musique à disque; XXIV, A tarvers le monde.—Le commerce des boitres à musique; XXV, Dans de récentes exposition; XXVI, La valeur artistique de la musique à peigne; XXVII, La boite à musique et les droits d'auteur. Bibliographical references in the notes.

962   Clark, John E. T. **Musical Boxes: A History and Appreciation.** London, Allen & Unwin, 1961. 264p. illus. index. LC 61-3223.

General history with emphasis on the mechanisms and particularly those made during the nineteenth century. Contents: 1, Small Musical Movements; 2, Large Musical Boxes; 3, Disc Machines; 4, Nicole-Freres; 5, Some Collectors; 6, Earlier Forms of Mechanical Music; 7, Various Types of Music Box; 8, A Word to Collectors; 9, Care of a Musical Box. Appendix with list of music box makers, those who exhibited at the Great Exhibition, 1851-53 and the Exhibition of 1862.

963   Mosoriak, Roy. **The Curious History of Music Boxes**. Chicago, Lightner Pub. Co., 1943. 242p. illus. index. LC 43-15244.
Popular history of music boxes and other musical clockwork from earliest times to 1905 with chapter on collecting (Expert Music Box Repairers, Points to Remember when Buying a Music Box, The Care of a Music Box, Repairing the Music Box by G. P. Heckert) and dictionary of makers and manufacturers of music works and music boxes. Emphasis is on pieces made in or imported into the United States. General bibliography, pp. 163-64.

964   Tallis, David. **Musical Boxes**. London, Frederick Muller, 1971. 142p. illus. index. LC 70-148834.
Popular history of European music boxes from the eighteenth century to the twentieth century directed to the collector. Equal emphasis placed on the case and clock work. Chapter on buying and repairing; appendices with directory of makers, glossary and general bibliography, pp. 137-38.

SCIENTIFIC INSTRUMENTS

Dictionaries

965   Mills, John F. **Encyclopedia of Antique Scientific Instruments**. New York, Facts on File, 1983. 255p. illus. ISBN 0871967995.
Comprehensive dictionary covering all aspects of the history of scientific instruments throughout the world. Includes clocks and watches. Entries cover: types of instruments, mechanisms, major makers, major scientists whose discoveries influenced instrumentations, styles and ornamentation. Directed to the needs of the average collector. Appendices with advice on care of the collection, fakes and forgeries and list of collections and museums. No bibliography.

Histories and Handbooks

966   Bennett, J. A. **The Divided Circle: A History of Instruments for Astronomy, Navigation and Surveying**. Oxford, Phaidon-Christie's, 1987. 224p. illus.index. ISBN 0714880388.
Comprehensive, well-illustrated history of astronomical, navigational, and surveying instruments from the sixteenth century to the end of the nineteenth century. Appendices with index of makers and glossary of technical terms. Comprehensive but unclassified bibliography, pp. 215-217.

967   Daumas, Maurice. **Scientific Instruments of the Seventeenth and Eighteenth Centuries**. New York, Praeger, 1972. 361p. illus. index. LC 77-112019.
Comprehensive, scholarly history of European scientific instruments of the seventeenth and eighteenth centuries. Emphasis is on the scientific rather than the artistic aspect, but many examples of artistically significant pieces are illustrated and the information provided on the general development of instrumentation is invaluable for the collector, curator, or scholar. Contents: Part One: Instrument-Making Industry in the Seventeenth Century; Part Two: Contributory

Factors in the Evolution of the Instrument-Making Industry; Part Three: The Instrument-Making Industry in the Eighteenth Century; Appendix: Description of the quadrant made for the Académie des Sciences by Chapotot the Younger. List of libraries, archives and collections. Comprehensive bibliography, pp. 342-48, and extensive bibliography in the notes. A standard work.

968   Michel, Henri. **Scientific Instruments in Art and History**. New York, Viking Press, 1967. 208p. index. illus. LC 67-4922.
   Well-illustrated survey of scientific instruments throughout the world and from earliest times to the twentieth century. Emphasis is on pieces noted for the artistic quality of their design and decoration. Contents: I, Basic Elements: Measuring Instruments, Drawing Instruments, Calculating Instruments; II, Measuring the Earth: Topography, Geography, Navigation; III, Measuring the Heavens; IV, The Measurement of Time: Gnomonics, Chronometry; V, Physical Measurements. Descriptive notes to the plates. Basic bibliography, pp. 201-02, and list of museums and other collections.

969   Turner, Gerard L. **Nineteenth-century Scientific Instruments**. London, Sotheby Publications; Berkeley, Calif., Univ. of California Pr., 1983. 320p. illus. index. ISBN 0520051602.
   Well-illustrated handbook/history of European scientific instruments of the nineteenth century directed to the collector. Contents: 1, Introduction; 2, Time; Weights & Measures; 4, Mechanics; 5, Hydrostatics; 6, Pneumatics; 7, Heat; 8, Sound; 9, Light; 10, Magnetism; 11, Electricity; 12, Chemistry; 13, Meteorology; 14, Surveying & Navigation; 15, Drawing & Calculating; 16, Recreational Science. Appendix with list of instrument makers. Good, selective bibliography, pp. 311-13.
   See also the museum catalog: *A Catalogue of European Scientific Instruments in the Department of Medieval and Later Antiquities of the British Museum*. by F. A. B. Ward. (London, Trustees of the British Museums, 1981. 152p. illus. index. ISBN 071411345X).

CHAPTER SEVEN

BIBLIOGRAPHIES, CATALOGS, AND INDEXES

970 Arnold, Janet, and Anthony Pegaret. **Costumes; Bibliography**. London, Victoria and Albert Museum in Association with the Costume Society, 1968. 49p. LC 76-357498.

A classified bibliography of about 400 books and periodical articles on the history of costume. Intended as an introduction for beginning students. The annotated entries cover exclusively Western dress from ancient times to the present, with an emphasis on English and French material. Useful reference tool for the beginner.

971 Berlin, Kunstbibliothek. **Katalog der Lipperheidischen Kostumbibliothek. Neubearbeitet von Eva Nienholdt und Gretel Wagner- Neumann.** Berlin, Mann, 1965. 2v. index. LC 67-73381r913.

First edition published in 1896-1905 in two volumes (Reprint: New York, Hacker, 1963). Catalog of the world's most important library of the history of costume, the bequest of Baron Franz Joseph von Lipperheide, comprising more than 12,000 books and 30,000 prints and other illustrations. Arranged in 25 subject divisions ranging from general works to works on particular periods and countries to special classes and types of costume. Complete bibliographical information provided in the entries with particular attention paid to descriptions of illustrations. Fully indexed. A standard reference work in the field of costume history.

972 Colas, Rene. **Bibliographie générale du costume et de la mode; description des suites, recuils, series, revues et livres francais et etrangers relatifs au costume civil, militaire et religieux, aux modes, aux coiffures et aux divers accessoires de l'habillement...** Paris, Colas, 1933. 2v. Reprint: New York, Hacker Art Books, 1963. LC 65-87490.

Comprehensive bibliography of 3,131 books and periodical articles in Western European languages arranged alphabetically by author with author, title, and subject indexes. Entries are descriptively annotated.

973 Hiler, Hilaire, and Meyer Hiler. **Bibliography of Costume, a Dictionary Catalog of about Eight Thousand Books and Periodicals...** New York, Wilson, 1939. 911p. Reprint: New York, B. Blom, 1967. LC 66-12285.

Classified and annotated bibliography of some 8,400 books and periodical articles on all aspects of costume and adornment in all languages. Interesting introductory essay, "Costumes and Ideologie." Easy-to-use source for older literature.

974 Monro, Isabel S., and Dorothy Cook. **Costumes Index; a Subject Index to Plates and to Illustrated Texts...** New York, Wilson, 1937. 338p. LC 37-7142.

Classified index to illustrations of costume in 615 titles (347 additional titles in a Supplement ([New York, Wilson, 1957, 210p.]). Classification follows country, class of person, types and items of costume, further subdivided by period. List of books indexed also gives locations in several major libraries. Does not include armor. A very useful reference tool.

975 Nordquist, Barbara K. E., Jean Mettam, and Kathy Jansen, eds. **Traditional Folk Textiles. Selected Readings and Bibliography**. Dubuque, Ia., Kendall/Hunt Pub. Co., 1986. 298p. illus. ISBN 0840338864.

Designed as a textbook. Selected and collected readings and bibliographies on textile production and dress in predominantly non-Western cultures. Contents: I, Africa; II, Middle East; III, Europe (peasant or folk costume); IV, Indian Sub-Continent; V, Asia; VI, Oceania; VII, North America (native American dress and textiles); VIII, South America.

DIRECTORIES

976 Centro Internazionale delle Art e del Costume, **Venezia: International Centre of Arts and Costume, Venice. Guida internazionale ai musei e alle collezioni pubbliche di costumi e di tessuti**. Venice, 1970. 594p. LC 73-310258.

Directory of 736 museums and public collections of costumes in countries throughout the world. Text in Italian, French, and English. Entries give address, name(s) of curator(s), description of the collection and a bibliography of published catalogs.

977 Huenefeld, Irene P. **International Directory of Historical Clothing**. Metuchen, N.J., Scarecrow Press, 1967. 175p. LC 67-10186.

Directory of over 2,000 collections of historical costume in North America and Europe. Includes museums, galleries, historical societies, libraries, and churches. Information was gathered by questionnaires. The collections are listed geographically, by title, and by clothing and clothing accessory.

DICTIONARIES AND ENCYCLOPEDIAS

978 Calasibetta, Charlotte M. **Fairchild's Dictionary of Fashion**. 2d ed. New York, Fairchild, 1988. 749p. illus. ISBN 0870056352.

Comprehensive dictionary of fashion comprised of brief entries relating to the history of costume and practical aspects of fashion of all periods. Emphasis is on modern fashion design. "Designers Appendix," pp. 547-98, is a repertory of leading contemporary fashion designers arranged by country.

979 Kybalova, Ludmilla, et al. **The Pictorial Encyclopedia of Fashion**. New York, Crown, 1968. 607p. illus. LC 70-415002.

Comprehensive encyclopedia of world costume from the fourth millennium B.C. to the 1960s. First part is a history: "4,000 Years in the History of Fashion." Second part is a dictionary of various types of costumes, garments and assessories. Includes hairstyles, headgear, etc. Illustrated from contemporary sources in all media.

980 Leloir, Maurice. **Dictionnaire du costume et de ses accessoires, des armes et des étoffes, des origines à nos jours...** Paris, Grund, 1951. 435p. illus. LC A52-6608.

Comprehensive, authoritative dictionary containing over 2,000 entries on all aspects of Western costume, including accessories and arms and armor. Entries vary in length from short definitions of terms to longer essays tracing the development of major pieces. Illustrated with 3,500 reproductions. No bibliography.

981 Picken, Mary B. **The Fashion Dictionary; Fabric, Sewing and Dress as Expressed in the Language of Fashion**. Rev. and enl. ed. New York, Funk & Wagnalls, 1973. 434p. illus. index. LC 72-83771.

First published in 1939 as *Language of Fashion*. Popular dictionary of short entries covering all aspects of costume, with special emphasis on construction, design and material. Illustrated with line drawings and plates reproducing actual pieces of costume and works of art depicting costume. No bibliography.

982 Planché, James R. **A Cyclopedia of Costume or Dictionary of Dress...** London, Chatto and Windus, 1876-79. 2v. illus. index. LC PO30-63r85.

Old, comprehensive dictionary/history of Western costume from 53 B.C. to circa 1700. Volume one is a dictionary of terms covering all aspects including arms and armor, ecclesiastical vestments and jewelry. Volume two is a general history, illustrated with line drawings, engravings, and color plates and emphasizing the general cultural content. A classic, pioneering work still a standard reference work in the history of costume.

983 Wilcox, Ruth T. **The Dictionary of Costume.** New York, Scribner's, 1969. 406p. illus. LC 68-12503.

Popular but comprehensive dictionary of world costume covering all aspects, including accessories, fabrics, colors and designers. Cross reference to foreign terms. Copiously illustrated with line drawings. Bibliography, pp. 404-06, lists books and periodical articles chiefly in English.

GENERAL HISTORIES AND HANDBOOKS

984 Allemagne, Henry Rene d'. **Les accessoires du costume et du mobilier depuis le treizième jusqu'au milieu du dix-neuvième siècle...** Paris, Schemit, 1928. 3v. illus. Reprint: New York, Hacker, 1970. 3v. in 2. LC 72-94899.

Comprehensive history of costume accessories, objets d'art, eating utensils and scientific instruments from the thirteenth through the nineteenth centuries. Contents: 1, La parure et la toilette; 2, Menus objets mobiliers; 3, Outlis, instruments et appareils de précision; 4, La table et la cuisine. Bibliography, pp. 565-67, lists books and periodical articles chiefly in French.

985 Arnold, Janet. **A Handbook of Costume.** London, Macmillan, 1973. 336p. illus. LC 74-154619.

Very useful handbook for the student of costume history. Has chapters on dating costume by construction technique, conservation, storage and display, costume for children and students, costume for the stage, and classified bibliography of books on costume and list of collections of costume in the British Isles. Bibliography gives directions on how to use sources in the study of costume.

986 Bell, Quentin. **On Human Finery.** 2d ed. London, Hogarth Press, New York, Schocken, 1976. 239p. illus. LC 77-370605.

Important theoretical study of the forces of change in fashion in Western society. Contents: I, Sartorial Morality; II, Sumptuosity; III, The Nature of Fashion; IV, Theories of Fashion; V, The Mechanism of Fashion; VI, Revolution; VII, Vicarious Consumption—Archaism; VIII, Recent History; IX, Deviations from Veblen. Appendices with essay on fashion and the fine arts and brief survey of fashion from the fifteenth to the sixteenth centuries. Basic bibliography, pp. 9-10.

987 Boehn, Max von. **Modes and Manners...** London, Harrap; Philadelphia, Lippencott, 1932-36. 4v. illus. index. Reprint: New York, B. Blom, 1970. 4v. in 2. LC 68-56493.

Comprehensive history of Western European dress as a manifestation of the general cultural development. Covers dress from the migrations to the end of the eighteenth century. Text divided into chapters on history, the arts and fashion. Excellent selection of illustrations derived from works of art depicting costume.

988   Boucher, Francois. **20,000 Years of Fashion: History of Costume and Personal Adornment**. New York, Abrams, 1967. 441p. illus. index. LC 66-12103.

Translation of *Histoire du costume en occident, de l'antiquité à nos jours* (Paris, Flammarion, 1965). Excellent, scholarly history of Western costume from prehistoric times to 1964 covering all aspects except arms and armor. Good coverage of accessories and jewelry. Excellent illustrations with notes of actual garments and works of art depicting costume. Useful maps, chronological tables, and glossary of terms. Specialized literature given at the end of each chapter, general bibliography including catalogs, 423p.

989   Bruhn, Wolfgang, and Max Tilke. **A Pictorial History of Costume; a Survey of Costume of All Periods and Peoples from Antiquity to Modern Times including National Costume in Europe and Non-European Countries...** New York, Praeger, 1955. 74p. (text), 200 plates. LC 55-11522.

Translation of *Kostümwerk*. Illustrated survey of world costume including arms and armor, military uniforms, ecclesiastical vestments, folk and native costume. Brief introductory text followed by good collection of plates based on facsimiles from the originals colored by Max Tilke and photographs in the Lipperheide Kostümbibliothek (971).

990   D'Assailly, Gisele. **Ages of Elegance: Five Thousand Years of Fashion & Frivolity**. Paris, Hachette, 1968. 251p. illus. LC 71-436253.

Popular survey of Western costume from the ancient world to the 1960s with emphasis on trends in high fashion. Good selection of illustrations. One-page bibliography of basic books.

991   Davenport, Millia. **The Book of Costume**. New York, Crown, 1948. 2v. illus. index. Reprinted 1962 in one volume. LC 48-9980.

Comprehensive history of Western costume from ancient Egypt and Mesopotamia through the nineteenth century. Large corpus of illustrations, mostly of works of art depicting costumed figures. Appendix, pp. 935-945, is a bibliography and index of sources for the illustrations, a valuable feature of the book. Treats ecclesiastical and military dress and armor as well as accessories. Most useful as a chronologically arranged corpus of illustrations.

992   Evans, Mary. **Costume Throughout the Ages**. Rev. ed. Philadelphia and New York, Lippincott, 1950. 360p. illus. index. LC 50-8475.

Comprehensive textbook history of Western costume from antiquity to 1900. Summaries of time periods at the beginning of each chapter, topics for discussion and bibliographical references at the end of each chapter. Comprehensive, classified bibliography, pp. 318-29.

993   Gorsline, Douglas W. **What People Wore: A Visual History of Dress from Ancient Times to Twentieth-Century America...** New York, Viking, 1952. 266p. illus. LC 52-12392.

Popular survey of Western dress with some Byzantine and Near Eastern costume. Covers military dress, including arms and armor. Large collection of illustrations, mostly line drawings adapted from art sources.

994   Kelly, Francis M., and Randolph Schawbe. **Historic Costume, a Chronicle of Fashion in Western Europe, 1490-1790...** London, Batsford, 1925. 284p. illus. Reprint: New York, B. Blom, 1968. 305p. illus. index. LC 67-13332.

Older history of costume directed to the needs of the theater. Contents: I, The Italiante Tendency (1490-1510); II, Puffs and Slashes: the German Element (1510-45); III, Spanish

Bombast (1545-1620); IV, Long Locks, Lace, and Leather (1620-55); V, Effects of the "Grand Règne" (1655-1715); VI, Paniers, Powder, and Queue (1715-90). Section with patterns of a cloak with hanging sleeves, a Spanish cape, a bodice and stomacher, a doublet and breeches, etc. Critically annotated bibliography, pp. 299-302, of books and periodical articles published before 1925.

995   Kelly, Francis M., and Randolph Schwabe. **A Short History of Costume and Armour...** London, Batsford, 1931. 2v. illus. index. Reprint: Newton Abbot, David & Charles, 1972. 261p. illus. index. LC 73-163461.

Older, comprehensive history of Western costume and armor from 1066 to 1866 with emphasis on English material. Useful diagrams of armor, glossary of terms, and good (for the older literature) general bibliography of books, periodical articles and catalogs.

996   Kohler, Karl. **History of Costume**. New York, Watt, 1928. 463p. illus. index. Reprinted: New York, Dover, 1963. LC 63-16328.

Concise but authoritative survey of Western costume from antiquity to circa 1870. Illustrated with plates and line drawings, some with useful construction details. Bibliography, pp. 457-58, is a limited list, chiefly of German books. Based on the author's *Praktische Kostumkunde in 600 Bildern und Schnitten,* Munich, Bruckmann, 1926. 2v. illus.

997   König, Rene, and Peter W. Schuppisser. **Die Mode in der menschlichen Gesellschaft**. Zurich, Modebuch-Verlag, 1958. 527p. illus. LC 59-37555.

Comprehensive history of Western costume from antiquity to the present illustrated with line drawings and photographs drawn from original costume designs and contemporary art works. Emphasis is on stylistic development. Good treatment of major fashion designers of the twentieth century. Bibliography, pp. 524-27, is a classified list of books and periodical articles mostly in German.

998   Laver, James. **The Concise History of Costume and Fashion**. New ed. New York, Oxford Univ. Press, 1983. 288p. illus. ISBN 0195203909.

Well-illustrated survey of Western costume from antiquity to the mid-twentieth century. Contents: 1, How It All Began; 2, Greeks and Romans; 3, The Dark Ages and the Middle Ages; 4, The Renaissance and the 16th Century; 5, The 17th Century; 6, The 18th Century; 7, From 1800 to 1850; 8, From 1850 to 1900; 9, From 1900 to 1939; 10, The Last 30 Years. Brief bibliography, p. 277.

999   Laver, James. **Costume**. New York, Hawthorn Books, 1964. 136p. illus. index. LC 64-13277.

Concise but authoritative history of Western costume from ancient Egypt to the twentieth century with chapters on Byzantine and Near Eastern dress. Illustrated mainly with art works or line drawings adapted from contemporary art works. No bibliography.

1000   Lester, Katherine M., and Bess V. Oerke. **Illustrated History of those Frills and Furbelows of Fashion Which Have Come to Be Known as: Accessories of Dress**. Peoria, Ill., Manual Arts Press, 1940. 587p. illus. index. LC 40-31572.

Comprehensive history of clothing accessories in the West from prehistoric Bronze Age to the early twentieth century, arranged by class or type of accessory. Good collection of illustrations with descriptive captions. Bibliographies at the end of each chapter and general bibliography, pp. 577-79, lists books chiefly in English.

1001   Norris, Herbert. **Costume & Fashion...** London, Dent, 1931-40. 3v. in 4. illus. index. LC 25-2565.

Comprehensive history of European dress up to 1600 with emphasis on the social context and on British developments. Contents: v. 1: Evolution of European Dress through the Earlier Ages; v. 2: Senlac to Bosworth, 1066-1485; v. 3, 1: The Tudors, 1485-1547; v. 3, 2: The Tudors, 1547-1603. Chapter on heraldry and feudalism in v. 2. No bibliography.

1002   Payne, Blanche. **History of Costume, from the Ancient Egyptians to the Twentieth Century.** New York, Harper & Row, 1965. 607p. illus. index. LC 65-10419.

Comprehensive history of European costume, well illustrated with drawings, plates and pattern drafts for garment construction. Sources for the illustrations given in the captions. Contents: 1, Egypt; 2, Mesopotamia; 3, The Bronze Age in Denmark; 4, Crete and Greece; 5, Etruscans and Romans; 6, The Byzantine Empire; 7, Western Europe to the 12th Century; 8, 12th and 13th Centuries; 9, The 14th Century; 10, Men's Costume of the 15th Century; 11, Women's Costume of the 15th Century; 12, High Renaissance: Men's Costume of the 16th Century; 13, High Renaissance: Women's Costume of the 16th Century; 14, The Baroque Period: Men's Costume of the 17th Century; 15, The Baroque Period: Women's Costume of the 17th Century; 16, 18th-century Fashions for Men; 17, Women's Costume of the 18th Century; 18, Men's Wear in the 19th Century; 19, Women's Fashions of the 19th Century. Basic bibliography, pp. 591-94.

1003   Racinet, Albert C. A. **Le costume historique...** Paris, Firmin-Didot, 1888. 6v. illus. LC 02-824.

Comprehensive, scholarly history of world costume from ancient times to the late nineteenth century. Volume one provides an introduction and catalog of the plates, tables of historical personalities, bibliography, pp. 113-24, glossary of terms and geographical and ethnographical indexes. Volume two covers Egyptian, Greek, Roman and Germanic, African and American Indian dress. Volume three treats Oriental dress; volume four, Western medieval, including amour, through the seventeenth century; volume five, European dress of the eighteenth century; volume six nineteenth-century European dress. An edited translation with excellent reproductions of Racinet's colored plates is: *The Historical Encyclopedia of Costumes.* Introduction by Aileen Ribeiro. New York, Facts on File, 1988. 320p. illus. index. ISBN 0816019762.

1004   Rubens, Alfred. **A History of Jewish Costume.** London, Funk & Wagnalls; New York, Crown, 1967. 221p. illus. index.

Comprehensive and authoritative history of Jewish costume. Contents: 1, Origins and Distinctive Features; 2, The Eastern World and the Influence of Islam; 3, The Western World—the Effects of Tradition and Restrictive Laws; 4, Poland and Russia; 5, The Western World—the Effects of Emancipation and Assimilation; 6, Rabbinical Dress. Appendices with essay on the costume of the Jewish high priest with extracts from Exodus and Josephus, extracts from sumptuary laws and dress regulations, and documents relating to the wearing of the yellow hat in the Comtat Venaissin. General bibliography, pp. 208-11, and additional bibliography in the notes.

1005   Rudofsky, Bernard. **The Unfashionable Human Body.** New York, Doubleday, 1974. 287p. illus. index. LC 74-160871.

Popular history of world costume with emphasis on the oddities and eccentricities of fashion and the aesthetics of human adornment. No bibliography.

1006   Russell, Douglas A. **Costume History and Style.** Englewood Cliffs, N.J.: Prentice-Hall, 1983. 544p. illus. index. ISBN 0131812149.

Comprehensive history of Western costume, Prehistoric times to the present, designed as a textbook. Clear chronological presentation. Illustrated with works of art, drawings of costume construction and for the later periods actual costume pieces. Supporting material from the history of interior design. Glossary and bibliography by chapters.

1007   Squire, Geoffrey. **Dress and Society, 1560-1970.** London, Studio Vista, 1974. 176p. illus. LC 73-11542.
    Survey of European dress from 1560 to 1970 as a manifestation of changing patterns of thought and belief. Well illustrated. Contents: The Eye of the Beholder; Style in the Dress of Thought; Clothes Make the Man, but Man Makes the Clothes; Mannerism; The Two Faces of Baroque 1600-1700; Rococo 1690-1770; Neo-classicism 1750-1815; From Romance to Materialism 1800-60; In All Directions 1860 and After. Basic bibliography, p. 173.

1008   Stibbert, Frederick. **Civil and Military Clothing in Europe: From the First to the Eighteenth Century.** New York, B. Blom, 1968. 217p. illus. LC 68-16212.
    Originally published in Italian (Bergamo, 1914). Pictorial survey with brief introductory text followed by excellent corpus of drawings adapted from art sources displaying special attention to details. Thorough coverage of armor. Bibliography of basic books.

1009   Truman, Nevil. **Historic Costuming...** 2nd ed. with additional chapters by Ruth Green. London, Pitman, 1966. 170p. illus. index. LC 66-72736.
    First published in 1936. Popular history/handbook of Western costume from ancient Greece and Rome to circa 1965, covering male and female dress and occasional treatment of clerical and military dress. Illustrated chiefly with line drawings. No bibliography.
    See also the exhibition catalog: *Weisse Westen, rote Roben: von den Farbordnungen des Mittelalters zum individuellen Farbgeschmack* by H. Nixdorff et al. (Berlin, Museum für Volkerkunde, 1983. 218p. illus. ISBN 3886091198).

ANCIENT COSTUME

1010   Abrahams, Ethel B. **Greek Dress: A Study of the Costumes Worn in Ancient Greece from Pre-Hellenic Times to the Hellenistic Age.** London, J. Murray, 1908. 134p. illus. index. LC 09-12608.
    Older, still-useful survey of ancient Greek dress from the Bronze Age to the end of the Hellenic period. Contents: I, Introduction; II, Homeric; III, Doric; IV, Ionic; V, The Maidens of the Acropolis—the Development of the Ionic Himation; VI, Materials and Ornamentation; VII, Hair and Head-dress; VIII, Footgear; IX, The Toilet—Conclusion. Bibliographical references in the footnotes. Greek and English indexes.

1011   Bieber, Margarete. **Entwicklungsgeschichte der griechischen Tracht von der vorgriechischen Zeit bis zum Ausgang der Antike.** 2d ed. Berlin, Mann, 1967. 61p. illus. index. LC 75-359074r87.
    Concise survey of the history of ancient Greek dress from Egyptian antecedents to Greco-Roman times. Contents: Einleitung; Die Technik der Gewandherstellung; Geschichte der griechischen Kleidung; I, Vorgriechische Zeit; II, Die archaische Zeit; III, Die klassische Zeit; IV, Die hellenistische Zeit; V, Die griechische-römische Zeit; VI, Modell und Kunstwerk bei griechischen Gewandstatuen. Updated bibliographies in each section.

1012   **Griechische Kleidung.** Berlin, De Gruyter, 1928. 100p. illus. index. Reprint: Berlin, de Gruyter, 1977. ISBN 3110048353.
    Important, scholarly history of ancient Greek costume as represented in works of art. Contents: Einleitung: Systematik der griechischen Gewänder; Übersicht über die Systematik mit

Beispielen; Beschreibung der Tafeln; I, Peplos; II, Chiton der Frauen; 2, Chiton der Männer; III, 1. Mantel der Frauen; III, 2. Mantel der Männer; IV, Modellaufnahmen; V, Harrtrachten; VI, Schmuck; VII, Fussbekleidung. Glossary of Greek terms with German equivalents. Bibliography, p. 95. A standard work by a leading specialist in Greek art.

1013   Bonfante, Larissa. **Etruscan Dress**. Baltimore, Md., Johns Hopkins Univ. Press, 1975. 256p. illus. LC 75-11344.
    Scholarly history/handbook of ancient Etruscan dress with 162 illustrations of Etruscan works of art depicting costumed figures with detailed descriptive captions. Contents: 1, Fabrics and Patterns; 2, Perizoma and Belts; 3, Chiton and Tunic; 4, Mantles; 5, Shoes; 6, Hats, Hair Styles, and Beards; 7, Foreign Influences and Local Styles. Appendix I: Strange Costumes and Special Problems; Appendix II: Vocabulary. Comprehensive bibliography, pp. 213-30, and bibliographical references in the notes.

1014   Gullberg, Elsa, and Paul Astrom. **The Thread of Ariadne. A Study of Ancient Greek Dress**. Goteborg, P. Astrom, 1970. 51p. illus. (Studies in Mediterranean Archaeology, v. 21). LC 72-583288.
    Scholarly study by an archaeologist and textile expert of the style and construction of ancient Greek dress. The authors posit that ancient Greek dress was actually pleated. Contents: Observation by E. Gullberg; What We Know about Ancient Fibres by P. Aström; Pictures and Text. Facts and Observations by E. Gullberg and P. Aström. Selected bibliography, pp.49-51, and further bibliography cited in the footnotes.

1015   Houston, Mary G. **Ancient Egyptian, Mesoptamian & Persian Costume and Decoration**. 2d ed. London, Black, 1954. 190p. illus. (A Technical History of Costume, 1). Reprinted 1972. LC 54-4264.
    History of ancient Near Eastern and Egyptian costume illustrated with drawings taken from depictions in works of art. Emphasis is on the construction of the garments. Classified bibliography, pp. 188-90.

1016   Houston, Mary G. **Ancient Greek, Roman and Byzantine Costume and Decoration**. 2nd ed. London, Black, 1947. 182p. illus. Reprinted 1963. (A Technical History of Costume, 2)
    Follows the same format as the first volume in the author's series (1015). Chapter on the Vestments of the Eastern Orthodox Church.

1017   Laver, James. **Costume in Antiquity**. New York, Potter, 1964. 139p. illus. LC 64-24791.
    Popular pictorial survey of ancient costume from Sumerian times through A.D. 500. Includes Bronze Age Europe. Brief introductory text is followed by line drawings derived from various historical art sources.

1018   Marinatos, Spyridon N. **Kleidung, Haar- und Barttracht**. Göttingen, Ruprecht, 1967. 113p. illus. (Archaeologia Homerica, Bd. 1, Kapitel A-B).
    Scholarly study of costume and hair style in Greece from Mycenean and Minoan times through the Geometric period based upon close study of costume depicted in art and literary evidence. Bibliographical footnotes.

MEDIEVAL DRESS

1019   Brooke, Iris. **Western European Costume, Thirteenth to Seventeenth Century & Its Relationship to the Theatre**. London, Harrap, 1939. 151p. illus. LC 39-27578.

Popular history/handbook illustrated with line drawings with descriptive notes. No bibliography.

1020   Evans, Joan. **Dress in Medieval France**. Oxford, Clarendon, 1952. 94p. (text), 84p. (plates). index.

Brief but authoritative history of Western European costume from 1060 to 1515 including clerical and military dress. Good selection of plates with descriptive notes. Bibliography, pp. 81-82, lists book in all languages.

1021   Houston, Mary G. **Medieval Costume in England & France; the 13th, 14th and 15th Centuries**. London, Black, 1939. 228p. illus. (A Technical History of Costume, 3). Reprinted, 1950. LC 46-13216.

Broad survey with emphasis on construction. Follows the format of the other volumes in the author's series (1015, 1016). Section of patterns. Glossary of terms. Classified bibliography, pp. 227-28.

1022   Scott, Margaret. **The Fourteenth & Fifteenth Centuries**. London, Batsford, 1986. 143p. illus. index. ISBN 0713448571.

In the series: A Visual History of Costume. Very useful, pictorial survey of costume in the West during the fourteenth and fifteenth centuries. Introductory essay discusses the sources and main features of the development of dress during the period and is followed by 150 plates of works of art illustrating costume. The plates are chronologically arranged and are accompanied by detailed descriptions. Glossary and select bibliography, pp. 139-40

1023   Scott, Margaret. **Late Gothic Europe, 1400-1500**. London, Mills & Boon, Atlantic Highlands, N.J., Humanities Press, 1980. 256p. illus. index. ISBN 0263064298.

In the series: History of Dress, in which no other volume has appeared. Comprehensive, insightful history of fifteenth century dress supported by large selection of illustrations from works of art, many of which are so poorly reproduced that they cannot support the points made in the text. Contents: 1, The Lilies, the Leopards and the Lion: An Historical Background; 2, The Gothic Nude; 3, Moralizing and Manufacturing; 4, International Gothic, c. 1380-c. 1420; 5, Sober Frivolity, c. 1420-c. 1440; 6, The Body Imprisoned, c. 1440-c.1460; 7, The Decline of the Gothic World, c. 1460-c. 1500; 8, The Last Refuge of the Gothic World. General bibliography, pp. 245, and some additional bibliography in the notes.

Ecclesiastical Vestments

1024   Bock, Franz. **Geschichte der liturgischen Gewänder des Mittelalters...** Bonn, Henry & Cohen, 1859-71. 3v. in 2. illus. Reprint: Graz, Akademische Druck- und Verlagsanstalt, 1970. LC 70-570381.

Pioneering history of medieval ecclesiastical vestments illustrated with engravings and color lithographs. Superseded by Braun (1025).

1025   Braun, Joseph. **Die liturgische Gewandung im Occident und Orient nach Ursprung und Entwicklung, Verwendung und Symbolik**. Freiburg im Breisgau, Herder, 1907. 797p. illus. index. LC 13-25792. Reprint: Darmstadt, Wissenschaftliche Buchgesellschaft, 1964.

Comprehensive, scholarly history of ecclesiastical dress in both Western and Eastern Christian traditions from early Christian times to the nineteenth century. The first of the great Jesuit art historian's magisterial works on Christian liturgical art. Contents: Erster Abschnitt: Die liturgischen Untergewänder: 1, Der Amikt; 2, Der Fanone; 3, Die Albe; 4, Das Cingulum; 5, Das Subcinctorium; 6, Rochett und Superpelliceum; Zweiter Abschnitt: Das liturgischen Oberwänder: 1, Die Kasel; 2, Dalmatik und Tunicella; 3, Das Pluviale; Dritter Abschnitt: Die liturgischen Bekleidungsstücke der Hände, der Fusse und des Kopfes: 1, Die Pontifikalhandschuhe; 2, Die pontifikalen Fussbekleidung; 3, Die Mitra; 4, Tiara, Pileolus, Birett; Vierter Abschnitt: Die Insignien: 1, Der Manipel; 2, Die Stola; 3, Das Pallium; 4, Das Rationale; Fünfter Abschnitt: Symbolik, Farbe und Segnung der liturgischen Gewänder: 1, Die mystische Deutung der liturgischen Gewänder; 2, Die liturgischen Farben; 3, Segnung der liturgischen Farben; Schlussabschnitt: Die liturgische Gewandung in ihrer Gesamtenwicklung. Extensive bibliographical footnotes. An indispensable and standard work.

1026   Chrysostomos, Archimandrite. **Orthodox Liturgical Dress: an Historical Treatment**. Brookline, Mass, Holy Cross Orthodox Press, 1981. 76p. illus. index. ISBN 091658643X.

Scholarly essays on the uniqueness and historical context of the development of Eastern Orthodox ecclesiastical dress. Contents: 1, Historiographical Problematics in the Study of the Origin of Liturgical Vesture; 2, Byzantine and Latin Vestments of Common Origin; 3, Vestments Unique to the Eastern Church; 4, The Social and Mystical Significance of Orthodox Liturgical Vesture. Bibliographical references in the footnotes. Illustrated with line drawings derived from works of art that are inadequately identified.

1027   Mayo, Janet. **A History of Ecclesiastical Dress**. New York, Holmes & Meier Pub., 1984. 192p. illus. ISBN 0841909830.

Concise survey of ecclesiastical dress from Early Christian times to the 1980s with emphasis on developments in England. Includes both Catholic and Protestant dress. Contents: 1, The Early Christians; 2, The Church in England 586-1066; 3, The Growth of Monasticism and the Beginnings of Opus Anglicanum; 4, The Great Age of Opus Anglicanum until the End of the Middle Ages, 1250-1509; 5, The Reformation 1509-1559; 6, The Elizabethan Settlement and the Birth of Protestantism 1559-1658; 7, The Establishment of Protestantism and the Anglican Church 1658-1829; 8, The Victorian Church, The Oxford Movement and After 1829-1914; 9, The Protestant Church in the Twentieth Century, 1914-1970; 10, Roman Catholic Vestments in the Twentieth Century, 1900-1980s. Illustrated glossary. Bibliography, pp. 183-84, lists books chiefly in English. Specialized, scholarly literature in the notes. A good introduction to the subject.

1028   Norris, Herbert. **Church Vestments, Their Origin & Development**. New York, Dutton, 1950. 190p. illus. index. LC 50-6481.

Survey history of ecclesiastical dress from Early Christian times to 1500. Contents: Brief Historical Data; Jesus Christus; Brief Sketch of the History of the Christian Church till 1500; Titles of Ecclesiastics; Vestments in General: 1, The Alb, 2, The Pallium, 3, Footgear, 4, The Chasuble, 6, The Amice, 7, The Stole, 8, The Maniple, 9, The Mitre, 10, The Tiara, 11, The Pastoral Staff or Crozier, 12, The Cross, 13, The Cross-staff, 14, The Halo or Nimbus, 15, Flabellum or Muscarium, Fan, 16, The Cope, 17, The Cassock, 18, The Surplice, 19, The Tunicle, 20, The Rochet, 21, The Almuce, 22, The Chinere, 23, The Tonsure and Headgear, 24, Rings and Gloves. Bibliographical references in footnotes. Older works in the same vein are: W. B. Wharton, *Vestiarium Christianum: the Origin and Gradual Development of the Dress of Holy Ministry in the Church*. London, Rivingtons, 1868. 252p. illus. LC 33-9891) and R. A. S. Macalister, *Ecclesiastical Vestments: Their Development and History*. (London, E. Stock, 1896. 270p. illus. LC 37-29677).

See also the museum catalog: *Catalogue of English Ecclesiastical Embroideries of the XII to XVI Centuries* (London, Victoria and Albert Museum, 1916. 47p. illus. LC 16-20420) and the exhibition catalog: *Raiment for the Lord's Service: A Thousand Years of Western Vestments*, by C. Mayer-Thurman (Chicago, Art Institute, 1975. 376p. illus.).

RENAISSANCE—MODERN COSTUME

1029   Boehn, Max von. **Modes & Manners of the Nineteenth Century as Represented in Pictures and Engravings of the Time...** New York, Dutton, 1927. 4v. illus. LC 28-3478.
Continuation of the author's *Modes and Manners...* (987). Published as volumes five through eight in the original German edition (*Die Mode. Menschen und Moden* first published in 1909; 6th ed. revised by Ursula von Kardoff; Munich, Bruckmann, 1963). Covers the period from 1790 to 1914. Its most valuable feature, the large collection of reproductions of works of art depicting costume, is marred in this set by a haphazard arrangement.

1030   Braun-Ronsdorf, Margarete. **Mirror of Fashion; a History of European Costume, 1789-1929.** New York, Mc Graw-Hill, 1964. 270p. illus. index. LC 64-22191.
Authoritative history of feminine high fashion from 1789 to 1929. Well illustrated with plates and line drawings with informative notes and catalog. Bibliography, p. 265, lists chiefly books in German.

1031   Ewing, Elizabeth. **History of Twentieth Century Fashion.** 3rd ed. London, Batsford, 1986. 278p. illus. index. ISBN 071344682X.
Popular survey of Western costume from 1900 to 1980 with emphasis on women's dress. General bibliography, pp. 271-74.

1032   Gernsheim, Alison. **Fashion and Reality, 1840-1914.** London, Faber, 1963. 104p. illus. index. LC 65-89180.
Authoritative survey of European and American costume from 1840 to 1914 with important collection of 235 illustrations taken from contemporary photographs. Contents: Notes on the Photographs; Part 1, The Rise and Fall of the Crinoline; Part II, Curves and Verticals. General bibliography, pp. 95-99, includes catalogs and periodicals. Further bibliography in the footnotes.

1033   Floerke, Hanns. **Die Moder der italienischen Renaissance.** Munich, Müller, 1924. 143p. illus. index.
Pictorial survey of dress in Italy from the fourteenth through the sixteenth centuries. Contains 132 plates of major works of art with notes describing the styles of the costumes depicted. Bibliographical footnotes.

1034   Laver, James, ed. **Costume of the Western World; the Tudors to Louis XIII.** London, Harrap; New York, Harper & Row, 1952. 390p. illus. LC 52-6679.
Comprehensive, authoritative history of Western costume from 1485 to 1650, consisting of essays on the major periods written by various British experts, followed by descriptive notes to the plates that are mostly derived from contemporary works of art. Bibliographies at the end of each chapter.

1035   Leloir, Maurice. **Histoire du costume de l'antiquité à 1914.** Paris, Ernst, 1933-49. v. 8-12. illus. index. LC 49-6746.
Monumental work by a leading authority; planned as a twelve-volume history of Western costume from antiquity to 1914 covering hairstyles, accessories and jewelry as well as all major

classes of costume. Only volumes 8 through 12 were published. Contents: v. 8: 1610-43; v. 9: 1643-78; v. 10: 1678-1725; v. 11: 1725-74; v. 12: 1775-1795. Well illustrated with many useful plates showing costumed figures in contemporary settings. Bibliographies at the end of each volume.

1036   Ribeiro, Aileen. **Dress in Eighteenth-Century Europe, 1715-1789**. London, Batsford, 1984. 220p. illus. index. ISBN 0713446501.

History of Western European dress of the upper classes during the eighteenth century. Illustrated with representations in paintings and prints. Bibliographical footnotes and alphabetical list of books and articles in all languages, pp. 207-12.

See also the exhibition catalog: *An Elegant Art: Fashion & Fantasy in the Eighteenth Century* (Los Angeles, Los Angeles County Museum of Art; New York, Abrams, 1983. 255p. illus. ISBN 0875871119).

AMERICAN COSTUME (U.S. and Canada)

1037   Earle, Alice. **Two Centuries of Costume in America, MDCXX-MDCCCXX**. New York, Macmillan, 1903. 2v. illus. index. Reprint: New York, Dover, 1970. LC 70-118167.

First comprehensive survey of early American costume that still contains a vast amount of valuable information. Dates and provenance of many illustrations must be checked against more recent scholarship. No bibliography.

1038   McClellan, Elisabeth. **Historic Dress in America: 1607-1800**. New York, B. Blom, 1969. 407p. illus. index. LC 70-81515.

Reprint of first edition of 1917 that was subsequently reprinted as: *History of American Costume, 1607-1870; with an Introductory Chapter on Dress in the Spanish and French Settlements in Florida and Louisiana...* New York, Tudor, 1937. 661p. illus. index.

Survey of early American dress including the Spanish and French settlements in Florida and Louisiana. Valuable source of information but must be used with the same caution as Earle (1037). Illustrated with redrawings from paintings and prints with inadequate references.

1039   Warwick, Edward, Henry C. Pitz, and Alexander Wykoff. **Early American Dress: The Colonial and Revolutionary Periods**. New York, Bonanza Books, 1965. 428p. illus. index. (The History of American Dress, v. 2). LC 64-14717.

Comprehensive history of dress from the earliest colonial times to circa 1800. Contents: I, The European Background; II, Virginia: 1607-1675; III, The New England Background: 1620-1675; IV, The Dutch in New York: 1623-1675; V, Growth and Change in the Colonies: 1675-1775; VI, Pennsylvania (and the Quakers); VII, The Revolution and the New Republic: 1775-1790; VIII, Children in Orth America: 1585-1790; IX, Frontier Life. Important corpus of plates of works of art illustrating early American dress. Comprehensive, annotated bibliography, pp. 389-98. No other volumes in the series published. A standard work.

1040   Wilcox, R. Turner. **Five Centuries of American Costume**. New York, Scribner's, 1963. 207p. illus. LC 63-9768.

Popular history from the earliest settlers to circa 1950. Includes military dress and American Indian costume. Illustrated with redrawings with inadequate documentation. Classified bibliography, pp. 203-07.

1041   Worrell, Estelle A. **American Costume, 1840 to 1920**. Harrisburg, Pa., Stackpole Books, 1979. 206p. illus. index. ISBN 0811701069.

Popular survey of costume in the United States between 1840 and 1920 illustrated with drawings by the author. Chronological arrangement with concluding chapter on design and construction. No bibliography.

See also the museum catalog: *Eighteenth-century Clothing at Williamsburg*, by L. Baumgarten (Williamsburg, Va., Colonial Williamsburg Foundation, 1986. 79p. illus. ISBN 0879351098).

See also the price guides: M. Dolan, *Vintage Clothing, 1880-1960: Identification & Value Guide*, (Florence, Ala., Books Americana, 1984. 201p. illus. ISBN 0896890392) and S. Malouff, *Collectible Clothing with Prices* (Des Moines, Ia., Wallace-Homestead, 1983. 160p. illus. ISBN 0870694235).

Native American Costume [*See also* Chapter Eighteen, Native American Textiles and Beadwork]

1042   Haire, Frances H. **The American Costume Book**. New York, Barnes, 1937. 164p. illus.

1043   Hofsinde, Robert. **Indian Costumes**. New York, Morrow, 1968. 94p. illus. LC 68-11895r85.

Popular survey of the traditional costume of the Apache, Blackfoot, Crow, Iroquois, Navaho, Northwest Coast Indians, Ojibwa, Pueblo, Seminole, Sioux and various Indian tribes of today.

1044   Koch, Ronald P. **Dress Clothing of the Plains Indians**. Norman, Okla., Univ. of Oklahoma Press, 1977. 219p. illus. index. ISBN 0806113723.

Survey of the traditional costume of the Indians of the Great Plains. Contents: 1, The People of the Plains; 2, Feathers; 3, Color and Painted Designs; 4, Quillwork; 5, Native Ornaments; 6, Trade: Beads; 7, Metal; 8, Cloth; 9, Hair and Headgear; 10, Skins and Shirts; 11, Dresses; 12, Leggings; 13, Footwear; 14, Dance and Group Costumes; 15, Comparisons Among Selected Tribes. Appendix with list of suppliers of materials for the creation of Indian costumes and list of museums with collections of Plains Indian costumes. General, classified bibliography, pp. 201-213, and additional literature in the notes.

1045   Minor, Marz. **The American Indian Craft Book**. Lincoln, Neb., Univ. of Nebraska Press, 1978. 416p. illus. index. LC 77-14075.

Popular survey of Native American costume and associated crafts. Contains 45 plates of costumes and objects in various museums and collections taken from photographs by the author; they are not adequately identified. Many line drawings in the text show construction of costumes, texts, masks and so on. Contents: I, Clothing and Personal Adornment; II, Indian Food; III, Ceremonies, Mysteries, and Medicine Men; IV, Home Is Where the Indian's Heart Is; V, Arts, Decorations, and Symbolism; VI, War Paint and Counting Coup; VII, Drums, Rattles, and Stamping Feet; VIII, Games, Sports, and Stories; IX, Indian Language. No bibliography.

1046   Noël, Michel. **Art Decoratif et vestimentaire des Amérindiens du Québec**. XVIe et XVIIe siècles. Ottawa, Les Éditions Leméac, 1979. 194p. illus. index. ISBN 2760952800.

Scholarly study of the costume of the Indians in Quebec during the first centuries of contact with Europeans. Includes basketery, barkwork as well as costume. Contents: Introduction: 1, L'origine asiatique des Amérindiens; 2, L'origine mythique des Amérindiens; Première partie: L'authenticitié au XVIe siècle: 1, L'inspiration tirée de l'environment; 2, Les interinfluences ethniques; 3, Les familles linguistiques; 4, Les vêtements et les parures. DeuxiEme partie. Recontre du quatrième groupe: 1, L'arrivée; 2, Le troc transforme l'art décoratif et vestimentaire. Troisième partie. L'acculturation: 1, Les conséquences de prêt-à-porter européen; 2, L'assimilation par la formation à l'eropéene; Conclusion: 1, Une nouvelle technologie déclasse l'ancienne; 2, Les Amérindiens deviennet dépendant. Bibliography, pp. 190-192, and further bibliography in the footnotes.

1047 Seton, Julia M. **The Indian Costume Book**. Sante Fe, N.M., The Seton Village Press, 1938. 220p. illus. index. LC 38-25886.

Popular history/handbook, still useful for its scope. Contents: Distribution of Tribes; Eskimo; Mackenzie; Northwest Coast; Woodlands: Plains Tribes; Plateau; California Indians; Southeast; Southwest; Mexico, Central and South America. Appendix with essay on Indian plays. Basic bibliography, pp. 215-220.

See also the museum handbook: *Indian Costumes in the United States: a Guide to the Study of the Collection of the Museum*, by C. Wissler (New York, American Museum of Natural History, 1928. 32p. illus.), the museum catalog: *Frontier America: Art and Treasures of the Old West from the Buffalo Bill Historical Center*, by P. Frees and S. E. Boehme (New York, Abrams, 1988. 128p. illus. ISBN 081090940).

EUROPEAN COSTUME

1048 Ribeiro, Aileen, and Valerie Cumming. **The Visual History of Costume: Original Research and Text for the 'Visual History of Costume' Series**. London, Batsford, 1989. 240p. illus. index. ISBN 0896761134.

Collection in one volume of the illustrations of the history of European costume from 1300 to 1984 found in the six individual volumes of the series (1022, 1023, 1036). Only the color plates—bound in the center—disturb the very useful continuous chronological flow of the illustrations. Descriptive captions to the plates. Selected bibliography, pp. 227-228.

France

1049 Renan, Ary. **Le Costume en France**. Paris, Librairie d'Education Nationale, 1890. 272p. illus. index. LC F01-3452.

Older history of costume in France from Gallo-Roman times to the end of the eighteenth century. Illustrated with drawings taken from works of art. Occasional bibliographical footnote.

1050 Trichet, Louis. **Le Costume du clergé. Ses origines et son évolution en France d'après les réglements de l'Eglise**. Paris, Les Editions du Cerf, 1986. 245p. illus. index. ISBN 2204024732.

Scholarly history of the everyday dress of the clergy—not liturgical costume—in France from the early Middle Ages to circa 1985. Emphasis is on the regulations of the Church regarding the dress of its clergy. Contents: Première Partie: La tradition (IVe-XIE s.): I, Aux origines de la discipline; II, Le costume traditionnel devient "clérical.". Deuxième Partie: "L'Honnêteté cléricale" (1950-1589): I, Une législation nouvelle (1050-1317); II, La discilpine et la mode de 1317 à 1490; III, La renaissance; IV, Les motifs et les moyens. Troisième Partie: La Soutane (1589-1984): I, De la Décrétrale de Sixte V à la révolution; II, De la révolution à nos jours (1790-1984). Comprehensive, classified bibliography, pp. 223-29.

Great Britain

1051 Brooke, Iris. **English Costume of the Early Middle Ages: The Tenth to the Thirteenth Centuries.** London, A. & C. Black, 1936. Reprinted 1948. 86p. illus.

———. **English Costume of the Age of Elizabeth: The Seventeenth Century.** London, A & C. Black, 1933. 87p. illus.

———. **English Costume of the Seventeenth Century.** London, A. & C. Black, 1934. 87p. illus.

———. **English Costume 1900-1950.** London, Methuen, 1951. 90p. illus.

Popular surveys of English costume illustrated with line and color drawings, chiefly by the author, that suffer from a penchant for over-dramatic poses. No bibliography. A concise version of all four volumes was published as: *A History of English Costume.* 4th ed. New York, Theatre Arts, 1972. 196p. illus. index. LC 72-85476.

1052 Buck, Anne. **Victorian Costume and Costume Accessories.** New York, Nelson, 1962. 215p. illus. index. LC 62-8330. Rev. 2d ed. London, Calton Bedford, 1984. 224p. illus. index. ISBN 0903585170.

Text is reprinted without alteration in the second edition, illustrations have been added, and the bibliography brought up to date. Important survey of costume and costume accessories of Great Britain during the Victorian period. Illustrations are unimpressive black and white plates but include instructive photographs of historic costume worn by contemporary models. Contents: 1, Dresses, 1837-50; 2, Dresses 1850-65; 3, Dresses 1865-70; 4, Dresses, 1875-90; 5, Dresses 1890-1900; 6, Underwear; 7, Outer Garments: cloaks, capes, mantles, coats, jackets, shawls and scarves; 8, Hats and Bonnets; 9, Caps and Headdresses; 10, Gloves and Mitten; 11, Aprons; 12, Stockings; 13, Shoes and Boots; 14, Bags and Boots; 15, Fans; 16, Handkerchiefs; 17, Muffs; 18, Parasols; 19, Men's Costume; 20, Children's Costume. Bibliography, pp. 218-20.

1053 Calthrop, Dion C. **English Costume, 1066-1820.** London, A. & C. Black, 1963. 463p. illus. LC 60-50250 rev.

Survey of English costume from the Norman Conquest to the Napoleonic Wars illustrated with line drawings and watercolors. No bibliography.

1054 Cunnington, Cecil W. **English Women's Clothing in the Present Century.** London, Faber, 1952. 312p. illus. index. LC 52-2960.

Comprehenive history of women's costume from 1900 to 1950 illustrated from contemporary fashion illustrations, photographs and drawings. Sequel to the author's: *English Women's Clothing in the Nineteenth Century.* Contents: 1, Changes in Half a Century; 2, The Edwardian or 'Flared Skirt' Period 1900 to 1908; 3, The 'Hobble Skirt' Period, 1909 to 1914; 4, 'First War Fashions', 1915 to 1918; 5, The 'Schoolboy Shape', 1919 to 1924; 6, The 'Schoolgirl Shape', 1925 to 1928; 7, 'False Dawn', 1930 to 1939; 8, 'Second War Fashions', 1940 to 1945; 9, 'Post-War Revival,' 1946 to 1950. Appendix with note on prices. No bibliography.

1055 Cunnington, Cecil W., and Phillis Cunnington. **Handbook of English Costume in the Nineteenth Century.** Philadelphia, Dufor, 1959. 606p. illus. index. LC A60-8603. Reprinted: Boston, Plays, Inc., 1971. LC 72-78805.

Comprehensive history of English costume in the nineteenth century divided into men, women and children; the first two further divided by decades. Illustrated with line drawings taken from contemporary works of art. Emphasis is on identifying the various types and parts of costume. Bibliography, pp. 588-93, includes sources, memoirs, letters, diaries, novels, essays together with literature on the history of costume.

1056   Cunnington, Cecil W., and Phillis Cunnington. **Handbook of English Costume in the Sixteenth Century**. New rev. ed. London, Faber, 1970. 244p. illus. index. LC 79-509836.

Comprehensive history of English costume of the sixteenth century. Follows the format of the authors' earlier volume on the nineteenth century (1024).

1057   Cunnington, Cecil W., and Phillis Cunnington. **Handbook of English Medieval Costume**. 2nd ed. London, Faber, 1969. 210p. illus. index. LC 73-442678.

Comprehensive history of English costume from Anglo-Saxon times to the early sixteenth century. Follows the format of the authors' earlier volume on the nineteenth century (1024).

1058   Dunbar, Joan T. **History of Highland Dress: A Definitive Study of Scottish Costume and Tartan, Both Civil and Military, Including Weapons**. 2d ed. London, Batsford, 1979. 248p. illus. index. ISBN 071341894X.

Comprehensive history of traditional Scottish costume with extensive use of documentary sources. Contents: 1, Documentary Accounts of Highland Dress; 2, Specimens of Tartan and Highland Dress; 3, Pictures of Highland Dress before 1745; 4, Pictures of Highland Dress during and after the '45; 5, Prince Charles Edward Stuart; 6, Women's Costume; 7, "The Costumes of the Clans"; 8, The "Vestiarum Scoticum"; 9, "Vestiarium Scoticum" Published; 10, Postscript on "Vestiarum Scoticum"; 11, Tartan Pattern Books; 12, Early Highland Military Uniform; 13, Highland Weapons; 14, Firearms; 15, The Powder Horn and Sporran; 16, Plaid Brooches. Appendix: Early Scottish Highland Dyes by A. Kok. Bibliographical references in the footnotes. A standard history of Scottish costume.

1059   Grange, Richard M. D. **A Short History of Scottish Dress**. New York, Macmillan, 1967. 120p. illus. index. LC 67-10516.

Popular survey of traditional Scottish costume. Contents: 1, Early Times; 2, The Saffron Tunic and the Tartan Plaid; 3, The Belted Plaid and the Sombre Broadcloth; 4, Tartan—the Symbol of Scotland. Anthology of quotes referring to Scottish dress from various literary sources, 1793-1948. Chronological bibliography, p. 115-116.

1060   Yarwood, Doreen. **English Costume from the Second Century B.C. to 1950**. 5th ed. London, Batsford, 1979. 302p. illus. index. ISBN 0713408537.

Survey history of dress in England illustrated with drawings with descriptive captions and a few plates of works of art showing costume. Text is clearly organized by periods and singles out specific parts by bold type. Bibliography of basic books, pp. xvii-xviii.

Italy

1061   Birbari, Elizabeth. **Dress in Italian Painting, 1460-1500**. London, Murray, 1975. 114p. illus. ISBN 0719524237.

Important study of the costumes depicted in Italian painting from 1460 to 1500. Contains 115 plates of details of costumes in paintings and drawings showing the construction of the various garments. Contents: 1, Introduction; 2, The Importance of Dress in Italy; 3, The Development of Fashion in Italy; 4, Textures, Layers and Linings; 5, The Man's Shirt; 6, The Woman's Chemise; 7, Doublet and Hose; 8, Women's Dresses; 9, Men's Sleeves; 10, Women's Sleeves; 11, Fastenings; 12, The Head-veil; 13, The Tailoring of Men's Clothes; 14, The Tailoring of Women's Clothes; 15, Adjustments and Arrangements of Dress; 17, Conclusion. Bibliographical references in the notes.

1062   Cappi Bentivegna, Ferruccia. **Abbligliamento e costume nella pittura italiana**. Rome, Bestelli, 1962-64. 2v. illus. index.

Pictorial survey of Italian costume from the fifteenth century to the end of the nineteenth century based upon representations in works of painting. Brief introductory text followed by plates with descriptive notes. Contents: v. 1: Il Quattrocento; Il Cinquecento; v. 2: Il Seicento; Il Settecento.

1063   Levi Pisetzky, Rosita. **Storia del costume in Italia**. Milan, Istituto Editoriale Italiano, 1964-69. 5v. illus. index. LC 65-50594.

Comprehensive history of Italian costume from the end of the Roman Empire to the end of the nineteenth century. Contains 1,096 plates with descriptive captions. Contents: v. 1: Il costume dopo la caduta dell'impero d'occidente; Il costume dei goti e il costume romano alla fine del V e durante il VI secolo; Il periodo bizantino del VI secolo; Il periode langobardo e gli ultimi domini bizantini; Il periodo carolingio; Il periodo ottoniano; Il secolo XI; Il secolo XII; Il secolo XIII. v. 2: Il Trecento; Il Quattrocento. v. 3: Il Cinquecento; Il Seicento. v. 4: Il Settecento. v. 5: L'Ottocento. Extensive bibliographical references in the footnotes. Standard work on Italian costume; the large corpus of plates are an essential resource for art, cultural and costume historians.

ORIENTAL COSTUME

1064   Ayer, Jacqueline. **Oriental Costume**. London, Studio Vista, 1974. 192p. illus. ISBN 0684140241.

Pictorial survey of costume in India, China and Japan from early historic times to the twentieth century, illustrated with drawings and watercolors taken from various sources including contemporary works of art. Although the sources are inadequately identified, the display of these drawings across several pages does convey the overall development of dress. Glossary of terms. No bibliography.

1065   Chandra, Moti. **Costumes, Textiles, Cosmetics & Coiffure in Ancient and Medieval India**. New Delhi, Oriental Publishers on behalf of the Indian Archaeological Society, 1973. 248p. illus. index. LC 73-905179.

Comprehensive history of Indian costume from the first century B.C. to the twelfth century. Illustrated with drawings taken from reliefs and other works of art. Bibliographical footnotes.

1066   Fairservis, Walter A. **Costumes of the East**. New York, Chatham, 1971. 160p. illus. index. LC 77-159783.

Popular survey of dress in the Near, Middle and Far East with emphasis on examples in the American Museum of Natural History in New York. General bibliography, p. 154.

1067   Ghurye, Govind S. **Indian Costume**. 2nd ed. Bombay, Popular Prakashan, 1966. 302p. illus. index. LC SA67-2291.

Comprehensive history of the traditional costume of India from the third century B.C. to the twentieth century. Contains 412 poorly reproduced illustrations. Contents: 1, Introduction; 2, Historical Background; 3, Up to 320 B.C. ; 4, From 320 B.C. to A.D. 320; 5, From A.D. 320 to A.D. 1100; 6, From A.D. 1100 to A.D. 1800; 7, Recent and Contemporary: Northern, Western and Central Regions; 8, Recent and Contemporary: Eastern, South-Central and West-Central Regions; 9, Recent and Contemporary: Southern, South-Eastern and South-Western Regions; 10, Resumé (summary). Valuable translation from Sanskrit of passages from Hindu and Buddhist sources regarding dress. Bibliography, pp. 287-93.

1068   Minnich, Helen B., and Shojiro Nomura. **Japanese Costume and the Makers of Its Elegant Tradition**. Rutland, VT, Tuttle, 1963. 374p. illus. index. LC 62-15063.

Popular, well-illustrated survey of Japanese traditional costume from earliest times to the twentieth century. Emphasis is on the Edo period. Illustrated with works of art depicting costumed figures and plates of actual examples in museums and private collections. General bibliography of books in English, French and Japanese, pp.361-64.

1069   Pandey, Indu Prabha. **Dress and Ornaments in Ancient India**. New Delhi, Bharatiya Vidya Prakashan, 1988. 232p. illus. index. ISBN 8121700329.

Scholarly history of dress in ancient India during the Kusana and Gupta periods, illustrated with drawings taken from works of art chiefly in the Mathura Museum. Extensive bibliography in the footnotes. Comprehensive but unclassified bibliography, pp. 219-27.

1070   Sahay, Sachidanand. **Indian Costume, Coiffure, and Ornament**. New Delhi, Munshiram Manoharial Publishers, 1975. 206p. illus. index. LC 75-902234.

History of traditional Indian dress from circa 325 B.C. to circa A.D. 1200 with particular reference to Bihar. Divided into chapters on male and female dress, hairstyle and ornament. Bibliographical footnotes and select bibliography, pp.177-183.

1071   Tilke, Max. **Oriental Costumes, Their Designs and Colors**. London, Paul, Trench, Trubner, 1923. 32p. (text), 128 plates.

Illustrated survey of mid-Eastern and Far Eastern ethnic dress. Illustrations show the garments lying flat (not worn by models), which is most useful for demonstrating how the pieces are made. No bibliography.

See also the exhibition catalogs: *Dragon Emperor: Treasures from the Forbidden City*, by M. A. Pang (Melbourne, National Gallery of Victoria, 1988. 138p. illus. ISBN 0724101357), *Robes of Elegance: Japanese Kimonos of the 16th-20th Centuries*, by I. Hayao and M. Nobuhiko (Raleigh, N.C., North Carolina Museum of Art, 1988. 246p. illus. ISBN 0882599550) and the museum catalog: *Decoding Dragons: Status Garments in Ch'ing Dynasty China*, by J. Vollmer (Eugene, Ore., Museum of Art, Univ. of Oregon, 1983. 224p. illus.).

AFRICAN AND AUSTRALIAN COSTUME

Bibliographies

1072   Eicher, Joanne B. **African Dress; A Select and Annotated Bibliography of Subsaharan Countries**. East Lansing, Mich., Michigan State University Press, 1969. 134p. illus. index. LC 73-731220.

Classified bibliography of 1,025 books and periodical articles on all aspects of traditional (tribal) dress and textile production in sub-Saharan Africa. Continued by Pokornowski (1073).

1073   Pokornowski, Ila M. et al., eds. **African Dress II. A Selected and Annotated Bibliography**. East Lansing, Mich., African Studies Center, Michigan State Univ. Press, 1985. 316p. index. LC 73-631220.

Continuation and expansion of the coverage of Eicher (1072). Contains 1,260 annotated books and periodical articles classified by region. Covers all aspects of native dress and textile production in sub-Saharan Africa.

Histories and Handbooks

1074 Flower, Cedric. **Duck and Cabbage Tree, a Pictorial History of Clothes in Australia, 1788-1914**. Sydney, Angus & Robertson, 1968. 157p. illus. index. LC 75-414017.

Popular history of Australian costume with a valuable collection of illustrations drawn mostly from contemporary works of art and photographs. Includes a chapter on the dress of Australian aborigines. No bibliography.

1075 Lazar, Vicky. **Costume and Fashion in South Africa 1652-1910; a Bibliography**. Cape Town, University of Cape Town, 1970. 30p. index. LC 79-573152.

Annotated bibliography of 152 titles relating to the history of the costume of the European settlers in South Africa from 1652 to 1910.

See also: Nordquist (975).

CHAPTER EIGHT

ENAMELS

BIBLIOGRAPHIES

1076   McClelland, Ellwood H. **Enamel Bibliography and Abstracts, 1928 to 1939, Inclusive, with Subject and Coauthor Indexes**. Columbus, Oh., American Ceramic Society, 1944. 352p. index.

Comprehensive bibliography of books and periodical articles in all languages covering all aspects of enamels and enameling. Subject index. Although concerned chiefly with technical aspects, lists a good sampling of works on the history of art enameling. Entries are presented in the form of brief abstracts.

See also Jean J. Marquet de Vasselot, *Bibliographies de l'orfèvrerie et de l'émaillerie française* (1957).

DICTIONARIES AND ENCYCLOPEDIAS

1077   Clouzot, Henri. **Dictionnaire des miniaturistes sur émail**. Paris, Morance, 1925. 243p. illus. LC 25-1106.

Comprehensive dictionary of European enamel miniaturists, providing basic biographical data and reference to major pieces. Bibliography of basic books and periodical articles, pp. 13-20.

1078   Molinier, Emile. **Dictionnaire des émailleurs depuis le moyen âge jusq'a la fin du XVIIIe siècle...** Paris, Rouam, 1885. 113p. illus. Reprint: Sala Bolognese, Forni, 1978.

Short-entry dictionary of enamelists working in Europe from the Middle Ages through the eighteenth century, with facsimiles of their marks and signatures. Contents: Dictionnaire; Essai d'une bibliographies des livre relatifs à l'histoire des émaux; Liste des principales collections publiques ou privées renfermant des émaux.

TECHNIQUE

1079   Clarke, Geoffrey, and Francis and Ida Feher. **The Technique of Enamelling**. rev. ed. London and New York, 1977. 112p.index. ISBN 0442242557.

Handbook of the techniques of modern enamelling. Although the emphasis is on painted enamel techniques, chapter seven on traditional techniques gives some basic information on champlevé and cloisonne techniques. Bibliography, p. 101, lists only works of interest to the contemporary artist working in enamel.

See also Maryon, *Metalwork and Enamelling...* (1796).

GENERAL HISTORIES AND HANDBOOKS

1080   Dawson, Edith B. **Enamels**. Chicago, McClurg, 1908. 207p. illus. index. LC 08-37675.
Popular survey of world enamels from antiquity to the twentieth century. Bibliography of basic books in English, pp. 199-201.

1081   Day, Lewis F. **Enamelling, a Comparative Account of the Development and Practice of the Art. The Course of Art and Workmanship**. London and New York, Batsford, 1907. 222p. illus. index. LC W8-71.
Popular history of world enamels with emphasis on technical development.

WESTERN ENAMELS

General Histories and Handbooks

1082   Burger, Willy. **Abendländische Schmelzarbeiten**. Berlin, Carl Schmidt, 1930. 222p. illus. index. (Bibliothek fur Kunst- und Antiquitätensammler, XXXIII). LC 30-13936.
Older, once-standard history of Western enamels from antiquity to the end of the nineteenth century. Still provides a good overview with a judicious selection of plates. Includes Byzantine enamels. Classified bibliography, pp. 215-220, is a good guide to the older literature including museum and exhibition catalogs.

1083   Garnier, Edouard. **Histoire de la verrerie et de l'émaillerie...** Tours, Mame, 1886. 573p. illus. index. LC 10-22596.
Older, once-standard history of Western enamels and glass from antiquity to the eighteenth century. Bibliographical references in the footnotes.

Byzantine Enamels

General Histories

1084   Amiranashvili, Shalva. **Medieval Georgian Enamels of Russia**. New York, Abrams, 1964. 126p. illus. LC 64-11576.
Concise survey of Georgian enamels from the seventh to the twelfth centuries with a collection of 122 color reproductions of pieces in the Georgian National Museum of Fine Arts, Tiflis, accompanied by a descriptive catalog.

1085   Kondakov, Nikolai P. **Geschichte und Denkmaler des byzantinischen Emails**. Frankfurt/Main, n.p. 1892. 412p. illus.

1086   Malle, Luigi. **Cloisonné buzantini. Con une introduzione all'arte dello smalto medioevale**. Turin, Stabilimento Grafico Impronta, 1973. 170p. illus. LC 73-361601.
Authoritative introduction to the history of Byzantine enamels from the fifth through the twelfth centuries with emphasis on technique. Contents: I, Introduzione alle ragioni espressive dell'arte dello smalto; II, Premessa per un orientamento bibliografico d'ordine generale—Regesti bibliografici essenziali generali; III, Regesti bibliografici essenziali specifici per gli smalti; IV, Profilo sommario d'una storia dello smalto dalle origini al tardo medioevo; V, I cloisonnés bizantini: A, Orientamenti di consultazione bibliografica, giudizio su alcuni principali contributi critici sugli smalti di Bisanzio; B, Lo smalto b1zantino e alcuni problemi generali; C, Le opere: 1, I secoli V-IX, 2, Sviluppi e capolavori del secolo X, 3, Il secolo XI, 4, La "Pala d'oro" di San marco a Venezia, 5, Smalti dell'estremo secolo XI e del XII secolo. Aooendici: I, Il trittico di

Chacl; II, La rilegatura d'Evangelario della Biblioteca degli Intronati di Siena; III, Cenni su aspetti tecnici dell'uso delle "cloisonné" e loro risoluzione sul piano stilistico. Bibliographical references in the text, comprehensive, chronologically arranged bibliography, pp. 25-32.

1087   Wessel, Klaus. **Byzantine Enamels**. Greenwich, Conn., New York Graphics Society, 1967. 211p. illus. index. LC 68-25736.

Concise survey of Byzantine enamels from the fifth century through the thirteenth century by a leading scholar in Byzantine art history. Introductory essay with bibliographical references in footnotes, followed by good selection of plates with catalog and references to the specialized literature. English translation has many inaccuracies, refer to the German edition: *Die byzantinische Emailkunst* vom 5. bis 13. Jahrhundert. (Recklinghausen, Bongers, 1967)

The Venetian Treasury

1088   Luigi-Pomorisac, Jasminka de. **Les émaux byzantins de la Pala d'Oro de l'Église de Saint Marc 'a Venise**. 2v. illus. Zurich, Keller, 1966. LC 67-96981.

Scholarly monograph on the complexity of the tenth through twelfth centuries Byzantine enamels assembled on the golden altar antependium and retable of the Cathedral of St. Mark's in Venice. Contents: vol. 1: I, Les émaux commandés à Constantinople pour l'autel de Saint-Marc à Venise; II, Les émaux byzantins ajoutés par le doge Pietro Ziani en 1209; Considérations sur les émaux byzantins de la Pala d'Oro; IV, Les remaniements du quatorzième siècle. Conclusion: La Pala d'Oro au cours des siècles. Comprehensive bibliography, pp. 81-82, and bibliographical references in the footnotes; vol. 2: plates.

1089   Hahnloser, Hans, ed. **Il tesoro di San Marco**. Florence, Sansoni, 1965-71. 2v. illus.

Contents: 1. La pala d'oro; 2, Il tesoro e il Museoy

Scholarly catalog of the important treasury in the Cathedral of San Marco, Venice. The first volume is dedicated to the gold and enamel antependium and retable on the high altar, the Pala d'Oro, which contains one of the most important groups of Byzantine enamels preserved today. Those Byzantine enamels are cataloged and discussed by W. F. Volbach. The second volume catalogs the other works of gold and silver and enamels in the treasury. Full scholarly apparatus including specialized bibliography cited in the catalog entries and footnotes of the text. General bibliographies at the end of both volumes.

Medieval Enamels

General Histories

1090   Gauthier, Marie-Madeleine. **Émaux du moyen âge occidental**. 2d ed. Fribourg, Office du Livre, 1972. 443p. illus. LC 73-351299.

Comprehensive, well-illustrated, scholarly history of western European enamels during the Middle Ages. Contents: 1, Les origines techniques: l'émail, Les métaux, l'émaillage; 2, Le haut moyen age, l'or: l'époque carolingienne de la fin du VIIIe siècle au Xe siècle, l'empire france et les royaumes européens, l'époque ottonienne, l'empire germanique vers 970-1030, les sources italiques de l'émaillerie romane; 3, Les émaux romans, le civre: l'aire méridionale, l'aire septentrionale; 4, L'époque 1200, l'émaillerie et l'art gothique: le "style 1200," L'émaillerie et l'art gothique français, la tradition royale et les émaux d'or; 5, Le Trecento, l'argent: La primauté toscane, les cours, les centres et les foyers; les villes libres germaniques; 6, La fin du moyen age, les joyaux: le gothique internatioanl, l'aube de la Renaissance. Catalog with full scholarly apparatus. Comprehensive, classified bibliography of books and periodical articles in all languages and specialized literature at the end of each entry in the catalog. The standard history and handbook on medieval enamels.

See also the catalog of the Kofler-Truniger Collection: *Email, Goldschmiede- und Metallarbeiten, europäisches Mittelalter*, by H. Schnitzler, P. Bloch and C. Ratton (Lucerne, Raber, 1965. 55p. 91 plates. LC 66-91151), the catalog of the Keir collection: *Medieval Enamels: Masterpieces from the Kier Collection*, by M. Gauthier and G. François (London, British Museum Publications, 1981. 40p. illus. ISBN 0714113581), the museum catalog: *Enamels & Glass: Catalog of Medieval Objects*, Boston Museum of Fine Arts by H. Swarzenski and N. Netzer (Boston, The Museum, 1986. 171p. illus. ISBN 0878462635), and the guide to the collection in the London Victoria and Albert Museum: M. Campbell, *An Introduction to Medieval Enamels* (London, H.M.S.O, 1983. 48p. ISBN 0112903851).

Forthcoming: G. Haseloff. *Email im frühen Mittelalter*. Marburg, Hitzeroth, 1990. 244p. illus. ISBN 3893980202.

National Histories

France

Limoges Enamels

1091   Gauthier, Marie Madeleine S. **Émaux limousins champlevés des XII, XIII & XIV siècles**. Paris, G. Le Prat, 1950. 164p. illus. LC A51-18151.

Concise history of Limoges enamels by a leading expert. Illustrated with 64 plates of objects exhibited in Limoges in 1948. Descriptive notes to the plates. Contents: 1, Les techniques; 2, L'évolution du décor: Fonds dorés a figures d'émail; Fonds émaillés; 3, Remarque sur le style et l'iconographie des émaux limousins: Des émaux limousins; Les éléments du décor; La composition; L'iconographie religieuse, l'iconographie civile. Bibliography, pp. 161-62.

1092   Gauthier, Marie-Madeliene. **Émaux meridionaux: catalogue international de l'ouvre de Limoges**. Paris, Éditions du Centre National de la Recherche Scientifique, 1987- illus. index.

Comprehensive, scholarly catalog of all known Limoges enamels. To date tome 1: *L'Epoque romane* (ISBN 222203650X) has appeared. Catalog entries have bibliographies. General bibliography, pp. 389-301.

1093   Rupin, Ernest. **L'öeuvre de Limoges**. Paris, Picard, 1890-92. 612p. illus. index. LC 12-21721.

The standard work on Limoges champlevé enamels, marred by a certain chauvinism— many illustrations in black and white. Contents: Première Partie: Histoire de l'Emaillerie Limousine; Second Partie: Les monuments. The second part has a discussion of a comprehensive catalog of various types of objects executed in Limoges enamels. Bibliographical references in the footnotes.

1094   Thoby, Paul. **Les croix limousines de la fin du XIIe siècle au début du XIVe siècle**. Paris, Picard, 1953. 175p. illus. index. LC A53-5016.

Scholarly history and study of the enameled crucifixes made in Limoges during the twelfth and the thirteenth centuries with a catalogue raisonné of 116 pieces. Contents: I, Généralités; II, Les Croix à revêtement de plaques d'émail, avec Christ champlevé et émaillé dans la plaque, sur un fond réservé et doré; III, Les Croix à revêtement de cuivre estampé ou gravé, avec Christ couronné en relief; IV, Les Croix à revêtement de plaques d'émail, avec crucifix en relief; V, Les Croix de cuivre entièrement métalliques; VI, Les Croix dans l'émaillerie limousine; VII, Les Croix à double traverse; VIII, Les Croiux étrangères. Bibliographical references in the footnotes and catalog entries.

Germany, Austria, and Switzerland

1095   Falke, Otto von, and Heinrich Frauberger. **Deutsche Schmelzarbeiten des Mittelalters.** Frankfurt/ Main, J. Baer, 1904. 151p. illus. LC 12-28921.

History of German medieval enamels from the eighth to the early sixteenth centuries based on works exhibited at the famous exhibition of German medieval art in Düsseldorf in 1902. Still useful for the collection of 130 black and white and 31 color plates in large format. Among the plates are illustrations of works in other media as well as enamels. Descriptive notes to the plates. Contents: I, Der Zellenschmelz auf Gold; II, Die Arbeiten des Rogerus von Helmershausen; III, Der Deutsche Kupferschmelz; IV, Gotischer Tiefschnittschmelz auf Silber. Bibliographical references in the footnotes.

1096   Guth-Dreyfus, Katia. **Transluzides Email in der Ersten Hälfte des. 14. Jahrhunderts am Ober-Mittel-und Niederrhein.** Basel, Birkhäuser, 1954. 132p. illus. (Baseler Studien zur Kunstgeschichte, Band IX).

Based on the author's dissertation. Scholarly history of Rhenish enamels during the first half of the fourteenth century with a catalog of 23 major works. Contents: Erster Teil: Oberrhein: I, Konstanz; II, Basel. Zweiter Teil: Mittelrehin: I, Speyer; II, Mainx; III, Unbestimmte Herkunst. Dritter Teil: Niederrhein: I, Köln; II, Aachen; III, Unbestimmte Herkunst. Comprehensive bibliography, pp. 123-28, and bibliography in the catalog entries and in footnotes.

Nicolas of Verdun

1097   Buschhausen, Helmut. **Der Verduner Altar. Das Emailwerk des Nikolaus von Verdun im Stift Klosterneuburg.** Vienna, Tusch-Druck, 1980. 170p. illus. index. ISBN 3850630439.

Well-illustrated, scholarly monograph on the enamels by Nicolas of Verdun on the Klosterneuburg altarpiece based, on a detailed examination of the physical evidence including the inscriptions as a basis for a reconstruction of the original ambo. Contents: Einführung; Stifterinschrift; Die Bildtafeln; I, Der Ambo des Nikolaus von Verdun; II, Der Stil des Nikolaus; III, Der Altar des Stephan von Sierndorf; IV, Das Program des Ambo. Comprehensive bibliography, pp. 165-66, and further bibliography in the notes.

1098   Drexler, Carl, and T. Strommer. **Der Verduner Altar im Stift Klosterneuburg bei Wien.** Vienna, 1903. 19p.(text), 52ls. (plates).

Scholarly description of the enamels decorating the Klosterneuburg altarpiece with large-size plates of each of the 51 plaques. Notes to the plates are both descriptive and analytical with particularly valuable analyses of the biblical inscriptions.

1099   Röhrig, Floridus. **Der Verduner Altar.** 2d ed. Vienna, Herold, 1955. 80p. illus. ISBN 3700801734.

Not a comprehensive monograph but an excellent description of the enamels by Nikolaus of Verdun and the fourteenth century paintings that make up the decoration of the high altarpiece of the Augustinian Cloister Church at Klosterneuburg. Emphasis is on the iconography of the enamels. All of the individual enamels are illustrated in good black and white plates, the inscription transcribed and translated into German, and the iconography fully described in notes that accompany the plates (Erklärung der einzelnen Bilder). Contents: Das Stift Klosterneuburg und der Verduner Altar; Die heutige Gestalt des Altars; Die Widmungsinschrift; Künstler und

Geschichte; Technik und Stil; Der Umbau von 1331; Der theologische Sinn; Erklärung der einzelnen Bilder. Comprehensive, classified bibliography, pp.78-80.

Great Britain

1100   Chamot, Mary. **English Medieval Enamels...** London, Methuen; New York, Putnam, 1906. 187p. illus. index. LC 31-1607.

Still the only study of the subject. Brief introductory essay sketches the development of enamels in England from the ninth century to the fifteenth century and is followed by plates—poor quality—with descriptive catalog that includes bibliographical references. Further bibliography in the footnotes.

1101   Dalton, M. **The Royal Cup in The British Museum.** London, British Museum, 1924. 11p. illus.

Scholarly monograph on the fourteenth-century gold enameled goblet in the British Museum. The author traces the provenance of the cup back to the French crown and concludes that it was made in Paris circa 1380. Bibliographical references in the footnotes.

Italy

1102   Hackenbroch, Yvonne. **Italienisches Email des frühen Mittelalters.** Basel, Holbein-Verlag, 1938. 68p. illus. index. (Ars Docta, Band II). LC A41-692.

Revision of the author's dissertation. Scholarly study of enamels made in Italy from the seventh century to the end of the twelfth century. Contents: I, Die Frühwerke; II, Die Mailänder Schmelzschule; III, Schmelz unbekannte Herkunft; IV, Die römische Schmelzschule; V, Die Schmelzschule von Monte Cassino; VI, Die sizilianische Schmelzschule. Within the chapters the major works are discussed in the format of a detailed catalog entry with references to specialized literature. Bibliography, p. 68 lists more general books referred to in the text.

1103   Petrassi, Mario. **Gli smalti in Italia.** Rome, Editalia, 1982. 302p. illus. index. ISBN 8870600203.

Well illustrated, comprehensive history of Italian enamels from the early Middle Ages to the sixteenth century. Brief introductory survey followed by plates with only short captions. Plates include many good details showing the technique of famous pieces. Concludes with the first, second, and third book of the *Diversarium Artium Schedula Theophili Presyteri et Monachi.* General bibliography, pp. 295-97.

1104   Elbern, Victor H. **Der karolingische Goldaltar von Mailand.** Bonn, Kunsthistorisches Institut der Universität Bonn, 1952. 123p. illus.(Bonn Beiträge zur Kunstwissenschaft, Band 2).

Scholarly study of the famous Carolingian gold and enamel altar antependium—the Paliotto—in San Ambrogio in Milan by a leading expert on early medieval metalwork. Contents: I, Zur Geschichte des Goldaltars; II, Form, Liturgische Gunktion und Name des Goldaltars; III, Zur Ikonographie der Bilderzyklus am Goldlaltar; IV, Ornamentik—Email—Edelsteine; V, Stilproblem; VI, Der Goldaltar und sein Ort in der frühmittelalterlichen Kunst. Specialized literature in the notes. General bibliography, pp. 122-23.

Low Countries

1105   Voelkle, William. **The Stavelot Triptych, Mosan Art and the Legend of the True Cross.** London and New York, Oxford Univ. Press, 1980. 45p. illus. LC 80-8970.

Pictorial monograph on the twelfth-century Mosan enamel triptych from Stavelot now in the Pierpont Morgan Library, New York City. Contents: The Stavelot Triptych; Mosan Art and Stavelot: A Brief Catalogue; The Legend of the True Cross: A Brief Catalogue. Selective bibliography, p. 26.

See also the exhibition catalog: *Wibald, abbé de Stavelot Malmedy et de Corvey (1130-1158)*, by J. S. Tiennon and J. Deckers (Stavelot, 1982).

Spain

1106 Hildburgh, W. L. **Medieval Spanish Enamels**. Oxford, Oxford University Press, 1936. 146p. illus. index. LC 37-12105.

Scholarly history and study of Spanish Romanesque enamels. The author argues that Spain was at least as prolific a center of production as Limoges, and should be credited with many of its products. Contents: I, General Considerations; II, Incertitude of the Limousin Hypothesis; III, Medieval Spanish Enamels on Gold; IV, The "Oriental" Elements of the Copper Champlevé Enamels; V, The Twelfth-century Copper Champlevé Enamels of Spain; VI, The Later Copper Champlevé Enamels of Spain. General bibliography, pp. 129-31, and bibliographical references in the footnotes.

1107 Juaristi Sagarzazu, Victoriano. **Esmaltes con especial mencion de los espanoles**. Barcelona, Labor, 1933. 286p. illus. index.

Survey history of world enamels from antiquity to the twentieth century with particular attention to developments in Spain: Segunda Parte: Los esmaltes en España: X, La Prehistoria. Los visigodos; XI, Esmaltes románicos en España; XII, Las obras de Limoges en España: 1, Los retablos, II, Las obras menores; XIII, El gótico en España; XIV, El Renacimento. El barroco; XV, Nuestro tiempo. Bibliography, pp. 264-270, is a comprehensive list with annotations of the older literature.

1108 Martin Ansón, Maria Luisa. **Esmaltes en España**. Madrid, Editorial Nacional, 1984. 170p. illus. ISBN 8427606354.

Authoritative survey of Spanish enamels from the early Middle Ages to the seventeenth century by a leading authority. Good selection of plates, unfortunately very poorly reproduced. Contents: Primeria: El Esmalte: I, El Esmalte; II, Origen y desarrollo de la esmaltería; Segunda Parte: El Esmalte en España: I, Periodo prerrománico; II, Período románico; III, Período gótico; IV, El Renacimento; V, El Barroco. Two excellent, classified bibliographies, the first, on the general history of Western enamels, follows the first part; the second, on the history of Spanish enamels, follows the second part.

Renaissance—Modern Enamels

1109 Marquet de Vasselot, Jean Joseph. **Les émaux Limousins de la fin du XVe siècle et de la première partie du XVIe: etude sur Nardon Pénicaud et ses contemporains**. 2v. illus. index. Paris, Picard, 1921. LC 31-22079.

Comprehensive history/handbook of late medieval Limoges enamels. Contents: Introduction (history of the various schools); Liste des émaux (descriptive notes to the plates); Appendixes: 1, Documents relatifs à Nardon et à Jean Fer Pénicaud; 2, Liste des émailleurs limousins; 3, Le groupe violet. Bibliography, 385-96.

See also the museum catalog: *Catalogue of the Painted Enamels of the Renaissance*, by P. Verdier (Baltimore, Md., The Walters Art Gallery, 1967. 423p. illus.).

ORIENTAL ENAMELS

1110   Cosgrove, Maynard G. **The Enamels of China and Japan: Champlevé and Cloisonné**.
New York, Dodd, Mead, 1974. 115p. illus. index. ISBN 0396606736.
   Well-illustrated, popular survey with a chapter on technique and manufacture. Bibliography of basic works in all languages, pp. 108-12.

1111   Garner, Harry M. **Chinese and Japanese Cloisonné Enamels**. 2nd ed. London, Faber and
Faber, 1970. 120p. illus. index. LC 71-587860.
   Authoritative survey of Chinese and Japanese cloisonné enamels from earliest times to the end of the Ch'ing dynasty in China and the end of the nineteenth century in Japan. Contents: The Nature of Enamels; The Early History of Enamels in the West; Chinese Enamels in the Pre-Ming Period; Methods of Assessment; Chinese Enamels of the 15th Century; The Chin-t'ai Myth; The 16th Century; The Traditional Period; The Ch'ing Dynasty; Japanese Cloisonné Enamels. Appendices with list of marks on cloisonné enamels and discussion of spit wires in Chinese cloisonné enamels. Classified bibliography of major books in Western languages, pp. 114-16. For criticism of Garner see bibliographical note in Liu (1112).

1112   Liu, Liang-Yu. **Chinese Enamel Ware: Its History, Authentication and Conservation**.
Taipei, Cyrgnus Publications, 1978. 94p. illus.
   Survey of Chinese enamels with useful chapters on technique and restoration. Contents: I, A Short History of the Development of Chinese Enamel Wares; II, Chinese Cloisonne Enamel: ts Authentication; III, The Authentication of Ch'ing Dynasty Painted Enamel with the Imperial Mark; IV, Preserving and Restoring Enamel Ware. Bibliography, pp. 89-90, lists 18 titles and is preceded by a bibliographical note challenging the reliability of H. Garner's *Chinese and Japanese Enamels* (1111).
   See also the catalog of the enamels in the National Palace Museum: *Enamelled Ware of the Ch'ing Dynasty* by Kuo li ku kung po wu yüan (Kowloon, Cafa Co., 1969. 2v. illus. LC 77-218086r85) and the exhibition catalog of the Pierre Uldry collection: *Chinesisches Cloisonné: die Sammlung Pierre Uldry* by H. Brinker and A. Lutz (Zurich, Museum Rietberg, 1985. 144p. illus. ISBN 3907070089).

CHAPTER NINE

FURNITURE

BIBLIOGRAPHIES

1113 **Furniture History**. London, Furniture History Society, v. 1 (1965)- ISSN 001-63058.

Annual bibliographies of books and periodical articles on all aspects of the history of furniture were published from 1965 to 1986 when five year retrospective bibliographies were introduced.

DICTIONARIES AND ENCYCLOPEDIAS

1114 Aronson, Joseph. **The New Encyclopedia of Furniture**. 3rd ed. New York, Crown, 1967. 484p. illus. LC 65-24334 rev.

Comprehensive dictionary of world furniture from ancient Egypt to the twentieth century but with emphasis on European furniture from the sixteenth century to the early nineteenth century. Contains 1,394 photographic illustrations and many figures. Comprehensive, classified bibliography, pp. 476-79.

1115 Bjot, Édouard. **Encyclopédie du meuble du XVe siècle jusqu'à nos jours...** Paris, Schmid, 1901-09. 8v. illus.

Corpus of 600 plates illustrating 2,000 pieces of furniture dating from the late Middle Ages to the early twentieth century, classified and arranged in alphabetical order. "Table analytique des planches" lists the pieces by type of furniture.

1116 Gloag, John. **A Short Dictionary of Furniture; Containing 1,767 Terms Used in Britain and America**. rev. 7 enl. ed. London, Allen &Unwin, 1969. 813p. illus. ISBN 047490039.

Comprehensive dictionary of terms and concepts related to the history of furniture. Includes furniture makers and designers. Entries vary from a few lines defining terms to several pages discussing styles and types of furniture. Illustrations feature reproductions of old illustrations of furniture. Contents: 1, The Description of Furniture; 2, The Design of Furniture; 3, Dictionary of Names and Terms; 4, Furniture Makers in Britain and America; 5, Books and Periodicals on Furniture and Design; Periods, Types, Materials, and Craftsmen from 1100-1950. Bibliography, pp. 779-83.

1117 Lockwood, Luke V. **The Furniture Collectors' Glossary...** New York, Walpole Society, 1913. 55p. illus. Reprint: New York, Da Capo, 1967. LC 67-27460.

An old, collector's glossary primarily of stylistic, ornamental and technical terminology. Illustrated with line drawings.

GENERAL HISTORIES AND HANDBOOKS

1118 Blaser, Werner. **Architektur im Möbel: vom Altertum zur Gegenwart. Furniture as Architecture: from Antiquity to the Present.** Zurich, Waser Verlag, 1985. 207p. illus. ISBN 3908080185.

History of world furniture from ancient times to the present with emphasis on the relationship between furniture and its architectural setting. Excellent plates often juxtaposing architectural details with furniture. Bibliography of works consulted, pp. 206-07.

1119 Boger, Louise A. **The Complete Guide to Furniture Styles.** Enl. ed. New York, Scribner's, 1969. 520p. illus. LC 73-85267.

Popular survey of world furniture from ancient times to the twentieth century with particular good coverage of English furniture. Selected bibliography of books in English, pp. 506-08.

1120 Evers, J. W. **Geschiedenis van het meubel.** Utrecht, Uitgeverij Ons Huis, 1962. 612p. illus. index. LC 66-54316.

Comprehensive, scholarly history of world furniture from ancient Egypt to the twentieth century with emphasis on the development of furniture styles in the West. Well illustrated with plates of museum pieces. Basic bibliography, pp. 609-10.

1121 Gloag, John. **A Social History of Furniture Design, from B.C. 1300 to A.D. 1960.** New York, Crown, 1966. 202p. illus. index. LC 66-20207.

Popular history of Western furniture from ancient times to the mid-twentieth century, with emphasis on furniture as a mirror of social change. Illustrated with museum pieces and illustrations from contemporary works of art. Period chapters are divided by type of furniture. Brief bibliography of books in English, p. 192.

1122 Hayward, Helena, ed. **World Furniture; an Illustrated History.** New York, McGraw-Hill, 1965. 320p. illus. index. LC 65-18175.

Popular history of world furniture from antiquity to the 1960s. Chapters are by various British experts. Well-illustrated with plates of museum pieces and views of period interiors in historic buildings and contemporary paintings and prints. Glossary, appendix on primitive furniture. Bibliography, p. 312, is a list of basic books.

1123 Hinckley, F. Lewis. **A Directory of Antique Furniture; the Authentic Classification of European and American Designs for Professionals and Connoisseurs.** New York, Crown, 1953. 355p. illus. LC 52-10776.

Comprehensive handbook for collectors. Brief introductory text followed by large corpus of plates arranged by country. The pieces illustrated are chiefly from private collections and, therefore, show what is accessible to the collector.

1124 **The History of Furniture. Introduction by Francis Watson.** New York, Morrow, 1976. 344p. illus. index. ISBN 0688030831.

Well-illustrated survey of the history of furniture in the West from antiquity to 1970. Contents: The Archaeological Record: Ancient and Medieval Furniture by James Wheeler; The Classical Revival, Europe's Renaissance by Geoffrey Beard; Formal Splendour: the Baroque Age by Gervase Jackson-Stops; The Line of Beauty: The Rococo Style by John Kenworthy-Browne; Purity of Form: The Neo-classical Reaction by Jonathan Bourne and Lucinda Fletcher; The Machine Age: The Nineteenth Century by Ian Grant; The Rebirth of Design: Arts and Crafts and Art Nouveau by Ian Bennett; The Triumph of Style: Art Deco by Martin Battersby; Innovation:

Furniture to the Present Day by Penny Radford. Glossary, list of collections, general bibliography, pp. 332-35.

1125 Lucie-Smith, Edward. **Furniture: A Concise History**. London, Thames and Hudson, 1979. 216p. illus. index. LC 79-4393.
　　　Popular survey of Western furniture from antiquity to the 1970s. Chapter on the meanings of furniture. Bibliography, pp. 208-209, is a alphabetical list of books in all languages.

1126 Mercer, Eric. **Furniture, 700-1700**. New York, Meredith, 1969. 183p. illus. index. LC 69-18425.
　　　History of furniture in western Europe from the early Middle Ages to the end of the seventeenth century, with emphasis on the cultural context of furniture design. Well illustrated with plates of furniture in various interiors. Bibliography, pp. 173-77, is a comprehensive but unclassified list of books in all languages.

1127 Müller, Sigrid Flamand (Christensen). **Alte Möbel von Mittelalter bis zum Jugendstil**. 9th ed. Munich, Bruckmann, 1981. 211p. illus. index. ISBN 3765418366.
　　　Concise but authoritative survey of Western furniture from the early Middle Ages to Art Nouveau. Well illustrated with museum pieces. Contents: Handwerkliche Voraussetzungen; Frühes Mittelalter; Italienische Renaissance; Französische Renaissance; Renaissance in den germanischen Ländern; Barock; Frankreich im 17. Jahrhundert; Hollands Blütezeit; Deutschland im 17. Jahrhundert; Frankreich und Italien im 18. Jahrhundert; Rokoko in Deutschland; England im 18. Jahrhundert; Klassizismus, Empire und Biedermeier; Das spätere 19. Jahrhundert, Jugendstil; Rückblick. Comprehensive, classified bibliography, pp. 235-38.

1128 Oates, Phyllis B. **The Story of Western Furniture**. London, Herbert Press, 1981. 253p. illus. index. ISBN 0906060093.
　　　Popular survey of furniture in the West from ancient Egypt to 1980. Illustrated with drawings from museum pieces and from representations of furniture in contemporary works of art. Select bibliography, pp. 243-44, lists book in English.

1129 Schmitz, Hermann. **The Encyclopedia of Furniture; an Outline History of Furniture Designs in Egypt, Assyria, Persia, Greece, Rome, Italy, France, the Netherlands, Germany, England, Scandinavia, Spain, Russia and in the Near and Far East up to the Middle of the Nineteenth Century** ... 2nd ed. London, Benn, 1956; New York, Praeger, 1957. 63p. (text), 320 plates. LC 57-9791.
　　　Pictorial survey of world furniture from antiquity to the middle of the nineteenth century. Brief introductory text is followed by good selection of plates with descriptive captions. No bibliography.

1130 Verlet, Pierre. **Styles, Meubles, décors, du moyen âge à nos jours**. Paris, Larousse, 1972. 2v. illus. index. LC 72-306820.
　　　Survey of Western furniture from the Renaissance to the twentieth century. Contributions by an international team of experts. Contents: Volume 1: Renaissance, Baroque, Louis XV; Volume 2: Louis XVI, Empire et XIXe siècle. Brief biographies of major makers and designers. Basic bibliography, pp. 255-56.

1131 Wanscher, Ole. **The Art of Furniture: 5000 Years of Furniture and Interiors**. New York, Van Nostrand Reinhold, 1967. 419p. illus. index. LC 66-25546.
　　　Comprehensive, authoritative survey of the history of world furniture from ancient times to the mid-twentieth century. Emphasis is on the aesthetic aspect and the relationship between

furniture and culture in the evolution of particular types such as the chair. Contents: Egypt; Classical Antiquity; The Middle Ages—Renaissance; 17th Century—Baroque; Rococo; China—Japan; 18th Century—England—America; 18th-19th Centuries—Classicism; 19th-20th Centuries—Traditions—Trends. General, classified bibliography, pp. 411-414.

Types of Furniture

Beds

1132 Juin, Hubert. **Le Lit**. Paris, Atelier Hachette/Massin, 1980. 123p. illus. ISBN 2010-075099.

Cultural history of the bed in Western civilization from antiquity to the twentieth century. Contains 244 illustrations of actual beds, contemporary designs, and advertisements for beds, and many useful plates of works of art of all periods showing beds and the activities that took place in them. Emphasis is on French examples. Basic bibliography, p. 120.

1133 Wright, Lawrence. **Warm and Snug: The History of the Bed**. London, Routledge & K. Paul, 1962. 360p. illus. LC 64-5045.

Broad cultural history of the bed in Western civilization from antiquity to 1960, illustrated with 341 reproductions of beds depicted in various media. General bibliography, pp. 342-46.

Chairs

1134 Frey, Gilbert. **The Modern Chair: 1850 to Today. Le siege moderne de 1850 a aujord'hui. Das moderne Sitzmöbel von 1850 bis Heute**. New York, Architectural Book Pub. Co., 1970. 187p. illus. LC 74-484355.

Pictorial survey of chair design from 1850 to 1970. Contains 95 line drawings of chairs, major designers from Thonet to Cini Boeri, with descriptive captions. Glossary of terms and short biographies of designers. Bibliography, pp. 186-87, includes literature on individual designers. Text in English, French and German.

1135 Gloag, John. **The Chair, Its Origins, Design and Social History**. South Brunswick, N.J., Barnes, 1964. 221p. illus. LC 67-13174.

Authoritative survey of the development of the chair in the West from antiquity to 1900, with emphasis on development in England. Large number of illustrations of museum pieces, works of art depicting chairs, and reproductions of advertisements. Contents: 1, Posture and Design; 2, Origins in the Ancient World and the Early Middle Ages, 3400 BC-AD 1300; 3, The Native English Style, 1300-1550; 4, The Taste of the New Rich, 1550-1630; 5, Puritan Interlude, 1630-1660; 6, The Restoration of Luxury, 1660-1690; 7, Curvilinear Design and the End of Rigidity, 1690-1730; The Great Chair-makers, 1730-1810; 9, Survival of the Native English Style, 1660-1900; 10, A Short History of the Rocking Chair, 1750-1900; 11, Design for Comfort, 1830-1900; 12, Craft Revivalists and Industrial Designers. Appendices with essays on gilding of chairs, painted furniture, and decoration of chairs. Short list of English designers and makers. Comprehensive, classified bibliography, pp. 201-204.

1136 Joy, Edward T. **Chairs**. rev. ed. London, Country Life Books, 1980. 127p. illus. index. ISBN 0600430707.

Popular survey history of English chairs from Roman times to the 1970s. Contains 104 illustrations with brief, descriptive captions. Useful glossary supplies clear definitions of the large variety of chair types and forms. No bibliography.

1137 Pollack, Pam. **Chairs through the Ages: a Pictorial Archive of Woodcuts & Engravings**. New York, Dover, 1982. 144p. illus. index. ISBN 0486243486.
Collection of illustrations of chairs taken from prints.

Choir-stalls [*See* Medieval Furniture]

Mirrors

1138 Hartlaub, G. F. **Zauber des Spiegels. Geschichte und Bedeutung des Spiegels in der Kunst**. Munich, Piper, 1951. 231p. illus. index. LC A52-2662.
Important history of the mirror and its representation in works of art from ancient times to the twentieth century. Contents: 1, Was der Mensch vom Spiegel lernte; 2, Spiegel und Seele; 3, Zur Kunstgeschichte des Spiegels; 4, "Das Mensch vor dem Spiegel" im Abbild der Malerei; 5, Kleine Geschichte des gemalten Spiegelbildes; 7, Der magische Spiegel in der Malerei; 7, Der Spiegel als Symbol: I, Sprache und Kunst; II, Der lauterer Spiegel; III, Spiegel der Vanitas; IV, Der Spiegel der Prudentia; Zum Beschluß. "Anmerkungen und Exkurse has extensive notes on the bibliography. A paradigmatic study of the history of the meaning of a decorative art object.

Writing Tables and Desks

1139 Dietrich, Gerhard. **Schreibmöbel vom Mittelalter zur Moderne**. Munich, Keyser, 1986. 231p. illus. index. ISBN 3874051714.
Comprehensive, typological history of furniture designed for writing from the Middle Ages to circa 1980. Contains 168 plates with descriptive captions. Contents: Romanik und Gotik: Vom mittelalterlichen Schreibbrett zum Kastenschreibtische: Möbel für Arbeit von Mönchen, Ratsschreibern und Kaufleuten; Renaissance: Tischpult, studiolo, vargueño, Kabinettsschrank: Schreibmöbel im Dienst von Humanisten, Schriftstellern und fürstlichen Sammlern; Barock: Bureau Mazarin, bureau plat, Pultschreibtisch und scriptor: Hof, Adel und Staatsverwaltung schaffen die Ahnen der modernen Schreibtische; Rokoko und Klassizismus: Wirksame Pracht und äußerste Eleganz: Im großen Jahrhundert des Absolutismus wird das Schreibmöbel zur Insignie der Macht; Vom Empire zum Art nouveau: Neuinterpretationen historischen Schreibmobiliars für Hof und Bürgertum und Aufbruch zu einer Möbelkultur; Werkbund und Bauhaus, Art déco und Design: Der Weg zum modernen Schreibmöbel. Comprehensive, classified bibliography, pp. 205-08.
See also L. L. Dewiel, *Tische und Schreibmöbel* (Munich, 1983).

ANCIENT FURNITURE

1140 Baker, Hollis S. **Furniture in the Ancient World: Origins and Evolution, 3100-475 B.C.** New York, Macmillan, 1966. 351p. illus. index. LC 66-23893.
Comprehensive history of furniture in ancient Egypt, the Near East, and the Aegean. Contents: Part I: Egypt: 1, The Early Beginnings: Dynasties I, II, and III; 2, The Old Kingdom; 3, Palace Furniture of the Eighteenth Dynasty; 4, The Furniture of King Tutankhamun; 5, The Egyptian Villa and Its Furnishings; 6, Household Furniture Types; Part II: The Near East: 1, Sumer; Furniture in the Early Periods; 2, From the Akkadian Period to the End of the Kassite Period; 3, The Assyrian and Neo-Babyloninan Periods in Mesopotamia; 4, The Peripheral Regions; Part III: The Aegean: 1, Introduction; 2, The Earliest Furniture; 3, The Minoan Ascendancy; 4, The Mycenaean Period in Greece; 5, The Early Greek Period; 6, The Continuing Influence. Appendix on techniques. Bibliographical references in the notes.

1141   Killen, G. **Ancient Egyptian Furniture**. Warminster, Wiltshire, England, Aris & Phillips, 1980- v. 1- ISBN 0856680958 (vol. 1).

Comprehensive, scholarly handbook of ancient Egyptian furniture. Volume 1 covers the period from 4000 to 1300 B.C. Contents: 1, Furniture Materials; 2, Tools; 3, Beds; 4, Stools; 5, Chairs; 6, Tables; 7, Vase Stands. Text consists of detailed catalogue-type notes to pieces in various museums around the world. Full scholarly apparatus is provided including references to specialized literature.

See also the exhibition catalog: *Vorm en geometrie in de Oud-Egyptische meubelkunst*, by P. de Bruyn (Ghent, Stadbestuur van Gent, 1982. 108p. illus.).

1142   Richter, Gisela M. A. **The Furniture of the Greeks, Etruscans and Romans**. London, Phaidon, 1966. 369p. illus. index. LC 66-2601.

Comprehensive, scholarly history of ancient furniture written by a leading scholar of ancient Greek art (*see* FA 887, 888). Contents: Aegean Furniture; Greek Furniture; Etruscan Furniture; Roman Furniture; Furnishings; Technique; Appendix: "Linear perspective in representations of Greek and Roman Furniture—short bibliography on perspective." Selected bibliography, pp. 341-43, and further bibliography in the footnotes. A standard work.

1143   Robsjohn-Gibbings, Terrence H., and Calton W. Pullin. **Furniture of Classical Greece**. New York, Knopf, 1964. 122p. illus. LC 63-17054.

Pictorial survey of ancient Greek furniture designs featuring modern reproductions from representations in works of ancient Greek art. Arrangement is by types, i.e., Klismoi, Diphoi, Trapezai, Klini and Kibotos. Note on fabrics. No bibliogrpahy.

1144   Steingräber, Stephan. **Etruskische Möbel**. Rome, Bretschneider, 1979. 384p. illus. ISBN 8885007295.

Revision of the author's thesis, *Cologne*, 1977. Scholarly history of ancient Etruscan furniture with a catalog of 791 pieces of furniture, fragments of furniture, and stone furniture in tombs. Catalog entries have bibliographical references. Contents: I, Systematischer Teil: 1, Typologie; 2, Denkmälergattungen; 3, Topografie; 4, Chronologie; II, Das Verhältnis Etruskischer Möbel zu Orientalischen, Griechischen und Römischen Möbelformen; III, Realitätscharakter, Funktion und Deutung. Bibliographical references in the footnotes.

1145   Williams, Caroline L Ransom. **Studies in Ancient Furniture: Couches and Beds of the Greeks, Etruscans and Romans**. Chicago, University of Chicago Press, 1905. 128p. illus. index. LC 5-5200.

Scholarly history of ancient Greek, Etruscan, and Roman couches based on a close examination of representations in art and references in documents. Contents: I, Chronological Survey of Forms; II, Materials, Technic, and Centers of Manufacture; III, Interlaced Filling of Couch Frames; IV, Furnishings—Mattresses, Pillows, Valances, and Draperies; V, Style. Bibliographical references in the footnotes.

MEDIEVAL FURNITURE

1146   Eames, Penelope. **Furniture in England, France and the Netherlands from the Twelfth to the Fifteenth Century**. London, Furniture History Society, 1977. 303p. (text), 72p. (plates). index. ISBN 0903335026.

Important history of medieval furniture with full scholarly apparatus. Contents: Part 1, Section A. Armoires, Buffets and Dressoirs; Section B, Beds and Cradles; Section C, Chests; Section D, Seating; Section E, Tables; Part 2. Style and Technique; Part 3, Conclusion. Extensive bibliographical references throughout. Comprehensive, unclassified bibliography of books and periodical articles, pp. 277-85.

1147 Wright, Arthur C. **Medieval Furniture**. Southend-on-Sea, Museums Service Borough of Southend-on-Sea, 1976. ISBN 0900690143.
Survey of medieval furniture illustrated with drawings made by the author from depictions of furniture in various medieval works of art. Arrangement is by type of furniture. Descriptive notes accompany the drawings. No bibliography.
See also F. Windisch-Graetz, *Möbel Europas* (1236).

Medieval Choir-stalls

1148 Kraus, Dorothy. **The Gothic Choirstalls of Spain**. London, Boston, Routledge & Kegan Paul, 1986. 218p. illus. index. ISBN 0710202946.
Survey of major Gothic choir-stalls in Spain with particular attention given to the restoration of the stalls in Oviedo Cathedral. Contents: Part One: Creation, Ruin, and Recreation of Oviedo's Choirstalls: I, Certificate of Birth; II, Iconoclasm by Subterfuge; III, Spains 'October' Destruction of the Upper Stalls; IV, The Lower Stalls Get 'Lost' in the Cathedral; V, Problems of the Restoration; VI, Piecing the New Choir Together; VII, A Museum of Four Hundred Carvings; VIII, A Kind of Consecration. Part Two: Spain's Choirstalls as a Mirror of Its History: IX, A Panorama of Styles and Origins; X, A Delicate Spiritual-Worldly Balance; XI, The Church's Artistic Reply to Heterodoxy; XII, Iconography of a 'Society at War'; XIII, Images of Spain's 'Far West'; XIV, Spain's Dwindling Patrimony of Choirstalls. Bibliographical references in the notes.

1149 Loose, Walter. **Die Chorgestühle des Mittelalters**. Heidelberg, Winter, 1931. 156p. illus.
Pioneering work on the medieval choir-stalls of western Europe with a catalog of hundreds of examples arranged by country, region and place. Contains 158 plates. Contents: Geschichtlicher Überblick; Bemerkungen über Kunstform und Weltanschauung; Die Einzelformen und ihre Geschichte; Der Schmuck; Die Herstellung; Die Erhaltung der gotischen Gestühle; Katalog; Bildliche Darstellungen. Comprehensive bibliography, pp. 67-70, and bibliographical references in the catalog entries.

1150 Remnant, G. L., and M. D. Anderson. **A Catalogue of Misericords in Great Britain**. Oxford, Clarendon, 1969. 221p. illus. index. LC 78-374990.
Important, scholarly catalog of medieval choir-stall misericords, i.e., the carvings beneath the seats, in Great Britain, arranged by place. Entries give detailed descriptions of the subjects depicted, probable date and bibliographical references. Essay on the iconography of British misericords by M. D. Anderson. General bibliography, pp. 201-05.

1151 Tracy, Charles. **English Gothic Choir-Stalls 1200-1400**. Woodbridge, Suffolk, Eng., Boydell Press, 1987. 82p. illus. index. ISBN 0851154689.
Important collection of scholarly essays on various aspects of choir-stalls in England dating between 1200 and 1400. Contents: I, The Choir-stalls in Thirteenth-century England with Particular Reference to Rochester and Salisbury Cathedrals, and Westminster Abbey; II, The Relationship between the Choir-stalls at St. Mary's Hospital, Chichester and Chichester Cathedral; III, The Winchester Cathedral Choir-stalls. An Analysis of the Monument and a Discussion of Outstanding Problems; IV, The Wells Cathedral Choir-stalls; V, The Hereford Cathedral Choir-stalls and the Bishop's Throne; VI, The Ely Cathedral Choir-stalls; VII, The Lancaster Church Choir-stalls; VIII, The Gloucester Cathedral Choir-stalls; IX, The Choir Furniture of St. Katherine's-

by-the-Tower and Its Position in the Stylistic Development of English Choir-stalls during the Second Half of the Fourteenth Century; X, Choir-stalls in English Collegiate Churches during the Last Quarter of the Fourteenth Century; XI, The Construction of Choir-stalls and the Craft of Joinery in the Thirteenth and Fourteenth Centuries. Glossary of terms. Appendices with extracts from documents referring to Winchester in 1308 and St. Stephen's Chapel, Westminster for 1351, 1352, and 1357. Select bibliography, pp. 73-76, and further bibliography in the notes.

RENAISSANCE—MODERN FURNITURE

1152   Duncan, Alastair. **Art Deco Furniture: The French Designers**. New York, Holt, Rinehart and Winston, 1984. 192p. illus. index. ISBN 0030000998.
    Pictorial survey of French Art Deco furniture. Contents: Art Deco and Modernism; The U.A.M.; The Scope of the Book; The 1920s/1930s Furniture Designers; Furniture Materials; The Paris Department Stores; The 1925 Exposition; Contemporary Collectors; Ocean Liners. Bibliographies of designers and select bibliography, p. 189.

1153   Garner, Philippe. **Twentieth-century Furniture**. New York, Van Nostrand Reinhold, 1981. 224p. ilus. index. ISBN 0442254210.
    Pictorial survey of furniture of the twentieth century in Europe and America. Contents: 1900: Art Nouveau; 1900-1920: Art and Crafts; The Twenties: Art Deco; The Twenties: International Modernism; The Thirties: Modernism and Eclecticism; The Forties/Fifties: New Materials, New Styles; The Fifties: The Contemporary Style; The Sixties: Neo-Modernism to Pop; The Seventies/Eighties: Past Craft and Future Technology. The chapters are further divided by country and designer. Glossary. Select bibliography, p. 220, lists books in all languages.

1154   Jervis, Simon. **Printed Furniture Designs before 1650**. London, The Furniture History Society, 1974. 54p. illus. LC 77-358751r85.
    Important collection of 449 plates illustrating designs for furniture from the sixteenth and early seventeenth centuries based on extensive research in the libraries and print rooms of Europe. Brief introduction has a bibliographical essay. Brief notes to the plates.

1155   Kjellberg, Pierre. **Art Deco: les maitres du mobilier**. Paris, Editions de l'amateur, 1981. 181p. illus. index. ISBN 2859170197.
    Pictorial survey of the furniture of the Art Deco movement. Brief introductory essay followed by brief biographies of the major designers and concluding with a chapter on the decor of the great Art Deco French Ocean Liners. Classified bibliography, p. 243.

1156   Madigan, Mary Jean, ed. **Nineteenth Century Furniture: Innovation, Revival, and Reform**. New York, Art & Antiques, 1982. 160p. illus. index. ISBN 0823080048.
    Survey of furniture design in the United States during the nineteenth century. Contents: The Empire Style: Philadelphia by K. M. Catalano; Hitchcock Furniture by R. Berenson; Rococo Revival: John Henry Belter by E. P. Douglas; Daniel Pabst by D. Hanks; Egyptian Revival by C. L. Bohdan; Eastlake-influenced Furniture by M. J. Madigan; Kimbel & Cabus by D. Hanks; Gallé and Majorelle by K. M. McClinton; American Art Nouveau Furniture by B. Telle, Charles F. A. Voysey by M. Page; Chicago Furniture by D. Hanks; Gustav Stickley by Barry Sanders; The Roycrofters by R. Edwards; Innovative Furniture by P. Talbott; Thonet and Bentwood by C. Wilk; George Hunzinger by R.W. Flint; Wicker by K. Menz; Cast Iron by E. Mippas; Adirondack Hickory by C. Gilborn. Selected bibliography, pp. 154-55.

1157   Mang, Karl. **The History of Modern Furniture**. New York, Abrams, 1979. 185p. illus. index. ISBN 0810910667.

Important history of modern furniture design with particular emphasis given to the major design developments. Contents: Anonymous Furniture in the Nineteenth Century—Harbingers of the Machine Aesthetic: Iron Furniture, The Mechanization of Furniture, Chiavari's "Campanino"; or, How to Improve on a Tradition Form, Anonymous Wicker Furniture, Michael Thonet and Bentwood Furniture; The Shakers: Beauty Rests on Utility; The Theories of William Morris and the Challenge of Industry: Art Nouveau—Overcoming Historicis, Beyond Art Nouveau— Antoni Gaudi, Frank Lloyd Wright, Otto Wagner, Adolf Loos, From Arts and Crafts to Werkbund—the Idea of Community, The Vienna School in the Interwar Period; From De Stijl to the International Style: De Stijl Furniture—Theory Become Concrete, The Bauhaus—Synthesis of Art, Craftsmanship, and Industry, Furniture of the International Style—Mies van der Rohe and Le Coubusier, Furniture for Housing Projects of the Interwar Period; Scandinavian Furniture— from Aninymity to World Renown: Developments in Sweden, Denmark's Teak Style, Alvar Aalto—Fantasy and Construction in Wood; Furniture Design After World War II: New Technologies: The United States, The International Style and Beyond, New Ideas from Italy, Plastic Furniture, From Chairs and Tables to Domestic Landscape, Education as a Chance for the Future. Bibliography, pp. 179-81.

1158   Payne, Christopher. **19th Century European Furniture**. 2d ed. Woodbridge, Antique Collector's Club, 1985. 506p. illus. ISBN 1851490019.

Comprehensive guide to the furniture produced in Europe and Turkey during the nineteenth century with the exception of Great Britain. Designed as a guide for sophisticated collectors. Arrangement is by country and then by type of furniture. Each country has a chapter with biographies of major designers and makers and a chapter on terminology peculiar to that country's furniture. Selected bibliography, p. 506.

1159   Sembach, Klaus, Jürgen H. Leuthäuse,r and Peter Gössel. **Twentieth-Century Furniture Design**. Cologne, Taschen, 1989. 255p. illus. ISBN 382280276X.

Well-illustrated survey of European and American furniture design from 1870 to 1980 with a biographical directory of major designers with portraits. Contents: A New Year's Eve Celebration; The Lady's Room; The Gentleman's Room; The Keep-fit Room; The Hotel Lounge; The Part Supporters' Room; Vernissage; Living Room with Dining Area and Serving Hatch; Cushion Landscape; Photo Studio; Finale. No bibliography.

1160   Stone, Anne. **Antique Furniture: Baroque, Rococo, Neoclassical**. New York, Exeter Books, 1982. 239p. illus. index. ISBN 0896731405.

Well-illustrated survey of European and American furniture from the seventeenth century to the middle of the nineteenth century. Emphasis is on the work of major designers. Many valuable plates of historic interiors. Glossary of terms, summary of the development of styles, bibliography of basic works in English, p. 236.

1161   Votteler, Arno, ed. **Wege zum modernen Möbel. 100 Jahre Designgeschichte**. Stuttgart, Deutsche Verlags-Anstalt, 1989. 143p. illus. index. ISBN 3421029563.

History of furniture design in western Europe and America from 1830 to 1987. Collaborative work of four German experts. Aim is to demonstrate the emergence of "modern" high design furniture. Contents: Die Biedermeierzeit; Die Gründerzeit; Die Weimarer Republik; Die Eusprünge des "modernen Möbels"; Jugendstil um 1900; Wendung zur "vernünftigen Sachlichkeit"; Die modische Moderne mit "elegant stilisiertem Dekor"; "Form ohne Ornament"; Form um 1930; Die Neue Sachlichkeit; Gediegen-heimatverbundene Schreinerkultur um 1940; Die gute Form; Neo-Funktionalismus und technische Ästhetik; Das dänische Möbel; Der

Internationale Stil 1960-1970; Der Kunststoff bringt eine neue Ästhetik; Klassiker der Moderne; Die Sehnsuch nach dem Natürlichen; Zitatmöbel für die Wohncollage; Conter-Design und Materialexpressionismus; Das "Solitär-Möbel" als Bedeutungsträger; Tendenzen zeitgeössischer Möbelgestaltung von 1945 bis 1987. Bibliographical notes and classified bibliography, pp. 132-33.

AMERICAN FURNITURE (U.S., Canada, and Latin America)

United States

Bibliographies

1162 Semowich, Charles J. **American Furniture Craftsmen Working Prior to 1920: An Annotated Bibliography**. Westport, Conn., Greenwood Press, 1984. 381p. illus. index. ISBN 031323275X.

Classified and annotated bibliography of 2,052 books and periodical articles on American furniture to 1920. Emphasis is on the furniture maker. The first section lists the literature on individual makers, the second section the literature on groups of furniture makers arranged by state, the third section lists general works on American furniture including a section on trade catalogs. Appendix with list of American furniture periodicals. Not all entries are annotated and the annotations are usually briefly descriptive.

Dictionaries

1163 Bjerkoe, Ethel H. and John A. Bjerkoe. **The Cabinetmakers of America...** Rev. and corrected ed. Exton, Pa., Schiffer Ltd., 1978. 272p. illus. LC 57-7278. First published in 1957 (Garden City, N.Y., Doubleday, 252p.)

Important biographical dictionary of furniture makers, designers, and manufacturers in the United States from early colonial times to the end of the nineteenth century. Brief biographies of some 3,000 craftsmen with bibliographical references at the end of larger entries. List of cabinetmakers by states, Glossary of terms and bibliography of books, pp. 270-72. Although superseded and corrected by much specialized literature of the past half-century, Bjerkoe is still the place to begin a search for information.

General Histories and Handbooks

1164 Bates, Elizabeth B., and Jonathan L. Fairbanks. **American Furniture, 1620 to the Present**. New York, Richard Marek Pub., 1981. 561p. illus. index. ISBN 0399900969.

Comprehensive pictorial history of American furniture from early Colonial times to 1980. Well-illustrated with pieces in museums and historical houses, and interiors showing furniture in contemporary settings. Chapters have brief historical sketches as introduction followed by descriptive notes to the plates. Contents: I, The Beginnings; II, The William & Mary Period 1690-1725; III, Queen Anne & Early Georgian 1725-1760; IV, Japanned Furniture 1710-1820; VI, Neoclassicism 1780-1835; VII, Away from the Mainstream; VIII, Victorian America 1830-1900; IX, The Frontier & Vernacular Traditions 1800-1850; X, Craft Revival, Reaction & Reform 1870-1930; XI, Moderne to Contemporary 1917-1980. Glossary. Comprehensive bibliography by W. Garrett and A. Eckardt, pp. 537-52.

1165 Butler, Joseph T., and Kathleen E. Johnson. **Field Guide to American Antique Furniture**. New York, Facts on File, 1985. 399p. illus. index. ISBN 0816010080.

Guide to identification of works of American furniture and furniture assessories from early Colonial times to 1930. First part is a survey history of furniture styles; second part is a handbook to the identification of pieces arranged by object class. Illustrated by line drawings made from pieces in museums, private collections and dealers. Selected bibliography, pp. 267-68.

See also the author's: *American Furniture from the First Colonies to World War I*. London, Triune, 1973. 144p. illus.

1166 Comstock, Helen. **American Furniture: Seventeenth, Eighteenth and Nineteenth Century Styles**. New York, Viking, 1962. 336p. illus. index. LC 62-18074. Reprint: Exton, Pa., Schiffer Publishing Co.,

Comprehensive survey of American furniture from 1650 to 1870 with emphasis on the characteristics of the styles and periods. Contents: 1, Jacobean—William and Mary : 1640-1720; 2, Queen Anne: 1720-55; 3, Chippendale: 1755-90; 4, Classical Period: 1790-1830; 5, Early Victorian: 1830-70. Selected bibliography, pp. 319-24.

1167 Fitzgerald, Oscar P. **Three Centuries of American Furniture**. Englewood Cliffs, N.J., Prentice-Hall, 1982. 323p. illus. index. ISBN 0139203710.

Comprehensive survey of American furniture from Colonial times to the end of the nineteenth century. Contents: I, The Jacobean Period: Joiners and Cabinetmakers in the New World; II, William and Mary: The Years of Transition; III, Queen Anne: The Line of Beauty; IV, The Chippendale Style; V, Furniture of the Federal Period; VI, American Empire; VII, The Country Cabinetmaker; VIII, Southern Furniture; IX, Furniture of the Folk: Shaker and Pennsylvania German; X, Victorian Furniture: The Gothic and Rococo Revivals; XI, Victorian Furniture: the Renaissance Revival; XII, The Eastlake and Other Revivals; XIII, The Connoisseurship of American Furniture. Appendix: Benjamin Lehman's "Prices of Cabinet & Chair Work" (1786); George Henkel's "Catalogue of Furniture in Every Style" (ca.1850). Comprehensive bibliograpby, pp. 304-15.

1168 Kaye, Myrna. **Fake, Fraud, or Genuine?: Identifying Authentic American Antique Furniture**. Boston, Little, Brown, 1987. 214p. illus. index. ISBN 082121666X.

Useful collector's guide to authenticity in American furniture from early Colonial times to circa 1830. Text is supported with many revealing photographs and drawings of construction details. General bibliography, pp. 204-08, and additional bibliography in the notes.

1169 Kirk, John T. **The Impecunious Collector's Guide to American Antiques**. New York, Knopf, 1982. 174p. illus. index. ISBN 0394496205

Introduction to collecting American furniture by a leading expert. The author employs an unusual but highly effective method of teaching connoisseurship by carefully describing the visual qualities that distinguish the genuine from the fake, the successful product of regional craftsmanship from aesthetically barren imitations, and by introducing the basics of good design by comparing common pieces of twentieth century industrial design. Emphasis is on "country" furniture of the East Coast. Contents: 1, Perception without Prejudice; 2, The Art of Looking; 3, Knowledge; 4, What Is It?; 5, Quality of Design—Comparisons; 6, Quality of Design—Sheer Line; 7, Buy It Ratty and Leave It Alone; 8, Fragments; 9, Shops; 10, Dealers and Auctions; 11, Quiz Yourself.

1170 Miller, Edgar G. **American Antique Furniture, a Book for Amateurs...** New York, Barrows, 1937. 2v. illus. index. Reprint: New York, Dover, 1966. 2v. illus. index. LC 66-20419.

Important collection of plates of American traditional furniture to 1870 arranged by type, e.g., volume one covers chairs, other seating furniture, and case furniture, and volume two covers mirrors, tables and stands, and clocks. Directed to collectors, the majority of pieces illustrated were in private collections. Many of the author's attributions no longer hold but the plates are still an important pictorial source, particularly for the collector.

See also the exhibition catalog: *American Furniture from the Kaufman Collection*, by J. M. Flanigan (Washington, D.C., National Gallery of Art, 1986. 263p. illus. ISBN 0894680994) and *American Furniture in Pendleton House*, by C. P. Monkhouse and T. S. Michie (Providence, R.I., *Museum of the Rhode Island School of Art*, 1986. 228p. illus. ISBN 0911517448).

Types of Furniture

1171 Bishop, Robert C. **Centuries and Styles of the American Chair, 1640-1970**. New York, Dutton, 1972. 516p. illus. LC 72-82702, Reprinted: New York, Bonanza Books, 1983. ISBN 0517413582.

Pictorial survey of chairs made in America from 1640 to 1970. Contains 923 plates with detailed descriptive captions. Selected bibliography, pp. 508-510.

1172 Forman, Benno M. **American Seating Furniture, 1630-1730: An Interpretative Catalogue**. New York, Norton, 1988. 397p. illus. index. ISBN 0393025160.

Important, scholarly history of early American seating furniture with catalog of the pieces in the Wintertur Museum. Contents: 1, Connoisseurship and Furniture History; 2, The Woods Used in American Furniture; 3, Seventeenth-Century Woodcarving Craftsmen and tTeir Crafts; The Catalogue: Seating Made by Turners; Seating Furniture Made by Joiners; Cromwellian-Style Upholstered Chairs and Couches; Cane Chairs and Couches; Carved Topp'd, Plain Topp'd, and Crook'd-Back Leather Chairs; Easy Chairs and Low Chairs. Appendices with the 1708 inventory of Charles Plumley, Philadephia Joiner, and "The Fourth Section" from Roubo's Menusier. Comprehensive bibliography, pp. 381-87.

See also the exhibition catalog: *300 Years of American Seating Furniture: Chairs and Beds from the Mable Brady Garvan and Other Collections at Yale University*, by P. E. Kane (Boston, New York Graphics Society, 1976. 319p. illus. index. ISBN 0821206788).

1173 Iverson, Marion D. **The American Chair, 1630-1890**. New York, Hastings House, 1957. 241p. illus. LC 57-11664.

History of American chairs from early colonial times to the end of the Victorian style. Text is arranged around 36 "styles" of chairs and is illustrated by drawings made from examples in museums and historic houses. Informative text with many extracts from or references to documentary sources. Chapter on the chairs and other furniture owned by George Washington. Appendix with list of museums and historic houses. Selected bibliography, pp. 231-32, and additional references in the footnotes.

1174 Ketchum, William C. **Chests, Cupboards, Desks & Other Pieces**. New York, Knopf, 1982. 476p. illus. index. ISBN 0394712706.

In the series: "The Knopf Collectors' Guides to American Antiques." Well-illustrated, pocket-sized guide to American antique furniture. Contains 334 color plates of well-selected pieces arranged by type and descriptive notes. Appendices have essays on identifying styles, construction and connoisseurship, types of woods and glossary. Basic bibliography, pp. 442-446.

1175   Schwartz, Marvin D. **Chairs, Tables, Sofas & Beds**. New York, Knopf, 1982. 478p. illus. index. ISBN 0394712692.

In the series: "The Knopf Collectors' Guides to American Antiques." Companion volume to Ketchum (1174). Contains 347 color plates with descriptive notes. Appendix with essay on upholstery.

1176 Williams, Henry L. **Country Furniture of Early America**. South Brunswick, N.J. A. S. Barnes, 1970. 138p. illus. index. Reprint: New York, Barnes, 1978. ISBN 0498020452.

Collector's handbook of American furniture made with simpler lines from early Colonial times to circa 1800. Contains 102 representative pieces grouped by type of furniture: benches, stools, chairs, settles, couches, cradles, tables, stands, boxes, racks, small cupboards and chests, chests, highboys, cupboards, dressers, dry sink, wardrobe, desks and secretary. Descriptive text includes measurements and drawings showing details of moldings, handles, construction, etc.

Windsor Chairs

1177 Nutting, Wallace. **A Windsor Handbook; Comprising Illustrations & Descriptions of Windsor Furniture of All Periods**. Southhampton, N.Y., Cracker Barrel Press, 1969. 192p. illus. LC 70-3749.

Collector's handbook of American chairs and a few tables of the Windsor type, dating between 1725 and 1825. Contains 116 illustrated pieces, most in private collections, and described in catalog fashion with emphasis on dating, provenance and rarity.

1178   Ormsbee, Thomas H. **The Windsor Chair**. New York, Deerfield Books, 1962. 223p. illus. LC 62-10516.

Collector's pictorial handbook of Windsor chairs made in Britain and America from the eighteenth century to the early twentieth century. Contains 80 illustrations with descriptive notes. Contents: I, Origin and Spread of the Windsor Chair; II, American Windsor Craftsmanship; III, Nine Types of American Windsor Chairs and Related Pieces; IV, Some Historic American Windsors; V, English Windsor Chairs; VI, Check List of Known American Chairmakers. The checklist provides basic biographical data and references to contemporary sources for major makers.

Colonial—Empire Furniture

1179   Comstock, Helen. **The Looking Glass in America 1700-1825**. New York, Viking, 1968. 128p. illus. index. LC 68-15480.

Pictorial survey of early American looking glasses. A 26-page introduction is followed by 85 plates with descriptive notes. Useful essay on makers and dealers with plates of labeled looking glasses. Bibliographical reference given in the text.

1180   Davidson, Marshall B. **The Bantam Illustrated Guide to Early American Furniture**. New York, Bantam, 1980. 421p. illus. index. ISBN 0553012223.

History/handbook of American furniture from early Colonial times to the beginning of the twentieth century directed to the collector. Illustrated with pieces in museums and historic houses. Introduction with survey history is followed by chapters devoted to types of furniture. Glossary, bibliography of basic books, pp. 407-08.

1181   Kirk, John T. **American Furniture and the British Tradition to 1830**. New York, Knopf, 1982. 397p. illus. index. ISBN 0394400380.

Important history of American furniture from early colonial times to 1830 with emphasis on the interdependence of American and British traditions. Takes a critical look at traditional concepts of native American qualities in furniture design. Contents: Issues Relating British to American Furniture: 1, Dependence & Levels of Sophistication; 2, Similarity of Designs, Role of Wood Identification & Ubiquity of Motifs; 3, Variations Available: Interpretations & Customers; 4, The Tradition of Painted Furniture; 5, English & American Carving; 6, The "Hadley" Composite Motif & Through Chamfering; 7, Significant Visual & Constructional Details; 8, What America Did Not Do; 9, Original American Statements. Visual Survey of British & American Furniture (arranged by type).

1182   Kirk, John T. **Early American Furniture: How to Recognize, Evaluate, Buy & Care for the Most Beautiful Pieces-High Style, Country, Primitive & Rustic**. New York, Knopf, 1970. 208p. illus. index. LC 71-111232. Paperback reprint, 1974. ISBN 0394706463.

Collector's handbook with emphasis on the visual qualities that categorize the various pieces as: "high style," "country," and "primitive and rustic." Author has a keen eye for design and quality distinctions. Contents: I, Taste, Design, Construction & Function; II, The Evolution of Style; III, Proportion & Organization; IV, The Role of Small Details; V, The Interpretation of Sources; VI, High-Style, Country, Primitive, & Rustic; VII, Evaluating & Collecting; VIII, Specialization; IX, Fakes, Reproductions, & Restorations; X, Care of Furniture.

1183   Lockwood, Luke V. **Colonial Furniture in America**. 3d ed. New York, Scribner's, 1926. 2v. illus. index. Reprint: New York, Castle, 1957. LC 26-22375.

Comprehensive history of American colonial furniture emphasizing the visual qualities of the many pieces illustrated. Contents: v. 1: Introduction, Chests of Drawers, Cupboards and Sideboards, Desks and Scritoires, Looking-glasses; v. 2: Chairs, Settees, Counches, and Sofas, Tables, Bedsteads, Clocks. Both volumes have a "supplementary chapter" with additional material from the second edition of 1913. Within the categories by type the pieces are arranged chronologically. A classic and pioneering work, Lockwood's corpus of plates is still a major reference source.

1184   Nutting, Wallace. **Furniture Treasury (Mostly of American Origin). All Periods of American Furniture with Some Foreign Examples in America, also American Hardware and Household Utensils**. Framingham, Mass., Old America Co., 1928-33. 3v. illus. index. Reprint in two volumes: New York, Macmillan, 1968. LC 29-560.

Comprehensive, pictorial dictionary of American furniture to the end of the Empire period. Arrangement is by type: volume one covers case furniture and tables; volume two chairs, clocks and other forms, and volume three (subtitled: Being a Record of Designers, Details of Designs and Structure, with Lists of Clock Makers in America, and A Glossary of Furniture Terms, Richly Illustrated) contains Nutting's idiosyncratic commentary with additional illustrations in line drawings. An old, standard work long viewed as the bible of American furniture collectors. Remains, in spite of numerous questionable attributions, an unsurpassed pictorial resource.

1185   Ormsbee, Thomas H. **Early American Furniture Makers, a Social and Biographical Study**... New York, Crowell, 1930. 183p. illus. index. Reprint: N.Y., Archer House, 1957. LC 57-13366.

Concise history of American furniture of the Colonial and Federal periods with emphasis on the relationship between furniture and furnituremakers and the general culture. Although inadequately referenced, there are useful quotes from contemporary sources and illustrations from advertisements. Contents: I, The Pilgrim Century; II, American Chippendales; III, Duncan Phyfe, the Great; Phyfe's Contemporaries; V, Plain and Fancy Chairmaking; VI, The Yankee Clockmakers;

VII, From Furniture to Politics. Appendix with pictorial outline of American furniture, list of furniture makers, and basic bibliography, pp. 179-81.

1186   Ormsbee, Thomas H. **Field Guide to Early American Furniture**. Boston, Little, Brown, 1952. 428p. illus. LC 52-9095. Reprint: New York, Crown, n.d.

Popular collector's handbook for the identification of American furniture from the early eighteenth century to circa 1850. Arranged by types and illustrated with line drawings of pieces typical of those accessible to the average collector. Glossary of terms, lists of furniture wood and types of hardware. List of basic books.

1187   Sack, Albert. **Fine Points of Furniture: Early American**. New York, Crown, 1950. 303p. illus. LC 50-1156. Reprinted 1969.

Important handbook on the connoisseurship of early (to circa 1800) American furniture. Introductory chapter on collecting is followed by a substantial corpus of illustrations grouped by types and arranged by levels of quality. Through the descriptive captions the author defines the visual qualities that place the pieces in "good", "better," or "best" categories. Final section lists the most often encountered restorations, replacements, and imperfections of various types of period American furniture. A classic collector's handbook by one of America's leading dealers in high quality period furniture.

1188   Singleton, Esther. **Furniture of Our Forefathers with Critical Description of Plates by Russell Sturgis**. New York, Doubleday, 1901. 2v. illus. index. Reprint: New York, Blom, 1970. 655p. LC 68-56505.

Early history of Colonial and Federal American furniture noteworthy for its references to inventories and price books, although frequently without indication of the specific source. Annotations to the plates by Sturgis, an architectural historian, are important sources for taste for early American furniture in the late nineteenth century.

Selected Regional and Special Studies

1189   Bivins, John, Jr. **The Furniture of Costal North Carolina, 1700-1820**. Winston-Salem, N.C., Museum of Early Southern Decorative Arts, 1988. 562p. illus. index. ISBN 0945578008.

Comprehensive, scholarly history of furniture made in the eastern third of what is now the state of North Carolina based upon a thorough examination of documentary sources and close scrutiny of pieces of furniture and historic settings. Contents: Part I: The Setting: 1, Towns and Transportation in Costal North Carolina, 2, Commerce, Society, and the Location of the Trade, 3, The Cabinet Trade: Structure, Shops, and Materials. Part II: The Furniture: 5, The Albemarle: Early Styles; the Chowan River Basin; 6, The Albemarle: The Roanoke River Basin; 7, The Pamlico and Cape Fear. Appendices with repertory of North Carolina cabinetmakers, 1700-1820, list of locations of artisans in the furniture trades, and series of maps showing the formation of North Carolina counties from 1700 to 1850. Comprehensive, classified bibliography, pp. 535-42. An excellent study of the development of an American regional style in furniture placed within a broad cultural historical perspective.

1190   Whitehill, Walter M., Jonathan L. Fairbanks, and Brock W. Jobe. **Boston Furniture of the Eighteenth Century**. Boston, Colonial Society of Massachusetts, 1974. 316p. illus. index. (Publications of the Colonial Society of Massachusetts, v. 48) Reprint: Charlottesville, Va., The University of Virginia Press, 1986. ISBN 0813911257.

Comprehensive, scholarly history of furnituremaking in Boston during the eighteenth century. Contents: The Boston Furniture Industry 1720-1740 by B. Jobe; Boston Japanned Furniture by D. A.. Fales; Boston's Colonial Japanners: The Documentary Record by S. H.

Hitchings; Boston Blockfront Furniture by M. M. Lovell; The Bombé Furniture of Boston by G. T. Vincent; Ornamental Carving on Boston Furniture of the Chippendale Style by M. E. Hayward Yehia; Benjamin Frothingham by R. H. Randall; New England Timbers with an annotated bibliography by G. Saltar; Appendices: A, Eighteenth-century Boston Furniture Craftsmen by M. Kaye; B, Readings on Individual Craftsmen (bibliography of books and periodical articles on individual designers and craftsmen).

1191   Dorman, Charles G. **Delaware Cabinetmakers and Allied Artisans, 1655-1855**. Wilmington, Del., Historical Society of Delaware, 1960. 107p. illus.

Biographical dictionary of furnituremakers active in Delaware between 1655 and 1855 based on information derived from written records, particularly directories and advertisements in newspapers. Illustrated with signed pieces of furniture. Appendices with pages from the workbook of John Janvier and the estate inventories of David Penny, Charles Trute, William Penny, and John White. Bibliography in the footnotes.

1192   Fabian, Monroe H. **The Pennsylvania-German Decorated Chest**. New York, Universe Books, 1978. 230p. illus. index. LC 77-91892.

Popular but informative introduction to the painted chest used by the Pennsylvania-Germans during the eighteenth and early nineteenth centuries. Contains excerpts from inventories and other documents. Good selection of plates with descriptive captions with further information in notes. Contents: The Pennsylvania-German Decorated Chest: The European Background; The Chest in Pennsylvania; Cabinetmaking and Woods; Construction; Hardware; Surface Decoration; Paint; Decoration and Decorators; Outside Pennsylvania. Selected bibliography, pp. 222-25.

1193   Fales, Dean A. **American Painted Furniture, 1660-1880**. New York, Dutton, 1972. 299p. illus. index. ISBN 0525053875.

Comprehensive history of American furniture with painted decoration from early Colonial times to circa 1890. Emphasis is on the rich tradition in New England during the eighteenth and early nineteenth centuries. Includes Shaker and Pennsylvania-German painted furniture. Comprehensive, classified bibliography, pp. 289-93, includes literature on regions and individuals.

1194   Honor, William M. **Blue Book, Philadelphia Furniture: William Penn to George Washington with Special Reference to the Philadelphia-Chippendale School**. 1935. Reprint: Washington, D.C., Highland House Pub., 1977. 340p. illus. index. ISBN 0918712009.

Comprehensive history of furniture made in Philadelphia during the second half of the eighteenth century. Extensive use of documentary evidence such as inventories and advertisements. Contents: I, Until Queen Anne; II, Queen Anne; III, An Introduction to Philadelphia-Chippendale; IV, Philadelphia Chippendale-Case Peices; V, Philadelphia-Chippendale—Tables, Sofas, Beds, Etc.; VI, Marlborough—A Refinement and Rival of the Cabriole; VII, Cabriole Chairs; VIII, Federal Fashions and Fabricators; IX, Looking-Glasses, Brackets, and Picture Frames; X, Windsor and Rush-Bottom Chairs. List of Philadelphia craftsmen in 1783 and 1786 indicating their listed trade(s) and amount of occupational tax.

1195   Kettell, Russell H. **The Pine Furniture of Early New England**. 1929. Reprint: New York, Dover, 1949. 447p. illus. LC 49-50212.

Pictorial handbook of furniture in pine made in New England before 1850. Introduction briefly discusses material, construction and hardware. Collection of 205 plates arranged by type of furniture has descriptive notes. Emphasis is on construction; dimensions are given for illustrated pieces and measured drawings for 55 pieces are provided in the appendix.

1196   Kirk, John T. **American Chairs: Queen Anne and Chippendale**. New York, Knopf, 1972. 208p. illus. index. ISBN 0394473280.

Important history of eighteenth-century chairs in the Queen Anne and Chippendale styles with emphasis on construction as a key to regional differences. Contents: I, The Regional Approach to American Furniture; II, Construction and Design Details; III, Regional Aesthetics. The "Pictorial Portfolio" contains 224 plates of chairs with detailed descriptive captions. Appendix discusses linguistic and other basis for regionalism in early America. Bibliographical references in the footnotes.

1197   Lyon, Irving W. **The Colonial Furniture of New England: A Study of the Domestic Furniture in Use in the Seventeenth and Eighteenth Centuries**. 1891. Reprint: New York, Dutton, 1977. 285p. illus. index. LC 76-52320.

Old history of furniture made in New England during the seventeenth and eighteenth centuries arranged by type of furniture: chests, cupboards, chest of drawers, desks, chairs, tables, clocks. Written by a collector. Still useful for the references to documents and illustrations of pieces now dispersed.

1198.   Theus, Mrs. Charlton M. **Savannah Furniture, 1735-1825**. n.p. (1967). 100p. illus. index. LC 67-7031.

History of furnituremaking in Savannah, Georgia, between 1735 and 1825 directed to the collector and regional historian. Extensive use of documentary evidence of the craft. Contents: Part I: Savannah—A Note of History; Woods; Inventories; Types of Furniture Made in Savannah; Cabinetmakers; Part II: Venture Furniture in Savannah. Chapter on cabinetmakers is a dictionary of some 50 names culled from records; no signed piece of Savannah furniture has survived. Chapter on inventories has both extracts and facsimiles.

See also the exhibition catalogs: *Plain & Elegant, Rich & Common: Documented New Hampshire Furniture, 1750-1850*. (Concord, N.H., New Hampshire Historical Society, 1979. 153p. illus. ISBN 0915916096), *Early Furniture Made in New Jersey, 1690-1870*. (Newark, N.J., Newark Museum, 1958. 89p. illus.), *Baltimore Painted Furniture, 1800-1840*, by W. V. Elder (Baltimore, Md., Baltimore Museum of Art, 1972. 132p. illus. ISBN 0912298251), *Kentucky Furniture* (Louisville, Ky., J. B. Speed Art Museum, 1974. 86p. illus.), *Early Furniture of Louisiana*, by J. J. Poesch (New Orleans, La., Louisiana State Museum, 1972. 85p. illus.), *Connecticut Furniture: Seventeenth and Eighteenth Centuries* (Hartford, Conn., Wadsworth Atheneum, 1967. 156p. illus.).

Victorian and Later Furniture

1199   Dubrow, Richard, and Eileen Dubrow. **Furniture Made in America, 1875-1905**. Exton, Pa., Schiffer Pub., 1982. 320p. illus. ISBN 0916838668.

Reproductions of more than 2,000 illustrations from the trade catalogs of nearly 80 furniture companies in the United States between 1875 and 1905. The illustrations are arranged by type and have no accompanying commentary. Designed as a guide to the identification of pieces of factory furniture, it is also a valuable source for serious research into the social and economic aspects of late nineteenth century American furniture.

See also the authors': *American Furniture of the 19th Century 1840-1880*. (Exton, Pa., Schiffer Pub., 1983. 247p. illus. index. LC 82-50615).

1200   Grotz, George. **The New Antiques: Knowing and Buying Victorian Furniture**. Garden City, N.Y., Doubleday, 1964. 224p. illus. index. LC 64-114000.

Popular collector's handbook of American Victorian furniture. Progression of style from 1815 to 1910 presented with line drawings of typical pieces. Chapter on refinishing Victorian furniture and "How the Antique Business Works." No bibliography.

See also K. McNerny. *Victorian Furniture, Our American Heritage.* (Paducah, Ky., Collector Books, 1981. 252p. illus. index. ISBN 0891451641).

1201   Ormsbee, Thomas H. **Field Guide to American Victorian Furniture**. Boston, Little, Brown, 1952. 428p. illus. LC 52-9095. Print: New York, Crown, n.d.

Popular collector's handbook of the identification of American furniture from 1840 to 1880. Arrangement is by type. Illustrated with line drawings of pieces accessible to the average collector. Brief bibliography of basic books.

Similar, updated guides, illustrated with photographs are: P. Dean, *Official Identification Guide to Victorian Furniture.* (Orlando, Fla., House of Collectibles, 1984. 310p. illus. ISBN 0876374151) and R and H. Swedberg, *Victorian Furniture: Styles and Prices.* (Des Moines, Ia., Wallace-Homestead, 1984. 2v. illus. ISBN 087069393X).

1202   Otto, Celia J. **American Furniture of the Nineteenth Century**. New York, Viking, 1965. 229p. illus. index. LC 65-21483.

Survey of American furniture of the nineteenth century emphasizing the importance of French sources. Arrangement is by styles, further divided by types. Includes musical instruments.

See also the exhibition catalogs: *Nineteenth-Century America: Furniture and Other Decorative Arts.* New York, Metropolitan Museum of Art, 1970. 232p. illus. index, and *Innovative Furniture in America from 1800 to the Present.* by David A. Hanks. New York, Horizon, 1981. 200p. illus. index.

See also the price guide: *The Collector's Encyclopedia of American Furniture. Volume One: The Dark Woods of the Nineteenth Century,* by R. W and H. Swedberg (Paducah, Ky., Collector's Books, 1991. ISBN 0891454411).

John Henry Belter, 1804-1863

1203   Schwartz, Marvin. **The Furniture of John Henry Belter and the Rococo Revival...** New York, E. P. Dutton, 1980. 88p. illus. index. ISBN 0525931708.

Published in conjunction with an exhibition by the Museum of Our National Heritage featuring pieces from the Gloria and Douglas Richard Manney Collection. Contents: Introduction; John Henry Belter: His Reputation through the Years; Distinguishing Belter as a Generic Term from Belter as a Cabinetmaker; Technical Observations; The Basic Facts and Some Theories about John Henry Belter's Origins; The Rococo Revival Style and the Work of John Henry Belter; A Gallery of Belter Furniture from the Collection of Gloria and Richard Manney. Bibliography, p. 86, contains references to nineteenth-century sources.

Twentieth Century

1204   Cathers, David M. **Furniture of the American Arts and Crafts Movement: Stickley and Roycroft Mission Oak**. New York, New American Library, 1981. 275p. illus. index. ISBN 0453003974.

Survey of American furniture made between 1900 and 1916 as part of the Arts and Crafts Movement. Contents: The History and Development of Arts and Crafts Furniture: 1, The Arts and Crafts Sources of Stickley's Design; 2, Gustav Stickley's Stylistic Development; 3, "Stamped in an Unobtrusive Place": How Gustav Stickley Marked His Furniture; 4, The L & J. G. Stickley Furniture Company; 5, The Roycroft Shops. "A Fine Plainness": Examples of Arts and Crafts Furniture: 6, Bookcases and China Closets; 7, Chairs and Settles; 8, Chests of Drawers; 9, Desks;

10, Servers and Sideboards; 11, Tables; 12, Individual Pieces. Appendix with transcript of interview with Barbara Wiles, Gustav Stickley's daughter and excerpt from the December 25, 1906, issue of the Tattler column in the *Furniture Journal* which was dedicated to the five Stickley brothers. General bibliography, pp. 261-63.

1205   Stone, Michael A. **Contemporary American Woodworkers**. Salt Lake City, Ut., G. M. Smith, 1986. 163p. illus. index. ISBN 0879050985.

Pictorial survey of the art furniture of 10 contemporary American woodworkers: Wharton Esherick, George Nakashimna, Bob Stockdale, Tage Frid, Sam Maloof, Arthur Espenet Carpenter, James Krenov, Wendell Castle, Garry Knox Bennet, and Jere Osgood. Bibliography of specialized literature on the 10 craftsmen, pp. 161-64.

See also the price guide: *Furniture of the Depression Era: Furniture and Accessories of the 1920s, 1930 and 1940s*, by R. W. and H. Swedberg (Paducah, Ky., Collector Books, 1987. 143p. illus. index. ISBN 0891453326).

Herman Miller Firm

1206   Caplan, Ralph. **The Design of Herman Miller**. New York, Watson-Guptill, 1976. 119p. illus. ISBN 0823071413.

Pictorial survey of the design, particularly office furniture, of the Herman Miller firm. Contents: The View from Madison Avenue; Zeeland: the Soil; D. J. De Pree: the Roots; Early Growth: Rohde; The Flowering of Design: Nelson, Eames, Girard; Branching Out: Propst; My Life in an Action Office; Redesigning the Family Tree; New Limbs; Shoptalk; Baptism and Chicken Soup; What Day Is It?: Frost; Collison Insurance. No bibliography.

Special Types of Furniture

1207 Andrews, Edward D., and Faith Andrews. **Religion in Wood: A Book of Shaker Furniture**. Bloomington, Ind., Indiana Univ. Press, 1966. 106p. illus. index. LC 66-12722.

Survey of Shaker furniture with introduction by Thomas Merton, chapter on "Spiritual Functionalism in Shaker Furniture" by Alan Gowans, and a collection of plates including many showing furniture in Shaker settings. Note on Shaker craftsmen lists comments on the individuals named in Isaac N. Youngs' registry of New Lebanon. General bibliography, pp. 105-06.

1208   Andrews, Edward D., and Faith Andrews. **Shaker Furniture: The Craftsmanship of an American Communal Sect**. 1937. Reprint: New York, Dover, 1950. 133p. illus. index. LC 37-6514.

Concise survey of furniture made by the Shakers in the eighteenth and nineteenth centuries with good selection of plates with detailed, descriptive notes. Frequent extracts from documents. Contents: Shaker Chronology; I, Shaker Craftsmanship; Its Cultural Background; II, Shaker Furniture; Its Essential Character; III, The Craftsmen of the Sect; IV, Shaker Houses and Shops; Plates. Appendices: A, The Shaker Chair Industry; B, Notes on Benjamin and Isaac Youngs, Shaker Clockmakers; C, Notes on Construction, Materials and Finishes. Comprehensive, classified bibliography, pp. 121-26.

See also J. V. Grant, *Shaker Furniture Makers*. (1210)

1209   Gilborn, Craig. **Adirondack Furniture and the Rustic Tradition**. New York, Abrams, 1987. 352p. illus. index. ISBN 0810918447.

Well-illustrated history of rustic furniture in the United States from the late eighteenth century to the present with emphasis on the rich tradition that developed in the Adirondack region in the late nineteenth and early twentieth centuries. Contents: The Background: Rustic Taste in

England and America; An Adirondack Aesthetic: From Shanty to Great Camp; Adirondack Tree Furniture; Cottage and Bungalow Furniture; From Old-Time Rustic Workers to Contemporary Craftsmen. Biographies of rustic furniture makers in the Adirondacks, pp. 317-27, comprehensive but unclassified bibliography, pp. 337-39, and bibliographical references in the notes.

1210   Grant, Jerry V., and Douglas R. Allen. **Shaker Furniture Makers**. Hanover, N.J., Univ. Press of New England, 1989. 180p. illus. index. ISBN 0874514886.

Scholarly history of Shaker furnituremakers with detailed biographies of 27 documented makers working between the 1830s and 1960s. Extracts from documentary sources and excellent illustrations of signed pieces and portraits of the late nineteenth century makers. Selected bibliography, pp. 176-78, and specialized bibliography in the notes.

1211   Kassay, John. **The Book of Shaker Furniture**. Amherst, Mass., Univ. of Massachusetts Press, 1980. 265p. illus. index. ISBN 0870232754.

Pictorial survey of Shaker furniture. Introductory chapters sketching the history of Shaker furniture are followed by plates of pieces arranged by type (beds, benches, etc.) with measured drawings and descriptive captions.

1212   Saunders, Richard. **Collecting and Restoring Wicker Furniture**. New York, Crown, 1976. 118p. illus. index. ISBN 0517526220.

Useful handbook/handbook of wicker furniture with emphasis on American production around 1900. Contents: 1, A Word about Wicker; 2, Early Wickerwork Furniture; 3, The Golden Age of Wicker; 4, The Turn of the Century; 5, Restoring Wicker Furniture. Appendices with list of minor American manufacturers and sources of supply for repair materials.

1213   Saunders, Richard. **Collector's Guide to American Wicker Furniture**. New York, Hearst Books, 1983. 150p. illus. index. ISBN 0878513078.

Popular history of wicker furniture with emphasis on that made for America in the late nineteenth and early twentieth centuries. Plates include photographs and advertisements depicting wicker furniture. Chapters on investing in wicker and repairing and caring for wicker furniture. Appendices with list of wicker repair specialists and suppliers of materials for the repair of wicker furniture. No bibliography.

See also the exhibition catalog: Ostergard, Derek E., ed. *Bent Wood and Metal Furniture, 1850-1946*. New York, American Federation of Arts, 1987. 366p. illus. index. ISBN 029596409X.

Regional Furniture

1214   Darling, Sharon. **Chicago Furniture: Art, Craft, and Industry, 1833-1983**. New York and London, Norton, 1984. 416p. illus. index. LC 83-25522.

Comprehensive history of furniture made in Chicago from 1833 to 1933 based on extensive use of documentary material. Contents: Part I: Introduction: 1, Frontier Furniture Makers, 1833-1851, 2, Steam-powered Manufactories, 1852-1872; Part II: Furniture for "The Million," 1873-1917: 3, The Dynamics of the Industry, 1873-1917, 4, Upholstered Parlor Furniture, 1873-1917, 5, Patent Furniture, 1873-1917, 6, Bedroom Furniture, 1873-1917, 8, Commercial Furniture, 1873-1917, 9, Cabinet Wares: Plain and Fancy, 1873-1917; Part III: Art Furniture, 1873-1917: 10, Modern Gothic, 1873-1880, 11, Special Designs for "The Sifted Few," 1880-1917, 12, Hand-carved Furniture and Period Reproductions, 1880-1917; 13, The Arts and Crafts Movement, 1889-1917; 14, Mission Furniture, 1895-1917, 15, A New Prairie Style, 1895-1917; Part IV: Modernism to Mies, 1918-1983: 16, What is Modern? 1918-1945, 17, The Great Central Market, 1918-1945, 18, The Postwar Years, 1946-1983. Appendix with "Other Chicago Designers and Manufacturers." Bibliography in the notes. An exemplar of local history in the decorative arts.

1215   Jenkins, Irving. **Hawaiian Furniture and Hawaii's Cabinetmakers, 1820-1940**. Honolulu, Editions Limited for the Daughters of Hawaii, 1983. 350p. illus. index. ISBN 0960793844.

Well-illustrated history of furniture made in Hawaii between 1820 and 1940. Illustrated with fine color plates of pieces, reproductions of photographs showing contemporary interiors, and portraits of personalities and drawings of construction details. Contents: I, The Early Timber Industry in Hawaii; II, Itinerant Carpenters and Missionary Furniture Makers in the Hawaiian Kingdom; III, Cabinetmakers in the Kamehameha Dynasty; IV, Cabinetmakers and Furniture Companies in the Kalakaua Period; V, Chinese Furniture Manufacturers from the Kalakaua Period into the Twentieth Century; VI, Twentieth-Century Cabinetmakers, Craftsmen and Designers; VII, Umeke, Hikiee and Kahili Stands: A Note on Three Distinctively Hawaiian Furnishings. Bibliography, pp. 343-44, has section listing manuscript sources.

See also the exhibition catalog: *Koa Furniture of Hawaii*, by Rhoda A. Hackler (Honolulu, Art Gallery, University of Hawaii at Manoa, 1981. 68p. illus.).

1216   Sikes, Jane E. **The Furniture Makers of Cincinnati, 1790 to 1849**. Cincinnati, Sikes, 1976. 264p. illus. LC 78-104982/r84.

Comprehensive history/handbook of furnituremaking in Cincinnati between 1790 and 1849, well illustrated with pieces in historical museums, reproductions of advertisements, the Book of Prices of the United Society of Journeymen Cabinet Makers of Cincinnati...(1836), furniture maker's labels and views of factories and workshops. Contents: 1, The Town as It Was; 2, Proof of Style; 3, The Furniture and Chair Industry; 4, (untitled: is a comprehensive biographical dictionary of furniture makers active in Cincinnati). Classified bibliography including unpublished sources, pp. 260-62.

1217   Taylor, Lonn, and David B. Warren. **Texas Furniture: The Cabinetmakers and Their Work, 1840-1880**. Austin, Tex., Univ. of Texas Press, 1975. 387p. illus. index. ISBN 02927-38013.

History/handbook of furniture made in Texas from circa 1850 to the twentieth century. Introductory chapters sketch the history and geography of early Texas furniture. These are followed by a catalog and plates of surviving pieces arranged by type. List of Texas cabinetmakers. Glossary of terms, and classified bibliography of books and periodical articles, pp. 355-360.

1218   Taylor, Lonn, and Dessa Bokides. **New Mexican Furniture, 1600-1940: The Origins, Survival, and Revival of Furniture Making in the Hispanic Southwest**. Sante Fe, N.M., Museum of New Mexico Press, 1987. 311p. illus. index. ISBN 0890131678.

Comprehensive history of furniture made in New Mexico from the Spanish conquest to the Second World War. Contents: Introduction; I, The Hispanic Tradition; II, Anglo-American Innovations; III. The Spanish Colonial Revival. Plates, which include tools, interiors, and portraits of furniture makers with the plates of pieces of furniture, have detailed descriptive captions. Comprehensive, classified bibliography, pp. 302-307, includes unpublished documents and interviews.

Canada

1219   Palardy, Jean. **The Early Furniture of French Canada**. 2nd ed. Toronto, Macmillan, 1965. 413p. illus. index. LC 65-22627.

Important history of French Canadian furniture of the seventeenth and eighteenth centuries in the form of a catalogue raisonné featuring 585 pieces. Contents: Introduction; History and

Catalogue Raisonné of the Early Furniture; Technical and Historical Aspects; Conclusion. Catalogue raisonné is divided into types of furniture. Appendix with summary of French regional influences and Canadian regional characteristics, lists of master-woodworkers, woodcarvers and carvers; list of master-locksmiths and locksmiths, and list of collectors. General bibliography, pp. 405-06, and further bibliography in the footnotes. A standard handbook of French-Canadian Colonial furniture.

1220   Stewart, Don R. **A Guide to Pre-Confederation Furniture of English Canada**. Dnon Mills, Longmans Canada, 1967. 150p. illus. LC 68-71836.

Collector's pictorial handbook of Canadian furniture made before 1867 illustrated with pieces in private collections. Contents: Search and Circa—An Introduction; The Heart of the House; Treen and Tole; The Summer Kitchen; The Beginning of Elegance; The Sitting-Room; The Dining-Room; The Bedroom; The Victorian Parlour. No bibliography.

1221   Webster, Donald B. **English-Canadian Furniture of the Georgian Period**. Toronto, McGraw-Hill Ryerson, 1979. 232p. illus. index. ISBN 007089802.

History of furniture made in English-speaking Canada from 1780 to 1850. Important, pioneering effort to chronicle the Canadian equivalent of American Colonial furniture. The "high" style Georgian furniture of Canada has long been neglected in favor of French-Canadian and primitive Canadian furniture. Contents: Introduction; Some General Considerations; Styles, Forms, and Fashions; The Question of Identification; Attribution and Makers; The Furniture (plates with descriptive captions arranged by type). Comprehensive, classified bibliography, pp. 227-29.

See also the exhibition catalog: *The Early Furniture of Ontario & the Atlantic Provinces: A Record of the Pieces Assembled for the Country Heritage Loan Exhibition from Private Collections across Canada* (Toronto, Feheley, 1976. 200p. illus.)

Latin America

1222   Aquiler, Carmen, et al. **El mueble mexicano: historia, evolucion a influencias**. Mexico, Fomento Cultural Banamex, 1985. 219p. illus. ISBN 9687009063.

Well-illustrated survey of furniture made in Mexico from pre-Columbian times to the twentieth century. Produced to accompany an exhibition in 1983 and 1984 at the Fomento Cultural Banamex in the Palacio de Iturbide. Contents: Mueble prehispánico by C. Aquilera; Mueble religioso by E. Vargas Lugo; Mueble civil by M. Martínez del Río de Redo; Taracea en México by J. Loyzaga; Mueble neoclásico by L. Ortiz Macedo; Mueble popular by T. Castelló Iturbide; Influencia Asiática by M. Carballo; Estudio sobre la Madera by C. Martínez López and F. Sánchez Martínez (with useful color plates and line drawings showing types of woods and cutting of timber); Geometrales de algunos de los Muebles Exhibidos (catalog with illustrations of the installation of the exhibit) by M. Enríquez, M. Figueroa, and A. Rubio. Glossary of terms. General bibliography, pp. 216-219.

1223   Bomchil, Sara, and Virginia Carreño. **El mueble colonial de los Americas y su circum-stancia historica**. Buenos Aires, Editorial Sudamerica, 1987. 919p. illus. ISBN 9500703866.

Comprehensive history of furniture in both North and South America from Colonial times to the end of the nineteenth century. Listed here because of the extensive coverage of the furniture history of Latin America. Illustrated with line drawings. Contents: Introduccion al estudio del mueble; Influencia oriental en el mobiliario americano; Bases españolas del mueble hispanoameri-cano; Mueble colonial ripolatense; Argentina; Uruguay;Paraguay; Chile; Brazil; Peru; Bolivia; Ecuador; Venezuela; Colombia o Nueva Granada; Panama; Costa Rica; Honduras; Guatemala; Cuba; Puerto Rico; Mejico; Mueble colonial estadounidense: Bases inglesas; Interpretacion estadounidense de los estilos ingleses; Canada. Comprehensive, classified bibliography, pp.899-908.

1224   Carrillo y Gabriel, Abelardo. **Evolucion del mueble en Mexico**. Mexico City, Instituto Nacional de Antropologia e historia, 1957. 166p. illus. index. LC 65-66407.

Survey of the stylistic development of furniture in Mexico from the Aztecs to the late nineteenth century. Contains 44 illustrations in the text, including a good selection of drawings taken from pre-Columbian monuments, plus 104 pages of plates of pieces of furniture with descriptive captions. No bibliograph6y.

1225   Duarte, Carlos F. **Muebles venezolanos; siglos XVI, XVII, y XVIII**. Caracas, Cuatro, 1966. 189p. illus. index. LC 77-277689.

Pictorial survey of furniture made in Venezuela during the sixteenth, seventeenth and eighteenth centuries. Brief introductory text has lists of carpenters and cabinet makers. Corpus of 218 pieces illustrated in black and white with descriptive captions. Bibliography, p.183.

1226   Gomez de Orozco, Federico. **El mobiliario y la decoracion en la Nueva España en el siglo XVI**. Mexico, Universidad Nacional Autonoma de Mexico, 1983. 111p. illus. (Instituto de Investigaciones Estéticas, Estudios y Fuentes del Arte en México, 44) ISBN 9685804915.

Scholarly history of furniture and interior decoration in Mexico during the sixteenth century based chiefly on documentary sources. Contents: I, Los factores; II, El palacio urbano fortificado en España y su equivalente en México; III, La mansion; IV, El mobiliario civil; V, El mobilario eclesiastico; VI, El mobiliario en general; VII, La ciudad de México en el siglo XVI; VIII, La vida en México en el siglo XVI. Apéndices: 1, Cocinas convetuales; 2, Torneos, juegos de cañas y ejercicios hipicos; 3, Ceteria o halconeria; 4, Inventario de Palacio de Cortés en Cuernavaca; 5, Una cena memorable; 6, Inventario de los bienes de la Parroquia de San Juan Xiquipilco, Estado de México, año de 1576. Bibliographical references in the footnotes.

1227   Santos, Jose de Almeida. **Mobiliario artistico brasiliero**. 2nd ed. Sao Paulo, Calecao Museu Paulista, 1963. 3v. illus. LC 64-6406 rev.

Comprehensive but poorly illustrated history/handbook of furniture in Brazil from early Colonial times to the end of the nineteenth century. Volume one is a history; volumes two and three are dictionaries of Brazilian furniture that include names of cabinetmakers. Bibliographical references in the footnotes.

1228   Taullard, A. **El mueble colonial sudamericano**. Buenos Aires, Ediciones Peuser, 1944. 286p. illus. LC 45-3028.

Comprehensive survey of furniture made in South America from the sixteenth to the early nineteenth centuries. Corpus of 391 illustrations of pieces of furniture including church furniture and accessories in wood. Descriptive captions to the plates. Contents: Del mueble en general; El mueble Español; El mueble Frances; El mueble Ingles; El mueble colonial Norteamericano; El mueble Rioplatense; El mueble Paraguayo; El mueble Luso-Brasileño; El mueble en Chile; El alto Peru; Peru; Ecuador; Colombia; Tipologia y evolucion de los muebles. General bibliography, pp 13-14, and further bibliography in the footnotes.

EUROPEAN FURNITURE

General Works

1229   Feulner, Adolf. **Kunstgeschichte des Möbels seit dem Altertum.** 2d ed. Berlin, Propy-
laen-Verlag, 1927. 654p. illus. index. LC 28-4644. Reprinted with introduction by Dieter Alfter:
Frankfurt am Main, Propylaen-Verlag, 1980. (Propylaen Kunstgeschichte. Supplement- und
Sonderbände, 2).
Comprehensive, scholarly history of European furniture from the Middle Ages to the
nineteenth century written by a leading art historian of the interwar years (*See* FA 1273, 1535).
Emphasis is on the history of furniture style and its relationship to contemporary painting,
sculpture and architecture. Contents: I, Einleitung; II, Mittelalter; III, Spätgotik; IV, Von der
Renaissance zum Barock; V, Spätbarock. Der Stil Louis XIV; VI, Rokoko; VII, Das Englische
Möbel im 18. Jahrhundert; VIII, Der Stil Louis XVI. Übergang zum Klassizismus; IX, Klassizismus. Empire und Biedermeier; X, Schluss. Das 19. Jahrhunderts. Comprehensive, classified
bibliography, pp. 613-616, and bibliographical references in the text.

1230   Grandjean, Serge. **Empire Furniture, 1800 to 1825.** New York, Taplinger, 1966. 120p.
illus. index. LC 66-11303.
Authoritative survey of French Empire furniture with emphasis on pieces made for the
general market. Directed to the collector and connoisseur. Contents: Chronological Table; The
Promoters of the Empire Style; Percier and Fontaine; Denon; Jacob-Desmalter; Cabinet Makers
of the Empire; Thomire and Other Workers in Bronze; The Emperor's Role as Maecenas; The
Empire Style in Furniture Becomes International; The Types of Furniture; Materials and Techniques. Ninety-six plates with descriptive notes. General bibliography, pp. 112-14, and further
bibliography in the footnotes.

1231   Ritz, Gislind M. **Alte bemalte Bauernmöbel Europa.** Munich, Callwey, 1970. 163p. illus.
ISBN 3766701916.
Comprehensive, well-illustrated, and authoritative survey of painted folk furniture through
Europe during the eighteenth and nineteenth centuries. Contents: Die nordische Länder; Deutsches
Sprachebiet; Die Alpenländer; Der Osten; Romanische Länder. Descriptive notes to the plates.
Comprehensive and classified bibliography, pp.158-162.

1232   Ritz, Gislind. **Alte geschnitzte Bauernmöbel.** Munich, Callwey, 1974. 200p. illus. index.
(Bauernmobel, Band III). 204p. illus. ISBN 3766703072.
Comprehensive, authoritative survey of European folk furniture with carved decoration
from the seventeenth century to the early nineteenth century with emphasis on the development
in German-speaking lands. Contents: Formen der Holzbehandlung; Geschichte-Erscheinung-Ver-
breitung; Norddeutschland; Mittel- und Süddeutschland; Alpenländer; Anhang; Exkurse: Dänemark und Schweden, Norwegen, Die Niederlande, Frankreich, Italien, Ungarn und Siebenbürgen;
Ornamente. Appendix (Anhang) has essay on conservation and a comprehensive, classified
bibliography, pp. 199-204.

1233   Schmidt, Robert. **Möbel.** 10th ed. Braunschweig, Klinkhardt & Biermann, 1975. 331p.
illus. index. LC 79-274946. (Bibliothek fur Kunst- und Antiquitätenfreunde, Band 5.).
Comprehensive, authoritative history of European furniture from the early Middle Ages
to Art Nouveau. Written by a former director of the Berlin Schlossmuseum and a leading expert
on the history of decorative arts, the text is outstanding for its even sweep and high level of aesthetic
sensitivity. Contents: I, Das Vorgotische Mittelalter; II, Gotik: Frühzeit (bis gegen 1400); Die
nördliche Spätgotik; Die südliche Spätgotik; III, Renaissance: Die romanische Länder; Die

germanischen Länder; VI, Barock: Frankreich; Italien; Deutschland; V, Rokoko: Frankreich; Italien; Deutschland; Holland; VI, Louis XVI: Frankreich; Deutschland; England; VII, Empire und Biedermeier; VIII, Historismus; IX, Jugendstil. Illustrations include important works destroyed in the Second World War. General bibliography, pp. 323-24, and further bibliography in the footnotes.

1234   Stürmer, Michael. **Handwerk und hofische Kultur: europäische Möbelkunst im 18.** Jahrhundert. Munich, Beck, 1982. 325p. illus. index. ISBN 340608284X.

Important history of the craft of the furniture artist in Europe during the eighteenth century, conceived in the broadest sense from technique and materials to the organization of the craft guilds, and influence of patronage and economics. Contents: I, Die Nahrung der Menschen; II, Fette Jahre, magere Jahre; III, Lebensformen der Zunft in Alteuropa; IV, Hobel und Rechenstift; V, Furniere, Farben, Polituren; VI, London—Die Macht des Marktes; VII, Paris—Les enfants de St. Anne; VIII, Berlin—Residenz- und Handelsstadt; IX, Die Mainzer Schreinerzunft; X, Die Macht und die Herrlichkeit—Hofhandwerker des 18. Jahrhunderts; XI, "Roentgen fecit a Neuwied"; Epolog: Ein Abschied von Arkadien. Bibliographical references in the notes and general bibliography, pp. 311-12.

1235   **Upholstery in America & Europe from the Seventeenth Century to World War I.** New York, London, W. W. Norton, 1987. 273p. illus. index. ISBN 0393024695.

Important collection of essays on the history of upholstered furniture chiefly in Britain and America. Contents: Upholstered Seat Furniture in Europe 17th and 18th Centuries by P. Thornton; 17th-Century Upholstery in Massachusetts by R. F. Trent; The Turkey-work Chairs of Holroodhouse by M. Swan; The Boston Upholstery Trade, 1700-1775 by B. Jobe; The Technique of 18th-Century Over-the-Rail Upholstery by W. Gusler, L. Graves, and M. Anderson; 18th-Century American Upholstery Techniques: Easy Chairs, Sofas, and Settees; Evidence from the Frame of a Late 18th-Century Sofa by E. S. Cooke; Richard Wevill, Upholsterer by P. C. O'Donnell; French Upholstery Practices of the 18th Century by J. Munger; Beyond the Fringe: Ornamental Upholstery Trimmings in the 17th, 18th, and Early 19th Centuries by L. W. Jackson; Some Notes on Western European Table Linen from the 16th through the 18th Centuries by C. A. Burgers; 18th-Century American Bed and Window Hangings by F. M. Montgomery; Bed and Window Hangings in New England, 1790-1870 by J. C. Nylander; Swedish Royal Curtain from the Early 19th-Century by E. Stavenow-Hidemark; F. A. Moreland's Practical Decorative Upholstery by M. G. Fales; Drapery Documents in the Study Exhibition by J. C. Nylander; The Re-Dressing of a Boston Empire Sofa by J. S. Ramirez; The A. H. Davenport Company of Boston: Notes on the Upholsterer's Trade in the Late-19th and Early 20th Centuries by A. Farnam; Spring Seats of the 19th and Early-20th Centuries by E. S. Cooke and A. Passeri; Upholstery Documents in the Collections of the Society for the Preservation of New England Antiquities by R. C. Nylander. Bibliographical references in the notes to each essay.

1236   Windisch-Graetz, Franz. **Möbel Europas. Von der Romanik bis zur Spätgotik mit einem Rückblick auf Antike und Spätantike.** Munich, Klinkhardt & Biermann, 1982. 2v. illus. index. ISBN 3781402126 (v.1), 3781402134 (v.2).

Comprehensive, scholarly history of Western furniture from the Romanesque to Renaissance. Illustrated with museum pieces. Contents: Band 1: I, Die Romanik; II, Die Früh- und Hochgotik; III, Die Spätgotik. Band 2 : I, Die Renaissance in Italien; II, Die Renaissance in Frankreich; II, Die Renaissance in Spanien; IV, Die Renaissance in den Niederlanden; V, Die Renaissance in England; VI, Die Renaissance in Süddeutschland; VII, Die Renaissance in der Schweiz; VIII, Die Renaissance in Norddeutschland; IX, Ausblick auf Dänemark und Schweden; X, Die Renaissance in Österreich; XI, Die Renaissance in Ungarn; XII, Ausblick auf die Renaissance in Böhmen und Polen. Bibliographical footnotes and classified bibliographies at the end of each volume. An exemplary work with thorough use of documentary sources and detailed consideration of decorative and technical aspects.

See also the price guides: C. Payne, *The Price Guide to 19th Century European Furniture* (excluding British) (Woodbridge, Antique Collectors' Club, 1981. 506p. illus. ISBN 09020-2891X) and J. Andrews, *The Price Guide to Antique Furniture* (Woodbridge, Antique Collectors' Club, 1982. 290p. illus. ISBN 0902028707).

France

Bibliographies

1237   Viaux, Jacqueline. **Bibliographie du meuble (mobilier civil français)**. Paris, Société des Amis de la Bibliothèque Forney, 1966. 589p. illus. LC 67-84648.

Comprehensive, classified bibliography of books and periodical articles on French civil furniture from the Middle Ages to 1966. Contents: I, Généralités; II, Meubles par époque; III, Meuble régional; IV, Artistes du meuble; V, Expositions; VI, Musées; VII, Collections; VIII, Inventaires; IX, Techniques; X, Corporations. Each section has bibliographical essay. Titles arranged chronologically. Thoroughly indexed. Supplement (Paris, Agence Culturelle de Paris, 1988. 624p. index) brings the coverage up to 1985.

General Histories and Handbooks

1238   Champeaux, Alfred de. **Le meuble**. Nouv. éd. Paris, Maison Quantin, 1885. 2v. illus. LC 32-23325.

Pioneering history of furniture in France from earliest times to the nineteenth century. The author assembled a portfolio of 960 important plates illustrating furniture and other decorative arts under the title: *Portfeuille des arts décoratifs*. (Paris, Calavas, 1889-98, 10v. in 5).

1239   Devinoy, Pierre. **Le siege en France du moyen age à nos jours**. Paris, Hartmann, 1948. 389p. illus. LC A49-2278.

History of the chair in France from the early Middle Ages to 1925. Contains 342 plates with brief, descriptive notes. Fifty-seven-page introductory essay. Appendix with drawings giving measurements for the major pieces. Bibliographical references in the notes.

1240   Felice, Roger de. **French Furniture under Louis XVI and the Empire**. London, Heinemann, 1920. 142p. illus. index.

————. **French Furniture under Louis XIV...** London, Heinemann, 1922. 142p. illus. index.

————. **French Furniture of the Middle Ages and under Louis XIII...** London, Heinemann, 1923. 152p. illus. index.

————. **French Furniture under Louis XV**. London, Heinemann, 1927. 132p. illus. index.

Series of pictorial surveys of French furniture from the Middle Ages to the end of the Empire style. Each volume has a brief introductory essay followed by a collection of plates illustrating major museum pieces, bibliography of basic books, and a glossary-index.

1241   Jarry, Madeleine. **Le siège français**. Fribourg, Office du Livre, 1973. 366p. illus. LC A49-2278.

Comprehensive, well-illustrated history of the chair and other pieces of seat furniture in France from the early Middle Ages to the Art Deco period. Emphasis is on the social and economic relationships.

1242   Kjellberg, Pierre. **Le mobilier français**. Paris, Editions Le Prat, 1978-1980. 2v. illus. ISBN 2852050455 (v. 1) ISBN 285205065X (v. 2).

Pictorial survey of French furniture from the Middle Ages to 1925 written by a well-known authority. Emphasis is on stylistic development and identification of major personalities. List of museums and general bibliographies at the end of each volume. Contents: Tome 1: 1, Le Moyen Age; 2, La Renaissance; 3, Le style Louis XIII; 4, Le style Louis XIV; 5, Le style Régence; 6, Le style Louis XV. Tome 2: 1, Le style Transition; 2, Le style Louis XVI; 3, Le style Directoire; 4, La formation du style Empire; 5, L'Empire; 6, La Restauration; 7, Le style Louis-Philippe; 8, La Seconde moitié du 19e siècle; 9, "L'Art Nouveau"; 10, "L'art Deco.".

1243   Viaux, Jacqueline. **French Furniture**. New York, Putnam, 1964. 200p. illus. index. LC 64-13023.

Popular survey of French furniture from the Middle Ages to 1960 by a leading expert. Chapters are devoted to the major periods and styles, and each has a good section on technique and ornament. Illustrated with museum pieces. Useful translator's glossary with definitions of French furniture makers. No bibliography.

See also the collection catalog: *Wallace Collection Catalogues. Furniture*, by F. J. B. Watson (London, W. Clowes. 1956. 360p. illus.).

Regional Furniture

1244   Boulanger, Gisele. **L'art de reconnaitre les meubles regionaux**. Paris, Hachette, 1966. 511p. illus. LC 66-82710.

Comprehensive, authoritative survey of the various regional styles of French provincial furniture from the Middle Ages to the middle of the nineteenth century. Includes ceramics, sculpture and textiles as part of interior decoration. Illustrated with many views of historic rooms in museums. Plates have descriptive captions. Contents: L'Alsace; L'Auvergne; La Bourgogne et la Bresse; La Bretagne; La Champagne; Flandres Artois Picardie; La Franche-Comté; La Guyenne et le Languedoc; Ile de France; La Lorraine; Le Lyonnais, la Savoie, le Dauphiné; La Normandie; La Provence; Le Val de Loire, Le Berry, Le Nivernais; La Vendée. No bibliography.

1245   Longnon, Henri, and Frances W. Huard. **French Provincial Furniture**. Philadelphia and London, Lippincott, 1927. 166p. illus. index. LC 27-6887.

Old, popular survey of the various regional styles of French furniture still useful as an introduction in English. Contents: I, The Sources of Its Styles; II, Flanders, Artois, and Picardy; III, Brittany and Normandy; IV, Alsace, Lorraine, and Champagne; V. Auvergne, Limousin, Poitou, Vendée, Angoumois, and Saintonge; VI, Burgundy, Charolias, Franche Comté, Bresse, Beaujolais, Lyonnais, Savoie, and Dauphiné; VII, Provence and Bas-Languedoc; VIII, Guienne, Gascony, Haut-Languedoc, and Le Pays Basque; IX, Textiles and Decoration; X, Conclusion.

1246   Salvy, Claude. **Dictionnaire des meubles region/aux**. Paris, Hachette, 1971. 291p. illus. LC 72-301263.

Popular handbook of French regional furniture and interior furnishings. Arrangement is by type of furniture subdivided by region. Concluding section on symbolism in the decoration of regional furniture. Basic bibliography, p. 291.

1247   Stany- Gauthier, Joseph. **La connaissance des meubles régionaux français; évolution, caractéristiques**. Paris, Moreau, 1952. 272p. illus. index. LC 53-30629.

History of French regional furniture written for the collector by a recognized authority. Contents: I, Considérations générales; II, Evolution du mobilier régional; III, La fabrication; IV, Le mobilier Breton; V, Le mobilier Auvergnat; VI, Le mobilier Vendéen, Poitevin, Saintongeois;

VII, Le mobilier Normand; VIII, Le mobilier Provençal; IX, Le mobilier Basque et Béarnais; X, Le mobilier du Languedoc et du Roussillon; XI, Le mobilier Bourguignon; XII, Le mobilier Dauphinois, Lyonnais et Savoyard; XIII, Le mobilier Bressau; XIV, Le mobilier Lorrain et Alsacien; XV, Le mobilier Ardennais et Champenois; XVI, Le mobilier du Nord, Flandres, Artois, Picardie; XVII, Le mobilier du Val-de-Loire et de l'Ile-de-France. Contains 188 poorly reproduced black-and-white illustrations. No bibliography.

1248 Tardieu, Suzanne. **Le mobilier rural traditionnel français**. Paris, Aubier-Flammarion, 1976. 217p. illus. index. ISBN 208210902X.
    Concise history of French provincial furniture styles of the eighteenth and nineteenth centuries. Contents: I, Domaine; II, Sources; III, Classifications; IV, Typologie; V, Caractères techniques; VI, Caractères stylistiques; VII, Caractères régionaux; VIII, Coutumes et croyances. General bibliography with introductory notes, pp. 197-205. List of museums with collections of regional furniture in France.
    See also the museum guides: *Le mobilier regional francais: Savoie, Dauphine*, by D. Gluck (Paris, Reunion des Musées Nationaux et Berger-Levrault, 1983. 297p. illus. ISBN 2701305160) and *Le mobilier regional français: Flandred, Artois, Picardie*, by S. Cuisenier (Paris, Reunie des Musées Nationaux et Berger-Levrault, 1984. 300p. illus. ISBN 2701305624).

Seventeenth Century

1249 Brunhammer, Yvonne. **Meubles et ensembles époque Directoire et Empire**. Paris, C, Massin, 1965.
    ———. **Meubles et ensembles époques Louis XIII et Louis XIV**. Paris, C. Massin, 1966.
    ———. **Meubles et ensembles époque Louis XV**. Paris, C. Massin, 1965.
    ———. **Meubles et ensembles époque Louis XVI**. Paris, C, Massin. 1965.
    ———. **Meubles et ensembles époques moyen-âge et Renaissance**. Paris, C. Massin, 1966.
    ———. **Meubles et ensembles époques Restauration et Louis-Phlippe**. Paris, C, Massin, 1966.
    Series of pictorial surveys of French furniture and interior decoration. Brief introductory essays followed by approximately 50 plates with descriptive captions. No bibliography.

1250 Ricci, Seymour de. **Louis XIV and Regency Furniture and Decoration**. New York, Helburn, 1929. 214p. illus. LC 30-8569.
    Pictorial handbook of French furniture in the Louis XIV and regency styles useful for the large selection of plates illustrating historic interiors and pieces of furniture in private collections. No bibliography.

Eighteenth Century

Biographical Dictionaries and Handbooks

1251 Béné-Petitclerc, Frederique. **Ebenisten der Louis-XVI-Mobel**. Braunschweig, Klinkhardt & Biermann, 1968. 43p. illus. LC 72-581346.
    Scholarly handbook of the chief furnituremakers of the Louis XVI period, with facsimiles of their marks, biographical data, and illustrations of signed pieces. Bibliographical references in the footnotes.

1252 Nicolay, Jean. **L'art et la manière des maitres ébénistes français au XVIIIe siècle**. Paris, Le Prat, 1956-59. 2v. illus. index. LC 56-40968 rev.
    Comprehensive handbook of French eighteenth-century cabinetmakers and furniture designers. Volume one is a biographical dictionary with rather full oeuvre catalogs of the major

designers. Volume two provides a dictionary of marks and signatures with an index by initials and a collection of documents on furniture manufacturing in eighteenth-century Paris.

1253 Salverte, Francois de. **Les ébénistes du XVIIIe siecle, leurs oeuvres marques**. 5th ed. Paris, De Nobele, 1962. 365p. illus. index. LC 24-26761.

First published in 1923. Comprehensive dictionary of French and some foreign cabinet-makers and designers of the eighteenth century. Alphabetically arranged, the entries give brief biography, list of works and facsimiles of their marks and signatures. Includes a few foreign makers associated with the French guilds. A standard reference work.

1254 Theunissen, André. **Meubles et sièges du XVIIIe siècle; menuisiers, ébénistes, marques, plans et ornementation de leurs oeuvres**. Paris, Editions "Le Document," 1934. 194p. illus. index. LC 35-10666.

Comprehensive dictionary of French eighteenth-century cabinet makers and their marks and signatures. Illustrated with plates and line drawings of decorative details of museum-quality pieces. Useful plates of marble used in French furniture. Contents: Tableau synoptique donnant de classement alphabetique et chronologique des ébénistes du XVIIIe siècle, Meubles et Siègnes du XVIIIe siècle classés par ordre alphabetique d'auteurs; Fac-similé d'une facture de Chartier, ébéniste et de Morel, maitre-sculpteur marbrier, en 1775, Marques d'inventaires, Marques et monogrammes de chateaux, Marque diverses; Liste des marbres utilisés au XVIIe siècle; Description (planche en couleurs); Bibliography, pp. 199-201. Glossary.

Histories and Handbooks

1255 Boutemy, André. **Analyses stylistiques et essais d' attribution de meubles français anonymes du XVIIIe siècle**. Brussels, Éditions de l'Université Bruxelles, 1973. LC 74-1926465.

Important study of French eighteenth-century furniture emphasizing the difference between "ebénistes" and "menuisiers" and, therefore, an important effort to pierce the anonymity of the unsigned works of furniture produced in Paris alongside the signed work commissioned by the crown. The author goes about his task by examining, with close stylistic scrutiny, a series of pieces in the Louis XV style in France, Britain, Germany and America. Bibliographical footnotes.

1256 Frégnac, Claude, ed. **French Cabinetmakers of the Eighteenth Century**. Paris, Hachette, 1965. 341 p. illus. LC 65-28468.

Popular, well-illustrated introduction to French eighteenth-century furniture and furniture makers. Contents: The Cabinetmakers and Their History in the Century of a Gentle Way of Life; The Evolution of Taste During the Regency; The Evolution of Taste During the Reign of Louis XV; The Evolution of Taste During the Reign of Louis XVI; Manufacturing Technique; Varieties of Furniture; The Stamps of the Paris Masters. No bibliography.

1257 Hinckley, F. Lewis. **A Directory of Antique French Furniture, 1735-1800**. New York, Crown, 1967. 220p. illus. index. LC 67-24767.

Pictorial survey of French furniture from Louis XV to the Empire period still useful for the collection plates illustrating pieces in museums and private collections arranged by type. Introduction discusses the major cabinet makers in Paris, followed by an alphabetical list of those active in the provinces. General bibliography, pp. 213-14.

1258 Souchal, Genevieve. **French Eighteenth Century Furniture**. New York, Putnam, 1961. 128p. illus. LC 61-12202.

Popular survey with emphasis on the development of the major types and classes of furniture. Illustrated with museum pieces (inadequately identified in the captions) and with works of eighteenth-century French painting depicting furniture and its use.

1259   Verlet, Pierre. **French Royal Furniture**. New York, C. Potter, 1963. 200p. illus. index. LC 64-20134.

Important history of furniture made for the French royal court from the time of Louis XIV to the end of the second Empire period written by a leading expert on French decorative arts. Contents: I, Manufacture: The Archives of the Garde-Meuble; The Crown Furniture; Ebénistes and Menuisiers; The Cabinet; Cucci and Gobelins Workshops; The Bureau and the Commode; Boulle and the Commode; Boulle and the Louvre Workshops; Gaudron and the Ebénistes of the Faubourg; Antoine Gaudreaux; The Bronze-Workers; B.V.R.B and the Marchands-Merciers; Gilles Joubert; The Secretaire; Oeben and the Mechanicians; Riesener; Benneman; Weisweiler; The Menuisiers of the Rue de Cléry; The Wood-Cravers; Drawings, Designs and Models; the Peintres-Doreurs; The Upholsterers; Sets of Furniture; Pliant and Tabourets; The Guéridon; The Pied-de-Table; The Silks of Lyons. II, Dispersal: The Example of Louis XIV; Removals of Furniture; Sales, Gifts and Destruction; Remaking and Transformation; The First Months of the Revolution; Revolutionary Sales; The Republic's Creditors; Autos-da-Fé and Vandalism; Offices and Residences; The Directory; Bonaparte and Napoleon I; Furniture for Everyday Use; The Musée du Garde-Meuble and the Louvre. III, Discovery: The First Collectors; Louis-Philippe and Versailles; The Efforts of the Empress Eugénie; First Identification; Methodical Research; Hunting Grounds; An Attempt at a Balance Sheet; The Refurnishing of Versailles. Bibliographical references in the notes.

1260   Verlet, Pierre. **Les meubles français au XVIIIe siècle**. Paris, L'Oeil du Connoisseur, 1956. 2v. illus. English Translation: Charlottesville, Va., Univ. of Virginia Press, 1991. ISBN 0813912903.

Important history of French eighteenth-century furniture with particular attention to technique including much valuable information on fakes and reproductions. Short dictionary of marks and signatures. Contents: v. 1, Menuiserie; v. 2, Ébénisterie. Ecah volume is subdivided by: 1, Généralities; 2, Écoles et styles; 3, Collections et collectionneurs. Important, annotated bibliography in v. 1, pp. 95-98, continued in v. 2, pp. 101-02. List of illustrations has commentaries. The standard work on French eighteenth-century furniture.

1261   Watson, F. J. B. **Louis XVI Furniture**. New York, Philosophical Library, 1960. 162p. illus. index. LC 61-4064.

Important introductory survey of French furniture made between 1760 and the French Revolution written by a leading British expert. Chapters on the development of style and forms, on techniques and materials, trade guilds and the influence of the major designers. Illustrated with museum pieces. Bibliography, p. 95 is an addendum to the bibliography in the author's catalog of Louis XVI furniture in the Wallace Collection (1243).

Paris

1262   Verlet, Pierre. **L'art du meuble à Paris au XVIIIe siècle**. 2d ed. Paris, Presses Universitaires de France, 1968. 128p. illus.

Concise but authoritative survey of Parisian furniture-making during the eighteenth century. Contents: I, La corporation des menuisiers-ébénistes; II, Menuisiers et ébénistes; III, La vie quotidienne; IV, L'atelier; V, La production. Summary bibliography, p. 127

Major Furniture Makers

André-Charles Boulle, 1642-1732

1263 Samoyault, Jean-Pierre. **André-Charles Boulle et sa famille: nouvelles recherches, nouveaux documents.** Geneva, Droz, 1979. 229p. illus. index. (Hautes études médiévales et modernes, 40). LC 80-122686r85.

Scholarly monograph on Boulle based on new archival information. Three new inventories, dated 1732, 1745, and 1754, are transcribed in full as is the acte de delaissement between Boulle and his children. Plates of plans of Boulle's shop, rooms in the Louvre decorated by Boulle, original designs and pieces of furniture by Boulle. Bibliographical references in the footnotes.

1264 Harvard, Henry. **Les Boulle.** Paris, L. Allison, 1893. 94p. illus.

Old, standard monograph on the furniture of André Boulle and his family. Description of the furniture illustrated with engravings is followed by biographical essays on the sons of André-Charles Boulle, Jean-Philippe Boulle, Pierre-Benoit Boulle, Charles-André Boulle, and Charles-Joseph Boulle. Bibliography, p. 91, lists important primary sources.

Charles Cressent, 1685-1768

1265 Ballot, Marie J. **Charles Cressent, sculpteur, ebéniste, collectionneur.** Paris, Champion, 1919. 385p. illus. index. Reprint: Paris, F. de Nobele, 1969. LC 72-573800.

Comprehensive monograph on the life and furniture of Cressent with extensive use of documentary sources. Contents: Première Partie—Biographie; Deuxième Partie—l'Oevure: Troisième Partie: Extraits des catalogues des ventes du XVIIIe siècle donnant des descriptions de meubles par Cressent; Cinquième Partie—Pièces justificatives (extracts of seventeen documents relating to Cressent's life and work); Note sur Jacques Cressent, sculpteur. Bibliography, pp. 369-74, is a classified list with important section on manuscript material.

Georges Jacob, 1739-1814

1266 Lafuel, Hector. **Georges Jacob, ebéniste du XVIIIe siècle.** Paris, Morance, 1923. 423p. illus. LC 25-1108.

Comprehensive monograph of the life and work of Jacob with extensive reference to documents. Contents: I, Importance de l'oeuvre de F.-H.-G. Jabob-Desmalter; II, Collaborateurs; III, Napoléon Ier; IV, Différentes sociétés et signateurs de F.-H.-G. Jacob-Desmalter;; V, Technique; VI, Fournitures pour les divers palais; VII, Travaux d'architecture et de menuiserie; VIII, Divers travaux d'ébénisterie; X, Montant des commandes impériales et royales. Comprehensive bibliography, pp. 441-46, with list of unpublished sources. List of marks with facsimiles.

See also Dumonthier, Ernest. *Chairs by Georges Jacob.* Paris, Morance, 1922.

Adam Weisweiler, 1744-1820

1267 Segoura, Maurice. **Weisweiler.** Paris, Editions d'Art Monelle Hayoy Vilo, 1983. 2300p. illus. ISBN 2903824037.

Well-illustrated monograph on the work of the German-born, French Neo-classical ebenenist, Adam Weisweiler, with a valuable appendix with extracts from documentary sources and catalogue raisonné. Contents: Introduction; Weisweiler: sa vie; étude technique du mobilier de Weisweiler; Weisweiler: de sa formation à sa collaboration avec Daguerre; Les différents types de meubles; Les ornements; Weisweiler et ses contemporains; Essai de chronologie de l'Oeuvre; Conclusion. Comprehensive, classified bibliography, pp. 192-95.

Nineteenth Century

1268 Ledoux-Lebard, Denise. **Les ebenistes du XIXe siècle: 1795-1889; leurs ouvres et leurs marques.** Paris, Editions de l'Amateur, 1984. 699p. illus. ISBN 2859170367.

Comprehensive dictionary of furnituremakers active in France from 1795 to 1889. In addition to basic biographical information, the entries for major figures make reference to participation in exhibitions, prizes won, major commissions, and append list of pieces sold at auction and list the museums which own pieces. Bibliographical references through notes. Comprehensive bibliography including archival material, pp. 690-99. A standard reference work intended as a complement to Salverte's dictionary of French eighteenth-century furnituremakers (1253).

Twentieth Century

Pierre Chareau, 1883-1950

1269 Vellay, Marc, and Kenneth Frampton. **Pierre Chareau Architect and Craftsman 1883-1950.** London, Thames and Hudson, 1985. 347p. illus. index. ISBN 0500234450.

Introductory, pictorial monograph on the furniture and interior designs of Pierre Chareau with extracts from Chareau's writing and other documentary sources. Good selection of illlustrations including many photographs on interiors that are now lost. Catalog of his designs and works with bibliographical references. General bibliography, pp. 340-44, contains a list of exhibitions of works by Chareau.

Emile-Jacques Ruhlmann, 1879-1933

1270 Camard, Florence. **Ruhlmann, Master of Art Deco.** New York, Abrams, 1984. 312p. illus. index. ISBN 0810915596.

Pictorial survey of the furniture and interior design of Ruhlmann, one of the great masters of Art Deco design. Well-illustrated with plates of extant pieces, reproductions of lost interiors and many sketches, all with descriptive captions. Contents: Ruhlmann as Furniture Designer; Elements of Style; Ruhlmann as Decorator; the Rhulmann Empire. No bibliography.

Paris

1271 Ledoux-Lebard, Denise. **Les ébénistes Parisiens du XIXe siècle (1795-1870).** 2d ed. Paris, F. de Nobele, 1965. 600p. illus. LC 66-77089.

Comprehensive, scholarly dictionary of Parisian furnituremakers active during the nineteenth century based upon extensive study of documentary records. Entries for major names give a facsimile of the makers' mark, lists of major pieces in museums today, lists of auctions and exhibitions, and bibliographical references through footnotes. The complicated genealogy of families of cabinetmakers like the Jacobs's is disentangled through family trees. Collection of plates of signed pieces.

Germany, Austria, and Switzerland

General Histories and Handbooks

1272 Falke, Otto von, and Hermann Schmitz, eds. **Deutsche Möbel vom Mittelalter bis zum Anfang des 19.** Jahrhunderts. Stuttgart, Hoffmann, 1923-24. 3v. illus. (Bauformen-Bibliothek, Band XIV, XVIII, XX)

Old, scholarly history of German furniture from the early Middle Ages through the nineteenth century. Concise text outlines the major periods and is followed by an excellent corpus of plates illustrating museum pieces and period interiors. Contents: I. Band: Vom Mittelalter bis zur Renaissance; II. Band: Deutsche Möbel des Barock und Rokoko; III. Band: Deutsche Möbel des Klassizismus.

1273 Kreisel, Heinrich, ed. **Die Kunst des deutschen Möbels. Möbel und Vertäfelungen des deutschen Sprachraums von den Anfängen bis zur Jugendstil.** Munich, Beck, 1970-74. 3v. illus. index. LC 68-121635.

Comprehensive, scholarly history of furniture in the German-speaking territories from the early Middle Ages to Art Nouveau. Illustrated with museum pieces. Text is arranged by periods, then by types, techniques, and centers. Excellent corpus of plates with accompanying descriptive captions. General bibliography (third volume), pp. 280-323, is an exhaustive, classified list of books and periodical articles. There are further bibliographical references in the footnotes. Does not include folk furniture or works by German furniture makers in foreign countries. Contents: Band 1: H. Kreisel, Von den Anfängen bis zum Hochbarock. 2nd ed., 1974; Band 2: H. Kreisel, Spätbarock und Rokoko. 1970; Band 3: G. Himmelheber, Klassizismus, Historismus, Jugendstil. 1973. An exemplary work. Supercedes the old, standard history: H. Schmitz, Deutsche Möbel von Mittelalter bis zum Anfang des 19. Jahrhunderts. 3v. illus. (Stuttgart, J. Hofmann, 1923-37).

1274 Schade, Gunter. **Deutsche Möbel aus Sieben Jahrhunderten.** Leipzig and Heidelberg, Schneider, 1966. 183p. illus. index. LC 67-75736.

Popular but authoritative survey of German furniture from the early Middle Ages through Jugendstil. Illustrations of museum pieces. Includes a glossary of terms and a bibliography of books in German, pp. 176-78.

Period Histories and Handbooks

Medieval and Renaissance

1275 Möller, Lieselotte. **Der Wrangelschrank und die verwandten süddeutsche Intarsien- mobel des 16.** Jahrhunderts. Berlin, Deutscher Verein fur Kunstwissenschaft, 1956. 194p. illus. index. LC A57-5068.

Scholarly study of south German intarsia furniture of the second half of the sixteenth century, illustrated with museum pieces with a thorough catalogue raisonné with bibliographical references. Comprehensive bibliography, pp. 156-76. A standard work in the field of Northern European Mannerist furniture and decorative arts.

1276 Trachsler, Walter. **Möbel der Frührenaissance aus der deutschsprachigen Schweiz, 1520 bis 1570.** 2d ed. Bern, P. Haupt, 1978. 16p. (text), 23 plates. ISBN 3258027137.

Survey history of Swiss furniture from 1520 to 1570 featuring examples in the Schweiz- erisches Landesmuseum in Zurich. A catalog with detailed descriptive entries and bibliographies accompany the plates illustrating 16 pieces, mostly large chests (Truhe) and cabinets (Schränke). Bibliography of basic works, p. 7.

Seventeenth and Eighteenth Centuries

1277 Brachert, Thomas, ed. **Beiträge zur Konstruktion und Restaurierung alter Möbel.** Munich, Callwey, 1986. 250p. illus. ISBN 3766708201.

Important collection of essays on the technique, materials, and restoration of German eighteenth-century furniture with particular attention given to the Roentgen workshop production.

Contents: Ein großer Rollschreibtisch von David Roentgen im Germanischen Nationalmuseum by H. W. Pape; Ein Toilettentisch von David Roentgen by E. Werwein; I Die Roentgen-Manufaktur: Markt, Technik und Innovation im 18. Jahrhundert by M. Stürmer; II Ein Pultschreibtisch von Abraham und David Roentgen im Germanischen Nationalmuseum; III Zwei Eckschränke von Abraham Roentgen aus den 1760er Jahren by M. Stürmer and E. Werwein; IV Ein Schreibschrank um 1775 von David Roentgen by T. Brachert; Technische Innovation der Roentgenwerkstatt by T. Brachert; Schildpatt—Verarbeitungstechniken und Imitationen by R. Vuilleumier; Schautullen und Kästchen von Abraham und David Roentgen by M. Stürmer and E. Werwein; Historische Klarlacke und Möbelpolituren by T. Brachert; Historische Holzbeizen by R. Vuilleumier; Historischen Holzbeizen by T. Brachert; Furniere und Farben der Ebenisten im 18. Jahrhundert by M. Stürmer; Werkstoff der Kunstschreinerei by R. Vuilleumier. Bibliographical references in the footnotes.

1278   Schaefer, Veronika. **Leo von Klenze: Möbel und Innenräume: ein Beitrag zur höfischen Wohnkultur in Spätempire.** Munich, R. Wolfle, 1980. 201p. illus. index. (Miscellanea Bavarica Monacensis, Heft 89) ISBN 3879131031.

Scholar study of the furniture and interior decoration designs by Leo von Klenze, architect for King Ludwig I of Bavaria. First part is an analysis of the historical background and influences on Klenze's furniture style. Second part is a detailed catalog of his furniture. Extensive use of documentary sources. General bibliography, pp. 187-198, and further bibliography in the notes.

Abraham and David Roentgen, 1711-1793, 1743-1807

1279   Fabian, Dietrich. **Roentgenmöbel aus Neuwied: Leben und Werk von Abraham und David Roentgen.** Bad Neustadt, Internationale Akademie für Kunstwissenschaft, 1986. 435p. illus. index.

Comprehensive, scholarly monograph on the furniture of Abraham and David Roentgen with an extraordinary collection of plates and measured drawings all with detailed descriptive notes. Contents: Neuwied im 18. Jahrhundert; Roentgen und die Herrnhuter Brüdergemeinde; Das Leben Abraham Roentgens; Das Leben David Roentgens; Das Werk Abraham und David Roentgens in Bilder und Beschreibungen: I, Mehrzwecktische; II, Tische und Flachschreibtische; III, Klapp- und Rollschreibtisch; IV, Kommoden und Kommodenschränke; V, Schreibkommoden und Aufsatzschreibkommoden; VI, Kabinettschränke; VII, Schreibschränke; VIII, Uhren, Spielwerke und Klaviere; IX, Eckschränkchen, Aufsatzschränkechen, Hundertschubladenschränke, Türmodell; X, Sitzmöbel; XI, Marketeriewandtafeln und Marketeriebilder; XII, Kästchen (Schatullen); XIII, Mitarbeiter und Nachfolger der Roentgenmanufaktur, Werke, Beschreibungen und Kurzbiographien; Stammbaum der Kunstschreinerfamilie Roentgen. Appendices with extracts from documents. An important catalogue raisonné.

1280   Greber, Josef M. **Abraham und David Roentgen. Möbel für Europa: Werdegang, Kunst und Technik einer deutschen Kabinett-Manufaktur.** Starnberg, J. Keller, 1980. 2v. illus. ISBN 3780801264. (Möbelkunst im 18. Jahrhundert, Band 1).

Comprehensive, scholarly monograph on the furniture of Abraham and David Roentgen. Band 1: Text; Band 2: plates. Contents to Band 1: Europäische Möbelkunst im 18. Jahrhundert by H. Jedding; Erste Arbeitsphase: Gründung einer kleinen Kunstschreinerei duruch Abraham Roentgen 1742 in der Herrnhutter Gemeine in Herrnhaag, Wetterau; Herstellung geschnizter und intarsierter Möbel nach englischem Vorbild, einfacher, holtstechnischer Innenausbau, Schließung der Werkstatt 1750; Zweiter Arbeitsphase: Ubersiedlung Abraham Roentgen nach Neuwied. Aufbau einer Kunstmöbel-Manufaktur zwischen 1750 und 1764; Modelle mit Schnizereien, Einlagen aus Furnieren, Elfenbein und Buntmetallen in reicherer Ausführung, Differenzierung der holztztechnischen Inneneinrichtungen und beweglichen Teile; Dritte Arbeitsphase: Finanzielle

Krise, Spannungen zwischen Roentgen und der Brüdergemiene, großen Hamburger Lotterie; neue Möbelformen, Weiterentwicklung der reichen Inneneinrichtungen, Aufkommen und Blüte farbig gravierter Intarisien; Vierte Arbeitsphase: Übernahmte der Leitung der Manufaktur duruch David Roentgen, 1779 Brechung der europäischen Vorrangstellung der Pariser Ebenisten, Heranziehung bedeutender Mitarbeiter wie Januarius Zick und Peter Kinzing; Möbel von höchsten Rang, komplizierte und vielseitige Inneneinrichtungen, Einführung neuer malerischer Instarsien im Mosaikverfahren; Fünfte Arbeitsphase: Höchste schöpferische Leistungsfähigkeit der Manufaktur zwischen 1780 und 1790; bisherige Möbelarten, Konstruktion und Inneausbau in gleicher Qualität und Bedeutung, künstlerische Instarsien und vergoldete Bronze als Oberflächenschmuck noch nebeneinander, später ohne Intarsien; Sechte Arbeitsphase: Auflösung der Manufaktur durch David Roentgen zwischen 1791 und 1795 aus vorwiegend religiösen Beweggründen und wegen kriegrischer Ereignisse, Nachfolge-Werkstätten in Berlin, in Weimer und in Barunschweig. Large corpus of plates with measured darwings is organized in the six "Arbeitsphase" of the text. General bibliography, pp. 280-283, and extensive bibliography in the notes and catalog. Standard work of Roentgen.

1281 Huth, Hans. **Roentgen Furniture**. London, Southeby Parke Bernet, 1974. 108p. illus. index. ISBN 0856670030.

First published as *Abraham und David Roentgen und ihre Neuwieder Möbelwerkstatt* (Berlin, Deutschen Verein für Kunstwissenschaft, 1928). Scholarly study of the furniture of Abraham and David Roentgen by a leading expert in European decorative arts of the eighteenth century. Contents: I, The Life of Abraham and David Roentgen; II, Neuwied Furniture; III, Workshop and Fabrique; Notable Workmen of the Roentgen Workshop (a dictionary of cabinet makers in Neuwied with bibliographical references at the end of the entries). Corpus of 273 pieces illustrated in excellent plates with descriptive notes. Appendix with extracts from documents including invoices of orders for furniture by Catherine II of Russia dated 1786 and Friedrich Wilhelm II dated 1786. Several excellent color plates have been added to this translation edition. Remains a standard monograph on the Roentgens.

Nineteenth Century

1282 Bahns, Jörn. **Biedermeier-Möbel. Entstehung-Zentren-Typen**. Munich, Keyser, 1979. 171p. illus. index. ISBN 3874051072.

Comprehensive history of Biedermeier-style furniture throughout the German-speaking countries. Contents: Biedermeier: Enstehung und Geschichte des Wortes; Biedermeier als Möbelstil; Typen-und Formengeschichte; Neo-Biedermeier um 1900. Glossary and selected bibliography, pp. 163-66.

1283 Bahns, Jörn. **Zwischen Biedermeier und Jugendstil. Möbel im Historismus**. Munich, Keyser, 1987. 219p. illus. ISBN 3874051781.

Sequel to (1282). Traces the history of furniture in the German-speaking countries from 1840 to 1900 with emphasis on the cultural context of the array of revival styles. Contents: Historismus in der Möbelkunst; Entwicklungslinien und Bedingungen; Die Situation um nach 1840; Die Weltausstellungen und ihre Auswirkungen; Die Rolle der Architekten und Entwerfer; Materialien und Surrogate—Luxus—und Massenproduktion; Möbelkunst 1840 bis 1900: Neugotik, Zweites Rokoko, Neorenaissance, Neubarock und Dittes Rokoko, Einflüsse jenseits der "klassischen" europäischen Stile: Exoticism, Volkskunst und Regionalstile; Wohungsausstattung; Abwehr vom Historismus. Bibliography, pp. 208-211, contains separate listing of contemporary catalogs.

1284 Himmelheber, Georg. **Biedermeier Furniture**. London, Faber and Faber, 1973. 115p. illus. index. LC 74-168702.

Concise history of Biedermeier furniture by a leading German expert. Contents: 1, Towards a Definition of the Biedermeier Style; 2, The Formal Vocabulary of the Biedermeier Style; 3, Cabinet-makers; 4, Regional Characteristics and Regional Cabinet-makers; 5, Upholstery; 6, Craftsmanship in Biedermier Furniture; 7, The Aftermath. Appendix: The Introduction of Freedom of Trade in Bavaria. Contains 115 plates with descriptive captions and bibliographical references. Bibliography, pp. 104-105.

1285 Pressler, Rudolf, and Robin Straub. **Biedermeier-Möbel**. 2d ed. Munich, Battenberg, 1989. 204p. illus. index. ISBN 387045220X.

Collector's handbook of German and Austrian furniture in the Biedermeier style. Collection of 430 illustrations of pieces with descriptive captions that include price ranges. Content: "Biedermeier"—Eine Karikatur gibt jener Zeit ihren Namen: Der Möbelstil, Das Möbel—Typen; Werterhalt durch Restaurierung und Pflege; Das Biedermeier-Möbel in der Auktion; Fachwortverzeichis; Anmerkungen zum Katalogteil und den Preisangaben; Katalog-Bildteil (arranged by type of furniture). Basic bibliography, p. 204.

1286 Luthmer, Ferdinand. **Empire-und Biedermeiermöbel aus Schlösser und Bürgerhäuser**. Frankfurt am Main, Frankfurter Verlags-Anstalt, 1923. 26p. 120ls (plates).

Survey of German furniture and interior decoration during the first half of the nineteenth century. Good collection of plates illustrating museum pieces and historic interiors.

1287 Zweig, Marianne. **Zweites Rokoko: Innenraume und Hausrat in Wien um 1830-1860**. Vienna, Schroll, 1924. 4p. (text). 46p. (plates). LC 25-810.

Pictorial survey of Viennese furniture and interior decoration in the neo-Rococo style that flourished between 1830 and 1860.

Thonet Furniture

1288 Bangert, Albrecht. **Thonet-Möbel; die Geschichte einer grossen Erfindung**. Munich, W. Heyne, 1979. 159p. illus. index. ISBN 3453413067.

Collector's history and handbook of the furniture made by the Thonet firm in the nineteenth century. Contents: Caféhausmöbel; Die Bugholztechnik schafft einen Möbeltyp; Die Geschichte des Hauses Thonet; Parktische Hinweise für den Sammler: Die Hölzer, Die Geflecte; Die Verschraubungen, Stuhlbeine und Verstrebungen, Rückenlehnen, Sitzflächen aus Holz, Restauriengungsfragen. Appendix with reproduction of pages from the 1904 Thonet catalog. Basic bibliography, p. 156.

1289 Mang, Karl. **Thonet Bugholzmöbel. Von der handwerklichen Ferigung zur industriellen Produktion**. Vienna, Brandstätter, 1982.159p. illus. ISBN 385447010X.

Well-illustrated, introductory monograph on the bentwood furniture of the Viennese firm of Thonet. Contents: 1, Michael Thonet und die Erfindung des Bugholzverfahrens; 2, Handwerkliche Fertigung und Beginnende Massenproduktion; 3, Das klassische Bugholzmöbel un 1870; 4, Gebrüder Thonet als Weltweite Unternehmer: Die Produktion zur Zeit des Historismus; 5, Das Bugholzmöbel und die Pioniere der Modernen Architektur; 6, Die Entwicklung seit 1918: Thonet-Mundus-Bugholzmöbel im sozialen Wohnbau—Die Auseinandersetzung mit der modernen Architektur—Die Stahlrohrmöbelproduktion—Thonet Heute; 7, Bugholzmöbel in der Kunst—Bugholzmöbel al Symbol Danksagung; Die "Klassiker" der Bugholztühle. Comprehensive, classified bibliography, pp. 157-58, and additional references in the notes.

1290   Vegesack, Alexander von. **Das Thonet Buch**. Munich, Bangert, 1987. 192p. illus. index. ISBN 3925560092.

Well-illustrated survey of the furniture produced by the Thonet firm from its beginnings to the 1930s. Contents: Frühe Jahre in Boppard/Auf der Suche nach neuen Techniken und Produkten/Die "Bopparder Möbel"/Thonets erste Patentanträge/Thonets Begegnung mit Metternich/ Thonets Reise nach Wien und erste Erfolge/Pfändung der Werkstatt in Boppard/Johann Heinrich Belter; Thonet in Wien: Neubeginn in Wien/Die Liechtensteiner Stühle/Die ersten Modelle aus der Gumpendorfer Werkstatt/Die Weltaustellung 1851/ Der Konsumsessel Nr. 14/Thonet und seine bisher unbekannter Konkurrenz; Gebrüder Thonet: "Gebr. Thonet" auf Erfolgskur/Die Erste Fabrik/ Die industriellle Möbelproduktion/Bistritz und weitere Neugründungen/Die Thonetsche Verkaufsstrategie/Kritische Anmerkungen zur Modellentwicklung auf der Basis von Anczeigen, historischen Fotos und Katalogen; Gründerzeit: August Thonet und eine neue Generation von Bugholzmöbel/Der Katalog von 1885/ Zurück in die Renaissance; Jugendstil; Zwanziger/Dreissiger Jahre: Von Bugholz zum Stahlrohr; Holzbiegetechnik. General bibliography, pp. 186-89.

1291   Wilk, Christopher. **Thonet: 150 Years of Furniture**. New York, Barron's, 1980. 143p. illus. ISBN 0812053842.

Concise survey of the production of the Thonet furniture company from 1830 to the 1970s. Contents: Bending Wood: 1830-1922; Wood and Steel: 1922-1945; Postwar Thonet: Europe and the United States. Plates include photographs of actual pieces, factory activities, and reproductions of catalog pages and advertisements. Comprehensive bibliography with introductory remarks about archives and other sources, pp. 140-43, and additional bibliography in the notes.

See also Bugholzmöbel, *Meubles en bois courbe: Bent Wood Furniture.* (Stuttgart, Kramer, 1980. 208p. illus. ISBN 3782804546).

Twentieth Century

1292   Müller, Dorothee. **Klassiker des modernen Möbeldesign**. Munich, Keyser, 1980. 175p. illus. index. ISBN 3874051358.

History of furniture design in Austria and Germany from 1900 to 1910 with emphasis on the works of Otto Wagner, Adolf Loos, Josef Hoffmann, and Koloman Moser directed to the collector and enthusiast. Contents: Voraussetzungen: Die Folgen der industriellen Revolution, Situation in Österreich; Stilwende; Konstruktiver Jugendstil; Die Künstler; Schüler und Mitarbeiter; Firmen; Ratschläge für Sammler. Classified bibliography, pp. 170-72.

See also the museum catalog: *Furniture of about 1900 from Austria & Hungary in the Victoria & Albert Museum* (London, Victoria and Albert Museum, 1986. 93p. illus. index. ISBN 0948107480).

Otto Koloman Wagner, 1841-1918

1293   Asenbaum, Paul, et al. **Otto Wagner. Möbel und Innenräume**. Salzburg, Residenz Verlag, 1984. 311p. illus. index. ISBN 3701703841.

Three essays on the furniture and interior designs of Otto Wagner with a comprehensive catalog and corpus of plates. Contents: Otto Wagners Interieurs: Vom Glaz der französischen Könige zur Ostentation der "moderne weckmäßigkeit" by P. Haiko; Modernität und Fotschrift bei Otto Wagner by H. Lachmayer; Die Möbel Otto Wagners by P. Asenbaum and R. Zettl; Katalog by P. Asenbaum and R. Zettle. Bibliographical references in the notes and the catalog entries.

Folk Furniture

1294 Baur-Heinhold, Margarete. **Alte Bauernstuben: Dösen, Küchen, Kammern von den Alpen bis zur See**. 2nd ed. Munich, Callwey, 1980. 215p. illus. index. ISBN 3766705482.

Comprehensive, well-illustrated survey of folk furniture in the context of folk interiors throughout the German-speaking territories. Sixty-page introduction followed by 330 plates illustrating furnished folk interiors. Descriptive captions to the plates. Contents: Einleitung; Die oberdeutsche Stube; Die niederdeutsche Stube; Schlußbetrachtung. Comprehensive, classified bibliography, pp. 210-212.

1295 Deneke, Bernward. **Bauernmöbel; ein Handbuch fur Sammler und Liebhaber**. 3rd ed. Munich, Keyser, 1979. 408p. illus. index. ISBN 3874050106.

Comprehensive, authoritative history/handbook of folk furniture in German-speaking countries. Contents: Erster Theil: Zur Entdeckung und Erforschung der Bauermöbel; Die Möbel in ihrer Beziehung zum Haus und zu Gewohnheiten häuslichen Lebens; Zusammensetzung des Möbelbestandes; Das Verhältnis von unbeweglicher zu beweglicher Ausstattung; Die Hersteller der Bauermöbel; Sitzmöbel—Bänke und Stühle; Tische; Schlafstätten; Wiege; Truhen, Schrankmöbel; Kommoden; Schenschive, Bankshrank, Hörnschapp; Borde und Anrichten; Kleinmöbel; Uhren; Zu den Ziertechniken; Motive der Auszier; Zur Auszier der Möbel in einzelnen Gebieten; Quellen der Textzeichungen; Zweiter Theil: Bildmonographie; Konstruktionszeichnungen. Comprehensive, classified bibliography, pp. 380-92.

See also Ritz (1231,1232).

1296 Schmidt, Leopold. **Bauernmöbel aus Sudeutschland, Oesterreich und der Schweiz**. Vienna and Hanover, Forum, 1967. 207p. illus. index. LC 68-92690.

Authoritative survey of south German, Austrian, and German-Swiss folk furniture of the eighteenth and nineteenth centuries. Includes 150 black-and-white plates and 42 color plates with descriptive notes. Contents: Hausen und Wohnen: Die oberdeutschen Möbellandschaften: Schweiz: Hochalpenbereich, Wallis, Graubünden, Innerschweiz, Bern, Nordostschweiz; Vorarlberg; Allgäu; Oberschwaben; Alt-Württemberg; Südbaden; Elsaß; Pfalz; Odenwald/Mainfranken; Mittelfranken; Rhön; Oberfranken; Egerland; Oberpfalz; Oberbayern; Niederbayern; Böhmerwald; Oberösterreich; Niederösterreich; Burgenland; Steiermark; Kärnten; Krain; Salzburg; Tirol. Comprehensive, classified bibliography, pp. 191-197.

Great Britain

Dictionaries

General

1297 Ash, Douglas. **Dictionary of English Antique Furniture**. London, Muller, 1970. 164p. illus. LC 78-537012.

Concise dictionary covering major English furnituremakers and designers, materials and techniques, styles and periods, and decoration illustrated with line drawings. A similar but older work is: Penderel-Brodhurst, James G., and Edwin J. Layton. *A Glossary of English Furniture of the Historic Periods...* London, Murray, 1925. 196p. illus.

1298 Edwards, Ralph. **The Shorter Dictionary of English Furniture; from the Middle Ages to the Late Georgian Period**. London, Country Life, 1964. 684p. illus. LC 66-43510.

One-volume condensation and revision of Macquoid and Edward's dictionary (1299). Comprehensive dictionary of English furniture from the Middle Ages to the nineteenth century.

Covers types of furniture, styles, materials and techniques, decoration, furniture assessories, and major British furnituremakers and designers. Illustrated with museum pieces. Although lacking bibliographic references, Edward's dictionary is an authoritative reference work.

1299   Macquoid, Percy, and Ralph Edwards. **The Dictionary of English Furniture from the Middle Ages to the Late Georgian Period.** Rev. and enl. ed. by Ralph Edwards. London, Country Life, 1954. 3v. illus. Reprint: Woodbridge, Suffolk, Baron Pub., 1983. ISBN 0907462375.

First published in 1904. Comprehensive dictionary covering terms, techniques, materials, ornament, types, periods, style, cabinet makers and designers. Larger entries are signed. Well illustrated. No bibliography. The standard dictionary of English period furniture. For a condensed version see Edwards (1298).

See also D. Yarwood, *English Interiors* (160).

Biographical Dictionaries

1300   Gilbert, Christopher, and Geoffrey Beard, eds. **Dictionary of English Furniture Makers 1660-1840.** London, Furniture History Society, 1986. 1046p. illus. index. ISBN 0901286184.

Comprehensive dictionary of English furnituremakers active between 1660 and 1840 including clock makers, barometer case makers, picture frame makers, box makers, spinning-wheel makers and inlayers. Based on thorough examination of directories, newspapers, trade cards, price books, sale catalogs, and the manuscript material in the Victoria and Albert Museum Furniture Archive and other archives. Collection of plates showing makers' marks, signatures and labels precedes the alphabetical dictionary. The majority of entries are short and refer to makers named in a few records. The longer entries on major figures also emphasize the information culled from records and do not, as a rule, refer to the style or other features of the maker's furniture.

1301   Heal, Ambrose. **The London Furniture Makers from the Restoration to the Victorian Era 1660-1840.** London, Portman Books, 1988. 276p. illus. index. ISBN 0713459840.

Reprint of 1953 edition (London, Batsford). Comprehensive dictionary of cabinetmakers active in London between 1660 and 1840. Includes gilders, carvers, and upholsterers. Based on registries and advertisements—many of which are illustrated—the entries are brief, often only giving the date and address. Appendix: "Old English Furniture and Its Makers: The Problem of Identification" by R. W. Symonds is illustrated with pieces bearing the name of the maker. No bibliography.

General History and Handbooks

1302   Beard, Geoffrey W. **The National Trust Book of English Furniture.** New York, Viking in association with the National Trust, 1985. 295p. illus. index. ISBN 0670801410.

Concise but authoritative survey of English furniture from circa 1500 to the 1930s. Emphasis is on the placement and use of furniture in various settings and on the trade of the furniture maker. Pieces and interiors illustrated are from the National Trust collections. Contents: Part One; The Trade: 1, The Craftsmen and the Workshops; 2, Methods and Techniques; 3, The Commission; 4, Decorative Styles. Part Two: The Furniture: 5, For the Crown and Court; 6, For Gentlemen; 7, For Servants; 8, Out of Doors. Appendices with dictionary of wood and list of cabinetmakers and designers. General bibliography, pp. 270-73, and additional bibliography in the notes.

1303   Beard, Geoffrey W., and Judith Goodison. **English Furniture, 1500-1840.** Oxford, Phaidon-Christie's, 1987. 302p. illus. index. ISBN 0714880299.

Well-illustrated collector's history/handbook of English furniture from 1500 to 1840 based on pieces sold at Christie's. Prices paid for the pieces illustrated are given in a list at the end. Each period is introduced by a brief historical sketch. This is followed by plates of pieces arranged by type of furniture. Detailed descriptive captions accompany the plates. General bibliography, pp. 285-86. Contents: 1, Oak and Walnut 1500-1700; 2, Queen Anne and Early Georgian 1700-1727; 3, Mahogany and Gilded Pine 1727-1754; 4, Chippendale and the Rococo 1754-1765; 5, Classical Origins 1765-1790; 6, Sheraton and Elegant Taste 1790-1805; 7, The Regency Style 1805-1840.

1304   Cescinsky, Herbert. **English Furniture from Gothic to Sheraton**. New York, Crown, 1958. 406p. illus. index. Reprint: New York, Dover, 1968. LC 68-19173.

An old, standard collector's history/handbook of English furniture and woodwork from the late Middle Ages through the eighteenth century. Includes chapter on lacquer ware and needlepoint. Comprehensive but poor quality collection of plates of buildings, interiors, drawings, and pieces of furniture (many representative of examples accessible to the collector).

1305   Fastnedge, Ralph. **English Furniture Styles from 1500 to 1830**. Baltimore, Md., Penguin, 1967. 321p. illus. index. LC 64-3941.

Comprehensive history of English furniture from the late Gothic period through the Regency style illustrated with plates and line drawings of museum quality pieces. Useful glossary and list of major cabinetmakers and designers. Notes to the chapters refer to further literature. Contents: 1, The Period of Oak (from the Early 16th Century to the End of the Commonwealth); 2, The Early Walnut Period (1600-90); 3, The Later Walnut Period (1690-1720); 4, Lacquer Furniture with Some Mention of Gilt and Silvered Furniture and Gesso; 5, The Early Georgian Period (1720-40); 6, The Pre-"Director" Period (1740-54); 7, The Post "Director" Period; 8, Robert Adam—the Classical Revival; 9, Hepplewhite: 'The Cabinet-maker and Upholsterer's Guide,' 3d ed., 1794; 10, Thomas Sheraton (1751-1806); 11, The Regency Period.

1306   Hayward, Charles H. **English Period Furniture**. Rev. and enl. ed. New York, Scribner's, 1971. 270p. illus. index. LC 77-155926.

First published in 1936. Concise history of English furniture from the Tudor period to 1880 with an outline of the development of French furniture from Louis XIV to the Empire period. Emphasis is on the construction of period furniture and a good collection of measured drawings and special analysis of chair construction is given in the appendices. Illustrated with black and white plates of documented pieces in museums and line drawings. Because of its emphasis, Hayward's history remains a useful work for the collector and restorer.

See also the author's craftsman handbook: *Antique Furniture Designs* (New York, Scribner's, 1979. 125p. illus. index. ISBN 0684163020).

1307   Learoyd, Stan. **A Guide to English Antique Furniture Construction & Decoration, 1500-1910**. New York, Van Nostrand Reinhold, 1981. 128p. illus. index. ISBN 0442259522.

Collector's handbook of English antique furniture with emphasis on materials and construction as a means to authentication and dating. Color illustrations of types of furniture woods on the fly leaves. No bibliography.

1308   Macdonald-Taylor, Margaret S. **English Furniture from the Middle Ages to Modern Times**. New York, Putnam, 1966. 299p. illus. index. LC 66-14485.

Concise, popular survey with chapters on historical development and major furniture types. Chronological table, glossary, and bibliography of basic books.

Similar works: Dean, Margery, *English Antique Furniture, 1450-1850.* (New York, Universe, 1969. 109p. illus. LC 69-17308), Stafford, Maureen, *British Furniture Through the*

Ages (New York, Coward-McCann, 1966. 112p. illus. index. LC 66-10846), Tomlin, Maurice, *English Furniture; an Illustrated Handbook* (London, Faber and Faber, 1972. 180p. illus.).

1309   Macquoid, Percy. **A History of English Furniture**. London, Lawrence & Bullen, 1904-08. 4v. illus. index. Reprint: New York, Dover, 1972. LC 76-158732.

Old, comprehensive history of English furniture from the Tudor period to the early nineteenth century. Many parts are out-of-date but the large collection of plates and the author's connoisseurship continue to recommend Marquoid's work as a standard history. Contents: v. 1, The Age of Oak; v. 2, The Age of Walnut; v. 3, The Age of Mahogany; v. 4, The Age of Satinwood.

1310   Sparkes, Ivan G. **An Illustrated History of English Domestic Furniture, 1100-1837: the Age of the Craftsman**. Bourne Ends, England, Spurbooks, 1980. 16p. illus. index. ISBN 0904978346.

Survey history of English domestic furniture directed to the collector. Arrangement is by types of furniture with chapters on furnituremaking and upholstery. Glossary of terms, bibliography, p. 155, lists books on specific furniture types.

1311   Strange, Thomas A. **A Guide to Collectors: 3,500 Illustrations: English Furniture, Decoration, Woodwork and Allied Arts...** London, McCorquodale & Co., and B. T. Batsford, 1986. 368p. illus.

Reprint of 1903 edition (London, Simpkin, Marshall, Hamilton. LC 03-17271). Large collection of illustrations in line drawing of pieces of English furniture and interior design dating from the seventeenth century to the early nineteenth century. Arrangement is chronological and then by designer and by type. The illustrations are largely taken from contemporary sources and the text often supplies extracts from the texts of those sources making Strange's compilation a valuable source for an overview of the history of design theory. The large number of illustrations also commends the work to collectors.

1312   Wills, Geoffrey. **English Furniture, 1550-1760**. Garden City, N.Y., Doubleday, 1971. 256 p. illus. index. LC 74-180909.

———. **English Furniture, 1760-1900**. Garden City, N.Y., Doubleday, 1971. 256p. illus. index.

Popular survey of English furniture from the time of Elizabeth I through the late Victorian period. Well illustrated with examples from museums and private collections.

See also the exhibition catalog: Brett, Gerard. *English Furniture and Its Setting*. Toronto, Univ. of Toronto Press, 1965. LC 65-9809.

Types of Furniture

1313   Cotton, Bernard D. **The English Regional Chair**. Woodbridge, Antique Collectors' Club, 1990. 511p. illus. index. ISBN 185149023X.

Comprehensive handbook of the varieties of chairs made in the various regions of England from the early eighteenth century to the early twentieth century. Large number of illustrations with descriptive captions designed to aid the collector in placing and dating antique chairs. Photographic reproductions of makers' marks and stamped names as well as views of workshops and portraits of chair makers. Contents: 1, Introduction; 2, Thames Valley and the Chilterns; 3, North East Region; 4, East Anglia; 5, South West Region; 6, West Midland; 7, North West Region. Index of Regional Chair Makers and Turners 1700-1900 (arranged by the same regions). Bibliography, pp. 510-11. Not only an invaluable collector's guidebook, but also a compilation of information of great importance to the issue of regionalism in furniture history.

1314   Hinckley, F. Lewis. **Queen Anne & Georgian Looking Glasses.** New York, Washington Mews Books, 1987. 254p. illus. index. ISBN 0814734472.

Collection of 332 plates of English and American looking glasses from the eighteenth century and the early nineteenth century. Introductory essays: "The Comparative Proving System"; "The Importance of Looking Glasses"; "The Development of Dublin Looking Glasses"; "Distributors of Colonial and Early Federal Looking Glasses." Bibliographical references in the footnotes.

1315   Sparkes, Ivan G. **The Windsor Chair: An Illustrated History of a Classic English Chair.** Bourne End, Spurbooks, 1975. 143p. illus. index. ISBN 0902875620.

See also the museum handbook: *English Chairs,* by R. Edwards. 3rd ed. (London, Victoria and Albert Museum, 1970. 29p. text, 130 plates. ISBN 0112900313).

Period Histories and Handbooks

Medieval to 1760

1316   Cescinsky, Herbert, and Ernest R. Gribble. **Early English Furniture and Woodwork.** London, Routledge, 1922. 2v. illus. index. LC 23-5371.

Comprehensive history of English furniture and carpentry from the fourteenth to the end of the seventeenth centuries. Contents: v. 1, The Dissolution of Monasteries; the Early Woodworker: His Life, Tools and Methods; The Plan of the Early Tudor House; The Development of the English Timber Roof; Gothic Woodwork and Colour Decoration; Timber Houses, Porches and Doors; The English Staircase; Wood Panellings and Mantels; Bedsteads and Their Development; v. 2, The Development of the Chest and Standing Cupboard; The Progression of English Oak Tables; The Development of the English Oak Chair; Walnut Chairs from 1660 to 1700; English Marqueterie; Domestic Clocks; English Lacquer Work. An old but still-standard history with a large collection of plates.

1317   Chinnery, Victor. **Oak Furniture.** Woodbridge, Antique Collectors' Club, 1979. 579p. illus. index. ISBN 0902028618.

Comprehensive history of English and New England furniture in oak from the Middle Ages to the eighteenth century designed for collectors but filled with much information of interest to scholars of the history of furniture. Contents: I, Time and Place—The Historical Context; 2, Makers and Methods—the Practical Context; 3, Form and Language—The Functional Types and Nomenclature; 4, The Stylistic Themes—A Decorative and Regional Chronology; Appendix I: Extracts from a Description of England by William Harrison; Appendix II: Extracts from an Academie or Store House of Armory & Blazon by Randle Holm; Appendix III: The Life of Humprehy Beckham of Salisbury; Appendix IV: Selections from the Probate Inventories of Provincial Woodworkers; Appendix V: Distribution of Population in the British Isles 1662; Appendix IV: The Private and Public Collector. Unclassified bibliography, pp. 570-71.

1318   Jourdain, Margaret. **English Decoration and Furniture of the Early Renaissance (1500-1650)...** London, Batsford, 1924. 305p. illus. index. LC 25-4332.

In the series: "The Library of Decorative Art." Continued by Lenygon (1319). Brief introductory text followed by a valuable collection of plates illustrating historic interiors, their decorative details, pieces of furniture, and other examples of interior decoration.

1319   Lenygon, Francis H. **Furniture in England from 1660 to 1760.** London, Batsford, 1920. 300p. illus. index.

Old, standard survey of English furniture dating between 1660 and 1760. Brief text with a large collection of still-valuable plates. Contents: I, The Dutch and French Influences, 1660-1715; II, The Venetian Influence, 175-1740 (The Early Georgian Period); III, The French Rococo, Chinese and Gothic Fashions, and the Classical Reaction, 1740-1760 (The Later Georgian Period); IV, Chairs, Stools, and Settees, with Their Upholstery; V, Beds, Window Corniches, and Curtains; VI, Tables; VII, Bookcases, Cupboards, and Writing Tables; VIII, Pedestals and Brackets; IX, Stands and Cabinets; X, Mirrors; XI, Clock-cases; XII, Veneer and Marquetry; XIII, Gesso; XIV, Silver and Silver-Mounted Furniture; XV, Lacquer. Occasional bibliographical footnote. Companion volume by the same author and in the same series ("The Library of Decorative Art") covers interior design and decoration in England during the same period: *Decoration in England from 1660-1770* (London, Batsford, 1920. 300p. illus. index).

1320   Lymonds, Robert W. **Veneered Walnut Furniture, 1660-1760**. London, Tiranti, 1946. 32p. illus. LC 47-2802.

Pictorial survey with brief introductory essay and descriptive notes to the plates.

1321   Wolsey, Samuel W., and R. W. Luff. **Furniture in England: The Age of the Joiner**. New York, Praeger, 1969. 104p. illus. index. LC 69-17082.

Handbook for the beginning collector of English furniture dating from 1550 to 1660. Chapters devoted to types of furniture follow a brief historical introduction. Glossary of terms. No bibliography.

1322   Symonds, Robert W. **English Furniture from Charles II to George II...** Woodbridge, Antique Collectors' Club, 1980. 269p. illus. index. ISBN 0902028952.

First published in 1929. History of English furniture from 1660 to 1760 designed to aid the collector. Important chapter on fakes. *See also* the author's *Furniture Making in Seventeenth and Eighteenth Century England: An Outline for Collectors*. London, Connoisseur, 1955. 238p. illus. index.

See also P. Eames. *Furniture in England, France and the Netherlands from the Twelfth to the Fifteenth Century* (1146).

1760 to 1830

1323   Edwards, Ralph, and Margaret Jourdain. **Georgian Cabinet-Makers**. 3rd ed. London, Country Life, 1955. 247p. illus. index. LC 55-13859. Reprinted 1962.

Important repertory of biographies of English cabinetmakers and allied craftsmen active during the eighteenth century with extensive use of and excerpts from documentary sources. Divided into Cabinet-makers, Joiners, and Carvers and Lesser-known and Minor Cabinet-makers, Joiners and Carvers. Bibliographical references in the footnotes. Collection of plates of signed or attributed pieces. Appendix with extracts from the Great Wardrobe Accounts relative to the work of Gerreit Jensen, Thomas Roberts, John Gumley and James Moore, William Vile, John Bradburn, William France, and William Gates.

1324   Hinckley, F. Lewis. **Hepplewhite, Sheraton & Regency Furniture**. New York, Washington Mews Book, 1987. 239p. illus. index. ISBN 0814734464.

Important corpus of plates of British furniture of the eighteenth and early nineteenth centuries. The introductory text puts forward the idea that the majority of the pieces of "period" furniture in the Hepplewhite, Sheraton and Regency styles were made in Dublin, not any center in England. This questionable premise does not diminish the usefulness of the plates for collectors of English furniture.

1325 Hughes, Therle. **Old English Furniture**. New York, Praeger, 1969. 201p. illus. index. LC 69-19858.

Concise survey of English furniture from the Middle Ages to the early nineteenth century. Directed to the collector with emphasis on stylistic and construction features as they relate to dating and authentication. Arrangement is by types, e.g., chests of drawers, chairs, tables, beds and cradles, cupboards, dining room display furniture, cabinets and bureaux, corner cupboards, mirrors, dressing tables, tripod furniture, long case clocks. Illustrated with pieces of the type accessible to the collector. No bibliography.

1326 Jourdain, Margaret. **English Decoration and Furniture of the Later XVIIIth Century (1760-1820): An Account of its Development and Characteristic Forms**. London, Batsford, 1922. 269p. illus. index. LC 23-2655.

In the series: "Library of Decorative Art," continuation of Lenygon (1319). Brief introductory text followed by a valuable collection of plates illustrating historic interiors and their decorative details and pieces of furniture and other interior furnishings. Bibliographical references in the footnotes.

1327 Musgrave, Clifford. **Regency Furniture, 1800 to 1830**. 2nd rev. ed. London, Faber and Faber, 1970. 157p. illus. index. LC 73-593790.

Concise but authoritative history of English furniture between 1800 and 1830. Contents: Henry Holland: French and Classical Origins; Thomas Sheraton and the New Influences; Thomas Hope and Classical Purity; George Smith and Fashionable Taste before 1811; The Egyptian Taste; The Chinese Taste; The French Taste in the Later Regency; Fashionable Taste after 1811; The Gothic Style; London and the Victorian Threshold; Types of Furniture; Processes and Materials. Glossary and appendix with entries from the Deepene sale catalog of 1917. General bibliography, p. 149.

1328 Collard, Frances. **Regency Furniture**. Woodbridge, Antique Collectors' Club, 1985. 346p. illus. index. ISBN 0907462510.

Comprehensive history of furniture in Britain from 1800 to 1830 intended for the sophisticated collector. Illustrated with many contemporary Regency designs and views of interiors. Contents: 1, Henry Holland, French Taste and Neoclassicism; 2, Thomas Sheraton and the Pattern Books of the Early Regency; 3, Thomas Hope and the Greek Revival; 4, French Influence in the Later Regency; 5, Historic Revivals; 6, Exotics and Rustics; 7, The Regency Revival; 8, Upholstery; 9, Techniques and Materials. Appendix with biographies of major designers and craftsmen. Bibliographical footnotes and comprehensive, classified bibliography including sources, pp. 335-37.

Chippendale

1329 Brackett, Oliver. **Thomas Chippendale, a Study of His Life, Work and Influence**. London, Hodder and Stoughton, 1924. 281p. illus. index. LC 25-3095.

Older, once-standard monograph. Contents: I, Social England in the Eighteenth Century; II, The Career of Thomas Chippendale; III, The Style in Vogue Previous to the Publication of the "Director"; IV, "The Gentleman and Cabinet-maker's Director"; V, The Chinese and Gothic Fashions; VI, The Influence of Robert Adam; VII, David Garrick and Madame Cornelys; VIII, Chippendale's Original Drawings; IX, Style, Workmanship and Material; X, Opinions and Criticism; Appendices with transcripts of documents relative to major commissions. Bibliography, pp. 142-44.

1330   Chippendale, Thomas. **The Gentleman and Cabinet-makers Director**. 3rd ed. New York, Towse Pub. Co., 1938. Reprinted New York, Dover, 1966. LC 66-24135.

Reprint of the third edition published by Chippendale in 1762. This reprint has a photographic supplement and biographical sketch by N.I. Bienenstock.

1331   Coleridge, Anthony. **Chippendale Furniture: The Work of Thomas Chippendale and His Contemporaries in the Rococo Taste: Ville, Cobb, Langlois, Channon, Hallett, Ince and Mayhew, Lock, Johnson and Others, circa 1745-1765**. London, Faber and Faber, 1968. 229p. illus. ISBN 0571084052.

In the series: "Faber Monographs on Furniture." Authoritative history of English furniture design between 1745 and 1765 emphasizing the lives and work of Thomas Chippendale and furniture makers in Chippendale's circle. Contains extensive extracts from documentary sources. Contents: I, Vile, Cobb, Langlois, Channon, and Hallet; II, English Rococo Designers (excluding Chippendale); III, Thomas Chippendale (1719-79): Part I: His Life, Part II: The Director; Part III: His Clients; IV, Some Leading Cabinet-makers Working in the Director Tradition. Includes 420 plates with descriptive notes. Select bibliography, pp. 216-19, specialized literature listed in the notes to the plates.

1332   Gilbert, Christopher. **The Life and Work of Thomas Chippendale**. London, Studio/Vista, 1978. 2v. illus. index. ISBN 0289708397.

Comprehensive, scholarly monograph on Chippendale. First volume contains text, the second, plates. Contents: Part I: Chippendale's Life and Business: 1, Biographical Essay, 2, Commercial Enterprise, 3, Branches of the Business; Part II, Chippendale's Furniture Designs: 4, The Director—promotion, publication and revision, 5, The Manuscript Designs, 6, Stylistic Development; Part III: Chippendale's Patrons and Furniture; Commisions in Chronological Order. Appendices with documents. Glossary of Terms used by Chippendale. Comprehensive, classified bibliography, pp. 310-15. A standard work on Chippendale.

Hepplewhite

1333   Hepplewhite and Company. **The Cabinet-maker and Upholsterer's Guide**. New York, Dover, 1969. 8p.(intro), 24p. 125 plates. LC 69-19164.

Facsimile reprint of the third edition (1794) of Hepplewhite's guide. Introduction by Joseph Aronson. General bibliography of twentieth-century works on Hepplewhite, p. ix.

1334   Musgrave, Clifford. **Adam and Heppelwhite and Other Neo-Classical Furniture**. London, Faber and Faber, 1966. 223p. illus. index. LC 66-72245.

Authoritative history of English furniture in the Neo-classical styles during the last third of the eighteenth century. Contents: The Adam Revolution; Adam's Furniture Designs and the Development of His Style; Adam and the French; Furniture in the Adam Houses; Hepplewhite and the Adam Dissemination; The Adam Craftsmen; Types of Furniture; Materials and Processes. Glossary. Bibliography, pp. 175-178, and bibliographical references in the notes. Detailed notes to the illustrations.

Thomas Johnson, 1714-c.1778

1335   Hayward, Helena. **Thomas Johnson and English Rococo**. London, Tiranti, 1964. 45p. (text), 191p. (plates). LC 64-55935.

Facsimile of Thomas Johnson's *Collection of Designs* (1758) with authoritative introduction. Contents of the introduction: I, Distortion and Prejudice; II, English Rococo: The First Phase; III, Thomas Johnson: A Fresh Vision; IV, Johnson's Influence as Designer; V, Thomas Johnson,

Carver; VI, The Last Years. Bibliographical references in the footnotes. Survey of medieval furniture illustrated with drawings made by the author from depictions of furniture in various medieval works of art. Arrangement is by type of furniture. Descriptive notes accompany the drawings. No bibliography.

Sheraton

1336   Fastnedge, Ralph. **Sheraton Furniture**. London, Faber and Faber, 1962. 224p. illus. index. Reprint: Woodbridge, Antique Collectors' Club, 1983. ISBN 0907462472.

Comprehensive monograph on the furniture in the Sheraton style made in England, and chiefly in London, during the last decade of the eighteenth century and early years of the first decade of the following century, based on a close examination of extant pieces and published and unpublished designs by Thomas Sheraton and others. Contents: Introduction; Thomas Sheraton, "The Drawing Book"; Some Contemporary Makers; Woods and Decorative Processes; The Furniture of the "Drawing Book"; Postscript. Detailed, descriptive notes on the plates. General bibliography, p, 115; specialized literature in the footnotes.

1337   **Sheraton Furniture Designs**, from the *Cabinet-maker's and Upholsterer's Drawing-book, 1791-94* with a preface by Ralph Edwards. London, Tiranti, 1949. 12p (text), 92p. (plates). LC 46-612.

Abridged edition of Sheraton's "Drawing Book" first published in 1791. A facsimile reprint of the 3rd edition, 1802, which contains the "Appendix" and "An Accompaniment" was published by Batsford in 1895.

1830 to 1915

1338   Agius, Pauline. **British Furniture, 1880-1915**. Woodbridge, Antique Collectors' Club, 1978. 195p. illus. index. LC 78-326810. ISBN 0902028766.

Comprehensive collector's guide to furniture made in Britain from 1880 to 1915. Contents: 1, The Scene 1880-1915 and Its Prehistory; 2, Continuing Victorian Forms; 3, Fashionable Reproduction Furniture 1880-1915; 4, Original Designs and Art Furniture; 5, Progressive Furniture c. 1885-1910; 6, Woods, Finishes and Some Fashions and Innovations; 7, Exact Copies and Fakes; 8, The Furniture Trade 1880-1915; Postscript 1915-40. Illustrated with pieces in museums, private collections and the antique trade. Large number of very valuable reproductions of contemporary sales catalogs. Comprehensive, classified bibliography, pp. 186-190.

1339   Aslin, Elizabeth. **Nineteenth Century English Furniture**. New York, Yoseloff, 1962. 93p. illus. index. LC 63-946.

History of furniture in Great Britain from late Regency to Art Nouveau, one of the first to attempt to set forth the originality of the works of the major Victorian designers by relating surviving pieces with records and other documentary evidence. Contents: Early Victorian Furniture; Exhibitions and Their Influence; Marble, Metal, Papier Maché and New Methods of Decoration; Woodcarving; William Morris and Company; Art Furniture and Aesthetic Movement; The Arts and Crafts; Art Nouveau; Cabinet-makers—A brief Guide. Bibliography, pp. 89-90, list books, periodicals, and contemporary exhibition catalogs.

1340   Joel, David. **Furniture Design Set Free. The British Furniture Revolution from 1851 to the Present Day**. London, Dent, 1969. 108p. illus. index. ISBN 060038117.

First published in 1953 as *The Adventure of British Furniture*. Important survey of British furniture design and manufacture from 1851 to the 1960s. Contents: The Victorian Background; William Morris, 1834-96; Ernest Gimson, 1864-1919, and the Barnsleys; L'Art Nouveau and

Some Commercial Pioneers; The Nineteen-Twenties; The Nineteen-Thirties; Furniture in War-time and Post-war Frustration; Design set Free; Recent and Contemporary British Furniture; The Designer Craftsmen. Appendices: Royal Influences; Some Diversions and Experiments; Notes on Some Furniture Timbers; Biographical Notes; We Beg to Differ. No bibliography.

1341   Joy, Edward. **English Furniture 1800-1851**. 2nd ed. London, Ward Lock, 1988. 318p. illus. index. ISBN 070636676X.

Comprehensive history of English furniture during the mid-Victorian period with emphasis on the relationship between furniture design and the history of taste. Contents: The Regency; 2, The Grecian, Egyptian and Chinese Tastes; 3, The Royal Furniture-Makers; 5, Interiors; 6, Patent Furniture; 7, The Structure of the Furniture Industry; 8, Materials and Methods; 9, The Great Exhibition, 1851. Well-illustrated with museum pieces, view of interiors, contemporary illustrations of manufacturing processes and designs. Bibliographical references in the notes.

1342   Symonds, Robert W., and B. B. Whineray. **Victorian Furniture**. London, Country Life, 1962. 232p. illus. index. LC 63-2076.

Survey of English furniture during the reign of Queen Victoria directed to the collector. Text includes many extracts from contemporary written sources. Contains 281 well-chosen illustrations with descriptive captions. Contents: 1, From Craft to Industry; 2, Furniture Styles up to 1867; 3, Furniture Styles after 1867; 4, The Victorian Home; 5, Techniques and Materials.

1915 to the Present

1343   Sparke, Penny. **Furniture: Twentieth-Century Design**. New York, Dutton, 1986. 112p. illus. index. ISBN 0525244131.

Pictorial survey of furniture design in Europe and America during the twentieth century. Contents: Part One: The Birth of the Modern Furniture Industry (1860-1914): 1, Britain and the Rise of the Mass Market; 2, Tradition and Mechanization in Europe; 3, The Democratization of Comfort in the USA; Part Two: Furniture for the Machine Age (195-1939): 4, Standard in European Furniture; 5, From Period to Modern Style in the USA; 6, British Furniture of Reaction; Part Three: Post-War Reconstruction (1940-1960): 7, America: Technique and Innovation; 8, Craft and Industry in Scandinavia; 9, The Birth of Designer Furniture; 10, From Utility to Contemporary; Part Four: Furniture for the Consumer Society (1961-1985): 11, The Challenge of Pop Culture; 12, From Conspicuous Consumption to "Anti-Furniture"; 13, Furniture in the Age of Pluralism. General bibliography, pp. 107-110.

Charles Rennie Mackintosh, 1868-1928

1344   Billcliffe, Roger. **Charles Rennie Mackintosh. The Complete Furniture, Furniture Drawings & Interior Designs**. 3rd ed. New York, Dutton, 1986. 272p. illus. index. ISBN 0525244964.

Important collection of illustrations of the furniture and interiors designed by Mackintosh. Brief introductory essay with bibliographical note, p. 23. 223, pages of plates arranged chronologically and with detailed descriptive captions that include bibliographies of the specialized literature. More important pieces have longer, catalog-like entries. An authoritative handbook.

Italy

General Histories and Handbooks

1345 Broscio, Valentino. **Il mobile italiano**. Rome, Editalia, 1971. 246p. illus. index. LC 72-877466.

Popular, pictorial handbook of Italian furniture from the Middle Ages to the twentieth century. Concise history and glossary of furniture terms are followed by section dedicated to particular types of furniture: cassoni, secretaries, credenzas, cabinets, tables, chairs, upholstered furniture. Bibliography of basic books, p. 237.

1346 Cera, Maurizio. **Il mobile italiano dal XVI al XIX secolo**. Milan, Longanesi, 1983. 294p. illus. LC 84-171149.

Pictorial handbook of Italian furniture from the sixteenth century to the end of the nineteenth century. Arrangement is by type of furniture. Plates of pieces that have recently been sold are featured with descriptive captions which include the price paid and date of auction. General bibliography, p. 291.

1347 Colombo, Silvao. **L'arte del legno e del mobile in Italia**. Busto Arsizio, Bramante, 1981. 335p. illus.

Well-illustrated survey of Italian furniture and interiors from the Middle Ages to the early nineteenth century with particular emphasis on the techniques of working and decorating wood (intarsia and marquetry). Large corpus of plates, many illustrating pieces of furniture accessible to the average collector. Appendices with glossary and bibliography, p. 335.

1348 Del Puglia, Raffaella, and Carlo Steiner. **Mobili e ambienti italiani dal gotico al floreale**. Milan, Bramate, 1963. 2v. illus. LC 67-120735.

Lavishly illustrated survey of Italian furniture from the Gothic period to the "floreale," i.e., Art Nouveau, style of the early twentieth century. Concise history followed by 621 plates with descriptive notes. No bibliography

1349 Eberlein, Harold D., and Roger W. Ramsdell. **The Practical Book of Italian, Spanish and Portuguese Furniture**. Philadelphia and London, Lippincott, 1927. 354p. illus. index. LC 27-25314.

An old, comprehensive survey of Italian, Spanish, and Portuguese furniture from the Renaissance to the end of the Neoclassical period. Contains 144 plates of pieces chiefly in private collections and with dealers. Descriptive captions. No bibliography.

1350 Ghelardini, Armando. **Il mobile italiano dal medioevo all'Ottocento**. Milan, Bramante, 1970. 154p. illus. index. LC 75-5512229.

Pictorial survey of Italian furniture from the Middle Ages to the end of the eighteenth century. Features 563 illustrations arranged by types. Contents: Cassoni e cassepanche; Credenze e cantonali; Cassettoni e cassettonicini; Cassettoni con alzata; Tavoli; Scrivanie; Armadi, liberie e vetrine; Ante e porte; Stipi e medaglieri; Letti; Mensole; Specchiere; Panche e divani; Seggiole e poltrone; Mobili diversi.

1351 Odom, William. **A History of Italian Furniture, From the Fourteenth to the Early Nineteenth Century**. Garden City, N.Y. Doubleday, 1918-19. 2v. illus. Reprint: New York, Archive Press, 1966. LC 67-10441.

Old, standard history of Italian furniture with an invaluable corpus of nearly 900 plates. Contents: Volume one: 1, Italian Gothic. The 14th and Early 15th Centuries; 2, The Early

Renaissance. The Second Half of the 15th Century; 3, The High Renaissance. The First Half of the 16th Century; 4, The Late Renaissance. The Second Half of the 16th Century. Volume 2: 1, The Baroque Style. The 17th Century; 2, The Rococo Styles. The First Half of the 18th Century; 4, The Empire Style. The Early 19th Century. No bibliography.

1352   Pinto, Piero. **Il mobile italiano dal XV al XIX secolo**. Novara, De Agnostini, 1981. 311p. illus. index.

General survey of Italian furniture from the fifteenth century to the beginning of the nineteenth century directed to the average collector. Illustrated with plates of museum pieces and line drawings of generic types. Arrangement is by region. Brief bibliography, p. 306.

1353   Puglia, Raffaello del, and Carlo Steiner. **Mobili e ambienti italiani dal gotico al floreale**. Milan, Bramante, 1963. 2v. illus.

Well-illustrated survey of Italian furniture from the Middle Ages to the Art Nouveau style (floreale style) of the early twentieth century. The 100-page introduction sketches the history of style in furniture and interior decoration. Features 621 plates with descriptive notes. No bibliography.

Period Histories and Handbooks

1354   Baccheschi, Edi. **Mobili intarsiati del sei e settecento in Italia**. Milan, Görlich, 1964. 131p. illus. LC 73-201244.

Pictorial survey of Italian furniture of the fifteenth and sixteenth centuries illustrated primarily with museum pieces and furniture in historic interiors. Plates with descriptive captions are arranged by types: Cassoni e cassapanche; Stalli corali; Sedie; Credenze; Armafdi; Letti; Porte; "Pezzi" diversi. No bibliography.

1355   Cito-Filomarino, Anna M. **L'ottocento: i mobili del tempo dei nonni dall'Impero al Liberty**. Milan, Gorlich, 1969. 255p. illus. index. LC 75-863251.

Pictorial survey of Italian furniture of the eighteenth century featuring museum pieces and historic interiors. Brief bibliography of basic books in Italian.

See also V. Broscio, *Mobili italiani dell' Ottocento*. Milan, Vallardi, 1964. 157p. illus. LC 67-57010.

1356   De Guttry, Irene. **Il mobile liberty italiano**. Bari, Laterza, 1983. 318p. illus. index. ISBN 8842022977.

Comprehensive history of Italian Art Nouveau furniture. Contents: Parte Prima: Storia del mobile italiano dell'eclettismo alla prima guerra: 1, Il mobile nell'Italia postunitaria; 2, La ricerca di un nuovo stile; 3, Gli anni Dieci; Appendice: Le reviste; Parte Seconda: Repertorio: 1, Ebanisti, mobilieri, disegnatoris; II, Anatlogia di mobili di artisti; III, Anonimi. The "Repertorio" contains detailed biographies of designers and craftsmen with bibliographical references. Comprehensive bibliography, pp.

1357   Mazzariol, Giuseppe. **Mobili italiani del Seicento e del Settcento**. Milan, Vallardi, 1963. 154p. illus. index. LC 66-80857.

Pictorial survey of Italian furniture and interiors of the seventeenth and eighteenth centuries. Contains a 30-page introduction followed by 106 pages of plates with descriptive captions. Basic bibliography, p. 153.

1358   Morazzoni, Giuseppe. **Il mobile neoclassico italiano**. Milan, Görlich, 1955. 62p. (text), 335 plates. LC A56-2182.

Authoritative survey history of Italian furniture from 1768 to 1820 arranged by place—i.e., Rome, Turin, Genoa, Parma, Florence, Naples, Milan and Venice. "Alcune caratteristiche del mobile neoclassico," pp. 48-56; "Album neoclassici," pp. 57-62, with a list of collected engravings depicting Italian Neoclassical furniture and interior decoration. Bibliographical footnotes.

1359   Pedrini, Augusto. **Italian Furniture: Interior Decoration of the Fifteenth and Sixteenth Centuries.** London, Tiranti, 1949. 24p. (text), 256 plates. index. LC 49-6923.

Popular, pictorial survey of Italian furniture and interior decoration during the Renaissance. No bibliography.

See also Pignatti, Terisio, *Mobili italiani del Rinascimento.* 2nd ed. Milan, Vallardi, 1962. 125p. illus. LC 72-201957.

1360   Schottmuller, Frida. **Furniture and Interior Decoration of the Italian Renaissance...** New York, Brentano, 1921. 246p. illus. LC 22-10616.

Pictorial survey of Italian Renaissance interior decoration and furniture. Brief introductory essay followed by 590 plates illustrating surviving interiors and contemporary paintings depicting interiors with descriptive notes. Bibliographical footnotes.

1361   Schubring, Paul. **Cassoni. Truhen und Truhenbilder der italienischen Frührenaissance. Ein Beitrag zur Profanmalerei im Quattrocento.** 2d ed. Leipzig, Hiersemann, 1923. 2v. illus. index. LC 25-13012.

Scholarly history/handbook of Italian painted marriage chests of the fifteenth century (Cassoni) by a leading historian of Italian Renaissance art. Emphasis is on the paintings decorating the sides of the chests. Contents: Band 1: Textband; Band 2: Tafelband. Contents Band 1: I, Einleitung. Allgemeines: Die Truhe in Frankreich, Der soziale Charakter der Truhe; II, Das florentiner Zimmer der Frührenaissance; III, Der Cassone; IV,Die literarische Grundlage und die Vermittler der antiken Stoffe; V, Truhen auf Bildern; VI, Die Entwicklung der Truhenmalerei und die Meister; VII, Der Inhalt der Darstellung; Katalog (arranged chronologically and then by region). Bibliographical references in the footnotes. A standard work.

See also the exhibition catalog: *Italian Cassoni: From the Art Collections of Soviet Museums*, by L. Faenson (Leningrad, Aurora Art Pub., 1983. 246p. illus.).

Regional Histories and Handbook

1362   Mannelli, Vinicio. **Il mobile regionale italiano.** Florence, Edam, 1964. 178p. illus. LC 67-58656.

Popular handbook of Italian regional furniture illustrated with pieces in private collections. General bibliography, pp. 177-78.

1363   **Mobile regionale italiani.** Milan, Görlich, 1969. illus.

Series of monographs on the furniture styles of various regions of Italy. Each has a brief introductory text followed by a collection of plates, mostly of pieces in private collections. To date the following have appeared:

Il mobile lombardo by C. Alberici (1969)
Il mobile umbro by G. Cantelli (1973)
Il mobile romano by G. Lizzani (1970)
Il mobile friulano by T. Miotti (1970)

Genoa

1364   Morazzoni, Giuseppe. **Il mobile genovese**. Milan, Libri Artistici, 1962. 213p. illus. LC 75-54749.

Authoritative survey of furniture in Genoa from the late Middle Ages to the end of the Neoclassical style circa 1850, based in part on archival and documentary sources. Contents: Elenco opere; Dal Quattrocento alla fine del Cinquecento; Dal Seicento al Barocchetto; Dal neoclassicismo all'Ottocento. Descriptive notes to the plates. Bibliographical references in the footnotes.

Venice

1365   Levy, Saul. **Lacche veneziane settecentesche**. Milan, Görlich, 1967. 2v. illus. index.

Pictorial survey of Venetian lacquered furniture of the eighteenth century. Contents: Introduzione; La lacche in Europa; Le lacche a Venezia. Repertory of nearly 500 plates of works arranged by type: Poltrone, divanti, sedie e panche; Cassettoni, credenze, comodini; Scrittoroi e cassettoni a ribalta; Armadi; Tavoli da parete, tavolini e trespoli; Specchiere e cornici; Porte; Strumenti musicali e accessori; Miscellanea. Includes illustrations of interiors of the lacquer decorated rooms in the Cà Bezzonico. Bibliography of basic works, v. 1, p. 24, and additional bibliography in the footnotes.

1366   Levy, Saul, and Giuseppe Morazzoni. **Mobile veneziano del settecento**. Milan, Görlich, 1964. 2v. illus. LC 76-410376.

Large corpus of plates of Venetian furniture of the eighteenth century. Brief introductory essay with glossary of terms. Plates are grouped by types: volume one: Poltrone, divani, sedie e sgabelli; cassettoni e comodini; Credenze. Volume two: Cassettoni con alzata; Armadi e mobili a libreria; Scrittori; Consolles; Tavoli e tavolini; Inginocchiatoi e trespoli; Specchiere; Testate di letto e letti; Mori, laccati dorati; Porte e un po' di tutto; Stoffe e carta stampata. No bibliography.

Low Countries

1367   Defour, Frans. **Belgische Meubelkunst in de XXe Eeuw. Van Horta tot Heden**. Tielt, Lannoo, 1979. 213p. illus. index. ISBN 9020907867.

Well-illustrated survey of furniture in Belgium from Art Nouveau to the 1970s. Brief biographies of the major personalities. Bibliography of basic books, p. 201. Summaries in French, German and English.

1368   Jonge, C. H. de, and Willem Vogelsang. **Hollandische Mobel und Raumkunst von 1650-1780**. The Hague, Nijhoff, 1922. 185p. illus. index.

Authoritative survey of Dutch furniture and interior decoration from 1650 to 1780. Introductory chapters discuss interiors as seen in paintings, historic buildings, and doll houses. Remaining chapters treat the principal types of furniture and rooms. Good collection of plates. Bibliography in the footnotes.

1369   Oliver, Lucile. **Mobilier des provinces Belges et des Flandres françaises**. Paris, Massin, 1977. 82p. illus. ISBN 2707209937.

Pictorial survey of the traditional furniture characteristic of the regions of Belgium and French Flanders (Départmwent du Nord). Includes both folk furniture and furniture made in provincial centers following prevailing "high" styles. Contents: Détermination géographique du mobilier des provinces Belges et des Flandres françaises; Historique: évolution du Mobilier Flandres et Wallonie; Le Mobilier Flamand: Le travail des artisans, Les garnitures métalliques, L'Habitat, Les meubles, Les petits meubles et ojets; Le mobilier Wallon; Le mobilier bourgeois, patricien et urbain; le mobilier rural. Good color plates showing pieces in rural domestic settings. Bibliography of basic books in French, p. 80.

1370   Philippe, Joseph. **Le mobilier liégeois (Moyen âge-XIXe siècle)**. Liège, Bénard et Central Reunies, 1962. 243p. illus. index. (Collection consacrée à l'art mosan, v. 2). LC 65-59331.

Comprehensive history of furniture in Liege and the Mosan Valley. Contents: 1, Le mobilier mosan et liègeois avant le XVIIIe siécle; 2, Le mobilier liègeois et mosan du XVIIIe siècle. Bibliography in the notes.

1371   Singleton, Esther. **Dutch and Flemish Furniture**. New York, McClure, Phillips, 1907. 338p. illus. index. LC 07-28525.

Popular history of furniture in the Low Countries from the Middle Ages through the mid-nineteenth century, with emphasis on the place of furniture in the overall history of interior design. Good chapter on the Dutch home and its furnishings with documented inventories. Illustrated with pieces in museums, interiors in historic buildings and contemporary prints and drawings. An old, standard work.

1372   **Thuis in de late middeleeuwen**. Zwolle, Waanders, 1980. 203p. illus. index. ISBN 9070072661.

Two essays on the history of domestic furniture and interior furnishings in the Netherlands from 1400 to 1535 and a catalog of the objects in an exhibition at the Provinciaal Overijssels Museum in 1980. Well-illustrated with interiors as represented in famous works of Early Netherlandish painting, e.g., the Merode altarpiece, drawings of the pieces of furniture shown in the paintings, and fine plates of the items of interior furnishing, e.g., ceramics, brass and copper, iron and pewter, shown in the exhibition. Contents: Het laatmiddeleeuwse burgerhuis in het Noorden en Osten van Nederland, by W. J. Wolters; Het huisraad in het Oostnederland bourger-woonhuis in de late middeleeuwen, by B. Dubbe; Catalogus by J. W. M. de Jong. Comprehensive, unclassified bibliography, pp. 192-95.

1373   Vogelsang, Willem. **Le meuble hollandais au Musee National d' Amsterdam**. Amsterdam, Van Rijkom, 1910. 13p. (text), 64 plates. LC 11-1264.

Concise survey of Dutch furniture from the Middle Ages to the nineteenth century based on pieces in the National Museum in Amsterdam.

See also the museum catalog: *Catalogus van meubelen en betimmeringen*. Amsterdam, Rijksmuseum. (Amsterdam, Rijksmuseum, 1952. 374p. illus. index).

Dutch Colonial Furniture

1374   Atmore, M. G. **Cape Furniture**. 3rd ed. Cape Town, Howard Timmins, 1976. 246p. illus. index. ISBN 0869780964.

Important history of the furniture of the European colonists in South Africa designed as a handbook for collectors. Contents: I, European Furniture Development; II, Colonial Furniture Development; III, The Cape—Historical Background; IV, The Method of Illustrations Used; V, Chairs; VI, Other Seating Furniture; VII, Tables and Sideboards; VIII, Short Cupboards—Corner Cupboards and Cabinets; IX, Armoires and Wardrobes; X, Display Cabinets and Cupboards—Wall Cupboards—Bureau Bookcases; XI, Bureaux—Bible Desks—Other Desks and Library Tables—Bookcases—Chests of Drawers; XII, Chest and Kists—Dough Troughs—Wagon Chests; XIII, Beds—Cradles and Cots—Washstands—Bidets—Linen Presses—Gueridons—Mirrors; XIV, Furniture Metalwork; XV, The Value of Cape Furniture and Some Hints on Where to Find It. Appendices with description of construction, restoration, refinishing, preservation and care. Bibliography, pp. 243-44, is a list of books and articles in English.

1375 Pearse, Geoffrey E. **Eighteenth Century Furniture in South Africa**. Pretoria, Van Schaik, 1960. 193p. illus. LC 61-41481.

Well-illustrated history of furniture made in South Africa during the eighteenth century with emphasis on the background in Holland. Contents: I, Historical Introduction; 2, The Seventeenth Century in Holland; 3, The Seventeenth Century at the Cape; 4, The Eighteenth Century in Holland; 5, The Eighteenth Century at the Cape; 6, Eighteenth Century Furniture at the Cape; 7, Timber; 8, Silver, China and Glass. Illustrated with plates and measured drawings with details of construction and ornament. Companion to the author's work on eighteenth century architecture in South Africa (ARCH 1353).

1376 Terwen-De Loos, Jeanne. **Het Nederlands koloniale meubel: studie over meubels in de voormalige Nederlandse kolonien Indonesie en Sri Lanka**. Franeker, T. Wever, 1985. 183p. illus. ISBN 9061353815.

History of furniture made in the European style in the former Dutch colonies in Indonesia and Sri Lanka (Ceylon) from the seventeenth century to the nineteenth century. Bibliographical footnotes, selected bibliography, pp. 163-65, and summary in English.

1377 Veenendaal, Jan. **Furniture from Indonesia, Sri Lanka and India during the Dutch Period**. Delft, Volkenkundig Museum Nusantara, 1985. 186p. illus. index. ISBN 9071423026.

Comprehensive, scholarly history of furniture made for Dutch colonists in Indonesia, Sri Lanka (Ceylon) and India from the seventeenth through the nineteenth centuries. The author emphasizes the interrelationship of the various centers. Contents: I, Introduction; II, Historical Background; III, The Initial Period; IV, Furniture with Low-Relief Carving, 1650-1680; V, Furniture with Half-Relief Carving, 1680-1720; VI, Furniture without Carving; VII, Chests; VIII, The Eighteenth Century; IX, Nineteenth Century Furniture; X, Sorts of Timber; XI, Inventories; XII, Glossary. Bibliographical references in the notes.

1378 Wall, Victor. **Het hollandsche koloniale barokmeubel...** Antwerp, De Sikkel; Amsterdam, Nijhoff, 1939. 231p. illus.

Comprehensive history of Dutch colonial furniture from the middle of the seventeenth to the beginning of the eighteenth centuries. Particular emphasis is given to furniture made of ebony and the production assumed to center in Batavia (Jakarta-Kota), Sri Lanka (Ceylon), the Coromandel Coast of India and the Moluccas. Bibliography, pp, 223-31, and specialized literature in the notes.

See also R.L. Bohier, *Furniture of the Dutch Period in Ceylon*. 2d ed. (Colombo, 1979).

Henry Van de Velde, 1863-1957

1379 Pecher, Wolf D. **Henry Van de Velde. Das Gesamtwerk: Gestaltung**. v. 1-. Munich, Factur, 1981-.

Comprehensive, scholarly monograph and catalogue raisonné of the applied and decorative arts designs of Henry Van De Velde. The first volume covers the interior and furniture designs to 1903; the second volume covers furniture and works of ceramics, textiles, metal, ivory, leather, basketry and costume dating after 1904. Planned are volumes on Van de Velde's architecture, painting and other designs. Comprehensive bibliography in volume two.

Russia

1380 Chenevière, Antoine. **Russian Furniture: The Golden Age 1780-1840**. New York, Vendom Press, 1988. 311p. illus. index. ISBN 0865650993.

Well-illustrated, comprehensive history of Russian furniture between 1780 and 1840.
Contents: 1780-1790: The Extent of Western Influence, The System of Production, Techniques
of Production, Planning and Cabinet-making, David Roentgen; 1790-1800: Christian Meyer,
Verre églomisé, Heinrich Gambs and His Early Work, The Russian Jacob Style; 1800-1810: The
Later Works of Heinrich Gambs, Andrei Voronikhin, Voronikhin at Pavlovsk, Other Pieces;
1810-1825: Examples, Carlo Rossi, Vasily Stasov; 1825-1840: Eclecticism, Historicism, Leo von
Klenze in St. Petersburg; Steel Furniture from Tula; Stone Cutting: Peterhof, Ekaterinburg,
Kolyvan, Other Stone-cutting Workshops. Dictionary of architects, artists and cabinet-makers.
Appendix with description of the Palace of Pavlovsk by the Grand Duchess Maria Feodorovna,
1795. Bibliography, pp. 304-308.

Scandinavia

1381   Andrén, Erik. **Möbelstilarna; en handbok i den svenska mobel-och inredningskon-
stens historia**. Stockholm, Saxon and Lindstrom, 1961. 279p. illus. index. LC 62-44178. Reprint:
Stockholm, Nordiska Museet, 1981. 254p. illus. index. ISBN 9171081992.
Authoritative survey of furniture in Sweden from the Middle Ages to the middle of the
sixteenth century. Contains 162 plates with descriptive captions. Contents: Förord; Medeltiden;
Den äldre vasatiden; Den yngre vasatiden; Den karolinkska tiden; Frederik I:s tid; Rokokotiden;
Den gustavianska tiden; Karl Johanstiden; Eklekticismen; Den senaste utvecklingen; Svenska
allmongemöbel; Ordförklaringar och konstnärsregister.

1382   Clemmensen, Tove. **Danske mobler; stiludviklingen fra renaessance til klunketid**. 3rd
ed. Copenhagen, Thaning and Appel, 1960. 97p. illus. LC 62-48467.
Popular history of Danish furniture from the Renaissance through the Empire styles.
Illustrated with museum pieces. Basic bibliography, pp. 967-97.

1383   Erixon, Sigurd. **Folklig mobelkultur i svenska bygder**. Stockholm, Nordisk, 1938. 288p.
illus. LC 41-3835. Reprint: Lund, Ekstrand, 1980. ISBN 974080547.
Comprehensive, authoritative history/handbook of Swedish folk furniture from the Middle
Ages to the nineteenth century. Divided into text and plates, both subdivided by types of furniture,
i.e., Sängar, Bänkar, Skåp, Bord, Stolar, Kistor, Smärre möbler och inredningsföremål. Comprehensive, classified bibliography, pp. 285-86. A standard work on Swedish folk furniture.

1384   Fischer, Ernst. **Svenska möbler i bild: Möbelformnerna från 1830-1930**. Stockholm,
Natur och Kultur, 1950. 272p. illus.
Concise survey of Swedish furniture from 1830 to 1930. Brief text followed by a collection
of 148 plates. Contents: Inledningh; Oscar I:s gotik; Karl XV:s rokoko; Oscar II:s klassicism: Ny
Louis XVI, Nybarocken och sadelmakarestilen; Nyrenässans; Jugenstilen; Tjugotalets klassicism.
No bibliography.

1385   Gjerdi, Trond. **Møbler i Norge**. Oslo, Aschehoug, 1976. 134p. illus. index. LC
77-461132.
Concise history of Norwegian furniture from 1600 to 1960. Illustrated with drawings,
many showing details of construction, as well as plates of actual pieces. Arrangement by types of
furniture and with a chapter on the stylistic history of twentieth century furniture. Good, classified
bibliography, pp. 130-33.

1386   Groth, Håkon. **Neoclassicism in the North. Swedish Furniture and Interiors 1770-
1850**. New York, Rizzoli, 1990. 224p. illus. index. ISBN 0847812731.

Sumptuously illustrated survey of Swedish furniture and interior decoration from 1770 to 1850. Excellent selection of plates, many in very high quality color, of major historic interiors. Historical introduction is followed by chapters on the major houses: Royal Palace, Stockholm, Gripsholm, Övedskloster, Sturehof, Hylinge, Gunnebo, Haga, Tullgarn, Princess Sophia Albertina's Palace, Stockholm, Bernshammar, Östanå; The Masreliez Rooms, Stockholm, Rosersberg, Vittskövle, Sperlingsholm, Elghammar, Skottorp, The Hazelius House, Stockholm, Högsjögård, Rosendal. Appendices with family tree of the Holstein-Gottorp and Bernadotte Dynasties; Catalogue of furniture types and styles, repertory of artists, architects, and craftsmen. Brief bibliography of basic works in English, p. 221.

See also T. Clemmensen, *Danish Furniture of the Eighteenth Century*. Copenhagen, Gyldendal, 1948. 35p. illus. LC 51-29893.

1387 Heinonen, Jorga. **Suomalaisia kansanhuonekaluja: Old Finnish Furniture**. Helsinki, Suomalaisen Kirjallisuuden Kirjapaino, 1969. 128p. illus.

Pictorial survey of Finnish furniture from the Middle Ages to the nineteenth century.

1388 Henschen, Ingegerd and Sten Blomberg. **Svenska möbellexikon**. Malmo, Norden, 1961-62. 3v. illus. LC 62-46920.

Comprehensive dictionary covering all aspects of the history of furniture in Sweden from the early Middle Ages to the 1950s. Entries include scholars, artists, designers and craftsmen, styles, periods, types, materials, and techniques. Broad scope of entries includes much on non-Swedish furniture. Longer entries have bibliographical references to literature in Swedish. Large collection of illustrations. One of the most comprehensive dictionaries on furniture in any language.

1389 Hernmarck, Carl. **Svenskt Sjuttonhundratal**. Stockholm, Almqvist & Wiksell, 1954. 200p. illus. index. (Nationalmusei Skriftserie, Nr. 1). LC A55-1367.

Scholarly history of Swedish furniture and interior furnishings of the eighteenth century. Includes silver, porcelain, and other decorative arts as they characterized aristocratic taste in interiors. Emphasis is on stylistic origins and development. Contents: Inledning: Arvet från 1600-talet; Förnuftet och upplysningen, Verklighetsflykten och sjuttonhundratalers exotism, Äkta material och imitation, Klassicismen under sjuttonhundratalet; De utländska impulserna och den ihemska traditionen: Inflytandet från Frankrike under den tessinska epoken, Den franska rokokon och Carl Hårleman, Louis seize och tidig gustaviansk stil, Inflytandet från England, Inflytandet från Tyskland, Den svenska traditionen; Övergångsformer och blandstilar: Övergången från senbarock till rokoko, Övergången mellan rokoko och klassicism, Äldre och yngre klassicism; Konstnärer och handverkare: Handverkarna och de direkta beställningarns, Konstnärerna och manufakturerna, Konstnärerna och skråhantverkarna; Beställarnas och köparnas roll: Ceremoniell konservatism, Konungamakten, de nya stilarnas inkörsport, Hur de högre stånden upptaga de nya stilnarna, Finns det en svensk stil?. Summary in French. Comprehensive bibliography, pp. 197-200.

1390 Hiort, Esbjorn. **Modern Danish Furniture**. New York, Architectural Book Pub. Co., 1956. 133p. illus. LC 56-59182.

Survey of Danish furniture from 1945 to 1955. Eighty-one plates with captions in English, French, German, and Danish. Fourteen-page introductory essay in the same languages. No bibliography.

1391 Lagerquist, Marshall. **Rokokomöbler signerade av ebenister och schatullmakare in Stockholm**. Stockholm, Nordiska Museet, 1949. 226p. illus. index. (Nordiska Museets Handlingar: 31).

Scholarly history of Swedish furniture in the Rococo style with particular attention to the distribution of works. Contents: Förord; Rokokon som modestil i svenskt möbelhantverk under 1700-talet; Fanermöblerna i Frankrike under rokokon; Individuella, korporativa och officiella stämplar; Mästarebestämda möbler i urval; Möbelexporten från Stockholm och den yrkesmässiga möbelhandeln; Bilaga A: Berättelse om svenska meuble-handelens första inrättning, och de öden, meuble-hanlaren Diedrich Tellerstedt uti 23 års tid undergådt; Bilaga B: Premierad möbelexport från Stockholm 1740-1780; Bilaga C: Värdefördelning av premierad möbelexport fån Stockholm 1740-1780; Noter till bilagorna; Förkortningar och citeringar; Källförteckning; Snickare i Stockholm 1740-1780. Contains 126 plates arranged by type of furniture.

1392   Lexow, Jan H. **Bergenske Empiremobler.** Bergen, J. Grieg, 1948. 72p. illus. LC 48-24872.
       Authoritative survey of Empire-style furniture made in Bergen. Contents: Stilen; Snekkerne; Møblene. Plates feature 29 pieces with details of inlay ornament. Bibliographical references in the notes.

1393   Møller, Viggo S. and Svend E. Møller. **Dansk Møbel Kunst.** Copenhagen, R. Naver, 1951. 117p. illus. LC 53-30482/r.
       Survey of Danish modern furniture produced in Copenhagen between 1927 and 1951. Introductory essay of 43 pages sketches the history from the late nineteenth century to 1951, followed by 61 pages of plates of both interiors and individual pieces. Repertory of modern Danish furniture makers with brief biographies. Summary in English. No bibliography.

1394   Steensberg, Axel and Grith Lerche. **Danske Bondemobler: Danish Peasant Furniture.** 4th ed. Copenhagen, A. Busck, 1989. 2v. illus. index. ISBN 8717059763.
       Comprehensive handbook/history of Danish folk furniture from the sixteenth century to the end of the nineteenth century, with particular attention given to the place of furniture in decorated interiors and the history of taste revealed in the provenance of major pieces. Bilingual text and captions to the 587 plates; however, the English text in the captions is an abbreviation of the Danish and often lacks the dating and technical information. Contents: Volume 1: Danish Peasant Furniture: Introduction, Definition, Sources of Peasant Wealth, Impact and Response, Placing of Furniture Inside the Farm, Permanence and Mobility; Tables and Benches; Chairs; Bedsteads; Chests; Travelling Boxes, Chests and Small Cases. Volume 2: Conservation of Painted Furniture: Techniques of Wood and Stone Imitation and Use of Stencils; Pressed Cupboards, Dressers and Wardrobes; Chest of Drawers and Bureau-cabinets; Shelves; Mirrors and Pictures; Clocks, Clock- and Watch-cases; Names of Craftsmen; List of Museums, Photographers, etc. General bibliography, pp. 116-117. A standard work on Danish folk furniture.
       See also the museum catalog: *Nordiska Museets möbler från svenska herrenmanshem.* Stockholm, Nordiska Museet (Stockholm, Museets Förlag, 1931-35. 3v. illus.).

Alvar Aalto, 1898-1976

1395   **Museum of Finnish Architecture, Finnish Society for Crafts and Design.** Alvar Aalto Furniture. Cambridge, Mass., M.I.T Press, 1985. 179p. illus. ISBN 0262132060.
       Three essays on the development of Alvar Aalto's furniture designs by Finnish experts. Contents: Early Furniture and Interior Designs by I. Herler; The Decisive Years by G. Schildt, Workshop Recollections by M-L. Parko; Fixed Furniture in Alvar Aalto's Architecture by E. Aalto and M-R Norri. Appendices with excerpts from Aalto's writings on interior and furniture design, chronology of mass-produced furniture, and selection of Artek's standard models.
       See also the exhibition catalog: *Alvar Aalto, Furniture and Glass*, by J. S. Johnson (New York, Museum of Modern Art, 1984. 24p. illus.).

Spain and Portugal

1396   Burr, Grace H. **Hispanic Furniture**. 2nd rev. and enl. ed. New York, Archive, 1964. 231p. illus. index. LC 64-22364.

First published in 1941. Survey of Spanish furniture from the Gothic period through the eighteenth century with emphasis on domestic furniture of the Spanish Renaissance and Baroque. Includes Spanish colonial furniture and a chapter on the excellent collection of furniture in the New York Hispanic Society of America. Notes to the plates with bibliographical references, general bibliography, pp. 215-19. Still the best history of Spanish furniture in English.

1397   Byne, Arthur and Mildred Byne. **Spanish Interiors and Furniture...** New York, Helbrun, 1921-22. 4v. illus. index. Reprint: New York, Dover, 1969. 330p. (plates). LC 70-97502.

Illustrated survey of Spanish interior decoration and furniture. A useful collection of plates.

1398   Claret Rubira, José. **Muebles de estilo español. Encyclopedia of Spanish Period Furniture Designs**. New York, Sterling Pub. Co., 1984. 352p. illus. index. ISBN 080697202X.

Contains 347 plates of line drawings of Spanish furniture from the fourteenth century to the late nineteenth century. No bibliography.

1399   Dalisi, Riccardo. **Gaudi, mobili e oggetti. Gaudi, Furniture & Objects**. Woodbury, N.Y., Barron's, 1979. 149p. illus. ISBN 0812053567.

Survey of Gaudí's activity as a designer of furniture and other interior accessories, written from the standpoint of a contemporary designer. Contents: Dalisi's Gaudí by A. Trimarco; Journey through Gaudí's Products, Objects, and Chairs; History-Dream/Mind-Body; Big-Small/Intellectual-Manual/Structure-Decoration; Emerging Techniques; Visit to Barcelona (1976); Evolution of Gaudí's Furniture; Geometry; Forms; Craftsman's Tools and Figurative Machines; A New Idea of Manuality. Appendices with essay on interpreting Gaudí, chronology of Gaudí's works and selected bibliography, p. 146.

1400   Domenech, Rafael, and Luis Perez Bueno. **Antique Spanish Furniture**. New York, Archive, 1965. 142p. illus. index. LC 64-25672.

Reprint of 1921 Spanish edition. Popular, bilingual history of Spanish furniture from the fourteenth through the seventeenth centuries, consisting of a brief introduction and notes to plates illustrating pieces in museums and private collections.

1401   Feduchi, Luis M. **Spanish Furniture**. New York, Tudor, 1969. 313p. illus.

Survey of furniture in Spain from its beginnings to the early twentieth century by a leading authority. Parallel texts in Spanish, English, French and German. Illustrated with pieces in Spanish museums and historic restorations. Bibliography pp. 308-13.

1402   Guimaräes, Alfredo, and Albano Sardoeira. **Mobiliário artistico português**. Porto, M. Abreu, 1924-35. 2v. illus. index. LC 91-112658.

Comprehensive history of furniture in Portugal from the Middle Ages to the end of the nineteenth century.

1403   Lozoya, Juan C. **Mubles de estilo español desde el gótico hasta el siglo XIX con el mueble popular**. Barcelona, Gili, 1962. 451p. illus. LC 65-88720.

Comprehensive survey of Spanish furniture from the Gothic period to the end of the nineteenth century. Arranged by periods, it consists of short chapters followed by measured line drawings. Brief bibliography, p. 451.

1404 Pinto Cardoso, Augusto. **Cadeiras portuguesas**. Lisbon, n.p., 1952. 121p. (text), 131p. (illus.). LC 53-33675.

Authoritative survey of Portuguese furniture from the Middle Ages to the early nineteenth century. Good collection of plates with descriptive notes illustrating museum-quality pieces. General bibliography, p. 129, and specialized literature in the footnotes.

1405 Sandao, Arthur de, **O móvel pintado em Portugal**. 2d ed. Porto, Livraria Civilizacao, 1984. 321p. illus. index.

First published in 1966 (LC 67-5803). Popular history of Portuguese painted furniture from the eighteenth century to the present. Most is folk furniture. Summary in French, English and German. Comprehensive bibliography, pp. 221-228.

1406 Smith, Robert C. **Samuel Tibau and Portugese Ivory Inlaid Furniture of the Seventeenth Century**. Coimbra, Universidade de Coimbra, 1962. 14p. illus.

Scholarly introduction to the furniture of Samuel Tibau active in Coimbra in the middle decades of the seventeenth century. Based on documentary evidence and study of the signed and dated pieces of case furniture, particularly in the church of Santa Cruz in Coimbra. Contains 20 black and white plates. Bibliographical references in the footnotes.

ORIENTAL FURNITURE

China

1407 Beurdeley, Michel. **Chinese Furniture**. Tokyo, Kodansha International, 1979. 199p. illus. index. ISBN 0870113879.

Well-illustrated survey of traditional Chinese furniture from the Han dynasty to the twentieth century. Contains 237 plates in the text plus 19 small illustrations of pieces that sold (prices given) at auctions in Paris, London, and New York in the 1960s and 1970s. Contents: I, Chinese Furniture before the Ming Dynasty; II, The Art of Living in China: The Scholars' Retreat, The Decorator Li Yu (1611-80), The Interior of a House in Canton in the Mid-18th Century "Of the Houses of the Chinese" by William Chambers; III, Chinese Furniture from the Ming Period (1368-1644) to the 20th Century: Hardwood Furniture, Lacquer Furniture, Furniture of Cloisonné Enamel, Furniture in So-Called Canton Enamel, Porcelain Seats and Furnishing, A Rehabilitation of Daoguang (Tao-kuang) Furniture, Metal Hinges, Locks and Handles. Appendices with essays on the influence of Chinese furniture on the applied and decorative arts of America, Britain, Germany and France. Glossary of terms and list of dynasty marks. General bibliography, pp. 197-98.

1408 Dupont, Maurice, and O. Roche. **Les meubles de la Chine**. Paris, A. Calavas, 1925. 6p. (text), 54 plates. Reprinted 1950.

Collection of plates of Chinese furniture in French museums with brief introduction. No bibliography.

1409 Ecke, Gustave. **Chinese Domestic Furniture**. Rutland, Vt., Tuttle, 1962. 49p. (text), 161p. (illus.). LC 62-21540.

First published in 1944 (Peking, Vetch). Collection of plates and measured drawings of Chinese furniture with details of construction.

1410 Ellsworth, Robert H. **Chinese Furniture, Hardwood Examples of the Ming and Early Ch'ing Dynasties**. New York, Random House, 1971. 299p. illus. index. LC 71-85592.

Comprehensive handbook/history of traditional Chinese furniture with particular emphasis on the methods of construction (joinery) and an important chapter on metal mountings. Contents: 1, Historical Background; 2, Ming Evidence for Dating of Chinese Furniture; 3, Woods Known to Have Been Used in Chinese Furniture; 4, Chinese Joinery; 5, Metal Mounts; 6, Chinese Furniture of the Ming and Ch'ing Dynasties; Notes on the Construction of the Illustrated Pieces; 7, The Change in Seating Furniture and Its Importance in the Dating of Chinese Furniture; 8, Conservation and Restoration. Appendices: "Random Talks on Chairs and Stools and the Method of Arrangement" by Chia-chun Chu and description of the O'an Tombs of the Ming Dynasty. Excellent, annotated bibliography, pp. 297-99.

1411   Kates, George N. **Chinese Household Furniture**. New York, Harper & Row, 1948. 125p. illus. LC 48-6567r48. Reprint: New York, Dover, 1962.

Concise survey of traditional Chinese furniture. Initial chapters treat Eastern and Western attitudes toward Chinese furniture, problems of dating, materials and techniques, and the general historical development; chapters follow on the major types and classes of Chinese domestic furniture. Descriptive notes to the plates. Basic bibliography, p. 125.

1412   Wang, Shih-Hsiang. **Classic Chinese Furniture: Ming and Early Quing Dynasties**. San Francisco, China Books & Periodicals, 1986. 327p. illus. index. ISBN 0835117693.

Well-illustrated history of furniture in China from the late fourteenth to the late eighteenth centuries. Features exquisite plates with multiple views and details of 162 pieces in museums and private collections. Measured drawings accompany the more elaborate pieces. Descriptive notes to the plates. Contents: I, The Golden Age; II, The Best Furniture Woods; III, The Origins of the Principal Furniture Forms; IV, The Types and Forms of Furniture; V, The Precision and Ingenuity of Joinery; VI, The Richness and Variety of Decorative Technique; VII, The Appreciation and Use of Furniture. Glossary, bibliography of books in Chinese and English, pp. 322-323.

India

1413   Krishna Murthy, K. **Ancient Indian Furniture**. Selhi, Sundeep Prakashan, 1982. 119p. illus. index. LC 82-907289.

Scholarly history of beds in India from the second century B.C. to the seventh century A.D. based on representations in works of art and written records. Contents: 1, Introductory; 2, Thrones: Asana (s); 3, Chairs; 4, Wheeled Furniture; 5, Seats and Moras; 6, Wicker Stands; 7, Tables; 8, Foot-stools or Foot-rests or Pada-pithas; 9, Bedsteads; 10, Pillows and Cushions; 11, Boxes; 12, Curtains; 13, Epilogue. Comprehensive, classified bibliography, pp. 103-112.

Japan

1414   Clarke, Rosy. **Japanese Antique Furniture: a Guide to Evaluating and Restoring**. New York, Weatherhill, 1983. 150p. illus. index. ISBN 0834801787.

Popular collector's handbook on traditional Japanese furniture with chapters on identification, evaluation, restoration, and care and maintenance. Appendix with list of antique shops in the Tokyo area and list of flea markets and antique fairs in Tokyo. General bibliography, pp. 141-42.

1415   Koizumi, Kazuko. **Wakagu: Traditional Japanese Furniture**. Tokyo, Kodansha International; New York, Harper & Row, 1986. 223p. illus. index. ISBN 087011722X.

Well-illustrated history of Japanese furniture from prehistoric times to the present with emphasis on the place of furniture in traditional Japanese life and techniques of joinery and carving. Contents: 1, Furniture and Furnishings; 2, The History; 3, Techniques. Appendices with repertory of abstract motifs in Japanese furniture. Many photographs and line drawings showing contemporary practices in making traditional furniture in Japan. Includes accessories such as mats and lighting fixtures.

Korea

1416   Wright, Edward R., and Man Sill Pai. **Korean Furniture: Elegance and Tradition.** Tokyo; New York, Kodansha International and Harper & Row, 1984. 192p. illus. index. LC 83-48878. ISBN 08701116525.

Pictorial survey of Korean traditional furniture with emphasis on nineteenth- and twentieth-century pieces and the place of furniture in traditional Korean domestic life. Chapters on wood, finishes, metal fittings, tools, and the art of joinery. No bibliography.

AFRICAN FURNITURE

1417   Sieber, Roy. **African Furniture and Household Objects.** Bloomington, Ind., Indiana Univ. Press, 1980. 279p. illus. ISBN 0253119278.

Important, authoritative introduction to the furniture and interior furnishing of sub-Sahara Africa published to accompany an exhibition of the same name organized by the American Federation of the Arts. Large number of illustrations of pieces of furniture and photographs showing the use and creation of furniture. Contents: House and Compound; Artisans; Implements; Furniture; Containers. Comprehensive bibliography, pp. 269-76.

See also the exhibition catalog: *Man at Rest: Stools, Chairs, Thrones, Foot-rests, Back-rests, Benches*, by E. A Dagan (Montreal, Centre Saidye Bronfman, 1985. 64p. illus. ISBN 0920473024).

CHAPTER TEN

GLASS

BIBLIOGRAPHIES

1418   Bush, Louise K. **The History and Art of Glass: Index of Periodical Articles, 1956-1979.** Boston, G. K. Hall, 1982. 876p. ISBN 0816113033.

Index of periodical articles on all aspects of glass culled from over 500 international periodicals, conference proceedings, and chapters in yearbooks. Organized in three broad categories: general, technology, history. The latter is subdivided by period and country. Continuation: *The History of Art of Glass: Index to Periodical Articles, 1980-1982* (Boston, G. K. Hall, 1984, 310p.)

1419 "Check List of Recently Published Articles and Books on Glass," in: **Journal of Glass Studies,** v. 1 (1959)-.

Annual, classified bibliography of articles in all languages published in the previous year. This material has been subsumed into Bush (1418).

1420 Duncan, George S. **Bibliography of Glass (from the Earliest Records to 1940).** Sheffield and London, Dawson of Pallmall, 1960. 544p. LC 59-9650.

Comprehensive, annotated and classified bibliography of nearly 20,000 titles consisting of books and periodical articles on all aspects of glass from antiquity to 1940. Detailed subject index.

DIRECTORIES

1421   **Répertoire international des musées et collections du verre: International Repertory of Glass Museums and Glass Collections.** Liège, Musée du Verre, 1966. 216p. LC 85-115718.

Directory of glass museums and collections arranged by country, city, and museum. Entries list personnel, origin, size, and nature of the glass collections with a brief bibliography.

TECHNIQUE

1422   Newton, Roy, and Sandra Davison. **Conservation of Glass.** London, Butterworths, 1989. 322p. illus. index. ISBN 0408106239.

In the series: "Butterworths Series on Conservation and Museology." Textbook for museum conservators but invaluable for any serious study of the techniques and materials of glass. Covers the earliest use of glass in antiquity to twentieth-century glass and includes stained glass. Contents: 1, The Nature of Glass; 2, Historical Development of Glass; 3, Technology of Glass Production; 4, Deterioration of Glass; 5, Materials Used for Glass Conservation; 6, Technical Examination of Glass; 7, Conservation of Glass. Glossary of terms. Exhaustive bibliography, pp. 284-309, annotated for conservation literature in the introduction.

DICTIONARIES AND ENCYCLOPEDIAS

1423   Elville, E. M. **The Collector's Dictionary of Glass.** London, Country Life, 1961. 194p. illus. LC 62-2440.
    Well-illustrated dictionary of glass from antiquity to the twentieth century directed to the collector. Emphasis is on British glass. Covers persons, styles, periods, techniques, and types of old glass. Introduction sketches the history of glass up to the Venetian period. Selected bibliography of books in English, pp. 193-194.

1424   Newman, Harold. **An Illustrated Dictionary of Glass** ... London, Thames & Hudson, 1977. 351p. illus. ISBN 0500232628.
    Well-illustrated, scholarly dictionary of world glass covering materials, techniques, production methods, decoration and styles, glass-makers, decorators, and designers from antiquity to the present. Contains 2,442 entries that provide very comprehensive coverage. Larger entries have bibliographical references. Introduction is a survey of the history of glass by Robert J. Charleston.

1425   Wilkinson, R. **The Hallmarks of Antique Glass.** London, Richard Madley, 1968. 220p. illus. ISBN 950022306.
    Collector's handbook covering European glass from ancient Egypt to the beginning of the twentieth century. Contents: 1, The Hallmark of Antique Glass—and How to Find Them; 2, Egyptian, Venetian and Syrian Glass; 3, 300 Years of English and Irish Tableware; 4, English Drinking Glasses and Engravings; 5, Chandeliers, Candelabra, Wall Brackets, Lustres and Candlesticks; 6, English Coloured Glass, from the 17th to the 20th Century; 7, French Glass, including Paperweights; 8, Bohemian Coloured and Engraved Glass; 9, Dutch Engraved and Stipple Engravings; 10, The Lampworker and His Art; 11, Collectable Items, Oddities and Figures; 12, The Repair, Restoration, Reproduction and Faking of Antique Glass. Glossary. No bibliography.

GENERAL HISTORIES AND HANDBOOKS

1426   Dexel, Thomas. **Gebrauchsgläser.** 2d ed. Braunschweig, Klinkhardt & Biermann, 1983. 301p. illus. index. ISBN 3781402088.
    Important history of everyday glassware from the late Middle Ages to the twentieth century with emphasis given to the formal development of types. Contains 403 high quality black and white plates and 6 color plates. Contents: Einleitung; Römisches und islamisches Glas; Becher; Römer; Teller, Schallen, Fußschalen und Dosen; Kelchgals und Pokal; Flaschen; Kannen und Krüge. Comprehensive bibliography, pp. 94-95. An authoritative work complimenting the author's histories of utilitarian vessels in other media (141, 532).

1427   Gros-Galliner, Gabriella. **Glass: A Guide for Collectors.** New York, Stein & Day, 1970. 175p. illus. index. LC 78-126973.
    Popular history of Western glass from ancient Egypt to the mid-twentieth century directed to collectors. Chapter on technique, list of museums, and glossary of terms. Bibliography of basic books, pp. 163-166. Similar is: Norma W. Webber, *Collecting Glass,. New York, Arco Pub. Co., 1972. 196p. illus.*

1428   Haynes, Edward B. **Glass Through the Ages.** Rev. ed. Baltimore, Md., Penguin, 1964. 309p. illus. index. LC 64-55875.

Popular history that provides a good introduction to the stylistic and technological aspects of the history of glass. Separate chapter on English eighteenth-century glass. Contents: I, The Glass of the Eastern World: 1, Beginnings, 2, The First Four Centuries, 3, The Second Four Centuries, 4, The Empty Ages, 5, The Rise and Fall of Venice, 6, The Revival in Western Europe, 7, German Glass, 8, Gilding the Lily, 9, Glassmaking in England, 10, Jacobite Glass; 11, English Glasses of the 18th Century. Bibliographies at the end of each chapter. An older history is: Dillon, Edward. *Glass*, London, Methuen; New York, Putnam, 1907. 373p. illus. index.

1429   Kampfer, Fritz, and Klaus G. Beyer. **Glass: A World History of 4000 Years of Fine Glass-Making**. Greenwich, Conn., New York Graphics Society, 1967. 314p. illus. LC 67-70992.
Well-illustrated survey of the history of world glass from ancient Egypt to the present. Brief historical essay is followed by plates with descriptive captions and good, comprehensive notes that include bibliographical references. Glossary of terms, techniques, types of glass and glass artists; many entries have bibliographical references. A good introduction for the general reader.

1430   Klein, Dan, and Ward Lloyd, eds. **The History of Glass**. London, Orbis, 1984. 288p. illus. index. ISBN 085613516X.
Well-illustrated survey of the history of glass in the Western World from antiquity to 1980. The work of a team of British experts. Glossary of terms. Bibliography of basic books and periodical articles, pp. 275-76.

1431   Mariacher, Giovanni. **Glass from Antiquity to the Renaissance**. London, Hamlyn, 1970. 157p. illus. LC 71-884683. Reprinted: London, Cassell, 1988. ISBN 0304321869.
Popular survey of Western glass written by a leading expert and illustrated with color plates of museum pieces. No bibliography. Similar work but including Oriental glass is: Savage, George. *Glass*, New York, Putnam, 1965. 128p. illus. LC 65-12438. Reprinted: London, Octopus, 1972.

1432   Mehlman, Felice. **Phaidon Guide to Glass**. Englewood Cliffs, N.J., Prentice-Hall, 1983. 256p. illus. index. ISBN 013663023X.
History of glass from antiquity to the early twentieth century. Designed as a collector's guide, the text is arranged by classes of objects, e.g., drinking vessels, lighting, serving food, etc. The broader categories are subdivided further by specific types and by countries. Chapter on collecting. Basic bibliography, pp. 246-47.

1433   Polak, Ada B. **Glass: Its Tradition and Its Makers**. New York, Putnam, 1975. 224p. illus. index. ISBN 0399115234.
Comprehensive, well-illustrated history of Western glass from the Middle Ages to circa 1870 with emphasis on the social and economic aspects. Bibliographies at the end of each chapter. Comprehensive bibliography, pp. 211-221.

1434   Schack, Clementine. **Die Glaskunst. Ein Handbuch über Herstellung, Sammeln und Gebrauch des Hohlglases**. Munich, Keyser, 1976. 344p. illus. index. ISBN 3874050971.
Comprehensive history/handbook of hollow glassware throughout the world from antiquity to the early twentieth century with emphasis on the techniques of production. Contents: 1, Glaserzeugung in Theorie und Praxis; 2, Die Zentren der Glasproduktion und ihre Geschichte; 3, Organisation der Glashütten; 4, Glas zu Kult- und Profanzwecken; 5, Bildthemen des Renaissance- und Barockglases; 6, Glasbildmotive im 19. und 20. Jahrhundert; 7, Gebrauchsgläser neuerer Zeit im Wandel von Form und Kunktion. Text is supported by a Bildkatalog with 328 examples in various museums around the world with full technical data and bibliographical references.

Bibliographical footnotes and classified bibliography, pp. 334-37. A standard work on the history of blown glass.

1435   Schlosser, Ignaz. **Das Alte Glas. Ein Handbuch fur Sammler und Liebhaber**. 3rd ed. Braunschweig, Klinkhardt & Biermann, 1977. 451p. ISBN 3781402401. (Bibliothek für Kunst- und Antiquitätenfreunde, 36).

Comprehensive history of world glass from ancient Egypt to the mid-twentieth century, directed to the series collector. Glossary of terms, chapter on collecting and restoring glass. Comprehensive, classified bibliography of books and periodical literature.

1436   Weiss, Gustav. **The Book of Glass**. New York, Praeger, 1971. 353p. illus. index. Glossary. LC 78-107151.

Comprehensive, scholarly history of glass in the West and in Islam from antiquity to the present with emphasis on technique. Contents: Glass in History; From the Earliest Beginnings to the Carolingian Period; From the Early Islamic Period to the Present Day; Technique and History of Glassmaking. Appendix with list of "Glasshouses: the Sites." Glossary. Comprehensive but unclassified bibliography, pp. 346-49.

See also the guides to major museum collections of glass: R. J. Charleston, *Masterpieces of Glass: A World History from the Corning Museum of Glass* (New York, Abrams, 1980. 239p. illus. index. ISBN 081091753X), *Glass from the Corning Museum of Glass: a Guide to the Collections* (Corning, N.Y., The Museum, 1974. 105p. illus. index.), *Art in Glass; a Guide to the Glass Collection* (Toledo, The Museum, 1969. 141p. illus. LC 72-108877). *Glass: a Handbook for the Study of Glass Vessels of All Periods and Countries & a Guide to the Museum Collection*, by W. B. Honey (London, Ministry of Education, 1946. 169p. illus. index), and the catalogs of major private collections: *Glass 500 B.C. to A.D. 1900: the Hans Cohn Collection* (Los Angeles, CA) by Axel von Saldern (Mainz, Zabern, 1980. 288p. illus. index. ISBN 3805304544), and Glassammlung Helfried Krug, *Beschreibender Katalog mit kunstgeschichtlicher Einführung von Brigitte Klesse* (Munich, Müller, Bonn, Habelt, 1965-(1973), v. 1-(2). LC 67-77578).

ANCIENT AND BYZANTINE GLASS

1437   Eisen, Gustav. **Glass, Its Origin, History, Chronology, Technic and Classification to the Sixteenth Century...** New York, Rudge, 1927. 2v. illus. index. LC 27-25827.

And old, standard history of Western glass from ancient Egypt and the Ancient Near East to the sixteenth century. Illustrated with 188 plates and 276 figures. Contents: I, General Reference to Origin: Matrices; Separate Parts; Decoration; Types and Their Nomenclature; II, Dates, Systems of Symmetry; Chronological Periods; III, Classification of Types: Egyptian Periods; IV, Sidonian Period and Its Types; V, Murrhina and Its Identification; VI, Mosaic Glass; Characteristics, Classifications, and Types; VII, Sidonian Rod-Glass, Ritual, Moulded, Lotus Cups; and Stratified Flasks; VIII, Sidonian Glass with Moulded Mythological and Symbolic Figures; IX, First Century A.D.: Pompeii, Tripoli, Sardinia, Syria; X, The Second Century A.D. Period of Glass; XI, Third Century Glass: Syria, Egypt, Germany, Gaul; XII, Third and Fourth Century Vases with Ground-Out and Engraved Designs; XIII, Domestic Glass of the Third and Fourth Centuries; XIV, The Constantinean Period of Ritual, Amuletic and Symbolic Glass; XV, Gold Glass of the Fourth and Fifth Centuries; XVI, Ritual and Symbolic Glass of the Fourth and Fifth Centuries; XVII, Late Sassanian Plain or Simply Decorated Glass; XVIII, Merovingian, Lombard, Frankish and Byzantine Glass; XIX, Egyptian and Arabic Glass; XX, Glass Representative of the Sacred Vessels in the Legends of the Holy Grail; XXI, Venetian and Other Late Glass; XXII, Chronology of the Origin and Progress of Glass Making. Chapters have brief introductory text followed by detailed notes to the numerous plates and figures. Comprehensive bibliography, pp. 751-61.

1438   Kisa, Anton. **Das Glas im Altertum.** Leipzig, Hiersemann, 1908. 3v. illus. index. LC 09-16578r56. Reprint: Rome, "L'Erma" di Bretschneider, 1968.

Comprehensive, scholarly history/handbook of glass from ancient Egypt through late Roman times. Chapters on technique including sculpture glasses, mosaics, enamels, etc. Appendix with marks and stamps. Bibliographical footnotes. A classic, pioneering standard work on ancient glass.

1439   Neuberg, Frederick. **Ancient Glass.** Toronto, University of Toronto Press, 1962. 110p. illus. index. LC 63-5593.

Comprehensive history of glass from ancient Egypt through the fourth century A.D. Illustrated with museum pieces with descriptive captions to the plates. Contents: I, The Material; II, Shape and Decoration; III, Glass Beads; IV, Egypt; V, Mesopotamia and Syria; VI, Palestine and the Jews; VII, Greece and Rome; VIII, The Western Roman Empire; IX, The Eastern Roman Empire; X, Final Thoughts. Chronological table, maps, classified bibliography of books and articles, pp. 106-107.

1440   Oppenheim, A. Leo, et al. **Glass and Glassmaking in Ancient Mesopotamia. An Edition of the Cuneiform Texts Which Contain Instructions for Glassmakers with a Catalogue of Surviving Objects.** New York, The Corning Museum of Glass, 1970. 242p. illus index. LC 75-131303.

Critical edition and translation of an important group of Mesopotamian cuneiform texts on glass and glassmaking. The first group from Nineveh is in the British Museum; the second, a middle Babylonian tablet, is also in the British Museum; the third, from the middle Kassite period, is in the Staatliche Museen in Berlin; and the fourth is a Hittite tablet likewise in the British Museum. Contents: A. Leo Oppenheim, The Cuneiform Texts: 1, Glasses in Mesopotamian Sources; 2, The Cuneiform Tablets with Instructions for Glassmakers; 3, The Technology of Mesopotamian Glassmaking. Robert H. Brill, The Chemical Interpretation of the Texts; Dan Barag, Mesopotamian Core-Formed Glass Vessels (1500-500 B.C.): 1, Geographical Survey; 2, Typological Survey; 3, Some Problems Related to the Archaeological History of Mesopotamian Glass. Axel von Saldern, Other Mesopotamian Glass Vessel (1500-600 B.C.). Full scholarly apparatus. A standard work on ancient Near Eastern glass.

See also the museum catalogs: *Ancient Glass in the Museum of Fine Arts* (Boston) by Axel von Saldern. (Greenwich, Conn., New York Graphics Society, 1968. 94p. illus.), *Ancient Egyptian Glass and Glazes in the Brooklyn Museum*, by Elizabeth Riefstahl (Brooklyn, N.Y., The Museum, 1968. 114p. illus.), *Glass from the Ancient World. The Ray Winfield Smith Collection* (Corning, N.Y., The Corning Museum of Glass, 1957. 298p. illus.), *Glass of the Roman Empire*, by David Whitehouse (Corning, N.Y., Corning Museum of Glass, 1988. 60p. illus. ISBN 0872901181), *Pre-Roman and Early Roman Glass in the Corning Museum of Glass*, by Sidney M. Goldstein (Corning, N.Y., The Museum, 1979. 312p. illus. ISBN 0872900673), *Glas der Antike*, by Ursula Liepmann (Hannover, Kestner-Museum, 1982. 143p. illus.), *La verre d'époque romaine au Musée archéologique de Strasbourg*, by Veronique Arveiller-Dulong and Jacques Arveiller (Paris, Ministere de la Culture, 1985. 320p. illus. index. ISBN 2711802728), *Katalog der römischen Gläser des Rheinischen Landesmuseum Trier*, by Karin Goethert-Polaschek (Mainz, Zabern, 1977. 352p. illus. ISBN 3805300980) and the exhibition catalog: *Glass of the Ceasars*, by D. B. Harden (Milan, Olivetti, 1987. 313p. illus.).

MEDIEVAL, BYZANTINE, AND ISLAMIC GLASS

1441   Philippe, Joseph. **Le monde byzantin dans l'histoire de la verrerie (Ve- XVIe siècle).** Bologna, Patron, 1970. 248p. illus. index. LC 72-553225.

Comprehensive, scholarly history of Byzantine glass from the fifth through the fifteenth centuries with emphasis on the role of glass and glass production in the general culture. Illustrated with museum pieces, line drawings, and views of glass in Byzantine painting and mosaics. Provided with many useful maps and plans of excavations and thorough bibliographical coverage in the footnotes.

See also the museum catalog: *Museum für Islamischer Kunst, Berlin. Glas,* by Jens Kroger (Mainz, Zabern, 1984. 242p. illus. ISBN 3805305745; Islamische Kunst, Band 1) and the exhibition catalog: *Phoenix aus Sand und Asche: Glass des Mittelalters* by Erwin Baumgartner and Ingeborg Krueger (Munich, Klinkhardt & Biermann, 1988. 459p. illus. ISBN 3781402789).

MODERN GLASS (19th and 20th Centuries)

1442   Arwas, Victor. **Glass: Art Nouveau to Art Deco.** New York, Rizzoli, 1977. 256p. illus. index. ISBN 0847801128.

Well-illustrated history of Art Nouveau glass in Europe and America designed for the collector and enthusiast. Introduction discussing techniques of fabrication, repairs, fakes and forgeries is followed by an illustrated dictionary of major designers and makers. Facsimiles of marks and signatures. Comprehensive bibliography of books and periodical literature, pp. 250-54.

1443   Bangert, Albrecht. **Glass. Art Nouveau and Art Deco.** London, Studo Vista, 1979. 160p. illus. index. ISBN 0289708699.

Collector's handbook of European and American art glass in the Art Nouveau and Art Deco styles. Chapter of information for the collector which includes "Building up a reference library" with annotated bibliography classified by language.

1444   Beard, Geoffrey. **International Modern Glass.** London, Barrie & Jenkins, 1976. 264p. illus. index. ISBN 0214200817.

Pictorial survey of glass throughout the world from 1870 to the 1970s. Emphasis is on art glass. Brief introductory essays sketch the development of modern glass. Corpus of plates arranged chronologically; dictionary of glass manufacturers; glossary of glass terms. Bibliography, pp. 254-56, is a classified list of books in all languages.

See also the author's: *Modern Glass* (London, Studio Vista, 1968. 160p. illus. index. LC 75-367713).

1445   Cooke, Fredrick. **Glass: Twentieth-Century Design.** New York, Dutton, 1986. 112p. illus. index. ISBN 0525244646.

Pictorial survey of twentieth-century glass, both art glass and utilitarian glassware, in western Europe and America. Contents: 1, The Nature of Glass; 2, The Formative Years: Art versus Industry; 3, The Decades of Modernism: 1905-1940; 4, Glass in the Design Age: 1940 to the Present. Bibliography of basic books in English with list of British and American periodicals.

1446   Grover, Ray, and Lee Grover. **Carved and Decorated European Art Glass.** Rutland, Vt., Tuttle, 1970. 244p. illus. index. LC 71-94025.

Pictorial handbook of European art glass with raised decoration. Gives facsimiles of marks and signatures. Contents: Austria: Loetz Witwe; Belgium: Val St. Lambert Glass Company; Czechoslovakia: Moser, L. Koloman; England: Cameo, Enamelled, Intaglio, Moss Agate, Overlay, Pull-up, Silveria, Threaded; France: Argy-Rousseau, Barbe, Brateau, Brocard, Copillet and de Caranza, Cros, Dammouse, Damon, D'Argental, Delatte and Arsall, Daum, Decorchemont, Despret, Ericot, Escalier de Cristal, G. de Feure, Emile Gallé, Genet and Michen, M. Goupy, Haligenstein, Indiana, A. Jean, Rene Lalique, August Legras, Louis Majorelle, Maurice Marinot, Christian Meisenthal, Edward Michel, M. Model, Muller Freres, Henru Navarre, Pantin, Eugene Rousseau and E. Leveille, St. Louis, Nacy, Salino, Schneider, Andred Thuret, Almeric Walter; Germany: Karl Koepping, F. Zach; Italy: Venice and Murano; Sweden: Kosta. List of museums with art glass collections. General bibliography, p. 239.

1447   Hilschenz-Mlynek, Helga, and Helmut Ricke. **Glass: Historismus, Jugendstil, Art Deco**. v. 1-, Munich, Prestel-Verlag, 1985-. (Materialen zur Kunst des 19. Jahrhunderts, Band 32) ISBN 3791307118.

Important, scholarly history of European art glass from the middle of the nineteenth century to the 1930s based on the collection of Helmut Hentrich now in the Kunstmuseum in Düsseldorf. Band 1 covers French glass. Contents: Der Sammler Helmut Hentrich; Anmerkungen über französisches Kunstglas: Exotische Einflüsse; Emile Gallé und die Ecole de Nancy; Die Pariser Weltausstellung 1900; Die Künstler der Pate de verre; Die Pariser Ausstellung 1925; Katalog. The catalog is arranged by maker and each is introduced by a comprehensive biography containing information on marks, list of exhibitions, list of museums where major pieces can be found and an extensive bibliography. The entries on the individual pieces have full technical data and references to specific literature. Glossary of technical terms, bibliography, pp. 438-40, facsimiles of signatures, and map showing location of factories at the end of the volume. The second, forthcoming volume will cover the art glass of all other countries.

See also the catalog: *The Art Nouveau and Art Deco Glass in the Österreichisches Museum für Angewandte Kunst in Vienna* (W. Neuwirth, Glas 1905-1925: vom Jugenstil zum Art Deco. Vienna, Neuwirth, 1985. ISBN 3900282102).

1448   Janneau, Guillaume. **Modern Glass**. London, The Studio; New York, W. E. Rudge, 1931. 184p. illus. index. LC 32-1528.

Pictorial survey of European and American art glass of the first quarter of the twentieth century. Includes table glass by major designers as well as lighting fixtures and other architectural glass. Important source for the taste for 'moderne' glass. Comprehensive bibliography by A. Fleming, pp. 54-56.

1449   Pazaurek, Gustav E., and Walter Spiegel. **Glas des 20. Jahrhunderts: Jugenstil, Art Deco**. Munich, Klinkhardt & Biermann, 1983. 263p. illus. index. ISBN 3781402193.

Edited reissue of two classic works by Pazaurek: *Moderne Gläser* (Leipzig, Seemann, 1910) and *Kunstgläser der Gegenwart* (Leipzig, Klinkhardt & Biermann, 1925). Comprehensive history of art glass from 1900 to circa 1930. Updated with new plates, references to recent literature in the footnotes, and new comprehensive bibliography, p. 256. Contents: Neue Formen und Dekors; Farbenfragen; Metallreflexe; Der Pariser Weltwettbewerb 1900; Nancy und die französischen Künstler; Österreich und Deutschland; Der Wiener Stil; Die Fachschulen und die Industrie ihres Wirkungskreises; Das Kunstglas in der Tschechoslowakei; Kunstgläser der übriger Länder; Die Malerei auf Hohlglas; Kristallstil und Glasstil; Das Schliffglas; Wilhelm von Eiff; Gläsermontierungen; Vor der Lampe geblasene Glasarbeiten; Beleuchtungskörper; Altertümeleien und Fälschungen; Nachwort.

1450   Pazaurek, Gustav E. **Gläser der Empire und Biedermeierzeit**. 2d ed. reworked by Eugen von Philippovich. Braunschweig, Klinkhardt & Biermann, 1976. 432p. illus. index. LC 81-471443.

First published in 1923 (Leipzig, Klinkhardt & Biermann)in the series: Monographien des Kunstgewerbes XIII/XV. Comprehensive and authoritative history/handbook of German, Austria, and Czechoslovakian glass of the first half of the nineteenth century. Contents: I, Allgemeiner Teil; II, Die Einzelnen Gruppen der Gläser: Der Glasschliff, In Metalformen geblasene und gepreßte Gläser, Der Glasschnitt im allgemeinen; Die Meister des Tiefschnitts, Der Hochschnitt; Kuglergraveurarbeiten; Farbengläser; Hyalith und Lithyalin nebst anderen Steingläser, Venetianisierende Tendenzen, Eingeglaste Pasten und Metall-Einglasungen, nebst Surrogaten; Doppel-wand-Medaillongläser und ihr vornehmster Vertreter J. J. Mildner; Andere Schmucktechniken; Kombinierte Dekore; Musterbücher der Biedermeierzeit; Vor der Lampe geblasene Arbeiten und Glasgepinste; Glasperlen-Dekor, Granatenzier; Sonstige Glasarbeiten; Datierte Gläser, Vorlagen zu Gläser; Gruppenbenennungen. Bibliographical references in the notes. A standard work on the great period of German nineteenth-century decorated glassware.

1451   Polak, Ada B. **Modern Glass**. New York, Yoseloff, 1962. 94p. illus. index. LC 62-10191.
   Survey of art glass in western Europe and America from 1875 to 1960 directed to the enthusiast and collector. Contents: 1, Fine-de-siècle, 2, Functionalism: 1915-40; 3, Neo-Functionalism: 1945-60. Appendix with list of glass marks. Selected bibliography, pp. 89-90.

1452 Revi, Albert C. **Nineteenth Century Glass: Its Genesis and Development**. Rev. ed. London and Camden, N.J., T. Nelson, 1967. 301p. illus. index. LC 67-103761.
   Handbook of nineteenth-century art glass with emphasis on the production of the last quarter of the century and particularly America. Directed to collectors and concerned chiefly with identification of the various types and manufacturers. Contents: Pearl Satinglass; Coralene; Amberina; Rose Amber; Pressed Amberina; Painted Amberina; Alexandrite; Shaded Opalescent Glassware; Flashed Glassware; Burmese; Peach Blow Glassware; Agata; Pomona; Frosted Glassware (Craquelle and Overshot Glassware); Crown Milano and Albertine; Royal Flemish, Napoli, and Verona Glass; Smith Brothers; The C. F. Monroe Company; Richardson & Atterbury Patents for Enameled Glassware; Venetian Techniques; Aventurine Glass; Peloton Glass; Threaded Glassware; Spun Glass; English Cameo Glass; Novelty-Type Cameo Glass; American Cameo Glass; Venetian Cameo Glass; French Cameo Glass; Cut, Engraved, and Etched Glassware; The Diatreta Technique; Vasa Murrhina, Spangled Glass, and Spatterglass; Clutha Glassware; Onyx Glassware; Silveria; Silvered Glass; Silver Deposit; Metal Encased Glassware; Lava Glassware; Stone Glasses; Iridescent Glassware; Pate de Verre; Cire Perdue; Tortise-Shell Glass; Applied Glass House Decoration; Cameo Incrustations; Paperweight Patents.

1453   Spiegl, Walter. **Glas des Historismus. Kunst-und Gebrauchsgläser des 19. Jahrhunderts**. Braunschweig, Klinkhardt & Biermann, 1980. 277p. illus. index.
   Comprehensive history of glass in western Europe during the second half of the nineteenth century. Emphasis is on vessels in the various historical revival styles. Complements the works of Pazaurek (1449, 1450) to form the most comprehensive history of European glass from Neoclassicism to Art Deco. Contents: Der Weg in die Stillosigkeit; Die Glasveredelung bis 1850 und ihre Auswirkungen auf die zweite Hälfte des 19. Jahrhunderts; Neugotik; Zweites Rokoko; Das farbige und bemalte Glas; Transparentbemalte Glas; Der antikisierende Stil; Neurenaissance; Tiefschnitt; Neubarock und Neurokoko; Doppelwand- und "Mildner" Gläser; Nachbildungen römischer, fränkischer und mittelalterlicher Gläser; Kunstgläser der Rheinischen Glashütten-Aktiengesellschaft Köln-Ehrenfeld; Der venezianische Stil; Überfangreliefschnitt; "Cameo" Glas; Rock Crystal; Emailbenmalte Gläser im altdeutschen Stil; Der orientalisierende Stil. Bibliography, pp. 273-75. List of exhibitions 1851-1900.
   See also the exhibition catalogs: *New Glass: A Worldwide Survey*, organized by the Corning Museum of Glass (Corning, N.Y., The Museum, 1979. 288p. illus. ISBN 087290069X),

La Verrerie Européene des années 50 (Marseille, M, Aveline, Musées de Marseille, 1988. 159p. illus. ISBN 2907010018).

AMERICAN GLASS (U.S. and Canada)

General Histories and Handbooks

1454   Barber, Edwin A. **American Glassware: Old and New**. Philadelphia, McKay, 1900. LC 00-6748.

Pioneering survey of glassware in the United States from Colonial times to the end of the nineteenth century directed to collectors. Concentrates on the types of glassware, particularly flasks, and major factories. Barber, like many early writers on American decorative arts, was greatly motivated by patriotism, which he saw in the scenes and motifs on glass plates and flasks and in the technological advance that culminated in Tiffany.

1455   King, Thomas B. **Glass in Canada**. Erin, Ontario, Boston Mills Press, 1987. 318p. illus. index. ISBN 0919783015.

Comprehensive, well-illustrated history of glass making in Canada from earliest times to 1980. Extensive use of documentary sources. Contents: 1, A Brief History of Glassmaking; 2, Then and Now—Glassblowing to Machine Production; 3, Early Canadian Glasshouses (c. 1839-1878); 4, The Establishment of the Canadian Glass Industry on a Permanent Basis (1878-1902); 5, Consolidation (1903-1913); 6, The Canadian Glass Industry Comes of Age (1913-1925); 7, The Troubled Years (1926-1945); 8, Expansion and Development (1946-1966); 9, Authentication, Attribution and Excavations; 10, Tableware and Industrial Ware in the Twentieth Century; 11, Flat Glass; 12, The Contemporary Scene (1967-1980; 13, Flameworking and Contemporary Glassblowing. Appendices with list of glass companies and their dates, list of bottle markings and closures, and repertory of pressed glass patterns. Glossary and selected bibliography, pp. 303-306. A standard work on Canadian glass.

1456   Knittle, Rhea M. **Early American Glass**. London and New York, Appleton, 1927. 496p. illus. index. Reprint: Garden City, N.Y., Garden City Pub. Co., 1948. LC 48-10807.

Survey history of glass in the United States from Colonial times to the middle of the nineteenth century. Until the work by the McKearins (1460, 1461) this was the best history and remains today a very readable and informative introduction. Bibliography of basic books and articles, pp. 449-53.

1457   Lee, Ruth W. **Victorian Glass: Specialties of the Nineteenth Century**. 12th ed. Wellesley Hills, Mass., Lee Publications, 1944. 608p. illus. Reprint: Rutland, Vt., Tuttle, 1985. ISBN 080487011X.

Pioneering handbook for collectors on American glassware made during the second half of the nineteenth century. Contents: I, Victorian Glass; II, Rarities in Pattern Glass; III, The Most Popular Patterns; IV, The Tree of Life; V, The Coin Pattern; VI, Pattern Glass Collectible in Sets—I; VII, Pattern Glass Collectible in Sets—II; VIII, Pattern Glass Collectible in Sets—III; IX, Pattern Glass Collectible in Sets—IV; X, Pattern Glass Collectible in Sets—V; XI, Shell and Jewel, or "Victor"; XII, Water Sets; XIII, Butter Dishes; XIV, "Opal Ware," or Milk-white Glass; XV, Table Settings; XVI, Figured Glass; XVII, Victorian Novelties; XVIII, Animal Dishes; XIX, Glass Hats; XX, Glass Slippers, Shoes and Boots; XXI, Victorian Vases; XXII, Peachbow, Burmese and Other Shaded Glass; XXIII, Sandwich Engraved, Cut, and Decorated Glass; XXIV, Development of Etched Glass. Illustrated with photographs and drawings of pieces. Notes to the plates. No bibliography.

1458   Lindsey, Bessie M. **American Historical Glass...** Rutland, Vt., Tuttle, 1966. 541p. illus. index. LC 67-11934.

Printed privately in 1948 and 1950. Illustrated handbook of pieces of American glass decorated with historical subjects from Colonial times to the early twentieth century. Contains 530 pieces, which are illustrated and described. Historical subject matter is very broadly defined to include virtually any representation so decorative pieces of glass in the form of recognizable objects are included. Roughly chronological arrangement. No bibliography

1459   McCain, Mollie H. **The Collector's Encyclopedia of Pattern Glass: A Pattern Guide to Early American Pressed Glass.** Paducah, Ky., Collector Books, 1982. 541p. illus. index. ISBN 0891452117.

Pocket-sized guide to the identification of patterns found in American pressed glass from the middle of the nineteenth century to the First World War. Arrangement is by pattern type, e.g., animals and birds, facets, ribs and columns, and representative pieces are illustrated in line drawings. Entries place date of manufacture with references to further information in list of books, p. 7, and price range. General bibliography, pp. 510-11.

1460   McKearin, George S., and Helen McKearin. **American Glass.** New York, Crown, 1941. 622p. illus. index. Reprint: New York, Bonanza, 1989. ISBN 0517682370.

Comprehensive history of glass in the United States from early Colonial times to the late nineteenth century. Chapters on the properties and techniques of glass are followed by a chronological survey emphasizing major centers of production and a detailed examination of the various types of decoration and objects. A corpus of nearly 2,000 plates and 1,000 line drawings accompany the text to produce the richest single source for the collector and historian of American glass. Bibliography, pp. 615-17, lists books and periodical articles. A standard work.

1461   McKearin, Helen, and George S. McKearin. **Two Hundred Years of American Blown Glass...** Rev. ed. New York, 1966. 382p. illus. index. LC 66-5563.

Comprehensive history of American blown glass from early Colonial times to the early twentieth century. Text discusses the European background, the development of glass blowing in the United States with emphasis on major factories and makers, and ends with a note on "the modern renaissance of the art of glass." Collection of 300 plates with descriptive notes accompany the text. Comprehensive bibliography of books and articles, pp. 615-617. Although superseded in regard to certain producers by more recent studies, still the most balanced overview of the history of American blown glass.

1462   Papert, Emma. **The Illustrated Guide to American Glass.** New York, Hawthorn Books, 1972. 289p. illus. index. LC 78-130722.

Collectors's handbook/history of American glass from early Colonial times to the 1970s. Contents: 1, Introduction to Glass Collecting; 2, The South Jersey Tradition; 3, Stiegel-Type Glass: The European Tradition; 4, Aristocratic Engraved Glass: Amelung and His Venture; 5, Midwestern Glass; 6, Glass Blown in Full-Sized Sectional Molds; 7, The Revolution of the Pressing Machine; 8, Wine Bottles and Whiskey Flasks; 9, Household Bottles and Jars; Pressed Pattern Glass; 11, Cut and Engraved Glass—The Middle and Brilliant Periods; 12, Late Nineteenth-Century Art Glass; 13, Twentieth-Century Glass; 14, Search Out, Caring For, and Displaying Antique Glass. Glossary. Bibliography of basic books, pp. 267-71.

1463   Schwartz, Marvin D. **Collector's Guide to Antique American Glass.** Garden City, N.Y. Doubleday, 1969. 150p. illus. index. LC 68-27138.

Popular, concise handbook of American glass from Colonial times to the end of the nineteenth century with chapters on collecting, art glass, and folk glass. No bibliography.

1464   Spillman, Jane S. **Glass Tableware, Bowls & Vases**. New York, Knopf, 1982. 478p. illus. ISBN 0394712722.

1465   ———. **Glass Bottles, Lamps & Other Objects**. New York, Knopf, 1983. 478p. illus. index. ISBN 0394715411.

In the series: "The Knopf Collectors' Guide to American Antiques." Pocket-sized guide books to American glass from earliest Colonial times to the twentieth century. Introductory chapters treat how to identify glass, history of the American glass industry, etc. Each volume has 350 plates of well-selected examples arranged by type with detailed descriptive notes. Prices of pieces are keyed to price guide in the appendix. Appendices have much practical information of interest to the collector including bibliographies of basic literature.

1466   Stevens, Gerald F. **Canadian Glass c.1825-1925**. Toronto, Ryerson, 1967. 262p. illus. index. LC 68-77094.

Concise history of Canadian glassware from 1825 to 1925 with emphasis on later industrial production. Reproduction of pages from catalogs are useful for the collector. Based on much archaeological information and emphasis is on identification of particular types and manufactories. Contents: The Factories; The Personnel; Documentation; Excavation; Cut Glass; The Lampworker. Preface has list of glass factories. Appendices with formulae for various glass works and additional information from documentary sources

1467   Unitt, Doris J., and Peter Unitt. **Treasury of Canadian Glass**. 2nd ed. Peterborough, Ontario, Clock House, 1969. 280p. illus. index. LC 75-480391.

Comprehensive collector's guide to Canadian glassware fromCcolonial times to circa 1920. Large collection of plates with brief descriptive captions. Arrangement is by manufacturer and/or type of pattern. Includes bottles, jars and other common utilitarian glassware, but the emphasis is on tableware with pressed decoration. Bibliography, p. 275.

1468   Watkins, Lura. **American Glass and Glassmaking**. New York, Chanticleer, 1950. 104p. illus. LC 50-6212.

Popular survey of glass in the United States from Colonial times to the middle of the twentieth century. List of important public collections and brief bibliography of basic books, p. 103. A similar work, but with chapter on collecting, is: *Valentine Van Tassel. American Glass.* New York, Gramercy, 1950. 128p. illus. index.

See also the exhibition catalog: *Masterpieces of American Glass* by Jane S. Spillman (New York, Crown, 1990. 100p. illus. ISBN 0517573245) and the museum catalog: *American and European Pressed Glass in the Corning Museum of Glass*, by Janes S. Spillman (Corning, N.Y., The Museum, 1979. 404p. illus. index. ISBN 0872901033).

See also the price guide: *The Official Price Guide to Glassware* (New York, House of Collectibles, 1986. 793p. illus. ISBN 0876373112).

Art Glass

1469   Lee, Ruth W. **Nineteenth-Century Art Glass**. New York, Barrows, 1952. 128p. illus. LC 52-10057.

Popular survey of the production of art glass in America during the last quarter of the nineteenth century directed to the collector. Contents: 1, Amberina, Plated Amberina, Rubena Verde, and Rubena Crystal; 2, Peachblow, Crown Milano, and Royal Flemish; 3, Pomona; 5, Satin Glass Coralene and Mother-of-Pearl; 6, Spangled, Vasa Murrhina, Spatter; 7, Agata; 8, Nikolas Lutz; 9, Mary Gregory; 10, Tiffany Art Glass; 11, Aurene; 12, Kew Blas; 13, Quezal; 14, Victor

Durand; 15, Iridescent Glass; 16, Cameo; 17, Collections in the Home. References to sales in the text. No bibliography.

1470   Revi, Albert C. **American Art Nouveau Glass**. Camden, N.J., Nelson, 1968. 476p. illus. index. LC 68-18778.

Comprehensive, illustrated handbook of American art glass in the Art Nouveau style. Emphasis is on identification of the products of the various designers and factories. Contents: Tiffany Glass Company; A. Douglas Nash Corporation; Quezal Art Glass & Decorating Company; Lustre Art Glass Company; Steuben Glass Works; Vineland Flint Glass; The Union Glass Company; Fostoria Glass Specialty Company; The Honesdale Decorating Company; The Imperial Glass Company; The H. C. Fry Glass Company; The Mt. Washington Glass Company; The C. F. Monroe Company; Handel & Company; A. J. Hall Company; Carl V. Helmschmied; H. E. Rainaud Company; Other Manufacturers of Art-Glass and Bent-Glass Lamps and Windows; Post-Art Nouveau Lamp Designs. Appendices with reproductions of catalogs of Steuben, Vineland Flint, Dorflinger and Carl V. Helmschmied. General bibliography, pp. 463-64. A standard handbook for collectors.

1471   Shuman, John A. **The Collector's Encyclopedia of American Art Glass**. Paducah, Ky., Collector Books, 1987. 335p. illus. index. ISBN 0891453555.

Well-illustrated, popular dictionary of American art glass. Emphasis is on the production of commercial houses between 1880 and the late 1930s. Includes cut glass as well as blown glass. Brief entries covering types, makers, designers and objects is followed by 250 pages of plates that illustrate representative pieces with descriptive captions including estimated prices, reproduction of the illustrations, stained glass windows and lamp shades from the *Art Glass Catalogue* (Chicago, 1910), reproductions of postcard views and advertisements of various factories. Appendices include glossary, advice for the collector, essay on silver plate accompanying art glass with facsimiles of marks, and forty-six pages of reproductions of advertisements. Bibliography, pp. 303-04. "Price Guide to American Art Glass Types Plus Other Glass" follows the index.

Cut and Engraved Glass

1472   Daniel, Dorothy. **Cut and Engraved Glass, 1771-1905: The Collector's Guide to American Wares**. 6th ed. New York, M. Barrow, 1950. 441p. illus. index. LC 50-8234.

Comprehensive collector's handbook of American cut and engraved glass from 1771 to 1905. The first serious effort to present the development of American cut glass and distinguish it from European, particularly Anglo-Irish, wares. Identifies 50 major patterns. Contents: I, Cut Glass: An American Heritage; II, How to Detect Imitations; III, The Making of Glass; IV, Cutting, Engraving, Etching; V, Cameo and Intaglio Glass; VI, Colored Cut Glass; VII, English Irish, or American?; VIII, The Early American Period, 1771-1830; IX, The Brilliant Period; XI, Patterns of the Brilliant Period; XII, Cut Glass, Today and Tomorrow; XIII, Candlesticks, Candelabra, Chandeliers; XIV, Lamps; XV, Decanters, Cologne Bottles, Condiment Sets; XVI, Boxes, Baskets, Knife Rests; XVII, Care of Cut Glass; XVIII, Advice to Collectors. Appendices with motif charts, list of known patterns, classification of Stiegel patterns, facsimiles of trademarks and chronological list of glass houses. Comprehensive, classified bibliography, pp. 420-29. A standard collector's handbook.

1473   Pearson, J. Michael. **Encyclopedia of American Cut and Engraved Glass, 1880-1917**. 3 vs. Miami Beach, Fla., By the Author, 1975-1978. ISBN 0916528014.

Comprehensive handbook of cut glass produced in the United States between 1880 and 1917. Nearly 2,000 examples are described and illustrated in a complex system organized around patterns and other prominent design features. Contents: Volume 1: Geometric Conceptions;

Volume 2: Realistic Patterns; Volume 3: Geometric Motifs. Designed as an identification guide for collectors; no effort is made to write the history of American Victorian cut glass.

1474   Revi, Albert C. **American Cut and Engraved Glass**. New York, Nelson, 1965. 497p. illus. index. LC 65-20016.

Comprehensive collector's handbook of American cut glass from circa 1850 and circa 1950. Arrangement is by state and then by manufacturer. Descriptive text with plates and line drawings. Appendices with list of members of the National Association of Cut Glass Manufacturers and repertory of trademarks and labels for cut glass wares. Standard collector's handbook. No bibliography.

1475   Swan, Martha L. **American Cut and Engraved Glass of the Brilliant Period in Historical Perspective**. Lombard, Ill., Wallace-Homestead Book Co., 1986. 328p. illus. index. ISBN 0870694308.

Popular but fact-filled handbook for collectors of American cut and engraved glass made between 1880 and 1915. Contents: 1, Learning about Glassmaking; 2, Our Glass Heritage in History; 3, Cut Glass in America: Early and Middle Periods; 4, Brilliant Period Cut Glass; 5, Social and Political Consequences of the Industrial Revolution; 6, Nomenclature of Motifs and Patterns; 7, Evolution of Pattern Styles; Patented Designs and Trademarks; 8, Advertising, Distribution, and Prices; 9, Evolution of a Glass Factory: Mount Washington/Pairpoint; 10, Life-Style of the Rich; 11, More Cut Glass Rarities; 12, Life-Style of the Middle Classes; 13, Cut Glassware in the Home; 14, Libbey Cut Glass; 15, Dorflinger, Hawkes, and Steuben; 16, Tuthill, Meriden, Bergen, and Niland; 17, Other Glassware Companies; 18, European Versus American; 19, Why and How to Build a Collection; 20, Choosing Glassware. Appendix with list of trademarks and signatures of American and Canadian glass makers and index of illustrated designs. Comprehensive, annotated bibliography, pp. 313-318. See separately published price guide below.

See also the price guides: *The Standard Cut Glass Value Guide*, by J. Evers (Paducah, Ky., Collector Books, 1981. 156p. illus. ISBN 0891450025) and *Value Guide to Cut and Engraved Glass of the American Brilliant Period in Historical Perspective*, by L. Swan (Lombard, Ill., Wallace-Homestead Book Co., 1986. 11p. ISBN 0870694472).

Pressed Glass

1476   Batty, Bob H. **A Complete Guide to Pressed Glass**. Gretna, La., Pelican Pub. Co., 1978. 261p. illus. index. ISBN 0882890573.

Collector's guide to the identification and evaluation of American pressed glass with emphasis on larger objects, particularly water pitchers from the second half of the nineteenth century. Arrangement is by type of pattern or distinctive pattern motif. The 300 patterns are described in detail and supported by drawings. Appendices have information on "states" series, reproductions, naming patterns of pressed glass, patterns of The U.S. Glass Company, and list of glass companies in America, 1888-1904. General bibliography, pp. 254-55.

1477   Heacock, William. **Encyclopedia of Victorian Colored Pattern Glass**. Marietta, Oh., Antique Publications, 1974-. v. illus.

Book I. *Toothpick Holders from A to Z.* (1974)
Book II. *Opalescent Glass from A to Z.*
Book III. *Syrups, Sugar Shakers & Cruets.* (1976)
Book IV. *Custard Glass from A to Z.*
Book V. *U. S. Glass from A to Z.* (1978)

Book VI. *Oil Cruets from A to Z* (1981)
Book VII. *Ruby-Stained Glass from A to Z.* (1986)
Book IX. *Cranberry Opalescent from A to Z.* (1987)
Comprehensive collector's handbook and price guide to American colored pattern glass of the late nineteenth century.

1478   Lee, Ruth W. **Ruth Webb Lee's Handbook of Early American Pressed Glass Patterns.** Rutland, Vt., C. E. Tuttle, 1984. 214p. illus. index. ISBN 0804870055.
First published in 1936. Pictorial collector's guide to the identification of American pressed glass dating between 1840 and the 1980s based upon the author's *Early American Pressed Glass.*

1479   McCain, Mollie H. **The Collector's Encyclopedia of Pattern Glass. A Pattern Guide to Early American Pressed Glass.** Paducah, Ky., Collector Books, 1982. 541p. illus. index. ISBN 0891452117.
Dictionary of patterns in American pressed glass from the middle of the nineteenth century to World War I. Arranged by type of pattern, e.g., animals, fruit, panels, and illustrated with drawings. Identifications of the individual pieces are keyed to list of reference works and to a table of price ranges.
See also the price guide: A. H. Matz. *Early American Pattern Glass: Values Revised 1978* (Paducha, Ky., Collector Books, 1978. 2v. illus. index. ISBN 0891450912).

1480   Revi, Albert C. **American Pressed Glass and Figure Bottles.** New York, Nelson, 1964. 446p. illus. index. LC 64-14510.
Comprehensive handbook of pressed glass made in America from the late eighteenth to the early twentieth centuries. Designed for the collector and emphasis is placed on identification of the various manufacturers. Many useful reproductions of pages from catalogues and advertisements. Contents: The Development of the Pressed Glass Industry in America; Adams & Company; The Atena Glass and Manufacturing Company; Atterbury & Company; Bakewell & Ensell; The Bay State Glass Company; Alexander J. Beatty Sons; The Beaumont Glass Company; The Beaver Falls Glass Company; The Bellaire Goblet Company; The Boston Sandwich Glass Company; The Brilliant Glass Works; Bryce, McKee & Company; Bryce, Higbee & Company; The Buckeye Glass Company; The Cambridge Glass Company; Campbell, Jones & Company; The Canton Glass Company; The Central Glass Company; Challinor, Taylor & Company, Limited; The Columbia Glass Company; The Co-Operative Flint Glass Company Limited; The Crystal Glass Company; Dalzell Brother & Gillmore; Dithridge & Company; Doyle & Company; The Dugan Glass Company; George Duncan & Sons; The Elson Glass Company; The Fenton Art Glass Company; The Findlay Flint Glass Company; The Fostoria Glass Company; The Franklin Flint Glass Company; The Greensburg Glass Company; The A. H. Heisey Glass Company; The Hemingray Glass Company; The Hipkins Novelty Mold Shop; Hobbs, Brockunier & Company; The Huntington Glass Company; The Imperial Glass Company; The Indiana Glass Company; The Indiana Tumbler & Goblet Company; The Jefferson Glass Company; King, Son & Company; The Kokomo Glass Company; The La Belle Glass Company; The Lancaster Glass Company; McKee & Brothers; The Model Flint Glass Company; The Mosaic Glass Company; The National Glass Company of Bellaire, Ohio; The National Glass Company; The New Brighton Glass Company; The New England Glass Company; The Nickel Plate Glass Company; The Northwood Glass Company; The O'Hara Glass Company; The Ohio Flint Glass Company; The Phoenix Glass Company; The Pioneer Glass Company; The Portland Glass Company; Richards & Hartley Flint Glass Company; Ripley & Company; The Riverside Glass Company; The Rochester Tumbler Company; Sweeney, McCluney & Company; The Thompson Glass Company; The Union Glass Company; The United States Glass Company; The Westmoreland Specialty Company; The West

Virginia Glass Company; The Windsor Glass Company; The Whitla Glass Company; Designs and Patents for Glassware; American Figure Bottles. General bibliography, pp. 413-14.

See also the exhibition catalog: *The Story of American Pressed Glass of the Lacy Period, 1825-1850,* by J. H. Rose (Corning, N.Y., Corning Museum of Glass, 1954. 163p. illus.).

See also the price guide: *Wallace-Homstead Price Guide to Pattern Glass,* by D. Miles (Lombard, Ill., Wallace-Homstead, 1986. 296p. illus. ISBN 0870694421).

Major Regions, Centers, and Factories

New England

1481   Wilson, Kenneth M. **New England Glass and Glassmaking.** New York, Crowell, 1972. 401p. illus. index. ISBN 0690580754.

Series: "Old Sturbridge Village Book." Comprehensive history of the production of glass and glassware in New England from earliest Colonial times to Art Nouveau. Includes industrial glass production, e.g., window glass, as well as glass tableware and charts the importation of glass into New England. Contents: 1, Heritage of New England Glass—Importations; 2, Seventeenth- and Eighteenth-Century Glassmaking Attempts in New England; 3, Nineteenth-Century New England Window Glasshouses; 4, Nineteenth-Century Connecticut Bottle Glasshouses; 5, Nineteenth-Century New Hampshire Bottle Glasshouses; 6, Nineteenth-Century Massachusetts Bottle Glasshouses; 7, The Flint Glass Industry in New England. Selective bibliography, pp. 385-87, and specialized literature in the notes. Chronological list of New England glasshouses and products.

See also the exhibition catalog: *The New England Glass Company, 1818-1888* (Toledo, Oh., Toledo Museum of Art, 1963. 80p. illus.).

Cambridge Glass

1482   Watkins, Lura W. **Cambridge Glass, 1818 to 1888: The Story of the New England Glass Company.** Boston, Marshall Jones, 1930. 199p. illus. index. LC 30-30210. Reprinted, 1953. LC 53-6027.

Contents: Introduction; The Story of the Factory; Materials and Characteristics; A Survey of the Products of the Factory; Pressed Glass; Molded Glass; Engraving and Cutting; Paper- weights; Lamps; Colored Glass of the Eighties; The Glass-Workers; Agents and Agencies; Other Cambridge Factories: The New England Crown Glass Company, The New England Glass Bottle Company, The Bay State Glass Company, The Boston Flint Glass Works; The Boston Silver Glass Company.

Sandwich Glass

1483   Barlow, Raymond E., and Joan F. Kaiser. **The Glass Industry in Sandwich: Volume 3.** Windham, N.H., Barlow-Kaiser Publishing Co., 1987. 280p. illus. index. ISBN 0887400817.

Comprehensive history/handbook of Sandwich glass most useful for the large corpus of plates grouped by time and type. Contents: 1, Boston and Sandwich Glass Company 1858-1882; 2, Vases and Flower Containers 1825-1908; 3, Cape Cod Glass Works 1858-1864; 4, Cape Cod Glass Company 1864-1869; 6, A Study of Stoppers 1825-1887; 7, The North Sandwich Industrial Area 1847-1895; 8, Which Balls Are Witch Balls? 1825-1887; 9, Covered Containers for Specialized Use 1830-1908; 10, Toys 1825-1897; 11, The Creations of Nicholas Lutz during his Years at Sandwich 1870-1892. Classified bibliography, pp.265-270, includes unpublished mate- rials. Note: Volumes 1 and 2 are planned. They will cover the early history of Sandwich glass. Volumes 3 and 4 roughly cover the periods 1858-1882 and 1882 and 1894 respectively. However, the arrangement of the catalogs by type has placed some early works in volume 4 and some later works in volume 3.

1484   Barlow, Raymond E., and Joan F. Kaiser. **The Glass Industry in Sandwich: Volume 4.** Windham, NH, Barlow-Kaiser Publishing Co., 1983. 381p. illus. index. ISBN 0961016604.

Comprehensive history/handbook of glass made in Sandwich most useful for the large corpus of plates grouped by time and type. Contents: 1, Boston and Sandwich Glass Company 1882-1894; 2, The Spurr Family in Sandwich; 3, Candlesticks 1825-1887; 4, Boston and Sandwich Glass Company Factory Site 1889-1920; 5, Insulators and Conduit 1851-1890; 6, Overshot (Frosted Ware) 1870-1887; 7, Cape Cod Glass Company Factory Site 1869-1922; 8, Vasa Murrhina Art Glass Company 1883-1885; 9, The Glass Cutting Enterprises of the Nehemiah Packwoods 1890-1922; 10, J. B. Vodon and Son, a Cutting and Engraving Shop 1895-1916; 11, Late Blown Ware 1870-1887; 12, Edward J. Swann, Master Decorator 1872-1895; 13, Threaded Glass 1880-1887; 14, The Decorating Work of Mary Gregory 1880-1884; 15, Epergnes 1870-1887; 16, Sandwich Co-operative Glass Company 1888-1891; 17, Trevaise 1907-1908. Classified bibliography, pp. 361-66.

1485   Chipman, Frank. **Romance of Old Sandwich Glass**. Sandwich, Mass., Sandwich Pub. Co., 1932. 158p. illus. index. LC 32-7881.

Collector's survey and handbook of old Sandwich glass. Contents: 1, Foreword; 2, From Sidon to Sandwich; 3, Deming Jarves goes Shooting; 4, Pressed Ware Distinctive; 5, Men and Women Who Wrought; 6, The Moulds—Acme of Skill; 7, Patterns and Types; 8, Colored Sandwich; 9, Notable Collections; 10, Late Sandwich; 11, Dictionary of Patterns (descriptions of 158 authenticated patterns and types of old Sandwich glass).

1486   Lee. Ruth W. **Sandwich Glass: The History of the Boston and Sandwich Glass Company**. 7th ed. rev. and enl. Nortborough, Mass., By the Author, 1947. 590p. illus. index. LC 47-23285.

Comprehensive history/handbook of Sandwich glassware directed to collectors and with emphasis on identification of patterns and dating. Contents: I, Deming Jarvis; II, Founding of the Boston & Sandwich Glass Company; III, Early Days at Sandwich; IV, The Pressing Machine and Jarves' Patents; V, First Types of Glass Produced; VI, The Middle Years. 1840-1858; VII, Later Years. 1860-1888; VIII, Interesting Early Blown Glass; IX, Blown Molded Glass; X, Cup Plates; XI, The Connecting Link; XII, Lacy Salts; XIII, Miniature Lacy Pieces; XIV, Sauce Dishes; XV, Small Lacy Bowls; XVI, Oblong Trays and Oval Dishes; XVII, Tea Plates; XVIII, Large Lacy Bowls and Plates; XIX, Lacy Compotes and Covered Dishes; XX, Lacy Sugar Bowls and Creamers; XXI, Pittsburg vs. Sandwich; XXII, Rarities in Lacy Glass; XIII, Octagonal Series of Lacy Plates; XXIV, Baccarat and Other Foreign Lacy Glass; XXV, Candlesticks; XXVI, Lamps; XXVII, Vases; XXVIII, Paperweights by Nicholas Lutz; XIX, Perfume Bottles and Jars; XXX, Pattern Glass; XXXI, Sandwich Engraved, Cut and Decorated Wares; XXXII, Closing Days.

1487   Williams, Lenore W. **Sandwich Glass: A Technical Book for Collectors**. New York, By the Author, 1922. 102p. illus. index. LC 22-2228.

Pioneering work on Sandwich glassware. Pocket-sized handbook of the decorative glass-ware made in Sandwich between 1825 and 1853. Contents: 1, Glass Cup Plates—Historical and Conventional; 2, Salts and Victorian Animals; 3, American Glass Candlesticks and Whale Oil Lamps; 4, Flat Ware of the Early Period; 5, Presentation and Commercial Pieces.

Middle Atlantic States

Corning Glass

1488   Farrar, Estelle S., and Jane S. Spillman. **The Complete Cut & Engraved Glass of Corning**. New York, Crown, 1979. 344p. illus, index. ISBN 0517534320.
    Series: "A Corning Museum of Glass Monograph." Comprehensive history of the production of cut and engraved glass in Corning from the late 1860s to the present. Contents: 1, Background; 2, The Cut-Glass Industry; 3, The Cutting and Engraving of Glass; 4, J. Hoare & Co.; 5, T. G. Hawkes & Co.; 6, Hunt Glass Works, Inc.; 7, O. F. Egginton Co.; 8, Engraving in Corning, 1868-1968; 9, Small Companies and Home Shops in Corning and Adjacent Villages; 10, Bronson Inkstand Co.; George W. Drake & Co.; 11, Corning Cut Glass Co.; 12, Giometti Brothers; 13, Steuben Glass Works (1903-18); Steuben Glass, Corning Glass Works (1918-33); 14, H. P. Sinclaire & Co.; 15, J. F. Haselbauer & Sons; Frederick Haselbauer, Engraver; 16, Thomas Shotton Cut Glass Works; 17, John N. Illig, Manufacturer of Artistically Engraved Glassware; 18, Corning's Ghost Companies; 19, Neighboring and Corning-Founded Companies; 20, Corning Today. Appendix with chronological list of cutting companies and home shops in Corning and immediate vicinity. Bibliographical references in the notes, selected bibliography, p. 328.

Steuben Glass

1489   Madigan, Mary J. S. **Steuben Glass: An American Tradition in Crystal**. New York, Abrams, 1982. 320p. illus. index. ISBN 0810916428.
    Lavishly illustrated history of Steuben glass from the founding of the firm in 1903 by Frederick Carder to the present. Contents: I, How Steuben Glass Is Made: Forming, Finishing, Decorating, Designing; II, Foundations: 1903-1929; III, The Troubled Years: 1929-1932; IV, A New Beginning: 1933-1937; V, World's Fair and World War: 1938-1946; VI, Gearing for Expansion: 1946-1950; VII, From America to the World: 1951-1961; VIII, Experiment and Change: 1958-1972; IX, Steuben Today: Innovation and Continuity; Epilogue by Thomas S. Buechner. Catalog with biographies of artists who worked for Steuben. Catalog of over 1,000 pieces of Steuben glass made between 1933 and 1981. Exhibition pieces are represented in plates with descriptive captions and stock pieces by line drawings. Bibliography, pp. 315-16, and bibliographical references in the notes.

1490   Plaut, James. **Steuben Glass: a Monograph**. 3rd ed. New York, Dover, 1972. 111p. illus. index. ISBN 0486228924.
    Pictorial survey of Steuben glass from its reorganization as an art glass maker in 1933 to 1971. Contents: The Evolution of Steuben Glass; How Steuben Glass Is Made; A Critical Estimate of Steuben Glass; Illustrations of Steuben Glass; Major Exhibitions; Public Collections. No bibliography.
    See also the exhibition catalog: *Steuben: Seventy Years of American Glassmaking* by Paul N. Perrot, Paul V. Gardner and James S. Plaut (New York, Praeger, 1974. 172p. illus. ISBN 0275443205).

Stiegel Glass

1491   Hunter, Frederick W. **Stiegel Glass**. Introduction and notes by Helen McKearin. 1914. 270p. illus. index. Reprint: New York, Dover, 1950. LC 67-4311.
    Pioneering work on an American glass factory. Comprehensive history of Stiegel glass produced during the eighteenth century with detailed biography of the founder, Henry William

Stiegel, transcripts of many valuable documents and analysis of the materials, techniques and products of the Stiegel factory. Although many of Hunter's attributions of pieces to Stiegel are now questionable, his history remains a basic source of information for collectors and scholars. Contents: Part I. Henry William Stiegel; Part II, Stiegel Glass: I, Glass in General, II, Early Glassmaking in America—Seventeenth Century, III, Early Glassmaking in America—Eighteenth Century; IV, Wistarberg; V, Siegel Glass: Sources of Information; VI, Stiegel Glass: Materials and Methods; VII, Stiegel Glass: Characteristics and Described Specimens. Bibliography, pp.263-65.

Tiffany Glass

1492   Duncan, Alastair, Martin Eidelberg, and Neil Harris. **Masterworks of Louis Comfort Tiffany**. New York, Abrams, 1989. 160p. illus. index. ISBN 0810924404.
   Richly illustrated survey of the art of Louis C. Tiffany published to accompany the exhibition: Masterworks of Louis Comfort Tiffany at the Renwick Gallery, Washington, D.C., and at the National Academy of Design, New York. Contents: Louis Comfort Tiffany: The Search for Influence by N. Harris; Tiffany and the Cult of Nature by M. Eidelberg; Stained Glass: Secular Windows and Ecclesiastical Settings by A. Duncan. Notes to plates with references to specialized literature.

1493   Koch, Robert. **Louis Tiffany, Rebel in Glass**. 3rd ed. New York, Crown, 1982. 246p. illus. index. ISBN 0517097346.
   Comprehensive monograph on the life and art of Louis Tiffany. Contents: Memories of Louis C. Tiffany by Comfort Tiffany Gilder and Dorothy Tiffany Burlingham; Introduction by Theodore Sizer; Part One: Artistic Interiors: Louis C. Tiffany as Painter and Decorator; Part Two: The Stained Glass Decades: Louis C. Tiffany as a Designer of Stained Glass Windows and Mosaics; Part Three: "Good Art in Our Homes": Louis C. Tiffany as the Creator of Favrile Glass, Tiffany Studios and Laurelton Hall; Part Four: "Afterword." Classified bibliography, pp. 217-230.
   See also the catalog: *The Tiffany Collection of the Chrysler Museum at Norfolk,* Norfolk, Va., Norfolk Museum, 1978. 159p. illus.

Midwestern States

Libbey Glass

1494   Fauster, Carl U. **Libbey Glass Since 1818**. Toledo, Oh., Len Beach Press, 1979. 415p. illus. index. LC 79-51116.
   Comprehensive history of Libbey glass and glassworks from 1818 to the 1940s. Large number of illustrations include reproductions of catalogs, advertisements, newspaper clippings, view of the plant and its personalities, as well as representative pieces of Libbey glass. Contents: Part One—Pictorial History: I, The First Half Century, 1818-1872; II, "Go West Young Man" The Early Years of Libbey Leadership, 1872-1893; III, The Year of Cut Glass Supremacy, 1893-1918; IV, Depression Year Failures Bring Reunion of Libbey and Owens Companies; V, Mid-Twentieth Century Expansion Years. Part Two—Collector's Guide: 1968 Toledo Museum Exhibition Cases; Individually Illustrated Section; Color Illustration Section. Part Three—Catalog Reprints: Cut Glass Catalog—1905; Cut and Engraved Glass Catalog c. 1920; Libbey-Nash Series Catalog—1933; Modern American Glassware Catalog. Selected bibliography, pp. 401-02.

EUROPEAN GLASS

General Works

1495 Davis, Frank. **Continental Glass**. New York, Praeger, 1972. 144p. illus. index. LC 79-180728.
Concise survey of European glass, excluding Great Britain, from antiquity to the twentieth century with emphasis on works of high, artistic virtuosity. Contents: 1, Introduction; 2, The Twilight of Rome; 3, Spain; 4, The Netherlands; 5, France; 6, Bohemia, Germany and Austria; 7, The Nineteenth Century and After. Appendix with essay on rock-crystal. General bibliography, p. 119.

1496 Middlemas, Keith. **Antique Glass in Color**. Garden City, N.Y., Doubleday, 1971. 120p. illus. LC 71-134442.
Concise survey of European glass from the Middle Ages to Art Nouveau illustrated with excellent color plates. No bibliography.

1497 Moore, Hannah H. **Old Glass, European and American**. New York, Tudor, 1935. 394p. illus. index. LC A35-1894.
Older survey of glassware from ancient Egypt to the middle of the nineteenth century with emphasis on British and American glass. Contents: Part I: The Art of Glass-making; Venetian Glass, Bohemian Glass, Dutch and Flemish Glass; Spanish Glass; French Glass; English Glass; Bristol Glass; Nailsea Glass; Irish Glass; Waterford Glass; Dublin and Cork Glass; Part II: American Glass; Wistarberg Glass; Stiegel Glass; Other Early Glass; Saratoga Glass; Bottles and Flasks; Three-Section Mould Glass; Stoddard Glass; Keene Glass; Pitkin Glass; Historic Cup Plates; Sandwich Glass; Mexican Glass; American Glass Factories (dictionaries of major manufactories). No bibliography.

1498 Schmidt, R. **Das Glas**. 2nd ed. Berlin, Leipzig, de Gruyter, 1922. 419p. illus. index. LC 13-9926.
An old, standard history of European glass from antiquity to the early nineteenth century with particular emphasis on German glass. Contents: I, Das Material und seine Bearbeitung; II, Das Glas im Altertum; III, Das mittelalerliche Glas Norwesteuropa; IV, Das orientalische Glas: Byzantnisches und sassanidisches Glas, Ägyptisches und syrisches Glas, Das emaillerte Glas des 13. und 14. Jahrhunderts, Das orientalische Glas seit dem 15. Jahrhundert; V, Das venezianische Glas; VI, Das Glas in Venezianer Art (Italy, Netherlands, Germany, Scandinavia); VII, Das deutsche Glas; VIII, Das gerissene punktierte holländische Glas; IX, Das spanische Glas; X, Das französische Glas; XI, Das englische Glas; XII, Das chinesische Glas. Bibliographical references in the notes.

1499 Schrijver, Elika. **Glass and Crystal**. New York, Universe, 1964. 2v. illus. index. LC 64-10342.
Concise but authoritative history of European glass from antiquity to 1950 with particularly clear explanations of technique. Contents: Volume I: 1, 'Born of Love'; 2, Glass and Crystal; 3, From 3500 B.C.; 4, The First Blown Glass; 5, After the Fall of the Roman Empire 400-800; 6, Islamic Glass; 7, Europe 800-1400; 8, Venice I; 9, Venice II; 10, Venice III; 11, Europe; 12, Decoration Techniques; 13, Germany and Bohemia; 14, France; 15, Spain; 16, The Netherlands; 17, England and Ireland; 18, Northern and Eastern Europe; 19, Europe from the End of the 18th to the Middle of the 19th Century. Volume II: Europe from the Middle of the Nineteenth Century to 1950.

1500   Steenberg, Elisa, and Bo Simmingskold. **Glas**. Stockholm, Natur och Kultur, 1958. 434p. illus. index. LC 58-46941.

Comprehensive history of glass from antiquity to the twentieth century with particular attention given to the techniques and materials of modern Swedish glass. Contents: Glasets historia by E. Steenberg: Inledning; Antikens glaskonst; Medeltidens gals i Mellaneuropa; Medeltidens orientaliska glaskonst; Venetiansk glaskonst; Spanskt glas; Tysk och böhmisk glaskonst; Engelsk glaskonst; Franskt glas; Holländskt glas; Danskt och norskt glas; Amerikanskt glas; Kinesisk glas; Modern utländsk glaskonsr; Gammalt svenskt glas; Modernt svenskt glas. Glas teknologi by B. Simmingsköld: Inledning; Vad är glas? Det Glasiga tillståndet; Glaskomponenter och råvaror; Glasets viskositet; De vanliga glasens kemiska sammanstättning; Fårglöst glas, avfärgning, solarisation; Färgglas och opalglas; Råvarulagring och mängberedning; Värme, temperatur-mätning, förbränning, bränslen; Glasugnar och eldfasta material; Smältprocessen; Ellektrisk glassmältning; Manuelle glastillverkning; Förädling av manuellt tillverkat glas; Maskinell glastillverkning; Spänningar i glas. Kylprocessen; Mågra av glasets fysikaliska egenskaper; Några nyara glasspecialiteter; Glastel; Elementär kemi för glasintresserade. Classified bibliography, pp. 427-29. Illustrated with 282 high quality black and white plates.

1501   Wilkinson, O. N. **Old Glass: Manufacture, Styles, Uses**. New York, Philosophical Society, 1968. 200p. illus. index. LC 68-6826.

Concise but authoritative history of European glass from antiquity to the early twentieth century with emphasis on developments in England during the eighteenth century. Contents: I, The Art of Glassmaking; 2, The Early Development of Glass; 3, The Supremacy of Venice; 4, The International Development; 5, The Birth of the English Industry; 6, The Monopolists; 7, The Eighteenth Century: 1; 8, The Eighteenth Century: 2; 9, English Commemorative Glass; 10, Notes on English Glass of the Eighteenth Century; 11, Glass after 1800. General bibliography, pp. 187-88, and specialized bibliographies at the end of each chapter.

See also the collection catalogs: *Glassammlung Helfried Krug. Beschreibender Katalog mit kunstgeschichtlicher Einführung*, by B. Klesse (Munich, Müller; Bonn, Habelt, 1965-73. 2v. illus. index. LC 67-77578), *European Glass from 1500-1800: the Ernesto Wolf Collection*, by B. Klesse and H. Mayr (Vienna, Kremayr & Scheriau, 1987. 151p. illus. ISBN 3218004659), and the museum guide: *Glass; a Handbook for the Study of Glass Vessels of All Periods and Countries & a Guide to the Museum Collection*, by W. B. Honey (London, Victoria and Albert Museum, 1946. 169p. illus.).

See also the price guide: *Glass*, by T. Curtis (New York, Coward, McCann & Geoghegan, 1982. 254p. illus. ISBN 0698111591).

France and Belgium

1502   Barrelet, James. **La verrerie en France**. Paris, Larousse, 1953. 207p. illus. LC 57-17943.

Concise history of glass in France from Gallo-Roman times to the twentieth century. Illustrations include works of art showing glass at various periods. Contents: I, Epoque Gall-Ro-maine; II, Epoche Préromane; III, Epoche Romane (du Xe au XIIe s.); IV, Epoque Gothique (du XIIIe au XVe s.), V, De la Renaissance à la Révolution; VI, De l'Empire à la IVe République. Glossary, maps with locations of glass houses, and comprehensive bibliography, pp. 189-192.

1503   Bloch-Dermant, Janine. **L'Art du verre en France, 1860-1914. The Art of French Glass, 1860-1914**. London, Thames & Hudson, 1980. 204p. illus. index. ISBN 08656550004.

Well-illustrated survey of French art glass from 1860 to 1914. Contents: The Technician and the Revival; Oriental Influences and the Search for New Forms: Philippe-Joseph Brocard, Auguste Jean, François-Eugène Rousseau, Amédée de Caranza; The Successors to François-Eugène Rousseau: Ernest-Baptiste Léveillé, Eugène Michel, Alphonse-Georges Reyen, Les

Frères Pannier; The School of Nancy: Emile Gallé, Les Frères Daum, Les Frères Muller; Pâte-de-Verre: Henri Gros, Albert Dammouse, Ringel d'Illzach, Georges Despret, François Décorchemont. Bibliography, pp. 199-200.

1504   Bloch-Dermatt, Janine. **La verre en France d' Emile Gallé a nos jours.** Paris, Editions de l'Amateur, 1983. 312p. illus. index. ISBN 2859170294.

Well-illustrated history/handbook of French art glass from 1860 to the present. Contents: L'art du verre en France de 1860 a 1914; L'école de Nancy et ses continuateurs: Émile Gallé, Daum, Les frères Muller, Paul Nicolas, André Delatte, Auguste Legras; Les maitres verriers: Maurice Marinot, André Thuret, Henri Navarre, Georges Dumoulin, Aristide Colotte, Dienvenu et Jean Sala; Les décorateurs sur verre: Auguste Heiligenstein, Marcel Goupy, Jean Luce; Les verriers artistiques: René Lalique, March Lalique, Marie-Claude Lalique, Baccarat: George Chevalier, Degué: Edouard Cazaux, Schneider, André Hunebelle, Marius Sabino; La pate de verre: François Décorchemont, Amalric Walter, Argy-Rousseau; Les éditeurs d'art; Verriers et décorateurs; Verriers d'aujourd'hui. Glossary and bibliography, pp. 311-312, which lists both books and periodical articles. This work is essentially an expansion to the present of the author's work on French glass of 1860-1914 (1503).

1505   Chambon, Raymond. **L'histoire de la verrerie en Belgique.** Brussels, Librairie Encyclopedique, 1955. 331p. illus. index. LC A56-1233.

Comprehensive, scholarly history of glassmaking in Belgium from the second century A.D. to 1950. Contents: I, Les périodes romaine et franque; II, La période féodale; III, La fin du Moyen Age; IV, Le régime espagnol: première période (jusqu'en 1621); V, Le régime espagnol: deuxième période (jusqu'en 1713); VI, Le régime autrichien; VII, L'industrie verrière aux points de vue économique et social de 1482 à 1790; VIII, De la mort de Joseph II à la Révolution Belge; IX, La Belgique indépendante (1ère période); X, La Belgique indépendante (2e période); XI, La Belgique indépendante (3e période); XII, La Belgique indépendante (4e période); XIII, Role économique et social de l'industrie verrière depuis 1790. Text illustrated with contemporary views of the use and making of glass. Collection of 158 illustrations of pieces of Belgian glass with descriptive notes. Bibliographical references in the footnotes and comprehensive bibliography, pp. 261-81.

Daum Frères

1506   Daum, Noël. **Daum. Maitres verriers.** Paris, 1980. 197p. illus. index. ISBN 2880010594.

Popular, well-illustrated survey of the art glass production of the Daum glasshouse from 1894 to 1960. Contents: Les Daum; La Genèse des styles; La Décoration à chaud; la Décoration à froid; Les pâtes de verre; Les Appareils d'éclairage; L'Entre-deux-guerres; Poésie du cristal; Les Services de table; Les Signatures. Classified bibliography, p. 195.

Émile Gallé, 1846-1904

1507   Duncan, Alastair. **Glass by Gallé.** London, Thames & Hudson, 1984. 224p. illus. index. ISBN 050023387X.

Well-illustrated monograph on Gallé as glass artist with emphasis on decorative and technical influences. Contents: 1, Enamelling; 2, Engraving; 3, Applied and Sculpted Decoration; 4, Marqueterie de verre; 5, Verreries parlantes; 6, Imitation Hardstones and Agates; 7, Verres hyalites and vases de tristesse; 8, Mounts. Appendix with signatures, review of prices, and classified bibliography, pp. 219-20.

1508   Garner, Philippe. **Emile Gallé**. London, Academy Editions; New York, St. Martin's Press, 1984. 167p. illus. index. ISBN 0312244169.

Well-illustrated monograph on Gallé covering his work in wood, ceramics, and glass, with emphasis on the overall artistic development of Gallé. Reproductions of significant pieces, photographs of Gallé's workshop and portraits of important persons. Contents: Biography; Influences; Faience; Wood; Glass; Le Chef des Odeurs Suaves; Conclusion; Le Décor Symbolique. General bibliography, p. 163, and more specialized literature in the notes.

1509   Newark, Timothy. **Emile Gallé**. Secaucus, N.J., Chartwell Books, 1989. 128p. illus. index. ISBN 1555214509.

Well-illustrated, popular survey of the art glass of Emile Gallé. Contents: 1, Paris 1900; 2, Growing Up; 3, Nature; 4, Technique; 5, Symbolism; 6, The School of Nancy. Includes plates of works of furniture with glass inlay decoration. Brief bibliography, p. 128.

René Lalique, 1860-1945

1510   Bayer, Patricia, and Mark Waller. **The Art of René Lalique**. London, Quintet Publishing Ltd., 1988. 192p. illus. index. ISBN 0747501823.

Sumptuously illustrated survey of the glass art of René Lalique written in a popular style and directed to collectors and the enthusiast. Contents: Lalique the Man; The Jewellery; Experiments with Glass; The Techniques; The Exhibitions; The Flacons and Powder Boxes; Boxes and Desk Accessories; Sculpture; Decorative Furnishings; Vases and Tableware; Architectural Work. General bibliography, p. 190.

1511   Dawes, Nicholas M. **Lalique Glass**. New York, Crown, 1986. 152p. illus. index. ISBN 0517558351.

Well-illustrated introduction to the glass of Lalique directed to the collector. Includes the work of René Lalique and his successors. Contents: 1, The Jeweler Who Discovered Glass (1860-1905); 2, The Dawn of an Empire (1905-1915); 3, The Irrepressible Creator (1915-1930); 4, "Le Style Lalique": Evolution of a Style; 5, A New Commercialism (1930-1945); 6, Lalique since 1945: The Tradition Continued; 7, Advice for the Collector: How to Avoid Defects, Fakes, and Forgeries. Glossary of terms, and good selected and classified bibliography, pp. 145-47.

1512   Mortimer, Tony J. **Lalique**. Secaucus, N.J., Chartwell Books, 1989. 128p. illus. index. ISBN 155521293X.

Popular, well-illustrated survey of the art glass of René Lalique. Includes major pieces of Lalique jewelry. Appendices with essay on Lalique hallmarks, list of collections in Europe and America, and brief bibliography, p. 125.

1513   Percy, Christopher V. **The Glass of Lalique: A Collector's Guide**. New York, Scribner's, 1977. 192p. illus. index. ISBN 0684156032.

Pictorial monograph on the glass of René Lalique with good collection of plates and with emphasis on identification and dating of pieces. Contents: 1, Introduction; 2, The Man and His Glass; 3, For the Collector; 4, Vases and Bowls; 5, Tableware; 6, Car Mascots and Paper-weights; 7, Scent Bottles and garnitures de toilette; 8, Illuminated Glass and Glass Fittings; 9, Glass in Architecture; 10, Small Objects: Statuettes, Ink-wells and Blotters, Clocks, Mirrors, Glass Jewelry, Boxes and Sweet-dishes; 11, Cire perdu; 12, Techniques; 13, Trademarks; 14, Design Numbers. Chapter on trademarks gives facsimiles; the chapter on design numbers provides a commentary and list from Lalique's factory catalog of 1932 with an index by object types. General bibliography, p. 187.

See also the exhibition catalog: *The Glass of René Lalique: the Magriel Collection, Mead Art Museum, Amherst College* (Amherst, Mass., The Museum, 1979. 36p. illus.).

Germany, Austria, and Switzerland, with Czechoslovakia

1514 Hettes, Karel. **Glass in Czechoslovakia**. Prague, SNTL, 1958. 64p. illus. LC 62-6801.

Pictorial survey of glass, both table glass and stained glass windows, in Czechoslovakia from the Middle Ages to 1950 with emphasis on the twentieth century. Contains 88 plates with descriptive captions. No bibliography.

1515 Pittrof, Kurt. **Böhmisches Glas im Panorama der Jahrhunderte: eine Kultur- und Wirtschaftsgeschichte**. Munich, Oldenbourg, 1987. 180p. illus. ISBN 3486544012. (Veröffentlichungen des Collegium Carolinum, Band 61).

Scholarly history/handbook of glass made in Bohemia from the fifteenth century to 1939. Extensive use of documentary sources and a small, yet excellent collection of plates. Contents: I, Der Glaz von sieben Jahrhunderten: 1, Zum Ursprung der Glaskunst und ihrer Verbreitung; 2, Handel und Wandel bis in die Zeit der Befreiungskriege; 3, Ein Jahrhundert der technischnen und künstlerischen Innovation; 4, Konjunktur, Krise, Kasatrophe. II. Meister der böhmischen Glaskunst in Ausland; II, Statistik. Comprehensive bibliography, pp. 161-66, and additional references in the footnotes.

See also the exhibition catalog: *Czechoslovakia Glass, 1350-1980*, Corning Museum of Glass (New York, Dover, 1981. 176p. illus. ISBN 0872901009), and *Bohemian Glass, 1400-1989*, S. Petrova and J-L. Olivie, eds. (New York, Abrams, 1990. 239p. illus. ISBN 0810912414), and *Lotz: Bohmisches Glas, 1880-1940*, H. Ricke et al. (Munich, Prestel-Verlag, 1989. 2v. illus. ISBN 3791309854).

1516 Rademacher, Franz. **Die deutschen Gläser des Mittelalters**. 2nd ed. Berlin, Verlag fur Kunstwissenschaft, 1963. 151p. illus. LC A33-1644.

Scholarly history of German medieval hollow table glass from the eighth century to circa 1500 based upon close examination of museum pieces and documentary sources. Contents: Der Stand der Hohlglaserzeugung in karolingischer Zeit; Die Quellen der Überlieferung für das Mittelalter; Das Glashütten; Die Glasfarben; Die Glasformen: I, Flaschen; II, Lampen; III, Becher; Ergebnisse. Appendix with extracts from documentary sources. Corpus of plates with descriptive notes. Bibliographical references in the footnotes. Included among the illustrations are representations of glass in medieval works of art. A standard work in medieval glass.

1517 Schade, Gunter. **Deutsches Glas von der Anfängen bis zum Biedermeier**. Leipzig, Koehler & Amelang, 1968. 219p. illus. LC 71-381541.

General survey of fine glass in Germany from the fifth century to the early nineteenth century. Illustrated with examples in the museum of the German Democratic Republic (East Germany). Bibliographical footnotes.

1518 Sellner, Christiane, ed. **Der Gläserne Wald: Glaskultur im Bayern und Oberpfälzer Wald...** Munich, Prestel, 1988. 160p. illus. index ISBN 3791308572.

Well-illustrated and well-documented history/handbook of the glassworks located in eastern Bavaria and active from the eighteenth century to the present. Includes essays by various experts on history, technique, decoration and education of the glassmakers, together with a description of tours following four routes through the east Bavarian glass country. Basic bibliography, p. 155.

See also the museum catalogs: *Das Glas des Jugendstils. Katalog der Sammlung Henrich im Kunstmuseum Düsseldorf*, by H. Hilschenz (2nd ed. Munich, Prestel, 1973. 535p. illus. index),

Das Glas des Jugendstils: Sammlung d. Österr. Musems f. Angewandte Kunst, by W. Neuwirth (Munich, Prestel, 1973. 435p. illus. index. ISBN 3791300490), and the exhibition catalogs: *German Enameled Glass: The Edwin J. Beinecke Collection and Related Pieces*, Catalog by Axel von Saldern (Corning, N.Y., Corning Museum of Glass, 1965. 474p. illus. LC 65-29139), *Glass in Germany: From Roman Times to the Present* (Opladen, Fr. Middelhauve, 1965. 82p. illus.), and *Loetz Austria, 1905-1918*, by W. Neuwirth (Cincinnati, Oh., Seven Hills Books, 1986. 400p. illus. ISBN 3900282277).

Lobmeyer Glass

1519   Rath, Stefan. **Lobmeyer. Vom Adel des Handwerks.** Vienna, Herold, 1962. 47p. (text),33p. (plates). LC 66-59634.

Introductory monograph on the glass art of the firm of Lobmeyer written by the leading designer. Foreword by Hermann Fillitz. Appendices with chronological table of the house of Lobmeyer from 1822 to 1960 and a family tree of the Hölzl, Lobmeyer, and Rath families. No bibliography.

See also: R. Schmidt. *100 Jahre österreichische Glaskunst. 1823 Lobmeyr 1923* (Vienna, Schroll, 1925. 115p. illus. LC 27-8496).

Great Britain

1520   Beard, Geoffrey W. **Nineteenth Century Cameo Glass.** Newport, Monmouthshire, Ceramic Book Company, 1956. 149p. illus. index. LC A57-2714.

Authoritative survey of British cameo glass during the nineteenth century with use of documentary sources. Contents: I, Cameo Glass in Classical Times; II, John Northwood (1826-1902), and the Revival of Cameo Glass Carving; III, The Followers of the Northwood Tradition: John Northwood II, Joshua Hodgetts, James Hill; IV, The Woodall Brothers and the Work of Thomas Webb and Sons, Storbridge; V, The Richardson Enterprise. Alphonse Lechwevrel and Joseph Locke. A Second Replica of the Portland Vase. Brief Biographies of Minor Producers of Cameo Glass. The "Cameo Incrustations" of Apsley Pellatt. Appendix with description of the Woodall pattern and price book. Contains 24 plates with descriptive captions. Bibliographical references in the text and notes.

1521   Charleston, Robert J. **English Glass and the Glass Used in England, circa 400-1940.** London, Boston, G. Allen & Unwin, 1984. 288p. illus. index. ISBN 0047480033.

Comprehensive and scholarly history of glass in England with emphasis on the relationship between glass and English society. Contents: 1, Conquest and Assimilation: The Anglo-Saxon Period, c. 400-1066; 2, Medieval Glass, c. 1066-1500; 3, The Rise of the English Glass Industry: Tudor and Stuart, c. 1500-1675; 4, The Dominance of Lead-Crystal, c. 1675-1825; 5, Tradition and Innovation: The Nineteenth Century; Epilogue: 1900-1939. Bibliographical footnotes and comprehensive bibliography, pp. 254-66. A standard history of English glass.

1522   Crompton, Sidney, ed. **English Glass.** New York, Hawthorn, 1968. 255p. illus. index. LC 68-14387.

Concise, pictorial, collector's handbook of English glass from the seventeenth century to 1964. First part gives a brief survey of English glass history by Euan Ross, outline of technique by E. M. Elville, and advice on collecting by Sidney Crompton. List of museums and collections, chronology, glossary, and basic bibliography, pp. 86-87. Second part is a repertory of 206 plates of pieces in groups of types arranged chronologically. Descriptive captions to the plates. Particularly rich in illustrations of stemware.

1523   Davis, Derek C. **English and Irish Antique Glass**. New York, Praeger, 1965. 151p. illus. index. LC 65-22886.

Concise survey of glass in England and Ireland from the Middle Ages to the early nineteenth century with emphasis on the eighteenth century and the identification and classifications of types of glassware by shape and decorative features. Contents: 1, Drinking Glasses and Their Classification; 2, Special Types of Glasses Attributed to Specific Drinks and Beverages; 3, Sweetmeat Glasses—Early Tapersticks and Candlesticks; 4, Development of the Wine Decanter; 5, Plain and Moulded Glass—Jacobite, Williamite and Hanoverian Glasses—Coin Glasses; 6, Engraved Glasses; 8, The Beilbys and Enamelled Glass—Gilding—Bristol and Other Coloured Glass; 9, Lustre Candlesticks—Candelabra and Chandeliers; 10, Miscellanea; 11, Old Glass in General. Appendices with glossary, chronology, list of public collections, list of glass houses, essay on glass paperweights, and selected bibliography, pp. 145-46.

1524   Hughes, George B. **English Glass for the Collector, 1660-1860**. New York, Praeger, 1968. 251p. illus. index. LC 68-21580.

Authoritative history of English glass from 1660 to 1860 with emphasis on identification of types. Contents: 1, The Story of Flint-Glass; 2, Wine-Glasses; 3, Flute-Glasses: Cider, Champagne and Strong Ale; 4, Rummers and Toddy-Lifter; 5, Cordial, Dram, Firing, Punch, Sham-Dram and Toast-Master Glasses; 6, Dessert Glasses; 7, Wine Bottles; 8, Decanters; 9, Candelabra and Lustres; 10, Candlesticks and Tapersticks; 11, Vase-Candlesticks and Girandoles; 12, Cut-Glass; 13, Moulded and Pinched Glass; 14, Pressed Glass; 15, Georgian Enamel, Bristol-Blue and Ruby-Red Glass; 16, Nailsea Glass; 17, Rolling-Pins, Reflecting Globes and Witch Balls; 18, Cristallo Ceramie; 19, Millefiori Work and Other Associated Paper-weights; 20, Cased and Overlay, Flashed, Stained, Spun, Mother-of-Pearl and Silvered Glass. Basic bibliography, p. 251.

1525   Hughes, George B. **English, Scottish and Irish Table Glass from the 16th Century to 1820**. Boston, Boston Book and Art Shop, 1956. 410p. illus. index. LC 56-58320.

Comprehensive, authoritative handbook of British glassware from the late sixteenth century to the early nineteenth century. Each chapter concludes with collection plates with descriptive notes. Contents: 1, Early History; 2, The Development of Flint-glass: 1660-1734; 3, The Development of Flint-glass: 1734-1820; 4, Stems: Anglicized Venetian, Baluster, Plain; 5, Stems: Incised-twist, Air-twist, and Cut; 6, Wineglasses: Bowls and Feet; 7, Decoration: Engraving; 8, Decoration: Cutting; 9, Decoration: Gilding; 10, Decoration: Enamelling; 11, Romers and Rummers; 12, Champagne Glasses; 13, Strong-ale Glasses; 14, Cordial, Dram, Firing and Toast-master Glasses; 15, Jacobite Glasses; 16, Serving Bottles, Decanter, Squares, and Carafes; 17, Sweetmeat Glasses and Salvers; 18, Wineglass Coolers and Finger-bowls; 19, Candlestick, Taper-sticks, Girandoles and Girandole-candlesticks; 20, Tumblers, Fruit and Salad Bowls; 21, Bristol-blue Glass; 22, Irish Glass; 23, Scottish Glass. General bibliography, p. 391

1526   Thorpe, William A. **English Glass**. 3rd ed. London, A. & C. Black, 1961. 304p. illus. index. LC 65-592.

First published in 1935. Concise history of glass in England from the second century A.D. to the twentieth century with emphasis on the place of glass in the general development of taste and fashion. Written by the leading expert of the pre-World War II years. Slights the production after 1830. Frequent quotes from documentary sources. Contents: I, The Northern Appropriation; II, The Medieval Slump; III, Mr. Jacob; IV, The Period of Monopolies; V, The Rise of English Crystal; VI, The Baroque Style; VII, The Baluster Style; VIII, Rococo; IX, Adam to Present. Appendix with note of advice for private collectors and list of British museums for glass. First edition has a general bibliography, pp. 263-71, and a useful introductory essay to the older literature.

1527 Thorpe, William A. **A History of English and Irish Glass**. London, Medici Society; Boston, Hale, Cushman & Flint, 1929. 2v. illus. index. LC 31-9501. Reprint: New York, Holland Pr., 1969. 2v. in 1.

An old, standard history of English and Irish "art" glass from the thirteenth century to circa 1845. Volume One: Text; volume two: 168 black and white plates. Contents of volume one: I, Principles of Technique: 1, The Excellence of a Glass Vessel; 2, Materials; 3, Fabrication; 4, Decoration; II, The Age of Adoption: 1, Sussex, 2, The Noble Vagabonds, 3, The Capture of Verselini; III, The Age of Assimilation: 1, The Pirate Patentees, 2, The Tyranny of Mansell, 3, The Restoration Revival; IV, The Ravenscroft Revolution; V, The Age of Design; VI, The Age of Ornament; VII, The Anglo-Irish Revival: Cut-glass. Appendices with essay on Abjects, Orts and Imitations; extracts from Thomas Betts' Accounts and Cardiff Ms 5.21, and essays on special types of antique glass. Comprehensive bibliography, pp. 341-50. The author has been faulted for not considering later manufactured glassware. In fact, he illustrates and comments on four pieces of Swedish and Viennese art glass of the earlier twentieth century which he presents as successful marriages between modern design and glass technique, and his account of the history of handcrafted glass is unmatched for its applications of the highest standards of connoisseurship. A standard work on antique English and Irish glass.

1528 Wakefield, Hugh. **Nineteenth Century British Glass**. 2d ed. London, Faber and Faber, 1982. 168p. illus. index. ISBN 057118054X.

First published in 1961. Pioneering history of British glass during the nineteenth century built around a framework of dated pieces and is particularly valuable for the Victorian period. Contents: 1, Cut Glass; 2, Earlier Coloured Glass and Novelties; 3, Engraved Glass; 4, Later Fancy Glass; 5, Mould-Blown and Press-Moulded Glass. List of marks. Selected bibliography, pp.162-63.

1529 Warren, Phelps. **Irish Glass: Waterford—Cork—Belfast in the Age of Exuberance**. 2d rev. ed. London and Boston, Faber and Faber, 1981. 264p. illus. index. ISBN 0571180280.

First published in 1970. Comprehensive, authoritative history of glassware made in Ireland from 1780 to 1835 with emphasis on the products of the Waterford Glass House. Contents: 1, England 1571-1745; 2, Ireland 1745-c. 1835; 3, The Glass House Cities and Their Factories: Dublin, Belfast, Waterford, Cork; 4, The Extent of the Industry and of Its Exports; 5, On Intrinsic and Applied Characteristics in Glass; 6, Survey of Marked Vessels; 7, Examples with Coins and Irish Silver Mounts; 8, Examples of Irish Luxury Glass; 9, Moulded Irish Glass; 10, Waterford and Cork Cutting Characteristics; 11, 'Waterford' Chandeliers and Other Lighting Fixtures; 12, Services; Appendices: A, Glossary of Irish Cutting Terms; B, A Note Concerning Vessels with Notched Rims; C, Excerpts from a Frenchman in England, 1784, François de La Rochefoucauld; D, "Receipts for Making Flint, Enamel, Blue & Best Green Glass, Always Used by John Hill—17th May 1786"; E, Excerpts from Sir Edward Thomason's Memoirs; F, The Marquess of Bute's Collection: An Historical Note. General bibliography, pp. 255-56, has not been up dated for the 2d ed.

1530 Wills, Geoffrey. **Antique Glass for Pleasure and Investment**. New York, Drake, 1972. 174p. illus. index. LC 73-93208.

Concise survey of English and Irish glass of the eighteenth and nineteenth centuries. Contains 116 plates, 16 in excellent color. Contents; 1, Composition and Manufacture; 2, Decoration; 3, The Start of the Industry; 4, George Ravenscroft; 5, The Eighteenth Century; 6, The Nineteenth Century; 7, Bottles; 8, Irish Glass. No bibliography.

1531 Wills, Geoffrey. **English and Irish Glass**. London, Guinness, 1968. 16 signatures of 16p. illus. index. LC 73-93208.

Survey of English glass from the sixteenth century to the twentieth century in the form of succinct essays on various types directed to the needs of the collector. Contents: 1, Commemorative Goblets; 2, Drinking Glasses: Part 1; 3, Drinking Glasses: Part 2; 4, Ewers and Decanters; 5, Table Wares; 6, Candlesticks and Lustres; 7, Chandeliers; 8, Irish Glass; 9, Bottles: to 1720; 10, Bottles: from 1720; 11, Enamelled and Engraved Glass; 12, 18th Century Coloured Glass; 13, Novelties and "Friggers"; 14, Victorian Glass: Part 1; 15; Victorian Glass: Part 2; 16, Modern Glass. General bibliography, p. iv.

William and Mary Beilby, 1740-1819, 1749-1797

1532   Rush, James. **The Ingenious Beilbys**. London, Barrie & Jenkins, 1973. 168p. illus. index. ISBN 0214654125.
    Comprehensive monograph on the life and work of theBeilby family of glassmakers noted for their romantic vignettes of English country life painted in white upon handblown drinking glasses and decanters. Contents: Part One: Newcastle upon Tyne: 1, Newcastle Glory, 2, The Huguenots, 3, Admiral Sir Robert Mansell, 4, The Closegate, 5, The Glass Dynasty of Dagnia, 6, The Tax on Glass and Coal, 7, The Newcastle Light Baluster, 8, The Era of Elegance, 9, A Beilby Glass Summary, 10, Belated Recognition; Part Two: The Beilbys: 11, The Beilby Family; 12, Ralph Beilby; 13, William Beilby; 14, A Beilby Masterpiece, 15, The Margaret and Winneford Bowl, 16, The Standard of Hesleyside, 17, Mary Beilby, 18, Thomas Bewick, 19, The Happy Glassmakers, 20, Decline and Glory. General bibliography, pp. 164-65.
    See also the exhibition catalog: *The Decorated Glasses of William and Mary Beilby* (Newcastle, 1980).

Italy

1533   Mariacher, Giovanni. **Italian Blown Glass from Ancient Rome to Venice**. New York, McGraw-Hill, 1961. 245p. illus. index. LC 61-15890.
    Survey of glass of Italy from the first century A.D. to the early nineteenth century. Sixty-page introduction is an authoritative outline of the history and technique of Italian glass. It is followed by a collection of 84 color plates of pieces chiefly in the Museo Vetrario in Murano. Descriptive captions to the plates. Classified bibliography, pp. 61-62, with especially full section on Venetian glass.

Major Regions and Centers

Florence

1534   Heikamp, Detlef. "Studien zur mediceischen Glaskunst: Archivalien, Entwurfszeichungen, Gläser und Scherben," **Mitteilungen des Kunsthistorischen Instituts in Florenz,** 30 (1986), pp. 12-423.
    Comprehensive, scholarly history of glass production in Florence in the sixteenth to early eighteenth centuries. Based on extensive study of documentary sources and extant pieces.

Venice

1535   Gasparetto, Astone. **Il vetro di Murano dall origini ad oggi**. Venice, Neri Pozza, 1958. 289p. illus. index.
    Comprehensive history of glass production in Murano from its beginnings. Contents: I, L'arte vetraria prima di Murano; II, L'industria vetraria muranese; III, Le tipiche produzione

muranesi; IV, Operai e maestri; V, Dizionarietto technico della vetraria. Contains 196 plates with descriptive captions. Bibliographical footnotes.

1536   Mentasti, Rosa B. **Il vetro veneziano**. Milan, Electa, 1982. 346p. illus. index. LC 83-111917.

Comprehensive, well-illustrated history of Venetian glass from the early Middle Ages to the twentieth century. Plates have descriptive captions. Comprehensive, classified bibliography, pp. 327-330.

See also exhibition catalogs: *Mille anni di arte del vetro a Venezia* (Venice, Albrizzi, 1982. 325p. illus.) and *Three Great Centuries of Venetian Glass*, Corning Museum of Glass (Corning, N.Y., The Museum, 1958. 116p. illus. LC 58-12443).

Scandinavia

1537   Jexlev, Thelma. **Dansk glas i renaessancetid 1556-1650**. Copenhagen, Nyt Nordisk, 1970. 189p. illus. index. LC 74-577288.

Comprehensive, scholarly history of Danish glass of the Renaissance with emphasis on glass production both artistic and commercial. Contents: De skriftlige kilders vidnesbyrd om dansk renaessanceglas by T. Lexlev; Glasvaerkstomter by P. Riismøller; Stoff og form by P. Riismøller; Vinduesglas by P. Riismøller; Rekonstruktion af ovnanlaeg by M. Schlüter; Andre tekniske forhold by M. Schlüter; Hvor langt er vi nået? by T. Jexlev; Kildefortegnelse og bibliografi (comprehensive, annotated bibliography).

1538   Larsen, Alfred, Peter Riismoller and Mogens Schluter. **Dansk Glas, 1825-1925**. 3rd ed. Copenhagen, Nyt Nordisk, 1979. 433p. illus. ISBN 8717025567.

Comprehensive, authoritative history of glass in Denmark from 1825 to 1925 with emphasis on the production of table glass. Contents: Traek af glasindustriens historie: Perioden før 1800; Perioden efter 1800; De enkelte vaerker: Holmegaards Glasvaerk, Kastrup Glasvaerk, Conradsminde Glasvaerk, Mylenberg Glasvaerk, Aalborg Glasvaerk, Hasle Glasvaerk, Helsingøor Glasvaerk, Nørrebro Glasvaerk, Lyngby Glasvaerk, Frederiksberg Glasveark, Fyens Glasvaerk, Arhus Glasvaerk. Vaerkernes produktion: Hundrede ørs stiludvikling; Danske art nouveau glas, Kildestoffet; Billedplancher og tekster (corpus of plates by type); Teknik og terminologi. Comprehensive, classified bibliography, pp. 431-432.

1539   Polak, Ada B. **Gammelt Norsk Glas**. Oslo, Gyldendal Norsk, 1953. 353p. illus. index. LC 54-25197.

Comprehensive authoritative history of glass in Norway from 1741 to 1843. Contents: I, En Nasjonalindustri forberedes og grunnlegges; II, Krystallverket på Nøstetangen 1753-1777; III, Krystalldrift ved Hurdals verk 1779-1808; IV, Krystalldrift ved Gjøovik verk 1809-1843; V, Verkstedarbeid ute og hjemme; VI, Heinrich Gottlieb Köhler; VII, Norsk Gravyr Ellers; VIII, Slipning, maling og forgylling; IX, Flasker og grøntglass, vindusglass og apotekerglass. Summary: "Old Norwegian Glass." Descriptive catalog of 272 pieces. Bibliographical references in the footnotes. A standard work on Norwegian glass.

1540   Seitz, Heribert. **Äldre svenska glas med graverad dekor...** Stockholm, Norstedt, 1936. 231p. illus. index. LC 36-34206. (Nordiska Museets Handlingar, 5).

Comprehensive, scholarly history of Swedish glassware with engraved decoration from the eighteenth and early nineteenth centuries featuring pieces in the Stockholm Noriska Museet. Contents: I, De betydelsefullaste faserna av gravyrens tidigare utveckling; II, Glastillverkningens allmänna tradition och situation e Sverige vid gravyrens införande; III, Till frågan om glasgravyrens första framträdande i vårt land; IV, Kungsholmsbruket, den äldre svenska glasgravyrens centrum; V, Skänska glasbruket (Henrikstorp); VI, 1700-talets övriga glas med graverad dekor. English summary. General bibliography, pp. 218-23, and specialized literature cited in the footnotes.

1541   Steenberg, Elisa. **Swedish Glass**. New York, Barrows, 1950. 168p. illus. LC 50-8734.
Concise but authoritative survey of Swedish glass from the seventeenth century to the middle of the twentieth century. Contents: I, Early Days and Melchior Jung's Glassworks, 1641; II, Kungsholm Glassworks, 1676-1815; III, Scania Glasswork, 1695-1762; IV, Kosta, Limmared, and Other Glassworks; V, Artistic Development; VI, Orrefors Glassworks; VII, Gate, Hald, Lindstrand; VIII, Örström, Landberg, Palmqvist; IX, Ollers, Nyblom, Hultröm; X, Skawonius, Elis Bergh, and the Strömbergs. No bibliography. Although illustrated with poor-quality black and white plates, it remains useful as the only overview of the important developments and personalities in Swedish glass.
See also the exhibition catalog: *Glas in Schweden, 1915-1960*, U. Gronert and H. Ricke, ed. (Munich, Prestel, 1986. 310p. illus. ISBN 3791307762).

Spain

1542   Frothingham, Alice W. **Spanish Glass**. London, Faber and Faber, 1963; New York, Yoseloff, 1964. 96p. illus. index. LC 64-3365.
Brief but authoritative guide from the twelfth century to the early nineteenth century. Contents: 1, Medieval Spanish Glass: Romanesque and Gothic Periods; 2, Cataluña and the Neighbouring Regions; 3, Southern Spain: Almería, Granada, Sevilla; 4, Castilla: Cadalso, Recuenco, Nuevo Baztán and Other Glass Centres of the Region; 5, The Royal Factory of La Granja de San Ildefonso. Comprehensive, classified bibliography, pp. 90-92, and further bibliography in the footnotes.

1543   Perez Bueno, Luiz. Vidros y vidrieras. Barcelona, A. Martin, 1942. 277p. illus. index. LC 44-24083.

ORIENTAL GLASS

1544   Blair, Dorothy. **A History of Glass in Japan**. New York, Kodansha International/USA, 1973. 479p. illus. index. ISBN 0870111965.
"A Corning Museum Glass Monograph." Comprehensive and scholarly history of glass in Japan from the Jomon period (c. 10,000 B.C. to c. 250 B.C.) to the 1970s. Important corpus of plates of museum pieces with descriptive notes and bibliographical references. Appendix: Chemical Considerations by R. H. Bill. Contents: Language Notes; Beginning of Glass in Japan; Period of the Great Tombs; Asuka and Hakuho Periods; Nara Period; Heian Period; Periods of Diminished Glass Production; Edo Period; Modern Perdion. Glossary, chronologies, maps and comprehensive, classified bibliography, pp. 461-69. Standard history of Japanese glass.

1545   Dikshit, Moreshwar G. **History of Indian Glass**. Bombay, Univ. of Bombay, 1969. 212p. illus. index. LC 73-911298.
Scholarly history of glass in India from earliest times to circa 1650. Contents: I, Early Indian Glass; II, Affluence of Glass in India; III, Glass of the Dark Period; IV, Mughal Glass; V, Documentary Evidence on Glass; VI, The Last Phase; Appendix I: Analysis of Ancient Indian Glass; Appendix II: Glass in Indian Literature. Bibliographical footnotes and classified bibliography, pp.183-190.

1546   Lamm, Carl J. **Mittelalterliche Gläser und Steinschnittarbeiten aus dem Nahen Osten.** Berlin, Reimer-Vohsen, 1929-30. 2v. illus. index. (Forschungen zur Islamischen Kunst, V). LC 31-1569.

Comprehensive and scholarly history of glass in the Near East from the twelfth through the fifteenth centuries. Volume of text and volume of plates illustrating museum pieces with descriptive notes. Exhaustive bibliography for its time, pp. 522-49. Still-standard history of the golden age of Islamic glass.

1547   Sen, S. N. (Samarendra Nath). **Ancient Glass and India.** New Delhi, Indian National Science Academy, 1985. 201p. illus. index. LC 85-904238.

History of glass in India from the second millennium B.C. to the fourteenth century A.D. based on archaeological and literary evidence. Emphasis is on materials and technique. Contents: I, Ancient Glass—Historical Background, General Characteristics, Properties, Compositions, Materials and Processes; II, Literary and Archaeological Evidence of Glass in Ancient India; III, Scientific Studies and Physio-Chemical Analyses of Indian Glass Specimens, Raw Materials and Sources; IV, Furnaces, Tools, and Techniques for Fashioning Glass Objects; V, Indian Glass as an Article of Trade. Bibliographical footnotes. Bibliography, pp.188-97, is divided into books and articles in Western languages and books—mostly source texts—in Sanskrit and Prakrit.

1548   Tsuchiya, Yoshio. **Glass of Japan.** Kyoto-shi, Shikosha, 1987. 254p. illus. ISBN 4879405027.

Pictorial survey of glass in Japan from the Edo Period to the present. Contains 146 plates of museum pieces followed by text in Japanese. Summary in English. No bibliography.

See also the exhibition catalog: *Clear as Crystal, Red as Flame: Later Chinese Glass*, by C. Brown (New York, China House Gallery, 1990. 103p. illus. LC 89-82709).

CHAPTER ELEVEN

IVORY

TECHNIQUE

1549 Cultler, Anthony. **The Craft of Ivory: Sources, Techniques, and Uses in the Mediterranean World, A.D. 200-1400**. Washington, D.C., Dumbarton Oaks, Research Library and Collection, 1985. 58p. illus. ISBN 01980262.

Scholarly introduction to the techniques and materials of Early Christian and medieval ivory carving featuring pieces in the Dumbarton Oaks Collection. Contents: 1, The Nature of Ivory; 2, Sources and Availability of Ivory; 3, Cutting and Carving Techniques; 4, Uses and Image of Ivory. Bibliography, pp. 55-58, includes primary sources.

1550 MacGregor, Arthur. **Bone, Antler, Ivory & Horn: The Technology of Skeletal Materials Since the Roman Period**. London, Croom Helm, Totowa, N.J., Barnes & Noble, 1985. 245p. illus. index. ISBN 0389205311.

Important, scholarly study of the use of bone, antler, ivory, and horn in western Europe from ancient Roman times to the end of the Middle Ages with emphasis on archaeological and art historical pieces in northwestern Europe to the ninth century. Contents: 1, Raw Materials; 2, Bone and Antler as Materials; 3, Availability; 4, Handicraft or Industry?; 5, Working Methods and Tools; 6, Artifacts of Skeletal Materials: A Typological Review. Bibliographical references in the notes, comprehensive bibliography, pp. 209-37.

GENERAL HISTORIES AND HANDBOOKS

1551 Beihoff, Norbert J. **Ivory Sculpture through the Ages**. Milwaukee, Wis., Public Museum, 1961. 93p. illus. index. LC 61-59507.

Concise, popular survey of world ivory carving with emphasis on use and manufacture. Brief reading list of books in English.

See also: Wills, Geoffrey. *Ivory*, South Brunswick, N.J., A. S. Barnes, 1969, 94p. illus. index. LC 68-27235.

1552 Burack, Benjamin. **Ivory and Its Uses**. Rutland, Vt., Tuttle, 1984. 240p. illus. index. ISBN 080481483X.

Useful handbook of world ivory carving directed to the collector with much valuable information on material and techniques in part one. Part One: History, Art, and Craft: I, Historical Development; II, Sources of Ivory; III, Ivory Substitutes; IV, Cutting and Carving; V, Coloration of Ivory; VI, Care and Cleaning; VII, Testing for Ivory; Part Two: Uses of Ivory (a dictionary of objects and classes of objects in which ivory was the principal material). List of museums with notable collections of ivory. Bibliographical references in the notes.

1553 Kunz, George F. **Ivory and the Elephant in Art, in Archaeology and in Science**. Garden City, N.Y., Doubleday, 1916. 527p. illus. index. LC 26-22438.

Older, comprehensive history of ivory carving throughout the world from prehistoric times to the nineteenth century. Particularly useful for the information it supplies about hunting elephants for ivory around 1900 and techniques used, especially in the Orient, to carve ivory. Contents: I, Prehistoric and Ancient Carved Ivories; II, Medieval and Modern Ivory Carvings; III, Oriental Ivory Carving; IV, Elephants, Historical; V, Elephant Hunting, etc.; VI, Sources, Composition, and Qualities of Ivory; VII, Working; VIII, Vegetable and Imitation Ivory; IX, Narwhal Horns, Walrus Tusks, etc; X, Elephants, Evolution of; also Mastodon, Mammoth, etc.; XI, Elephant Tusks; XII, The Commerce of Ivory. Appendix with repertory of ivory carvers, chiefly nineteenth century. Bibliographical references in the footnotes.

1554   Tardy (firm). **Les ivoires, évolution décorative du Ier siècle à nos jours**. Paris, Tardy, 1966. 319p. illus. index. LC 67-71291. (Collection Tardy, v. 112)

Comprehensive, pictorial history of ivory carving throughout the world from antiquity to the nineteenth century. Contents: Europe et Byzance: subjets religieux; Europe et Byzance: sujets profanes; Islam et influence: siculo-arabe, hispano-mauresque; Inde-Ceylon, Chine, Japon, Afrique; Les faux gothiques. Appendices with list of ivory carvers and dictionary of netsuke marks. Bibliography, pp. 279-80, lists basic books in all languages. Most useful for quick identification of ivories.

1555   Vickers, Michael et al. **Ivory: A History and Collector's Guide**. London, Thames & Hudson, 1987. 352p. illus. index. ISBN 0500235058.

Comprehensive, well-illustrated survey of ivory carving throughout the world from antiquity to the present with chapters on collecting and care of ivory objects of art. Includes carving in walrus, narwhal, bone, scrimshaw, and other ivory-like materials.Contents: I, Early Civilizations; 2, Rome and the Eastern Empire; 3, Europe; 4, Africa; 5, The Far East, South-Asia; 7, North America; 8, Central and South America; 9, Contemporary Carvers. Glossary and list of museums with important collections of ivory. Classified bibliography of books and periodical articles, pp. 344-45.

WESTERN IVORY

General Histories and Handbooks

1556   Maskell, Alfred. **Ivories**. London, Methuen; New York, Putnam, 1905. 551p. illus. index. Reprint: Rutland, Vt., Tuttle, 1966. LC 66-20572.

Pioneering work on the history of ivory carving throughout the world from prehistoric times to the end of the nineteenth century. Contains a great deal of useful information and is still a balanced and comprehensive overview. The many pieces illustrated are presented in tabular form in the appendix. Bibliography, pp. 539-45, is an excellent guide to the older literature.

1557   Molinier, E. **Ivoires**. Paris, Librairie Centrale des Beaux-Arts, 1896. 245p. illus. (Histoire gènèrale des arts appliqués a l'industrie, I) LC 01-22039R28.

Old, once-standard history of Western ivories from the fifth century to the end of the eighteenth century. Useful for the thorough coverage of the older literature through references in the footnotes. Contents: Les ivoires de la décadence romaine; Les ivoires byzantins; Les ivories de l'époque carolingienne; L'époque romane; Les ivoires de l'époque gothique; La Renaissance; Le XVIIe et le XVIIIe siècle.

1558   Philippovich, Eugen von. **Elfenbein**. 2d ed. rev. and enl. Braunschweig, Klinkhardt & Biermann, 1982. 480p. illus. index. ISBN 3781401677. (Bibliothek fur Kunst- und Antiquitätenfreunde, XVII)

Comprehensive history/handbook of Western ivories from antiquity to Art Deco. Supersedes: Pelka, Otto. *Elfenbein.* 2nd ed. Berlin, Schmidt, 1923. 419p. illus. index. (Bibliothek fur Kunst- und Antiquitäten Sammler, XVII). Contents: Einhorn; Walrosszahn; Geschichte des Elfenbeins; Etruskisches Elfenbein; Frühchristliches Elfenbein; Byzantinisches Elfenbein; Die Konsulardiptychen; Elfenbein der Karolingerzeit; Ottonisches Elfenbein; Byzantinisches Elfenbein nach dem Bilderstreit; Charakteristika aus dem 11. Jahrhundert; Frankreich' Italien; England; Skandinavien; Schweiz; Spanien und Portugal; Holland und Belgien; Deutschland; Österreich; Russland; Das 19. und 20. Jahrhundert—Art Deco. This historical section is followed by a catalog of pieces by subject: figures groups, medallions and a discussion of techniques, fakes, forgeries, photographing and caring for ivories. Classified bibliography, pp. 467-71, with separate list of exhibition catalogs. Although directed to the collector, the historical section goes beyond the superficial sketch usually found in such works.

Ancient Ivories

Ancient Near East

1559 Barnett, Richard D. **Ancient Ivories in the Middle East.** Jerusalem, Institute of Archaeology, Hebrew University of Jerusalem, 1982. 99p. (text), 67p. (illus.) LC 83-3213576.
Authoritative survey of ivory carving in Egypt and the Near East from earliest times to Roman imperial times. Contents: I, The Elephant; II, Ivory Working and Ivory Workers; III, Egypt; IV, Ancient Palestine and Syria in the Late Chalcolithic Period and Bronze Age; V, Anatolia; VI, Crete and the Aegean World; VII, Mesoptamia, Urartu and Iran; VIII, Syria and Phoenicia in the Iron Age; IX, Classical Greece and Etruria; X, The Hellenistic World, India and Rome. Extensive bibliography in the notes.

1560 ———. **A Catalogue of the Nimrud Ivories with Other Examples of Ancient Near Eastern Ivories in the British Museum.** London, Trustees of the British Museum, 1957. 252p. illus. index.
Scholarly catalog of the large collection of ivories excavated at Nimrud by Layard and Loftus in the middle of the nineteenth century. Contents: The City of Nimrud; The Excavations and Excavators of Nimrud; Syrian and Phoenician Art: Their Origins and Development; The Loftus Group: Shapes and Motifs; The 'Layard Series': Their Original Function; The Evidence of Similar Collections of Ivories; The Date and Origin of the Layard Group; Technique; Inscriptions; Elephants and Ivory; Catalogue. Contains 132 plates. Extensive bibliography in the notes to the text and the catalog entries.

1561 Crowfoot, J. W., and G. M. Crowfoot. **Early Ivories from Samaria.** London, Palestinian Exploration Fund, 1938. 62p. (text), 25ls. (plates). LC 40-11130.
Scholarly description of the ancient Israelite ivory fragments excavated from Samaria between 1931 and 1933 and presented as coming from the Ahab's ivory house described in I Kings and dated in the tenth century B.C. Contents: 1, The Find and Identification of the Ivories; 2, The Composition of the Collection; 3, Description of the Plates; 4, Conclusions; Appendix 1, The Origin of the Ivory; 2, The Character of the Insets. Bibliographical references in the footnotes.

1562 Huls, Yvette. **Ivoires d'Etrurie.** Brussels, Palais des Académies, 1957. 238p. illus. (Etudes de philologie, d'archéologie et d'histoire anciennes, tome 4.) LC 59-41656.
Scholarly history of ancient Etruscan ivories. Contents: Introduction: Ivoires du Proche Orient et ivoires orientalisants de la méditerranée oriental; I, Inventaire: A, Catlogue des ivoires et des os figurés étrusques; B, Instrumentum; Deuxième partie: I, Le travail de l'os en Italie avant l'arrivéee des Étrusque; II, Les origines étrusques et le travail de l'ivoire en Étrurie; III, Le cycle

orientalisant. Étrurie centrale et méridonale; IV, Le cycle orientalisant. Étrurie septentrionale; V, Le cycle archaique; VI, Le cycle classique; VIII, La période hellénistique; VIII, Conclusion. Bibliography in the footnotes and general bibliography, pp.13-15.

1563 ———. **The Nimrud Ivories**. London, British Museum Publications, 1978. 63p. illus. ISBN 0714180009.

Introduction to the ivories excavated from the Assyrian Palace of Ashurnarsipal II (883-859 B.C.) at Nimrud (Calah) from 1849 to 1974 and now in the British Museum, London. Authoritative text by archaeologists directing the excavations between 1963 and 1974, Contents: Introduction; The Assyrian Style; The Phoenician Style, The Syrian Style. Short bibliography, p. 61.

1564 Huls, Yvette, and Leri G. Davies. **Ivories in Assyrian Style: Commentary, Catalogue and Plates**. London, British School of Archaeology in Iraq, 1970. 60p. (text), 23 plates. index.

Scholarly catalog with commentary on the ancient Assyrian ivories excavated from Nimrud and now in the British Museum. Full scholarly apparatus including bibliographies at the end of each catalog entry.

See also the museum guide: *Assyrian Reliefs and Ivories in the Metropolitan Museum of Art*, by V. E. Crawford (New York, The Museum, 1980).

Greece

1565 Freyer-Schauenburg, Brigitte. **Elfenbeine aus dem samischen Heraion: Figürliches, Gefässe und Siegel**. Hamburg, Cram, de Gruyter, 1966. 155p. illus. (Universität Hamburg. Abhandlungen aus dem Gebiet der Auslandskunde, Band 70.)

Scholarly study of 32 ivory carvings from the Heraion of Samos. The pieces include most of the figurative pieces and are attributed to a number of ancient centers including Greece, Egypt, Phoenicia, and the Near East and chiefly date from the seventh and eighth centuries B.C. Contents: Katalog der Elfenbeine aus dem samischen Heraion; Fundumstände; Stilistisch-chronologische Untersuchung; Zur Bedeutung der Elfenbeine von Samos. Bibliographical references in the notes.

1566 Marangou, Evangelia-Lila I. **Lakonische Elfenbein- und Beinschnitzereien**. Tübingen, Wasmuth, 1969. 332p. illus. LC 74-581175.

Revision of author's dissertation, *Tübingen*. Scholarly history of ancient Greek ivory carving of the sixth and seventh centuries B.C. with focus on the so-called Laconian ivories. Author's aim is to date and group the pieces through detailed examination of style and iconography. Contents: I, Die Denkmäler der lakonischen Elfebein- und Beinschnitzereien: Beschreibung, Zeitbestimmung und Bedeutung; II, Die Stellung der lakonischen Schnitzereien. Fully indexed. Complete scholarly apparatus including bibliographical references in the footnotes and catalog entries.

Early Christian Ivories

1567 Cechelli, C. **La cattedra di Massimiano ed altri avori romano-orientali**. Rome, Libreria dello Stato, 1936-1944. illus. LC A41-2818.

Scholarly description of the Early Christian/Byzantine ivory reliefs decorating the famous cathedral of Maximian (545-53) in the Archiepiscopal Museum, Ravenna. Contents: Bibliografia (comprehensive, classified bibliography); I, Storia esterna della cattedra; II, Di Una cattedra donata as Ottone II e del probabile officio della cattedra Ravennate.

1568 Delbrueck, Richard. **Die Consulardiptychen und verwandte Denkmäler**. Berlin, De Gruyter, 1929. 295p. illus. index. (Studien zur spätantiken Kunstgeschichte, Band 2). LC AC-34-953.

Scholarly study of ivory consular diptych dating from the fifth and sixth centuries A.D. with a detailed catalog of 71 examples. Contents: I, Bibliographie und Schriftquellen; II, Einleitung: 1, Allgemeines, 2, Das normale Kostüm, 3, Das Togakostüm, 4, Konsulare Geschenke und Festlichkeiten; III, Katalog; IV. Verzeichnis der Texttafeln und Textabbildungen. The standard work on this important genre of Early Christian ivory carving.

1569 Kollwitz. Johannes. **Die Lipsanothek von Brescia**. Berlin, De Gruyter, 1933. 2v. illus. (Studien zur spätantiken Kunstgeschichte, Band 7). Reprinted 1978. ISBN 3110057018.
    Scholarly monograph on the famous ivory casket circa 360 in Brescia. Contents: Einleitung; Ikonographische Untersuchung; Formale Beschreibung; Die Heimat der Lipsanothek; Die Enstehungszeit der Lipsanothek. Bibliographical footnotes and a list of major works, pp. ix-xiii.

1570 Metz, Peter. **Elfenbein der Spätantike**. Munich, Hirmer, 1962. 40p. (text), 24 plates.
    Introductory essays survey ivory carving during the fourth and fifth centuries followed by 48 excellent plates of major pieces with descriptive notes and bibliographical references.

1571 Natanson, John. **Early Christian Ivories**. London, Tiranti, 1953. 34p. illus. LC 53-11097.
    Introduction to Early Christian ivory carving of the fourth through the sixth centuries. Brief historical sketch followed by informative notes to the well-chosen plates. General bibliography, p. 23.
    See also the museum catalog: *Elfenbeinarbeiten der Spätantike und des frühen Mittelalters*, 3rd ed. by Wolfgang F. Volbach. (Mainz, Zabern, 1976. 156p. illus. LC 76-471665).

Byzantine Ivories

1572 Goldschmidt, Adolf and Kurt Weitzmann. **Die byzantinischen Elfenbeinskulpturen des X.-XIII. Jahrhunderts**. 2d ed. Berlin, Deutscher Verlag für Kunstwissenschaft, 1979. 2v. illus. index. ISBN 3871570753. (Die Elfenbeinskulpturen, Band 5-6).
    First published in 1930-34 (Berlin, Cassirer) as volumes 5 and 6 in series: "Denkmaler Deutschen Kunst." Scholarly history and catalog of Byzantine ivory carvings dating from the tenth through the thirteenth centuries. Contents: Erster Band: Kästen: I, Zusammenfassung: 1, Die technische Behandlung und Verwendung der Kästen, 2, Der Werkstattbetrieb, 3, Die Rosetten-Ornamentik, 4, Die Stoffgebiete und ihre Vorbilder, 5, Das Verhältnis der Kästen zur allgemeinen Stilentwicklung, 6, Das Problem der Lokalisierung, 7, Die Sitentwicklung der einzelnen Gruppen; Teil II: Kritischer Katalog. Zweiter Band: Reliefs: I, Teil: Orientierungen und Zusammenfassung: 1, Allgemeines, 2, Die malerische Gruppe, 3, Die Romanos-Gruppe, 4, Die Triptychon-Gruppe, 5, Die Nikephoros-Gruppe, 6, Die Rhamengruppe, 7, Ikonographie; II. Teil: Kritischer Katalog. Bibliographical references at the end of the catalog entries and in the footnotes of the essays. A standard work on Byzantine ivories.

Medieval Ivories

1573 Beckwith, John. **Ivory Carvings in Early Medieval England**. London, Harvey, Miller and Medcalf, 1972. 168p. illus. index. LC 73-158589.
    Well-illustrated and authoritative survey of ivory carving in England from the seventh through the twelfth centuries. Detailed descriptive and analytical notes to the 128 plates with full bibliographies of the specialized literature. Further bibliography in the notes to the text.
    See also the exhibition catalog: I*vory Carvings in Early Medieval England, 700-1200*, (London, Arts Council of Great Britain, 1974. 100p. illus. index. LC 74-189032).

1574   Beigbeder, Olivier. **Ivory.** New York, Putnam, 1965. 128p. illus. LC 64-16768.

Pictorial survey of Western ivories from prehistoric times through the eighteenth century. Brief introductory text followed by good selection of pieces illustrated in color and black and white with descriptive captions. Appreciative text serves as a good introduction.

1575   Gaborit-Chopin, Danielle. **Ivoires du moyen age.** Fribour, Office du Livre, 1978. 232p. illus. index. LC 78-381830.

Comprehensive, scholarly history of ivories in eastern and western Europe from the fourth through the fifteenth centuries. Contents: I, De l'ivoire; II, L'héritage antique: la survivance de l'art classique. Thèmes paiens et chrétiens, L'Occident au Ve siècle, La Méditerranée orientale; III, Le haute moyen age: L'époque des Invasions, L'art aulique: les ivoires carolingiens; IV, Le temps des clercs: les ivoires romans: l'an mil, la floraison romane; V, Les princes et les bourgeois: les ivoires gothiques: Les prémices, le style monumental, Paris sous le regne de Philippe le Bel et des premiers Valois, Les ateliers non parisiens, l'ivoirerie sous Charles V, le gothique international, la fin du moyen age. Catalog of the 270 illustrated pieces with bibliographies. General bibliography, pp. 215-221.

1576   Cust, Anna Maria. **The Ivory Workers of the Middle Ages.** London, Bell, 1902. 170p. illus. index. LC 70-178523.

Older, concise history of European ivories from the Early Christian period to the early fifteenth century. Still a useful overview. Contents: I, Consular and Other Secular Diptychs; II, Latin and Byzantine Ivories; III, Lombardic, Anglo-Saxon, Carlovingian and German Ivories; IV, Romanesque and Gothic Ivories. Appendix with a list of diptychs and a list of collections of ivories. Bibliographic references in the footnotes.

1577   Goldschmidt, Adolph. **Die Elfenbeinskulpturen aus der romanischen Zeit, XI.-XII. Jahrhundert.** Berlin, Deutscher Verlag für Kunstwissenschaft, 1923-26. 2v. illus. index. (Die Elfenbeinskulpturen, Band 3-4). Reprint: Berlin, Deutscher Verlag für Kunstwissenschaft, 1972, 1975. ISBN 3871570516 (v. 2).

Scholarly history and catalog of ivory carvings of western Europe during the Romanesque period. Continuation of the author's work on early medieval ivories (1578). First volume covers German ivories, the second volume covers the ivories produced in England, France, Belgium, Spain, and Italy with a chapter on chess figures in ivory. Both volumes present the material in introductory essays followed by detailed, critical catalogs of the major pieces. Bibliographical references at the end of the catalog entries and in the footnotes of the essays. Fully indexed. A monumental and standard work not only for ivory carving but for the history of early Medieval sculpture as well.

1578   Goldschmidt, Adolph. **Die Elfenbeinskulpturen aus der Zeit der Karolingischen und Sächsischen Kaiser, VIII.-XI. Jahrhundert.** Berlin, Deutscher Verlag fur Kunstwissenschaft, 1914-18. 2v. illus. index. Reprint: Berlin, Deutscher Verlag fur Kunstwissenschaft, 1969-70. LC 72-365274 (Die Elfenbeinskulpturen, Band 1-2).

Scholarly history and catalog of Carolingian and Ottonian ivories with emphasis on distinguishing the various schools and describing the stylistic development. Contents: Band 1: Die Adagruppe; Die Liuthardgruppe; Die Metzer Gruppe; Jungere Metzer Schule; Kleine Gruppen und Einselstücke. Contents Band 2: In both volumes the material is presented in introductory essays followed by detailed, critical catalogs of the major pieces. Bibliographical references at the end of the catalog entries and in the footnotes of the essays. The standard work on early medieval ivories. Continued into the Romanesque period (1577).

1579   Grodecki, Louis. **Ivoires francais**. Paris, Larousse, 1947. 157p. illus. index.
Survey of French ivory carving from the early Middle Ages to the end of the eighteenth century by a major authority on French medieval art.

1580   Koechlin, Raymond. **Les ivoires gothiques francais**. Paris, Picard, 1924. 2v. plus folder of plates. LC 24-28948.
Standard handbook of French Gothic ivories with an invaluable corpus of plates. Covers both sacred and secular ivories. Introductory chapter treats technique, manufacture, and patronage. Volume one, text; volume two, critical catalog of 1,328 pieces with separate bibliographies for each entry; volume three, plates. Appendix with list of dated examples. Bibliographical footnotes.

1581   Longhurst, M. H. **English Ivories**. London, Putnam, 1926. 123p. illus. index. LC 27-20558.
Survey of ivory carving in England from the early Middle Ages to the end of the nineteenth century with descriptive catalog of well-chosen pieces. Contents: Historical Introduction: I, The Pre-Conquest and Romanesque Period; II, The Gothic Period; III, The Renaissance and Latter Periods. Ascriptions; Catalogue. List of collections of English ivories and general bibliography, pp. 117-18, and further bibliography in the notes.

1582   Natanson, John. **Gothic Ivories of the Thirteenth and Fourteenth Centuries**. London, Tiranti, 1951. 40p. illus. LC 51-13487.
Concise survey of western European ivories of the thirteenth and fourteen centuries. Brief introductory essay followed by good selection of plates with descriptive notes.
    See also the exhibition catalog: *Elfenbeinarbeiten von der Spätantike bis zum hohen Mittelalter*, by A. von Euw. (Frankfurt am Main, Liebieghaus, 1976), the museum catalog: *Masterpieces of Ivory from the Walters Art Gallery*, by R. H. Randall, Jr. (New York, Hudson Hills Press, 1985. 338p. illus. index. ISBN 0933920423), and the Victoria and Albert Museum guide: *P. Williamson. An Introduction to Medieval Ivory Carvings* (Owings Mills, Md., Stemmer House Pub., 1982. 47p. illus. ISBN 0880450061).

Renaissance—Modern Ivories

1583   Arwas, Victor. **Art Deco Sculpture: Chryselephantine Statuettes of the Twenties and Thirties**. rev. & enl. ed. London, Academy Editions; New York, St. Martin's Press, 1984. 107p. illus.ISBN 0312052510.
Pictorial survey of European Art Deco statuettes of ivory and metal. Brief introductory essay followed by 82 pages of plates of examples with descriptive captions. No bibliography.

1584   Scherer, Christian. **Studien zur Elfenbeinplastik der Barockzeit**. Strassburg, 1897. 139p. illus. (Studien zur Deutschen Kunstgeschichte, 12).
Scholarly history of German ivory carving of the seventeenth century. Contents: I, Ignaz Elhafen; II, Balthasar Permoser; III, Der Monogrammist PI; IV, Die Familie Lücke; V, Der Monogrammist HE; VI, Jacob Dobbermann; VII, Theophilus Wilhelm Frese. Bibliographical references in the footnotes.

1585   Theuerkauff, Christian. **Studien zur Elfenbeinplastik des Barock**. Freiburg in Breisgau, Rota Druck J. Krause, 1964. 402p. illus. LC 74-225257.
Dissertation, Freiburg. Important history of German Baroque ivories with emphasis on the work of Matthias Rauchmiller and Ignaz Elhafen. Detailed catalog of 153 pieces with specialized bibliographies.

See also the exhibition catalog: *Elfenbeinkunst des 19. ynd 20. Jahrhunderts*, by H. W. Hegemann. (Erbach/Odenwald, Elfenbeinmuseum, 1971. 64p. illus.).

ORIENTAL IVORY (including Netsuke)

Islamic

1586 Kühnel, Ernst. **Die islamischen Elfenbeinskulpturen. VII.-XIII Jahrhunderts**. Berlin, Deutscher Verlag fur Kunstwissenschaft, 1971. 103p. illus. LC 73-327439.

Important, scholarly history and catalog of Islamic ivory carving from the seventh through the thirteenth centuries. Essential corpus of 112 large-size plates with detailed, analytical and descriptive catalog entries with specialized bibliographies. Contents: Einleitung und Zusammenfassung: I, Frühislamische Arbeiten; II, Die spanisch-arabische Gruppe; III, Die sarazenischen Olifante und Kästen; IV, Fatimidische Elfenbeinplatten. Kritischer Katalog. Appendix with essays on sources and treasury inventories. A standard work on Islamic ivories.

India

1587 Dwivedi, Binod P. **Indian Ivories: A Survey of Indian Ivory and Bone Carvings from the Earliest to Modern Times**. New Delhi, Agam Prakashan, 1976. 152p. illus. index. LC 76-904534.

Comprehensive history of ivory carving in India based on the author's dissertation. Contents: I, Material and Technique; II, Bone and Ivory in Epigraphs and Literature; III, The Harappan Bone and Ivory Carvings; IV, Neolithic and Chalcolithic Bone and Ivory Carvings; V, Pre-Christian Era Bone and Ivory Carvings; VI, Kusana Bone and Ivory Carvings; VII, Gupta and Post-Gupta Bone and Ivory Carvings; VIII, Early Mediaeval Bone and Ivory Carvings; IX, Mediaeval Ivory and Bone Carvings. Comprehensive, classified bibliography, pp.137-145, including sources. Further, specialized literature in the footnotes.

China

1588 Cox, Warren E. **Chinese Ivory Sculpture**. New York, Bonanza Books, 1966. 118p. illus. index. LC 46-267.

Survey of Chinese ivory carving with emphasis on Ch'ing ivory statuettes and reliefs. Contents: I, Sources of Ivory; II, Elephants and Their Ancestor; III, Elephants and Ivory in Pre-Han China; IV, Han, T'ang and Sung Periods; V, Ming Ivories; VI, Ch'ing to Modern Ivories; VII, The Working of Ivory. A useful introduction that gives some attention to the significance of ivory carving in early China. No bibliography.

1589 Eastham, Barry C. **Chinese Art Ivory**. rev. & enl. ed. Ann Arbor, Mich., Ars Ceramica, 1976. 86p. illus. index. ISBN 0893440035.

First published in 1940 in Tientsen. Survey of Chinese ivory carving directed to the collector. Contents: I, The Fine Arts of China; II, Some Preliminary Discussion; III, Three Types of Carving; IV, Ivory Economy; V, The Ivory Carver's Subjects; VI, Beauty and Use; VII, Religious Influences; VIII, Place of Origin; IX, Time of Origin; X, Development of Types; XI, Critical Estimate. No bibliography.

1590 Laufer, Berthold. **Ivory in China**. Chicago, Field Museum of Natural History, 1925. 78p. illus. LC 45-53010REV.

Older, authoritative introduction to Chinese ivory carving. Illustrated with six plates of pieces obtained by the Marshall Field expedition to China in 1923. Contents: Ivory in China; The

Elephant in China and Trade in Elephant Ivory; Folk-lore of the Mammoth and Trade in Mammoth Ivory; Trade in Walrus and Narwhal Ivory; Objects Made of Ivory. General bibliography, p. 78.

See also the exhibition catalog: *Chinese Ivories: from the Shang to the Qing*, (London, The Oriental Ceramic Society, 1984. 200p. illus. ISBN 0903421224).

Japan

1591   Brockhaus, Albert. **Netsuke. Versuch einer Geschichte der Japanischen Schnitzkunst.** 2d ed. Leipzig, Brockhaus, 1909. 482p. illus. index. LC 06-1084.

Pioneering work on netsuke illustrated with 325 plates in black and white and color gravure of pieces in the author's collection. Contents: I, Netsuke-Kunst; II, Geschichte der Netsuke-Kunst; III, Netsuke-Künstler (List of netsuke artists with references to the type of netsuke they carved and their dates); IV, Beschreibender Katalog der Sammlung Brockhaus.

See also the author's shorter history, translated into English: *Netsuke* (New York, Duffield, 1924. 175p. illus. Reprint: New York, Hacker, 1975).

1592   Bushell, Raymond. **Collectors' Netsuke.** New York, Walker-Weatherhill, 1971. 199p. illus. index. LC 70-139687.

Important collector's handbook of Japanese ivory carving focusing on schools and individual artists. Contents: I, The Soken Kisho Carvers; II, Other Eighteenth Century Carvers; III, Early Nineteenth Century Carvers; IV, Middle Nineteenth Century Carvers; V, Mejii-Taisho Carvers; Vi, Contemporary Carvers. Within these chapters the subdivision is by artist. Illustrations include details of marks and signatures. Classified bibliography of books in English, French, German, and Japanese.

See also the author's: *An Introduction to Netsuke* (Rutland, Vt., Tuttle, 1964. 71p. illus. LC 64-24948).

1593   Kinsey, Miriam. **Contemporary Netsuke.** Rutland, Vt., Tuttle, 1977. 261p. illus. index. ISBN 0804811598.

Survey of netsuke carving in Japan from 1925 to the present designed for the collector and enthusiast. Contents: 1, Background; 2, Contemporary Netsuke; 3, Subject Matter; 4, Collecting Contemporary Netsuke; 5, Techniques; 6, A Netsuke in the Making (A Photographic Series); 7, Contemporary Carvers. Appendices with lists of makers, their signatures, and a list of netsuke dealers. Bibliography, pp. 249-51, is an alphabetical list of books in English.

See also the author's: *Living Masters of Netsuke* (New York, Kodansha International, 1984. 232p. illus. index. ISBN 0870116797).

See also the catalog of the British Museum's collection of netsuke: *Netsuke: The Miniature Sculpture of Japan*, by R. Barker (Woodbury, N.Y., Barron's, 1979. 184p. illus. index. ISBN 0812051823), the catalog of the Hindson Collection: *Netsuke:a Comprehensive Study Based on the M. T. Hindson Collection*, by N. K. Davey (London, Totowa, N.J., Sotheby Publications, 1982. 566p. illus. index. ISBN 0856671169), and the guide to the Netsuke in the Victoria and Albert Museum: *An Introduction to Netsuke*, by J. Earle (Owings Mills, Md., Stemmer House, 1980. 47p. illus. ISBN 0880450045).

JADE

Chinese Jade

Bibliographies

1594   Born, Gerald M. **Chinese Jade: An Annotated Bibliography**. Chicago, Celadon Press, 1982. 431p. index. LC 82-135282.
Comprehensive bibliography of books and periodical articles in English published between 1880 and 1981 on Chinese jade . Bibliographical essay on sources in Chinese and English introduces the bibliography, arranged by name of the author. Entries are fully described in the annotations.

Histories and Handbooks

1595   Capon, Edmund, and William MacQuitty. **Princes of Jade**. New York, Dutton, 1973. 192p. illus. index. LC 73-14410.
Popular but informative and effectively illustrated survey of ancient Chinese jade with particularly good coverage of the discoveries of Han dynasty funerary jade in the Wei Valley. Contents: I, Prince of Han; 2, China before the Han Dynasty; 3, Mind over Matter: From Confucius to Lao Tzu; 4, The Han Dynasty; 5, The Court of the Son of Heaven; 6, Everyday Life in Han China; 7, Han Imperialism: China and the West; 8, Art and Culture: The Age of Realism; 9, The Legacy of Han. Includes works in other materials, particularly ceramics and bronze, recovered from Han dynasty tombs. Select bibliography, p. 188.

1596   Hansford, S. Howard. **Chinese Carved Jades**. Greenwich, Conn., New York Graphics Society, 1968. 131p. (text), 96 plates. LC 68-11278.
Scholarly history of Chinese jade based in part on archaeological evidence. Contents: 1, Introduction; 2, The Material and Its Sources; 3, Progress of the Craft; 4, Design, Purpose and Usage: Neolithic, Shang and Chou; 5, Design Purpose and Usage: Han to Ch'ing; 6, Archaeology. Bibliography of 127 annotated titles in Chinese and Western languages.

1597   Laufer, Berthold. **Jade: A Study in Chinese Archaeology and Religion**. Chicago, Field Museum of Natural History, 1912. 370p. illus. index. LC 12-15552. (Publication of Field Museum of Natural History, 154. Anthropological Series, vol. X) Reprint: New York, Dover, 1974. LC 74-81085r892.
Pioneering work on Chinese jade carving with emphasis on the religious significance of ancient jades. Contents: Jade and Other Stone Implements; Jade Symbols of Sovereign Power; Astronomical Instruments of Jade; Jade as Writing Material; Jade in Religious Worship—the Jade Images as the Cosmic Deities; Jade Coins and Seals; Personal Ornaments of Jade; Jade Amulets of the Dead; Jade Objects Used in Dressing the Corpse; Jade Carvings of Fishes, Quadrupeds and Human Figures in the Grave; Vases of Jade; Jade of the Eighteenth Century. Bibliography, pp. 355-60.

1598   Nott, Stanley C. **Chinese Jade throughout the Ages...** London, Batsford, 1936. 198p. illus. index. Reprint: Rutland, Vt., Tuttle, 1962. LC 62-8839.
Old, once-standard collector's handbook of Chinese jade still useful for information on types of jade objects, particularly those accessible to the collector. Contents: I, Mineralogical Characteristics and Occurrence of Jade; II, Archaic Carvings in Jade; III, Archaic Ritual Symbols and Imperial Emblems up to the Han Dynasty; IV, Archaic Jade Carvings Possessing Astronomical Characteristics; V, Archaic Jade Symbols of Worship; VI, Archaic Jade Carvings from the

Han to the Ming Dynasties, 206 B.C.-A.D. 1368; VII, Archaic Vessel Forms in Jade from the Chou to the Ming Dynasty; VIII, Jade Carvings of the Ming Dynasty; IX, Jade Carvings of the Ch'ing Dynasty; X, Style in Jade Carving from the Shang-Yin Dynasty to the Present Day; XI, The Ju-i or Sceptre; XII, Animal Carvings in Jade; XIII, Bird, Fish and Insect Carvings in Jade; XIV, Designs Embodying Symbolic Emblems and Characters; XV, Plant and Flower Forms in Jade Carvings; XVI, Vase Forms in Jade; XVII, Jade Objects for the Writing Table; XVIII, Divinities and Other Celestial Forms Carved in Jade. Bibliographies of Chinese works and works in Western languages, pp. 166-174, and additional references in the footnotes.

1599   Salmony, Alfred. **Carved Jade of Ancient China**. Berkeley, Calif., Gillick Press, 1938. 85p. (text), 72 plates. Reprint: London, Han-Shan Tang, 1982. ISBN 0906610036.

Important scholarly study of Chinese jade with emphasis on the stylistic relationships between jades and other works of Chinese art. Contents: Jade; Ancient Texts; Neolithic; Shang; Early Western Chou; Late Western Chou; Early Eastern Chou; Late Eastern Chou; Han; Three Kingdoms and Six Dynasties; T'ang; Conclusion. Plates accompanied by descriptive catalog with bibliographical references.

1600   Salmony, Alfred. **Chinese Jade through the Wei Dynasty**. New York, Ronald Press, 1963. 287p. illus. index. LC 62-17538.

First part of a planned two-volume comprehensive history of Chinese jade carving. Text is interspersed with plates accompanied by detailed catalog entries. Contents: 1, Introduction; 2, Pre-Anyang; 3, Shang; 4, Early Western Chou; 5, Middle Chou; 6, Late Eastern Chou; 7, Han; 8, Wei. Bibliographical references in the footnotes and the catalog entries.

1601   Savage, George. **Chinese Jade: A Concise Introduction**. New York, October House, 1965. 72p. illus. index. LC 65-11507.

Concise survey of Chinese jade carving from prehistoric times to the end of the eighteenth century directed to the collector. Illustrated with museum pieces and pieces from the London art market. Bibliographical references in the footnotes and list of basic books, p. 69.

1602   Whitlock, Herbert P., and Martin L. Ehrmann. **The Story of Jade**. New York, Sheridan House, 1965. 222p. illus. index.

Popular history of Chinese jade directed to the collector with emphasis on identification of images in later jade and featuring illustrations of many pieces from the Drummond jade collection in the American Museum of Natural History in New York. Bibliographical note in the introduction.

See also the exhibition catalog: *Chinese Jade Throughout the Ages: An Exhibition* (London, Oriental Ceramic Society, 1975. 152p. illus.).

New Zealand Jade

1603   Beck, Russell J. **New Zealand Jade**. Wellington, A. H. & A. W. Reed, 1984. 173p. illus. index. ISBN 0589015443.

Comprehensive history of jade carving in New Zealand from Maori times to the present, written from the point of view of a contemporary artist-gem cutter. Contents: 1, Terminology; 2, New Zealand Jade Locations; 3, Bowewnite or Tnangiwani; 4, Maori History and Legends; 5, Maori Lapidary; 6, Jade Maori Artefacts; 7, European Lapidary; 8, Lapidary Hints. Appendices: I, The Origin of Nephrite; II, Physical Properties of New Zealand Nephrite; III, Jade Substitutes; IV, World Sources of Jade. Glossary. Bibliography, pp. 165-169.

1604   Pearce, Gilbert L. **The Story of New Zealand Jade, Commonly Know as Greenstone.** Auckland, Collins, 1971. 109p. illus. LC 72-176652.

Popular survey of jade carving in New Zealand from Maori times to the present, with emphasis on modern carving. Contents: 1, The Crucible of Time; 2, Jade Casts Its Spell; 3, The Mists of Legend; 4, The Greenstone Revolution; 5, The Craftsman and the Stone; 6, Changing Days; 7, New Methods and Ancient Skills. Appendices with essays on the chemical nature of jade and its imitations. General bibliography, pp. 103-104.

See also the exhibition catalog: *The Armytage Collection of Maori Jade,* by K. Athol Webster (London, Cable Press, 1948. 79p. illus.).

Pre-Columbian Jade

1605   Digby, Adrian. **Maya Jades**. rev. ed. London, British Museum Publications, 1972. 32p. illus. ISBN 0714115320.

Concise introduction to jade carving by the ancient Maya featuring pieces in the British Museum, London. Contents: The Background to Maya Jades; Dating of Jade Ornaments; Sources of Jade; Methods of Working; Beads; Ear Ornaments; Inlay; Nose Ornaments; Minor Pendants and Amulets; Flat Pendants with Human Faces or Figures; Early Pendants from Copan; Naturalistic Pendants in the Round; Some Outstanding Jade. General bibliography, pp. 31-32.

1606   Easby, Elizabeth K. **Pre-Colombian Jade from Costa Rica**. New York, A. Emmerich, 1968. 103p. illus. LC 68-55753.

Well-illustrated survey of Pre-Columbian jades from Costa Ricca. Contains 68 plates, most in color, with brief descriptive captions. Contents: Introduction; Costa Rica; Axe Gods; Figure Pendants; Beak Birds; Human and Composite Figures; Animals; Winged Pendants and Bats; Beads and Bar Pendants; Ear Ornaments; Club Heads and Minor Forms; Chronology. Basic bibliography, pp. 102-3.

1607   Tibon, Gutierre. **El jade de Mexico: el mundo esotérico del "chalchihuite."** Exico, D. F. Panoram Editorial, 1983. 157p. illus. ISBN 9683801056.

Popular introduction to jade carving in Pre-Columbian Mexico. Contents: 1, Jade y Chalchihuite; 2, Raices de la scralidad del jade; 3, El jade en los nombres miticos; 4, El jade no es esmeralda; 5, Los tresoros de jade; 6, Jaderos y lapidaros; 7, El jade; 8, El jade, espejo adivinatorio; 9, El jade Americano y el jade chino; 10, De donde procede nuestro jade?; 11, El jade en los nombres lugares; 12, El jade en los nombre de personas; 13, exegesis de un glifo misterioso; 14, el jade incrustado en los dientes. General bibliography, pp.153-57.

See also the exhibition catalog: *Jade precolombino de Costa Rica,* by C. Balser (San Jose, Costa Rica, Instituto Nacional de Seguros, 1980. 130p. illus.).

AMBER

1608   Fraquet, Helen. **Amber**. London and Boston, Butterworths, 1987. 176p. illus. index. ISBN 0408030801.

Gemological handbook on amber with survey of its use from antiquity to the present. Particularly useful for information on various types of amber and tests for authenticity. Contents: 1, Profile: Summary of Characteristics; 2, The Use of Amber in Antiquity; 3, Unsettled Europe; 4, European Renaissance Amber; 5, Medicinal Usage of Amber; 6, Adulteration: Amber of the Nineteenth and Twentieth Centuries; 7, Composition and Plastics; 8, Amber and Asia; 9, Amber from Sicily; 10, Amber from Romania; 11, Amber from the Dominican Republic; 12, Amber from Mexico; 13, Resins Confused with Amber; 14, Gemological Tests for the Identification of Amber;

15, Laboratory Techniques for the Identification of Amber; 16, Resins and Their Botanical Parentage; 17, Inclusions; Appendix 1: Geological Ages; 2: Amber in the USA; 3: Infra-red Spectra of Amber Samples.

See also: P. C. Rice. *Amber, the Golden Gem of the Ages* (New York, Kosciuszko Foundation, 1987. 289p. illus. index. ISBN 0917007205).

1609   Laufer, Berthold. **Historical Jottings on Amber in Asia.** Millwood, N.Y., Kraus Reprint Co., 1964. 31p. illus.
    Reprint from *Memoirs of the American Anthropological Association.* v. 1, pt. 3, pp. 213-244.

1610   Pelka, Otto. **Bernstein.** Berlin, R. C. Schmidt, 1920. 148p. ilus. (Bibliothek für Kunst-und Antiquitätensammler, Band 18). LC 23-12211.
    Older collector's history and handbook of European amber carving from the Middle Ages to the nineteenth century.

1611   Reineking von Bock, Gisela. **Bernstein: Das Gold der Ostsee.** Munich, Callwey, 1981. 185p. illus. index. ISBN 3766705571.
    Well-illustrated, comprehensive history of amber from prehistoric times to the 1980s. Includes amber carvings and amber jewelry. Contents: Entstehung und Verbreitung von Ostsee-bernstein; Verbreitung von Bernstein auf Erde; Paläontologie und Bernsteininklusen; Gewinnung von Bernstein; Bernsteinhandel und Bernsteingesetze; Entwicklung der Bernsteinkunst; Verwit-terung des Bernsteins; Pressbernstein; Nachweis von echtem Bernstein. Comprehensive bibliog-raphy, pp. 170-182.

1612   Rohde, Alfred. **Bernstein, ein deutscher Werkstoff: seine künstlerische Verarbeitung vom Mittelalter bis zum 18. Jahrhundert.** Berlin, Deutscher Verein für Kunstwissenschaft, 1937. 83p. illus.
    In the series: "Denkmäler deutscher Kunst." Standard history of the artistic use of amber from the Middle Ages to the eighteenth century with emphasis on German works in the Baltic territories. Contents: Einleitung; I, Mittelalter, Der Bernstein im Deutschordenslande; II, Renais-sance. Der Bernstein unter den Herzögen von Preußen; III, Das 17. und 18. Jahrhundert. Corpus of 317 plates with descriptive notes. Bibliographical references in the footnotes.

1613   Williamson, G. C. **The Book of Amber.** London, Benn, 1932. 268p. illus. index. LC 32-22051.
    General history of amber and its use in art. Contents: On Amber Generally; Classical Allusions to Amber; Nomenclature; The Amber Routes; Amber Considered from the Point of View of Anthropology; Amber Considered as a Mineral; The Home of Succinite; The Zoology and Botany of Amber; Amber in Art; The Locality in Which Amber Is Found; English Amber; Amber Considered from the Point of View of Medicine and Folklore; Sicilian Amber or Simetite; Rumanite or Roumanian Amber; Burmite or Burmese Amber; Ambergris; Gedanite and Pseudo-Amber; Amber Varnish; Ambroid or Pressed Amber. General bibliography, pp. 239-248.
    See also the museum catalogs: *Jewelery and Amber of Italy: A Collection in the National Museum in Naples*, by R. Siviero (New York, McGraw-Hill, 1959. 153p. illus. index), *Catalogue of the Carved Amber in the Department of Greek and Roman Antiquities*, by D. E. Strong (London, The British Museum, 1966), guide: *Jade, Amber, and Ivory*, by H. P. Whitlock (New York, American Museum of Natural History, 1934. 16p. illus. LC 36-10267).

SHELL

1614 Critchley, Paula. **The Art of Shellcraft**. New York, Praeger, 1975. 96p. illus. ISBN 0275515400.

Popular survey on the use of shells for various decorative purposes with emphasis on contemporary craft applications. Interspersed among the illustrations are some historic, chiefly late nineteenth and early twentieth centuries, shell decorated boxes, picture frames, etc. No bibliography.

1615 Pazaurek, Gustav E. **Perlmutter**. Berlin, Gbr. Mann, 1937. 79p. illus.

Handbook of objects made of carved or inlaid mother-of-pearl with emphasis on German works of the sixteenth and seventeenth centuries.

1616 Ritchie, Carson I. A. **Shell Carving: History and Techniques**. South Brunswick, N.Y., A.S. Barnes, 1974. 208p. illus. index. ISBN 0498079287.

Popular survey of shell carving throughout the world from prehistoric times to the present, with emphasis on the mother-of-pearl inlay work and shell cameo carving of Europe from the seventeenth century to the present. Contents: 1, Faces of the Gods; 2, The Talking Shell: Wampum; 3, Foundation of the Universe: Tortoiseshell and Nacre in the Far East; 4, Heavenly Trumpets: The Sacred Chank; 5, Barbaric Pearl and Gold: Shell Carving in the South Seas; 6, Scallop of Salvation: Mother-of-Pearl in the Near East; 7, The Gates of Heaven: Mother-of-Pearl Carving in Europe; 8, The Ship of Pearl: The Nautilus Shell; 9, The Sounding Shell: Tortoiseshell in Europe; 10, The Gem from the Sea: The Cameo.

1617 Suarez Diez, Lourdes. **Tipologia de los objetos prehispanicos de concha**. Mexico, Instituto Nacional de Antropologia e Historia, SEP, 1977. 209p. illus. (Instituto Nacional de Antropologia e Historia, Coleccion Cientifica, Arquelogia, 54).

Scholarly, archaeological study of shell carving in Pre-Colombian Central America aimed at identification of various mollusks used, and the techniques employed in fashioning and carving shell to establish a catalog of types of shell art. Contents: Agradecimientos; Introduccion; Generalidades sobre la concha; Tecnicas de manufactura; Analysis de material y tipologia; Resumen y conclusiones. Illustrated with line drawings. General bibliography, pp. 199-200.

See also the author's work on the technique of Pre-Columbian shell carving: *Tecnicas prehispanica en los objetos de concha*, (Mexico, Instituto Nacional de Antropologia e Historia, SEP, 1974. 69p. illus. LC 80-512229r852).

CORAL

1618 Liverino, Basilio. **IL Corallo, esperienze e ricordi di un corallaro**. Bologna, Luigi Parma, 1983. 229p. illus.

Comprehensive history of coral as a material in jewelry and other works of art with particular attention given to the sources of coral in Italian waters. Contents: I, Il Mondo del corallo; 2, Il Corallo de Pacifico; 3, La Pesca nel Mediterraneo; 4, Dati tecnici; 5, Storia della lavorazione del corallo; 6, Usi e impieghi; 7, Attività attuale; 8, Torre del Greco e il corallo. Glossary and basic bibliography, p. 229.

1619 Putaturo Murano, Antonella, and Alessandra Perriccioli. **L'arte del corallo: le manifatture di Napoli e di Torre del Greco fra Ottocento e Novecento**. Naples, Gaetano Macchiaroli, 1989. 145p. index. ISBN 888582305X.

Scholarly essays on the history of carving in coral and mother-of-pearl in Naples and Tore del Greco from the seventeenth through the nineteenth centuries. Well-illustrated with 150 plates—many in high-quality color—of jewelry and small-scale carvings. Contents: L lavorazione del coraqllo nei centri del Mediterraneo by A. P. Murano; Dalla promulgazione del Codice corallino all'Unità by A. P. Murano; Dall'Unità all'apertura della Scuola d'incisione sul corallo by A. P. Saggese; La Sculo del corallo e le manifatture locali by A. P. Saggese. Chronologically arranged bibliography, pp. 99-103, and further bibliography in the footnotes.

See also: Tescione, Giovanni. *Il corallo nella storia e nell'arte* (Naples, 1965. 405p. illus. index).

CHAPTER TWELVE

JEWELRY

DICTIONARIES

1620 Newmann, Harold. **An Illustrated Dictionary of Jewelry**. London, Thames & Hudson, 1981. 334p. illus. LC 81-50797.

Comprehensive dictionary of world jewelry from ancient times to the present. Over 2,500 entries cover materials, techniques, types, styles, makers, and famous pieces of jewelry. The longer entries have bibliographical references. Numerous illustrations support the informative text.

1621 Mason, Anita. **An Illustrated Dictionary of Jewellery**. New York, Harper & Row, 1974. 390p. illus. LC 73-11590.

General dictionary of world jewelry covering tools and techniques, precious and non-precious gemstones and metals, history of jewelry from ancient times to the present, and biographical entries for a number of notable jewelers and jewelry-making firms. Illustrated with line drawings.

GENERAL HISTORIES AND HANDBOOKS

1622 Barth, Hermann. **Das Geschmeide; Schmuck- und Edelsteinkunde**. Berlin, A. Schall, 1903. 2v. illus. index.

Older, comprehensive history/handbook of Western jewelry. Volume one provides a history from antiquity through the nineteenth century; volume two is a good handbook of jewelry-making and lapidary technique. Bibliographical footnotes.

1623 Biehn, Heinz. **Juwelen und Preziosen**. Munich, Prestel, 1965. 415p. illus. index. LC 66-80680.

History of European jewelry from the Middle Ages to the twentieth century with emphasis on gem stones, their cutting and polishing, setting, symbolism, and value. Contents: Glaz und Magie der Edelsteine; Zauber der Perle; Amulett und Talisman; Sammler und Liebhaber; Geschenke und Ehrengaben; Schatzkammern und Schmucktrousseaus; Repraesentatio; Verpfändung und Verkauf; Diebstahl und Raub; Epilog; Tafel der Diamantenschnitte und Gewichte. Selected bibliography, pp. 410-15.

1624 Bott, Gerhard. **Ullstein Juwelenbuch, Abendlandische Schmuck von der Antike bis zu Gegenwart**. Berlin, Frankfurt; Vienna, Ullstein, 1972. 305p. illus. index. LC 73-33552.

Well-illustrated, authoritative survey of Western jewelry from the ancient Greek to the immediate post-World War II periods. Contents: Schmuck der Spätantike; Schmuck des Mittelalters; Schmuck der Renaissance; Schmuck der Barockzeit; Schmuck des 19. Jahrhunderts; Schmuck der Stilbewegung um 1900; Schmuck des 20. Jahrhunderts. Appendices with essays on the history of precious metal by I. Schneider, the characteristics and methods of working on the various precious stones, pearls and coral by R. Heil, and essay on purity standards and marks. Excellent, comprehensive, classified bibliography, pp. 284-293.

1625 Egger, Gerhart. **Generations of Jewelry from the 15th through the 20th Century.** West Chester, Pa., Schiffer, 1988. 219p. illus. index. ISBN 0887401244.

History of Western jewelry from the Renaissance to the 1970s. Superb plates from photographs by Helga Schmidt-Glassner including many portraits illustrating the use of jewelry at various times. Contents: The Concept: Amulet Character of Jewelry; Goldsmith's Art and Ornamentation as Expressions of the Times; Types of Jewelry; Rise of the Bourgeoisie-Jewelry as a Status Symbol. The Facts: Chronological Development of Middle-Class Jewelry; Ornamental Designs. The Examples (436 plates with descriptive captions). Bibliography of basic books in all languages, p. 217. An excellent history; both insightful and useful.

1626 Gregorietti, Giovanni. **Jewelry through the Ages.** New York, Crescent, 1969. 319p. illus. LC 74-83809.

Well-illustrated history of world jewelry from ancient Egypt to the 1960s. Included among the illustrations are works of art depicting figures wearing jewelry. Contents: I, Gold: Its Physical Properties and Methods of Working; The Use of Gold in the Ancient World; The Use of Gold in Pre-Columbian America; The Use of Gold in Africa; II, Coloured Stones in Jewelry: India, Pearls, Precious Stones in Ancient Egypt; Precious Stones in Greece and Rome; Archaeological Discoveries; III, The Middle Ages: Byzantium; Early Medieval Europe; Supersition, Amulets and Talismans; The Gothic Era; IV, The Renaissance: The Age of Elaborate Jewels; V, The Baroque Period: The Age of Stone Cutting; The Diamond; Coral; The Far East; VI, The 18th Century: The Period of French Influence; VII, The 19th Century: The Industrial Revolution; Diamonds; VIII, 1870 to the Present Day. Comprehensive bibliography, pp. 314-16.

1627 Kuntzsch, Ingrid. **A History of Jewels and Jewelry.** New York, St. Martin's Press, 1981. 263p. illus. index. ISBN 0312380887.

Translation of: *Glanz und Zauber des Schmucks* (Leipzig, Editions Leipzig, 1981). Comprehensive, well-illustrated survey of jewelry throughout the world from antiquity to the 1970s. Chronologically and geographically arranged text is followed by collection of 229 plates with descriptive captions. Bibliography of basic books in all languages, pp. 255-56.

1628 Lanllier, Jean, and Marie-Anne Pini. **Five Centuries of Jewelry in the West.** New York, Leon Amiel, 1983. 327p. illus. index. ISBN 0814807291.

Well-illustrated survey of jewelry in western Europe and America from the Renaissance to the 1970s. Emphasis is on gem set jewelry. First chapter is an introduction to gemology. Last chapter treats jewelry designed by modern artists. Bibliography of basic books in all languages, pp. 325-326.

1629 Tait, Hugh, ed. **Jewelry, 7000 Years. An International History and Illustrated Survey from the Collections of the British Museum.** New York, Abrams, 1986. 255p. illus. index. ISBN 0810911574.

Richly illustrated survey of world jewelry from antiquity to circa 1950 based on pieces in the British Museum, London. Work of a team of British experts. Select bibliography, p. 244.

See also the exhibition catalogs: *Jewelry Ancient to Modern,* A. Garside, ed. (Baltimore, Md., Walters Art Gallery, 1979) and *Objects of Adornment: Five Thousand Years of Jewelry from the Walters Art Gallery* (Baltimore, New York, American Federation of Arts, 1984. 190p. illus. ISBN 091748176X), and the museum catalog: *The Art of the Jeweller, a Catalogue of the Hull Grundy Gift to the British Museum,* by H. Tait and C. Gere (London, British Museum, 1984. 2v. illus.).

ANCIENT JEWELRY

General Works

1630   Ogden, Jack. **Jewellery of the Ancient World**. London, Trefoil Books, 1982. 185p. illus. index. ISBN 0862940087.

Survey history of jewelry in antiquity from ancient Sumer to the end of the Roman periods, with emphasis on the methods and materials of the ancient goldsmiths and jewelers. Contents: Jewellery and the Archaeologist; Gold and Silver; Metals Other Than Gold and Silver; The Gemstones; Organic Gem Materials; Glass, Enamel and Faience; Ancient Imitation and Altered Gemstones; Stone Working; Forgeries; The Jeweller. Comprehensive bibliography classified by chapters, pp. 182-185.

1631   Rosenthal, Renate. **Jewellery in Ancient Times**. London, Cassel, 1973. 96p. illus. index. LC 75-300473r85.

Popular, illustrated survey from ancient Egypt through the early Middle Ages. No bibliography.

See also the guide to the collection of the Staaliche Museen Preussischer Kulturbesitz Berlin, *Schmuck der alten Welt*, by A. Greifenhagen (Berlin, Mann, 1974. 70p. illus. ISBN 3786122237) and the exhibition catalog: *Gold Jewelry: Craft, Style, and Meaning from Mycenae to Constaninoplis*, Museum of Art, Rhode Island School of Design (Louvain-la-Neuve, Erasme, 1983. 227p. illus. LC 83-212591).

Egypt and the Ancient Near East

1632   Aldred, Cyril. **Jewels of the Pharaohs; Egyptian Jewelry of the Dynastic Period**. New York, Praeger, 1971. 256p. illus. index. LC 72-108266.

Well-illustrated history of ancient Egyptian jewelry with emphasis on stylistic development and technique. Contents: 1, The Recovery of Ancient Egyptian Jewellery; 2, The Uses of Ancient Egyptian Jewellery; 3, The Materials; 4, The Craftsmen and Their Tools; 5, Techniques; 6, The Forms; Epilogue. Chronological table, detailed descriptive notes to the plates. Classified bibliography, pp. 246-49, including excavation reports, technical studies, exhibition and museum catalogs, and literary sources.

1633   Maxwell-Hyslop, K. R. **Western Asiatic Jewellery, c. 3000-612 B.C.** London, Methuen, 1971. 286p. illus. index. LC 75-874454.

Comprehensive and scholarly history of jewelry in the ancient Near East from early historic times to the rise of ancient Persia. Contents: 1, Mesopotamia: The Early Dynastic period; 2, Mesopotamia: The Argonid period c. 2370-2200 B.C.; 3, Anatolia 2500-2000 B.C.; 4, The Guti-Gudea Period, Third Dynasty of Ur to Isin and Larsa Dynasties 2250-1894 B.C.; 5, Babylonia, Mesopotamia and Iran 2017-1750 B.C.; 6, Anatolia c. 1950-1750 B.C.: Kültepe-Kanesh and the Assyrian Karum; 7, Phoenicia, Syria and Palestine c. 2000-1550 B.C., Asiatic-Cypriote Relations c. 1550-1450 B.C.; 8, Syria and Palestine c. 1550-1300 B.C.; 9, Iran in the Mid-second Millennium B.C.; 10, The Kassite Period in Babylonia and the Mid-Assyrian Period in Assyria; 11, Assyria and Iran: Twelfth to Seventh Centuries B.C.; 12, Urartu: Ninth to Seventh Centuries B.C.; 14, Palestine and Syria:Twelfth to Sixth Centuries B.C.; 15, Assyria and Iran: Ninth to Seventh Centuries B.C. Bibliographical footnotes and comprehensive, classified bibliography, pp. 271-73. A standard work.

1634   Sargon, Odette. **Les bijoux préhelléniques**. Paris, Librairie Orientaliste Paul Geuthner, 1987. 386p. illus. index. (Bibliothèque archéologique et historique, tome 108) ISBN 2705303367.

Scholarly history and study of ancient Aegean jewelry. Contents: P Découvertes et techniques des métaux précieux: I, La préparation des métaux précieux, II, L'orfèvre; Bijoux: III, Couronnes, diadèmes, bandeaux et motifs décoratifs d'une destination peut-être apparentée; IV, Pendants d'oreilles; V, Perles, éléments de colliers; VI, Pendentifs; VII, Bracelets et cercles; VIII, Petits anneaux décorés; IX, Epingles. Comprehensive, classified bibliography, pp. 225-86, and further bibliography in the notes.

1635   Vilimková, Milada. **Egyptian Jewelry**. London and New York, Hamlyn, 1969. 141p. illus. index. LC 70-436451.

Survey of ancient Egyptian jewelry illustrated with pieces in the Cairo Museum. First seven chapters outline the stylistic development of Egyptian jewelry design. Eighth and ninth chapters discuss the decoration and materials and techniques of ancient Egyptian jewelry. Catalog of 94 pieces with descriptive notes. Bibliographical references to list of abbreviations, p. 52.

1636   Wilkinson, Alex. **Ancient Egyptian Jewellery**. London, Methuen, 1971. 266p. illus. index. LC 79-874376.

Scholarly history of jewelry in pharonic Egypt. Introductory chapter on the craft of ancient Egyptian jewelry followed by chapters dedicated to the main periods. Contents: 1, Craftsmen; 2, Predynastic Period; 3, Early Dynastic Period; 4, Old Kingdom; 5, Middle Kingdom; 6, New Kingdom: 1—17th-18th Dynasties; 7, New Kingdom: 2—19th-20th Dynasties; 8, 21st-26 Dynasties; 9, Kushite Period; 10, Late Period—23rd-26th Dynasties; 11, Conclusion. Bibliographical footnotes. Fully indexed. A standard work.

Greek and Roman

1637   Becatti, Giovanni. **Oreficerie antiche dalle minoiche alle barbarische**. Rome, Istituto Poligrafico dello Stato, 1955. 255p. illus. index. LC 55-42867.

Comprehensive history of gold jewelry from the ancient Aegean civilizations of the second millennium B.C. to the Germanic invasions of the fifth through seventh centuries. Includes other objects in gold such as drinking vessels. Chronologically arranged text is followed by a collection of 590 plates and catalog. Catalog entries include bibliographies. General bibliography, pp. 229-34.

1638   Coraelli, Filippo. **Greek and Roman Jewellery**. London, Methuen, 1961. 236p. illus. index. LC 63-4648.

Pictorial survey of ancient Greek, Etruscan and Roman gold jewelry from the Geometric period to the fourth century A.D. Sixty-four color plates with descriptive captions. No bibliography.

1639   Pfeiler, Bärbel. **Römischer Goldschmuck des ersten und zweiten Jahrhunderts n. Chri. nach datierten Funden**. Mainz, P. von Zabern, 1970. 136p. illus. LC 77-585018.

Based on the author's dissertation, *Frankfurt am Main,* 1968.

Scholarly history of ancient Roman gold jewelry from the first and second centuries A.D. based on dated examples. Emphasis on development of decorative styles and types. Chronological arrangement subdivided by sites. Catalog of the dated examples with bibliographical references. Bibliographical references in the footnotes and bibliography of basic books in all languages, pp. 127-31.

See also the exhibition catalog: *Greek Gold: Jewelry from the Age of Alexander*, by H. Hoffmann and Patricia F. Davidson (Mainz, Zabern, 1965. 311p. illus.).

GERMANIC JEWELRY

1640   Haseloff, Günter. **Die germanische Tierornamentik der Völkerwanderungszeit: Studien zu Salin's Stil I**. Berlin, New York, Walter de Gruyter, 1981. 3v. illus. (Vorgeschichtliche Forschungen, Band 17). ISBN 3110047608.

Important, scholarly study of the zoomorphic ornament on jewelry and other metalwork falling into Bernard Salin's first style of Germanic ornament (FA965) and dated by Haseloff in the late fourth and fifth centuries A.D. Contents: Band I: Einleitung; I, Eine jütländische Fibelgruppe und ihre Verwandten; II, Stiphasen im nordischen Stil I; III, Früher Stil auf Schnallen des Namurois und vom Niederhein; Band II: IV, Stil I auf Fibel des nordischen Typs vom Kontinent; V, Stil I aud Fibel vom kontientalen Typ; Schluß Band III: Zu den Filigranblechen der Bügelfibeln aus Donzdorf, Grab 78 by B. Arrhenius; Bifrons Grave 41 by Sonia C. Hawkes; Zur Inschrift der Runenfibel von Nonzdorf by W. Krause; Die Münzanhänger aus dem Frauengrab Kirchheim unter Teck, Grab 85 by E. Nau; Zur Datierung von Grab 5 und 129 des alemannischen Gräberfeldes von Bopfingen, Kreis Aalen by D. Reimann; Nachtrag: Das Fibelfragment aus Idstedt, Kreis Schleswig by G. Haseloff. Full scholarly apparatus including extensive bibliographical references in the footnotes. A standard work on Germanic jewelry and metalwork.

1641   Haseloff, Günther. **Kunststile des frühen Mittelalters: Völkerwanderungs- und Merowingerzeit**. Stuttgart, Württembergisches Landesmuseum, 1979. 112p. illus.

Concise but authoritative survey of jewelry in Europe from the period of the Germanic invasions to the end of the seventh century based upon pieces in the Württembergisches Landesmuseum, Stuttgart, therefore emphasizing Alemannic material. Contents: Die Anfänge der Kunst bei den Alamannen; Nordische Tierornamentik bei den Alemannen; Der Beginn einer eigenen Tierornamentik bei den Alemannen; Flechtbandornamentik; Die Verschmelzung von Flechtband und Tierornamentik: Stil II; Der farbigen Stile; Goldblechschiebenfibeln; Die goldene Reiterscheibe von Pliezhausen; Christliche Motive in der Kunst des 7. Jahrhunderts; Brakteatenfibeln und Brakteatenanhänger. General bibliography, pp. 108-09.

1642   Holmqvist, Wilhelm. **Tauschierte Metalarbeiten des Nordens aus Römerzeit und Völkerwanderung**. Stockholm, Wahlström & Widstrand, 1951. 158p. illus. (Kungl. Vitterhets historie och antikvtets akademiens. Handlingar, 70, nr. 2).

Important, scholarly history of late-Roman and early-Germanic metalwork, chiefly jewelry, with inlay ornament. Major contribution to the question of the relationship of Germanic and Roman art. Contents: Vorwort; Die römische Kunstindustrie; Die kontinental-germanische Entwicklung; Die angelsächsische Entwicklung; Nordische Metalleinlagen aus der römischen Eisenzeit; Nordische Metalleinlagen aus der Völkerwanderungszeit. Comprehensive biblkiography, pp. 153-58, and further bibliography in the footnotes.

1643   Jenny, Wilhelm A. **Germanischer Schmuck des frühen Mittelalters**. Berlin, Verlag für Kunstwissenschaft, 1933. LC 34-19379.

Important corpus of 64 plates illustrating major pieces of Germanic metalwork dating from the fourth through the early eleventh centuries. Authoritative introduction with comprehensive bibliography, pp. 33-36. Descriptive notes to the plates with bibliographical references.

See the exhibition catalog: *Arts of the Migration Period in the Walters Art Gallery*, (Baltimore, Md., The Gallery, 1961. 173p. illus. LC 61-65213).

Sutton Hoo Treasure

1644 Bruce-Mitford, Rupert L. S. **The Sutton Hoo Ship-Burial**. London, British Museum Publications, 1975-1983. 3v. in 4. illus. ISBN 071411331X.

Comprehensive, scholarly catalog and study of the objects discovered in the seventh century A.D. ship burial in Sutton Hoo, East Anglia. Contents: v. 1: Excavations, Background, the Ship, Dating, and Inventory; v. 2: Arms, Armour and Regalia; v. 3: Late Roman and Byzantine Silver, Hanging Bowls, Drinking Vessels, Cauldrons and Other Containers, Textiles, the Lyre, Pottery Bottle and Other Items (2 vs.).

1645 Grohskopf, Bernice. **The Treasure of Sutton Hoo; Ship-burial for an Anglo-Saxon King**. New York, Atheneum, 1970. 168p. illus. LC 74-86555.

Popular introduction to the Sutton Hoo treasure. Contents: I, The Dig; 2, The Treasure; 3, The Questions; 4, Sutton Hoo and the Age of Beowulf; 5, Sutton Hoo Now. Selected bibliography, pp. 153-155.

MEDIEVAL JEWELRY

1646 Earle, John. **The Alfred Jewel, an Historical Essay**. Oxford, England, Clarendon, 1901. 196p. illus. LC 01-12925.

Comprehensive study of the ninth-century jewel pendant long associated with King Alfred the Great of England. Written from an antiquarian point of view, it nonetheless has much useful information and insights. Contents: I, Description of the Alfred Jewel; II, The Epigraph or Legend; III, Early Speculations about Its Design and Manner of Use; IV, Bishop Clifford's Theory; V, A Jewel in the Crown; VI, The Boar's Head; VII, The Figure in Enamel and the Engraved Plate at the Back of It; VIII, Alfred in Somerset beyond Pedrida; IX, Newton Park and Fairfield House; X, Gold Rings Contemporaneous; XI, Some Closing Reflections. Appendices with documents relevant to the early history of the jewel. Occasional bibliographical footnotes.

1647 Hinton, David A. **Medieval Jewellery from the Eleventh to the Fifteenth Century**. Aylesbury, Shire Publications, 1982. 48p. illus. index. ISBN 0852635761.

Introductory history of medieval jewelry in England from the Norman Conquest to the end of the fifteenth century designed as a handbook for enthusiasts of archaeology. Sequel to Jessup (1648). Description of the chief museum collections. Illustrations of major museum pieces with good descriptive captions. Basic bibliography, p. 24.

1648 Jessup, Ronald. **Anglo-Saxon Jewellery**. New York, Praeger, 1953. 148p. illus. index. LC 52-13579.

Survey of gold, silver and bronze Anglo-Saxon jewelry (fifth through eighth centuries) with emphasis on the burial treasures. Introduction sketches the history of the Anglo-Saxon, their burial customs, jewelry uses and manufacture. Forty plates of major pieces have detailed, descriptive notes with bibliographies.

See also the author's: *Anglo-Saxon Jewellery* (Aylesbury, Shire Publications, 1974. 96p. illus. index. ISBN 0852632614).

See also the exhibition catalogs: *L'Or des Vikings, exposition du Musée des Antiquités Nationales de Suède* (Bordeaux, Musée d'Aquitaine, 1969. 308p. illus).

RENAISSANCE JEWELRY

1649   Hackenbroch, Yvonne. **Renaissance Jewellery**. London, Sotheby Parke Bernet; Munich, Beck, in association with The Metropolitan Museum of Art, New York, 1979. 424p. illus. index. ISBN 0856670561.

Comprehensive and scholarly history of jewelry in the late fifteenth and sixteenth centuries. Arrangement is by country. Extensive bibliographical references in the notes, comprehensive bibliography, pp. 379-384, and appendix with excerpts of documents, mostly inventories, related to the collecting and use of jewelry during the Renaissance. A standard work.

See also the exhibition catalog: *Princely Magnificence: Court Jewels of the Renaissance, 1500-1630* (London, Debrett's Peerage, 1980. 140p. illus. and the collection catalog: *The Thyssen-Bornemisza Collection: Renaissance Jewels, Gold Boxes and Objets de Vertu* (London, Philip Wilson for Sotheby Publications, 1984. 384p. illus. ISBN 0865650446).

MODERN JEWELRY (19th and 20th Centuries)

1650   Becker, Vivienne. **Antique and Twentieth Century Jewellery: A Guide for Collectors**. New York, Van Nostrand Reinhold, 1982. 301p. illus. index. ISBN 0442214006.

Comprehensive history/handbook of European and American jewelry of the nineteenth and the early twentieth centuries. Illustrated with pieces in private collections and in the trade. Contents: 1, Diamond Brooches; 2, Coral Jewellery; 3, Nineteenth Century Gold-Work; 4, Piqué; 5, Silver of the Late Nineteenth Century; 6, Collecting in Unusual Materials; 7, Mourning Jewellery; 8, Scottish Jewellery; 9, Flowers in Jewellery; 10, Animals in Jewellery; 11, Stick-pins; 12, Cameos and Engraved Gems; 13, Mosaics in Jewellery; 14, Egyptian Revival Jewellery; 15, Signed Jewellery of the Mid-nineteenth Century; 16, The Famous Jewel Houses; 17, Signed Art Nouveau Jewellery; 18, Pendants at the Turn of the Century; 19, Arts and Crafts Jewellery; 20, Liberty and his Rivals; 21, Edwardian and Art Deco Jewellery. General bibliography, p. 291. A fact-filled, very useful handbook for the collector.

1651   Becker, Vivienne. **Art Nouveau Jewelry**. London, Thames & Hudson, 1985. 240p. illus. index. ISBN 0500234337.

Well-illustrated survey of jewelry in the Art Nouveau style in Europe and the United States. Biographical dictionary of major jewelers, guide to makers' marks and signatures, and bibliography of books, periodicals, and exhibition catalogs, p. 237.

1652   Cartlidge, Barbara. **Twentieth-century Jewelry**. New York, Abrams, 1985. 238p. illus. index. ISBN 0810916851.

Sumptuously illustrated survey of European and American jewelry from 1900 to 1984 with emphasis on avant garde art jewelry and the contribution of women. Contents: 1, 1900-1920: Art Nouveau and the Arts and Crafts Movement; II, 1920-1950: Art Deco; Arts and Crafts; Australia; Jewellery Industry; World War II; III, 1950-1970: Education: United States, Australia, and Japan, Europe; The Craft Revival; Is Jewellery Art ?; Women in Gold- and Silversmithing; From Royal Regalia to 'Op' Jewellery; IV, 1970-1984: Internationalism; Contemporary Views on the Old Argument; Etiquette; Other Original Ideas: Australia, Canada, Europe; Developments in Eastern Europe; France: A Special Case; The 1980s. Appendices with biographies of major jewelry makers and designers, list of exhibitions, and general bibliography, p. 231.

1653   Dewiel, Lydia-Lida. **Schmuck vom Klassizismus bis zum Art Deco**. Munich, Mosaik, 1979. 160p. illus. index. ISBN 3570024679.

Collector's handbook of European jewelry from the French Revolution to 1925. Illustrated with pieces of the type accessible to the serious collector with price ranges in German marks. Chapter with information for the collector with a classified bibliography of books in all languages.

1654   Gabardi, Melissa. **Art Deco Jewellery 1920-1949**. Woodbridge, Antique Collectors' Club, 1989. 329p. illus. index. ISBN 1851490655.

Well-illustrated survey of jewelry in the Art Deco style produced in Europe and the United States. Contents: I, The Explosion of Art Deco; II, The Emancipation of Women's Fashion; III, Art Deco Jewellery by Artist Jewellers: Jean Despres, Jean Dunand, Georges Fouquet, Jean Fouquet, Gustave Miklos, Gerard Sandoz, Raymond Templier, Paul Brandt, Other Creative Jewellers; IV, High Fashion Jewellery of the 1920's: Boucheron, Cartier, Chaumet, Mellerio dits Meller, Noury-Maubouisson, Van Cleef and Arpels, Other Jewellers; V, Jewellery of the 1930's; VI, The Second Generation of 1930's Jewellery; VII, Gold Jewellery of the 1930's; VIII, Jewellery of the 1940's; 1950-The End of the Period of Crisis. General bibliography, p. 329.

1655   Gere, Charlotte. **European and American Jewellery, 1830-1914**. London, Heinemann, 1975. 240p. illus. index. ISBN 04334288004.

American edition: *American and European Jewelry* (New York, Crown, 1975). Survey of European and American jewelry from Neoclassicism to Art Nouveau. Contents: Part 1: Fashions and Styles (1830-50, 1851-75, 1876-1914); Part 2: Materials, Techniques and Marks; Part 3: Jewellers and Designers (120 biographies of jewelers, designers and firms). Glossary of jewelry terms. Selected bibliography, pp. 233-34.

1656   Gere, Charlotte, and Geoffrey C. Munn. **Artists' Jewellery: Pre-raphaelite to Arts and Crafts**. Woodbridge, Antique Collectors' Club, 1989. 244p. illus. ISBN 1851490248.

Well-illustrated survey of the jewelry designed by famous artists from the middle of the nineteenth century to the end of the first quarter of the twentieth century with emphasis on Britain. Illustrated with actual pieces, designs for jewelry, paintings by the various artists featuring their jewelry and photographs of persons—usually the artist's family—wearing the jewelry. All illustrations have descriptive captions. Contents: I, Art and Fashion; II, Art and Commerce; III, From Romanticism to Aestheticism; IV, Dante Gabriel Rossetti and the "Pre-Raphaelite" Fashion; V, The Craft Revival; VI, Art Nouveau and Jugendstil; VII, Post-War Postscript; IX, Enamelling Revival. Classified bibliography, including good list of exhibition catalogs, p. 240

1657   Hinks, Peter. **Nineteenth Century Jewellery**. London, Faber and Faber, 1975. 120p. illus. index. ISBN 057116501.

Well-illustrated, comprehensive history of jewelry in Europe and America during the nineteenth century. Includes peasant, i.e., European folk jewelry. Chapter on collecting. Appendix with lists of gold and silver marks of ten countries.

1658   Hughes, Graham. **Modern Jewelry: An International Survey, 1890-1967**. rev. ed. London, Studio Vista, 1968. 256p. illus. ISBN 0289277094.

Pictorial survey of European and American jewelry from 1890 to 1960 with emphasis on designers working for commercial production. Contents: 1, Introduction; 2, Value—the Essence; 3, Style; 4, Structure of the Trade; 5, Gems; 6, Technical History; 7, Advertising and Display; 8, Wearers and Fashion; 9, Evolution of Design; 10, The Main Picture Sequence; 11, Epilogue. Appendices with biographies of leading designers and firms and selected bibliography, pp. 253-55. Useful collection of reproductions of advertisements and photographs of women wearing jewelry.

1659   Raulet, Sylvie. **Jewelry of the 1940s and 1950s**. New York, Rizzoli, 1988. 332p. illus. index. ISBN 0847809358.

Translation of: *Bijoux des années 1940-1950* (Paris, Editions du Regard, 1987). Lavishly illustrated survey of high-fashion jewelry in Europe and America between 1937 and 1961 with emphasis on France. Biographies of major designers and firms. Select bibliography of books and articles, p. 327.

See also the exhibition catalogs: *Ornamenta: Internationale Schmuckkunst*, Schmuckmuseum Pforzheim (Munich, Prestel, 1989. 319p. illus. ISBN 3791310151), *International Exhibition of Modern Jewellery, 1890-1961*. (London, Worshipful Company of Goldsmiths, 1961. 2v. illus.).

AMERICAN JEWELRY

1660   Proddow, Penny and Debra Healy. **American Jewelry: Glamour and Tradition**. New York, Rizzoli, 1987. 208p. illus. index. ISBN 084780830.

Lavishly illustrated survey of jewelry in the United States from early Colonial times to the 1980s. Contents: 1, Early American Jewelry Establishments: North, East, South, and West; 2, The Establishment of Tiffany & Co.; 3, Tiffany and Co. and The International Expositions, 1867-1900; 4, Art Nouveau; 5, Platinum Jewelry; 6, The New York Jewelry Establishment: World War I to 1929; 7, From the Depression to World War II; 8, World War II; 9, Van Cleef & Arpels in New York; 10, Harry Winston, Inc.; 11, Texas and the West; 12, The 1960s; 13, Tiffany & Co. and Bulgari, New York. Glossary of more common terms, few bibliographical references in the notes and general bibliography, p. 206.

Native American Jewelry

1661   Bedinger, Margery. **Indian Silver. Navajo and Pueblo Jewelers**. Albuquerque, Univ. of New Mexico Press, 1973. 264p. illus. index. LC 72-94659.

Scholarly history of jewelry making by the Navajo and Pueblo Indians from the early historic period to the present. Contents: Part I: The Navajos: 1, Malleable Stone; 2, Metal of the Moon; 3, Silver Ornaments from Silver Dollars; 4, The Classic Era: 1880-1900; 5, The Craft at the Turn of the Century; 6, The Esthetics of Navajo Silverwork; 7, From Craft to Curio. Part II: The Pueblos: 8, Out of the Stone Age; 9, The Zuni; 10, The Hopis; 11, The Rio Grande Pueblos; 12, Change and Innovation; 13, Modern Indian Silver: From Craft to Art. Comprehensive bibliography, pp. 243-55, and bibliographical references in the notes.

1662   Frank, Larry. **Indian Silver Jewelry of the Southwest 1868-1930**. Boston, New York Graphics Society, 1978. 214p. illus. index. ISBN 0821207407.

Pictorial collector's handbook to the classic era of Southwest Indian jewelry making. Illustrations and many valuable historic photographs showing Indians wearing native costumes and jewelry. Features pieces in the Smithsonian Institution, Field Museum of Natural History, Museum of the American Indian, Museum of New Mexico, Heard Museum, Wheelwright Museum, Millicent Rogers Museums, Lynn D. Trusdell Collection, Graham Foundation for Advanced Studies in the Fine Arts, and private collections. Selected bibliography, p. 207.

EUROPEAN JEWELRY

France

1663   Vever, Henri. **La bijouterie française au XIX siècle**. Paris, H. Floury, 1908. 3v. illus. index. LC 10-27886. Reprint: Florence, S.P.E.S., 1976.

Early, comprehensive history of French jewelry during the nineteenth century. Illustrated with actual pieces and numerous fashion illustrations showing jewelry worn with contemporary dress. Chronological arrangement. Volume one covers the consulate, empire, restoration, and Louis-Philippe periods. Bibliographical references in the footnotes. Contents: Tome I: L'Empire; Tome II, La Second Empire; Tome III, La Troisième République. Bibliographical references in the footnotes.

Major Jewelers

Boucheron

1664   Néret, Gilles. **Boucheron: Four Generations of a World-renowned Jeweler**. New York, Rizzoli, 1988. 223p. illus. index. ISBN 0847809870.

Lavishly illustrated, popular survey of the jewelry of the firm of Boucheron from the last decade of the nineteenth century to the 1980s. Descriptive captions to the plates. General bibliography, p. 219.

Cartier

1665   Nadelhoffer, Hans. **Cartier, Jewellers Extraordinary**. New York, Abrams, 1984. 293p. illus. index. ISBN 0810907704.

Sumptuously illustrated survey of the jewelry production of the firm of Cartier from its founding in 1854 to the Second World War. Contents: 1, From Apprentice to Court Jeweler; 2, Rue de la Paix; 3, The Garland Style; 4, Tiaras; 5, Art Nouveau—Religious Art—The War Years; 6, Under the Spell of Fabergé; 7, In St. Petersburg; 8, Pearls; 9, Charles Jacqueau and the Ballets Russes; 10, Pharaohs, Sphinxes and Pyramids; 11, Le Indes galantes; 12, "1925": The Preparation of a Style; 13, Vanity Fair: Toilet and Cosmetic Articles—The Chinese Influence—Department 'S'; 14, Chinaeras, Dragons and the Great Cats; 15, The Great Necklaces—The London Workshops—Dealers; 16, "The Jeweled Flight of Time"; 17, Swords for Academicians—Cartiers Patents—The Second World War; 18, Great Transactions. Appendices with Cartier family tree and chronology. General bibliography, 303.

Peter Carl Fabergé, 1846-1920

1666   Bainbridge, Henry C. **Peter Carl Fabergé**. London, Spring Books, 1966. 167p. illus. index. Reprint: New York, Crescent Books, 1979. ISBN 0517066572.

Comprehensive monograph on the life and work of Fabergé first published in 1949. Contents: I, The Family and House of Fabergé; II, Peter Carl Fabergé, the Man; III, The Art and Craft of Fabergé; IV, The Imperial Russian Easter Eggs; V, Fabergé in the Edwardian Era and the Sandringham Animals and Flowers; VI, The Fabergé Figurines in Russian Stones of Colour; VII, The Workmasters of Fabergé; VIII, The Marks of Fabergé. Chapter 7 has a comprehensive dictionary of the many craftsmen working for Fabergé. Bibliographical references in the footnotes.

1667   Habsburg-Lothringen. **Géza von and A. von Solodkoff**. Fabergé, Court Jeweler to the Tsars. New York, Rizzoli, 1979. 171p. illus. index. ISBN 0847802442.

Popular survey of the jewelry made by the firm of Fabergé from 1870 to 1915 with valuable chapter on the market for Fabergé works to 1979. Contents: The Family and the Development of the Firm; The Foundation of Fabergé's Success; The Fabergé Style; Art, Craftsmanship or Kitsch?; Workshops and Craftsmen; Materials and Techniques; Fabergé's Easter Eggs; Fabergé and His Competitors; Collectors and Collections; Fabergé's Market and Prices; Fabergé and Fake Fabergé; Hallmarks and Signatures on Fabergé Objects. Appendices with glossary, catalog of Fabergé's Easter eggs, and general bibliography, p. 167.

1668   Ross, C. Marvin, and Marjorie M. Post. **The Art of Karl Fabergé and His Contemporaries**. Norman, Okla., Univ. of Oklahoma Press, 1965. 238p. illus. index. LC 65-14804.

History of the jewelry made by Karl Fabergé and his assistants based on the collection of Marjorie Merriweather Post at Hillwood in Washington, D.C. Contents: Part I: Fabergé and His Master Craftsmen: 1, Karl Fabergé, 2, Mikhail Evlampievich Perkhin, 3, Agathon Fabergé, 4, Erik August Kollin, 5, Henrik Wigstrom, 6, Johann Viktor Aarne, 7, August Wilhelm Holström, 8, Albert Holmström, 9, Karl Gustav Hjalmar av Armfelt, 10, A.R. 11, Vladimir Solovev, 12, Julius Aleksandrovich Rappaport, 13, Carvings in Hardstones, 14, Fabergé's Moscow Branch, 15, Fabergé's Fitted Boxes; Part II: Fabergé's Russian Followers and Imitators: 1, Introduction, 2, Karl Karlovich Hahn, 3, I. Britzin, 4, Nichols and Linke, 5, Unidentified Goldsmiths; Part III: The Pan-Slavic Movement in Metalwork and Enamel: 1, Introduction, 2, Paul Akimovich Ovchinnokov, 3, Fedor I. Ruckert, 4, Ivan Petrovich Khlebnikov, 5, G. P. Grachev, 6, Sazykov Firm, 7, Ivan Saltykov, 8, I. Ozeritskii, 9, Gregory Sbitnev, 10, The Mishukov Family, 11, J. Vasilev, 12, Anton Kuzmichev, 13, Orest Fedorovich Kurliukov, 14, Nikolai Vasilevich Alekseev, 15, Vasilii Agafanov, 16, Maria Semenova, 17, The Artels, or Co-operatives, 18, Unidentified Pan-Slavic Silversmiths, 19, Small Easter Eggs in Silver, Enamel, and Hardstone. Part IV: Russian Imperial Portraits; Part V: Russian Imperial Mementoes; Part VI: Russian Imperial Orders, Decorations, and Prizes; Part VII: Decorations for Ladies at Court; Part VIII: Russian Imperial Watches. Comprehensive, classified bibliography, pp. 229-33.

1669   Snowman, Abraham K. **Carl Fabergé: Goldsmith to the Imperial Court of Russia**. New York, Viking, 1979. 160p. illus. index. ISBN 0670204862.

Pictorial survey of the work of Carl Fabergé. Contents: Introduction; Metals, Enamels and Stones; A Restless Imagination; Stone Carvings; Flower Studies; Imperial Easter Eggs; In Retrospect; Marks and Standards; Wrong Attributions, Pastiches & Forgeries. Appendix with chronology. Plates have descriptive captions.

See also the author's *The Art of Carl Fabergé* (London, Faber and Faber, 1953).

See also the exhibition catalogs: *Fabergé and His Contemporaries: The India Early Minshall Collection of the Cleveland Museum of Art*, by H. Hawley (Cleveland, The Museum, 1967. 139p. illus. LC 67-28951) and *Fabergé, Jeweler to Royalty: From the Collection of Her Majesty Queen Elizabeth II and Other British Lenders*, by A. K. Snowman (Washington, D.C., Smithsonian Institution, 1983. 112p. illus.).

René Lalique 1860-1945 [See also Chapter Ten—European Glass, France and Belgium]

1670   Barten, Sigrid. **René Lalique: Schmuck und Objets d'art, 1890-1910: Monographie und Werkkatalog**. Munich, Prestel, 1977. 592p. illus. index. ISBN 3791303872. (Materialien zur Kunst des. 19. Jahrhunderts, Band 22).

Scholarly monograph of René Lalique as jeweler featuring a comprehensive catalog of his signed and attributed works. Contents: Einleitung; Biographie und historische Voraussetzungen: Biographie, Der Schmuck in der zweiten HÄlfte des 19. Jahrhunderts, Lucien Falize und Oscar Massin, Abgrenzung von Juweler- und Künslerschmuck; Die Abschnitte der künstlerischen sance—Juwelier- und Goldschmuck, 1896-1901 Höhepunkt des Art Nouveau-Schmuckes—Neue Materialien, 1902-1905 Gemässigte Formgebung—Objets d'art, 1905-1910 Kristallglas-Schmuck; Das Werk Laliqiues: Svchmuckstücke, Material und Verarbeitung, Atelier und Vertrieb, Signatur und Stempel, Motive, Kompositione, Farbigkeit, Zeichnungen, Datierung, Das 'Genre Lalique', Die Farbabbildungen 1-104, Schmuck und Gesellschaft, Die Krise im Kunstgewerbe, Schlussbetrachtung, Anmerkungen. Werkkatalog (divided by types). Full scholarly apparatus including bibliographies of specialized literature in the catalog entries, bibliographical footnotes to the text and comprehensive bibliography, pp. 156-164.

1671   Marcilhac, Félix. **René Lalique, 1860-1945, Maitre-Verrier**. Paris, Editions de l'Amateur, 1989. 1047p. illus. ISBN 2859170820.

Comprehensive monograph on the art of René Lalique in glass and other materials with a catalogue raisonné of hundreds of works including original sketches and designs. Contents: I, Analyse historique de l'oeuvre de verre; II, Analyse technique de l'oeuvre de verre; III, Analyse raisonnée de l'oeuvre de verre: Objects d'art, Bijoux de verre, Eclairage, Verrerie de Table, Oeuvres diverses. The numerous works illustrated are not accompanied by a detailed catalog entry but instead basic information is given in captions. A valuable resource for the identification of pieces by Lalique and his firm. No bibliography.

See also the exhibition catalogs: *Art Nouveau Jewelry by René Lalique*, by M. T. Gomes Ferreira (Washington, D.C., International Exhibitions Foundation, 1986. 11p. illus. ISBN 0883970864) and *René Lalique*, by V. Becker (London, Goldsmiths' Hall, 1987).

Germany

1672   Clifford, Anne. **Cut-Steel and Berlin Iron Jewellery**. London, Adams & Dart, 1971. 95p. illus. ISBN 0498079074.

Popular collector's history/handbook of the iron and steel jewelry made in Germany (chiefly Berlin) during the late eighteenth and early nineteenth centuries. Contains 57 plates with brief descriptive captions. General bibliography, p. 33.

1673   Egger, Gerhart. **Bürgerlicher Schmuck: 15. bis 20. Jahrhundert**. Munich, Callwey, 1984. 222p. illus. index. LC 87-63484.

Survey of jewelry made for the German upper-middle-class from the fifteenth to the twentieth centuries. Illustrated with pieces in museums and portraits.

1674   Hase, Ulrike von. **Schmuck in Deutschland und Österreich, 1895-1914: Symbolismus, Jugendstil, Neohistorismus**, Munich, Prestel, 1977. 430p. illus. index. ISBN 3791303856. (Materialien zur Kunst des 19. Jahrhunderts, Band 24).

Comprehensive, scholarly history of jewelry in the German-speaking lands between 1895-1914 with a chapter on jewelry in Hungary and Bohemia. Contents: Tendenzen im Schmuckschaffen der 2. Hälfte des 19. Jahrhunderts; Von der Einheitlichkeit des Lebens. Bemerkungen zum Ornament und zum Symbolismus; Deutschland; Das Elsass: Eine Übersicht; Österreich; Die K. K. Staaten Ungarn un Böhmen. Large corpus of plates with descriptive captions. Glossary of marks and signatures. Specialized bibliography in the notes, general bibliography, pp. 423-425.

1675   Marquardt, Brigitte. **Schmuck: Klassizismus und Biedermeier 1780-1850; Deutschland, Österreich, Schweiz**. Munich. Verlag fur Kunst & Antiquitäten, 1983. 332p. illus. index. ISBN 3921811260.

Comprehensive history/handbook of jewelry in German-speaking lands from 1780 to 1850. Particularly useful is the long series of portraits used to illustrate the development of jewelry styles and the use of the various pieces. Contents: Schmuck—Eine besondere Kunstform;

Schmuck im Wandel der wirtschaftlichen und sozialen Verhältnisse; Handwerkliche Herstellung—Grundung von Schmuck-Fabriken; Schmuck des Klassizismus; Biedermeierschmuck—Vielfalt von Stiltendenzen 1820-1850. Catalog of representative pieces arranged by type. Bibliography, pp. 323-25.

Great Britain

1676 Armstrong, Nancy. **Jewellery: An Historical Survey of British Styles and Jewels.** London, Butterworth, 1973. 304p. illus. index. ISBN 0718819772.

Comprehensive history of British jewelry from the Middle Ages to the twentieth century directed to the general reader, dealer, and collector. Contents: 1, A Background of Belief; 2, A Background of Events; 3, The Offshore Islands; 4, Medieval England; 5, The House of Tudor; 6, The House of Stuart; 7, Georgian Glitter; 8, Neo-classical Restraint; 9, Victorian Sentimentality; 10, The Art Nouveau; 11, The Twentieth Century; 12, The Present Day. Appendices with discussion of care of jewelry, determining value, advise on a career in the jewelry trade, and lists of the National Association of Decorative and Fine Arts societies. Basic bibliography, pp. 273-75.

1677 Bradford, Ernle D. S. **English Victorian Jewellery.** New ed. London, Spring, 1967. 141p. illus. index. LC 68-111095.

Concise survey of English jewelry made from the 1830s to the early twentieth century. Contents: 1, The Eighteenth-century Background; 2, Early Victorian and High Victorian Styles; 3, Gold Filagree Jewellery and the Etruscan Style; 4, Semi-precious Jewellery of the Nineteenth Century; 5, Popular Jewellery: Its Ancestry and Its Development in the Nineteenth Century; 6, Techniques and Materials; 7, The End of an Epoch. General bibliography, pp. 133-34.

1678 Evans, Joan. **English Jewellery from the Fifth Century A.D. to 1800.** New York, Dutton, 1921. 168p. illus. index.

Comprehensive, authoritative history of jewelry in England from the early Middle Ages to the nineteenth century. Contents: I, Anglo-Saxon and Celtic Jewellery; II, English Jewellery of the Middle Ages; III, English Jewellery of the Early Renaissance; IV, Elizabethan Jewellery; V, English Jewellery of the XVII Century; VI, English Jewellery of the XVIII Century. Bibliographical references in the footnotes. Emphasis is on major pieces and the relationship between jewelry and society.

1679 Flower, Margaret C. **Victorian Jewellery.** Rev. ed. South Brunswick, N.J., A. S. Barnes, 1973. 271p. illus. index. LC 72-6463.

Comprehensive, authoritative history/handbook of British jewelry from 1837 to 1901. Contents: I, Introduction; II, The Early Victorian, or Romantic Period; III, The Mid-Victorian, or Grand Period; IV, The Late Victorian, or Aesthetic Period; V, Early Victorian Jewellery; VI, Mid-Victorian Jewellery; VII, Late Victorian Jewellery. Chapters II-IV are brief historical sketches; chapters V-VII form a catalog of Victorian jewelry by types with summaries listing materials and decorative motifs common in each period. Glossary. General bibliography, pp. 259-60. Introductory chapter on collecting jewelry by Doris L. Moore. Appendix with list of jewelers.

1680 Hinks, Peter. **Twentieth Century British Jewellery, 1900-1980.** Boston, Faber and Faber, 1983. 192p. illus. ISBN 0571108016.

Concise but fact-filled history of British jewelry from 1900 to 1800 covering both commercial products and products of the craftsman jewelers. Directed to the collector and fancier with a good collection of illustrations in color and black and white with descriptive captions. Contents: 1, The Edwardian Period—1900 to 1914; 2, The Great War; 3, Arts and Crafts; 4, The

Twenties; 5, The Thirties; 6, The Second World War and After—1939 to 1960; 7, The Sixties; 8, The Seventies. General bibliography, pp. 186-87.

1681 Oman, Charles C. **British Rings, 800-1914.** London, Batsford, 1974. 146p. illus. LC 74-165686.

Authoritative survey of British rings made between 800 and 1914 with 815 plates and descriptive notes. Contents: Part I: Rings, Their Materials and Uses: Introduction; 1, The Wearing of Rings; 2, The Makers & Markings of Rings; 3, Decorative Rings; 4, Signet Rings; 5, Love Rings & Rings Given at Weddings; 6, Investiture & Ceremonial Rings; 7, Religious, Magical & Medicinal Rings; 8, Political & Portrait Rings; 9, Mourning Rings; 10, Rings with Miscellaneous Inscriptions & Rings of Sergeants-at-Law; 11, Scientific Rings. Part II: Catalogue of Illustrations. Appendices with extracts from Tudor inventories and list of surviving rings of sergeants-at-law. Extensive bibliography in the notes.

Italy

1682 Rossi, Filippo. **Italian Jeweled Arts.** London and New York, Abrams, 1958. 233p. illus. index. LC 58-3307.

Pictorial survey of Italian jewelry and jeweled goldsmiths' works from the twelfth to the nineteenth centuries. Bibliographical footnotes and general bibliography, p. 223.

Netherlands

1683 Gans, M. H. **Juwelen en mensen; de geschiedenis van het bijou van 1400 tot 1900, voornamelijk naar Nederlandse bronnen.** Amsterdam, de Bussy, 1961. 479p. illus. index. LC 66-55674.

Comprehensive history of jewelry in the Netherlands from the fifteenth century to 1900. Emphasis is on jewelry as personal adornment with many illustrations of portraits. Contents: 1, Bijou-geschiednis. Inleiding; 2, Bourgondische Rijkdom; 3, Het Manierisme; 4, Hof en burgerij in Neerlands Gouden Eeuw; 5, De achttiende eeuw. Brillantflonkering; 6, Negentiende eeuws individualisme; 7, Diamant en mens. Appendices with lists of inventories. Bibliographical footnotes and general bibliography, pp. 477-79

Spain

1684 Muller, Priscilla E. **Jewels in Spain 1500-1800.** New York, New York Hispanic Society, 1972. 195p. illus. index.

Comprehensive history of Spanish jewelry from 1500 to 1880 with extensive use of documentary evidence and illustrations of contemporary paintings. Many inventories are published for the first time. Covers jewelers and their patrons, stylistic, and iconographic aspects. Contents: I, The Reign of Ferdinand and Isabella; II, Interlude: Spain and the New World; III, The 16th Century: Renaissance and Mannerism; IV, The 17th Century; V, The 18th Century. A standard work.

ORIENTAL JEWELRY [See also Chapter Sixteen, Oriental Gold and Silver Work]

1685　Eudel, Paul. **Dictionnaire des bijoux de l'Afrique du Nord.** Paris, E. Leroux, 1906. 242p. illus. LC 08-29322.

Comprehensive dictionary of the types of traditional jewelry of Morocco, Algeria, Tunisia, and Libya. Arranged by the transliterated Arabic names and illustrated with line drawings. The entries are descriptive and make reference to regional differences. No bibliography.

See also the exhibition catalogs: *Islamic Jewelry in the Metropolitan Museum of Art*, by M. Jenkins and M. Keene (New York, The Museum, 1983. 160p. illus.), *Power and Gold: Jewelry from Indonesia, Malaysia, and the Philippines from the Collection of the Barbier-Muller Museum, Geneva*, by S. Rodgers (New York, Asia Society, 1985. 369p. illus.), and *Pracht und Geheimnis: Kleidung und Schmuck aus Palastina und Jordanien: Katalog der Sammlung Widad Kawar aus einer Ausstellung des Rautenstrauch-Joest-Museums der Stadt Köln...*, G. Volger, ed. (Cologne, Rautenstrauch-Joest-Museum, 1987. 432p. illus. ISBN 3923158157).

GEMS, CAMEOS, AND INTAGLIOS [See also Chapter Eleven, Ivory, Jade, Amber, and Shell Carving]

General Works

1686　Babelon, Ernest. **La Gravure en pierres fines, camées et intailles.** Paris, Quantin, 1894. 318p. illus. index.

Old, once-standard history of cameos and intaglios from antiquity through the nineteenth century. Contents: Chapitre Premier: I, La matière; II, La technique; Chapitre II: I, Les populations préhistoriques; II, L'Egypte; III, Les Caldéo-Assyriens; IV, Les Arméniens, les Elamites, les Mèdes et les Perses; V, Les Héthéens; VI, Les Phéniciens, les Araméens et les Juifs; VII, Cypre et Carthage; Chapitre III: I, Les intailles mycéniennes et crétoises; II, La glyptique grecque archaïque; III, La glyptique étrusque; Chapitre IV: I, La glyptique aux Ve et IVe siècles; II, La période hellenistique; Chapitre V: I, Les pierres gravées sous la République et le Haut Empire; II, Les pierres gravées avec signatures d'artistes; III, Grylles, abraxzs, sujets chrétiens; Chapitre VI: I, La glyptique byzantine; II, Les Parthes Arsacides et Sassanides; III, Les Arabes et l'Orient moderne; Chapitre VII: I, Destination des pierres gravées antiques durant le moyen âge; II, Les pierres magiques et les lapidaires; III, Les pierres gravées par les artistes du moyen âge; Chapitre VIII: I, La gravure en pierres fines dans la Renaissance italienne; II, La Renaissance française; Chapitre IX: I, Les XVIIe et XVIIIe siècles; II, Le XiXe siècle. Bibliographical references in the footnotes.

1687　Gebhardt, Hans. **Gemmen und Kameen.** Berlin, R. C. Schmidt, 1925. 232p. illus. index. (Bibliothek fur Kunst- und Antiquitäten Sammler, Bd. XXVII). LC 26-16794.

Older but still-useful overview of cameos and intaglios for the collector. Introductory chapter defining the field of glyptics is followed by a history from ancient Babylonia to the nineteenth century and dictionary of artists' names and signatures. Bibliography, pp. 226-228.

1688　Davenport, Cyril J. H. **Cameos.** London, Seeley; New York, Macmillan, 1900. 66p. illus. index. LC 02-18733.

Survey history of gem cameos from ancient Greece and Rome to the end of the sixteenth century, illustrated with pieces mostly in British museums. Useful chapter on materials and techniques. No bibliography. An old work by a leading British expert.

1689 King, Charles W. **Handbook of Engraved Gems**. 2d ed. London, G. Bell, 1885. 287p. illus. index.

An old, standard history of Western intaglio gems from antiquity to the Renaissance with emphasis on ancient Greek and Roman gems. Contents: I. History of the Glyptic Art; II, Famous Rings and Signets; III, Cabinets of Gems; IV, Description of the Plates; V, Catalogue of Artists. The 76 plates are in line drawing. Chapter III is a highly informative description of the collections of engraved gems in collections in London, Florence, Paris, Naples, Vienna. Chapter V is a repertory of ancient gem engravers with lists of their signed pieces. Bibliographical references in the footnotes.

1690 Lippold, Georg. **Gemmen und Kameen des Altertums und der Neuzeit**. Stuttgart, J. Hoffman, 1922. 190p. illus. index. LC 24-1691.

Pictorial history of intaglios from ancient Greece to the end of the eighteenth century. Introductory essay followed by an important corpus of plates grouped by subject with detailed descriptive notes with bibliographical references. Standard work.

1691 Osborne, Duffield. **Engraved Gems, Signets, Talismans and Ornamental Intaglios, Ancient and Modern...** New York, Holt, 1912. 424p. illus. index. LC 12-37310.

Comprehensive history of intaglios from antiquity to the end of the nineteenth century. Part one gives a historical survey, part two covers the subjects depicted in intaglios, part three discusses the techniques and materials of historical intaglios. Thirty-two plates. Older works still useful as a source for the iconography of intaglios.

1692 Sutherland, Beth B. **The Romance of Seals and Engraved Gems**. New York, Macmillan, 1965. 174p. illus. index. LC 65-10403.

Popular and informative introduction to the history of intaglio gems engraving written by a gem carver. Contents: 1, My Apprenticeship; 2, The History of Glyptic Tools and Materials; 3, Gem Engraving in the Ancient World; 4, Seals of the Ancient World after the Development of Writing; 5, The Seals of the Ancient Far East; 6, The Classical Age; 7, The Glyptic Arts in the Early Christian Era; 8, European Seals of the Middle Ages; 9, Renaissance Seals and Gems; 10, Early Industrialization and the Glyptic Arts; 11, Seals and Gems in Modern Times. Appendices with list of tools and techniques, stones and their hardness, and synoptic calendar. Classified bibliography of books in English.

Ancient Gems, Cameos, and Intaglios

1693 Boardman, John. **Archaic Greek Gems: Schools and Artists in the Sixth and Early Fifth Centuries B.C.** Evanston, Ill., Nortwestern Univ. Press, 1968. 236p. illus. LC 68-25581.

Scholarly history of ancient Greek intaglio gems during the Archaic Period. Contents: I, Introduction and Notes to the Reader; II, Beetles and Borders; III, Phoenician Gems and Greece; IV, Sixth-Century Orientalising and Excursus on Gorgons and the East; V, Scenes of Narrative; VI, The Satyr Groups; VII, The Sphinx-and-Youth Groups; VIII, The Dry Style; IX, The Group of the Leningrad Gorgon, Epimenes and Others; X, The Latest Archaic Styles; XI, Island Carabs; XII, Lions and Lion-Fights; XIII, Other Animals and Monsters; XIV, Pseudo-Scarabs; XV, Summary and Conclusions. Bibliographical references in the notes.

1694 Boardman, John. **Greek Gems and Finger Rings: Early Bronze Age to Classical**. London, Thames & Hudson, 1970. 458p. illus. index. LC 72-569570.

Authoritative history of ancient Greek gem engraving with particular emphasis on the relationship between gem engraving and contemporary art. Contents: I, Introduction; II, Minoans and Myceneans; III, The Geometric and Early Archaic Periods; IV, Archaic Gems and Finger

Rings; V, Classical Gems and Finger Rings; VI, Greeks and Persians; VII, Hellenistic Greece and Rome; VIII, Materials and Techniques. Extensive bibliography in the notes, pp. 386-449.

1695 Boardman, John. **Island Gems: A Study of Greek Seals in the Geometric and Early Archaic Periods.** London, Society for the Promotion of Hellenic Studies, 1963. 176p. illus. index. (Society for the Promotion of Hellenic Studies. London. Supplementary Paper, no. 10) LC 66-95157.

Scholarly history of early Greek intaglio seals. Contents: Part I: Island Gems: 1, Introduction; 2, Materials, 3, Classification by Technique, 4, Lentoids and Amygdaloids, 5, Other Shapes, 6, The Artists, 7, Chronology, 8, Island Gems and the Bronze Age, 9, Provenences and Centres of Production, 10, Island Gems and Coins, 11, Early Melos. Part II: Other Groups of Archaic Greek Seals: 1, Stone Seals; 2, Other Materials and Types; Part III: 1, Seal Usage; 2, Summary. Extensive bibliography in the footnotes. Fully indexed.

1696 Furtwängler, Adolf. **Die antiken Gemmen. Geschichte der Steinschneidekunst im classischen Altertum.** Leipzig and Berlin, Gieseke & Devrient, 1900. 3v. illus. index. LC 2-26047. Reprint: Amsterdam and Osnabrück, Hakkert and Zeller, 1965.

Authoritative, comprehensive history of engraved gems and cameos in ancient Greece and Rome with background history from ancient Egypt and the ancient Near East through the Mycenean and Minoan periods. Contents of Band I: Einleitung: Der Orient; 1, Die Mykenische Epoche; 2, Das Griechische Mittelater; 3, Der Ausgang des Mittelalters. Das Siebente Jahrhundert; 4, Die Periode des archaischen Stiles; 5, Die griechischen Gemmen des frühen Stiles vor Alexander; 6, Die griechischen Gwemmen der hellenistischen Epoche; 7, Die etruskischen Skarabäen; 8, Die italischen Gemmen während der letzten Jahrhunderte der römischen Republik; 9, Die griechisch-römischen Gemmen der Augusteischen Epoche und der früheren Kaiserzeit; 10, Die spätere Kaiserzeit und das Ende der antiken Glyptik; Anhang: 1, Überblick die Glyptik im Mittelalter und in den neueren Zeiten; 2, Überblick über die in der Antiken Glyptik verwendeten Steinarten und die Technik ihrer Bearbeitung; 3, Überblick über die von antiken Gemmen handelnde neuere Litteratur; Nachträge (additions to the first nine chapters). Appendix 3 is a comprehensive, annotated bibliography of the nineteenth century literature. Extensive bibliography in the footnotes. Band II is a catalog and Band III a corpus of 67 plates with photographic reproductions of hundreds of examples. Additional pieces illustrated in the text volume. A standard work on ancient gems and cameos.

1697 Richter, Gisela M. A. **The Engraved Gems of the Greeks, Etruscans and Romans.** 2v. London, New York, Phaidon, 1968-71. illus. index. LC 68-27417.

Comprehensive history of engraved gems in classical antiquity illustrated with actual size reproductions of actual gems and enlarged reproductions of cast impressions. Comprehensive bibliography, v. 1, pp. 327-32 and v. 2, pp. 291-96.

1698 Vollenweider, Marie-Louise. **Die Porträtgemmen der römischen Republik.** Mainz, P. von Zabern, 1972-74. 2v. illus. index. LC 72-345986.

Comprehensive, scholarly history and catalog résumé of Roman gemstones engraved with portraits dating from the Republican period. First volume contains text; second volume contains catalog and 168 plates. Full scholarly apparatus including specialized bibliographies in the catalog entries. Contents: I. Teil: Die italienischen Vorstufen der römischen Gemmenporträts: I, Ursprünge und Anfang der Steinschneidekunst in Italien; II, Köpfe auf italischen Skarabäen; III, Der Kubismus als ein Stil element der italischen Bildniskunst; IV, Das überlange Profil als Merkmal eines italischen Porträttypus; V, Das frontale Bildnis; VI, Die Verschmelzung von italischen Grundtypen mit hellenistischen Formen. II. Teil: Bildnisse römischer Principes. Fully indexed. The standard work on early Roman intaglios.

1699 Vollenweider, Marie-Louise. **Die Steinschneidekunst und ihre Künstler in Spätrepublikanischer und Augusteischer Zeit**. Bade-Baden, Grimm, 1966. 148p. illus. index. LC 67-70754.

Scholarly history of ancient Roman intaglio art during the first century before Christ. Contents: Hellenistische Cameen mit en face Bildnissen; Die Blüte der Steinschneidekunst in Rom und ihr politischer und sozialer Hintergrund; Die Steinschneider der spätrepublikanischen und frühaugusteischen Zeit (chronologically subdivided then by artist); Gemmenschneider des Augustus: Solon, Dioskurides; Die kaiserliche Gemmenwerkstatt: Die Söhne des Dioskurides, Schuler des Dioskurides; Der blaue Saphircameo. Full scholarly apparatus including bibliographical footnotes. A standard work on the golden age of ancient intaglio and cameo art.

1700 Zazoff, Peter. **Die Antiken Gemmen**. Munich, Beck, 1983. 446p. (text), 132p. (plates). index. ISBN 3406088961.

In the series: "Handbuch der Archäologie." Scholarly history/handbook of ancient glyptics from Minoan times to the end of the Roman period, with postscripts on medieval and Renaissance intaglios. Chapters dedicated to the various civilizations and periods are each introduced with a survey of the state of research with exhaustive bibliography, discussions of principal sites, stylistic development, types of stones used, etc. References to the specialized literature in the footnotes. A standard work; worthy successor to the works of Furtwängler (1696) and Lippold (1690).

1701 Zazoff, Peter and Hilde Zazoff. **Gemmensammler und Gemmenforscher: von einer noblen Passion zur Wissenschaft**. Munich, Beck, 1983. 285p. illus. index. ISBN 3406088953.

Comprehensive and scholarly history of collecting glyptics and gems in German-speaking countries from the seventeenth century to 1937. Concentrates on the careers of Philipp von Stosch (1691-1757), Johann Joachim Winckelmann (1717-1768), Philipp Daniel Lippert (1702-1785), Adolf Furtwängler (1853-1907) and Paul Arndt (1865-1937) as chief representatives of collecting in their times. Extensive bibliographical footnotes.

See also the museum catalogs: *Antike Gemmen in deutschen Sammlungen*. (Munich, Prestel, 1968-1975. 5v. illus.), *Die antiken Gemmen des Kunsthistorischen Museums in Wien* (Munich, Prestel, 1973-. v. 1-), and *Catalogue of the Engraved Gems and Finger Rings. Ashmolean Museum*, by J. Boardman and M. Vollenweider (Oxford, New York, Clarendon, 1978- v. 1. Greek and Etruscan. ISBN 019813195X).

Medieval Gems, Cameos, and Intaglios

1702 Evans, Joan. **Magical Jewels of the Middle Ages and the Renaissance, Particularly in England**. Oxford, England, Clarendon Press, 1922. 264p. illus. index. Reprint: New York, Dover, 1975. ISBN 0486233677.

Important study of the meanings attached to jewels from antiquity through the eighteenth century. Contents: I, Magical Jewels and Gems in the Ancient World; II, The Earlier Christian Lapidaries; III, The Lapidaries of Spain and the Nearer East; IV, Western Mediaeval Lapidaries; V, Mediaeval Astrology: Lapidaries of Engraved Gems; VI, Magical Jewels of the Middle Ages; VII, The Renaissance: Lapidaries of the Sixteenth and Seventeenth Centuries; VIII, Magical Jewels of the Renaissance; IX, The Age of Criticism: The Seventeenth and Eighteenth Centuries. Appendix with transcriptions of texts from medieval manuscript sources. Bibliographical footnotes. Superseded by Meier (1705).

1703 Friess, Gerda. **Edelsteine im Mittelalter; Wandel und Kontinuität in ihrer Bedeutung durch zwölf Jahrhunderte (in Aberglauben, Medizin, Theologie und Goldschiedekunst)** Hildesheim, Gerstenberg Verlag, 1980. 206p. index. ISBN 3806708339.

Scholarly study of the meaning attached to gems in the Middle Ages through detailed study of texts. Contents: I, Kenntnis und Bewertung von Edelsteinen in der Literatur des Mittelalters (im Zeitraum von Plinius—1200); II, Edelstein auf mittelalterlichen Goldschmiedearbeiten des 8.-12. Jahrhunderts. Appendices with source material on the 17 biblical gems and author indexes to both primary and secondary literature.

1704   Hahnloser, Hans R., and Susanne Brugger-Koch. **Corpus der Hartsteinschliffe des 12.-15.** Jahrhunderts, Berlin, Deutscher Verlag für Kunstwissenschaft, 1985. 278p.(text), 466p. (plates). index. ISBN 3871571016.

Comprehensive, scholarly corpus of works of medieval applied and decorative art—reliquaries, crosses, vessels, etc.—made in part or whole of cut and polished quartz. The first part explores in detail the types of quartz used in the Middle Ages, the techniques employed, the centers of production, and the inventories of treasuries from the eleventh to fifteenth centuries. The second part classifies and describes the various objects made of or decorated with cut quartz. The third part is a catalog of 573 objects dating from the twelfth through the fifteenth centuries. Excellent plates. Full scholarly apparatus including bibliographical references in text and catalog. Comprehensive bibliography including exhibition catalogs, pp. 257-262. A monumental and standard work.

1705   Meier, Christel. **Gemma Spiritualis: Methode und Gebrauch der Edelsteinallegorese vom frühen Christentum bis ins 18. Jahrhundert.** Munich, Fink, 1977-. (Münstersche Mittelalter-Schriften, Band 34/1) ISBN 3770512510.

Comprehensive history of the meaning attached to gems from the Early Christian period to the end of the eighteenth century. To date only the first part has appeared. Index to both parts will be in the second part. Contents of Teil I: I, Voraussetzungen und Anfänge der christlichen Edelsteinallegorese: 1, Die Methode der Steinallegorese, 2, Die antike Lithologie, 3, Die Anfänge der christlichen Edelsteinallegorese; II, Die Eigenschaften der Edelsteine als Deutungsantsätze: 1, Farben, 2, Lichtwirkungen, 3, Die übrigen physikalischen und die chemischen Merkmale, 4, Entstehung, 5, Fundort/Fundzeit, 6, Gewinnung, 7, Besitzer, 8, Medizinische Wirkungen, 9, Fassung, 10, Geschlect, 11, Alter, 12, Wert/Rang, 13, Varietäten, 14, Fehler, 15, Fälschung, 16, Praktisch-technische Verwendung, 17, Name, 18, Platz/Zahl. Extensive bibliographical footnotes and exhaustive bibliography, pp. 510-542. Second part will treat the place of gems in allegory, in particular the allegories of heaven. Promises to be not only the standard work on the meaning of gems but also a paradigmatic study in the history of allegory and especially the relationship between literary allegory and the visual arts.

Renaissance—Modern Gems, Cameos, and Intaglios

1706   Kris, Ernst. **Die Meister und Meisterwerke der Steinschneidekunst in der italienischen Renaissance.** Vienna, Schroll, 1929. 2v. illus. index. Reprinted, 1979. ISBN 370310404X.

Comprehensive, scholarly history of Italian Renaissance intaglios. Contents: I, Einleitung und Beiträge zur Geschichte der Technik; II, Zur burgundisch-französischen Glyptik des späten Mittelalters; III, Die Sammlungen antiker Gemmen im Quattrocento, Kopien, Fälschungen und Erneuerungen—Die Plaketten; IV, Gemmenbildnisse—Vorbilder der Gemmen. Die oberitalienische Glyptik bis zum Anfang des Cinquecento; V, Die Glyptik in der ersten Hälfte des Cinquecento—Matteo dal Nassaro, Valerio Belli, Giovanni dei Bernardi, Alessandro Cesati und ihr Kreis; VI, Gemmen- und Kameenschneider der zweiten Hälfte des Cinquecento; VII, Die Prunkgefässe aus Bergkristall und Halbedelstein; VIII, Annibale Fontana ald Steinschneider; IX, Die Werkstatt der Sarachi und die Mailänder Prunkgefässe der Spätrenaissance; X, Die Glyptik in Florenz am Ausgang des Cinquecento; XI, Die Werksatt der Miseroni und die Steinschneidekunst am kaiserlichen Hofe. Full scholarly apparatus including critical catalog of the pieces illustrated in the 200 plates. A standard work.

CHAPTER THIRTEEN

LACQUER

GENERAL HISTORIES AND HANDBOOKS

1707   **Lacquer: An International History and Illustrated Survey.** New York, Abrams, 1984. 256p. illus. index. ISBN 0810912791.

Lavishly illustrated survey of world lacquer art with useful appendices on collecting and restoring. Written by a team of British experts. Contents: I, China; 2, Korea; 3, Japan; 4, The Ryukyu Islands; 5, South East Asia; 6, The Near East, the Middle East and India; 7, Europe and Russia; 8, The United States; 9, The Twentieth Century. Comprehensive bibliography, pp. 249-51, includes titles in Oriental languages.

WESTERN LACQUER

1708   Holzhausen, Walter. **Lackkunst in Europa: Ein Handbuch für Sammler und Liebhaber.** Braunschweig, Klinkhardt & Biermann, 1959. 320p. illus. index. (Bibliothek für Kunst- und Antiquitätenfreunde, Band 38). LC 59-44866.

Comprehensive, authoritative history of lacquerware produced in Europe from antiquity to the middle of the eighteenth century. Contents: Die Anfänge der Lackmalereii in Europa; Zwischenspiel; Die Blütezeit der Lackmalerei; Deutschland; Die Spätzeit der Lackmalerei; Variationen über das Thema Lackmalerei. Directed to collectors, there is particular attention paid to lacquered furniture and small-scale objects such as the boxes by Strobwasser of Braunschweig. Bibliographical references in the notes.

1709   Huth, Hans. **Lacquer in the West: The History of a Craft and Industry 1550-1950.** Chicago and London, Univ. of Chicago Press, 1971. 158p.(text), 364 plates. index. LC 73-130185.

Comprehensive, authoritative history of western European and American lacquer from the seventeenth century to 1950 with emphasis on the lacquer furniture of the eighteenth century. Contents: I, Lacquer in the Seventeenth Century; II, Lacquer in the Eighteenth Century; III, Lacquer in England and the North American Colonies; IV, Italian Lacquer; V, German Lacquer; VI, French Lacquer; VII, Lacquer in the Netherlands, Scandinavia, Russia; VIII, The Lacquer Industry. Large corpus of 364 plates with descriptive notes. Selected bibliography, pp. 136-38, is a comprehensive, chronological list of primary and secondary works. A standard history of Western lacquer by a leading expert on eighteenth-century decorative arts.

ORIENTAL LACQUER

1710   Herbert, Kurt. **Oriental Lacquer: Art and Technique.** New York, Abrams, 1962. 513p. illus. index. LC 66-22168.

Pictorial survey of Oriental lacquerware with collection of 236 plates grouped by types, i.e., carved lacquer, gray lacquer, incised lacquer, inlaid mother-of-pearl, various inlays, various surfaces, lacquer on other materials, gold and silver grounds, Togidashi, Hiramakie, Takamakie, smooth grounds of coloured lacquer and painted lacquer. Descriptive captions to the plates.

Appendices with essay on the history of Oriental lacquer key to the groupings used in the collection of plates, glossary of terms, note on Japanese lacquer artists by W. Speiser, list of Japanese lacquer artists, and comprehensive bibliography, pp. 502-508, which is both classified by subject and listed in chronological order.

1711 Luzzato-Bilitz, Oscar. **Oriental Lacquer**. London and New York, Hamlyn, 1969. 158p. illus. LC 77-457134 Reprint: London, Cassell, 1988. ISBN 0304321842.

Popular, pictorial survey of Far Eastern lacquer, including furniture, from the fourth century B.C. through the nineteenth century. Color plates of major museum pieces. No bibliography.

1712 Yu-kuan, Lee. **Oriental Lacquer**. New York, Weatherhill, 1972. 394p. illus. LC 74-157275.

Comprehensive history of Far Eastern lacquerware from before the Han dynasty to the early twentieth century. Emphasis is on technique and information from documentary and literary sources. Text followed by a corpus of 264 plates with very detailed descriptive and analytical notes that include bibliographical references. Contents: Part One: Notes on the Study of Oriental Lacquerware: 1, Introductory; 2, On Materials and Techniques; 3, On Identification and Dating; 4, On Chinese Texts; Part Two: Plates and Commentaries. Appendices with chart and description of the sexagenary cycle; map of Chinese lacquerware production sites; chronologies of China, Korea, and Japan; selected bibliography for Chinese lacquerware (literary texts in Chinese) with note on lacquer connoisseurs and scholars; list of Chinese lacquer artisans by dynasty; glossary of Chinese lacquer terms; essay of lacquer of the Ryukyu Islands by J. Kreiner, history of Ryukyuan lacquer by Y. Kamakura; glossary of Chinese designs and the proceedings of the Yuan Art Symposium, lacquer section held at the Cleveland Museum of Art, 1968; reproductions of pages from the various editions of the Ko Ku Yao Lun prefaces; essay on Sung lacquer at the Engaku-Ji by J. Okada; Romanized readings for names of objects shown in the plates. A standard work on Oriental, particularly Chinese, lacquerware.

Burma

1713 Fraser-Lu, Sylvia. **Burmese Lacquerware**. Bangkok, The Tamarind Press, 1985. 164p. illus. index. ISBN 9748622088.

Popular survey of Burmese lacquerware with emphasis on contemporary production. Contents: I, Background of Burmese Lacquer (traces history from Pagan dynasty—1044-1287—to the twentieth century); II, The Lacquer Process; III, Techniques of Lacquer Decoration and Moulding; IV, Design Motifs; V, Lacquerware Objects for Secular Use; VI, Lacquerware Objects for Religious Use; VII, Lacquer Craft Centres in Burma; VIII, Lacquerware Collections (good descriptions of collections of Burmese lacquerware in museums in Burma and abroad); IX, Conclusion (with advise on care of lacquerware). General bibliography, pp. 154-157, a few additional titles in the footnotes of chapter I.

See also the exhibition catalog: *Meisterwerke Burmanischer Lackkunst*, by G. Prunner (Hamburg, Museum für Volkerkunde, 1966).

China

1714 Feddersen, Martin. **Chinesische Lackkunst: ein Brevier**. Braunschweig, Klinkhardt & Biermann, 1958. 46p. illus. LC A58-6098.

Concise but authoritative survey of Chinese lacquer, including furniture from the third century B.C. through the middle of the nineteenth century. Brief bibliography of basic books and periodical articles.

1715   Wang, Shih-hsiang. **Ancient Chinese Lacquerware**. Beijing, Foreign Languages Press, 1987. 237p. illus. ISBN 7119001485.

Pictorial survey of Chinese lacquer from neolithic times to the Ching (Qing) dynasty. Brief introductory essays sketches the outlines of the historical development with particular attention to techniques. Collection of 106 color and 48 black-and-white plates with descriptive notes. Selected bibliography, pp. 28-30, has useful translations of and brief comments on Chinese language material.

See also the exhibition catalogs: *Chinesische Lackarbeiten*, by K. J. Brandt. Linden Museum Stuttgart (Stuttgart, Das Museum, 1988. 159p. illus.) and Krahl, Regina, *From Innovation to Conformity: Chinese Lacquer from the 13th to 16th Centuries* (London, Bluett & Sons, 1989. 92p. illus.).

Japan

1716   Jahss, Melvin, and Betty Jahss. **Inro and Other Miniature Forms of Japanese Lacquer Art**. Rutland, Vt., Tuttle, 1971. 488p. illus. index. LC 76-109406.

Comprehensive history and collector's handbook of Japanese lacquer with particularly full treatment of technique. Contents: 1, Characteristics of Japanese Lacquer Art; 2, History of Japanese Lacquer; 3, Lacquer Manufacture and Technique; 4, Miniature Lacquer Art Forms; 5, The Netsuke as an Art Form; 6, Subject Matter of Japanese Art; 7, Lacquer Artists. Appendices with list of miniature lacquer artists, list of their signatures and genealogical charts of lacquer artists' families. Glossary and comprehensive bibliography, pp. 479-482.

1717   Ragué, Beatrix von. **A History of Japanese Lacquerwork**. Toronto, Univ. of Toronto Press, 1976. 303p. illus. index. ISBN 0802021352.

Translation of: *Geschichte der japanischen Lackkunst* (Berlin, De Gruyter, 1967), which was published in the series: "Handbücher der Staatlichen Museen." Comprehensive, authoritative history of Japanese lacquer from the fourth century A.D to the present. Contents: 1, Origins and Apprentice Years; 2, Early Heian Period: The Rise of an Indigenous Style; 3, Eleventh and Twelfth Centuries: The Golden Age of Heian Lacquerwork; 4, Kamakura Period; 5, Muromachi Period I: Nambokucho Period to the Higashiyama Period; 6, Muromachi Period II: from the End of the Higashiyama Period to 1567; 7, Momoyama Period; 8, Early Edo Period; 9, Mid- and Late Edo Period; 10, From the Meiji Period to the Present Day. Comprehensive bibliography, pp. 267-71, and further bibliography in the notes. Appendices with list of dated lacquer objects, Japanese names and terms with written characters, period table and map. A standard history of Japanese lacquer.

1718   Shimizu, Christina. **Les laques du Japon: Urushi**. Paris, Flammarion, 1988. 297p. illus. ISBN 2080120883.

Lavishly illustrated survey of the history of lacquer in Japan from the second century to the present. Contents: Introduction; Technique des laques japonais; L'art du laque a l'aube de la civilisation japonaise; Importation et création: L'ipact chinois a l'époque de Nara; La japonisation des formes et des techniques: L'époque de Heian; La recherche du réalisme: L'époque de Kamakura; La patronage des Shogun Ashikaga: L'époque de Muromachi; Les débuts de la modernité: l'époque de Momoyama; Les laques des seigneurs et des marchands: L'époque d'Edo; Les laques modernes de l'ère Mejii a nos jours. General bibliography, pp. 279-81.

See also the collection catalog: *Japanese Lacquer*, by P. F. Schneeberger. (Geneva, Collections Baur, 1984. 193p. illus. ISBN 2880310059).

CHAPTER FOURTEEN

LEATHER AND BOOKBINDING

LEATHER

Technique

1719 Waterer, John Williams. **A Guide to the Conservation and Restoration of Objects Made Wholly or in Part of Leather**. New York, Drake Pub., 1972. 60p. illus. ISBN 0877491801.

Although specifically concerned with conservation, this concise survey contains much information on the history of materials and techniques in leather art. Particularly valuable is the glossary of leather terms which is divided into: Leather Made from Hides, Leather Made from Skins; Untanned Materials; Glossary of Processes and Technical Terms, and American Terms. Classified bibliography, pp. 59-60, and further bibliography in the footnotes.

1720 Attwater, W. A. **The Technique of Leathercraft**. rev. ed. London, Batsford, 1983. 144p. illus. index. ISBN 0713423455.

Thorough guide to the techniques and materials of leathercraft. Although directed to the contemporary craftsman, the hand techniques described are applicable to traditional work in leather. Excellent, detailed photographs illustrating the various steps. Useful guide for the historian and restorer. General bibliography, p. 142.

General Histories and Handbooks

1721 Clouzot, Henri. **Cuirs décorès**. Paris, A. Calavas, 1928. 2v. illus.

Important corpus of plates of tooled, gilt and painted leather ranging from small objects such as caskets and bookbindings to saddles and wall coverings. Brief introductory essays followed by plates with descriptive captions. Contents: tome 1: Cuirs exotiques; tome 2: "Cuirs de Crodoue." Includes examples of European and Oriental leatherwork. No bibliography.

1722 Gall, Günter. **Leder im europäischen Kunsthandwerk. Ein Handbuch fur Sammler und Liebhaber**. Braunschweig, Klinkhardt & Biermann, 1965. 406p. illus. index. (Bibliothek für Kunst- und Antiquitätenfreunde, 44). LC 66-67495.

Comprehensive, authoritative history of leather in the applied and decorative arts of Europe from the early Middle Ages to the beginning of the twentieth century. Contents: Das Material: Gerbung, Geschichte des Gerbens; Frühes Mittelalter: Koptische Lederarbeiten, Irische und angelsächsische Lederarbeiten; Der Lederschnitt: Prager Werkstätten, Frankreich, Nordfrankreich und Flandern, Österreich, 15. Jahrhundert, Lederpanzer, Goldlederschnitt; Der Lederschnitt in Italien: Prunkschilde; Sonderformen des Lederschnitts: Spanische Arbeiten, Mexikanische Arbeiten; Die Handvergoldung: Einfluß des Orients, Spiralstil, Italienische Sondergruppe, Entwicklung nach 1600; Die Werkstätten; Entwicklung in 17. und 18. Jahrhundert; Truhen; Pergamentarbeiten, Mosaikarbeiten, Arbeiten für Napoleon I.; Ledertapeten: Herstellung, Entwürfe, Liturgische Gewänder; Lederplastiken und Reliefs: Pietadarstellungen, Reliefarbeiten; Ledergefäße; Das 19. Jahrhundert: Fabriken und Manufakturen, Preßvergoldung, Übertragbarkeit der Form, Lederpressung, Historismus, Jugendstil. Bibliographical references in the notes. A standard work on the history of leatherwork.

1723   Waterer, John William. **Leather Craftsmanship**. London, Bell; New York, Praeger, 1968. 121p. illus. index. LC 68-25991.

General survey of the art of leatherwork, arranged in two parts. Part I discusses the properties and preparation of leather; part 2 encompasses the craftsmanship aspects by technique: molding, lamination, without reinforcement, and with decoration. Articles covered include bookbindings, shoes, upholstery, saddles, armor, and cases from the Iron Age to circa 1965.

See also the author's *Leather in Life, Art and Industry* (London, Faber and Faber, 1946. 320p. illus. index. LC 47-17923).

See also the museum catalog: *Deutsches Ledermuseum, Deutsches Schuhmuseum, Offenbach*, by G. Gall and R. Wente-Lukas (Braunschweig, Westermann, 1981. 128p. illus. ISBN 03418634).

Spanish Leather

1724   Waterer, John W. **Spanish Leather: A History of Its Use from 800 to 1500 for Mural Hangings, Screens, Upholstery, Altar Frontals, Ecclesiastical Vestments, Footwear, Gloves, Pouches, and Caskets.** London, Faber and Faber, 1971. 130p. illus. index. LC 72-179775r86.

Survey of Spanish leather art from 800 to 1800 with discussion of origins in Moorish Spain, dissemination, gilding and other decorative techniques, uses, and centers of production. Appendices with glossary, chronological table, ordinances and list of extant hangings.

BOOKBINDING

Bibliographies

1725   Brenni, Vito J. **Bookbinding, a Guide to the Literature**. Westport, Conn., Greenwood Press, 1982. 199p. illus. index. ISBN 0313237182.

Comprehensive, classified bibliography of 1,527 books and periodical articles on all aspects of bookbinding. Contents: 1, Reference Works; 2, Bookbinding Design, Methods, and Other Writings on Technique; 3, Materials; 4, Binding Machinery and Tools; 5, Decoration; 6, History of Bookbinding from Ancient Times to the Present; 7, History of Bookbinding in the Countries of the World; 8, Care and Repair of Bookbindings; 9, Study of Bookbinding; 10, Audio Visual Aids; 11, Bookplates; 16, Bookjackets. Brief annotations for a few titles.

1726   Mejer, Wolfgang. **Bibliographie der Buchbinderei- Literatur**. Leipzig, Hiersemann, 1925. 208p. index. LC 26-10760.

Mejer, Wolfgang, and Hermann Herbst. **Bibliographie der Buchbinderei- Literatur, 1924-1932**. Leipzig, 1933. LC 26-10766r342.

Comprehensive, retrospective, classified bibliography of 2,691 items. Includes books and selected major articles from the major journals of bookbinding. The supplement is more exhaustive in coverage for the years 1924-32. Fully indexed. Continued for the years 1933 to 1937 in *Jahrbuch der Einbandkunst*, 4, 1937, pp. 189-215.

Technique

1727 Roberts, Matt T. **Bookbinding and the Conservation of Books: A Dictionary of Descriptive Terminology.** Washington, D.C., Library of Congress, 1982. 296p. illus. ISBN 0844403660.

Authoritative dictionary of the terminology used in the repair and conservation of historic bookbindings. Contains much information on the history of bookbinding. Illustrated with line drawings and 13 excellent color plates of historic bindings and endpapers. Longer entries have bibliographical references to a list at the end of 373 books and articles.

General Histories and Handbooks

1728 Adam, Paul. **Der Bucheinband; seine Technik und seine Geschichte.** Leipzig, Seemann, 1890. 268p. illus. index. (Seemanns Kunsthandbücher 6).

An old, standard history of bookbinding with a thorough description of techniques, both modern/mechanized and historic/hand techniques. Contents: I, Die Technik der Buchbinderei: I, Die Anfertigung des Buches bis zum Beschneiden; 2, Das Buchschnitt und die weietere Bearbeitung bis zur äusseren Verzierung; 3, Das Verzieren der Einbanddecke; II, Geschichte der Buchdecke: 1, Der mittelalterliche Einband; 2, Der Lederband mit Goldverzierung (Renaissanceband). General bibliography, pp. 262-63.

1729 Bogeng, Gustav A. E. **Der Bucheinband.** Halle a. S., Knapp, 1913. 382p. illus. index. LC 73-437430.

A standard history of European bookbinding written from the point of view of the bibliophile. Contents: Einleitung; Die Gebrauchsform des Bucheinbandes; Die Bucheinbandstoffe; Die Einbandverzierung; Buchbinder und Büchersammler. Basic bibliography, pp. 193-98.

1730 Brassington, William Salt, ed. **A History of the Art of Bookbinding.** London, Elliot Stock, 1894. 277p. illus. index.

An old, standard history of Western bookbinding from antiquity to the end of the nineteenth century with particular attention given to the development of English binding. Contents: Part I: Books of the Ancients: I, The Earliest Records of Prehistoric Man; II, Records of the Earliest Nations—The Babylonian and Assyrian Books; III, The Records of the Ancient Egyptians; IV, Books in the Times of the Greeks and Romans. Part II: A History of the Art of Bookbinding: V, First Bookbindings—Ivory Diptychs—Early Christian Bookbindings—Byzantine Bindings; VI, Carolingian Period—Bookbindings in Ivory—Goldsmiths' Work and Enamel; VII, Celtic Bookbinding—Irish Book-Satchels—Book-Shrines—Metal Bindings and Ornamental Leather Bookbindings; VII, Monastic Bookbinding—English and Continental Bookbinding up to the Invention of Printing; IX, English Stamped-Leather Bookbinding in the Twelfth and Thirteenth Centuries; X, Continental Bookbinding in the Fifteenth Century—Patrons of Literature—Leather Bookbinding, English Guilds—German, Italian, Netherlandish, and French Bindings; XI, English Stamped-Leather Binding, Trade Binding, Fifteenth and Sixteenth Centuries; XII, Bookbinding in the Sixteenth Century—Signatures—Forwarding—Price of Bindings Restricted by Law in England—Book in Chains—Ornamented Edges—Embroidered Bookbindings; XIII, Gold-Tooled Bindings—Italian—French—Great Collectors and Famous Bookbinders; XIV, English Royal Bindings—Bindings in Velvet, Gold, Silver, and Enamel—English Gold-Tooled Bindings from the Reign of Henry VIII to that of Queen Anne; XV, Modern English Bookbinding. Appendices with ordinance of the Bookbinders' Guild, London, 1403, an extract of a 1311 court case against the burglars of a Dionisia woman bookbinder in Fleet Street, and an extract from an act of 1483 granting free import for books into England. Bibliographical references in the footnotes.

1731 Diehl, Edith. **Bookbinding, Its Background and Technique.** New York, Rhinehart, 1946. 2v. illus. index. Reprint: New York, Dover, 1980. ISBN 0486240207.

Comprehensive, scholarly history/handbook of Western bookbinding from ancient times to the twentieth century. Volume I is the history; volume II a detailed handbook of the techniques of hand bookbinding. Contents: Volume I: I, Primitive Records and Ancient Book Forms; II, The Book of the Middle Ages; III, Renaissance and Modern Times; IV, Early Methods of Production and Distribution of Books; V, Bookbinding Practices; VI, National Styles of Book Decoration; VII, Miscellanea. Volume II: I, Craftsmanship; II, Workshop Appointments, Equipment and Record Keeping; III, Flexible Binding; IV, Guarding, Mending, and Mounting; V, Folding and Gathering; VI, End Papers; VII-XVIII, Forwarding; XIX-XX, Miscellanea; XXI, Materials; XXII-XXIII, Finishing; XXIV, Lettering; Glossary. Comprehensive bibliography, v. I, pp. 205-219. A standard work on bookbinding.

1732 Gruel, Leon. **Manuel historique et bibliographique de l'amateur de reliures.** Paris, Gruel & Englemann, 1887. 186p. illus. index. LC 03-14630.

————. **Deuxième Partie.** Paris, Gruel & Leclerc, 1905. 186p. illus. index.

A general history of fine binding treating the origin of formats and styles of decoration from the Middle Ages through the eighteenth century. A dictionary of binders, patrons, collectors, and terms forms a major part of both volumes. Part two begins with a section on bookbinding oddities. Comprehensive bibliography of the older literature in part one, pp. 179-86, and extensive bibliography in the footnotes.

1733 Helwig, Hellmuth. **Einführung in die Einbandkunde.** Stuttgart, Hiersemann, 1970. 278p. illus. index. LC 77-51605.

Authoritative introduction to the field of rare bookbindings with excellent chapters on the history, conservation, research, and the literature of bookbinding. Contents: I, Die Einbandtechnik und die Einbandarten mit besonderer Berücksichtigung des Bibliothekseinbandes; II, Die Technik und die stilistische Entwicklung der Einbanddekoration; III, Das Sammeln von Bucheinbänden, die Bewertung historischer Bucheinbände und die Einbandfälschung; IV, Die Einbandforschung und ihre Methoden; V, Das Katalogisieren von Bucheinbänden; VI, Die Reproduktion historischer Bucheinbände mit Hilfe der Photographie und der Durchreibung; VII, Die Literatur zur Einbandkunde; VIII, Die Konservierung, Restaurierung und Verfälschung von Bucheinbänden. Appendices with examples of descriptions of book bindings and glossary of foreign, i.e., non-German, terminology used in writing on book bindings. Extensive bibliographies at the end of sections and chapters. Chapter VII is a critically annotated bibliographic essay with 139 numbered citations.

1734 Helwig, Hellmuth. **Handbuch der Einbandkunde.** n.p., Maximilian-Gesellschaft, 1953-55. 3v. illus. index. LC 54-35934.

Comprehensive, scholarly dictionary of European bookbinders from the sixteenth through the first half of the nineteenth centuries. Arrangement is by country subdivided by century. The entries give basic biographical data with references to a list of 160 reference works plus specialized literature. Basic reference work on the history of bookbinding.

1735 Loubier, Hans. **Der Bucheinband von seinen Anfang bis zum ende des 18. Jahrhunderts.** 2nd rev. and enl. ed. Leipzig, Klinkhardt & Biermann, 1926. 272p. illus. index. (Monographien des Kunstgewerbes, 21/22). LC 28-18759.

Authoritative survey of European bookbinding from antiquity to circa 1900. Still essential for the methodology. Contents: 1, Grunzüge der Technik; Das Schriftwesen im Altertum; 3, Der kirchliche Prachtband des frühen Mittelalters; 4, Der Prachtband des späten Mittelalters; Der mittelalterliche Lederschnittband; 6, Der mittelalterliche Ledereinband mit Blindpressung; Der Orientalische Einband; 8, Der Renaissance-Band in Italien und Frankreich; 9, Der Renaissance-

Band in Deutschland und England; 10, Der Einband im XVII. und XVIII. Jahrhundert; 11, Der Einband im XIX. Jahrhundert und in der neuesten Zeit. Bibliographical references in the footnotes.

1736   Prideaux, Sarah T. **An Historical Sketch of Bookbinding**. London, Lawrence & Bullen, 1893. 303p. index. Reprint: New York, Garland, 1989. ISBN 0824040244.

Important early history of bookbinding from the early Middle Ages to circa 1830. Contents: 1, Historical Sketch of Bookbinding; 2, Table of Contemporaneous Sovereigns in France and England; 3, Technical Terms in Ordinary Use; 4, Embroidered Book-Covers; 5, The Use of Metal in Bound Books; 6, Book-Edge Decoration; 7, Early Documents Relating to the Craft; 8, Bibliography of Works Relating to Binding. The last two chapters contain still-useful information.

1737   Schreiber, Heinrich. **Einführung in die Einbandkunde**. Leipzig, Hiersemann, 1932. 277p. index. LC 32-20781.

Scholarly history/handbook handicapped only by the lack of illustrations. Aspects treated include the phenomena of bookbinding, the literature of bookbinding (an excellent formal bibliography for this chapter appears as an appendix, pp. 256-59), the many facets of technique, forms of bookbinding materials, decoration by types and nationality, and the state of research to 1930. Appendices include models for descriptive cataloging of bookbinding and a polyglot glossary of bookbinding terms. A standard, classic work on bookbinding.

See also the exhibition catalog: *The History of Bookbinding, 525-1950 A.D.*, Baltimore Museum of Art (Baltimore, Md., Trustees of the Walters Art Gallery, 1957. 275p. illus. index. LC 58-1915r82), and the museum catalogs: *Bookbindings*, 3rd ed. Victoria and Albert Museum (London, H.M.S.O., 1985. 152p. illus. ISBN 011290226X), and *Österreichischen Nationalsbibliothek, Europäische Einbandkunst aus Mittelalter und Neuzeit*, by Otto Mazal (Graz, Akademische Druck- und Verlagsanstalt, 1970. 94p. illus.).

Medieval Bookbinding

1738   Bollert, M. **Lederschnittbände des XIV. Jahrhunderts**. Leipzig, Hiersemann, 1925. 77p. illus. LC 26-5254.

Important collection of 36 plates of fourteenth-century leather bookbindings with carved decoration with scholarly catalog. Bibliographical references in the footnotes.

1739   Federici, Carlo, and Konstantinos Houlis. **Legature buzantine vaticane**. Rome, Fratelli Palombi, 1988. 154p. illus. ISBN 88766215816.

Important, scholarly history of Byzantine bindings based on the collections of the Vatican. Bibliographical references in the footnotes.

1740   Goldschmidt, Ernst P. **Gothic & Renaissance Bookbinding**. 2d ed. London, E. Ph. Goldschmidt, 1928. 2v. illus. index. LC 28-13156. Reprint: Niewkoop, de Graaf, 1967. LC 67-97089.

Important history of European bookbinding from the thirteenth to sixteenth centuries based on the author's famous collection. First volume text; second plates. The 126-page introduction is a pioneering history of the period. Catalogue raisonné is a scholarly catalog of 268 bookbindings in Goldschmidt's collection. Entries have complete bibliographies. Fully indexed. A standard work.

1741   Kyriss, Ernst. **Verzierte gotische Einbande im alten deutschen Sprachgebiet**. Stuttgart, Hettler, 1951. 160p. index.
————. **Tafelband 1.**, 1953
————. **Tafelband 2.**, 1956
————. **Tafelband 3.**, 1958
Scholarly catalogue raisonné of mainly fifteenth- and sixteenth-century bindings produced in German-speaking countries. Grouped according to locations, binders, initials, armorials, and workshops. The three columns of plates illustrate the catalog in sequence. An important scholarly reference checklist and catalog.

1742   Mazal, Otto. **Buchkunst der Gotik**. Graz, Akademische Druck- und Verlagsanstalt, 1975. 253p. illus. (Buchkunst im Wandel der Zeiten, Band 1). ISBN 3201009490.
Sequel to the author's work on the art of the Romanesque book. Covers the period from 1250 to 1500. Contents: 1, Die gotischen Buchschriften; 2, Die gotische Buchmalerei; 3, Gotische Buchkunst im frühen Buchdruck; 4, Der gotischen Bucheinband. Comprehensive, classified bibliography, pp. 211-223, with list of facsimiles of major Gothic books.

1743   ————. **Buchkunst der Romanik**. Graz, Akademische Druck- und Verlagsanstalt, 1978. 366p. illus. (Buck Kunst im Wandel der Zeiten, Band 2/2). ISBN 3201010561.
Comprehensive, scholarly history of the art of the book in western Europe from 1000 to circa 1250, which includes bookbinding. Contents: 1, Die romanische Buchschrift; 2, Die romanische Buchmalerei; 3, Der romanische Bucheinband. Comprehensive, classified bibliography, pp. 317-328.

1744   Steenbock, Frauke. **Der kirchliche Practheinband im fruhen Mittelalter, von den Anfangen bis zum Beginn der Gotik**. Berlin, Deutscher Verlag fur Kunstwissenschaft, 1965. 238p. (text), 176 plates. illus. index. LC 70-209568.
Scholarly history of the great sumptuous bindings made for church use in the early Middle Ages. Book covers are discussed by types, symbolism, relationship to liturgy, and other specialized approaches. The bulk of the work is an excellent scholarly catalog of 127 bindings from the fifth to the thirteenth centuries, each entry with literature for the binding discussed. Bibliography, pp. 233-37.
See also the exhibition catalog: *Twelve Centuries of Bookbindings, 400-1600* (New York, Pierpont Morgan Library: Oxford Univ. Press, 1979. 338p. illus. index. ISBN 0192115804).

Renaissance—Modern Bookbinding

1745   Duncan, Alastair, and Georges de Bartha. **Art Nouveau and Art Deco Bookbinding**. New York, Abrams, 1989. 200p. illus. index. ISBN 0810918811.
Sumptuously illustrated survey of French bookbinding from 1880 to 1940. Brief introductory essay is followed by plates of bindings by: Rose Adler, René Aussourd, Charles Benoit, Henri Blanchetière, Paul Bonet, Robert Bonfils, André Bruel, Georges Canape, Emile Carayon, Georges Cretté, Henri Creuzevault, Geneviève de Léotard, Jean Dunand, Max Fonèsque, Franz, Louis-Denise Germain, Jean Goulden, Madeleine Gras, Léon Gruel, François Horclois Kauffmann, René Kieffer, Clovis Lagadec, Charles Lanoë, Pierre Legrain, Jacques Anthoine-Legrain, Leprêtre, Georges Levitsky, Marius Magnin, André Mare, Marianne, Mme Marot-Rodde, Emile Maylander, Georges Mercier, Charles Meunier, Marius-Michel, Thérèse Moncey, Henri Noulhac, Louise Pinard, A. Pinard-Lefort, Victor Prouvé and Camille Martin, Ralli, Petrus Ruban, François-Louis Schmied, Marcellin Semet and Georges Plumelle, J. K. Van West, Vermoel, René Wiener, Yseux. Biographical dictionary follows the plates. Entries have specialized bibliographies. General, classified bibliography, pp. 197-198.

1746   Hobson, Anthony. **Humanists and Bookbinders: The Origins and Diffusion of the Humanistic Bookbinding 1459-1559, with a Census of Historiated Plaquette and Medallion Bindings of the Renaissance**. Cambridge, England, Cambridge Univ. Press, 1989. 296p. illus. ISBN 0521355362.

Important scholarly history of early Renaissance gilt bookbindings in Italy and France. Contents: 1, The Paduan Antiquaries; 2, Italy: the Fifteenth Century; 3, The Humanistic Binding: Islamic Sources; 4, The Humanistic Binding: Classical Sources; 5, Coins, Medals and Plaquettes: Italy; 6, Medals and Plaquettes: Northern Europe; 7, Fligree, Facades and Fortune; 8, The Bindings of the Fontainebleau Library; Census of Historiated Plaquette and Medallion Bindings of the Renaissance. Comprehensive bibliography, pp. 273-277.

1747   Lewis, Roy H. **Fine Bookbindings in the Twentieth Century**. New York, Arco, 1984. 151p. illus. index. ISBN 0668060840.

Survey of art bookbinding in Europe and America in the twentieth century. Contents: 1, The Background; 2, The Early Days of the Country; 3, The Individual Comes into His Own; 4, Attitudes to Modern Binding; 5, Innovation; 6, Out in Front: Philip Smith and Ivor Robinson; 7, The Names to Note; 8, Collecting Bindings—Fine, Fanciful and Freakish. Chapter 7 is a biographical dictionary of major modern bookbinders with bibliographical references. Glossary and selected bibliography, p. 148.

American Bookbinding

1748   French, Hannah D. **Bookbinding in Early America: Seven Essays on Masters and Methods**. Worcester, Mass., American Antiquarian Society, 1986. 230p. illus. index. ISBN 0912296763.

Essays by the leading authority on American bookbinding of the Colonial Period. Contents: Scottish-American Bookbindings; The Amazing Career of Andrew Barclay, Scottish Bookbinder of Boston; "Bound in Boston by Henry B. Legg"; Caleb Buglass, Binder of the Proposed Book of Common Prayer, Philadelphia, 1786; John Roulstone's Harvard Bindings; Full Gilt and Extra Gilt; Thomas Jefferson's Last Bookbinder: Frederick August Mayo. Bibliographical footnotes.

1749   Lehmann-Haupt, Hellmut, ed. **Bookbinding in America: Three Essays**. New York, Bowker, 1967. 293p. illus. index. LC 67-13796.

First published in 1941. Contents: Early American Bookbinding by Hand, by H. D. French; The Rise of American Edition Binding, by J. W. Rogers; On the Binding of Old Books, by H. Lehmann-Haupt. Bibliographical footnotes.

1750   Thompson, Lawrence S. **Kurze Geschichte der Handbuchbinderei in den Vereinigten Staaten von Amerika**. Stuttgart, M. Hettler, 1955. 111p. illus. (Meister und Meisterwerke der Buchbinderkunst, Heft 3). LC A58-5432.

Concise survey of bookbinding in the United States from Colonial times to the mid-twentieth century with emphasis on the art of bookbinding of the twentieth century. No bibliography.

See also the exhibition catalogs: *Bookbinding in America, 1680-1910: From the Collection of Frederick E. Maser*, by W. Spawn (Bryn Mawr, Pa., Bryn Mawr College Library; Charlottesville, Va., Univ. of Virginia Press, 1983. 122p. illus. index. ISBN 0813910137) and *Early American Bookbindings from the Collection of Michael Papantonio*, 2d ed. (Worcester, Mass., American Antiquarian Society, 1985. 120p. illus. index. ISBN 0912296755).

European Bookbinding

Denmark

1751   Larsen, Sofus, and Anker Kyster, eds. **Danish Eighteenth Century Bindings, 1730-1780**. Copenhagen, Levin & Munksgaard, 1930. 53p. (text), 101 plates, illus. LC 31-4533.
    Survey of Danish bookbinding with emphasis on the renowned binders of the eighteenth century. Good selection of plates. No bibliography.

France

1752   Devauchelle, Roger. **La reliure en France de ses origines a nos jours**. Paris, Rousseau-Girard, 1959-61. 3v. illus. index. LC 59-41734r.
    Comprehensive history of European and French bookbinding. Volume one covers European bindings from antiquity to the end of the seventeenth century, with French bindings exclusively after the Renaissance. Volume two covers French bindings from 1700 to 1850; volume three French bindings from 1850 to circa 1950. Each volume is indexed separately and has its own bibliography.

1753   Marius Michel (firm). **La reliure française. Depuis l'invention de l'imprimarie jusqu'a la fin du XVIIIe siècle**. Paris, Morgand & Fatout, 1880. 144p. illus. LC 3-19218.
    Older, popular history of French bindings by a prominent Parisian firm of the late nineteenth century. Lavish illustrations of the most important French bindings. Appendix with documents from the seventeenth and eighteenth centuries relating to the regulations of the trade of bookbinding by the crown and the University of Paris. Bibliographical references in the footnotes.

1754   Michon, Louis-Marie. **La reliure française**. Paris, Larousse, 1951. illus. index. LC 51-33279.
    Authoritative survey of French bookbinding from the ninth and tenth centuries to contemporary bindings. Emphasis is almost wholly stylistic. Contents: I, Les reliures d'orfèvrerie et d'ivoire du moyen âge; II, La reliure de cuir, des origines au XVe siècle; III, La reliure estampée au XVe siècle et au début du XVIe; IV, La reliure de luxe à ornements dorées de 1500 à 1547; V, La reliure de 1547 à 1565; VI, La reliure de 1565 à 1635; VII, La reliure de 1635 à 1715; VIII, La reliure de 1715 à la fin du XVIIIe siècle; IX, La reliure au XIXe siècle et au début du XXe; X, La reliure contemporaine. Appendix with list of major binders and collectors. General bibliography, p. 140.

1755   Thoinan, Ernest (pseud.). **Les reliures français (1500-1800)**. Paris, Paul, Huard, Guillemin, 1893. 416p. illus. LC 03-27015.
    Important history of bookbinding in France treated as a social history and history of styles by Antoine Ernest Roquet. The first section is a history of the profession in Paris; the second is a stylistic history of French bindings. Appendix with repertory of bookbinders and their marks. Bibliographical references in the footnotes.

Germany

1756   Helwig, Hellmuth. **Das deutsche Buchbinder-Handwerker. Handwerks- und Kulturegeschichte**. Stuttgart, Hiersemann, 1962-65. 2v. illus. LC 63-58587.
    Scholarly history/handbook on German bookbinding from the early Middle Ages to the 1960s. Chiefly a social history, the craft is traced from the cloister to the modern workshop, with

sections on guilds, the apprentice, journeyman, and master. Large compendium of sayings, songs, superstitions, and beliefs by and about bookbinders and their art. Bibliography of frequently cited sources, v. 1, pp. xvii-xx and v. 2, pp. xviii-xxiii, and frequent references throughout the text. A standard work on German bookbinding.

Great Britain

1757 Ball, Douglas. **Victorian Publishers' Bindings**. London, Library Association, 1985. 214p. illus. index. ISBN 0853659362.
    Scholarly history of the design and decoration of cloth publishers b'indings in Britain from 1830 to 1902. Contents: 1, The Start of the Nineteenth-Century; 2, The Introduction of Cloth; 3, Binding Technology; 4, The Decoration and Graining of Cloth and Its Bibliographical Importance; 5, The Climate of Design; 6, Development of Cover Design 1: to 1850; 7, Development of Cover Design 2: from 1850; 8, Designer and Design; 9, John Leighton; 10, Other Binding Designers: a Synopsis; 11, Publisher and Binder; 12, Binder's Signatures and Their Potential Use; 13, An End...and a Beginning? Appendices with essay on identification of cloth grains, chronological list of types of cloth bindings, chronological synopsis of the use of papier maché and relievo bindings, chronological list of bindings by major designers, and repertory of binders' signatures. Comprehensive bibliography, pp. 193-97, and special bibliographies at the ends of the chapters.

1758 McLean, Ruari. **Victorian Publisher's Book-bindings in Paper**. London, G. Fraser, 1983. 112p. illus. index. ISBN 0860920658.
    Illustrated survey of British books with decorated paper bindings between 1830 and 1902. Introduction sketches the history of paper bound books under the headings: French Romantic Bindings; Papier-mâché; Children's Books; Fin-de-Siècle and Art Nouveau. Introduction followed by 93 pages of illustrations mostly in color of bindings and slip cases with descriptive captions. General bibliography, p.6.
    See also by the same author: *Victorian Book Design*, 2nd ed. (London, G. Fraser, 1972) and *Victorian Publishers' Book-Bindings in Cloth and Leather* (Berkeley, Calif., Univ. of California Press, 1973. 160p. illus. index. LC 73-80741).
    See also the exhibition catalog: **Modern British Bookbinding, Bibliotheca Wittockiana**, Brussels; Koninklijke Bibliotheek, The Hague (London, Designer Bookbinders, 1985. 44p. illus. ISBN 0950076546).

Oriental Bookbinding

1759 Martinique, Edward. **Chinese Traditional Bookbinding: A Study of Its Evolution and Techniques**. 1983. 87p. (text), 24p. (plates) ISBN 0896445968. (Chinese Materials Center. Asian Library Series, no.19).
    Brief survey of the evolution of the binding of Chinese books from the seventh century to the early twentieth century. Contents: 1, The Study of Chinese Bookbinding; 2, Early Chinese Bookbinding; 3, The Change from Roll to Flat Format; 4, The Protection and Preservation of Chinese Double-Leaved Books; 5, Conclusion. Comprehensive bibliography, pp. 69-79, with titles in Chinese translated.

1760 Sarre, Friedrich P. T. **Islamic Bookbindings**. London, Keagan Paul, 1923. 167p. illus. LC 24-27670.
    Collection of 36 plates of Islamic bookbindings dating between the fourteenth and eighteenth centuries in private and public collections in Berlin. Descriptive notes to the plates. Bibliographical references in the footnotes. Twenty-page introductory essay sketches the history and characteristics of west Islamic bookbinding.

1761 Weisweiler, Max. **Der islamische Bucheinband des Mittelaltars**. Wiesbaden, Harrasowitz, 1962. 193p. (text), 42 plates. (Beiträge zum Buch- und Bibliothekswesen, 10). LC 63-33419.

Important, scholarly history of Islamic medieval bookbinding based on examples in German, Dutch, and Turkish collections. Contents: A. Allgemeiner Teil: I, Ziel, Weg, Mittel; II, Aufbau und Einteilung; III, Der Buchdeckel; IV, Die Klappe; V, Der Steg; VI, Der Innenspiegel; VII, Die Stempel; VIII, Verzeichnis der Deckeltypen; IX, Verzeichnis der Klappentypen; X, Verzeichnis der Stempel. B. Besonderer Teil (catalog of 387 examples). C. Chronologisches Verzeichnis der Handscriften. Full scholarly apparatus including specialized bibliographies in the catalog entries. Plates are of rubbings of bindings.

See also the exhibition catalogs: *Islamic Bindings and Bookmaking*, by G. Bosch, et al. (Chicago, Oriental Institute, 1981. 235p. illus.), *A Jeweler's Eye: Islamic Arts of the Book from the Vever Collection*, by G. D. Lowry and S. Nemazee (Washington, D.C., Smithsonian Institution, 1988. 240p. illus. ISBN 0295966769), and the museum catalog: *Islamic Bookbindings in the Victoria and Albert Museum*, by D. Haldane (London, World of Islam Festival Trust in association with the Victoria and Albert Museum, 1983. 205p. illus. LC 84-141245).

CHAPTER FIFTEEN

MEDALS AND SEALS

BIBLIOGRAPHIES

1762   Grierson, Philip. **Coins and Medals: A Short Bibliography.** London, G. Philip, 1954. 88p. LC 55-35035.

Useful, classified bibliography of basic books, chiefly in English, on coins and medals of the Western World.

DICTIONARIES

1763   Forrer, Leonard. **Biographical Dictionary of Medalists; Coin, Gem, and Seal-engravers, Mint-masters, Etc....** London, Spink, 1902-30. 8v. illus. index. Reprint: New York, B. Franklin, 1970. (Burt Franklin: Bibliography & Reference Series, 319). LC 71-118749r892.

Comprehensive, scholarly dictionary with references to bibliographical sources at the end of most entries. General bibliography, v. 1, pp. xxxix-xlviii, and v. 8, p. 368. Volumes 7 and 8 are supplements. Standard references.

MEDALS

General Histories and Handbooks

1764   Bernhart, Max. **Medaillen und Plaketten. Ein Handbuch für Sammler und Liebhaber.** 3. von Tyll Kroha völlig neubearb. Aufl. Braunschweig, Klinkhardt und Biermann, 1966. 245p. illus.index. LC 67-72200.

Comprehensive and authoritative history of European medals and plaquettes from the fifteenth to the twentieth centuries. Contents: I, Vorwort; II, Einleitung: Begriff und Vorläufer der Medaille; III, Die italienische Renaissancemedaille: Das Quattrocento; IV, Die italienische Renaissancemedaille: Das Cinquecento; V, Die Renaissancemedaille in Deutschland und den Niederlanden; VI, Die Renaissancemedaille im übrigen Europa: Vom Frühbarock zum Klassizismus; VII, Die italienische Medaille im 17. und 18. Jahrhundert; VIII, Deutsche Medaillenkunst in Barock und Rokoko; IX, Schweizer Medailleure; X, Die französische Barockmedaille; XI, Die Barockmedaille in den Niederlanden; XII, Die Barockmedaille im übrigen Europa; XIII, Klassizismus und Empire; XIV, Vom Historismus zum Jugendstil; XV, Die Medaille im 20. Jahrhundert; XVI, Das Sammeln von Medaillen und Plaketten. Appendices with repertory of marks and signatures, list of collections, and basic bibliography, pp. 239-40.

1765   Lnormant, Francois. **Monnaies et medailles.** Nouv. ed. Paris, Quantin, 1885. 328p. illus. index. LC F01-3444r28.

Old, still-useful survey of medallions from antiquity to the end of the Renaissance with emphasis on the relationship between medallions and medals and coins. Contents: Première Partie—L'Antiquité: I, Origine et propogartion de l'art monétaire; II, Les métaux monétaires; III, Procédes de fabrication des monnaies; IV, Les monnaies coulées; V, Les ateliers monétaires; VI,

Les graveurs des monnaies; VII, Principes de la composition des types monétaires; VIII, Les types monétaires et leur choix; IX, L'imitation dans les types monétiares; X, Les médaillons impériaux romains; XI, Les médaillon contorniates; XII, Tessères thèatrales et jetons. Deuxième Partie.—Les Temps modernes: I, L'art monétaire au moyen âge; II, Les médailleurs italiens de la Renaissance; III, Les médailles allemandes de la Renaissance; IV, Les médailles et monnaies françaises; V, Les procédés de monnayage des anciens et des modernes, comparés au point de vue de leur résultat artistique. Appendices with lists of medalists and medallion engraves. Bibliographical references in the footnotes.

See also the exhibition catalog: *Les Graveurs d'acier et la medaille, de l'Antiquité a nos jours.* (Paris, Muséé de la Monnaie, 1971. 731p. illus.).

Ancient Medals [*See also* Chapter Twelve, Ancient Gems, Cameos, and Intaglios]

1766   Gnecchi, Francesco. **Il medaglioni romani descritti ed illvstrati...** Milan, Hoepli, 1912. 3v. illus. Reprint: Bologna, Forni, 1968. LC 12-16174.

Important corpus of ancient Roman medals. Contains 333 plates illustrating over 1,000 examples with descriptive catalog entries that include references to specialized literature. Contents: v. 1. Oro ed argento; v. 2. Bronzo. pte. 1. Gran modulo; v. 3. Bronzo. pte. 2. Moduli minori. pte. 3. Medaglioni del Senato. In each volume the text and catalog is proceeded by essays discussing the metallic content of the medals, stylistic and iconographic features, and inscriptions. Bibliographical references in the footnotes. Still an essential pictorial resource for the study of Roman medals.

1767   Toynbee, J. M. C. **Roman Medallions**. New York, American Numismatic Society, 1944. 268p. illus. index. (Numismatic Studies, no. 5). Reprinted, 1986. ISBN 0897222121.

Comprehensive, scholarly history from Augustus to Justinian, written by a leading classicist. Important corpus of 49 plates. Contents: Part I. Medallions and Coins: 1, The Definition of the Term "Roman Medallion"; II, The Classification of Roman Medallions; III, Coins Incorrectly Classed as Medallions. Medallic Coins. Border-line Pieces; Part II. Mints and Provenances: I, Mints; II, Provenances; Part III: The Purpose of Roman Medallions: I, The Occasions of Medallion Issues (1); II, The Occasions of Medallion Issues (2); III, Medaillons and Their Recipients; Part IV: The Historical Development: I, Introduction; II, Augustus to Commodus; III, Septimus Sverus to Carinus and Numerianus; IV, Diocletian to Justinian; Part V: Medallions and Imperial Life: I, Medallions and Politics; II, Medallions and Religion; III, Medallions and Art. Appendices with essay of forgeries, casts, lead medallions, contorniates. Select bibliography, pp. 240-43, and bibliographical references in the footnotes.

Renaissance Medals

General Histories and Handbooks

1768   Hill, George F. **Medals of the Renaissance**. rev. & enl. ed. by Graham Pollard. London, British Museum Publications, 1978. 230p. illus. ISBN 071410843X.

First published: Oxford, Clarendon Press, 1920. Authoritative history of European medals of the fifteenth and sixteenth centuries with emphasis on the identity and activity of the major artists. Contents: I, Medallic Technique; II, Northern Italy in the Fifteenth Century; III, Rome and Florence in the Fifteenth Century; IV, The Italian Medal in the Sixteenth Century; V, German Medals; VI, Medals of the Netherlands; VII, French Medals; VIII, England and Scotland. Updated, comprehensive bibliography, pp. 189-93, and further bibliography in the notes.

1769 Weber, Ingrid. **Deutsche, niederländische und französische Renaissanceplaketten, 1500-1650: Modelle für Reliefs an Kult, Prunk und Grebrauchsgestanden.** Munich, Bruckmann, 1975. 2v. illus. ISBN 376541462X, 3765414921.

Comprehensive, scholarly catalog of Renaissance plaquettes made in Germany, the Netherlands, and France from 1500 to 1650. Within the chronological sections the plaquettes are arranged by place and designer. Full, scholarly apparatus including detailed descriptions of the pieces, biographies of the designers, and bibliographies of the specialized literature. Contents: Band 1: 15. Jahrhundert: 1. Hälfte 16. Jahrhundert; 2. Hälfte 16. Jahrundert; 17. Jahrhundert. Band 2 is a corpus of 1,058 pieces on 302 plates.

See also museum guides: *Medaillen der Renaissance und des Barock: eine Auswahl aus den Beständen des Badischen Landesmuseum*, (Karlsruhe, Das Museum, 1969. unpaged text, 58 plates) and *Renaissance Medals from the Samuel H. Kress Collection at the National Gallery of Art*, (London, Phaidon, 1967. 307p. illus. index. LC 67-105399).

French Renaissance Medals

1770 Mazerolle, F. **Les Médailleurs français du XVe siècle au milieu du XVIIe siècle.** 3v. illus. Paris, Imprimerie Nationale, 1902-04. LC 14-11854.

Comprehensive handbook of French medalists of the Renaissance. Contents: Tome 1: Introduction et documents; tome 2: Catalogue des médailles et des jetons; tome 3: Album. The catalog in volume 3 contains 1,021 medals mostly from the Cabinet de France des Médailles, Bibliothèque Nationale. Plates in volume three are from plaster casts.

German Renaissance Medals

1771 Grotemeyer, Paul. **"Da ich het die gestalt." Deutsche Bildnismedaillen des 16. Jahrhunderts.** Munich, Prestel, 1957. 56p. illus. (Bibliothek des Germanischen National-Museums Nurnberg zur deutschen Kunst- und Kulturegeschichte, Band 7).

Authoritative introduction to German Renaissance medals with a selection of relevant documents and excellent plates illustrating 72 masterpieces with descriptive notes. Bibliography in the notes.

1772 Habich, Georg. ed. **Die deutschen Schaumünzen des XVI. Jahrhunderts...** Munich, Bruckmann, 1929-34, 5v. illus, index. LC A33-2761.

Monumental handbook of German medals of the sixteenth century arranged by schools and masters. The nearly 4,000 catalog entries contain bibliographical references. Introduction on technique in volume one. Third volume contains extensive indexes by artist, sitter, inscriptions and subjects. The standard reference work on German Renaissance medals. The author published a concise handbook: *Die deutschen Medailleure des XVI. Jahrhunderts* (Halle, Reichmann, 1916. 292p. illus.).

Italian Renaissance Medals

1773 Armand, Alfred. **Les médailleurs italiens des quinzième et seizième siècles...** 2nd ed. Paris, Plon, 1883-87. 3v. illus. index. LC 14-17771. Reprint: Bologna, Forni, 1966.

Dated but still an indispensable handbook of Italian medalists of the fifteenth and sixteenth centuries. The 2,600 medals are divided into two parts: pieces by known medalists and anonymous pieces. Entries give full descriptions including references to reproductions and locations of unpublished medals. Volume three contains a supplement to both parts and indexes.

1774   Fabriczy, Cornelius von. **Italian Medals**. New York, Dutton, 1904. 223p. illus. index. LC 05-9663.

Translation of *Medaillen der italienschen Renaissance* (Leipzig, Seemann, 1903). Concise survey of Italian Renaissance medals with emphasis on attribution. Introduction on technique is followed by chapters on Pisano and other North Italian medalists, Venetian and Bolognese medalists, Florentine medals, Roman medalists, the medals of the Medicean court, the Papal mint, and Paduan and Milanese medalists. Bibliographical footnotes.

1775   Friedländer, Julius. **Die italienischen Schaumünzen des funfzehnten Jahrhunderts (1430-1530). Ein Beitrag zur Kunstgeschichte...** Berlin, Weidmann, 1882. 223p. illus. index. LC 10-11095. Reprint: Bologna, Forni, 1976.

Comprehensive, scholarly history of Italian Renaissance medals with a corpus of 62 plates. Text is arranged around major medalists grouped by place. Bibliographical references in the footnotes.

1776   Habich, Georg. **Die Medaillen der italienischen Renaissance...** Stuttgart and Berlin, Deutsche Verlags-Anstalt, 1923. 168p. illus. index. LC 24-17218.

Authoritative history of Italian Renaissance medals with important corpus of 100 plates with descriptive notes. Contents: I, Allgemeines; II, Vorgeschichte; III, Pisano und seine Schule; IV, Francesco Laurana und Pietro da Milano; V, Sperandio; VI, Ausläufer von Pisanos Stil in Venedig; VII, Bellano und andrere; VIII, Florentiner Erzgiesser; IX, Niccolo Fiorentino und seine Schule; X, Ausläufer der Florentiner Medaille; XI, Talpa; XII, Goldschmiede, Siegel- und Stempelschneider; XIII, Übergang zum Cinquecento; XIV, Andere Meister der Prägemedaille: Die Cavalli; XV, Francia; XVI, Die neue Anschauung im XVI. Jahrhundert; XVII, Meister der Kardinallegeten; XVIII, Dekorative Tendenz; XIX, Mosca, Caraglio und Domenico Veneziano; XX, Antikisiende Stein- und Stempelschneider; XXI, Prägemedaillen; XXIII, Venetianische Bildhauer; XXIV, Leone Leoni und seine Schule; XXV, Spätere Manieristen. Bibliographical footnotes.

1777   Heiss, Alois. **Les Médailleurs de la Renaissance**. 8 vs. in 9, Paris, J. Rothschild, 1881-92.

Pioneering work in the history of Italian Renaissance medals. Contents: 1: Vittore Pisano (1881); 2: Francesco Laurana, Pietro da Milano (1882); 3: Niccolò, madio da Milano, Marescotti, Lixignolo, Petrecino, Baldassre Estense, Corradini, anonymes travaillant à Ferrare au XVe siècle (1883); 4: Léon-Baptiste Iberti, Matteo de' Pasti, et anonyme de Pandolphe IV Malatesta (1883); 5: Niccoló Spinelli, Antonio del Pollaiuolo, Giovanni delle Comiole, les Della Robbia, Bertoldo, Gentile Bellini, Costanzo, et anonymes d'Alphonse Ier d'Este, de Charles VIII, d'Anne de Bretagne, de Lucrèce Borgia, de Larent-le-Magnifique et de Mahomet II (1885); 6: Sperandio de Mantoue et les médailleurs anonymes des Bentivoglio, seigneurs de Bologne (1886); 7: Venise et les vénetiens du XVe ou XVIIe siècle. (1887); 8, 1: Florence et les Florentins du XVe au XVIIe siècle (1891); 8, 2: Florence et la Toscane sous les Médicis (1892).

1778   Hill, George F. **A Corpus of Italian Medals of the Reniassance before Cellini...** London, British Museum, 1930. 2v. illus. index. LC 31-13120. Reprint: Florence, Studio per Edizioni Scelte, 1984.

Standard handbook on Italian Renaissance medals with 1,333 entries of medals made between 1390 and 1530. Arrangement is by city of origin. Medals are reproduced to scale and display both obverse and reverse sides (unfortunately from plaster casts). Entries have comprehensive bibliographies. A standard reference work.

1779 Middeldorf, Ulrich A., and Dagmar Stiebral. **Renaissance Medals and Plaquettes: Catalogue**. Florence, Studio per Edizioni Scelte, 1983. 250p. illus. index. LC 83-207513.

Catalog of 89 medals and 8 plaquettes, mostly Italian, from unnamed private collections written by a leading authority on Italian Renaissance art.

See also the museum catalog: *Medaglie italiane del Rinascimento nel Museum Nazionale del Bargello: Italian Renaissance Medals in the Museo Nazionale del Bargello*, by J. Graham Pollard (Florence, Studio per Edizioni Scelte, 1984-85. 3v. illus.).

Major Medallists

1780 Lawrence, Richard H. **The Paduans: Medals by Giovanni Cavino**. Chicago, Atgonaut, 1967. 31p. illus. LC 65-3344.

Catalog of 113 medals by Giovanni Cavino (1499-1570), who created highly skilled imitations of ancient Roman medals. Entries contain bibliographical references. Only a few medals are reproduced by line drawing.

1781 Weiss, Roberto. **Pisanello's Medallion of the Emperor John VIII Palaeologus**. London, British Museum, 1966. 32p. illus. LC 66-74437.

Scholarly monograph on Pisanello's cast bronze medallion of Emperor John VIII Palae-ologus, one of the most important medallions of the Early Renaissance. Contents: I, The Beginnings of the Italian Renaissance Medal; II, Pisanello the Medallist; III, Pisanello and the Emperor John VIII; IV, Pisanello's Medal of the Emperor John VIII; V, The 'Fortuna' of Pisanello's Medal of John VIII. Bibliographical appendix with useful comments on the literature of Renaissance medals.

SEALS

General Histories and Handbooks

1782 Berchem, Egon von. **Siegel**. 2nd ed. Berlin, R. C. Schmidt, 1923. 222p. illus. index. (Bibliothek fur Kunst- und Antiquitätensammler, Bd. II). LC 19-562.

Authoritative introduction to European seals of the Middle Ages and Renaissance largely superseded by Kittel (1788). Contents: 1, Bedeutung der Siegel für Kunst und Wissenschaft; 2, Der Begriff "Siegel," ihr Alter und Verwendung; 3, Die Siegelstempel: Material, Herstellung, Stempelschnitt, Vererbung, Vernichtung, Verwahrung, Verschiedene Arten von Stempeln; 4, Die Siegelstoffe: Metall, Wachs, Siegellack, Oblate; 5, Die Anfertigung und Befestigung der Siegel; 6, Die Form und Größe der Siegel; 7, Die Siegeltypen: Schrift-, Bild-, Porträt- und Wappensiegel; 8, Die Siegelinhaber: Kaiser und Könige, Geistlichkeit, hoher Adel, niederer Adel, Bürger, Frauen, Gemeinden, Zünfte; 9, Die Inschriften der Siegel; 10, Anlegen und Ordnen von Siegelsammlun-gen; 11, Anfertigung von Siegelsammlungen; 12, Siegelsammlungen; 13, Literatur.

1783 Birch, Walter de Gray. **Seals**. London and New York, Methuen, 1907. 327p. illus. index. LC 08-2185.

Old, once-standard survey of European seals from the early Middle Ages to the early twentieth century. Emphasis is placed particularly on English seals of the Middle Ages. Contents: I, The Earliest Seals; II, Development of the Art of Seals—Study of the Seals of England; III, Seals of Royal Offices and Officers; IV, Ecclesiastical and Capitular Seals of England and Wales; V, Seals of English Monasteries, Abbey, Priories and Monastic Orders; VI, Local Seals of Cities, Towns, Corporations, Boroughs, Honours, Hundreds, Liberties, Universities, Schools, etc.; VII, Some Official Seals Relating to Wales; VIII, Some Equestrian Seals and Seals of Noble Ladies

Some Official Seals Relating to Wales; VIII, Some Equestrian Seals and Seals of Noble Ladies of England and Wales; IX, English Heraldic Seals; X, Colonial and Company Seals; XI, Miscellaneous Designs and Devices of English Seals; XII, Royal Seals of Scotland; XIII, Episcopal Seals of Scotland; XIV, Scottish Monasteries, Colleges, and Ecclesiastical Foundations; XV, Local Seals of Scotland; XVI, Scottish Heraldry and Devices; XVII, Some Seals Relating to Ireland; XVIII, Bullae of the Byzantine Empire; XIX, Seals of Italy—Bullae of Popes and Doges of Venice, etc.; XX, Seals of France; XXI, Miscellaneous European and Other Seals—Denmark, Germany, The Netherlands, Norway, Poland, Russia, Spain, Sweden, the East, America, etc. Appendix with glossary of heraldic and conventional terms. No bibliography.

1784   Brugmans, Hajo. **Corpus sigillorum neerlandicorum. De nederlandsche zegels tot 1300...** The Hague, Nijhoff, 1937-40. 3v. illus. index.
    Scholarly handbook/history of seals of the Netherlands dating after 1300. Bibliographical references in the footnotes. A standard work on Dutch seals.

1785   Ewald, Wilhelm. **Siegelkunde.** Munich and Berlin, Oldenbourg, 1914. 244p. illus. index. (Handbuch der mittelalterlichen und neuren Geschichte, v.4, 1). Reprint: Munich, R. Oldenbourg, 1969. LC 73-411821.
    Comprehensive, authoritative, and scholarly history/handbook of European seals from the early Middle Ages to the end of the nineteenth century. Forty plates illustrate seal impressions, facsimiles of impressions, actual seals and apparatus, and documents with seals attached. Contents: I, Quellen zur Siegelkunde; II, Die Bedeutung und der Gebrauch des Siegels im allgemeinen; III, Aufkommen und Verbreitung des Siegelbrauches im Mittelalter. Die rechtliche Bedeutung des mittelalterlichnen Siegels; IV, Zeitpunkt der Vornahme der Siegelung: die Verfertiger der Siegelabdrücke; die Kontrolle der Besiegelung; Siegeltaxe; Zeitpunkt der Siegelung; V, Verwendung mehrer Siegelstempel durch einen Siegelführer; VI, Gemeinschaftliche Siegelstempel, Abnutzung, Vernichtung, Vererbung und Veränderung von Siegelstempel; VII, Die Siegelstemmpel; VIII, Die Siegelstoffe; IX, Anfertigung und Befestigung der Siegelabdrücke; X, Das Äussere der Siegel; XI, Siegelbetrug. Extensive bibliography in the footnotes.

1786   Gandilhon, René. **Bibliographie de la sigilloraphie francaise.** Paris, Imprimerie nationale, 1955. 187p. Reprint: Paris, Picard, 1982. 222p. ISBN 2708400770.
    Comprehensive bibliography of the literature on the history of French seals. Contains 2,542 books and periodical articles broadly classified. Brief annotations attached to titles that are not self- evident.

1787   Grandjean, Poul-B. **Dansk sigillographi.** Copenhagen, Schultz, 1944. 374p. illus. index. LC A49-5150.
    Scholarlyhistory/handbook of Danish seals from the early Middle Ages through the nineteenth century. Comprehensive, classified bibliography, pp. 333-43. Standard work on Danish seals.

1788   Kittel, Erich. **Siegel.** Braunschweig, Klinkhardt & Biermann, 1970. 530p. illus. index. LC 76-545573. (Bibliothek für Kunst- und Antiquitätenfreunde, Band II).
    Comprehensive and authoritative history of Western seals from ancient times to the sixteenth century. Contents: I. Die antike Welt: 1, Alter Orient; 2, Kreta; 3, Griechenland; 4, Rom; 5, Die Bibel; 6, Vom Altertum zum Mittelalter. Merowinger; 7, Rückblick; II, Siegelkunde. Allegmeiner Teil: Siegel und Urkunde. Siegelrecht; 2, Siegelstempel und Siegelarten; 3, Siegelstoffe. Anbrigung der Siegel; 4, Siegelformen und Siegelbilder allegemein; 5, Sieglinschriften; III, Siegelkunde. Besonderer Teil: 1, Köngige und Kaiser; 2, Landfriedenssiegel; 3, Hoher Adel und Länder; 4, Damensiegel; 5, Niederer Adel; 6, Städte; 7, Schöffengerichte Dörfer; 8, Zünfte

und sontige Körperschaften. Hospitäler, Universitäten; 9, Bürger und Bauern; 10, Päpste; 11, Bischöfe, Äbte, Sonstige geistliche Würdenträger; 12, Stifter und Kloster. Kirchengemeinden; 13, Amst- und Bohördensiegel. Appendices with essay on inscriptions on seals, list of collections, and very comprehensive, classified bibliography, pp. 468-509. A standard work on European seals.

See also: Seyler, Gustav A. *Geschichte der Siegel* (Leipzig, P. Friesenhahn, 1894. 383p. illus. index. LC 18-8613) in the series "Illustrierte Bibliothek der Kunst- und Kulturgeschichte."

1789   Roman, Joseph H. **Manuel de sigillographie française.** Paris, Picard, 1912. 401p. illus. index. LC 20-1942.

Comprehensive, scholarly, history/handbook of French seals of the Middle Ages. Contents: I, Histoire du sceau; II, Utilité de l'étude des sceaux; III, Étude et conservation des sceaux; IV, De l'emploi du sceau; V, Diverses sortes de sceaux; VI, Matière des sceaux; VII, Forme et dimension des sceaux; VIII, Mode d'apposition des sceaux; IX, Types des sceaux; X, Des légendes; XI, Des signets; XII, De l'emploi des intailles ou pierres gravées; XIII, Sigillographie régionale, bibliographie et caractéristique; XIV, L'art et les artiste graveurs de sceaux; XV, De la conservation et la reproduction des sceaux. Bibliographical references in the footnotes.

See also the museum catalogs: *I sigilli dell'Archivo Vaticano,* by Pietro Sella. (Vatican City, Bibliotheca Apostolica Vaticana, 1937-64. 3 vs. text, 3 vs. plates), *Catalogue of Seals in the Department of Manuscripts in the British Museum,* by W. D. Gray. (London, Trustees of the British Museum, 1887-1900. 6vs. illus.), *Das Siegel der deutschen Kaiser und Könige von 751 bis 1913,* by O. Posse (Dresden, W. Baensch, 1909-1913. 5v. in 3. Reprint: Leipzig, Zentralantiquariat der Deutschen Demokratische Republik, 1981), *Das Siegel im Altertum: Gebrauchsgegenstand und Kunstwerk: Staatliche Museen Berlin, Ägyptisches Museum, Islamisches Museum, Antikenmuseum, Vorderasiatisches Museum,* by V. Enderlein (Berlin, Die Mussen, 1986. 32p. illus. LC 87-420851), and the exhibition catalog: *Il sigillo nella storia e nella cultura,* ed. S. Ricci (Rome, Società Editoriale Jouvence, 1985. 264p. illus.).

Ancient Seals [*See also* Chapter Twelve, Ancient Gems, Cameos, and Intaglios]

1790   Amiet, Pierre. **La Glyptique mesopotamienne archaique.** Paris, Centre National de la Recherche Scientifique, 1961. 455p. illus. LC 66-54320.

Comprehensive, scholarly handbook/history of ancient Mesopotamian engraved cylinder seals. Contents: Première partie: I, Les origines de la glyptique; II, Les origines de la glyptique en Basse Mésopotamie. Les cachets prédynastiques; III, La glyptique prédynastique d'Uruk; IV, La glyptique prédynastique en dehors d'Uruk; V, La glyptique susienne; VI, La glyptiqye prédynastique. Essau de Synthèse; VII, La période de transition entre l'époque prédynsatique et l'époque dynastique archaique; VIII, L'époque Dynastique Archaique—I: La phase ancienne de l'Epoque Dynastique; IX, L'époque Dynastique Archaique—II: La période Présargonique; Deuxième partie: L'interpretation du Répertoire Iconographique: I, La glyptique primitive; II, L'époque prédynastique; III, L'époque prédynastique—Le culte et la mythologie; IV, La vie quotidienne a l'époque prédynastique; V, La glyptique proto-Elamite; VI, La periode de Transition; VII, La période de Transition—La mythologie et le culte; VIII, L'époque dynastique archaique—La scènes de la vie quotidienne et la Cérémonie du banquet; IX, L'époque dynastique archaique—La mythologie animalière: héros, animaux et monstres; X, Le culte et la mythologie a l'Epoque dynastique archaique. Corpus of drawings taken from cylinder seal impressions. Extensive bibliographical footnotes and general bibliography, pp. 195-198. A standard work.

1791   Dignard, Françoise. **Répertoire analytique des cylindres orientaux: publiés dans des sources bibliographiques éparses (sur ordinateur)**. Paris, Editions du Centre National de la Recherche Scinetifique, 1975. 3v. illus. ISBN 2222018242.

1792   Forman, Werner, and D. J. Wiseman. **Cylinder Seals of Western Asia**. London, Batchworth Pr., 1959. 118p. illus. index.
Survey of cylinder seals in the Ancient Near East with valuable collection of 118 plates of seals reproduced in actual size and enlarged. Contents: Classification; The Uses of Seals; Technique; Inscriptions; The Protoliterate Period; The Early Dynastic Period; Akkadian; The Third Dynasty of Ur; Old Babylonian; Peripheral Styles; Middle Assyrian; Neo-Assyrian and Neo-Babylonian; Achaemenian. General bibliography, pp. 46-47.

1793   Matz, Friedrich. **Die Frühkretischen Siegel. Eine Untersuchung über das Werden des minoischen Stiles**. Berlin and Leipzig, de Gruyter, 1928. 277p. illus. index.
Important, scholarly history of ancient Minoan seals with corpus of 25 plates with photographic reproductions of seals. Text integrates the seals into the overall development of Minoan art. Contents: I, Umgrenzungen der Aufgabe; II, Das Material—A, Katalog der Stemplesiegel, B, Die Prismen, C, Die Abdrücke; III, Stand der Forschung und Fragestellung; IV, Die ägyptischen Knopfsiegel; V, Die hittischen Stempelsiegel; VI, Die frühkretischen Siegel; VII, Das subneolithische Südosteuropa; VIII, Die Ägäis und Anatolien in der frühen Bronzezeit; XI, Zusammenfassung der Ergebnisse. Extensive references to the literature in the footnotes.

Oriental Seals

1794   Bowes, James L. **Japanese Marks and Seals**. Ann Arbor, Mich., Ars Ceramica, 1976. 379p. illus index. ISBN 0893440027.
First published in 1882. Comprehensive dictionary of seals, i.e., marks, found on Japanese ceramics, illuminated manuscripts and printed books, metalwork, lacquer, enamels, metal, wood, ivory, etc. Appendix with lists of zodiacal cycle and year period marks.

1795   Lai, T. C. **Chinese Seals**. Seattle, Wash., Univ. of Washington Press, 1976. 200p. illus. ISBN 0295955171.
Popular introduction to the history of traditional Chinese seals. Illustrations include both seal impressions and works of art on which seals are impressed. Contents: Introduction by Jiu-fong L. Chang; Two Poems; Of Seals and Kings; Seal Artists; The Aesthetics of Seals; Hsien Chang: Leisure Seals; Some Seal Scripts; Pictographic Seals. Glossary is a list of romanized Chinese names with their equivalents in Chinese characters.

1796   Veit, Willibald. **Siegel und Siegelschrift der Chou-, Chin- und Han-Dynasties**. Stuttgart, F. Steiner, 1985. 297p. illus. ISBN 3515044892. (Studien zur ostasiastischen Schriftkunst, Bd. 4).
Comprehensive, scholarly study of ancient Chinese seals from the Chou to the Han dynasties based on both literary and art historical evidence. Contains 198 plates illustrating both seals and seal impressions. Contents: 1, Einleitung; 2, Die Bedeutung des Siegels in China an Hand von Beispielen aus der Literatur der Chou-, Ch'in- und Han-Dynastie; Die Enstehung des Siegels; 3, Die Entwicklung der chinesischen Schrift bis zur Han-Dynastie einschließlich, mit der Chau-shu seit der Ch'un-ch'iu-Zeit als Schwerpunkt der Betrachtung; 4, Terminologie; 5, Die Siegel der Chan-kuo-Zeit, der Ch'in- und der Han-Dynastie; Die Schrift aud Siegeln und ihre Entwicklung. Comprehensive bibliography that includes works in Chinese and Japanese as well as Western languages, pp. 205-217.

1797   Wang, Chi-chien, comp. **Seals of Chinese Painters and Collectors of the Ming and Ching Periods, Reproduced in Facsimile Size and Dechipered**. Hong Kong, Hong Kong Univ. Press, 1966. 726p. illus. LC 66-84760.

Comprehensive dictionary of the seals used by Chinese painters and collectors. First published in 1940 in Chinese and German, the 1966 edition reprints the large corpus of over 9,000 seals with text in Chinese and German and adds, as an appendix: "American Supplement. Further Seals Found on Chinese Paintings in American and Public Collections." The seals are given in facsimile impression and arranged according to the *Chinese Biographical Dictionary* (23rd edition. Shanghai, 1934). Alphabetical index affords access by Wade-Giles romanization. A standard work designed primarily as a means of determining authenticity of Chinese paintings.

See also the exhibition catalog: *Kuo kung hsi yin hshuan ts'ui: Masterpieces of Chinese Seals in the National Palace Museum*, (Taipei, National Palace Museum, 1974. 111p. illus.).

CHAPTER SIXTEEN

METALWORK

TECHNIQUE

1798   Braun-Feldweg, Wilhelm. **Metal; Design and Technique.** New York, Van Nostrand Reinhold, 1975. 296p. illus. index.

Translation of: *Metall—Werkformen und Arbeitsweisen* (Ravensburg, Maier, 1968). Survey of the chief techniques and materials of metalwork directed to the interested layman rather than the contemporary craftsman. Contents: 1, Metalcrafts in the Past and Present; 2, Objects; 3, Raw Materials; 4, Techniques of Forming; 5, Decorating Techniques; 6, Metallic Raw Materials and Expendable Materials; 7, Calculation of Alloys; 8, Precious Stones; 9, Historical and Stylistic Survey; 10, Basic Terms of Heraldry. Comprehensive, classified bibliography, pp. 287-88.

1799   Maryon, Herbert. **Metalwork and Enamelling: A Practical Treatise on Gold and Silversmiths' Work and Their Allied Crafts.** 5th rev. ed. New York, Dover, 1971. 347p. illus. LC 76-130881.

Handbook to the techniques and materials used in metalwork and enameling designed as a guide to modern craftsmen but with frequent reference to older, traditional practice. Illustrated by pieces in the British Museum and with excellent explanatory drawings. Contents: I, Materials and Tools; II-V, Soldering; VI-VII, Filigree and Other Small Work; VIII-X, The Setting of Stones; XI, Raising and Shaping; XII, Spinning; XIII-XIV, Repoussé Work; XV, Mouldings; XVI, Twisted Wires; XVII, Hinges and Joints; XVIII, Metal Inlaying and Overlaying; XIX, Niello; XX, Japanese Alloys and Stratified Fabrics; XXI-XXVII, Enamelling, XXVIII-XXXII, Metal Casting; XXXIII, Construction; XXXIV, Setting Out; XXXV, Polishing and Colouring; XXXVI, The Making and Sharpening of Tools; XXXVII, Design; XXXVIII, Benventuto Cellini; XXXIX, Assaying and Hallmarking; XL, Various Tables and Standards; XLI, Gauges. Notes to the plates. Bibliography, p. 318.

GENERAL HISTORIES AND HANDBOOKS

1800   Baer, Eva. **Metalwork in Medieval Islamic Art.** Albany, N.Y., State University of New York Press, 1983. 371p. illus. index. ISBN 0873956028.

Scholarly handbook/history of Islamic metalwork from the seventh through the fourteenth centuries. Does not include arms and armour. Contents: I, The Craft: Materials and Techniques; II, Groups of Metal Objects: 1, Lighting Devices, 2, Thurification Vessels; 3, Inkwells and Pen-boxes; 4, Caskets and Boxes; 5, Ewers and Pitchers; 6, Cups, Bowls, and Basins; III, The Decoration: 1, Ornaments, 2, Epigraphy, 3, The Thematic Repertoire; IV, Stylistic Developments; V, The Excellence of Metalwork. Comprehensive bibliography, pp. 351-62, and additional references in the notes.

1801   Branigan, Keith. **Aegean Metalwork of the Early and Middle Bronze Age.** Oxford, Clarendon, 1974. 216p. illus. index. ISBN 0198132131.

Scholarly history of the metalwork, bronze weapons and implements, and gold and silver jewelry in the ancient Aegean from 3000 to 1700 B.C. Contents: I, The Typological Study; II, The Metallurgical Study; II, The Historical and Cultural Study; Appendix 1, Analyses of Aegean Copper/Bronze Artefacts; Appendix 2, Catalogue Index to Hoards of the Aegean EBA and MBA; The Catalogue. The catalog lists 3,453 pieces. Bibliographical references in the footnotes.

1802   Clouzot, Henri. **Les arts du metal...** Paris, Laurens, 1934. 524p. illus. index. LC 38-29851.
Old, once-standard history of world metalwork from ancient times to the twentieth century. Includes gold and silver, bronze and brass, iron and steel including arms and armor. Unmatched today for its scope. Contents: Livre Premier: Les métaux précieux; Livre Second: Le bronze et le cuivre; Livre Troisième: Le plomb, l'étain et le zinc; Livre Quatrième: Le fer; Livre Cinquième: Les armes; Livre Sixième: La parure. Excellent comprehensive bibliography of the older literature, pp. 484-94.

1803   ———. **Le travail du metal.** Paris, Rieder, 1921. 116p. illus. LC 21-13431.
Concise survey of European metalwork of the first two decades of the twentieth century valuable for its insight into contemporary tastes of the great French jewelers like Henri Becker and René Lalique. Contents: I, Le Fer; II, Le Bronze d'éclairage; III, Le Bronze d'appartement; IV, l'étain; V, Cuivre repoussé et repercé; VI, Orfèvrerie civile; VII, Orfèvrerie religieuse; VIII, Bijouterie et joaillerie; IX, Conclusion. No bibliography.

1804   Collon-Gevaert, Suzanne. **Histoire des arts du métal en Belgique.** Brussels, Palais des Académies, 1951. 476p. illus. index. (Académie royale de Belgique, Classe des Beaux-Arts, Mémoires, t. 7). LC A52-5580.
Comprehensive, scholarly history of metalwork in Belgium from 2000 B.C. to the end of the eighteenth century. Particularly valuable for the development during the Middle Ages and especially the enameled metalwork of the Mosan Valley during the twelfth century. Contents: I, Age du bronze (2,000-900 av. J.C.); II, Age du fer (900 à 50 av. J.-C.); III, Les industries et les arts du métal pendant la période belgo-romaine (500 av.-400 ap. J.C.); IV, Orfèvrerie barbare (Ve-VIIIe siècles); V, IXe, Xe, XIe siècles. Les siècles pauves de l'orfèvrerie; VI, Le XIIe siècle ou l'âge d'or mosan: Renier de Huy, Godefroid de Huy et Nicolas de Verdun; VII, Hugo d'Oignies et l'orfèvrerie du XIIIe siècle; VIII, Le travail du ciuvre du XIVe au XVIIIe siècle; IX, L'orfèvrerie sous le régime corporatif (XIVe-XVIIIe s.); X, La feronnerie d'art; XI, L'étain; XII, Le plomb en art.. Bibliographical essay, pp. 425-445, and specialized bibliography in the footnotes.
        See also A. Riegl, *Spatrömische Kunstindustrie* (FA 944), B. Salin, *Die altgermanische Thierornamentik* (FA 965), C. R. Dodwell, *Anglo-Saxon Art...* (FA1081), H. Swarzenski, *Monuments of Romanesque Art* (FA1131), P. Lasko, *Ars Sacra: 800-1200* (FA1072).

1805   Haedeke, Hanns-Ulrich. **Metalwork.** New York, Universe, 1970. 227p. illus. index. LC 75-90382.
        Comprehensive history of copper, bronze, brass, iron, and pewter from the early Middle Ages to Art Nouveau with emphasis on the social dimension. Contents: I, Copper: 1, Mining and Processing, 2, Domestic Utensils; II, Bronze and Brass: 1, Production of Bronze and Brass, 2, The Carolingian Period to the Romanesque, 3, The Gothic Period, 4, The Renaissance, 5, Domestic Metalwork from the Gothic Period to the Nineteenth Century; III, Iron: 1, Iron-mines and Foundries, 2, Weapons and Cutlery, 3, Armour and Firearms, 4, Wrought-ironwork during the Romanesque and Gothic Periods; 5, Wrought Ironwork in the Renaissance, Baroque and Rococo Periods, 6, Cast-iron; IV, Pewter: 1, Tin-mining and the Making of Pewter; 2, Antiquity to the Gothic Period, 3, Pewter Ware in the Fifteenth and Sixteenth Centuries, 4, Pewter Ware from the Seventeenth Century to the Period of Art Nouveau. Comprehensive bibliography of books in many languages, pp. 213-18.

1806   Jenny, Wilhelm A. von. **Keltische Metallarbeiten aus heidnischer und christlicher Zeit.** Berlin, Verlag fur Kunstwissenschaft, 1935. 62p. illus. index. LC 35-2055.

Important collection of 64 plates with scholarly catalog of pieces of Celtic metalwork dating between the fifth century B.C. and A.D. 1123 written by a leading scholar of early medieval decorative arts. Brief introduction sketches the development of Celtic metalwork. General bibliography, p. 62, and additional bibliography in the notes and the catalog entries.

1807   Lüer, Hermann, and Max Creutz. **Geschichte der Metallkunst.** Stuttgart, Ferdinand Enke, 1904-1908. 2v. illus. index.

Comprehensive history of European metalwork from antiquity to the early twentieth century. Although out-of-date in many details, Lüer and Creutz remains unrivaled for its scope. Contains 845 illustrations and mention of nearly three times as many pieces in the text. Contents: Band 1: Kunstgeschichte der unedlen Metalle: Die Schmiedeeisenkunst; Die Bronzekunst; Blei-, Zinn- und Zinkkunst. Band 2: Kunstgeschichte der edlen Metalle. Within the media subdivided by time and then by place. Band 2 has appendix with thirty-page history of jewelry. Bibliographical references, usually to works mentioned, but not illustrated, in the text.

BRASS, BRONZE, AND COPPER

General Histories and Handbooks

1808   Lockner, Hermann P. **Messing: Ein Handbuch über Messinggerät des 15.—und 17. Jahrhunderts.** Munich, Klinkhardt & Biermann, 1982. 188p. illus. index. ISBN 3781402010.

Comprehensive collector's handbook/history of European brass and bronze utensils from the fifteenth through the seventeenth centuries. Contents: I, Der Werkstoff; II, Der Messingguss von Kirchen- und Hausgerät; III, Die Drehbank; IV, Das figürliche Giegefäss Aquamanile; V, Becken, Beckenschlägerschüsseln; VI, Die Kanne; VII, Der Eimer; VIII, Der Lavabokessel; IX, Der Mörser; X, Der Leuchter; XI, Das Réchaud und der Schüsselring. Information on fakes and forgeries. Bibliographical references in the footnotes.

1809   Moore, Hannah. **Old Pewter, Brass, Copper, and Sheffield Plate.** Rutland, VT, Tuttle, 1972. 224p. illus. LC 75-104206.

First published in 1905. Collector's history of western European and American pewter, brass and Sheffield plate wares. Emphasis is on England and American in the eighteenth century and on the description of types of vessels. Text has frequent extracts from documentary sources which are still useful but inadequately referenced. Appendices with list of makers with some facsimiles of marks.

1810   Schiffer, Peter, Nancy Schiffer, and Herbert Schiffer. **The Brass Book: American, English and European, Fifteenth Century through 1850.** Exton, PA, Schiffer, 1978. 447p. illus. index. ISBN 091683817X.

Illustrated collector's handbook of antique brass objects with emphasis on American pieces of the eighteenth and early nineteenth centuries. Brief introductory essay followed by large collection of plates with descriptive captions. The plates are grouped by type of object, e.g., andirons, bells, boxes, candle holders, scientific instruments, etc. Bibliography of collector's books, p. 444.

1811   Turner, Eric. **An Introduction to Brass.** Owings Mills, MD, Stemmer House Pub., 1982. 48p. illus. ISBN 088045007X.

In the series: "Victorian and Albert Museum Introductions to the Decorative Arts." Introduction to the history of European brass from the fourteenth to the twentieth centuries based on pieces in the Victoria and Albert Museum collections. Objects include: cauldrons, dishes, mortars, holy water buckets, ewers, weights, candlesticks, aquamanile, etc. Selected bibliography, p. 48.

1812 Verster, A. J. C. **Bronze: altes Gerät aus Bronze, Messing und Kupfer**. Hanover, Fackeltrager-Verlag, 1966. 71p. (text), 94 (plates). LC 67-97478.

First published in Dutch as: *Brons in den tijd* (Amsterdam, Bussy, 1956). Survey history of bronze, brass and copper bells, door knockers lavaboes, mortars, censers, chalices, etc., from the fifteenth through the seventeenth century. Directed to the collector. Selected bibliography, pp. 71-72.

1813 Wills, Geoffrey. **The Book of Copper and Brass**. London, Country Life, 1968. 96p. illus. index. ISBN 600430324.

Popular collector's handbook of English and American everyday copper and brass ware of the eighteenth and nineteenth centuries. Introduction discusses mining, smelting, manufacture and trade, and is followed by a dictionary of copper and brass objects illustrated with pieces accessible to the average collector. Brief bibliography of books in English.

Particular Periods and Countries

1814 Burgess, Fred W. **Chats on Old Copper and Brass**. ed. and rev. by C. G. E. Bunt. London, Benn, 1954. 183p. illus. index. LC 55-24142. Reprinted: East Ardsley, EP Pub. Limited, 1973. ISBN 054098305.

First published in 1914 (New York, Stokes). Old collector's handbook of British copper and brass with introductory chapters on the history of bronze from prehistoric times to the Middle Ages. Chapters dedicated to types of objects: Church Brasswork, Domestic Utensils, Candlesticks and Lamps, Bells and Bell-Metal Castings, Civic Emblems and Weights and Measures, Sundials, Clocks, and Brass Instruments. Brief discussions of Oriental bronzes and brasses and primitive, i.e., African, bronzes. No bibliography.

1815 Gentle, Rupert, and Rachel Feild. **English Domestic Brass, 1660-1810, and The History of Its Origins**. New York, Dutton, 1975. 204p. illus. index. LC 75-327278. ISBN 0525098356.

Comprehensive history/handbook of English domestic brass from the Elizabethan age to 1810 designed for the collector and antiquarian. Since large quantities of English brassware were exported to America in Colonial times, this work is an essential source for American collectors and historians of early American material culture. Contents: 1, Brass—the Two-Faced Metal; 2, The Mines and the Mines Royal; 3, The Mineral and Battery Works; 4, Fuel and Fire: Brass in the Interregnum; 5, The Makers: the Genesis of the English Brass Industry; 6, The Methods: The Machinery of Eighteenth-Century Brass-Making; 7, Birmingham and the Merchants; 8, Patterns and Pattern Books; 9, The Borrowed Lines of Brass. Appendixes with dates of events affecting the brass industry in England, list of marks and signatures found on English brass, discussion of processes and materials used in working brass, definitions of metals and alloys sympathetic with brass, e.g., paktong, latten, ormolu. Collection of plates arranged by category of object with introductory essays sketching the history of the objects. Detailed, descriptive captions to the 366 plates. Bibliography of basic books in English, p. 87.

1816 Kauffman, Henry J. **American Copper & Brass**. Camden, N.J., T. Nelson, 1968. 288p. illus. index. LC 68-13938. Reprint: New York, Bonanza Books, 1979. ISBN 0517303507.

Popular handbook for collectors—useful to the scholar also—for the large number of illustrations and frequent quotes from period documents. Contents: 1, The Metals—Copper and Brass; II, The Trades—the Coppersmith and the Brass Founder; III, Products of the Coppersmith; IV, Products of the Brass Founder; V, William Bailey—A Craftsman; VI, Documented List of Coppersmiths; VII, Documented List of Brass Founders. Bibliography, pp. 282-83, is an unclassified list of books and periodical articles.

1817   Perry, John T. **Dinanderie; a History and Description of Medieval Art Work in Copper, Brass and Bronze...** New York, Macmillan; London, Allen, 1910. 238p. illus. index. LC 11-18821.

Comprehensive history of the production of works in copper and brass during the Middle Ages with emphasis on Dinant and the neighboring towns of the Mosan Valley in Belgium. Contents: Part 1: Introductory: I, General View, II, Dinant and the Mosan Towns; III, The Origins; IV, The Materials; V, The Processes. Part 2, Historical: VI, The Schools; VII, Germany; VIII, The Netherlands; IX, France; X, England; XI, Italy and Spain. Part 3, Descriptive: XII, Preliminary; XIII, Portable Altars; XIV, Pyxes, Ciboria and Monstrances; XV, Shrines; XVI, Reliquaries; XVII, Crosses; XVIII, Censers; XIX, Candlesticks and Lightholders; XX, Crosiers; XXI, Holy Water Vats; XXII. Lecterns; XXIII, Book-covers; XXIV, Fonts; XXV, Ewers and Water Vessels; XXVI, Bronze Doors; XXVII, Sanctuary Rings or Knockers; XXVIII, Bells; XXIX, Tombs; XXX, Monuments. Selected bibliography, pp. 221-222.

1818   Pettorelli, Arturo. **Il bronze e il rame nell'arte decorative italiana.** Milan, Hoepli, 1926. 314p. illus. index. LC 44-12938.

Older survey of bronze casting in Italy from ancient Etruscan times to the end of the nineteenth century covering monumental as well as decorative pieces; most valuable for the 303 plates arranged in chronological order and comprehensive bibliography of the older literature, pp. 5-8.

1819   Schiffer, Peter, Nancy Schiffer, and Herbert Schiffer. **The Brass Book: American, English and European, Fifteenth Century through 1850.** Exton, Pa., Schiffer, 1978. 447p. illus. index. ISBN 091683817X.

Illustrated collector's handbook of antique brass objects with emphasis on American pieces of the eighteenth and early nineteenth centuries. Brief introductory essay followed by large collection of plates with descriptive captions. The plates are grouped by type of object, e.g., andirons, bells, boxes, candle holders, scientific instruments, etc. Bibliography of collector's books, p. 444.

Particular Objects

1820   Falke, Otto von, and Erich Meyer. **Romanische Leuchter und Gefässe.** Giessgefässe der Gotik. Berlin, Deutscher Verein für Kunstwissenschaft, 1935. 121p. illus. index. (Bronzegeräte des Mittelalters, I Band). Reprinted 1983. ISBN 3871570931.

Comprehensive, scholarly history of Romanesque bronze candlesticks, candelabra and other lighting fixtures, crucifix bases and Romanesque and Gothic aquamanile. Contents: I, Leuchter und Kreuzständer; A, Kirchenleuchter des 11. Jahrhunderts; B, Rankenleuchter und Kreuzfüße aus Lothringen und Sachsen; C, Altarleuchter aus Lothringen; D, Westdeutsche, meist rheinische Leuchter; E, Altarleuchter und Kreuzständer aus Fritzlar und Westfalen; F. Skandinavische Leuchter; G, Süddeutsche Leuchter; H, Drachenleuchter; I, Figürlicher Leuchter; K, Simsonleuchter. II, Gießfeäße oder Aquamanilien: A, Gießgefäße in Drachenform; B, Reiteraquamanilien, Kentauren und Statuetten; C, Gießgefäße und Reliquiare in Kopf- und Büstenform; D, Romanische Gießlöwen; E, Frühgotischen Gießlöwen; F, Hochgotische Gießlöwen des 14.

Jahrhunderts; G, Spätgotische Gießlöwen; H, Gießgefäße in verschieden Tierformen. Catalog with plates of 611 pieces. Extensive bibliography in the footnotes and the catalog entries. A pioneering work in the field of medieval bronzes and a standard work on aquamanile. Springer (1825) supplements the material on crucifix bases.

1821   Mende, Ursula. **Die Türzieher des Mittelalters**. Berlin, Deutscher Verlag fur Kunstwissenschaft, 1981. 342p. illus. index. ISBN 3871570869. (Bronzegeräte des Mittelalters, Band 2).

Comprehensive, scholarly history of medieval bronze door handles from the ninth century to the end of the fifteenth century. Contents: I, Einführung; II, Die Formen und ihre Entwicklung; III, Ikonographie; IV, Technik. Catalog with bibliographies to the 212 pieces illustrated in the plates. Comprehensive bibliography including museum and exhibition catalogs, pp. 299-323. A standard work and worthy addition to the series begun by von Falke and Meyer.

1822   Michaelis, Ronald F. **Old Domestic Base-Metal Candlesticks from the 13th to 19th Century Produced in Bronze, Brass, Paktong and Pewter**. Woodbridge, Antique Collectors' Club, 1978. 139p. illus. index. ISBN 0902028278.

Handbook of European candlesticks in brass, etc.,with emphasis on British pieces from the Middle Ages to 1820. Introductory chapters on candles and candlemakers, materials and techniques of manufacture, followed by chapters on the forms of candlesticks typical of the major periods. Appendix with tables showing the varying constituents of brass/bronze from 800 to 1840. Bibliography of books and articles, p. 139.

See also John R. Grove, *Antique Brass Candlesticks 1450-1750* (Queen Anne, Md., n.p., 1967. 140p. illus).

1823   Spear, Nathaniel, Jr. **A Treasury of Archaeological Bells**. New York, Hastings House Pub., 1978. 281p. illus. index. ISBN 0803871821.

Handbook for collectors of bells from ancient cultures around the world. Arrangement is by geographic area and then by country or civilization. Numerous illustrations have descriptive captions that include dimensions. Text summarizes archaeological finds and offers information and conjectures concerning the use to which ancient bells were put. Although not a scholarly work—there are no footnotes and the bibliography, pp. 276-77, is an alphabetical list of archaeological reports—Spear's work presents a large body of material on a little known subject.

1824   Springer, L. Elsinore. **The Collector's Book of Bells**. New York, Crown, 1972. 244p. illus. index. LC 76-168319.

Popular collector's handbook of bells. Includes bells in materials other than metal. Contents: 1, Oldest of Collectibles; 2, Oriental Bells, Gongs, and Rattles; 3, Indian, Asian, and African Bells; 4, European Favorites; 5, The Search for Americana; 6, Beast of Burden Bells; 7, The Figural Bell; 8, Bells as Toys; 9, Dual-Purpose Bells; 10, On Starting a Collection; 11, Related Regalia. Price Guide to Antique Bells. General bibliography, p. 234.

1825   Springer, Peter. **Kreuzfüsse: Ikonographie und Typologie eines hochmittelalterlichen Gerätes**. Berlin, Deutscher Verlag für Kunstwissenschaft, 1981. 255p. illus. index ISBN 3871570850. (Denlmäler deutscher Kunst: Bronzegeräte des Mittelalters, Band 3).

Comprehensive, scholarly history of medieval bronze cross bases. Contents: Einleitung; Liturgie, Ikonologie und Kreuzfuss; Formale Entwicklung und Typologie; Masstab und Bedeutung; Zusammenfassung; Katalog. Catalog contains 56 pieces dating from the eleventh through the thirteenth centuries. Entries provide detailed information concerning material, dimensions, provenance, dating, condition, and summarizes the literature—with complete bibliographies—on each piece. Bibliographical references in the notes and comprehensive bibliography of works cited, pp. 223-35.

1826 Theuerkauff-Liederwald, Anna-Elisabeth. **Mittelalterliche Bronze- und Messingefässe: Eimer, Kannen, Lavabo, Kessel.** Berlin, Deutscher Verlag für Kunstwissenschaft, 1988. 508p. illus. index. ISBN 3871570990 (Denkmäler deutscher Kunst: Bronzegeräte des Mittelalters, Band 4).

Comprehensive, scholarly history of medieval vessels of bronze and brass. Contents: Material und Technik; "Dinanderie"; Produktionszentren der "Dinanderie"; Archivalische Quellen zum Handwerk; Archivalische Quellen zur Formenbezeichnung; Eimer; Kannen; Lavabokessel. For each class of object, i.e., Eimer (buckets), Kanne (pitchers), and Lavaboes, there is a detailed catalog with plates. Included with the plates of actual pieces are illustrations of the use of such pieces in contemporary paintings and other works of art. Catalog entries have bibliographical references. Exhaustive, classified bibliography, pp. 477-490. A definitive work on medieval bronze vessels with the exception of aquamanile.

1827 Wittop Koning, Dirk A. **Bronzemörser.** Frankfurt am Main, Govi-Verlag, 1975. 66p. illus. LC 76-471639.

Pictorial survey of bronze mortars from the twelfth century to the present.

1828 Middeldorf, Ulrich. **Fifty Mortars: A Catalogue.** Florence, S.P.E.S, 1981. 195p. illus. LC 81-178747.

Important, scholarly catalog of the mortars in the Giorgio Corsi Collection. The pieces date chiefly from the fifteenth and sixteenth centuries. Ground-breaking work with basic information on size, form, material, finish, etc., that is applicable to the subject as a whole. Excellent, comprehensive bibliography.

1829 Thurm, Sigrid. **Deutscher Glockenatlas....** Munich and Berlin, Deutscher Kunstverlag, 1959-. LC A60-1332r87.

Comprehensive census of church bells from all periods in Germany. Each volume has an introduction discussing the history of the bells in the region followed by a catalogue of more than 1,000 bells arranged by place. Fully indexed by founders, coats of arms, and iconography. Extensive bibliographical references in the notes. To date the following have appeared, each as separate titles:

Württemberg und Hohenzollern, 715p. (1959)
Bayerisch-Schwaben, 611p. (1967)
Mittelfranken, 497p. (1973)

Chinese Bronze Vessels and Mirrors

Technique

1830 Barnard, Noel. **Bronze Casting and Bronze Alloys in Ancient China.** Canberra, Australian National Univ. and Monumenta Serica, 1961. 336p. illus. (Monumenta Serica. Monograph Series, 14). LC 62-6942.

Important, scholarly study of the materials and techniques of ancient Chinese bronzes. Although a chief aim of the author was to provide technical approaches to the problem of forgeries, the study is rich in important insights into the ancient methods, particularly the use of piece molds. Contents: 1, Preliminary Remarks; 2, Bronze Casting and the Literary Evidence; 3, Bronze Casting Techniques in the Light of Iron Foundry Practices; 4, Origins and Techniques of Bronze Casting; 5, Sectional Molds and the Significance of 'Sectionalism'; 6, Analyses of Bronzes; 7, Study of Patina and Corrosive Effect; 8, Concluding Remarks. Appendices include further notes on casting with piece molds and the lost wax process, with extracts from early and modern descriptions. Comprehensive, classified bibliography, pp. 308-324.

1831 Barnard, Noel, and Sato Tamotsu. **Metallurgical Remains of Ancient China**. Tokyo, Nichósha, 1975. 343p. illus. index. LC 76-372970.

Important, scholarly study of ancient Chinese metallurgy with particular reference to the relationship between bronze casting and other metallurgic techniques. The authors posit the independent development of bronze casting in China and concentration of that development in the Yangtse River Valley. Numerous detailed maps show distribution of finds and excellent drawings illustrate techniques. Contents: Origins of Bronze Casting in Ancient China: 1, Evidence Preserved in pre-Anyang Archaeological Artifacts; 2, The Present Significance of the Distribution of pre-Anyang Bronze Age Sites and Aeneolithic Sites; 3, Some Remarks on Theories of Western Origins; 4, Alloy Constituents and Ore Distribution; 5, Pottery Kilns and Bronze Casting Furnaces; 6, The Crucible—Smelting and Melting; 7, Master-patterns, Models, and Molds; 8, Iron, Foundry, and Forge; 9, Techniques and Metals. Distribution Maps. Table of Sites and Remains. Fully indexed. Bibliographical references in the footnotes.

See also v. 2: *Technical Studies* by R. J. Gettens in the museum catalog: *The Freer Chinese Bronzes*, by J. A. Pope, R. J. Gettens, James Cahill, and Noel Barnard (Washington, D.C., Smithsonian Institution, 1967-69. 2v. illus.).

Histories and Handbooks

1832 Bulling, A. **The Decoration of Mirrors of the Han Period, a Chronology**. Ascona, Artibus Asiae, 1960. 116p. LC 62-2188.

Important scholarly history of bronze mirrors of the Han dynasty. Collection of 81 plates of pieces in American museums and collections. Contents: Introduction; Western Han Period; Time of Transition and the Eastern Han Period; Conclusions. Comprehensive bibliography of the literature in Western languages and Chinese and Japanese, pp. 105-108, and additional bibliography in the footnotes.

1833 Bussagli, Mario. **Chinese Bronzes**. London, Cassell, 1969. 150p. illus. index. LC 69-473121. Reprinted: London, Cassell, 1987.

Concise survey of ancient Chinese bronzes from earliest examples to those dating from the seventh century A.D. Brief text with 70 illustrations in color. No bibliography.

1834 Deydier, Christian. **Chinese Bronzes**. New York, Rizzoli, 1980. 252p. illus. index. ISBN 0847803236.

Well-illustrated, up-to-date introduction to the history of Chinese bronzes from the Shang dynasty to the Ming dynasty. Contents: The Shang Dynasty; The Zhou Dynasty; Inscriptions; Weapons, Fibulae, Mirrors; The Han Dynasty; The Six Dynasties; The Sui Dynasty; The Tang Dynasty; The Song, Yuan and Ming Dynasties. Appendices with chart of shapes, essay on ancient bronze casting technique, advice to the collector, glossary, chronological table, map and list of museums. There are 152 pieces illustrated in the text; an additional 102 pieces are shown in small illustrations in the separate catalogue in the appendices. All of the illustrations have descriptive captions.

1835 Hentze, Carl. **Bronzegerät, Kultbauten; Religion im ältesten China der Shang Zeit**. Antwerp, De Sikkel, 1951. 273p. illus. LC A52-8146.

Important, scholarly history of Chinese bronzes during the Shang dynasty with particular emphasis on the ritual purposes. Contents: I, Einleitung; II, Die Dämonenmasken mit den Pilzhorn; III, Die Stangeaufsätze an den Chia- und Chüeh-Gefässen; IV, Der älteste chinesische Kultbau zur Shang-Zeit; V, Ornamentik einiger Kultbauten und ihre Bedeutung; VI, Die Kuang-Gefässe und die gegensätzlichen Dämonen; VII, Weitere ikonographische Einzelheiten der Bronzegefässe;

Anschliessende Ergebnisse und Auswertugen. Bibliographical references in the footnotes. Corpus of 103 plates with descriptive notes.

1836 Heusden, Willem van. **Ancient Chinese Bronzes of the Shang and Chou Dynasties**. Tokyo, private pub. 1952. 193p. illus.
    Survey of ancient Chinese ritual bronzes based on the author's collection with emphasis on the function of ancient bronzes. Information, dating, and technique are now inaccurate, but discussions of connoisseurship is still worth reading today. Contents: Chronology of Early Chinese Dynasties; The People; The Ritual; The Bronzes: Technique of Casting, Types of Objects, The Origin of the Types, Decorative Motifs, The Origin of the Motifs, Inscriptions, Patina, The Dating of Bronzes, Imitation Ancient Bronzes, The Appreciation of Chinese Bronzes. Appendix with note on bronze disease. Detailed catalog of the author's collection. General, annotated bibliography, pp. 70-73.

1837 Koop, Albert J. **Early Chinese Bronzes**. London, Benn, 1924. 84p. (text), 110 plates. index. Reprint: New York, Hacker, 1971. ISBN 0878170472.
    Older survey of ancient Chinese bronze vessels still useful for the plates that include many pieces in private collections that have since disappeared from view. Out-of-date and inaccurate in matters of technique and dating, the comments in the text on decorative styles and use of early ritual vessels are still valuable. General bibliography, pp. 77-78.

1838 Li, Hsüeh-ch'in. **The Wonder of Chinese Bronzes**. Beijing, Foreign Languages Press, 1980. 80p. illus. LC 80-129182.
    Survey of the history of ancient Chinese bronzes with a useful overview of archaeological discoveries that took place in mainland China from the 1950s to 1980. Contents: The Origin of Chinese Bronzes; Classification of Bronzes; "The Earth Cherishes No Treasure"; A Long History of Development; Testaments of Ancient History; From Pictographs to Seals and Clerical Scripts; Myth and Reality; Technique of Bronze Casting; Bronze Mirrors, Belt Hooks, Seals and Coins; The Spread of Bronze Culture from the Central Plain. Includes a map of places mentioned in the text where bronzes were unearthed. Bibliographical references in the footnotes.

1839 Ma, Cheng-yuan. **Chung-kuo tai ching: Ancient Chinese Bronzes**. New York, Oxford Univ. Press, 1986. 206p. illus. ISBN 0195837959.
    Authoritative handbook of bronzes from the Shang through the Han dynasties based in large part on the pieces from mainland China exhibited in the United States in 1980 at the Metropolitan Museum of Art, New York (*see* note at the end of this section). Contents: Part I: A General Survey of Shang and Zhou Bronzes: Bronze Casting, Bronze Tools and Weapons, Ritual Bronzes of Shang and Zhou Slave-owning Aristocrats, The Forms and Decoration of Shang and Zhou Bronzes, Bronze Objects of the Early 'Feudal Society.' Part II: Selected Examples of Ancient Chinese Bronzes: Bronze Tools, Bronze Weapons, Bronze Ritual Vessels, Musical Instruments and Other Articles, Bronze Coins. Part III: Nomenclature: Food Vessels, Wine Vessels, Water Vessels, Musical Instruments. The 85 pieces illustrated and described in Part II are all from mainland Chinese collections. Descriptions are particularly thorough in translating and interpreting inscriptions.

1840 Rupert, Milan. **Chinese Bronze Mirrors; a Study Based on the Todd Collection...** New York, Paragon Book Co., 1966. 259p. illus. LC 66-30335.
    Reprint of a "work first published in 1935" (Peiping, San Yu Press, 1935). General survey of Chinese bronze mirrors from pre-Han dynasty times to the Ching dynasty based on a collection of 1,000 examples found in the five northern provinces of Suiyuan, Shensi, Shansi, Honan, and Hopei. The catalog describes 429 mirrors; approximately a third are illustrated in the plates.

Descriptions provide translations of inscriptions on the mirrors. Contents: Uses of Mirrors; Casting and Design Technique; Metal Content of Mirrors; Patina; Shapes and Ornamentation; Inscriptions; Mythology; "Magic" Mirrors; Forgeries; Dynastic Periods. General bibliography, pp. 83-84.

1841 Swallow, Robert W. **Ancient Chinese Bronze Mirrors**. Peiping, H. Vetch, 1937. 84p. illus. Reprinted: Ann Arbor, Mich., Ars Ceramica, 1977. LC 76-28881.

Pioneering work on ancient Chinese bronze mirrors with 621 illustrations, many of pieces in the former collection of H. Lambert. Reprint has a new introduction by F. Bleicher and expanded bibliography. Contents: I, "After the Ch'in Nothing Can Be Accounted Old"; II, Mirror in Ancient Times; III, Classification According to the Dynasties; IV, Shapes, Sizes, and Variation in the Knob or Boss; V, Designs and Decorations; VI, The Story of a Mirror; VII, Characters and Inscriptions on Mirrors; VIII, Mirrors: Perfect and Otherwise; IX, The Great Ch'in Mystery; X, Mirrors of the Six Dynasties; XII, Mirrors of the T'ang Dynasty; XIII, Sung Reproductions; XIV, Some Rare and Peculiar Mirrors. Selected bibliography, pp. 59-64.

1842 Trübner, Jörg. **Yu und Kuang zur Typologie der chinesischen Bronzen**. Leipzig, Klinkhardt & Biermann, 1929. 32p. illus. index. LC 42-4233.

Important collection of 69 plates of ancient Chinese bronze Yu and Kuang vessels with an introductory essay presenting a chronology of Chou bronzes on the basis of close stylistic classification. Descriptive notes to the plates. No bibliography.

1843 Watson, William. **Ancient Chinese Bronzes**. 2d ed. Rutland, Vt., Tuttle, 1977. 117p. illus. index. LC 77-379502.

Authoritative history of Chinese bronze vessels and mirrors from the second millennium B.C. to the end of the second century A.D. Contents: I, Introduction; II, The Ritual Vessels; III, Ornament; IV, Inscriptions on Vessels; V, Mirrors. Appendix with note on bronze technique. Bibliography, pp. 104-06, has an introductory paragraph summarizing sources for more specialized literature. Notes to the text have bibliographical references. Carefully chosen collection of 104 plates with descriptive captions. Although there have been important archaeological discoveries since 1975, Watson's work is still a balanced overview.

1844 Weber, George W. **The Ornaments of Late Chou Bronzes**. New Brunswick, N.J., Rutgers Univ. Press, 1973. 631p. illus. index. LC 72-163965.

Important, scholarly study of the genesis and development of ornamental designs on Chou dynasty—sixth and fifth centuries B.C.—bronzes with special attention to the motif of interlace. Bulk of the text takes the form of highly detailed catalog entries of selected pieces. These entries feature drawings of ornamental designs keyed to their positions on the vessel. Full scholarly apparatus including general bibliography, pp. 625-31, and further bibliographical references in the notes and in the catalog entries.

1845 White, William. **Bronze Culture of Ancient China**. Toronto, Univ. of Toronto Press, 1956. 219p. illus. LC 57-4556. (Museum Studies. Royal Ontario Museum of Archaeology, no. 5).

Scholarly, archaeological catalog of a group of ritual bronze vessels and other bronzes of the Honan province dating between 1400 B.C. and 771 B.C. (Shang and Early Chou dynasties). Contents: Bronze in Ancient China; Ten Groups of Ceremonial Objects: I, The Elephant Tomb Set; II, The Halberd-Bearer Set; III, The Disk-Bearer Set; IV, The Ancestor Hsin Set; V, The Mang Shan Set; VI, The Ch'en-Ch'en Set; VII, The Prince Kung of Sung Set; VIII, The Sha-wan Set; IX, The Marquis K'ang of Wei Set; X, Various Small Units. Appendices with chronology of Shang kings, list of names of vessels, ceremonial graphs on oracle bones, essay on the date of the

Elephant Tomb, essays on relationship of bronze and Iron Age in China and archeological work in China. Bibliographical references in the footnotes.

See also the collection catalogs: *Ancient Chinese Bronzes in the Avery Brundage Collection*... by R. Y. Lefevre d'Argencé (Berkeley, Calif., Diablo Press for the De Young Museum Society, 1967. 132p. illus. LC 68-2529), *Chinese Bronzes from the Collection of Chester Dale and Dolly Dale* by E. von Erdberg Consten (Ascona, Artibus Asiae, 1978. 250p. illus. Artibus Asiae: Supplementum, 35. LC 79-321709), and the exhibition catalogs: *Ritual Vessels of Bronze Age China*, by M. F. J. Loehr (New York, Asia Society; New York Graphics Society, 1968. 183p. illus.), *Treasures from the Bronze Age of China* (New York, Metropolitan Museum of Art; Ballatine Books, 1980. 192p. illus. LC 80-11099), *Chinese Bronzes: Art and Ritual*, by J. Brown (London, British Museum, 1987. 120p. illus. ISBN 0714114391), *Ancient Indonesian Bronzes*, by P. C. M. Lunsingh Scheurleer (Leiden, N.Y., Brill, 1988. 179p. illus. ISBN 9004088202).

GOLD AND SILVER [*See also* Chapter Twelve—Jewelry]

Technique

1846   Staton-Bevan, William N. **The Goldsmith's and Silversmith's Handbook**. 2d ed. London, Technical Press, 1968. 109p. illus. index. ISBN 0291394043.

Practical handbook on the techniques of working in silver, gold, platinum, palladium and rodium. Chapter on assaying silver and gold.

1847   Brepohl, Erhard. **Theorie und Praxis des Goldschmieds**. 5th ed. Leipzig, Fachbuchverlag, 1978. 451p. illus. LC 80-463100.

Comprehensive handbook of the materials and techniques of gold and silversmiths' work. Contents: 1, Werkstoffe; 2, Arbeitstechniken; 3, Herstellung einzelner Teile von Schmuckstücken. Bibliography, p. 500.

1848   Goodden, Robert Y., and Philip Popham. **Silversmithing**. London and New York, Oxford Univ. Press, 1971. 128p. illus. LC 72-175094.

Handbook of techniques used by silversmiths and goldsmiths. Since handcraft procedures are featured and illustrated, this handbook is valuable for understanding traditional techniques. Contents; 1, Design; 2, The Materials; 3, Shaping Processes; 4, Soldering; 5, Construction and Strengthening; 6, Boxmaking; 7, Investment Casting; 8, Finishing; 9, Embellishment. Brief bibliography, p.123.

1849   Grimwade, Mark. **Introduction to Precious Metals**. London, Newnes Technical Books, 1985. 131p. illus. index. ISBN 0408014512.

Handbook of the properties of silver, gold, and platinum and the techniques used to work them. Directed to the jeweler, collector, and craftsman as well as to the student of metallurgy. Contents: 1, Introduction; 2, Occurrence, Extraction and Refining; 3, Physical Properties of the Precious Metals; 5, Chemical Properties of the Precious Metals; 6, Silver and its Alloys; 7, Alloys of Gold: the Carat Golds; 8, The Platinum-Group of Metals and Their Alloys; 9, Melting, Alloying and Casting; 10, Working and Annealing Practice; 11, Joining Techniques; 12, Assays and Hallmarking; 13, Coatings and Surface Decoration; 14, Electroplating and Allied Processes; 15, Other Uses of Precious Metals. General bibliography, pp. 127-28.

1850   Rosenberg, Marc. **Geschichte der Goldschmidekunst auf technischer Grundlage**. Frankfurt am Main, Baer, 1908-25. 7v. illus. index. Reprint: Osnabruck, Ohms, 1972. ISBN 3535012554.

Comprehensive history of Western gold and silversmiths' art with emphasis on technique and on the development to 1000. Volume one is an introduction treating material and general procedures and processes, volume two covers the technique of granulation, volumes three through five cover enamel, volumes six and seven cover niello. Illustrated with museum pieces. Bibliographical references in the footnotes. A standard work on the techniques of the goldsmith.

General Dictionaries of Marks [*See also* individual countries for national dictionaries]

1851 Beuque, Émile. **Dictionnaire des poinçons officels français et étrangers, anciens et modernes.** Paris, C. Courtois, 1925- 28. 2v. illus. index. Reprint: Paris, de Nobele, 1988. ISBN 2851890166.

Comprehensive dictionary of gold and silver marks arranged in two parts: marks in the form of figurines and objects, and marks consisting of letters or numbers. Marks are given in facsimiles.

1852 Ris-Paquot, Oscar E. **Dictionnaire des poinçons, symboles, signes figuratifs, marques et monogrammes des orfèvers français et etrangers, fermiers généraux, maitres des monnaies, controleurs, vérificateurs, etc.** Paris, Laurens, 1890. 382p. illus. Reprint: New York, Garland, 1978. LC 78-50278.

Comprehensive dictionary of marks found on gold and silver including jewelry marks. Emphasis is on France with special sections devoted to the goldsmiths and jewelers of France, and specifically of Paris. Although a century old, Ris-Paquot's dictionary is still a valuable reference work for the history of French precious metalwork.

1853 Rosenberg, Marc. **Der Goldschmide Merkzeichen.** 3rd ed. Frankfurt am Main, Frankfurter Verlags- Anstalt, 1922- 28. 4v. illus. index. LC 30-15709. Reprinted 1955.

Comprehensive dictionary of gold and silversmiths' marks with particular emphasis on the German-speaking countries. Arranged by city and then by artist. Contents: Band 1-3: Deutschland; Band 4: Ausland und Byzanz. Entries give the dates of the artist, list of examples of his work—often with dimensions—, bibliographical references, and a facsimilies of his mark(s). First published in 1890, Rosenberg's dictionary remains the standard and indispensable reference. Superseded by many later specialized dictionaries—German dictionaries of silversmiths' marks have been devoted to regions since Rosenberg—it remains the sole reliable guide for many areas such as Byzantine marks.

1854 Tardy (firm). **Les poinçons de garantie internationaux pour l'argent.** 13th ed. Paris, Tardy, n.d (1980). 545p. illus. index.

Pocket-sized comprehensive dictionary of silversmiths' marks arranged by country then by city. English table of contents, pp. 484-486, general, classified bibliography, pp. 389-404.

1855 ———. **Les poinçons de garantie internationaux pour l'or.** 6th ed. Paris, Tardy, 1967. 326p. illus. index. LC 68-86688.

Pocket-sized, comprehensive dictionary of gold hallmarks arranged by country. Identification of individual figurative marks is facilitated by the subject index.

General Histories and Handbooks

1856   Blair, Claude, ed. **The History of Silver**. New York, Ballantine Books, 1987. 256p. illus. index. ISBN 0345345762.

General history of silver and gold art in Europe and America from antiquity to the present. Well-illustrated with museum pieces with descriptive captions. Contents: 1, The Ancient World by K. Painter; 2, The Migration Period and the Middle Ages by r. Lightbown; 3, The Renaissance and Mannerism by T. Schroder; 4, Baroque Silver, 1610-1725 by A. S. Cocks; 5, The Rococo by E. Barr; 6, Neoclassicism by E. Barr; 7, The Nineteenth and Early Twentieth Centuries by S. Bury; 8, Art Deco and After: 1920-60 by P. Garner; 9, Contemporary Silver by G. Hughes. Appendix I: The Craft of the Silversmith by C. Blair; Appendix 2: The Metals, Hallmarking and Methods of Assay by J. Forbes. Comprehensive, classified bibliography of books and periodical articles in all languages, pp. 243-45.

1857   Blakemore, Kenneth. **The Book of Gold**. New York, Stein and Day, 1971. 224p. illus. index. LC 73-16034.

Well-illustrated, worldwide survey of the place of gold in society and the fabrication of objects made of gold from earliest times to the present. Part one is a chronological survey; part two has chapters on the golden regalia of Europe, gold coins and refining gold and its hallmarks. Basic bibliography, p. 219.

See also Sutherland, Carol H. *Gold: Its Beauty, Power and Allure* (New York, McGraw-Hill, 1959. 196p. illus. index. LC 66-16097).

1858   Brett, Vanessa. **The Sotheby's Directory of Silver, 1600-1940**. London, Philip Wilson for Sotheby's Publications, 1986. 432p. illus. index. ISBN 0856671932.

Comprehensive collector's handbook of European and American silver dating from 1600 to 1940, based on the catalogs of silver sales at Sotheby's between the 1920s and the spring of 1984. Introductory essays discusses the silver trade, styles of silver, and tips on collecting. The directory features 2,000 pieces of silver sold at Sotheby's, arranged by country and then by silversmith in roughly chronological order. Captions give the date of the pieces, their weights and sizes, and lists the sale dates and prices paid. Basic biographical data is supplied for each silversmith with bibliographical references (chiefly for marks). Appendix with family trees of Augsburg goldsmiths, currency conversion table for pounds into dollars from 1925 to 1984, and annual average prices for silver pieces in London per troy ounce for the same period.

1859   Brunner, Herbert. **Old Table Silver: A Handbook for Collectors and Amateurs**. New York, Taplinger, 1967. 223p. illus. index. LC 67-16593.

Translation of *Altes Tafelsilber* (Munich, Bruckmann, 1964). Concise but authoritative history of European domestic hollowware and other large or highly decorated pieces of silver for use at table from the late Middle Ages to the early nineteenth century. Valuable for the information on the relationship between forms and functions. Contents: Silver and Table Silver; The User; Production; Marks and Guild Regulations; Short History of Forms: Hollow Forms, Standing Vessels, Flat Forms, Knives, Forks and Spoons, Candlesticks for the Table, Table and Travelling Services; Short History of Ornament; Form and Decoration, A Chronological Survey; European Workshops. Concise repertory of principal city hallmarks. Plates arranged to form a typological survey. Bibliography, pp. 160-63, with separate, comprehensive list of museum and exhibition catalogs.

1860   Dombi, Istvan et al. **Bruckmann's Silber-Lexikon**. Munich, Bruckmann, 1982. 340p. illus. ISBN 3765417556.

Comprehensive, well-illustrated dictionary on all aspects of silver, particular continental European silver, from ancient times to the present. Brief entries cover places, styles, persons, decoration, techniques, and types of silver objects. Comprehensive bibliography, pp. 334-39, with separate sections on dictionaries of marks, exhibition and museum catalogs.

1861   Houart, Victor. **L'Argenterie miniature**. Fribourg, Office du Livre, 1981. 236p. illus. index. LC 81-148055.
    Comprehensive, well-illustrated history of silver miniatures made in Europe and America during the seventeenth and eighteenth centuries. Contents: Les figurines des nefs d'argent; Le jouets d'argent des princes de France; L'argenterie miniature en France, en Allemagne, en Russie, aux Etats-Unis et ailleurs; Les Pays-Bas; Le Grande-Bretagne. General bibliography, p. 230. Descriptive captions to the 175 plates. Facsimiles of marks at the ends of each section.

1862   Honour, Hugh. **Goldsmiths and Silversmiths**. New York, Putnam, 1971. 320p. illus. index. LC 77-14221.
    Survey history of European gold and silversmiths from the Carolingian period to the early twentieth century. Richly illustrated with signed or attributed works and designs by the smiths.

1863   Jones, Edward A. **Old Silver of Europe & America from Early Times to the Nineteenth Century...** Philadelphia, Lippincott, 1928. 376p. illus. index. LC 29-1922.
    An old, comprehensive survey of silver in Europe and America from the sixteenth century to the early nineteenth century. Illustrated with 96 plates. Arrangement is alphabetical by country. For several countries, e.g., Austria, Baltic States, Belgium, Czechoslovakia, Hungary, Norway, Poland, Portugal, Spain, Sweden, and Switzerland, these chapters remain the only introductions in English. Bibliographical references in footnotes.

1864   Link, Eva M. **The Book of Silver**. New York, Praeger, 1973. 301p. illus. index. LC 75-107153.
    Comprehensive history of silver from antiquity to the present, with emphasis on the appreciation of the artistic merits of major pieces and the development of style. Useful features: outlines of types of table plate, list of principal cities with their marks, glossary of terms, and a good chapter on techniques and the history of silversmiths' guilds and hallmarks. Bibliography, pp. 291-96, is a thorough but unclassified list of books in many languages.

1865   Steingräber, Erich. **Der Goldschmied. Vom alten Handwerk der Gold- und Silberarbeiter**. Munich, Prestel, 1966. 96p. illus. (Bibliothek des Germanischen Nationalmuseums Nürnberg, Band 27). LC 75-553006.
    Introduction to the history of European gold and silversmiths from the Middle Ages to the eighteenth century written by a leading expert. Excellent selection of plates illustrating tools and techniques. Contents: Prolog; Vom Aufsteig des alten Hand-Werks; Der heilige Eligius und seine Jünger in der bildenden Kunst; Von der Wiege bis zum Grabe; Uomini illustri; Der Goldschmied am Werk. Comprehensive bibliography, pp. 82-83.

1866   Taylor, Gerald. **Art in Silver and Gold**. New York and London, Dutton, 1964. 160p. illus. LC 64-4439.
    Popular survey of the art of the gold and silversmith from the ancient Near East to 1950 illustrated with 150 black-and-white plates of major museum pieces. No bibliography.

Ancient Gold and Silver [*See also* Chapter Twelve—Ancient Jewelry]

1867   Baratte, F. **Römisches Silbergeschirr in den gallischen und germanischen Provinzen**. Aalen, Gessellschatt für Vor—und Frühgeschichte in Würtlemberg und Hohenzollern. 1984. 100p. illus.

Scholarly study of Roman silver from the provinces of Gaul and Germania dating from the second through the fourth centuries A.D. Contents: Geschichte der Funde; Der Schatz von Trier; Der Schatz von Wettingen; Versteckfunde in Notzeiten; Silbergeschirr—Zeugnisse der Geschichte; Tempelschätze; Silberschätze von Berthouville und von Notre-Dame d'Allençon; Kirchenschätze; Tischgeschirr; Techniken und Künstler; Eine Sonderform: die Kragenschüssel; Gallo-römische Werkstätten: Geschirr in Niellotechnik; Silbergeschir des 1. Jahrhunderts n. Chr.; Formen des 2. und 3. Jahrhunderts n. Chr.; Niellotechnik—Relieftechnik; Silberarbeiten in Gallien im 4. Jahrhundert n. Chr.; Die Funde; Silberschatz von Kaiseraugst; Mode des 4. Jahrhunderts n. Chr. in Form und Ornament; Silberschmiede und Werkstätten; Kaiserliche Werkstätten—Verbreitungen der Silbergefässe; Kunden bestimmen den Geschmack. Detailed English summary. Catalog to the plates with references to the specialized literature. General bibliography, p. 95. Since the literature on ancient Roman silver is widely scattered in archaeological periodicals, this survey by a major expert is a valuable introduction and overview.

1868   Carducci, Carlo. **Gold and Silver Treasures of Ancient Italy**. Greenwich, Conn., New York Graphics Society, 1964. 85p. illus. LC 63-22472.

Pictorial survey of ancient Etruscan and Roman gold and silver based on pieces exhibited in Turin in 1961. Good plates with descriptive notes. Basic bibliography, pp. xxx-xxxiii.

1869   Coarelli, Filippo. **L'oreficeria nell'arte classica**. Milan, Fabbri, 1967. 158p. illus. index. LC 68-110814. Reprint: London, Cassell, 1988. ISBN 0304321745.

Popular, pictorial survey of gold and silver in the ancient world from the Greek Geometric period through late Roman times. List of basic books, p. 155.

1870   Cristofani, Mauro, and Marina Martelli, eds. **L'Oro degli Etruschi**. Novara, Agostino, 1983. 343p. illus. index. LC 87-173525.

Richly illustrated history of ancient Etruscan gold. Introductory essays sketch the history of Etruscan goldsmiths' work in four periods: L'età dell ferro; l'orientalizzante; l'arcaismo; l'età classica ed ellenistica. A catalog of objects follows arranged by archaeological site. Bibliographies conclude each catalog entry. General bibliography, pp. 334-40, and further bibliography in the notes to the text.

1871   Duval, Noël, and François Baratte. **Argenterie romaine et byzantine**. Paris, De Boccard, 1988. 237p. illus. index. ISBN 2701800382.

Collected essays on various aspects of ancient Roman and Byzantine silver based on a symposium held in Paris in 1983. Contents: The Gilding of Roman Silver by W. A. Oddy; The Gilding of Roman on Late Roman Silver by J. Lang; Etudes analytiques d'objets en argent romains, Bilan et perspectives (à propos du trésor de Boscoréale) by T. Berthoud, L. Hurtel and M. Menu; The Silver from the Thetford Treasure by C. Johns; Anse en argent, du 1ers. de notre ère découverte sur l'oppidum d'Ambrussum by M. Feugere; Le trésor d'argenterie gallo-romain de Thil dit "trésor de Caubiac" by M. Feugere and M. Martin; Remarques préliminaires à l'établissement d'un inventaire de la vaisselle d'argent gallo-romain, origine et datation by F. Baratte; Roman Silver Hoards: Ownership and Status by K. S. Painter; Les largesses impériales et l'émission d'argenterie du IVe au VIe siècle by R. Delmaire; L'argent des Vandales: plats et monnaies by C. Morrisson, C. Brenot and J. Barrandon; Spätantike und frühbyzantinische Silbergegenstände im mittleren Donaugebiete, innerhalb und ausserhalb der Grenze des

Römerreiches by E. S. Thomas; Sasanian Silver: Internal Developments and Foreign Influences by P. O. Harper; The Origins of the Syrian Ecclesiastical Silver Treasures of the Sixth-Seventrh Centuries by M. Mundell Mango; A propos du curateur Mégas by D. Feissel; Zwei silberne Tetrachenportraits im Römisch-Germanischen Zentralmuseum Mainz by E. Künzl; A Bishop's Gift: Openwork Lamp from the Sion Treasure by S. Boyd; Zum Gewicht des römischen Pfundes by M. Martin; La toreutique byzantine du VIe siècle by V. N. Zalesskaja. Bibliographies at the end of each essay.

1872   Harper, Prudence I. **Silver Vessels of the Sasanian Period.** Volume One: *Royal Imagery.* New York, Metropolitan Museum of Art, 1981. 256p. illus. index. ISBN 0870992481.

First volume is a comprehensive, scholarly handbook of silver in Iran during the reign of the Sasanian dynasty (226-651 A.D.) Contents: Part One: Catalogue and Interpretation by P. O. Harper. I, Historical Outline; II, Medallion Bowls with Human Busts; III, Vessels with Hunting Scenes; IV, Thrones and Enthronement Scenes; V, Interpretation and Conclusions. Part Two: Technical Study by P. Meyers. Appendixes with tabulation of iconographic details according to style; data on inscriptions and provenance, discussion of a hunting plate in the Guennol Collection and the Touroucheva Plate with Shapur II hunting lions. Full scholarly apparatus including an exhaustive bibliography, pp. 242-250.

1873   Overbeck, Bernhard. **Argentum Romanum; ein Schatzfund von spätrömischen Prunkgeschirr.** Munich, K. Thiemig, 1973. 64p. illus. ISBN 3521040453.

Authoritative introduction to the nine silver bowls buried circa A.D. 324 in an unknown East Roman site and today in Munich. Contents: Die historischen Grundlagen; Das Inventar des Schatzfundes; Die Datierung; Die Werkstätten; Die Beamten; Die Gewichte; Der offizielle Charakter der mit kaiserlichen Inschriften oder dem kaiserlichen Bilde versehenen Schalen. Selected bibliography, p. 64, and references to specialized literature in the notes.

1874   Strong, Donald E. **Greek and Roman Gold and Silver Plate.** 2d ed. Ithaca, N.Y., Cornell University Press; London, Methuen, 1979 235p. illus. index. ISBN 0416725104.

Comprehensive, scholarly handbook on ancient Greek and Roman gold and silverwork. Covers techniques, functions, and stylistic development from the Bronze Age to the fifth century A.D. with frequent reference to documentary sources. Contents: 1, General Background; 2, Bronze Age; 3, Archaic Greece and Etruria; 4. Classical Greece, 480-330 B.C.; 5, The Hellenistic Age: Early Hellenistic, 330-200 B.C.; 6, The Hellenistic Age: Late Hellenistic, after 200 B.C.; 7, The Roman Empire; 8, The Roman Empire: 1st Century A.D.; 9, The Roman Empire: 2d and 3d Centuries; 10, The Roman Empire: 4th and 5th Centuries A.D.. Appendixes: I, The Treasure of Trier; II, List of Decorated Drinking-cups of the Hellenistic-Roman Class; III, Analyses of Ancient Silver Plate; IV, The Finds from Dherveni. Bibliographical footnotes. A standard work on ancient silver.

See also exhibition catalog: *Silver of the Gods: 800 Years of Greek and Roman Silver* (Toledo, Ohio, Toledo Museum of Art, 1977).

Boscoreale Treasure

1875   Baratte, Francois. **La Trésor d'orféverie romaine de Boscoreale.** Prais, Ministèrè de la Culture, 1985. 96p. illus. ISBN 2711820483.

Sumptuously illustrated and authoritative introduction to the Roman treasure of 109 pieces of silver discovered in the ruins of a villa in Boscoreale in 1895 and now in the Louvre. Contents: Le domaine de Boscoreale; Le Trésor et son possesseur; Vaisselle d'argent et service de la table; Les techniques décoratives; Les objets de toilette, La vaisselle de table et son décor; Argenterie et politique; Orfèvres et ateliers; Catalogue sommaire du Trésor. Bibliography, p. 95.

Gundestrup Cauldron

1876   Pittioni, Richard. **Wer hat wann und wo den Silberkessel von Gundestrup angefertigt?** Vienna, Verlag der Österreichischen Akademie der Wissenschaft, 1984. 51p. illus. ISBN 37001-06696. (Österreichische Akademie der Wissenschaften, Phliosophisch-Historische Klasse, Bd. 178).

Authoritative introduction to the famous Bronze Age—"Celtic"?—silver cauldron in Copenhagen. Bibliographical references in the footnotes.

Kaiseraugst Treasure

1877   Cahn, Herbert A., and Annemarie Kaufmann-Heinimann, eds. **Der spätrömische Silberschatz von Kaiseraugst.** Derendingen, Habegger Verlag, 1984. 2v. illus. index. ISBN 3857-231479.

Scholary essays on and catalog of the fourth century A.D. treasure of Roman silver discovered in 1962 in Kaiseraugst. First volume text, second plates. Contents of Band I: Fundgeschichte und Restaurierung by J. Ewald; Die Zeitumstände: 337-357 n. Chr. by H. A. Cahn; Katalog by M. Martin et al; Herstellungstechnik by E. Foltz et al.; Stempel, Gewichtsangaben un Inscriften by M. Martin; Römisches Tafelsilber: Form- und Funktionsfragen by S. Martin-Kilcher; Vermutungen über Funktion und Besitzer des Silberschatzes by H. Wrede and H. A. Cahn; Der Silberschatz und seine Stellung in der spätantiken Kulturgeschichte by K. Scheffold. Comprehensive bibliography, pp. 15-19, and bibliographical references in the notes. The standard work on the Kaiseraugst treasure and a paradigm among monographs on ancient silver treasures.

See also Laur-Belart, R. *Der spätrömische Silberschatz von Kaiseraugst* (Aargau). Basel, 1967, and Instinsky, H. U., *Der spätrömischen Silberschatzfund von Kaiseraugst.* (Wiesbaden, 1971. (Abhandlungen Akad. Wissenschaft. Lit Geistes-und sozialwiss. Kl. 5).

Mildenhall Treasure

1878   Brailsford, J. W. **The Mildenhall Treasure.** London, Trustees of the British Museum, 1955. 23p. illus.

Provisional catalog of the late-Roman silver found at Mildenhall and acquired by the British Museum in 1946. Contents: Introduction; Inventory; Technical; Date and Origin. Brief bibliography, p. 24.

Oxus Treasure

1879   Dalton, O. M. **The Treasure of the Oxus: With Other Examples of Early Oriental Metal-work.** 3rd ed. London, Trustees of the British Museum, 1964. 75p. illus. LC 75-16513.

First published in 1905. Scholarly catalog with a comprehensive introduction of the hoard of Sassanian gold and silver found along the Oxus River in the Hindu Kush in 1877 and now in the British Museum. Catalog entries of the 211 objects have bibliographical references. Literature that appears between 1905 and 1960 is listed at the end of the preface to the third edition by R. D. Barnett.

Medieval and Byzantine Gold and Silver
[*See also* Chapter Twelve, Medieval Jewelry]

1880   Belli Barsali, Isa. **Medieval Goldsmiths' Work.** London and New York, Hamlyn, 1969. 157p. illus. LC 77-481903.

Popular survey of medieval gold and silverwork, enamels, and jewelry from the fourth through the fifteenth centuries. Illustrated with museum pieces with descriptive captions. No bibliography.

1881   Busch, Harald, and Bernard Lohse, eds. **Wunderwelt der Schreine: Meisterwerke mittelalterlicher Goldschmiedekunst**. Frankfurt/Main, Umschau, 1959. 19p. (text), 80p. (plates).

Pictorial survey of medieval gold and silver reliquary shrines from the twelfth to the sixteenth centuries. Notes to the plates with bibliographical references.

1882   Dodd, Erica C. **Byzantine Silver Stamps**. With an Excursus on the Comes Sacrarum Largitionum by J. C. Kent. Washington, D.C., Dumbarton Oaks Research Library Collection, 1961. 283p. illus. index. (Dumbarton Oaks Studies, 7). LC 61-16953.

Comprehensive, scholarly study of stamps on Byzantine silver. Contents: Part I: Classification and Analysis of the Stamps; Part II: The Question of Provenance and Controls; Part III: Catalogue of Stamped Objects. List of Stamped Objects and Illustrations. Thorough index. Bibliographical references in footnotes. General bibliography in the list of abbreviations, pp. 279-80.

The author published a supplement: "Supplement I: New Stamps from the Reigns of Justin II and Constans II" in *Dumbarton Oaks Papers*, no. 18 (1964), pp. 237-48.

1883   Ebersolt, Jean. **Les arts somptuaires de Byzance; etude sur l'art imperiale de Constantinople**. Paris, Leroux, 1923. 164p. illus. index. LC 24-24005.

Scholarly history of Byzantine sumptuary arts from the fourth through the fifteenth centuries. Emphasis is on gold and silver work and enamels, other sumptuary arts like silk textiles, ivory carving, and manuscript illumination are also included. Concentrates on the products of the imperial workshops in Constantinople. Chapters on the classical tradition and Oriental influences. Bibliographical references in the footnotes.

1884   Elbern, Victor H. **Die Goldschmiedekunst im frühen Mittelalter**. Darmstadt, Wissenschaftliche Buchgesellschaft, 1988. 155p. illus. index. ISBN 3534031423.

Comprehensive, authoritative survey of gold and silverwork in Europe during the early Middle Ages, the distillation of a lifetime of study particularly in the relationship between precious metal art and the liturgy. Contents: I, Einführung und allgemeine Fragen; 2, Von der merowingischen zur karolingischen Goldschmiedekunst; 3, Im Lichte der karolingischen "Renovatio"; 4, Rom-Mailand-Aachen: Der Goldaltar von Sant' Ambrogio; 5, Liturgische Kunst in edlen Metallen und die Zeit Karls des Kahlen; 6, Vom Sinn des Golds in der Kunst des frühen Mittelalters. Excellent, comprehensive, classified bibliography, pp. 125-40.

1885   Fritz, Johann M. **Goldschmiedekunst der Gotik in Mitteleuropa**. Munich, Beck, 1982. 377p. illus. index. ISBN 3406090907.

Comprehensive, scholarly study of the work of gold and silversmiths during the thirteenth through the early sixteenth centuries in the territory of the former Holy Roman Empire. Contents: Einleitung: Funktion und Bedeutung von Goldschmiedewerken in der mittelalterlichen Welt; Verlorenes und Erhaltenes; Von den Goldschmieden und ihrem Handwerk; "Swas die goltscmid machent"; Das Zurschaustellen gotischer Goldschmiedewerke—zugleich ein Beitrag zu ihrer Verwendung; Vom geistlichen und weltlichen Sinn eines Schatzes; Möglichkeiten und Probleme einer kunsthistorischen Einordnung; Versuch eines kunstgeschichtlichen Überblicks. Corpus of 975 plates with detailed notes including bibliographies. Comprehensive, classified bibliography, pp. 346-55, with section on exhibition catalogs.

1886   Grimme, Ernst G. **Goldschmiede im Mittelalter: Form und Bedeutung des Reliquiars von 800 bis 1500.** Cologne, DuMont Schauberg, 1972. 190p. illus. index. LC 72-363845.

Authoritative introduction to the gold and silverwork of the Middle Ages from the ninth century to the early sixteenth century. Text concentrates on famous reliquaries and has a lengthy appendix with extracts from contemporary documents relating to relics and reliquaries. Contents: 1, Auf den Pilgerstraßen Europas; 2, Reliquiare als Ausdruck des Imperium Christianum in der Zeit der karolingischen Herrscher; 3, 'Redende' Reliquiare im Zeitalter der ottonischen Herrscher—Die Trierer Egbertwerkstatt; 4, 'In hoc signo'—Kreuzreliquiare des Ostens und des Westens; 5, Beim Zeugnis der Reliquien... Reliquiar und Herrschaftszeichen; 6,Abbild der Himmelsstadt—Schreine und Architekturreliquiare; 7, 'Kunstwer' und Selbstbespiegelung—Reliquiare des späten Mittelalters; Text Dokumente. Bibliographical references in the notes.

See also the author's *Abglaz des Ewigen: mittelalterliche Goldschmiedekunst* (Munich, Thiemig, 1980. 68p. illus. ISBN 3521041093).

1887   Lightbown, R. W. **Secular Goldsmiths' Work in Medieval France: A History.** London, Society of Antiquaries of London, 1978. 136p. ilus. index. ISBN 0500990271 (Reports of the Research Committee of the Society of Antiquaries of London, no. 36).

Comprehensive, scholarly history of secular gold and silverwork made in France during the Middle Ages (13th-15th centuries) with a corpus of plates illustrating all known examples. Contents: I, Early Records of Secular Goldsmiths' Work in France. The Organization of the Craft; II, The Principal Sources of Information for Medieval Secular Plate. Types of Plate, I; III, Types of Plate, II; IV, The Social Distribution and Social Functions of Plate; V, Design and Style; VI, Mounted Vessels of Crystal, Hardstones, Glass, Shells, Nuts, and Ostrich Eggs. Their Presence in Collections. The Taste of Jean, Duc de Berry; VII, Techniques of Decoration, I. Precious Stones. Cloisonné, Champlevé and Basse-taille Enamelling. Plique àjour Enamel. Email en ronde bosse; VIII, The Motifs of Enamelled Decoration on Plate; IX, Techniques of Decoration and the Motifs Used in Them, II. Niello, Engraving, Pouncing, Figurated Decoration and Ornament. The Royal Gold Cup; X, Goldsmiths in Relation to Specialist Craftsmen and Designers. The Goldsmiths of Paris and the Royal Courts. The Goldsmiths of Avignon and the Provinces; XI, The Fifteenth Century. The Plate of the Last Years of King Charles VI. The Introduction of the Date-letter and Other Supervisory Regulations. Gold Plate. Types of Plate—Simplicity of Design. Types of Decoration. Painted Enamel. Mounted Vessels. King René of Anjou. Late Fifteenth-Century Royal Patronage. Select bibliography, pp.128-29, and references to the specialized literature in the notes.

1888   Lipinsky, Angelo. **Oro, argento, gemme e smalti; technologia delle arti dalle origini alla fine del medioevo, 3000 a.C.-1500 d.C.** Florence, Olschki, 1975. 516p. illus. (Arte e archeologia, 8). LC 76-508152.

Comprehensive history of gold and silversmiths' work from ancient Egypt to the end of the Middle Ages. Includes enamel and gems. Emphasis is on the technique of the goldsmith. Contents: I,L'uomo ed i metalli preziosi nelle religioni, nella vita sociale, nell'economia; II, I giacimenti auriferi ed argentifieri nel mondo antico e medievalee, Italia compresa; III, I metodi dell'estrazione e dell'affinamento; IV-V, Le diverse technologie della lavorazione artistica; VI, le gemme note nell'antichità, nelle religioni e folklore; loro provenienza e lavorazione; VII, Gli smalti, inventari nell'ambiente mediterraneo e la loro differenziata evoluzione. Bibliographies at the end of each section.

1889   Lüdke, Dietmar. **Die Statuetten der gotischen Goldschmiede: Studien zu den "autonomen" und vollrunden Bildwerken der Goldschmiedeplastik und den Statuettenreliquiaren in Europa zwischen 1230 und 1530.** Munich, Tuduv-Verlagsgesellschaft, 1983. 2v. illus. ISBN 3880731284.

Scholarly history of full-round gold and silver statuette-reliquaries in western Europe from 1230 to 1530. The author seeks to show a continuum between the earliest medieval reliquary statues like the Essen Madonna (10th century) and the late medieval type, and to describe the morphology of the later type. Contents: I, Die Typen der gotischen Goldschmiedestatuetten, ihre Enstehung und ihre Voraussetzungen; II, Die Goldschmiedestatuetten zwischen 1230 und 1530; III, Künstlerischer Entsehungsproceß und stilistische Erscheinung der gotischen Goldschmiedestatuetten; Zweiter Teil: Katalog. The catalog contains 364 examples. Full scholarly apparatus including comprehensive, classified bibliography, pp. 228-92, specialized literature in the catalog entries and notes.

1890   Scheffler, Wolfgang. **Gemalte Goldschmiedearbeiten: kostbaren Gefässe auf den Dreikönigsbildern in den Niederlanden und in Deutschland, 1440-1530: ein typologischer Beitrag zur Goldschmiedekunst.** Berlin, W. de Gruyter, 1985. 293p. illus. index. ISBN 3110101165.

Important study of the representations of goldsmiths' work in German and Netherlandish paintings of the Adoration of the Magi dating between 1440 and 1530. The representations of 40 paintings are described and analyzed in detail and compared with existing pieces of goldsmiths' work. General bibliography, pp. xi-xiii.

1891   Steenbock, Frauke. **Der Kirchliche Prachteinband im frühen Mittelalter. von den Anfängen bis zum Beginn der Gotik.** Berlin, Deutscher Verlag für Kunstwissenschaft, 1965. 237p. (text), 176p. (plates). LC 70-209568.

Comprehensive, scholarly study of luxury ecclesiastical book covers decorated with ivories, precious metals and gems in western Europe from the fifth century to the first half of the thirteenth century. Important exploration of the typology of book covers and the relationship between the decoration on covers and the liturgical function of the books. Detailed catalog of 127 examples with full bibliographies. Contents: Das fünfteilige Diptychon; Das Diptychon; Der Kreuztypus; Bild-oder Rahmentypus; Buch und Liturgie; Symbol und Darstellung; Darstellung und Liturgie; Tradition und Eigenständigkeit; Einbandschmuck und Manuskript; Antike Steinschneidearbeiten und Antikenimitationen. Comprehensive bibliography, pp. 233-237.

See also the museum catalog: *Anglo-Saxon Ornamental Metalwork 700-1100 in the British Museum*, by D. M. Wilson (London, British Museum, 1964. 248p. illus. index) and the exhibition catalog: *L'Or des Vikings, exposition du Musée des Antiquités National de Suède, Bordeaux, Musée d'Acquitaine, 196* (Bordeaux, Musée d'Aquitaine, 1969. 308p. illus.).

Pre-Columbian Gold and Silver

1892   Mujica, Gallo M. **The Gold of Peru.** 2nd ed. Recklinghausen, Aurel Bongers, 1967. 294p. illus. LC 68-72927.

Pictorial survey of ancient Inca gold. Introductory essay followed by collection of 144 plates of gold objects and pieces of jewelry, most in private collections. Appendix with transcripts of documents relative to Inca gold in the archives of the Indies in Seville. General bibliography, pp. 285-86.

1893   Perez de Baradas, Jose. **Orfebreria prehispanica de Colombia.** Estilos tolima y muisca. Madrid, Banco de la Republica, 1958. 2v. illus. index. LC 59-48283.

Comprehensive handbook to ancient Inca gold based on objects in the Museo del Oro, Bogota. Volume of text and volume of plates. Text is arranged in two parts: Estilo tolima and Estilo musica, the individual pieces are organized by site. Bibliographical references in the catalog entries. General bibliography, pp. 351-58.

See also the museum catalog: *Museo del Oro*, Colombia; *Gold Museum*, Colombia by Luis Duque Gomez (Bogota, Delroisse, 1982. 238p. illus. ISBN 285518083X) and the exhibition catalog: *The Art of Precolumbian Gold: The Jan Mitchell Collection* edited by Julie Jones (Boston, Little, Brown, 1985. 248p. illus. ISBN 0821215949).

Renaissance and Baroque Gold and Silver
[*See also* Chapter Twelve, Renaissance Jewelry]

1894   Hayward, J. F. **Virtuoso Goldsmiths and the Triumph of Mannerism 1540-1620**. London, Sotheby Parke Bernet, 1976. 751p. illus. index. ISBN 0856670057.

Comprehensive history of gold and silversmiths' work in western Europe from 1540 to 1620. Emphasis is on stylistic development. Well-illustrated with major museum pieces, designs and comparative works in other media. Contents: Part I, Text: 1, The Study of Silver; 2, Patrons, Goldsmiths, and Guilds; 3, The Craft of the Goldsmith; 4, The Renaissance; 5, The Renaissance Goldsmiths; 6, Mannerism; 7, Italy; 8, France; 9, Spain and Portugal; 10, South Germany; 11, Erasmus Hornick; 12, North and Western Germany, Switzerland, Saxony; 13, The Habsburg Family Dominions: Hungary and Poland; 14, The Netherlands; 15, England; 16, The Goldsmith as Armourer and Base Metal Worker. Part 2: Catalogue of Plates; Part 3: Plates. General bibliography, pp. 729-31, specialized bibliography in the notes at the end of each chapter.

1895   Hernmarck, Carl. **The Art of the European Silversmith 1430-1830**. London and New York, Sotheby Parke Bernet, 1977. 2v. illus. index. ISBN 0856670340.

Comprehensive history of European gold and silver from the late Gothic period to the end of the Neoclassical style with emphasis on style, design, decoration, and form. Volume one text, volume two a corpus of 1,000 plates. Contents: Part I, Culture and Countries (divided by country); Part II: Styles: Late Gothic and Renaissance, Mannerism, Late Sixteenth Century Neo-gothic, The Herrera Style, Baroque, Régence and Rococo, Back to Antiquity; Part III, Secular Silver: Vessels for Wine and Beer, Vessels for Serving Drinks, Tea, Coffee and Chocolate Sets, Table Silver, Furniture and Ornaments, Ewers and Basins, Silver for the Dressing Table, Candlesticks and Candelabra, Treasury Pieces, Special Pieces; Part IV, Church Silver: Chalices, Patens and Cruets, Vessels to Contain the Host, Altars, Processional Crosses, Altar Crosses and Candlesticks, Croziers, Vessels for Holy Water, Thuribles and Incense Boats, Paxes, Baptismal Vessels, Reliquaries, Special Pieces; Part V, Some Decorative Techniques: Engraving, Flat-chasing, The Etched Moresque, Filligree, Le Style Rustique, Sheffield Plate and Other Cost-saving Methods. Comprehensive, classified bibliography, pp. 376-387. Index of gold and silversmiths with birth and death dates and references to the illustrations. A standard work by a leading scholar and connoisseur.

Modern Gold and Silver [*See also* Chapter Twelve, Modern Jewelry]

1896   Krekel-Aalberse, Annelies. **Art Nouveau and Art Deco Silver**. New York, Abrams, 1989. 272p. illus. index. ISBN 0810918927.

Well-illustrated, comprehensive history of silver in Europe and the United States from 1880 to 1940. Geographical arrangement. Biographies of artists and silversmiths with dictionary of silvermarks. Bibliographical references to specialized literature in the notes and general bibliography, pp. 269-270.

1897   Culme, John. **Nineteenth-Century Silver**. Feltham, Hamlyn, 1977. 232p. illus. index. ISBN 0600391345.

History of silver in Great Britain during the nineteenth century. Contents: I, The Industry: Workshops and Operatives: Introduction, Sheffield Plate and Industrialization, The Assay Offices,

Master and Men; 2, The Trade: Styles and Retailers: Rundell's and the Early Nineteenth Century, Historicism, Naturalism, Medievalism and Gothicism, Testimonials; 3, The Exhibitions: Showmen and Craftsmen: National Taste and the Early Exhibitions; Electroplate and the Exhibitions to 1851; The International Exhibition of 1862; The Japanese Influence and Foreign Competition; Multi-medium Pieces and the Exhibits of 1889; Novelties; Liberty's and the Arts and Crafts Movement. Sources, pp. 225-26, list books and periodical literature. Illustrations include numerous reproductions of contemporary trade advertisements, designs, and views of factory and craft operations.

1898   Grandjean, Serge. **L'orfèverie du XIXe siècle en Europe**. Paris, Presses Universitaires de France, 1962. 161p. illus. index. LC 63-55026.

Survey history of silver and gold in nineteenth-century Europe. Contents: Pt. 1: Généralités et techniques: 1, Le XIXe siècle et l'orfèvererie en Europe; 2, Poinçons et technique; 3, Les principaux types d'objets. Part 2: Le style et ses particularités. Part 3: Collections et collectionneurs: 1, Le marché et les collections; 2, Les principales collections publiques. Lists of principal makers and marks. Classified and partly annotated bibliography, pp. 121-27, includes books and periodical articles.

1899   Hughes, Graham. **Modern Silver Throughout the World 1880-1967**. New York, Crown, 1967. 256p. illus. index. LC 67-26050.

Popular survey of European and American gold and silver from 1880 to 1967. Includes some works of jewelry. Discussion of techniques. Dictionary of major makers. Selected bibliography, p. 255.

AMERICAN GOLD AND SILVER (U.S., Canada, and Latin America)

United States

Dictionaries of Marks

1900   Currier, Ernest M. **Marks of Early American Silversmiths...** Portland, Me., Southworth-Anthoensen Press; London, Quaritch, 1938. Reprint: Harrison, N.Y., R. A. Green, 1970. 179p. illus. index. LC 74-111387.

Early dictionary of American silversmiths and their marks to 1840, arranged by name of maker and illustrated with facsimiles. General bibliography, pp. 177-79.

1901   Ensko, Stephen G. C. **American Silversmiths and Their Marks III**. New York, Ensko, 1948. 285p. illus. Reprint: New York, Dover, 1983. ISBN 0486244288.

Third edition of a still-standard handbook of marks on American silver dating before 1850. First part is list by name, giving basic biographical data, locations of businesses, records of training, etc. Second part treats marks illustrated by line drawings. Bibliography, pp. 281-85, is a chronological listing of basic works on American silver. Enhanced over previous editions by the addition of maps showing locations of silversmiths' shops in Boston, New York, and Philadelphia. Ensko's dictionary is built upon the earlier work of French (1902) and Currier, but itself has not been superseded as a general dictionary of early American silver. *Early American Silver Marks*, by James Graham (New York, n.p. 1936. 81p. illus.) is an abridged, pocket-sized dictionary based on the first edition of Ensko.

1902   French, Hollis. **A Silver Collector's Glossary and a List of Early American Silver-smiths and Their Marks**. New York, Walpole Society, 1917. 164p. illus. Reprint: New York, DaCapo, 1967. LC 67-27454.

Pioneering work on early-American silver marks. All of the information on makers and their marks was absorbed into the dictionaries by Currier (1900) and Ensko (1901). The glossary, pp. 133-64, is still useful for basic definitions.

1903   Kovel, Ralph M. **American Silver Marks, 1650 to the Present**. New York, Crown, 1989. 421p. illus. index. ISBN 0517568829.

Comprehensive dictionary of marks on American silver directed to the needs of the average collector. Expands the material in Ensko by addition of marks on silver after 1850. Entries give basic biographical data and referral to reference books listed at the end, a feature that makes the work a useful bibliographical tool for specialized literature on individual makers.

1904   Rainwater, Dorothy T. **Encyclopedia of American Silver Manufacturers**. 3rd ed. rev. West Chester, Pa., Schiffer, 1986. 266p. illus. ISBN 0887400469.

First published in 1966 as: *American Silver Manufacturers*. Comprehensive dictionary of marks on American manufactured silver dating from the middle of the nineteenth century to circa 1920. There are more than 2,000 marks representing over 1,400 firms. Includes facsimiles of the marks and short histories of the firms. Glossary and general bibliography, pp. 261-66. Useful guide designed for the collector but necessary for any research into industrial production of silverware in America.

1905   Thorn, C. Jordan. **Handbook of American Silver and Pewter Marks**. New York, Tudor, 1949. 289p. illus. LC 50-5385.

Popular dictionary illustrating in facsimile 3,500 marks, arranged by name of maker.

See also the exhibition catalog: *Marks of American Silversmiths in the Ineson-Bissell Collection*, by L. C. Belden (Charlottesville, Virg., Univ. of Virginia Press, 1980. 505p. illus. ISBN 0813907985).

General Histories and Handbooks

1906   Fennimore, Donald L. **Silver & Pewter**. New York, Knopf, 1984. 478p. illus. index. ISBN 0394715276.

In the series: "The Knopf Collectors' Guides to American Antiques." Authoritative collector's guide to American silver, silver-plated and pewter ware from Colonial times to the present. Contains 338 pieces arranged by type of object illustrated with good color plates and described in detail with special commentary on the value of the piece to the collector. Estimated retail prices of the pieces are given in a list at the end. Has a concise repertory of marks. General bibliography, pp. 466-69.

1907   Hood, Graham. **American Silver: A History of Style, 1650-1900**. New York, Praeger, 1971. 255p. illus. index. LC 77-124854. Reprint: New York, Dutton, 1989. ISBN 0525482172.

Survey of the stylistic development of American silver characterized by a deepened aesthetic sensibility. Contents: 1, Society, Silversmiths, and tTeir Wares; 2, The 17th Century; 3, Baroque Silver of the William and Mary Period; 4, Queen Anne Silver; 5, Fully Developed Rococo Silver; 6, The Classical Taste of the Early Republic; 7, The Empire Style; 8, Later 19th-century Styles. Illustrates most of the great masterpieces of American silver art. Classified bibliography, pp. 247-50.

1908   Phillips, John Marshall. **American Silver**. New York, Chanticleer Press, 1949. 128p. illus. LC 49-10604.

Survey of American silver from the seventeenth through the nineteenth centuries by a leading connoisseur. Introductory chapter on the craft of the early American silversmith followed by stylistic history. Illustrated with museum pieces. Bibliography, pp. 127-28, lists basic books.

1909   Schwartz, Marvin D. **Collectors' Guide to Antique American Silver**. New York, Bonanza Books, 1982. 174p. illus. index. ISBN 0517320924.

First published in 1975 (New York, Doubleday). Popular history/handbook of American silver from the seventeenth century to the early twentieth century. Contents: I, Silver-making Techniques for the Connoisseur; II, Seventeenth- and Early Eighteenth-Century Forms; III, Eighteenth-Century Design: Rococo; IV, The Neo-classical as an American Silver Style; V, Victorian (or Nineteenth Century) Is Different; VI, Revival Style: 1830-70; VII, Eclectic and Academic Design: 1870-1900; VIII, Twentieth Century Possibilities; IX, Identifying American Silver. Appendix with a list of major American silversmiths and manufacturers giving dates and localities. Select bibliography, p. 169.

1910   Wenham, Edward. **The Practical Book of American Silver**. Philadelphia, Lippincott, 1949. 275p. illus. index. Reprint: New York, Garland, 1978. ISBN 0824033779.

Concise history of silver in America from Colonial times to circa 1830, noted for its clarity in sketching the stylistic development and its sensitivity to the place of silver in early American life. Illustrated with line drawings showing the development of shapes and decoration of major types of silver flat and hollowware. Chapter on collecting and repertory of major marks. General bibliography, pp. 265-67.

Colonial and Federal Periods

1911   Avery, Clara L. **Early American Silver**. New York and London, Century, 1930. 378p. illus. index. LC 30-30325. Reprint: New York, Russell and Russell, 1968.

Pioneering history of American silver from earliest Colonial times to the middle of the nineteenth century. Emphasis is on the development of style and the influence of Europe on American silver design and the regional styles of Massachusetts and New York. Although superseded in breadth and depth of information by Fales (1913) and Hood (1907) it remains unmatched for quality of stylistic description and connoisseurship. Bibliographical notes, pp. 361-64.

1912   Bigelow, Francis H. **Historic Silver of the Colonies and Its Makers...** New York, Macmillan, 1917. 476p. illus. index. LC 17-25629. Reprint: New York, Tudor Publishing Co., 1948.

Pioneering work on early American silver sparked by the Colonial revival of 1900. Arranged by types of object. Demonstrates a wide knowledge of public and private collections and is still a valuable reference guide. Index of silversmiths.

1913   Fales, Martha G. **Early American Silver**. Rev. and enl. ed. New York, Dutton, 1973. 336p. illus. index. ISBN 0525472991.

Comprehensive history of American silver from 1675 to 1825. Contents: Part I: Artistry in American Silver: 1, Stylistic Development and Quality, 2, The Development of Forms, 3, Design Sources, 4, Regional Contributions; Part II: The Historical Significance of American Silver: 5, Domestic Silver, 6, Church Silver, 7, Official Silver, 8, Presentation Silver; Part III: The Role of the American Silversmith: 9, The Men and Their Training, 10, The Shops, Equipment, and Methods, 11, Business Procedures, 12, Allied Crafts; Part IV: Special Features of American Silver: 13, The Metal, 14, Engraving, 15, Reading the Marks, 16, Dating American Silver; Part

V: Special Aids: 17, Cautions, 18, Care of Silver. Comprehensive, classified bibliography with introduction, pp. 309-320.

1914   Jones, E. Alfred. **The Old Silver of American Churches**. Letchworth, Alden Press for the National Society of the Colonial Dames of America, 1913. 2v. illus. index LC A14-812r34.

    Large and important corpus of over 1,000 pieces of silver dating before 1825 in American churches. Arrangement is by place and entries give detailed physical descriptions of the pieces, including facsimiles of marks and record information from archives. Index of churches by state and index of donors as well as general index. An indispensable reference work for the study of early American ecclesiastical plate.

1915   Kauffman, Henry J. **The Colonial Silversmith: His Techniques & His Products**. New York, Galahad Books, 1969. 176p. illus. index. ISBN 08836516X. LC 71-101526.

    Popular introduction to Colonial American silver with particular attention given to the craft of the silversmith. Useful drawings show techniques. Contents: The Metal; The Workshop; Forks and Spoons; Plates and Basins; Cups and Beakers; Porringers and Bowls; Mugs and Tankards; Teapots and Coffeepots; Other Objects. Selected bibliography, p. 173.

    See also the exhibition catalogs: *Masterpieces of American Silver* (Richmond, Virg., Virginia Museum of Fine Arts, 1960. 99p. illus.), and *Silver in American Life: Selections from the Mabel Brady Garvan and Other Collections at Yale University* (New Haven, Conn., Yale University Art Gallery, 1979. 193p. illus. index), *Colonial Silversmiths, Masters, and Apprentices* (Boston, Museum of Fine Arts, 1956. 98p. illus. LC 57-1355), and the museum guide: *Colonial Silver in the American Wing*, by F. G. Safford (New York, Metropolitan Museum of Art. 1983).

John Coney, 1655-1722

1916   Clarke, Hermann F. **John Coney, Silversmith 1655-1722**. Boston, Houghton Mifflin, 1932. 59p. illus. Reprint: New York, Da Capo Press, 1971. LC 71-87562.

    Introductory monograph on the Colonial Boston silversmith John Coney with a detailed catalog of his marks and 31 plates of his works. Bibliographical references in the footnotes.

Jeremiah Dummer, 1645-1718

1917   Clarke, Hermann, and Henry W. Foote. **Jeremiah Dummer: Colonial Craftsman & Merchant 1645-1718**. Boston, Houghton Mifflin, 1935. 205p. illus. Reprint: New York, Da Capo Press, 1970. LC 75-87563.

    Well-researched monograph on the life and work of the Colonial New England silversmith, Jeremiah Dummer. Includes a detailed catalog of his marks and a catalog of his portrait paintings similar in style to the portraits of Dummer and John Coney, which have been attributed to Jeremiah Dummer. Bibliographical references in the footnotes.

Jacob Hurd, 1703-1758

1918   French, Hollis. **Jacob Hurd and His Sons, Nathaniel and Benjamin, Silversmiths**. Cambridge, Mass., 1939. 148p. illus. Reprint: New York, Da Capo Press, 1972. ISBN 0306-704064.

    Scholarly monograph on the Boston silversmith Jacob Hurd and his two sons, based on examination of marked pieces and documentary sources. Detailed description of the marks used by the three silversmiths. Reprint edition contains the Addenda published in 1941. Bibliography, p. 147.

Myer Myers, 1723-1795

1919 Rosenbaum, Jeanette W. **Myer Myers, Goldsmith 1723-1795**. Philadephia, Jewish Publication Society of America, 1954. 141p. illus. index. LC 54-5666.

Introductory monograph on the life and work of the Colonial New York silversmith. Contents: 1, Craftsman and Patriot; 2, Contemporary Newspaper Notices Concerning Myer Myers; 3, Colonial Court Records by Herbert A. Fogel; 4, Genealogy; 5, Plates; 6, Technical Notes by Kathryn C. Buhler. Bibliography, pp. 139-41, has list of manuscript sources.

Paul Revere, 1735-1818

1920 Buhler, Kathryn C. **Paul Revere, Goldsmith, 1735-1818**. Boston, Museum of Fine Arts, 1956. 46p. illus.

Authoritative description of works in silver by Revere in the Boston Museum of Fine Arts. Good plates of the 65 pieces and portraits of Revere and his family with descriptive captions. Appendix with facsimiles of Revere's touchmarks.

See also the exhibition catalog: *Paul Revere, 1735-1818: The Events of His Life Painted*, by A. Lassell Ripley and *Some Examples of His Silver and Prints*, by M. M. Tymeson (Worcester, Mass., Art Museum, 1965. 86p. illus.) and the biography: *L. Martin. Paul Revere* (New York, F. Watts, 1987. 95p. illus. ISBN 0531103129.).

Nineteenth and Twentieth Centuries

1921 Burke, James H. **The Warner Collector's Guide to American Sterling Silver and Silver-plate Holloware**. New York, Warner Books, 1982. 256p. illus. index. ISBN 0446976342.

Collector's guide to American sterling and silver-plated hollowware of the late nineteenth and early twentieth centuries. The 420 pieces are arranged in 50 categories. Entries are brief and have references to a scale of availability. No bibliography.

1922 McClinton, Kathryn C. **Collecting American 19th Century Silver**. New York, Scribner's, 1968. 280p. illus. index. LC 68-27784.

Handbook/history of American silver—not silverplate—from 1800 to 1910 directed to the needs of the collector. Contents: I, Collecting American Nineteenth Century Silver: I, Marks; II, The Late Classic Federal and Empire (1800-1840): 1, Federal, 2, Empire; III, American Victorian Silver (1840-1900): 1, Rococo (1840-1850), 2, Renaissance Revival (1851-1870), 3, Eclecticism (1870-1900); IV, Art Nouveau Silver (1895-1910): 1, Martelé, 2, Silver Deposit Ware and Silver-Mounted Cut Glass; V, Presentation Pieces and Trophies; VI, Presentation Swords; VII, American Navy Battleship and Cruiser Silver; VIII, American Church Silver; IX, Silver Masonic Jewels and Medals; X, Small Silver Collectibles: Late Victorian Match Boxes, 2, Silver-Headed Canes, 3, Inkstands and Desk Furnishings, 4, Snuffboxes and Other Small Boxes, 5, Tea Bells, Tea Balls and Strainers, Tea Caddies, 6, Open Salts and Mustard Pots, 7, Fish Knives, 8, Ladies' Chatelaines, Belt Buckles and Hatpins, 9, Coffee Spoons, 10, Children's Silver, 11, Silver Thimbles and Scissors, 12, Indian Peace Medals and Trinkets, 13, Medals of Scholarship. Glossary. Classified bibliography, pp. 274-276, includes a few references to newspaper articles, list of exhibition catalogs, and list of periodicals.

See also Snell, Doris. *American Silverplated Fatware Patterns* (Des Moines, Ia., Wallace-Homestead, 1980. 228p. illus. index. ISBN 0870692240.

1923 Rainwater, Dorothy T., and H. Ivan Rainwater. **American Silverplate**. Nashville, Tenn., Thomas Nelson; Hanover, Pa., Everybodys Press, 1968. 480p. illus. index. LC 72-7998. ISBN 084074322X.

Comprehensive history/handbook of silver-plated wares made in the United States from circa 1840 to circa 1940 with emphasis on Victorian pieces. Contents: I, Historical Background; II, Early Electroplating and the Rise of Factories; III, Manufacturing and Marketing; IV, Patented Processes; V, Development of Styles; VI, Exhibition and Presentation Silver and Ornamental Art Works; VII, Silverplate for Table and Household Use; VIII, Small Silverware and Novelties; IX, Lighting Devices; X, Flatware; XI, Care and Restoration. Appendices with glossary and general bibliography, pp. 461-65. Directed to the collector and, therefore, concerned primarily with identification of pieces. Rainwater's work contains a wealth of information for the historian of industrial age decorative arts. Illustrations include a large number of reproductions from contemporary catalogs and advertisements.

1924   Turner, Noel D. **American Silver Flatware, 1837-1910.** South Brunswick, N.J., A. S. Barnes, 1972. 473p. illus. index. LC 68-27217.

Comprehensive history of manufactured silver flatware—sterling and electroplated—in the United States and Canada from 1837 to 1910 with emphasis on use in the home, in hotels, steamships, etc. Large section devoted to the identification of flatware patterns with illustrations forms manufacturers' catalogs and comprehensive dictionary of trademarks and trade names of American, Canadian, and British manufacturers. Comprehensive bibliography of books and periodical articles, pp. 413-22.

See also the price guide: *The Official Identification and Price Guide to Silver and Silverplate*, by J. Schwatz (New York, House of Collectibles, 1989. 467p. illus. ISBN 08763-77843).

Gorham Silver

1925   Carpenter, Charles H. **Gorham Silver, 1831-1981.** New York, Dodd, Mead, 1982. 332p. illus. ISBN 0396080685.

Comprehensive, authoritative, and well-illustrated history/handbook of the silver and related metalware produced by the Gorham Company and its predecessor companies of Providence, Rhode Island, from 1831 to 1981. Contents: 1, Introduction; 2, The Beginnings; 3, Coin Silver Spoons; 4, John Gorham: The Expansionist; 5, The Post-Civil War Years; 6, Innovation and Fantasy; 7, Antoine Heller and the New Academy; 8, The Bronzes; 9, Presentation Pieces; 10, Souvenir Spoons; 11, Holbrook and Codman; 12, Martelé; 13, Art Deco; 14, After World War II. Appendices with repertory of Gorham marks, Gorham flatware patterns, catalog of well-known bronzes cast by Gorham, and list of Gorham presidents from 1865-1981. Comprehensive bibliography, pp. 315-19, with essay on Gorham source material.

Tiffany Silver

1926   Carpenter, Charles H. **Tiffany Silver.** New York, Dodd, Mead, 1984. 296p. illus. index. ISBN 0396083382.

Scholarly monograph based on close examination of documentary sources. Contents: I, George Wickes; II, The Goldsmith's Wife; III, The Goldsmith's Business; IV, The Appentices; V, The Workshop; VI, The Journeymen and Sub-Contractors; VII, The Associates; VIII, The Associates Ledger; IX, The Designers and Modellers; X, The Influence of William Kent; XI, The Clients; XII, The Patronage of the Prince of Wales; XIII, The Prince's Silver; XIV, Epilogue; Appendix I: Duty and Drawback; Appendix II: The Leinster Dinner Service. General bibliography, p. 206, and specailized bibliographical references in the footnotes. Comprehensive survey of the silver produced by Tiffany & Co. from 1837 to 1976. Illustrations include contemporary advertisements, views of the factory, and details of pieces showing marks. Contents: 1, Changing Views on Victorianism; 2, The Early Years: 1837-1867; 3, The Leading Silversmiths; 4, The

Sumptuous Table 1: Hollow Ware; 5, The Sumptuous Table 2: Flatware; 6, Silver Out of the Dining Room; 7, Presentation Silver; 8, Presentation Swords and Guns; 9, Yachting and Other Sporting Trophies; 10, The Japanese and Other Exotic Influences; 11, Electroplated Silver; 12, The Making of Tiffany Silver; 13, Tiffany Marks; 14, The Twentieth Century—a Postscript. Bibliography, pp. 285-88.

New England Silver

1927   Bohan, Peter, and Philip Hammerslough. **Early Connecticut Silver, 1700-1840.** Middletown, Conn., Wesleyan Univ. Press, 1970. 288p. illus. index. LC 76-82543.

Comprehensive, scholarly handbook of Connecticut silversmiths active between 1700 and 1840. Introductory essays: "The Connecticut Silversmith," and "Tradition and Innovation in Connecticut Silver," followed by a corpus of 184 plates of signed pieces with descriptive notes. "Biographical Notes on the Silversmiths" is a short entry dictionary of Connecticut silversmiths. Comprehensive, classified bibliography, pp. 279-84.

1928   Flynt, Henry N., and Martha Gandy Fales. **The Heritage Foundation Collection of Silver, with Biographical Sketches of New England Silversmiths, 1625-1825.** Old Deerfield, Mass., Heritage Foundation, 1968. 391p. illus. index. LC 67-26102.

History/handbook of New England silver from the seventeenth century to the middle of the nineteenth century based on the collection given to the Heritage Collection, Old Deerfield, by Henry R. Flynt. First part: "The New England Silver Climate" contains essays by various experts on the silver of Maine, New Hampshire, Vermont, Massachusetts, Rhode Island, and Connecticut. Second part is an essay on the Heritage Collection by M. G. Fales. Third part, the most useful part, is a comprehensive biographical dictionary of New England silversmiths with photographic reproductions of their touchmarks. Comprehensive bibliography, pp. 367-82.

See also the exhibition catalog: *The New England Silversmith: An Exhibition of New England Silver from the Mid-Seventeenth Century to the Present, Selected from New England Collections* (Providence. R.I., Museum of Art, Rhode Island School of Design, 1965. 141p. illus.) and Volume 1, New England Museum catalog: *American Silver: Garvan and Other Collections in the Yale University Art Gallery* (New Haven, Conn., Yale University Press, 1970. 344p. illus.).

New York Silver

1929   von Khrum, Paul. **Silversmiths of New York City, 1684-1850.** New York, By the author, 1978. 155p. LC 78-111515.

Directory of more than 2,500 silversmiths active in New York between 1684 and 1850. Based on city directories and other written sources as well as actual objects. Introduction discusses the nature and history of date marks, sources and fineness of silver and other technical aspects of silverwork in New York City.

See also the exhibition catalogs by V. Isabelle Miller: *Silver by New York Makers: Late Seventeenth Century to 1900* (New York, Museum of the City of New York, 1937. 71p. illus.) and *New York Silversmiths of the Seventeenth Century* (New York, Museum of the City of New York, 1962), and Volume 2, Middle Colonies and the South, museum catalog: *American Silver: Garvan and Other Collections in the Yale University Gallery* (New Haven, Conn.,Yale Univ. Press, 1970. 300p. illus.).

Pennsylvania Silver

1930   Gerstell, Vivian S. **Silversmiths of Lancaster, Pennsylvania, 1730-1850.** Lancaster, Pa., Lancaster County Historical Society, 1972. 145p. illus. LC 72-86855.

Comprehensive, scholarly history and handbook of the silversmiths active in Lancaster County, Pennsylvania between 1739 and 1850. Brief introductory essay sketching the history of the craft of the silversmith in Pennsylvania is followed by alphabetically arranged entries on the maker silversmiths. Basic biographical data in footnotes to secondary sources. Hallmarks and pieces are illustrated through photographic reproductions. Appendices have extracts, many in facsimiles, of inventories related to the silversmiths: John Getz, Peter Getz, William Glenn, Charles Hall, Lewis Heck and Abraham Le Roy. Excellent, classified bibliography including manuscript sources, pp. 143-45.

Maryland Silver

1931   Pleasants, J. Hall, and Howard Sill. **Maryland Silversmiths, 1715-1830, with Illustrations of Their Silver and Their Silver Marks and with a Facsimile of the Design Book of William Faris.** Baltimore, Md., Lord Baltimore Press, 1930. 324p. illus. index. Reprint: Harrison, N.Y., R. A. Green, 1972. LC 72-195417

Comprehensive, authoritative history/handbook of early silversmiths active in Maryland. Particularly useful is the unusually large collection of plates illustrating marked pieces and original designs by major silversmiths, especially the Design Book of William Faris. Contents: Introduction; A Survey of Maryland Silver andIits Makers; Silversmiths' Marks (given in facsimile); The Baltimore Assay Office and Its Marks; Annapolis Silversmiths; Baltimore Silversmiths; Eastern Shore Silversmiths; Western Maryland Silversmiths; Silversmiths of Harford, Charles, and St. Mary's Counties; William Faris and His Shop; Apprentices; Indentured Immigrant Silversmiths; Maryland Watch and Clock Makers Not Known to Have Worked as Silversmiths; A Table of Initials of Maryland Silversmiths, Watch and Clock Makers, and Allied Craftsmen.

See also the exhibition catalogs edited by Jennifer F. Goldsborough: *Eighteenth and Nineteenth Century Maryland Silver in the Collection of the Baltimore Museum of Art* (Baltimore, Md., Baltimore Museum of Art, 1975. 204p. illus.) and *Silver in Maryland* (Baltimore, Museum and Library of Maryland History, 1983. 300p.).

Southern Silver

1932   Burton, E. Milby. **South Carolina Silversmiths, 1690-1860.** Charleston, S.C., Charleston Museum, 1942. 311p. illus. index. LC 42-18172. Reprint: Rutland, Vt., Tuttle, 1968.

Biographies of 320 silversmiths active in South Carolina from the founding of the colony to the Civil War, arranged by place. Much information drawn from written records.

1933   Cutten, George B. **Silversmiths of North Carolina, 1696-1850.** 2d ed. Raleigh, N.C., North Carolina Department of Cultural Resources, 1984. 301p. illus. index. LC 85-107646.

Revised by Mary R. Peacock. Authoritative dictionary of silversmiths active in North Carolina between 1696 and 1850. Entries give excerpts from documentary and published sources and photographic reproductions of hallmarks and marked pieces. Appendices with extracts of North Carolina documents referring to silver. Bibliographical references in the notes.

1934   ——. **Silversmiths of Virgina, 1694-1850.** Richmond, Virg., The Dietz Press, 1952. 259p. illus. index. LC 52-14077.

Comprehensive dictionary of silversmiths active in Virginia between 1694 and 1850 based on archival and other documentary sources. Arrangement is by town or city and entries for major personalities give reproductions of portraits, documents, signed pieces, and marks. Extensive bibliography furnished through notes, pp. 221-45.

1935 ———. **Silversmiths of Georgia, 1733-1850**. Savannah, Ga., Pigeonhole Press, 1958.
Comprehensive dictionary of silversmiths active in Georgia between 1733 and 1850 based on archival and other documentary sources. Arrangement is by town or city and entries for major personalities give reproductions of portraits, documents, signed pieces, and marks. Extensive bibliography in the footnotes.
See also exhibition catalogs: *Southern Silver: An Exhibition of Silver Made in the South prior to 1860* (Houston, Tex., Museum of Fine Arts, 1968. 90p. illus.).

Mid-West and Western Silver

1936 Beckmann, Elizabeth D. **Cincinnati Silversmiths, Jewelers, Watch and Clockmakers**. Cincinnati, Oh., B.B. & Co., 1975. 168p. illus. index. LC 75-24983.
Dictionary of silversmiths, jewelers, watch and clockmakers active in Cincinnati between 1851 and 1900. Entries for the major personalities have illustrations of signed pieces, reproductions of advertisements, and facsimiles of marks. All entries have references to and often extracts from documentary sources. Comprehensive, classified bibliography, pp. 156-160.

1937 Boultinghouse, Marquis. **Silversmiths, Jewelers, Clock and Watch Makers of Kentucky 1785-1900**. Lexington, Ky., n.p., 1980. 368p. illus. index. LC 85-243093.
Comprehensive, well-illustrated dictionary of silversmiths, jewelers, and clock and watch makers active in Kentucky between 1785 and 1900. Biographies include excerpts from documentary sources, portraits, and reproductions of advertisements as well as plates of signed pieces by major craftsmen. Glossary of marks has photographic reproductions of hallmarks. Comprehensive bibliography, pp. 353-55.

1938 Darling, Sharon S. **Chicago Metalsmiths: A Illustrated History**. Chicago, Chicago Historical Society, 1977. 141p. illus. index. ISBN 0913820067.
Informative, pictorial history of silversmiths, coppersmiths, and bronze casters active in Chicago from 1904 to 1970. Illustrations include large numbers of contemporary views, portraits, and reproductions of advertisements, as well as pieces of silver with details of hallmarks. Contents: From Trinketmakers to Tastemakers 1804-1890; A Renaissance: The Arts and Crafts Movement 1890-1918; Chicago's Modern Metalsmiths 1918-1970; Other Shops and Individuals 1844-1970. Comprehensive bibliography, pp. 137-38.

1939 Hiatt, Lucy F., and Noble W. Hiatt. **The Silversmiths of Kentucky, 1785-1850**. Louisville, Ky., The Standard Printing Co., 1954. 135p. illus. index. LC 54-25276.
Dictionary of silversmiths, watchmakers, and jewelers active in Kentucky from 1785 to 1850, arranged alphabetically by silversmith's name. Entries provide basic biographical information and references to marked pieces. Entries on major personalities include extracts and references to documentary sources. Brief repertory of marks in drawings, pp. 113-18. Comprehensive bibliography, pp. 121-126, includes archival and published sources.

1940 Knittle, Rhea M. **Early Ohio Silversmiths and Pewterers, 1787-1847**. Cleveland,Oh., n. p., 1943. 63p. illus. LC 43-10754.
Valuable history and handbook on silver and pewter made in Ohio between 1787 and 1847. Contents: Early Ohio Silver: The Ohio Indians, Their Silver Ornaments and Crosses, Concerning the Scarcity of Silver Coin in Ohio, Methods Employed in Making Silver; Historical Data Concerning the Early Ohio Silversmiths, Silversmiths in the Muskingum Valley, Silversmiths in the Upper Hocking Valley, The Finest Silversmiths in Gallipolis; Early Cincinnati Silversmiths, Check-list of Early Ohio Silversmiths; Early Ohio Pewter; Check-List of Early Ohio Pewterers

and Makers of Britannia Ware. Checklists are arranged by place; the information was culled from documentary sources. No illustrations of marks or signatures. Basic bibliography, p. 63.

1941   Morse, Edward W., ed. **Silver in the Golden State: Images and Essays Celebrating the History and Art of Silver in California**. Oakland, Calif., Oakland Museum of History Department, 1986. 119p. illus. LC 87-402523.

Collected essays on silver and silverware in California from the earliest colonists to the present. Contents: Introduction by L. T. Frye; Dedication: Interview with Elliot Evans by E. Evans and D. Cooper; Silver in the Golden State by E. W. Morse; Arts and Crafts Silversmiths: Friedell and Blanchard in Southern California by L. G. Bowman; Big Bonanza: the Comstock and California Silver; Cerro Gordo by D. Chaput; Icons of Continuity and Change: Some Thoughts on Silver and the California Experience by G. W. R. Ward; X-ray Fluorescence of California Silverware: Some Preliminary Findings by J. W. Burke. Appendices with essays on northern California flatware and marks on California silver. Bibliographical references in the notes.

Canada

1942   Langdon, John. **Canadian Silversmiths 1700-1900**. Toronto, Stinehour, 1966. 145p. illus. index. LC 66-28195.

Comprehensive, scholarly history/handbook of Canadian silversmiths active between 1700 and 1900. Historical sketch discusses the use of silver, forms of silver, fashions in silver, Indian trade silver, quality controls, marking of silver, techniques and hints on identification of silversmiths. Repertory of makers with photographic reproductions of their marks. Entries for the individual silversmiths often give extracts from and references to contemporary sources. Seventy-six plates illustrate major signed pieces. Comprehensive, classified bibliography, pp. 231-33. Standard work on Canadian silversmiths.

1943   Langdon, John. **Guide to Marks on Early Canadian Silver, 18th and 19th Centuries**. Toronto, Ryerson, 1968. 104p. illus. LC 72-392416.

Pocket-sized dictionary of Canadian silversmiths' marks arranged alphabetically by makers' name and illustrated with photographs of actual marked pieces. Has supplement of Robert Hendery and Hendery & Leslie punch marks.

1944   Unitt, Doris J., and Peter Unitt. **Canadian Silver, Silver Plate and Related Glass**. Peterborough, Ontario Clock House, 1970. 256p. illus. index. LC 76-888154.

Popular collector's handbook of Canadian sterling silver and silverplated ware including those combining glass and silver. Some of the chapters were previously published in antiques magazines. Contents: The Silver Thread Through Canadian History by A. Gatrill; Early Silver from Private Collections with Photographs from Henry Birks' Collection; Early Silver from Private Collections; Craftsmanship a Family Tradition; They Set a Tradition of Quality; Silver Plate, Mass Produced Craftsmanship; They Made Their Mark in 1847—The Rogers Bros.; The Meriden Britannia Company in Canada; W. Rogers Mfg. Company; Ontario Silver Company; Acme Silver Company; Standard Silver Plate Company; Simpson, Hall, Miller & Company, Montreal; The International Silver Company of Canada; Toronto Silver Plate Company; Flatware Patterns; The Ice Pitcher by Howard Hogan; Napkin Rings; Butter Dishes; Victorian Tea-Time; Silversmith, Manufacturers, Merchants, Marks; Related Glass; Glossary of Terms. Illustrated with photographs of pieces including details of marks and many contemporary advertisements, catalog pages and views of factories. Index of makers and manufacturers by province. General bibliography, pp. 250-51.

See also exhibition catalog: *Silver in New France. by Jean Trudel* (Ottawa, National Gallery of Canada, 1974. 237p. illus. ISBN 0888842562) and the companion volume of sources:

Les orfèvres de Nouvelle-France: Inventaire descriptif des sources, by R. Derome (Ottawa, Galerie Nationale du Canada, 1974. 243p. index).

Latin America

1945   Anderson, L. L. **The Art of the Silversmith in Mexico, 1519-1936.** New York, Oxford University Press, 1941. 2v. illus. index. Reprint: New York, Hacker, 1975. LC 73-81683.
   Comprehensive history of silver in Mexico during the colonial and early modern periods. Discusses silver production, organization of silversmiths, their marks and the development of style. Introductory chapter on preconquest silverwork. Well-illustrated and with a good list of silversmiths' marks. Appendix with ordinances relative to the silversmith's art. Bibliography, v. 1, pp. 435-51, is a comprehensive but unclassified list of books and periodical articles.

1946   Boylan, Leona D. **Spanish Colonial Silver.** Sante Fe, N.M., Museum of New Mexico, 1974. 202p. illus. index. LC 74-82799.
   Effort to distinguish the silver made in New Mexico during Spanish colonial rule from silver made elsewhere in Spanish America. Based on 329 pieces in five museum collections in New Mexico: The Morley Collection, The IBM Collection, the Mrs. Henry Lyman Collection and the Museum of New Mexico Collection. Contents: I, The Collection; II, Historical Background in New Mexico; III, Ecclesiastic Silver; IV, Domestic Silver; V, Accessories and Gear; VI, Provincial Styles. Plates and catalog of the pieces which were exhibited together at the New Mexico Museum. Appendix with reproductions of Mexican and Guatemala-Chipas hallmarks and transcripts of significant documents. Comprehensive bibliography, pp. 159-162, and further references in the notes.

1947   Duarte, Carlos F. **Historia de la orefebreria en Venezuela.** Caracas, Monte Avila, 1970. 513p. Illus. index. LC 82-186991.
   Authoritative history/handbook of silver and goldwork in Venezuela from early colonial times to the beginning of the nineteenth century with extensive use of documentary evidence. Contains 205 poorly reproduced plates with descriptive notes. Appendix with biographical dictionary of gold and silversmiths. Basic bibliography, pp. 493-95.

1948   Saville, Marshall H. **The Goldsmith's Art in Ancient Mexico.** New York, Museum of the American Indian-Heye Foundation, 1920. 264p. illus. (Indian Notes and Monographs, Miscellaneous, No. 7). LC 21-1836r.
   Old but still-useful survey of pre-Columbian gold of Mexico with many useful extracts from inventories. Contents: Introduction; The Loot Obtained by the Spaniards in the Conquest of Mexico; Inventories; Sources of Gold; Uses of Gold; The Aztec Goldsmiths and Their Work; Gold Jewels from the State of Oaxaca; Nahuan Region; Tarascan Region; Totonacan Region; Conclusion. Bibliographical references in the footnotes.

1949   Taullard, Alfredo. **Plateria sudamericana...** Buenos Aires, Peuser, 1941. 285p. illus. LC 42-17124.
   Comprehensive history of silver in South American from pre-Hispanic times through the nineteenth century. Contents: Plateria prehispá; las minas del Peru, el cerro de Potosi; Plateria peruana; Plateria religiosa; La tarja de Potosi, y lámina de Oruro; La plateria en el virreinato del Rio de la Plata; El mate; Plateria de apero guacho; Las minas de Chile, Atacama, La Rioja y otras regiones; Plateria pampa; Plateria araucan. Collection of 387 plates and list of silversmiths. Brief bibliography, pp. 708, references to more specialized literature in the footnotes.

1950   Torre Revello, José. **La orfebreria colonial en Hispanoamérica y particularamente en Buenos Aires.** Buenos Aires, Editorial Huarpes, 1945. 112p. illus. LC 46-18824.

Concise history of gold and silverware in colonial Latin America with particular emphasis on the production in Buenos Aires. Contents: Introccíon; I, La orfebreria en la América Precolombina; II, La orfebreria en Europa; III, La orfebreria en Hispanoamérica; IV, Los plateros de Bueonos Aires. Appendices with extracts from regulations governing gold and silversmiths in Mexico from 1538-1543. Poorly reproduced illustrations with short descriptive captions. Bibliographical references in the footnotes.

1951   Valladares, Jose G. **Ourivesaria.** Rio de Janiero, Ouro, 1968. 208p. illus. index. LC 68-131074.

Concise history of gold and silverwork in Brazil during the eighteen and nineteenth centuries. Contents: I, A matéria-prima; II, Os artistas; III, Contrastes e ensaiadores; IV, A obra. Appendix with repertory of silversmiths and their marks. Bibliographical references in the notes.

1952   Valle-Arizpe, Artemio de. **Notas de plateria.** Mexico, Herrero Hermanos, 1961. 427p. illus. index. LC 62-2637.

Comprehensive, scholarly history of gold and silverwork in Mexico from early colonial times to the end of the nineteenth century based in part on documentary sources. Introductory chapter on pre-Columbian gold and silverwork. Contains 126 poorly reproduced plates. Contents: I, La platería precortesiana; II, Cómo trabajaban la plata y el oro los indios mexicanos; III, Las vajillas de don Hernando y sus regalos al César; IV, Más presentes a Carlos V; V, Regalos de Hernán Cortés a iglesias y monasterios de España y a personas particulares de allá; VI, El ex-voto; VII, Primeros tiempos de la platería en la colonia; VIII, Generalidades sobre gremios y cofradías, su formatión y estado jurídicio en Castilla; IX, Gremios y cofradías; X, Ordenanzas de tiradores de oro y plata de batihojas y del noble arte de la Plateria; XI, El auge de la plateria, la riqueza y el lujo en México; XII, Historia de la antigua calle de los plateros; XIII, En la calle de los plateros; XIV, Instrumentos de trabajo de los plateros y de cómo trabajaban la plata y la doraban; XV, Fiestas de los plateros; XVI, El tesoro de la catedral de México; XVII, Que es continuació del anterior; XVIII, Mentalidad cretina; XIX, Saqueo de la catedral de México; XX, Plata en la Puebla de los Angeles, en el Santuario de Guadalupe y en otras iglesias de México; XXI, Plateros famosos; XXII, Ladrones sacrílegos y plateros inquisitoriados; XXIII, Leyes, pragmáticas y ordenanzas de la plateria. Basic bibliography, pp. 421-27, and bibliographical references in the footnotes.

See also exhibition catalogs: *Plateria Sudamerica de los Siglos XVII-XX* (Munich, Bayerisches Nationalmuseum and Staatliche Museum für Völkerkunde, 1981) and *Three Centuries of Peruvian Silver* (Washington, D.C., Smithsonian Institution and New York, Metropolitan Museum of Art, 1968).

EUROPEAN GOLD AND SILVER

1953   Gruber, Alain. **Silverware.** New York, Rizzoli, 1982. 305p. illus index. ISBN 08478-04402.

Richly illustrated history of European silverware from the sixteenth to the nineteenth centuries. Emphasis is not on identification but upon the use of silver. Rare collection of views of interiors showing the historic use and place of silverware. Contents: I, The Silver Sideboard; II, Table Silver: Illustrations of Table Settings from the Sixteenth to the Nineteenth Century; III, A Typology of Silver Objects: The Table, The House. Bibliography, pp. 291-97.

See also: Hernmarck, Carl. *The Art of the European Silversmith 1430-1830* (1892).

See also the price guide: *Silver.* by T. Curtis. (New York, Coward, McCann & Geoghegan, 1982. 254p. illus. ISBN 0698111605).

Belgium

1954 Stuyck, R. **Belgische Zilvermarken/Poinçons d'argenterie belges**. Antwerp, Brussels, Erasme, 1984. 314p. illus.

Comprehensive dictionary of over 5,000 Belgian town and makers' marks used by silversmiths from the fifteenth to the nineteenth centuries. List of silversmiths with cross-references to localities.

Denmark

Dictionaries of Marks

1955 Bøje, Christian A. **Dansk guld og sølv smedemaerker før 1870**. Copenhagen, Nyt Nordisk, 1946. 589p. illus. index. Reprint: Copenhagen, Politikens Forlag, 1979. ISBN 87567-32880.

Comprehensive dictionary of over 3,000 marks found on Danish gold and silver from the fourteenth to the nineteenth centuries. Arranged by place—Copenhagen first—and then chronologically. Compact editions with introductory material in English published in 1969 by Politiken Forlag.

Histories and Handbooks

1956 Bøje, Christian A. **Gammelt dansk sølvtøj**. 2nd ed. Copenhagen, Thaning & Appel, 1960. 102p. illus. index. LC 56-22999.

Concise survey of Danish silver from the sixteenth century to the early nineteenth century with brief note on hallmarks. No bibliography. English translation of first edition (1948) published as: *Old Danish Silver*.

1957 Boesen, Gudmund, and Christian A. Bøje. **Old Danish Silver**. Copenhagen, Hassing, 1949. 35p. (text), 496 plates. index. LC 49-49539.

Pictorial survey of Danish domestic plate from 1550 to 1840 arranged by type of object, e.g., tankards, goblets, wine jugs, coffee-, chocolate-, and teapots, etc. Plates with descriptive notes. Bibliography of basic books, pp. 36-41.

1958 Lassen, Erik. **Dansk sølv**. Copenhagen, Thaning & Appel, 1964. 294p. illus. index. LC 66-80842.

Comprehensive, authoritative history of Danish silver from the early Middle Ages to the middle of the nineteenth century. Contents: Middelalder: Jelling, Gyldne altre og helgenskrin, Heilige kar, Absalons skatte, Gotiske alterkalke i det 14 århundrede, Drikkehorn, Kirkesølv fra højgotisk tid, Det oldenborgske horn; Renaissance: Christian I i Italien, Det gyldne løvvaerk, Segl og medalje, Florisstilen, Gotiske former—Renaissancens ornamentik, Omkring Rosenblommen, Kongens krone, Skattefunde og arevesølv, Drikkekander, stobe og baegre, Kongens bestillinger, sensrenaissancens sølvarbejeder; Barok: Bruskornamentik, Enevaelens majestaetssymboler, Lukus, Sølve til daglig, Lys på bordet, Filigran, Kirkesølve fra baroktiden, Te, kaffe of chokolade, Lø- og båndveark, Ligeknaekket sølve, Sølvmøbler; Rokoko: Pringdelse og oversigtt, Mester-stykket, Rokoko-sølv i hovedstad og provins, Sidste fase, Nye signaler; Klassicisme: Kritik af rokoko-sølvet, Overgangsstilen, Sølvtøjet tegnes, Den engelske indflydelse, Abildgaards sukker-skål, Tejøj, Slutning; Stempling af sølve (essay on the history of Danish silvermarks). Bibliographical references in the notes.

See also the exhibition catalog: *George Jensen Silversmithy: 77 Artist, 75 Years* (Washington, D.C., Renwick Gallery of the National Collection of Fine Arts, 1980. 127p. illus. ISBN 0874748003).

Finland

1959   Borg, Yra. **Guld-och silversmeder i Finland deras stämplar och arbeten 1373-1873.** Helsinki, Tilgmann, 1935. 528p. illus. index.
Comprehensive handbook of Finnish gold and silversmiths' work from 1373 to 1873 arranged by place and then by artist.

France

Bibliographies

1960   Marquet de Vasselot, Jean Joseph. **Bibliographie de l'orfèverie et de l'émaillerie françaises...** Paris, Picard, 1925. 293p. index. (Société Française de Bibliographie, Publications, t. 12) Reprint: New York, Garland, 1978. ISBN 0824033671.
Comprehensive, classified bibliography of more than 2,700 books and articles on French gold and silverwork and enamels published up to 1923. Contents: 1, Généralités; 2, Technique; 3, Métier; 4, Poinçons; 5, Modèles, sujets; 6, Époques; 7, Localités; 8, Musées; 9, Expositions; 10 Collections privées; 11, Trésors; 12, Artistes; 13, Objets.

Dictionaries of Marks

1961   Beuque, Émile. **Dictionnaire des poinçons officiels francais et étrangers, anciens et moderns de leur création (XIVe siècle) à nos jours.** 2v. Paris, Courtois, 1925-28. illus. index. Reprint: Paris, Nobele, 1988. LC 89-159547.
Comprehensive dictionary of nearly 6,000 control marks on platinum, gold, and silver from all over the world, but with emphasis on French marks dating from the fourteenth to the twentieth centuries. Both volumes are divided into marks in the form of figures and objects, and marks in the form of letters, numbers, and signs. Marks are illustrated in line drawings.

1962   Beuque, Émile and M. (F.) Frapsauce. **Dictionnaire des poinçons des maitres orfevres français du XIVe siècle a 1838.** Paris, Beuque-Frapsauce, 1929. 343p. illus. index. Reprint: Paris, Nobele, 1964.
Comprehensive dictionary of French gold and silversmiths' marks, illustrated with facsimiles. Supplements (1961) which emphasizes control marks. Part one covers marks containing symbols and initials; part two has marks with symbols but without initials, and part three covers marks in lozenge form.

1963   Carré, Louis. **A Guide to Old French Plate...** London, Chapman & Hall, 1931. 270p. illus. index. LC 31-30211. Reprint: London, Eyre & Spottiswoode, 1971.
Concise handbook of French gold and silver marks. Contents: I, The Marks on French Plate from the 13th Century to the End of the 18th Century: 1, The Three Kinds of Marks, 2, Glossary of Marks; II, The Marks on French Plate from the Law of 19. Brumaire, Year VI, until the Present Time: 1, The Standards and Marks, 2, Glossary of Marks. Part I is an abridged version of (1964).

1964 Carré, Louis. **Les poinçons de l'orfèverie françiase du quatorzième siècle jusqu'au debut du dix-neuvième siècle**. Paris, Carre', 1928. 355p. illus. index. Reprint: New York, B. Franklin, 1968. LC 69-19033.

Comprehensive dictionary of French gold and silver marks from the fourteenth to the early nineteenth centuries. Part one is a survey history of French silver and silver marks; part two deals with marks of master goldsmiths, assay marks, control marks, marks of confraternities, cities, and state officials, ;part three covers marks of cities with Paris first with others following in alphabetical order. Part I of (1963) is an abridged version of the work.

1965 **Dictionnaire des poinçons de l'orfèverie provinicial française**. Geneva, Droz, 1976-. V. 1-. LC 77-565816r85.

Comprehensive handbook of the marks found on French silver and gold produced outside of Paris from the Middle Ages to the nineteenth century. Each volume has an historical essay as an introduction describing the history of the gold and silversmiths' craft in the particular region, with references to and extracts from inventories, accounts, ordinances and regulations. Following is a directory of masters by place with facsimiles of their marks. When completed the dictionary will greatly supersede Helft (1966). To date the following volumes have appeared:

1. *Les Orfèvres de Franche-Comté et de la Principauté de Montbéliard du Moyen Age au XIXe siècle.* (1976). 1,088p. LC 77-562116.
2. *Les Orfèvres du ressort de la Monnaie de Bourges.* (1977). 501p.
3. *Les Orfèvres du Dauphiné du Moyen Age au XIXe siècle.* (1985). 606p. LC 85-208564.
4. *Les Orfèvres de Troyes en Champagne.* (1986). 356p.

1966 Helft, Jacques. **Le poinçon des provinces françaises**. Paris, De Nobele, 1968. 612p. illus. LC 68-111690.

Comprehensive dictionary of French provincial gold and silver marks. Arrangement is by region (place de jurisdictions) and marks are reproduced in both facsimile and photographs. Dictionary section is followed by an excellent corpus of plates illustrating major pieces. Comprehensive bibliography, pp. 600-607. Thoroughly indexed. The standard reference work on French provincial silver.

General Histories and Handbooks

1967 Babelon, Jean. **L'orfèverie française**. Paris, Larousse, 1946. 124p. illus. index.

Popular survey history of gold and silver in France from ancient Gaul to the early twentieth century. Illustrated with museum pieces. Selected bibliography, pp. 116-20.

1968 Bouilhet, Henri. **L'orfèverie française aux XVIIIe et XIXe siècle**. Paris, H. Laurens, 1902-1912. 3v. illus. index.

Comprehensive history of French gold and silver of the eighteenth and nineteenth centuries. Illustrated with pieces in museums, private collections, and dealers.

1969 Brault, Solange and Yves Bottineau. **L'orfèverie française du XVIIIe siècle**. Paris, Presses Universitaires de France, 1959. 189p. illus. index. LC 61-43045.

Popular pictorial survey of French eighteenth century featuring major museum pieces. Bibliography of books and periodical articles, pp. 109-114.

1970 Cripps, Wilfred J. **Old French Plate; Its Makers and Marks...** 3rd ed. London, Murray, 1920. 115p. illus. index. LC 10-25617.

Survey history of French silver from the seventh century to circa 1838. List of principal hallmarks. Useful appendix with pieces with makers' names and marks.

1971   Davis, Frank. **French Silver, 1450-1825**. New York, Praeger, 1970. 104p. illus. index. LC 72-516592.
Popular history directed to the collector, yet illustrated with museum pieces. Bibliography of basic books in French and English, pp. 99-100.

1972   Dennis, Faith. **Three Centuries of French Domestic Silver**. New York, Metropolitan Museum of Art, 1960. 2v. illus. index. LC 60-9288.
Comprehensive history/handbook of French domestic plate from the seventeenth to the early nineteenth centuries based on a loan exhibition at the Metropolitan Museum of Art in 1938. Contents: v. 1, Introduction by P. Remington; Illustrations of Parisian Silver; Illustrations of Provincial Silver. V. 2, Introduction; The Marks on Paris Silver; The Marks on Provincial Silver; Chronological Table of the Paris and Provincial Silver; Goldsmiths' Marks by First Initial; Devices used in Silver Marks; Illegible Marks. Classified bibliography, v. 2, pp. 189-92.

1973   Havard, Henry. **Histoire de l'orfèverie française**. Paris, May & Metteroz, 1896. 472p. illus. LC F01-2443.
Old, once-standard history of French gold and silver from the earliest times through the nineteenth century. Includes jewelry and enamels. Bibliographical footnotes.

1974   Helft, Jacques, ed. **French Master Goldsmiths and Silversmiths from the Seventeenth to the Nineteenth Century**. New York, French and European Publications, 1966. 333p. illus. LC 66-9055.
Survey history of French gold and silversmiths' art from the seventeenth to the nineteenth centuries illustrated with major museum pieces. Contents: Introduction by J. Babelon; The Age of Louis XIV and Its Splendors by Y. Bottineau; The Triumph of Rocaille by Y. Bottineau; The Return of Antiquity by Y. Bottineau; The Splendors of the Imperial Epoch by O. Lefuel. List of major hallmarks of Paris. Basic bibliography, p. 333.
See also the exhibition catalog: *Three Centuries of French Domestic Silver; Its Makers and Its Marks*, by F. Dennis (New York, Metropolitan Museum, 1960. 2v. illus. index).

Aix-en-Provence

1975   Jordan-Barry, Raymond. **Les orfèvres de la généralité d'Aix-en-Provence du XVe siècle ay début du XIXe siècle**. Paris, Nobele, 1974. 483p. illus. LC 75-508323r85.
Comprehensive handbook of gold and silversmiths active in Aix-en-Provence from the late Middle Ages to the early nineteenth century. Facsimiles of hallmarks and list of 124 pieces in various collections. Comprehensive bibliography, pp. 475-78.

Languedoc

1976   Thuile, Jean. **Histoire de l'orfèvrerie du Languedoc de Montpellier et de Toulouse. Répertoire des orfèvres depuis de moyen-âge jusqu'au début du XIXe siècle**. Paris, Schmied, 1964-69. 3v. illus. LC 76-443643.
Comprehensive, scholarly handbook/history of gold and silversmiths active in Montpellier and Toulouse from the end of the Middle Ages to the early nineteenth century. Contents: v. 1: A à C; v. 2: D à L; v. 3: M à Z.

Paris

1977   Nocq, Henry. **Le poinçon de Paris, répertoire des maitres-orfèvres de la jurisdiction de Paris depuis le moyen-âge jusqu'à la fin du XVIIIe siècle.** Paris, Floury, 1926-30. 5v. illus. index. Reprint: Paris, Laget, 1967. LC 70-351667.

Comprehensive dictionary of Parisian gold and silversmiths' marks. Contains over 5,500 marks of masters active between the thirteenth and eighteenth centuries. Alphabetical arrangement by initials: v. 1, A-C; v. 2, D-K; v. 3, L-R; v. 4, S-Z. Volume 5: errata and addenda. Volume 4 also contains: Résumé chronologique, Brèves indications, Liste des gardes, Poinçons des fermiers, Itinéraire des gardes, Notice sur les orfèvres de la généralité de Paris, Principales sources de l'histoire des orfèvres de Paris. The standard reference work for the history of Parisian silver.

Germany, Austria, and Switzerland

Dictionaries of Marks

1978   Scheffler, Wolfgang. **Berliner Goldschmiede: Daten, Werke, Zeichen.** Berlin, Hessling, 1968. 647p. illus. index. LC 74-416236.

Comprehensive, authoritative handbook of the gold and silversmiths active in Berlin from the fifteenth century to the end of the nineteenth centuries based upon extensive examination of documentary sources and actual pieces. Entries are arranged chronologically and give full biographical data including extracts from documents and facsimiles of marks and a list of signed pieces in public collections. Contains entries for over 2,500 gold and silversmiths plus coin and medal engravers, gem engravers, enamelers, embroiderers using pearls, gold and silver, and workers in mother-of-pearl and amber. Fully indexed. Comprehensive bibliography, pp. xiii-xvi. A paradigm of a scholarly dictionary of silversmiths. The author's dictionaries on other German centers and regions form, with this volume on Berlin, an unmatched work of reference. Scheffler has written similar handbooks of the gold and silversmiths of other regions of Germany. They include:

> *Goldschmiede Hessens: Daten, Werke, Zeichen.* Berlin and New York, de Gruyter, 1976. 848p. illus. index. LC
>
> *Goldschmiede am Main und Neckar: Daten, Werke, Zeichen.* Hanover, Verlag für Kunst und Antiquitäten, 1977. 119p. illus. index. LC
>
> *Goldschmiede Mittel- und Nordostdeutschlands von Wernigerodebis Lauenburg in Pommern: Daten, Werke, Zeichen.* Berlin and New York, de Gruyter, 1980. 666p. illus. index. ISBN
>
> *Goldschmiede Niedersachsens: Daten, Werke, Zeichen.* Berlin, DeGruyter, 1965. 2v. illus. index. LC 66-50161.
>
> *Goldschmiede Ostpreussens: Daten, Werke, Zeichen.* Berlin andNew York, de Gruyter, 1983. 346p. illus. index. Goldschmiede Rhineland-Westfalens: Daten, Werke, Zeichen.Berlin, De Gruyter, 1973. 2v. illus. index. LC 72-81568.

Histories and Handbooks

1979   Braun, Joseph. **Meisterwerke der deutschen Goldschmiedekunst der vorgotischen Zeit.** Munich, Riehn and Reusch, 1922. 2v. illus. (Sammelbande zur Geschichte der Kunst und des Kunstgewerbes, Band VIII). Reprint: New York, Garland, 1979. ISBN 082403354X.

Pictorial survey of gold and silver work made in the German-speaking countries from the eighth to the early thirteenth centuries. Includes major pieces in mixed media such as the great reliquary shrines of the twelfth century. Contains 192 plates arranged in chronological order with detailed notes that include bibliographical references. General bibliographies appear at the beginning of the notes in each volume.

1980   Heuser, Hans-Jörgen. **Oberrheinische Goldschmiedekunst im Hochmittelalter.** Berlin, Deutscher Verlag für Kunstwissenschaft, 1974. 250p. illus. index. ISBN 3871570410.

Comprehensive, scholarly history of goldsmiths' art in the region of the upper Rhineland from 1200 to 1350. Includes seals and engraved gems and cameos. Catalog of 177 pieces. Contents: 1, Strassburg um 1200; 2, Strassburger Siegel und Verwandtes; 3, Der Onyx von Schaffhausen und die staufischen Kronenteile in Stockholm; 4, Eine Deckelschale mit Strassburger Beschau; 5, Die Johannes-Werkstatt in Freiburg; 6, Freiburger Ateliers seit der Jahrhundertwende; 7, Meister Konrad von Hausen in Konstanz; 8, Der Goldschmiede des Katharinentaler Konventsiegels; 9, Das Ziborium von Klosterneuburg; 10, Versenktes Relief und Email in der Hochgotik; 11, Die grossen Meister in Konstanz seit der Jahrhundertwende; 12, Werkstätten zwischen Breisgau und Bodensee; 13, Die sogennanten Wiener: Schmelze des 14. Jahrhunderts; 14, Konstanz oder Zürich; 15, Zürcher Siegel und andere Goldschmiedearbeiten aus der Stadt; 16, Basel. Der Münsterschatz und Siegel der Stadt; 17, Membra disiecta; 18, Werkkatalog; 19, Siegelkatalog; 20, Urkunden; 21, Abgekürzt zitierte Literatur; 22, Register. Full scholarly apparatus.

1981   Leitermann, Heinz. **Deutsche Goldschmiedekunst; das Goldschmiedehandwerk in der deutschen Kunst- und Kulturgeschichte.** Stuttgart, Kohlhammer, 1953. 156p. illus. index. (Urban Bucher, 8). LC A55-2431.

Concise history of gold and silver in German-speaking lands from the early Middle Ages to the twentieth century. Contents: I, Schätze aus germanischer Zeit; II, Monumentale Schöpfungen des Mittelalters; III, Gotik in Gold und Silber; IV, Meister und Werke der renaissaance; V, Von der Barockzeit bis zur Gegenwart; VI, In der Werkstatt des Meisters; VII, Zwischen Arbeittisch und Zunfstube; VIII, Neue Zeit—neue Möglichkeiten. Descriptive notes to the plates include bibliographical references. Further bibliography in the notes.

1982   Overzier, Claus. **Deutsches Silber: Formen und Typen, 1550-1850.** Munich, Klinkhardt & Biermann, 1987. 185p. illus. index. ISBN 3781402630.

Comprehensive history/handbook of German silverware from the late Middle Ages to circa 1830 by type of object. Contents: Pokale; Humpen, Kannen, Krüge; Becher; Kannen und Becken; Deckelschüsseln; Terrinen; Scraubflaschen; Teedosen; Kaffeekannen; Schokoladekannen; Teekannen; Sahnekännchen; Dosen: Toilettedosen, Zuckerdosen; Kleine Deckelschälchen (Salbdöschen); Gewürzdosen; Tellem, Platten, Tablettes, Schüsseln; Fußplatten; Saucieren; Schalen; Henkelschälchen; Leuchter; Reiseservice und Bestecke; Salzschälchen; Senfgefäße; Zuckerstreuer; Tafelaufsätze und andere Tischgeräte; Schreibzeuge; Räuchergefäße und Riechdosen; Fälschungen und Verfälschungen. General bibliography, pp. 173-74, and further bibliography in the notes.

1983   Schade, Gunter. **Deutsche Goldschmiedekunst.** Leipzig, Koehler and Amelang, 1974. 241p. illus. index. LC 75-571246r883.

Authoritative survey of German gold and silver art from the early Middle Ages to the early nineteenth century. Emphasis is on the works of highest aesthetic quality and the relationship between art in gold and silver and the general culture. Contents: Gold und Silber; Attribute von Reichtum und Macht; Die berühmtesten Schatzfunde in Deutschland; Gold und Silber: Vorkommen, Abbau, Eigenschaften; Maße und Gewichte; Die handwerklichen Techniken des Goldschmieds; Die Goldschmiede und ihre Stellung in der Gesellschaft; Meisterwerke der karolingischen Zeit; Die mittelalterliche Reliquienverehrung und ihre Bedeutung für die Goldschmiedekunst; Die Goldschmiedekunst in ottonischer Zeit; Goldschmiedearbeiten der romanischen Zeit; Die Goldschmiedekunst der Gotik; Die Rolle der Zünfte und die Organization des Goldschmiedehandwerks; Die Goldschmiedekunst im Zeitalter der Renaissance; Die Goldschmiedekunst im Klassizismus. Glossary and short repertory of major city hallmarks. General bibliography, pp. 230-32.

Aachen

1984 Grimme, Ernst G. **Aachener Goldschmiedekunst im Mittelalter von Karl dem Grossen bis zu Karl V.** Cologne, Seemann, 1957. 211p. illus. index. LC 57-34253.

History of gold and silversmiths' art in Aachen from the eighth to the middle of the sixteenth centuries based largely on examples in the treasury of the Cathedral of Aachen and other church treasuries.

Augsburg

1985 Seling, Helmut. **Die Kunst der Augsburger Goldschmiede 1529-1868: Meister, Marken, Werke.** 3v. Munich, Beck, 1980. illus. index. ISBN 3406057292.

Comprehensive history of the gold and silver art of Augsburg between 1529 and 1868. Includes both secular and ecclesiastical work. Volume one is an authoritative history based on documentary sources as well as detailed knowledge of the over 1,000 pieces presented in a scholarly catalog in the second volume. Third volume is a dictionary of town and makers' marks. A standard work on the history of Augsburg silver and a paradigm for all regional histories in the applied and decorative arts.

Lübeck

1986 Warncke, Johs. **Die Edelschmiedekunst in Lübeck und ihre Meister.** Lübeck, Max— Schmidt-Römhild, 1927. 368p. illus.

History of gold and silver art in Lübeck from the thirteenth to the nineteenth centuries with biographical data and marks of 665 masters.

Munich

1987 Frankenburger, Max. **Die alt-Münchner Goldschmiede und ihre Kunst.** Munich, Bruckmann, 1912. 558p. illus. index.

Comprehensive history of the art of the gold and silversmiths of Munich from 1292 to 1805. First part is a history of Munich gold and silver; part two a chronological listing of biographies with transcriptions of archival documents and list of marks.

Nuremberg

1988 Kohlhaussen, Heinrich. **Nürnberger Goldschmiedekunst des Mittelalters und der Dürerzeit 1240 bis 1540.** Berlin, Deutscher Verlag für Kunstwissenschaft, 1968. 590p. illus. index. LC 77-377748.

Authoritative essays on major aspects of the history of gold and silversmiths' art in Nuremberg between 1240 and 1540. Contents: Nürnberger Siegel um 1240-1530; Reliquienträger des 14. und 15. Jahrhunderts und Verwandtes; Nürnberger Buchbeschläge 14.-16. Jahrhundert; Frühe Kelche um 1330-1430; Greifenklaue, Strausseneier; Glattwandige Gefässe; Späte Kelche zwischen 1430 und 1530; Monstranzen; Reliquiare um 1500; Dürer und die Tischbrunnen; Silberschiffe; Das gebuckelte Gefäss; Der Einbruch von Naturformen, Dürer und die Krug-Werkstatt; Melchior Baier d. Ä. und Peter Flötner; Der Meister ME und 1535; Weitere Goldscmiede nach Ludwig Krug und neben Melchior Baier; Die Meister; Die Beschau; Die Meistermarken, Signaturen; Beziehungen. All of the essays end with a scholarly catalog of the works with references to the specialized literature. Comprehensive bibliography, pp. 532-34.

See also the exhibition catalog: *Wenzel Jamnitzer und die Nürnberger Goldschmiedekunst 1500-1700...* by G. Bott, ed. (Munich, Klinkhardt & Biermann, 1985. 531p. illus. index. ISBN 3781402533).

Vienna

1989 Neuwirth, Waltraud. **Lexikon Wiener Gold- und Silberschmiede und ihre Punzen, 1867-1922**. Vienna, Neuwirth, 1976, 1977. 2v. illus. index. ISBN 3900282005.

Comprehensive dictionary of gold and silversmiths active in Vienna between 1867 and 1922. Includes jewelers. Arranged alphabetically by name. Volume one covers A-K, volume two, L-Z. Entries give the makers' marks in facsimile, basic biographical data, and references to work in major exhibitions. Illustrated with drawings and photographs. Volume one has "Annals of the Viennese Goldsmiths," a chronological list of events from 1170 to 1965 affecting the work of gold and silversmiths in Vienna. Volume two has the essay "Modern Austrian Jewelry" by W. Fred reprinted from the Studio of 1908.

Zurich

1990 Lösel, Eva-Maria et al. **Zürcher Goldschmiedekunst vom 13. bis zum 19. Jahrhundert**. Zurich, Buchverlag Berichthaus, 1983. 503p. illus. index. ISBN 3855720479.

Comprehensive history/handbook of gold and silversmiths' work in Zurich from the thirteenth to the nineteenth centuries. First part is a history; second part a dictionary of 693 artists with short biographies, list of works, and facsimiles of their marks.

Johann Melchior Dinglinger

1991 Watzdorf, Erna von. **Johann Melchior Dinglinger der Goldschmied des deutschen Barock**. Berlin, Mann, 1962. 2v. illus. index. LC 63-38407.

Comprehensive, authoritative, scholarly monograph on the most outstanding goldsmith of the baroque period. Contents: Band I: I. Leben; II, Werke: Das Georgskleinod; Die Juwelengarnituren Augusts des Starken; Kabinettstücke. Pretiosen. Band II: III, Brüder und Sohn: Georg Friedrich Dinglingers Leben und Werke; George Christoph Dinglingers Leben und Werke; Johann Friedrich Dinglingers Leben und Werke; IV, Würdigung. Appendices with documents in extract, catalog of the potraits of the Dinglingers, and catalog of the works of the Dinglingers. Comprehensive bibliography, pp. 423-27, includes lists of unpublished sources. Standard work on Dinglinger and a model monograph on a major goldsmith.

Great Britain

Dictionaries of Marks and Signatures

1992 Banister, Judith, ed. **English Silver Hall Marks Including the Marks of Origin on Scottish & Irish Silver Plate, Gold, Platinum & Sheffield Plate**. 2d ed. London, W. Foulsham & Co., 1983. 118p. ISBN

Pocket-sized dictionary of major British (over 500) assay, hallmarks and makers' marks arranged by city and by maker. Historical introduction. Similiar works without the Scottish material are Bradbury, Frederick. *Guide to Marks of Origin on British and Irish Silver Plate from Mid-16th Century to the Year 1959,*. 10th ed. (Sheffield, Northend, 1959. 93p. illus.), Bradbury,

Frederick. British and Irish Silver Assay Office Marks, 1544-1954... 9th ed. (Sheffield, Northend, 1955. 90p. illus.).

1993 Chaffers, William. **Hall Marks on Gold & Silver Plate...** 10th ed. London, Reeves, 1922. 395p. illus. index. LC 22-12010.

Comprehensive dictionary of hallmarks on English, Scottish, and Irish silver and gold with table of ordinances affecting hallmarks, chronological list of English plate, and table of London gold and silversmiths. Bibliography of the older literature, pp. 373-83. An old standard work largely superseded by Jackson (1995).

1994 Cripps, Wilfred J. **Old English Plate; Ecclesiastical, Decorative and Domestic: Its Makers and Marks.** 11th ed. London, Murray, 1926. 540p. illus. index. Reprint: Wakefield, Eng., E. P. Pub., 1977. ISBN 071581236X.

First published in 1878. Older dictionary/handbook of British silver makers and marks with a useful appendix of pieces used as authority for London date-letters and makers' marks, plus tables of date-letters on other English silver and on Irish and Scottish silver. A similar work is Howard, Montague, *Old English Silver: Its History, Its Makers and Its Marks,* (New York, Scribner's; London, Batsford, 1903. 421p. illus.), but with a useful section on the evolution of particular types of silver, e.g., spoons, knives, forks, cups, tankards, salvers, candlesticks, etc.

1995 Jackson, Charles J. **English Goldsmiths and Their Marks; a History of the Goldsmiths and Plate Workers of England, Scotland, and Ireland...** 2nd ed. London, Macmillan, 1921. 747p. illus. index. Reprint: New York, Dover, 1964. LC 64-18852. 3rd rev. ed. is titled *Jackson's Silver & Gold Marks of England, Scotland & Ireland.* Edited by Ian Pickford. Woodbridge, Antique Collectors' Club, 1989. 766p. illus. ISBN 0907462634.

First published in 1905. Comprehensive handbook of British gold and silversmiths and their marks. Introductory chapters treat legislation concerning goldsmiths and standards for gold and silver in Great Britain and Ireland. Dictionary of over 13,000 assay, year, town, and makers' marks is arranged by place and illustrated with facsimiles. The standard reference work for British gold and silver marks.

General Dictionaries and Encyclopedias

1996 Ash, Douglas. **Dictionary of British Antique Silver.** New York, Hippocrene Books, 1972. 189p. illus. LC 72-80991.

Popular dictionary with short entries for types of silverware, techniques, and styles, each illustrated with line drawings. Emphasis is on British silver of the seventeenth through the early nineteenth centuries. Brief selected bibliography, p. 189.

1997 Clayton, Michael. **The Collector's Dictionary of Silver and Gold of Great Britain and North America.** 2d ed. Woodbridge, Antique Collectors' Club, 1985. 481p. illus. index. ISBN 090746257X.

Comprehensive dictionary of silver in Great Britain and North America from 1180 to 1880 covering silversmiths and other artists who designed silverwork, types of objects, decorative motifs, materials, techniques, and places. Very well illustrated with 730 plates, many with more than one object. The longer entries have bibliographies at the end. The classified bibliography, pp. 472-480, is the most comprehensive list of books in English available. A standard collector's handbook.

General Histories and Handbooks

1998 Banister, Judith. **English Silver**. New York, Hawthorn, 1966. 251p. illus. LC 66-16161.

Popular history/handbook covering English silver from 1500 to 1960. Part one covers technique, hallmarks, and collecting and includes a glossary of terms and brief bibliography of basic works. Part two consists of short essays on the characteristics of the major periods in the history of English silver.

See also English Silver by J. M. Dennis (New York, Walker, 1970. 83p. illus.), *Three Centuries of English Domestic Silver, 1500-1820* by G. B. and Therle Hughes (New York, Praeger, 1968. 248p. illus. index.), and *Silver for Pleasure and Investment* by G. Wills, (New York, Arco, 1969. 169p. illus. index).

1999 Clayton, Michael. **Christie's Pictorial History of English and American Silver**. Oxford, Phaidon-Christie's, 1985. 319p. illus. index. ISBN 0714880183.

Comprehensive history of silver in England and North America from the fifteenth century to 1860. Compliments the author's *Dictionary . . .* (1994). Contents: 1, Elizabethan; 2, Jacobean, Carolean and Commonwealth; 3, Restoration, Charles II, James II; 4, William and Mary; 5, Queen Anne and George I; 6, George II; 7, George III; 8, Regency, George V, William IV; 9, Victorian. Within the periods the chapters are subdivided by type or class of object. Well-illustrated with pieces sold at Christie's with prices paid in appendix. Brief bibliography of basic books, pp. 305-306, with note to seek fuller bibliography in the author's *Dictionary. . .*(1994).

2000 Glanville, Philippa. **Silver in England**. London, Unwinm & Allen; New York, Holmes & Meier, 1987. 366p. illus. index. ISBN 0047480041.

In the series: "English Decorative Arts." Comprehensive history of silver in England from the Middle Ages to the present. Part one provides a six-part history; part two a three-part analysis of the craft, organization, and clientele of silversmiths; part three is a three-part examination of the history of design and ornament in English silver; part four is a two-part history of attitudes toward collecting and the sociology of silver, i.e., the uses of silver. Comprehensive, classified bibliography, pp. 338-355, and specialized literature in the notes. A well-rounded history of English silver.

2001 Grimwade, Arthur. **Rococo Silver, 1727-65**. London, Faber and Faber, 1974. 96p. illus. index. LC 74-188299.

In the series: "Faber Monographs on Silver." Authoritative survey of English silver made between 1727 and 1765 in the Rococo style. Particular attention is given to large pieces of hollowware and the work of Paul de Lamerie. Contents: I, The Rise and Fall of the Style; II, Development of the Craft; III, Frederick, Prince of Wales, As Patron of Rococo Silver; IV, The Forms of Plate; V, The Cost of Plate; VI, Engraving. Basic bibliography, pp. 68-69.

2002 Holland, Margaret. **Old Country Silver: A Account of English Provincial Silver, with Sections on Ireland, Scotland and Wales**. New York, Arco, 1971. 240p. illus. index. LC 79-160142.

Important addition to the literature on British silver as it covers the provincial work often ignored in other histories. Arranged by region and town. Well-illustrated with museum pieces and pieces accessible to the average collector, plus facsimiles of major hallmarks. Classified bibliography of books and periodical articles, pp. 227-230.

2003   Jackson, Charles J. **An Illustrated History of English Plate, Ecclesiastical and Secular...** London, Country Life, 1911. 2v. illus. index. Reprint: New York, Dover, 1969. ISBN 0486-223345.

Comprehensive history/handbook of English, Irish, and Scottish silver from the early Middle Ages to the end of the Georgian period. Designed as a collector's handbook to complement the author's dictionary of marks (1995). In spite of its antiquity, still the most informative source for the identification of the numerous types of silverware, particularly of the eighteenth century. Contents: Volume I: Part I: Chronological: I, The Early British Period. Native Work in Britain and Ireland (1500 B.C.-A.D. 200); II, The Roman Period; III, The Anglo-Saxon Period; IV, The Art of the Goldsmith in Ireland in the Middle Ages; V, The Norman Period; VI, The Gothic Period; VII, The Period of the Renaissance; VIII, The Early Stuart and Commonwealth Period; IX, The Late Stuart Period; X, The Period of the Enforced High Standard for Plate; XI, The Rococo Period; XII, The Late Georgian Period; Part II: Ecclesiastical Plate; XIII, Chalices and Patens; XIV, Altar-Cruets, Spoons, Pyxes, and Ciboria, Monstrances, Censers, Bells, Shrines, Candlesticks, Paxbredes, Chrismatories, Croziers, Mitres, Processional Crosses, Reliquaries, Diptychs, Triptychs, and Other Articles; XV, Post-Reformation Communion Plate. Communion Cups and Patens; XVI, Communion Flagons, Ewers and Basins, Altar Dishes, Altar Candlesticks, and Alms Dishes. Volume II: Part III: Secular Plate; XVII, The Spoon and Its History with References to the Table-knife and Table-fork; XVIII, The Salt or Salt-Cellars; XIX, Rose-water Dishes and Ewers; XX, Silver-Mounted Horns; XXI, Mazers and Vessels of Mazer-like Form Constructed of Silver or Having Silver Mounts; XXII, Hanaps, or Standing Cups; XXIII, Beakers, Font and Tazza-Shaped Cups, Goblets, Small Wine-cups, and Tumblers; XXIV, Two-Handled Cups, Including Porringers and Candle Cups, Tasters, Saucers, Sweetmeat Dishes, and Quaichs; XXV, Flagons, Pilgrim Bottles, Tankards and Mugs, Silver-Mounted Jugs of Stoneware, Earthenware, Marble, Glass and Ostrich-Egg, Black Jacks and Leathern Bottles; XXVI, Wine-Fountains and Wine-Coolers, Punch-Bowls, Monteiths and Punch-Ladles; XXVII, Plates and Dishes; Skillets, Broth-Bowls, Soup-Tureens, Sauce-Boats, Sauce-Tureens and Argyles, Salvers, Boxes for Spice and Sweetmeats, Casters and Muffineers, Cruets, Cruet-Frames and Mustard-Pots; XXVIII, Candlesticks, Including Scones and Candelabra, Snuffers, Snuffer-trays, and Stands; XXIX, Andirons or Fire-Dogs, Vases and Beaker-Shaped Ornaments, Furniture, Toilet-sets, Standishes or Ink-Stands, Tobacco-Boxes, Snuff-Boxes, Freedom-Boxes, Pomanders and Vinaigrettes; XXX, Articles Formed Mainly of Pierced Sheet Metal and Wire-Work; XXXI, Tea-Pots, Coffee-Pots, Chocolate-Pots, and Jugs for Hot Water and Milk, Tea-Caddies, Tea-Kettles, Tea-Urns, and Tea-Cups, Sugar-Bowls, Sugar-Tongs, and Cream-Jugs; XXXII, Ceremonial and Official Plate.

2004   Okie, Howard P. **Old Silver and Old Sheffield Plate, a History of the Silversmith's Art in Great Britain and Ireland....** 2nd ed. New York, Doubleday, 1952. 420p. illus. index.

First published in 1928. Older history/handbook of British silver designed for the collector. Useful chapter on Sheffield plate. Provides lists of British, American, and some continental silver date-letters, place marks, and makers marks.

2005   Taylor, Gerald. **Silver**. 2nd ed. Baltimore, Md.,Penguin, 1963. 301p. illus. index. LC 63-25568.

Survey of British and American silver from the Middle Ages through the Regency period, with epilogue on Victorian and modern silver. Illustrated with museum pieces (mostly domestic silver). Glossary of terms, table of major hallmarks, and note on how to clean silver. Good, classified bibliography of books, pp. 286-96.

2006   Wardle, Patricia. **Victorian Silver and Silver-plate**. New York, Universe, 1963. 238p. illus. index. LC 67-20988.

Survey history of silver and silver-plated ware in Britain from 1830 to 1900. Contents: 1, 1837-50; 2, Sheffield Plate; 3, Electro-plate; 4, The Society of Arts, Henry Cole and Felix Summerly; 5, The Great Exhibition of 1851; 6, Silver Sculpture; 7, 1851-62; 8, The International Exhibition of 1862; 9, Racing Trophies and Testimonials; 10, Armstead, Morel, Ladeuil and Wilms; 11, 1862-80; 12, Christopher Dresser; 13, 1880-1901; 14, New Developments in 1890s. Appendices with marks. General bibliography, pp. 227-28.

2007   Wenham, Edward. **Domestic Silver of Great Britain and Ireland**. New York, Oxford University Press, 1935. 186p. illus. index. LC 32-31287.

Collector's history of domestic silver made in Great Britain and Ireland from circa A.D. 500 to circa 1930 with emphasis on hollowware from 1725 to 1830. Contents: I, Anglo-Saxon and Gothic; II, From the Renaissance to the Enforced High Standard; III, The Georgian Period; IV, The Victorian Period and After; V, The Traditions of Table Silver; VI, The Silversmiths of Scotland; VII, The Silversmiths of Ireland; VIII, Marks on English Silver; IX, Sheffield Plate; X, Methods of Forging Old Silver; XI, Recent Auction Prices. Chapter V is a fairly detailed description of the major types of domestic silver, e.g., spoons, forks, knives, and skewers, standing-salts and salt-cellars, ewers, basins, salvers, and trays, drinking-horns, mazers, standing-cups, candle-cups, goblets, beakers, and tumblers, pilgrim bottles, flagons, black-jacks, tankards, and mugs, tasters and saucers, wine-fountains, wine-cisterns, wine-coolers, punch-bowls, and Monteiths, skillets, broth-bowls, and saucepans, soup-tureens, entré and covered dishes, sauce-boats, sauce-tureens, and argyles, small-boxes, pomanders, and vinaigrettes, muffineers, casters, cruet-frames, and mustard-pots, dishes, plates, and dish-crosses, candlesticks, candelabra, taper-sticks, and snuffers, vases, scones, and furniture, toilet services, standishes and inkstands, pierced articles, cake-baskets, sweetmeat-baskets, and cruet-frames, decanter stands, centre-pieces and espergnes, teapots, tea caddies, cream-jugs, sugar-bowls, and sugar-tongs, tea-services, coffee-pots, chocolate-pots, and biggins, hot-water kettles and urns, tea-cups. Brief bibliography, p. 176.

England

2008   Oman, Charles C. **Caroline Silver, 1625-1688**. London, Faber and Faber, 1970. 73p. illus. ISBN 0571094422.

Introduction to English silver from 1625 to 1688. Contents: I, The Artistic Climate; II, The Crown and the Goldsmiths; III, Trends and Techniques; IV, Brief Lives of Some Eminent Goldsmiths; V, Dining Room Plate; VI, Plate about the House. Appendix with list of plate given to the Duchess of Portsmouth. General bibliography, pp. 66-67, and further bibliography in the notes. Index of gold and silversmiths with facsimiles of their marks, pp. 72-73.

2009   Oman, Charles C. **English Church Plate, 597-1830**. London, Oxford University Press, 1957. 326p. illus. index. LC 58-445.

Comprehensive history of Roman Catholic and Anglican ecclesiastical silver from the early Middle Ages to 1830 with special attention to the history of patronage and liturgical function. Illustrated with museums pieces chiefly from the provinces of Canterbury and York. Contents: Part I: The Middle Ages: I, The Church and the Goldsmiths; II, The Plate of the Churches; III, The Plate of the Private Chapels; IV, Security in Medieval Times; V, Mass Plate; VI, Altar Plate; VII, Miscellanea. Part II, Church Plate and King: I, The King as Donor; II, The King as Spoiler;. Part III: Since the Reformation: I, The Church and the Goldsmiths, II, The Plate of the Churches; III, The Plate of the Private Chapels; IV, Security in Post-Reformation Times; V, Communion Plate, VI, Altar Plate, VII, Miscellanea. Part IV: The Catholic Recusants: I, The Catholic Recusants and the Goldsmiths, II, Mass Plate, III, Miscellanea; Conclusion. Comprehensive, classified bibliography, pp. 291-297. appendices with a list of medieval chalices and patens, list of Edwardian communion cups, distribution of communion cups and paten-covers made by

Elizabethan goldsmith IP, list of Anglican seventeenth-century Gothic chalices, lists of goldsmiths who worked for the Catholic Recusants to 1697. Thorough index. A standard work.

2010   Oman, Charles C. **English Domestic Silver**. 7th ed. London, A. & C. Black, 1968. 240p. illus. index. LC 79-406854.

Companion volume to the author's history of church silver (2009) but with a more popular tone and directed to the needs of the collector. Chapters treat the goldsmith and his craft, development of style, major classes of plate, hallmarks, heraldic engraving and fakes. Illustrated with museum pieces. General bibliography, pp. 233-234.

2011   Oman, Charles C. **English Engraved Silver 1150 to 1900**. London and Boston, Faber and Faber, 1978. 158p. illus. index. ISBN 0571104983.

Survey of the technique, style and iconography of English silver with engraved decoration. Covers church and domestic silver. Chronological arrangement. Appendices with catalog of works attributed to the engravers P over M and a list of apprentices and their masters taken from the records of the Goldsmiths' Company. Bibliographical references in the notes; select bibliography, p.154.

2012   Row, Robert. **Adam Silver, 1765-1795**. London, Faber and Faber; New York, Taplinger, 1965. 94p. illus. index. LC 65-20355.

In the series: "Faber Monographs on Silver." History of silver made in England in the style introduced by Robert Adam. Contents: I, Introduction: the Artistic Climate; II, Robert Adam: the Composition of a Style; III, London Made; IV, Birmingham and Sheffield I: A Revolution in Method; V, Birmingham and Sheffield II: The Provinces Established; VI, London and the Second Phase of Neo-Classicism; VII. Marketing, Competition and Pieces. Short bibliography of basic books, p. 89, further bibliography in the footnotes.

2013   Schroder, Timothy. **The National Trust Book of English Domestic Silver 1500-1900**. New York, Viking, 1988. 338p. illus. index. ISBN 0670802379.

Comprehensive history of English domestic silver from the early Tudors to the end of the Victorian Era with emphasis on the use of silver. Contents: 1, Silver: The Metal and the Craft; 2, The Early Tudors; 3, The Elizabethan Age; 4, The Early Seventeenth Century; 5, The Restoration; 6, The Huguenot Contribution; 7, The Rococo Period; 8, Neo-Classicism and Industrialization; 9, The Early Nineteenth Century; 10, The Victorian Era: Craft and Industry. Appendix with biographies of major English goldsmiths. Brief bibliography, p. 319, but specialized bibliography in the notes. The organization of this work belies the innovative, sociological, and economical approaches used by the author in writing the history of English silver.

2014   Watts, W. W. **Old English Silver**. New York, Scribner's, 1924. 179p. illus. index. LC 24-30749.

Older, classic comprehensive history/handbook of English silver from the eighth to the early nineteenth centuries. Text is useful today for the many references to silver in life of the times and the corpus of 134 plates is one of the most extensive. Contents: I, The Goldsmiths' Guilds and Societies; II, Causes of Disappearance of Old Silver; III, The Anglo-Saxon Period; IV, The Medieval Period; V, The 16th Century. The Tudor Period; VI, The 17th Century, to the End of the Commonwealth Period; VII, The 17th Century, from the Restoration until the Year 1700; VIII, The 18th Century, to the End of the Reign of George II; IX, The 18th and 19th Centuries, the Reigns of George III and George IV; X, Ecclesiastical Plate: Pre-Reformation; XI, Ecclesiastical Plate: Post-Reformation, to the End of the Commonwealth Period; XII, Ecclesiastical Plate: from the Restoration to Charles II. Appendix with essay on hallmarks. Bibliographical references in the footnotes.

See also the exhibition catalog: *Women Silversmith, 1685-1845: Works from the Collection of the National Museum of Women in the Arts*, by P. Granville, J.F. Goldsborough (New York, Thames & Hudson, 1990. 176p. illus. ISBN 0500235783).

Sheffield Plate

2015   Bradbury, Frederick. **History of Old Sheffield Plate: Being an Account of the Origin, Growth, and Decay of the Industry and of the Antique Silver and White or Britannnia Metal Trade...** Sheffield, 1968. 539p. illus. LC 74-417915.

First published in 1912. Comprehensive history of Sheffield plate with an important repertory of marks. Contents: I, The Invention; II, The Earliest Manufacturers of Sheffield Plate; III, History of the Trade; IV, Processes, Practices and Inventions; V, Surviving Methods, with Illustrations of Workshops, Tools, and Materials; VI, Innovation That Revolutionized the Old Trade; VII, Locality of Manufacture; VIII, Advice to Collectors—Designers; IX, Ascertaining Dates of Specimens; X, List of Makers and Their Marks; XI, Other Industries Connected with Old Sheffield Plate. The Manufacturer of Silver; XII, The Britannia Metal Industry.

2016   Hughes, George B. **Sheffield Silver Plate**. New York, Praeger, 1970. 303p. illus. index. LC 72-114296.

Comprehensive history/handbook of Sheffield plate directed to the collector. Contents: I, Introduction: Silver Plating on Steel; 2, The Discovery of Sheffield Plate; 3, Identifying Sheffield Plate 4, Manufacturing Processes; 5, Decoration and Finishing Techniques; 6, Edges and Mounts; 7, Makers' Marks; 8, British Plate; 9, Domestic Lighting I; 10, Domestic Lighting, II; 11, The Service of Wine, I; 12, The Service of Wine, II; 13, The Tea Equipage; 14, The Service of Coffee; 15, Epergnes; 16, Dinner Ware; Breakfast and Supper Dishes; 17, Dish Rings; Dish Crosses and Stands; 18, Sauce and Gravy Vessels; Boats, Tureens; Argyles; Saucepans; 19, Cruets and Soy Frames; 20, Mustard Pots and Salt-cellars; 21, Egg-cup Stands, Egg-boilers and Toast Racks; 22, Fish Slices; Asparagus Servers; Mazarines; 23, Waiters and Trays; 24, Inkstands; 25, Snuff-boxes; Patch-boxes and Bonbonnieres; Nutmeg Graters; 26, Buttons; 27, Wire-work; 28, Miscellaneous. Contains 269 plates with descriptive notes. Basic bibliography, p. 267.

2017   Robertson, Richard A. **Old Sheffield Plate**. London, Benn, 1957. 190p. illus. LC 57-4785.

Concise survey of Sheffield plate with particular attention given to the evolution of the technique of manufacture. Contents: I, Introductory; II, Close Plating. French Plating and Fused Plate; III, The Pioneers and the Things They Made; IV, The Industry Established. Bradbury, Roberts, Nicolson and Boulton; V, About Techniques—Die-sinking. Flat Hammering. Swaging. Wire Edging. Spinning. Piercing. Soldering and Burnishing; VI, Techniques Continued—Flat Chasing. Engraving. Soldered-in Shields. Rubbed-in Shields. Tea-urn Taps. Fakes; VII, Where Old Sheffield Plate was Made. The Establishment of Assay Offices at Sheffield and Birmingham. Registration of Platers' Marks; VIII, Makers' Marks; IX, Silver Design during the Period of Old Sheffield Plate Manufacture; X, Old Sheffield Plate in the Dining-room; XI, Old Sheffield Plate on the Breakfast and Tea Tables; XII, The Part of Old Sheffield Plate in Domestic Lighting. Conclusion. Appendix with list of museums in Great Britain, Ireland, and the United States with notable collections of Sheffield plate. No bibliography.

2018   Wyler, Seymour B. **The Book of Sheffield Plate**. New York, Crown, 1949. 188p. illus. index. LC 49-9252.

Collector's handbook/history of Sheffield plate with a useful repertory of hallmarks that include later, i.e., Victorian, silver-plate, all given in facsimile. Contents: 1, Definition of Sheffield Plate—Discovery of the Process; 2, Laws Regulating the Production of Sheffield Plate; 3, The

Problems of Manufacture and How They Were Overcome; 4, Other Countries Where Sheffield Plate was Produced; 5, Outstanding Makers of Sheffield Plate; 6, Articles Made in Sheffield Plate—I; 7, Articles Made in Sheffield Plate—II; 8, Articles Mmade in Sheffield Plate—III; 9, History of Electroplating; 10, Identification of Originals and Recognition of Spurious Pieces; 11, The Collecting of Sheffield Plate; 12, The Care and Cleaning of Sheffield Plate.

See also the price list: Thomas Price, *The Price Guide to Old Sheffield Plate* (Woodbridge, Antique Collector's Club, 1978. 396p. illus.).

London

2019   Culme, John. **The Directory of Gold & Silversmiths, Jewellers & Allied Traders 1838-1814 from the London Assay Office Registers.** 2v. illus. index. Woodbridge, Antique Collectors' Club, 1987. ISBN 0907462464.

Comprehensive dictionary of the gold and silversmiths, jewelers, watch and clock makers, etc. registered with the London Assay Office between 1838 and 1914. Continues Grimwade (2019). The biographic data of over 4,000 individuals and firms is provided in volume one, their marks in volume two. The biographical information comes mostly from the registers of the London Assay Office with trade and street directories as supplemental sources. Marks are photographic reproductions of those on the strike plates of the assay office. Biographical entries have references to secondary literature.

2020   Grimwade, Arthur G. **London Goldsmiths, 1697-1837: Their Marks and Lives from the Original Registers at Goldsmiths' Hall and Other Sources.** London, Faber and Faber, 1976. 728p. illus. ISBN 0571180655.

Comprehensive dictionary of London goldsmiths. Supplements Jackson (1995). Part one is a dictionary of nearly 4,000 marks of London goldsmiths active between the 1697 and the accession of Queen Victoria in 1837. Includes both the registered marks and unregistered marks taken from pieces. Includes marks of provincial goldsmiths registered in London and the marks of jewelers, watchcase makers and other specialists working in gold and silver. Part two is a biographical dictionary covering 2,500 London gold and silversmiths. The standard handbook on London silver and gold. Continued by Culme (2019). A concise dictionary of the major London silversmiths' marks of the same period is: Fallon, John P. *Marks of London Goldsmiths and Silversmiths, Georgian Period* (Newton Abbot, David & Charles, 1972. 420p. illus.).

2021   Heal, Ambrose. **The London Goldsmiths, 1200-1800: a Record of the Names and Addresses of the Craftsmen, Their Shop-Signs and Trade Cards...** London, Cambridge Univ. Pr., 1935. 279p. illus. Reprint: Newton Abbot, David & Charles, 1972. LC 35-34464.

Supplement to Jackson (1995) but not superseded by Grimwade (2020) as it covers a broader period—over 7,000 names are listed—and includes special material, e.g., names of bankers and pawnbrokers (350) and shop-signs (1,500).

2022   Reddaway, Thomas F. **The Early History of the Goldsmiths' Company, 1327-1509...** London, Arnold, 1975. 378p. illus. ISBN 0713157496.

Scholarly history of the first 200 years of the London Goldsmiths' Company based on an analysis of the company's records. Contents: 1, The Company Established; 2, London in 1341; 3, The Years of Consolidation, 1341-92; 4, The Second Charter (1392) and Its Results; 5, Years of Prosperity, 1404-44; 6, 15th-century Problems; 7, New Beginnings, 1478-1509; Appendixes: I, The Book of Ordinances; II, Biographical notes; III, Assay and Touch: the Background to the Reforms of 1478; IV, Wardens of the Company. Comprehensive, classified bibliography, pp. 342-49.

Paul Lamerie, 1688-1751

2023   Phillips, P. A. S. **Paul de Lamerie**. London, Batsford, 1935. 115p. illus. LC 35-34262.

Comprehensive, authoritative monograph on the life and work of the London gold and silversmith Paul de Lamerie. Contents: I, Paul De Lamerie's Nationality; II, The De Lamerie Family in England; III, History of the Plate Family; IV, Paul De Lamerie as a Master-man; V, Paul De Lamerie's Children; VI, De Lamerie's Admission to the Livery of the Goldsmiths' Company...; VII, De Lamerie's Property Deals; Trial of the Pyx; VIII, De Lamerie's Father Dies a Pauper...; IX, De Lamerie's Daughter's Marriage...; XI, De Lamerie Makes His Will; XII,, De Lamerie's Will and Its Conditions; XIII, Paul De Lamerie Invoices; XIV, Paul De Lamerie and William Hogarth; XV, Paul De Lamerie as a Craftsman. Appendices with transcripts and extracts of inventories, correspondence and other documents. Corpus of 164 plates of signed pieces with detailed, descriptive notes.

See also the exhibition catalog: *The Work of Paule de Lamerie*. Stirling and Clark Art Institute. (Williamstown, Mass., The Institute, 1953. 35p. illus.).

George Wickes, 1698-1761

2024   Barr, Elaine. **George Wickes, 1698-1761, Royal Goldsmith**. New York, Rizzoli, 1980. 210p. illus. index. ISBN 0847803260.

Well-illustrated monograph on the life and work of George Wickes. Contents: I, George Wickes; II, The Goldsmith's Wife; III, The Goldsmith's Business; IV, The Apprentices; V, The Workshop; VI, The Journeymen and Sub-Contractors; VII, The Associates; VIII, The Associates's Ledger; IX, The Designers and Modellers; X, The Influence of William Kent; XI, The Clients; XII, The Patronage of the Prince of Wales; XIII, The Prince's Silver; XIV, Epilogue. General bibliography, p. 206.

Ireland

2025   Bennett, Douglas. **Irish Georgian Silver**. London, Cassell, 1972. 369p. illus. index. LC 73-159885. ISBN 0304290289.

Comprehensive history of silver from 1714 to 1830 with emphasis on the identity of the individual gold and silversmiths, their hallmarks, and their organization based on close examination of written records and large numbers of pieces of silver. Contents: Part I, The Company of Goldsmiths of Dublin: 1, The History of the Goldsmiths Company, 2, Acts of Parliament Controlling the Manufacture and Sale of Gold and Silver Wares in Ireland from 1637-1825; Part II, The Work of the Goldsmiths of Dublin: 1, The Early Georgian Period, 2, The Rococo Period, 3, The Adam or Neo-classical Period, 4, The Regency Period; Part III, Other Irish Goldsmiths: 1, Cork Goldsmiths, 2, Limerick Goldsmiths, 3, Other Provincial Goldsmiths; Part IV, Fakes, Forgeries and Sub-standard Good; Part V, Guide to Hall-marks. Appendices with lists of makers and their marks. Bibliography of basic sources, p. 357.

2026   Ticher, Kurt. **Irish Silver in the Rococo Period**. Shannon, Irish University Press, 1972. 28p. (text), 105 plates. LC 73-152334.

Pictorial survey of Irish eighteenth-century silver with Rococo forms and decoration arranged by type of object. Brief text followed by plates with descriptive captions. No bibliography.

See also exhibition catalogs: *Irish Silver, An Exhibition of Irish Silver from 1630-1820* (Dublin, Trinity College, 1971) and *Irish Silver from the Seventeenth to the Nineteenth Century* (Washington, D.C., Smithsonian Institution, 1982).

Scotland

2027   Finlay, Ian. **Scottish Gold and Silver Work**. London, Chatto & Windus, 1956. 178p. illus. index. LC 57-73.
   Survey of gold and silversmiths' work in Scotland from the pre-Christian Celtic period to the early nineteenth century directed to the collector and enthusiast. Contents: I, The Earliest Celtic Gold and Silver Work; II, The Christian Celtic Period; III, The Middle Ages; IV, Brooches, Medieval and Later; V, The Reign of James V; VI, The Standing Mazers; VII, The Reformation; VIII, Early Communion Plate; IX, Secular Plate, Early Seventeenth Century; X, Seventeenth Century Provincial Work; XI, The Later Seventeenth Century; XII, Edinburgh—The Golden Age; XIII, Highland Jewellery and Weapons; XIV, Edinburgh—the Later Eighteenth Century; XV, The Burgh Craftsmen. The last chapter is a history of the guild and craftsmen of Edinburgh with references to documentary sources including extracts from inventories and registries. Bibliographical references in the footnotes.

British Colonial Silver

2028   Heller, David. **A History of Cape Silver, 1700-1870**. Cape Town, D. Heller, 1949. 276p. illus. index. LC A 50-4836.
   Pictorial survey of Colonial silver made in South Africa with list of major hallmarks. General bibliography, p. 270.

2029   Wilkinson, Wynyard R. T. **Indian Colonial Silver: European Silversmiths in India, 1790-1860, and Their Marks**. London, Argent Press, 1973. 171p. illus. index. ISBN 0903-869004.
   Handbook of silversmiths working under British direction in India between 1790 and 1860. Entries supply basic information and illustrations of pieces by the makers with photographic reproduction of the marks. Bibliography of books referred to in the entries, p. viii.

Hungary

2030   Köszeghy, Elemér. **Magyarszagi ötvösjegyek a középkortol 1867-ig: Merkzeichen der Goldschmiede Ungarns vom Mittelalter bis 1867**. Budapest, Kiraly Magyar Egyetemi Nyomda, 1936. 432p. illus.
   Dictionary of over 2,000 marks on gold and silver made in the territory of the former kingdom of Hungary from the Middle Ages to 1867. Arrangement is by place. Indexes by monograms, figurative marks, numbers, and names. Hungarian/German text.

2031   Kolba, Judit H. and Annamaria T. Németh. **Goldsmith's Work**. Budapest, Corvina, 1973. 46p. (text), 72p. (plates). LC 75-307054r852.
   Pictorial survey of gold and silversmiths' art in Hungary based on a selection of 72 objects dating from the eleventh to the nineteenth centuries.

Italy

Dictionaries of Marks

2032   Bulgari, Constantino G. **Argentieri gemmari e orafi d'Italia...** Rome, Lorenzo del Turco, Ugo Bozzi and Fratelli Palombi, 1958-74. 5v. illus.
   Comprehensive dictionary of the gold and silversmiths and gem engravers in Italy from the fourteenth to the nineteenth centuries. Includes makers of jewelry. Each volume has an

introductory essay describing the history of events and laws relating to the trade of the jeweler and precious metal smiths in the particular province followed by directory of artists with biographical data and facsimiles of marks. Also provides references to documentary sources. To date the following have appeared:

Parte 1: *Roma* 2v. (1958-59)
Parte 2: *Roma; Lazio-Umbria* (1966)
Parte 3: *Marche-Romagna* (1969)
Parte 4: *Emilia* (1974)

The standard reference work for the history of Italian gold, silver, and jewelry artists.

Histories and Handbooks

2033   Bunt, Cyril G. E. **The Goldsmiths of Italy: Some Account of Their Guilds, Statutes, and Work**. London, Martin Hopkinson, 1926. 197p. illus. index. Reprint: New York, Garland, 1979. ISBN 0824033574.

History of Italian gold and silversmith art from the fourteenth to the nineteenth centuries compiled from the notes of Sidney J. A. Churchill.

2034   Churchill, Sidney J. A. **The Goldsmiths of Italy....** London, Hopkinson, 1926. 182p. illus. index. Reprint: New York, Garland, 1979. ISBN 0824033574.

Important study of the organization, patronage, and activities of gold and silversmiths in Italy from the Middle Ages to the nineteenth century. Contents: I, The Goldsmiths of Rome: Their Statutes; II, Papal Patronage of the Goldsmiths; III, Cellini, Caradosso, and Other Master-Craftsmen; IV, The Goldsmiths of Tuscany: Statutes of Siena and Florence; V, The Work of Pistoiese, Sienese, and Aretine Artists; VI, The Work of Florentine Artists: The Medici Wardrobe Accounts; VII, The Goldsmiths of Perugia and Bologna; VIII, The Goldsmiths of Milan, Turin, and Bergamo; IX, The Statutes of Naples, the Abruzzi, and Aquila; X, The Goldsmiths of Venice; XI, The Sumptuary Laws and Peasant Jewellery. Appendices with extracts from early statues of Rome, bibliography on the goldsmithery of Rome, bibliography of published sources for the goldsmithery outside Rome, and a general bibliography, pp. 168-173.

2035   Denaro, Victor F. **The Goldsmiths of Malta and Their Marks**. Florence, L. S. Olschki, 1972. 241p. illus. index. (Arte e Archeologia, 3). LC 73-154306r85.

Authoritative history of the Goldsmiths of Malta from the sixteenth century to circa 1970 with comprehensive repertory, by periods, of the assay and makers' marks. Contents: I, The Goldsmiths Under the Order of St. John; II, The Confraternity of St. Helen; III, Plate in the Hospitals; IV, The Goldsmiths During the French Occupation (1798-1800); V, The Goldsmiths Under British Rule; VI, The Goldsmiths and Their Work; VI, Church Plate; VIII, Domestic Silver; IX, Marks on Maltese Silver. Appendices with discussions on assay standards. General bibliography, pp. 235-36, and further bibliography in the footnotes.

2036   Gregorietti, Guido. **Italian Gold, Silver and Jewelry: Their History and Centres**. Milan, Alfieri & Lacroix, 1971. 178p. illus. index. LC 72-190525.

Pictorial survey of Italian gold and silver work with emphasis on twentieth century studio jewelry and handcrafted silver tableware. Many of the plates are not adequately identified. General bibliography, p. 177.

See also the exhibition catalog: Morassi, Antonio, *Antica oreficeria italiana* (Milan, Hoepli, 1936. 128p. illus. index).

Rome

2037 Fornari, Salvatore. **Gli argenti romani**. Rome, Edizioni del Tritone, 1968. 316p. illus.
Comprehensive history of the art of Roman gold and silversmiths from antiquity to the end of the nineteenth century. Contents: I, Premessa. Argenterai pagana e cristiana; II, Storia degli statuti. Instituzione dell'Università degli Orefici, Nascita del "Nobil Collegio degli Orefici e Argentieri di Roma"; III, Capolavori poco noti del Quattrocento e Cinquecento romano. Celebri dinastie di orefici e argentieri del Rinascimento al Seicento; IV, Argenteria romana dei secoli quattordicesimo e quindicesimo. Tesori romani a Lisbona; V, Sviluppi e varietà degli argenti romani settecenteschi. Gusto neoclassico nell'argenteria del primo Ottocento; VI, Giulio Romano ed altri grandi ideatori di argenterie; VII, Gli argenti inediti fra il 1700 e il 1870. Well illustrated. Bibliography of basic works, pp. 315-16.

Southern Italy

2038 Accascina, Maria. **I marchi delle argenterie e orefichie siciliane**. Busto Arizio, Bramante, 1976. 244p. illus. LC 77-561556r85.
Comprehensive dictionary of marks of gold and silverwork from Sicily. Arranged by place and then chronologically; includes assay, town, and makers' marks. Much information gleaned from documents.

2039 Accascina, Maria. **Oreficeria di Sicilia dal XII al XIX secolo**. Palermo, Flaccovio, 1974. 507p. illus. index. LC 75-585531.
History of gold and silversmiths' work in Sicily from the twelfth to the nineteenth centuries with emphasis on religious pieces.

2040 Catello, Elio, and Corrado Catello. **Argenti napoletani dal XVI al XIX secolo**. Naples, Giannini, 1973. 452p. illus. index.
Comprehensive history of gold and silversmiths' work in Naples from the sixteenth to the nineteenth centuries. Contents: La corporazione degli orefici; L'argenteria a Napoli; La punzonatura; Gli argenteri. Dictionary of marks. Bibliography of basic works, pp. 425-28, and further bibliography in the notes.

2041 Catello, Elio and Corrado Catello. **L'oreficeria a Napoli nel XV secolo**. Naples, Di Mauro, 1975. 166p. illus. index. LC 77-461724r85.
Companion work to the authors' (2040) covering the fifteenth century.

Northern Italy

2042 Zastrow, Oleg. **L'oreficeria in Lombardia**. Milan, Electa, 1978. 237p. illus. index. LC 77-457385.
Survey of gold and silversmiths' art in Lombardy from the Middle Ages to the nineteenth century based on masterpieces in museums and church treasuries in Lombardy.

Netherlands

General Dictionaries of Marks

2043 **Meestertekens van Nederlandse goud- en zilversmeden**. The Hague, Staatsdrukkerij-en Uitgeverijbedrijf, 1963-67. 2v. illus. LC 75-279479r85.

Comprehensive dictionary of marks found on Dutch gold and silver between 1814 and 1966. Includes masters,' place, and assay marks. First volume covers the marks of 1814-1963 with over 600 pages devoted to masters. Volume two covers the marks used after 1963 and was designed to receive loose-leaf supplements but they ceased in 1967.

2044   Voet, Elias, Jr. **Nederlands goud- en zilvermerken 1445-1951.** 10th ed. s'Gravenhagen, Nijhoff, 1977. 77p. illus. ISBN 9024791421.

General dictionary of marks found on Dutch gold and silver between 1445 and 1951. Concentrates on the assay marks of 43 centers. Alphabetical arrangement. For Dutch makers' marks see the author's various regional handbooks (2046-2048).

General Histories and Handbooks

2045 Duyvene de Wit- Klinkhamer, Th. M. and M. H. Gans. **Dutch Silver.** London, Faber and Faber, 1961. 97p. illus. index. LC 70-356237.

General history of the art of the Dutch silversmiths from the sixteenth century to circa 1830. Chapters on marks, values, fakes and use. Thorough bibliography of books and articles, pp. 89-93. An authoritative introduction for the collector.

2046   Frederiks, J. W. **Dutch Silver.** The Hague, Nijhoff, 1952- 1961. 4v. illus. index. LC 52-67706rev.

Comprehensive handbook/history of Dutch antique silver arranged by types of object and then by style. Within the stylistic division the objects are grouped by place and by master. Full scholarly apparatus including bibliographical references for each piece. Contents: Vole 1, Embossed Plaquettes, Tazze and Dishes: I, The Renaissance Style; II, The Period of Transition; III, The Baroque Style; IV, The 18th Century. Volume 2, Wrought Plate of North and South-Holland from the Renaissance until the End of the Eighteenth Century: I, Print Engravers; II, Silversmiths. Volume 3, Wrought Plate of the Central, Northern and Southern Provinces from the Renaissance until the End of the Eighteenth Century. Volume 4, Embossed Ecclesiastical and Secular Plate from the Renaissance until the End of the Eighteenth Century. Thorough indexes in each volume. General bibliography supplied through la ist of abbreviations at the beginning of each volume.

2047   Schrijver, Elka. **Netherlands Zilver.** Bussum, van Dishoeck, 1971. 104p. illus. LC 72-306046.

Popular history of Dutch silver from the Middle Ages through the mid-nineteenth century. Bibliography of basic works, p. 102.

See also the exhibition catalog: *Nederlands Zilver/ Dutch Silver 1580-1830*, by A. L. den Blaawen (Amsterdam, Rijksmuseum, 1979. 390p. illus. ISBN 9012025710).

Amsterdam

2048   Citroen, Karel A. **Amsterdam Silversmiths and Their Marks.** Amsterdam, North-Holland; New York, Elsevier, 1975. 280p. illus. index. (North Holland Studies in Silver, v. 1). ISBN 0720492017.

Comprehensive dictionary of over 1,000 marks on silver produced in Amsterdam between 1550 and 1800. Entries give biographical information, types of objects in which the makers specialized and trade affiliations. Introductory text in English; dictionary entries in Dutch. Two-page Dutch/English glossary. Index to makers' marks.

2049   Voet, Elias, Jr. **Merken van Amsterdamsche goud- en zilvermeden**. The Hague, Nijhoff, 1966. 170p. illus. index. LC 68-99895.
Dictionary of 1,473 marks of Amsterdam gold and silversmiths from 1509 to 1813.

Haarlem

2050   Voet, Elias, Jr. **Haarlemsche goud- en zilversmeden en hunne merken**. Haarlen, De Erven F. Bihn, 1928. 361p. illus. index.
Comprehensive dictionary of gold and silversmiths active in Haarlem between 1550 and 1814 with facsimiles of their marks. Biographies include quotes from archival sources.

Northern Holland

2051   Voet, Elias, Jr. **Merken van Friesche goud- en zilversmeden**. The Hague, Nijhoff, 1931. 340p. illus. index. LC 75-572100r852.
Comprehensive dictionary of Frisian gold and silversmiths and their marks from the sixteenth to the eighteenth centuries.

Norway

General Histories and Handbooks

2052   Polak, Ada. **Gullsmedkunsten in Norge for og nå**. Oslo, Dreyers Forlag, 1970. 178p. illus. index.
Concise but authoritative history of Norwegian silver from pre-Christian times to the twentieth century. Contents: I, Gull og sølv; II, Gullsmeden og hans håndverk; III, Edelmetall og stempling; IV, Hedensk og kristent; V, Laugstiden; VI, Fra laugsoppløsningnen til 1914; VII, Fra 1914 til i dag. English summary includes translations of the captions of the plates. Comprehensive bibliography with list of exhibition catalogs, pp. 172-74.

2053   Polak, Ada. **Norwegian Silver**. Oslo, Dreyers Forlag, 1972. 155p. illus. index. ISBN 8209010484.
Authoritative survey of silver made in Norway from pre-Christian times to the middle of the twentieth century with particular attention to silver between 1600 and 1900 which has been collected by foreigners—chiefly English—on holiday in Norway, since the mid-nineteenth century. Contents: Pre-Christian Times; The Middle Ages; The Guild Period 16th-19th Centuries: Origins and Organization of the Guilds; Domestic Silver of the Guild Period; Church Plate; Peasant Silver; From 1830-1930: Mechanization, 19th Century Types, Old and New, Trends of Style, Three Fine Masters, Break-down of the Guild System, Modernization of the Training-Programme; Yesterday and Today; Marks; Norwegian Goldsmiths and Designers. Selected bibliography, p. 156.

2054   Kielland, Thor B. **Norsk guldsmedkunst i middelalderen**. Oslo, Steenske, 1927. 511p. illus. index. LC 36-5429.
Comprehensive history of Norwegian gold and silver from Viking times to the end of the Middle Ages. Contents: 1, Indledning; 2, Guldsmedenes Haandverksforhold; 3, Sen Vikingetid og Tidlig Kristentid; 4, Romansk; 5, Unggotik; 6, Hoigotik; 7, Sengotik. Bibliographical references in the notes. An old standard work.

Bergen

2055   Krohn-Hansen, Thorvald, and Robert Kloster. **Bergens gullsmedkunst 1550-1850**. Oslo, Bergen, Universitetsforlaget, 1963. 202p. illus. index.
Comprehensive history of the gold and silversmiths of Bergen from 1568 to 1840. Summary in English.

Oslo

2056   Grevenor, Henrik, and Thor B. Kielland. **Guldsmedhaanverket i Oslo og Kristiania**. Lauget, arbeidern, mestrene. Kristiania, 1924. 449p. illus.
Comprehensive dictionary of the marks of silversmiths active in Oslo from the late Middle Ages to the twentieth century.

Trondheim

2057   Krohn-Hansen, Thorvald. **Trondhjems gullsmedkunst, 1550-1850**. Oslo, 1963. 202p. illus. (Scandinavian University Books). LC 64-46574r832.
Comprehensive history/handbook of silver made in Trondheim (Trodhjem) from 1550 to 1850 with repertory of silversmiths and their marks and an excellent corpus of 241 plates. Contents: Historisk innledning; Trondhjems renessansegullsmedkunst gjenoppdaget; Kirkesølv; Bordsølv; Spisebestikk og Serveringsbestikk; Sølv til personlig bruk; Sluttord.
See also Brodahl, Johan E. *Trondhjems guldsmeder*, 5v. (Trondjem, 1923-1947 illus. index; Trondhjems historiske forening. Skrifter).

Portugal

Dictionaries of Marks

2058   Vidal, Manuel G. **Marcas de contrastas e ouvrives portugueses; desde o seculó XV a 1950**. Lisbon, Casa da Moeda, 1958. 560p. illus. LC 59-30601.
Comprehensive dictionary of marks on Portuguese silver from the fifteenth century to 1950. Collection of plates of major signed pieces.

Histories and Handbooks

2059   Couto, Joaó and António M. Gonçalves. **A ourivesaria em Portugal**. Lisbon, Livros Horizonte, 1960. 186p. illus. index.
History of Portuguese gold and silver from the fourteenth to the eighteenth centuries.

Russia

Dictionaries of Marks

2060   Postnikova-Loseva, M. M. **Russian Gold- and Silversmithing: Its Centers and Masters of the 16th-19th Centuries**. Moscow, Izdatel'stvo Nauka, 1974. 372p. illus. LC 74-348421.
Dictionary of Russian gold and silversmiths with facsimiles of their marks. Text in Russian, summary in English.

Histories and Handbooks

2061   Solodkoff, Alexander von. **Russian Gold and Silver**. London, Trefoil Books, 1981. 238p. illus. index. ISBN 0862940044.
   Well-illustrated survey of gold and silver in Russia, including the Baltic provinces and Finland, from the beginning of the seventeenth to the end of the nineteenth centuries. Contents: Organization of the Goldsmith's Trade in Russia; Styles and Influences in the Goldsmith's Art in Russia; Materials, Techniques and Typical Objects; Marks on Russian Gold and Silver Objects; Centres of Gold and Silverwork; Important Masters, Workshops and Firms: Ador, Bolin, Fabergé, Grachev, Han, Keibel, Khlebmikov, Morozov, Nicholls & Plincke, Ochinnikov, Pauzié, Sazikov; List of Masters; Russian Town Marks; Index to Marks and Signatures. Select bibliography, pp. 231-233 with translations of Russian titles.

Spain

Dictionaries

2062   Fernández, Alejandro, Rafael Munoa, and J. Rabasco. **Enciclopedia de la plata española y Virreinal americana**. San Sebastian, Rafael Munoa, 1984. 566p. illus. LC 85-133898.
   Comprehensive handbook/history of gold and silver of Spain and the Spanish Viceroyal territories in the New World. Part one is a history of Spanish silver; part two a dictionary of marks; part three covers silver in Spanish-dominated Mexico, California, Florida, Peru, Brazil, Paraguay, and Chile. A standard reference work for the history of Spanish gold and silver.

Histories and Handbooks

2063   Davillier, Charles. **Recherches sur l'orfévrerie en Espagne au moyen age et a la Renaissance...** Paris, Quantin, 1879. 286p. illus. index. LC 10-13504.
   Comprehensive history of Spanish gold and silver from the fifth to the end of the sixteenth centuries. Still valuable for the frequent references to documentary sources. Bibliographical footnotes.

2064   Johnson, Ada M. **Hispanic Silverwork...** New York, Hispanic Society, 1944. 308p. illus. index. LC 45-1901.
   History of Spanish silver from the fourteenth to the nineteenth centuries with emphasis on the role of princely patronage and foreign influences. References inventories and other documents. Contents: I, Gothic Silverwork in the 14th Century; II, Gothic Silverwork in the 15th Century; III, Renaissance Silverwork; IV, 17th-Century Silverwork; V, 18th- and 19th-Century Silverwork; VI, Catalogue of Silverwork in the Collection of the Hispanic Society of America.
   See also museum catalog: *Golden Age of Hispanic Silver, 1400-1655* (South Kensington, Victoria and Albert Museum, 1968. 71p.(text), 180p. (plates) catalog by Charles Oman).

Los Arfes

2065   Sanchez Caton, F. J. **Los Arfes. Escultores de plata y oro**. Madrid, Editorial "Saturnino Calleia," 1920. 79p. illus. LC 22-15498r44.
   Survey of the art of the Arfe family (Enrique de Arfe, Antonio de Arfe, Juan de Arfe) active in Spain between 1501 and 1603. Text includes excerpts from documentary sources. Bibliographical references in the table of contents, pp. 76-79.

Sweden

Dictionaries of Marks

2066   Upmark, Gustaf. **Guild- och silversmeder i Sverige, 1520- 1850**. Stockholm, Froleen, 1943. 951p. illus. index.

Comprehensive dictionary of Swedish gold and silver marks from 150 to 1850. Arranged by place and illustrated with facsimiles. Standard reference work for the history of Swedish silver to be used with volume four of (2067).

Histories and Handbooks

2067   Berg, Gosta, et al., eds. **Svenskt Silversmide, 1520-1850**. Stockholm, Nordisk Roto-gravyr, 1941- 63. 4v. illus. LC 49- 34806 rev.

Comprehensive handbook/history of Swedish gold and silver from 1520 to 1850. Contents: v. 1, Renässans och barock. 1520-1700 by O. Källström and C. Hernmarck; v. 2, Senbarock, Frederik I:s stil och rokoko, 1700-1780 by C. Hernmarck, A. Stavenow and G. Munthe; v. 3, Gustaviansk stil, empire och romantik, 1780-1850 by C. Hernmarck and E. Andrén. Äldre guldsmedsteknik by B. Bengtsson; v. 4, Guld- och Silverstämplar by E. Andrén, B. Hellner, C. Hernmarck and K. Holmquist. Volume 4 has over 9,000 facsimiles of marks and over 3,000 biographies of gold and silversmiths. English summaries at end of volumes 3 and 4. Bibliographies in each volume and further bibliography in the notes. A standard work on Swedish gold and silver. The dictionary of marks in volume 4 largely supersedes that by Upmark (2066).

ORIENTAL GOLD AND SILVER

2068   Al-Jadir, Saad. **Arab & Islamic Silver**. London, Stacey International, 1981. 216p. illus. index. ISBN 0905743237.

Comprehensive, well-illustrated survey of silverware and silver jewelry of the Islamic world from the earliest times to the present. Contents: Introduction; The Early History of Silverwork; The Functions of Silverwork; Types of Silverwork; The Silversmith and His Craft; The Revival of Folk Art and Its Importance; The Silverwork of North Africa and Spain; The Silverwork of the Arabian Peninsula; The Silverwork of the Levant, Mesopotamia, Persia, Turkey and Caucasia; The Silverwork of Central and South-east Asia; Conclusion. Bibliography, p. 213, list books in all languages. Titles in Arabic and Russian are translated.

See also the museum handbook: *From Silver to Ceramic: The Potter's Debt to Metalwork in the Greco-Roman, Oriental and Islamic World*, by M. Vickers et al (Oxford, Ashmolean Library, 1986. 102p. illus. ISBN 0907849156).

2069   Forbes, Henry A., John D. Kernan, and Ruth S. Wilkins. **Chinese Export Silver, 1785 to 1885**. Milton, Mass., Museum of the American China Trade, 1975. 303p. illus. index. LC 75-12401r852.

Comprehensive history/handbook of Chinese export silver as it related to trade to England and America. Contents: Part 1, Silver; a New Category of Chinese Export Art: I, Definition and Scope; II, Loss and Recovery. Part 2, Historical Background: III, The Indigenous Tradition; IV, Sources of Silver; V, Fineness and Cost; VI, Demand; VII, Manufacturing Centers; VIII, Packaging, Supply, and Delivery. Part 3, Identification: IX, Style; X, Form; XI, Technique, Structural Elements, and Decoration; XII, Makers; XIII, Marks. Plates grouped by types; catalog arranged by makers. Appendices with list of Chinese dynasties and epochs, analyses of Chinese export silver, list of Chinese export silver masters, and comment on the difficulties of translating makers' names. Comprehensive, classified and annotated bibliography, pp. 261-76. A standard work on an important but little-researched aspect of the history of silver.

2070   Roth, Henry L. **Oriental Silverwork, Malay and Chinese; a Handbook for Connoisseurs, Collectors, Students and Silversmiths**. Kuala Lumpur, University of Malaysia Press, 1966, 300p. illus. index. LC 67-8882.

Popular collector's handbook of traditional Malay and Chinese silver featuring 142 pieces in the collection of C. Wray with brief descriptive captions. No bibliography.

See also the exhibition catalog: *Chinese Gold & Silver in the Carl Kempe Collection. A Catalogue by Bo Gyllensvärd* (Stockholm, 1953. 255p.) and *The Chait Collection of Chinese Export Silver*, by J. Dvereaux Kernan (New York, Ralph Chait Galleries, 1985. 269p. illus. index).

IRON AND STEEL

American Iron and Steel [*See also* Lindsay, 2090]

2071   Kauffmann, Henry J. **Early American Ironware Cast and Wrought**. Rutland, Vt., Tuttle, 1966, 166p. illus. index. LC 65-16743.

Popular collector's survey of Colonial and nineteenth-century American iron and steelware useful for the many illustrations of collectible items. Contents: I, The Blast Furnace; 2, The Forge; 3, The Iron Foundry; 4, The Blacksmith; 5, The Whitesmith; 6, The Farrier; 7, The Edge Toolmaker; 8, The Cutler; 9, The Locksmith; 10, The Gunmsmith; 11, The Nailer; 12, The Wheelwright; 13, The Tinsmith. No bibliography.

2072   Schiffer, Herbert, Peter Schiffer, and Nancy Schiffer. **Antique Iron: Survey of American and English Forms, Fifteenth through Nineteenth Centuries**. Exton, Pa., Schiffer, 1979. 348p. illus. index. ISBN 0916838269.

History/handbook of American and English antique wrought and cast ironwork. Particularly useful for the collector is the large number of illustrations of typical objects. Contents: 1, Architectural Hardware; 2, Armament; 3, Boxes; 4, Conestoga Wagon; 5, Decorated Tin; 6, Fireplace Equipment; 7, Fire Marks; 8, Furniture; 9, Garden Ornaments; 10, Kitchen Utensils; 11, Lighting; 12, Miscellaneous; 13, Stoves; 14, Tools; 15, Toys; 16, Weathervanes. General bibliography, pp. 347-48.

2073   Sonn, Albert H. **Early American Wrought Iron**. New York, Scribner's, 1928. 3v. illus. index. Reprint: New York, Bonanza Books, 1979. ISBN 051727793X.

Comprehensive history/handbook of American wrought ironwork from Colonial times to 1850. Useful for the large collection of detailed sketches of thousands of iron objects with descriptive captions. Volume 1 covers door hardware such as knockers, latches, and locks; volume 2 covers door bolts, hinges, hasps, etc.; volume 3 covers architectural ironwork such as balconies, braces, railings, newels, grates, grills, weather vanes, wall anchors, gutter supports, foot scrapers, and various types of iron domestic objects such as andirons, kitchen utensils, and lighting equipment.

European Iron and Steel

2074   Ayrton, Maxwell and Arnold Silcock. **Wrought Iron and Its Decorative Use**. London, Country Life, 1929. 196p. illus. index. LC 29-18650.

Survey of wrought ironwork throughout the world but with particular attention given to the work of English and Welsh smiths. Contains 239 plates with descriptive captions. Contents:

I, General History; II, Introductory; III, Fourteen to Seventeenth Centuries; IV, Seventeenth Century Developments; V, Jean Tijou; VI, The Welsh Smiths; VII, The West of England Smiths; VIII, The Midland Smiths; IX, Miscellaneous Examples; X, The Decay and Revival of Smith-Craft. General bibliography, p. 188.

2075 Ffoulkes, Constance J. **Decorative Ironwork; the Craftsman and His Art**. London, Methuen, 1913. 148p. illus. LC 14-968. Cambridge, Mass., Harvard University Press, 1950. 221p. illus. index.

Older survey of European wrought ironwork from the early Middle Ages through the Baroque. Contents: Hinges and Door Ornaments; Grilles, Railings, and Gates; Exterior Decorations; Furniture, etc.; Locks, Keys, and Bolts; Handles, Knockers, etc.; Chests and Caskets; Clocks, Mirrors, Jewellery, etc.; Names of Smiths and Ironworkers (alphabetical list with references to work and date). At the end of each chapter there is a list by place of additional examples. General bibliography, pp. xix-xx.

2076 Gardner, John S. **Ironwork**. revised by W. W. Watts. London, Victoria and Albert Museum, 1978. 3v. illus. index. ISBN 0905209001 (pt.1). Rev. ed. London, Board of Education, 1922-30. 3v. illus. index. (Victoria and Albert Museum, Publication nos. 131, 195).

Comprehensive history of European wrought iron from prehistoric times to the end of the nineteenth century based on pieces in the Victoria and Albert Museum. Contents: Part I, From the Earliest Times to the End of the Medieval Period; Part II, Continental Ironwork of the Renaissance and Later Periods; Part III, A Complete Survey of the Artistic Working of Iron in Great Britain from the Earliest Times. Bibliographies of books in the Museum library at the end of each volume. A standard history by a leading designer and museum curator.

2077 Hoever, Otto. **An Encyclopedia of Ironwork; Examples of Hand Wrought Ironwork from the Middle Ages to the End of the 18th Century...** New York, Weyhe, 1927. 29p. (text), 320 plates. Reprint: New York, Universe, 1962. LC 62-12006.

Important collection of plates illustrating European artistic wrought ironwork from the Middle Ages to the end of the 18th century. Brief historical essay introduces the plates.

2078 Robertson, E. Graeme, and Joan Robertson. **Cast Iron Decoration: A World Survey**. New York, Watson-Cuptill, 1977. 336p. illus. index. LC 77-361564r85.

Comprehensive pictorial survey of cast iron architectural ornament. Introductory essay followed by a good selection of plates. Contents: 1, Introduction; 2, The British Isles; 3, The Continent; 4, U.S.A.; 5, Australia and New Zealand; 6, Empires and Influences. Comprehensive, classified bibliography, pp. 324-31.

See also J. Gloag and D. Bridgwater, *A History of Cast Iron in Architecture* (ARCH 872).

2079 Zimelli, Umberto, and Giovanni Vergerio. **Decorative Ironwork**. London, Hamlyn, 1969. 159p. illus.

Popular, pictorial survey of Western wrought iron from antiquity through the Baroque. No bibliography.

France

2080 Blanc, Louis. **La fer forgé en France. La régence: aurore, apogée, déclin. Oeuvres gravéés des anciens maïtres serruriers, architectes, dessinateurs et graveurs**. Paris and Brussels, van Oest, 1930. 96 plates. index.

2081 ———. **La fer forgé en France aux XVIe et XVIIe siècles. Oeuvres gravées des anciens maîtres, serruriers, architectes, dessinateurs et graveurs**. Pars, van Oest, 1928. 27p. 96 plates. index.

Collection of plates of French engravings illustrating design for works in wrought iron dating from the sixteenth century through the Regency period. Both volumes have brief biographies of the most important masters of the period.

2082 D'Allemagne, Henri R. **Les anciens maitres serruriers**. Paris, Grund, 1943. 2v. illus. Reprinted, 1983. LC NUC87-315888.

Comprehensive, scholarly history of the wrought iron work in France and especially the guild of blacksmiths of Paris from the Middle Ages to the nineteenth century. Contents: Première Partie: La Corporation des serruriers Parisiens: 1, Histoire générale de la cammunauté, II, Les finances de la communauté, III, La confrérie, IV, L'appretissage, V, Le compagnonnage, VI, Le chef-d'oeuvre, VII, Réception a la maitrise, VIII, La maitrise, IX, Régelementation du travail, X, Le jurés, XI, Les juridictions successives, XII, Les enclos privilégiés, XIII, Nomenclature des serruriers admis a la maitrise de 1585 a 1611 et de 1742 a 1779; Deuxiéme Partie: Les meilleurs travaux des serruriers: I, Mines de fer et fonderies, II, Les ateliers des serruriers, III, pentures, IV, grilles, V, Rampes d'escalier—chaires a prêcher—grilles de fenêtres—balcons, VI, Serrures et entrées de serrures, VII, Clefs, VIII, Marteaux de portes—guichets—verrous, IX, Enseignes—potences—porte-étendard, X, Lurins, XI, Meubles en bois et en fer, Appareils de chauffage—appareils d'orthopédie, Instruments de chirugie, XII, Les marveilleuses inventions d'Agostino de Ramellis. Corpus of 177 plates illustrating pieces and scenes of the activities of blacksmiths and culters. Bibliographical references in the footnotes.

2083 Frank, Edgar B. **Old French Ironwork; The Craftsman and His Art**. Cambridge, Mass., Harvard Univ. Press, 1950. 221p. illus. LC 50-9903.

Translation of *Petite ferronnerie ancienne* (Paris, SELF, 1948).

Collector's introduction to French small-scale wrought ironwork from the Middle Ages to the nineteenth century. Contents: I, The Craftsmen; II, Tools and Inventions; III, Locks of the Fifteenth and Sixteenth Centuries; IV, Locks of the Seventeenth and Eighteenth Centuries; V, Padlocks; VI, Key; VII, Hinges, Bolts, Escutcheons, Knockers, Grilles, Nails; VIII, Caskets; IX, Tobacco Devices, Nutcrackers, Knives, Scissors, Sewing Accessories; X, Bag Frames, Rings, Bonbonnières, Seals, Corkscrews, Mio Chin Figurines; XI, Candlesticks, Lecterns, Statues, Miscellany. Basic bibliography, pp. 217-18.

Jean Lamour, 1698-1771

2084 France-Lanord, Albert. **Jean Lamour. Serrurier du Roi 1698-1771**. Nancy, Université de Nancy, 1977. 108p. illus. LC 79-358489.

Introductory monograph on the life and work of Jean Lamour, one of the greatest wrought iron artists of all time. Contents: I, Le Maitre Serrurier; II, Le travail du fer au XVIIIe siècle; III, Le Surrurier du Roi: Notre Dame de Bonsecours, La Malgrange, L'Hotel des Missions royales, Château de Laneuville, Chanteheaux, Château de Commercy, La Primatiale; IV, La Place Royale; V, Les derières années; En guise de conclusion: vie et mort des ouvrages en fer. General bibliography, p. 105.

Germany

2085 Baur-Heinhold, Margarete. **Geschmiedetes Eisen vom Mittelalter bis um 1900**. Konigstein, Langewies, 1963. 112p. illus. LC 68-120905.

Popular, pictorial survey of German wrought iron from the Middle Ages to 1900. Introductory essays sketch the history and techniques. No bibliography.

2086   Hefner-Alteneck, J. H. von. **Eisenwerke oder Ornamentik der Schmiedekunst des Mittelalters und der Renaissance**. Tübingen, Wasmuth, 1870. 39 p. (text), 84p. (plates). Reprint: Tübingen, Wasmuth, 1984. ISBN 3803050502.

Collection of measured drawings—reproduced in lithography—of examples of German medieval and Renaissance wrought ironwork arranged chronologically with descriptive notes.

2087   Schmidt, Eva. **Der preußische Eiesenguss. Technik, Geschichte, Werke, Künstler**. Berlin, Mann, 1981. 325p. illus. index. ISBN 378611308.

Comprehensive, scholarly history of the production of artistic cast iron in Prussia during the nineteenth century. Includes large-scale architectural and sculptural cast iron as well as various small-scale objects for the interior and cast iron jewelry. Contents: Allgemeine Einführung in die Geschichte des Eisenkunstgusses; Zu den technischen Verfahren des Eisengusses; Eisenguß im preußischen Brückenbau des 18. und 19. Jahrhunderts; Die Verwendung des Eisengusses für Großbauten und bei Monumentalbildwerken; Die Entwicklung des Lauchhammerwerkes und seine Bedeutung für die Denkmalsplastik der Königlichen Eisengießerei Berlin; Die Königliche Eisengießerei Gleiwitz; Die Paulinenhütte in Neusalz a.d. Oder; Die Königliche Eisengießerei Berlin; Aus der Tätigkeit der Knappschaft; Die künstlerische Produktion des Klassizismus; Die Bildhauer des Klassizismus; Die Bildner der Königlichen Eiesengießerei Berlin: Modelleure, Medailleure, Former, Gießer, Ziseleure; Karl Friedrich Schinkel und der Eisenkunstguß; Das Kreuzbergdenkmal; Das Eiserne Kreuz und die vaterländischen Gedenkgüsse; Gedächtnismonumente; Ausstattugsstücke; Grebrauchs- und Ziergegenstände; Eisenschmuck; Die künstlerische Produktion von etwa 1835 bis 1874; Der Bronzxeguß der Königlichen Eisengießerei Berlin; Der Anteil der Berliner Privatgießereien; Der Einfluß des preußischen Einsengusses auf deutsche und außerdeutsche Gießereien; Versuch zur Wiederbelebung des Eisenkunstgusses im 20. Jahrhunderts. Appendices with extracts from documents. Comprehensive, classified bibliography, pp. 293-98, and further bibliography in the notes. A major contribution to the history of artistic cast iron.

2088   Stuttmann, Ferdinand. **Deutsche Schmiedeeisenkunst**. Munich, Delphin-Verlag, 1927-30. 5v. illus.

Important corpus of mounted plates of German wrought ironwork from the Middle Ages to the 1920s. Brief introductory essays and a descriptive list of the plates proceed each volume. No bibliography.

Great Britain

2089   Gardner, John S. **English Ironwork of the XVIIth and XVIIIth Centuries; an Historical & Analytical Account of the Developement of Exterior Smithcraft...** London, Batsford, 1911. 336p. illus. index. Reprint: New York, Blom, 1970. LC 69-16319.

Comprehensive history of English wrought ironwork of the seventeenth and eighteenth centuries. Contents: Medieval Ironwork; The Evolution of Gates; Railings, Balustrades, Balconies, Stair-ramps and Grilles; Lampholders, Brackets, Signs and Vanes; List of Smiths and Designers. Important work in the history of English artistic wrought ironwork.

2090   Lindsay, J. Seymour. **Iron and Brass Implements of the English and American House**. Rev. and enl. ed. Bass River, Mass., Carl Jacobs, 1964. 88p.(text), 473p. (plates).

Popular survey of English and American domestic brass and iron from the late Middle Ages to the early nineteenth century illustrated with drawings by the author. Contents: Part One,

The Hearth; Part Two, Cooking and Other Kitchen Utensils; Part Three, Various Articles Employed in Obtaining and Maintaining Artificial Light; Part Four, Metal Work Dealing with Tobacco Smoking; Part Five, Those Examples That Cannot Be Included in Any of the Previous Classes; Part Six, Some Examples of American Colonial Implements. Text contains some useful extracts from inventories and other documentary sources. No bibliography.

2091   Lister, Raymond. **Decorative Wrought Ironwork in Great Britain**. Rutland, Vt., Tuttle, 1970. 267p. illus. index. LC 72-113903.
        Concise but informative history of artistic wrought ironwork in Great Britain from the early Middle Ages to the twentieth century. Emphasis is on technique. Contents: I. Introductory; 2, Technique; 3, Architectural Wrought Ironwork; 4, Domestic Ironwork; 5, The Blacksmith. Glossary. Comprehensive, classified and annotated bibliography, pp. 245-57, and additional bibliography in the footnotes.

Italy

2092   Ferrari, Giulio. **Il ferro nell' arte italiana...** Milan, Hoepli, 1927. 197p. illus.
        Pictorial survey of artistic wrought ironwork in Italy from the eleventh century to the beginning of the nineteenth century. Contains 170 plates arranged chronologically following a 13-page introduction. No notes to the plates. No bibliography.

Spain

2093   Byne, Arthur, and Mildred Byne. **Spanish Ironwork...** New York, Hispanic Society, 1915. 143p. illus. index. LC 16-2612.
        Older survey of Spanish decorative wrought ironwork from the early Middle Ages to the seventeenth century. Contents: I, Spanish Ironwork Previous to the Gothic Period;; II, Gothic Rejas and Pulpits; III, Gothic Hardware and Domestic Utensils; IV, The Development of the Reja; V, Renaissance Church Rejas; VI, Smaller Renaissance Productions; VII, The Last Spanish Ironwork. Appendix with catalog of the ironwork in the Hispanic Society of America. No bibliography.

Cutlery

2094   Hayward, John F. **English Cutlery, Sixteenth to Eighteenth Century**. London, H.M.S.O., 1957. 44p. illus.
        Brief survey of English cutlery from the sixteenth century to the end of the eighteenth century based upon pieces in the collections of the Victoria and Albert Museum. Twenty-four plates are accompanied by good descriptive notes. No bibliography.

2095   Lloyd, Godfrey I. H. **The Cutlery Trades: an Historical Essay in the Economics of Small-scale Production**. London, Cass, 1968. 493p. illus. LC 68-102951.
        First published in 1913. Economic and social history of the cutlery trade in Great Britain with particular reference to Sheffield. Contains much valuable information relative to the history of technique. Contents: I, The Older Forms of Industry; II, The Process of Cutlery Manufacture: III, The Raw Material; IV, The Rise and Localization of the Industry; V, The Rule of the Company; VI, The Workers of Hallamshire: Their Numbers and Standard of Comfort; VII, Industrial Organization; VIII, Earnings and Employment; IX, The Health of the Workers; X, The Early Days of Trade-Unionism in Sheffield; XI, The Trade Outrages; XII, The Sectional Trade Societies; XIII, Commercial Development; XIV, The Industry Abroad; XV, Comparisons. Appendices with excerpts from documentary sources. Bibliographical references in the footnotes.

2096   Pagé, Camille. **La coutellerie depuis l'origine jusq'à nos jours**. Châtellerault, Impr. H. Rivière, 1896-1904. 6v. illus. LC 08-15390.

Comprehensive history of cutlery of all types from antiquity to 1900. Particular emphasis is placed on the history of French cutlery. Contents: Tome I: Pemière Partie: La Coutellerie ancienne. I, Origine du couteau; II, Couteaux de table; III, Coutellerie de luxe; IV, Couteaux communs; V, Objets de coutellerie; Deuxième Partie: Les Couteliers. I, Les Premiers couteliers; II, Les Couteliers de Paris du XIIIe au XVIIIe siècle; III, Les Couteliers de province du XIIIe au XVIIIe siècle; IV, Les Couteliers de Chatellerault; V, Jurandes maitrises; VII, La Corporation des couteliers; VII, La Fin des corporations; VIII, La Fabrication ancienne; IX, L'art du coutelier; X, Divers procédés de fabrication; Notes Complementaires. Tome II: Troisième Partie: La Coutel-lerie moderne. I, La Coutellerie et les couteliers; II, La coutellerie de Paris; III, La Coutellerie de Province; IV, La Coutellerie Chatelleraudaise; V, Les Maitières premières; VI, Matières animales; VII, Les Bois et autres substances; Notes Complémentaires. Tome III: Quatrième Partie: La Fabrication de la Coutellerie. VIII, Matières et outils; IX, Les Procédés mécaniques; X, La Coutellerie d'art; XI, Les Fabriques de coutellerie de Chatellerault; XVIII (misplaced from tome IV), L'industrie coutelière a Thiers et a Nogent; XIX, La Taillanderie. Tome IV: Quatrième Partie: Le Commerce de la Coutellerie. Les Ouvrages coutelier. XII, Revue de la coutellerie; XIII, Les Accessoires de la coutellerie; XIV, La Gainerie; XV, Le Commerce de la coutellerie; XVI, Reasseurs et marchands; XVII, La Classe ouvrière au XIXe siècle; Notes complémentarires. Tome V. Cinquième Partie. La Coutellerie étrangère: Ocèamnie, Amèrique, Afrique, Asie. Introduction; I, L'Ocèanie; II, L'Amèrique; III, La Coutellerie en Amérique; IV, L'Afrique; V, Le Commerce de la coutellerie en Afrique; VI, L'Asie; VII, La Coutellerie en Asie; Notes complémentaires. Tome VI. Cinqième Partie. Europe. VIII, Les premiers ages du fer; IX, L'industrie des barbares; X, Rasoirs, ciseaux; XI, Coutelas, dagues, poignards du XIIIe au XVIIIe siècle; XII, La Coutellerie dans l'Europe meridonale; XIII, La Coutellerie dans l'Europe septentrionale; XIV, La Coutellerie dans l'Europe centrale; XV, La Coutellerie a l'exposition de 1900; XVII, Armoires—Mariques—Carantie; XVIII, Termes usités en coutellerie; Epiloque: Notes complémentarires du tome VI. Illustrated with numerous cuts and a few color graveur plates. Extensive references to specialized literature in the footnotes. Although out-of-date in many details, Page's work is unequaled today in scope of information and illustrations.

See also the exhibition catalog: *Masterpieces of Cutlery and the Art of Easting. Victoria and Albert Museum* (London, The Museum, 1979. 55p. illus.).

American Cutlery

2097   Peterson, Harold L. **American Knives: The First History and Collector's Guide**. New York, Scribner's, 1958. 178p. illus. index. LC 58-7523. Reprint: Highland Park, N.J., Gun Room Press, 1980.

Popular history of American knives from colonial times to the twentieth century. Contents: I, Knife Names; II, Knives of the Explorers and Colonists; III, The Bowie and Its Associates; IV, Army Knives; V, Naval Dirks and Other Knives; VI, The Indian and His Knife; VII, Pocket Knives; VIII, The Manufacture and Sharpening of Knives. Appendix with list of makers includes descriptions of their marks.

See also J. Sargent, *American Premium Guide to Pocket Knives*, 2d ed. (Florence, Ala., Books Americana, 1989. 481p. illus. ISBN 0896890678) and J. B. Voyles, *The American Collectors Association Price Guide to Antique Knives* (Chattanooga, Tenn., American Blade, Inc., 1990. 480p. illus. index. ISBN 0911881123).

Locks and Keys

2098   Curtil-Boyer, Charles. **L'Histoire de la Clef de l'époque romaine au XVIIIe siècle.** Paris, Editions Vilo, 1968. 95p. illus. LC 76-390648.

Well-illustrated survey of European keys from the late Roman period to the eighteenth century in the form of brief descriptions of classes of keys and specific keys in the collections of various French and Swiss museums and private collections. No bibliography.

2099   Buehr, Walter. **The Story of Locks.** New York, Scribner's, 1953. 45p. illus. LC 53-12882.

Popular survey of lockmaking from ancient times to the mid-twentieth century with drawings of the major types of lock mechanisms. No bibliography.

2100   Eras, Vincent J.M. **Locks and Keys Throughout the Ages.** Folkestone, Bailey and Swinfen, 1974. 176p. illus. ISBN 0561002231.

Popular survey of locks from antiquity to the twentieth century with emphasis on the mechanisms. Contents: I, What Is a Lock?; II, Metallurgy; III, The First Metal Locks; IV, Locks and Keys and Their Manufacture; V, Modern Locks and Their Applications; VI, Permutations in Locks and Keys; VII, Locks for Safes and Strong Room Doors; VIII, Safe Deposit Box Locks; IX, Some General Remarks on Keyless Combination Locks.

2101   Holtmeier, Ludwig. **Truhen, Schlösser und Tresore: mechanische Sicherungstechnik im Wandel der Zeit.** Bad Wörishofen, Hans Holzmann, 1989. 148p. illus. ISBN 3778302698.

Well-illustrated survey of locks, strong boxes, safes and other security devices from prehistoric times to the present, written from the perspective of general cultural history. Emphasis is on Germany for later periods. Illustrations include works of art from various times showing use of locks, etc., and reproductions of advertisements of lock and safe manufacturers and clippings from newspapers on famous safe-crackings (mostly in Germany). Contents: Von der Steinzeit zu den Hochkulturen vorchristlicher Zeit; Die Entstehung der ersten Schlösser; Bedeutung von Schlösser in frühen Kulturen; Die Kelten verbreiten das Schmiedehandwerk; Das Römische Reich—Endstation der alten Hochkulturen; Übergang in die nachantike Welt des Mittelalters; Die Entwicklung und Verbreitung des Münzgeldes gibt entscheidende Anstöße; Das Spätmittelalter— Entscheidende Veränderungen im Leben der Menschen führen zu ersten Schritten in ein neues Zeitalter; Die mittelalterliche Burg—ein Beispiel integrierter Sicherheitstechnik; Der Stand des Geldwechsler fordert und fördert mechanische Sicherheit; Der mittelalterliche Schlösser als Kunsthandwerker; Das Jahrhundert der Schloßindustrie; Die industrielle Revolution verändert die Welt—Die ersten Firmen des Geldschrank- und Tresorbaues werden gegründet; Die Gründungs- swelle von Banken und Sparkassen im 19. Jahrhundert fördert die Entstehung weiterer Geld- schrankfabrikken; Grundsätzliches zum Geldschrank und seine Konstruktionsprinzipien; Wettkampf der System; Der Einbrecher—Gegenspieler des neuen Industriezweiges; Ein neuer Entwicklungsschub für Geldschrank- und Tresortürschlösser; Der Weg in das 20. Jahrhundert— Die ersten Tresorraumanlagen werden installiert; Der zweite Weltkrieg bricht aus; Die Entwick- lunge seit 1948; Welle von Einbrüchen in den 60er und 70er Jahren; Sicherheit wird meßbar. General bibliography, p. 147.

2102   Monk, Eric. **Keys: Their History and Collection.** Aylesbury, Shire Publications, 1974. 64p. illus. index. ISBN 0852632541.

Useful survey of the history of locks and keys from ancient Egypt to the end of the nineteenth century. Contents: From Latch to Lock and Key; Warded Locks and Elaborate Keys; Innovations versus the Lock-picker; The Trade and the Collector. Incomplete citations in the general bibliography, p. 62.

See also the museum catalog: *Alte Schlosserkunst aus den Sammlungen des Bayerischen Nationalmuseum* (Munich, Die Versicherungskammer, 1976. 72p. illus. LC 85-166844).

PEWTER

Bibliographies

2103 Denman, Carolyn. **A Bibliography of Pewter**. Boston, Pewter Collectors' Club of America, 1945. 21p. (Bulletin, no. 15).

Comprehensive, classified bibliography of books and periodical articles on all aspects of the history of pewter throughout the world. List of museums containing collections of pewter, pp. 20-21.

Dictionaries of Marks

2104 Stara, Dagmar. **Pewter Marks of the World**. London, New York, Hamlyn, 1977. 260p. illus. index. ISBN 0600370908.

Comprehensive dictionary of nearly 2,000 marks on pewter from around the world. Arrangement is by symbol type and, therefore, is a useful first place to look in deciphering pewter marks. Brief discussion of marking practices in various countries with bibliographical references.

General Histories and Handbooks

2105 Boucaud, Philippe and Claude Fregnac. **Les Étains. Des origines au début de XIXe siècle**. Fribourg, Office du Livre, 1978. 339p. illus. index. LC 79-381004.

Comprehensive history of pewter in Europe and North America from antiquity to the early nineteenth century. Contents: I, L'étain dans l'Antiquité et le Haut Moyen Age; II, Les étains religieux; III, Les étains médiévaux à usage domestique; IV, Les étains corporatifs et municipaux aux XVe et XVIe siècles; V, Edelzinn: les étains bobles; de la Renaissance; VI, Les étains corporatifs et municipaux aux XVIIe et XVIIIe siècles; VII, Les pichets et mesures aux XVIIe, XVIIIe et XIXe siècles; VIII, Les étains à usage domestique aux XVIIe, XVIIIe et XIXe siècles; IX, Les étains à usage médical; X, Quelques notes à l'usage des collectionneurs; XI, Les poinçons. Directory of pewter marks is arranged by country. Each country is introduced by a general comment with bibliographical references. Marks are given in photographs and facsimile drawings. Classified bibliography of books in all languages, pp. 330-31.

2106 Brett, Vanessa. **Phaidon Guide to Pewter**. Oxford, Phaidon Press, 1981. 256p. illus. index. ISBN 0136620493.

Popular, well-illustrated history/handbook of pewter in Europe and North America from the Middle Ages to the present. Useful section on pewter marks giving a good overview of the complex history of marks illustrated with some excellent photographs of marks. General bibliography, pp. 246-47, indicates those titles most useful for deciphering marks.

2107 Cotterell, Howard H., Adolphe Riff, and Robert M. Vetter. **National Types of Old Pewter**. Rev. and exp. ed. Princeton, N.J., Pyne Press, 1972. 152p. illus. index. LC 72-76871.

Collection of articles by the authors that appeared in the magazine *Antiques* before 1933. They provide a useful introduction in English to non-American pewter. Emphasis is on identification of nationality by form or shape of common objects. Occasional bibliographical reference in the footnotes.

2108   Cotterell, Howard H. **Pewter Down the Ages; From Medieval Times to the Present Day...** London, Hutchinson, 1932. 237p. illus. index. LC 33-7395.

Survey of European pewter from the early Middle Ages to the twentieth century with many useful illustrations of pewter depicted in contemporary works of art. Contents: I, Pewter Evolution; II, Early Mediaeval Pewter; III, Mediaeval and Sixteenth-Century Pewter; IV, Pewter of the Seventeenth Century; V, Pewter of the Eighteenth Century and After. Particularly comprehensive glossary. Short list of British pewterers and their marks. No bibliography.

2109   Haedeke, Hanns-Ulrich. **Zinn. Ein Handbuch fur Sammler und Liebhaber.** 3rd ed. Braunschweig, Klinkhardt & Biermann, 1984. 498p. illus. index. LC 84-141902.(Handbuch fur Kunst- und Antiquitätensammler, XVI).

Comprehensive survey of history of European pewter from antiquity to the early twentieth century with separate chapter on German pewter. Illustrated with museum pieces. Contents: I, Vorkommen, Gewinnung; II, Die Verarbeitung des Zinns; III, Die Zünfte; IV, Zinn in Vorgeschichtlicher Zeit und der Antike; V, Mittelalter; VI, Renaissance und Manierismus; VII, Das Zinngerät der deutschen Landschaften; VIII, Klassizismus und Biedermeier; IX, Historismus und Jugendstil; X, Das Zinngerät ausserhalb Deutschlands; XI, Das Sammeln von Zinn. Bibliography, pp. 351-56, is a comprehensive but unclassified list of books and periodical articles in all languages.

2110   Hornsby, Peter R. G. **Pewter of the Western World, 1600-1850.** Exton, Pa., Schiffer, 1983. 381p. illus. index. ISBN 0916838838.

Comprehensive history of pewter made in Europe and North America from 1600 to 1850 directed to the collector. Bulk of the work consists of chapters on types of pewter with brief introduction and large collection of plates with descriptive captions. Content: 1, Background: What Is Pewter?, Tin Resources, How Was Pewter Made?, The Guilds; 2, History of the Pewter Industry; 3, Decoration on Pewter; 4, Marks on Pewter; 5, Religious Pewter; 6, Institutional Pewter; 7, Medical Pewter; 8, Pewter for Eating; 9, Pewter for Drinking; 10, Domestic Pewter; 11, Miscellaneous Pewter. Appendix with guide to dating pewter, fakes and forgeries, and care of pewter. Brief bibliography of basic books in English, pp. 375-76.

See also the price guide: *Pewter*, by T. Curtis (Galashiels, Scot., Lyle Pub., 1978. 125p. illus. ISBN 0902921541).

American Pewter (U.S. and Canada)

Dictionaries of Marks

2111   Jacobs, Carl. **Guide to American Pewter.** New York, McBride, 1957. 216p. illus. index. LC 56-12017.

Dictionary of American pewter marks arranged alphabetically by name of the maker. Introduction sketches the history and collecting of pewter in the United States. Short biographies of the makers includes prices—now very out-of-date—of selected works bearing the maker's mark. Marks are illustrated by line drawings. Appendix with drawings of the characteristic forms of pewter objects. No bibliography. For an updated and pocket-sized dictionary *see:* Celia Jacobs, *Pocket Book of American Pewter; the Makers and the Marks.* 2d ed. rev. and enl. (Boston, Herman, 1970. 93p. illus. LC 70-111761. Reprint: Brattleboro, Vt., Stephen Greene Press, 1981. ISBN 082890460X).

See also: R. M. Kovel, *A Directory of American Silver, Pewter, and Silver Plate (1903).*

General Histories and Handbooks

2112   Coffin, Margaret. **The History & Folklore of American Country Tinware, 1700-1900.** Camden, N.J., T. Nelson, 1968. 226p. illus. index. LC 68-25512.

Popular history/handbook of decorated tinware in America from 1700 to 1900. Contents: Introduction; A Dictionary on Tinware Shapes; Early Tinsmithing in Massachusetts; Apprentices, Toolmakers, Decorators, and Peddlers in Connecticut; The Stevenses of Steven Plains, Maine; Other Maine Smiths and Peddlers; Spread of Tin Industry to New York and Vermont; Tinmen and Peddlers in Pennsylvania and Further West; Leaves from the Journals of a Smith, a Peddler, and a Tinker; Peddler Folklore; Identification and Care of Old Tinware. Appendices with discussion of material and techniques of tinware before 1700 and outside America. Comprehensive bibliography, pp. 212-15.

2113   Ebert, Katherine. **Collecting American Pewter.** New York, Scribner's, 1973. 163p. illus. index. LC 72-12147.

Popular history/handbook tracing American pewter in two periods: 1700-1825 and 1825-1860 with short biographies on the principal pewterers and sections on lamps, cleaning pewter, and pewter fakes and reproductions. List of American pewterers and their marks. Selected bibliography at the end of each chapter.

2114   Gould, Mary E. **Antique Tin & Tole Ware: Its History and Romance.** Rutland, Vt., Tuttle, 1958. 136p. illus. index. LC 57-8796.

Popular history of American tinware to the middle of the nineteenth century with chapters on technique and the life of the tin peddler. No bibliography.

2115   Kauffman, Henry. **The American Pewterer; His Techniques & His Products.** Camden, N.J., T. Nelson, 1970. 158p. illus. index. LC 77-113170.

Popular history of American pewter of the eighteenth and nineteenth centuries. Section on techniques is based on efforts to reproduce traditional pewter work rather than on close examination of actual pieces or molds and, therefore, is unreliable. Appendix with reprint of *Metropolitan Museum's American Pewterers and Their Marks* (New York, 1942) is valuable from the historiographical standpoint for the marks, derived from rubbings, but is less reliable than those in other works.

2116   Kerfoot, John Barett. **American Pewter...** New York, Houghton Mifflin, 1924. 239p. illus. index. LC 24-30174. Reprint: Detroit, Gale, 1976.

Pioneering work on American pewter of the Colonial period and early nineteenth century based on extensive personal observation and written with a pronounced patriotism. The author is much concerned with establishing rarity, and gives "statistical tables" of the productivity of particular pewterers. Unusual grouping of makers by the type of pieces they commonly made.

2117   Laughlin, Ledlie I. **Pewter in America, Its Makers and Their Marks.** Barre, Mass., Barre Pub., 1969-71. 3v. illus. index. LC 77- 86912. Reprint in one volume: New York, American Legacy Press, 1981. ISBN 0517350637.

Volumes 1 and 2 were first published in 1941. Volume 3, first issued in 1971, follows the same arrangement of chapters as in the first two volumes and was intended as a revision and correction. Because of this it is necessary to check all three volumes.

Comprehensive history/handbook of American pewter from early colonial times to circa 1850 containing a wealth of documentary material and the most complete repertory of American pewter marks. Contents: v. 1: The European Background; Problems of the Colonial Pewterer; The Business of a Pewterer; The Marks on Pewter; Pewter-making in America; Household Pewter;

Ecclesiastical Pewter; The Pewterers of Massachusetts Bay; The Rhode Island Pewterers; The Pewterers of the Connecticut Valley. V. 2: The Pewterers of New York City; Albany Pewterers; The Pewterers of Pennsylvania; The Pewterers of the South; The Initialed Porringers; Unidentified American Touches; The Britannia Period; Dethroned Pewterers; Fakes; the Cleaning and Care of Pewter. Appendices with checklist of American makers of pewter, Britannia or block tin, and inventories of American pewter shops. Fully indexed. The standard work on American pewter.

2118   Montgomery, Charles F. **A History of American Pewter**. 2d ed. rev and enl. New York, Dutton, 1978. 307p. illus. index. ISBN 0525474676.
       Comprehensive, authoritative history of American pewter from the early colonial period to 1880. Contents: 1, Pewter in Everyday Life; 2, The American Pewterer and His Craft; 3, Connoisseurship; 4, Church Communion Tokens; 5, Lighting: Candlesticks, Lamps, and Sconces; 6, Drinking Vessels: Mugs and Tankards; 7, Pitchers; 8, Plates, Dishes and Basins; 9, Porrigers; 10, Spoons and Ladles; 11, Utensils for Tea and Coffee; 12, "Any Uncommon Thing in Pewter." 13, The Collecting of American Pewter before 1950, Incorporating 100 Great Examples of American Pewter. Appendices with lists of public collections of American pewter, plates and dishes in the Winterthur Museum, the composition of American pewter, and hints—now obsolete—on cleaning pewter. Prepared as a catalog of the Winterthur Museum collection, the addition of "100 Great Examples of American Pewter before 1850" in the second edition considerably expands the scope of this well-rounded standard history.

2119   Smith, Carolyn A., and Peggy R. Hixon. **The Mystery Era of American Pewter, 1928-1931**. Oklahoma City, Okla., Universal Press, 1979. 67p. LC 80-100088.
       Introduction to American pewter ware made between 1928 and 1931 when the metal was revived in imitation of colonial wares. Directed to the collector, sections are devoted to major manufacturers with illustrations of characteristic pieces and trademarks. Index of manufacturers.
       See also D. H. Fennimore, *Silver and Pewter* (1903) the museum catalogs: *American Pewter* (Brooklyn, N.Y., Brooklyn Museum, 1949. 36 p.), *American Pewter in the Museum of Fine Arts, Boston* (Boston, Museum of Fine Arts, 1974. 119p.), and the exhibition catalogs: *Pewter in American Life* (n.p., Pewter Collector's Club of America, 1984. 159p.).

Regional Histories and Handbooks

2120   Calder, Charles A. **Rhode Island Pewterers and Their Work**. Providence, R.I., E. A. Johnson, 1924. 38p. illus.
       Brief history with biographies of pewterers active in Rhode Island between 1749 and 1856 with illustrations of marked pieces and hallmarks. Appendices with alphabetical list of American pewterers that gives basic biographic data and description of their marks.

2121   Thomas, John C. **Connecticut Pewter and Pewterers**. Hartford, Conn., Connecticut Historical Society, 1976. 194p. illus. LC 76-24380.
       Comprehensive, scholarly history of pewter and pewterers in Connecticut from circa 1750 to circa 1870. Contents: The Pewter: The Metal, Manufacturing, Selling Pewter, The Pewter of Connecticut, The New York Influence on Connecticut Pewter, The Spoon Makers, Mass Production; The Pewterers (presented in chronological order with illustrations of marked pieces and hallmarks with special attention given to the Danforth family of pewterers). Appendix with checklist of Connecticut pewterers. Comprehensive, classified bibliography, pp. 189-90, and further bibliography in the text.

European Pewter

General Histories and Handbooks

2122   Mory, Ludwig. **Schönes Zinn; Geschichte, Formen und Probleme**. 3rd ed. Munich, Bruckmann, 1972. 335p. illus. index. LC 72-312843.

Concise survey of pewter throughout the world from prehistoric times to the twentieth century with emphasis on the relationship of pewter to society and on the production in German-speaking lands. Good selection of 332 plates with descriptive notes and 14 color plates illustrating pewter in historic settings. Repertory of 433 hallmarks. Contents; Die Bedeutung von Zinn in früher Zeit; Vom Handwerk der Zinngießer; Das späte Mittelalter; Barock und Rokoko; Klassizismus, Biedermeier, Jugendstil, Wende zu neuen Formen; Zinngeräte der Gegenwart; Das ausländische Zinngießergewerbe; Marken-Tafeln. Appendices with essays and illustrations on pewter "disease," fakes and forgeries, stylistic change in pewter, and collecting and use of pewter. General bibliography, pp. 317-18.

See also the author's: *Zinn in Europa. Bildkarte der regionalen Krug und Kannentypen* (Munich, Bruckmann, 1972. 21p. illus. LC 73- 303721).

2123   Nadolski, Dieter. **Old Household Pewterware: Its Appearance and Function in the Course of 6 Centuries...** New York, Holmes & Meier, 1987. 328p. illus. index. ISBN 0841-91088X.

Comprehensive history of domestic pewter in Europe from the fifteenth century to the middle of the nineteenth century with emphasis on German works and written from a sociological or cultural historical point of view. Although the text tends to be descriptive rather than analytical, the numerous references and quotes from documentary sources provide an important basis for further study of the significance and uses of pewter. Contents: 1, The Pewterers' Trade; 2, Tableware; 3, Pouring Vessels for Serving; 4, Drinking-vessels; 5, Kitchenware and Storage Vessels; 6, Measurers; 7, Lighting Devices; 8, Equipment for Hygiene and the Sick-bed; 9, Miscellaneous Articles for Persons and Households. Table of 685 pewter marks. Classified bibliography, pp. 312-320.

2124   Verster, A. J. G. **Old European Pewter**. London, Thames & Hudson, 1958. 80p. illus. index. LC 59-3356.

Concise but authoritative survey of European pewter from the Middle Ages to the nineteenth century. Contents: Pewter in Home and Tavern; Pewter in Church and Cloister; Pewterers and Their Guilds; Marking and Finishing; Collectors and Counterfeiters. Comprehensive, classified bibliography, pp. 67-70; 107 plates with descriptive captions.

National Histories and Handbooks

Czechoslovakia

2125   Tischer, Friedrich. **Böhmishes Zinn und seine Marken**. Leipzig, Hiersemann, 1928. 329p. illus. index. Reprint: Osnabrück, Ohms, 1973. ISBN 3535012872.

Comprehensive, scholarly handbook of Bohemian pewter from the late Middle Ages to the twentieth century with emphasis on the production of the golden age of Bohemian pewter, 1550 to 1750. Marks are arranged by place and then by masters listed chronologically. Fully indexed. Bibliographical references in the text.

France

2126   Tardy (firm). **Les Étains francais**. Paris, Tardy, 1959. 843p. illus. index. LC 61-33100.
    Comprehensive, authoritative handbook/history of French pewter from the Middle Ages to the twentieth century. The bulk of the work is a dictionary of pewter by place with entries on place marks and marks of pewterers illustrated with facsimiles of marks and plates (poor quality, black-and-white) of marked pieces. Contents of introductory text: Provenance; Alliages; Fonté; Soudures; Dorage, argentage; Nettoyage; Maladies; Répartions; Fraudes; Décors; Essais; Lois générales; Destructions; Poinçons; Étains parisiens; Poinçons de la marque; Potiers parisiens du XIIIe siècle; XIVe siècle; XVe siècle; XVIe siècle; XVIIe siècle; XVIIIe siècle; XIXe siècle; XXe siècle; Notes complémentaires sur le lois, ordannances; Carte des généralités. The dictionary of marks was published separately as: *Les poinçons des étains français* (Paris, n.p. 1968. 284p. illus. LC 68-113754. Reprinted, 1985. ISBN 2901622151).

Germany

Dictionaries of Marks

2127   Hintze, Erwin. **Die deutschen Zinngiesser und ihre Marken...** Leipzig, Hiersemann, 1921- 31. 7v. illus. index. Reprint: Aalen, Zeiler, 1964-65. LC 65-42721.
    Comprehensive dictionary of German pewter marks. Geographical arrangement with towns listed alphabetically and the makers chronologically. Entries provide biographical data and facsimiles of their marks. Contains 6,800 pewter marks. Contents: Band 1: Sächsische Zinngiesser; Band 2: Nürnberger Zinngiesser; Band 3: Norddeutsche Zinngiesser; Band 4: Schlesische Zinngieser; Band 5-7: Süddeutsche Zinngiesser: 1, Aalen-Kronach, 2, Kunzelsau-Sulzbach, 3, Tauberbischofsheim bus Zweisel mit Anhang Elsass, Österreich, Schweiz, Ungarn. Indexes by name of master, marks (separate indexes for combined master and town marks, city marks, masters' marks, marks of quality) and owners of the pieces illustrated. A standard work with extraordinary scope and depth.
    See also Haedeke (2109) and Nadolski (2123).

Great Britain

Dictionaries of Marks

2128   Cotterell, Howard H. **Old Pewter, Its Makers and Marks in England, Scotland and Ireland...** London, Batsford, 1929. 432p. illus. index. Reprint: Vt., Tuttle, 1963. LC 63-4599.
    Comprehensive handbook of British pewterers and their marks. Introduction with historical sketch of pewter-making in Britain with references to documentary sources. Alphabetical list of 5,374 pewterers with illustrations of their marks. Indexes of marks by initials, devices and hallmarks. A standard reference work for research on British pewter.

2129   Jackson, Radaway. **English Pewter Touchmarks, Including the Marks of Origin of Some of the Scottish and Irish Pewterers**. London and New York, Foulsham, 1970. 123p. illus. LC 77-866555.
    Pocket-sized dictionary of major British pewter marks with introduction covering the history of touchmarks in England. General bibliography, pp. 121-23.

2130   Markham, C. A. **The "New" Pewter Marks and Old Pewter Ware; Domestic and Ecclesiastical...** London, Reeves & Turner, 1928. 355p. illus. index. LC 28-25363.

Comprehensive handbook of British pewterers and their marks with emphasis on London. Covers the period from the late fifteenth century to the early nineteenth century. Chapters on history, types, manufacture, collecting and repair. No bibliography.

Histories and Handbooks

2131   Hatcher, John, and T. C. Barker. **A History of British Pewter**. London, Longman, 1974. 363p. illus. index. LC 73-93118.

Comprehensive history of pewter in Britain from the early Middle Ages to the present with emphasis on social and technological aspects and use of documentary sources. Contents: Part 1, Pewter before 1700 by J. Hatcher: 1, From Early Times to the Norman Conquest; 2, The Middle Ages; 3, The 16th and 17th Centuries; 4, Pewterers' Guilds and the Regulation of the Industry; 5, Manufacturing and Marketing. Appendix A, Data Extracted from the London Company Records: 1451-1700, Appendix B, The Retail Price of Pewterware, before 1700. Part 2, Pewter in Modern Britain by T. C. Barker: 6, The Decline of Pewter; 7, The Company and the Craft. Bibliographical footnotes and comprehensive, classified bibliography, pp. 333-40.

2132   Michaelis, Ronald F. **Antique Pewter of the British Isles**. London, Bell, 1955. 118p. illus. index. Reprint: New York, Dover, 1071. LC 74-138387.

Comprehensive history of pewter in Britain from the thirteenth century through the early nineteenth century with emphasis on the information in documentary sources. Chapters treat history, types of pewter ware, decoration, marks and collecting; each chapter has a separate bibliography. List of basic books, p. 114.

2133   Peal, Christopher A. **Pewter of Great Britain**. London, John Gifford, 1983. 247p. illus. index. ISBN 0707106354.

Revised, updated and augmented version of the author's: *British Pewter and Britannia Metal: For Pleasure and Investment* (London, Gifford, 1971. 200p. illus. index. LC 79-854003).

Comprehensive history of pewter in Britain from Roman times to the early nineteenth century. Contents: 1, Introduction; 2, The Pewterers' Company; 3, Collecting; 4, Cleaning and Repairing; 5, Marks; 6, Romano-British, Early Medieval—to End Sixteenth Century; 7, 1600-1660; 8, 1660-1710; 9, 1710-1825; 10, 1825-1900; 11, Scottish Pewter by P. Spencer Davies; 12, Welsh, Irish and Channel Isles Pewter; 13, British Pewter in New England by Ian D. Robinson; 14, Recognizing European Pewter by D. A. Mundill; 15, Britannia Metal—Its History, Alloy and Manufacture by J. L. Scott; 16, Notes on Fakes and Repros. Bibliography of books and articles, pp. 235-36.

Scotland

2134   Wood, Ingleby. **Scottish Pewterware and Pewterers**. Edinburgh, Morton, 1905. 223p. illus. index. Reprint: New York, Garland. 1976. LC 78-50314.

Old but still -aluable survey of pewter in Scotland with emphasis on the seventeenth and eighteenth centuries. Chapter on the history of the guilds of pewterers in various centers. Repertory of touchmarks. No bibliography.

Netherlands

2135   Dubbe, B. **Tin en tinnegieters in Nederland**. Lochem, De Tijdstroon BV, 1978. 470p. illus. index. LC 72-222357.

Comprehensive, scholarly history of Dutch pewter from the late Middle Ages to the twentieth century with emphasis on the training of pewtersmiths and position of pewter manufacture in Dutch society. Contents: 1. Inleiding: Vindplaasten van tin. Tinhandel; 2, Gilden, Bestuur, Financien, Inkomsten van het gilde; 3, Toelatingseisen, Leerling en knechten, Proef. Gezamenlijk vormenbezit; 4, Sammenstelling verschillende tinalliages. Merken, Merkenplaat Haarlemse tinnegieters; 5, Enige opmerkingen over de techniek van het tinnegieten. Tinpest; 6, Toepassing van tinwerk in de menselijke samenleving to het jaar 1600. Bespreking van een aantal in deze periode gebruikte boorwerpen; 7, Toespassing van tinwerk in de menselijke samenleving na het jaar 1600. Verval van het ambacht. Bespreking van enige in deze periode gebruikte voorwerpen. Negentiende-eeuwse tinnegieters; 8, Vals of echt. Besluit. Comprehensive bibliography, pp. 152-55, and further literature in the notes.

Russia

2136   Gahlnbäck, Johannes. **Russisches Zinn. Leipzig, Hiersemann, 1928- 1932.** 2v. illus. index.
    Comprehensive history of pewter in Russia of the seventeenth and eighteenth centuries based on extensive study of documentary sources and close study of marked pieces. Illustrated with line drawings, facsimiles of hallmarks, photographic reproductions of pieces, and details of ornament and inscription taken from rubbings. First volume covers Moscow pewter; second volume covers the pewter of St. Petersburg. Extensive bibliography in the footnotes.

Scandinavia

2137   Bruzelli, Birger. **Tenngjutare i Sverige...** Stockholm, Forum, 1967. 606p. illus. index.
    Comprehensive, scholarly history and handbook of Swedish pewter and pewterers. Standard source for facsimiles of marks.

2138   Möler, Johan. **Tennsamlarens uppslagsbok, Forteckning over tenngjutare i Sverige och Finland fran 1600- talets borjan- till ar 1900...** 3rd ed. Stockholm, Natur och Kultur, 1969. 151p. illus. index. LC 70-576665.
    Popular, pocket-sized handbook of Swedish pewter marks from 1600 to 1900. Marks are given in facsimile and include place and master marks. Introductory text gives practical advice to collectors. Good, classified bibliography, pp. 120-122.

Switzerland

2139   Bossard, Gustav. **Die Zinngiesser der Schweiz und ihr Werk.** Zug, Strubin, 1920-34. 2v. illus. index. Reprint: Osnabrück, Zeller, 1978. ISBN 3535024226.
    Comprehensive dictionary of Swiss pewter marks dating from the fourteenth to the nineteenth centuries. Volume one has facsimiles of 866 marks arranged geographically; volume two discusses local styles, lists town marks. Biographical data on the pewtersmiths with illustrations of their work.

2140   Schneider, Hugo, and Paul Kneuss. **Zinn: Die Zinngiesser der Schweiz und ihre Marken.** Olten and Freiburg im Breisgau, Walter Verlag, 1983. 382p. illus. LC 72-565650r852.
    Comprehensive dictionary of Swiss pewter marks arranged by town and then chronologically. The iconographical dictionary of marks is one of the most effective indexes yet devised for pewter marks.
    See also the catalog of the pewter collection in the Schweizerisches Landesmuseum, Zurich compiled by H. Schneider and titled: Zinn. *Olten and Freiburg im Breisgau*, Walter Verlag, 1970. 396p. illus.

CHAPTER SEVENTEEN

MUSICAL INSTRUMENTS

BIBLIOGRAPHIES

2141 Coover, James. **Musical Instrument Collections: Catalogues and Cognate Literature**. Detroit, Information Coordinators, 1981. 464p. illus. index. ISBN 0899900135.

Comprehensive, very useful, classified and annotated bibliography of catalogs of collections and exhibitions of musical instruments of all times and places. Includes literature about the collections. Arrangement is by place for institutions and by name of owner for private collections. Annotations are brief but often indicate locations of copies using Library of Congress abbreviations. Appendices with chronological list of early inventories (to 1825), expositions, and exhibitions.

DIRECTORIES

2142 Jenkins, Jean L., ed. **International Directory of Musical Instrument Collections**. Buren, Knuf, 1977. LC 78-319779/MN.

Scholarly directory of collections of musical instruments in museums throughout the world. Entries are grouped by country and place and include address and hours, description of the size, type, and history of the collection, and bibliography of catalogs and other guides (published before 1972).

DICTIONARIES

2143 **The New Grove Dictionary of Musical Instruments**. London, Macmillan Press; New York, Grove's Dictionaries of Music, 1987. 3v. illus. ISBN 0943818052.

Comprehensive, scholarly dictionary of world musical instruments. Many entries have been taken from the *New Grove Dictionary of Music*. Large number of new entries, particularly on the musical instruments of the Third World. Bibliographies of specialized literature are provided at the ends of the larger entries. A standard reference work on musical instruments.

2144 Marcuse, Sibyl. **Musical Instruments: A Comprehensive Dictionary**. New York, Norton, 1975. 608p. illus. LC 64-19290.

Comprehensive dictionary of world musical instruments. Entries vary from one- or two-line definitions to several pages dedicated to major instrument types. Bibliographical references to a list of 206 reference works, pp. 603-608.

2145 Sachs, Curt. **Real Lexikon der Musikinstrumente**. Enlarged and corrected edition. New York, Dover, 1964. 452p. illus. LC 63-19505.

First published in 1913 when it was a pioneering work in the history of organology. Enlarged edition has a new introduction by Emanuel Winternitz.

Comprehensive, authoritative dictionary on all aspects of the history of musical instruments around the world from ancient times to the twentieth century. Illustrated with line drawings. Larger entries have bibliographies and often extracts from earlier works. General bibliography provided in the list of abbreviations, pp. xv-xx. Still a useful reference work, particularly for the references to terminology in non-Western languages and for the extracts.

2146   Wright, Rowland. **Dictionnaire des instruments de musique: étude de lexicologie.** London, Battley, 1941. 196p.

Dictionary of musical instruments important for the extensive references to printed sources attached to the brief definitions. General bibliography, pp. xi-xiv, is a valuable guide to the older literature.

GENERAL HISTORIES AND HANDBOOKS

2147   Baines, Anthony, ed. **Musical Instruments through the Ages.** New York, Walker, 1966. 244p. illus. index. LC 66-22505.

Authoritative survey of world musical instruments consisting of essays on the major classes of instruments, written by various specialists. Useful glossary of technical and acoustic terms. Basic bibliography, pp. 223-32.

2148   Bragard, Roger, and Ferdinand J. De Hen. **Musical Instruments in Art and History.** New York, Viking, 1968. 281p. illus. index. LC 68-15484.

Comprehensive survey of Western musical instruments from prehistoric times to the twentieth century with particular attention given to instruments of artistic merit and the representation of musical instruments in works of art. Good collection of color plates, mostly of instruments in The Conservatoire Royal de Musique, Brussels. Contents: I, The Prehistoric Age; II, The Middle Ages; III, The Renaissance; IV, From Monteverdi to J. S. Bach; V, The Classical Period; VI, Romanticism and Impressionism; VII, The Twentieth Century. Each chapter is subdivided by types of instruments. Classified bibliography of titles in English, pp. 277-78.

2149   Buchner, Alexander. **Colour Encyclopedia of Musical Instruments.** London, New York, Hamlyn, 1980. 352p. illus. index. ISBN 0600364216.

Pictorial survey of world musical instruments featuring excellent color plates of major museum pieces with descriptive captions.

2150   Galpin, Francis W. **Old English Instruments of Music.** 4th ed. London, Methuen, 1965. 254p. illus. index. Reprint: Clair Shore, Scholarly Prrss, 1978. LC 74-181161/MN.

Comprehensive, authoritative history of musical instruments in England from the early Middle Ages to the end of the nineteenth century based upon the study of actual instruments, representations of instruments in works of art, and documentary references. Particularly thorough for Medieval and Renaissance instruments. Contents: I, Rote and Harp; II, Gittern and Citole; III, Mandore and Lute; IV, Psaltery and Dulcimer; V, Crowd, Rebec and Viol; VI, Orgaistrum and Symphony; VII, Clavichord and Virginal; VIII, Recorder and Flute; IX, Shawm and Pipe; X, Horn and Cornett; XI, Trumpet and Sackbut; XII, Organs Portative and Positive; XIII, Tabors and Nakers; XIV, Cymbals and Chimes; XV, The Consort.

2151   Galpin, Francis W. **A Textbook of European Musical Instruments, Their Origin, History, and Character.** London, Williams and Norgate, 1937. 256p. illus. index. LC 56-58142.

Older survey of world musical instruments from prehistoric times to 1937 arranged by class of instrument with emphasis on technical features. Poor-quality illustrations. General bibliography, pp. 19-22.

2152 Geiringer, Karl. **Instruments in the History of Western Music**. 3rd ed. New York, Oxford Univ. Press, 1978. 318p. illus. index. ISBN 0195200578.

First published as: *Musical Instruments: Their History in Western Culture from Stone Age to the Present Day* (London, Allen & Unwin, 1943). Comprehensive, authoritative history of Western musical instruments. Contents: Prehistory and Antiquity; II, The Middle Ages (to 1300); III, Ars Nova and the Early Renaissance (1300-1500); IV, High Renaissance (sixteenth century); V, The Baroque Era; VI, The Classical Period (1750-1810); VII, From Romanticism to Avant-Garde (1810-1960). Appendix: "Rudiments of the Acoustics of Musical Instruments." Comprehensive bibliography, pp. 301-308. An old standard history.

2153 Meer, John Henry van der. **Musikinstrumente: von der Antike bis zur Gegenwart**. Munich, Prestel-Verlag, 1983. 301p. illus. index. ISBN 3791306561 (Bibliothek des Germanischen Nationalmuseums Nürnberg zur deutschen Kunst-und Kulturgeschichte, N.F. Band 2).

Comprehensive, scholarly history of Western musical instruments from the Middle Ages to the twentieth century based upon the world-renowned collections of the Germanisches Nationalmuseum, Nuremberg. Contents: Die europäischen Musikinstrumente bis 1500: Das Erbe der Antike und der Einzug des Orients; Das 16. Jahrhundert: Spezialisierung, Familienbildung und Schmelzklang; Von 1600 bis 1750: Harmonisches Denken, Einschränkung der Instrumentenfamilien und Spaltklang; Von 1750 bis 1914: Bildung der heute am meisten verbreiten Musikpraxis; 1914 bis 1980. Illustrated with actual instruments and many illustrations showing musical instruments being played from contemporary works of art. Comprehensive, classified bibliography, pp. 287-91.

2154 Ott, Alfons. **Tausend Jahre Musikleben, 800-1800**. Munich, Prestel, 1961. 95p. illus. (Bibliothek des Germanischen National-Museums zur deutschen Vergangenheit, Band 18/19). LC 62-32867.

Introductory survey of German musical instruments, well illustrated with plates of major museum pieces and works of art illustrating musical instruments and their use. Brief bibliography of books in German.

2155 Remnant, Mary. **Musical Instruments: an Illustrated History: From Antiquity to the Present**. London, Batsford, 1989. 240p. illus. index. ISBN 0713451696.

Popular but informative pictorial survey of European musical instruments from the ancient world to the present. Arrangement is by type of instrument. Contains 240 useful illustrations of instruments and depictions of musical instruments in works of art. Classified bibliography of works in English, pp. 229-34.

2156 Sachs, Curt. **The History of Musical Instruments**. New York, Norton, 1940. 505p. illus. index. LC 41-559.

Comprehensive history of world musical instruments from prehistory to the twentieth century by a leading musicologist. Contents: First Part: The Primitive and Prehistoric Epoch: I, Early Instruments: Motor Impulses, Ritual Functions, Melodic Impulses; 2, The Chronology of Early Instruments. Second Part: Antiquity: 3, Sumer and Babylonia; 4, Egypt; 5, Israel; 6, Greece, Rome and Etruria; 7, India; 8, The Far East; 9, America (pre-Columbian period). Third Part: The Middle Ages: 10, The Far East; 11, India; 12, Southeast Asia; 13, The Near East; 14, Europe. Fourth Part: The Modern Occident: 15, The Renaissance (1400-1600); 16, The Baroque

(1600-1750); 17, Romanticism (1750-1900); Epilogue: The Twentieth Century. Comprehensive bibliography, pp. 469-88. A standard work.

2157   Stauder, Wilhelm. **Alte Musikinstrumente in ihrer vieltausendjährigen Entwicklung und Geschichte.** Braunschweig, Klinkhardt & Biermann, 1973. 461p. illus. index. LC 73-308790.
   Comprehensive, authoritative history of Western musical instruments from ancient Egypt to the end of the eighteenth century. Factual and insightful text supported by an excellent collection of plates illustrating musical instruments in contemporary works of art and actual historic instruments. Contents: Altertum: A, Vorderer Orient; B, Ägypten; C, Griechenland; D, Italien; E, Nord- und Mitteleuropa; Mittelalter: A, Saiteninstrumente; B, Blasinstrumente; C, Schlaginstrumente; Die Musikinstrumente der neueren Zeit: A, Saiteninstrumente; B, Die Blasinstrumente; C, Die Trommelinstrumente; D, Die Selbstklinger (Idiophone); E, Musikautomaten. Appendices with repertory of major musical instrument makers, glossary of terms, list of collections, and classified bibliography, pp. 450-52. A standard work.

2158   Stauder, Wilhelm. **Einführung in die Instrumentenkunde.** Wilhelmshaven, Heinrichshofen, 1974. 191p. LC 73-92255. (Taschenbücher zur Musikwissenschaft, 21).
   Research guide to the history of musical instruments emphasizing Western instruments from the Middle Ages to the end of the nineteenth century with a comprehensive, classified bibliography, pp. 130-187. Contents: Die Ordnung; Die akustischen Instrumentenuntersuchungen; Die Geschichte der Musikinstrumente; Die Instrumentensammlung und der Nachbau alter Instrumente; Instrumentensammlungen; Kataloge von Instrumentensammlungen; Die Namen der Musikinstrumente und ihre Etymologie; Die Beziehungen zwischen Musikinstrument und Gesellschaft; Die Abendländischen Musikinstrumente: Siteninstrumente; Blainstrumente; Fellisntrumente; Selbsklinger; Elektronische Musikinstrumente; Musikautomaten; Schifttum: Zur Instru- mentenkunde allgemein; Zur Ordnung; Zur Akustik; Zur Geschichte der Musikinstrumente.

2159   Winternitz, Emanuel. **Musical Instruments of the Western World.** New York, McGraw-Hill, n.d. 259p. illus. index. LC 66-24889.
   Concise but authoritative survey of Western musical instruments from the early Middle Ages to the nineteenth century featuring plates and a descriptive catalog to 100 major pieces. Contents of introductory text: Form and Function; Historical Aspects; History of Collecting; Organological Literature; Classification. Comprehensive, classified bibliography, pp. 254-55, and additional bibliography in the notes.
   See also the museum catalogs: *American Musical Instruments in the Metropolitan Museum of Art,* by L. Libin (New York, Metropolitan Museum of Art; Norton, 1985. 224p. illus. index. ISBN 0870993798), *Catalogue of Musical Instruments. Victoria and Albert Museum,* by R. Russell and A. Baine (London, H.M.S.O., 1968. 3v. illus.), *Catalogue of the Crosby Brown Collection of Musical Instruments of All Nations* (New York, Metropolitan Museum of Art, 1902-07. 4v. in 5. illus.), *Die europäischen Musikinstrumente im Germanischen Nationalmuseum Nürnberg,* by J. H. van der Meer (Wilhelmshaven, Heinrichshofen, 1979-), *Die Sammlung alter Musikinstrumente; beschreibendes Verzeichnis* by J. Schlosser (Kunsthistorisches Museum in Wien, Publikationen aus den Sammlungen für Plastik und Kunstgewerbe, Band III; Vienna, Schroll, 1920. 143p. illus. Reprint: Hildesheim, New York, Olms, 1974), *Catalogue déscriptif & analtytique du Musée instrumentale du Conservatoire royal,* by V. Mahillon (Ghent, Hoste, 1880-1912. 5v. illus. Reprint: Paris, Les Amis de la Musique, 1979. 5v. in 2), and the museum guide—to the largest collection of musical instruments in the world—with bibliographical references to the several specialized catalogs-*Musikinstrumenten-Sammlungen Berlin. Eine Übersichte,* by A. Berner (Berlin, Das Museum, 1963).

ANCIENT MUSICAL INSTRUMENTS

2160   Schmidt-Colinet, Constanze. **Die Musikinstrumente in der Kunst des Alten Orients: archäologisch-philologische Studien**. Bonn, Bouvier, 1981. 55p. (text), 58p. (plates). ISBN 3416016173 (Abhandlungen zur Kunst-, Musik- und Literaturwissenschaft, Band 312).

Scholarly study of the musical instruments of the various ancient Near Eastern civilizations based upon representations in works of art and descriptions in documentary sources. Contents: I, Die Typen der altorientalischen Musikinstrumente: 1, Saiteninstrumente; 2, Schlaginstrumente; 3, Blasinstrumente. II, Die schriftliche Überlieferung: 1, Zur Benennung der Instrumente; 2, Zum musikalischen Brauchtum; 3, Zur Notation. Bibliographical references in the notes.

2161   Vorreiter, Leopold. **Die schönsten Musikinstrumente des Altertums**. Frankfurt amd Main, Verlag Das Musik Instrument, 1983. 216p. illus. index. ISBN 3920112946.

Well-illustrated, authoritative introduction to the history of musical instruments from ancient Egypt to the fall of Rome. Introductory essay followed by illustrations of instruments based upon archaeological finds and representations in works of art. Illustrations match ancient representations with watercolor drawings reconstructing the pieces. Bibliography of 120 titles, pp. 210-212, and additional bibliography in the notes.

2162   Wegner, Max. **Die Musikinstrumente des alten Orients**. Münster in Westfalen, Aschendorff, 1950. 73p. illus. (Orbis Antiquus, Hefte 2). LC 53-31561.

Pictorial survey of musical instruments of the ancient Near East. Plates of instruments and representations of instruments in works of art. No bibliography.

See also the museum catalogs: *Catalogue of Egyptian Antiquities in the British Museum. III. Musical Instruments*, by R. D. Anderson (London, The British Museum, 1976. 86p. illus.), *Ancient Musical Instruments of Western Asia*, by J. Rimmer (London, The British Museum, 1969. 51p. illus.), *Les instruments à musique égyptiens au Musée de Cluny*, by C. Ziegler (Paris, Édition del la Réunion des Musée Nationaux, 1979. 135p. illus.).

MEDIEVAL AND RENAISSANCE MUSICAL INSTRUMENTS

2163   Bornstein, Andrea. **Gli strumenti musicali del Rinascimento**. Padua, F. Muzzio, 1987. 315p. illus. index. ISBN 8870213870.

Scholar history of European musical instruments of the fifteenth and sixteenth centuries with emphasis on the musical rather than the artistic aspect. Comprehensive bibliography, pp. 296-305, and bibliographical references in the footnotes.

2164   Crane, Frederick. **Extant Medieval Musical Instruments; a Provisional Catalogue by Types**. Iowa City, Ia., Univ. of Iowa Press, 1972. 105p. illus. ISBN 0877450226.

A catalog of extant medieval musical instruments arranged according to the classification system of Hornbostel-Sachs ("Systematik der Musikinstrumente," Zeitschrift für Ethnologiee, 46, 1914, 553-590), based largely on published references. Entries are descriptive and supply bibliographical references. Illustrated with line drawings. Comprehensive bibliography, pp. 91-105.

2165   Montagu, Jeremy. **The World of Medieval and Renaissance Musical Instruments**. Woodstock, N.Y., Overlook Pr., 1976. 136p. illus. index. ISBN 0715372807.

Survey of western European musical instruments from the early Middle Ages to circa 1600 with many illustrations of depictions of musical instruments in contemporary works of art.

Contents: 1, The Early Middle Ages; 2, The Crusades; 3, The Hundreds Years' War; 4, The Renaissance. General bibliography, pp. 132-33.

2166   Munrow, David. **Instruments of the Middle Ages and Renaissance**. London, Oxford Univ. Press, 1976. 95p. illus. index. ISBN 0193213214.
Concise, pictorial survey of European musical instruments of the Middle Ages and the Renaissance. Good selection of plates showing instruments in Medieval and Renaissance works of art. Chapters treat the various classes of instruments: woodwind, keyboard, brass, strings, and percussion in the two periods. Bibliographical references in the notes.

BAROQUE—MODERN MUSICAL INSTRUMENTS

2167   Baines, Anthony. **European and American Musical Instruments**. New York, Viking, 1966. 174p. illus. index. LC 66-25611. Reprint: London, Chancellor, 1983. ISBN 0907486282.
Authoritative introduction to the history of keyboard instruments in western Europe and America from the fifteenth through the mid-nineteenth centuries. Plates with descriptive notes. Comprehensive, classified bibliography, pp. 161-66.

2168   Montagu, Jeremy. **The World of Baroque and Classical Musical Instruments**. Woodstock, N.Y., Overlook Press, 1979. 136p. illus. index. LC 78-25814.
Concise, pictorial survey of European musical instruments during the seventeenth, eighteenth and early nineteenth centuries. The three periods are subdivided by types of instruments. General bibliography, p. 130-31.

CHAPTER EIGHTEEN

TEXTILES

BIBLIOGRAPHIES

2169 "Bibliographie" in **Bulletin de Liason du Centre International d'Etude des Textiles Anciens**. v. 21- Lyon, 1965-.

Annual bibliography of books and periodical articles on the history, restoration and preservation of all kinds of textiles, including costume. A standard reference tool for serious study in the history of textiles.

2170 Wilckens, Leonie von. "Textilen in Westeuropa. Literatur von 1945-1965." **Zeitschrift fur Kunstgeschichte**, v. 24, 1961, pp. 261-75.

Scholarly essay critically evaluating the scholarly literature, books, and periodical articles that appeared on all aspects of Western textiles between 1945 and 1961. The works are cited in the footnotes.

DIRECTORIES

2171 Lubell, Cecil. **Textile Collections of the World**. New York, Van Nostrand Reinhold, 1976-(1977) v. 1- (3) illus. index.

Comprehensive directory of the textile collections directed more to the contemporary designer than to the art historian or collector. Each volume has a guide to the collection arranged by city, a brief essay sketching the history of textile design in the particular country, and a repertory of plates intended to serve as a source of ideas for textile designers. The information provided under the individual collections in the guide section is quite full and includes addresses and telephone numbers, names of the curatorial staff, detailed descriptions of the range and size of the collections, descriptions of the galleries, study rooms, archives and libraries, and concludes with comments on the publications of the museums that include uneven references to exhibition and museum catalogs. To date (the series appears to have ceased with v. 3) the following have appeared:

   v. 1. *United States & Canada* (1976. 336p. illus. ISBN 0442248962)

   v. 2. *United Kingdom-Ireland* (1976. 240p. illus. ISBN 0442248954)

   v. 3. *France* (1977. 240p. illus. ISBN 0442248946)

DICTIONARIES AND ENCYCLOPEDIAS

2172 **A F Encyclopedia of Textiles**, by the Editors of *American Fabrics Magazine*. 2nd ed. Englewood Cliffs, N.J., Prentice Hall, 1972. 636p. illus. index. LC 70-167915.

Comprehensive encyclopedia with emphasis on materials and techniques. Part two, covering the history and origin of textiles, has a section on inventors and inventions in textile manufacture. Part eight treats textile terminology.

2173   Heiden, Max. **Handwörterbuch der Textilekunde aller Zeiten und Volker fur Studier-ende, Fabrikanten, Kaufleute, Sammler und Zeichner der Gewerbe, Stickerein, Spitzen, Teppische...** Stuttgart, Enke, 1904. 664p. illus. LC 05-10476r90.

Older, comprehensive dictionary of textiles covering mechanized textile manufacture as well as terms applicable to the history of traditional, handwoven textiles.

2174   Linton, George E. **The Modern Textile Dictionary**. 4th rev. enl. ed. Plainfield, N.J., Textile Book Service, 1973. 716p. illus. LC 72-96456.

General dictionary of textile terms with particular attention given to modern materials and techniques. Useful for concise definitions of most traditional fabrics from the technical standpoint. Appendix with "Selected List of the Better Semitechnical and Technical Books on Textiles."

TECHNIQUE

2175   Landi, Sheila. **The Textile Conservator's Manual**. London, Butterworths, 1985. 202p. illus. index. ISBN 0408106247.

Authoritative handbook of textile conservation with much information on the technique of historic textiles. Features case histories of the treatment of various historic textiles in the Victoria and Albert Museum. Contents: 1, The Profession; 2, Technology: Fibres, Textiles, Dyes, Degra-dation, The Chief Fibres; 3, The Object: Examination, Options and Choice; 4, Recording, Handling and Preparation; 5, Chemicals and Their Uses; Cleaning; 7, Support and Consolidation; 8, Reassembly and Finishing; 9, Display, Storage and Transportation; 10, Equipment and the Workroom. Appendices include glossary of weaving terms and basic bibliography with annota-tions, pp. 197-200.

GENERAL HISTORIES AND HANDBOOKS

2176   Birrell, Verla L. **The Textile Arts**. New York, Harper & Row, 1959. 524p. illus. index. LC 58-8363.

Comprehensive history of textile weaving, braiding, dyeing and painting illustrated with 217 plates of pieces of textile, drawings of looms and other equipment, and photographs of activities associated with textile-making throughout the world. Contents: Introduction: Fabric Formation and Design; I, History of Weaving; II, Textile Fibers and Yarns and Their Uses; III, Simple Looms and Their Uses; IV, Belt Looms and Belt Weaves; V, Rug Looms and Rug-Making Techniques; VI, Mechanically Operated Looms; VII, Basic Weaves; VIII, Nonwoven Fabrics— The Single-Element Processes; IX, Embroidery and Needlework; X, Dyes and Dyeing Processes; XI, Textile Painting Processes; XII, Textile Stamping and Printing Processes. Comprehensive, classified bibliography, pp. 493-500, of books in English.

2177   Dreger, Moriz. **Kunstlerische Entwicklung der Weberei und Stickerei**. Vienna, K. K. Hof- und Staatsdruckerei, 1904. 3v. illus. index. LC 10-34198.

An old, standard history of textiles in Europe from antiquity to the early nineteenth century. Although out-of-date in many places, Dreger is still a valuable overview and contains many excerpts from documentary sources not found in other similar histories. First volume is text, the second and third are an important collection of plates. Contents of Textband: I. Abschnitt: Das Auslaufen der spätantiken Überlieferungen; II. Abschnitt: Die Spaltung der östlichen Mittel-meerkultur und die byzantinische Kunst; III. Anschnitt: Die Begründung der süditalienischen Textilkunst; IV. Abschnitt: Die Begründung der oberitalienischen Textilindustrie; V. Abschnitt: Das Granatapfelmuster; VI. Abschnitt: Die Stickerei der nördlichen Länder im Mittelalter; VII. Abschnitt: Weberei und Stickerei der Renaissancerichtung; VIII. Abschnitt: Weberei und

Stickerei der Barockrichtung; IX. Abschnitt: Weberei und Stickerei der Rokokorichtung; X. Abschnitt: Weberei und Stickerei in der Richtung des Klassizismus und Naturalismus. Bibliographical references in the footnotes.

2178   Geijer, Agnes. **A History of Textile Art: A Selective Account**. Totowa, N.J., Sotheby Parke Bernet, 1982. 317p. (text), 95p. (plates), index. ISBN 0856670553.
    Comprehensive, scholarly history of textiles throughout the world from antiquity to the present with emphasis on technical aspects and developments in Scandinavia. Contents: I, Materials; II, Weaving Implements; III, Woven Fabrics and Weaving Techniques; IV, Development of Plain Weaving; V, Individually Patterned Weaves; VI, Mechanical Patterning; VII, Silk Weaving in Asia; VIII, Silk Weaving in Europe; IX, Silk Weaving in Scandinavia; X, Linen Damask and Other Table Linens; XI, Knotted Pile Fabrics and Other Fleecy Textiles; XII, Dyeing, Textile Printing and Pattern Dyeing; XIII, Miscellaneous Textile Techniques; XIV, The Textile Trade with The Orient; XV, Textiles and Textile Crafts in the Scandinavian Countries; XVI, When and How Textiles Have Been Preserved—and Should Be Preserved; XVII, Concluding Remarks. Bibliographical notes and comprehensive bibliography, pp. 290-305.

2179   Glazier, Richard. **Historic Textile Fabrics, a Short History of the Tradition and Developement of Pattern in Woven and Printed Stuffs...** London, Batsford; New York, Scribner's, 1923. 119p. illus. index. LC 23-17634.
    Concise but comprehensive history of the techniques of producing textiles with woven and printed figurative decoration from ancient times to the twentieth century. Contents: I, Introduction; II, Materials Used by the Weaver; III, The Loom; IV, The Evolution of Pattern; V, Woven Patterns; VI, Early Tapestries; VII, Woven Fabrics; VIII, The Printed Pattern; IX, Dyed and Printed Fabrics; X, Ecclesiastical Vestments. General bibliography, pp. 115-116.

2180   Hunter, George L. **Decorative Textiles; an Illustrated Book on Coverings for Furniture, Walls and Floors...** Philadelphia and London, Lippincott; Grand Rapids, Mich., The Dean-Hicks Co., 1918. 457p. illus. index. LC 18-23397.
    Comprehensive history of textile, paper, and leather coverings used on the floors and walls and as upholstery in the West from the late Middle Ages to the nineteenth century. Still useful for its scope and integration of textiles for interiors and furniture. Contents: I, Damasks, Brocades and Velvets—Part I; II, Damasks, Brocades and Velvets—Part II; III, Damasks, Brocades and Velvets—Part III; IV, Fundamentals and Modern Weaves; V, Laces; VI, Embroideries; VII, Carpets and Rugs; VIII, Carpets and Rugs; IX, Chinese and Bokhara Rugs; X, Caucasian and Turkish Rugs; XII, Persian and Indian Rugs; XII, Tapestries and Their Imitations; XIII, Gothic Tapestries; XIV, Renaissance Tapestries; XV, Gobelins, Beauvais, Mortlake Tapestries; XVI, Tapestry Furniture Coverings; XVII, Chintzes and Cretonnes; XVIII, Tooled and Illuminated Leathers; XIX, Wall Papers; XX, Drapery and Furniture Trimmings; XXI, Working Bibliography of Decorative Textiles lists books in the library of the Metropolitan Museum of Art in New York with comments and annotations.

2181   Jaques, Renate, and Ernst Flemming. **Encyclopedia of Textiles; Decorative Fabrics from Antiquity to the Beginning of the 19th Century Including the Far East and Peru**. New York, Praeger, 1958. 32p. (text), 500 illus. LC 58-8171.
    Brief, introductory text followed by valuable, carefully chosen corpus of plates. Text and plates are arranged as follows: ancient Egypt and Syria, Byzantium, Islamic textiles of Mesopotamia: Baghdad, Iraq; Italy: Sicily, Italy: Lucca, Genoa, Florence, Venice; Spain; Germany: Regensburg, Cologne, Scandinavia; Switzerland, Netherlands, Germany; France; China; Persia; Poland; Turkey; Japan; South America: Peru. Focus is on woven textiles. No bibliography.

2182 Migeon, Gaston. **Les arts du tissu**... Nouv. ed., revue et aumentee. Paris, Renouard, 1929. 468p. illus. LC 14-12818.

Older, once-standard history of world textile arts from antiquity to the nineteenth century. Contents: Première Partie: Les Tissus de soie décorés: 1, Tissus d'origine sassanide, II, Tissus d'origine byzantine; III, Les tissus coptes; IV, Les tissus musulmans; V, Tissus allemands; VI, Tissis italiens; VII, Tissus flamands; VIII, Tissus français; IX, Le Tissu de soie en Chine et au Japon; Deuxième Partie: La Broderie: I, Broderies byzantines; II, La Broderie en occident; III, La Broderie en Allemagne; IV, Broderies Anglais. Opus Anglicanum; V, La Broderie en Italie; VI, La Broderie en Espagne; VII, La Broderie dans les Flandres; VIII, La Broderie en France; Troisième Partie: La Tapisserie: I, Technique; II, Historique; III, Période archaique; IV, La Tapisserie en France et en Flandre aux XIVe siècle—Paris et Arras; V, La Tapisserie en Flandre au XVe siècle; VI, Les Ateliers de Bruxelles au XVe et au XVIe siècles; VII, La Tapisserie en Italie et en Espagne; VIII, La Tapisserie en Allemagne; IX, La Tapisserie en Angeterre jusqu'au XVIIe sècle; X, La Tapisserie en France aux XVe et XVIe siècles; XI, Les Ateliers de la Marche, Felletin et Aubusson; XII, L'organisation des manufactures royales en France au XVIe siècle; XIII, L'Atelier de Mortlake en Angleterre; XIV, La Tapisserie en France au XVIIe et au XVIIIe siècles—La Manufacture des gobelins sous Louis XIV; XV, La Manufacture de Beauvais; XVI, Les Tapis de pied en Orient; XVII, Les Tapis de pied en France; Quatrième Partie: La Dentelle: I, La Dentelle a l'aiguille; II, La Dentelle aux fuseaux. Occasional bibliographical footnote.

2183 Thomas, Michel, et al. **Textile Art**. New York, Rizzoli, 1985. 279p. illus. index. ISBN 0847806405.

Well-illustrated survey of the history of world textiles with emphasis on tapestry and the revival of tapestry in the twentieth century. Contents: I, World Centers of Textile Art by Sophie Pommier: Archaeology, The Fabrics of Ancient Peru, The Mediterranean Basin, Coptic Fabrics, Moslem Fabrics, Italian and French Fabrics, Chinese Fabrics, Japanese Fabrics, Indian Fabrics, South-Asian Fabrics, Central Asian Fabrics, African Fabrics, Myths and Rituals; II, The Primacy of Tapestry in the West by Michel Thomas and Christine Maingay: Tapestry and embroidery, The Great Centers of Tapestry; The Late Nineteenth and Twentieth Centuries; III, The Revival of Textile Art by Michel Thomas: The Sources of Contemporary Textile Art, Textile Materials and Modern Art; Perspectives by Michel Thomas. Comprehensive, classified bibliography, pp. 259-63.

2184 Weibel, Adele Coulin. **Two Thousand Years of Textiles; the Figured Textiles of Europe and the Near East**. New York, Pantheon, 1952. 169p. illus. Reprint: New York, Hacker Art Books, 1972. LC 77-143367.

Concise, authoritative introduction to European and Near Eastern (Islamic) textiles with figurative decoration from prehistoric times to the nineteenth century. Contents: Introduction: I, Material: 1, The Fibers; 2, The Dyes; II, Technique: 1, Spinning; 2, Weaving; 3, The Weaves; 4, The Weavers. History: I, Precursors of Woven Fabrics; II, The Earliest Textiles; III, Tapestry Weaving in Egypt and Syria; IV, The Early Silk Trade; V, The Earliest Western Silk Fabrics; VI, The Sassanian Empire; VII, Byzantine Silks; VIII, Islamic Textiles; IX, European Textiles. Selected pieces in American museums with descriptive catalog. Basic bibliography, pp. 165-67.

TYPES OF DECORATED TEXTILES

Pattern Dyed Textiles

2185 Bühler, Alfred. **Ikat, Batik, Plangi. Reservenmusterungen auf Garn und Stoff aus Vorderasien, Zentralasien, Südösteuropa, und Nordafrika.** Basel, Pahros-Verlag, H. Schwabe, 1972. 3v. illus. index. ISBN 3723000932.

Important, scholarly history of itak, batik, and plangi woven textiles in central Asia, the Near East, North Africa, and southeast Europe. First volume is text, second has statistical tables of the various weaves and a comprehensive bibliography, pp. 35-49, third volume is a large important corpus of plates. Contents of Band 1: Erster Teil: Alte Ikatstoffe aus Ägypten. Übersicht der Ikatformen. Vergleichende Untersuchungen; Zweiter Teil: Ikat in Arabien, Vorder- und Zentralasien, Südosteuropa und Nordafrika; Dritter Teil: Reservenmusterungen auf Stoff in Nordafrika, Vorder- und Zentralasien, Ost- und Südosteuropa; Vierter Teil: Ergebnisse der Reservierungsverfahren: I, Wurzelgebiete der Reservierungsverfahren; II, Die Frage einmaliger Enstehung der Reservierungsverfahren. A monumental work, not only the standard work on pattern dyed textiles but, in addition, a model of scholarly study in the history of textile technique.

2186 Larsen, Jack L., et al. **The Dyer's Art: Ikat, Batik, Plangi.** New York, Van Nostrand Reinhold, 1976. 272p. illus. index. ISBN 0442246854.

Well-illustrated, popular survey of dyed textiles throughout the world from early times to the present. Contents: Introduction; Plangi; Batik; Ikat; Some Contemporary Implications of Resists; Dyes and Dyeing; Notes on Sources for the Study of Resists. Comprehensive, annotated bibliography, pp. 247-57.

2187 Nabholz-Kartaschoff, Marie-Louise. **Ikatgewerbe aus Nord- und Südeuropa.** Basel, 1969. 286p. illus. index. (Basler Beiträge zur Ethnologie, Band 6). LC 77-464713.

Comprehensive, scholarly history of ikat woven textiles in Europe from the seventeenth century to the present with emphasis on technique, which is examined in great detail. Contents; A. Technischer Teil: I, Material; II, Bindungen; III, Motive; IV, Musteranordnung; V, Hauptyypen. B. Beschreibender TeiL: Arbeitsgänge und Fertiggewebe. C. Vergleichender Teil. D, Zusammenfassung. Comprehensive bibliography, pp. 285-86, and further bibliography in the footnotes.

2188 Robinson, Stuart. **A History of Dyed Textiles: Dyes, Fibres, Painted Bark, Starch-resist, Discharge, Tie-dye, Further Sources for Research.** Cambridge, Mass., M.I.T. Press, 1969. 112p. illus. index. LC 77-98039.

Authoritative survey of dyed textiles throughout the world from antiquity to the present century. Contents: The Ancient World: 1, Fibres Used in Antiquity; 2, Earliest Examples of Dyed and Dye-patterned Cloths; 3, Preservation and Identification of Ancient Fibres; 4, Colouring Substances and Dyes; Further Developments: 1377-1856: 5, Medieval Dyers and Dyes; 6, Scientific Developments; Nineteenth and Twentieth Centuries: 7, Synthetic Dyes; 8, Modern Fibres; Resist Processes: 9, Batik; 10, Tie and Dye; 11, Other Resist Methods. Appendices with list of museums with collections of textiles; libraries and booksellers, and bibliographical essay, pp. 89-98.

Printed Textiles

2189 Blackshaw, H., and R. Brightman. **Dictionary of Dyeing and Textile Printing.** New York, Interscience Publishers, 1961. 221p. illus. LC 61-65748.

General dictionary of the technology of textile dyeing and printing. Although modern techniques are featured, there is much useful information on basic materials and techniques. Classified bibliography of works in English, pp. 202-205.

2190   Brunello, Franco. **The Art of Dyeing in the History of Mankind**. Vicenza, N. Pozza, 1973. 467p. illus. index. LC 74-169032.

Important, scholarly history of the techniques and materials used in textile production from prehistoric times to the early twentieth century. Contents: I, Prehistory and Primitive Peoples; II, Ancient Egypt Extra-European Civilizations; III, The Classical Period; IV, The Middle Ages; V, The Renaissance and the Seventeenth Century; VI, The XVIIIth Century and the First Half of the XIXth Century; VII, The Revolution of Synthetic Dyestuffs. Appendix with dictionary of natural dyestuffs used before the discovery of synthetic dyes. Plates illustrate historic dye processes. Comprehensive, classified bibliography, pp. 395-422. The standard work on the history of textile dyes.

2191   Percival, Maciver. **The Chintz Book**. London, Heinemann, 1923. 103p. illus. LC 23-18154.

Older, popular survey of printed cotton textiles in India and Europe from the seventeenth century to the early nineteenth century, still useful as an overview and for the discussion of the uses of printed cotton in the Georgian period. Contents: I, Introductory—A Sketch of the History of Printed Cottons, with Some Account of How They were Produced; II, Indian "Chints" and How They Were Made; III, Indian "Chints"—How They Were Used in England in the Seventeenth and Eighteenth Centuries; IV, How English Cottons Were Printed in the Eighteenth Century, Before the Invention of Machinery; V, Pioneers of English Cotton Printing; VI, The Days of Freedom; VII, How Chintzes Were Used in England during the Georgian Period; VIII, Printed Cottons in France—Oberkampf and the "Toiles de Jouy"; IX, Dates and Landmarks in the History of Chintzes and Printed Cottons. Bibliographical essay, pp. 79-80, and additional bibliography in the footnotes.

2192   Robinson, Stuart. **A History of Printed Textiles**. Cambridge, Mass., M.I.T. Press, 1969. 152p. illus. index. LC 71-98040.

Authoritative survey of printed textiles in Europe and America from 1750 to the twentieth century with a chapter on the earlier background. Contents: Origins; Great Britain: 1750 to the Present Day: Copper-plate and Wood-block Prints; Roller and Rotary Printing; The Discovery of Mauveine; The Aftermath of the Industrial Revolution: The Great Exhibition; William Morris and the Influence of the Arts and Crafts Movement; Screen Printing; Other Processes Developed during the Nineteenth Century; Textile Design from 1939 to the Present Day; Heal's, Liberty's and Sanderson's; Developments Abroad (by countries). Appendices with list of museums, libraries and booksellers, and comprehensive bibliography, pp. 124-36, with useful annotations.

Silks

2193   Algoud, Henri. **La soie, art et histoire**. Paris, Payot, 1928. 255p. illus. Reprint: Lyon, La Manufacture, 1986. ISBN 290463858X.

Old, standard history of European decorative silks from the Middle Ages to the nineteenth century with authoritative chapters of French silk weaving. Contents: L'âge antique et des hautes époques; La floraison italienne du Moyen Age et de la Renaissance; Le métier de la soie en France du XVe au XVIIIe siècle; L'ère française de la soie au XVIIIe siècle; Les temps modernes. Updated, general bibliography, pp. 197-98.

2194   Cole, Alan Summerly. **Ornament in European Silks**. London, Debenham & Freebody, 1899. 220p. illus. index. LC 09-1341.

An old, still-useful introduction to the history of woven silk patterns from ancient Persia to the end of the eighteenth century in Europe. Contents: I, Introductory; II, The Manufacture of Silken Stuffs in Europe; III, Materials and Processes in Weaving Silks, Embroideries and Tapestries; IV, Principles Which Have Been Observed in the Designing of Ornament; V, Silk Patterns of Sassanian, Egypto-Persian, and Byzantine Origin; VI, Silk Patterns of Saracenic, Spanish, Sicilian, and Italian Origin; VII, 15th and 16th Century Italian Patterns; VIII, 16th Century Ottoman and Italian Patterns; IX, 17th and 18th Century Patterns; X, Ornament in Embroidery. Bibliographical references in the footnotes.

2195   Falke, Otto von. **Decorative Silks...** New ed. New York, Helburn, 1922. 47p. (text) 126 plates. LC 22-23056.

Authoritative introduction to the history of patterned silk textiles from antiquity to 1800 with an important collection of plates with descriptive notes. Contents: Weaving in Antiquity; I, Silken Tissues of the Late Antique Period; II, Silk-Weaving in the Early Mediaeval Period from the 8th to the 13th Century; III, Silk-Weaving of the Late Mediaeval Period from 1300 to 1500; IV, Main Currents in Silk-Weaving from 1500 to 1800. Bibliographical references in the footnotes.
See also the author's: *Kunstgeschichte der Seidenweberei* (Berlin, 1913, 2v. illus.).

2196   Schmidt, Heinrich J. **Alte Seidenstoffe; ein Handbuch fur Sammler und Liebhaber.** Braunschweig, Klinkhardt & Biermann, 1958. 483p. illus. index. (Bibliothek fur Kunst- und Antiquitätenfreunde, Bd. 10). LC 58-45287.

Comprehensive, authoritative history of world decorative silk from antiquity to the end of the eighteenth century directed to the collector. Contains 399 plates illustrating pieces of silk fabric, works of art illustrating silks, and many valuable diagrams and drawings showing the techniques and weaves of antique silks. Contents: Einleitung: Zu Werkstoff und Technik der Weberei; Das Altertum: Der Alte Orient, Griechisches, Römisches, Christliches Altertum, China unter der Handynastie, Iran unter den Sasaniden; Das Mittelalter: Byzanz, Die islamischen Länder, Iran und Iraq, China, Ost- und Mittel- und Vorderasien unter den Mongolen, Ägypten, Syrien und Kleinasien, Spanien, Sizilien, Italien, Florenz und Lucca, Venedig, Deutschland und Frankreich; Die Neue Zeit: China, Japan und Indien, Persien und die Türkei, Italien, Florenz, Venedig, Genua, Mailand und andrere Orte Italiens, Spanien, Frankreich und andere Länder nördlich der Alpen. Comprehensive bibliography, pp. 434-49, and additional bibliography in the notes.

2197   Thornton, Peter. **Baroque and Rococo Silks**. New York, Taplinger, 1965. 209p. illus. index. LC 65-14391 rev.

Important, scholarly history of figured silks produced in Europe between 1640 and circa 1770 with emphasis on the historical art significance of the patterns. Contents: I, Fashion and Silk-Patterns: The Demand for Fresh Patterns; France the Leader of Fashion; The Importance of the Silk-Designer; The Copying of Silk-Designs; Dating the Successive General Styles; II, The Centres of Silk-Weaving: France (Tours, Lyons, Other Centers); Italy; England (Spitalfields, Other Centers); Ireland; Holland; Spain; Sweden; Denmark; Germany; Austria; Switzerland; Russia; Poland; Summary; III, Figured Silks—Their Sale and Their Use: The Silk-mercers and Their Shops, The Cost of Silk Materials, Furnishing Silks; I, The Silks of the Baroque Period; II, The Bizarre Silks; III, The Early Stages of Naturalism; IV, The 'Lace-Pattern' Silks; V, Naturalism Achieved; VI, The Retreat from Naturalism; VII, Furnishing Silks. Contains 120 plates with descriptive notes including bibliographical references. General bibliography, p. 198, and further bibliography in the notes.

PREHISTORIC TEXTILES

2198   Hald, M. **Ancient Danish Textiles from Bogs and Burials**. 2d ed. Copenhagen, National Museum of Denmark, 1980. 398p. illus. ISBN 8748003123. (Publications of the National Museum. Archaeological-Historical Series, v. 21).

Comprehensive, scholarly history and analysis of rich finds of prehistoric textiles from Denmark. Contents: I, Textiles and Skins from Peat Bogs (by place); II, Textiles from Settlements and Graves (by place); III, Raw Materials and Spinning; IV, Woven Fabrics and Their Construction; V, Dating Prehistoric Danish Weaves; VI, Looms and Fabrics; VII, Tablet Weaving; VIII, Braiding and Sprang; IX, Needle and Sewing; X, Prehistoric Costume in Denmark; XI, Material, Shape and Parallelism. Comprehensive bibliography, pp. 394-98, and further bibliography in the notes. A standard work on this the single, most important group of prehistoric textiles.

2199   Jorgensen, Lise B. **Forhistoriske textiler i Skandinavien—Prehistoric Scandinavian Textiles**. Copenhagen, Kongelige Nordiske Oldskriftselskab, 1986. 390p. illus. index. ISBN 8787483467. (Nordiske fortidsminder, Serie B-in quarto, Bd. 9).

Scholarly history of the rich finds of prehistoric and early Medieval textiles from Scandinavia with particular attention to the details of weave and distribution of types of textiles. Text in Danish and English. Contents: I, Introduction; II, Bronze-Age Textiles; III, Pre-Roman Iron Age Textiles; IV, Roman Iron Age Textiles; V, Migration Period Textiles; VI, Merovingian Period Textiles; VII, Viking Age Textiles; VIII, The Development of Textiles from the Early Bronze Age to the Viking Age; IX, Comparative Material in North and Central Europe; X, Conclusions. Comprehensive, unclassified bibliography, pp. 367-375.

2200   Schlabow, Karl. **Textilefunde der Eisenzeit in Norddeutschland**. Neumunster, K. Wachholtz, 1976. 100p. illus. ISBN 3529015156. (Göttinger Schriften zur Vor- und Frühgeschichte, Bd. 15).

Scholarly study of the rich finds of Germanic textiles from the moors of northern Germany with detailed descriptions directed to reconstruction of Germanic dress around the time of Christ's birth. Contents: I, Erhaltungsmöglichkeiten von Textilen aus der Vorzeit; II, Geborgene Textilien der Eisenzeit und ihre Fundberichte; III, Rohmaterial zum Weben in der Vorzeit; IV, Naturfarben der Schafwolle und künstliche Färbung; V, Das Spinnen des Webgarns; VI, Die komplizierte Webetechnik der Eisenzeit erfordert einen Webstuhl von besonderer Eigenart; VII, Die Kleidung der Germanen in den Jahrhunderten um Christi Geburt: A, Die Kleidung der Germanen nach den überlieferten römischen Denkmälern der Eisenzeit, B, Die Kleidung der Germanen nach den Untersuchungsergebnissen erhaltener Kleidungsstücke aus den Mooren Norddeutschlands. Comprehensive bibliography, pp. 98-100, and further bibliography in the footnotes.

PRE-COLUMBIAN TEXTILES

2201   Anton, Ferdinand. **Ancient Peruvian Textiles**. New York, Thames & Hudson, 1987. 236p. illus. index. ISBN 0500014027.

Well-illustrated and authoritative introduction to pre-Columbian textiles. Contains 183 plates with descriptive notes. Contents: 1, The Language of Textiles; 2, The Devine Image in the Chavín Cilture; 3, From Paracas to Nazca; 4, Naturalism to Abstraction; 5, Gods, Spirits, and Beasts; 6, The Inca Empire. Select bibliography, pp. 231-33, and bibliographical references in the notes.

2202   Bird, Junius, and Louisa Bellinger. **Paracas Fabrics and Nazca Needlework**. Washington, D.C., National Publishing Co., 1954. 126p. illus. index. LC 54-9410.

Important, scholarly catalog of the collection of the Paracas and Nazca textiles in The Textile Museum, Washington, D.C. The scholarly catalog is followed by authoritative chapters on design and techniques and technical analysis. Annotated bibliography, pp. 117-122.

2203　Feltham, Jane. **Peruvian Textiles**. Aylesbury, Shire, 1989. 72p. illus. index. ISBN 0747-800146.

In the series: "Shire Ethnography." Introduction to the ancient pre-Columbian textiles of Peru with references to the continuation of techniques and decoration of present-day Indians of Peru. Contents: Chronology; 1, The Land and the People; 2, Materials and Tools; 3, Techniques; 4, Characteristics of Peruvian Textiles; 5, The Development of Peruvian Weaving; 6, Dress Ancient and Modern; 7, Textiles and Society; 8, Museums; 9, Further Reading (books in English).

2204　Harcourt, Raoul d'. **Textiles of Ancient Peru and Their Techniques**. Seattle, Wash., University of Washington Press, 1962. 186p. illus. index. LC 62-17150. Reprinted, 1987. ISBN 0295953314.

Scholarly study of pre-Columbian textiles of Peru with emphasis on technique and materials. Contains 117 black-and-white plates with detailed notes. Contents: Part I: Woven Textiles: 1, Plain Weave; 2, Fabrics of Varied Weave; 3, Fabrics with Supplementary Decorative Warp or Welft Yarns; 4, Double Cloth; 5, Gauzes; 6, Open-work Fabrics; 7, Fabrics with Wrapped Warp; 8, Fabrics Made of Twisted Warp or Welft; 9, Dyed or Tie-Dyed Woven Fabrics. Part II: Nonwoven Fabrics: 10, Plaiting or Braiding; 11, Network; 12, Felt. Part III: Ornamentation and Trimming of Fabrics: 13, Embroideries; 14, Trimmings. General bibliography, pp. 141-146.

See also O'Neale, Lila M., *Textile Periods of Ancient Peru* (Berkeley, Calif., University of California Press, 1930-1950. 3v. illus. index, University of California, *Berkely University of California Publications in American Archaeology and Ethnology*, v. 28, no. 2; v. 39, no. 2; v. 40, no. 4).

2205　Paul, Anne. **Paracas Ritual Attire: Symbols of Authority in Ancient Peru**. Norman, Okla., Univ. of Oklahoma Press, 1990. 170p. illus. index. ISBN 08606122307.

Scholarly study of the ancient textile costumes from Paracas with emphasis on the decoration of the textiles and the form of the costumes as symbols of rulership. Full catalog of the textiles from the Paracas Necropolis Mummy Bundle 378 and 310. Contents: 1, Paracas: A Cultural Legacy Preserved in Cloth; 2, Paracas Textiles Within the Andean Weaving Tradition; 3, The Ancient Desert Community of Paracas; 4, The Anatomy of Paracas Burial Bundles; 5, Paracas Ritual Attire; 6, Style as a Component of Meaning in Paracas Textile Iconography; 7, Paracas Textile Iconography: the Reflection of Social Identities and a World View; 8, Conclusions. Comprehensive bibliography, pp. 159-165.

2206　Rowe, Ann P. **Costumes & Featherwork of the Lords of Chimor: Textiles from Peru's North Coast**. Washington, D.C., Textile Museum, 1984. 190p. illus. ISBN 0814050235.

Scholarly study of the woven textile and featherwork costumes of the pre-Columbian Chimu civilization of Peru. Contains 29 color plates and 197 black and white illustrations. Contents: Introduction: The Kingdom of Chimor, Cotton Fiber Processing, The Mystery of Chimu Textiles; The Bird Lot Style; The Toothed Crescent Headdress Style; The Pelican Style; The Plain Crescent Headdress Style; Featherwork. Comprehensive bibliography, pp. 188-190, and bibliographical references in the notes.

2207   Vanstan, I. **The Fabrics of Peru**. Leigh-on-Sea, England, F. Lewis, 1966. 16p. (text), 60p. (illus). LC 67-79078.

Introductory survey of pre-Columbian fabrics of Peru with collection of 60 plates with briefly descriptive notes. No bibliography.

See also the museum handbooks: *Means, Philip A. Peruvian Textiles* (New York, Metropolitan Museum of Art, 1930. 27p. (text), 24 plates), and *Paracas Textiles*, by A. Paul (Goteborg, Goteborgs Etnografiska Museum, 1979. 56p. illus.).

ANCIENT TEXTILES

2208   Hall, Rosalind M. **Egyptian Textiles**. Aylesbury, Shire, 1986. 72p. illus. index. ISBN 0852638000.

Introduction to the ancient textiles of Egypt with reference to the continuation today of traditional techniques. Contents: 1, The Archaeological Importance of Textiles; 2, Woven Fabrics and Dyeing; 3, Spinning and Weaving; 4, Representations of Costume; 5, Garments for Life and Death; 6, Tutankhamun's Wardrobe; 7, The Egyptian Laundry; 8, Sewing and Darning; 9, Dress and Rank in Ancient Egypt; 10, Museums to Visit.

2209   Petzel, Florence E. **Textiles of Ancient Mesopotamia, Persia, and Egypt.** Corvallis, Ore., Cascade Print Co., 1987. 226p. illus. ISBN 0961847603.

Study of the development of textiles in ancient Egypt and the ancient Near East with particular references to fibers and weaving techniques. Useful as a source of information and for bibliographies that appear at the end of the three chapters: I, Mesopotamia; II, Persia; III, Egypt.

2210   Volbach, Wolfgang F. **Early Decorative Textiles**. London, New York, Hamlyn, 1969. 157p. illus. LC 79-437236.

Concise but authoritative survey of Coptic and Byzantine textiles from the fourth through the ninth centuries. Contains 71 pieces illustrated with rather poor-quality color plates with accompanying descriptive notes. No bibliography.

COPTIC AND BYZANTINE TEXTILES

2211   Baerlocher, Martin. **Grundlagen zur systemaischen Erfassung koptischer Textilen**. Basel, Graphische Betriebe Coop Basel, 1983. 314p. illus. Phd. dis.

Scholarly study of the weaving technique used in ancient Coptic textiles. Contents: Einleitung; Stoffbildungsgrundlage; Die Forschungssituation; Merkmale koptischer Wirkereien; Vor der Rekonstruktion der koptischen Textilien. Illustrated with drawings showing details of weaving. Comprehensive bibliography, pp. 312-313.

2212   Kybalova, Ludmilla. **Coptic Textiles**. London, Hamlyn, 1967. 157p. illus. LC 68-98613.

General survey of ancient and medieval Coptic textiles with a good collection of 113 plates of pieces in European museums with descriptive captions. Contents: Introduction; 1, The Background of the Copts; 2, The History of the Copts; 3, Architecture, Painting and Sculpture, 4, Textiles: Tombs, and Clothing, Iconography, Symbolism and Ornament, Technique and Technology; 5, Conclusion. Brief bibliography, p. 48.

See also the museum catalogs: *Spätantike und koptische Textilen*, by E. Eggebrecht (Mainz/Rhein, P. von Zabern, 1978- illus. Hildesheim, Pelizaeus-Museum, Katalog ägyptischer Altertümer, 2. ISBN 3805303386), *Die Spätantiken und Koptischen Textilen im Hessischen Landesmuseum*, by D. Renner (Wiesbaden, Marrassowitz, 1985. 116p. illus. ISBN 3447025409), *Die koptischen Textilen in den vatikanischen Museen*, by D. Renner-Volbach (Wiesbaden, Steiner,

1982. 154p. illus. ISBN 3515035478. Kataloge/Pinacoteca vaticana, Bd. 2), *Les tissus coptes: catalogue raisonne du Musée des Beaux-arts de Dijon; suivi oar le catalogue de la collection du Museum d'Histoire Naturelle de Dijon*, by P. Cauderlier (Dijon, Musée des Bauex-arts de Dijon, 1985. 125p. illus.), *Textiles coptes: des Musées Riyaux d'Art et d'Histoire*, by J. La Fontaine-Dosogne (Brussels, Musées Royaux d'Art et d'Histoire, 1988. 98p. illus.), *Looms and Textiles of the Copts: First Millennium Egyptian Textiles in the Carl Austin Rietz Collection of the California Academy of Sciences*, by D. L. Carroll (San Francisco, California Academy of Sciences, 1988. 201p. illus. ISBN 0295966726), *Koptische Textilkunst im spätantiken Ägypten: die Sammlung Rautenstrauch im Städtischen Museum Simeonstift Trier*, by C. Nauerth (Trier, Spee-Verlag, 1978. 98p. illus. ISBN 3877604129), Lyon, *Musée historique des tissus: soieries sassanides, coptes et byzantines Ve -XIe siècles*, by M. Martiniani-Reber (Paris, Éditions de la Reunion des Musées Nationaux, 1986. 129p. illus. index. ISBN 2711820092), *Textiles from Medieval Egypt, A.D. 300-1300*, by T. K. Thomas (Pittsburgh, Penn., Carnegie Museum of Natural History, 1990. 66p. illus. ISBN 0911239200).

AMERICAN TEXTILES (U.S. and Canada)

Bibliographies

2213   Gordon, Beverly. **Domestic American Textiles: A Bibliographic Source-book**. Pittsburgh, Penn., Center for the History of American Needlework, 1978. 217p. index. LC 78-108861.
Annotated bibliography of 574 entries published between 1876 and 1976.

Dictionaries

2214   Montgomery, Florence M. **Textiles in America, 1650-1870**. New York, Norton, 1984. 412p. illus. ISBN 0393017036.

Directories

2215   Lubell, Cecil, ed. **United States & Canada: An Illustrated Guide to the Textiles in the United States and Canadian Museums**. New York, Van Nostrand Reinhold, 1976. 336p. illus. index. ISBN 044224892. (Textile Collections of the World, v. 1). *See* (2171).

General Histories and Handbooks

2216   Little, Frances. **Early American Textiles**... New York and London, Century, 1931. 267p. illus. index. LC 31-32892.
An old, standard history of textiles in America from the seventeenth century to the early nineteenth century. Contents: 1, Beginnings; 2, The South in the 17th Century; 3, Early New England and the North; 4, Development of the Industry; 5, The Beginning of the Machine Age; 6, The Story of American Silk; 7, Spinning and Weaving; 8, Embroidery in America; 9, Early Cotton-Printing in America; 10, Textiles Used in Early American Houses.

2217   Pettit, Florence H. **America's Printed and Painted Fabrics; 1600-1900**. New York, Hastings House, 1970. 256p. illus. index. LC 76-113770.
Popular and informative survey of printed and painted fabrics in America between 1600 and 1900. Contents: I, How Do They Print a Fabric: Basic Methods; Hand Printing Processes; Machine Printing Processes; A Complete History of World Fabric Prints. III, Jamestown Colony to the Revolution, 1607-1775; IV, From the Revolution to 1900. Bibliography of 103 titles, pp. 245-247.

2218   Schoeser, Mary, and Celia Rufey. **English and American Textiles**. New York, Thames & Hudson, 1989. 256p. illus. ISBN 0500014736.

Well-illustrated, authoritative history of textiles made in England and America from 1790 to the present. Among the illustrations are many views of historic interiors and designs. Particular attention is given to recently restored historic interiors and their fabrics. Contents: 1, Basic Cloths; 2, Revolution (1790-1825); 3, Exuberance (1825-1860); 4, Renaissance (1860-1890); 5, Towards Simplicity (1890-1920); 6, Contrast and Variety (1920-1950); 7, Individuality (1950-1980); 8, Retrospection (1980-1990). Comprehensive, classified bibliography, pp. 247-50, and additional bibliography in the notes.

Canada

2219   Burnham, Harold B., and Dorothy K. Burnham. **"Keep Me Warm One Night": Early Handweaving in Eastern Canada**. Toronto, Univ. of Toronto Pess., 1972. 387p. illus. index. LC 72-83388.

Comprehensive history of weaving, woven textiles, and costumes made of woven textiles in eastern Canada from early colonial times to the middle of the nineteenth century, with special emphasis on coverlets. Catalog of 400 pieces in the Royal Ontario Museum. Contents: The Background; 2, Tools and Equipment; 3, The Basic Weaves, Tabby, Twill, and Simple Patterns; 4, Costume; 5, Carpets, Blankets, Linens; 6, An Introduction to Coverlets; 8, Overshot Coverlets; 9, "Summer and Winter" Coverlets; 10, Multiple-shaft Coverlets; 11, Twill Diaper Coverlets; 12, Doublecloth Coverlets; 13, Jacquard Coverlets. Appendix with list of pieces in the Royal Ontario Museum. Select bibliography, pp. 379-380.

2220   **La fabrication artisanale des tissus: appareils et techniques**. Quebec, Musée du Québec, Ministère des Affaires Culturelles, 1974. 103p. illus. LC 75-509822r79.

Handbook of the techniques of traditional textile weaving in French Canada illustrated with plates of tools and other implements and views of weavers at their work. Contents: I, Le Lin; II, La leine; III, Le filage; IV, Le dévidage; V, La teinture et l'ébouillantage de la laine; VI, Le blanchiment du lin; VII, Le bobinage; VIII, L'ordissage; IX, Le tissage; X, Le foulage; XI, Le produits du tissue; XII, La récupération des produits usagés; XIII, Le lavage. Classified bibliography, pp. 101-02.

See also the exhibition catalog: *The Comfortable Arts: Traditional Spinning and Weaving in Canada*, by D. K. Burnham (Ottawa, National Gallery of Canada, 1981. 238p. illus.).

Native American Textiles and Beadwork

2221   Dockstader, Frederick J. **Weaving Arts of the North American Indian**. New York, Crowell, 1978. 223p. illus. index. ISBN 0690017391.

Authoritative survey of the weaving of Native Americans from the earliest times, i.e., circa 1250, to the twentieth century. Contents: 1, The Fibers of Native American Weaving: A Historical Background; 2, The Warp of Technique: Method and Manner in Weaving; 3, The Social Weft: Effects of Weaving upon Indian Life; 4, The Economic Brocade: Trade and Commerce; 5, The Web of the Fabric: A Survey of Textile Production by Region; 6, The Contemporary Scene: Influences, Personalities, and Markets Today; 7, Conservation and Preservation: How to Care for Woven Textiles. Comprehensive bibliography, pp. 210-19.

Navajo Textiles

2222   Amsden, Charles A. **Navaho Weaving: Its Technic and History**. Santa Ana, Calif., The Fine Arts Press, 1934. 263p. illus. Reprint: New York, Dover, 1991. ISBN 0486265374.

Pioneering work on the history and technique of Navajo weaving. Contents: Part I—The Technic of Navaho Weaving: I, Finger Weaving; II, Loom Development in America; III, The Navaho Loom; IV, Weaves of the Navaho; V, Native Dyes: Development; VI, Native Dyes: Methods and Formulas; VII, Types and Uses of Navaho Textiles. Part II—The History of Navaho Weaving: VIII, The First Sheep; IX, Early Navaho Weaving; X, Bayeta—1800-1863; XI, Taming the Navaho—1863-1868; XII, Blanket to Rug—The Transition Period—1870-1890; XIII, The Rug Business—1890-1932; Chapter XIV, The Growth of Design—1800-1920; XV, The Revival—1920 to Present. Bibliographical references in the footnotes. A standard work.

2223   Dedera, Don. **Navajo Rugs: How to Find, Evaluate, Buy and Care for Them**. 2d ed. Flagstaff, Aria., Northland Pub., 1990. 123p. illus. index. ISBN 0873581385.

Collector's guide to contemporary Navajo rugs illustrated with 83 color and black and white plates showing pieces—one from 1803—and scenes of spinning and weaving. Useful chapters on buying, fakes, and care. Selected readings, pp. 119-20.

2224   James, George W. **Indian Blankets and Their Makers**. Glorieta, N.M., Rio Grande Press, 1970. 213p. Illus. ISBN 087380015X.

First published in 1927. Early history and handbook of Navajo blanket weaving with important reproductions of early twentieth-century photographs of weaving activities and plates of blankets in the author's collection. Contents: I, Where Navaho Blankets Are Made, Navaho Houses and Their Songs of Blessing; II, The Birth and Growth of the Art of Navaho Blanket-Weaving; III, The Early History of the Navaho Blanket-Weaving; III, The Early History of the Navaho Blanket; IV, The Bayeta Blanket of the Navaho; V, Old Style Native Wool Blankets; VI, Navaho and Pueblo Squaw Dresses; VII, The Song of Blessing of the Blanket; VIII, The Temporary Deterioration of the Art of Navaho Blanket Weaving; IX, Improving the Art of Navaho Blanket Weaving; X, The Significance and Symbolism of Color in the Navaho Blanket; XI, Dyeing with Native and Aniline Dyes; XII, The Origin and Symbolism of Navaho Blanket Designs; XIII, A Navaho Weaver at Work; XIV, The Designs on Modern Navaho Blankets; XV, Navaho and Pueblo Belts, Garters, and Hair Bands; XVI, The Outline Blanket; XVII, Kachina or Yei Blankets; XVIII, The Classification of Modern Blankets; XIX, Imitation Navaho Blankets; XX, Pueblo Indian Weavers; XXI, The Chimayó Blanket; XXII, Cleaning the Navaho Blanket. Occasional bibliographical reference in the footnotes.

2225   Kaufman, Alice, and Christopher Selser. **The Navajo Weaving Tradition: 1650 to the Present**. New York, Dutton, 1985. 150p. illus. ISBN 0525242996.

Well-illustrated survey of Navajo weaving featuring 220 mostly color plates of rugs and tapestries with descriptive captions. Contents: 1, A Brief Introduction to Navajo Weaving; 2, The First Weavers; 3, The Classic Period; 4, Bosque Redondo and the Aftermath; 5, The Reservation Traders; 6, Contemporary Navajo Weaving; 7, The Weaving Process—Tools, Techniques and Materials. Selected bibliography, pp. 145-46.

2226   Rodee, Marian E. **Old Navajo Rugs: Their Development from 1900 to 1940**. Albuquerque, N.M., Univ. of New Mexico Press, 1981. 113p. illus. index. ISBN 0826305679.

Concise survey of Navajo rugs, e.g., wall hangings, dating between 1890 and the beginning of World War II. Contains 77 plates with brief descriptive captions. Contents: 1, Navajo Weaving before 1890; 2, The Transitional Period, 1890 to 1920; 3, Fiber: the Key to Identification; 4, J. B. Moore and the Crystal Trading Post; 5, George Bloomfield and Two Gray Hills; 6, Lorenzo

Hubbell of Ganado and His Trading Empire; 7, Wheelwright, McSarron, and the Chinle Revival; 8, Tees Nos Pos, Red Lake, and Tuba City; 9, Pictorial and Ceremonial Rugs. Select bibliography, pp. 107-09.

See also the exhibition catalogs: *Navajo Textiles: The William Randolph Hearst Collection*, by N. J. Blomberg (Tuscon, Ariz., University of Arizona Press, 1988. 257p. illus. index. ISBN 0816510784) and *The Song of the Loom: New Traditions in Navajo Weaving*, by F. T. Dockstader (New York, Hudson Hills Press in association with the Montclair Art Museum, 1987. 130p. illus. index. ISBN 0933920881).

Beadwork

2227 Orchard, William C. **Beads and Beadwork of the American Indians: A Study Based on Specimens in the Museum of the American Indian, Heye Foundation**. 2d ed. New York, The Museum, 1975. 168p. illus. (Contributions from the Heye Foundation, v. 11, 1975).

First published in 1929. Classic reference work on American Indian beadwork. Contents: Shell Beads; Pearl Beads; Boen Beads; Stone Beads; Drilling; Metal Beads; Wampum; Odd Forms and Materials; Trade Beads; Woven Beadwork; Sewing Techniques; Edgings; Bead Inlays; Beaded Baskets. Contains 41 plates and 136 figures. Bibliographical references in the footnotes.

2228 Wildschut, William. **Crow Indian Beadwork:Aa Descriptive and Historical Study**. New York, Museum of the American Indian, Heye Foundation, 1959. 55p. illus. (Contributions from the Museum of the American Indian, Heye Foundation, vol. 16). Reprint: Ogden, Utah, Eagle's View Pub., 1985. ISBN 0943604079.

Coverlets

2229 Heisey, John W. **A Checklist of American Coverlet Weavers**. Williamsburg, Virg., Colonial Williamsburg Foundation, 1978. 149p. illus. index. ISBN 0879350482.

Index to the coverlets woven by 942 jacquard weavers in nineteenth-century America. Entries supply basic biographical data including the geographic area in which the weaver was active, the weavers ethnic origin, and a list of the signed and dated examples. Includes over 2,500 coverlets. Concluding chapter is a repertory of weavers' trademarks. An essential reference tool. For a recent, comprehensive bibliography of the literature on American coverlets *see*: C. Anderson, "Coverlet Bibliography," in *Ars Textrina, 2* (1984), pp. 203-215.

2230 Wilson, Sadyne T., and Doris F. Kennedy. **Of Coverlets: The Legacies, the Weavers**. Nashville, Tenn., Tunstede, 1983. 494p. illus. index. LC 83-90885.

Important, scholarly history of coverlets made in Tennessee from the nineteenth century to the present. In addition to much information on the technique and style of old coverlets, this excellent work includes interviews and photographs of contemporary weavers of coverlets. The work of a team from the Handweavers Guild of Nashville from 1978 to 1983. Bulk of the work is a directory of the work of named weavers giving biographical data, photographs when available, and color plates of the work with diagrams showing the nature of the woven decoration. Contents: Tennessee Textile History Project 1978-1983; Weave Structure of the Overshot Coverlet; Motif Classification System; The Legacies, The Weavers; The Tradition Lives; The Educators; Preview—A History of Textiles in Tennessee. Appendices with index of motifs, cross-reference index to pattern names, and index of documented textiles by owner. Comprehensive bibliography, pp. 469-70.

See also the exhibition catalogs: *Coverlets: A Handbook on the Collection of Woven Coverlets in the Art Institute of Chicago,* by Mildred Davison and C. Mayer-Thurman (Chicago, The Art Institute, 1973. 228p. illus. LC 73-82570), *American Hand-Woven Coverlets in the Newark Museum,* by M. E. White (Newark, N.J., The Museum, 1947. 83p. illus.), *American Coverlets of the Nineteenth Century, from the Helen Louise Allen Textile Collection* (Madison, Wis, Elvehjem Art Center, 1974. 95p. illus.), and *Heirlooms from Old Looms; a Catalogue of Coverlets Owned by the Colonial Coverlet Guild of America and Its Members* (Chicago, 1955, 406p. illus.).

Quilts

Dictionaries

2231   Khin, Yvonne M. **The Collector's Dictionary of Quilt Names and Patterns.** Washington, D.C., Acropolis Books, 1980. 489p. illus. index. Reprint: New York, Portland House, 1988. ISBN 0517669145.

Comprehensive dictionary of the patterns used in quiltmaking. Arrangement is in broad geometric categories. Over 2,400 patterns are identified and the source of the pattern is given in the caption. Brief bibliography, pp. 17-18.

Histories and Handbooks

2232   Bishop, Robert, William Secord, and Judith P. Weissman. **Quilts, Coverlets, Rugs, and Samplers.** New York, Alfred A. Knopf, 1982. 477p. illus. index. ISBN 0394712714.

In the series: "The Knopf Collector's Guides to American Antiques." Pocket-sized but comprehensive and authoritative handbook of American quilts, coverlets, rugs, and samples dating from colonial times to the present. Contains 343 pieces illustrated in color. Accompanying text provides a description, analysis of the materials and technique employed, provenance and date, paragraph relating the piece to others of the same general type, hints for collectors that give practical advice concerning provenance, dating, and estimation of the interest in the piece by collectors, and gives a general price range for the piece. Appendices with quilt pattern guide, quilt stitches guide, coverlet pattern guide, and sampler and needlework stitches guide. Glossary of terms. General bibliography, pp. 447-50, includes list of collector's publications with addresses. An excellent collector's guide.

2233   Colby, Averil. **Quilting.** New York, Scribner's, 1971. 212p. illus. index. ISBN 0684-100797.

Comprehensive history of quilts from the late Middle Ages to the present with emphasis on Great Britain. Although the illustrations are all in black-and-white, they are supported by many instructive drawings that together give an effective explanation of the stylistic and technical features. Contents: 1, Origins; 2, Materials; 3, Tools and Equipment; 4, Patterns: Wadded Quilting; 5, Patterns: Flat, Cord and Stuffed Quilting; 6, The Sixteenth Century; 7, The Seventeenth Century; 8, The Eighteenth Century; 9, The Nineteenth Century; 10, The Twentieth Century; 11, Gathered Patchwork. Appendices have detailed descriptions of the major techniques. Comprehensive, classified bibliography, pp. 206-210, and additional bibliography in the notes. A scholarly and authoritative work on the history of quilts.

2234   Findley, Ruth E. **Old Patchwork Quilts and the Women Who Made Them.** Philadelphia, Lippincott, 1929. 202p. illus. index. Reprint: Newton Centre, Mass., Ct. Branford, 1970. LC 78-20748.

Older, once-standard history of American quilts from colonial times to the end of the nineteenth century instrumental in the revival of quilting in the twentieth century. Contents: I, Patchwork in Early America; II, The Quilting Bee; III, How Quilts Are Made; IV, Development of Quilt Designs; V, The Four-Patch; VII, The Nine-Patch; VIII, Diamonds; IX, The Migration of Patterns; X, Origin of Quilt Names; XI, Appliqué; XII, Set, Borders and Wadding; XIII, Quilting and Quilting Designs; XIV, Wash-Goods—Mostly Calico; XV, Colors, Dyes and Dyeing; XVI, The Decline of Handicraft.

See also Webster, Marie D. *Quilts: Their Story and How to Make Them.* New ed. (Santa Barbara, Calif., Practical Publications, 1990. ISBN 0962081159. First published in 1915).

2235   Haders, Phyllis. **The Warner Collector's Guide to American Quilts.** New York, Warner Books, 1981. 255p. illus. ISBN 0446976369.

Pocket-sized collector's handbook of American quilt patterns. Forty-seven patterns are described, illustrated, and arranged in the broad categories of pieced quilts, appliquéd quilts, and white work. Each type of pattern is described in an introductory paragraph. This is followed by catalog entries describing and illustrating actual pieces. Price ranges are given for each piece. Selected bibliography, pp. 15-16, has a section of books on textile preservation.

2236   McKendry, Ruth, and Blake McKendry. **Quilts and Other Bed Coverings in the Canadian Tradition.** Toronto, New York, Van Nostrand Reinhold, 1979. 240p. illus. index. ISBN 0442-297785.

Well-illustrated, comprehensive survey of Canadian quilts and coverlets from early colonial times to the twentieth century. Contains 441 illustrations including many valuable details of patterns and weaves; all have descriptive captions. Useful discussions of the functional aspects of bedclothes. Contents: 1, Immigrants and Imports: The Loyalists and After; 2, Making Cloth at Home; 3, The Bedstead; 4, Bed Furniture; 5, The Feather Bed; 6, Blankets, Sheets and Pillowcases; 7, Quilts, Counterpanes and Coverlets; 8, The Fabrics Used in Making Quilts; 9, Sets, Borders and Batts; 10, Quilt Names; 11, Symbolism in Quilts; 12, Dates, Origins and Styles; Epilogue. General, classified bibliography, pp. 233-34.

2237   Orlofsky, Patsy, and Myron Orlofsky. **Quilts in America.** New York, McGraw-Hill, 1974. 368p. illus. index. LC 74-6160.

Popular but comprehensive history of quiltmaking in America with useful chapters on the types of quilts and dating and provenance. Content: 1, The History of Quilts in America; 2, The Quilt; 3, Quilting; 4, Tools and Equipment; 5, Stenciled, All-White, and Embroidered Quilt Tops; 6, The Whole-Cloth Quilted Spread; 7, Types of Quilts; 8, Patterns and Pattern Names; 9, Signing and Initialing; 10, The Age of a Quilt; 11, Care; 12, Where to See Quilts. Comprehensive bibliography, pp. 351-57.

2238   Safford, Carleton L. **America's Quilts and Coverlets.** New York, Bonanza Books, 1985. 313p. illus. index. ISBN 0517143917.

First published in 1973. Well-illustrated survey of American quilts and coverlets from the early eighteenth century to the present. Contents: The Bed Rug; Linsey-Woolsey; The Whole-Cloth Spread; The "Work" Spread; "White Work"; The Patchwork Quilt; The Appliqué Quilt; The Overshot Coverlet; The Double Weave Coverlet; The Summer and Winter Coverlet; The Jacquard Coverlet; The Candlewick Spread; The Stencil Spread; The Crazy Quilt; The Derivatives. Plates have descriptive captions. General bibliography, p. 310.

2239   Strickler, Carol. **American Woven Coverlets.** Loveland, Colo., Interweave Press, 1987. 200p. illus. index. ISBN 0934026300.

Useful, popular survey of American woven coverlets from colonial times to the end of the nineteenth century, with particular attention to the techniques used by home weavers. Contents: What Are Coverlets?; Why Were Coverlets Woven?; When Were Coverlets Woven?; Who Wove Coverlets?; Where Were Coverlets Woven?; How Were Coverlets Woven?; Handling a Coverlet; How to Care for a Coverlet; A Gathering of Coverlets (illustrations of and detailed descriptions of weave of 50 coverlets). General bibliography, pp. 195-96.

EUROPEAN TEXTILES

General Histories and Handbooks

2240 Walton, Perry. **The Story of Textiles; a Bird's-eye View of the History of the Beginning and the Growth of the Industry by Which Mankind Is Clothed**. New York, Tudor, 1937. 274p. illus. index.

Older survey of textile production in the West from prehistoric times to the early twentieth century. Still useful as an overview of the development of weaving techniques, especially in the United States. Contents: I, The Beginning of Textiles; II, Flax, Linen, Wool, Cotton, and Silk; III, Factory System; IV, Era of Invention; V, American Industry before the Revolution; VI, American Industry after the Revolution and Before Slater; VII, Era of Samuel Slater; VII, Era of Lowell, Applelton, Moody, Jackson, and Boott; IX, Other Textile Centres.

2241 Weigert, Roger-Armand. **Textiles en Europe sous Louis XV: The Most Beutiful Specimens in the Richelieu Collection**. Greenwich, Conn., New York Graphics Society, 1964. 168p. illus. LC 65-87993.

Catalog of the samples of textiles dating between 1715 and 1736 that were collected by Marshall Duke de Richelieu and now in the Département des estampes, Bibliothèque Nationale, Paris. Samples are of textiles produced in France and abroad. High-quality, tipped in, color plates with descriptive captions in French. Summary in English. Excellent glossary. Few bibliographical references in the notes to the French preface.

2242 Ysselsteyn, G. T. van. **White Figurated Linen Damask from the 15th to the Beginning of the 19th Century**. The Hague, Van Goor Zonen, 1962. 255p. illus. index. LC 63-24089rev.

Authoritative introduction to white linen damask cloth woven with figure decoration from the fifteenth to the early nineteenth centuries written by and for the collector. Scholarly catalog of 425 pieces, 100 of which are illustrated in the plates. Extensive bibliography in the footnotes of the introductory essay and in the catalog entries.

France

2243 Brédif, Josette. **Toiles de Jouy: Classic Printed Textiles from France 1760-1843**. London, Thames & Hudson, 1989. 184p. illus. index. ISBN 0847811352.

Well-illustrated, authoritative history of printed textiles in France from the early eighteenth century to the middle of the nineteenth century with emphasis on the production of Oberkampf at Jouy-en-Josas. Postscript carries the development into the twentieth century. Contents: The History of Printed Textiles; Oberkampf and the Jouy Factory; The Factory in Operation; The Patterns; Printed Textiles from 1760 to the Present. Appendices with note on Indian calico printed textiles, list of personnel at the Jouy factory, survey of the extant pattern books of the Jouy factory. Comprehensive, classified bibliography, pp. 178-180, includes a list of exhibition catalogs.

2244 Clouzot, Henri. **Painted and Printed Fabrics; the History of the Manufactory at Jouy and Other Ateliers in France 1760-1815...** New Haven, Conn., Yale University Press, 1927. 108p. illus. index. Reprint: New York, Arco, 1974. LC 76-168418. ISBN 0405022565.

Old, standard history of French printed textiles of the eighteenth century with a useful chapter on the history of cotton printing in *England and America* by F. Morris. Contents: History of the Manufactory at Jouy; Other Important Centers of Cotton Printing in France, 1760-1815; Notes on the History of Cotton Printing, Especially in England and America. Appendix with a list of cotton-printing centers in France. General bibliography, pp. xv-xvii.

Germany

2245 Jaques, Renate. **Deutsche Textilkunst; ihrer Entwicklung bis zur Gegenwart...** Berlin, Rembrandt Verlag, 1942. 319p. illus. index. LC 54-19803.

Concise but authoritative survey of German textiles from the early Middle Ages to the twentieth century. Emphasis is on woven textiles, particularly tapestry. Contents: Die Romanische Zeit: Der Zeugdruck, Die Weberei, Die Stickerei; Die Gotik: Die Wirkerei, Der Oberrhein, Das Elsass, Der Mittelrhein, Middeldeutschland, Franken, Eichstätt, Niederdeutschland, Die Stickerei, Stickerei in Gold, Seide, Leinen und Wolle, Die Tuchapplikation, Niederrheinische Stickerei der Spätgotik, Westfälische Leinenstickereien; Die Weberei: Kölner Borten, Spätmittelalterliche Halbseidenstoffe, Deutsche Wollstoffe, Der Zeugdruck; Das 16.-18. Jahrhundert: Die Wirkerei des 16. und der ersten Hälfte des 17. Jahrhunderts, Die Wirkerei der zweiten Hälfte des 17. und des 18. Jahrhunderts; Strickteppiche, Der Zeugdruck, Die Seidenweberei, Deutsche Leinen- und Seiden-Damaste, Beiderwand, Die Stickerei. No bibliography.

Great Britain

2246 Hunton, W. Gordon. **English Decorative Textiles; Tapestry and Chintz, Their Design and Developement from the Earliest Times to the Nineteenth Century.** London, Tiranti, 1930. 9p. (text), 18 plates.

Pictorial survey with brief introductory essay and plates with descriptive captions. Basic bibliography, p. 10.

2247 Kendrick, Albert F. **English Decorative Fabrics of the Sixteenth to Eighteenth Centuries...** Benfleet, England, Lewis-on-Sea, 1934. 88p. illus. index. LC 05-29072r883.

Authoritative survey of English embroidery, carpets, and tapestry from the sixteenth through eighteenth centuries. Contains 52 black and white plates. Contents: 1, Introductory; 2, 16th Century: 1, Embroideries, 2, Carpets; 3, 17th Century: 1, Embroideries, 2, Carpets and Turkey-work, 3, Tapestries, 4, Embroidery in the Latter Half of the Century; 4, 18th Century: 1, Tapestries, 2, Carpets, 3, Embroideries. Few bibliographical references in the footnotes.

2248 Montgomery, Florence M. **Printed Textiles; English and American Cotton and Linens, 1700-1850.** New York, Viking, 1970. 379p. illus. index. LC 69-17973.

Authoritative survey of American and British printed fabrics from 1700 to 1850 with an important catalog of major pieces. Contents: Part I: 1, English Printed Textiles; 2, Trade with the Colonies; 3, Furnishing in American Homes; 4, Textile Printing in America in the Eighteenth Century. Part II: Catalogue: Blue-Printed Textiles; China-Blue and Blue-Resist Textiles; Copperplate-Printed Textiles; Roller-Printed Textiles; American Plate- and Roller-Printed Textiles; Appliqué and Patchwork Quilts. Comprehensive bibliography, pp. 361-70.

2249 Parry, Linda. **Textiles of the Arts and Crafts Movement.** New York, Thames & Hudson, 1988. 160p. illus. index. ISBN 0500274975.

History of all aspects of textiles exhibited by the Arts and Crafts Exhibition Society between 1888 and 1916. Contents: 1, The Artistic and Industrial Background; 2, The Evolution of a Style; 3, Textiles in the Arts and Crafts Exhibitions; 4, Designers, Manufacturers and Shops. Dictionary of designers, craftsmen and organizations. Bibliography, p. 156, and references to specialized literature in the notes.

Italy

2250   Podreider, Fanny. **Storia dei tessuti d'arte in Italia, secolo XII-XVIII**. Bergamo, Istituto Italiano d'Arti Grafiche, 1928. 312p. illus. index.

Pioneering history of Italian woven textiles from the twelfth through the eighteenth centuries illustrated with pieces of textile and works of art in which textiles are depicted. Contents: I, La technica delle stoffe antiche; II, Inizio della tessitura italiana nel sec. XII; III, Diffusione dell'arte serica nelle repubbliche italiane nel secolo XIII; IV, Cenni storici e statistici sullo sviluppo dell'arte serica italiana nel sec. XIV—Lucca, Genova, Firenze, Bologna, Venezia; V, La vita del quattrocento e l'arte tessile italiana; VI, La vita del cinquecento e la diffusione dell'arte tessile in Italia—Piemonte, Veneto, Lombardia, Liguria, Emilia, Romagna e Lazio, Toscana, Basilicata, Sicilia; VII, L'inizio della concorrenza franchese e le condizioni dell'industria tessile italiana nel sec. XVII—Veneto, Lombardia, Toscana, Lazio; VIII, Il settecento e l'inizio della nuova organizzazione dell'arte tessile italiana—Piemonte, Liguria, Veneto, Toscana, Lombardia. Bibliographical references in the footnotes.

2251   Santangelo, A. **Treasury of Great Italian Textiles**. New York, Abrams, 1964. 239p. illus. index. LC 64-14691.

Translation of: *Tessuti d'arte italiani dal XIIo al XVIIIo secolo* (Milan, Electra, 1959. 241p. illus. index. LC A60-2242). Well-illustrated, authoritative survey of Italian textiles from the late Middle Ages to the eighteenth century. Brief introductory text followed by excellent, tipped-in color plates. Contents: I, Twelfth Century Textile Production: Islamic Influences at Palermo; II, The Dominance of Luccan Production in the Thirteenth and Fourteenth Centuries; III, Venetian Textiles during the Fourteenth Century; IV, Individual Artists and the International Gothic Style: Fifteenth Century; V, Textiles of Florence and Milan: Sixteenth Century; VI, New Developments in Venetian Textile Art; VII, Textiles of Rome and Genoa during the Seventeenth and Eighteenth Centuries: The Shift from Italy to France. Comprehensive bibliography, pp. 235-37.

Spain and Portugal

2252   Réal, Daniel. **Tissus espagnoles et portugais**. Paris, Calavas, 1925. 9p. (text), 49 plates.

Brief essay on the history of nonfigurative textiles of Spain and Portugal from the ninth to the twentieth centuries. Plates with descriptive captions. No bibliography.

Scandinavia

2253   Branting, Agnes, and Andreas Lindblom. **Medieval Embroideries and Textiles in Sweden**. Stockholm, Almquist & Wiksells Boktryck, 1932. 2v. illus. index.

Comprehensive, scholarly history of woven and embroidered textiles, both foreign and Swedish, from the tenth to the mid-fifteenth centuries. Excellent collection of plates with descriptive captions. A standard work.

Eastern Europe

2254   Majkowski, Karol. **Polish Textiles**. Leigh-on-Sea, Lewis, 1968. 62p. illus. LC 74-356-498r90.
Pictorial survey of Polish textiles from the Middle Ages to the twentieth century. No bibliography.

2255   Potrescu, Paul. **Romanian Textiles**. Leigh-on-Sea, Lewis, 1966. 71p. illus.
Pictorial survey of Romanian textiles from the Middle Ages to the twentieth century. No bibliography

ORIENTAL TEXTILES

Islamic Textiles

2256   Bunt, Cyril, G. E. **Persian Fabrics**. Leigh-on-Sea, England, F. Lewis, 1963. 9p. (text), 55p. (illus.). LC 66-46996/M.
Pictorial survey of ancient, medieval, and modern Persian textiles. No bibliography.

2257   Lombard, Maurice. **Les textiles dans le monde musulman VIIe-XIIe siècles**. Études d'économie médiévale. Paris, The Hague, New York, Moton, 1978. 316p. illus. index. ISBN 2719304457.
Scholarly history of textile production in the Islamic world from the seventh through the twelfth centuries. Focus is on production and trade rather than decoration. Illustrated with maps showing spread of influences. Contents: I, Les progrès de deux textiles anciens: la laine et le lin; II, L'avènement de deux textiles nouveaux: le coton et la soie; III, Les textiles secondaires ou rares; IV, Les teintures et les produits nécessaires a la préparation des étoffes; V, Un exemple de centre textile: le delta égyptien; VI, Volume et qualité de la production textile; VII, Travail et techniques; Une civilisation du textile. Excellent, comprehensive, classified bibliography, pp. 262-279.

2258   Oz, Tahsin. **Turkish Textiles and Velvets**. Ankara, Turkish Press Broadcasting and Tourist Department, 1950. 119p. illus. LC 51-26434.
Authoritative introduction to the history of Turkish textiles, particularly velvet, from the fourteenth century through the sixteenth century in the form of brief introductory essays on the three centuries, followed by detailed descriptions of plates that illustrate both actual textiles and works of art showing the use of textiles as costume and furnishings. Bibliographical references in the footnotes.

2259   Reath, Nancy A., and Eleanor B. Sachs. **Persian Textiles and Their Techniques from the Sixth to the Eighteenth Centuries**. New Haven, Conn., Yale Univ. Press; London, Milford, 1937. 133p. illus. index. LC 37-14436.
Scholarly history of Persian woven textiles from the sixth to the eighteenth centuries with emphasis on identification of types of weaves. Contents: Table of Textile Classification; Introduction; 1, Distinctive Persian Types; 2, Sasanian and Early Islamic Weaves; 3, Seljuk Weaves; 4, 14th and 15th Centuries; 5, Safavid Weaves; 6, Post-Safavid Weaves; 7, Conclusion; pt. 2. Definition of Terms; pt.3. Analyses of Textiles; pt. 4. Diagrams and Plates.

2260   Rogers, Clive ed. **Early Islamic Textiles**. Brighton, Rogers & Podmore, 1983. 47p. illus. ISBN 095088751X.

Collected essays on various aspects of early Islamic decorative textiles. Contents: Textile Techniques of the Near East at the Time of the Arab Conquest; The Construction of Tunics by H. Granger-Taylor; Some Aspects of the Octagon by S. Crosby; Early Islam—an Historical Background by C. Rogers; The Tiras Issue by C. Rogers; The Influence of Persian Textile Motifs by C. Rogers; Cotton and Silk in the Early Islamic World by H. Granger-Taylor; Textiles from Quseir al-Qadim by G. Eastwood. General bibliography, p. 47.

2261   Reswick, Irmtraud. **Traditional Textiles of Tunisia and Related North African Weavings**. Los Angeles, Craft & Folk Art Museum; Seattle, Wash., Univ. of Washington Press, 1985. 242p. illus. index. ISBN 029596281X. (Folk Art Monographs, 1).

Survey of traditional weaving and rugmaking in Tunisia, Algeria, Morocco and Libya. Twenty-seven color plates of rugs, seven color pattern plates, and many drawings illustrating weaving techniques. General bibliography, pp. 225-31.

2262   Riefstahl, Rudolf M. **Persian and Indian Textiles from the Late Sixteenth to the Early Nineteenth Century**. New York, Weyhe, 1923. 14p. (text), 36 plates. LC 43-47984.

Collection of black-and-white plates illustrating 289 pieces of Persian and Indian textiles from the second half of the sixteenth century to the early nineteenth century. No bibliography.

2263   Wiet, Gaston. **Soieries persanes**. Cairo, Institut Francais d'Archeologie Oriental, 1947. 251p. illus. index. LC 50-159.

Scholarly history of ancient and medieval Persian silks with particular emphasis given to the relationship between textiles and Persian culture. First three chapters are in the form of detailed catalog entries to the 20 plates. Contents: Deux soieries Sassanides; Soieries de Raiy; Une aiguière bouyide; Le milieu historique: La conquête arabe, Choc en retour, L'iranisation du califat. Les principautés, Les révoltes religieuses, Les Guèbres et leurs pyrées, Les sectes musulmanes, Les dihkans, Le role de la Perse dans la civilisation musulmane; Histoire de Raiy; Date et localisation des tissus: L'épigraphie, L'époque probable des tissus; La valeur historique et artistique du trésor de Raiy. General bibliography, pp. xi-xix, and extensive references to the specialized literature in the footnotes. A standard work.

See also the museum catalogs: *Catalogue of Muhammadan Textiles of the Medieval Period*, by A. F. Kendrick (London, Victoria and Albert Museum, 1924. 74p. illus. LC 24-20062), *Catalogue of Dated Tiraz Fabrica: Umayayd, Abbasid*, Fatimid by E. Kühnel (Washington, D.C., Textile Museum; National Pub. Co., 1952. 137p. illus.)

Far Eastern Textiles

India

Bibliographies

2264   Singh, Iqbal Bahadur. **Indian Textiles: a Select Bibliography**. Varanasi, Bharat Kala; Bhavan, Baranas Hinu Uni., 1986. 59p. index. LC 87-904266.

Classified bibliography of 768 titles in English based on the holdings of the "various specialized libraries in Varabasi." Covers the history, technology, and conservation of Indian textiles.

Histories and Handbooks

2265   Irwin, John, and Katherine B. Brett. **Origins of Chintz. With a Catalogue of Indo-European Cotton Paintings in the Victoria and Albert Museum**. London, H.M.S.O., 1970. 134p. illus. index. LC 73-484119.

Scholarly history of Indo-European painted cotton fabrics (chintz) based on the collections of the Victoria and Albert Museum and the Royal Ontario Museum. Contents: 1, The Significance of Chintz; 2, The Pattern of Trade; 3, Technique and Conditions of Manufacture; 4, Early Coromandel Group: 1600 to 1650; 5, The Flowering Tree; 6, Furnishing Fabrics; 7, Costume. Appendix 'A': Beaulieu's account of the technique of Indian cotton-painting, c. 1734; Appendix 'B' Father Coeurdoux's letters on the technique of Indian cotton-painting, 1742 and 1747; Appendix 'C' The Roxburgh account of Indian cotton-painting: 1795. Comprehensive, classified bibliography, pp. 59-63. Detailed catalog entries with bibliographies for 188 pieces. A standard work.

See also the museum catalogs: *Indian Painted and Printed Fabrics*. by J. Irwin and M. Hall (Bombay, Bastikar, 1971. 203p. illus. Historic Textiles of India at the Calico Museum, v. 1) and *Indian Tie-dyed Fabrics* by A. Buhler, E. Fischer, M. Nabholz (Ahmedabad, Calico Museum of Textiles, 1980. 159p. illus. Historic Textiles of India at the Calico Museum, v. 4.).

2266   Watson, John F. **The Textile Manufactures and the Costumes of the People of India**. Varanasi, Indological Book House, 1982. 173p. illus. LC 82-903695.

First published: London, 1866. Important early survey of the textiles and costume of India during the mid-nineteenth century. It was written to accompany a collection of 700 samples of textiles distributed in 18 volumes to various sites in Britain and India. These samples are referred to throughout the text and in many cases they are described in table format indicating type of weave, length, width, weight, cost and place of manufacture. These tables represent an extraordinary resource for the textile historian. The text also contains valuable plates reproducing contemporary photographs of Indians in traditional dress. Contents: Introduction; Costume of the People of India; Loom-made Articles of Male Attire: I, Turbans, II, Loongees and Dhotees, III, Kummerbunds; Loom-made Articles of Female Attire: I, Sarees, II, Kerchiefs for Head and Shoulders; Piece Goods: Made-up Garments, Dacca Muslins, Muslins, Calicoes, Canvas—Cotton, Coloured Cotton Goods, Printed Cotton Goods, Cotton—Miscellaneous, Silk, Wild Silks, Loom Embroidery, —Gold and Silver, Gold and Silver Tissues, Hand Embroidery, Lace, Wool, Camel Hair, Yak Hair, Carpets and Rugs, Fabrics from Central Asia and Russia.

See also the exhibition catalog: *Treasures of Indian Textiles* (Ahmedabad, Calico Museum, 1982. 145p. illus.) and the museum catalog: *Trade Good: A Study of Indian Chintz in the Collection of the Cooper-Hewitt Museum of Decorative Arts and Design*, by A. B. Beer (Washington, D.C., Smithsonian Institution Press, 1970. 133p. illus.).

The Kashmir Shawl

2267   Ames, Frank. **The Kashmir Shawl: And Its Indo-French Influence**. Woodbridge, Antique Collectors' Club, 1986. 347p. illus. index. ISBN 0907462626.

Well-illustrated collector's history/handbook of Kashmir from the its origins in the Mughal period through the development of machine-made imitations in nineteenth-century Europe. Contents: 1, Classification of the Kashmir Shawl; 2, Structure and Composition; 3, Manufacturing Techniques up to the Present Day; 4, Symbolism and the Boteh; 5, Shawl Trade and Shawl Fashions in the Orient; 6, Shawl Weaving in France; 7, The French School of Shawl Design; An Illustrated Guide Showing the Chronological Development of the Kashmir Shawl Patterns from the 17th to the 19th Century. Appendices with essays on the style of French painting during the

Empire, on the similarity between Kashmir shawls and Oriental carpets, and the reversible shawl. Comprehensive bibliography, pp. 340-43, has sections devoted to design albums and archives.

See also the museum handbook: Irwin, John. *The Kashmir Shawl* (London, H.M.S.O., 1973. 61p. illus. index. LC 74-194845. ISBN 0112901646. Victoria and Albert Museum, Museum Monograph, no. 29).

See also the exhibition catalog: *The Kashmir Shawl* (New Haven, Conn., Yale Univ. Art Gallery, 1975. 52p. illus.).

Japan

2268   Blakemore, Frances. **Japanese Design through Textile Patterns**. New York, Weatherhill, 1979. 272p. illus. index. ISBN 0834801329.

2269   Gunsaulus, Helen C. **Japanese Textiles**. New York, Japan Society of New York, 1941. 94p. illus. LC 41-15160.

Pictorial survey of Japanese textiles of the seventeenth and eighteenth centuries. Contains a 29-page introduction followed by 16 plates, each proceeded by several pages of description. Basic bibliography, pp. 93-94.

2270   **Textile Designs of Japan**, compiled by the Japan Textile Color Design Center. Tokyo, New York, Kodansha International, 1980. 3v. illus. ISBN 0870113968.

Sumptuously illustrated survey of Japanese textiles from prehistoric times to the end of the Edo Period. Volume one covers free-style textiles; volume two geometric-style textiles. Total of 35 plates with brief descriptive notes and introductory essay.

See also the exhibition catalog: *Japanese Textiles; The Marjorie and Robert Graff Collection* (Newark, N.J., The Newark Museum, 1978. 26p. illus.) and *Kosode, 16th-19th Century Textiles from the Nomura Collection*, by A. M. Stinchecum (New York, Japan Society, 1984. 234p. illus. ISBN 0870114298).

Southeast Asia

2271   Elliot, Inger M. **Batik, Fabled Cloth of Java**. New York, C. N. Potter, 1984. 240p. illus. index. ISBN 0517551551.

Well-illustrated and informative survey of Indonesia Batik textiles from the earliest contacts with traders from the West to the present day. Contains 119 color plates of examples of Batik and costumes. Appendix with an additional 143 illustrations and descriptive notes of pieces of Batik in various museums and collections in Europe and America. Contents: I, Tales of a Trade Route Island; II, Batik in the Royal Courts; III, Journey to Pekalongan; IV, Journey to Gresik; V, Modern Batik. Useful, annotated bibliography, pp. 230-35.

2272   Gittinger, Mattiebelle. **Splendid Symbols: Textiles and Tradition in Indonesia**. Washington, D.C., Textile Museum, 1979. 240p. illus. LC 79-50373.

Authoritative survey of the traditional textiles of the various peoples of Indonesia with particular emphasis given to the role of textiles in social customs and religion. The 184 illustrations include pieces of textiles and scenes of textilemaking. Contents: Introduction; Textiles as Gifts and Items of Prestige; Textiles in Their Ceremonial and Ritual Context; Design as Message; Textiles as Costume; Geographic Areas. Detailed descriptive captions to the plates. Comprehensive bibliography, pp. 235-40.

2273   Langewis, Laurens, and Fritz A. Wagner. **Decorative Art in Indonesian Textiles**. Amsterdam, Van der Peet, 1964. 211p. illus. LC 65-6590.

Pictorial survey of contemporary Indonesian textiles. Contains 216 plates keyed to a classification system described in the introduction together with a informative essay on technique and design of traditional Indonesian textiles. Basic bibliography, pp. 44-45.

2274 Warming, Wanda. **The World of Indonesian Textiles**. Tokyo, New York, Kodansha International, 1981. 200p. illus. index. ISBN 0870114328.

Survey of Indonesian textiles with emphasis on the continuation of traditional textile techniques. Contents: 1, Warp Ikat: Craft of the Ancient Peoples; 2, Warp Ikat: A Myriad of Motifs; 3, Other Ikat Cloths and Tie-Dyeing; 4, Weaving and Woven Patterns; 5, Batik Craft of Java; 6, Batik: Patterns Old and New. Excellent photographs of present-day textile techniques. General bibliography, p. 191.

See also the museum guide: *Batiks*, by J. Irwin (London, Victoria and Albert Museum, 1969. 50p. illus. ISBN 0112900518) and the exhibition catalogs: *Treads of Tradition: Textiles of Indonesia and Sarawak*, ed. by J. Fischer (Berkeley, Calif., University Art Museum, 1979. 98p. illus.), *Textile Traditions of Indonesia*, by M. H. Kahlenberg (Los Angeles, Los Angeles County Museum of Art, 1977. 116p. illus. ISBN 087587083X), *Indonesische Textilien: Wege zu Göttern und Ahnen: Bestandkatalog der Museen in Nordrhein-Westfalen*, by B. Khan Majlis (Cologne, Wienand, 1984. 373p. illus. ISBN 392315805X).

AFRICAN TEXTILES

2275 Boser-Sarivaxevanis, Renee. **Les tissus de l' Afrique Occidentale**. Tome 1: Senegal, Gambie, Mali, Haute-Volta, Niger, Guinee portugaise, Guinee, Sierre Leone, Liberia, Cote d'Ivoire, Ghana. Basel, 1972. 227p. illus. index. (Basler Beiträge zur Ethnologie, 13). LC 73-310716.

Scholarly handbook of the traditional textiles of western Africa with a catalog of 252 examples of textiles of Senegal, Gambia, Mali, Upper Volta, Niger, Portuguese Guinea, Guinea, Sierra Leone, Liberia, Ivory Coast, and Ghana. Introduction presents a detailed analysis of the weaves that characterize the various ethnic groupings. Full scholarly apparatus including extensive bibliography in the footnotes.

2276 Picton, John, and John Mack. **African Textiles**. New York, Harper & Row, 1989. 208p. illus. ISBN 0064301907.

First published in 1979 (London, British Museum Publications). Important, comprehensive survey of traditional decorative textiles of Sub-Saharan Africa. Contents: 1, Introduction; 2, The Raw Materials; 3, The Loom; 4, The Single-Heddle Loom; 5, The Double-Heddle Loom; 6, Weaving in Madagascar; 7, Pattern Dyeing; 8, Drawn, Painted, Printed and Stencilled Patterns; 9, Appliqué and Related Techniques; 10, Embroidery. Comprehensive bibliography, pp. 202-05, was updated for this edition.

2277 Polakoff, Claire. **African Textiles and Dyeing Techniques**. London, Routledge & Kegan Paul, 1982. 265p. illus. index. ISBN 0710009089.

Informative survey of African textiles with emphasis on west Africa and traditional dyeing. Contents: 1, American Interest in African Fabrics; 2, African Textiles; 3, The Art of Tie Dye in Africa; 4, Wax and Paste Resist Patterning—"Batik"; 5, The Hand-printed Adinkra Cloth of Ghana; 6, Bokolanfini—The Mud Cloth of Mali; 7, Korhogo Cloth of Ivory Coast; 8, Traditions/Transitions: Working with African Textiles Today. Appendix: Indigo—The Legend and Technique. Comprehensive, classified bibliography, pp. 243-50, and additional bibliography in the notes.

2278   Plumer, Cheryl. **African Textiles; an Outline of Handcrafted Sub-Saharan Fabrics**. East Lansing, Mich., African Studies Center, Michigan State Univ. Press, 1971. 146p. LC 76-633408r90.

Scholarly monograph on the traditional fabrics of sub-Saharan Africa with emphasis on distinguishing the various tribal textiles. Contents: West Africa: Cameroons; Dahomey; Ghana; Guinea; Ivory Coast; Liberia; Mali; Nigeria; Senegal; Sierra Leone; Upper Volta; Central Africa: The Congosd; South Central Africa: Angola; Rhodesia; Zambia; East Africa: Ethiopia; Kenya; Ruwanda; Sudan; Tanzania; Uganda; Southeran Africa: Republic of South Africa. Each of the national chapters is subdivided by tribe. Bibliographical references in the footnotes.

2279   Sieber, Roy. **African Textiles and Decorative Arts**. New York, Museum of Modern Art, 1972. 239p. illus. LC 72-76268.

Important essay on African textiles and related decorative arts of sub-Saharan Africa written by a leading scholar to accompany an exhibition. Useful selected bibliography by R. Walker Randall, pp. 229-39.

See also the exhibition catalogs: *African Textiles*, by B. Wass and B. Murnane (Madison, Wis., Elvehjem Art Center, Univ. of Wisconsin, 1978), *Textilhandwerk in West-Afrika. Führer durch das Museum für Völkerkunde und Schweizerisches Museum für Völkskunde, Basel* (Basel, Das Museum, 1972).

CARPETS AND RUGS

General Histories and Handbooks

2280   Black, David ed. **The Macmillan Atlas of Rugs & Carpets**. New York, Macmillan, 1985. 255p. illus. index. ISBN 0025111205.

Pictorial handbook of Oriental and non-Oriental carpets and rugs written by a team of experts. Introductory chapters discuss technique, production and design, and history of carpets. Gazetteer gives introductions to the various regional types of carpets made in Turkey, the Caucasus, Persia, Baluch, Turkestan, Tibet, China, India, Morocco, Europe, North America (Navajo) and concludes with advice on buying and caring for carpets. General bibliography, p. 249.

2281   Hubel, Reinhard G. **The Book of Carpets**. New York, Praeger, 1970. 347p. illus. index. LC 71-107152.

Comprehensive handbook of traditional rugs and carpets throughout the world with emphasis on Oriental carpets. Contents: Early History and the Spread of the Knotted Carpet; Production, Structure and Material; Colours and Dyeing; Design and Pattern; Names and Terms for Carpets; Turkish Carpets; Caucasian Carpets; Persian (Iranian) Carpets; Turcoman Carpets; The Carpets of East Turkestan; Chinese Carpets; Carpets from Other Countries; Age and Authenticity; Purchase, Laying, Care; On Collecting Oriental Carpets. Glossary index, list of museums with collections of carpets and classified bibliography, pp. 345-46.

European and American Carpets and Rugs

2282   Campana, P. Michele. **European Carpets**. Feltham and New York, Hamlyn, 1969. 158p. illus. LC 70-550059.

Popular survey of the carpets of England, France, Spain and Portugal with emphasis on the eighteenth and nineteenth centuries. Illustrated with color plates of museum pieces. No bibliography.

2283   Faraday, Cornelia. **European and American Carpets and Rugs...** Grand Rapids, Mich., Dean-Hicks, 1929. 383p. illus. index. Reprint: Woodbridge, Antique Collector's Club, 1990. 484p. illus. ISBN 1851490922.

Comprehensive, well-illustrated history of hand-woven decorative floor coverings and machine-made carpets and rugs in Europe and America from the fifteenth century to the 1940s. The 112 color plates have descriptive captions. Large number of black and white illustrations of additional examples and views of factory procedures. Reprint addition is augmented by additional color plates, addition of descriptive captions to all the color plates, and a new classified, comprehensive bibliography, pp. 475-79. Contents: I, The Rugs of Spain; II,The Rugs of France; III, Rugs of the British Isles; IV, Rugs of the North Countries: Scandinavia, Finland, Russia; V, The Rugs of Poland and the Balkan Countries; VI, The Rugs of Germany, Austria and Czecho-slovakia; VII, The Rugs of Belgium, Holland and Italy; VIII, Technique; IX, American Hand-Made Rugs, Rugs of the North American Indians; X, American Machine-made Carpets; XI, Carpets and Rugs to Order; XII, Modern Carpets and Rugs. An invaluable source of information on many aspects of European rugs and carpets, but especially so for machine-made carpets of the nineteenth and early twentieth centuries.

2284   Weeks, Jeanne G., and Donald Treganowan. **Rugs and Carpets of Europe and the Western World**. Philadelphia, Chilton, 1969. 251p. illus. index. LC 70-99605.

Popular survey history of rugs and carpets made in Europe and America from the fifteenth century to 1900 with a chapter on Native American rugs and blankets. Contents: 1, Spain; 2, France; 3, Great Britain; 4, Scandinavia; 5, Greece; 6, America; 7, American Indian. General bibliography, pp. 243-44. Broad selection of plates—many poorly reproduced—with brief captions.

America

2285   Von Rosenstiel, Helene. **American Rugs and Carpets from the Seventeenth Century to Modern Times**. New York, Morrow, 1978. 192p. illus. index. ISBN 0688033253.

Comprehensive survey of American carpets and rugs. Includes floorcloths, mats and other forms of floor covering. Contents: 1, Alternate Floor; 2, Matting; 3, From Rags to Riches; 4, Floorcloths, Oilcloths and Linoleums; 5, From Hand to Mechanized Loom; 6, Flatwoven Carpets; 7, Brussels, Wilton and Tapestry; 8, Turkey Work, Axminster and Chenille; 9, Tufted Carpets; 10, Embroidered Carpets; 11, Custom Carpets. Appendices with illustrated chronologies of ingrain patterns and Brussels, Wilton and tapestry patterns. Comprehensive bibliography, pp. 184-187.

See also the exhibition catalog: *America Underfoot: A History of Floor Coverings from Colonial Times to the Present*, by A. N. Landreau (Washington, D.C., Smithsonian Institution Press, 1976. 76p. illus.).

Hooked Rugs

2286   Kent, William W. **The Hooked Rug; a Record of Its Ancient Origin, Modern Development, Methods of Making, Sources of Design, Value as Handicraft, the Growth of Collections, Probable Future in America, and Other Data**. Detroit, Mich., Tower Books, 1971. 210p. illus. LC 78-172437.

First published in 1941. Informative survey of American hooked rugs from colonial times to the 1930s. Contains 172 poorly reproduced illustrations with descriptive captions. Contents: I, The First Traces of Origin Abroad; II, The Very Probable Origin Given; III, The Simplicity of the Process; IV, Suitable Materials and Dyeing; V, The Source and Decadence of Designs; VI, Classification of Designs and Rugs Contemporary with Hooking in America; VII, Rapid Development in America; VIII, Artistic, Economic and Intrinsic Values; IX, A Hunt for Rugs in Canada; X, Careful Collecting, Using, Cleaning and Repairing; XI, Various Sizes, Age, Modern and Future Production and Development; XII, Scotch Rugs; XIII, Possible Sources of Rug Design; XIV, General Consideration of the Art.

2287   Ketchum, William C. **Hooked Rugs: A Historical and Collector's Guide: How to Make Your Own**. New York, Harcourt Brace Jovanovich, 1976. 164p. illus. index. ISBN 0151421684.

Combination of a collector's introduction to American hooked rugs and a how-to-do-it manual for those interested in imitating historical hooked rug techniques. The former has a good selection of plates illustrating rugs from the nineteenth and twentieth centuries with descriptive captions, the latter has many of the same and other rugs with drawings of their design features. Brief bibliography, p. 164.

2288   Kopp, Joel. **American Hooked and Sewn Rugs: Folk Art Underfoot**. 2d ed. New York, Dutton, 1985. 141p. illus. index. ISBN 052524316X.

Popular and well-illustrated history of American hooked rugs of the nineteenth and twentieth centuries. Contains 213 illustrations with descriptive captions. Contents: Bed Rugs; Yarn-Sewn Rugs; Shirred Rugs; Embroidered and Braided Rugs; Hooked Rugs—Part I: Nineteenth Century: Shaker Rugs; Patterns; Hooked Rugs—Part II: Twentieth Century: Grenfell Rugs; Illustrations on Techniques; Cleaning, Storage, and Display. Selected bibliography, p. 128.

See also the exhibition catalog: *Canadian Hooked Rugs, 1860-1960: Le tapis crochete canadien, 1860-1960* (Toronto, Canadian Museum of Carpets and Textiles, 1977. 12p. illus.).

France

2289   Jarry, Madeliene. **The Carpets of Aubusson**. Leigh-on-Sea, F. Lewis, 1969. 65p. illus. ISBN 0853171211.

Survey history of Aubusson carpets from the eighteenth century to the present. Introductory essay written by a leading French textile historian. Contains 92 plates with descriptive notes. No bibliography.

2290   Jarry, Madeliene. **The Carpets of the Manufacture de la Savonnerie**. Leigh-on-Sea, F. Lewis, 1966. 47p. illus. LC 67-109861.

Survey of the carpets manufactured at Savonnerie from the seventeenth century to circa 1950. Introductory essay by a leading French textile historian. Seventy plates with descriptive notes. No bibliography.

2291   Verlet, Pierre. **The Savonnerie. Its History**. The Waddesdon Collection. Fribourg, Office du Livre, 1982. 535p. illus. index. ISBN 070780082.

Magisterial history of the carpets manufactured at the Savonnerie factory based upon the pieces in the Waddesdon Collection with a complete scholarly catalog of that collection. Contents: General Introduction: The Savonnerie Factory: The History of the Savonnerie Factory, Bourbon Family Tree; I, The Savonnerie in the Seventeenth and Eighteenth Centuries: 1, The Louvre, 2, Chaillot, 3, The Dupont-Lourdet Partnership, 4, The Royal Factory, 5, The Factory Buildings at Chaillot; II, Technique: 1, Looms and Equipment, 2, Weaving, 3, Raw Materials, 4, Colours and Dyes; III, The Personnel; IV, Production and Outlets; V, The Cartoons; VI, Imitations. The Catalogue. Appendices with list of carpets for the Long Gallery of the Louvre, presents given by the King, and private purchases at the Savonnerie between 1750 and 1793. General bibliography, pp. 13-19, and references in the notes and the catalog entries.

Great Britain

2292 Mayorcas, Manda J. **English Needlework Carpets; 16th to 19th Centuries**. Leigh-on-Sea, F. Lewis, 1963. 64p. illus.

Collector's history and handbook of English needlework carpets. The only work on the subject. Contains 94 plates dating between circa 1520 and circa 1890 with descriptive notes. Contents: Introduction; English Needlework Carpets; Recognition and Identification; Stitches. Bibliographical references in the footnotes.

2293 Tattersall, Creassey E. C. **A History of British Carpets from the Introduction of the Craft until the Present Day**. New ed. rev. and enl. by Stanley Reed. Leigh-on-Sea, F. Lewis, 1966. 139p. illus. index. LC 67-73474.

Comprehensive, authoritative history of British carpets. Contents: 1, Carpets in General; 2, Carpets in Britain—16th & 17th Century Developments; 3, A Diversion into Turkey Work; 4, 18th Century Onwards; 5, Embroidered or Needlework Carpets; 6, Descriptive Notes on the Historical Carpets; 7, Machine Made Carpets; 8, Some Carpet Manufacturers. Chapter six is a descriptive catalog of the pieces illustrated in the work and includes bibliographies. Additional bibliography in the footnotes. A standard work in the field of Western carpets.

See also the museum catalog: *Catalogue of Spanish Rugs, 12th Century to 19th Century*, b. E. Kühnel (Washington, D.C., Textile Museum, 1953. 64p. illus.).

Oriental Carpets and Rugs

General Histories and Handbooks

2294 Bausback, Peter. **Antike Orientteppiche**. Braunschweig, Klinkhardt & Biermann, 1979. 544p. illus. index.

Comprehensive, authoritative collector's handbook of oriental carpets and rugs dating before the end of the nineteenth century. Introductory essays on design, color and technique are very informative and extraordinarily clear photographs show the various knots and weaves of antique carpets. Essays are followed by a catalog of nearly 500 examples illustrated in color with detailed descriptive notes. Catalog entries are organized by broad region: Turkey, Caucasus, Persia, India, Turkomania, East Turkestan, China and subdivided by type, e.g., Bergama, Daghestan, Bidjar, Beschir, etc. No bibliography.

2295 Dilley, Arthur U. **Oriental Rugs and Carpets; A Comprehensive Study**. New York and London, Scribner's, 1931. 303p. illus. index. Reprint: Philadelphia, Lippincott, 1959. LC 59-13247.

Older, once-standard history of Oriental carpets in English still useful for the perspective it brings to the interest in Oriental carpets in America in the early twentieth century. Contents: I, Rugs Have a Beginning; II, Rugs of Kings, Caliphs and Shahs; III, Persia's Great Rugs; IV, Persia's Semi-antique and Modern Rugs; V, India's Great Rugs; VI, Rugs of Turkey; VII, Rugs of the Caucasus; VIII, Western Turkestan, Afghanistan, Beluchistan Rugs; IX, Chinese Rugs; X, Chinese Turkestan Rugs; XI, Rugs of Spain; XII, Fibres and Dyes; XIII, The Weaver's Work; XIV, The Significance of Names. Occasional bibliographical reference in the footnotes.

2296 Erdmann, Kurt. **Oriental Carpets: An Essay on Their History**. New York, Universe, 1960. 78p. illus. index. LC 60-14504.

Introduction to the history of Oriental carpets by a leading authority with emphasis on the earliest carpets through the seventeenth century. Contents: The Oriental Rug and Europe; The Earliest Knotted Rugs; The Genesis of the Knotted Rug; The Knotted Rug of the Seljuks; Early

Ottoman Rug Design; Mamluk Carpets; The Knotted Rug's Production Methods; Revolutioniza-
tion of the Design; The Persian Carpet; The Persian Carpet in Later Years; The Caucasian-North-
west Persian Carpet; Ottoman Carpets; Ushak Carpets; The Anatolian Prayer Rug; The Oriental
Rug's Fringe Areas: China, India, Spain. Comprehensive bibliography, pp. 59-69, includes many
periodical articles.

2297   Erdmann, Kurt. **Seven Hundred Years of Oriental Carpets**. Berkeley, Calif., University
of California Press, 1970. 238p. illus. index. LC 69-12473.
     First published as *Siebenhundert Jahre Orientteppich* in 1966 and based upon 51 articles
published in the journal *Heimtex*. Assembled here and edited by Hanna Erdmann. Essays on many
central issues on the history of the Oriental carpet by a leading scholar, and highly informative
descriptions of many of the major collections of Oriental carpets in Turkey and Germany.
Contents: The Beginnings of Carpet Studies: Early Carpets in Western Paintings, Oriental Carpets
in Paintings of the Renaissance and the Baroque, Carpets in Oriental Miniatures, The Discovery
of the Antique Carpet, The 'Holy' Carpet of Ardebil, Carpet Exhibitions since 1890; Individual
Groups of Carpets: Turkish Carpets, The Small Silk Carpets of Kashan, Garden Carpets, Figure
Carpets, Persian Carpets of Turkish Provenance, A Carpet 'Unmasked'; Some Collections and
Museums: The World's Carpets, Carpets as Turkish Booty, Venice and the Oriental Carpet,
Carpets in Turkish Mosques, The Türk ve Islam Museum in Istanbul, Carpets in German
Museums, A New German Carpet Collection: Hamburg; The Berlin Carpet Collection: The War
Losses of the Berlin Museum, Carpets in East Berlin at the End of the War, Carpets in West Berlin
at the End of the War, New Acquisitions of the Berlin Museums; Peripheral Problems: Verses in
Carpets, Dated Carpets of the Sixteenth and Seventeenth Centuries, Dated Carpets of the
Eighteenth and Nineteenth Centuries; Carpet Fragments, Carpet Pairs, Carpet Cartoons, Wagirehs,
Carpets of Unusual Shape; European Production: Carpets with European Blazons, Spanish
Carpets, European Peasant Rugs. Extensive bibliography given in the notes to the illustrations and
text. An indispensable work for any serious study of the history of Oriental carpets.

2298   Grote-Hasenbalg, Werner. **Der Orientteppisch. Seine Geschichte und seine Kultur**.
Berlin, Scarabaeus, 1922. 3v. illus. index. Lc 23-6794.
     Older collector's handbook of Oriental carpets emphasizing the classic period from the
fifteenth through the eighteenth centuries. Important corpus of 120 color plates of carpets mostly
in private collections and three water color sketches of contemporary, i.e., 1920s, interiors with
Oriental carpets coordinated with other furnishings. Contents: I, Technisches zur Herstellung der
Teppiche; II, Von der Ästhetik des Orientsteppich; III, Die Verwendung der Orientteppiche im
Innenraum; IV, Über die Behandlung und das Reparieren der Teppiche; V, Ratschläge für das
Studium und den Einkauf von Teppichen; VI, Hinweise auf das Sammeln von Teppichen und
Alterkennzeichen; VII, Zur Enstehung der islamischen Kunst; VIII, Zur Geschichte des Islams
bis zum Ende der Mongolherrschaft; IX, Zur Neuzeitlichen Geschichte Persiens; X. Zur
neuzeitlichen Geschichte der Türkei; XI, Zur Vorgeschichtliche des Knüpfteppichs; XII, Die
Teppichzentren: 1, Kleinasiatischen Teppiche, 2, Kaukasische Teppiche, 3, Persische Teppiche,
4, Transkaspische Teppiche, 5, Indische Teppiche, 6, Ostturkestanische und Chinesische Teppiche. Bibliographical references in the footnotes.

2299   Hawley, Walter A. **Oriental Rugs, Antique and Modern**. New York, Tudor, 1937. 320p.
illus. index. Reprint: New York, Dover, 1970. LC 79-105665.
     First published in 1913 (London, John Lane). An old, comprehensive history/handbook
of Oriental carpets with emphasis on the work of the great centers in Iran. Contents: I, Introduction;
II, Physical Features and History of Rug-Producing Lands; III, Materials; IV, Dyeing; V, Weaving;
VI, Designs and Symbols; VII, Rug Weaving before the Eighteenth Century; VIII, Classification
of Modern Rugs; IX, Persian Rugs; X, Asia Minor Rugs; XI, Caucasian Rugs; XII, Central Asiatic

Rugs; XIII, Indian Rugs; XIV, Chinese Rugs; XV, Kilims; XVI, How to Distinguish Rugs; XVII, Purchasing Rugs. Particularly valuable today for the detailed information on rugs imported to the West in the decades around 1900 which have become, in the last decades of the twentieth century, highly sought -fter pieces by collectors. No bibliography.

2300   Jacobsen, Charles W. **Oriental Rugs, a Complete Guide**. Rutland, Vt., Tuttle, 1962. 479p. illus. LC 62-14117.
Comprehensive handbook on Oriental carpets written by a leading American importer. Contents: Part I: General Discussion: 1, In General; 2, General Classification; 3, Persian Rugs; 4, Caucasian Rugs; 5, Turkish Rugs; 6, Turkoman or Bokhara Family Rugs; 7, Indian Rugs; 8, Chinese Rugs; 9, Afghanistan Rugs; 10. Japanese Rugs; 11, Pakistan, Bulgarian, and Grecian Rugs; 12, Antique Oriental Rugs; 13, Designs; 14, Materials and Methods; 15, Dyes; 16, The Chemical Treating or Bleaching of Oriental Rugs; 17, Changes of Color and Irregularities in Shape; 18, The Difference between the European and American Markets; 19, Oriental Rugs vs. Domestic Rugs; 20, Used Rug Sales; 21, Care of Rugs; 22, About Rug Books; 23, Advice for the Rug Purchaser; 24, The Outlook for the Future; Part II: Description of Types; Part III: Plates. Informative text, useful for the types of rugs imported into the United States in the first half of the twentieth century that fall into the semi-antique category.

2301   Kühnel, Ernst, and Wilhelm von Bode. **Antique Rugs from the Near East**. rev. ed. Ithaca, N.Y., Cornell Univ. Press, 1984. 187p. illus. index. ISBN 0801416523.
Important scholarly history of Near Eastern carpets from the fifteenth through the seventeenth centuries. First published in 1902, Kühnel and Bode's work is still a standard on the history of the classic Oriental carpet. Contents: Introduction; The Carpets of Turkey: Early Anatolian Rugs, The So-called Holbein Rugs, The Carpets of Ushak, Other Rugs of the 16th and 17th Centuries; Rugs of the Caucasus: the So-called Dragon Rugs—Other Patterns; Egyptian Carpets: Mamluk Carpets—Ottoman Design Schemes—So-called Checkerboard Rugs; The Carpets of Persia: Early Persian Rugs, Medallion Carpets, Vine Scroll Patterns, Compartment Designs, Rugs with Progressive Designs: So-called Vase Carpets—Shrub and Tree Rugs—Garden Rugs; Pictorial Rugs; The So-called Polonaise Rugs; Prayer Rugs; Rugs from India; Concluding Remarks. General bibliography, pp. 176-79, with an additional list for 1984 edition. A standard work.

2302   Martin, Frederick Robert. **A History of Oriental Carpets before 1800**. Vienna, 1908. 159p. illus. index.
Authoritative and pioneering survey of Oriental carpets from the fifteenth century to 1800 published as a supplement to: *Oriental Carpets* (London, Cousins, 1892-96. 3v. illus.), which is a pioneering history of Oriental carpets of the nineteenth century. Both are based in large part on the superb collection in the Österreichisches Museum für Kunst und Industrie in Vienna. Contents of *Oriental Carpets*: 1, Modern Turkey Carpets, a Monograph by J. M. Stoeckel; 2, Decorative Animal Figures in Old Oriental Carpets by W. Bode; 3, Indian Carpets by V. J. Robinson; 4, Notes on the History of Oriental-Carpet-Weaving in France by M. Gerspach; 5, The Present State of the Carpet Industry in Persia by S. T. A. Churchill; 6, Oriental Manufacture of Sumptuary Carpets by G. Birdwood; 7, Monograph on Oriental Carpets by C. Rudaon Clarke. Both works were reworked and updated with an important, comprehensive bibliography by K. Erdmann as: *Old Oriental Carpets,* issued by the Austrian Museum for Art and Industry with text by Friedrich Sarre and Hermann Trenkwald, translated by A. F. Kendrick. (Vienna, Schroll, 1926-29. 2v. illus. LC 29-12885).

2303   Mumford, John K. **Oriental Rugs...** New York, Scribner's, 1929. 278p. illus. index. Reprint: New York, Bramhall House, 1981. ISBN 0517339358.

An old introduction first published in 1900. Contents: I, Introduction; II, History; III, The Rug-Weaving Peoples; IV, Materials; V, Dyers and Dyes; VI, Design; VII, Weaving; VIII, Classification; IX, Caucasian; X, Turkish; XI, Persian; XII, Turkoman; XIII, Khilims; XIV, Indian. Appendix with textile tables which tabulate the knot, warp, weft, pile, sides, ends, and knots-to-inch of the various types of Oriental carpets and rugs.

2304   Neff, Ivan C., and Carol V. Maggs. **Dictionary of Oriental Rugs: With a Monograph on Identification by Weave**. New York, Van Nostrand Reinhold, 1979. 238p. illus. ISBN 0442206178.

A two-part work; the first is a valuable study of the weaving techniques and materials characteristic of the various regions and places of oriental rug and carpet manufacture; the second part is a dictionary of brief entries defining the styles associated with the various places and regions. Good collection of color plates with close-up details of the weave as seen from the back. These details are an especially valuable feature. Bibliography of basic books in English, pp. 148-51.

2305   Neugebauer, Rudolf, and Siegfried Troll. **Handbuch der orientalischen Teppichkunde**. Leipzig, Hiersemann, 1930. 111p. illus. index. (Hiersemanns Handbücher, Band IV). LC 31-6893.

Important early history/handbook of Oriental carpets from the fifteenth century to the early twentieth century. Contents: 1, Der orientalische Teppich vor 1800; 2, Der orientalische Tepich nach 1800; 3, Der Technik des orientalischen Teppichs; 4, Die orientalischen Teppiche als Kunstwerk; 5, Einkauf und Behandlung des Orientteppichs.

2306   Orendi, Julius. **Das Gesamtwissen uber antike und neue Teppiche des Orients**. Vienna, Julius Orendi, 1930. 2v. illus. LC 31-12955.

Important, older collector's handbook on Oriental carpets, a product of Viennese scholarship and connoisseurship. Second volume contains 1,260 illustrations of carpets dating from the fifteenth to the early twentieth centuries. Text of first volume contains still-valuable technical data concerning weaves and knots. No bibliography.

2307   Ropers, Hinrich. **Morgenländische Teppiche; ein Handbuch fur Sammler und Liebhaber**. 9th ed. Braunschweig, Klinkhardt & Biermann, 1961. 331p. illus. index. (Bibliothek fur Kunst- und Antiquitätenfruende, Bd. 19). LC 66-75973.

Authoritative handbook of Oriental carpets with emphasis on those made in the period from 1850 to 1950 and reflecting the taste of European collectors. Introduction covers techniques and materials, motifs and ornament, purchasing and care of Oriental carpets. Bulk of the text is a description of the various types arranged under the broad regional headings: Türkei, Kaukasus, Persien, Turkmenien. Many of the carpets illustrated are with private collections and dealers. General bibliography, p. 326.

2308   Schürmann, Ulrich. **Oriental Carpets**. rev. and exp. ed. London, Octopus Books, 1979. 247p. illus. ISBN 0706410173.

Collector's guide to Oriental rugs and carpets. Contents: Designs—straight or curved lines; Colours—bold or subtle; Animals and floral motifs; Symbolism; Depth of Pile and Density of Knotting; Ways of Determining the Age; The Significance of Names; Building up a Collection; Tales from the Orient; Capital Investment and the Future. Collection of color plates of pieces, mostly in German private collections, with descriptive notes. No bibliography.

See also the museum catalogs: *Oriental Rugs in the Metropolitan Museum of Art*, by M. S. Dimand (New York, Metropolitan Museum of Art, distrib. by New York Graphics Society, 1973. 353p. illus.), *Oriental Carpets in the Philadelphia Museum of Art* (Philadelphia, The Museum, 1988. 304p. illus.), the museum guide books: *Orientteppiche, 16.-19*, Jahrhundert

(Hanover, Kestner-Museum, 1966. 87p. illus.), *Guide to the Collection of Carpets*, 2d ed. (London, Victoria and Albert Museum, 1920. 88p. illus.), and the exhibition catalog: *Antike orientalische Knüpfkunst: Ausstellung*, by P. Bausback (Manheim, Frank Bausback, 1976. 325p. illus. LC 78-353937).

Caucasian and Central Asian Carpets and Rugs

2309   Bidder, Hans. **Carpets from Eastern Turkestan, Known as Khotan, Samarkand and Kansu Carpets**. New York, Universe, 1964. 96p. illus. LC 64-22109.

Authoritative history/handbook of carpets woven in Eastern Turkestan from the Han dynasty to the twentieth century with emphasis on the production in Khotan and Kansu during the eighteenth and nineteenth centuries. Contents: I, Historical Survey of Carpet Manufacture in Khotan; II, The Carpet Craft in Khotan; III, The Khotan Carpets; IV, The So-called Chinese Carpets (Kansu, Suiyuan, Ninghsia and Paotou Carpets). Contains 46 plates with descriptive captions. Bibliographical references in the footnotes.

2310   Gans-Ruedin, Erwin. **Caucasian Carpets**. New York, Rizzoli, 1986. 369p. illus. index. ISBN 0847807509.

Pictorial handbook of Caucasian rugs and carpets from the seventeenth century to the present. Twenty-four page introduction surveys geography, language, and culture of the region and characteristics of the carpets. This is followed by a collection of good-quality color plates with descriptive notes. Arrangement is by traditional tribal types: Kazak, Karabakh, Genje, Shirvan, Kuba, Dagestan and has separate chapter on kilims. General bibliography, pp. 365-66.

2311   Kerimov, Liatif. et al. **Rugs and Carpets from the Caucasus: The Russian Collections**. Harmondsworth, Penguin Books; Leningrad, Aurora Art Pub., 1984. 151p. illus. ISBN 0713-915056.

Pictorial collector's handbook of Caucasian carpets from the eighteenth century to the twentieth century featuring color plates of examples in museums in the former Soviet Union, most of which have not been published before. Brief introductions concentrate on describing the various types. The 124 plates have descriptive captions that include details of weave, material, dyes, finish and ornament. Contents: Rugs and Carpets of Azerbaijan by L. Kerimov; Rugs and Carpets of Daghestan by L. Kerimov; Carpets of Armenia by N. Stephanian; Georgian Pardaghi Carpets by T. Grigoliya. Bibliography, pp. 150-151, lists books and articles in Russian (titles translated) and Western European languages.

2312   Kuloy, Hallvard K. **Tibetan Rugs**. Bangkok, White Orchid Press, 1982. 233p. illus.

Collector's handbook of the traditional rugs and carpets of Tibet and the adjacent areas of Nepal, Bhutan, and Tsinghai. Illustrations of 258 pieces, most in private collections. Contents: I, General Introduction: 1, Rug-making and Usage, 2, Raw Materials Employed, 3, Production Techniques, 4, Traditional Dyeing Materials, 5, Elements of Design, 6, The Age of Tibetan Rugs; II, The Tibetan Rug; III, Rugs Used for Sitting and Sleeping; IV, Rugs Used in Monasteries and for Ritual and Ceremonial Purposes; V, Saddlery Rugs; VI, Rugs Used for other Purposes. Bibliography of books in Western languages, pp. 10-11.

See also the exhibition catalogs: *Temple, Household, Horseback: Rugs of the Tibetan Plateau*, by D. K. Myers (Washington, D.C., Textile Museum, 1984. 111p. illus.), *The Tiger Rugs of Tibet*, ed. by M. Lipton (Stuttgart, H. Mayer, 1988. 191p. illus. ISBN 1853320250).

2313   Schurmann, Ulrich. **Central-Asian Rugs**. London, Allen & Unwin, 1970. 176p. illus. LC 70-569162.

Handbook of the rugs of Turkestan with 99 color plates of examples, mostly in European private collections. Descriptive captions to the plates. Contents: I, The Gul; II, Determination of Age; III, Characteristics of the Products of the Individual Rug Areas: Turkoman, Turkoman Rugs from Afghanistan and Beloch Rugs, East Turkestan Rugs; IV, Historical Background by H. König; V. Color Plates. List of reference books, p. 176, list titles chiefly in German.

2314 Schurmann, Ulrich. **Caucasian Rugs: A Detailed Presentation of the Art of Carpet Weaving in the Various Districts of the Caucasus during the 18th and 19th Century.** Accokeek, Md., Washington International Associates, 1974. 359p. illus. ISBN 09150360002.

Handbook of Caucasian rugs with a brief introduction outlining characteristics of weave, color, design and with comments on dating and stylistic changes. Introduction is followed by 359 color plates illustrating Caucasian carpets arranged by region or place with descriptive notes.

2315 Stone, Peter F. **Rugs of the Caucasus: Structure and Design.** Chicago, Greenleaf Co., 1984. 188p. illus. index. ISBN 0940582015.

Informative handbook of rugs and carpets made in the Caucasus with unusually detailed treatment of the technique of weaving and knotting. No illustrations of actual rugs. Contents: 1, The Method; 2, Technical Analysis; 3, Caucasian Rugs and the Caucasus; 4, Baku; 5, Dagestan, Derbend and Lesghistan; 6, Genje; 7, Karabagh; 8, Kazak; 9, Kuba; 10, Moghan; 11, Shirvan; 12, Talish and Lenkoran. Comprehensive bibliography, pp. 179-81.

2316 Tschebull, Raoul. **Kazak; Carpets of the Caucasus.** New York, Near Eastern Art Research Center, 1971. 104p. illus. LC 78-165292.

Introduction to Kazak rugs and carpets woven in the nineteenth and early twentieth centuries. Contains 40 plates of pieces in museums and private collections with detailed descriptive notes. General bibliography, pp. 100-101.

2317 Yetkin, Serare. **Early Caucasian Carpets in Turkey.** London, Oguz Press, 1978. 2v. illus. LC 78-316277.

Comprehensive history of rugs and carpets woven in the Caucasian regions of Turkey to the end of the nineteenth century. Volume I text; volume II catalog and plates. Contents of volume I: 1, Dragon Carpets; 2, The Transitional from Dragon to the Floral Carpets; 3, Floral Carpets; 4, Geometric Carpets; 5, Medallion Carpets; 6, Prayer Rugs; 7, Borders; 8, Iranian Influence on Caucasian Carpets; 9, Anatolian Influence on Caucasian Carpets. Bibliographical references in the notes and cataloge entries.

See also the exhibition catalog: *Early Caucasian Rugs*, by C. G. Ellis (Washington, D.C., Textile Museum, 1975. 112p. illus.).

Chinese Carpets and Rugs

2318 Gans-Ruedin, Erwin. **Chinese Carpets.** Tokyo, New York, Kodansha International, 1981. 200p. illus. index. ISBN 0870114859.

Pictorial survey of Chinese carpets from 1850 to 1980. Introduction sketches the earlier history of Chinese carpets and describes the characteristics and production of modern Chinese carpets. This is followed by plates of carpets by regions with descriptive notes. Particularly useful are the large number of plates illustrating very recent carpets made in China following Persian designs. General bibliography, pp. 196-98.

2319 Eiland, Murray L. **Chinese and Exotic Rugs.** Boston and New York, New York Graphics Society, 1979. 246p. illus. index. ISBN 0821207458.

Comprehensive and informative collector's handbook of Chinese, Indian, North African, Balkan, and Central Asian carpets with particularly close examination of materials and techniques (the appendices have essays on laboratory identification of dyes, microscopic examination of fibers, and the weight of silk fibers). Contents: I, The Rugs of China; II, The Tibetan Carpet; III, The Rugs of Mongolia; IV, The Rugs of Eastern Turkestan; V, The Rugs of India; VI, The Carpets of North Africa; VII, Flat Weaves of the Balkans. Bibliographical references in the notes.

2320   Hackmack, Adolf. **Chinese Carpets and Rugs**. Tientsin, China, Librarie Francaise, 1924. 78p. illus. index. Reprint: New York, Dover, 1973. LC 72-93765.
Older, popular collector's handbook of traditional Chinese carpets still useful for its information and illustrations (poor quality) of rugs made around 1900. Contents: I, The Development of Carpet Weaving; II, Carpet Designs; III, The Colours of Chinese Carpets; IV, The Weaving of the Carpet. No bibliography.

2321   Hyman, Virginia D., and William C. C. Hu. **Carpets of China and Its Border Regions**. Ann Arbor, Mich., Ars Ceramica, 1982. 290p. illus. ISBN 0893440302.
Comprehensive survey of Chinese carpets from the Han dynasty to the present with emphasis on the relationship between carpets and Chinese art and life. Contains many excerpts from documents referring to carpets and illustrations of works of art showing carpets. Contents: History; Colours and Dyes; Carpet Materials; Symbolism; Rug Construction; Rug Shapes and Usage; The Border Regions. General bibliography, pp. 283-290, and further bibliography in the footnotes.

2322   Lorentz, H. A. **A View of Chinese Rugs from the 17th to the 18th Century**. London and Boston, Routledge Kegan Paul, 1972. 194p. illus. index. LC 72-95682.
Comprehensive, authoritative handbook/history of early Chinese rugs. Contents: Part One: Rugs from Eastern Turkestan: The Vase-Pomegranate Pattern, The Medallion Design, The Gül Pattern, Other Designs, Prayer Rugs, Saddle Rugs; Part Two: Chinese Rugs: I, The Geographical and Historical Background of Chinese Rugs; II, The Colours of Chinese Rugs; III, The Use of Colour in Chinese Rugs; IV, Patterns in Chinese Rugs: Their Symbolism and Origin; V, Patterns in Chinese Rugs: Specific Symbols; VI, The Use of Pattern; VII, A Discussion of Western and Other Influences; VIII, Development of Colour and Pattern: Selected Examples; IX, Summing Up; X, Modern Chinese Rugs: the Twentieth Century, Survival of Traditional Styles; XI, The Materials of Chinese Rugs; XII, The Making of a Chinese Rug; XIII, Uses and Sizes of Chinese Rugs; XIV, Origins and Centres of Production: Ninghsia, Kansu and Suiyuan, Paotou, Tibet, Mongolia; Conclusion. Comprehensive bibliography, pp. 185-88, and additional bibliography in the notes.

2323   Rostov, Charles I., and Jia Guanya. **Chinese Carpets**. New York, Abrams, 1983. 223p. illus. index. ISBN 0810907852.
Well-illustrated survey of Chinese rugs and carpets from the Han dynasty to the present with emphasis on the relationship between carpets and Chinese culture in general, and on the revival of traditional carpet design and technique since 1970. Features many older carpets now in the Textile Museum, Washington, D.C. Contents: 1, History; 2, Symbols and Symbolism; 3, Weaving Methods and Techniques; 4, Materials; 5, Identification and Dating. Appendices with essays on Chinese classics, Chinese measurements, Chinese calendars, and a note on Pinyin spelling. Bibliography, p. 222, lists both Chinese and English-languages sources.

Indian Carpets and Rugs

2324 Gans-Ruedin, Erwin. **Indian Carpets**. New York, Rizzoli, 1984. 318p. illus. index. ISBN 0847805514.

Well-illustrated handbook/history of carpet weaving in India from the seventeenth century to 1980. Introduction sketches the history and describes the centers of production. Chronologically arranged catalog of pieces illustrated in color with detailed descriptive notes under the group headings: Mughal Carpets, Antique Agra, Kashmir, Amritsar, Agra, Jaipur, Bhadohi, Mirzapur. Basic bibliography, pp. 307-08.

Persian (Iranian) Carpets and Rugs

2325 Edwards, A. Cecil. **The Persian Carpet**. 4th ed. London, Duckworth, 1974. 384p. illus. index.

First published in 1953. Comprehensive, informative handbook/history of handknotted carpet production in Iran with emphasis on production in the major centers during the late nineteenth century and the first half of the twentieth century. Contents: I, Retrospect; II, Carpets of the Great Period; III, The Weaver's Craft; IV, The Craft of the Dyer; V, Some Notes on Design; VI, Tabriz, the Heriz Weaving Area; The So-Called Zenjan Rugs; VII, Hamadan and Its Environs; with a Note on Malayer; VIII, The Kurdish Weaves: Senneh, Bijar and the Kurdish Tribal Rugs; IX, Arak (Sultanabad) and Its Environs; with a Note on Seraband; X, The Turkoman Rugs of the Persian Steppe; XI, Meshed, the Qainat and Turshiz (Kashmar); XII, The Baluchi Tribal Rugs of Khurasan; XIII, Kerman and Its Environs; the Afshari Rugs; a Note on Yezd; XIV, The Tribal and Village Rugs of Fars; XV, Isfahan and the So-called Bakhtiari Weaves; Joshaqan; and a Note on Nain; XVI, Kashan and Qum; XVII, The Future of the Industry. Appendices with chronology of the Persian carpet, export statistics of carpets from Persia between 1923 and 1973 and list of Persian measures and their approximate equivalents. Bibliographical references in the footnotes.

2326 Gans-Ruedin, Erwin. **The Spendor of Persian Carpets**. New York, Rizzoli, 1978. 546p. illus. index. ISBN 0847801799.

Pictorial handbook of Persian carpets from earliest times to the present with emphasis on the period from 1800 to the present. Good quality color plates of representative pieces are accompanied by descriptive notes that include size, type of knot, number of knots per square inch, material used for warp, weft and knots. Arrangement is by traditional regions and centers: Azerbijan, Hamadan, Kurdistan, Arak Region, Qum, Kashan, Isfahan, Chahar Mahal, Shiraz, Kerman, Turkoman, Mashhad, Laluchi. General bibliography, pp. 541-42. Text in English and Arabic.

See also Tanavoli, Parviz, *Shahsavan Iranian Rugs and Textiles* (New York, Rizzoli, 1985. 435p. illus. index. ISBN 084780626X).

See also the exhibition catalog: *Carpets of Central Persia: With Special Attention to Rugs of Kirman*, by M. H. Beattie (London, World of Islam Pub. Co., 1976. 104p. illus. ISBN 090503516X), *Woven from the Soul: Spun from the Heart: Textile Arts of Safvid and Oajar Iran, 16th-19th Centuries*, ed. by C. Bier (Washington, D.C., Textile Museum, 1987. 336p. illus. ISBN 0874050278), *Turkmenische Teppiche und die ethnographische Bedeutung ihrer Ornament*, by A. Siawosch (Hamburg, Museum für Völkerkunde, 1970. 68p. illus. English translation: Fishgard, Crosby Press, 1975. ISBN 0903580306).

Turkish Carpets and Rugs

2327 Erdmann, Kurt. **The History of the Early Turkish Carpet**. London, Oguz Press, 1977. 101p. illus. ISBN 0905820029.

Translation of: *Der türkische Teppich des 15. Jahrhunderts.* (Istanbul, Maarif Basimevi, 1957). Updated provenance of the rugs with several new plates. Important, pioneering, scholarly history of Turkish rugs and carpets from the thirteenth to the end of the seventeenth centuries. The work of a leading scholar, Erdmann's history not only charts the stylistic development and differentiates the major types, but presents Turkish carpets as the pinnacle of textile art as opposed to the Persian carpet that is appraised as a derivative of painting. Illustrated with major carpets and fragments, and many European paintings illustrating Turkish carpets, most notably the so-called Holbein carpets. Contents: Foreword by Hanna Erdmann; Translator's Preface by Robert Pinner; Introduction; I, The 13th and 14th Centuries; II, The 16th and 17th Centuries; III, Conclusions on the 15th Century; Bibliography of Kurt Erdmann on Carpets compiled by Hanna Erdmann. Bibliographical references in the notes.

2328   Yetkin, Serare. **Historical Turkish Carpets**. Ankara, Turiye Is Bankasi Cultura Publications, 1981. 171p. illus. LC 83-225119.
       Scholarly history of Turkish carpets from the fourteenth through the seventeenth centuries. Encompasses both surviving examples and representations of Turkish rugs and carpets in works of Western art. Poor quality plates. Contents: Seljuk Rugs: a, Konya carpets, b, Beysehir carpets, c, Fostat (Old Cairo), carpets; Animal Figured Carpets; The First Ottoman Rugs; Rugs in Flemish Paintings; Ottoman Rugs of the Classical Period; Usak Rugs; Other Usak Types; Bergama Rugs; Ottoman Court Carpets; Rugs Belonging to Nonspecific Group. Comprehensive but unclassified bibliography, pp. 141-62.
       See also the museum catalog: *Topkapi Saray Museum: Carpets*, by J. M. Rogers and H. Tezcan (London, Thames & Hudson, 1987. 240p.).

Turkoman Carpets

2329   Loges, Werner. **Turkoman Tribal Rugs**. Atlantic Highlands, N.J., Humanities Press, 1980. 204p. illus. ISBN 0391017365.
       Collector's pictorial handbook of antique, i.e., nineteenth century, Turkoman rugs. Brief introductory essays followed by color plates with descriptive notes. Contents: 1, The Turkoman People; 2, Turkoman Rugs and Carpets; 3, Tekke Carpets; 4, Salor Carpets; 5, Aryk Carpets; 6, Yomut Carpets; 7, Chodor Carpets; 8, Kizilayak Carpets; 9, Ersari Carpets; 10, Arabatshi Carpets; 11, Other Central Asian Carpets. General bibliography, p. 204.

2330   O'Bannon, George W. **The Turkoman Carpet**. London, Duckworth, 1974. 168p. illus. index. ISBN 0715607405.
       Pictorial handbook of carpets made by Turkoman tribes in Central Asia, Afghanistan, Iran, and imitations made in Pakistan and India. Emphasis is on twentieth-century pieces. General bibliography, pp. 164-65.

Kilims

2331   Justin, Valerie. **Flat-woven Rugs of the World: Kilim, Soumak, and Brocading**. New York, Van Nostrand Reinhold, 1980. 224p. illus. index. ISBN 0442242115.
       Pictorial survey of kilim and other flat-woven floor coverings from around the world. Contents: The Kilim; Materials; Methods; Turkey; Iran; Afghanistan; USSR; Europe; Africa; The Near East; India; China; South America; Middle America; North America. Basic bibliography, pp. 187-89.

2332   Petsopoulos, Yanni. **Kilims, Flat-woven Tapestry Rugs**. New York, Rizzoli, 1979. 394p. illus. index. ISBN 0847802450.

Well-illustrated survey of Oriental kilims with emphasis on identification of various regional types. Contents: Geographical and Social Background; The Study and Classification of Kilims; The Structure of Kilims; Designs, Patterns and Compositions; Symbolism and Tradition; Anatolia; Caucasus; Persia; India and China.

See also the exhibition catalog: *From the Bosporus to Samarkand; Flat-woven Rugs*, by A. N. Landreau and W. R. Pickering (Washington, D.C., Textile Museum, 1969. 112p. illus.) and the museum catalogs: *Flatweaves of the Vakiflar Museum, Istanbul* (Istanbul, Belkis Balpinar, Udo Hirsch, 1982. 295p. illus. ISBN 3923185022), and *Flat-woven Textiles*, by C. Cootner (Washington, D.C., Textile Museum, 1981. 223p. illus. The Arthur D. Jenkins Collection, v. 1).

EMBROIDERY

Bibliographies

2333   Sestay, Catherine J. **Needle Work: A Selected Bibliography with Special Reference to Embroidery and Needlepoint**. Metuchen, N.J., Scarecrow Press, 1982. 153p. index. ISBN 0810815540.

Classified and annotated bibliography of 475 titles on needlework with emphasis on technique and the contemporary revival of traditional craft techniques and designs.

Dictionaries and Encyclopedias

2334   Caulfield, Sophia F. A., and Blanche C. Saward. **The Dictionary of Needlework, and Encyclopedia of Artistic, Plain and Fancy Needlework...** 2nd ed. London, Gill, 1885. 528p. illus. LC A15-802. Reprinted under the title: *Dictionary of Needlework: Enyclopedia of Victorian Needlework*. New York, Dover, 1972. 2v. illus. LC 72-2139.

Older, comprehensive dictionary of embroidery, lace, and other forms of needlework with particular attention to those popular in the Victorian period in England. Copiously illustrated with many details of stichery patterns and techniques. In its day, Caulfield's dictionary was instrumental in popularizing needlework as an activity in middle-class households and today it is an important source for the historian. The color plates in the original are reproduced in black and white in the reprint.

2335   Clabburn, Pamela. **The Needleworker's Dictionary**. New York, William Morrow, 1976. 296p. illus. ISBN 0688030548.

Popular dictionary of needlework, e.g., embroidery, lace, and applique from around the world and from ancient times to the present directed to the needlework artist. Excellent collection of illustrations with many in color. Bibliography of works in English, pp. 288-292. Appendix with list of museums and collections in Great Britain and America.

2336   Dillmont, Therese de. **Encyclopedia of Needlework**. New ed. rev. and enl. New York, Crescent Books, 1987. 789p. illus. ISBN 0517631806.

Comprehensive dictionary of needlework covering materials and techniques under the following main headings: Plain Sewing; The Sewing and Embroidering Machine; Machine Sewing and Embroidering; Embroidery on White Materials; Linen Embroidery; Embroidery on Silk and Velvet; Gold Embroidery; Appliqué Work; Tapestry; Knitting; Crochet; Tatting; Filet Lace; Openwork Lace; Embroidered Lace; Needle-made Lace; Pillow Lace; Needlework Trimmings; Miscellaneous Directions (contains valuable advice on care and restoration). Although directed chiefly to the handworker and textile artist, Dillmont's work is an authoritative source for the history of needlework techniques.

General Histories and Handbooks

2337 Antrobus, Mary S., and Louisa Preece. **Needle Work Through the Ages; a Short Survey of Its Development in Decorative Art...** London, Hodder and Stoughton, 1928. 413p. illus. index. LC 24-23722.

An old, standard history still valuable for its great scope and large number of illustrations (103 plates with descriptive notes). Contents: Part I: Prehistoric to Second Century A.D.: I, Introductory; II, Origin and Development of Stitches and Material; III, Egypt; IV, Chaldea and Assyria; V, Aegean; VI, Discoveries in Turkestan and Mongolia. Part II: Second Century to Present Day: VII, Peru; VIII, Second to Sixth Centuries; IX, The Development of Silk through Embroidery and Weaving; X, Tenth to Twelfth Centuries; XI, Twelfth and Thirteenth Centuries; XII, Fourteenth Century; XIII, Fifteenth Century; XIV, Sixteenth Century; XV, Seventeenth Century; XVI, Eighteenth Century; XVII, Nineteenth Century and the Present. General bibliography, pp. 391-98, and further bibliography in the notes.

2338 Cavallo, Adolph S. **Needlework**. New York, Cooper-Hewitt Museum, 1979. 128p. illus. index. LC 78-62725.

In the series: The Smithsonian Illustrated Library of Antiques.

Concise history of needlework throughout the world from earliest times to the present with a chapter on studying and collecting. Contents: Introduction; 2, Techniques of Needlework; 3, Mainstreams in the West; 4, Mainstreams in the East; 5, Western Asia and the Near East; 6, Needlework of the Indigenous Peoples of Africa and America; 7, About Studying and Collecting Needlework. Illustrated chiefly with pieces in American collections. General, classified bibliography of works in English, p. 124.

2339 Christie, Grace. **Embroidery and Tapestry Weaving; a Practical textbook of Design Workmanship...** London, Hogg, 1096. 414p. illus. index. 4th ed. London, Putnam, 1933. 403p. illus. index. Reprint: London, Pitman; New York, Taplinger, 1979. ISBN 08000824016.

Handbook of the techniques of traditional European and American embroidery and tapestry weaving from the Middle Ages to 1930. Illustrated with drawings, many showing in detail various stitches. Contents: I, Introduction; II, Tools, Appliances, and Materials; III, Pattern Designing; IV, Stitches; V, Stitches (continued); VI, Stitches (continued); VII, Canvas Work and Stitches; VIII, Methods of Work; IX, Methods of Work (continued); X, Methods of Work (continued); XI, Embroidery with Gold and Silver Threads; XII, Lettering, Heraldry, and Emblems; XIII, The Garniture of Work; XIV, Practical Directions; XV, Tapestry Weaving; XVI, Necessary Appliances and Materials; XVII, Preparations for Work; XVIII, The Technique of Weaving. No bibliography.

2340 Christie, Grace. **Samplers and Stitches; a Handbook of the Embroiderer's Art...** London, Batsford; New York, Dutton, 1929. 144p. illus. 4th ed. New York, Hearthside Press, 1959. 152p. illus. LC 59-15824.

Handbook of stitches and other techniques used in embroidery illustrated with numerous line drawings and a good selection of photographic plates of modern embroidery. Christie's handbooks are useful for several purposes. They reflect the revival of traditional needlework after 1920 and are clear in their description of technical aspects that are common to both modern and earlier embroidery. Contents: I, Introductory; II, Flat Stitches; III, Looped Stitches; IV, Chained Stitches; V, Knotted Stitches; VI, Composite Stitches; VII, Canvas Stitches; VIII, Drawn Fabric Stitches; IX, Black Work—Lace Stitch Fillings—Darning; X, Cut and Drawn Work and Insertion Stitches; XI, Couching and Laid Work; XII, Applied and Inlaid Work—Quilting. No bibliography.

2341 Farcy, Louis de. **La broderie du XIe siècle jusqu'à nos jours d' après des specimens authentiques et les anciens inventaires**. Angers, Belhomme, 3 portfolios. 1890-1900. LC 10-22600.

Important, pioneering history of embroidery from the eleventh century to the nineteenth century. Corpus of 214 large-format plates . Bibliographical references in the footnotes.

2342 Gostelow, Mary. **A World of Embroidery**. New York, Scribner's, 1975. 512p. illus. index. ISBN 0684142309.

Wide-ranging survey of embroidery, particularly useful for the inclusion of many Third World countries and emphasis on contemporary work. First part is arranged by country; the second is an illustrated dictionary of types of stitches and techniques. Bibliography, pp. 451-63.

See also Drury, Elizabeth, ed., *Needlework: an Illustrated History*. (New York, Paddington Press, 1978. 363p. illus. ISBN 0448220660).

2343 Groves, Sylvia. **The History of Needlework Tools and Accessories**. London, Country Life, 1966. 136p. illus. index. Reprint: New York, Arco, 1973. LC 72-97034.

Comprehensive, authoritative history of European needlework tools. Contains a great deal of information on the technique place of needlework in the social history of Europe during the eighteenth and nineteenth centuries. Contents: 1, Needles and Needle-case; 2, Thread and Thread-winders; 3, Thimbles, Yard Measures, and Miscellaneous Sewing Accessories; 4, Scissors and Knives; 5, Pins, Pinchusions and Pin-boxes; 6, Needlwork Clamps; 7, Sewing Caskets, Chatelaines, Work-boxes and Work-tables; 8, Knitting; 9, Netting, Net-Work and Needle-made Lace; 10, Knotting and Tatting; 11, Embroidery and Cord-making; 12, Tambouring and Crochet; 13, Purse-making, Beadwork, Braid- and Mat-weaving; 14, Pillow Lace; 15, Patterns and Pattern Books; 16, The Practice of Parfilage. No bibliography but the text contains many quotes from sources.

2344 Jones, Mary E. **A History of Western Embroidery**. London, Studio Vista; New York, Watson-Guptill, 1969. 159p. illus. index. LC 77-83369.

Broad but informative survey of embroidery in western Europe and America from ancient Greece to circa 1950. Emphasis is on the history of the art of embroidery rather than on the technique of embroidery. Contains 85 well-chosen plates. Contents: 1, The Technique of Embroidery; 2, The Evolution of Embroidery; 3, The Embroidery of Antiquity; 4, English Embroidery; 5, France; 6, Germany; 7, Swiss Linen Embroidery; 8, Italy; 9, Spain and Portugal; 10, Flanders; 11, Eastern Europe; 12, Northern Europe; 13, America; 14, Modern Embroidery. Basic bibliography, p. 156.

2345 Lotz, Arthur. **Bibliographie der Modelbücher; beschreibendes Verzeichnis der Stich- und Spitzenmusterbücher des 16. und 17. Jahrhunderts**. Leipzig, Hiersemann, 1933. 274p. illus. index. LC 34-13466.

Important, scholarly catalog of model books for patterns in embroidery and lace printed during the sixteenth and seventeenth centuries. Arrangement is by country and then chronologically. Thoroughly indexed.

2346 Parker, Rozsika. **The Subversive Stitch: Embroidery and the Making of the Feminine**. New York, Routledge, 1989. 247p. illus. index. ISBN 0415902061.

Important feminist history of European embroidery from the Middle Ages to the 1980s. Emphasis is on English examples. Contents: 1, The Creation of Femininity; 2, Eternalising the Feminine; 3, Fertility, Chastity and Power; 4, The Domestication of Embroidery; 5, The Inculcation of Femininity; 6, From Milkmaids to Mothers; 7, Femininity as Feeling; 8, A Naturally Revolutionary Art? Select bibliography, pp. 233-39.

2347 Ring, Betty, ed. **Needlework: An Illustrated Survey**. New York, Main Street/Universe Books, 1975. 174p. illus. index. LC 75-10933.
Collection of articles that appeared in *Antiques* between 1922 and 1975.

2348 Rogers, Gay A. **An Illustrated History of Needlework Tools**. London, John Murray, 1983. 243p. illus. index. ISBN 0719540216.
Comprehensive history of European and American needlework tools from the eighteenth century to circa 1940 directed to the collector. Contents: I, Fitted Needlework Boxes; 2, Sewing Cases and Chatelaines; 3, Needles and Needlecases; 4, Thimbles and Thimble Cases; 5, Scissors; 6, Tape-Measures, Emeries and Waxers; 7, Pin Cushions; 8, Thread Containers; 9, Needlework Clamps; 10, Handwork Tools; 11, Plain Sewing and Handwork Gadgets. General bibliography, pp. 232-36, and further bibliography in the notes.

2349 Schuette, Marie, and Sigrid Muller-Christensen. **A Pictorial History of Embroidery**. New York, Praeger, 1964. 336p. illus. index. LC 64-13379.
Contains 464 well-chosen plates with descriptive catalog including bibliographies of specialized literature. Covers European embroidery, including Byzantine, from the fifth century B.C. to the early twentieth century. Excellent introductory essays: "Materials and Technique" by S. Muller-Christensen; Historical Introduction by M. Schuette.
See also the museum catalog: *Three Hundred Years of Embroidery 1600-1900: Treasures from the Collection of the Embroiderers' Guild of Great Britain*, by P. Johnstone (East Molesey, Embroiderer's Guild, 1987. 95p. illus. ISBN 094926881X).

Byzantine and Medieval Embroidery

2350 Brel-Bordaz, Odile. **Broderies d'ornements liturgiques: XIIIe-XIVe siècle**. Paris, Nouvelles Editions latines, 1982. 204p. illus. LC 82-237458. ISBN 2723301789.
Scholarly history of Western medieval liturgical embroideries of the thirteenth and fourteenth centuries with valuable catalog of thirteen pieces that update and supplement Christie (2360). Poor-quality illustrations. Contents: Introduction; I, Les broderies et leurs techniques; II, Les programmes iconographiques; III, approches stylistiques: Composition général, L'opus Anglicanum dans le context de l'art anglais au XIVe siècle; Problèmes d'attribution et de datation des broderies. Appendix with extracts from documents. Comprehensive, classified bibliography, pp. 187-98, and extensive bibliography in the footnotes and catalog entries.

2351 Johnstone, Pauline. **The Byzantine Tradition in Church Embroidery**. London, Tiranti, 1967. 144p. illus. index. LC 67-17572.
Informative introduction to the history of Byzantine ecclesiastical embroidery. Contents: I, The Byzantine Background; II, Textiles and Embroidery; III, Vestments; IV, Iconography; V, Ornament; VI, Inscriptions; VII, Workers and Workrooms; VIII, Technique; IX, Embroidery and History; X, Pieces Illustrated (commentary on the 120 plates). Comprehensive bibliography, pp. 132-135, and bibliographical references in the footnotes.

2352 Millet, Gabriel. **Broderies religieuses du style Byzantin**. Paris, Presses Universitaires de France, 1947. 117p. illus.
Authoritative, scholarly history of Byzantine ecclesiastical embroidery with important corpus of 216 plates. Contents: L Livre Premier—Costume Liturgique. I, Epitrachilia, médaillons; II, Epitrachilia arcades; III, Epitrachilia, style de la croix gammée; IV, Epitrachilia et ovaria, champ rectangulaire; V, Costume liturgique, pièces diverses. Livre II.—Voiles. I, Voiles byzantins et serbs; II, Voiles moldaves et valaques; III-IV, Epitaphioi, ensemble et détails. General bibliography, pp. 110-14, and bibliographical references in the notes.

2353   Wagner, Margarete. **Sakrale Weisstickereien des Mittelalters**. Esslingen, Burgbücherei Wilhelm Schneider, 1963. 44p. illus.

Authoritative introduction to medieval ecclesiastical white-on-white embroidered textiles. Bibliographical references in the footnotes. For a comprehensive, authoritative history of the important group of lower Saxon medieval embroideries *See:* R. Kroos, *Niedersächsische Bildstickereien des Mittelalters* (Berlin, Deutscher Verlag für Kunstwissenschaft, 1970. 211p. illus. index. ISBN 3871570109).

American Embroidery and Needlework

2354   Bath, Virginia C. **Needlework in America. History, Designs, and Techniques**. New York, Viking, 1979. 336p. illus. index. ISBN 0670505757.

Comprehensive history of American needlework from early Colonial times to the twentieth century. Includes chapter on American Indian needlework including beadwork. Plates include drawings of patterns and diagrams of stitches. Contents: I, North American Indian Needlework; II, Surface Embroidery in Woolen Thread; III, Bed Rugs and Pile Embroidery; IV, Surface Embroidery in Silk; V, Thread-Counted Embroidery; VI, Patchwork, Appliqué, and Quilting; VII, Rug Hooking; VIII, White Embroidery and Lace. General bibliography, pp.

2355   Hanley, Hope. **Needlepoint in America**. New York, Scribner's, 1969. 160p. illus. LC 74-78283.

General pictorial survey of American needlepoint from early colonial times to 1960. Illustrations include tools and drawings of stitches. Contents: European Origins; Colonial America; The Berlin Period; Some Old Stitches Revived; Epiloque: From 1900 On. Appendices with descriptions of types of canvas used in nineteenth-century needlepoint. General, classified bibliography, pp. 153-57, includes catalogs and pamphlets, magazines and newspapers.

2356   Harbeson, Georgiana B. **American Needlework: The History of Decorative Stitchery and Embroidery from the Late Sixteenth to the Twentieth Century**. 1938. LC 38-290098. Reprint: New York, Bonanza Books, n.d. 232p. illus. index.

An old, standard history covering Native American textiles and beadwork as well as American embroidery and decorative stitchery from early Colonial times to the early twentieth century. Contents: I, American Indian Porcupine-Quill Embroidery; II, Indian Bead Needlework; III, Indian Appliqué, Alaskan Fishskin Needlework; IV, Early Stump Work, Silk and Wool Needlepoint Pictures; V, Crewel Embroidery in the Colonies; VI, Early Quilting, Candlewicking and Turkey Work; VII, Early Samplers; VIII, Philadelphia Type Samplers, Quaker Needlework and Pennsylvania Dutch Embroidery; IX, Later Samplers; X, Embroidered Wedding Gowns and Waistcoats; XI, Needle Lacework: Darning and Tambour; XII, White Work, Costume Embroideries and Accessories; XIII, Moravian Work: Memorial Samplers and Silk on Satin Embroideries; XIV, Embroidered Maps and Needlework Rugs; XV, Embroidered Coats of Arms, Banners, Flags and Flag Preservation; XVI, Needlepoint Pictures and Upholstery; XVII, Godey's, Leslie's, and Peterson's Needlework Patterns; XVIII, Fashionable Berlin Wool-work; XIX, Canvas Lacework and Raised Wool-work; XX, Embroidery on Paper: Bookmarks and Mottoes; XXI, Braiding, Velvet-work and Chenille Stitchery; XXII, Applique Arascene Embroidery and Ribbon-work; XXIII, Beadwork with Wool Combinations; XXIV, Sewing Accessories; XXV, Deerfield Blue and White Work Revival, Candlewicking and Netting; XXVI, The Transition Period; XXVII, Religious Needlework; XXVIII, The Return to Silk Embroideries; XXIX, New Uses of the Sampler; XXX, Modern Crewel Embroidery; XXXI, Contemporary Needlepoint Embroidery: Screens and Covers; XXXII, Contemporary Needlepoint Embroidery: Miscellaneous Furnishings, Accessories, Petit-Point Pictures; XXXIII, Needlework of the Future. General bibliography, pp. 225-26.

2357   Kassell, Hilda. **Stitches in Time: The Art and History of Embroidery.** New York, Duell, Sloan and Pearce, 1967. 108p. illus. LC 67-2273.

Concise history of American embroidery from Colonial times to the twentieth century. Appendix with introduction to the craft of modern embroidery. Basic bibliography, pp. 107-08.

2358   Swan, Susan B. **Plain and Fancy: American Women and Their Needlework, 1700-1850.** New York, Holt, Rinehart & Winston, 1977. 240p. illus. index. ISBN 003015121X.

Important history of needlework in relationship to the sociological position of women in American society from 1700 to 1850. Contains 123 plates with descriptive captions. Contents: 1, Plain Sewing, Plain Housewives; 2, Molding the Accomplished Miss; 3, The Golden Years of Needlework: The Age of Craftsmanship; 4, Diversions for Genteel Ladies: the Age of Accomplishments; 5, To Make a House a Home: The Age of Domesticity. Comprehensive, partly annotated bibliography, pp. 235-37.

2359   Wheeler, Candace. **The Development of Embroidery in America.** New York and London, Harper & Row, 1921. 151p. illus. LC 21-20517.

General survey of embroidery in America from colonial times to the twentieth century. Contents: Introductory—the Story of the Needle—Beginnings in the New World; The Crewelwork of Our Puritan Mothers; Samplers and a Word about Quilts; Moravian Work, Portraiture, French Embroidery and Lacework; Berlin Woolwork; Revival of Embroidery, and the Founding of the Society of Decorative Art; American Tapestry; The Bayeux Tapestries. Bibliographical references in the notes.

See also the museum handbook: *A Winterthur Guide to American Needlework,* by S. B. Swan (New York, Crown, 1976. 144p. illus.).

Samplers

2360   Bolton, Ethel S., and Eva J. Coe. **American Samplers.** Boston, Society of the Colonial Dames of America, 1921. 416p. illus. index. Reprint: Princeton, N.J., Pyne Press, 1973. LC 72-88732.

Important catalog of American embroidered samplers dating between 1660 and 1830. Includes 126 poorly reproduced plates. Divided by periods, i.e., 1600-1700, 1700-1799, 1800-1830, introductory essays are followed by lists of samplers arranged by the name of the embroiderer. Brief descriptions of the pieces form the entries. Separate chapter, "An Anthology of Sampler Verse," is a chronological list of verses. Bibliographical references in the footnotes. A standard handbook.

2361   Krueger, Glee. **New England Samplers to 1840.** Sturbridge, Mass., Old Sturbidge Village, 1978. 227p. illus. index. LC 79-107906.

Survey of New England embroidered samplers from the late eighteenth century to circa 1840 with an important collection of 93 plates in various private collections and a directory of schools and teachers offering needlework instruction, 1706-1840. Comprehensive, classified bibliography, pp. 209-220.

See also the exhibition catalogs: *A Gallery of American Samplers: The Theodore H. Kapnek Collection,* by G. F. Krueger (New York, Dutton, 1978. 96p. illus. ISBN 0517455927), *American Needlwork Treasures: Samplers and Silk Embroideries from the Collection of Betty Ring,* by B. Ring (New York, Dutton, 1987. 112p. illus. index).

European Embroidery and Needlework

Germany

2362   Schuette, Marie. **Gestickte Bildteppiche und Decken des Mittelalters**. Leipzig, Hiersemann, 1927-30. 2v. illus. LC 31-24701.

Scholarly history and catalog of German medieval embroidered wall hangings and covers. Only two volumes covering the famous pieces in north Germany have been completed. Contents: Band 1, Die Klöster Wienhausen und Lüne; Das Lüneburgische Museum (1927); Band 2, Braundschweig; Die Klöster Ebstorf und Isenhagen; Wernigerode; Kloster Drubeck; Halberstadt (1930). Each has an authoritative introduction followed by detailed catalog. Catalog entries have bibliographies and additional references in the footnotes. A standard work and a paradigmatic scholarly catalog.

Great Britain

2363   Christie, A. G. I. **English Medieval Embroidery, a Brief Survey of English Embroidery Dating from the Beginning of the Tenth Century until the End of the Fourteenth...** Oxford, Clarendon, 1938. 206p. illus. index. LC 38-22979.

Comprehensive, scholarly history and catalog of English medieval embroidery with particular emphasis on Opus Anglicanum. Contents: Introduction: Importance of Embroidery in the Middle Ages, Fame of Opus Anglicanum Abroad, Characteristics of Opus Anglicanum, Nature of Surviving Examples, Causes of Destruction; Design, Designers, Workers, and Work Centres, Materials, Technique, Scope of Inquiry. Appendix I: Some Embroidery Workers and Purchases of Embroideries Recorded in Medieval Documents; Appendix II: Contemporary Records of Medieval Embroideries; Descriptive Catalogue of Existing English Medieval Embroideries. Detailed catalog entries with bibliographies. A standard work.

See also the exhibition catalog: *Opus Anglicanum; English Medieval Embroidery*, by D. King (London, Arts Council, 1963. 64p. illus.).

2364   Digby, George Wingfield. **Elizabethan Embroidery**. New York, Yoseloff, 1964. 151p. illus. index. LC 64-54751.

Authoritative history of embroidery in England during the sixteenth and early seventeenth centuries. Extensive use of documentary sources. Contents: Part I: 1, General; 2, Domestic and Professional Embroidery; 3, The Inspiration of Gardens and Flowers; 4, Emblems; 5, Design Sources; 6, Two Noble Needlewomen; Part II: 1, Embroidery of Dress; 2, Embroidery for Furnishing. Appendix with list of inventories. Comprehensive and classified bibliography, pp. 142-46.

2365   Gostelow, Mary. **Art of Embroidery: Great Needlework Collections of Britain and the United States**. New York, Dutton, 1979. 256p. illus. index. ISBN 0525930647.

Pictorial survey of works of embroidery in various museums and historic houses in Great Britain and America. Illustrations include, together with overall and detailed views of the various pieces of embroidery, views and portraits of persons associated with the historic houses. Contents: I, The American Museum in Britain: American Coverlets; II, Blair Castle: Lady Evelyn's Whitework; 3, Colonial Williamsburg: Embroideries for the Home; 4, Daughters of the American Revolution Museum: Family Records, Pictures and Samplers; Glamis Castle: A Royal Miscellany; 6, Hardwick Hall: Bess Hardwick's Embroideries; 7, The Helen Allen Collection: Internationalism and Variety; 8, The Henry Ford Museum: Faces of the Past; 9, The Henry Francis du Pont Winterthur Museum: Canvaswork; 10, Historic Deerfield: Crewel Embroidery; 11, Mellerstain: A Children's Masterpiece; 12, Milton Manor House: An Exquisite Needlework Box; 13, The

National Cathedral: Ecclesiastical Decoration; 14, Ohio Historical Society: Local Heritage; 15, Old Sturbridge Village: New England Costume; 16, Parham Park: Seventeenth-century Bible Pictures; 17, Traquair House: Flowers of Profusion; 18, The Valentine Museum: Beautiful Needleworks amid Elegance; 19, The Washington Family: Patriotic Embroideries; 20, Wells Cathedral: The Quire Canvasworks; 22, The Continuing Heritage. General bibliography, pp. 251-52, and additional bibliography in the notes.

2366   Hughes, Therle. **English Domestic Needlework, 1660-1860**. London, Butterworths, 1961. 255p. illus. index. LC 61-19567.
     Concise history of embroidery and other forms of decorative needlework made in England for domestic use between 1660 and 1860. Directed to the collector and enthusiast, emphasis is placed on style and function. Contains 48 black-and-white and four-color plates with descriptive captions. Contents: 1, Historical Background: General Trends; 2, Historical Background: Eastern Influences; 3, Wool Work; 4, Metal Work; 5, Black Work and White Work; 6, Pictorial Embroidery; 7, Book Covers; 8, Furniture Embroidery; 9, Bed Hangings and Pillows; 10, Cushions; 11, Quilting and Patchwork; 12, Samplers; 13, Raised or Stump Work; 14, Pinchusions; 15, Beadwork; 16, Costume Embroideries; 17, Gloves; 18, Other Dress Accessories: Aprons, Bags and Purses, Pockets, Muffs; 19, Patterns and Their Sources; 20, Old Embroidery Tools. No bibliography.

2367   Kendrick, Albert F. **English Needlework**. 2nd ed. revised by Patricia Wardle. London, Black, 1967. 212p. illus. index. LC 67-87510.
     First published in 1933. Authoritative survey of English embroidery and other decorative needlework from the early Middle Ages to the nineteenth century written by former Keeper of the Department of Textiles at the Victoria and Albert Museum. Contents: I, The Middle Ages: 1, Anglo-Saxon Embroidery, 2, The Bayeux Tapestry, 3, Opus Anglicanum, 4, Other Pre-Reformation Ecclesiastical Work; 5, Secular and Domestic Work; II, The Sixteenth Century: 1, Henry VIII to Mary, 2, Elizabeth; III, The Seventeenth Century: 1, Early Stuarts and Commonwealth, 2, The Restoration; IV, The Eighteenth Century; V, The Nineteenth Century. Selected bibliography, pp. 200-202, is a classified list updated to 1960.

2368   Morris, Barbara J. **Victorian Embroidery**. New York, Universe, 1970. 238p. illus. index. ISBN 0876631243.
     Authoritative survey of the revival of needlework in Great Britain during the reign of Queen Victoria. Extensive use of documentary sources. Contents: 1, Berlin-work, Bead-work and Cross-stitch Embroidery; 2, Whitework; 3, Patchwork and Appliqué; 4, Machine Embroidery; 5, Church Embroidery; 6, "Morris" Embroideries; 7, Art Needlework; 8, The Arts and Crafts Exhibition Society; 9, The Glasgow School; 10, "Fancy-work" and Miscellaneous Types of Embroidery; 11, Embroidery in America. Appendices with lists of embroidery work societies, list of natural objects suitable to embroidery, and extracts from a report by Alan Cole upon his visits to Irish lace-making and embroidery schools in 1897. Bibliography, pp. 219-225, includes list of Victorian periodicals.
     See also the museum catalog: *Catalogue of English Domestic Embroidery of the Sixteenth & Seventeenth Centuries*, Victoria and Albert Museum (London, H. M. Stationery Off., 1950), *Catalogue of English Ecclesiastical Embroideries of the XIII to XVI Centuries*, Victoria and Albert Museum (London, Board of Education, 1930).

Italy

2369   Ricci, Elisa. **Ricami italiani antichi e moderni**. Florence, Felice le Monnier, 1925. 310p. illus.

Comprehensive, authoritative history of Italian embroidery from the Middle Ages to the early twentieth century. Brief essays on the development in the various periods followed by detailed notes to 65 plates. Contents: Ricami antichi: Nell'Antichità; Nel Medio Evo; Nel Rinascimento; I libretti di modelli; Dal seicento all'Impero.Ricami moderni: La Rinascita; I laboratori; Burano; Signore e operale; Le ciociare; I nuovi ricami; Le "industrie femminili." Bibliographical references in the footnotes.

Oriental Embroidery

2370   Chung, Young Yang. **The Art of Oriental Embroidery: History, Aesthetics, and Techniques**. New York, Scribner's, 1983. 183p. illus. index. ISBN 0684180405.

Popular survey of traditional Chinese, Korean and Japanese silk embroidery. Contents: 1, The Foundations of Oriental Silk Embroidery; 2, Home Accessories; 3, The Chinese Dragon Robe; 4, The Japanese Kimono; 5, The Korean Bridal Robe; 6, Costume Accessories; 7, Scrolls, Screens, and Banners; 8, Oriental Embroidery Design. Appendix with catalog of design and symbolic motifs. Bibliography, pp.175-78, lists books in Chinese and English.

See also the author's *The Origins and Development of the Embroidery of China, Japan, and Korea*. (New York, 1977).

LACE

Bibliographies

2371   Overloop, E. van. **Catalogue des ouvrages se rapportant a l'industrie de la dentelle**. Brussels, H. Lamertin, 1906. 433p. illus. index.

Comprehensive bibliography of books and periodical articles in all languages on all aspects of lace published before 1905. Titles are listed alphabetically in two parts: Première partie: Ouvrages et publications se rapportant directement à la dentelle; Deuxième partie: Ouvrages et publications ne traitant pas directement de la dentelle, mais pouvant être utiliement consultés à son sujet. Répertoire méthodique, pp. 127-403, classifies the same titles by subject and type of publication. Invaluable source for the older literature.

Dictionaries and Encyclopedias

2372   Brooke, Margaret L. **Lace in the Making with Bobbins and Needle...** London, Routledge, 1923. 164p. illus. index. LC 24-2482. Reprint: McMinnville, Ore., Robin & Russ Handweavers, 1975.

Detailed and comprehensive handbook of lacemaking covering the techniques and patterns of both bobbin and needle lace. Illustrated with plates of pieces of old lace in the Victoria and Albert Museum. Contents: I, Pillow Lace; II, Outfit; III, Elementary Instruction; IV, How to Begin; V, Edges; VI, Raised Work; VII, Ornamental Clothwork; VIII, Hanging on and Fastening off for Bars, Nets and Fillings; IX, Bars; X, Nets: Plain; XI, Fillings; XII, Special Kinds of Lace; XIII, The Development of Hand-made Lace, Laces and Their Centres. Chronologically arranged bibliography, pp. 156-58.

2373   Clifford, Chandler R. **The Lace Dictionary**. New York, Clifford & Lawton, 1913. 156p. illus. index. Reprint: Detroit, Gale, 1981. ISBN 0810343118.

Popular dictionary covering terms used in all aspects of lacemaking illustrated with many photographs and drawings of details and structures. Particularly useful for identification of particular types of historic lace. No bibliography.

2374 Whiting, Gertrud. **A Lace Guide for Makers and Collectors; with Bibliography and Five-Language Nomenclature...** New York, Dutton, 1920. 415p. illus. LC 20-2109.

Valuable handbook of the techniques of lacemaking with polyglot list of terms and a comprehensive bibliography of 1958 titles, which is a valuable source for early titles and manuscripts.

General Histories and Handbooks

2375 Bath, Virginia C. **Lace.** Chicago, Regnery, 1974. 320p. illus. index. LC 73-20671.

Popular survey of lacemaking with emphasis on contemporary production and advice for amateur lacemakers. Has large number of useful plates of historic examples. Arrangement is by types of lace: Network; Needle Lace; Bobbin Lace; Mixed Lace. General bibliography, pp. 313-316.

2376 Caplin, Jessie F. **The Lace Book.** New York, Macmillan, 1932. 166p. illus. index. LC 32-25123.

Handbook for the identification of lace with good black and white plates and drawings. Contents: I, Laces, Their Importance, Identification, Forms, and Uses; II, Hand-made Lace; III, Machine-made Lace; IV, Materials Used in Making Lace. Tests; V, Real or Imitation Lace; VI, Identifying Laces. Lace Chart; VII, Care of Lace. Glossary of Lace Terms. Basic bibliography, pp. 163-64.

2377 Earnshaw, Pat. **Lace in Fashion: From the Sixteenth to the Twentieth Centuries.** London, Batsford, 1985. 144p. illus. index. ISBN 0713446420.

Survey history of the use of lace in European costume from the sixteenth to the twentieth centuries. Chapters on the five centuries on lace for children, lace on underwear, and peasant laces. Glossary of terms and sources of recommended reading, pp. 164-65.

2378 Frauberger, Tina. **Handbuch der Spitzkunde. Technisches und Geschichtliches uber die Nah-, Kloppel- und Maschinenspitzen.** Leipzig, Seemann, 1894. 272p. illus. index. LC 49-38757.

Old handbook/history of European lace and lacemaking with still-valuable information on techniques with surprisingly good plates of pieces of lace and extraordinary drawings illustrating the complicated manipulations in bobbin and pillow lace. Contents: I, Die Technik: 1, Die Vorläufer der Spitzen; 2, Die Technik der Nadelspitze; 3, Die Technik der Klöppelspitze; 4, Die Technik der Maschinenspitze; II, Geschichtliches. Bibliographical references in the footnotes.

2379 Head, Mrs. R. E. **The Lace & Embroidery Collector; a Guide to Collectors of Old Lace and Embroidery.** London, Barrie & Jenkins, 1922. Reprint: Detroit, Gale, 1974. 252p. illus. index. LC 74-2031.

Important early history of European lace and embroidery directed to collectors. Pieces illustrated are representative of the type accessible to the collector. Contents: I, The Developemnt of Lace; II, Italy (I)—Needle-point Lace; III, Italy (II)—Bobbin-Laces; IV, France (I)—Needle-point Laces; V, France (II)—Bobbin-Lace; VI, The Low Countries—Belgium, Flanders, Holland; VII, Germany and Northern Europe; VIII, Spain and Portugal; IX, England and Ireland; X, Lace Bobbins; XII, Lace in Relation to Costume; XII, The Identification of Lace; XIII, On Collecting Embroideries; XIV, Needlework prior to the Tenth Century; XV, From 900 to 1500; XVI, From

1500 to 1625; XVII, From 1625 to 1700; XVIII, From 1700 to 1820; XIX, Samplers. Appendices with glossary of terms, list of ecclesiastical embroidery in English provincial churches and museums, and bibliography.

2380   Henneberg, Alfred von. **Stil und Technik der alten Spitze**. Berlin, Wasmuth, 1931. 181p. illus.
An authoritative introduction to the history of European lace from the sixteenth century through the eighteenth century with an important collection of 181 plates with captions in German, English, French, and Italian, and descriptive notes in German. Plates include overall and detailed photographic illustrations of specimens, drawings illustrating techniques, and reproductions of works of art showing lace as costume. Contents: I, Allgemeine Geschichte der Spitze; II, Beschreibende Untersuchung der Alten Spitze: 1, Das Ornament, 2, Die Textur, 3, Die Technik; III, Zur Entwicklungsgeschichte der Spitze: 1, Die Stilepochen, 2, Stil und Zeitbestimmung, 3, Die Rolle der Persönlichkeit: Françoise Badar (1624-1677), 4, Schlußworte. Comprehensive, classified bibliography, p. 52.

2381   Jackson, Emily N. **A History of Hand-Made Lace**. London, Upcott Gill; New York, Scribner's, 1900. 245p. illus. index. Reprint: Detroit, Tower Books, 1971. LC 70-136558.
An old, standard history/handbook still useful for the detailed dictionary of lace appended to the text. Contents: I, The Evolution of Lace; II, Anecdotal History of Medieval Lace; III, Anecdotal History of Lace in the Seventeenth Century; IV, Anecdotal History of Lace in the Eighteenth Century; V, Anecdotal History of Lace in the Nineteenth Century; VI, Ecclesiastical Lace; VII, Lace Fans; VIII, Peasant Laces; IX, The Transport of Lace; X, The Care of Lace; XI The Literature of Lace (a useful bibliographical essay); A Dictionary of Lace.

2382   Jourdain, Margaret. **Old; a Handbook for Collectors...** London, Batsford, 1907. 121p. illus. index. Reprint: Detroit, Gale, 1981. ISBN 081034310X.
An older, once-standard survey of the history of European lace for the collector. Still a useful overview. Contents: I, Introduction; II, Lacis or Darned Netting; III, Cutwork (Reticella) and Punto in Aria; IV, Early Italian Bobbin Lace; V, Venetian Needlepoint and Burano Lace; VI, Milanese Lace; VII, Cretan; VIII, Flanders; IX, Belgian Lace; X, Mechlin and Antwerp Lace; Valenciennes and Dutch Lace; XII, Alençon and Argentan; XIII, Lille and Arras; XIV, Chantilly; XV, English Needlepoint; XVI, English Bobbin Lace; XVII, English Bobbin Laces; XVIII, Irish Laces; XIX, Blondes. Bibliographical references in the footnotes.

2383   Kraatz, Anne. **Lace: History and Fashion**. New York, Rizzoli, 1989. 192p. illus. index. ISBN 0847810291.
Lavishly illustrated history of lace in European fashion from the sixteenth century to the twentieth century. Contents: The Sixteenth Century: Openwork; The Seventeenth Century: Masculinity; The Eighteenth Century: Femininity; The Nineteenth Century: Virtuosity and Mechanics; The Twentieth Century: Art and Fashion; The Future; Laces of the World; The Making of Lace. Glossary of terms, select bibliography, pp. 190-191.

2384   Levey, Santina M. **Lace: A History**. London, Victoria and Albert Museum in association with W. S. Many & Sons, 1983. 140p. illus. index. ISBN 090128615X.
Authoritative, well-illustrated history of lace, lacemaking, and lace in costume in Europe from the sixteenth century to circa 1914. Contains 500 plates of pieces of lace and works of art depicting lace. Contents: I, The Origins of Lace; II, The Age of Cutwork: c. 1560 to c. 1620; III, The Triumph of Bobbin Lace: c. 1620 to c. 1675; IV, Baroque Lace: c.1650 to 1710; V, The Classic Laces: c. 1690 to c. 1789. Part I: The Laces and Their Technique; VI, The Classic Laces: c. 1690 to c. 1789. Part II: Fashion and Design; VII, The Neo-Classical Period: c. 1780 to c. 1815;

VIII, Lace of the Romantic Period: 1810 to 1851; IX, The Mid-century Lace Boom: 1851 to 1867; X, Lace in a Period of Instability: 1867 to 1914. Glossary and general bibliography, pp. 129-132.

2385   Moore, H. Hudson. **The Lace Book.** New York, Tudor, 1937. 206p. illus. index. LC S40-34.

Older, popular history of European lace. Contents: I, The Growth of Lace; II, Italian Lace; III, Flemish Lace; IV, French and Spanish Lace; V, English and Irish Lace. No bibliography.

2386   Morris, Frances, and Marian Hague. **Antique Laces of American Collectors.** New York, William Helburn for the Needle and Bobbin Club, 1920-26. 5v. illus. index. LC 20-12867.

Important catalog of lace made in various European centers and owned by various public and private collections in the United States. The majority of the pieces date from the seventeenth and eighteenth centuries. Introductory essays on lace used by American colonists in the seventeenth and eighteenth centuries. Detailed, descriptive catalog entries with bibliographical footnotes.

2387   Palliser, Fanny M. **History of Lace, Entirely Revised, Rewritten and Enlarged Under the Editorship of M. Jourdain and Alice Dryden...** London, Sampson Low, Marston, 1919. 536p. illus. index. Reprint: (3rd ed.). Detroit, Tower Books, 1971. LC 75-78219. (4th ed.). New York, Dover, 1984. ISBN 0486247422.

First published in 1875. Classic, pioneering history of lace. Still valuable for its scope and great number of references to and extracts from documentary sources. Contents: I, Needlework; II, Cut-Work; III, Lace; IV, Italy; V, Greece—Crete—Turkey—Malta; VI, Spain; VII, Flanders—Brussels (Brabant)—Mechlin—Antwerp—Flanders (West)—Franders (East)—Hainault; VIII, France to Louis XIV; IX, Louis XIV; X, Louis XIV (cont.); XI, Louis XV; XII, Louis XVI to the Empire; XIII, The Lace Manufactures of France—Alençon (Dép. Orne), Normandy; XIV, Agentan (Dép. Orne); XV, Isle de France—Paris (Dép. Seine)—Chantilly (Dép. Oise); XVI, Normany—Sein Inférieure—Clavados—Bretagne; XVII, Valenciennes (Dép. du Nord)—Lille (Dép. du Nord)—Arras (Artois) (Dép. Pas-de-Cailais)—Bailleul (Dép. du Nord); XVIII, Auverge and Vélay—Le Puy (Dép. Haute-Loire)—Aurillac and Murat (Dép. Cantal); XIX, Limousin—Lorraine—Champagne—Burgundy—Lyonnois—Orléanois—Berry—Poitou; XX, Holland, Germany, Switzerland, Austria and Hungary—Holland—Saxony—Germany (North and South)—Switzerland; XXI, Denmark—Sweden—Russia; XXII, England to Queen Elizabeth; XXIII, Queen Elizabeth; XXIV, James I to the Restoration—James I—Charles I—The Commonwealth; XXV, Charles II to the House of Hannover—Charles II—James II—William III—Queen Anne; XXVI, George I—George II; XXVII, Smuggling; XXVIII, George III; XXIX, The Lace Manufactuers of England; XXX, Bedfordshire—Buckinghamshire—Northamptonshire—Suffolk; XXXI, Wiltshire and Dorsetshire; XXXII, Devonshire—Honiton—Tolly Lace—Japan; XXXIII, Scotland; XXXIV, Lace Manufacturers of Scotland; XXXV, Ireland; XXXVI, Bobbin Lace and Machine Lace—Bobbin Net— France—Belgium—Machinery Lace. Bibliographical references in the footnotes.

2388   Powys, Marian. **Lace and Lace-making.** Boston, Branford, 1953. 219p. illus. index. LC 52-14187. Reprint: Detroit, Gale, 1981. ISBN 0810343126.

Survey history of lace written by a lacemaker and, consequently, useful for its explanation of techniques and materials. Contents: I, The Beauty of Lace; II, The Naming of Lace; III, The Pedigree of Lace (useful "family tree" of lace techniques); IV, The Key to Lace; V, Lace Design; VI, Ecclesiastical Lace; VII, Lace for Personal Adornment; VIII, Lace in Decoration; IX, Bridal Laces; X, Lace Collecting; XI, Directions for Making Lace; XII, Lace Mending, Cleaning and Care. Brief selected bibliography, p. 217.

2389 Schuette, Marie. **Alte Spitzen: Nadel- und Kloppelspitzen. Ein Handbuch fur Sammler und Liebhaber**. 4th ed. Braunschweig, Klinkhardt & Biermann, 1963. 247p. illus. index. (Bibliothek fur Kunst- und Antiquitätenfruende, Bd. 6).

Comprehensive, authoritative history of European needle and bobbin lace by a leading scholar in the history of textiles. Contents: I. Teil. Technik der Spitz; I, Ursprung und Vorläufer der Spitze, die deknüpfte Spitze; II, Vorstuffen der Nadelspitze; III, Nadelspitze: 1, Falche Nadelspitze mit quadritischen Steg-Grund; 2, Flache Nsadelspitze und Relief Nadelspitze und Reliefnadelspitze ohne Stege; 3, Grundspitze; 4, Technische Abaraten und Nachahmungen; IV, Klöppelspitze: 1, Flechtspitze; 2, Formenschlagspitze—Genua, Venedig; 3, Leienschlag mit und ohne Stege; 4, Leinenschlag mit Netzgrund; 5, Ziernetzspitze; 6, Kombinierte Spitzen—Bnadspitze. II. Teil. Geschichte der Spitze: V, Italien; VI, Franreich; VII, Die Niederlande; VIII, Spanien; IX, Deutschland; X, Egngland. Comprehensive bibliography, pp. 237-39. A standard work.

2390 Seguin, Joseph. **La dentelle. Histoire description- fabrication- bibliographie**. Paris, J. Rothschild, 1875. 214p. illus. index. LC 11-21534.

2391 Wardle, Patricia. **Victorian Lace**. New York, Praeger, 1969. 286p. illus. index. LC 69-11863.

Comprehensive history of European lace and lacemaking during the nineteenth century with important chapters on early machine-made lace. Contents: 1, Fashions in Lace in the Nineteenth Century; 2, France; 3, Belgium; 4, England; 5, Ireland; 6, Miscellaneous; 7, Machine-made Lace in England; 8, Machine-made Lace in France and Elsewhere. Appendix with summary of the basic techniques of lacemaking. Comprehensive bibliography, pp. 267-70.

National Histories and Handbooks

Belgium

2392 Paulis, L. **Pour connaitre la dentelle**. Antwerp, De Nederlandsche Boekhandel, 1947. 135p. illus. index.

Authoritative history/handbook of European lace with particular attention given to Belgian lace. Contents: Première Partie: Généralités; Deuxième Partie: Le Point a l'aiguille; Troisième Partie: La Dentelle aux fuseaux; Quatrième Partie: Dentelles "Tissées" a fils continus. Contains 48 plates of pieces of lace chiefly in Belgian museums. Bibliographical references in the footnotes.

Italy

2393 Ricci, Elisa. **Old Italian Lace**. Philadelphia, Lippincott, 1913. 2v. illus. LC 14-11605.

An old, standard history published in a limited edition of 300 copies. Emphasis is on works of the sixteenth, seventeenth and eighteenth centuries. Contains 757 high-quality plates illustrating pieces of lace and works of art depicting costumes featuring lace. Contents: v. 1: 1, Modano or lacis, drawn-thread work, Buratto; 2, Punto a reticello; 3, Punto in aria; v. 2: Bobbin laces: Venice, Genoa, Milan, Abruzzi. Bibliographical references in the footnotes.

Spain

2394 May, Florence L. **Hispanic Lace and Lace Making**. New York, Hispanic Society of America, 1939. 417p. illus. index. LC 39-13996.

Older but authoritative history of Spanish lace from the Middle Ages to the early twentieth century. Illustrations include works of art depicting lace. Contents: I, Origins of Lace. Some Types of Passementiere and Their Uses; II, Drawn Work and Cutwork. Network. Macramé; III, Needle and Bobbin Laces. Gold and Silver Laces—Punto de España; IV, Foreign Influences. The Ruff. Lace in the Seventeenth Century. Popular Designs; V, Silk Laces. Mantillas. Nineteeenth-Century Laces. Machine-made Laces; VI, Lace-making Centres in Spain: Andalucía. Castilla. Cataluña, Galicia. Valencia and Alicante. The Balaeric Islands. The Canary Island; VII, Hispanic Lace-making: Portugal and the Azores. The Philippine Islands. Mexico. South and Central America. Comprehensive bibliography, pp. 400-405.

United States

2395 Vanderpoel, Emily N. **American Lace and Lace-makers...** New Haven, Conn., Yale University Press, 1924. 14p. (text), 110 plates.

Important collection of 110 plates of American lace from early Colonial times to 1920 with a few examples of Native American beadwork and lacework bags. Descriptive notes to the plates. No bibliography.

TAPESTRY

Bibliographies

2396 Guiffrey, Jules M. J. **La tapisserie; bibliographie critique de la tapisserie dans les differents pays de l'Europe, depuis ses origines jusqu a nos jours.** Paris, Picard, 1904. 128p. index. LC 05-9286.

Comprehensive classified bibliography of 1,083 entries covering books, catalogs, and periodical articles on all aspects of European tapestry published to 1904. More important titles are annotated.

General Histories and Handbooks

2397 Ackerman, Phyllis. **Tapestry, the Mirror of Civilization...** New York, Oxford University Press, 1933. 451p. illus. index. Reprint: New York, AMS, 1970. ISBN 040400279X.

Comprehensive survey of tapestry from antiquity to the end of the nineteenth century. Contents: I, The Ancient Near East; II, The Empires of Rome; III, The Norseman and Their Descendants; IV, The Fourteenth Century; V, The Fifteenth Century; VI, The Fifteenth Century Weavers and Designers; VII, The Tapestry of the Reign of Marguerite of Austria; VIII, The Fontainebleau Looms; IX, The Flemish Renaissance; X, Catherine De'Medici and Henri III; XI, Rubens and the Seventeenth Century; XII, The Lesser Looms; XIII, The Far and Middle East; XIV, Peru and Mexico; XV, The Period of Louis XIV; XVI, The Period of Louis XV; XVII, The Tapestries of Goya; XVIII, The Nineteenth Century. Appendices with discussion of techniques, collections, collectors, and guild regulations. Bibliographical references in the notes and basic bibliography, pp. 431-33.

2398 Coffinet, Julien. **Arachne: ou l'art de la tapisserie.** Geneva, Office du Livre, 1971. 245p. illus. index. LC 72-325093.

History of Western tapestry from the Middle Ages to 1970 with emphasis on the technical aspects. Illustrations include many details of major works. Bibliographical footnotes.

2399 Göbel, Heinrich. **Wandteppiche. Leipzig, Klinkhardt und Biermann, 1923-24.** 3v. in 6. illus. index. LC 24-23990.

Standard history of western European tapestry from the Middle Ages to the end of the eightenth century. Contents: Teil I: Die Niederlande; Teil II, Die romanischen Länder; Teil III:

Die germanischen und slavischen Länder. Teil I and II have separate text and plates volumes; Teil III has text and plates in both volumes. Teil I also published in English: *Tapestries of the Lowlands* (New York, Brentano, 1924. Reprint: New York, Hacker Art Books, 1974). Comprehensive bibliography provided in the footnotes.

2400   Guiffrey, Jules M. J., et al. **Histoire générale de la tapisserie**. Paris, Societe Anonyme de Publications Periodiques, 1878-85. 3v. illus. index. Reprint: Osnabrück, Zeller, 1971. ISBN 3535015715.

An old, once-standard history of European tapestry from the Middle Ages to the eighteenth century. Extensive use of documentary sources, many of which are included as extracts in the text or in full in the appendices. Still indispensable. Corpus of 105 unmounted plates (some in color). Contents: v. 1 (pt. 1) by J. Guiffrey: Tapisseries françaises. Première période: Moyen Age (1302-1515); Deuxième période: Renaissance (1515-1660); Troisième période: Les Manufactures royales de tapisserie depuis Louis XIV jusqu'à nos jours (1660-1880); Appendices: Les Ateliers provincaux de la France: Aubusson, Felletin et Bellegarde; Lyon, Amiens; Cambrai, Limoges; Montpellier, Tours; Orléans, Bretagne; Châtillon, Cadillac, Béarn, Reims; Charleville; Angers, Gisors, Nancy; Troyes, Beauvais, Rouen; Marseille, Boulogne, Torcy. v. 2 (pt.2): Tapisseries italiennes, allemandes, russes, etc. by E. Müntz. Italie: Sienne; Pérouse; Urbin; Correggio; Modène; Vigevano; Gènes; Rome; Ferrare; Florence; Mondone; Venise; Naples; Turin. Allemagne: Le moyen âge; La Renaissance; L'atelier de Lauingen; Les ateliers de Frankenthal et de Clèves; La première manufacture de Munich; Autres ateliers allemands du XVIIe siècle; Le XVIIIe siècle. Manufactures de Munich, de Berlin, de Dresde, de Heidelberg; Suisse; Angleterre: Le moyen âge; La Renaissance; La manufacture de Mortlake; Le XVIIIe siècle; Espagne; Danemark; Hongrie, Pologne, Russie, Turquiie, Extr'me Orient. v. 3 (pt. 3): Tapisseries flamandes by A. Pinchart: Arras; Valenciennes; Lille; Douai; Ypres; Evirons de Lille; Bruges; Middelbourg (en Flabdres); Tournai; Mons; Binche; Enghien et les environs; Audenarde; Grammont; Lessines, Ath et Courtrai; Gand; Alots; Bruxelles. Extensive bibliographic references in the footnotes.

2401   Hunter, George L. **The Practical Book of Tapestries...** Philadelphia and London, Lippincott, 1925. 302p. illus. index. LC 25-25285.

Comprehensive history of European tapestries from the Middle Ages to the twentieth century. Once a standard work in English but still useful as a broad overview. Contents: I, Introduction; II, Primitive Tapestries; III, Early Gothic Picture Tapestries; IV, Gothic Religious and Allegorical Tapestries; V, Gothic Historical and Romantic Tapestries; VI, Gothic Country Life Tapestries; VII, Gothic Tapestries Rich in Gold; VIII, Flemish and French Renaissance Tapestries; IX, Gobelin Tapestries of the Seventeenth Century; X, Flemish Tapestries of the Seventeenth and Eighteenth Centuries; XI, Beauvais Tapestries; XII, Gobelin Tapestries of the Eighteenth Century; XIII, Aubusson Tapestries; XIV, German and Swiss Tapestries; XV, Italian Tapestries; XVI, English, Spanish, and Russian Tapestries; XVII, Tapestry Texture; XVIII, Tapestry Design; XIX, Tapestry Manufacture; XX, Tapestry Furniture Coverings; XXI, Modern Tapestries; XXII, Public Collections and Tapestry Literature. Bibliographical references in the footnotes. Complements the author's earlier work: *Tapestries, Their Origin, History and Renaissance* (2402).

2402   Hunter, George L. **Tapestries, Their Origin, History and Renaissance**. New York, Lane, 1913. 438p. illus. index. LC 13-90.

Still-useful survey of European and American tapestry with emphasis on techniques and chapters on care and exhibition. Contents: I, The Renaissance of Tapestries; II, Gothic Tapestries; III, Renaissance Tapestries; IV, Flemish and Burgundian Looms, Arras, Brussels, Tournai, Bruges, Enghien, Oudenarde, Middlebourg, Lille, Antwerp, Delft; V, English Looms. Mortlake, Merton, Barcheston, Windsor; VI, The Gobelins, Beauvais and Aubusson; VII, Other Looms.

American, Italian, German, Spanish, Russian, Swedish, Norwegian; VIII, The Texture of Tapestries. Arras Tapestries. Greek and Roman Tapestries. High Warp and Low Warp. The Process of Weaving; IX, Designs and Cartoons. Portraits in Tapestries. Counterfeit Arras. Animals in Tapestries. Verdures; X, Tapestry Signatures. Tapestry Captions, Tapestry Borders, Tapestry Shapes and Sizes and Measurements; XI, The Bible in Tapestries; XII, History and Romance in Tapestries; XIII, Tapestry. Point of View and Perspective, Tapestry Light and Shade; XIV, Care of Tapestries. How to Hang, Clean, Repair of Them; XV, Tapestry Museums, Collections, Expositions, Inventories, Sales and Books; XVI, Tapestries at the Metropolitan Museum of Art.

2403 Jarry, Madeline. **World Tapestry, from Their Origins to the Present**. New York, Putnam, 1969. 358p. illus. LC 68-22257.

Well-illustrated survey of European tapestries from the late Middle Ages to the twentieth century by a leading French expert. Contents: I, The Origins of Tapestry; II, Europe in the Fourteenth Century; III, The Arras and Tournai Workshops in the Fifteenth Century; IV, Tapestry at the Dawn of the Renaissance; V, The Sixteenth Century: Tapestry during the Renaissance; VI, The Seventeenth Century: From Rubens to Le Brun; VII, French Workshops in the Eighteenth Century; VIII, Tapestry Outside of France in the Seventeenth and Eighteenth Centuries; IX, Tapestry in the Nineteenth and Twentieth Centuries: Decline and Revival. Concluding essay on technique includes photographs of present-day practices. Comprehensive, classified bibliography, pp. 349-54.

2404 Müntz, Eugene. **A Short History of Tapestry: From the Earliest Times to the End of the 18th Century...** London and New York, Cassell, 1885. 399p. illus. LC 12-3923.

An old, standard survey written by a leading expert. Contents: I, Tapestry in Ancient Times; II, Tapestry amongst the Greeks; III, Tapestry in Rome before the Triumph of Christianity; IV, Tapestry in the East from the Beginning of the Christian Era to the Crusades; V, The Lower Empire; VI, Tapestry in the West, from the Ninth to the Twelfth Century; VII, The Thirteenth Century; VIII, The Fourteenth Century; IX, The Fifteenth Century; The Sixteenth Century; X, The Sixteenth Century; XI, The Sixteenth Century (continued); XII, The Seventeenth Century; XIII, The Seventeenth Century (continued); XIV, The Eighteenth Century; XV, The Eighteenth Century (continued); XVI, The Technique of Tapestry. Appendix with hints for collectors and repertory of marks. Bibliographical references in the footnotes.

2405 Schmitz, Hermann. **Bildteppiche; Geschichte der Gobelinwirkerei**. 3rd ed. Berlin, Verlag fur Kunstwissenschaft, 1922. 352p. illus. index. LC 47-35509.

Older, scholarly history of European tapestries from antiquity to the end of the eighteenth century with emphasis on stylistic development. Contents: Vorwort: Technik und Stil der Bildwirkerei, Bildwirker, Kartonzeichner und Maler; Die Verwendung der gewirkten Bildteppiche; Altertum, Byzanz und Islam; Deutsche gewirkte Teppiche des romanischen Stils; Französische und deutsche gewirkte Teppiche des 14. Jahrhunderts; Blütezeit der Bildwirkerei seit dem Anfang des 15. Jahrhunderts: Deutschland, Die Niederlande; Frankreich; Verschiedene Länder; Schluß. Stilentwicklung der Bildwirkerei im Zusammenhang. Appendix with facsimiles of marks on tapestries. Basic bibliography, pp. 349-52, and additional bibliography in the notes.

2406 Thomson, Francis P. **Tapestry, Mirror of History**. New York, Crown, 1980. 224p. illus. index. ISBN 0517534150.

Survey history of Western tapestry from antiquity to 1980. Written as an abridged and updated version of the author's father's work (2404). Contents: 1, The Nature of Tapestry; 2, The Founding of Western Tapestry Industries; 3, The Renaissance of the Sixteenth Century; 4, The Seventeenth Century; 5, From the Eighteenth to the Mid-Nineteenth Century; 6, A Century of British Tapestry Renaissance; 7, A Century of World Tapestry Renaissance. Appendices on tapestry identification with facsimiles of marks and signatures, glossary of terms, and essay on the art of dyeing. Bibliographies at the end of each section.

2407　Thomson, William G. **A History of Tapestry from the Earliest Times until the Present Day.** Rev. ed. New York, Putnam, 1931. 550p. illus. index. Reprint: Wakefield, E. P. Publishing, 1973. LC 74-157028.

First history of tapestry in English. Written by a man influential in the revival of tapestry weaving in Britain (Dovecot Tapestry Studios in Corstorphine). Contents: I, Pre-Christian Tapestry; II, Later Egyptian or Coptic Tapestries; III, Tapestry in Europe until the 14th Century; IV, The Parisian Tapestry Workshop in the 14th Century; V, Tapestries of Arras, Germany and England in the 14th Century; VI, Tapestries of Arras in the 15th Century; VII, Tapestry-Weaving in the Smaller Flemish Towns, France, Germany, Italy and Spain, 15th Century; VIII, Tapestries in England and Scotland during the 15th Century; IX, 15th and Early 16th Century Tapestries; X, Tapestry-Weaving in the Low Countries in the 16th Century; XI, 16th Century—Tapestry-Weaving in France, Italy, Germany, Sweden, Etc.; XII, 16th Century—England, Scotland and Ireland; XIII, 17th Century—England, Scotland and Ireland; XIV, Tapestry-Weaving in Flanders, Italy, Germany, Etc., in the 17th Century; XV, 17th Century—Workshops in France—Formation of the Goblins; XVI, The Gobelins and Manufactories in France and Italy; XVII, A Sketch of Tapestry-Weaving in Flanders, Germany and England from 1700 to the Present Day; XVIII, Tapestry Marks. Bibliographical references in the footnotes.

2408　Verlet, Pierre, et al. **Great Tapestries: The Web of History from the 12th to the 20th Century.** Lausanne, Edita S. A., 1965. 278p. illus. index. LC 67-2729.

Well-illustrated, popular survey of European tapestry by a team of French experts. Brief introductory essay for each period followed by color plates of major pieces with descriptive notes. Contents: Gothic Tapestry by P. Verlet; Classical Tapestry by M. Florisoone; Contemporary Tapestry by A. Hoffmeister; The Weaver's Art by F. Tabard. Basic bibliography, pp. 269-70.

2409　Ysselsteyn, Gerardina T. van. **Tapestry: the Most Expensive Industry of the XVth and XVIth Centuries...** The Hague, Van Goor Zonen, 1969. 232p. illus. index. LC 72-398050.

Important history of European tapestry making during the fifteenth and sixteenth centuries with emphasis on the economic questions of why and for whom tapestries were made. Contents: I, Introduction and Technic; II, The Burgundian Power; III, Paris; IV, Arras; V, Tournay; VI, Brussels; VII, The Country-side, Edingen, Audenarde; VIII, Tours, Touraine; IX, Bruges; X, Die Burg Rötteln; XI, Italy. Comprehensive, classified bibliography, pp. 204-215, and additional bibliography in the footnotes.

See also the museum catalogs: *Tapestries of Europe and of Colonial Peru in the Museum of Fine Arts, Boston* by A. S. Cavallo (Boston, The Museum, 1967. 2v. illus.).

Medieval Tapestries

2410　Heinz, Dora. **Europäische Wandteppische; ein Handbuch für Sammler und Liebhaber.** Band I: Von den Anfangen der Bildwirkerei bis zum Ende des 16. Jahrhunderts. Braunschweig, Klinkhardt & Biermann, 1963. 338p. illus. index. (Bibliothek fur Kunst- und Antiquitätenfruende, Band 37). LC 64-6573.

Authoritative survey of European tapestries from antiquity to the end of the sixteenth century with emphasis on distinguishing the work of various centers. Contents: Technik der Bildweberei; Die Anfange der Bildwirkerei im Altertum und ihre Geschichte bis zum 11. Jahrhundert; Die Wanteppiche der Romanik; Deutsche Wandteppiche des 14. Jahrhunderts; Die Französische und Niederländische Tapisseriekunst bis zum Ende der Spätgotik; Die deutschen Bildteppich der Spätgotik; Die Tapisseriekunst der Niederlande in der Renaissance und

Spät-renaissance; Die Manufaktur von Fontainebleau; Die italienische Tapisseriekunst bis zum Ende des 16. Jahrhunderts; Die deutsche Bildwirkerei im 16. Jahrhundert; Die Bild-wirkerei in den nordischen Ländern und in England bis zum Ende des 16. Jahrhunderts. Comprehensive, classified bibliography, pp. 319-31.

See also the author's introductory essay: *Medieval Tapestries*. (New York, Crown, 1967. 14p. (text), 20 plates. LC 67-15642).

See also the museum catalog: *La tapisserie medievale au Musée de Cluny*, by F. Joubert (Paris, Ministere de la Culture et de la Communciation, 1987. 224p. illus. index. ISBN 2711-820947).

Angers Apocalypse Tapestry

2411 Auzas, Pierre-Marie, et al. **L'Apocalypse d'Angers: chef-d'ouvre de la tapisserie medievale.** Fribourg, Suisse, Office du Livre, 1985. 195p. illus. index. ISBN 2826400134.

Well-illustrated, authoritative introduction to the Angers Apocalypse tapestry with stunning details as well as overall views of the series. Contents: La tenture de l'Apocalypse et la galerie du château d'Angers by P. M Auzas; Du Livre à la tenture de l'Apocalypse by F. Muel; Histoire de la tenture de l'Apocalypse by A. Ruais; Emblématique et histoire de l'art by C. de Mérindol; Conservation et restauration de la tenture de l'Apocalypse by C. de Maupeou; La tenture de l'Apocalypse by A. Ruais. Basic bibliography, p. 194, with list of nine earlier monographs.

Bayeux Tapestry

Bibliographies

2412 Brown, Shirley A. **The Bayeux Tapestry: History and Bibliography.** Woodbridge, Boydell Press, 1988. 186p. index. ISBN 085115509X.

Annotated bibliography of 465 titles on all aspects of the Bayeux tapestry arranged chronologically. Annotations are detailed and descriptive with particular attention given to the array of opinions concerning the date, provenance, and use of the famous embroidery. Two essays proceed the bibliography. The first traces in detail the history of the Bayeux tapestry from the listing of it in the inventory of the treasury of the Cathedral of Bayeux in 1476 to the installation in the Centre Guillaume le Conquérant in 1983. The second essay is a chronological review of the literature on the Bayeux Tapestry. Appendices with extracts from manuscript sources.

2413 Bernstein, David J. **The Mystery of the Bayeux Tapestry.** Chicago, Univ. of Chicago Press, 1987. 272p. illus. index. ISBN 0226044009.

Comprehensive, scholarly study of the style and iconography of the Bayeux Tapestry that underlines the English origin of the work by attempting to show an underlying theme of "resistance" through references to the Old Testament story of the Babylonian captivity. Contents: Part One: The Making of the Tapestry: I, The Patron; II, Provenance; III, Canterbury; from Anglo-Saxon to Norman; IV, The Englishness of the Tapestry: Style; V, The Englishness of the Tapestry: the Borders; VI, Continuous Narrative, Distinctive Format and the Idea of Triumph; Part Two: Iconography: Mixed Messages: VIII, The Politics of Art; IX, Visual Polyphony: Animals in the Borders; X, Centre Stage: King or Bishop?; XI, Victory at Hastings and the Death of Harold; XII, Conclusion to Part Two; Part Three: 'By the Waters of Babylon': XIII, The Bayeux Tapestry and the Hebrew Scriptures; XIV, A Story Frought with Meaning; XV, Conclusion of Part Three. Bibliographical references in the notes.

2414 Bertrand, Simone. **La tapisserie de Bayeux et la manière de vivre au onzième siècle.** Saint-Léger-Vauban, Yonne, Zodiaque, 1966. 317p. illus. index. (Introductions à la Nuit des Temps, 2). LC 66-7316.

Important, scholarly monograph on the Bayeux tapestry written by the conservator in charge of the work. Contents; 1, Matière et forme. Etude technique: A, Analyse des éléments textiles, B, Laine des broderies, C, Technique d'exécution, D, Les cartons ou le dessin, E, Caractère unique de la tapisserie; 2, Contexte historique; 3, Les inscriptions de la tapisserie; La vie au XIe siècle. Appendix with excerpts from documents on the Bayeux Tapestry dating from 1066 to 1966. Basic bibliography, p. 320.

2415 Levé, Albert. **La Tapisserie de la Reine Mathilde, dite la Tapisserie de Bayeux.** Paris, Laurens, 1911. 212p. illus. index. LC 33-32162.

Older study of the Bayeux Tapestry that seeks to establish that it was made in France and commissioned by Queen Mathilde as a gift to mark the consecration of the Cathedral of Bayeux in 1077.

2416 Parisse, Michel. **La tapisserie de Bayeux.** Paris, Denoël, 1983. 140p. illus. ISBN 2207-228665.

Study of the Bayeux Tapestry as work of propaganda analyzing the narrative from the point of view of modern cinematic techniques. Contents: I, Le récit en images; II, Lecture de la tapisserie: 1, Normandie et Angleterre face à face, 2, Une oeuvre de propogande, 3, Le choix d'un support, 4, Une conception filmique; III, Un documentaire du XIe siècle: 1, Les hommes et les femmes, 2, Les combattants, 3, La vie des nobles, 4, Les relations entre les hommes, 5, Les constructions, 6, L'artisanat, 7, le bestiaire; Annexe I. Sources et bibliographue; Annexe II. La Tapisserie de Bayeux devant les historiens; Annexe III. Fiche technique sur la Tapisserie.

2417 Stenton, Frank M., ed. **The Bayeux Tapestry: A Comprehensive Survey.** 2d ed. New York, Phaidon, 1965. 194p. illus. LC 65-28977.

Important collection of essays by British scholars on various aspects of the Bayeux Tapestry. Contents: The Historical Background by F. Stenton; Style and Design by F. Wormald; Technique and Production by G. W. Digby; Arms and Armour by J. Mann; The Costumes by J. L. Nevinson; History of the Tapestry by S. Bertrand; Inscriptions by F. Wormald; The Architecture by R. A. Brown. Select bibliography, pp. 87-83, is a classified and annotated list of books in all languages.

2418 Wilson, David M. **The Bayeux Tapestry.** New York, Alfred A. Knopf, 1985. 234p. illus. LC 85-40219.

Scholarly and authoritative study of the Bayeux Tapestry with illustrations based on new photographs with particular attention to the artistic background of the work and especially the similarities with contemporary English and Scandinavian art. Contents: I, The Inscriptions; II, The Commentary; III, The Story Told in the Tapestry; IV, Style, Art and Form; V, Buildings, Dress and Objects. Bibliographical references in the notes.

Unicorn Tapestry (Cloisters Museum, New York)

2419 Freeman, Margaret B. **The Unicorn Tapestries.** New York, Metropolitan Museum of Art; distributed by Dutton, 1976. 244p. illus. ISBN 0870991477.

Authoritative monograph on the early sixteenth-century Unicorn Tapestry series in the Cloisters. Thoroughly illustrated with detailed views of the seven pieces and many illustrations of other works of art used as stylistic and iconographical comparisons. Contents: 1, The Unicorn in Ancient and Medieval Texts; 2, The Unicorn in Medieval and Early Renaissance Art; 3, The

Birds and the Beasts of the Tapestries; 4, The Hunt; 5, The Groves of Trees, the Flowery Field, and the Gardens; 6, The AE the FR and Other Problems Relating to the Original Ownership of the Tapestries; 7, The Making of the Tapestries; 8, The Tapestries in the Inventories, Their Treatment During the French Revolution, and Their History in Later Years. Bibliographical references in the footnotes.

2420   Williamson, John. **The Oak King, the Holly King, and the Unicorn: The Myths and Symbolism of the Unicorn Tapestries.** New York, Harper & Row, 1986. 260p. illus. ISBN 0060155302.

Wide-ranging and not completely convincing analysis of the iconography of the Cloisters' tapestry. Contents: Part One. Seeing Old Art with New Eyes: 1, The History of the Unicorn Tapestries; 2, France in Transition: A Perspective of the Period; 3, The Fusion of Classical and Christian Gods; 4, Iconography and Its Meaning; 5, Myths of Death and Resurrection: The Oak King, the Holy King, the Wild Man, and Christ. Part Two: The Unicorn Tapestries: I, The Start of the Hunt; II, The Unicorn at the Fountain; III, The Unicorn Crossing the Stream; IV, The Unicorn Defends Himself; V, The Unicorn Is Killed and Brought to the Castle; VII, The Unicorn in Captivity; Conclusion; Diagrams Identifying the Flora of the Unicorn Tapestries. Selected bibliography, pp. 241-52.

Unicorn Tapestry (Cluny Museum, Paris)

2421   Erlande-Brandenburg, Alain. **La Dame à la Unicorne.** Paris, Editions de la Réunion des Musées Nationaux, 1977, n.p. ISBN 2711800881.

Well-illustrated introduction to the Cluny Museum Unicorn Tapestries by a leading medieval art historian. Offers a thorough summary of the various theories concerning the provenance, patronage and symbolism of the famous series. Contents: La Vue; L'Ouïe; Le Gout; L'Odorat; Le Toucher; A mon seul désir; La Dame à la Licorne Etude: I, Historique; II, L'iconographie; III, Les problèmes stylistiques. No bibliography.

2422   Jossua, Jean-Pierre. **La Licorne: Histoire d'un Couple.** Paris, Cerf, 1985. 133p. illus. ISBN 2204022993.

Scholarly monograph on the Cluny Unicorn tapestries with emphasis on the iconography. The author seeks to prove that the series was commissioned as a wedding gift and its iconography is chiefly concerned with marriage. Contents: Première partie: Repères historiques: I, Présentation de la licorne; II, La pucelle et la licorne dans l'art. Deuxième partie: Les Figures et le rêve: I, Tendre couple; II, Animal merveilleux; III, Corne sensible; IV, Miroir tendu, espace clos; Conclusion; Princiipaux témoins iconographiques. Bibliographical references in the footnotes.

Renaissance—Modern Tapestries

2423   Jarry, Madeleine. **La Tapisserie. Art du XXème siècle.** Freibourg, Office du Livre, 1974. 357p. illus. index. LC 75-509302.

Comprehensive, well-illustrated history of world tapestries from Art Nouveau to 1973 written by a leading French expert. Contents: Technique: La haute lisse; La basse lisse; Matériaux; La teinture; Transcription du carton par le tissage; Autres techniques; I, Préliminarires d'un renouveau: L'Agnleterre et les Ateliers de William Morris; La Tradition aux Gobelins; Recherches textiles de Nabis; Tapisseries de Maillol; Manzana-Pissarro; Scandinavie et Art Nouveau; Le Jugendstil: Les Ateliers de Scherrebek; Le Bauhaus; Sophie Taeuber-Arp; L'Italie et le groupe futuriste; Les expressionnistes allemands; Marie Cuttoli; Aubusson et Lurçat; Guillaume Janneau aux Gobelins; La Belgique; La Hongrie: Noémi Ferenczy; La Tchécoslovaquie et la Pologne; Les Etats-Unis; Le Japon; II, La Renaissance de la tapisserie française: Jean Lurçat et son oeuvre;

L'association des peintres cartonniers de tapisserie et l'école de Lurçat; Dufy, Gromaire, Dubreuil; La Compagnie des arts français: Jacques Adnet et la tapisserie, art d'intérieur; Les rustiques; Surréalisme et humour; Les exceptionnels; Le role de Pierrte Baudouin; La groupe de Denise René; La tapisserie abstraite; III, La tapisserie—art mondial 1963-1973: Conception et réalisation; La France; La Belgique et la Hollande; La Suisse, L'Allemagne, l'Autriche; La Grande-Bretagne; Les Pays scandinaves; Les Pays de l'Est; L'Espagne et le Portugal; L'Italie et le basin méditerranéen; L'Afrique; Les Amériques; Le Japon; L'Australie. Extensive, comprehensive bibliography in the notes classified by the table of contents.

2424 Kuenzi, Andre. **La nouvelle tapisserie**. Geneva, Les Editions de Novent, 1973. 303p. illus.
Survey of tapestry and related fiber art works from 1945 to 1970. Contents: La tapisserie classique; La nouvelle tapisserie; L a nouvelle tapisserie et le mur; La nouvelle tapisserie, l'espace et l'environnement. Appendix with brief biographies of major artists.

2425 Viale, Mercedes. **Tapestries: from the Renaissance to the 19th Century**. London, Cassell, 1988. 155p. illus. ISBN 0304321850.
Originally published: London, Hamlyn, 1969. Popular, pictorial survey of European tapestries from the sixteenth century to the nineteenth century. Color plates with descriptive notes.
See also the museum catalog: *European Post-medieval Tapestries and Related Hangings in the Metropolitan Museum of Art*, by E. A. Standen (New York, The Museum, 1985. 2v. illus. index. ISBN 0870994069).

National Histories and Handbooks

France

Bibliographies

2426 Marquet de Vasselot, Jean J., and Roger-Armand Weigert. **Bibliographie de la tapisserie, des tapis et de la broderie en France**. Paris, Colin, 1935. 354p. index. (Archives de l'art francais. Nouv. per., t. XVIII).
Comprehensive, classified bibliography of 2,700 books and periodical articles on all aspects of French tapestries, embroidery, and rugs published to 1932. Supplemented by bibliography in Weigert (2431). A standard reference work.

Dictionaries

2427 Viallet, Nicole. **Tapisserie; méthode et vocabulaire. Inventaire général des monuments et des richesses artistiques de la France**. Paris, Inventaire Général des Monuments et des Richesses Artistiques de la France, 1971. 148p. illus. LC 74-168740.
Part of the "Principes d'analyse scientifique" subseries of the Inventaire général des monuments et des richesses artistiques de la France (FA1523). Comprehensive, authoritative handbook of the techniques and materials of French tapestry from earliest times to the twentieth century. Contents: Introduction; Bibliographie; 1, Définition du domaine de la tapisserie; 2, Méthode d'analyse; 3, Instructions pratiques pour la consitution d'un dossier d'inevantaire; 4, Vocabulaire méthodique. Bibliography, pp. 2-5, is a classified list that includes works on non-French as well as French tapistries. A standard reference work.

Histories and Handbooks

2428 Kurth, Betty. **Gotische Bildteppiche aus Frankreich und Flandern**. Munich, Riehn & Reuch, 1923. 12p. (text). illus. (Sammelbande zur Geschichte der Kunst- und des Kunstgewerbes, Band 7).

Pictorial introduction to French and Flemish tapestries of the fourteenth through the sixteenth centuries. Brief but informative introductory essay is followed by well-selected plates with descriptive captions.

2429 Lestocquoy, Jean. **Deux siècles de l'histoire de la tapisserie, 1300-1500**. Paris, Arras, Lille, Tournai, Bruxelles. Arras, Commision départements des monuments historiques du Pas-de-Calais, 1978. 140p. illus. (Commission départementale des monuments historiques du Pas-de-Calis, Memoires, t. 19\19). LC 79-370381r85.

2430 Salet, Francis. **La tapisserie francaise**. Paris, Vincent, Freal, 1946. 23p. (text), 103 illus. LC 47-23909.

Pictorial survey of French tapestries from the Middle Ages to the twentieth century. Introductory essay written by a well-known French historian.

2431 Weigert, Roger-Armand. **French Tapestry**. London, Faber and Faber, 1962. 214p. illus. index. LC 62-1841/L/r883.

Translation of *La tapisserie française* (Paris, Laurens, 1956). Concise but authoritative survey of French tapestries from the fourteenth century to the twentieth century with glossary of terms, dictionary of designers and manufacturers, and classified bibliography, pp. 206-12, designed to supplement (up to 1955) the standard bibliography of Marquet de Vasselot (2426). Contents: I, Generalities; II, The Origins and Early History of Tapestry in the West, The Paris Workshops in the 14th Century; III, Franco-Flemish Tapestry down to 1450; IV, Franco-Flemish Tapestry from 1450 Onwards; V, French Tapestries of the 15th and Early 16th Centuries; VI, The Tapestries of the Renaissance; VII, The Paris Workshops in the 17th Century. The Gobelins Factory: 1662-1793; VIII, The Beauvais Factory in the 17th and 18th Centuries; IX, Aubusson and Other Factories in the 17th and 18th Centuries; X, The 19th and 20th Centuries.

See also the exhibition catalog: *Masterpieces of Tapestry from the Fourteenth to the Sixteenth Century*, by G. Souchal (New York, The Metropolitan Museum of Art, 1974. 222p. illus.).

Germany

2432 Kurth, Betty. **Die deutschen Bildteppiche des Mittelalters**. Vienna, Scholl, 1926. 3v. illus. index.

Scholarly history and catalog of German medieval tapestries written by a leading textile historian. Band 1: Text; Band 2, 3: Plates. Contents of Band 1: Die Technik; Vorgotische Bildwirkereien; Gotische Bildwirkereien; Katalog; Qullenanhang (collection of 56 documents related to tapestries). Catalog describes, with extensive bibliographical references, the works illustrated in the plates in Band 2 and Band 3. A standard work.

Great Britain

2433 Marillier, Henry C. **English Tapestries of the Eighteenth Century. A Handbook of Post-Mortlake Productions of English Weavers**. London, The Medici Society, 1930. 128p. illus. index.

Important handbook/survey of English tapestry weaving during the eighteenth century in the form of descriptions of major examples and sets arranged by subjects, e.g., Acts of the Apostles, Ovid's Metamorphoses, Months and Seasons, etc. Contains 48 small-scale plates. Occassional bibliographical reference in the footnotes.

Italy

2434   Grazzini, Nello Forti. **L'arazzo ferrarese**. Milan, Electa, 1982. 239p. illus. index.

Well-illustrated, scholarly history of Ferrara tapestries of the fifteenth and sixteenth centuries with a detailed description of the series attributed to Nicola Karcher in Lisbon. Contents: 1, L'età di Nicolò III d'Este; 2, L'età di Lionello e Borso d'Este; 3, Tra Quattrocento e Cinquecento; 4, Da Ercole II ad Alfonso II d'Este. Gli arazzi di Ferrara: Le Pietà, Le Metamorfosi, Le Pergoline, Le Storice di Ercole, Le Storie di San Giorgio e San Maurello, I Giochi di putti, Le Storie di Mosè, Le Storie della Vergine. Appendix with extracts from the D'Este inventories 1457-1469. Comprehensive bibliography, pp. 228-231.

2435   Viale, Mercedes. **Arazzi italiani**. Milan, Electa, 1961. 259p. illus. LC 66-57659.

Scholarly, survey/history of tapestry in Italy from the fifteenth century to the nineteenth century. Well-illustrated with descriptive captions to the plates, which include many color details. Text is divided by centuries. Glossary of technical terms, list of marks of manufacture, and classified bibliography, pp. 75-78.1469. Comprehensive bibliography, pp. 228-231.

Low Countries

2436   D'Hulst, Roger A. **Flemish Tapestries from the Fifteenth to the Eighteenth Century**. New York, Universe, 1967. 324p. illus. index. LC 67-12503.

Pictorial survey of Flemish tapestries. A 31-page introduction followed by 30 tapestries dating between 1373 and 1717 presented with introductory text, plates and descriptive notes. Basic bibliography, pp. 295.

2437   Göbel, Heinrich. **Tapestries of the Lowlands**. New York, Brentano, 1924 98p. illus. Reprint: New York, Hacker, 1974. LC 73-79046.

Translation of *Wandteppiche. pt. 1. Niederlande. See* (2396).

2438   Ysselsteyn, G. T. van. **Geschiedenis der Tapijtweverijen in de noordelijke Nederlanden...** Leiden, Leidische Uitgevermaatschappij, 1936. 2v. illus. index.

Comprehensive, scholarly, and authoritative history of tapestry weaving in the Northern Netherlands from the sixteenth to the eighteenth centuries with an important collection of 966 extracts from documents. Contents: Volume One: I, Benaming; II, Techniek en materiaal; III, Bewknopt geschiedkunig overzicht van de ontwikkeling der tapijtnijverheid; IV, De tapijtwerkers in vlaandeeren gedurende de 16e eeuw en hun uittocht naar den vreemde; V, De geschiedenis der tapijtwevererijen in de noordelijke Nederlanden; VI, De economische en sociale structuur van het bedrijf; VII, Ontwerpers, wevers en tapijten; VIII, Merken—Slot. Volume Two:Inleiding; Lijst van debruikte archieven; Lijst van afkortingen; General ordonnantie van Karel V; Uittreksels uit nederlandsche archieven de tapisserie betreffende; Tapitsiersregister; Lijst van geraadpleegde boeken; Merkentabellen; Voorloopige catalogus van noordnederlandsche tapijten. A three-page English summary concludes volume two. Comprehensive bibliography, pp. 471-76, and numerous references in the footnotes.

Spain

2439   Castellanos y Díaz, María. **Historia y técnica ornamental y decorativa de los bordados españoles**. Madrid, Antonio G. Izquierdo, 1922. 107p. illus.

Important history of embroidery and tapestry weaving in Spain from the fifteenth to the end of the seventeenth centuries with an appendix essay on the technique of the Goya tapestries. Contents: Ornamentación; Composiciones ornamentales; Ritmos; Decoración; Lienzos bordados: Bordados que decoran los ornementos liturgicos; Bordados populares; Bordados que decoran los ornementos liturgicos; El bordado en siglo XVI: Italia—España—El Escorial—Ornamentos liturgicos de El Escorial—Bordados que se exhiben en las Salas Capitulares; Breve reseña de los principales bordados que conservan nuestras Catedrales y Museos; Metodologia de la asignatura de Labores, en la Escuela primaria y en la Escuela Norma; La Tapiceria en España: Historia y técnica de la tapiceria de alto lizo; Tapices de Goya; Técnica de la tapiceria de alto y bajo lizo; Telar: Material—Operaciones—Cartón—Grabados reproduciendo el tapiz que hice para estudiar la técnica de la tapiceria de alto lizo. Bibliographical references in the footnotes.

2440   Valencia de Don Juan, Juan Bautista Crooke y Navarrot, conde de. **Tapices de la corona de España**. Madrid, de Blass, 1903. 2v. illus.

Important, early contribution to the history of Spanish tapestry based on pieces in the possession of the crown. Bibliographical references in the footnotes.

See also the exhibition catalog: *Tapestries and Carpets from the Palace of the Prado: Woven at the Royal Manufactory of Madrid* (New York, Putnam, 1917. 24p. illus. Publication of the Hispanic Society of America, no. 111, LC 17-29784).

Goya Tapestries

2441   Arnáiz, José M. **Francisco Goya, cartones y tapices**. Madrid, Espasa Calpe, 1987. 320p. illus. ISBN 842395843.

Scholarly monograph on Goya's work as a tapestry designer with a catalogue raisonné of 67 oil paintings, sketches and cartoons. Contents: I, La Real Fábrica de Santa Báarbara; II, Goya hasta su llegada a la Real Fábrica; III, Los primeros catones: Comedor de los principes de Asturias en El Escorial (mayo-octubre de 1775); IV, Comedor de los principes de Asturias en el Palacio de El Pardo: primera seie (octubre de 1776-enero de 1778); V, Dormitorio y antedormitorio de los principes de Asturias en El Pardo (mayo de 1778-enero de 1780); VI, La suspensión de los trabajos en Santa Bárbara (1780-1786); VII, Comedor de los principes de Asturias en el Palacio de El Pardo: segunda serie (1787); VIII, Ultimos trabajos (1788-1792); IX, Los bocetos. Appendix with documents in extract and facsimile. General bibliography, pp. 228-229, and further bibliography in the footnotes and catalog.

CHAPTER NINETEEN

TOYS AND DOLLS

BIBLIOGRAPHIES

2442   Lutz, Nacie A. **Dolls. A Complete Bibliography**. Newport, Calif., The Doll Works, 1981. 286p. illus. index. ISBN 0940070006.
   Annotated and classified bibliography of 779 mostly popular books in English on dolls and doll collecting. Useful for literature on collecting.

DICTIONARIES AND ENCYCLOPEDIAS

2443   Coleman, Dorothy E., and Evelyn J. Coleman. **The Collector's Encyclopedia of Dolls**. New York, Crown, 1968. 697p. illus. LC 68-9101.

2444   Coleman, Dorothy E., Elizabeth A. Coleman, and Evelyn J. Coleman. **The Collector's Encyclopedia of Dolls**. Volume Two. New York, Crown, 1986. 1266p. illus. index. ISBN 0517557967.
   The two Coleman dictionaries constitute the most comprehensive dictionary of American and European dolls covering types, styles, materials, construction, and makers and manufacturers. Emphasis is on dolls of the late nineteenth and early twentieth centuries with information on all major manufacturers including facsimiles of their marks. The second volume should be consulted first, as it has references back to the information in the first in the text and in the indexes. Both dictionaries have comprehensive, classified bibliographies before the indices. The bibliography in volume two is especially valuable for the list of catalogs of manufacturers and distributors. A standard work for collectors and students of the history of dolls.

2445   Coleman, Elizabeth A. **Dolls: Makers and Marks Including Addenda**. 2d ed. Washington, D.C. n.p., 1966. 161p. illus. LC 66-25627.
   Dictionary of dollmakers active between 1850 and 1880 with facsimiles of marks. Most of the information has been subsumed by the author's subsequent encyclopedia (2441).

HISTORIES AND HANDBOOKS

2446   Allemagne, Henry R. d'. **Histoire des jouets...** Paris, Hachette, 1902. 316p. illus. index. LC 20-14745.
   Comprehensive history of toys from prehistory to the end of the nineteenth century. Occasional bibliographical footnotes.

2447   Bachmann, Manfred, and Claus Hansmann. **Dolls the Wide World Over**. New York, Crown, 1973. 240p. illus. LC 72-94617.

Pictorial survey of world dolls from prehistoric times to the twentieth century with emphasis given to the general cultural context. Illustrated with pieces chiefly in the museums of the former German Democratic Republic. Contents: 1, Primitive Forms of the Doll; 2, Craftsmen-made Dolls; 3, The Doll as a Mirror of Social Realities; 4, The Doll Culture of the Eighteenth Century; 5, The Doll in the Nineteenth Century; 6, The Doll in the Twentieth Century, the 'Century of the Child'; 7, Dolls from East and South-East Asia; 8, Souvenir Dolls—Ambassadors of Good Will. Bibliography, pp. 200-02.

2448   Barenholtz, Bernard, and Inez McClintock. **American Antique Toys, 1830-1900**. New York, Abrams, 1980. 286p. illus. index. ISBN 0810906686.

Well-illustrated survey of toys made in America between 1830 and 1900 with emphasis on the ways toys were used. Contents: The Barenholtz Collection; Historical Background; Toys to Grow On; Symbols of Freedom; Familiar Animals; Race and Chase; Fairy Tales and Fantasy; Strictly for Pleasure; The Circus; The Workaday World; Identification and Trademarks; The Manufacturers. General bibliography, p. 282.

2449   Boehn, Max von. **Dolls and Puppets**. New York, Cooper Square, 1966. 521p. illus. index. LC 65-25496.

Translation of: *Spielzeug und Puppen*. Comprehensive, pioneering history of Western dolls and puppets from antiquity to the twentieth century. Contents: Part I: Dolls. I, Prehistoric Dolls; II, Ancestor Images; III, Fetishes, Amulets, and Talismans; IV, Image Magic; V, Votive Images; VI, Funeral and Other Images; VII, Waxworks and the Mannequin; VIII, Toy Dolls in Ancient Times; IX, Early Toy Dolls in Europe; X, The Fashion Doll; XI, The Toy Doll in the Nineteenth Century; XII, The Toy Doll in the Modern Period; XIII, Dolls of Exotic Peoples; XIV, Dolls Used for Decorative Purposes; XV, Porcelain Figures; XVI, Utensils in Doll Form; XVII, The Doll and the Stage; XVIII, Edible Dolls; XIX, The Doll in Literature. Part II: Puppets: I, Automata and Movable Images; II, The Origin of the Puppet-Show; III, Table Decorations and the Christmas Crib; IV, The Tin Soldier; V, The Puppet-Show in Antiquity; VI, Marionettes in the Sixteenth to the Eighteenth Century; VII, Marionettes in the Nineteenth Century; VIII, The Shadow Theatre in the Orient; IX, Occidental Shadow Theatres; X, Marionettes in the Far East; XI, The Puppets of To-day; XII, How Our Marionette Theatre Started, The Puppet-play of Doctor Faust (text). Bibliography, pp. 481-506, is an expanded version of the bibliography in the German edition and is a major resource for the literature in all languages to 1930.

2450   King, Constance E. **The Collector's History of Dolls**. London, R. Hale; New York, St. Martin's Press, 1978. 608p. illus. index. ISBN 0312150253.

Comprehensive history of dolls throughout the world from ancient Egypt to the twentieth century. Chapters one through eight provide a survey history, chapters nine through eighteen deal with dolls made of particular materials (bisque, wax, cloth, etc.) and made in certain countries (Germany, France, England, America), chapter nineteen gives practical advice on collecting dolls. Glossary, list of doll museums, and basic bibliography, pp. 599-601. A standard collector's handbook.

2451   King, Constance E. **Antique Toys and Dolls**. New York, Rizzoli; South Kensington, Christie's, 1979. 256p. illus. index. ISBN 0847802787.

Richly illustrated survey of toys and dolls from antiquity to the present. Contents: Early Toys; The Toy Horse; Tin Toys; Political Toys and the Model Theatre; Dolls in Adult Form; Child-like Dolls; Soft Toys; The Miniature World; Board Games and Jigsaw Puzzles; Toy Animals and Their Settings. Appendix with advice to collectors. Bibliography of basic books, pp. 250-251.

See also the exhibtion catalog: *First Collections: Dolls and Folk Toys of the World*, by M. Longenecker, ed. (La Jolla, Calif., Mingei International Museum of World Folk Art, 1987. 158p. illus. ISBN 0914155059).

See also the price guide: *Dolls & Toys*, by T. Curtis (Galashiels, Selkirshire, Lyle Pub., 1982. 254p. illus. ISBN 0698111923).

AMERICAN TOYS AND DOLLS

2452　McClintock, Inez, and Marshall McClintock. **Toys in America**. Washington, D.C. Public Affairs Press, 1961. 480p. illus. index. LC 59-13657.

Comprehensive history of American toys from Colonial times to 1950. Illustrations include reproductions of old advertisements as well as actual examples. Includes games. Contents: 1, Colonial Play; 2, New Nation, New Games; 3, Toy Craftsmen; 4, Early Toy Manufactories; 5, Games, Books and Other Amusements; 6, Christmas Rush—Early 19th Century Style; 7, "The Child's Benefactor"; 8, Ingenious Pigs and Acrobats; 9, Sports and Vehicles (1850-1875); 10, New Dolls and Books (1850-1875); 11, Metal Toys and Board Games (1850-1875); 12, On the Move—With Sound Effects (1875-1900); 13, More Toys That Really Worked (1875-1900); 14, Old Favorites Change (1875-1900); 15, The Teddy Bear Story; 16, Big Toys and Big Names; 17, Toy Trusts, War, and Competition; 18, A Billion Dollars' Worth of Toys; 19, The Future of American Toys. Appendix with list of American toy manufacturers before 1900. Comprehensive bibliography, pp. 465-69.

See also the author's *Antiques of American Childhood* (New York, Potter, 1970).

2453　Lavitt, Wendy. **Dolls**. New York, Knopf, 1983. 478p. illus. index. ISBN 039471542X.

In the series: "The Knopf Collectors' Guides to American Antiques." Pocket-size guide to American antique dolls. Includes dolls in a variety of materials, including folk and Indian dolls and dolls imported into the United States. Contains 357 pieces arranged in rough chronological order. Entries give descriptions, materials, marks and dimensions, makers, origin and period, comments, and hints for the collector. Price guide and repertory of marks given in the appendix.

2454　Whitton, Blair. **Toys**. New York, Knopf, 1984. 478p. illus. index. ISBN 0394715268.

In the series: "The Knopf Collectors' Guides to American Antiques." Authoritative, comprehensive collector's guide to American toys of the nineteenth and twentieth centuries. Includes examples of European-made toys commonly imported into the United States. The 351 toys are arranged into groups by type. The pieces are illustrated by good-quality color plates and have detailed descriptions with special commentary on the value of the pieces to the collector. Price list giving estimates of the retail value of pieces around 1980 is provided at the end. Useful chapter on how to evaluate toys and repertory of major manufacturers and their marks. General bibliography, pp. 454-56.

See also the exhibtion catalog: *The Stuff of Dreams: Native American Dolls*, by M. J. Lenz (New York, Museum of the American Indian, 1986. 96p. illus. ISBN 0934490430).

See also the price guides: *Long, Ernest and Ida Long. Dictionary of Toys Sold in America*, 2v. (Mokelumne Hill, Calif., n.p. 1971, 1978), and Friz, Richard, *The Official Price Guide to Collectible Toys*, 5th ed. (New York, House of Collectibles, 1988. 432p. illus. index. ISBN 0876370881).

EUROPEAN TOYS AND DOLLS

2455   Cieslik, Jürgen, and Mariann Cieslik. **German Doll Encyclopedia**. Cumberland, Md., Hobby House, Inc., 1985. 356p. illus. index. ISBN 0875882382.

Comprehensive dictionary of German dolls and dollmakers produced with extensive use of documentary sources. Entries give documentary history of the firm or maker, facsimiles of marks, reproductions of advertisements, and illustrations of actual pieces. German dollmaking was a major export industry in the nineteenth and early twentieth centuries and the American and British markets were especially large. There were, in addition, numerous independent—often women—artists who designed and made "art dolls" alongside the mass produced wares of Thuringia. Glossary of German terms, bibliography of source material, pp. 355-56. General index and indexes by mold marks and numbers.

2456   Fawcett, Clara H. **Dolls**. Boston, Charles T. Branford, 1964. 282p. illus. index. LC 64-16263.

Popular history with emphasis on nineteenth century and modern dolls. Chapter on early history, restoration and repair, list of doll museums in the United States, and list of collector's dolls patented in America. Classified list of books, pp. 268-73.

2457   Fawdry, Kenneth, and Marguerite Fawdry. **Pollock's History of English Dolls & Toys**. London, Ernest Benn, 1979. 214p. illus. index. ISBN 0510000495.

Popular history of English dolls and toys from the earliest time to 1975. Contents: My Toys 1975-1950; Mama's Toys 1950-1925; Grandma's Toys 1925-1900; Queen Victoria's Dolls 1900-1800; Queen Anne's Toys 1800-1700; King Charles, Queen Bess and Beyond. An unusual feature is the use of autobiographical quotes by various individuals recalling their playthings. Illustrated with contemporary scenes of toys in use, advertisements by toy manufacturers, as well as actual pieces. Bibliography, pp. 208-09, arranged by chapters.

2458   Fraser, Antonia. **Dolls**. New York, Putnam, 1963. 128p. illus. index. LC 63-15526.

Authoritative survey of world dolls from antiquity to the present with emphasis on English and American dolls of the nineteenth century. Brief bibliography of basic books.

2459   Fraser, Antonia. **A History of Toys**. New York, Delacorte, 1966. 256p. illus. index. LC 66-20120. Another edition: New York and London, Spring, 1972. LC 72-170632.

Authoritative survey/history of toys and dolls from antiquity to the mid-twentieth century illustrated with 290 plates of representative pieces and contemporary advertisements and representations of toys and dolls in works of art. Contents: 1, The Nature of Toys; 2, Ancient and Primitive Playthings; 3, Toys of the Greeks and Romans; 4, Medieval Childhood; 5, Toys in the Age of the Renaissance; 6, The Expanding Eighteenth-Century World; 7, Movable Toys; 8, Optical Toys and the Juvenile Theatre; 9, More Nineteenth-Century Toys; 10, The Doll and Her Belongings; 11, The Nursery Before the First World War; 12, Toy-making as an Industry; 13, Toys in the Twenties and Thirties; 14, Modern Times. Select bibliography, pp. 249-50, and additional bibliography in the notes.

2460   Fritzsch, Karl E., and Manfred Bachmann. **An Illustrated History of Toys**. London, Abbey, 1965. 194p. illus. Reprint: New York, Hastings House, 1978. LC 66-31982.

Survey of German toys, mostly from the eighteenth to the twentieth centuries, illustrated with 104 plates of examples in museums of the former German Democratic Republic. Contents: A Contribution to the History of Toy Making in Germany: Home-made Toys; Toys from the Guild's Workshops; Nuremberg's Importance in the Toy Trade; Oberammergau Carvings;

Berchtesgaden Ware; Toys from the Gröden Valley; Sonneberg and the Meiningen Uplands; Toy Country of the Erzgebirge. Bibliography, pp. 193-94, lists chiefly works in German.

2461   Gordon, Lesley. **Peepshow into Paradise, a History of Children's Toys**. London, Harrap, 1953. 264p. illus. index. LC 54-9928.
       American edition published by De Graff (New York, 1954). Popular history of world dolls from prehistory to the twentieth century. Illustrations chosen from museum pieces and a selection of pieces of types accessible to the collector.

2462   Gröber, Karl. **Kinderspielzeuge aus alter und neuer Zeit**. 2nd ed. Edited by Juliane Metzger. Hamburg, M. von Schröder, 1965, 221p. illus. index. LC 66-57981.
       Comprehensive and authoritative survey of toys, dolls, and other playthings from antiquity to the beginnings of the mass-produced wares of the nineteenth century. Contains 100 pages of plates with particular attention given to German dolls and dollhouses of the eighteenth and nineteenth centuries. Comprehensive bibliography, p. 211. Appendix: "In Memoriam Karl Gröber" contains a bibliography of the author's writings.

2463   Hildebrandt, Paul. **Das Spielzeug im Leben des Kindes**. Berlin, G. Söhlke, 1904. 421p. illus. index. Reprint: Düsseldorf, Diedrichs Verlag, 1979. ISBN 3424006556.
       Pioneering study of toys in relationship to the life of children in the eighteenth and nineteenth centuries. Contents: 1, Künstlerische Speile; II, Hand-und Kunstfertigkeitspiele; III, Maschinen-Spielzeug und mechanische Kunstwerke; IV, Wissenschaftliche Spiele; V, Gesellschaftsspiele; VI, Kampf-, Kriegs-, Soldaten- und Heldenspiele; VII, Figurenspiele, besonders mit Tieren; VIII, Das Puppen-oder Kinderfigurenspiel; IX, Das Kinderzimmer; X, Bilderbücher, Märchen, Sagen und Erzählungen. Bibliography, pp. 411-414.

2464   Hillier, Mary. **Dolls and Doll Makers**. New York, Putnam, 1968. 256p. illus. index. LC 68-20629.
       Popular history from prehistoric and ancient times to the present, including primitive and Oriental dolls. Chapter on folk dolls and useful list of dollmakers and their marks. Brief bibliography of basic books.

2465   Kollbrunner, Curt F. **Figurines d'étain; soldats de collection**. Fribourg, Office du Livre, 1979. 228p. illus. index.
       Comprehensive, authoritative history of European tin soldiers and other figurines from 1700 to the First World War with emphasis on Swiss manufacturers. Contents: Les figures d'étain en tant que jouets, de 1700 environ jusqu'au- delà de la Première Guerre mondiale (essay by P. M. Mäder); Fabrication des figurines; Présentation des figurines; Deux exemples historiques; Figurines, groups et dioramas; Expositions dans les musées; Catalogue des fondeurs et graveurs de figurines d'étain (by P. M. Mäder). Comprehensive, classified bibliography, pp. 219-27.

2466   Tosa, Marco. **Classic Dolls**. New York, Abbeville Press, 1989. 272p. illus. ISBN 0896-599728.
       Translation of *Effetto bambolla* (Milan, Ideallibri, 1987). Richly illustrated survey of European dolls from ancient times to 1920 with emphasis on porcelain dolls of the nineteenth and early twentieth centuries. Contents: 1, The Early Years; 2, The Golden Age; 3, The Great French Doll-makers; 4, German Genius and the Bébé Caractère; 5, The Invention of the Mechanical Doll; 6, Promoters of Fashion; 7, The Italian Scene; 8, Art and the Doll. Collection of 87 plates of dolls, mostly in private collections, with descriptive captions.

2467   White, Gwen. **Antique Toys and Their Background**. New York, Arco, 1971. 260p. illus. index. LC 74-153651.

Popular history/handbook covering games and novelties as well as toys, with emphasis on the nineteenth century. Useful chapter on earlier history, section on marks with index, and a bibliography of basic books, pp. 254-55.

2468   ———. **European and American Dolls and Their Marks and Patents**. London, Batsford; New York, Putnam, 1966. 274p. illus. index. LC 66-24567.

Comprehensive handbook/history of European and American dolls by a leading expert. Chapter on marks has repertory of facsimiles. Contains 353 well-selected plates with descriptive captions. Contents: I, Materials: Wood, Papier Maché and Other Compositions, Ceramics, Leather, Wax, Rag, Rubber, Metals, Celluloid; II, Details: Hair, Eyes, Joints, Dress, White Work; III, Noveltier: Pedlar Dolls, Talking and Singing Dolls, Walking and Crawling Dolls, Feeding Dolls, Swimming Dolls, Oddities, Upside-down Dolls and Skipping Dolls, Dolls with More Than One Face, Paper Dolls; IV, Marks; V, Makers Name. Basic bibliography, p. 268.

CHAPTER TWENTY

WALLPAPER

BIBLIOGRAPHIES

2469　Entwisle, E. A. **A Literary History of Wallpaper**. London, Batsford, 1960. 211p. illus. LC 61-19420.

Comprehensive bibliography of books and periodical articles on wallpaper published between 1509 and 1960 listed chronologically by date of publication. Includes many general works, often of a literary nature, that mention wallpaper in passing and those passages are reprinted with the citation. Contains 127 plates illustrating wallpaper manufacture and use of wallpaper.

GENERAL HISTORIES AND HANDBOOKS

2470　Entwisle, E. A. **The Book of Wallpaper; A History and an Appreciation**. London, A. Barker, 1954. 151p. illus. index. LC 55-19718.

Authoritative survey of wallpaper in Europe from the seventeenth century to the twentieth century. Contents: 1, The First Wallpapers; 2, Chinese Wallpapers; 3, London Paperhanging Makers; 4, Papier Maché, Painted Papers and Print Rooms; 5, Growing Popularity of Wallpapers; 6, Wallpapers at the Great Exhibition; 7, William Morris and Other Wallpaper Designers; 8, Twentieth Century Achievements. No bibliography.

2471　Greysmith, Brenda. **Wallpaper**. New York, Macmillan, 1976. 208p. illus. index. LC 76-3384/r84.

Survey of European wallpaper from the sixteenth century to circa 1950. Contains 151 plates with descriptive captions. Appendix with advice on how to search for and uncover old wallpaper. Basic bibliography, pp. 202-04.

2472　McClelland, Nancy V. **Historic Wall-papers; from Their Inception to the Introduction of Machinery**. Philadelphia, Lippincott, 1924. 458p. illus. index. LC 24-25785.

Older history of wallpaper in Europe and America from the seventeenth century to the middle of the nineteenth century. Still useful as an overview. Contents: I, Scope of This History; II, Period I. The Earliest Block-printed Papers in France; III, Period I. The First Block-Stamped Papers in England; IV, Period II. Papers Imitating Tapestries and Woven Stuffs; V, Period III. Paper Imitating Printed Fabrics; VI, Chinese, Anglo-Chinese, and Franco-Chinese Papers; VII, Period IV. Paper Imitating Painted Panels—French; VIII, Period IV. Paper Imitating Painted Panels—English; IX, Period V. The Epoch of Scenic Papers; X, Painted Scenic Papers, Fireboards, Borders, Overdoors and Screens; XI, Early American Wall-papers; XII, Some Famous Scenic Papers and Their Owners; XIII, Translation from Dufour's Booklet on the Captain Cook Wall-paper; XIV, Conspectus of Biography of Wall-paper Designers, Manufacturers, and Dealers from 1500 to 1840; XV, Wall-papers Issued by Some of the French Fabricants of the Eighteenth and Nineteenth Centuries. Comprehensive, classified bibliography, pp. 447-449. A classic work still useful as an overview and as a mine of information contained in the numerous extracts from documents in the text.

2473 Olligs, Heinrich, ed. **Tapeten. Ihre Geschichte bis zur Gegenwart**. Braunschweig, Klinkhardt & Biermann, 1969-1970. 3v. illus. index. LC 74-578679.

Comprehensive, scholarly history of wallpaper and other decorative wall coverings from the late Middle Ages to the twentieth century. Essays by various experts. Contents: Bd. 1: Tapeten-Geschichte; Bd. 2: Fortsetzung Tapeten-Geschichte; Bd. 3: Technik und Wiltschaftliche Bedeutung.

2474 Oman, Charles C. **Wallpaper: an International History and Illustrated Survey from the Victoria and Albert Museum**. New York, Abrams, 1982. 486p. illus. index. ISBN 0810917785.

Comprehensive, authoritative history of wallpaper based on the great collections of the Victoria and Albert Museum, London. Contents: Part One by C. C. Oman; Part Two by J. Hamilton; Catalogue; Anonymous Wallpapers and Wallpaper Designs; Pattern Books; Designers. Comprehensive bibliography, pp. 457-66.

2475 Teynac, Francoise, Pierre Nolot, and Jean-Denis Vivien. **Wallpaper, a History**. New York, Rizzoli, 1982. 251p. illus. index. ISBN 0847804348.

Well-illustrated survey of wallpaper from earliest times to the present. Excellent descriptions and illustrations of techniques. Contents: Part I: From the Origins of Wallpaper to the Age of Printing: 1, The Ancestors of Wallpaper; 2, Influences and Discoveries; 3, The Golden Age: Johan Baptist Jackson (1701-77), Georgian and Regency Papers, German Wallpaper Makers, Jean-Baptiste Réveillon (1725-1811), After the Revolution, Panoramic or Landscape Wallpapers; American Wallpapers; 4, Grandeur and Decadence: Technical and Artistic Refinements in France (1815-30), The Industrial Age and the Great Exhibitions, The Union of Art and Industry, The Floral Motif; Part II: The Industrial Age: 1, The Last Great Styles: William Morris, a New Spirit in Wallpaper, Art Nouveau, Young America, Artistic Influences in France, From Jugendstil to Bauhaus; 2, Contemporary Wallpapers: The New German School, New Work in America, England: Old and New Themes; France between the Wars, France Today, Publishers of Wallpaper, Important Wallpaper Exhibitions. Part III: Wallpaper and the Arts: 1, Wallpaper and Literature, 2, Wallpaper and Painting; Part IV: Manufacturing Techniques: 1, Early Techniques; 2, Industrial Techniques. Comprehensive bibliography, pp. 235-38.

See also the Victoria and Albert Museum handbook: *An Introduction to Wallpaper* (London, M.S.S.O., 1983. 48p. illus. ISBN 011290386).

See also the museum catalogs: *Wallpapers: A History and Illustrated Catalogue of the Collection of the Victoria and Albert Museum*, by C. C. Oman and J. Hamilton (London, Sotheby, 1982. 486p. illus. index. ISBN 0856670960) and *Deutsches Tapetenmuseum Kassel*, by E. W. Mick (Kassel, Thiele & Schwartz, 1984. 144p. illus. ISBN 3878160445).

AMERICAN WALLPAPER

2476 Lynn, Catherine. **Wallpaper in America: From the Seventeenth Century to World War I**. New York, W.W. Norton, 1980. 533p. illus. index. ISBN 0393014487.

Well-illustrated, scholarly history of wallpaper in America from colonial times to the early twentieth century. Contents: Part One: The Seventeenth and Eighteenth Centuries. 1, The Earliest American Wall Hangings; 2, How Wallpaper Was Made; 3, Eighteenth-Century English Wallpaper Style; 4, Eighteenth-Century French Wallpaper Styles; 5, Oriental Wallpapers; 6, Eighteenth-Century American Wallpapers; 7, The Paper Hanger's Stock in Trade; 8, Color Schemes and the Use of Wallpapers. Part Two: The Nineteenth Century: 9, French Scenic Wallpapers; 10, French Wallpaper Ornaments of the Early and Mid-Nineteenth Century; 11, French Wallpapers and the Development of the American Craft; 12, Repeating Patterns of the Early Nineteenth Century; 13,

Bandboxes; 14, Making Wallpaper by Machine; 15, 1840 to 1870: The Imprint of Machines, the Elaboration of Styles; 16, The 1870s and 1880s: A Major Change in Taste; 17, 1890 to 1915: Revivals and the Pursuit of Novelty. Appendices with dictionary of colors used in eighteenth and nineteenth century wallpaper, checklist of American manufacturers, list of wallpaper reference collections, and essay on sources. Selected bibliography, p. 514, and extensive coverage of the literature in the notes.

2477   Nylander, Richard C., Elizabeth Redmond and Penny J. Sander. **Wallpaper in New England: Selections from the Society for the Preservation of New England Antiquities.** Boston, The Society, 1986. 283p. illus. LC 85-61849.

Scholarly hsitory of wallpaper in New England from the early eighteenth century to the early twentieth century with a catalog of the examples in the collections of the Society for the Preservation of New England Antiquities. Well illustrated with color and black and white plates of specimens and reproductions of photographs showing historic interiors. Contents: Part One: Essays. I, The Use and Manufacture of Wallpaper in New England, 1700-1820 by A. L. Cummings; II, From Paper Stainer to Manufacturer: J. F. Bumstead & Co., Manufacturers and Importers of Paper Hangings by K. A. Guffey. Part Two: Catalogue (79 categories). Selected bibliography, pp. 275-76.

See also the pamphlet: *Wallpapers in Historic Preservation*, by C. L. Frangiamore (Washington, D.C., Dept of Interior, National Park Service, Office of Arcaheology and Historic Preservation, 1977. 56p. NPS Publication; 185).

EUROPEAN WALLPAPER

France

2478   Clouzot, Henri. **Histoire du papier peint en France**. Paris, C. Moreau, 1935. 272p. illus. LC 35-14294.

Important, scholarly history of French wallpaper from the early eighteenth century to the middle of the nineteenth century. Twenty-six tipped-in, color plates of wallpaper and many black and white plates and figures illustrating wallpapers, manufacture of and use of wallpaper. Contents: I, Atelier du Dominotier—Les Papillon; II, Tontisses sur toile.—Papier bleu d,Angleterre—Imitations en France; III, Réveillon tontissier; IV, Apogée de Réveillon; V, L'Oeuvre de Réveillon; VI, Pillage et incendie de la folie Titon; VII, Dernières années de Réveillon; VIII, Emules de Réveillon a Paris et en Province; IX, Jacquemart et Bénard; X, Révolution et Empire; XI, Dufour et Leroy; XII, Les Zuber; XIII, Restauration; XIV, Gouvernement de Louis-Philippe et Second Empire. Appendix with list of participants in the expositions of 1878 and 1889. Basic bibliography, pp. 255-56, and specialized literature in the footnotes.

2479   Entwisle, E. A. **French Scenic Wallpapers, 1800-1860**. Leigh-on-Sea, F. Lewis, 1972. 63p. illus. index. ISBN 0853170088.

Authoritative history of French wallpaper, 1800-1860, with panoramic scenes. Contents: 1, The Early French Wallpaper Makers; 2, Origins: The Rotondes and the Dioramas; 3, Characteristics, Methods of Manufacture, Application; 4, The Zubers and Their Wallpapers; 5, Joseph Dufour and Amable Leroy; 6, Jacquemart et Bénard and other Makers; 7, Comments. Contains 70 black and white plates. Appendix with list of titles of scenic wallpapers. Authorities consulted, p. 57.

2480   Nouvel, Odile. **Wallpapers of France, 1800-1850**. New York, Rizzoli, 1981. 130p. illus. index. ISBN 0847803961.

Survey of French wallpaper of the first half of the nineteenth century, particularly valuable for the 600 color illustrations of samples with descriptive captions. Text in French, English, and German. Appendix with extract from Michel Spoerlin's *Fabrication du papier peint dit Iris ou Irisé* (Mulhouse, n.d.). Basic bibliography, p. 30.

See also the exhibition catalog: *Toiles de Nantes, des XVIIIe et XIX siècles* (Mulhouse, Musée de l'Impression sur Etoffes, 1978. 159p. illus.).

Great Britain

2481   Entwisle, E. A. **Wallpapers of the Victorian Era**. Leigh-on-Sea, Lewis, 1964. 55p. illus.

Authoritative introduction to wallpaper in Britain during the nineteenth century. Forty-eight black and white plates with brief descriptive captions. Contents: I, Mawre Cowtan and J. G. Crace; 2, Critics of Wallpaper Design; 3, Two Great Exhibitions, 1851, 1862; 4, Manufacturing Processes and Working Conditions; 5, Wallpaper Novelties; 6, Pioneering Paperstainers; 7, William Morris and Later Designers; 8, Rosamund M. Watson & C. F. A. Voysey; 9, Fin de Siécle and Art Nouveau; 10, France and Other Countries. No bibliography.

2482   Sugden, Alan V., and John L. Edmondson. **A History of English Wallpaper, 1509-1914**. London, Bt. Batsford, 1925. 281p. illus. LC 26-14045.

Comprehensive history of English wallpaper. Contents: I, Wallpaper's Ancestry; II, Early Wallpapers; III, Eighteenth Century Developments; IV, Famous Pioneers; V, Chinese Papers and English Imitations; VI, Late Georgian Achievements; VII, The Coming of Machinery; VIII, How Wallpaper "Found" Itself; IX, The Coming of William Morris; X, Developments in Taste and Technique. Important appendix with mill records arranged by company name and essay on raised materials used for relief decoration. A standard work.

See also the exhibition catalog: *A Decorative Art: 19th Century Wallpapers in the Whitworth Art Gallery* (Manchester, Whitworth Art Gallery, 1985. 67p. illus.).

AUTHOR-TITLE INDEX

Reference is to item number. Authors and titles discussed in the annotations in this bibliography have been indexed along with the authors and titles that constitute the main entries. Those items from the annotations are distinguished by an "x" at the end of the item number. Exhibition and museum catalogs are also listed by title and in the subject index by name of institution.

Morse, Edward W., 1941
Mortimer, Tony J., 1512
Mory, Ludwig, 2122
Mosca, Luigi, 829
Mosoriak, Roy, 963
Moss, 109
Mountfield, David, 24
Mrlian, Rudolf, 279
Mudge, Jean M., 714
Mueble colonial de los Americas, 1223
Mueble colonial sudamericano, 1228
Mueble mexicano: historia, evolucion a influencias, 1222
Muebles de estilo español, 1398
Muebles de estilo español desde el gótico, 1403
Muebles venezolanos; siglos XVI, XVII, y XVIII, 1225
Muhe, Richard, 895
Mujica, Gallo M., 1892
Müller, Dorothee, 1292
Müller, Heide, 796
Muller, Heinrich, 386
Muller, Priscilla E., 1684
Müller, Sigrid Flamand (Christensen), 1127, 2349
Mumford, John K., 2303
Mundt, Barbara, 70, 588
Mundy, R. G., 806
Munn, Geoffrey C., 1656
Munoa, Rafael, 2062
Munroe, A., 720
Munrow, David, 2166
Munsterberg, Hugo, 320, 322, 565
Müntz, Eugene, 2404
Muraoka, Kageo, 321
Murayama, T., 568
Murnane, B., 2279
Museo del Oro, Gold Museum Colombia, 1893x
Museo delle porcellane di Doccia, 684
Museum of Finnish Architecture, 1395
Musgrave, Clifford, 1327, 1334
Musical Boxes, 964
Musical Boxes: A History and Appreciation, 962
Musical Instrument Collections, 2141
Musical Instruments in Art and History, 2148
Musical Instruments of the Western World, 2159
Musical Instruments through the Ages, 2147
Musical Instruments: A Comprehensive Dictionary, 2144
Musical Instruments: an Illustrated History, 2155
Musical Instruments: Their History in Western Culture, 2152
Musikinstrumente des alten Orients, 2162
Musikinstrumente in der Kunst des Alten Orients, 2159

Musikinstrumente: von der Antike bis zur Gegenwart, 2153
Musikinstrumenten-Sammlungen Berlin, 2159
Muth, Marcia 755
Mycenaean Pictorial Vase Painting, 451
Mycenaean Pottery: Analysis and Classification, 450
Myer Myers, Goldsmith 1723-1795, 1919
Myers, 105
Myers, D. K., 2312
Mystery Era of American Pewter, 1928-1931, 2119
Mystery of the Bayeux Tapestry, 2413

Nabeshima, 568
Nabholz, M., 2265
Nabholz-Kartaschoff, Marie-Louise, 2187
Nadelhoffer, Hans, 1665
Nadolski, Dieter, 2123
Nagatake, T., 568
Nakagawa, Sensaku, 721
Nakazato, T., 568
Nance, Ernest M., 662
Napoli e l'arte ceramica dal XII al XX secolo con marche e piante'di antiche fabbriche, 829
Natanson, John, 1571, 1582
National Handicrafts and Handlooms Museum, New Delhi, 319x
National Trust Book of English Domestic Silver 1500-1900, 2013
National Trust Book of English Furniture, 1302
National Types of Old Pewter, 2107
Native Arts of Norway, 301
Nauerth, C., 2212
Navaho Weaving: Its Technic and History, 2222
Navajo Pottery: Traditions & Innovations, 765
Navajo Rugs: How to Find, Evaluate, Buy, 2223
Navajo Textiles: The William Randolph Hearst Collection, 2226x
Navajo Weaving Tradition: 1650 to the Present, 2225
Naylor, Gillian, 71, 151
Nederlands goud- en zilvermerken 1445-1951, 2044
Nederlands klokken- en horloge makers van af 1300, 948
Nederlands koloniale meubel, 1373
Nederlands Porselein, 685
Nederlands Zilver/Dutch Silver 1580-1830, 2047x
Nederlandse interieur: Binnenhuis, meubelen, tapijten, koper, 184
Nederlandse majolica, 835
Needle Work Through the Ages; a Short Survey, 2337
Needle Work: a Selected Bibliography, 2333
Needlepoint in America, 2355

SUBJECT INDEX

References are to item number, not page number. Where primary and secondary references occur, the former are distinguished by bold type. The subjects discussed in the annotations in this bibliography have been indexed here along with the subjects that constitute the major headings. The benefit of this is quick access to many specific subject designations that are included in the classification system of the bibliography. These subjects range from particular artists, works of the applied and decorative arts, sites, and types of objects.